The
Psychology
of
GENDER

The
Psychology
of
GENDER

Vicki S. Helgeson

Prentice
Hall

Upper Saddle River, New Jersey 07458

Library of Congress Cataloging-in-Publication Data

Helgeson, Vicki S.
   The psychology of gender / Vicki S. Helgeson.
      p.   cm.
   Includes bibliographical references and index.
   ISBN 0-13-028769-5
   1. Sex role.   2. Sex differences (Psychology)   I. Title.
HQ1075.H45 2001
305.3—dc21

                                        2001018548

Editorial Director: *Laura Pearson*
Managing Editor: *Sharon Rheinhardt*
AVP, Director of Manufacturing and Production: *Barbara Kittle*
Director of Marketing: *Beth Gillet Mejia*
Managing Editor, Production: *Mary Rottino*
Production Liaison: *Fran Russello*
Project Manager: *Publications Development Company of Texas*
Manufacturing Manager: *Nick Sklitsis*
Prepress and Manufacturing Buyer: *Tricia Kenny*
Art Director: *Jayne Conte*
Cover Designer: *Bruce Kenselaar*
Cover Image Credit: *Roxanne Villa/SIS, Inc.*
Marketing Manager: *Sharon Cosgrove*

This book was set in 10/12 Trump by Publications Development
Company of Texas and was printed and bound by RR Donnelly.
The cover was printed by Phoenix Color Corp.

Printed in the United States of America

10   9   8   7   6   5   4   3   2

ISBN 0-13-028769-5

Prentice-Hall International (UK) Limited, *London*
Prentice-Hall of Australia Pty. Limited, *Sydney*
Prentice-Hall Canada Inc., *Toronto*
Prentice-Hall Hispanoamericana, S.A., *Mexico*
Prentice-Hall of India Private Limited, *New Delhi*
Prentice-Hall of Japan, Inc., *Tokyo*
Pearson Education Asia Pte. Ltd., *Singapore*
Editora Prentice-Hall do Brasil, Ltda., *Rio de Janeiro*

To Mark, my husband and my best friend

CONTENTS

6 Communication   228

11 Multiple Roles and Health

12 Mental Health   **500**

PREFACE

The purpose of this text is to provide a review of the empirical research and conceptual discussions surrounding gender and to examine the implications of gender for relationships and health. The focus of this book goes beyond sex alone—whether one is biologically male or female—to explore the roles that society has assigned to men and women and the other variables that co-occur with sex, such as status and gender-related traits. The implications of social roles, status, and gender-related traits for relationships and health are examined. This is why the book is titled *The Psychology of Gender* rather than *The Psychology of Sex*. Gender is a term that represents the social and cultural forces that influence men and women in our society. The book discusses the "psychology" of gender because the focus is on the individual in the social context. The primary focus is not on biology and anthropology, although their contributions to the study of gender are included.

Rather than review every single topic related to gender, I examine the implications of gender for two broad domains of research: relationships and health. These domains are chosen, first, because they are central to our lives. Friendships, romantic relationships, and relationships at work have a great impact on our day-to-day functioning. Psychological well-being and physical health are important outcomes in their own right. A second reason for the focus on relationships and health is that these are domains in which clear sex differences have been documented. These sex differences cannot be attributed to biology alone; thus, relationships and health are domains for which gender, the social category, may play a role.

The book is divided into three sections, with each section building on the previous one. First, the nature of gender and the development of gender roles is presented. In the first chapter, I provide a brief overview of the scientific method and discuss the difficulties in conducting research on gender, including the philosophical and political issues that pervade this arena. I then provide a brief history of the psychology of gender, which includes discussions of the various instruments used to study gender (Chapter 2). I also discuss our attitudes toward gender and gender roles, as well as gender-role stereotypes (Chapter 2). I then turn to the research literature to provide the current data (Chapter 3) and theory (Chapter 4) on sex differences in cognitive, emotional, and social domains. In Chapter 4, I also discuss different theories of gender-role development, such as evolutionary theory, social learning theory, social role theory, and gender schema theory. In Chapter 5, I discuss the implications of gender and gender roles for achievement. Thus, in this first section of the book, I provide important information on the similarities and differences between men and women and the theories that explain any observed differences. The data and the theories are important for understanding the subsequent sections of the book that address the implications of gender for relationships and health.

The second section of the book begins with a discussion of men's and women's communication and interaction styles (Chapter 6). These findings have implications for the specific relationships discussed: friendship (Chapter 7) and romantic relationships (Chapter 8). Recent research on cross-sex friendship and gay and lesbian relationships are included in these chapters. The role of gender in relationships is critical to understanding the third section of the book, how gender influences health.

The third section begins with an overview chapter documenting sex differences in mental and physical health and theories as to their origins (Chapter 9). Health is broadly construed in this book to reflect specific physical health problems such as coronary artery disease, but also to encompass mental health problems (e.g., depression, eating disorders) and behavioral problems, such as aggression. In Chapter 10, I investigate the implications of gender as a health resource in relationships, in particular marriage. The effects of marriage and marital quality on health are reviewed in Chapter 10, whereas the effects of work and parenting on health are reviewed in Chapter 11. Subsequent chapters focus on two specific health issues: Chapter 12 focuses on depression and Chapter 13 focuses on aggression (including rape, domestic violence, and sexual harassment).

Multiple perspectives on the development of differences between men and women are offered, but the primary perspective that I emphasize is a social psychological one. I examine gender as an individual difference variable but focus on the influence of the context—the situation, the environment, the culture—on gender. I have drawn from research in the areas of psychology, sociology, anthropology, medicine, and public health.

I do not merely itemize sex differences in this text. In many domains, sex differences are more elusive than people believe. I highlight both similarities and differences and remind the reader about the magnitude of differences throughout the chapters. I also point out methodological flaws or difficulties that may bear on the observance of sex differences. The focus of the book is on the explanations for men's and women's thoughts, feelings, and behavior—not simply a summary statement of the similarities and differences between men and women.

This text can be used for an undergraduate course on the psychology of gender, preferably for more advanced students. This text also could be supplemented with empirical readings for a graduate-level course. The book should have widespread appeal to students in the sciences and humanities. Students certainly do not have to be psychology majors to read this text, but some knowledge of research methods would be helpful. Because social psychological theories are so widely discussed in this text, a student who has taken such a course will find the book especially appealing and be able to grasp many of the concepts quite quickly. However, theories are explained in sufficient detail that students without a background in social psychology or psychology should understand the material.

Gender is a topic with which all of us are familiar, regardless of the scientific literature. Thus, it is sometimes difficult to mesh personal experiences with the research literature. To help students integrate the two, each of the chapters includes exercises—mini-experiments—for students to conduct to test some of the research ideas presented. The results of these experiments will not always work out as intended, partly because the sample sizes will be small, partly because the samples will not be representative, and partly because the best ideas do not always translate into the best research designs. The purpose of the exercises is to allow students to gain experience with some of the methods used to study gender and to learn firsthand about how people experience gender in their lives. Other aids to learning include key terms in boldface throughout the chapters and a summary of key terms and definitions at the end of the chapter; summaries of the main points at the end of the chapter; a list of thought-provoking discussion questions; and a list of suggested readings accompanying each chapter.

VICKI S. HELGESON

ACKNOWLEDGMENTS

I would like to thank the anonymous reviewers of this book as well as the people who gave so generously of their time to read and comment on chapters of the book: Rosalind Barnett, Kay Deaux, Alice Eagly, Barbara Gutek, Judith Hall, Susan Sprecher, and Ingrid Waldron. I would like to extend a special thanks to an "anonymous" reviewer who revealed her identity to me, Letitia Anne Peplau. These people's comments and suggestions have greatly enhanced this book.

I owe a great deal of gratitude to the many staff and students at Carnegie Mellon University who have helped me in this endeavor, including Zeljka Buturovic Bradaric, Todd Crouch, Tiffany Durish, Nicole Emery, Ping-szu (Sylvia) Huang, Elizabeth Page-Gould, Renee Rhodes, and Pamela Snyder. I especially appreciate the efforts of Jill Holtz, Antonina Karaczun, Germaine Marnell, and Susan McClellan, who, among other things, had to decipher my writing as they made suggestions to this manuscript. I am indebted to Denise Janicki, who went through every page of this book with a fine-toothed comb, asked questions about statements that were less than sensible, and provided creative ideas to bring the book to life. I also want to thank the students in the Psychology of Gender classes that I taught in fall 1999 and spring 2000 for reading drafts of the chapters in this text.

I would like to thank Eric Stano for seeking me out and persisting in getting me to write this book. His enthusiasm for the work inspired me. I am also grateful to Sharon Rheinhardt and others at Prentice Hall who have patiently answered all of my questions and guided me through this process. I also wish to acknowledge the following Prentice Hall reviewers: Mary Ballard, Appalachian State University; Ann Fuehrer, Miami University of Ohio; and Christina Maslach, University of California at Berkeley.

Finally, I would like to thank my family: my mother and father for all of their love and support over the years; my husband, Mark, for reading parts of the book, providing comments, and especially for coming home early one day after reading Chapter 8 because, as he said, "that's just the kind of egalitarian guy I am"; and my daughter, Katja, not necessarily for aiding in the completing of this book (to the contrary), but for providing me with vivid examples of gender-role socialization.

V. S. H.

1

Introduction

In 1998, my daughter was born and so was my own personal experience with the psychology of gender. As an advocate of equal opportunities and equal treatment for men and women, I thought this practice should begin with infancy. To start, my husband and I tried not to let gender be the overriding principle by which we chose Katja's toys and clothes. This proved to be far more difficult than we thought. In infancy, there are a fair number of "gender-neutral" clothes and toys. But by 1 year of age, the boys' toys and clothes are in one section, the girls' in another, and there is little common ground. I finally figured out why there are gender-neutral clothes for infants: because many parents-to-be and gift-givers make purchases before the baby is born and don't know the sex of the newborn. By 1 year of age, everyone knows.

By dressing Katja in gender-neutral clothes, I learned that the default assumption of others was that she must be a boy. Any infant girl in her right mind (or her parents' right mind) would wear pink or ruffles or have bows in her hair or have her ears pierced! Because I personally hated pink, Katja had a lot of blue, yellow, purple, and red. When we carried her around as an infant, people in the grocery store or the shopping mall would comment on what a cute boy we had. When we mentioned that he was a she, people often subtly reprimanded us for not providing the appropriate cues: the pink, the ruffles, the hair bows. Some people remarked that of course she was a girl because she had so much hair. I know of no evidence that girls are born with more hair than boys. I found it an interesting paradox that the biological default is female (i.e., at conception, the embryo is destined to become female unless exposed to male hormones), but that the social default is male. When in doubt, assume the baby is a boy—unless there are strong social cues indicating the baby is a girl. It is not nearly as offensive to assume that a girl is a boy as to assume that a boy is a girl. And people do expect you to be offended. When someone did mistake Katja for a boy, I wasn't surprised. How can you tell at that age? But the person who made the remark

1

was always extremely apologetic, as if she had insulted me by assuming that Katja was of the other sex.

Now that Katja is beyond 1 year old, the shopping becomes more difficult. Boys' and girls' clothes have even less in common. Blue jeans that are plain in the boys' section are decorated with flowers or ruffles in the girls' section. A simple pair of shorts in the boys' department is elaborated with a flap in the girls' department so that it looks like a skirt. Girls' clothes are covered with an amazing assortment of flowers. Girls also are expected to wear dresses. How practical is it to play in the sand, climb a tree, and run around in a dress? You can't even buy socks that are for both boys and girls; there are boy socks and girl socks. Guess which ones have the ruffles?

The point I am trying to convey by my experience is that sex is a very important category to us as a society. It is very important that we know an infant's sex. Because infant boys and girls do look alike, parents are expected to provide clues to society. An infant's sex is one of the first things that you try to figure out about him or her and is one of the first things that you notice about a child or an adult. Have you ever found yourself in a situation where you didn't know the sex of a person? You look for clues in the person's dress, in the face, the physique, and the voice. Why does it bother you so much? Why do you need to know the person's sex to interact with her—or him? A person's sex—really, a person's gender (I explain the distinction next)—has implications for our feelings, our beliefs, and our behavior toward the person. Your own gender has implications for how others feel about you, what others think about you, and how others behave toward you.

Gender has been the subject of scientific scrutiny for an entire century. Scientists have debated the similarities as well as the differences between men and women: Are men better at math than women? Are men more aggressive than women? Are women more emotional than men? Do men and women have the same capacities to be nurses, doctors, and lawyers? Scientists also have examined the implications of being male and female for one's relationships and one's health: Are women's relationships closer than those of men? Does marriage provide more health benefits for men compared to women? Are women more depressed than men? Are men less willing than women to seek help for health problems?

You have probably found yourself asking some of these questions. You probably are fairly confident that you know the answers to some of them. Gender is a topic with which we all feel intimately familiar. What woman doubts that men are less likely than women to ask for directions? What man doubts that women are more likely than men to dwell on their problems? We have many experiences that we bring to bear on these issues, but our anecdotal observations are not the same as observations gained from well-established scientific methods. In fact, our anecdotal observations may be biased in favor of sex differences when differences do not really exist. When evaluating the literature, you will see that the answer to the question of sex differences is usually fairly complicated. The appearance of sex differences depends on myriad factors: the place, time, person, audience, and characteristics of the one making the observation.

In this text, I evaluate the literature on the psychology of gender, paying special attention to the implications that gender has for our relationships and our health. I begin this first chapter by defining the terminology that is used in the study of gender. Next, I comment on how gender is construed in other cultures. Then, I review the scientific method on which the majority of the research presented in this text is based and examine the unique difficulties that researchers face when studying gender. I conclude the chapter by providing an overview of the various political and philosophical viewpoints that many researchers have taken when studying gender.

DEFINITION OF TERMS

This textbook is called *Psychology of Gender.* Why not *Psychology of Sex?* What is the difference between sex and gender? Is gender just the more politically correct term? One of our first tasks is to define these terms and other sex-related and gender-related ideas.

The first distinction to make is between sex and gender. **Sex** refers to the biological categories of male and female, categories distinguished by genes, chromosomes, and hormones. Culture has no influence on one's sex. Sex is a relatively stable category that is not easily changed, though recent technology has allowed people to change their biological sex. **Gender,** by contrast, is a much more fluid category: it refers to the social categories of male and female. These categories are distinguished from one another by a set of psychological features and role attributes that society has assigned to the biological category of sex. What are some of the psychological features that we assign to sex in the United States? Emotionality is a trait that we ascribe to women and competitiveness is a trait that we ascribe to men. These traits are features of gender rather than sex. Whereas sex is defined in the same way across cultures, gender differs because each society has its own prescriptions for how men and women ought to behave. Unger (1990) defines gender as "the cognitive and perceptual mechanisms by which biological differentiation is translated into social differentiation" (pp. 109–110). A feature of the male sex category includes the Y chromosome; regardless of whether a male

wears a baseball cap or barrettes, is competitive or empathetic, he is of the male sex because he possesses the Y chromosome. Personality and appearance are related to the gender category. In the United States, a feature of the female gender category is nurturance; a person who is nurturant is behaving in a way consistent with the social category for women. Another feature of the female gender category in the United States is to wear a skirt; typically, if you encounter someone in this country wearing a skirt, you can assume the person is psychologically female as well as biologically female. However, in other countries, such as Scotland, wearing a skirt or a kilt is quite normal for a person who is of the biological male sex; thus, one would not want to use wearing a skirt as a feature of the male or female gender category in Scotland. It is American culture that views a kilt as a skirt; a person from Scotland does not view a kilt as a skirt. The content of gender categories—but not sex categories—is influenced by society, culture, and time.

Now that this important distinction has been made, I must point out that the distinction is rarely employed in practice. Laypersons as well as scientists often use the terms interchangeably; articles in the newspaper as well as articles in scientific journals do not use the terms consistently. Even the American Psychological Association is not consistent in its employment of these terms. For example, when submitting an article to be published in a scientific journal, the editor often replaces the phrase "sex differences" with "gender differences." There is a good chance that the author is simply referring to differences between people who are biologically male versus biologically female without any thought to their psychological attributes; that being the case, the correct term would be sex differences. However, some people argue that the phrase "sex differences" implies that the basis of the difference is biological (McHugh, Koeske, & Frieze, 1986). Yet, if you conduct a study of men and women and find that men outperform women on a video game or that women have better recall on a memory task than men, do you have any evidence that the difference is biological? No. A better term to use to describe these differences is **sex-related behavior.** This term implies that the behavior corresponds to sex but it does not say anything about the cause or the etiology of the difference.

A term that better captures society's influence on the biologically based categories of male and female is **gender role** rather than gender. A **role** is a social position that is accompanied by a set of norms or expectations. For example, one role that you most certainly possess is the role of student. What are some of the expectations that go along with this role? One expectation is that you study for class; another might be that you socialize and stay up late at night with friends. In this instance, there may be a conflict between the expectations within a given role.

Gender role refers to the expectations that go along with being male versus female. We typically expect men to be strong, to refrain from crying, to be independent and competitive. These are features of the male gender role. By contrast, we typically expect women to be caring, emotionally expressive, polite, and helpful: features of the female gender role. In other words, we expect men to be **masculine** and we expect women to be **feminine.** Masculinity includes the traits, behaviors, and interests that society has assigned to the male gender role. A masculine trait is self-confidence; a masculine behavior is aggression; and a masculine interest is watching sports. Femininity includes the traits, behaviors, and interests that are assigned to the female gender role. A feminine trait is emotional; a feminine behavior is helping someone; and a feminine interest is cooking. In Chapter 2, we will discuss the content of masculinity and femininity in more detail.

When expectations within a role conflict, such as in the example of the student above, we experience **intrarole conflict.** How might women experience intrarole conflict within their gender role? Women are expected to be emotional and express their feelings but also to be sensitive to the needs of others. So, should a woman who is unhappy with her marriage express those feelings to her husband? If she expresses her feelings, she is adhering to her role in terms of expressing emotion but she is contradicting her role by expressing feelings that might upset someone else. How might men experience intrarole conflict within the male gender role? One expectation of the male gender role is to achieve; another is to be independent and not ask for help. What should a man who desires to adhere to his gender role do if he is stumped on a homework assignment that his buddy has completed? If he asks for help, he will further his achievement goal but at the expense of another goal: appearing independent. Just because a given role has a set of guidelines does not mean that those guidelines might not conflict with one another from time to time. Gender roles are no exception.

When the expectations of one role conflict with the expectations of another role, we experience **interrole conflict.** You possess other roles besides your gender role. What roles conflict with your gender role? There are times when the expectations of the role of student may conflict with both the male gender role and the female gender role. In a large lecture class, the expectation of a student is to sit quietly in the class and listen, a passive role that may conflict with the active aspects of the male gender role. In a small seminar, the expectation of a student is to actively participate in class discussion, which may include some debate; this active, possibly argumentative role, may conflict with the female gender role. Think about some of your relationship roles. Does your role as a friend, son or daughter, boyfriend or girlfriend ever conflict with your gender role? A male student involved in a group project may experience conflict between the male gender role norm to be independent and the student role norm to work together with classmates on group projects. The difficulty here is that the norms for the two different roles clash.

In part due to role conflict, there are times when we violate the norms associated with our roles. What are the consequences of behaving in ways that violate norms? The consequences could be minor or severe; it will depend on how central that norm is to the role and how strongly the situation calls for adherence to the role. What are the consequences for a male's not being independent? There may be only minor repercussions for this behavior. What are the consequences for a male wearing a dress—unless it is a costume party? These consequences might be more severe. A central feature of the male gender role is to not appear feminine. What are the consequences for a male being cooperative instead of competitive? Cooperative behavior may be accepted in the classroom but not well at all on the football field. Do football players ever suggest talking to the other team about the best strategy for both teams to perform well? What are the consequences for a female not being emotional or being active? Again, it will depend on the situation. A female who fails to express feelings at an emotional event, such as a funeral, may be judged quite harshly; today, a female who is active in sports will not necessarily be viewed negatively.

Think about the consequences for violating the norms that go along with your gender role. Try violating a norm to see

what the effect is. There are some examples in Exercise 1.1. Who do you think suffers more for violating gender role norms, men or women? Many people maintain that it is men who suffer more. Today, women who behave "like men" are often accepted and even applauded. It is acceptable for women to dress like men by wearing pants, suits, and even ties; it is acceptable for women to have jobs that were traditionally held by men, such as doctor, lawyer, even construction worker. But is it acceptable for men to dress like women by wearing a dress or nylons? (It is more acceptable for men to wear earrings.) Are men who possess jobs traditionally held by women, such as nurse or secretary, encouraged or applauded? It is

---

EXERCISE 1.1
Views of Gender-Role Incongruent Behavior

Try adopting some behavior that does not fit your gender role and see how people respond—verbally and nonverbally.

For example, if you are male, try:

Wearing a dress.

Wearing makeup.

Calling for an escort service when you walk across campus in the dark.

Going into a salon and having your fingernails painted.

If you are female, try:

Chewing tobacco in public.

Joining a group of guys to play football or basketball.

Working on your car with a man standing by (changing the oil, changing a tire).

Going into a barbershop and getting your hair cut.

How did you feel?
How did others respond?

interesting that a little girl who behaves like a boy is called a "tomboy" but a little boy who behaves like a girl is called a "sissy." Sissy has more negative connotations than tomboy. Today, parents have no problem giving their little girls trucks to play with and encouraging girls to play sports. But how do parents feel about giving their little boys dolls and encouraging them to play "house"?

Most scientists believe that men suffer more negative consequences for gender-role violations than women. The reason? Status. Women who take on characteristics of the male gender role are moving toward a higher status, whereas men who take on characteristics of the female gender role are moving toward a lower status. We applaud the move up but not the move down. The relation of gender to status will be elaborated on later in the chapter.

The term gender role is used interchangeably with the term sex role. Personally, I don't know what to make of the latter term. Sex role really does not make sense because it confuses a biological category, sex, with a social category, role. Thus, it is peculiar that one of the leading scientific journals in this area is called *Sex Roles* instead of "Gender Roles." I prefer to use the term sex when referring to the biological categories of male and female, and to use the terms gender and gender role when referring to the psychological attributes and expectations we have for those categories.

Now we can ask whether people accept the psychological category that accompanies their biological sex. **Gender identity** is one's perception of the self as psychologically male or female. You have probably heard of people who are biologically male but feel as if they are female and wish that they were female, or vice versa. **Transgendered** individuals are said to have a gender identity problem, meaning that their biological sex is incongruent with their psychological sex

(S. Cole, Denny, Eyler, & Samons, 2000). A transgendered person may be biologically female but feel psychologically like a male and choose to live a life as a male. This transgendered individual may dress and behave like a man, that is, take on the male gender role. In some cases, transgendered people will seek to have surgery to change them biologically to the other sex. A person whose sex has been biologically changed is a **transsexual** (S. Cole et al., 2000).

Gender identity is not to be confused with **sexual orientation.** Sexual orientation refers to whether people prefer to have other-sex or same-sex persons as partners for love, affection, and sex. **Heterosexuals** prefer other-sex partners; **homosexuals** prefer same-sex partners; and **bisexuals** are accepting of other-sex and same-sex partners.

Sex typing (which really should be referred to as gender typing) is the process by which sex-appropriate preferences, behaviors, skills, and self-concept are acquired. How does a boy become masculine? A girl feminine? We will review the different theories of sex typing in Chapter 4. The point here is that people who adhere to the gender role assigned to them by society are sex-typed. A male who thinks, feels, and behaves in masculine ways and a female who thinks, feels, and behaves in feminine ways are each **sex-typed.** A male who acts feminine and a female who acts masculine are each said to be **cross-sex-typed.** Someone who incorporates both masculine and feminine qualities is not sex-typed and is often referred to as **androgynous.** Androgyny will be discussed in more detail, also in Chapter 4.

Thus far, we have been discussing attributes that define a person's sense of self. Gender also comes into play when we think about other people. One's own personal view about how men and women should behave is called a **gender-role attitude.** You might believe that women should be caring and nurturant, whereas men should be independent and assertive; you might also believe that women should have primary responsibility for raising children and men should have primary responsibility for earning money to take care of the family. If so, then you have a traditional gender-role attitude; that is, your view fits the expectations that society in general has for how men and women should behave. Alternatively, you might believe that both men and women should be assertive and caring and that both should be equally responsible for working inside and outside the home; in this case, you have a more egalitarian gender-role attitude. Many people hold what Hochschild (1989) refers to as a "transitional attitude," which fits somewhere between traditional and egalitarian. You may believe that both men and women should participate in work inside the home and outside the home, but that women should give the home their primary attention and men should give work their primary attention. This person is striving for an egalitarian philosophy but some residual traditional gender-role attitudes remain.

There are three other terms that reflect one's attitude to the category of sex. Each term maps onto one of the three components of an attitude: affect, cognition, and behavior. The affective (feeling) component of one's attitude toward the sex category is called **sexism** or prejudice toward people based on their sex. Typically, we think of sexism as involving a negative attitude or negative affect, but it could entail positive affect. If you dislike the person whom your wife hired to take care of your children because the person is male, you are showing sexism. Likewise, if you like the person your wife hired merely because she is female, you also are showing sexism. The cognitive component of one's attitude toward sex is a **sex stereotype** or **gender-role stereotype.** These terms refer to one's beliefs

about the features of the biological or psychological categories of male and female. If you perceive that the male nanny would not be competent because he lacks the required nurturant qualities, you are engaging in gender-role stereotyping. The behavioral component of one's attitude toward men and women is **sex discrimination.** Sex discrimination involves the differential treatment of people based on their biological sex. If you fire the male nanny because you dislike men as nannies and you doubt his competence because he is a man, you are engaging in sex discrimination. Sex discrimination is often a result of both sexism and gender-role stereotyping.

Finally, one last term that must be introduced is **feminism.** What image did that term conjure up for you? The definitions of feminism are vast and varied. At the most fundamental level, a feminist is someone who believes that men and women should be treated equally. You are probably thinking, "Is that all there is to feminism? If so, I must be a feminist." In fact, over the years, I have had many students in class tell me that they did not realize that they were feminists until taking my class. And several students have told me that their parents did not realize that they were feminists until the students took my course. Renzetti (1987) conducted a study of female college students in the 1980s and found that only 27% of them labeled themselves as feminists; despite their lack of endorsement of the feminist label, the vast majority rejected traditional roles for women and endorsed feminist attitudes.

A defining feature of feminism is a high regard for women. Most people in our society would agree that women should be valued. The disagreement lies in the current status of women in our society: whether they are currently valued or devalued. Feminism also can include the belief that society needs to make changes for the equal treatment of men and women to occur and can include the impetus to take action to make these changes. It is these latter ideas that are more controversial.

Crosby, Todd, and Worell (1996) conducted a study in which they interviewed 77 female academic psychologists who were feminists. They asked the women, "When you say 'I am a feminist,' what do you mean?" The most common response was the belief in gender equality. Fewer than half (41%) of the respondents spontaneously mentioned activism as part of the definition. However, when the women were provided with a list of features and asked to check which ones were part of the definition of feminism, 92% checked "works actively to change social structures." The investigators also found that participants who labeled themselves feminists spontaneously mentioned activism. Some examples of their activism are shown in Table 1.1. You probably expected to see much more radical behaviors than the ones listed in the table. You can see that the examples of activism shown in Table 1.1 are ones that promote women or ones in which causes important to women, such as day care, are promoted. Do you participate in similar activities? If so, do you identify yourself as a feminist?

Thus, it appears that the belief in gender equality is the central feature of feminism, but that activism is an important feature of feminism for those whose identities are most strongly tied to it. Try Exercise 1.2 to find out how feminism is viewed at your institution.

TABLE 1.1   Examples of Feminist Activism

Working in women's center on campus.
Developing a course on women's studies.
Helping to set up day care programs.
Promoting women's sports.
Taking a leadership role in the university.
Working at a rape crisis center.
Promoting women political candidates.
Donating money to women's organizations.
Increasing awareness of sexual harassment.
Participating in pro-choice rally.

Source: Crosby et al. (1996).

EXERCISE 1.2
Definition of a Feminist

Ask 10 men and 10 women to describe the first things that come to mind when they think of the term "feminist." This will tell you a couple of things: first, you will learn whether people view the term favorably or unfavorably; second, you will learn the content of this category. Construct a frequency distribution of the features listed. The features that are most often listed by these people are features that are central to the feminist category; the features that are listed least often are peripheral to the category and probably more reflective of that particular individual. What percentage of features is negative versus positive? Do men or women view a feminist in more positive or negative terms? To address this question, calculate the number of positive and negative features identified by the group of men and the group of women.

Ask these same 20 people two more questions. Ask whether they believe men and women should be treated equally, the defining feature of a feminist. You could ask people to respond on a 5-point scale: 1 = Definitely not, 2 = Probably not, 3 = Unsure, 4 = Probably should, 5 = Definitely should. Then ask whether each person is a feminist. Do answers to these two questions correspond?

CULTURAL DIFFERENCES IN THE CONSTRUAL OF GENDER

I have defined the terminology that is used in the psychology of gender. All of these terms, however, have diverse meanings and are construed at least slightly differently by people of different ethnic backgrounds in the United States and more differently by people from other cultures. Ramet (1996) proposes the idea of a **gender culture,** which reflects "society's understanding of what is possible, proper, and perverse in gender-linked behavior" (p. 2). In other words, each society generates its own standards for gender-linked behavior.

Because the majority of research that has been conducted and is examined in this book interprets gender—the roles of men and women in society—in similar terms, it might be interesting to step outside of our cultural view and consider how gender is construed in a few different cultures around the world.

Cultures with Multiple Genders

One assumption about gender shared by many cultures is that there are two genders: male and female. Did it ever occur to you that there could be more than two genders? In several Native American cultures, there are four genders (Lang, 1996). For these cultures, gender does not map onto biological sex; instead, gender is based on people's social roles. The four categories are man, woman, woman-man, and man-woman. A man who is biologically male but adopts many, if not all, of the social role characteristics of a female is known as a woman-man. A female who is biologically female but adopts many, if not all, of the social role characteristics of a male is known as a man-woman. Because the notion of two genders is so strongly ingrained in us, people

often leap to the conclusion that the man-woman and woman-man must be homosexual. This is not at all true. In fact, a woman-man is likely to marry a woman; he is simply drawn to the social role of women. He may dress like a woman and adopt the language and mannerisms of a woman. Sometimes, the woman-man and man-woman categories stem not from personal choice but from a family's needs. Perhaps a family needs someone to do male work but has only female children; one of the female children may be designated a man-woman so that she can adopt the male social role. It also is important to point out that the woman-man and man-woman genders are not categories that are inferior to the traditional man and woman genders.

The appearance of multiple genders also occurs in the Balkans (Ramet, 1996). In this case, people primarily take on the other gender role to serve society's needs. For example, some biological females are raised as males when the society is in need of those functions that are best served by men. In the Balkans, these women assume a male social identity and perform the work of men. They are not allowed to marry and are sworn to virginity. These people are *highly* respected.

In Western cultures, gender is defined by one's genitals (Lang, 1996). We have no culturally defined category for people who are uncomfortable with their sex or who would like to combine elements of both male and female gender roles. We are very uncomfortable when we cannot determine someone's sex and we are very uncomfortable with people who try to create new gender categories (e.g., transsexuals).

Morocco

In Morocco, there are only two genders but the two are very distinct (Hessini, 1994). The distinction between the male gender role and the female gender role manifests itself in terms of physical space. Private space, which is the space reserved for the family inside a home, is female space. Public space, which is basically everything outside of the home, is male space. The duties of men and women are distinct and take place in their separate physical spaces. The women fulfill their roles in female space, inside the home, and the men fulfill their roles in male space, outside the home. It is clear that public space is men's space as only men are found in coffee shops and theaters, and only men hang out in public places. If women are in public, they are usually scurrying from one place to the next.

The distinct roles of men and women are not questioned in Morocco (Hessini, 1994). The man is the leader of the family and works outside the home to provide for the family; the woman is responsible for the household, which includes the education and religious training of children. Even in modern Morocco, women are not concerned with equality. The Moroccan people believe that the two sexes complement one another. Although the cultural code is for men to financially support the family, there is an increasing trend for women to work outside the home, largely due to economic necessity. This is creating some tension because both men and women maintain the belief that women should not work outside the home and that women's primary responsibility lies inside the home.

One way in which women are able to work and enter into public spaces is by wearing the *hijab* and *djellaba* when they go out in public (Hessini, 1994). The hijab is a large scarf that covers a woman's head, neck, and shoulders so that only her face is seen. The hijab provides a sense of Muslim identity and security for women; it is a veil that women view as shielding them from the outside world so that they can feel as if they are still in their private space. The

djellaba is a long, loose-fitting gown, which hides the shape of the body. Women believe that these articles of clothing protect them from men and help to preserve the social order. A woman who does not wear the hijab and djellaba is viewed as naked. Other clothing shows the outline of the female body, which provokes and attracts men, leading to adultery. Women are held more responsible for adultery than men; thus, in a sense, the hijab and djellaba are viewed as avenues to freedom in that they allow the woman to go into public spaces.

People from the West, however, hardly view the hijab as liberating (Hessini, 1994). Instead, the hijab is viewed as an indication of women's oppression and male domination. The hijab perpetuates the stereotype of women as sexual temptresses whom men are unable to resist.

The Agta Negrito

Some people have maintained that women's and men's distinct social roles are rooted in biology. As evidence, they cite the distinct roles of men and women in hunter-gatherer societies. Women are biologically predisposed to gather and men are biologically predisposed to hunt. Women can't hunt because hunting would reduce their ability to bear and take care of children. In most hunter-gatherer societies, the division of labor is as predicted: men hunt and women gather.

The Agta Negrito is a society in the Phillipines that challenges this idea (Goodman, Griffin, Estioko-Griffin, & Grove, 1985). In this society, women hunt and they are as successful as men. Hunting doesn't impair women's fertility. Women who hunt do not differ from women who do not hunt in age at menarche, age at first pregnancy, or age of the youngest child. Women who hunt also are able to take care of children.

How is it that women are able to hunt in this society? There are two reasons. One is physical, having to do with the Agta terraine: women can hunt close to home. The second is social: other people help with child care. Women hunters either take nursing infants with them or leave toddlers at home where they are cared for by other family members. The structure of this culture shows that there is no biological reason that women cannot hunt and that the division of labor between the two sexes is not drawn in stone.

Tahiti

There is evidence that men's and women's roles can be similar. Tahiti is an example of a truly androgynous society (Gilmore, 1990). The social roles of men and women are very much the same. Women have the same status as men and have the same opportunities as men in domestic, occupational, and recreational spheres. Not only are men's and women's roles similar, but men and women share similar personalities. There is no pressure on men and women to behave differently or to behave in accordance with traditional gender roles. Men are not worried about proving their masculinity, for example, and do not feel the need to take risks. This similarity of men and women is even reflected in their language; there is no word for gender in language, no male or female pronouns. The society is based on cooperation rather than competition; perhaps because resources are available to people, there is no economic reason to compete. There is little aggression, no war, and no hunting; that is, there is nothing for men to defend. Thus, there is no basis for an ideology of masculinity to have evolved. The people in this society truly seem to function without thinking about gender.

Status and Culture

With the exception of Tahiti and probably a few other cultures, one commonality in the way gender is construed around the world is that men have higher status than women (Chisholm, 2000). How is men's higher status compared to women's, or male dominance, manifested?

There are a number of indices of gender inequality. The higher illiteracy rates of women, less access to medical care for women, a lower earnings ratio of women compared to men, and the legitimization of physical abuse of women in some countries are all manifestations of men's higher status relative to women's (Chisholm, 2000). In India and China, some female fetuses are aborted because they are less valued than males.

The dominant group in a society has rights and privileges that are not available to the subordinate group (Ostenson, 1996). In our society, we can talk about male privilege, White privilege, heterosexual privilege, class privilege, and even attractiveness privilege. People who have the privilege are often unaware of it; those who lack the privilege are aware. For example, heterosexual privilege entails the right to marry, to have a public ceremony that entails celebration and gifts from family and friends, and to have children without being questioned. Heterosexuals do not view this as a privilege because it has come to be expected. Homosexuals, however, who do not have these privileges, certainly recognize heterosexual privilege.

What is male privilege? Historically, women were not allowed to vote or own property. More recent examples of male privilege include only men being allowed to serve in the military and men having greater access than women to certain jobs, to higher levels of education, and to political office (Ostenson, 1996). Until 1972, only men could run the Boston Marathon (Rosenbloom, 2000). The first two women who ran the marathon, in 1966 and 1967, disguised themselves, one by dress and one by name; upon recognition, their completion of the race was dismissed, questioned, and not officially recognized. Until a few years ago, women were not allowed to enter the all-male military schools the Citadel and the Virginia Military Institute. Shannon Faulkner applied to the Citadel in 1993 by omitting any reference to her gender; she was admitted, but on learning of her gender, the Citadel withdrew their offer of admission.

Today, great strides have been made in the United States toward gender equality. Obviously, women can vote, run for political office and win elections, and have gained in occupational status. However, women are not nearly as prevalent in government as men, and women rarely are found in the highest occupational statuses, such as chief executive officers of industry. We have yet to see a female president or even a serious female presidential candidate. The similarities and differences in the treatment and behavior of men and women will appear in numerous chapters throughout the book. The important point to keep in mind is whether a sex difference in behavior is due to something inherent about being male or female or to something about status.

THE SCIENTIFIC METHOD

In this text, I review the scientific literature on gender and its implications for relationships and health. I also make reference to some of the more popular literature on gender. You already may be familiar with books such as Deborah Tannen's (1990) *You Just Don't Understand: Women and Men in Conversation* and John Gray's (1992) *Men Are*

from Mars, Women Are from Venus. I include these more popularized views of gender because I want you to be familiar with them. You will read about sex differences in the newspaper and hear about sex differences on television, especially on news shows such as *Dateline* and *20/20*. In this text, we evaluate these popularized notions about gender and sex differences from the point of view of the scientific literature. You will be able to judge which differences are real and which are not, which differences are exaggerated, and which comparisons between men and women have not been studied adequately. You will also know what questions to ask when faced with a report on sex differences.

Before moving on to the literature, both popular and scientific, it is important for you to understand the scientific method on which research is based and the difficulties inherent in conducting research on gender. If you have taken a research methods course, you are familiar with the scientific method and you know that there are always trade-offs in conducting good research. The study of gender has some unique difficulties that other research domains do not face. Other difficulties inherent in scientific research are particularly problematic in the study of gender. First, I turn to the scientific method. There are a number of terms introduced in this section; they are summarized in Table 1.2.

The scientific method rests on **empiricism.** Empiricism means that information is collected via one of our major senses, usually sight. One can touch, feel, hear, or see the information. This information, referred to as **data,** usually takes the form of thoughts, feelings, or behaviors. For example, I will examine the way in which men and women think about themselves and the world, the way men and women experience and express emotions, the way men and women interact with other people, and the

TABLE 1.2 Key Terms Used in Scientific Method

Age effect: an effect due to the age of the respondent.

Cohort effect: an effect due to the cohort or generation of the respondent.

Correlational study: a study in which one observes the relation between two variables, often at a single point in time.

Cross-sectional study: a study in which the data are collected at one point in time, usually a cross-section of different age groups.

Data: information (e.g., thoughts, feelings, behaviors) that is collected for the purpose of scientific examination.

Demand characteristics: the ways participants of an experiment can influence the outcome of a study.

Dependent variable: the variable that is expected to be influenced by manipulation of the independent variable; the effect.

Empiricism: basis of scientific method that involves the collection of information via one of the major senses (usually sight).

Experimental method: research method in which the investigator manipulates one variable and observes its effect on another variable.

External validity: the confidence that the results from an experiment generalize to the real world.

Facts: statements made about data.

Field experiments: experiments in which the investigation is taken into the environment where the behavior to be studied naturally occurs.

Hypothesis: a prediction that a certain observation will occur under a specific set of conditions.

Independent variable: the variable that is manipulated during an experiment; the cause.

Internal validity: the confidence that the true cause of the effect is being studied.

Longitudinal study: a study in which the data are collected at multiple time points.

Negative correlation: correlation in which the level of one variable increases and the level of the other variable decreases.

Positive correlation: correlation in which the levels of both variables increase or the levels of both variables decrease at the same time.

Random assignment: method of assignment in which each participant has an equal chance of being exposed to each condition.

Random selection/random sampling: method of selecting a sample in which each member of the population has an equal chance of being a participant in the study.

Replication: the repeating of a study, often with different measures of the independent variable and the dependent variable.

Selection bias: result of participants not being randomly sampled or not being randomly assigned to condition.

Stimulus/target variable: a variable that can be manipulated in an experiment.

Subject variable: a variable that is a permanent characteristic of the person (subject), and that may affect the person's response to another variable.

Theory: an abstract generalization that provides an explanation for a set of facts.

way men's and women's bodies respond to stress. Statements about these observations, or data, are called **facts.** A collection of facts can be used to generate a **theory,** or an abstract generalization that provides an explanation for the set of facts.

For a theory to be scientific, it must be falsifiable, meaning there must be the possibility that it can be disproved. Creationism, for example, is not a scientific theory because there is no way to disprove it. Some theories are not scientific because they are circular. For example, a theory about gender roles could be circular. If you define the male gender role as the traits, interests, and behaviors exhibited by men but modify the traits, interests, and behaviors included in the theory so that it fits all men, the theory is circular. You start out by defining the male gender role as active, independent, and competitive. Then you come across a male who is cooperative, so you change the definition to omit competitive. You come across another male who is honest, so you add that trait. In this case, there would never be a way to disprove the theory. All men would fit the male gender role. However, this isn't the case with gender role theories. We first define the male gender role and then measure it among a group of men. We find that some men adhere more strongly and some men adhere less strongly to the male gender role. Some men do not adhere to the male gender role at all; they are still men but they do not take on the male gender role.

A theory is used to generate a **hypothesis,** a prediction that a certain observation will occur under a specific set of conditions. A hypothesis is tested by creating those conditions and then collecting data. The statements made from the data, facts, may either support the hypothesis and thus, the theory, or suggest that the theory needs to be modified.

Each of these steps in the research process is shown in Figure 1.1.

Let's take an example. One theory of the origin of sex differences is social role theory. According to social role theory, any differences in behavior that we observe between men and women are due to the different social roles they hold in society. We can apply this theory to the behavior of nurturance. One hypothesis would be that women are more nurturant than men because their social roles of mother and caretaker require more nurturant behavior than the social roles that men possess. This hypothesis suggests that men and women who are in the same social roles will show similar levels of nurturance. There are a couple of ways that we could test this hypothesis. We could compare the levels of nurturance among men and women who have similar roles in society—men and women who are parents and in the same occupation, say, nursing. If we study nurses, we could measure nurturance by the number of minutes spent with patients while *not* performing specific nursing duties. The number of minutes of free time with patients is the data. Let's say that we find that male and female nurses (who are also parents) spend the same number of minutes with patients in a nonworking capacity. This is a fact and it supports our hypothesis that men and women who possess the same social roles behave in similar ways.

Another way that we could test our hypothesis would be to assign males and females to one of two social roles in the laboratory, a caretaker or a noncaretaker role, and observe nurturant behavior. In the

FIGURE 1.1 Steps in the research process.

caretaker condition, we would ask participants to play with and take care of a puppy; in the noncaretaker condition, we would ask participants to teach the puppy some tricks. If both men and women show the same high level of nurturant behavior in the caretaker condition and the same low level of nurturant behavior in the noncaretaker condition, our hypothesis that social role rather than sex leads to differences in nurturance would be supported and our theory substantiated. If women are observed to show greater levels of nurturance than men in both conditions, regardless of the instructions received on how to interact with the puppy, we would have to revise our theory. This observation would suggest that there is something about being female, aside from social role, that leads to nurturance.

The two studies just described are quite different in design. The first is a correlational study and the second an experimental study. These are the two kinds of studies primarily described in this text. Let me describe the differences.

Correlational Study

A **correlational study** is one in which you observe the relation between two variables, usually at a single point in time. For example, we could correlate job characteristics with nurturant behavior. We would probably observe that people who held more people-oriented jobs displayed more nurturance. The problem would be that we would not know if the job caused nurturance or if being a nurturant person caused people to choose those jobs. Does being a social worker lead to nurturance, or do more nurturant people choose social work? We also could correlate sex with job characteristics. We would probably find that women are more likely than men to hold people-oriented jobs. The problem here

isn't exactly the same as the one identified above. Here, we know that job characteristics do not cause someone's sex. However, we still do not know that someone's sex caused him or her to have a certain kind of job. There may be a third variable that is responsible for the relation between sex and people-oriented jobs. That third variable could be salary. Perhaps the pay of people-oriented jobs is lower than that of other jobs and women are more likely to be hired into low-salary positions. There are often a number of explanations for a correlation.

The value of a correlation can range from −1 to +1. Both −1 and +1 are referred to as perfect correlations. You can perfectly predict one variable from the other variable. In the examples above, there will not be perfect correlations. It will not be the case that all nurturant people are in people-oriented jobs or that all women are in people-oriented jobs. An example of a perfect correlation can be found in physics. There is a perfect correlation between how fast you are driving and how far your car takes you. If you drive 60 mph, you will travel 60 miles in one hour or 120 miles in two hours; if you drive 100 mph, you will travel 100 miles in one hour or 200 miles in two hours. For every 1 mph you increase your speed, you will travel 1 mile further in an hour. That is, you can perfectly predict distance from speed. As you might guess, in psychological research, we cannot perfectly predict one variable from another. Most correlations reported in psychology will fall in the .3 to .4 range.

A **positive correlation** is one in which the levels of both variables increase or decrease at the same time. For example, you might find that women who hold more traditional gender-role attitudes are more likely to perform the majority of household chores; that is, as women's gender-role attitudes become more traditional, the amount of household chores performed increases. This is depicted in the left half of Figure 1.2. A **negative correlation** occurs when the level of one variable increases and the level of the other decreases. This is depicted in the right half of Figure 1.2. An example of a negative correlation would be the amount of household chores performed by a man with traditional gender-role attitudes: the more traditional his attitude, the fewer household chores he performs.

Correlational studies are often conducted with surveys or by making observations of behavior. It is important how you choose the people to complete your survey or to be the subject of observation; they need to approximate or be representative of the population to whom you wish to generalize your findings. I once had a student in my class conduct an observational study of touching to see if sex is related to who initiated and received touch. She conducted the study on the bus and concluded that nobody touches anyone. This study suffered from a **selection bias;** people on the bus are not a representative sample, especially during the morning commute to work. To ensure a representative sample, the researcher should **randomly select** or **randomly sample** the participants from the population. Random selection ensures that each member of the population has an equal chance of being a participant in the study. You could randomly select a sample by putting the names of all the people in the population in a hat and drawing out a sample of names. You could assign every member of the population an identification number and randomly select a set of numbers. Imagine that you want a representative sample of 100 adults in your community and everyone in your community has a phone number that

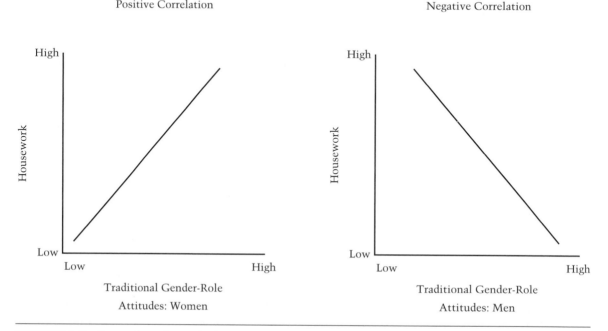

FIGURE 1.2   Examples of correlations.

begins with the same first three digits. You could have a computer generate a series of four-digit random sequences and call those phone numbers with those sequences. Would this procedure result in a random sample? Close—but the sample would be biased in one way: you would not be representing the people in your area who do not have telephones.

Although random selection is important for the validity of correlational research, it is difficult to achieve and rarely is employed. Often, we want to make inferences that generalize to the entire population, or at least the population of our country. It would be difficult to place 250 million names in a hat; thus, we approximate and randomly select from a community that we believe is fairly representative of the population. The important point to keep in mind is that we should generalize our findings only to the population it truly represents. This is particularly important in the study of gender because the vast majority of research has been conducted on White, middle-class Americans and findings may not generalize to people of other races, other classes, or other cultures.

You are probably wondering how a research participant pool at a university fits into the random selection process. The answer is: not very well. Do you have a research participant pool at your institution where you are asked to participate in a certain number of experiments? Or, are there postings that request volunteers to participate in research? In either case, you are probably choosing to participate in a particular experiment; that is, you were not randomly selected from the entire population of college students. Worse yet, the kinds of people who choose to participate in a certain experiment may not be representative of the entire population of students. One must keep this research limitation in mind when generalizing from the results of our studies.

Experimental Study

The second research method that we will discuss in this text is the **experimental method.** In an experiment, the investigator manipulates one variable, called the **independent variable,** and observes its effect on another variable, called the **dependent variable.** To keep these two concepts straight, remember that the dependent variable "depends on" the independent variable. In the experiment described previously, the instructions on how to interact with the puppy were the independent variable (caretaker vs. noncaretaker condition) and the behavior of nurturance was the dependent variable. Table 1.3 lists more examples of independent variables and dependent variables.

How do we know that other variables besides the independent variable—the instructions—aren't responsible for the effect on nurturance? Maybe the students in the caretaker condition were more nurturant with the animals than students in the noncaretaker condition because they had pets in their homes when they were growing up. This is possible but unlikely, because in an experiment participants are randomly assigned to condition. **Random assignment** means that each participant has an equal chance of being assigned to each condition. Because of random assignment, on average, the people in one condition will be comparable to the people in the other condition, with the exception of how they are treated with regard to the independent variable. Random assignment is a key feature of the experimental method.

Random assignment can be accomplished by flipping a coin or drawing numbers out of a hat. Random assignment means

TABLE 1.3   Examples of Independent and Dependent Variables

Research Question	Independent Variable	Dependent Variable
Is employment harmful to women's health?	Employment	Health
Does testosterone increase aggression?	Testosterone	Aggression
Is rumination a source of depression?	Rumination	Depression
Which relationships are closer—same-sex or other-sex?	Relationship type	Closeness
Are men or women smarter?	Sex	Intelligence
Does commitment in a relationship decrease power?	Commitment	Power
Are lesbians more masculine than heterosexual women?	Sexual orientation	Gender role
Is touching a function of status?	Status	Touching
Is housework divided more evenly among egalitarian couples?	Egalitarian vs. traditional	Division of labor
Do we smile more at male or at female infants?	Infant sex	Smiling

that there is no systematic way of assigning people to conditions. Dividing the classroom in half so that people on the right are in one group and people on the left are in another group would *not* be random. Theoretically, there could be differences between the kinds of people who sit on the right versus the left side of the classroom. In the classroom in which I teach, students who sit on the left side of the seminar table can look out the window, whereas students who sit on the right side have a view of the wall, so they might as well look at me. Imagine that you had asked participants to decide whether they wanted to play with the puppy or teach it tricks. If you let people choose their condition, the people in the two conditions would be different; nurturant people are likely to choose to play with the puppy. Differences in nurturant behavior between the two conditions would be due to a **selection bias** because people selected their own groups and were not randomly assigned to the condition.

Notice that some of the independent variables in Table 1.3 are changeable and some are not; that is, one can manipulate employment, testosterone, rumination, and relationship commitment to study their effects. In a true experiment, one must be able to manipulate the independent variable to study its effects. Other independent variables are not changeable, the most important of which is sex. When sex is a characteristic of a person, as in the research question "Are men or women smarter?" sex is referred to as a **subject variable.** Studies in which sex is a subject variable are not true experiments because someone cannot be randomly assigned to be male or female. The majority of research that compares men and women—evaluating similarities and differences between men's and women's behavior—is not experimental. We observe in the laboratory or in the real world how men and women think, feel, and behave. This research is correlational because we cannot manipulate a person's sex.

Is there any way that we can make sex comparisons in the context of an experimental design? We can make sex a **stimulus** or **target variable,** meaning that it is the characteristic of something to which people respond. Let's take the research question "Do we smile more at male or at female infants?" One way to answer that question is to compare how often adults smile at male and female infants. However, this would be a correlational study; we would be correlating infant sex with smiling, and sex would be a subject variable. We wouldn't know if infant sex caused the smiling or something else about the infant caused the smiling; for example, infant girls are more likely to wear pink and perhaps pink causes smiling. A better way to address this research question is by conducting an experimental study in which infant sex is a target variable. We could show people pictures of the same child and randomly tell one group that the infant is "Joe" and the other group that the infant is "Joelle." Then we can tell if people smile more at infants they perceive to be female compared to those they perceive to be male. When sex is a target variable, random assignment can take place and a true experiment can be conducted.

There are advantages and disadvantages to both correlational and experimental methods. The major ones are identified in Table 1.4. The advantage of the experimental

method is that cause and effect can be determined. The reason that cause and effect can be determined is that all other variables in the experiment are held constant except for the independent variable (the cause). Thus, any differences in the dependent variable (the effect) can be attributed only to the differences in the way the groups were treated. One point on which philosophers of science agree about causality is that the cause must precede the effect. In an experiment, the cause, by definition, precedes the effect. This is not always the case in a correlational study. Thus, the strength of the experimental method is **internal validity,** that is, being confident that you are measuring the true cause of the effect.

The disadvantage of the experimental method is that experiments are usually conducted in an artificial setting, such as a laboratory, so the experimenter can have control over the environment. Recall the experiment where people were interacting with a puppy. The experiment was set up to observe nurturant behavior. Do interactions with a puppy in a laboratory where people are told how to behave generalize to how adults on the whole interact with their own pets? Or to how they interact with their children? Results from these kinds of experiments may be less likely to generalize to the real world; that is, they are low in **external validity.** In the real world, men and women may be given very different messages about how to interact with puppies, babies, and adults. In addition, in the real world, people do not think that their behavior is being observed by an experimenter.

By contrast, a strength of the correlational method is external validity. You can observe behavior in a real-world setting so that you are studying the true behavior. You could ask people to report their true nurturant behavior on a questionnaire or you could unobtrusively observe nurturant

TABLE 1.4 Experimental Method versus Correlational Method

	Experimental	Correlational
Strength	Internal validity	External validity
Weakness	External validity	Internal validity

behavior by studying mothers and fathers with their children at school or during a doctor's visit. Recording the amount of time nurses spend with patients is a good indication of nurturant behavior.

Correlational studies can be easy to conduct. A quick survey allows one to collect a large amount of information at one time on a range of variables. The major disadvantage of the correlational method is that one cannot determine cause and effect because the variables are measured simultaneously. Recall the nursing study where sex differences in nurturant behavior were measured. If women spend more time than men with patients, can we conclude that women are more nurturant than men? Because people are not randomly assigned to sex, the male and female nurses may differ on a host of other variables aside from their sex. Perhaps the male nurses have positions of greater authority that do not allow time to talk to patients once nursing duties are completed; perhaps the patients spend more time talking to female than male nurses because they expect the female nurse to be more nurturant. In this case, it is the patient's behavior rather than the nurse's sex that is causing displays of nurturance. The problem with the correlational method is that you do not know which of these possibilities is correct. The correlational method lacks internal validity.

FIELD EXPERIMENT. There are rare occasions when the experimental method is taken into the real world, into what we call the field where the behavior under investigation naturally occurs. These are **field experiments.** Field experiments can be ideal because they have both internal and external validity. However, field experiments are difficult to conduct; it is much easier to control the environment of the laboratory than the real world. An example of a field experiment on gender and nurturance is randomly assigning men and women managers in a

business organization to receive different instructions on how to interact with their employees: to either teach them new information and technology (noncaretaker condition), or to make sure they all get along with one another and are happy (caretaker condition). The experiment has internal validity because people are randomly assigned to condition. On average, the only difference between the two groups of managers will be the instructions they received. The experiment will have external validity because we are observing actual nurturant behavior in a real-world setting: the organization. We could measure nurturant behavior in terms of offers to help the employee or time spent with the employee talking about likes and dislikes about the job. Now, imagine how likely an organization would be to let you randomly assign their managers to have different kinds of interactions with their employees. In addition, imagine how difficult it would be to ensure that *only* the independent variable differs between the two groups. There are many other variables that could influence managers' behavior that would be difficult to control: the way the manager is treated by his or her own boss, the nature of the employee's job (whether it involves working with others, whether it involves technology), and the number of employees that a single manager has. Would you be able to randomly assign a manager to focus on technology with one employee but focus on relationships with the other employee? Because field experiments do not have the same kind of controls over behavior that laboratory experiments do, they are difficult to conduct.

CROSS-SECTIONAL VERSUS LONGITUDINAL DESIGNS. Aside from conducting a field study, there is another way to enhance the internal validity of correlational studies. Recall that a correlational study usually measures the relation between two variables at a single point in time. This is not always the case. When a single time point is used, we say that the study is **cross-sectional.** However, we may measure the independent variable at one time and the dependent variable later; this is a **longitudinal** study. In a longitudinal study, there are multiple time points of study. Can we discern cause and effect with a longitudinal study? Remember that a key principle to establishing causality is that the cause precedes the effect. A longitudinal study helps to establish causality but does not ensure it. Let's take an example.

We could survey a group of women from the community to see if employment is related to health. If we conduct one survey at a single point in time, we are conducting a cross-sectional study. Let's say that we find a correlation: employment is associated with health. The problem is that we do not know if employment leads to better health or if healthier people are more likely to be employed. A longitudinal study may help to solve this problem. We could measure employment at one time (Time 1) and measure health six months later (Time 2). If employment at Time 1 is associated with health at Time 2, can we conclude that employment caused health? Only if we take into consideration Time 1 health. Time 1 employment must be associated with a change in health between Time 1 and Time 2.

Longitudinal studies help to establish causality and also help to distinguish **age effects** from **cohort effects.** A cohort refers to a group of people of similar age, such as a generation. In the cross-sectional study previously described, let's say that we find a relation between age and employment, such that older women are employed for fewer hours outside the home. Can we conclude that women decrease the amount of hours they spend in employed work as they get older? If so, this would be an age effect. However, in a cross-sectional design, one cannot distinguish age effects from cohort

effects, effects due to the generation of the people. Older women were raised at a time when women were less likely to be employed. Thus, the fact that older women work fewer hours outside the home might be due to the fact they held traditionally female jobs that require fewer hours. With a longitudinal design, one would take a single cohort of women (age 20 to 25) and follow them for years to see if their employment and health changed over time.

DIFFICULTIES IN CONDUCTING RESEARCH ON GENDER

Now that you understand the basic components of the research process, we can examine the difficulties that arise when applying this process to the study of gender. At each stage of the research process, the researcher, who is sometimes the experimenter, can intentionally or unintentionally influence the outcome. This influence can occur from the question asked, the way the study is designed, how the data are collected, how the data are interpreted, and how the results are communicated. Participants in experiments also can influence the outcome by their awareness of gender-role stereotypes, their desire to fit or reject gender-role norms, and their concerns with self-presentation. That is, participants care about how they appear to the experimenter and to other participants. Below, I first review the ways that the experimenter can influence the outcomes of studies and then the ways that the participant can influence those same outcomes.

Experimenter Effects

Experimenter effects refer to the ways the experimenter, or the person conducting the research, can influence the results of a study. Eagly (1978) reviewed studies on sex differences in conformity and found that the sex of the author influenced the results! It turned out that male authors were more likely than female authors to report sex differences in conformity (that women were more conforming than men), and female authors were more likely than male authors to report no sex differences in conformity. How can this be? One explanation is that people published studies that fit their expectations. Another explanation is that men and women experimenters designed different kinds of studies, with one design showing a sex difference and one not.

The experimenter can influence the outcome of a study at many levels. Each of these is described below and shown in Figure 1.3.

QUESTION ASKED AND STUDY DESIGN. First, the experimenter can influence the outcome of a study by the nature of the question asked and the subsequent design of the study. For example, a researcher could be interested in determining the effects of women working outside the home on children's well-being. One researcher may believe that it is harmful for women to work outside the home while they have small children. To test this hypothesis, the researcher could design a study in which children in day care are compared to children at home in terms of the number of days that they are sick in a year. Because the children at day care will be exposed to more germs, they will experience more sick days the first year than children at home. In this case, the experimenter's theory about mothers working outside the home being harmful to children will be supported. However, another experimenter may believe that mothers working outside the home is beneficial to children. This experimenter examines the reading level of kindergartners and finds that children whose mothers worked outside the home have higher reading levels than children whose mothers did not work outside the home. The problem here: the mothers who worked outside the home were more highly educated than the mothers who worked inside the home, and this education may have been transmitted to the children. In both cases, the experimenter's preexisting beliefs influenced the specific question asked and the way the study was designed to answer that question.

Most scientists are very interested in the phenomenon that they study and do have expectancies about the results of their work. In an area as controversial as gender, it is difficult to find a scientist who does not have a belief about the outcome of the study. It is all right to have an expectation, or hypothesis, based on scientific theory,

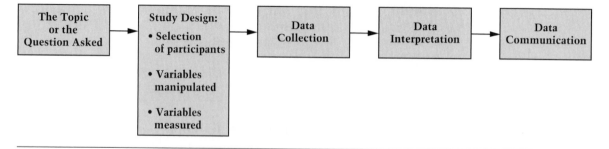

FIGURE 1.3   Stages of the research process that can be influenced by the experimenter.

but one must be cautious about hunches based on personal experiences and desires. The best situation is one in which the scientist conducting the research does not care about the outcome of the study and has little invested in it. But most of us do care about the outcomes of studies and are invested in those outcomes. As a mother who works outside the home, what would I do if I conducted a study and found that children whose mothers worked suffered? The task that the scientist must confront is to set aside preexisting beliefs and biases to conduct a study in as objective a way as possible. **Replication,** or the repeating of a study, by different investigators with different measures of the independent variable and the dependent variable helps to enhance our confidence in a finding.

STUDY DESIGN: PARTICIPANTS.   The experimenter can influence the outcome of the study by the specific participants who are chosen. Obviously, experimenters who limit their studies to all males or all females should question whether their findings generalize to the other sex. Experimenters who study both men and women should also be sensitive to other variables besides sex that could distinguish the two groups. For example, several decades ago, an experimenter who compared the mental health of men and women might have been evaluating employed men and nonemployed women because most men worked outside the home and most women did not. If such a study showed women to be more depressed than men, one might wonder whether this finding was attributable to being female or to not having a job outside the home. Today, any studies conducted of men and women would want to take into consideration employment status. There are other variables that may co-occur with sex and be responsible for any observed sex differences, such as income, occupational status, and even

health. Investigators should make sure they are studying comparable groups of men and women.

STUDY DESIGN: VARIABLES MANIPULATED AND MEASURED.   The experimenter can influence the outcome of a study through the variables that are manipulated and measured. McKenna and Kessler (1977) discovered that the way a variable was manipulated in an experiment differed depending on whether the participants were male or female. They examined studies on aggression and found that aggression as an independent variable took a more passive form among studies of women than among studies of men. That is, aggression was manipulated in studies of women by having people read about a frustrating situation. Aggression was more likely to be manipulated in studies of men by having people treated in a hostile manner. Would it surprise you if these studies showed that males responded more aggressively to being ridiculed than females did to reading about being stuck in a traffic jam? When aggression was a dependent variable, the behavior recorded was likely to be passive in the case of female participants and active in the case of male participants. Aggression was more likely to be measured by overt behavior, such as shocking another person, in studies of men, and by more passive behavior, such as ratings of aggressive feelings on a self-report questionnaire, in studies of women.

Dependent measures, in particular, can be biased in favor of males or females. A study that compares male and female mathematical ability by asking children to make calculations of baseball averages is biased against females to the extent that boys and girls have different experiences with baseball. A study that evaluates sex differences in helping behavior by measuring how quickly a person responds to an infant's cries is biased against males to the extent that men and women have different experiences with children. During the teenage years, girls are more likely than boys to baby-sit as a way to earn extra money, so it may be that females feel more comfortable than males in picking up a crying infant. A helping situation that is biased in the direction of males is assisting someone with a flat tire on the side of the road. Here, you may find that men are more likely than women to provide assistance, because men may have more experience changing tires than women. It is unlikely that men have a "tire-changing" gene that women do not possess, just as it is unlikely that women have a "diaper-changing" gene that men do not possess. Men are provided with more opportunities to change tires just as women are provided with more opportunities to console a crying infant. Thus, in generalizing across studies, one has to ensure that the different ways a dependent variable is measured do not account for the different findings.

DATA COLLECTION. The experimenter can influence the outcome of a study by how the data are collected. The experimenter may treat men and women differently in a way that supports the hypothesis. Rosenthal (1966) found that male and female experimenters smiled more and glanced more at same-sex participants than other-sex participants while giving the experimental instructions. He concluded that men and women are not in the same experiment when the experimenter is aware of their sex.

For example, an experimenter may be examining sex differences in communication and want to test the hypothesis that women make more eye contact than men. The experimenter may inadvertently make more eye contact with female than with male participants, which leads to greater reciprocation by the women. The experimenter also can influence participants'

behavior by giving subtle cues like nodding of the head to indicate that the correct response is being given. An experimenter might believe women self-disclose more than men; the experimenter could engage male and female participants in a conversation in a way that elicits more self-disclosure on the part of females by revealing more personal information to female participants than to male participants. As you will see in Chapter 7, both men and women feel more comfortable disclosing to women than to men. The experimenter might provide subtle nonverbal cues that encourage female disclosure (e.g., head nodding, open posture, smiling, looking attentive) and subtle cues that discourage male disclosure (e.g., looking bored, not paying attention, shifting around anxiously in one's seat).

The experimenter's beliefs can influence his or her own behavior, which then encourages participants to respond in a way that confirms the experimenter's beliefs. That is, the participant's behavior becomes a **self-fulfilling prophecy.** In these cases, experimenters are probably not intentionally influencing the outcome, but their beliefs are subtly influencing their own behavior and, consequently, the participant's behavior. It may be difficult for experimenters to treat male and female participants equally because most experimenters are aware of gender-role stereotypes and the norms for male and female behavior. One way to minimize this bias is for the investigator to hire an experimenter who is blind to the purpose of the study, especially the hypotheses. In this situation, your only concern is that the experimenter brings to the study his or her lay perceptions of how men and women differ. A better solution is to have the experimenter blind to the participant's sex. This can be accomplished by providing standardized instructions or questions to participants via an audiotape or intercom, so that the experimenter cannot see the participant.

DATA INTERPRETATION. The experimenter can influence the outcome of the study by the way he or she interprets the data. When I was in graduate school, a fellow student and I set out to resolve an ongoing debate in the literature about whether women fear achievement and men fear affiliation. (This research will be discussed in more depth in Chapter 5.) We had college students write stories in reaction to scenes of men and women. We then coded the stories for themes of violence, which were taken to be indications of fear. Coding stories is subjective; pushing someone off a bridge is certainly an act of violence, but should "dreaming of falling" be categorized as a theme of violence? This is a difficult judgment, and a judgment that one would not want to be influenced by knowing the respondent's sex. Thus, we guarded against bias by removing the participant's name and sex from the stories. However, if you read a story, do you think that you can determine the sex of the author? There still may have been subtle cues, such as handwriting and jargon, that could have conveyed the person's sex to us.

In many cases, it is difficult to be blind to the participant's sex, especially if you are conducting a study where you are observing a behavior. This is especially problematic because the same behavior may be interpreted differently when it is displayed by a male versus a female. Imagine that you observe someone screaming. If the person screaming is female, you may interpret the behavior as hysteria; if the person screaming is male, you may interpret the behavior as anger. If someone asserts an opinion at a business meeting, we may interpret this behavior as assertive if male and aggressive if female. The following study illustrates how people can interpret the same behavior differently depending on an individual's sex.

A study was conducted in which college students were shown a videotape of an infant playing with a teddy bear, a doll, a buzzer, and a jack-in-the-box (Condry & Condry, 1976). Students were asked to rate the intensity of the infant's emotional responses to each object. Students were randomly assigned to one of two conditions in which they were told that the infant was a girl, "Dana," or a boy, "David." The infant's emotional responses to the teddy bear and the doll were consistently positive, and the infant's emotional responses to the buzzer were consistently negative, regardless of whether the infant was seen as Dana or David. Students perceived the infant's response to the jack-in-the-box differently, however, depending on the infant's sex: if the infant was thought to be a male, his crying was viewed as showing anger; if the infant was thought to be a female, her crying was viewed as showing fear. Thus, the same behavior—crying—was interpreted as fear in one case and anger in the next. In addition, the male students showed larger differences in their ratings of the infant's response to the jack-in-the-box. The authors concluded that people view behavior similarly when it is clear-cut, but that under conditions of ambiguity, such as the situation with the jack-in-the-box, behavior may be interpreted differently depending on whether it is displayed by a male or a female. This study has far-reaching implications for our behavior as adults. Just think how differently you would respond to someone who was afraid versus someone who was angry.

The idea that behavior is interpreted differently when it is displayed by a male versus a female is the subject of a sex discrimination case described in Chapter 2. A female accountant displayed stereotypical masculine behavior by being assertive, behavior that was normative for the accountant role but not for the female gender role. Her behavior was construed in negative terms and led to her failure to become a partner in the firm.

Even when the interpretation of a behavior in an experiment is clear, the overall outcome of an experiment may be subject to different interpretations. For example, one behavior that has received a great deal of attention in the gender literature is conformity. The question is: Are women more conforming than men? But why isn't the question Are men more independent than women, or Are men less compliant than women? If more women than men agree with a group of people and more men than women disagree with a group of people, are women conforming or are men being independent? A study by Eagly and colleagues manipulated the conditions that surrounded conformity and found that men's being more independent than women was a more accurate statement of the results than women's being more conforming than men (Eagly, Wood, & Fishbaugh, 1981). Eagly manipulated whether participants indicated their agreement or disagreement with other people publicly or privately; the results are shown in Table 1.5. In the public condition, women showed more conformity than men; in the private condition, however, there were no sex differences in conformity and men's and women's behavior was more like that of women in the public

condition. Thus, the deviant cell in this study was when men expressed their public opinion. Instead of showing that women are more concerned with appearing agreeable in the presence of other people, the study showed that men are more concerned with appearing independent in the presence of other people.

COMMUNICATION OF RESULTS. Finally, the experimenter can influence the impact of a study by how the findings are communicated. Experimenters may report only results that support their hypotheses. That is, experimenters who believe there are sex differences may conduct a dozen studies until a difference appears and then report that one difference. Experimenters who believe there are no differences between men and women may conduct a dozen studies, slightly altering the situation in each one, until no difference appears and then report that study. This is a problem for the study of gender because, as you will see later, there are two political philosophies: that there are only a few small sex differences and that there are major sex differences that pervade our lives.

Another problem with the communication of results is that sex differences are inherently more interesting than sex similarities; thus, studies of differences are more likely to be published. A researcher who designs a study that does not involve issues of gender may routinely compare men's and women's behavior in the hope that no differences are found. In this case, the investigator considers sex to be a nuisance variable. If no differences are found, gender is probably not mentioned in the article, so there is no record of the similarity! If differences are found, gender may become the focus of the study. Some people argue that sex differences should be routinely examined in all research (e.g., Eagly, 1987a). Others suggest that sex differences should be examined *only* when there is theoretical

TABLE 1.5   Conformity or Independence?

	Women	Men
Public	8.51	6.92
Private	8.55	8.12

Note: Numbers reflect the extent of agreement with the confederate, or degree of conformity.
Source: Adapted from Eagly, Wood, and Fishbaugh (1981).

justification for doing so, and that sex differences not grounded in theory should be replicated before being published (McHugh et al., 1986).

The scientific bias of publishing differences is perpetuated by the media, who are not likely to pick up a story on a study that shows sex similarities. A study that shows differences is going to gather the attention of the media and will be placed in a prominent place in the newspaper.

Susan Faludi (1991) published a book entitled *Backlash: The Undeclared War Against American Women* in which she describes somewhat questionable research findings that are published by the media even when refuted by other scientific research—according to Faludi, because they support the culture of the time. For example, a story in the newspaper appeared showing that the chances of a single college-educated woman getting married at age 30 was 20%, at age 35 was 5%, and at age 40 was 1.3%. The study made front page news, despite questionable methods and a small sample size. A follow-up study that used actual census data showed quite different statistics: at age 30, 58% to 66%; at age 35, 32% to 41%, and at age 40, 17% to 23%. The follow-up study, however, was not picked up by the media. Faludi reports another example having to do with the effect of divorce on income. The study received a great deal of media attention because it showed that divorce led women to experience a 73% decline in their standard of living and men to experience a 42% increase in their standard of living. By contrast, another study showed the decrease for women was much smaller, 30%, and the increase for men was much smaller, 10% to 15%. It did not receive publicity. Finally, a study of infertility widely noted in newspapers and on radio and television talk shows showed that women between the ages of 31 and 35 had a 40% chance of becoming infertile. Reporters did not note, however, that

this study was based on a very unique sample: women receiving artificial insemination because their husbands were sterile. A subsequent study based on a more representative sample showed that the infertility rate for women between the ages of 30 and 34 was 14%, only 3% more than women in their early 20s.

Faludi's position, obviously, is that research findings showing adverse effects of the women's movement on women's economics, fertility, and relationships are being highlighted, whereas research findings showing positive effects of the women's movement are stifled. Regardless of whether Faludi's overall claim is correct, these examples show that the media are more likely to sensationalize the more outrageous research findings and are less likely to highlight findings that are less interesting. Sex differences are interesting; sex similarities are not. One of the skills you will gain from reading this text is being able to evaluate reports about sex differences that you read in the popular press. Start now by trying Exercise 1.3.

In summary, we need to be alert to how experimenter expectancies can shape the results of studies. One remedy is to have a team of scientists with opposing beliefs conduct research on a topic. Why do you think this does not happen very often? Social psychologists have shown that we are attracted to people who are like us, people who share our beliefs and values. Thus, it is more likely that we will find ourselves collaborating with people who share our beliefs about the outcome of a study. Replication is another strategy that we have built into science as a check on the influence experimenters have on research findings. Before taking a finding seriously, we make sure that it has been repeated—repeated with different samples, repeated with different measures of both the independent and dependent variables, and repeated by different investigators. We can be more

---

EXERCISE 1.3
Comparing Media Reports to Scientific Reports

Find a news article on gender, most likely on sex differences, in the newspaper or news magazines. Find one that refers to the original source of the study; that is, it gives the reference to a scientific journal. Compare the news version of the study to the scientific report of the study. Answer the following questions:

1. Did the news article accurately reflect the findings of the scientific study?

2. What did the news article leave out, if anything?

3. What did the news article exaggerate, if anything?

4. Was there anything in the news article that was misleading?

5. What did you learn by reading the scientific article that you wouldn't have learned by reading the news article?

6. Why did this particular study appear in the news? Was it important? Was the finding "catchy"?

---

confident of similarities or differences between male and female behavior when we see them emerge repeatedly and over a wide variety of contexts. As shown in Chapter 3, however, changing the context usually alters how men and women behave.

Participant Effects

The ways in which participants of an experiment can influence the outcome of a study are referred to as **demand characteristics.** There are certain demands or expectations about how to behave as a participant in an experiment. Participants often conform to or react against these demands. The **social desirability response bias** is one example of a demand characteristic. That is, people want to behave in socially desirable ways, ways in which they appear normal and likable. In our society, it is socially desirable for men to appear masculine and women to appear feminine. On self-report inventories of masculinity and femininity, men typically will rate themselves as high on masculinity and women will rate themselves as high on femininity regardless of how they really score on traits that define those concepts. That is, regardless of whether a man rates himself as independent or self confident (traits we ascribe to masculinity), most men will rate themselves as masculine. Thus, participants may behave in ways that fit their gender role, especially if they realize the purpose of the experiment.

If I asked the students in my class for a show of hands as to who is emotional, more women than men would raise their hands. If I asked the students for a show of hands as to who is aggressive, more men than women would raise their hands. Does this mean that men are more aggressive than women and women more emotional than men? Certainly not—not on the basis of that hand showing. It is socially desirable for men to say they are aggressive and women to say they are emotional. The design of the study is poor because the public behavior increases the chance of introducing a social desirability response bias. One precaution that you can take to guard against demand characteristics is to have responses be private—anonymous and confidential—rather than public. Another precaution is to disguise the purpose of the experiment.

One study showed that men's and women's behavior conformed to gender-role expectations when the behavior was public but not when the behavior was private. Men and women college students were asked to look at pictures of infant monkeys and to rate the animal's "emotional appeal" (P. Berman, 1975, cited in Tavris & Wade, 1984). The men and women were randomly assigned to one of two conditions: public or private. The study showed that women gave higher ratings of attraction in the public than the private condition, whereas men gave higher ratings of attraction in the private than the public condition. Why? It is socially desirable for women to be attracted to small, fuzzy animals but not so for men, and so their behavior conformed to this norm in the public condition where people could view their responses.

In a review of the literature on responsiveness to infants, women were found to be more responsive to infants than men when self-report measures were used (P. Berman, 1980). For example, women reported being more upset by an infant's cries than did men. However, when physiological measures of responsiveness were taken, no sex differences in responsiveness appeared. If physiological measures of heart rate, blood pressure, and skin conductance reflect our true responses (which is debatable), the self-reported sex differences could merely reflect men and women adhering to their gender roles. Men and women may simply be reporting behavior that confirms your and their expectancy.

This problem may have surfaced in a study I conducted on the kind of support men and women provide (Mickelson, Helgeson, & Weiner, 1995). There is a strong popular notion, which has less scientific basis, that women provide more emotional support than men. Emotional support involves listening, expressions of caring, and sympathy. To test this idea, we had men and women disclose a problem to a stranger, another male or female college student. We audiotaped the responses of the stranger to examine whether men and women provided different kinds of support. When we coded the anonymous transcripts of these conversations for type of support, we were surprised to find that men and women were equally likely to provide emotional support. However, we also asked the listeners to indicate the kinds of support they provided. Female listeners reported providing more emotional support than male listeners. One interpretation of this finding is that there truly are no sex differences in provision of emotional support, but men and women expect there to be a difference and so perceive a difference. The men and women in the study could have been reporting behavior that fits their gender roles.

One remedy to the problem of participant effects is to have multiple measures of a behavior. For example, if you want to know how men and women compare in terms of assertiveness, you could examine self-reports of assertiveness, you could set up an experiment to elicit assertive behavior, and you could obtain other people's reports of participants' assertive behavior. In studies of aggression among children, a frequently used measure of other people's reports is peer nomination. All of the children in the class nominate the most aggressive child, the child most difficult to get along with, or the child who makes them afraid. When one person is named by the majority of the children, we can have a great deal of confidence that the child is exhibiting some kind of behavioral problem.

The Setting: Laboratory versus Field

Much of our research on gender is conducted in the laboratory rather than the field, or the real world. There are a number of problems in applying the conclusions from research on gender conducted in the laboratory to our everyday lives, specifically, problems with external validity. In the laboratory, everything is held constant except the independent variable, which is usually participant's sex. Thus, men and women come into the laboratory and face equal treatment and equal conditions. The problem is that men and women do not face equal conditions in the real world. Thus, one might be more likely to find similar behavior in the laboratory than in the real world. If that is the case, the differences in behavior observed in the real world might be due to the different situations in which men and women find themselves.

For example, if you bring men and women into the laboratory and then provoke them, they may display similar levels of anger. However, in the real world, women are more likely than men to hold low status positions where displays of anger are inappropriate and often punished. In addition, in the real world, men are provoked more often than women. Thus, men may display more anger than women in the real world because men are more often provoked than women and women are more often punished for displays of anger compared to men. Self-disclosure is another example of a behavior that may appear more similar between men and women in the laboratory than in the real world. If you ask men and women similar kinds of questions in a similar manner in the laboratory, you may find men and women equally likely to self-disclose. But, in the real world, men and women are more likely to encourage self-disclosure in women because people are uncomfortable with men self-disclosing. Laboratory studies show that women and men are equally capable of expressing anger and self-disclosing under similar conditions; however, men and women do not face similar conditions in the real world.

Another difficulty with laboratory research is that it is often conducted on college students (Sears, 1986). College students differ from the general population in a number of ways. They are more likely to be White, upper to middle class, higher in education, and homogeneous on a number of dimensions. The college experience is one in which the roles of men and women and the statuses of men and women are more similar compared to their situations after college. Thus, it is questionable whether one can generalize the similarities observed among college students to the general population.

Variables Confounded with Sex

A fundamental problem for the study of gender is that one cannot randomly assign a person to be male or female. As mentioned earlier, sex is usually a subject variable rather than a true independent variable that can be manipulated. You can manipulate sex when you are leading respondents to believe that the sex of a target person is what you want them to believe it is. Here, sex is a target variable. However, when comparing men's and women's feelings, thoughts, and behavior, we cannot be certain that any differences found are due to sex alone; men and women come into the laboratory with their own values, histories, and experiences. Most important, sex is confounded with status.

We cannot separate the effects of sex from status. Is it that women smile more than men, or is it that low-status people smile more than high-status people? We will see in Chapter 6 that many of the sex differences observed in verbal and nonverbal communication seem to be due to status. When men and women are randomly assigned to a high-status or low-status position in the laboratory, high-status persons of both sexes typically display "male" behavior and low-status persons of both sexes typically display "female" behavior.

If you are questioning whether men have a higher status than women in the United States, ponder the following. One piece of evidence could be reflected in childbearing. Pohlman (1969) found that people waited longer to have a second child if the first child was a boy than a girl. People also were more likely to have a third child if the first two were girls than if they were boys. More recent data suggest that people still prefer their firstborn to be a boy (Gilroy & Steinbacher, 1983; McDougall, DeWit & Ebanks, 1999). This preference is stronger among men than women (Gilroy & Steinbacher, 1983). In 1997, a Gallup Poll was conducted of around 1,000 adults in each of 16 countries across Asia, Europe, North America, and Latin America. Respondents were asked which sex they would prefer if they could have only one child. In 13 of the 16 countries, the preference was for a boy over a girl. In the United States, 35% preferred a boy, 23% preferred a girl, and 42% expressed no preference. These preferences are shown in Table 1.6.

It appears that children are all too aware of the status difference between men and women. In the early 1980s, over 2,000 children, ranging from third to twelfth grade, were asked to imagine what it would be like to wake up as the other sex. Some sample responses are shown in Table 1.7. You can see that the transition for girls to boys is not all bad; girls say they would have more freedom, would have a closer relationship with their father, and wouldn't have to think as much about appearance. The transition for boys to girls, however, is much more harsh; boys now have new sources of worry: appearance, sexual abuse, and more restrictions.

In the 1990s, I asked over 300 college students to write essays on the same question, and similar themes resulted. Men and women were able to identify positives and negatives in considering the transformation. Women noted several advantages:

TABLE 1.6 Preference for Child's Sex, in Percentages

	Boy	Girl	No Opinion
Canada	26	16	58
Colombia	35	27	38
France	41	31	28
Germany	21	19	60
Great Britain	31	26	43
Guatemala	23	13	64
Hungary	25	12	63
Iceland	12	16	72
India	40	27	33
Lithuania	33	34	33
Mexico	31	24	45
Singapore	19	11	70
Spain	20	27	53
Taiwan	29	9	62
Thailand	44	27	29
United States	35	23	42

Source: Gallup News Service (1997).

they would be less afraid, more adventurous, and more independent; but also several disadvantages: they would have more difficulty receiving support, they would have less meaningful conversations. Some aspects of life were considered to have mixed effects. Women said that having to work would be a negative, but this would be offset by more opportunities for advancement. On the positive side, women said that they would be taken more seriously as men, but on the negative side this meant more would be expected of them. Men noted primarily negatives in their hypothetical transformations to women; becoming more nervous, more self-conscious, and more concerned about appearance, worrying about men coming on to them, and worrying about walking alone at night. One of the advantages men noted was similar to the disadvantage women noted: as women, the men said they would have more friends and be

TABLE 1.7   Schoolchildren's Perceptions of Life as the Opposite Sex

As Boys, Girls Would Expect to	Representative Responses (Grade Level in Parentheses)
Be more assertive and self-reliant	"I think I would be more outspoken and confident." (tenth)
Show less emotion	"I would have to stay calm and cool whenever something happened." (tenth)
Become more aggressive	"I could beat up people." (sixth) "I'd probably need to start cussing." (eleventh) "I'd have to be more (rowdy, macho, smart-alecky, noisy, etc.)." (various) "I'd kill my art teacher, instead of arguing with him as I do now." (eighth)
Have more freedom	"I could stay out later." (unspecified) "There would be fewer rules." (unspecified) "I'd be trusted more when driving." (unspecified)
Think less about appearance	"I wouldn't have to be neat." (fourth) "I wouldn't have to worry how I look." (sixth) "If I woke up tomorrow and I was a boy . . . I would go back to bed since it would not take one very long to get ready for school." (tenth)
Be freed from treatment as a sex object	"[I'd no longer have to experience] leers while walking down the street." (eleventh) (Many girls noted that they would not have to worry about rape.)
Perform different duties at home	"I would take out the garbage instead of doing the ironing." (twelfth) "I wouldn't have to babysit." (sixth)
Spend more time with and be closer to their fathers	"I could go hunting and fishing with my dad." (sixth) "My dad would . . . teach me how to work with wood." (sixth) "My father would be closer because I'd be the son he always wanted." (sixth) "If I were a boy, my Daddy might have loved me." (third)

TABLE 1.7   (continued)

As Girls, Boys Would Expect to	Representative Responses (Grade Level in Parentheses)
Be quieter and more reserved	"[I'd have to] . . . wait for others to talk to me first." (tenth) "I'd have to be (nicer, more polite, goodie-goodie, like a lady, etc.)." (various)
Be less active	"Instead of wrestling with my friends, I'd be sitting around discussing the daily gossip." (unspecified) "I would play girl games and not have many things to do during the day." (unspecified) "I would have to hate snakes. Everything would be miserable." (unspecified) "I couldn't climb trees or jump the creek." (unspecified)
Be more restricted	"I'd have to come in earlier." (unspecified) "I couldn't have a pocket knife." (unspecified) "I couldn't throw spit wads." (unspecified)
Worry more about appearance	"I couldn't be a slob any more. I'd have to smell pretty." (eighth) "I'd have to shave my whole body!" (sixth) "I would use a lot of makeup and look good and beautiful, knowing that few people would care for my personality." (twelfth)
Be treated as sex objects	"If I were gorgeous, I would be jeered at and hear plenty of comments." (twelfth) "I'd have to watch out for boys making passes at me." (third)
Worry about violence against females	"I'd have to know how to handle drunk guys and rapists." (eighth) "I would have to be around other girls for safety." (eleventh)
Perform different duties at home	"I would dust the house instead of vacuuming." (fourth) "I would be the one who has the kid." (eighth)
Do fewer things with their fathers	"I would not help my dad wash the car or gas up the car." (fourth) "I would not be able to help my dad fix the car and truck and his two motorcycles." (sixth)

Source: Alice Baumgartner, "My dad might have loved me." Student perceptions of differences between being male and being female. Paper published by the Institute of Equality in Education, Denver, 1983.

more sociable. Conduct your own experiment on this issue in Exercise 1.4.

Another variable besides status that is confounded with sex is gender role. When we observe a sex difference in a behavior, is it due to the biological category of male or female, or is it due to the psychological category of gender? Too often, we fail to examine whether the difference is due to sex or to gender role. One area of research where there is substantial agreement as to whether a sex difference exists is aggression. Even aggression, however, may be partly due to biological sex and partly due to gender role, that is, our encouragement of aggression among males and discouragement of aggression among females. As described in Chapter 13, features of the male gender role have been linked to aggression. Throughout this book, we will be very attentive to the impact that gender roles have in areas of sex differences.

Situational Influences

Even if we examine personality traits in addition to participant's sex, we often find that in some situations we observe a difference and in some situations we do not observe a difference. Some situations are high in behavioral constraints, meaning that the behavior required in the situation is clear and not very flexible; in this case, sex may have little to do with behavior. A graduation ceremony is such a situation. Men and women are usually dressed alike in robes, march into the ceremony together, and sit throughout the ceremony quietly until their name is called to receive the diploma. The behavior in this situation will be determined more by the situation than by characteristics of the people, including their sex. There are other situations that are low in behavioral constraints that would allow the opportunity for men and women to display different behaviors; informal social gatherings are an example of such a situation.

There also are situations that make gender especially salient. A wedding is such a situation. Here, the norms for men's and women's attire are very different; no one expects men and women to dress the same at a wedding. The dress is formal; it would be unusual for a man to attend a wedding in a dress or a woman to attend a wedding in a tuxedo. There are traditions that make sex salient. The bride does not throw the bouquet to the entire crowd, only to eligible women; likewise, the groom throws the garter to eligible men. This is an occasion that may make differences in the behavior of men and women more likely to appear.

There also may be specific situational pressures to behave in accordance with or in opposition to one's gender role. Being raised in a traditional family, I have often found myself behaving in ways more consistent with the female gender role when I am with my family than when I am at home. During large family gatherings at holidays, it is customary for the women to tend to the dishes and the men to tend to the football. Do I help with the dishes? Of course. It would be rude not to. Besides, I don't really like football. Would my

EXERCISE 1.4
Life as the Other Sex

Select an age group. Ask 10 males and 10 females to answer the following question: "Imagine that you woke up tomorrow and were the other sex. Go through your entire day and describe how your life would be different."

Read through the stories and identify themes, such as the ones shown in Table 1.7. Construct a frequency distribution of those themes.

husband help with the dishes? Probably not. He likes football and would be shooed out of the kitchen.

There may be other situations in which behaving in opposition to gender roles is attractive. I remember the first time I went to look for a car by myself. The salesperson guided me to the cars with automatic transmissions and made some remark about women not being able to drive cars with a manual transmission. The worst part was that he was right; I had tried and couldn't drive a stick shift. But that incident inspired me. I was determined to learn how to drive a stick shift and to buy a car with a manual transmission—to do my part in breaking down that stereotype. I drive a car with a manual transmission and probably always will because of that salesperson's remark. In this case, the situation made gender roles salient, but the effect was to create behavior inconsistent with gender roles.

The situational forces that shape behavior are a dominant theme in this book. One cannot study gender outside of the context in which it occurs, the situations in which men and women find themselves and the people with whom they interact. This is the social psychological perspective and a perspective that is emphasized throughout this book.

PHILOSOPHICAL AND POLITICAL ISSUES SURROUNDING GENDER

The last issue that is important to address in an introductory chapter to the psychological study of gender is the philosophical and political debates that have taken place. The study of gender, in particular the study of sex differences, is a politically charged topic. With gender, scientists are often in one of two camps: those who believe that there are important differences between the sexes and those who believe that the two sexes are fundamentally the same. There are also investigators who believe that we should or should not compare men and women for a variety of reasons. I address each of these debates and then turn to the political movements that have influenced the study of gender: the women's movements and the men's movements. Finally, I conclude this section by providing some hints on how to write in a nonsexist manner.

The Sex Difference Debate

The people who believe the two sexes are fundamentally the same are known as the **minimalists.** The minimalists believe that there are very few differences between men and women and that if the context was held constant, differences would vanish. That is, any differences in behavior observed between men and women might be due to the roles they hold or the situations in which they find themselves.

By contrast, the **maximalists** believe that there are fundamental differences between men and women. Historically, the maximalists believed that male traits were more highly valued (Bohan, 1997). One concern with work on sex differences is that male behavior has been viewed as the norm, so women are always compared to men. Recall the previous example where women were said to be more conforming than men rather than men being more independent than women. More recently, theorists such as Carol Gilligan and Nancy Chodorow have argued in favor of sex differences, but point out that women's views of the world and ways of relating to the world are not inferior to those of men. In 1982, Gilligan published *In a Different Voice,* in which she claimed that men and women have fundamentally different ways of viewing morality. Here, the emphasis was on maximizing differences between the sexes. The key point that Gilligan made—and the novel point—is that "difference" does not mean "deficit." That is, women's view of morality is different from that of men but equally valuable, not deficient in any way. These maximalists argue that there are two very different and equally valuable ways of relating to the world.

You may be wondering, Why should I care about this debate? The reason you should care is that one's political philosophy determines how one interprets a research finding. Take the sex difference in math. There is a sex difference and the difference is statistically significant. The difference is also small. One group of researchers will emphasize that the size of the effect is small, that most men and women have similar aptitudes in math, and that only a small percentage of highly gifted men account for this difference. These people also might argue that we should ignore the difference. Another group of researchers will emphasize the fact that the difference is real and that even small differences can have large effects. These investigators will devote time and economic resources to understanding the cause of the difference and how to eliminate the difference.

Whether someone is a minimalist or a maximalist also has implications for whether gender is worth studying. A maximalist would certainly find gender worth studying, whereas not all minimalists would agree.

Should We Study Gender?

Now let us turn to the question of whether comparing men and women is a legitimate domain of study. Quite a debate has emerged over this issue. McHugh and her colleagues (1986) argued that sex comparisons could be made but that results should not be reported unless there is a theoretical rationale to explain them. This approach would eliminate the problem of investigators routinely testing for sex differences without cause and publishing differences when they find them. McHugh et al. believe that sex differences that do not have a theoretical rationale should be replicated before being published.

Eagly (1987a), however, disagrees. She responded to McHugh et al.'s (1986) request by suggesting quite the opposite approach: that investigators routinely report the results of sex comparisons in their research whether they are hypothesized or not. Eagly argued that McHugh et al.'s ideas would bias the literature in favor of differences because most theories are about differences. Eagly also was concerned that McHugh et al.'s idea of publishing only the results of sex comparisons that are theoretically based would bias the literature in favor of research that upholds rather than challenges existing theories. If an investigator happened on a finding that there was a domain of math ability in which women outperformed men (which turns out to be true, by the way, as will be seen in Chapter 3), the investigator wouldn't be able to publish the finding because it didn't fit with previous research. Because the finding isn't published, there wouldn't be the opportunity for others to find out about the result and try to replicate it.

McHugh et al. (1986) suggested that a cautionary note about the small size of the difference should be attached to sex difference reports. Eagly (1995) argues against this idea because such a note would need to be attached to all psychological research. Eagly argues that most sex differences are in the small to moderate range but that the size of the effects are similar to most variables examined in psychological research: "The magnitude and the consistency across studies of sex-difference findings show a range of values that is probably fairly typical of the range of values produced for many other areas of inquiry in psychology" (p. 154). She also noted that the impact of most psychological variables is affected by context. Eagly suggests that the minimalists avoid asking the question Are there sex differences? because they are afraid that the observance of differences will justify the unequal treatment of women.

Roy Baumeister (1988) responded to both Eagly (1987a) and McHugh et al. (1986) by suggesting that the entire field of comparing men and women should be completely abandoned. He said that the reason the field of sex differences emerged was to raise people's consciousness about the exclusion of women from research. Because women are now routinely included in studies, there is no longer any need to compare men and women. He argued that the study of sex comparisons perpetuates stereotypes and, in agreement with McHugh et al., can legitimize discrimination: "By reporting and discussing sex differences, psychology contributes to the persistence of discrimination" (p. 1093). He disagreed with Eagly that the routine investigation of differences would reveal similarities that would challenge stereotypes because the media are not as interested in similarities as in differences. Because people are not randomly assigned to sex, the study of sex differences is not about sex per se, according to Baumeister; it is about some other variable that is related to sex, such as status. Baumeister argued that scientists should spend their energies focused on these other variables rather than sex.

Social Construction of Gender

The **constructionists** no doubt would agree with Baumeister's (1988) position. They maintain that it is fruitless to study gender because gender cannot be divorced from its context (Marecek, 1995). Constructionists maintain that gender is created by the perceiver: facts about gender do not exist, only interpretations. The constructionists challenge the use of the scientific method to study gender because they maintain that you cannot view the world objectively; our history, experiences, and beliefs affect what we observe (Unger, 1990). Marecek argues that the empirical method is not untainted by social forces, and that science is not as value-free as some expect.

Constructionists argue that psychologists should not study sex differences because such studies assume that gender is a static quality of an individual (Hare-Mustin & Marecek, 1998). They maintain that gender is a dynamic social construct that is ever changing, a social category created by society. Bohan (1997) nicely illustrates the difference between the perspective of people who study sex differences and the constructionists. Sex difference researchers would describe a person as friendly; constructionists would describe an interaction as friendly. The people who perceive the interaction as friendly have a shared definition of friendliness. Now, we can translate this line of thinking to the study of sex comparisons. Researchers who make sex comparisons might describe women as more empathic than men. Constructionists would focus on the empathy involved in the interaction, the factors that contributed to the empathy, and how empathy becomes linked to women more than men. The constructionists would examine the explanations as to why empathy was illustrated more in women in this particular situation.

Constructionists are concerned that the study of sex comparisons ignores the variability within women and within men. The study of sex comparisons also ignores the situations and circumstances that influence men's and women's behavior. Constructionists argue that the question of whether men and women are similar or different is the wrong question to ask. Questions that ought to be asked revolve around how social institutions, culture, and language contribute to gender and to gendered interactions.

In Chapter 3, I review the literature that has compared men and women, being careful to point out the size of the effects, the variability within sexes, the extent to which the situation or context influences sex differences, and the potential for researcher biases. As we have seen, people can influence research by the questions asked and the way studies are designed. Many of the concerns raised by the constructionists are addressed in that chapter.

Women's Movements

It is a common misconception that the women's movement in the United States first began in the 1960s (Murstein, 1974). Women's movements first emerged in the 1800s. The issues that these women confronted, however, were different from those of contemporary women. These women believed men and women were fundamentally different, and they did not seek to equalize the roles of men and women. Instead, women aimed for greater respect for their domestic role (Murstein, 1974). Women in the 1800s and early 1900s were concerned with abolition, temperance, and child labor laws. These issues became "women's issues" because women were the ones to raise them. But these women discovered that their low-status position in society kept their voices from being heard. In 1920, women finally gained the right to vote. After that, the women's movement remained fairly silent until the 1960s.

In 1963, Betty Friedan published *The Feminine Mystique,* in which she discussed "the problem that has no name."

The problem was that women's delegation to the domestic sphere of life inhibited their opportunities for personal development. Women were not active in the workforce nor in the political community. Friedan organized the National Organization for Women, or NOW, in 1966. The goal of this women's movement differed from the earlier movements. Here, women were concerned with their subordinate position in society and sought to establish equal rights for women. The purpose of NOW was to "take action to bring women into full participation in the mainstream of American society now, exercising all the privileges and responsibilities thereof, in truly equal partnership with men" (Friedan, 1963, p. 384). In the epilogue to *The Feminine Mystique,* Friedan explains that NOW stood for the National Organization *for* Women rather than the National Organization *of* Women because men must be included to accomplish these goals.

NOW is the largest women's rights organization in the United States. To date, it includes more than 0.5 million members and is represented in all states. NOW seeks the elimination of sex discrimination, sexual harassment, racism, and homophobia. NOW has taken on issues of economic equality, reproductive rights, and violence against women. Since its formation, NOW has successfully challenged protective labor laws that kept women from high-paying jobs as well as the sex classification of job advertisements in newspapers. Did you know that there used to be a "Help Wanted–Men" column and a "Help Wanted–Women" column? See Table 1.8 for some sample advertisements. Can you imagine an advertisement for a receptionist today that requested an "attractive young lady"? Can you imagine that an accountant position be available only to men? In recognition of the work that women perform inside the home, NOW popularized the phrase "women who work

TABLE 1.8 Job Advertisements

Help Wanted-Female

Assistant to Executive: Girl Friday.

Asst Bkpr-Biller: Young, some steno preferred, but not essential; bright beginner considered.

Asst. Bookkeeper-Typist: Expd. all-around girl.

Secty-Steno: Age 25–35 Girl Friday for busy treasurer's office.

Receptionist, 5 day wk: Attractive young lady, good typist, knowledge of monitor board.

Help Wanted-Male

Pharmacist: To manage large chain-type indep. drug store.

Refrigeration: Shop servicemen, experienced.

Maintenance: Foreman, mach. shop exp.

Accountant-Sr.: For medium-sized firm, heavy experience, auditing, audit program preparation, report writing and federal and state income tax.

Source: New York Times, June 11, 1953.

outside the home." Most of us feel rightly embarrassed when we ask a woman if she works and she says, "Yes, I work at home all day taking care of two kids, a cat, a dog, and a husband." In 1967, NOW endorsed the Equal Rights Amendment (ERA), which was passed by Congress in 1972 but failed to be ratified by enough states in 1982. More recently, NOW organized a campaign to elect women and feminist persons to political office in 1992, which helped to send a record-breaking number of women and feminists to Congress and to state governments.

The women's movement in the United States has been criticized as a movement of White middle-class women (Margolis, 1993). However, the U.S. women's movement also is perceived to serve a larger portion of women compared to the movements in other countries, which are perceived to be more radical and less cohesive. For example,

in India, the women's movement poses a threat to people's national identity because traditional roles are so grounded in culture. There is a core of commonality to the women's movements around the world: they are focused on improving the position of women in society, equality in the labor force, and economic independence for women (Margolis, 1993).

Men's Movements

More recently, a series of men's movements have appeared, partly in response to the women's movement of the 1960s. None of the men's movements, to date, has had the cohesion or impact on society of this women's movement. Some men's movements endorse the women's movement and share some of the concerns the women's movement raised about the harmful aspects of the male gender role. These men refer to themselves as feminists and are likely to agree that society does not treat men and women equally, that men and women should be paid for equal work, and that features of the male gender role, such as competitiveness, homophobia, and emotional inhibition, are not good for men's relationships. In a sense, this movement has encouraged men to behave in more communal ways. The National Organization for Changing Men, founded in 1983, is just such a movement. These men are pro-feminist.

Other men's movements are a reaction against the women's movement and seek to restore traditional male and female roles. Two recent movements are the mythopoetic movement and the Promise Keepers. Both of these movements view men and women as fundamentally different. Both encourage men to rediscover their masculinity and to reject the "feminization" of men. The movements are referred to as pro-masculinist.

The mythopoetic movement was organized by Robert Bly (1990), who wrote the national best-selling nonfiction book, *Iron John: A Book about Men.* The concern of the mythopoetic movement is that the modernization of society has stripped men of the rituals of tribal society that bound men together. The movement involves rituals, ceremonies, and retreats, with the goal of reconnecting men with one another.

The Promise Keepers is a Christian fundamentalist movement. The Bible is used to justify the differences between men and women and to justify the natural state of men's superior position over women. The first meeting of the Promise Keepers was held in 1990 and 72 men attended (Messner, 1997). Attendance peaked in 1996 with 1.1 million men participating in 22 cities nationwide. Participation has dropped off more recently, as less than .5 million men participated in Promise Keepers gatherings in 1998. The Promise Keepers urge men to keep their promises to be responsible fathers and husbands and to renounce alcohol and sexual temptations. But, to do so, the Promise Keepers encourage men to reclaim their high-status position in society and their position as head of the household in the family. One Promise Keeper reported in a local newspaper, "As the man of the house goes, so goes the house" (Levin, 2000). An interesting facet of the Promise Keepers' conventions is that more than half of the volunteers who put the conferences together are women, yet women are not allowed to attend. This organization is viewed as antifeminist because men and women are not viewed as equals.

Other men want to move beyond gender equality for women to gender equality for both sexes. One man, Warren Farrell (1993), began as a feminist, became a masculinist, and then said that neither really apply. He wrote the book *The Myth of Male Power*, in which he outlines the ways in which men lack power in our society. He is in agreement that there are obvious sources of female powerlessness, such as women's lower pay, women's lack of freedom to walk alone at night, and our lack of respect for women as they age. However, he also says that there are indicators of male powerlessness in our society that ought to be recognized. For example, men are the ones drafted into the military. In addition, society instills in men the notion that they are the breadwinners of the family; whereas women have the option of working or staying home to raise children if they can afford it, society does not endorse this option for men. Men also have been socialized to not ask for help, one result of which is that men commit suicide more frequently than women. Men are much more likely to be in prison compared to women. It is well-known that men commit more acts of violence than women, but do people recognize that men are more likely than women to be victims of violence? He argues that violence against women is repudiated by society, but violence against men is accepted, if not glorified, in the form of sports. Farrell claims that films call attention to violence against women but that the vast majority of victims of violence in films are men. Try Exercise 1.5 to see if Farrell's claims about violence in the media are valid. Finally, and most important, men die six years earlier than women. The fact that African Americans die earlier than Caucasians in the United States is taken as evidence of African Americans' powerlessness compared to Caucasians'. Why isn't men's lower life expectancy compared to women an indicator of men's powerlessness?

Should we consider men's lower longevity compared to women to be an indicator of men's powerlessness, as Farrell (1993) suggests? According to Michael Messner (1997), it does not make sense to say that both men and women are

<table>
<tr><td>

EXERCISE 1.5
Depictions of Women in Film

Warren Farrell (1993) maintains that films call attention to violence against women, but 95% of the people killed are men. He argues that women are not killed in movies, with the exception of a few conditions: (1) when the viewer does not really get to know the woman because she appears in no more than three scenes; (2) when she is not a "real" woman, meaning she is either an alien being or is crazy. Test his hypothesis:

1. Choose a representative sample of movies: comedy, drama, action-adventure, mystery, etc.
2. Come up with a way to measure violence.
3. Record all acts of violence; include the sex of the perpetrator and the sex of the victim.
4. How did the viewer feel about the victim? Did the viewer "like" him or her, "get to know" him or her (number of scenes)?
5. Can you determine whether the conditions surrounding male violence differ from the conditions surrounding female violence?

</td></tr>
</table>

A Note on Language

In 1972, an article appeared in *Ms.* magazine that began with the following story:

> On the television screen, a teacher of first-graders who had just won a national award is describing her way of teaching. "You take each child where you find him," she says. "You watch to see what he's interested in, and then you build on his interests." A five-year-old looking at the program asks her mother, "Do only boys go to that school?" "No," her mother begins, "she's talking about girls too, but . . ." (C. Miller, Swift, & Maggio, 1997, p. 50)

But what? Is it acceptable to use the male pronoun to imply male and female? In 1983, the American Psychological Association proclaimed that scientists must refrain from using sexist language in their writing. This means that we cannot use the generic he to mean both men and women in our scientific writing. The statement was issued nearly 20 years ago. Even today, it is common to find the use of the generic he in books in other disciplines. I find that many college students use "he" to refer to men and women in their writing. When I correct students' papers (changing he to he/she or they), some are quite offended and cast me as an extremist. Many people will say that everyone knows "he" refers to "he and she," so what's the harm? "He" is more efficient. When you write the word "he" or "him," do you think of both men and women? The answer is clear: No.

The concern with sexist language is that people do not really perceive "he" as representing "he or she." Several studies have shown that this is a legitimate concern. Nancy Henley (1989) reviewed 20 studies in which participants were given sentences with the generic "he" or unbiased language ("he/she" or "they"). All of

oppressed in society; for oppression to occur, one group must be oppressed and the other must be the oppressor. Instead, Messner argues that the difficulties men face are the price they pay for being the group in power. In either case, we can agree that there are relational, mental, and physical health hazards associated with aspects of the female and the male gender roles in our society. This is why this book emphasizes the implications of gender and gender roles for relationships and health.

the studies clearly showed that the generic he is more likely to call to mind male names, male persons, and male images. Although female participants were less vulnerable to this bias than male participants, women, too, were more likely to think of men when reading the generic he. For example, in one study, male and female college students were exposed to either a sexist or a nonsexist paragraph taken from an ethics manual for psychologists (Briere & Lanktree, 1983). In the sexist version, the male pronoun was used to represent all people, whereas in the nonsexist version, "he" was replaced with "he or she." After reading the paragraph, participants exposed to the sexist version viewed psychology as less suitable for women than participants exposed to the nonsexist version; the two groups did not differ in their perceptions of how suitable psychology was for men. Other studies have students read or speak passages that contain sexist or gender-neutral language and find that sexist language leads people to conjure up more images of male than female figures compared to gender-neutral language (Gastil, 1990; Hamilton, 1988). Henley asks, "So, does *man* embrace *woman*? According to these findings, *man* most readily embraces *man*" (p. 65). See how language influences perception at your school with Exercise 1.6.

Is there any reason to believe that the climate is changing, that nonsexist language is becoming more acceptable and sexist language is becoming more maligned? In a fairly recent study, a person who used sexist language was perceived negatively (M.E. Johnson & Dowling-Guyer, 1996). College students evaluated the transcript of an occupational counseling session in which the counselor used exclusive (e.g., referring to all secretaries as she and all physicians as he) versus inclusive (e.g., using he or she or they to describe persons)

EXERCISE 1.6
Effects of Sexist Language on Male and Female Images

Ask 10 people to read one of two sentences. The sentences must be identical, with the exception that one version uses sexist language (e.g., "A student should place his homework in a notebook") and one version uses gender-neutral language (e.g., "Students should place their homework in a notebook" or "A student should place his or her homework in a notebook"). (If possible, compare the two gender-neutral conditions.) Ask readers to visualize the sentence while reading it. Then ask them to write a paragraph describing their visual image. At the very end of the task, ask if the image was male or female or unclear.

---

language. Students rated the counselor who used exclusive language as more sexist than the counselor who used inclusive language. In addition, students were less inclined to see the counselor who used exclusive compared to inclusive language. However, this latter finding really applied only to women who had less traditional attitudes toward gender.

Using nonsexist language in your writing is not as difficult as you might think. The easiest way to get around the he/she issue is to use the plural they. Other tips are shown in Table 1.9.

THIS BOOK'S APPROACH TO THE STUDY OF GENDER

According to Deaux (1984), there are three approaches to the study of gender. First, sex is used as a subject variable. This is the

TABLE 1.9   Tips for Nonsexist Writing

1. Replace pronouns (he, his, him) with he or she.

   The student should raise his hand.   *The student should raise his or her hand.*

2. Delete pronouns (he, his, him) by rewriting sentence in the plural.

   The student sits quietly at his desk.   *Students sit quietly at their desks.*

3. Delete pronouns entirely from the sentence.

   The teacher read the folder on his desk.   *The teacher read the folder on the desk.*

4. Change pronouns to "you."

   A person should wash his own clothes.   *You should wash your own clothes.*

5. Change pronouns to "one."

   Tell the student that he can write a letter.   *Tell the student that one can write a letter.*

6. Replace "man" with "someone" or "no one."

   No man is an island.   *No one is an island.*

7. Replace "mankind" or "ancient man" with "our ancestors" or "men and women" or "humanity."

   This is a giant step for mankind.   *This is a giant step for men and women.*
       This is a giant step for humanity.

   Ancient man developed the . . .   *Our ancestors developed the . . .*

8. Replace "men" with "humans."

   Men have always . . .   *Humans have always . . .*

9. Replace "manmade" with "artificial."

   It is a manmade reservoir.   *It is an artificial reservoir.*

10. Replace "spokesman" with "spokesperson" or "representative."

    The spokesman for the client's family has arrived.   *The representative for the client's family has arrived.*

11. Replace "chairman" with "chairperson" or "chair."

    The chairman called the meeting to order.   *The chair called the meeting to order.*

12. Replace "Englishmen" or "Frenchmen" with "the English" or "the French."

    Englishmen always serve tea with scones.   *The English always serve tea with scones.*

13. Replace "steward" and "stewardess" with "flight attendant."

    The stewardess served the meal.   *The flight attendant served the meal.*

14. Replace "salesman" with "salesperson," "salespeople," "sales representative," or "sales clerks."

    Mary is a traveling salesman.   *Mary is a traveling salesperson.*

Source: Adapted from C. Miller and Swift (1980).

most traditional approach to research and is represented in the studies of sex comparisons. The idea here is that sex is an attribute of a person; investigators compare the thoughts, feelings, and behaviors of men and women. Deaux (1984) concludes that this approach has shown that most sex differences are qualified by interactions with context; for example, sex differences in conformity appear in some situations (e.g., public) but not others (e.g., private). A second approach has been to study the psychological differences between men and women: masculinity and femininity. This second approach is still an individual differences approach, but the subject is the social category of gender roles rather than the biological category of sex. Here, we examine how gender roles influence people's thoughts, feelings, and behaviors. Is being female associated with providing help, or is being empathic a better predictor of helping behavior? If the latter is true, both men and women who are high in empathy will be helpful. Third, sex is examined as a stimulus or target variable. Researchers examine how people respond to the categories of male and female. An example of this approach is finding that people rate pictures of infants as more attractive when the infant is thought to be a female and stronger when the infant is thought to be a male. Only with this latter approach can sex be randomly assigned.

All three of these approaches are represented in this text. I examine gender as an individual difference variable but am careful to note how the context influences behavior. I highlight both similarities and differences between men and women. Most important, I focus on the explanations for the source of any observed sex differences, for example, whether other variables that co-occur with sex, such as status or gender-related personality traits, are the causal source of the behavior.

I focus on two domains of behavior: relationships and health. Relationships are an important subject in their own right. Relationships contribute to the quality of one's life as well as to one's mental and physical health. The impact of relationships on our psychological and physical well-being, the prevalence of violence in relationships, and the high rate of relationship dissolution in the form of divorce in the United States are reasons that relationships require our attention. Health also is an important subject in and of itself. Over the past century, we have extended our life span by decades but now are more likely to live with health problems for longer periods of time. We have been made increasingly aware of the role that psychological and social factors play in our health. Gender has implications for those psychological and social forces.

Summary

First, I identified some important terms in the psychological study of gender. Sex, the biological category, was distinguished from gender, the psychological category. An important term that was introduced is gender role, which refers to the expectations that society has for being male or female; we expect men to be masculine and women to be feminine, in other words, to act in accordance with their gender role. Other terms that were defined include gender identity, sexual orientation, sex or gender typing, sexism, gender-role stereotype, and sex discrimination. I discussed the multiple meanings of feminism, concluding that equality for men and women was the most central component of the definition and activism a more peripheral component. Because each society has its own definitions of gender and ways of defining male and female roles, I also described several cultures that have alternative ways of constructing gender.

Next, I reviewed the features of the scientific method that is used to study gender. The scientific method rests on empiricism; it includes the collection of data that are used to make statements, develop theories, and generate hypotheses. Two scientific methods were discussed: the correlational method and the experimental method. The advantage of the experimental method is internal validity and the advantage of the correlational method is external validity. The importance of random selection and random assignment was explained. I also described the differences between cross-sectional and longitudinal studies; longitudinal designs may provide stronger tests of causality and are able to distinguish cohort effects from age effects.

Then, I reviewed the difficulties one faces in the scientific study of gender. There are a number of ways in which the experimenter can be a source of bias: by influencing the question asked, the way a study is designed (including the participants chosen and the way variables are manipulated and measured), the way the data are collected, how the data are interpreted, and whether the data are reported. Participants also can influence the outcome of a study, in particular by demand characteristics and concerns with self-presentation. Other difficulties that researchers encounter when studying gender include the problem of generalizing from the laboratory to the real world, isolating the effects of participant's sex from variables that are confounded with sex such as status and gender role, and consideration of how the context influences behavior.

Finally, I concluded the chapter by presenting various political and philosophical debates in the study of gender. The minimalists, who emphasize the similarities between men and women, were distinguished from the maximalists, who emphasize the differences. I provided an overview of the issues that have arisen when people discuss whether sex differences should be examined, reported, and/or interpreted. A brief history of the women's movements was provided along with a description of the more recent men's movements. I also made suggestions on how to write in a nonsexist manner.

DISCUSSION QUESTIONS

1. What is the distinction between "sex" and "gender"? How do you think this distinction should be employed in practice?
2. How is gender portrayed in other cultures?
3. Describe a scientific theory with which you are familiar. It doesn't have to be from psychology; it could be from biology or physics, for example. Go through the stages of the research process shown in Figure 1.1.
4. What is the difference between random assignment and random sampling? How is each related to internal and external validity?
5. Identify behaviors that you think might be interpreted differently when displayed by a male versus a female. For each one, explain why.
6. If you have ever been in an experiment, discuss some of the ways that just knowing you were in an experiment influenced your behavior.
7. What are some of the ways that we can determine whether men have higher status than women in a given culture?
8. Do you think we should be comparing men and women? Why or why not?
9. Why hasn't any one men's movement gained the strength of the women's movement?
10. How can the use of sexist language be harmful?

Suggested Reading

Eagly, A. (1995). The science and politics of comparing women and men. *American Psychologist, 50*, 145–158.

Marecek, J. (1995). Gender, politics, and psychology's ways of knowing. *American Psychologist, 41*, 162–163.

Messner, M.A. (1997). *Politics of masculinities: Men in movements.* Thousand Oaks, CA: Sage.

McHugh, M.C., Koeske, R.D., & Frieze, I.H. (1986). Issues to consider in conducting nonsexist psychological research: A guide for researchers. *American Psychologist, 41*, 879–890.

Miller, C., & Swift, K. (1988). *The handbook of nonsexist writing.* New York: Harper and Row.

Key Terms

Androgynous—Term describing one who incorporates both masculine and feminine qualities.

Bisexual—Individuals who accept other-sex and same-sex individuals as sexual partners.

Constructionist perspective—Perspective that maintains that gender cannot be divorced from its context.

Cross-sex-typed—Condition of possessing the biological traits of one sex but exhibiting the behaviors characteristic of the gender that corresponds with the other sex.

Feminine—Description of trait, behavior, or interest that is assigned to the female gender role.

Feminism—Belief that men and women should be treated equally.

Gender—Term used to refer to the social categories of male and female.

Gender culture—Each society's or culture's conceptualization of gender roles.

Gender identity—One's perception of oneself as psychologically male or female.

Gender role—The expectations that go along with being male or female.

Gender-role attitude—One's personal view about how men and women should behave.

Heterosexuals—Individuals who prefer other-sex sexual partners.

Homosexuals—Individuals who prefer same-sex sexual partners.

Interrole conflict—Experience of conflict between expectations of two or more roles that are assumed simultaneously.

Intrarole conflict—Experience of conflict between expectations within a given role.

Masculine—Description of a trait, behavior, or interest that is assigned to the male gender role.

Maximalism—Perspective that maintains that there are important differences between the two sexes.

Minimalism—Perspective that maintains that the two sexes are fundamentally the same.

Role—A social position that is accompanied by a set of norms or expectations.

Sex—Term used to refer to the biological categories of male and female.

Sex discrimination—Behavioral component of one's attitude toward men and women that involves differential treatment of people based on their biological sex.

Sexism—Affective component of one's attitude toward sex that is characterized by demonstration of prejudice toward people based on their sex.

Sex stereotype/gender role stereotype—The cognitive component of one's attitude toward sex.

Sex-related behavior—Behavior that corresponds to sex, but is not necessarily caused by sex.

Sex-typed—Condition of possessing the biological traits of one sex and exhibiting the behaviors characteristic of the gender that corresponds with that sex.

Sex typing—The acquisition of sex-appropriate preferences, behaviors, skills, and self-concept (i.e., the acquisition of gender roles).

Sexual orientation—The preference to have other sex or same-sex persons as sexual partners.

Transgendered—Descriptive term referring to individuals whose psychological sex is not congruent with their biological sex.

Transsexual—A person whose biological sex has been surgically changed.

2

Conceptualization and Measurement of Gender Roles and Gender-Role Attitudes

Take the quiz in Exercise 2.1. If you answered "a" to each of these questions, you are high in psychological masculinity; if you answered "b" to these questions, you are high in psychological femininity—at least according to one way that masculinity and femininity used to be measured. These are sample items from the Attitude Interest Analysis Survey (1936), one of the first measures of gender roles.

In the previous chapter, I provided a very abstract definition of gender roles. Where did this concept come from? What did it mean 100 years ago, and what does it mean today? Is it better to be masculine or feminine? Or does it depend on whether you are male or female?

The first goal of this chapter is to provide an overview of the history of the psychology of gender. In reviewing the history of the field, I examine the different ways that people conceptualized and measured gender roles. The study of gender roles includes not only how we expect men and women to behave, but also how we view the actual behavior of men and women—that is, our gender-role attitudes. Thus, in

the second half of the chapter, I examine people's attitudes toward gender roles and toward the category of gender. Attitudes consists of feelings, such as prejudice toward men or women; cognitions, such as gender-role stereotypes; and behaviors, such as sex discrimination.

HISTORY OF THE PSYCHOLOGY OF GENDER

I have divided the field into four time periods that approximate those identified by Richard Ashmore (1990). Each time period is marked by one or more key figures in the field.

1894–1936: Sex Differences in Intelligence

The focus of the first period was on the differences between men and women. This period was marked by the publication of a book by Ellis (1894) titled *Man and Woman*, which called for a scientific

---

EXERCISE 2.1
Quiz

Choose the correct answer to each question.

1. Which of the following words most comes to mind when you see the word "date"?

   a. fruit   b. appointment

2. Tokyo is a city in:

   a. Japan   b. China

3. How disgusted are you by seeing someone chew gum?

   a. not at all   b. very much

4. How wicked is excessive drinking?

   a. somewhat bad   b. extremely wicked

5. Would you like to be a forest ranger?

   a. yes   b. no

6. Do you like or dislike Christopher Columbus?

   a. dislike   b. like

7. Is the following statement true or false: Love at first sight is usually the truest love.

   a. false   b. true

8. Do people ever say that you talk too much?

   a. yes   b. no

---

approach to the study of the similarities and differences between men and women. No consideration was yet given to personality traits or roles that were associated with sex. Thus, gender roles were not part of the picture. The primary goal of this era was to examine if (really, to establish that) men were intellectually superior to women. To accomplish this goal, scientists turned to the anatomy of the brain (Shields, 1975).

First, scientists focused on the size of the human brain. Because women's heads and brains are smaller than those of men, there seemed to be conclusive evidence that women were intellectually inferior. However, men also were taller and weighed more than women; when body size was taken into account, the evidence for sex differences in intelligence became less clear. If one computed a ratio of the weight of the brain to the weight of the body, women appeared to have the relatively larger brains. If one computed the ratio of the surface area of the brain to the surface area of the body, men appeared to have the relatively larger brains. Thus, brain size alone could not settle the question of sex differences in intelligence.

Next, researchers turned to specific areas of the brain that could be responsible for higher levels of intellectual functioning. The frontal cortex was first thought to be responsible for higher levels of mental functioning, and men were observed to have larger frontal lobes than women. Then it appeared that men did not have larger frontal lobes; instead, men had larger parietal lobes. Thus, thinking shifted to the parietal lobe as the seat of intellectual functioning. All of this research came under sharp methodological criticism because the scientists observing the anatomy of the brain were not blind to the sex associated with the particular brain; that is, the people evaluating the brain knew whether it belonged to a male or a female. This situation was ripe for the kinds of experimenter biases described in Chapter 1. Obviously, scientists could have developed hypotheses based on what they already observed to be true. If they found that one part of a brain was larger in men than women, than that part of the brain was assumed to hold the key to intellectual powers.

The period ended with the seminal work of *Sex and Personality* published by Lewis Terman and Catherine Cox Miles in

1936. They concluded that there were no sex differences in intellect: "Intelligence tests, for example, have demonstrated for all time the falsity of the once widely prevalent belief that women as a class are appreciably or at all inferior to men in the major aspects of intellect" (p. 1).

1936–1954: M/F as a Global Personality Trait

During this next period, researchers shifted their focus from sex differences alone to consider the notion of gender roles. The construct of masculinity/femininity, or M/F, was introduced during this period. Terman had concluded that the differences between men's and women's intelligence were small and possibly nonexistent. Instead, he argued that the real mental differences between men and women could be captured by measuring masculinity and femininity. He and Miles stated, "The belief is all but universal that men and women as contrasting groups display characteristic sex differences in their behavior, and that these differences are so deep seated and pervasive as to lend distinctive character to the entire personality" (1936, p. 1).

They developed a 456-item instrument to measure masculinity-femininity. It was called the Attitude Interest Analysis Survey (AIAS, 1936) to disguise the true purpose of the test. The AIAS was the first published M/F scale. The items chosen were based on statistical sex differences observed in elementary, junior high, and high school children. This meant that items on which the average female scored higher than the average male were labeled feminine, and items on which the average male scored higher were labeled masculine, regardless of the content of those items. The M/F scale was also bipolar, which meant that masculinity and femininity were viewed as opposite ends of a single continuum. The sum of the feminine items was subtracted from the sum of the masculine items to yield a total M/F score.

The instrument was composed of seven subject areas: (1) word association, (2) ink blot association, (3) information, (4) emotional and ethical response, (5) interests (likes and dislikes), (6) admired persons and opinions, and (7) introversion-extroversion, which really measured superiority-subordination. Sample items from each subject area are shown in Table 2.1; some items also appeared in Exercise 2.1. Several of these subscales are quite interesting. The information scale was based on the assumption that men have greater knowledge than women about some areas of life, such as sports and politics, and women have greater knowledge about other areas of life, such as gardening and sewing. Thus, giving a correct response to an item about which women are supposed to know more than men would be scored as feminine; conversely, giving a correct response to an item about which men are supposed to know more than women would be scored as masculine. For example, consider the first item on the information subscale shown in Table 2.1. Answering that a marigold is a flower would be scored as feminine, whereas answering that a marigold is a stone would be scored as masculine. The emotional and ethical attitudes subscale was scored such that being feminine meant getting angry when seeing others treated unfairly and being masculine meant getting angry when being disturbed at work.

There were no assumptions about the basis of these sex differences. Terman and Miles (1936) left the cause of the sex differences—biological, psychological, or cultural—unspecified.

Other M/F scales followed, including one subscale contained in a vocational

TABLE 2.1   Sample Items from the Attitude Interest Analysis Survey

Responses with a + are indicative of masculinity, responses with a – are indicative of femininity, responses with a 0 are neutral and not scored as either.

Word Association

Look at the word in capital letters, then look at the four words which follow it. Draw a line under the word that goes best or most naturally with the one in capitals; the word it tends most to make you think of.

1. POLE   barber (0)   cat (+)   North (–)   telephone (+)
2. DATE   appointment (–)   dance (+)   fruit (+)   history (+)

Ink-Blot Association

Here are some drawings, a little like inkblots. They are not pictures of anything in particular but might suggest almost anything to you, just as shapes in the clouds sometimes do. Beside each drawing four things are mentioned. Underline the one word that tells what the drawing makes you think of most.

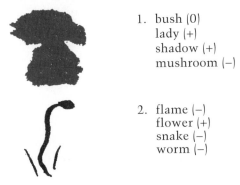

1. bush (0)
   lady (+)
   shadow (+)
   mushroom (–)

2. flame (–)
   flower (+)
   snake (–)
   worm (–)

Information

In each sentence draw a line under the word that makes the sentence true.

1. Marigold is a kind of	fabric (+)	flower (–)	grain (–)	stone (+)
2. Tokyo is a city of	China (–)	India (–)	Japan (+)	Russia (0)
3. A loom is used for	cooking (+)	embroidering (+)	sewing (+)	weaving (–)
4. The number of players on a baseball team is	7 (–)	9 (+)	11 (–)	13 (0)

Emotional and Ethical Response

Below is a list of things that sometimes cause anger. After each thing mentioned draw a circle around VM, M, L, or N to show how much anger it causes you.
   VM means VERY MUCH; M means MUCH; L means A LITTLE; N means NONE.

1. Seeing people disfigure library books	VM (–)	M (–)	L (+)	N (+)
2. Seeing someone trying to discredit you with your employer	VM (+)	M (0)	L (+)	N (–)

(continued)

TABLE 2.1 (continued)

Below is a list of things that sometimes cause disgust. After each thing mentioned draw a circle around VM, M, L, or N to indicate how much disgust it causes you.
    VM means VERY MUCH; M means MUCH; L means A LITTLE; N means NONE.

1. An unshaven man	VM (–)	M (–)	L (+)	N (+)
2. Gum chewing	VM (–)	M (–)	L (+)	N (+)

Below is a list of acts of various degrees of wickedness or badness. After each thing mentioned draw a circle around 3, 2, 1, or 0 to show how wicked or bad you think it is.
    3 means EXTREMELY WICKED; 2 means DECIDEDLY BAD; 1 means SOMEWHAT BAD; 0 means NOT REALLY BAD.

1. Using slang	3 (–)	2 (–)	1 (+)	0 (+)
2. Excessive drinking	3 (–)	2 (+)	1 (+)	0 (0)

Interests

For each occupation below, ask yourself: Would I like that work or not? If you would like it, draw a circle around L. If you would dislike it, draw a circle around D. If you would neither like nor dislike it, draw a circle around N. In deciding on your answer, *think only of the kind of work.* Don't consider the pay. Imagine that you have the ability to do the work, that you are the right age for it, and that it is equally open to men and women.

1. Forest ranger	L (+)	D (–)	N (0)
2. Florist	L (–)	D (+)	N (+)

Personalities and Opinion

Below is a list of famous characters. After each name draw a circle around L, D, or N to indicate whether you like that character.
    L means LIKE; D means DISLIKE; N means NEITHER LIKE NOR DISLIKE.

1. Daniel Boone	L (+)	D (–)	N (–)
2. Christopher Columbus	L (–)	D (+)	N (+)
3. Florence Nightingale	L (–)	D (+)	N (+)

Read each statement and consider whether it is mostly true or mostly false. If it is mostly TRUE draw a circle around T. If it is mostly FALSE draw a circle around F.

1. The world was created in six days of twenty-four hours each.	T (+)	F (0)
2. Love "at first sight" is usually the truest love.	T (+)	F (–)

Introvertive Response

Answer each question as truthfully as you can by drawing a line under YES or NO.

1. Did you ever have imaginary companions?	YES (–)	NO (+)
2. Do you worry much over possible misfortunes?	YES (–)	NO (+)
3. As a child were you extremely disobedient?	YES (+)	NO (–)
4. Do people ever say that you talk too much?	YES (+)	NO (–)

Source: Terman and Miles (1936).

interests instrument called the Strong Vocational Interest Blank (Strong, 1936). The entire instrument measures one's likes and dislikes and is used to help people choose a career. The M/F scale was based on the small subset of items, 13%, in which men and women had different likes and dislikes. The fact that men and women endorsed similar levels of interests on 87% of the items was not regarded as important. The following areas of interests were designated masculine: mechanical, scientific, athletic, legal, political, and sales; the following areas were designated feminine: musical, artistic, literary, clerical work, teaching, and social work.

A few years later, Hathaway and McKinley (1940) developed the Minnesota Multiphasic Personality Inventory (MMPI), of which you have probably heard. It eventually included an M/F scale that consisted of items reflecting liking certain occupations, altruism, emotional sensitivity, sexual preference, and gender identity questions. The most notable feature in the development of this scale is that the femininity items were validated on 13 homosexuals. Homosexual men were compared to heterosexual male soldiers; at that time, heterosexual male soldiers epitomized masculinity and homosexual men were considered feminine. In fact, feminine traits were considered to be a predisposing factor to homosexuality in men (Terman & Miles, 1936). Women were not even involved in research to evaluate femininity. Thus, there are at least two major problems with this instrument: first, women were not involved in the conceptualization of the female gender role; second, there were only 13 homosexual men involved in the study, which is hardly sufficient to validate an instrument even if they had been the appropriate population.

Some researchers became concerned about the self-report methodology that was used to assess M/F. The purpose of the tests might have been obvious, which could lead men and women to give socially desirable rather than truthful responses. The concern focused on demand characteristics. Thus, several projective tests of M/F were developed, including one by Franck and Rosen (1949). They developed a test that consisted of incomplete drawings, like the stimuli shown in the first column of Figure 2.1. Franck and Rosen began with 60 stimuli, asked men and women to complete the drawings, and found sex differences in the way that 36 of the 60 were completed. These 36 stimuli then comprised the test. How did men and women differ in their drawings? Men were found to be more likely to close off the stimuli, make sharper edges, include angles, and

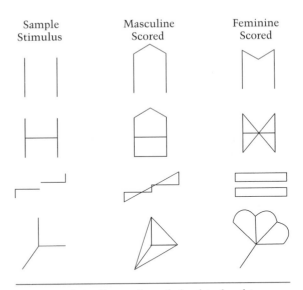

| Sample Stimulus | Masculine Scored | Feminine Scored |

FIGURE 2.1 Examples of the kinds of incomplete drawings that appeared on Franck and Rosen's (1949) projective test of masculinity/femininity. How the drawings were completed was taken as an indication of masculinity or femininity. The second column represents masculine ways of completing the drawings and the third column represents feminine ways of completing the drawings. *Source:* Adapted from Franck and Rosen (1949).

focus on unifying objects rather than keeping them separate. Women were found to leave a stimulus open, to make round or blunt edges, and to make lines that pointed inward. The content of the objects men and women drew also was found to differ: men drew nude women, skyscrapers, and dynamic objects, whereas women drew animals, flowers, houses, and static objects. Franck and Rosen also suggested that men's and women's drawings could be linked to their own sex's body parts. In regard to men's drawings, they said, "Expansion, upward motion, angular position and oneness are characteristics of the male sex organ, and in a sense, of masculine body build" (p. 254). In regard to women's drawings, they said, "Accessibility, emphasis on the inside of the body, roundness, symmetry and two-ness are female body characteristics" (p. 254).

Interestingly, Franck and Rosen (1949) did not conclude that a male and a female who receive the same score on the test are the same in terms of masculinity and femininity. In fact, they argued that the drawings of a male who receives a feminine score are quite bizarre and very different from the drawings of a female who receives a feminine score. They applied the same logic to a female who receives a masculine score. If the instrument does not measure psychological masculinity and femininity among both men and women, one wonders about the purpose of the test. Franck and Rosen suggested that their instrument measures acceptance of one's gender role rather than the degree of masculinity and femininity. Males who scored masculine and females who scored feminine were considered to have accepted their gender roles.

All of the M/F scales that were developed up to this point suffered from a number of conceptual weaknesses. First, the tests did not distinguish between more or less masculine and more or less feminine people; they merely distinguished men from women, a distinction that did not need to be made. Second, any item that revealed sex differences was taken as evidence of masculinity and femininity, regardless of its relevance to these constructs; this can be seen from the fact that knowing a marigold is a flower was an indicator of femininity. Third, femininity and masculinity were assumed to be opposite ends of a single continuum; all of the scales were bipolar, such that masculinity represented one end and femininity represented the other. Finally, gay men were equated with feminine women. There seemed to be some confusion among masculinity, femininity, and sexual orientation. An assumption at the time was that psychologically healthy men were masculine and psychologically healthy women were feminine.

1954–1982: Sex Typing and Androgyny

One focus of this period was on sex typing, that is, how boys and girls developed sex-appropriate preferences, personality traits, and behaviors. Theories ranged from Freud's theory of gender identification, which states that women learn their roles by identifying with their mothers and men learn their roles by identifying with their fathers, to sociology's societal norm theory, which states that society has rules or norms for the way men and women are expected to behave. This period was marked by Eleanor Maccoby's (1966) publication of *The Development of Sex Differences*, which reviewed important theories of sex typing, such as social learning theory and cognitive development theory. Many of these theories will be reviewed in detail in Chapter 4.

In 1973, Anne Constantinople published a major critique of the existing M/F instruments. She questioned the use of sex differences as the basis for defining masculinity and femininity; she also questioned whether masculinity-femininity was really a unidimensional construct that could be captured by a single bipolar scale. The latter assumption, in particular, was addressed during this period by the publication of instruments that distinguished masculinity and femininity as independent constructs.

INSTRUMENTAL VERSUS EXPRESSIVE DISTINCTION. A distinction brought to the study of gender roles that helped to conceptualize masculinity and femininity as separate dimensions was the distinction between an instrumental and an expressive orientation. In 1955, Parsons, a sociologist, and Bales, a social psychologist, distinguished between instrumental or goal-oriented behavior and expressive or emotional behavior in their studies of male group interactions. They discovered that men had two different leadership styles: the instrumental leader was focused on getting the job done and the expressive leader was focused on maintaining group harmony.

Parson and Bales (1955) extended the instrumental/expressive distinction to gender. They saw a relation between superior power and instrumentality and a relation between inferior power and expressivity. They believed the distinction between the husband role and the wife role was both an instrumental/expressive distinction as well as a superior/inferior power distinction. The instrumental orientation became linked to the male gender role and the expressive orientation became linked to the female gender role.

Two instruments were developed during this period that linked orientation to gender role. In 1974, Sandra Bem published the Bem Sex Role Inventory (BSRI) and Spence, Helmreich, and Stapp published the Personal Attributes Questionnaire

(PAQ). They are still the most commonly used inventories to measure masculinity and femininity. The innovative feature of both instruments was that masculinity and femininity were conceptualized as two independent dimensions rather than a single bipolar scale; thus, a person received a masculinity score and a femininity score. Masculinity and femininity were no longer viewed as opposites.

The BSRI (Bem, 1974) was developed by having undergraduates rate how desirable it is for a man and a woman to possess each of 400 attributes. Items that students rated as more desirable for a male to possess were indicators of masculinity and items that students rated as more desirable for a female were indicators of femininity. Items were not based on respondents' views of how *likely* men and women are to have these traits but on their views of how *desirable* it is for men and women to have the traits.

The BSRI consists of 60 items: 20 masculine, 20 feminine, and 20 neutral items. The neutral items are included in the instrument to disguise the purpose of the scale. Consistent with Parsons and Bales's (1955) distinction, the masculine items have an instrumental orientation, focusing on getting the job done, and the feminine items have an expressive orientation, focusing on being concerned for others. Scores on the masculinity and femininity scales are generally uncorrelated, reflecting the fact that they are two independent dimensions.

In contrast to the BSRI, the PAQ (Spence, Helmreich, & Stapp, 1974) was developed by focusing on the perception of how likely men and women are to possess certain traits. College students were asked to rate the typical adult male and female, the typical college male and female, and the ideal male and female. The items on this instrument are shown in the top half of Table 2.2. The masculinity scale included

TABLE 2.2   Personal Attributes Questionnaire

Masculinity (M+)	Femininity (F+)	Masculinity-Femininity (M/F)
Independent	Emotional	Aggressive
Active	Able to devote self to others	Dominant
Competitive	Gentle	Excitable in major crisis
Can make decisions	Helpful to others	Worldly (vs. home-oriented)
Never gives up	Kind	Indifferent to others' approval
Self-confident	Aware of others' feelings	Feelings not easily hurt
Feels superior	Understanding of others	Never cries
Stands up well under pressure	Warm in relations to others	Little need for security

Source: Spence et al. (1974).

Extension of Personal Attributes Questionnaire

Unmitigated Agency (M−)

Arrogant	Dictatorial
Boastful	Cynical
Egotistical	Looks out for self
Greedy	Hostile

Source: Spence, Helmreich, and Holahan (1979).

items that students viewed as more characteristic of men than women but also as ideal for both men and women to possess. "Independence" was a masculinity item; the typical college male was viewed as more independent than the typical college female, but independence was perceived to be equally desirable in both men and women. The femininity scale included items that were more characteristic of women but also viewed as ideal in both women and men. "Understanding of others" was a femininity item; the typical college female was rated as more understanding of others than the typical college male, but respondents viewed being understanding of others as a socially desirable trait for both women and men. Spence and colleagues (1974) also created a third scale, called the masculinity-femininity scale. These were items on which college students believed the typical college male and the typical college female differed, but they

also were items that students viewed as socially desirable for one sex to possess but not the other. The masculinity-femininity subscale was a bipolar scale in which one end represented masculinity and the other femininity; for example, the typical college male was viewed as worldly, whereas the typical college female was viewed as home-oriented. In addition, respondents viewed it as more socially desirable for men than women to be worldly and more socially desirable for women than men to be home-oriented.

Like the BSRI, the items on the masculinity scale were thought to reflect an instrumental or agentic orientation and the items on the femininity scale to reflect an expressive or communal orientation. Because the meaning of the masculinity-femininity scale was, and still is, unclear, it is seldom included in research. The BSRI and the PAQ masculinity scales are highly correlated, as are the femininity scales.

When these scales were developed, consistent sex differences appeared. Men scored higher on the masculinity scales and women scored higher on the femininity scales. But the scales were developed over 25 years ago. Do sex differences still appear today? Research that has compared masculinity and femininity scores over time (1970s, 1980s, 1990s) has shown that femininity scores have not changed, meaning that there are still consistent sex differences (Spence & Buckner, under review; Twenge, 1997b). Women's masculinity scores, however, have increased over time, which has had the effect of reducing the overall sex difference (Spence & Buckner, under review; Twenge, 1997b). The fact that women's masculinity scores have increased but men's femininity scores have remained the same probably reflects the greater changes in the female than the male gender role over the past several decades. Women have been encouraged to become agentic, but men have not been as encouraged to become communal.

ANDROGYNY.   One outgrowth of these two M/F inventories (the BSRI and the PAQ) was the conceptualization of and research on **androgyny.** Androgyny emerged from the operationalization of masculinity and femininity as unipolar, independent dimensions. The androgynous person was one who displayed both masculine and feminine traits. Androgyny was first measured with the BSRI by subtracting the masculinity score from the femininity score. Positive difference scores reflected femininity and negative difference scores reflected masculinity. Scores near zero reflected androgyny, signifying that people had a relatively equal amount of both traits. A male who scored masculine and a female who scored feminine were referred to as **sex-typed.** A masculine female and a feminine male were referred to as **cross-sex-typed.**

One problem with this measurement of androgyny is that the score did not distinguish between people who endorsed many masculine and feminine qualities from people who endorsed only a few masculine and feminine qualities. Someone who endorsed 10 masculine and 10 feminine traits received the same score (0) as someone who endorsed 2 masculine and 2 feminine traits; both were viewed as androgynous.

Spence et al. (1974) had an alternative system for scoring androgyny. They divided scores on the masculinity and femininity scales in half to create the four groups shown in Figure 2.2. Someone who possessed a high number of masculine features and a low number of feminine features was designated masculine; someone who possessed a high number of feminine and a low number of masculine features was designated feminine. These people were referred to as sex-typed if their sex corresponded to their gender role. The androgynous person was someone who possessed a high number of both masculine and feminine features. A person who had few masculine or feminine traits was referred to as undifferentiated. To this day, most researchers still do not know the meaning of this last category, yet

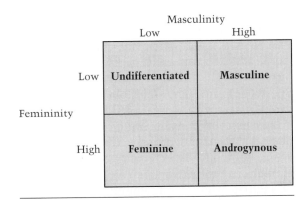

FIGURE 2.2 This is a sex-typing typology based on people's scores on masculinity and femininity.

they often create these four categories when using either the PAQ or BSRI.

Androgyny was put forth by Bem (1974, 1975) as an ideal: the androgynous person was one who embodied the socially desirable features of both masculinity and femininity. It was no longer believed that the most psychologically healthy people were masculine men and feminine women; instead, the healthiest people were thought to be those who possessed both attributes. Androgynous people were supposed to have the best of both worlds and to demonstrate the greatest behavioral flexibility and the best psychological adjustment. Unfortunately, subsequent research revealed that the masculinity scale alone predicts behavioral flexibility and psychological adjustment as well as and sometimes better than the androgyny score (W. Jones, Chernovetz, & Hansson, 1978; S. Taylor & Hall, 1982). In hindsight, this finding is not so surprising because the traits included on the BSRI and PAQ masculinity scales are those that are valued by American society. Bem actually conceptualized androgyny to be much more than the sum of masculine and feminine traits. Androgyny had implications for how one thought about the world. This will be elaborated on in Chapter 4 in the discussion of gender-schema theory.

UNDESIRABLE ASPECTS OF MASCULINITY AND FEMININITY.   One criticism of the PAQ, and of the BSRI to some extent, is that the attributes are all socially desirable. In 1979, Spence, Helmreich, and Holahan set out to develop scales that paralleled the original M and F scales in content but differed in social desirability. Conceptually, the masculinity scale, which they referred to as M+, was thought to reflect a positive instrumental or agentic orientation, whereas the femininity scale, which they referred to as F+, was thought to reflect a positive expressive or communal orientation. Spence and colleagues were looking to develop scales that

measured socially *undesirable* aspects of agentic and communal orientations.

They turned to the work of David Bakan (1966), who richly developed the ideas of agency and communion. Bakan argued that there were two principles of human existence: an agentic one that focused on the self and separation, and a communal one that focused on others and connection. Bakan also suggested that agency was the male principle and communion the female. Bakan argued that it was important for agency to be mitigated by communion and that **unmitigated agency** would be destructive to the self and society. Unmitigated agency reflected a focus on the self to the neglect of others. Drawing on this work, Spence and colleagues (1979) developed a negative masculinity scale that reflected unmitigated agency; the scale included in the Extension of the Personal Attributes Questionnaire (EPAQ) is shown in the bottom of Table 2.2.

The scale is agentic like the earlier positive masculinity scale, is more common in men than in women, and is socially undesirable in both men and women. Most important, it conceptually reflects the construct of unmitigated agency: a focus on the self to the exclusion of others. It includes a hostile attitude toward others and self-absorption. The scale is positively correlated with the M+ scale, reflecting the focus on the self, and negatively correlated with the F+ scale, reflecting the absence of a focus on others (Helgeson & Fritz, 1999).

Spence and colleagues (1979) also wanted to capture socially undesirable aspects of the female gender role. Turning to Bakan (1966) again, they noted that communion also ought to be mitigated by agency. Although Bakan never used the term **unmitigated communion,** he noted that it would also be unhealthy to focus on others to the exclusion of the self. Spence and colleagues had more difficulty coming up with traits that conceptually reflected unmitigated communion. They developed a couple of negative femininity scales, but neither conceptually captured the construct of unmitigated communion (Spence et al., 1979). Later, I developed an unmitigated communion scale (Helgeson, 1993; Helgeson & Fritz, 1998), shown in Table 2.3. The unmitigated communion scale has two components: overinvolvement with others and neglect of the self (Fritz & Helgeson, 1998). It is positively correlated with F+, reflecting the focus

on others, and negatively correlated with M+, reflecting the absence of a focus on the self (Helgeson & Fritz, 1999).

Both unmitigated communion and unmitigated agency have been shown to be important constructs in the area of gender and health and account for a number of sex differences in health. This research will be reviewed in later chapters of the book that focus on health.

SUMMARY. The period between 1954 and 1982 brought with it major innovations in the conceptualization and measurement of gender roles. First, the distinction between the instrumental and expressive orientation was made and then linked to gender. This led to the development of two instruments, the PAQ and the BSRI, which are still the most widely used instruments to measure psychological masculinity and femininity. The unique feature of both of these instruments that set them apart from previous measures was the idea that masculinity and femininity were not bipolar ends of a single continuum but two independent dimensions. This led to the development of the androgyny construct. In its most rudimentary form, androgyny was captured first by similar scores on masculinity and femininity and then by high scores on masculinity and femininity. The most recent advance during this period was the idea that there were socially undesirable aspects of gender roles that ought to be considered and measured. This led to the concepts of unmitigated agency and unmitigated communion.

1982–Present: Gender as a Social Category

In the past two decades, research on gender and sex differences has proliferated. To demonstrate the increased interest in this area of research, Worell (1996) conducted

---

TABLE 2.3   Unmitigated Communion Scale

Instructions: Using the scale below, place a number in the blank beside each statement that indicates the extent to which you agree or disagree. Think of the people close to you—friends or family—in responding to each statement.

Strongly Disagree	Slightly Disagree	Agree nor Disagree	Slightly Agree	Strongly Agree
1	2	3	4	5

____ 1. I always place the needs of others above my own.

____ 2. I never find myself getting overly involved in others' problems.*

____ 3. For me to be happy, I need others to be happy.

____ 4. I worry about how other people get along without me when I am not there.

____ 5. I have no trouble getting to sleep at night when other people are upset.*

____ 6. It is impossible for me to satisfy my own needs when they interfere with the needs of others.

____ 7. I can't say no when someone asks me for help.

____ 8. Even when exhausted, I will always help other people.

____ 9. I often worry about others' problems.

* Items are reverse scored.

Source: V.S. Helgeson and H.L. Fritz (1998). A theory of unmitigated communion. *Personality and Social Psychology Review, 2,* 173–183.

a literature search with the key words "women," "gender," and "sex differences" for a single year in each of the past three decades: 1974, 1983, and 1993. As shown in Figure 2.3, the literature on sex differences has shown a steady increase across the three decades, whereas the literature on women and gender has shown a dramatic increase since 1983.

There have been two recent trends in the psychological study of gender. The first has been to view gender as a multifaceted or multidimensional construct, meaning that the two-dimensional view of masculinity and femininity is not sufficient to capture gender roles. The development of the unmitigated agency and unmitigated communion scales was a first step in this direction. The second research direction has been to emphasize the social context in which gender occurs. The research on gender diagnosticity addresses this issue. Emphasis on the social context led to research on gender-role constraints, the difficulties people face due to the limits a society

places on gender-role-appropriate behavior. I examine each of these research directions.

GENDER ROLE AS MULTIFACETED.   In 1985, Spence and Sawin called for the renaming of the PAQ masculinity and femininity scales. They stated that these scales reflect only one aspect of masculinity and femininity—instrumentality or agency and expressiveness or communion—and that the names of the scales should reflect these aspects. They argued that masculinity and femininity were multidimensional constructs that could not be captured by a single trait instrument.

What else is involved in masculinity and femininity besides the traits that appear on the BSRI and the PAQ? Researchers began to realize that lay conceptions of masculinity and femininity included more diverse content, such as physical characteristics and role behaviors, in addition to personality traits. A. Myers and Gonda (1982) asked 747 visitors to a museum to define the terms masculine and feminine. They

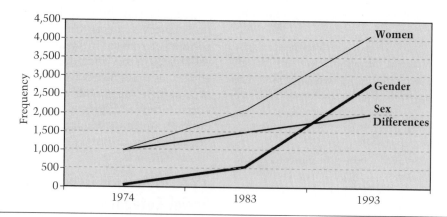

FIGURE 2.3   Frequency of gender-related references over three decades. The results of a literature search show that the frequency with which articles on sex differences have appeared has steadily increased over the past several decades, whereas the frequency with which articles on gender and on women have appeared have substantially increased. *Source:* Adapted from Worrell (1996).

concluded that people's responses did not correspond to the ways masculinity and femininity were measured with traditional trait inventories; instead, the most frequently cited attributes focused on physical appearance.

In 1994, I adopted a different approach to identify the content of masculinity and femininity (Helgeson, 1994b). Rather than viewing masculinity and femininity as clear-cut categories composed of a set of necessary and sufficient features, I viewed them as fuzzy categories, or prototypes. A **prototype** is an abstract set of features commonly associated with a category, such that features vary in their representativeness of the category.

Before I explain the prototypes of masculinity and femininity, let's take an example of a prototype of another category. Take the category *chair*. What are some features of this category? One feature is "seat" or "something you sit on." This is a central feature of the category chair. If you can't sit on it, can it be a chair? However, the feature "seat" is not sufficient to define the category chair because you can sit on a sofa and you can sit on the floor. Other features of the category chair include arms, legs, and a back. These features are less central to the category chair than seat because a chair, for example, a beanbag chair, can exist without legs or arms. Applying the prototype approach to the categories of masculinity and femininity would provide us with the features that constitute these categories as well as indicators of how central or peripheral the features are to the categories.

In my prototype study, 223 college students and 182 of their parents were asked to describe one of six target persons: a masculine man, a masculine woman, a masculine person, a feminine man, a feminine woman, or a feminine person (Helgeson, 1994b). Slightly less than half of the sample was Caucasian; thus, the sample was diverse in terms of age as well as ethnicity. The idea was to discern the features of masculinity and femininity independent of a target's sex. The 20 most commonly identified features of a masculine male and a masculine female are shown in Table 2.4, and the 20 most commonly identified features of a feminine female and a feminine male are shown in Table 2.5. Items that are capitalized are common to both male and female targets, meaning that they are features of masculinity and femininity that are not tied to sex. I ended up not analyzing the data in response to a masculine person or feminine person because the majority of people applied a sex to the target, so people were not necessarily responding to a person who could be either male or female. Interestingly, the masculine person was either assumed to be male (79%) or sex was unspecified (21%). The feminine person was designated female about half of the time (47%), designated male part of the time (21%), or sex was unspecified (32%).

Notice that the features of masculinity and femininity shown in Tables 2.4 and 2.5 fall into one of three categories: personality traits (P), interests (I), or physical appearance (A). Unlike the Myers and Gonda (1982) study, the majority of features did not refer to physical appearance. The average person identified 5 personality traits, 2 interests, and 3 physical appearance features for each target. In addition, many of the identified personality traits are reflected on conventional M/F inventories, suggesting that lay conceptions of M/F do fit the scientific literature. For example, feminine items that were identified by at least 10% of the respondents and included on the PAQ are *emotional, passive, not aggressive, cries easily,* and *helpful. Likes kids, soft-spoken,* and *shy* are feminine items that appear on the BSRI. The masculine items *aggressive, competitive,* and *dominant* are included on both the PAQ

TABLE 2.4   Prototypical Features of Masculinity

		Masculine Male				Masculine Female	
1.	A*	MUSCULAR	71.4	I	LIKES SPORTS		64.7
2.	I	LIKES SPORTS	52.9	A	MUSCULAR		50.6
3.	A	TALL	51.4	A	short hair		37.1
4.	P	SELF-CONFIDENT	50.0	A	dress casually		38.8
5.	A	dark	30.0	A	deep voice		30.6
6.	P	arrogant	28.6	P	SELF-CONFIDENT		30.6
7.	I	dates women	28.6	P	aggressive		30.6
8.	I	FITNESS	27.1	A	no makeup		30.6
9.	P	caring	25.7	A	big		24.7
10.	A	attractive	21.4	I	FITNESS		23.5
11.	P	strong convictions	21.4	P	homosexual		20.0
12.	I	CONCERN W/ WORK	20.0	P	DOMINANT		16.5
13.	P	intelligent	18.6	A	TALL		14.1
14.	P	DOMINANT	15.7	I	CONCERN W/ WORK		14.1
15.	P	emotionally strong	14.3	I	CARS		14.1
16.	A	HAIRY FACE	14.3	I	drinks alcohol		14.1
17.	I	CARS	14.3	I	men friends		14.1
18.	P	honest/fair	14.3	A	ugly		14.1
19.	P	intense/persistent	14.3	A	HAIRY FACE		12.9
20.	P	good manners	14.3	P	not caring		11.8
21.	A	rugged	14.3	A	fat		11.8
22.	A	well-dressed	14.3				

* P: personality; A: appearance; I: interests.

Source: V.S. Helgeson. (1994). Protypes and dimensions of masculinity and feminity. *Sex Roles, 31*, 653–682. Copyright 1994. Reprinted by permission.

and the BSRI; *adventurous, ambitious, strong convictions,* and *interested in fitness and sports* are included on the BSRI; *self-confident* is on the PAQ; and *hostile, arrogant,* and *selfish* are on the unmitigated agency scale of the EPAQ. Let's take a closer look at the prototypes of masculinity and femininity.

Masculinity. It is interesting to note that features unique to the masculine male are socially desirable (e.g., well-dressed), but features unique to the masculine female are socially undesirable (e.g., not caring, ugly). Physical appearance features were named more often in response to a masculine

female than a masculine male. What does this mean? When we think of a masculine woman rather than a masculine man, we especially focus on physical appearance. Among the masculine personality traits identified, the ones attributed to a female were negative (aggressive, unsocial, uncaring, hostile). The masculine female was viewed more negatively all around than the masculine male. The traits ascribed to the masculine female were more indicative of unmitigated agency than agency.

Femininity. With a feminine target, physical appearance features came to mind when thinking of a female more than a male.

TABLE 2.5 Prototypical Features of Femininity

		Feminine Female				Feminine Male	
1.	P*	CARING	37.5	P	homosexual		48.3
2.	P	good manners	35.9	A	thin		46.6
3.	A	wears a dress	34.4	P	insecure		31.0
4.	A	long hair	29.7	P	emotional		31.0
5.	A	WELL-DRESSED	28.1	I	LIKES ART		29.3
6.	P	self-confident	26.6	P	CARING		27.6
7.	I	CONCERN W/ APPEAR	26.6	I	women friends		27.6
8.	A	attractive	23.4	A	WELL-DRESSED		25.9
9.	P	SOFT-SPOKEN	23.4	I	dislikes sports		24.1
10.	I	family-oriented	21.9	I	interest in fashion		22.4
11.	I	likes music	21.9	A	gesticulates		22.4
12.	P	SOCIAL	21.9	I	CONCERN W/ APPEAR		22.4
13.	A	makeup well done	20.3	A	high-pitched voice		20.7
14.	P	DELICATE	20.3	P	SOCIAL		19.0
15.	A	small	20.3	P	SHY		19.0
16.	P	SHY	18.8	P	DELICATE		17.2
17.	I	LIKES ART	18.8	P	weak		17.2
18.	I	books	17.2	P	sensitive		17.2
19.	P	friendly	17.2	P	creative		15.5
20.	P	intelligent	15.6	P	talkative		15.5
21.	P	traditional	15.6	P	SOFT-SPOKEN		15.5
22.	A	smiles	15.6				
23.	A	manicured nails	15.6				

* P: personality; A: appearance; I: interests.

Source: V.S. Helgeson. (1994). Protypes and dimensions of masculinity and femininity. *Sex Roles, 31,* 653–682. Copyright 1994. Reprinted by permission.

This is similar to the finding for the masculine targets. Thus, physical appearance comes more to mind when thinking of a female than a male, regardless of whether the target is masculine or feminine. Feminine physical appearance features included wears a dress, wears frills, wears heels, wears makeup, and has long hair. Some personality features were distinct to the feminine male; some of these were positive (e.g., talkative, emotional, creative) and some negative (e.g., insecure, weak).

One limitation of this research is that the conceptions of masculinity and femininity are limited to the people who have been studied: typically, White, middle-class American men and women. It would

be interesting to know more about conceptions of masculinity and femininity across people of different races, classes, religions, and more diverse age groups, such as younger children and the elderly. Try Exercise 2.2 to see if you can broaden your understanding of people's views of masculinity and femininity.

THE SOCIAL CONTEXT SURROUNDING GENDER. An emphasis during this period, and today, is on how the social context influences the nature of gender. Social psychologists, in particular Kay Deaux and Brenda Major (1987), have examined gender as a social category by emphasizing the situational forces that influence whether sex

---

EXERCISE 2.2
Prototypes of Masculinity and Femininity

Construct your own prototypes of masculinity and femininity by asking 20 people, 10 men and 10 women, to describe a masculine and a feminine person and consider the following questions in their descriptions.

1. What does a masculine (feminine) man (woman) look like?

2. What personality traits does a masculine (feminine) man (woman) possess?

3. How does a masculine (feminine) man (woman) behave?

4. What is a masculine (feminine) man (woman) interested in?

5. What does a masculine (feminine) man (woman) think about?

List all of the features mentioned, and construct a frequency distribution for each feature. Identify the most frequently named features and indicate what percentage of your respondents named each feature.

To make your study more interesting, focus on a specific group of people that you think are underrepresented in this research. You might choose children, the elderly, people of a minority race such as Asian Americans, Hispanic Americans, or African Americans, or people of a unique occupation. Then compare the responses you receive to those shown in Tables 2.4 and 2.5. Use only one target sex, male or female, so that you can compare the responses you receive to those shown in the tables.

---

interactions with people (Bohan, 1997; Tavris, 1999). According to the constructionist viewpoint, there is no essence to masculinity and femininity; instead, masculinity and femininity are categories constructed by society (Bohan, 1997; Tavris, 1999). Masculinity and femininity reside in the eyes of the perceiver.

Social constructionists distinguish themselves from the **essentialists,** who view gender as an attribute of a person. Constructionists criticize the essentialist viewpoint for leading to false universals. Essentialists compare men and women and make conclusions about differences in general. Social constructionists ask Which men? Which women?, emphasizing the diversity of human experience (Bohan, 1997). Another concern that constructionists raise is the assigning of qualities that are associated with women to the female sex rather than to the context in which women find themselves (Bohan, 1997). For example, should a lack of assertiveness be ascribed to the female sex or to the subordinate role that women inhabit? Constructionists are concerned that qualities that result from societal forces, such as oppression, are being ascribed to the female gender. They also are concerned that recent essentialists, such as Carol Gilligan, are encouraging women to value qualities that emerge from oppression. Gilligan applauds women's different, but equally important, way of viewing morality: by focusing on relationships. According to Bohan (1997), it is a very effective strategy for the oppressor to encourage the oppressed to value their qualities. The problem in the area of gender is that society does not value the qualities associated with women to the extent that society values the qualities associated with men.

Constructionists are concerned that the experiences women have are being attributed to the women themselves rather

differences in behavior are observed. Their model of sex differences is discussed in more detail in Chapter 4. Another approach has been the movement by the **social constructionists,** who argue that gender does not reside inside a person but resides in our than society. As an example, Bohan (1997) makes the point that women today take self-defense classes to prepare them for the violence of society. This strategy focuses on women rather than society as the problem. It is easier to change individuals than it is to change social institutions.

There is support for the social constructionist viewpoint. The studies reviewed in Chapter 3 that compare men and women in a number of domains may appear to take an essentialist viewpoint, but the research results in a constructionist conclusion. Most of the reviews of sex comparisons lead to the conclusion that the situation, the context, has a large influence on the size of any differences that appear between men and women. I review in this chapter some studies on stereotyping that show how others' expectations influence behavior, such that the behavior reaffirms the stereotypes that people hold. In these cases, the perceiver is creating the situation. The literature on gender and communication reviewed in Chapter 6 leads to the conclusion that many of the differences in behavior between men and women are more a function of status than of sex; when men and women have the same status, behavior is more similar.

In conclusion, social constructionists emphasize the diversity of human experience and view gender as the effect of an interaction rather than the cause of the interaction. We, the perceivers, create gender by our expectations, by our behavior, and by what we decide to include in this category.

A newer approach to the study of gender roles takes into consideration both of the issues raised in this section: the multifaceted view of gender and the social context surrounding gender. This new approach to the measurement of gender-related individual difference variables is known as **gender diagnosticity** (GD; Lippa & Connelly, 1990). GD estimates the probability that a person is male or female given a set of gender-related indicators (e.g., wears a dress, likes football). Items that discriminate men from women are assigned weights, which depend on the magnitude of the discrimination. GD is a weighted combination of the indicators that discriminate men from women. Indicators may include occupational preferences, personality characteristics, attitudes, cognitive abilities, and leisure interests. Thus, GD can be applied to a broad range of gender-related phenomena and is multidimensional in nature. One advantage over traditional measures of M/F is that GD is tailored to the specific population; in one group of people, being achievement-oriented may be a construct that discriminates between the sexes, but in another group of people, such as college students, this variable may not discriminate between men and women very well. Because GD is not a static category, it does not "reify" the constructs of masculinity and femininity, according to Lippa (1991, 1995). Thus, GD pays special attention to the social context. GD also can change over time as gender-related preferences change. For example, wearing earrings used to be diagnostic of the female sex, but not so today; similarly, wanting to be a medical doctor is no longer diagnostic of sex, as similar numbers of men and women attend medical school. Lippa has shown that GD is more strongly related than traditional M/F scores (defined by the PAQ and BSRI) to gender-related behaviors, such as smiling, spatial skills, and SAT scores (Lippa, 1991; Lippa & Connelly, 1990). The major advantage of the GD measure is that it can change with time and place so that new measures of masculinity and femininity do not have to be continually reinvented.

GENDER-ROLE STRAIN. By viewing gender as a social category, greater attention was given to the influence society has on the nature of gender roles. One outgrowth of this recognition was the research on **gender-role**

strain. This occurs when the expectations that accompany one's gender role have negative consequences for the individual. Gender-role strain is likely to occur when gender-role expectations conflict with one's naturally occurring tendencies or personal desires. A male who is uncoordinated or a female who is athletic may experience gender-role strain in physical education classes. A male who wants to pursue dance or a female who does not want to have children also may suffer some gender-role strain.

I asked the undergraduates in my Psychology of Gender class to identify sources of gender-role strain, that is, situations in which what they wanted to do conflicted with what they were expected to do based on their sex. The women identified three areas of conflict. First, they wanted to be assertive and independent but felt they were expected to be dependent, especially on men. Second, some women said they were expected to be nurturant and to "mother" but were not interested in children. Third, women expressed that they were held to a double standard by society, especially their parents and grandparents: they were expected to get an education but not at the expense of finding a good man to marry.

The men identified four areas of strain. First, some men expressed the desire to talk about inner feelings and problems, but felt this conflicted with the male image, especially the fraternity male. Second, some men felt strain because they were not athletic. Third, some men said they felt conflicted during sports when they were expected to be aggressive and competitive but also wanted to be a "good sport." Fourth, men expressed displeasure over the idea that they were expected to be the dominant force in relationships with women, the one to initiate activities and the one to take charge; they would prefer a more equal relationship.

Obviously, these ideas are only a few examples of gender-role strain—and certainly not from a representative sample. The men and women who gave these examples were enrolled in a Psychology of Gender course. How might their ideas differ from those of other college students? Examine sources of gender-role strain at your college in Exercise 2.3.

Joseph Pleck (1995) describes two theories of gender-role strain. **Self-role discrepancy** theory suggests that strain arises when you fail to live up to the gender role society has constructed. This describes the man who is not athletic, the man who is unemployed, the woman who is not attractive, and the woman who does not have children. **Socialized dysfunctional characteristic** theory states that strain arises because the gender roles that society instills contain inherently dysfunctional personality characteristics. For example, the male gender role includes the inhibition of emotional expression, which is not healthy; similarly, the female gender role includes dependency, which also may not be adaptive. The first four questions in Exercise 2.3 assess self-role discrepancies and the last four questions assess socialized dysfunctional characteristics.

The concept of gender-role strain has largely been applied to men. The ideas were inspired by popular books on men that appeared in the 1970s and the 1980s, such as Goldberg's (1976) *The Hazards of Being Male*, Nichols's (1975) *Men's Liberation: A New Definition of Masculinity*, Tolson's (1977) *The Limits of Masculinity*, and Naifeh and Smith's (1984) *Why Can't Men Open Up?* These books, based largely on anecdotal evidence collected by men interviewing men, outline how some of the features of the male gender role limit men's relationships and are potentially harmful to men's health. These books largely adopt Pleck's (1995) socialized dysfunctional

EXERCISE 2.3
Gender-Role Strain

Interview 10 men and 10 women at your college. Identify common sources of gender-role strain.

1. Think about how men (women) are expected to *behave*. How does your behavior differ from how men (women) are expected to behave?

2. Think about how men (women) are expected to *look*. How does your appearance differ from how men (women) are expected to look?

3. Think about the *personality characteristics* that men (women) are expected to have. How does your personality differ from the personality men (women) are expected to have?

4. Think about the things that are supposed to *interest* men (women). How do your interests differ from the interests that men (women) are expected to have?

5. Think about the ways in which your *behavior* matches the behavior that society expects of men (women). Do you feel that any of these behaviors are harmful?

6. Think about the ways in which your *physical appearance* matches the way society expects men (women) to look. Do you feel that any of these expectations are harmful?

7. Think about the ways in which your *personality* matches the personality society expects men (women) to have. Do you feel that any of these personality traits are harmful?

8. Think about the *interests* that you have that correspond to the interests society expects men (women) to have. Do you feel that it is harmful to have any of these interests?

characteristic theory. Collectively, they identified a number of sources of gender-role strain among men:

1. *Homophobia*, the fear of homosexuality or being considered a homosexual, limited men's abilities to connect with other men.

2. *Competitiveness* limited men's relationships with other men by keeping them from revealing vulnerabilities.

3. *Emotional inhibition* limited men's relationships with both men and women by keeping them from expressing their feelings.

4. *Physical strength* kept men from admitting pain or seeking help for physical problems.

5. An *achievement-orientation* made men goal-oriented at the expense of considering or enjoying the process to reach the goal.

6. *Dominance and aggression* harmed men's relationships with men and women and with society as a whole.

7. *Independence and self-reliance* kept men from asking for needed help.

As you can see, each of these aspects of male gender-role strain has implications for men's relationships and men's health, the two emphases of this text. Do the sources of gender-role strain identified by the men that you interviewed in Exercise 2.3 fit into these seven categories?

Male Gender-Role Strain Instruments. A variety of instruments measure the kinds of male gender-role strain described above (see Table 2.6). Notice that each instrument has a number of subscales reflecting the different sources of strains, and each has a subscale that measures inhibiting emotions. Thus, the inability to express emotions must be one of the most prominent sources

TABLE 2.6   Sample Items from Male Gender-Role Strain Scales

Brannon Masculinity Scale (Brannon & Juni, 1984)

(Indicate extent of agreement)

No sissy stuff—avoiding femininity
It bothers me when a man does something that I consider feminine.

No sissy stuff—concealing emotions
When a man is feeling a little pain he should try not to let it show very much.

Big Wheel—being the breadwinner
Success in his work has to be a man's central goal in this life.

Big Wheel—being admired and respected
It's essential for a man to have the respect and admiration of everyone who knows him.

Sturdy Oak—toughness
I like for a man to look somewhat tough.

Sturdy Oak—male machine
A man should always try to project an air of confidence even if he doesn't really feel confident inside.

Give 'em Hell—violence and adventure
A real man enjoys a bit of danger now and then.

Masculine Gender Role Stress (MGRS; R.M. Eisler & Skidmore, 1987)

(Rate stressfulness of each situation)

Physical inadequacy
Feeling that you are not in good physical condition.
Not being able to find a sexual partner.

Emotional inexpressiveness
Telling your spouse that you love her/him.
Admitting that you are afraid of something.

Subordinate to female
Being outperformed at work by a woman.
Having a female boss.

Intellectual inferiority
Having to ask for directions when you are lost.
Working with people who seem more ambitious than you.

Performance failure
Being unemployed.
Not making enough money.

Gender-Role Conflict Scale (O'Neil, Helms, Gable, David, & Wrightsman, 1986)

(Indicate extent of agreement)

Success, power, competition
Moving up the career ladder is important to me.
Winning is a measure of my value and personal worth.

TABLE 2.6 (continued)

Restrictive emotionality
I have difficulty expressing my emotional needs to my partner.
I have difficulty telling others I care about them.

Restrictive affectionate behavior between men
Hugging other men is difficult for me.
Being very personal with other men makes me feel uncomfortable.

Conflicts between work and family relations
My needs to work or study keep me from my family more than I would like.
My career, job, or school affects the quality of my leisure or family life.

Masculine Role Inventory (Snell, 1986)

(Indicate extent of agreement)

Success preoccupation
There are career drawbacks associated with investing oneself in a relationship.
Strong involvement in a love relationship will ultimately interfere with career activities.

Restrictive emotionality
If people thought of me as a sensitive person, they might exploit me.
In order to become a successful person, it's important not to show emotional weakness.

Inhibited affection
I prefer not to be emotionally involved with another person.
I don't devote too much time to personal relationships.

Masculine Gender-Role Ideology (Pleck, Sonenstein, & Ku, 1993b)

(Indicate extent of agreement)

It is essential for a guy to get respect from others.
A young man should be physically tough, even if he's not big.

of strain for men. The achievement orientation and the repercussions that follow when a man fails to achieve is captured in each of the scales. Concerns with physical strength and elements of homophobia appear on some of the scales.

These instruments have been associated with poor mental health and poor physical health. The Masculine Gender Role Stress scale (MGRS) has been associated with alcohol abuse (Isenhart, 1993) and psychological distress (McCreary et al., 1996). The Gender-Role Conflict Scale has been associated with lower psychological well-being, including lower self-esteem and higher depression among college men (Good & Mintz, 1990; Sharpe & Heppner, 1991). The Gender-Role Conflict Scale also has been associated with negative attitudes toward seeking psychological help and reports of less help seeking from a variety of sources (friends, family, professionals) for personal or academic problems (Good, Dell, & Mintz, 1989). Thus, men who score high on gender-role conflict are in a double bind because they are more likely to be depressed but less likely to seek help for depression.

Another way to view gender-role strain is to examine the prescriptions that society has for the male gender role. Pleck, Sonenstein, and Ku (1993b) argued that men behave as they do not because of biology, but because of society's conception of masculinity. This represents a social constructionist perspective. They created a masculine gender-role ideology scale to represent the extent to which men endorse society's prescriptions for the male gender role. Whereas the PAQ and BSRI masculinity scales measure whether one possesses culturally defined masculine traits, masculine gender-role ideology measures whether one believes the self *should* have masculine traits. The Brannon Masculinity Scale, shown at the top of Table 2.6, reflects masculine ideology and formed the basis for Pleck's own masculine ideology scale; sample items from Pleck et al.'s (1993b) scale are shown at the end of Table 2.6. The scale includes the ideas that men are always ready to have sex, that men should not have to do housework, that men deserve respect, that men should not self-disclose, that men should be physically tough, and that men should not act like women. Each of these ideas is represented in other instruments on male gender-role strain.

In a 1988 national survey of 1,880 adolescent males ages 15 to 19, Pleck and colleagues (1993b) linked masculine ideology to a variety of problem behaviors, including difficulties with school, substance abuse, sexual activity, and delinquency. One limitation of this study is that the data were correlational; thus, we do not know if masculine ideology led to the problem behavior or the problem behavior led to masculine ideology.

Part of the social constructionist view of gender is that different social forces will affect different groups of men—not only men in different cultures, but men of different age groups and men of different racial backgrounds. Thus, the nature of gender-role strain will differ. One ethnic group in which gender-role strain has been studied is the African American community.

Male Gender-Role Strain among African Americans. African American men face a dilemma because in the United States the male gender role is associated with high power and high status but the African American race is associated with a lack of power and low status. American culture does not provide African American men with legitimate pathways to validate their masculinity. Thus, gender-role strain arises among African American men in part due to self-role discrepancy theory, the idea that African American men are not given the opportunity to achieve the male gender role ideal as articulated by American culture. The central features of the masculine gender role are achievement and success; racism and poverty make it difficult for African American men to be economically successful, and they are more likely to be unemployed and are less educated than Caucasian men. Staples (1978) suggests that African American men's lack of opportunity to pursue legitimate pathways to masculinity leads them to resort to other avenues, in particular, violence.

This issue was depicted in a scene from the 1991 movie, *Grand Canyon*. The car of a White man, Kevin Kline, breaks down on the way home from a Lakers game in Los Angeles. No sooner has Kline called a towing company than he is accosted by several young African American men. As the men are about to rob Kline, Danny Glover (another African American man) shows up in a tow truck. Glover tries to talk the leader of the African American men into doing him a "favor" and letting the two of them (Glover and Kline) go on their way. The leader grants the favor but only after getting Glover to admit that he was asking for a "favor" rather than making a demand, *not* out of respect for the man but because he had a gun. The African American leader says, "No gun, no respect—that's why I always got the gun." The threat of violence is one way to get respect.

An avenue that African American men are encouraged to pursue to validate masculinity is athletics; this has been referred to as the "manhood hustle" (Doyle, 1995). A focus on athletics can be healthy, but African American men may neglect their education to spend time on athletics. The reality is that very few African American men, or men in general, will be able to make a living as successful athletes. African American men also may face gender-role strain when the norms for the male gender role clash with the norms for African American culture. The male role in our society emphasizes "doing, competing, and achieving," whereas the African American role emphasizes "feeling and cooperation" (S. Harris & Majors, 1993).

One study explored whether African American and Caucasian men face different sources of gender-role strain. I. Harris, Torres, and Allender (1994) identified 30 messages that American culture provides to men about how they should behave. White men and African American men between the ages of 18 and 74 were asked how much influence each message had on them. More African American men said the message to be a "warrior" had been influential; the warrior message involves identifying with war heroes and risking one's life to prove oneself. More Caucasian men said the message to be "stoic" (i.e., ignore pain, not admit weakness) and the message to be "self-reliant" (i.e., asking for help implies weakness) were influential. These findings support the idea that Caucasian men are less likely than African

American men to emphasize cooperation and feelings.

Female Gender-Role Strain. Gender-role strain has rarely been studied in women. In 1992, Gillespie and Eisler identified five areas of strain for women: (1) fear of unemotional relationships, (2) fear of physical unattractiveness, (3) fear of victimization, (4) fear of behaving assertively, and (5) fear of not being nurturant. Sample items from their scale are shown in Table 2.7. This female gender-role strain scale was associated with depression and was largely distinct from the PAQ femininity scale.

One instance in which gender-role strain may be prevalent among women is when they find themselves in traditionally male settings, such as medical school or law school. D. McIntosh, Keywell, Reifman, and Ellsworth (1994) found that

TABLE 2.7 Sample Items from Female Gender-Role Stress Scale

Fear of Unemotional Relationships
Feeling pressured to engage in sexual activity.
Being taken for granted in a sexual relationship.

Fear of Physical Unattractiveness
Being perceived by others as overweight.
Feeling less attractive than you once were.

Fear of Victimization
Hearing a strange noise while you are home alone.
Having your car break down on the road.

Fear of Behaving Assertively
Bargaining with a salesperson when buying a car.
Supervising older and more experienced employees at work.

Fear of Not Being Nurturant
Having someone else raise your children.
A very close friend stops speaking to you.

Source: Gillespie and Eisler (1992).

women experienced greater strains than men during law school. Over the course of the first year of law school, women's health declined and levels of depression increased relative to men. The investigators identified two major sources of strain among women: sexism, the idea that the women felt they were treated differently, and a lack of free time and a lack of time with one's partner or spouse. The latter source of strain may reflect a conflict that women face between pursuing achievement and tending to their relationships. Partners may be less supportive of women than men putting their personal lives on hold to pursue a career.

SUMMARY. There have been two shifts in the most recent thinking about gender roles. First is the realization that gender roles are multifaceted constructs that cannot be fully captured by single trait measures of agency and communion. Masculinity and femininity are broad categories that include personality traits, physical appearance, and occupational interests and role behaviors. Second, researchers have paid increasing attention to the idea that gender roles are influenced by the social context, the time, place, or culture; thus, conceptualizations of gender roles will change as the social context changes. Measures of gender diagnosticity are one way to take the changing social context into consideration. One outgrowth of the emphasis on the social context in studying gender has been to consider the strains people face from the gender roles society imposes. Strains arise when one's behavior is discrepant from the role that society has set forth, and when the behaviors required of the role are not compatible with mental and physical health. Numerous instruments exist to measure gender-role strain among men and demonstrate relations to poor health. There has been less investigation of female gender-role strain, but one promising avenue to explore is when

women are placed in traditionally masculine settings.

GENDER-ROLE ATTITUDES

In the first half of this chapter, I provided a brief history of how gender roles have been conceptualized and measured. This research was devoted to identifying the features of gender roles. In the next half of the chapter, I investigate people's attitudes toward gender roles. Do you view the traditional male favorably or unfavorably? How do you behave when confronted with people who do not conform to gender-role expectations? First, I examine research on attitudes toward men's and women's roles, that is, whether you believe men and women should have distinct and separate roles or whether you believe they should have similar and equal roles. Then, I review the literature on the three components of attitudes toward the category gender: affect (feelings), cognition (beliefs), and behavior. People's feelings toward gender are described by the term sexism; people's beliefs about gender are referred to as gender-role stereotypes; and people's behavior toward others based on gender is known as sex discrimination.

Attitudes toward Men's and Women's Roles

Do you find it acceptable for women to work outside the home? To serve in the military? Acceptable for men to take the same amount of time off from work as women to have a child? To stay home and take care of children? If you find all of these ideas acceptable, then you have an egalitarian view of gender roles. Most people find that they agree in principle with some of these ideas but not all, or they only partly agree with each of the ideas. For example, most people find it acceptable for women to work outside the home—which is a good thing, because most women do. Fewer people find it acceptable for a woman to work outside the home when she has a 3-month-old child and there is no financial need for her to work.

Attitudes toward men's and women's roles have been referred to as **gender ideologies** (Hochschild, 1989). A **traditional** gender ideology maintains that men's sphere is work and women's sphere is the home. The implicit assumption is that men have greater power than women. An **egalitarian** gender ideology maintains that power is distributed equally between men and women and that men and women identify equally with the same spheres. There could be an equal emphasis on home, on work, or on some combination of the two. Most people's attitudes toward men's and women's roles lie somewhere between the two. Thus, Hochschild identified a third gender ideology, **transitional.** A typical transitional attitude toward gender roles is that it is acceptable for women to devote energy to both work and family domains, but women should hold proportionally more responsibility for the home and men should focus proportionally more of their energy on work.

Perhaps the most widely used instrument to measure attitudes toward gender roles is the Attitudes Toward Women Scale (ATWS; Spence & Helmreich, 1972). The ATWS was developed during the women's movement of the 1960s and assessed beliefs about the behavior of men and women in domains that have traditionally been divided between them, such as raising children, education, and paid employment. Although the scale's title specifies attitudes toward women, many of the items really measure attitudes toward both women's and men's roles. Sample items from the 15-item scale include:

Swearing and obscenity are more repulsive in the speech of a woman than a man.

Women should worry less about their rights and more about becoming good wives and mothers.

It is ridiculous for a woman to run a locomotive and for a man to darn socks.

Sons in a family should be given more encouragement to go to college than daughters.

There are many jobs in which men should be given preference over women in being hired or promoted (Spence & Helmrich, 1972).

Using measures such as the ATWS, it has been shown that women have less traditional attitudes toward gender roles compared to men (Deaux & LaFrance, 1998). This sex difference appears to be an almost universal phenomenon. In a study of adolescents' attitudes toward women in 46 countries, women held less traditional attitudes than men across cultures (Gibbons, Stiles, & Shkodriani, 1991). The authors also divided the countries into two groups: the individualistic and wealthier, such as the United States and Germany, and the collectivist and less wealthy, such as Mexico and India. They found that individualistic cultures were less traditional than collectivist.

Not surprisingly, attitudes toward men's and women's roles have become more liberal over time. Twenge (1997a) conducted a meta-analysis of studies that used the ATWS between 1970 and 1995. Although women's attitudes have always been more egalitarian than men's, the size of the sex difference seems to be getting smaller over time. Both men's and women's attitudes became more liberal during the late 1970s. Women's attitudes continued to become more liberal during the early 1980s; however, men's attitudes did not change any further until the early 1990s.

You probably noticed that some of the items on the ATWS are quite outdated. For example, it is quite common for daughters to go to college and "run a locomotive." The problem with this scale is that today nearly everyone agrees or disagrees with an item. Who wouldn't agree at least on a self-report instrument that men and women should have similar job opportunities? If everyone responds in a similar fashion, it will be more difficult to detect individual differences in gender ideology with the ATWS. The ATWS fails to capture some of the contemporary issues about men's and women's roles, such as whether women should serve in the military, whether men and women should be paid equally for the same work, and whether women have the right to an abortion.

More recently, a feminist attitude and ideology scale was developed that reflects issues more relevant to women today (Morgan, 1996). The Liberal Feminist Attitude and Ideology Scale (LFAIS) has a gender role subscale that reflects relations between men and women and responsibilities at work versus home. Sample items include: "It is insulting to the husband when his wife does not take his last name" and "An employed woman can establish as warm and secure a relationship with her children as a mother who is not employed." The scale also has a subscale devoted to the goals of feminism, in particular, equal opportunities for men and women, but also issues such as violence against women and reproductive rights. The third subscale reflects feminist ideologies: the belief that women are subject to discrimination and that action should be taken to improve the status of women. The LFAIS is correlated with one's perception of oneself as a feminist, with more liberal general political attitudes, and with lower religiosity scores. Women, but not men, who score liberal on this scale are more likely to have a mother who was employed during their childhood.

Just as expectations for gender roles are dependent on the context, there are ethnic and cultural differences in attitudes toward men's and women's roles. Most of the research has focused on African Americans, but there are some studies of Hispanics and Chinese.

AFRICAN AMERICANS. It is not clear whether African Americans have more or less traditional attitudes toward gender compared to Caucasians. Binion (1990) compared 123 adult African American women with 45 Caucasian women. The women were recruited from an employment office, and all were of lower socioeconomic status. Binion measured participants' gender-role traits (using the PAQ) and gender-role attitudes. She found that African American women were more likely than Caucasian women to be classified as androgynous and masculine. Yet, African American women reported more traditional attitudes toward men's and women's roles than Caucasian women; African American women were more likely than Caucasian women to believe that women are responsible for raising the children, that men should not have to do housework, and that men do not take women seriously.

Why are African American women less traditional on measures of gender-role traits but more traditional on measures of gender-role attitudes? Binion (1990) argues that African American women, unlike Caucasian women, are socialized to be independent, self-reliant, and hard-working, traits that conflict with traditional female gender-role norms to be dependent and emotional. One reason African American women possess stereotypical masculine traits is that they have been employed outside the home for a longer period of time than Caucasian women due to economic necessity (Sanchez-Hucles, 1997). According to Binion, African American women need the stereotypical masculine traits to survive in American society, but hold traditional attitudes about gender roles so that they can get along more easily with African American men. Attempts by African American women to gain equality in the home may be especially threatening to African American men, who, unlike Caucasian men, are not viewed as the more powerful group by society. Thus, African American women face a predicament in aligning themselves with the women's movement because doing so puts them at odds with men who are their allies in the race movement.

One way to resolve the contradictions within African Americans is to consider that these attitudes are multidimensional. African Americans tend to have a positive attitude toward women working, which may appear to be a nontraditional gender ideology. However, African Americans also have a conservative attitude about women's role in the home. In a longitudinal study conducted between 1967 and 1981 of over 500 mother and son pairs, African American mothers and sons were more liberal than Caucasian mothers and sons over the course of the study in terms of their attitudes toward women working (e.g., It is all right for wives to work outside the home; Blee & Tickamayer, 1995). Yet, African American mothers and sons were more conservative than Caucasian mothers and sons in their attitudes toward women's role in the home (e.g., Men should not have to perform housework; A woman's place is in the home).

HISPANICS.   Gender-role attitudes are more traditional among Hispanics. In a review of 10 studies that used the ATWS to compare the gender-role attitudes of African Americans, Caucasians, and Hispanics, Caucasian women were the most nontraditional and Hispanic women the most traditional (Vazquez-Nuttall, Romero-Garcia, & de Leon, 1987). Participants in these studies were college students and other adults, largely from the United States. Hispanic women who were more acculturated into the United States expressed more liberal attitudes toward women.

CHINESE.   Historically, men and women in China have held very traditional roles. The Confucian doctrine of the Chinese culture emphasizes the lower status of women compared to men; one doctrine is "The virtue of a woman lies in three obediences: obedience to the father, husband, and son" (cited in Chia, Allred, & Jerzak, 1997, p. 138). In a study comparing students from Taipei, Taiwan, to students in North Carolina, Chinese students had more conservative attitudes toward marital roles in terms of who should make the decisions within the family (Chia, Moore, Lam, Chuang, & Cheng, 1994). Chinese male students thought it more inappropriate for men to express emotion than did American students. Using the ATWS, female students in both countries held more liberal attitudes toward women than did men.

Cross-cultural research on attitudes toward gender can be difficult to conduct because the definition of a traditional gender role differs across cultures. One study found that American women were more conservative than Chinese women because American women preferred more masculine males (Chia et al., 1994). However, the American definition of a masculine male was used in this study; Chinese men are socialized to value poetry, reading, rituals, and music, as well as interdependence and cooperation. No wonder it appeared that American women preferred independent, competitive men compared to Chinese women. But, this doesn't mean that American women are more traditional; they are simply expressing a cultural preference.

There also may be more mundane issues of response bias when comparing cultures. For example, the Chinese emphasis on moderation may explain why they choose responses that are in the middle of the scale rather than at the extremes, in comparison to Americans (Chia, Allred, et al., 1997). Demand characteristics may be especially problematic in studies of the Chinese because the Chinese value interdependence and collectivism over independence (Chia, Allred, et al., 1997).

In this section of the chapter, I examined people's attitudes toward gender roles: beliefs about whether males and females should hold traditional roles where men are more powerful than women, or whether males and females should have egalitarian roles where the power distribution between the sexes is more equal. In examining attitudes toward gender, one can also consider how people *feel* about men and women, how people *think* about men and women, and how people *behave* toward men and women.

Affective Component: Sexism

Sexism is one's attitude or feeling toward people based on their sex alone. Disliking a doctor because she is female or a nurse because he is male are examples of sexism. Instruments that measure sexism often consist of people's beliefs about men and women but contain an affective component to these beliefs. That is, the beliefs reflect either a high or low regard for someone because of his or her sex.

You might expect that sexism has declined over the past several decades, and

perhaps it has. But today there is a more subtle version of sexism. Swim, Aikin, Hall, and Hunter (1995) distinguished between traditional and modern sexism. Traditional sexism includes endorsement of traditional roles for men and women, differential treatment of men and women, and the belief that women are less competent than men. Traditional sexism reflects an open disregard for the value of women. Few people today would publicly express such feelings. Modern sexism, by contrast, includes the denial of any existing discrimination toward women, an antagonism to women's demands, and a resentment of any preferential treatment for women. In short, modern sexism implies that one is not sympathetic to women's issues. Sample items from Swim et al.'s traditional and modern sexism scales are shown in Table 2.8. The two sexism scales are positively correlated, meaning that people who score high on one scale are likely to score high on the other scale. One way that the authors validated the modern sexism scale was to ask respondents to estimate the number of women who held certain jobs. Modern sexism is correlated with overestimating the percentage of women who hold male-dominated jobs; thus, people who endorse modern sexism underestimate women's difficulties in obtaining jobs traditionally held by men.

An example of modern sexism is the perception that African American women have preferred status in the workforce. Some people believe that an African American woman somehow counts twice in terms of affirmative action: once for being female and once for being African American, which gives her a special advantage in acquiring a job. However, the truth of the matter is that African American women are not advantaged (Sanchez-Hucles, 1997). African American women are paid less than White women, African American men, and

TABLE 2.8 Sample Items from Sexism Scales

Traditional Sexism (Swim et al., 1995)

Women are generally not as smart as men.

It is more important to encourage boys than to encourage girls to participate in athletics.

Modern Sexism (Swim et al., 1995)

Discrimination against women is no longer a problem in the United States.

Society has reached the point where women and men have equal opportunities for achievement.

Over the past few years, the government and news media have been showing more concern about the treatment of women than is warranted by women's actual experiences.

Hostile Sexism (Glick & Fiske, 1996)

Women exaggerate problems they have at work.

Once a woman gets a man to commit to her, she usually tries to put him on a tight leash.

Most women fail to appreciate all that men do for them.

Benevolent Sexism (Glick & Fiske, 1996)

A good woman should be set on a pedestal by her man.

Women should be cherished and protected by men.

Many women have a quality of purity few men possess.

Every man ought to have a woman he adores.

White men, and have the lowest-status positions in the workforce. Although there has been an increase in the number of African American women who have attained professional positions, the percentage of White women in professional positions is over 10 times that of African American women. According to Sanchez-Hucles (1997): "The myth of African American women's advantage allows privileged individuals to deny their own privilege and minimize the oppression that African American women and others with unprivileged status face in their work lives" (p. 576).

You probably are thinking of sexism as a negative feeling toward women. But sexism, like any affective attitude, can consist of *negative* or *positive* feelings. This is reflected in the distinction that Glick and Fiske (1996) made between hostile sexism and benevolent sexism. **Hostile sexism** is just as it sounds: feelings of hostility toward women. It reflects the idea that women exaggerate discrimination and take advantage of and manipulate men. **Benevolent sexism,** by contrast, reflects positive feelings toward women, including a prosocial orientation toward women (e.g., the desire to help women). Benevolent sexism is still a harmful attitude, however, because it is rooted in the belief that women are less competent than men and are in need of men's help. Benevolent sexism can be detected in the following remark made by a Promise Keeper: "One of the greatest messages Promise Keepers teaches is how to serve your wife, how to really treat your wife like a queen" (Levin, 2000). Sample items from the hostile and benevolent sexism scales are shown in Table 2.8. Although these two scales reflect two very different affective states in regard to women, the two are positively correlated, meaning that people who endorse items on one scale also endorse items on the other. This positive correlation underscores the idea that both hostile sexism and benevolent sexism are based on negative images of women.

Although sexism can be exhibited toward both men and women, it is typically studied and measured as a negative feeling toward women. People also may have negative feelings toward a person because the person is male. Feminists have certainly been accused of this. The idea of "male-bashing" illustrates our concern with people derogating men. Jokes about women drivers and "dumb blondes" are regularly perceived as examples of sexism. But aren't jokes about men's incompetence at being fathers or men not asking for directions also examples of sexism? I came across the following cartoon in a recent issue of the *New Yorker* (June 5, 2000; see Figure 2.4). I am embarrassed to admit that I laughed. And my husband laughed. Now, imagine that the sex of the characters was reversed: the joke wouldn't be funny and the joke wouldn't be published. See if you can construct a sexism scale that is relevant to men in Exercise 2.4.

Sexism or prejudice may lead to stereotyping and stereotyping may lead to prejudice. However, there is not a one-to-one relation (Stephan, Ageyev, Coates-Shrider, Stephan, & Abalakina, 1994; Stephan & Stephan, 1993). People may hold

"There's an article in here that explains why you're such an idiot."

FIGURE 2.4 People do not always recognize this kind of cartoon as sexism, but if the sexes were reversed, it would easily be labeled as sexism. © The *New Yorker* collection 2000 William Haefeli from cartoonbank.com. All rights reserved.

EXERCISE 2.4
Creating a Sexism Scale

Construct a sexism scale that reflects one's attitude toward men. Remember that the scale can reflect either a positive or a negative feeling about a man based on his sex. Thus, you might have two subscales, one to reflect positive feelings and one to reflect negative feelings. You also might want to create a traditional subscale that reflects how people (say, your parents or grandparents) felt toward men years ago and a more modern subscale that reflects how people feel about men now. Remember, the key is that one has this feeling or belief about someone just because he is male.

Guidelines

Make sure you have at least four items for each subscale.

Administer the scale to a set of 30 college students: 15 men and 15 women.

Administer the scale to a set of 30 older adults (e.g., your parents): 15 men and 15 women.

Find out if the items within each subscale are correlated with one another.

Find out if the subscales are correlated with each other.

Test for sex differences. Are men or women more sexist in regard to their attitudes toward men?

Test for age differences. Are college students or older adults more sexist?

---

stereotypes about men and women without having negative feelings. In the next section, I examine the beliefs that people have about both men and women—really, about men's and women's roles.

Cognitive Component: Gender-Role Stereotyping

The following is a description of a famous person:

> This individual is an accomplished twentieth-century political figure who, prior to entering politics, worked as a research chemist and as a tax attorney.

Who do you think this person is? Can you picture the person? Now read the next description of a famous person:

> This internationally recognized public figure was known to be a loving and involved parent, and had gained a reputation for always being well-coifed and tastefully dressed.

Who do you think this person is? Can you picture the person? Does this description bring to mind a different image than the first one? Are the traits described in the second passage incompatible with those described in the first passage? You might be surprised to know that both passages refer to the same person: Britain's former prime minister, Margaret Thatcher. Gender-role stereotypes probably led you to picture the first person as a man and the second person as a woman.

What Is a Gender-Role Stereotype? A stereotype is a schema or a set of beliefs about a certain group of people. **Gender-role stereotypes** are the features we assign to men and women in our society, features that are not assigned due to biological sex but due to the social roles that men and women hold. Thus, I refer to these stereotypes as gender-role stereotypes rather than sex stereotypes. One reason that it may not have occurred to you that the descriptions

in the previous paragraph were of the same person is that the first description fits our male gender-role stereotype and the second fits our female gender-role stereotype.

Stereotypes have descriptive and prescriptive components. The descriptive component identifies the features of the stereotype. The trait features of the male and female stereotypes are likely to be those found on the PAQ and BSRI masculinity and femininity inventories. The prescriptive component of a stereotype says that we *should* have those features.

Gender-role stereotypes are especially powerful because of their prescriptive component (Fiske & Stevens, 1993). The prescriptive component of a stereotype is enforced by other people; it is our representation of how other people think we ought to behave. For example, you may be a man who doesn't want a career but would prefer to stay home and take care of a family. What will other people's reactions be? Your male friends? Your female friends? Your girlfriend? There is a great deal of pressure from other people to adhere to one's gender role.

Gender-role stereotypes have other unique features. Gender as a category is activated immediately on meeting someone, because one of the first things that you notice about a person is his or her sex. Imagine that you see a baby, such as the one in Figure 2.5 on page 80. The baby has long hair, so it must be a she. But the baby is in a blue car seat, which implies that it is a he. You become extremely uncomfortable because you do not know which pronoun to use. You certainly do not want to refer to the baby as the wrong sex!

Components of Gender-Role Stereotypes. What are the features of the male and female gender-role stereotypes? In 1972, Broverman, Vogel, Broverman, Clarkson,

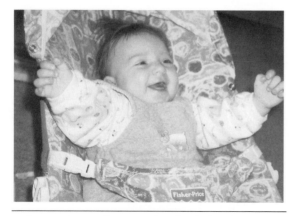

FIGURE 2.5 Photograph of a baby dressed in blue with a lot of hair. Is it a boy or a girl?

and Rosenkrantz developed a questionnaire to assess people's perceptions of masculine and feminine behavior. They administered this questionnaire to over 1,000 people, and concluded that there was a strong consensus as to the characteristics of men and women across age, sex, religion, marital status, and education.

They defined a stereotypical feature as one in which 75% of both males and females agreed that the trait described one sex more than the other. This definition rule led to the 41 items shown in Table 2.9. The male characteristics (listed in the right column) focused on competence, rationality, and assertion. The female characteristics (listed in the left column) focused on warmth and expressiveness. These traits are very similar to the ones found on conventional M/F inventories.

Broverman and colleagues (1972) also found that the male characteristics were more highly valued than the female characteristics. You can see in Table 2.9 that more of the masculine characteristics are socially desirable (top half). The investigators also asked samples of men and women to indicate which of these traits are most desirable in an adult, without specifying the adult's sex; more masculine than feminine items were endorsed. Mental health professionals also rated the masculine items as more healthy than the feminine items for an adult to possess. In fact, when mental health professionals were asked to identify which items fit a healthy female, a healthy male, and a healthy adult, their ratings of the healthy adult and the healthy male did not significantly differ. However, clinicians differed in their ratings of the healthy adult and the healthy female. The stereotype of the healthy adult more closely approximated the stereotype of the adult male than the adult female. Clinicians appear to have different standards of mental health for men and women. The greater value attached to the male stereotype compared to the female stereotype is reminiscent of the greater value attached to the male gender role. Are the features of the male gender role still valued more highly than the features of the female gender role? Answer this question by conducting the experiment in Exercise 2.5, on page 82.

Not only is the stereotype of an adult the stereotype of a male, but apparently, the stereotype of an entire country more closely approximates the stereotype of a male than a female. In one study, college students rated their perceptions of 28 countries, as well as their perceptions of adult men and women from those countries, using 41 agentic and communal traits (Eagly & Kite, 1987). The investigators wanted to determine whether the stereotype of a nation was more similar to the stereotype of the nation's men or the nation's women. College students rated countries with which they would be familiar, such as Iran, Cuba, Israel, Japan, Denmark, and India. The investigators predicted that the stereotype of the nation would be more similar to the stereotype of the nation's

TABLE 2.9   Stereotypic Sex-Role Items (Responses from 74 College Men and 80 College Women)

Competency Cluster: Masculine pole is more desirable

Feminine	*Masculine*
Not at all aggressive	Very aggressive
Not at all independent	Very independent
Very emotional	Not at all emotional
Does not hide emotions at all	Almost always hides emotions
Very subjective	Very objective
Very easily influenced	Not at all easily influenced
Very submissive	Very dominant
Dislikes math and science very much	Likes math and science very much
Very excitable in a minor crisis	Not at all excitable in a minor crisis
Very passive	Very active
Not at all competitive	Very competitive
Very illogical	Very logical
Very home-oriented	Very worldly
Not at all skilled in business	Very skilled in business
Very sneaky	Very direct
Does not know the way of the world	Knows the way of the world
Feelings easily hurt	Feelings not easily hurt
Not at all adventurous	Very adventurous
Has difficulty making decisions	Can make decisions easily
Cries very easily	Never cries
Almost never acts as a leader	Almost always acts as a leader
Not at all self-confident	Very self-confident
Very uncomfortable about being aggressive	Not at all uncomfortable about being aggressive
Not at all ambitious	Very ambitious
Unable to separate feelings from ideas	Easily able to separate feelings from ideas
Very dependent	Not at all dependent
Very conceited about appearance	Never conceited about appearance
Thinks women are always superior to men	Thinks men are always superior to women
Does not talk freely about sex with men	Talks freely about sex with men

Warmth-Expressiveness Cluster: Feminine pole is more desirable

Feminine	*Masculine*
Doesn't use harsh language at all	Uses very harsh language
Very talkative	Not at all talkative
Very tactful	Very blunt
Very gentle	Very rough
Very aware of feelings of others	Not at all aware of feelings of others
Very religious	Not at all religious
Very interested in own appearance	Not at all interested in own appearance
Very neat in habits	Very sloppy in habits
Very quiet	Very loud
Very strong need for security	Very little need for security
Enjoys art and literature	Does not enjoy art and literature at all
Easily expresses tender feelings	Does not express tender feelings at all easily

Source: I.K. Broverman, S.R. Vogel, D.M. Broverman, F.E. Clarkson, and P.S. Rosenkrantz. (1972). Sex-role stereotypes: A current appraisal. *Journal of Social Issues, 28*(2), 59–78.

EXERCISE 2.5
Comparisons of Ideal Adult with Ideal Male and Ideal Female

List the personality traits and interests identified in Tables 2.4 and 2.5 for the prototypical male and prototypical female. These features represent more recent conceptualizations of male and female gender roles. Place each feature on a 5-point scale, such as:

Not at
all caring   1   2   3   4   5   Very
                                  caring

Ask a sample of your friends to rate the ideal person on each of these features. On the next page, ask the same friends to rate the ideal male on each of these features. On the third page, ask the same friends to rate the ideal female on each of these features. Always make sure the "ideal person" is the first page so as to disguise the nature of the research. Counterbalance the order of the second and third pages. That is, ask half of your participants to rate the ideal male second and the other half to rate the ideal female second.

For each item, examine the mean response for the ideal person, the ideal male, and the ideal female. Does the ideal person more closely resemble the ideal male, the ideal female, or both equally?

---

men than the nation's women to the extent that men and women had unequal roles in that country. They reasoned that in countries where men have a higher status than women, the women are less likely to hold prominent roles in the nation and are less visible to outsiders. Indeed, the authors found that students' perceptions of a country were more similar to their perceptions of the men than the women who inhabited that country. This trend was especially strong in countries that students viewed as not emphasizing equality for men and women.

Ethnic and Cultural Views of Men and Women. One of the problems with research on gender-role stereotypes is that the stereotypes are often generated by middle-class Caucasians about middle-class Caucasians. Do people of different races have the same stereotypes of male and female gender roles? The gender-role stereotypes of Caucasian and African American adults who attended vocational schools, community colleges, and universities were examined (P. Smith & Midlarsky, 1985). Participants rated how characteristic 239 traits and behaviors were of men and women. There were more similarities than differences in African Americans' and Caucasians' conceptions of men and women, suggesting that there is some consensus as to the components of gender-role stereotypes. The most frequent characteristics ascribed to the female gender role by both African Americans and Caucasians were "homemaker" and "mother." Both viewed the male gender role as "breadwinner," "leader," and "money manager."

There also were several interesting differences between African Americans' and Caucasians' conceptions of men and women. First, African Americans were less likely to stereotype; that is, they perceived fewer differences between men and women compared to Caucasian persons. Second, there were some interesting ethnic differences in perceptions of men and women. Caucasians were more likely to see women as passive, status-conscious, and interested in shopping, whereas African Americans were more likely to view women as involved with church activities. In regard to the perception of men, Caucasians were more likely to view men as unexpressive, aggressive, competitive, and status-conscious, whereas African Americans were more likely to view men as fathers, family-oriented, and factory workers.

Some of these differences between African Americans' and Caucasians' gender-role conceptions may have to do with socioeconomic status rather than race. Is the Caucasian person's stereotype of the woman as a shopper due to her race or to the likelihood that she has more money than the African American woman? Is the African American person's stereotype of the man as a factory worker due to his race or to the fact that African Americans are more likely than Caucasians to hold blue-collar positions? Other differences, however, may have to do with the cultural values of African Americans and Caucasians. African Americans' view of the female as attending church and the male as family-oriented may reflect a greater attachment to these activities in the African American community than in the Caucasian community.

A major cross-cultural study of gender-role stereotypes was undertaken by J. Williams and Best (1990). They examined the gender-role stereotypes of people in 30 countries, including Nigeria, England, Spain, Australia, India, Thailand, Bolivia, Peru, and the United States. Williams and Best were surprised at the similarities in gender-role stereotypes across such a diverse set of cultures. In all 30 countries, the male stereotype was more active and stronger than the female stereotype. Men were more likely to be viewed as dominant, critical, logical, and unemotional, whereas women were more likely to be viewed as affectionate, helpful, anxious, and dependant. Men were viewed as more instrumental and women were viewed as more relationship-oriented.

Surprisingly, these stereotypes were unrelated to socioeconomic status or the educational level of women in the country. Instead, religion seemed to have a greater influence on stereotypes. Men and women were viewed as more different from one another in predominantly Protestant countries, such as the United States and England, compared to predominantly Catholic countries, such as Ireland and Brazil. Women also were viewed more positively in Catholic than Protestant countries. The authors attributed these findings to the greater prominence that women are given in Catholic compared to Prostestant theology; specifically, in the Catholic Church, the Virgin Mary is held in high regard, as are the many female saints. The investigators also compared the Muslim religion in Pakistan, where all significant religious figures are male, to the Hindu religion in India, which includes both gods and goddesses. The people in Pakistan were more likely than the people in India to differentiate between men and women; in addition, Pakistanis viewed women less favorably than Indians.

Views of Men and Women Who Vary in Ethnicity or Culture. People from a wide variety of cultures may share similar gender-role stereotypes, but do people's stereotypes of men and women depend on the ethnic group to which the target person belongs? In one study, 259 college students (half of whom were Caucasian) indicated their perceptions of Anglo-American, African American, Asian American, and Mexican American men and women (Niemann, Jennings, Rozelle, Baxter, & Sullivan, 1994). The most frequently generated descriptors for each racial group are shown in Table 2.10.

One can see that race certainly influences the content of male and female stereotypes. Both Anglo and African American males are described as athletic, but Asian American and Mexican American are not, and African American females are. Anglo and African American men are described as tall, but Asian American and Mexican American men and women are

TABLE 2.10   Most Frequent Features of Each Category

Anglo American Males	African American Males	Asian American Males	Mexican American Males
Intelligent	Athletic	Intelligent	Lower class
Egotistical	Antagonistic	Short	Hard worker
Upper class	Dark skin	Achievement-oriented	Antagonistic
Light skin	Muscular	Speak softly	Dark skin
Pleasant	Criminal	Hard worker	Noncollege
Racist	Speak loudly	Pleasant	Pleasant
Achievement-oriented	Tall	Dark hair	Dark hair
Caring	Intelligent	Good student	Ambitionless
Attractive	Unmannerly	Small build	Family-oriented
Athletic	Pleasant	Caring	Short
Sociable	Lower class	Slender	Criminal
Blond hair	Ambitionless	Family-oriented	Poorly groomed
Tall	Noncollege	Upper class	Unmannerly
Hard workers	Racist	Shy	Intelligent
Ambitionless	Sociable	Speak with accent	Alcohol user

Anglo American Females	African American ·Females	Asian American Females	Mexican American Females
Attractive	Speak loudly	Intelligent	Dark hair
Intelligent	Dark skin	Speak softly	Attractive
Egotistical	Antagonistic	Pleasant	Pleasant
Pleasant	Athletic	Short	Dark skin
Blond hair	Pleasant	Attractive	Overweight
Sociable	Unmannerly	Small build	Baby makers
Upper class	Sociable	Achievement-oriented	Family-oriented
Caring	Intelligent	Caring	Caring
Light skin	Attractive	Shy	Intelligent
Achievement-oriented	Lower class	Dark hair	Sociable
Fashion-conscious	Egotistical	Slender	Noncollege
Light eyes	Ambitionless	Hard worker	Ambitionless
Independent	Caring	Passive	Passive
Passive	Humorous	Good student	Short
	Honest	Well mannered	Antagonistic

Source: Adapted from Niemann et al. (1994).

described as short. Sociable is an attribute used to describe all groups of women except Asian American, but sociable also is used to describe Anglo and African American men. Caring is an attribute shared by all four groups of women but also Anglo American and Asian American men.

One can also find contradictory features within a given gender-role stereotype, which likely reflect individual differences in perceptions. Mexican American women are viewed as attractive yet overweight. Anglo American men are viewed as hard workers yet ambitionless. African American men and women and Mexican American men and women are viewed as antagonistic yet pleasant.

Another researcher found that stereotypes of women varied by race and social class (Landrine, 1985). College students described stereotypes of lower-class African American women, middle-class African American women, lower-class White women, and middle-class White women. White women were described as more dependent, passive, and emotional than African American women. African American women were described as dirty, hostile, and superstitious compared to White women. Middle-class women were described as ambitious, happy, warm, and intelligent compared to lower-class women. Lower-class women were described as confused, dirty, hostile, inconsiderate, and irresponsible compared to middle-class women. Clearly, the stereotypes of White women were more positive than the stereotypes of African American women, and the stereotypes of middle-class women were more positive than the stereotypes of lower-class women. Landrine (1985) concluded from her research that the traditional stereotype of women in our culture is really a stereotype of middle-class White women.

Thus, the content of gender-role stereotypes appears to be affected by the race and social class of the target. People of different ethnic backgrounds may have some commonality in their conceptions of gender-role stereotypes. However, the specific content of stereotypes appears to depend on the race and class of the target.

THE STRUCTURE OF GENDER-ROLE STEREO-TYPES. Gender-role stereotypes, like perceptions of masculinity and femininity, consist of role behaviors (e.g., being the head of the household or the primary child caretaker), physical features (e.g., muscular or thin), and occupations (e.g., truck driver or nurse). In addition to describing these diverse features of gender-role stereotypes, researchers have begun to look at how the components of stereotypes are related to one another. If you know someone has a masculine occupation, such as construction worker, do you then infer masculine traits, masculine role behaviors, and masculine physical features? For example, if you discover that a woman is an auto mechanic, will you infer that she is independent or emotional? Will you assume she is the person in the house who takes care of finances or of household chores?

In a series of experiments, Deaux and Lewis (1984) examined if one component of gender-role stereotypes implicated the other components. They provided college students with one set of information about a target person, such as feminine traits, and asked them to judge the likelihood that the person would have feminine versus masculine role behaviors, occupations, and physical features. Results showed that one component of gender-role stereotypes did implicate the other components. More important, the stereotype component was more important than the sex of the person in determining the other judgments. This means that if you know a person is a nurse, you are more likely to infer a feminine trait, such as kind, rather than a masculine trait, such as self-confident, even if the target person is male.

When it came to inferring the target person's sexuality, however, college students did use information about both the person's sex and gender-role stereotypes. Homosexuality was most likely to be inferred when one component of gender-role stereotypes, role behavior, was incongruent with the target's sex, for example, a male who decorates the house or a female who climbs mountains.

This research suggests that there is cohesion to gender-role stereotypes and that a person's sex is not as important as traits, role behaviors, and physical features in implicating the stereotype. Thus, if you see a female and know nothing about her, you are likely to assume features of the female gender role. However, if you are provided with other gender-role information about this female, for example, that she exhibits masculine role behavior or is in a masculine occupation, you are more likely to use that information than her biological sex to draw inferences about her personality. Thus, aspects of gender-role stereotypes hang together, but the person's sex does not have to be part of the stereotype.

Physical characteristics were especially likely to lead one to infer other stereotype components (Deaux & Lewis, 1984). That is, when you learn that a female is thin, has a fair complexion, and blonde hair, you are highly likely to infer feminine personality traits (e.g., passive and emotional), role behaviors (e.g., likes to cook and takes care of children), and occupations (e.g., homemaker and nurse). Knowing a person's traits, role behaviors, or occupation has some influence on our inference of other stereotype components but not as large an influence as that of physical characteristics.

To what extent do people rely on stereotypes when other information is available about the person? If you do not know anything about your neighbor's 10-year-old except that the child is a girl, you may buy her a doll for her birthday. What if you know that your neighbor's 10-year-old girl is always climbing trees in the backyard? Would you still buy her a doll, or would something more active seem appropriate? How much you know about a person determines if you use category-based expectancies or target-based expectancies. **Category-based expectancies** occur when you do not know much about a person except the category to which he or she belongs. In that case, you rely on the category to make a judgment. In the absence of any other information aside from sex, you might assume sex-related traits and sex-related preferences. **Target-based expectancies** are the perceptions you have about a person based on individuating information. Once you acquire more information about a specific target, besides the person's sex, you will use that information to make judgments.

There is evidence that individuating information can overcome category-based information. Studies that provide participants with only a modest amount of information about a target person, usually sex, age, and occupation, find that a piece of individuating information is a better predictor of the traits college students assign to the target than the target's sex. That is, in the presence of individuating information, target-based expectancies override category-based expectancies.

Another study showed that role was more important than sex in determining people's perceptions of men and women (Eagly & Steffen, 1984). College students read one of several vignettes in which the sex of the person was varied as was the person's role: employed person versus homemaker. Students rated the character in the vignette on 18 characteristics that were adapted from the PAQ. As shown in Figure 2.6, homemakers were perceived as more communal than employed persons, regardless of the person's sex. As shown in Figure 2.7, employed persons were viewed as more agentic than homemakers, regardless of sex. Figures 2.6 and 2.7 show that there were no differences in perceptions of how communal or agentic men and women homemakers were. Although there was no

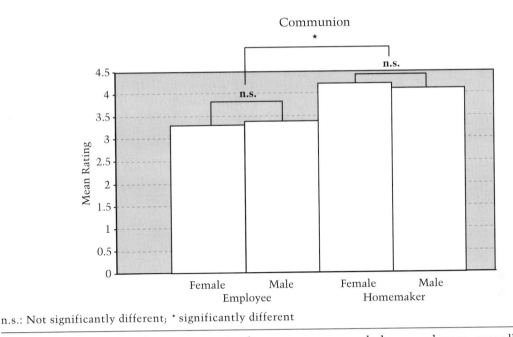

Communion

n.s.: Not significantly different; * significantly different

FIGURE 2.6   Homemakers are perceived as more communal than employees, regardless of sex. *Source:* Adapted from Eagly and Steffen (1984).

difference in perceptions of how communal men and women employees were (Figure 2.6), employed women were rated as *more* agentic than employed men (Figure 2.7). With the exception of this latter finding, the study showed that perceptions of men and women were similar when their roles were similar.

SUBCATEGORIES OF GENDER-ROLE STEREOTYPES.   As men's and women's roles have changed, we have created multiple categories for men and women. That is, we create subcategories of gender-role stereotypes. For example, our stereotype of a male businessman is not the same as our stereotype of a male construction worker; likewise, our stereotype of a female homemaker is not the same as our stereotype of a female doctor. Two studies have examined subtypes of the female stereotype; both

showed that people have a traditional and a nontraditional subtype for women (Clifton, McGrath, & Wick, 1976; Six & Eckes, 1991). The traditional woman included being a housewife and being maternal. The nontraditional woman was a feminist and a career woman. A third subtype reflected woman as sex object, vamp, tart, and Playboy bunny. One of the studies investigated subtypes of men (Six & Eckes, 1991). The categories that emerged were less distinct than the categories of women. There were two tough-minded subtypes: the career man and the cool playboy; the other subtype reflected a quieter, softer, philanthropist man.

Is having subcategories within one general stereotype helpful? It may seem that subtyping is beneficial because it detracts from the power of the overall stereotype. However, subtyping is merely a way

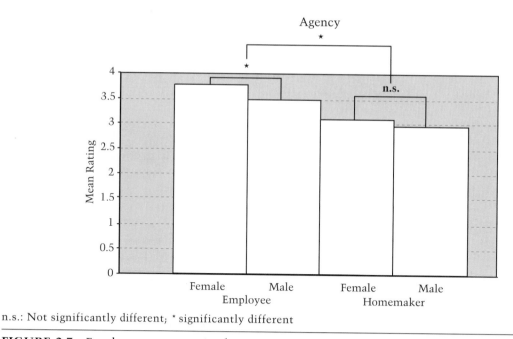

n.s.: Not significantly different; * significantly different

FIGURE 2.7 Employees are perceived as more agentic than homemakers. There is no sex difference in how agentic male and female homemakers are perceived to be. However, female employees are perceived to be *more* agentic than male employees. *Source:* Adapted from Eagly and Steffen (1984).

to create an exception and leave the overall stereotype intact (Fiske & Stevens, 1993). How many of you know someone who is extremely prejudiced against African Americans but manages to adore Michael Jordan? Jordan is viewed as an exception to the African American stereotype and a member of the subtype "successful African American athlete" or "successful athlete." Thus, subtyping does not necessarily reduce the power of stereotypes.

DO GENDER-ROLE STEREOTYPES SERVE ANY FUNCTION?   A stereotype is a belief about someone based on his or her membership in a category. Categorizing people and objects simplifies our world. Think about when you first meet someone. You place that person into a number of categories, each of which leads you to draw a number of inferences.

You notice whether the person is male or female, a student or a professor, Catholic or atheist, athletic or nonathletic. You then use these categories to make certain inferences. For example, you might feel more comfortable swearing in front of an atheist than a Catholic because expletives often have religious connotations. But who is to say that the atheist would not be offended or that the Catholic hasn't a foul mouth? You may assume the student is about 20 years old and the professor about 50. There are exceptions here, too, as you may find a 50-year-old return-to-school student and a 30-year-old professor. Although there are exceptions, categories generally simplify information processing.

The danger of stereotyping is that it influences our perception and recollection of events in a way that can be harmful to men and women. For example, gender-role stereotypes can lead people to perceive men and women differently when they are displaying the same behavior (Aries, 1996). In one study (Newcombe & Arnkoff, 1979), men and women in a conversation used the same number of tag questions (i.e., ending a sentence with phrases such as "isn't it?") and qualifiers (i.e., using words that convey uncertainty such as "I guess" or "I think"). Although men's and women's behavior was identical, respondents perceived that women used more tag questions and qualifiers than men, consistent with the female stereotype. Why is this important? As you will see in Chapter 6, women are perceived to use less powerful language than men, and women's language has implications for judgments of their competence. Thus, misperceiving women's language can lead to misperceptions of competence.

Another problem with stereotypes is that they can lead us to treat people differently when we should not. That is, we may discriminate against people based on their sex. Stereotyping can be harmful when our beliefs influence our behavior toward others in such a way that others confirm the stereotype. Imagine you believe that boys are not good at reading and do not like to read, so you don't give your male preschooler any books to read. Is it a surprise that he has more difficulty than the girls in kindergarten when it comes to reading? No, your stereotype will have created the situation. This is known as a **self-fulfilling prophecy.**

A self-fulfilling prophecy was demonstrated in a study that showed female college students behaved in ways that fit the stereotype a hypothetical male held of them (Zanna & Pack, 1975). Female participants were told that they had the opportunity to interact with a male who was made to appear desirable (had no girlfriend, was tall, attended their college) or undesirable (had

a girlfriend, was short, attended another college). In addition, the female students read a description of this male in which he expressed either traditional or nontraditional views of women. Three weeks before the experiment and then during the experiment, the female students were asked to rate themselves on a series of masculine and feminine traits, which they knew would be shown to the hypothetical male partner. The investigators found that female respondents changed their self-description to be more traditional or less traditional depending on the male's preferences, but only when he was presented as desirable. As shown in the left side of Figure 2.8, women displayed themselves as more nontraditional when the hypothetical male expressed nontraditional rather than traditional views of women. When the hypothetical male was not presented as a desirable partner, the male's views did not affect how women portrayed themselves (right half of Figure 2.8).

Finally, another study showed that people conform to others' stereotypes in terms of the tasks and chores they are willing to perform (Skrypnek & Snyder, 1982). Previously unacquainted pairs of college students were told to negotiate which person would perform each of 24 pairs of tasks. The negotiation took place via a signaling system, as students were placed in separate rooms so that they could not see or hear each other. In all cases, a male interacted with a female. The men, however, were led to believe that they were either interacting with a female or a male, and they behaved differently depending on whether they thought the person was male or female. The women who were perceived to be female chose more feminine tasks, whereas the women who were perceived to be male chose more masculine tasks. The men probably encouraged partners thought to be female to perform feminine chores and

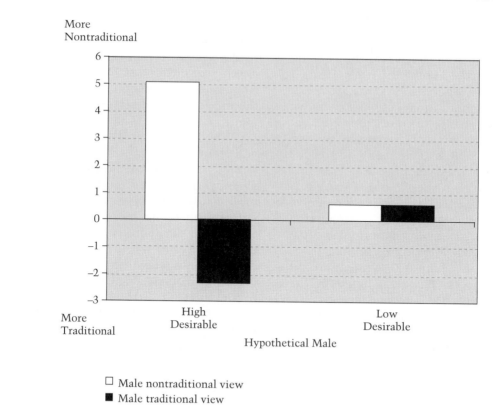

More
Nontraditional

More
Traditional

□ Male nontraditional view
■ Male traditional view

FIGURE 2.8 When a hypothetical male was presented as a desirable partner, females changed their self-descriptions to be more nontraditional if he expressed nontraditional views of women and more traditional if he expressed traditional views of women. When the hypothetical male was presented as low in desirability as a partner, the male's views of women did not affect the women's self-descriptions. *Source:* Adapted from Zanna and Pack (1975).

partners thought to be male to perform masculine chores. Toward the end of the experiment, the women themselves came to initiate these kinds of choices. That is, the men's expectations actually influenced the behavior of the women partners.

Up to this point, the impact of the self-fulfilling prophecy on stereotypes has sounded mostly negative. Can the self-fulfilling prophecy ever help performance? If I believe that boys are quite skilled at reading and give a boy a lot of books to read, will he develop superior reading skills?

Quite possibly. Shih, Pittinsky, and Ambady (1999) investigated whether stereotypes can help as well as hinder performance. They studied quantitative skills among Asian women because of the contradictory stereotypes for Asians and women in this domain: females are depicted as having inferior quantitative skills, whereas Asians are depicted as having superior quantitative skills. The investigators found that Asian women's performance on a math test improved when their racial identity was made salient but deteriorated when their gender identity was made salient. Thus, it appears that stereotypes can influence performance in both positive and negative ways.

ALTERING GENDER-ROLE STEREOTYPES. If we make exceptions for cases that do not fit our stereotypes and treat people in ways to confirm our stereotypes how, if possible, can stereotypes ever be altered? It is true that stereotypes are difficult to change. We tend to notice information that confirms our stereotype and to ignore information that disconfirms it or to create a special subtype for those disconfirming instances. We also make dispositional or trait attributions for behavior that confirms the stereotype but situational attributions for behavior that disconfirms the stereotype. Let's take an example. We expect women to show an interest in children. Therefore, if we see a woman playing with a baby, we are likely to make the dispositional attribution that she is nurturant rather than the situational attribution that she is bored and looking for a way to distract herself. Conversely, if we see a man playing with a baby, we are more likely to decide that situational forces constrained his behavior (i.e., someone told him to play with the baby) because attentiveness to children is not consistent with the male gender-role stereotype. Test this idea yourself by coming up with stereotype-consistent and stereotype-inconsistent behaviors in Exercise 2.6 and asking people to make attributions for those behaviors.

There are circumstances in which stereotypes can be changed. First, it is easier to disconfirm stereotypical traits when the behavior that reflects the trait is clear rather than ambiguous (Rothbart & John, 1985). For example, it would be easier to disconfirm the stereotype that a woman is talkative rather than the stereotype that a woman is emotional, because it is easier to observe talking or not talking than

---

EXERCISE 2.6
Attributions for Stereotype-Consistent and Stereotype-Inconsistent Behavior

Identify a set of five behaviors that are stereotype-consistent for men and five behaviors that are stereotype-inconsistent for men. An example of a stereotype-consistent behavior is "Joe watches football on television." An example of a stereotype-inconsistent behavior is "Joe is washing the dishes." Now, do the same for women. An example of a stereotype-consistent behavior is "Maria is sewing a shirt." An example of a stereotype-inconsistent behavior is "Maria is changing the oil in her car."

Now, ask 10 men and 10 women to explain each of the behaviors. Categorize each explanation as dispositional (due to something about the person, a trait) or situational (due to something about the environment, such as luck, chance, or the force of an external agent). It is best to be blind to the sex of the person who gave you the response.

---

emotionality. It also is easier to disconfirm positive traits than negative traits (Rothbart & John, 1985). Thus, your favorable impressions of people are more easily changed than your unfavorable impressions; it is easier to change people's beliefs that a woman is kind than to change people's beliefs that a woman nags. Rothbart and John (1985) remark, "Favorable traits are difficult to acquire but easy to lose, whereas unfavorable traits are easy to acquire but difficult to lose" (p. 85).

The prototype approach has been applied to stereotyping to understand how stereotypes can be altered (Rothbart & John, 1985). The likelihood of a target being associated with a category depends on how well the target fits the category overall. When faced with a target person, we try to find the closest match between the target person's features and the features of a specific category, or stereotype. How good the match is depends on how prototypical, or how good an example, the target is of the category. Disconfirmation of a feature of a stereotype is more likely to occur if the target person otherwise closely matches the category. That is, we are more likely to change a feature of a stereotype if the disconfirming behavior is in the context of other behavior that fits the stereotype. Let's take an example. The feature "not emotional" is part of the male stereotype. How might we decide that being emotional is acceptable for men? We will be more persuaded by an emotional male who watches football than by an emotional male who reads poetry; similarly, we will be more persuaded by a successful competitive businessman who is emotional than an emotional male hairdresser. What would have to happen for us to view the traditionally masculine occupations, such as lawyer and doctor, as acceptable for women? We will be more convinced by a female doctor who is married and has a family than by a single female doctor with no family in the area. We are more likely to view disconfirming behavior as acceptable if it is displayed by someone who otherwise fits the gender-role stereotype.

Sometimes we do not have to alter our stereotype because a target person calls to mind more than one stereotype; then, we can choose which stereotypes to invoke. When thinking of Martina Navratilova, do you apply the category "lesbian" or "successful athlete"? To someone who likes Navratilova but has a negative stereotype of lesbians, she will more closely approximate the stereotype of successful athlete. For prejudiced people, she does not represent a disconfirming instance of the stereotype of lesbians; instead, she is an example of the stereotype for "successful athlete."

VIEWS OF STEREOTYPE-INCONSISTENT INFORMATION. What happens when a person of one sex displays behavior that corresponds to the other sex? Earlier, I said that we might fail to notice the behavior, ignore the behavior, or make a situational attribution for it. When faced with gender-role-incongruent behavior that we cannot ignore, we may view the behavior as more extreme. For example, assertiveness may be viewed as more extreme when displayed by a woman than a man. In one study, job applicants who used power in their speech were perceived as more aggressive than job applicants who did not use power in their speech, *especially* when the applicant was female (Wiley & Eskilson, 1985). As shown in Figure 2.9, women who used power in their speech were viewed as more aggressive than men.

Correspondent inference theory (Jones & Davis, 1965) can explain why we make more extreme judgments for stereotype-inconsistent behavior. **Correspondent inference theory** is a theory about dispositional attributions for behavior that specifies the conditions that foster more extreme or stronger dispositional attributions. According to this theory, we are more likely to make dispositional attributions for behavior that is not normative, but unique. We are more likely to infer that a person is emotional if that person cries during a comedy than during a sad movie. Because many people cry during sad movies, this behavior is considered to be normative; so, crying during a sad movie does not say anything about an individual's personality. Crying during a comedy, however, is not normative and leads to stronger trait attributions for behavior. Similarly, we are more likely to infer that a person is religious if he or she goes to church on a Tuesday rather than a

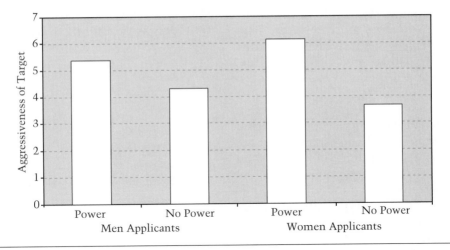

FIGURE 2.9 Aggressiveness of women applicants. Job applicants who used power in their speech were perceived as more aggressive than job applicants who did not use power in their speech. This was especially the case for female applicants. *Source:* Adapted from Wiley and Eskilson (1985).

Sunday. And we are more likely to infer aggression in a woman who uses power in her speech than in a man who uses power in his speech because the woman's behavior is more unique.

In addition to viewing gender-role-inconsistent behavior as more extreme, we also view this behavior in more negative terms than gender-role-consistent behavior. In a review of the literature on leadership, female leaders were viewed less favorably than male leaders because the behavior expected of a leader more closely approximates expectations for the male gender role than the female gender role (Eagly, Makhijani, & Klonsky, 1992). The investigators found that females were judged especially harshly if they demonstrated a stereotypical masculine style of leadership (autocratic) or if they held a male-dominated role. Eagly and colleagues also found a positive correlation between this bias and the year the study was published, meaning that the bias is increasing rather than decreasing over time.

Thus, women are faced with a dilemma when taking positions of leadership: if they adhere to the leader role, they violate the female gender role; if they adhere to the female gender role, they are not living up to the leader role. Men may be faced with the same dilemma when they take on traditionally female roles, such as child caretaker: if they adhere to the caretaker role and leave work to tend to a sick child, they violate the male gender role; if they adhere to the male gender role and put their work first, they are not living up to the caretaker role.

DO STEREOTYPES REFLECT REALITY? Stereotypes reflect society's beliefs about the features that men and women possess, about which there is widespread agreement. But do stereotypes reflect reality? Some people argue that stereotypes exaggerate the differences that are observed between men and women. In 1972, Broverman and colleagues found that men and women differed in their self-perceptions but viewed the differences between the stereotypical man and the stereotypical woman as more extreme. That is, women viewed themselves as feminine and men viewed themselves as masculine, but women viewed themselves as less feminine than the female stereotype, and men viewed themselves as less masculine than the male stereotype. This study suggested that there was some correspondence between people's perceptions of others and themselves, but that stereotypes of others were more extreme than views of self.

Gender-role stereotypes are an exaggeration in that they do not take into consideration any overlap between men and women. It is certainly not the case that all men are independent and all women are emotional. There will be some women who are more independent than the average man, and some men who are more emotional than the average woman. Our perceptions of men and women reflect this awareness. In one study, men and women were asked to estimate the likelihood that a male and a female possessed a trait, a behavior, or a physical feature (Deaux & Lewis, 1983). There were numerous sex differences; however, people did not perceive that all men and no women possessed masculine attributes. As shown in Table 2.11, men were rated as more likely to be independent than women, but students still thought women had a 58% chance of being independent. Similarly, students thought women were more likely than men to take care of the children in the family, but that men had a 50% likelihood of taking care of children. Thus, our beliefs about men and women are not mutually exclusive.

Consistent with this research, other investigators have suggested that our gender-role stereotypes are rooted in reality and do not exaggerate the differences between men and women. Swim (1994) compared college students' perceptions of the magnitude of 17 differences in men's and

TABLE 2.11 Perceived Likelihood That the Target Would Possess the Attribute, in Percentages

	Men	Women
Sample Traits		
Independent	.78	.58
Emotional	.56	.84
Sample Behaviors		
Takes the initiative with the opposite sex	.82	.54
Cares for the children	.50	.85
Sample Physical Features		
Muscular	.64	.36
Small-boned	.39	.62

Source: Adapted from Deaux and Lewis (1983).

women's personalities to the results of research findings. If people perceived the same size difference on an attribute, such as empathy, as the research found, the stereotype would be accurate. Swim concluded that there was *not* a consistent tendency for students to overestimate the differences between men and women. Overestimation of the size of sex differences occurred for only two behaviors, aggression and verbal skills. Students thought the size of the difference between men's and women's aggression and women's and men's verbal skills was greater than research findings have shown to be true. More recently, Hall and Carter (1999) conducted a similar analysis of 77 traits and behaviors among five samples of college students. They also concluded that students are quite accurate; however, students who viewed themselves as more stereotypical were less accurate in their beliefs about men and women.

In sum, people's beliefs about the difference between men and women are fairly good representations of the actual differences. One problem with this area of research is that it is difficult to test the accuracy of many components of gender-role stereotypes. Obviously, one can determine objectively that men, on average, are taller than women. But how does one determine whether men are truly more independent than women? How does one determine whether women are more empathic than men? This may be an impossible task because of the **shifting standard** (Deaux & LaFrance, 1998). The shifting standard is the idea that we might have one standard for defining a behavior for one group but another standard for defining the behavior in another group. Recall that stereotype-inconsistent information was viewed as more extreme than stereotype-consistent information. For example, if you learn that a woman drives across the country alone, you might classify that behavior as highly independent. However, this same behavior displayed by a man may be less noteworthy. The same behavior is viewed as more extreme when displayed by a woman than a man. Because we presume men to be more independent than women, it may take more "independent behavior" to judge a man as equally independent as a woman. Similarly, it may take more displays of helpfulness by a woman than a man to label the person "helpful." You might consider a man who takes care of an infant to be quite helpful but not even notice a woman who cares for an infant.

The shifting standard makes it difficult to compare men's and women's behavior because we have different standards for defining a behavior that is displayed by a man versus a woman. Behavior that is similar may appear to be different because of shifting standards. Recall the research that showed that when men and women used the same language, differences were perceived (Newcombe & Arnkoff, 1979). Behavior that actually differs between men and women also may appear similar

because of shifting standards. For example, you might believe that men are helpful because they will stop and help someone with a flat tire. You might also believe women are helpful because people are more likely to seek support from a woman than a man. But the behaviors are different and not necessarily comparable.

Taken collectively, these studies show that it is difficult to assess the accuracy of stereotypes. We may perceive men and women to behave differently because sex differences in behavior truly exist. Or, it may be that our stereotypes about men and women affect our interpretation of the behavior.

STATUS OF STEREOTYPES TODAY. Have stereotypes changed over time? Bergen and Williams (1991) investigated this question by comparing the stereotypes of male and female college students in 1972 to those in 1988. In each of the two years, 100 students (50 male, 50 female) were asked to rate how frequently each of 300 items was associated with men and women. The correlation of the ratings across the two years was high (.90). The investigators also wondered whether people's perceptions of men and women had become more variable over time, but there was no difference in the standard deviation of the ratings—a measure of variability—across the two years. Bergen and Williams were careful to point out that just because students' stereotypes of men and women had not changed, this did not mean that their self-perceptions were unchanged. Recall the earlier discussion on self-perceptions of masculinity and femininity: recent research showed that women had become more masculine or agentic over time.

Another way to learn whether society's stereotypes of men and women have changed is to examine depictions of men and women on television. Three of the most poplar sitcoms in the 1980s reflected the new emphasis on androgyny: *Family Ties, Growing Pains,* and *The Cosby Show.* All three depicted feminine-looking, dedicated mothers who were professionals in male-dominated fields (architect, writer, lawyer). The shows also featured devoted fathers who were professionals in fields that required sensitivity and concern for others (educational program producer for a PBS station, psychiatrist, obstetrician). The influence of the media on gender roles is discussed in Chapter 4 when we review gender-role socialization theories of sex differences. Try Exercise 2.7 to see if you think stereotypes have changed.

EXERCISE 2.7
Stereotypes Obtained from Media Portrayals of Men and Women

Examine a set of television shows to see if and how the stereotypes of men and women have changed. You may focus on a particular type of program or sample across a variety of programs (e.g., drama, comedy, cartoon). Then, examine one episode of 10 different programs and record the following for each character:

1. Character's sex.
2. Character's appearance.
3. Character's role (housewife, doctor, detective).
4. Character's personality traits.
5. Character's behavior.

If you are really energetic, conduct the same kind of experiment on a similar set of shows that appeared on television 20 or 30 years ago. Then, compare the two sets of stereotypes. A variation of this experiment is to review television commercials or magazine advertisements.

CHILDREN'S STEREOTYPES. Gender-role stereotyping begins at an early age. In a study of 3- and 5-year-olds, Haugh, Hoffman, and Cowan (1980) found that children rated male and female infants in gender-role-stereotypical ways. They showed the children videotapes of two infants, one labeled a boy, "Bobby," and the other labeled a girl, "Lisa." Children were asked to choose which infant matched a given trait (e.g., strong or weak, smart or dumb, nice or mean, quiet or loud). Even children this young were clearly aware of gender-role stereotypes. They were more likely to choose the girl infant as weak, dumb, nice, and quiet, and the boy infant as strong, smart, mean, and loud.

Young children have more rigid stereotypes about men and women than do adults (Golombok & Fivush, 1994), probably because children's thinking in general is more rigid (Donaldson, 1976). Young children are more likely than adults to rely on target sex than individuating information when making a judgment about a person. That is, children rely more on category-based expectancies than target-based expectancies in comparison with adults. Attention to individuating information appears to increase with age. For example, in one study, children ages 4 through 10 were asked to choose which toy a target child would like to play with (C. Martin, 1989). Each child was given a description of a boy or a girl who had stereotypical, nonstereotypical, or neutral interests. A stereotypical interest would be a boy who likes to play with airplanes or a girl who likes to play with a makeup kit; a nonstereotypical interest would be a boy who likes to play with an iron or a girl who likes to play baseball. The child was then asked how much the target child wanted to play with the following four sex-typed toys: a car, a train engine, a sewing machine, and a doll. The younger children, on average 4½, chose the toy that matched the target child's sex, regardless of the target child's interests. For example, when told that the target girl likes to play baseball, younger children still believed the girl would prefer to play with a sewing machine than a car. Older children, on average 8½, paid attention to both kinds of information, the target child's sex and the target child's interests. They thought that a boy who likes to play with an iron would be interested in the train engine because he was a boy but also a doll because of his feminine interests. Another study also found an increase in the use of individuating information and less reliance on target sex as the age of the child increased (Biernat, 1991).

At first glance, it may seem that increasing age leads to decreasing use of gender-role stereotypes because people are using the individuating information instead of the target's sex to make judgments. Yet, I pointed out earlier that gender-role stereotyping increases with age. How do these two ideas fit together? Older students may be less likely to rely on target sex to infer behavior, but they use their knowledge of gender-role stereotypes to generalize from one aspect of gender-role behavior to another. The older students are taking into consideration the individuating information rather than target sex, but that individuating information comes from gender-role stereotypes. Beliefs about gender roles— masculinity and femininity—may be more rigid than beliefs about sex (Biernat, 1991).

Among the components of a stereotype, it appears that children acquire the role-related components before the trait components (Ruble & Ruble, 1982). That is, children are more likely to perceive that boys play with trucks, grow up to be doctors, and climb trees, whereas girls play with dolls, grow up to be nurses, and play hopscotch, *before* they ascribe independence and competitiveness to boys and emotionality and helpfulness to girls.

The perception of masculinity and femininity as opposites takes time to develop in children. Biernat (1991) asked kindergartners, third-, seventh-, and tenth-graders, and college students to judge targets on features of masculinity and femininity. She found that masculinity and femininity had a small positive correlation among the kindergartners, were uncorrelated among the third-, seventh-, and tenth-graders, and were negatively correlated among the college students. Thus, it seems that it takes time for our conceptions of masculinity and femininity as opposites to appear.

Do children's stereotypes reflect those of their culture? Zammuner (1987) studied the stereotypes of children, ranging in age from 5 to 12, in Holland and Italy. Because Italy has more traditional gender roles than Holland, Zammuner expected that the children in Italy would have stronger gender-role stereotypes than the children in Holland. Zammuner found a great deal of consistency in the stereotypes of both sets of children. Both Italian and Dutch children perceived men to be more lazy, superficial, absent-minded, and violent, yet also more clever and stronger than women. Italian and Dutch children perceived women to be more gossipy, vain, and weak, but also more patient, sensitive, and comforting than men. Zammuner also found evidence of an egocentric bias in both boys and girls, that is, the tendency to ascribe positive traits to one's own group and negative traits to the outgroup. Traits that girls assigned to themselves, such as patient, were perceived by boys not to be linked to one sex. Traits that boys assigned to themselves, such as clever, were perceived by girls not to be linked to one sex.

Despite these similarities, Italian children were more likely than Dutch children to perceive sex differences in personality traits. In studies of toy preferences, Dutch children were more likely to perceive toys as gender-neutral and less likely to choose a sex-appropriate toy to play with compared to Italian children. In addition, girls from both countries chose more "incorrect" toys (i.e., toys that are not congruent with their gender role) than boys. This finding fits with the literature in English-speaking countries, suggesting that the male gender role is more rigid than the female gender role.

Behavioral Component: Sex Discrimination

In 1993, Shannon Faulkner applied to an all-male military school, the Citadel (Lacayo, 1995). She was accepted because she made no reference to her sex on the application. When the Citadel discovered that they had admitted a female, they withdrew the offer. A U.S. District Court ruled that the all-male admissions policy was unconstitutional and Faulkner entered the Citadel in August 1995. She lasted five days and then withdrew. Whether the fight was lost due to a lack of physical preparation for the Citadel, or to the emotional stress of death threats and classmates clad in T-shirts bearing the slogan "1,952 bulldogs and 1 bitch," no one can be sure (Lacayo, 1995). Her departure was marked by cheers and honking horns.

Several months later, in January 1996, lawyers from the Virginia Military Institute (VMI) argued before the U.S. Supreme Court that the VMI was not suitable for women because a woman's aspirations in the South are largely to marry, women's ethics revolve around care more than justice, even "macho" women cry, and only "bad girls" would want to attend an all-male military school (Carlson, 1996). The Court, however, ruled that the school would have to admit women.

Discrimination is the differential treatment of individuals based on their membership in a category. Sex discrimination, the subject of the above cases, is the differential treatment of persons based on their sex. As shown by the remarks made to the Supreme Court, gender-role stereotyping and prejudice or sexism can lead to sex discrimination. In a noteworthy case on sex discrimination, social psychological research on gender-role stereotyping was presented to the Supreme Court and played a critical role in the Court's decision. Thus, I next describe the situation in some detail.

The case involved Ann Hopkins, who was denied partnership at Price Waterhouse, one of the top eight accounting firms in the United States. Hopkins maintained that she was denied partnership because of her sex. Price Waterhouse maintained that she had some "interpersonal skills" difficulties: "According to some evaluators, this 'lady partner candidate' was 'macho,' she 'overcompensated for being a woman, and she needed a 'course at charm school.' A sympathetic colleague advised that Hopkins would improve her chances if she would 'walk more femininely, wear make-up, have her hair styled, and wear jewelry'" (Hopkins v. Price Waterhouse, 1985, p. 1117, cited in Fiske, Bersoff, Borgida, Deaux, & Heilman, 1991).

A notable feature of this case is that the literature on gender-role stereotyping was presented to the Supreme Court and became an important factor in its decision. Susan Fiske, a social psychologist and an expert on stereotyping, testified to the conditions that foster stereotyping. One condition is when an individual is unique in his or her membership in a given category. A single man in a class of 30 women or a single Asian person in a class of 20 Caucasians is more likely to become a victim of stereotyping. Only 1% of the partners (7 of 662) at Price Waterhouse were female at the time

(Fiske & Stevens, 1993). Thus, Hopkins's sex was salient. Salience draws more attention to the person and, as a consequence, leads to more extreme or polarized evaluations (Fiske & Taylor, 1991). Another condition that fosters stereotyping is when the group to which an individual belongs is incongruent with the person's role, in this case, the person's occupation. For example, male nurses are more likely to be viewed in terms of gender-role stereotypes than female nurses. In the 1980s, a woman who was a manager of a Big 8 accounting firm was in a nontraditional occupation for women, an occupation incongruent with the female gender role. Recall that stereotype-inconsistent behavior, such as being in a nontraditional role, is viewed as more extreme; thus, assertive behavior on the part of Hopkins was likely to have been viewed as aggressive.

One feature of stereotyping is that people perceive and interpret a situation in accordance with their beliefs. Recall the study from Chapter 1 in which an infant crying in response to a jack-in-the-box was interpreted as fear if the infant was thought to be female and anger if the infant was thought to be male (Condry & Condry, 1976). In the case of Hopkins, some maintained that her clients viewed her aggressive behavior in positive terms: behavior that implied she could get the job done. The partners, however, viewed her aggressive behavior in more negative terms: as that of someone who was difficult to get along with. Citing the literature on gender-role stereotyping, Fiske et al. (1991) maintained that Hopkins's behavior may have been viewed differently because she was female. Recall the research on the shifting standard.

The Supreme Court took the scientific literature on gender-role stereotyping seriously and found in favor of Hopkins. The Court noted that the situation presented to Hopkins by Price Waterhouse was a no-win situation: the job required the trait of "aggressiveness" in order to succeed, yet objected to women possessing this trait. The Court responded:

> Indeed, we are tempted to say that Dr. Fiske's expert testimony was merely icing on Hopkins' cake. It takes no special training to discern sex stereotyping in a description of an aggressive female employee as requiring "a course in charm school." Nor . . . does it require expertise in psychology to know that, if an employee's flawed "interpersonal skills" can be corrected by a soft-hued suit or a new shade of lipstick, perhaps it is the employee's sex and not her interpersonal skills that has drawn the criticism. (*Price Waterhouse v. Hopkins,* 1989, p. 1793, cited in Fiske et al., 1991)

Fiske later stated that she could not decide if this comment meant the court was dismissing psychology as "common sense" or that the stereotyping was so blatant that expert testimony was not needed.

If we remove gender-role stereotypes, will sex discrimination disappear? Not necessarily. Some research has shown that sex discrimination can occur in the absence of gender-role stereotypes. For example, Glick, Zion, and Nelson (1988) found that they could alter managers' and business professionals' perceptions of but not their behavior toward male and female job applicants. When they provided professionals with the same information about male and female applicants—that they possessed features of the male gender role—professionals perceived men and women to be equally aggressive. However, the professionals still indicated they would be more likely to interview male than female applicants for a masculine job and more likely to interview female than male applicants for a feminine job. Thus, regardless of a person's traits, we may still view a receptionist as "female" and a construction worker as "male." It is the occupational stereotypes that could lead to sex discrimination.

When people think of sex discrimination, they typically think of women as being treated unfairly compared to men, especially in regard to employment situations. This topic is reviewed in more depth in Chapter 11. Can you think of any ways that we treat men unfairly? When the military draft was still in effect and only men were chosen, was that sex discrimination? When two working parents divorce and custody is automatically awarded to the mother, is that sex discrimination? Remember that sex discrimination refers to the differential treatment of either men or women due to their sex.

SUMMARY

In the first part of the chapter, I reviewed the history of the psychology of gender. The field began by addressing the question of whether women were intellectually inferior to men. When there was insufficient evidence to support this claim, the field shifted to focus on the mental or psychological differences between men and women, that is, masculinity and femininity. The first comprehensive measure of masculinity and femininity was the AIAS, but numerous other inventories soon followed. A major shift in the conceptualization and measurement of masculinity and femininity occurred in 1974 with the development of the BSRI and the PAQ. These two instruments challenged the bipolar assumption that masculinity and femininity were opposites and the view that the healthiest people were masculine men and feminine women. Instead, the model of mental health was embodied in the androgynous

person, someone who incorporates both masculine and feminine traits.

The most recent approaches to the conceptualization of masculinity and femininity have emphasized their multiple components. We now realize that masculinity and femininity consist of behaviors, roles, and physical characteristics as well as personality traits. Researchers also have emphasized how the social context influences the display of sex differences and the meaning of gender. Gender diagnosticity is one approach that has taken the social context into account. An area of research that emphasizes the role that society plays in shaping gender-role norms is gender-role strain. Gender-role strain is experienced when the norms for one's gender role conflict with one's naturally occurring tendencies or with what would be psychologically adaptive. This area of research has largely been applied to men.

In the second half of the chapter, I moved beyond conceptions of gender roles to the study of attitudes toward gender roles and to the category of gender. Attitudes consist of three components: affective, cognitive, and behavioral. With respect to gender, the affective component is sexism, the cognitive component is gender-role stereotyping, and the behavioral component is sex discrimination. I reviewed instruments that measure traditional and modern sexism as well as sexism that includes both favorable and unfavorable attitudes toward women. I presented the components of gender-role stereotypes and discussed how the components are related to one another. I presented data on the problems with gender-role stereotypes, including how they affect perception and behavior. There are difficulties in changing gender-role stereotypes, in particular because stereotype-inconsistent behavior is often unnoticed, attributed to situational causes, or viewed as more extreme. Sexism and gender-role stereotyping are antecedents to sex discrimination, which I discussed in the context of a recent Supreme Court ruling that utilized data on gender-role stereotyping in reaching its decision.

DISCUSSION QUESTIONS

1. What are some of the weaknesses and strengths of the instruments that have been used to measure masculinity and femininity?
2. Discuss the concepts of agency, communion, unmitigated agency, and unmitigated communion. How would you expect these constructs to be related to one another?
3. What are some areas of gender-role strain for men and women today?
4. In what areas have attitudes toward men's and women's roles become less traditional over time, and in what areas have they remained unchanged?
5. How do gender-role stereotypes relate to self-perceptions of gender role?
6. Why is it difficult to change gender-role stereotypes? How would you go about trying to change someone's gender-role stereotype?
7. The majority of studies on gender-role stereotypes have been conducted on Caucasian, middle-class adults, typically college students. In what ways have these samples limited our research?
8. How would our lives be different if gender-role stereotypes were erased from our minds?

SUGGESTED READING

Ashmore, R.D. (1990). Sex, gender, and the individual. In L.A. Pervin (Ed.), *Handbook of*

personality: Theory and research (pp. 486–526). New York: Guilford Press.

Bakan, D. (1966). *The duality of human existence.* Chicago: Rand McNally.

Deaux, K., & Kite, M. (1993). Gender stereotypes. In F.L. Denmark & M.A. Paludi (Eds.), *Psychology of women: A handbook of issues and theories* (pp. 107–139). Westport, CT: Greenwood Press.

Fiske, S.T., Bersoff, D.N., Borgida, E., Deaux, K., & Heilman, M.E. (1991). Social science research on trial: Use of sex stereotyping research in Price Waterhouse v. Hopkins. *American Psychologist, 46,* 1049–1060.

Spence, J.T., & Helmreich, R.L. (1978). *Masculinity and femininity: The psychological dimensions, correlates, and antecedents.* Austin: University of Texas Press.

Thompson, E.H., Jr., & Pleck, J.H. (1995). Masculine ideologies: A review of research instrumentation on men and masculinities. In R.F. Levant & W.S. Pollack (Eds.), *A new psychology of men* (pp. 129–163). New York: Basic Books.

KEY TERMS

Androgyny—Displaying both masculine and feminine traits.

Benevolent sexism—Positive feelings toward women that are coupled with the notion that women are less competent than men and are in need of men's help.

Category-based expectancies—Assumptions about individuals that are based on characteristics of general categories to which they belong.

Correspondent inference theory—Idea that people are more likely to make dispositional attributions for behavior that is unique or extreme rather than normative.

Cross-sex-typed—Exhibiting gender-role characteristics that correspond with the other sex.

Egalitarian gender ideology—Maintains that power is distributed equally between men and women and that men and women identify equally with the same spheres.

Essentialism—Perspective that gender is a permanent attribute of the person.

Gender diagnosticity—Estimation of the probability that a person is male or female given a set of gender-related indicators.

Gender-role stereotypes—Features that individuals assign to men and women in their society; features that are not assigned due to one's biological sex but due to the social roles that men and women hold.

Gender-role strain—The tension that develops when the expectations that accompany one's gender role have negative consequences for the individual.

Hostile sexism—Feelings of hostility toward women that are reflected by negative assumptions about women.

Prototype—An abstract set of features commonly associated with a category, such that features vary in their representative of the category.

Self-fulfilling prophecy—Situation in which expectations influence behavior toward someone so that the person behaves in a way to confirm one's expectations.

Self-role discrepancy—The strain that arises when one fails to live up to the gender role society has constructed.

Sexism—Feeling toward people based on their sex alone.

Sex-typed—Exhibiting the gender-role characteristics that correspond with one's sex.

Shifting standard—Idea that there is one standard for defining the behavior of one group but another standard for defining the behavior of another group.

Social constructionist approach—Suggests that masculinity and femininity are categories constructed by society and that each society may have a different definition of masculinity and femininity.

Socialized dysfunctional characteristics—Inherently dysfunctional personality characteristics that are fundamental to the gender roles instilled by society.

Target-based expectancies—Perceptions of a person based on individual information about that person.

Traditional gender ideology—Maintains that men's sphere is work and women's sphere is home.

Transitional gender ideology—Maintains that it is acceptable for women and men to identify with the same spheres, but that women should devote proportionately more time to matters at home and men should devote proportionately more time to work.

Unmitigated agency—Personality orientation that is characterized by a focus on the self to the exclusion of others.

Unmitigated communion—Personality orientation that is characterized by a focus on others to the exclusion of the self.

3

Sex-Related Comparisons: Observations

INTRODUCTION TO THE SUBJECT OF SEX-RELATED COMPARISONS

> "Are Boys Better at Math?" (*New York Times*, December 7, 1980)
>
> "New Study Shows Boys Outnumber Girls 13 to 1 as Top Math Scorers" (*Christian Science Monitor*, December 6, 1983)
>
> "Male Hormones Linked to Math Ability in Junior High School Boys, Study Finds" (*Toronto Star*, May 30, 1986)

These are the eye-catching headlines of stories about a study on sex-related differences in math. Differences are interesting. Differences are eye-catching. And, as you will see in this chapter, differences are often exaggerated and overinterpreted—especially the one referred to in the headlines above.

As mentioned in Chapter 1, the subject of sex comparisons is controversial. Scientists continue to debate whether sex comparisons should be made. Regardless of one's philosophy on this issue, one cannot ignore the fact that a vast literature exists on this topic. Many sex comparisons have been made in cognitive abilities: Who has better spatial abilities? Who has greater aptitude in math? Are men or women better with language? Sex comparisons also have been made in social domains: Is one sex more empathic? Who helps more? Who is more aggressive? There is also research on whether men or women are the more "emotional" sex: Do men and women view morality and interact with the world in the same way? I review each of these areas of research. Other areas in which sex comparisons have been made, particularly those having to do with relationships and health, are addressed in subsequent chapters. The primary goal of this chapter is to evaluate the results of sex comparisons in cognitive, social, emotional, and developmental domains.

Before reviewing the results of the sex comparisons that have been made, you should realize that there are more similarities than differences between men and women. However, there are some obvious, incontestable differences. For example, men, on average, are taller than women; men, on average, are stronger than women; women, by contrast, have a higher proportion of body fat than men. These are biological facts. However, even within the realm of biology, there are a great number of similarities between men and women. Most men and women have two eyes, two arms, and two legs; most men and women have a heart, lungs, and vocal cords with which they can speak. The same logic applies to the cognitive and social domains. Although there may be some differences, by far, men and women have more in common in the way that they think and in the way that they behave.

If there are so many similarities between men and women, why do we focus on differences? Belle (1985) suggested that we tend to focus on differences when we are confronted with two of anything. For example, parents with two children are more likely than parents of three or more children to emphasize the differences between the children: "Mary is good in math but not geography; Johnny is good in geography but not math." Parents with three children, however, are more likely to describe each child individually without making a comparison to the other children: "Mary is good in math, Johnny is good in geography, Paul is good in English." Belle also reported that the same phenomenon occurs among anthropologists studying two kinds of cultures. Whereas two cultures are often described in comparison to one another, anthropologists who study more than two cultures emphasize the diversity of human nature. Thus, we would be less likely to emphasize sex differences if there were at least *three* sexes!

If there are more similarities than differences between men and women, why does it seem that men and women are so different? Why is John Gray's (1992) book *Men Are from Mars, Women Are from Venus* a best-seller if men and women are not opposites? One reason is that differences are more salient, more eye-catching, than similarities. I mentioned in Chapter 2 that sex is a very salient attribute of a person. Thus, when two people perform differently on a task and we look for an explanation, we can easily draw the inference that sex must be the distinguishing factor. Second, we have stereotypes about men's and women's behavior that are quite distinct. Under certain conditions, we tend to recall information that confirms our stereotypes and disregard information that disconfirms our stereotypes. This is called **confirmatory hypothesis testing.** We are most likely to do this when we have strong expectations, when the stereotype is about a group, and when the stereotype is about a trait (Stangor & McMillan, 1992). For example, one stereotype about babies is that males are more active than females. Several years ago, my husband and I were visiting some neighbors. There was a male infant and a female infant, both of whom seemed intent on tearing up the house! The mother of the male infant remarked, "Isn't it true about how much more active boys are than girls? Look at Justin compared to Emily." My husband, who does not pay attention to gender as much as many people do, disappointed the mother by failing to confirm her hypothesis. He said, "They both seem pretty active to me!" The mother was clearly disappointed in this response. If a male and a female take a math test and the male outperforms the female, most people will remember this incident. But if the female outperforms the male, we will either forget the incident, decide that the female or male was "different" and not representative of their group, or make a situational attribution (e.g., Maria had seen the test before; Matthew didn't get much sleep last night).

As you will see, a sex difference has been documented in some domains. Unfortunately, a significant difference in performance between males and females is often misunderstood to mean that all males are better at task X than all females or all females are better at task Y than all males. An example of a significant difference in performance is shown in Figure 3.1. You can see that the mean score for men is slightly (and could be significantly) higher than the mean score for women. But you also should notice that there is a great deal of overlap in the distributions of men's and women's scores. Only a small number of men are performing better than all of the women, and only a small number of women are performing worse than all of the men. Thus, even though a sex difference exists, most men and women are performing about the same. Keep this in mind when you read

through the chapter. When you read about a sex difference that does not fit with your personal experience, remember that a sex difference does not imply that *all* men differ from *all* women.

I begin my review on the sex comparison research by discussing the early work of Maccoby and Jacklin, who published the first comprehensive review of sex differences in 1974. Although this book had a great impact on the field, it also was subjected to serious criticism, which I discuss. Then, I review the more recent work on the sex comparisons that have been made in several important cognitive and social domains.

Maccoby and Jacklin's *Psychology of Sex Differences*

Maccoby and Jacklin's (1974) *Psychology of Sex Differences* entailed a comprehensive review of the ways men and women differ psychologically. They examined intellectual or cognitive domains as well as social abilities. Their conclusions were surprising to many people: there were few domains in which sex differences existed, and many stereotypes had no basis in fact. They identified sex differences in only four domains: verbal ability (advantage girls), visual-spatial ability (advantage boys), mathematical ability (advantage boys), and aggression (greater in boys). They found no sex differences in self-esteem, sociability, analytic ability, or achievement motivation, and it was unclear whether there were sex differences in activity level, competitiveness, dominance, or nurturance.

One limitation of Maccoby and Jacklin's (1974) work is that it was a **narrative review.** In a narrative review, authors decide which studies are included and come to their own conclusions about whether the majority of studies provide evidence for or against a sex difference; basically, a

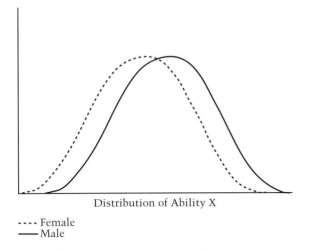

Distribution of Ability X

---- Female
—— Male

FIGURE 3.1 Sample distribution of a hypothetical ability (ability X) for males and females. You can see that there is a great deal of overlap between the two distributions. Yet, the average of ability X is slightly higher for males than females. This illustrates the fact that a sex difference on an ability does not mean that all men differ from all women. In fact, a statistically significant sex difference can exist even when most of the men and women are similar in their ability level.

tally is made of the number of studies that report a difference versus no difference. There are several difficulties with this kind of review. One problem is that the authors decide how many studies are enough to show that a difference does or does not exist. If 12 of 12 studies show a difference, a difference must exist. But what about 10 of 12? Or 8 of 12? Or even 6 of 12? How many is enough? A second difficulty with narrative reviews is that the pattern of results may be disproportionately influenced by findings from small samples. Perhaps the majority of studies show men and women have equal verbal ability but all of these "no difference" studies have sample sizes under 30, and the few studies that report women have greater verbal skills than men are based on sample sizes of over 100. Should we still conclude that there is no sex difference in verbal ability? The power to detect a significant difference between men and women when one truly exists is limited in small samples. Thus, a review of an area of research that contains many small sample studies may lead to the conclusion that no difference exists when in fact there is a true sex difference.

In 1976, Jeanne Block wrote a response to Maccoby and Jacklin's (1974) review of sex differences that was virtually ignored. J. Block reviewed the same literature and arrived at conclusions very different from the ones reached by Maccoby and Jacklin. She examined their review in detail and found several serious problems. First, she noted that Maccoby and Jacklin did not censor the studies they included; that is, they averaged across all studies, whether methodologically sound or not. A number of the studies had very small samples, a problem noted above. Some studies used unreliable instruments; other studies used instruments that lacked **construct validity,** meaning there was not sufficient evidence

that the instruments measured what they were supposed to measure.

Second, J. Block (1976) noted that there was a tremendous age bias in the studies reviewed. She found that 75% of the reviewed studies were limited to people age 12 and under; 40% used preschool children. The reason so many studies were conducted with children is that comparisons between males and females first became popular in developmental psychology. Developmental psychologists compared males and females in their studies, hoping that no differences would be found so that they could combine boys and girls when analyzing their data. Why is it a problem that Maccoby and Jacklin's (1974) review focused so heavily on children? Because they did not take into consideration the fact that some sex differences might not appear until adolescence and later; in fact, the three cognitive differences that Maccoby and Jacklin noted did not appear until adolescence. Adolescence is sometimes referred to as a time of **gender intensification,** a time when boys and girls are concerned with adhering to gender roles. Thus, sex differences that arise as a result of socialization pressures might not appear until adolescence. Even sex differences thought to be influenced by hormones might not appear until puberty. When Block categorized the studies into three age groups (under 4, between 5 and 12, and over 12), she found that sex differences in many domains became larger with increasing age.

Third, J. Block (1976) noted that Maccoby and Jacklin (1974) had omitted some key studies. Block agreed with the sex differences that Maccoby and Jacklin found but also found evidence of other sex differences. She concluded that boys, compared to girls, were better on insight problems, showed greater dominance, had a stronger self-concept, were more active, and were more impulsive. Girls, in comparison to boys, expressed more fear, showed more anxiety, had less confidence on tasks, maintained closer contact with friends, sought more help, scored higher on social desirability, and were more compliant with adults.

The conclusions of Maccoby and Jacklin (1974) and of J. Block (1976) were obviously not the same. Both, however, relied on narrative reviews of the literature. In the 1980s, a new method was developed to review the literature that led to more objective conclusions: meta-analysis. Much of the recent literature on sex comparisons, which is described in this chapter, has relied on meta-analysis. I now describe the meta-analytic approach to sex comparisons.

Meta-Analysis

Meta-analysis is a statistical tool that quantifies the results of a group of studies. In a meta-analysis, one takes into consideration not only whether a significant difference is found in a study but the size of the difference, or the **effect size.** The effect size is calculated by taking the difference between the means of the two groups (in this case, men and women), and dividing this difference by the variability in the scores of the members of these two groups (i.e., the standard deviation). As the size of the sample increases, the estimate of the mean becomes more reliable. This means that the variability around the mean, the standard deviation, often becomes smaller in larger samples. A small difference between the means of two large groups will result in a larger effect size than a small difference between the means of two small groups. Hence, a study that shows men score 10 points higher than women on the math SAT will result in a larger effect size if there are 100 women and men in the study than if there are 20 women and men in the study. The size of an effect is measured with the

d statistic. The rule of thumb used to interpret the d statistic is that .2 is a small effect, .5 is a medium effect, and .8 is a large effect (J. Cohen, 1977). A .2 effect size means that sex accounts for less than 1% of the variance in the outcome; a .5 effect means that sex accounts for 6% of the variance; a .8 effect means that sex accounts for 14% of the variance (J. Cohen, 1977).

If a large effect accounts for only 14% of the variance, is a small effect even worth discussing? As you will discover in this chapter, many sex differences have a small effect size. Whether small means trivial is an issue that continues to be hotly debated. On the one hand, the finding that sex accounts for 1% of the variance in an outcome does not appear to be earth-shattering. However, 1% can be quite meaningful (Rosenthal, 1994): it depends on the outcome. For example, small effects in medical studies can have enormous implications. In a study to determine whether aspirin could prevent heart attacks, participants were randomly assigned to receive aspirin or a placebo. The study was called to a halt before it ended because the effects of aspirin were so dramatic (Steering Committee, 1988). The investigators deemed it unethical to withhold aspirin from people. In that study, aspirin accounted for less than 1% of the variance in heart attacks. What about outcomes that are relevant to gender? Bringing the issue closer to home, R.E. Martell, Lane, and Emrich (1996) used computer simulations to examine the implications of a small amount of sex discrimination on promotions within an organization. They assumed that promotions were based on performance evaluations, but they found that an equal number of men and women at entry-level positions resulted in 65% of men holding the highest-level positions when only 1% of the variance in performance ratings was attributable to sex. So here, a very small bias had large consequences. Keep this in mind when considering the sizes of the effects in this chapter.

There are several advantages to using meta-analysis rather than narrative reviews to understand an area of research. As mentioned previously, meta-analysis takes into consideration the size of the effects; thus, all studies showing a significant difference will *not* be weighted similarly. Another advantage of meta-analysis is that researchers can examine how other variables influence, or moderate, the size of the effect. A **moderating variable** is one that alters the relation between the independent and the dependent variable. I often refer to a moderating variable as an "it depends on" variable. When sex comparisons are made, a difference may "depend on" the age of the respondents, the gender role of the respondents, or the year the study was published. Recall that J. Block (1976) found that many sex differences were apparent only among older participants; thus, age was a moderator variable. Another potential moderating variable is the year of publication. If a sex difference appeared in the 1970s but disappeared by the 1990s, perhaps men's and women's behavior became more similar over time. One can even ask if the results of a sex comparison depend on the sex of the author; men or women may be more likely to publish a certain result. Age, gender role, author's sex, and year of publication are frequently tested as moderator variables in the following meta-analyses.

There is one way that meta-analysis is limited in the same way that narrative reviews are: researchers still make subjective decisions about what studies to include in the review. Researchers conducting a meta-analysis often will come up with a set of criteria to decide whether a study is included in the review. Criteria may be based on sample characteristics (e.g., restrict to English-speaking samples) or on methodological requirements (e.g., participants must be randomly assigned to condition). One difficulty with any kind of review, meta-analytic or narrative, is that studies that fail to detect a difference are unlikely to be published. In meta-analysis, this is referred to as the **file drawer problem** (Hyde & McKinley, 1997): studies that do not find sex differences are not published and end up in investigators' file drawers, so the published studies represent a biased sample of the studies that have been conducted. The file drawer problem is addressed in a meta-analysis by estimating the number of studies having a zero effect that would have to exist for the meta-analysis effect to no longer be significant. When this number is large (i.e., 1,000 studies finding no sex difference would have to exist), one can be more confident in the effect size determined by a meta-analysis. The file drawer problem may not be as significant in studies of sex comparisons as in other research because some of the sex comparison data come from studies whose primary purpose was not to evaluate sex. Investigators may be studying aggression, empathy, or math ability for other reasons aside from sex but report the results of sex comparisons as a matter of routine.

SEX COMPARISONS IN COGNITIVE ABILITIES

Many people assume that men have greater spatial and math abilities than women. Isn't that why men don't have to ask for directions, and why men are so often put in charge of family finances? Probably not. People also assume that women have greater verbal skills than men. Does this translate into women talking more than men? Also, probably not. As the literature below shows, these assumptions are overly simplistic. This area of research is highly controversial because a sex difference in an area of cognition could lead people to assume that one sex is more suitable for a career field that requires that ability. This could ultimately lead to sex discrimination. Thus, it is important that we evaluate this research carefully. For each cognitive ability that I discuss, one or more meta-analyses exist. So that you understand the meaning of a difference, I report the effect size, the d in parentheses for the major findings. As shown in Figure 3.2, a d that is positive indicates that men outperform women and a d that is negative indicates that women outperform men.

Spatial Ability

Spatial ability is not a single construct. Think of all the activities that involve spatial skills: reading maps, doing jigsaw puzzles, locating simple figures in more complex figures (i.e., embedded figures), and mentally rotating three-dimensional objects. Given the diversity of tasks that involve spatial skills, it is no surprise that the results of sex comparisons depend on the type of spatial skill.

Linn and Petersen (1985) conducted a meta-analysis on three distinct spatial skills, shown in Figure 3.3. They found that the size of the difference heavily depended on the type of spatial skill. Men outperformed women on tests of spatial perception ($d = +.44$), which require the respondent to

Men Outperform Women			Women Outperform Men		
.8	.5	.2	0	−.2	−.5	−.8
Large	Medium	Small		Small	Medium	Large

FIGURE 3.2 Indication of the strength of effect sizes (d).

orient an object in space with respect to his or her own body. Men also outperformed women on mental rotation tasks ($d = +.73$), which involve mentally rotating a three-dimensional object that is depicted in two dimensions to match a target object. Men outperformed women on spatial visualization tasks, such as the embedded figures task, which requires one to locate a simple figure in a complex figure, but the difference was very small ($d = +.13$). The size of the effects for mental rotation and spatial visualization was stable across age. The size of the effect for spatial perception increased with age: under 13 ($d = +.37$), 13 to 18 ($d = +.37$), over 18 ($d = +.64$). What does this mean? One possibility is that the difference between boys and girls increases with age due to biological maturation. Another possibility is that the difference between boys and girls increases with age because there is a greater diversity in experiences that involve spatial skills among older children than among younger children. For example, an experience that involves spatial skills is driving a car, and adolescent boys are more likely than adolescent girls to drive cars. Yet another possibility is that the age trend reflects a cohort effect. People from one cohort, or age group, may differ from people in another cohort in spatial perception because the two groups were raised differentially. Older males and females may have been raised in more traditional families where less equal opportunities to develop spatial perception were provided. Because the age comparisons across studies are cross-sectional, we cannot distinguish among these explanations.

Another meta-analysis, conducted in 1995 by Voyer, Voyer, and Bryden, reached similar conclusions. They found moderate sex differences for spatial perception ($d = +.44$) and mental rotation ($d = +.56$), but only a small difference for spatial visualization ($d = +.19$). Thus, the size of the sex

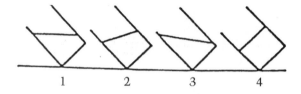

A spatial perception item. Respondents are asked to indicate which tilted bottle has a horizontal water line.

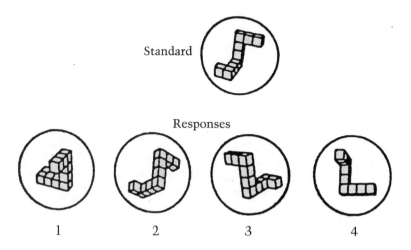

A mental rotation item. Respondents are asked to identify the two responses that show the standard in a different orientation.

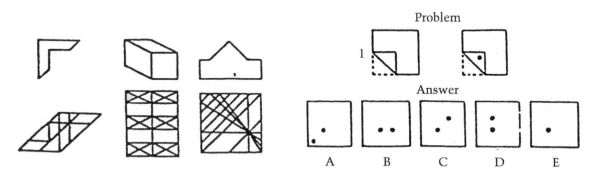

Spatial visualization items. Left, Embedded Figures: Respondents are asked to find the simple shape shown on the top in the complex shape shown on the bottom. Right, Paper Folding: Respondents are asked to indicate how the paper would look when unfolded after a hole is punched.

FIGURE 3.3 Sample items from tests that measure spatial perception, mental rotation, and spatial visualization. *Source:* M. C. Linn and A. C. Petersen (1985). Emergence and characterization of sex differences in spatial ability: A meta-analysis. *Child Development, 56,* 1479–1498. © 1985 Society for Research in Child Development.

difference in spatial skills ranged from very small to large, depending on the particular skill. Similar to the previous meta-analysis, Voyer et al. also found that the size of the sex difference increased with age. In children under 13, sex differences ranged from zero to small. In children over 18, sex differences ranged from small to large. However, Voyer et al. averaged across tasks when they examined age as a moderator variable.

The stability of sex differences in spatial abilities over time appears to depend on the specific spatial ability. Masters and Sanders (1993) conducted a meta-analysis of sex differences on the mental rotation task between 1975 and 1992 and found no relation of the effect size to the year of publication. Thus, sex differences in one domain of spatial ability, mental rotation, has been relatively stable over time.

There is a very consistent and sizable sex difference in one skill that requires spatial ability: aiming at a target (Kimura, 1999). Men are consistently better than women in their accuracy at throwing objects at a target, whether shooting or throwing darts. Physical factors such as reaction time, height, and weight do not account for this sex difference. Differences in experiences with target shooting also do not account for the sex difference (Kimura, 1999). The sex difference can be observed in children as young as 3 years old. Performance on this task seems to be unrelated to performance on other spatial ability tasks, such as mental rotation (Kimura, 1999). (There are other motor skills in which women excel that are not linked to spatial ability, such as fine motor skills that involve the movement of fingers.)

Up to this point, the size of the sex difference in spatial skills has been variable but the effects have always been in the direction of men. Can we at least conclude that the direction of the effect is consistent across spatial tasks? No. A spatial domain

in which women appear to have greater skill than men is spatial location memory (Eals & Silverman, 1994). Women are more likely than men to notice if an object has been moved from its original location, and women are better than men at finding lost objects. If you show men and women a picture that contains a number of objects, such as the one shown in Figure 3.4, and remove or move one object, women will be more likely than men to notice the change. How quickly can you figure out which objects have been moved from the top of Figure 3.4 to the bottom? If you place men and women in a room with objects, after leaving the room, women will be more accurate than men in recalling which objects were in the room and where those objects were located. Women also seem to excel at a game that requires object location (McBurney, Gaulin, Devineni, & Adams, 1997). In a memory game, a set of illustrated cards is presented with the pictures turned face down. There are pairs of cards with the same picture, and each person may turn over any two cards to try to find a match. Women are better than men at finding the matches. Thus, the direction of the sex difference in spatial skills is not even consistent across all tasks.

One conclusion is that men are better at manipulating objects in space and women are better at locating objects. These differences could lead men and women to give directions differently. One study found that women are more likely to use landmarks and men are more likely to use distances and north/south/east/west terminology when giving directions (Dabbs, Chang, Strong, & Milun, 1998). A parallel finding has been shown with rats: female rats are more likely than male rats to rely on landmarks and male rats are more likely than female rats to use geometric cues when solving problems (Kimura, 1992). Look at the map shown in Figure 3.5. How would you get from the Town Hall to Flag Park? Conduct your own

FIGURE 3.4 Example of a test used to measure spatial location memory. Cover the bottom figure and study the top figure. Now, cover the top figure and examine the bottom figure. Which items are in a different location?

FIGURE 3.5   Research has suggested that men and women give directions differently: that men use north/south/east/west terminology and women use landmarks. How would you get from the Town Hall to Flag Park?

survey on how men and women give directions in Exercise 3.1 to see if this is true.

In summary, it is difficult to draw one conclusion about the results of sex comparisons in spatial abilities because the results depend on the specific task. The size of the difference ranges from small to large and is usually, but not always, in favor of men. The size of some differences, in particular spatial perception, seem to increase with age, but the size of other differences, such as mental rotation, seem to remain stable over time.

Mathematical Ability

Certainly, math ability is one domain in which sex differences are clear-cut, right? Recall the headlines at the beginning of the chapter. Two meta-analytic reviews concluded that there was a small sex difference in math ability favoring males. Hyde, Fennema, and Lamon (1990) conducted a meta-analysis of 100 studies on math skills

---

EXERCISE 3.1
Sex Comparisons in Directions

Choose one location that is across the town or city where you live and one location that is not very far away. Ask 10 men and 10 women to give you directions to each of these. Then have them write out the directions. Record use of landmarks, estimates of distance, use of street names, and north/south/east/west terminology to see if there are sex differences.

that involved 254 independent samples. The overall effect size was small, $d = +.15$, favoring males over females. Hedges and Nowell (1995) conducted a meta-analysis of large samples of high school students. They found effect sizes that ranged from $+.03$ to $+.26$, with an average of $+.16$. Thus, both reviews concluded that the overall sex difference in math skills is small.

Like spatial skills, math ability also encompasses an array of distinct skills and results of sex comparisons depend on the specific skill. Results also depend on the age of the participants. In one meta-analysis, men outperformed women on mathematical problem solving $(d = +.08)$, but this difference was limited to older children, specifically high school $(d = +.29)$ and $(d = +.32)$ college students (Hyde, Fennema, & Lamon, 1990). The authors suggested that this sex difference may appear among older students because women take fewer math and science courses than men in high school and college. However, other research has shown that differences in math courses cannot account for men's superior performance in math (Bridgeman & Wendler, 1991). In one domain, math computations, females outperformed males $(d = -.14)$, but this difference was limited to elementary and middle school children $(d = -.20$ and $-.22$, respectively; Hyde, Fennema, & Lamon, 1990). There were no sex differences in understanding of mathematical concepts $(d = -.03)$ at any age. The investigators also noted that sex differences in math skills appear to be decreasing over time. The effect size in studies published before 1974 was $+.31$, whereas the effect size in studies published from 1974 onward was $+.14$. Thus, as men and women are provided with more similar math-related opportunities and are equally encouraged to pursue math, differences may be diminishing.

The small sex difference in math aptitude certainly challenges prevailing stereotypes. Where does the idea come from that men outperform women in math by leaps and bounds? One source is studies of select samples of individuals who are highly talented in math. In Hyde, Fennema, and Lamon's (1990) meta-analysis, the effect sizes for select samples ranged from $+.33$ to $+.59$. This means that among very talented math people, men have greater ability than women. In fact, when these select samples were excluded from the meta-analysis, the effect size was near zero $(d = +.05)$. A major study of talented adolescents showed a sizable advantage for men over women in math. This was the Study of Mathematically Precocious Youth (SMPY) that attracted the headlines at the beginning of the chapter. This study examined nearly 10,000 12- and 13-year-olds who were talented in math (Benbow & Stanley, 1980). To be eligible for the study, students had to have scored in the upper 2% to 5% on a national standardized math test. The study involved six separate samples evaluated between 1972 and 1979. These students completed the math and verbal SAT tests. Although there was no sex difference on the verbal portion of the SAT, a medium-size sex difference appeared on the math portion $(d = +.39)$. The size of the difference was even larger when the extreme high end of this already highly select sample was examined. Specifically, two times as many boys as girls scored above 500, four times as many boys as girls scored above 600, and 12 times as many boys as girls scored above 700 on the math SAT (Benbow, 1988). Benbow noted that the size of the sex difference did not seem to be changing over time.

It is important to realize that the findings from the SMPY study are not representative of the general population: this was a highly select sample. Unfortunately, the results of the study were highly publicized and the selectness of the sample often was not noted or was lost in the content of the news articles. This explains why people seem to believe that there is a larger sex difference in math skills than there really is.

Is nature or nurture responsible for the sex difference in math? Benbow and Stanley (1980) argued that the large sex difference in the SMPY that persisted across time suggests a biological basis. They suggested that this sex difference in math could not have come from boys and girls taking different courses, because they have had similar educational backgrounds at this point in their education (seventh and eighth grade). Others argue that men and women do not have similar experiences with math by seventh or eighth grade in terms of which activities are reinforced by parents, teachers, and peers (J.S. Eccles & Jacobs, 1986). This idea is elaborated on in Chapter 5.

Some people believe that men and women have different attitudes toward math. At some point, math becomes labeled as a masculine domain. A meta-analysis of attitudes toward math and math anxiety on 126 independent samples revealed that sex differences in most attitudes toward math were small, except that men were much more likely than women to view math as a male domain ($d = +.90$; Hyde, Fennema, Ryan, Frost, & Hopp, 1990). The authors found that the size of the difference in attitudes toward math seemed to increase with age; in particular, there were larger sex differences among high school students compared to elementary school children. Thus, if attitudes toward math were to account for sex differences in performance, it would do so only among older students. This fits with the one domain in which a substantial sex difference has been documented in the normal population, problem-solving ability, a difference that appears only among older students. Thus, part of the reason men perform better on math tasks compared to women

among older students is because men are more confident than women in math.

Other investigators considered the possibility that men's greater math ability was linked to men's greater spatial ability. In one study, math ability was linked to a measure of spatial skills that typically reveals consistent sex differences: the mental rotation task (Casey, 1996). Men's higher mental rotation ability accounted for sex differences in math SAT scores in two high-ability samples. In another study, a variety of explanations for men's superior math ability was tested: math anxiety, math self-confidence, and spatial skills (Casey, Nuttall, & Pezaris, 1997). The investigators found that men had higher SAT math scores than women, that men performed better on the mental rotation task, and that women had higher math anxiety. There were no sex differences in math self-confidence. Men's mental rotation abilities, rather than women's math anxiety, accounted for most of the sex difference in the SAT math score. The participants in this study were the top third of college-bound students.

The linking of mental rotation to math ability is correlational in these studies and also limited to high-ability samples. Recall from Chapter 1 that correlation does not imply causation. There may be some third variable that explains men's higher mental rotation and math ability. It is interesting, however, to know that the two are connected.

In summary, sex differences in math for the general population are small and may be decreasing over time. In addition, sex differences in math are not consistent across all math domains. Men have higher problem-solving ability, but women have greater computational skills. There is cross-cultural support for these differences: similar trends have been identified in samples from Thailand, Taiwan, and Japan (Kimura, 1999). Sex differences in math ability among the highly talented are substantial; these differences may relate to men's advantage in spatial skills, in particular mental rotation.

Verbal Ability

Of all the cognitive domains, sex differences in verbal ability are the first to emerge in children (Halpern, 2000). On average, girls talk earlier than boys and develop larger vocabularies and better grammar than boys. Some of these sex differences diminish with time.

Hyde and Linn (1988) conducted a meta-analysis of 165 studies that evaluated sex differences in verbal ability. They found a very small effect ($d = -.11$), in the direction of women outperforming men. The investigators examined several types of verbal ability, including vocabulary, analogies, reading comprehension, and essay writing. All of the effect sizes were small, except for speech production; in that case, there was a moderate effect of female superior performance ($d = -.33$). Sex differences also were consistent across age groups, from 5-year-olds to adults over 26. However, sex differences appeared to decrease over time. In studies published before 1974, the effect size was $d = -.23$; in studies published in 1974 and after, the effect size was $d = -.10$. There also was a trend for articles whose first author was male to report smaller effect sizes than in articles whose first author was female; this reminds us of the potential for investigators to influence their results. More recently, another meta-analysis appeared that was limited to studies of high school students (Hedges & Nowell, 1995); all effects for verbal ability were near zero.

There is one verbal ability in which a large sex difference exists: writing. Standardized tests have neglected to include a writing component because it is difficult to score. However, the Educational Testing Service (1994) administered a writing proficiency exam to fourth-, eighth-, and eleventh-graders in 1984, 1988, 1990, and 1992. Females outperformed males at all ages and at all times of assessment. Thus, the sex difference in writing ability has been stable over time.

Like math ability, sex differences in verbal skills also depend on the population studied. Sex differences are larger when people with verbal difficulties are examined (Hyde & McKinley, 1997). Boys are 10 times more likely than girls to have severe dyslexia and 3 to 4 times more likely than girls to stutter (Halpern, 1992). Several people question whether boys have more verbal difficulties than girls or if boys are more likely to be referred for special services than girls. S. Shaywitz, Shaywitz, Fletcher, and Escobar (1990) followed 445 kindergartners in the state of Connecticut through third grade. They evaluated the prevalence of reading disabilities among children in second and third grade in two different ways. First, they identified reading disabled children by using objective performance criteria; these were referred to as "research-identified" disabled students. Second, they noted whether teachers referred students for special education services for reading disability; these were referred to as "school-identified" disabled students. As shown in the right half of Figure 3.6, schools were two to four times more likely to identify boys as reading disabled compared to girls—a significant difference. As shown in the left half of Figure 3.6, researchers identified similar percentages of boys and girls as reading disabled using objective criteria. Why the discrepancy? Specifically, why are boys who are not objectively determined to have a reading disability labeled so by teachers? Investigators also had teachers rate students on a host of other characteristics. Teachers

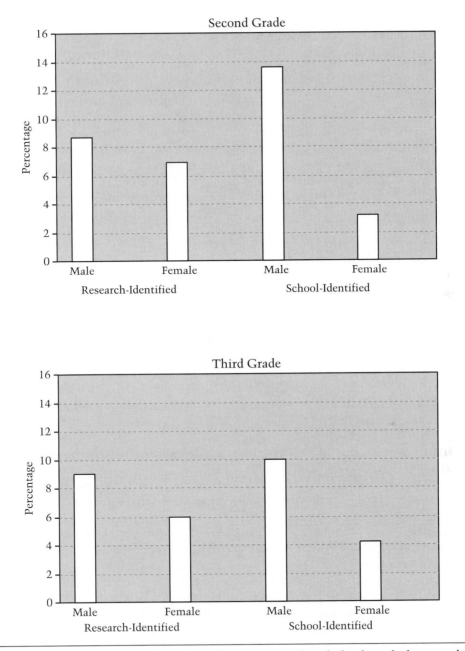

FIGURE 3.6 Identification of reading disability in second and third grade boys and girls. Researchers were equally likely to identify boys and girls as having a reading disability using objective criteria. Teachers at the school, however, were more likely to refer boys than girls for a reading disability using their own subjective criteria. *Source:* Adapted from Shaywitz et al. (1990).

viewed reading disabled boys as overactive and having more behavioral problems compared to non-reading disabled boys. Teachers' views of boys' behavior may have influenced their judgments of the boys' reading ability.

Again, researchers have concluded that sex differences in verbal ability depend on the specific domain. Most differences are small, but some, such as differences in writing ability, are more substantive. The sex difference may be larger when people with verbal difficulties are considered.

Two Studies in Cognitive Abilities

Before winding up this section, there are two recent major studies that evaluate sex differences and similarities for a wide range of cognitive abilities. Let's take a look at these studies and see if they agree with the findings from the previous meta-analyses.

The first is a study conducted by Hedges and Nowell (1995) in which they analyzed data from six nationally representative samples of adolescents and young adults between 1960 and 1992. Between 11,000 and 25,000 people were surveyed in each study. A strength of this report is the representativeness of the samples; too often, studies of sex differences in cognition use select samples, such as highly gifted individuals or even college students. On average, women outperformed men on reading comprehension, perceptual speed, and associative memory, but these effect sizes were small. Men outperformed women on math, social studies, and spatial abilities, but these effect sizes also were small. There were two moderate effects: women performed better in writing, and men performed better in science. The largest effects were for vocational aptitude domains, such as mechanical reasoning, electronic information, and automobile shop information,

where men outperformed women. Although sex differences in math and science narrowed over time, the sex difference in reading and writing appeared to be stable over the 32 years.

Hedges and Nowell (1995) also found that men's scores were more variable than women's on almost all of the cognitive domains examined. There were more men than women in both the bottom and top 10% of the distributions; this explains why sex differences in math are small in nationally representative samples but larger in select, talented samples where only the upper portion of the distribution is examined.

The second recent study on cognitive abilities was conducted by the Educational Testing Service (ETS; Cole, 1991) in 1997. It included over 400 different tests from over 1,500 data sets that involved millions of students from fourth grade through graduate school. The primary conclusion of this study was that sex differences in performance across the different domains were small; most were close to zero. Figure 3.7 shows the size of the differences for 15 domains. The size of a given difference is again represented by the d statistic. In this figure, a positive d means that girls outperformed boys, whereas a negative d means that boys outperformed girls. Notice that the vast majority of the differences are small, between −.2 and +.2. Notice also that the differences within the various kinds of math ability and verbal ability are not consistent. For two verbal abilities (writing and language) there are sizable differences favoring females; the other two verbal skills (reading and vocabulary reasoning) show very small differences in the direction of females. There are two categories of math ability, one of which favors males (concepts) and one females (computation); in both of these cases, the difference is small. Among the other domains, there is a small advantage for boys in geopolitical subjects

12th Grade Profile: Gender Difference and Similarity for 15 Types of Tests

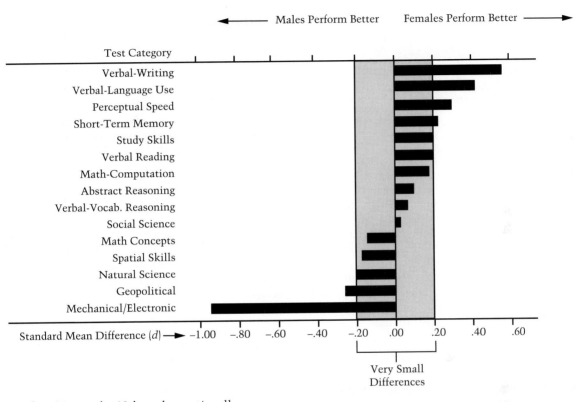

◄—— Males Perform Better   Females Perform Better ——►

Test Category
- Verbal-Writing
- Verbal-Language Use
- Perceptual Speed
- Short-Term Memory
- Study Skills
- Verbal Reading
- Math-Computation
- Abstract Reasoning
- Verbal-Vocab. Reasoning
- Social Science
- Math Concepts
- Spatial Skills
- Natural Science
- Geopolitical
- Mechanical/Electronic

Standard Mean Difference (d) ——► −1.00 −.80 −.60 −.40 −.20 .00 .20 .40 .60

Very Small
Differences

Based on 74 tests for 12th graders nationally.

FIGURE 3.7 Results of hundreds of studies of tests of men's and women's academic abilities. As you can see, most of the sex differences are very small. *Source:* N. S. Cole (1997). *The ETS gender study: How females and males perform in education settings.* Copyright 1997. Reprinted by permission of Educational Testing Service, the copyright owner.

(e.g., history, economics, and geography) and a large advantage for boys in mechanical/electronic subjects. There are small advantages for girls in perceptual speed and short-term memory.

Consistent with previous reports, differences were more likely to be found among older than younger students. There were virtually no differences in any subject area for fourth-graders. Differences in language abilities began to emerge by grade 8, whereas differences in mathematical abilities began to emerge by grade 12. The study also showed that over the past 30 years, the sex difference in mathematical ability has decreased, whereas the sex difference in language has virtually remained unchanged.

Like Hedges and Nowell (1995), the ETS (1997) study showed that males have more variability in their distribution of scores than females. This is shown in Figure 3.8. Thus, there are slightly more males

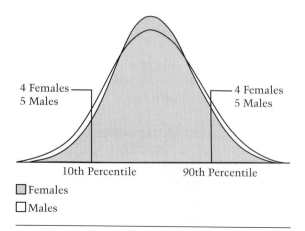

4 Females
5 Males

4 Females
5 Males

10th Percentile   90th Percentile

◻ Females
◻ Males

FIGURE 3.8 Score distributions. On many tests of academic ability, males have more variability in their scores than females, meaning that there are more males at the high end and low end of the distribution. Below the 10th percentile and above the 90th percentile, there are 4 females for every 5 males. *Source:* N. S. Cole (1997). *The ETS gender study: How females and males perform in education settings.* Copyright 1997. Reprinted by permission of Educational Testing Service, the copyright owner.

than females at both the higher and the lower ends of the distribution. The explanation for this finding is not clear. Again, the greater male compared to female variability has implications for studies in which select populations are evaluated, such as only those attending college. Those studies may be sampling from the right half of the distribution in Figure 3.8, making it look like there is more of a male advantage than there really is in the general population.

Finally, the ETS (1997) study noted that, regardless of test scores, females outperform males on nearly all major subject areas when it comes to school grades. High school grades are important because they predict college performance, even when test scores are taken into consideration. The authors suggest that grades may reflect

other domains besides aptitude, such as effort and class participation.

Conclusions

The results of the meta-analyses and the two large-scale studies are similar: most sex comparisons in cognition reveal small differences. Again, keep in mind that a small difference may have meaningful implications. More important than the size of the difference is the variability of the differences. It's much too simplistic to talk about sex differences in spatial skills, math ability, or verbal skills because each domain consists of a number of distinct skills. For example, in the spatial domain, there is a sizable male advantage for one skill, mental rotation. In the verbal domain, there is a sizable sex difference in writing, favoring females. The size of the differences also depends on the sample. There are substantial sex differences in math among highly talented samples and substantial sex differences in verbal skill among those with verbal difficulties. There also seems to be evidence that there is greater male compared to female variability in quantitative, spatial, and verbal skills (Hyde & McKinley, 1997).

The size of the sex difference in math skills appears to be decreasing, but it is not as clear if the size of the sex difference in verbal skills is decreasing. Why would sex differences decrease? If the decrease is real, who is changing? Are women's math skills improving, or are men's math skills deteriorating? Are men's verbal skills improving, or are women's skills deteriorating? It also is possible that it only appears as if the sex difference is changing over time; what may in fact be changing is the methodology of the studies and the political climate. Perhaps the studies conducted more recently are more methodologically sound and less biased. Could methodological flaws explain why the earlier studies showed larger sex differences? Standardized tests may be less sex-biased today than they were 20 or 30 years ago. If more objective testing is responsible for smaller sex differences, then the earlier differences were not real. It also is possible that the political climate has contributed to the decrease in sex differences. The atmosphere has shifted from emphasizing to minimizing sex differences. The political environment may be a cause or an effect of the recent trend toward finding no sex differences in cognitive abilities. The political climate may be a reaction to a true decline in differences, or this climate may contribute to a greater publication of studies that show no differences. Socialization practices also have shifted over time as sex differences in cognitive abilities have diminished. Parents may be more likely to encourage girls to perform well in math and science and to encourage boys to perform well in reading and writing. Explanations for sex differences are elaborated on in Chapter 4.

SEX COMPARISONS IN SOCIAL DOMAINS

Cognitive abilities were easily assessed by standardized tests and measures. Social abilities are a little trickier. How do we judge which sex is more helpful, more sexual, more empathic, or more aggressive? Should we rely on self-report measures? Do people know their own abilities, or will they distort them in the direction of the ability they ought to have? Perhaps observing behavior is a better method to assess social abilities. But are observers truly unbiased in their perceptions and interpretations of a behavior? There are advantages and disadvantages to each method; thus, in social domains, we look for consistency in findings across methodologies.

Empathy

Crying at a sad film, saying "I understand" to a friend who has disclosed a problem, and putting yourself in someone else's shoes are all different ways of empathizing. There are many definitions of **empathy,** but at its core, empathy seems to involve feeling the same emotion as another person or feeling sympathy or compassion for another person. In their review of the literature on empathy, Eisenberg and Lennon (1983) concluded that sex differences in empathy, like sex differences in cognition, depend on how empathy is measured.

Many studies measure empathy in children with the picture-story technique: children are shown a picture and told a story about another child's emotion, then each child is asked what emotions he or she is experiencing. Matching of emotions indicates empathy. There were enough studies using this technique to employ meta-analysis. Eisenberg and Lennon (1983) found a very small effect in the direction of girls scoring higher than boys $(d = -.10)$. Interestingly, there was also a sex of experimenter effect for this measure of empathy: girls were more empathic than boys when the experimenter was female (and most of the experimenters were female), whereas boys were more empathic when the experimenter was male. Thus, the prevalence of female experimenters in these studies could have contributed to the overall sex difference in empathy.

When empathy was measured by self-report, a narrative review of the literature revealed large sex differences favoring females. In other words, women report being more empathic than men. When empathy was measured with physiological measures (e.g., heart rate or skin conductance) or by unobtrusive observational measures of nonverbal behavior, no sex differences in empathy appeared.

How does one make sense of these different findings on sex differences in empathy? Which way of measuring empathy is more accurate? Self-report measures are easily influenced by response biases. Undoubtedly, men and women realize that women are supposed to be more empathic than men. Men and women may distort their self-reports of behavior in the direction of gender-role norms. If this means that physiological measures of empathy are more accurate than self-report measures, then the evidence for sex differences in empathy is relatively weak. However, physiological measures of empathy are not without problems. If your heart starts racing when you watch a woman in a film get raped, what does this mean? Is it empathy, the actual experiencing of another person's distress? Is it compassion? Or is it discomfort at witnessing such a violent act? Thus, the status of sex differences in empathy is unclear.

Helping Behavior

Although I have convinced you that the evidence that women are more empathic than men is weak, you probably have every confidence that women are more helpful than men. But is this true? Not according to Eagly and Crowley's (1986) meta-analysis of helping behavior. The 172 studies in this review measured actual helping behavior or the self-report of a commitment to engage in a helping behavior; in other words, self-reports of general helpfulness were not included. The effect was in the direction of males helping more than females ($d = +.34$). The direction of this sex difference may seem surprising because helping is central to the female gender role. The sex difference was limited to a certain kind of help, however. That is, the situation was a moderator variable: males were more likely than females to help in situations of danger.

Another important moderator variable was the sex of the person in need of help. The sex of the recipient influenced whether a male helped but not whether a female helped. Males were more likely to help females than males, whereas females were equally likely to help males and females. There also was a sex difference in receipt of help. Women were more likely than men to receive help in general ($d = -.46$). In addition, women were more likely to receive help from men than women, whereas men were equally likely to receive help from men or women. Thus, men helping women seems to be an especially prevalent kind of helping.

The investigators found that many of these sex differences were stronger under public conditions, where others could view the behavior, than under private conditions, where the behavior was anonymous. Males and females may behave differently in the presence of others because they are concerned with gender-role norms. In situations of danger, we expect men to provide help and women to receive help. In Eagly and Crowley's (1986) review, the publication year was inversely correlated with the size of the effect, indicating that the sex difference was getting smaller over time. Perhaps our expectations of men's and women's roles in situations of danger have changed over the years.

One of the limitations of this literature is that most of the situations involved strangers. In the real world, most helping behavior occurs in the context of relationships. Thus, the kind of helping that is central to the female gender role may not have been tapped in these studies. Helping behavior that occurs in relationships is discussed in Chapters 7 and 8. In that context, there is a great deal of evidence that both men and women turn to women for help.

Sexuality

Are men the more "sexual" sex, or did the sexual revolution and the women's movement place men and women on more equal ground in the sexual arena? Again, the answer depends on how sexuality is defined. Oliver and Hyde (1993) conducted a meta-analysis on sexual attitudes and sexual behaviors. They evaluated 177 articles published between 1974 and 1990 that contained data from 239 independent samples. Most of the respondents were college students and young adults. Not surprisingly, men were more liberal in their overall attitudes toward sex, but the size of the effects depended on the specific attitude and behavior. Men were more liberal in their attitudes toward premarital sex, especially when it was casual $(d = +.81)$. There were small effect sizes on other attitudes toward sex: men were more accepting of extramarital sex $(d = +.29)$, more likely to have had sex $(d = +.33)$, and had had a larger number of sexual partners $(d = +.25)$. Although there was a very small sex difference in attitudes toward masturbation $(d = +.09)$, there were very large sex differences in the incidence of masturbation $(d = +.96)$, with men reporting a higher incidence than women. The authors found no differences in sexual satisfaction, incidence of kissing, incidence of oral sex, or attitudes toward homosexuality. This latter finding was later contested. Whitley and Kite (1995) located some additional studies on homosexuality and reported a small sex difference $(d = +.26)$, such that males held more negative attitudes than females. The sex of the target was critical: men were significantly more negative than women about gay men $(d = +.51)$ but there was no sex difference in attitudes toward lesbians. The effect sizes for sexual attitudes and behavior were inversely correlated with the year of publication. Thus, many of the sex differences had

diminished over time. Sex differences also decreased as the age of the respondent increased, meaning that there were fewer sex differences among adults than among younger people.

Studies of sexual behavior are difficult to conduct, and many reports have been based on convenience samples (i.e., people who volunteer to participate in a study or people who are interested in the topic of sexual behavior). In 1994, Laumann, Gagnon, Michael, and Michaels reported the results of one of the first national probability samples of sexual behavior, called the National Health and Social Life Survey. Over 3,000 people participated. The study is important because a representative sample of adults ages 18 to 59 was obtained to report on their sexual behavior. Some of the findings correspond to the meta-analysis. There were sex differences in the frequency of masturbation over the prior year: whereas 37% of men said that they never masturbated, the corresponding figure for women was 58%; over three times as many men as women reported masturbating in the prior week (27% vs. 8%). One similarity was in the frequency of sex. Men and women reported that they had sex equally often during the prior year; however, over half of the men (54%) but only 19% of women reported thinking about sex every day or several times a day. Consistent with the meta-analysis, men reported more sexual partners during the prior year and during the prior five years. When respondents were asked how many sexual partners they had had since age 18, over 50% of the men but only 30% of the women identified more than five partners. During the prior year, 23% of men and 12% of women reported having more than one partner.

These latter findings are puzzling. If men and women are having sex with each other, it would seem that they should report the same number of partners. What are some of the reasons that men might report more sexual partners than women? Laumann et al. (1994) offer some possible explanations. First, there are more women than men in the United States, so it is possible for men to have more partners than women. The size of the sex ratio in the population, however, is unlikely to account for such a large sex difference in the number of sexual partners. Second, it is possible that there are a few women having sex with a large number of men. Third, the homosexual population could account for these findings; if gay men have more partners than do lesbians, there would appear to be an overall sex difference in the number of partners. The explanation that the authors favor and the explanation that makes the most sense to me is a response bias: it is socially desirable for men to exaggerate and women to underreport the number of sexual partners.

One problem with research on sexuality is that the data, for obvious reasons, are gathered via self-report rather than observation. Thus, the conclusion that we reach is that men and women *report* differences in sexual attitudes and behaviors. One must be cautious in interpreting these findings because demand characteristics (i.e., men's and women's desire to adhere to their gender roles) may influence the reports. It would be consistent with the male gender role to exaggerate sexual activity and express more liberal attitudes, and it would be consistent with the female gender role to underreport sexual activity and express more conservative attitudes.

Another way to think about sex differences in sexual behavior is to focus on the variability in behavior rather than the average level of behavior. According to Baumeister (2000), women's sexual behavior is more variable than men's. He refers to this idea as **erotic plasticity,** the extent to which one's sex drive is influenced by social and cultural factors. Baumeister argues that women's sexual behavior is more variable than men's and responds to changing

circumstances. For example, he points out that the women's movement had a large effect on women's sexual behavior but not much effect on men's sexual behavior. He uses the survey data that Laumann et al. (1994) collected to illustrate his point. The percentage of men who had five or more sexual partners by age 30 was similar for the oldest cohort of men (38%) and the youngest cohort of men (49%). The behavior of women, however, had obviously undergone a change: the percentage of women who had five or more sexual partners by age 30 was 2.6% for the oldest cohort and 22.4% for the youngest cohort. Baumeister also points out that cultural and social factors have a greater influence on women's sexual behavior compared to men. For example, religion is more closely tied to the sexual behavior of women; a very religious woman may not have sex outside of marriage, whereas a man might be willing to have sex outside of marriage regardless of his religious beliefs. There also is greater variation in women's sexual behavior across cultures. Furthermore, immigration studies show that women's sexual behavior changes as they become more acculturated into their new country, but men's sexual behavior remains the same. Data on sexual behavior among homosexuals also supports Baumeister's theory: lesbians report more heterosexual sex than gay men; there also are more bisexual women than men. Finally, the last piece of evidence that Baumeister uses to support his theory is the finding that there is less consistency between sexual attitudes and sexual behaviors among women than men. In other words, aspects of the situation or the environment have more of an influence on women's sexual behavior. For example, whether a man uses a condom can be predicted from his attitudes about condoms; whether a woman asks a man to use a condom will be determined by a variety of other factors aside from her attitudes about condom usage, such as the characteristics of the particular man.

Although there seems to be a great deal of evidence in support of women's greater erotic plasticity, the evidence is largely circumstantial. In other words, no study has been conducted to actually test the theory. Instead, Baumeister (2000) looked to the literature and examined whether the results from previous studies fit this theory. The theory is certainly provocative.

Why might women's sexual behavior be more variable than men's? One theory is that men have more power than women and that it is more adaptive for low-power people (women) to change their behavior to fit the desires of high-power people (men).

Activity

As I chase my 2-year-old daughter around the yard for the fiftieth time, I find it difficult to convey the stereotype that boys are believed to be more active than girls. Eaton and Enns (1986) conducted a meta-analysis of 90 articles that included 127 comparisons of boys' and girls' activity levels, typically measured either by an objective instrument or by observation. They found that males were more active than females and the effect size was moderate ($d = +.49$). The effect size seemed to increase with age: small among infants ($d = +.29$), medium among preschoolers ($d = +.44$), and large among older children ($d = +.64$). The increase in the effect size due to age could be due to biological maturation or differential socialization pressures. The size of the effect also depended on the presence of peers: when peers were present, the effect was larger ($d = +.62$) than when they were absent ($d = +.44$). This finding supports some kind of social influence. Either boys and girls are changing their behavior to fit peers' expectations or peers are exacerbating boys' and girls' preexisting tendencies.

Aggression

Aggression involves behavior that is intended to harm someone; it is not just the extreme of assertiveness. Although the topic of aggression is evaluated in depth in Chapter 13, I report the general findings on sex differences in aggression here. Eagly and Steffen (1986) conducted a meta-analysis on adult studies of aggression. They reviewed 63 studies that included 81 independent samples. They restricted their analysis to studies that included behavioral measures of aggression and excluded those that relied on self-report alone; the self-report studies would be vulnerable to the same kinds of problems mentioned when I discussed the empathy and sexuality studies. Laboratory studies of aggression typically use the teacher-learner paradigm: the participant is assigned the role of teacher and is instructed to shock the learner (who is a confederate working with the experimenter) for giving incorrect responses. The shocks are an indicator of aggression. Field studies of aggression typically expose people to a frustrating event and then observe their behavior.

The meta-analysis showed a small effect in the direction of men being more aggressive than women ($d = +.29$). The sex difference was larger in laboratory than in field studies and was larger for physical than psychological measures of aggression. The effect size also was larger in those studies where female respondents estimated there would be greater harm to the victim, said they would experience greater guilt and anxiety when aggressing, and said they would face greater danger from aggressing compared to men.

The authors also found a sex of target effect, such that respondents were more aggressive to men than to women ($d = +.13$). This effect also was larger in laboratory than in field studies and larger for physical than psychological measures of aggression. Thus, men are more likely than women to be the perpetrators and the recipients of aggression.

A meta-analysis by Hyde (1986) reported a larger sex difference in aggression ($d = +.50$), but that review included studies of children. Sex differences in aggression appear to be larger among children than adults; different theories may account for this (Eagly & Steffen, 1986). For example, sex differences in aggression may be driven more by biology in younger children but more by the environment in adults; adults have learned that aggression is not appropriate, and adults can better control their impulses than children.

One limitation of the studies on aggression, especially those conducted in the laboratory, is that nearly all involve interactions between strangers. The studies fail to include more real-world examples of aggression, such as someone actually assaulting another individual. A central feature of psychologists' definition of aggression is the intent to harm; one wonders if an intent to harm is present in the laboratory studies of aggression. Real-world aggression is addressed in more detail in Chapter 13.

General Personality Attributes

Up to this point, I have examined sex comparisons of some specific behaviors, but are there general differences in men's and women's personalities? A meta-analysis is available to address this question. Feingold (1994) conducted a meta-analysis on the studies reviewed by Maccoby and Jacklin (1974) and then conducted a meta-analysis that included more recent studies. Both reviews reached the same conclusions. There were no sex differences in self-esteem or locus of control. Men were more assertive than women ($d = +.38$ in first analysis, $d = +.17$ in second analysis), and women were more anxious than men ($d = -.29$ in first

analysis, $d = -.15$ in second analysis). Feingold also examined whether the method of assessing personality affected the results. Most studies of personality rely on self-report measures; as mentioned previously, the problem with those studies is that men and women are often aware of gender-role-appropriate behavior and may respond in ways to fit their gender roles. So, are men really more assertive than women? Or, do men know that they should be assertive, and women know that they should not be so assertive, and so they behave accordingly? Interestingly, an examination of studies that relied on behavioral measures of assertiveness found no sex differences ($d = +.04$), whereas studies that relied on self-report measures showed the expected difference, although it was small ($d = +.23$).

Feingold (1994) conducted a second study that examined markers of the more traditional domains of personality: neuroticism, conscientiousness, agreeableness, extroversion, and openness to experience. Large sex differences appeared on two traits, assertiveness ($d = +.50$) and nurturance ($d = -.97$), the two traits that map onto Bakan's (1966) notions of agency and communion. Men were more assertive than women, and women were more nurturant than men.

Conclusion

Sex differences in the domains of social behavior seem to be strongly influenced by the way the behavior is measured. Demand characteristics, specifically, men's and women's desire to adhere to gender roles, are likely to influence whether sex differences are observed. For empathy, sex differences on self-report measures were large and sex differences on physiological measures were nonexistent. Sex differences in sexual attitudes and behavior are difficult to evaluate because studies rely exclusively on self-report. Sex differences in helping behavior were larger under public than private conditions, and sex differences in children's activity levels were larger when peers were present than when they were not. All of these findings suggest respondents' behavior is influenced by their concern with how they appear to others.

Even when the behavior itself is studied, it too often takes place by observing interactions among strangers. Thus, the question of whether men or women are more empathic, more helpful, or more aggressive with friends, family, and acquaintances is largely unknown. More field research is needed in these areas.

SEX COMPARISONS IN EMOTION

Two people receive news that an accident has caused a neighbor to lose her baby. One cries, the other does not. You probably imagine that the one who cries is female, the more emotional sex. Two people witness some teenagers "soaping" their car on Halloween. One yells at the teenagers and chases them down the street, the other ignores the incident. You probably imagine that the one yelling is male, the more . . . the more what? Yes, anger, too, is an emotion. So, who is the more emotional sex?

There is certainly a stereotype that women are more emotional than men. In fact, one of the items on the PAQ femininity scale is "very emotional." However, the femininity scale is really a measure of communion or expressiveness rather than emotionality. How should we decide whether men or women are more emotional, or whether the sexes are equally emotional? There are three primary sources of information that researchers have examined to address this issue: people's self-reports of their experience of emotion, people's nonverbal expressions of emotion, and people's

physiological responses to emotion stimuli. Unfortunately, there is not a consistent pattern of findings across these three modalities as to whether one sex is more emotional than the other. I review each source of information.

In this section, I examine emotionality at a broad level. I devote some attention to specific emotions, but greater coverage of specific emotions is found in subsequent chapters; for example, sadness is examined more closely in Chapter 12 on depression, and anger is examined more closely in Chapter 13 on aggression.

The Experience of Emotion

First, we can ask whether men and women experience emotions similarly. Many investigators argue that men and women have similar emotional experiences. Ekman (1992) points out that there is a universal set of emotions that both men and women experience and that there are common facial expressions that generalize across the two sexes as well as across different cultures. When individual emotions are examined, it appears that men and women experience the emotion similarly. For example, similar incidents provoke men and women to anger (Averill, 1982). However, there may be more subtle sex differences in the experience of emotion. Although the causes of anger are similar for men and women, women are more often angered by the behavior of close others, whereas men are more often angered by the behavior of strangers (Fehr, Baldwin, Collins, Patterson, & Benditt, 1999).

Do men and women experience emotions with the same frequency? We typically address this question by asking men and women to provide direct reports as to how often they experience a particular emotion. Studies that use direct self-report methods typically reveal that women report greater emotion than men (LaFrance & Banaji, 1992), even in the context of close relationships (Sprecher & Sedikides, 1993). This leads to the conclusion that women are more emotional than men. Other studies measure emotionality through indirect self-report methods. For example, participants might be asked to describe an emotional experience, or conversations of participants could be recorded; these verbalizations are then coded for the number of emotion words used, which is taken to be an index of emotionality. Such indirect self-report methods typically do not reveal sex differences (LaFrance & Banaji, 1992). In other words, men and women use the same amount of emotion words when describing an emotional event.

One concern that has been raised about research showing sex differences in emotion is that these differences are a function of a recall bias (Larson & Pleck, 1998). Much of the data come from self-report methodologies that ask men and women to recall emotions over a period of time, and it is possible that women are better than men at recalling their emotions. To address this issue, in one study, married couples carried electronic pagers so that they could report their current emotional state "online" whenever they were beeped (Larson & Pleck, 1998). Men and women reported similar emotional states. Other studies of college students and adults have confirmed this finding with the same methodology (Larson & Pleck, 1998). One exception is a study of adolescents: when adolescents carried electronic pagers, women reported more positive affect (happy, cheerful, excited) and more anxiety than men.

The *frequency* of experiencing an emotion is not the same as the *intensity* of an emotional experience. "How often do you feel nervous?" is a measure of the

frequency with which one experiences anxiety. The intensity of anxiety would be measured with an item such as "When I am nervous, I get shaky all over." Many instruments confound frequency and intensity. The following item confounds the two: "I often cry when I am sad." "Often" indicates the frequency of experiencing sadness, whereas the act of crying describes the intensity of the sadness. When frequency was distinguished from intensity, there were few sex differences in frequency but consistent sex differences in intensity (Fujita, Diener, & Sandvik, 1991): females reported more intense positive and negative emotions. The female gender role also has been associated with experiencing emotions more intensely (Grossman & Wood, 1993). Distinguish between the frequency and intensity of emotions in a survey of your peers with Exercise 3.2.

Another intriguing source of evidence that woman are more emotional than men,

---

EXERCISE 3.2
Frequency versus Intensity of Emotion

Choose four emotions and identify three synonyms for each. For example, anger could be indicated by angry, frustrated, irritated. Ask 10 men and 10 women to indicate "how often" (frequency) they have experienced each emotion over the past week. Then ask them to indicate "how strongly" (intensity) they experienced each emotion during the past week. Counterbalance the frequency and intensity measures so that there is no order effect. Average across the three indicators of each emotion to come up with a frequency and intensity measure. Do men and women differ in the frequency and intensity of these emotions?

or that emotion is more central to the lives of women, is that women seem to have better recall for emotional events. In a series of studies on autobiographical memory, children were asked to report events and college students to recall events from their childhood in which they experienced a particular emotion (P. Davis, 1999). Across five studies, females were able to recall more events than males in response to each of the emotion cues (e.g., happiness, sadness, anger, fear). In addition, it took females less time to recall the first event for each emotion. There were no sex differences in the recall of events that were not emotional. Thus, it is not that females have superior recall in general; it appears that females are better able to recall events that are linked to particular emotions.

In summary, it appears that men and women experience emotions similarly but that women may experience emotions more intensely. This latter finding might explain why women have better "emotion memories" than men.

The Expression of Emotion

Despite men's and women's similar experiences of emotion, there is considerable evidence that there are sex differences in the expression of emotion (Brody & Hall, 1993; Sprecher & Sedikides, 1993). Women report that they are more emotionally expressive than men. For example, female undergraduates rated themselves higher on spontaneous expressions of emotions and emotional sensitivity (recognizing and responding to others' emotions), whereas male undergraduates rated themselves higher on emotional control (i.e., regulating emotions; Guerrero & Reiter, 1998). Self-report data are hardly convincing, however, because men and women are clearly aware of the stereotypes that women are emotional and expressive and men are not so emotional and inexpressive.

Observational data also support the claim that women are more expressive than men. Sex differences in the expression of emotion have been found as early as infancy. A study of 2-year-olds showed that girls were more expressive than boys during play (Malatesta, Culver, Tesman, & Shepard, 1989). Even observational data are not without their limitations, however. Coders are typically not blind to respondent sex and may rate the same face as more expressive if believed to be female rather than male. Try Exercise 3.3 to see how knowledge of sex could influence perceptions of emotion. However, other observational and physiological data are more compelling. Both men and women can more easily identify the emotion of a female than of a male (LaFrance & Banaji, 1992), suggesting that women's faces are more emotionally expressive than men's faces. When men and women express emotions, physiological measures reveal greater facial activity in the female face (Grossman & Wood, 1993; LaFrance & Banaji, 1992).

Females are not more likely than males to express all emotions. Women are more likely to express emotions such as

---

EXERCISE 3.3
Perception of Emotion in Boys and Girls

Videotape an infant or child playing. Make sure the sex of the child is not obvious. Tell 10 people that the child is male and 10 people that the child is female. Ask them to rate how emotional the child is, how expressive the child is, and what emotion the child is experiencing. Does the sex of the child influence these reports?

happiness, sadness, fear, guilt, and shame, whereas men are more likely to express anger, pride, and contempt (Brody & Hall, 1993). College students' beliefs about emotions seem to confirm these findings. College students were asked to estimate the frequency with which males and females experience and express emotions (Fabes & Martin, 1991). The investigators found that students believed men and women were equally likely to experience emotions but that women were more likely to express fear, sadness, and love and men were more likely to express anger.

One study compared college students' experiences of love, joy, sadness, fear, and anger to their gender-role stereotypes about these same emotions (Grossman & Wood, 1993, Study 1). In terms of personal experiences, women reported more intensely experiencing and expressing all of the emotions except anger. In terms of stereotypes, both male and female students believed the typical female more intensely experiences and expresses all of the emotions but anger and that the typical male more intensely experiences and expresses anger. Interestingly, there was a correspondence between personal experiences and stereotypes: the people who had the strongest stereotypes were the ones who had the most different experiences. That is, a female with strong stereotypes reported more intense emotions and a male with strong stereotypes reported less intense emotions, unless the emotion was anger.

One emotion that has received much research attention is anger. Do men and women respond to anger in the same ways? Women are more likely than men to cry and to express hurt feelings when angry (Fehr et al., 1999). Men realize this, as they report that their romantic partners express hurt feelings when angry (Fehr et al., 1999). Are women's responses more passive? When men and women were presented with the same anger-provoking incident in

the laboratory, they responded similarly (Biaggio, 1989). However, when men and women recorded how they responded to anger-provoking incidents in their daily lives over a two-week period, men were more likely to respond with physical and verbal antagonism, whereas women reported more passive responses. Recall that one limitation of laboratory research is that men and women have a similar status and are treated the same, which may limit the extent to which findings generalize to the real world.

Crying is one behavior in which sex differences in emotional expression are thought to exist. College women report being more likely than college men to cry in response to anger, fear, sadness, and disappointment (Timmers, Fischer, & Manstead, 1998). Women also report crying more often and with more intensity than men (Lombardo, Cretser, Lombardo, & Mathis, 1983). In the latter study, students were provided with a list of different stimulus situations (e.g., wedding, breakup of a relationship). Women, on average, were more likely to cry across the situations. The one situation in which men and women reported that they were equally likely to cry was the death of a close other. There is similarity in the pattern of men's and women's crying behavior, however, because the two sexes ranked the situations similarly in terms of which situations would result in the least and most crying.

It is difficult to study sex differences in the expression of emotion because the same expression may be interpreted differently, depending on whether it is displayed by a male or a female. For example, women's crying in response to anger may be misunderstood as sadness. Recall the study from Chapter 1 in which the child was crying after seeing the jack-in-the-box (Condry & Condry, 1976); people perceived a female child as afraid and a male child as angry. The sex of the person displaying the behavior also influences perceptions of aggression (Condry & Ross, 1985). College students rated the aggressiveness of a child playing in the snow with another child. The sex of the two children was disguised by snowsuits; students were led to believe they were viewing a girl with a girl, a boy with a girl, a girl with a boy, or a boy with a boy. The behavior of the child was rated as significantly less aggressive when students thought it was a boy playing with another boy compared to the other three dyads. The authors explained that aggressive behavior is expected of boys: respondents rated gender-congruent behavior as less extreme than gender-incongruent behavior. This fits with the research reported in Chapter 2 that gender-incongruent behavior is often viewed as extreme.

In total, it appears that women are more likely than men to express emotions, with the exception of anger. The counterpart to emotional expression may be emotional inhibition. Are there times when women don't want to express emotions, other than when they are angry? One such time may be when experiencing disappointment. There is evidence that girls are particularly good at hiding disappointment compared to boys. In two studies of first- and third-graders, boys had more difficulty than girls hiding their disappointment when receiving a gift they didn't want (T. Davis, 1995). The author argued that girls are socialized to be nice, and part of being nice is pretending to like an unwanted gift.

Gender roles also have been related to the expression of emotion, and often show stronger relations than respondent's sex. Femininity or communion, specifically, has been associated with emotional expression (Brody & Hall, 1993). Two studies have associated androgyny with emotional expression. In a study that compared androgynous, masculine, and feminine persons, androgynous persons were found to be more emotionally expressive than masculine persons, and feminine persons fell between the two groups (Kring & Gordon, 1998). In another study, androgynous individuals more frequently expressed happiness, sadness, love, and hate compared to masculine, feminine, or undifferentiated groups (Ganong & Coleman, 1984). The relation of androgyny to the expression of such a variety of emotions may have to do with the fact that androgyny incorporates both femininity and masculinity, which are each linked to the expression of different emotions: androgyny includes femininity, which is associated with expressions of love, happiness, and sadness, along with masculinity, which is associated with expressions of hate.

Gender roles have been specifically linked to the expression of anger. A series of 17 different instruments that reflected anger, hostility, and aggression were administered to undergraduates (Kopper & Epperson, 1996). These instruments reflected three categories of anger: aggressive acting-out anger, anger proneness (which includes uncontrollable verbal expressions of anger), and anger suppression (which includes passive-aggressiveness and resentment). Sex was related to only one of the measures of anger: males scored higher than females on the aggressive acting-out anger. However, male and female gender roles were more strongly related than sex to all of the measures of anger. Femininity was inversely related to all three measures of anger; masculinity was associated with greater aggressive acting-out anger and greater anger proneness.

Physiological Measures of Emotion

Given the limitations of self-report methods of emotion, one might hope that physiological methods would provide a more definitive answer to the issue of sex differences in emotions. Unfortunately, physiological indicators of emotionality are controversial. Researchers find it difficult to agree on which physiological measure best taps emotion: heart rate, blood pressure, galvanic skin response? Even within a given physiological measure, findings are inconsistent. For example, studies that examine galvanic skin response show that sometimes males and sometimes females are more responsive to emotional stimuli (LaFrance & Banaji, 1992). When multiple measures of physiological reactivity are used, findings within a study are often inconsistent across these measures. Despite these difficulties, a couple of findings have emerged. One consistent finding is that women show greater facial activity compared to men, as measured by electromyograph (EMG) responses. EMG response is a facial muscle movement that is especially sensitive to negative emotion. With the exception of EMG responses, it appears that there is slightly more evidence that men are more physiologically reactive to emotions than women (LaFrance & Banaji, 1992).

How do we reconcile the different conclusions reached by self-report and physiological data? One answer is that women are more outwardly expressive and men are more internally reactive to emotional stimuli. This idea was supported by a study in which college students viewed a film depicting one of three emotions (sadness, fear, happiness; Kring & Gordon, 1998). There were no sex differences in the self-report of an emotion. However, videotaped documentation showed that women were more emotionally expressive than men, and physiological measures evidenced that men were more reactive to some of the films. The investigators suggested that men were more likely to be internalizers with respect to emotions, by experiencing them physiologically but not expressing them, and that women were more likely to be externalizers with respect to emotions, by

expressing them outwardly but not reacting physiologically.

Basis of Emotion

If women express emotions outwardly and men express emotions inwardly, the basis of an emotion may differ for men and women. That is, men and women may base their emotions on different sources of information. Pennebaker and Roberts (1992) have made a compelling case that men infer their emotion from internal physiology and women infer their emotion from environmental cues. Men seem to be more sensitive to internal physiology than women: in laboratory studies, men can be more easily trained than women to predict their heart beats (Katkin, Blascovich, & Goldband, 1981). In their natural environment, however, men and women are equally adept at predicting their physiology. In the real world, information from internal physiology and external stimuli are both available. When men and women have been brought into the laboratory where external cues are held constant and physiological cues are manipulated, men are better than women at predicting the physiological changes within their body.

For example, Pennebaker and Watson (1988) asked people with normal-range blood pressure to come into the laboratory and carry out a series of tasks. Blood pressure was measured throughout the tasks and estimated by participants. Respondents also carried a portable blood pressure monitor at home and estimated their blood pressure once a day over a period of two weeks. Men and women were equally accurate in estimating their blood pressure at home, where internal and external information was available. Men and women also were more accurate at home than in the laboratory. However, in the laboratory, where the external cues were held constant and only internal physiological information was available, men were more accurate than women.

In another study, Cox and colleagues (1985) asked a group of insulin-dependent diabetics to estimate their blood glucose levels about four times a day for 10 days at home, and about 54 times over a 24-hour period in the hospital, where blood glucose levels were manipulated. Men and women were equally accurate in estimating their blood glucose levels at home and more accurate at home than in the laboratory. However, men were more accurate than women in the laboratory. Again, in the natural environment, two sources of information are available to people with diabetes: how they are feeling physiologically and environmental information, such as time of day, nature of food eaten, time of last insulin injection, and stressfulness of current circumstances. These studies suggest that in the natural environment, women attend to environmental cues and men attend to internal cues.

Pennebaker and Roberts (1992) offer a variety of explanations for this phenomenon, but do not favor any particular one. It is possible that there are biological differences between men and women that make physiological information more available to men. It also is possible that the lower status of women leads them to pay more attention to their environment, even in the case of determining their own emotions.

Conclusions

To determine which sex is more emotional is an oversimplification of a more complex phenomenon. Men and women largely experience emotion similarly. The expression of emotion differs depending on the emotion. Women are more likely than men to express the majority of emotions; the one exception is anger, which men express more than women. The bases of emotion also may differ for men and women, such that women attend more to the environment and men attend more to internal physiology. If the environment has more of an impact on women, it makes sense that they show more observable expressions of emotion.

SEX COMPARISONS IN MORAL DEVELOPMENT

Imagine the following dilemma: Heinz has a wife who is dying and he is unable to get a drug that would save her life. The only pharmacist who sells the drug is asking an exorbitant amount of money for it, and Heinz is poor.

This is the famous "Heinz dilemma." The question we are faced with is: Should Heinz steal the drug? It is not the answer to that question that determines the extent of someone's moral development. Rather, it is the reasoning one uses to arrive at an answer that is used to classify someone's stage of moral reasoning.

This dilemma was used by Lawrence Kohlberg (1981) in his creation of a six-stage theory of moral development. Kohlberg evaluated people's stages of moral development by presenting them with a series of hypothetical moral dilemmas and coding their responses. The first two stages of moral development are called *preconventional* and emphasize the physical consequences of behavior. In other words, people decide for or against a behavior out of a fear of punishment or a desire to be rewarded. The third and fourth stages are called the *conventional* stages and emphasize the importance of rules and laws; the third stage emphasizes conformity to rules and others' expectations, whereas the fourth stage emphasizes the importance of maintaining law and order. The fifth and sixth stages are referred to as *postconventional* and involve developing one's own internal standards, separate from those of society.

Kohlberg (1981) based his theory on a longitudinal study of boys, following them from elementary school through adulthood. Because Kohlberg's study excluded females, one questions whether his theory generalizes to girls. In 1982, Carol Gilligan criticized Kohlberg's work, arguing that his stages did not fairly represent women's views of moral reasoning. Gilligan said that women often ended up being classified as having a lower stage of moral development than men when using the Kohlberg scheme. Girls often were being classified at only the third stage of development, which emphasizes how others feel about the situation, pleasing others, and gaining approval from others. Boys were more likely to be classified at the fourth stage, which emphasizes rules and duties, or the postconventional stage, which emphasizes individual rights and personal standards.

Gilligan (1982) took issue with this classification hierarchy. She argued that women did not have an inferior moral orientation but an orientation different from men's. Gilligan challenged Kohlberg's theory with the information she gained from interviews of women describing real-life moral dilemmas. The results from her interviews with women, in particular a group of women deciding whether or not to have an abortion, led her to conclude that women have a **morality of responsibility** that emphasizes their connection to others, whereas men have a **morality of rights** that emphasizes their separation from others. Women are concerned with their responsibilities to others, others' feelings, and the effect their behavior has on relationships, whereas men are concerned with their rights, rules, and standards of justice. Gilligan stated,

"While she places herself in relation to the world . . . he places the world in relation to himself" (p. 35). Kohlberg's stages of moral development emphasize the importance of developing a sense of justice, whereas Gilligan emphasizes the importance of a responsibility or care orientation. Gilligan and Attanucci (1988) distinguish between the two: "A justice perspective draws attention to problems of inequality and oppression and holds up an ideal of reciprocal rights and equal respect for individuals. A care perspective draws attention to problems of detachment and abandonment and holds up an ideal of attention and response to need" (pp. 224–225). Gilligan argued that Kohlberg's theory identifies the male way of moral reasoning as superior to the female way.

The Kohlberg (1981) and Gilligan (1982) procedures to assess moral development have some commonalities and some differences. Both evaluate the content of people's responses to moral dilemmas, that is, the way people make their decision rather than the decision itself. In Gilligan's procedure, often the entire interview is coded as either reflecting a justice or a care orientation (Lyons, 1983). The primary way in which Gilligan's procedure differs from that used by Kohlberg is that the respondent gets to choose his or her moral dilemma. Respondents are typically asked to describe a moral conflict, a time in which they had difficulty deciding what was the right thing to do. The interviewer responds by asking questions to elicit more information about how the person resolved the dilemma. By contrast, Kohlberg presents people with a series of hypothetical dilemmas and asks them to describe how they would resolve the dilemma.

The difference between the two procedures is important because sex differences in moral development are more likely to be found in studies where people describe real-life moral dilemmas than in studies where people respond to standardized hypothetical dilemmas (Gilligan & Attanucci, 1988; L.J. Walker, de Vries, & Trevethan, 1987). It is possible that the women in Gilligan's studies are choosing to describe moral dilemmas that are different in nature from the ones men describe. Perhaps the moral dilemmas that women describe are ones that are more likely to elicit a care orientation. Rothbart, Hanley, and Albert (1986) tested this idea. They gave people the Heinz dilemma, which they argued called for a justice orientation, but also a dilemma that involved physical intimacy, which they argued called for a care orientation. The results of the study showed that both men and women responded with a justice orientation to the Heinz dilemma but a care orientation to the physical intimacy dilemma. The participants also were asked to generate their own dilemma in this study. Just as they expected, women generated more relationship dilemmas than men, which were more likely to be scored as having a care than a justice orientation.

One study compared the Kohlberg and Gilligan procedures (Pratt, Golding, Hunter, & Sampson, 1988). Both Kohlberg's standardized interview protocol and Gilligan's procedure were used to determine the stage of moral development among young adults (age 18 to 24), middle-age adults (30 to 45), and older adults (60 to 75). There were no sex differences using Kohlberg's procedure. Sex differences were found using Gilligan's procedure but only among the middle-aged adults. Among middle-aged adults, women were more likely to adhere to a care orientation and men to adhere to a justice orientation. With Gilligan's procedure, the investigators also found that women were more likely to describe relationship problems and men to describe nonrelational problems. All respondents who described a

nonrelational problem used a justice orientation. This is further evidence that one reason Gilligan's procedure elicits different moral orientations between men and women is that women are more likely than men to describe relationship dilemmas that call for a care rather than a justice orientation. By contrast, the Kohlberg procedure uses standard dilemmas that focus more on legality and rights than on personal relationship conflicts (Pratt et al., 1988).

In a second study, respondents described two moral dilemmas using Gilligan's procedure to see if there was some stability in the orientation that respondents used (Pratt et al., 1988). Sixty percent of the respondents used the same orientation when faced with two different dilemmas; this number is not significantly different from chance, which is 50%. Thus, the reliability of Gilligan's procedure is somewhat questionable. Other factors may determine whether sex differences in moral orientations are observed. In the latter study, sex differences in moral orientations were found in married parents but not married nonparents (Pratt et al., 1988). As shown in Figure 3.9, mothers were more likely to adopt the care orientation and fathers to adopt the justice orientation, but male and female nonparents were equally likely to adopt a care or a justice perspective. In this case, being a parent or nonparent was a moderator of sex differences. As you will see in Chapter 11, men's and women's roles diverge more when they become parents.

Do men and women really think about morality differently? In 1984, Walker conducted a review of the studies on moral development that used Kohlberg's procedure and concluded that there was little support for sex differences in moral development. She evaluated three age groups: children and early adolescents, late adolescents, and adults. For each group, there were proportionately

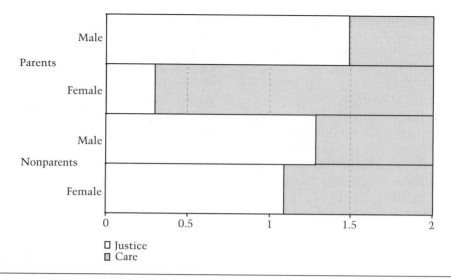

FIGURE 3.9 Sex differences in care and justice orientations. Among parents, men were more likely to adopt the justice orientation than the care orientation, and women were more likely to adopt the care orientation than the justice orientation. There was no sex difference in the orientation that nonparents adopted. Men and women may come to have different moral orientations when they become parents, or people who become parents may differ in moral orientation from those who do not become parents. *Source:* Pratt et al. (1988).

few samples that revealed sex differences. Of 108 samples, only 8 showed clear sex differences, in the direction of men being more morally advanced than women. A meta-analysis of the studies revealed no overall effect for sex. More recent studies have also refuted the notion that Kohlberg's methodology yields sex differences (L.J. Walker et al., 1987; Wark & Krebs, 1996).

Other procedures besides Kohlberg's and Gilligan's have been used to assess moral development. In one study, fifth-, eighth-, and eleventh-graders were asked to describe three situations in which they felt guilty (C. Williams & Bybee, 1994). The investigators hypothesized that boys would feel more guilt over breaking rules if they emphasize a justice and rule orientation, and that girls would feel more guilt over inconsiderate behavior in relationships if they emphasize a care orientation reflect-

ing a concern for others. The results indicated that boys were more likely than girls to describe situations in which they damaged property, were fighting with others, and victimized animals. Girls were more likely to describe situations of lying and inconsiderate behavior. Thus, Gilligan's theory was largely supported. Use this methodology in Exercise 3.4 to see if college students' experiences of guilt correspond to Gilligan's theory.

Moral development was coded more objectively by having college students read four moral dilemmas and rate the importance of 12 statements in making their decisions (Friedman, Robinson, & Friedman, 1987). Six statements focused on Kohlberg's concern with justice (e.g., "Consider the rights of the individual") and six statements focused on Gilligan's concern with a care orientation (e.g., "Consider the

> **EXERCISE 3.4**
> **Experiences of Guilt**
>
> Ask 10 men and 10 women to describe a time when they felt guilty. You could have them choose the most recent incident or the most severe incident. Code responses into a justice orientation or a care orientation. Are there sex differences in guilt experiences? Administer the PAQ from Chapter 2 to find out if agency and communion are related to guilt experiences.

effects on the relationship"). There were no sex differences on either the justice statements or the care orientation statements. Although these statements may be more objective indicators of the kinds of orientations people use to resolve moral dilemmas, the use of objective statements also may have primed people to consider aspects of the dilemmas they normally would not have considered.

There are advantages and disadvantages to all of the procedures used when evaluating moral development. Coding open-ended responses is more likely to provide an accurate view of how respondents really make decisions, but also is likely to leave out information that respondents may consider but not necessarily articulate. Closed-ended responses to objective questions provide standardized information that can be used for comparison between the sexes but is more likely to lead respondents to consider information that they might not ordinarily consider.

It also is possible that moral orientation is tied to gender roles rather than sex per se. In one study, adults were asked to describe themselves (Pratt et al, 1988). The descriptions were classified as focusing more on connection (i.e., self in relationship with others) or on individuation (i.e., self as separate from others). People who were classified as having connection self-concepts were more likely to adopt the care orientation, whereas people who were classified as having individuation self-concepts were more likely to adopt the justice orientation using Gilligan's procedure.

Similarly, standard measures of gender roles have been associated with moral reasoning. In one study, college students responded to three moral dilemmas: an unplanned pregnancy, marital infidelity, and caring for a parent (Sochting, Skoe, & Marcia, 1994). Moral reasoning was classified as self-oriented (one's own comfort and discomfort as guiding principle), as other-oriented (others' welfare as guiding principle), and self-and-other-oriented (balancing both the needs of self and of others as guiding principle). They found that masculinity, as measured by the PAQ, was associated with a self-orientation, femininity was associated with an other-orientation, and androgyny was associated with the combined self-and-other-orientation.

Sex differences in morality also are likely to be influenced by ethnicity and culture. For example, C. Stack (1997) constructed a set of moral dilemmas and gave them to African American adolescents to resolve. Boys' and girls' dilemmas were equally likely to be classified as care- or justice-oriented. C. Stack argued that African American men and women have more similar views of themselves in relationship to others because they jointly face prejudice and discrimination from the environment.

In summary, Kohlberg's (1981) theory of moral development was criticized for the exclusion of women during its creation; the concern was that women emerged as morally inferior to men. More recent data, however, have suggested that there really

are no sex differences in moral development using Kohlberg's procedure. However,
the controversy sparked the concept of two
different views of morality, one emphasizing individual rights (justice) and the other
emphasizing responsibility to others (care).
It is not so much that men and women view
morality differently as that men and women
face different kinds of moral dilemmas.
Men seem to face moral dilemmas that
focus on justice and women seem to face
moral dilemmas that focus on relationships.

SEX COMPARISONS IN SOCIAL DEVELOPMENT

Think of the "Who am I?" task. Your responses to this question indicate how you
define yourself. The crux of the debate
on sex differences in social development
centers on the achievement of identity.
Erikson's (1950) stage theory of social development suggests that one must successfully resolve the issues in one stage of
development before proceeding to the next
stage. His theory also states that the
achievement of an identity precedes the
achievement of intimacy. If true, how do
we explain the person who achieves his or
her identity in part by connection to others? Some researchers have argued that
Erikson's sequence may describe men's social development better than women's social development (Gilligan, 1982; Marcia,
1993) because women are more likely to experience identity and intimacy simultaneously. That is, part of women's identity is
their relationship with others.

Early research on adolescents supported this theory (Douvan & Adelson,
1966). Boys formed their identities by
making concrete occupational plans; by
contrast, girls' future plans were unclear—
their identity would be shaped by who they

married. Thus, girls' identities were a consequence rather than an antecedent of intimacy. Did this mean that boys had reached
a higher level of social development than
girls? No. At that time, boys and girls were
socialized in ways that made for very different identity formations.

Even today, there is evidence that
men's and women's social development follows different courses. Studies have shown
that there is a stronger relation between
identity and intimacy development in men
than in women because in women, intimacy is as likely to precede as to follow
identity development (Orlofsky, 1993). In a
study of male and female college undergraduates, nearly all of the males who
had achieved intimacy had also achieved
identity, whereas one-third of the high-
intimacy females had not achieved identity
(Schiedel & Marcia, 1985). These findings
suggest that identity is not necessarily a
prerequisite for the development of intimacy in women. A recent study of high
school students showed that identity issues
were more salient than intimacy issues in
both male and female decision making (Lacombe & Gay, 1998). However, female students were more likely than male students
to merge the two concerns.

In a longitudinal study of college students, a strong relation between identity
achievement in college and intimacy
achievement (defined as marriage) 18 years
later was found among men but not women
(Kahn, Zimmerman, Csikszentmihalyi, &
Getzels, 1985). Nearly all of the unmarried
men scored below average on the measure
of identity achievement. In addition, there
were few high-identity men who had not
married. Thus, the achievement of identity
seemed to be necessary for the achievement
of intimacy in men. There was little difference in the identity scores of married and
unmarried women, however. Thus, for

women, identity achievement was unrelated to whether they achieved intimacy.

Again, one can ask whether gender roles rather than sex per se are related to the social stages of development. In one study, masculinity, as assessed by the BSRI, was associated with the achievement of identity in both males and females (Scheidel & Marcia, 1985). Femininity was associated with the achievement of intimacy in males but not females. Other research has linked masculinity to identity achievement and femininity to intimacy achievement (Marcia, 1993).

In conclusion, the traditional theory of social development has been challenged as applying more to men than women. The theory suggests that identity precedes intimacy in a stage sequence. There is some evidence that identity and intimacy concerns are more fused in women than in men, which makes women appear to reach a lower level of social development.

SUMMARY

I reviewed the evidence for sex differences in cognitive abilities, specifically spatial skills, math skills, and verbal skills. Overall, most of the differences are small. For each domain, the size of the sex difference varies with how the ability is assessed. For example, in the spatial skills domain, there is a more substantial sex difference favoring males for one particular skill, the mental rotation task, but negligible differences for the other spatial skills. In terms of verbal skills, many differences are small, but the female advantage in writing is an exception. The size of the sex difference also depends on the nature of the population. Sex differences in math are minimal among general populations; among individuals highly talented in math, males clearly outperform females. Sex differences in verbal skills also are influenced by the population studied; among children with verbal difficulties, there is a preponderance of boys over girls. For many of these areas of cognition, the differences seem to be getting smaller with time.

I also reviewed the evidence for sex differences in a number of social behaviors. Many of the domains show larger sex differences when self-report methods are used compared to more objective measures of behavior. For example, self-reports of empathy demonstrate a substantial sex difference favoring women, but observational and physiological measures are less clear. Other sex differences in social behavior are influenced by the environment; for example, boys' higher activity level compared to girls' is exacerbated by the presence of peers. One limitation of much of this research is a lack of external validity because social behavior is often studied in the laboratory, where the natural context is removed.

In general, men and women seem to experience emotion similarly, although women may experience emotions more intensely. Sex differences in emotional expression depend on the specific emotion: women are more likely to express sadness, love, and fear, whereas men are more likely to express anger and pride. There is some evidence that emotion for women has a more external focus; women express emotion externally and use cues from the environment to determine internal states. By contrast, emotion for men has a more internal focus; they react to emotion physiologically but do not necessarily express it outwardly. Men also rely on internal states rather than external cues to determine feelings.

Two stage theories of development, moral development and social development, may differ for men and women. It has been suggested that men define morality in terms of justice and women in terms of responsibility or connection to others. If true, previous theories of moral development may unfairly represent women as inferior. However, it appears that men and women have similar views of morality but face different moral dilemmas that call for construing morality differently. The problem with previous theories of social development is that the sequence of establishing an identity *before* achieving intimacy may describe men's experiences more than women's.

Discussion Questions

1. Have each person in the class read one of the meta-analytic reviews of sex comparisons in this chapter and provide more detail on the procedures used and the specific findings.
2. For which of the cognitive domains is there the most evidence of sex differences? Sex similarities?
3. What does the sex difference in "variability" refer to?
4. Which cognitive differences between men and women seem most likely due to environmental factors, and which seem most likely due to biological factors?
5. What are some of the methodological problems in making sex comparisons in social behavior?
6. What is the evidence for women having greater erotic plasticity than men?
7. Is there a sex difference in emotionality?
8. How does the social environment influence men's and women's expression of emotion?
9. Do men and women define morality differently?

10. How are identity and intimacy related for men and women today? Should Erikson's theory be modified?

Suggested Reading

Block, J. (1976). Issues, problems, and pitfalls in assessing sex differences: A critical review of the psychology of sex differences. *Merrill-Palmer Quarterly, 22*(4), 283–308.

Gilligan, C. (1982). *In a different voice: Psychological theory and women's development.* Cambridge, MA: Harvard University Press.

Halpern, D.F. (2000). *Sex differences in cognitive abilities.* (3rd ed.). Mahwah, NJ: Erlbaum.

Kimura, D. (1999). *Sex and cognition.* Cambridge, MA: MIT Press.

Maccoby, E.E., & Jacklin, C.N. (1974). *The psychology of sex differences.* Stanford, CA: Stanford University Press.

Key Terms

Aggression—Behavior that is intended to harm someone.

Confirmatory hypothesis testing—Process of noticing information that confirms stereotypes and disregarding information that disconfirms stereotypes.

Construct validity—Evidence that a scientific instrument measures what it was intended to measure.

Effect size—The size of a difference that has been found in a study.

Empathy—The ability to experience the same emotion as another person, or feel sympathy or compassion for another person.

Erotic plasticity—The extent to which one's sex drive is influenced by social and cultural factors.

File drawer problem—A difficulty encountered when compiling a review of scientific literature due to the fact that studies showing null results are unlikely to be published.

Gender intensification—Concern on the part of girls and boys with adherence to gender roles; applies to adolescence.

Meta-analysis—A statistical tool that quantifies the results of a group of studies.

Moderating variable—A variable that alters the relation between the independent variable and the dependent variable.

Morality of responsibility (care orientation)—Moral reasoning that emphasizes connections to others, responsibilities, and others' feelings.

Morality of rights (justice orientation)—Moral reasoning that emphasizes separation from others, rights, rules, and standards of justice.

Narrative review—A review of scientific literature wherein the authors reach their own conclusions about whether the majority of studies provide evidence for or against the topic of the review (e.g., sex differences).

4

Sex-Related Comparisons: Theory

Now the opposite of the male is the female. . . . in human beings the male is much hotter in its nature than the female. On that account, male embryos tend to move about more than female ones, and owing to their moving about they get broken more, since a young creature can easily be destroyed owing to its weakness. And it is due to this self-same cause that the perfecting of female embryos is inferior to that of male ones. . . . we should look upon the female state as being as it were a deformity, though one which occurs in the ordinary course of nature. (Aristotle, 1953; pp. 391, 459, 461)

Aristotle had one theory of sex differences. More recently, John Gray has set forth another theory in *Men Are from Mars, Women Are from Venus:*

One day long ago the Martians, looking through their telescopes, discovered the Venusians. Just glimpsing the Venusians awakened feelings they had never known. They fell in love and quickly invented space travel and flew to Venus. The Venusians welcomed the Martians with open arms. . . . The love between the Venusians and the Martians was magical. They delighted in being together, doing things together, and sharing together. Though from different worlds, they reveled in their differences. . . . Then they decided to fly to Earth. In the beginning everything was wonderful and beautiful. But the effects of Earth's atmosphere took hold, and one morning everyone woke up with a peculiar kind of amnesia. . . . Both the Martians and Venusians forgot that they were from different planets and were supposed to be different. . . . And since that day men and women have been in conflict. (pp. 9–10)

These two theories about the origin of sex differences are quite different and hardly comparable. But both theories have one thing in common: that men and women are opposites.

In this chapter, I discuss a number of theories that might shed light on the sex-related differences reviewed in Chapter 3. These theories are often applicable to both the origin of sex differences in cognition and social behavior, and to the development of gender roles. Gender-role socialization, in fact, is one explanation for sex differences in cognition and social behavior. I discuss biology, including the role of genes, hormones, and brain anatomy, and evolutionary theory, an emerging field that applies biological principles to the understanding of social behavior. I examine psychoanalytic theory, social learning theory, cognitive development theory, and gender schema theory. I end the chapter by discussing Deaux and Major's (1987) comprehensive model of sex differences. They focus on the role of situational factors and the gender-role attributes of the people involved in the situation. I conclude with some remarks about the constructionist and postmodern perspectives on this area of research.

As you will see, there is no one correct theory. Each offers some contribution to discussions of gender. Undoubtedly, the origin of sex differences and the development of gender roles can be explained by pieces of each of the theories outlined below. Descriptions of these theories, as well as the key concepts, are presented in Table 4.1 on page 144.

BIOLOGY

Biological theories of sex differences identify genes and hormones, as well as the structure and function of the brain, as the causes of observed differences in physical appearance, cognition, behavior, and even gender roles.

Genes

Could gender roles be hard-wired? Are there specific genes linked to masculinity and femininity? Mitchell, Baker, and Jackson (1989) examined the contribution of genes to masculinity and femininity by studying twins. They examined 38 monozygotic and 32 dizygotic twins. Monozygotic twins, also known as identical twins, share 100% of their genes; dizygotic twins, or fraternal twins, share 50% of their genes. That is, fraternal twins share the same number of genes as nontwin siblings. The theory behind these kinds of twin studies is that genes explain the greater similarity in behavior between identical twins compared to fraternal twins because the environment for both sets of twins is the same, but the genes differ. Mitchell and colleagues found a greater correspondence in self-reports of masculinity and femininity between identical twins than fraternal twins. They concluded that genes explained from 20% to 48% of the differences and environment explained from 52% to 80% of the differences in masculinity and femininity. Thus, genes may partly contribute to the development of some aspects of gender roles.

One question to raise here is whether the environment of identical twins is really the same as the environment of fraternal twins. I have twin nephews who are identical. One of people's first responses to them when they were born was to look for similarities. In fact, people sent them all sorts of newspaper stories depicting bizarre twin coincidences. Investigate how people respond to identical and fraternal twins with Exercise 4.1 on page 145.

Hormones

Hormones are chemicals produced by the endocrine system that circulate throughout the body. There are two classes of sex-related hormones: androgens and estrogens. The male sex hormones are **androgens** (e.g., testosterone) and the female sex hormones are **estrogens.** This does not

TABLE 4.1   Theories of Sex Differences

Theory	Description	Key Terms
Biological	Identifies genes and hormones as well as the structure and function of the brain as the cause of observed physical appearance, cognition, behavior, and gender roles.	androgens estrogens corpus collosum lateralization
Evolutionary	An extension of Darwin's theory of evolution that states that different social behaviors may have evolved in men and women because it was adaptive for their survival.	adaptive challenges maternal investment interactionism
Psychoanalytic	Original theory suggested that gender roles are acquired by identification with the same-sex parent. Modern versions emphasize the importance of all early relationships.	Oedipal complex unconscious processes identification object-relations theory
Social learning	Contends that all behaviors, including those specifically related to gender role, are learned through reinforcement and/or modeling.	reinforcement observational learning environmental influence
Gender-role socialization	States that people and objects in the child's environment shape behavior to fit gender-role norms.	differential socialization parental influence sex typing
Social role	Variant of gender-role socialization theory that suggests that differences in men's and women's behavior are a function of the different roles men and women hold in our society.	conformity differential status nurturance egoistic dominance
Cognitive development	Assumes that the child is an active interpreter of the world, and that observational learning occurs because the perceiver cognitively organizes what he or she sees. Social cognitive theory extends this position by suggesting that gender role acquisition is influenced by social as well as cognitive factors.	gender identity gender constancy categorization
Gender schema	Contends that children acquire gender roles due to their propensity to process information into sex-linked categories.	gender-role schema gender aschematic androgyny

mean, however, that males have only androgens and females have only estrogens; men and women have both classes of hormones but in different amounts. Sex hormones affect the brain, the immune system, and overall health. There is no doubt that hormones also influence behavior. The question is, to what extent?

How can we evaluate the effects of hormones on men's and women's behavior?

Could we randomly assign one group of women to receive testosterone and one group of women to receive a placebo? Some ethical issues arise in manipulating people's hormone levels. One solution is to study the relation of different levels of hormones across men and women to some behavior. This would be a correlational study. Another solution is to manipulate the hormones of other species, such as rats, and

EXERCISE 4.1
**The Environments of Identical
and Fraternal Twins**

Can we presume that the greater similarity in behavior of identical twins compared to fraternal twins is due to genes alone because both sets of twins share the same environment? The question you are investigating in this exercise is whether they do share the same environment. Ideally, you should interview a pair of identical twins and a pair of fraternal twins. If you don't have access to both, perhaps you can interview one set and the class can pool the results. Ask the twins, their siblings, and their parents questions such as the following:

1. Do you dress alike?
2. Do you share the same room?
3. Do people refer to you as "The Twins"?
4. Does everyone know that you are a twin?
5. Do you share the same friends?
6. Do you play together?
7. Do you play with the same toys?
8. Do people comment on how much alike the two of you are in personality?
9. Do people seem to look for similarities in your behavior?
10. Do people seem to look for differences in your behavior?
11. How are the two of you similar? Different?

The goal of this exercise is to examine similarities and differences in the physical and social environments (i.e., how parents, teachers, and peers respond) of the two kinds of twins. I argue that the environment of identical twins is not the same as the environment of fraternal twins because people expect to see more similarities in identical than in fraternal twins. Recall the power of our expectancies!

observe their behavior. Indeed, research has shown that if male or female rats are deprived of sex hormones, sex-related behavior is affected (Kimura, 1992, 1999). For example, male rats who are deprived of androgens show less mounting behavior. Can we extrapolate from this research that human sexual behavior is determined by hormones? Maybe in part, but certainly not exclusively. There are many other factors that influence the frequency of human sexual behavior.

Has there been any link between hormones and sex-related differences in cognitive abilities? It would certainly be a straightforward theory if we found that androgens were linked to spatial skills and estrogens were linked to verbal skills. However, the relation of hormones to cognition is more complicated than that. One source of information on this issue comes from studies of girls with congenital adrenal hyperplasia (CAH). This is a genetic disorder resulting from a malfunction in the adrenal gland that results in prenatal exposure to high levels of male hormones. Some studies have found that girls with CAH perform better on tasks of spatial abilities compared to girls without CAH (Kimura, 1992). This would seem to be conclusive evidence for a link of male hormones to spatial abilities. However, another study showed that higher levels of testosterone were associated with superior spatial skills among women but inferior skills among men (Kimura, 1987); if testosterone was the key to spatial abilities, men with high levels of testosterone also should have greater spatial ability. In a review of the literature, Collaer and Hines (1998) concluded that there is very little evidence that prenatal exposure to sex hormones influences cognitive abilities.

Perhaps hormones are related to the more social aspects of behavior. In a study of female college students, testosterone levels were linked to gender roles (Baucom, Besch, & Callahan, 1985). Feminine women had lower levels of testosterone than masculine and androgynous women. However, undifferentiated women—those who scored low on both masculinity and femininity—had the highest levels of testosterone. The link between hormones and gender-role behavior is not a simple one. It is not the case that androgens correspond to male gender-role behavior and estrogens correspond to female gender-role behavior.

The linking of hormones to gender-role behavior has largely been studied by examining the effects of prenatal exposure to sex hormones. In a review of the literature, Collaer and Hines (1998) concluded that there were effects, but that the effects depended on the specific hormone and the specific domain of behavior. There is a clear relation between prenatal exposure to androgens and masculine gender-role behavior among women but not men. Across the studies, the most evidence for effects of exposure to prenatal androgens on gender-role behavior in women is in the domain of type of play (Collaer & Hines, 1998). For example, researchers have compared girls with CAH to their healthy sisters on gender-related behavior and attitudes. One study found that CAH girls demonstrated more masculine play, activities, and physical appearance than their sisters (Dittmann et al., 1990). Studies also have shown that CAH girls show less interest in infants, less desire to have children, and more desire to have a career (Dittmann et al., 1990; Leveroni & Berenbaum, 1998; Udry, Morris, & Kovenock, 1995) Berenbaum and Hines (1992) found that at ages 3 and 8, girls who were exposed to high levels of prenatal androgens were more likely to play with male toys (e.g., helicopter, cars, blocks) and less likely to play with female toys (e.g., dolls, kitchen equipment, telephone) than girls who had not been exposed. There were no differences in toy preferences between boys who were and were not exposed to high levels of prenatal androgens. The authors admit, however, that this study does not prove that prenatal hormones cause masculine toy preferences; there could be another variable that is influenced by the hormone and responsible for toy preferences, for example, activity level. Perhaps prenatal androgens make children more active, which then leads them to prefer more active toys.

Exposure to prenatal androgens also has been linked to homosexuality or bisexuality in women (Collaer & Hines, 1998). However, the size of this effect is small, meaning that the majority of CAH women are heterosexual. The most recent research has shown stronger links of CAH to homosexual fantasy rather than homosexual behavior in women (Dittmann, 1997; Veniegas & Conley, 2000).

Most of the evidence for the influence of prenatal androgens on masculine gender-role behavior in girls comes from the studies of girls with CAH (Collaer & Hines, 1998). These studies are problematic because girls with CAH are often born with male genitalia, a condition that is usually altered with surgery. Thus, the parents and the children are aware of the influence of this particular prenatal androgen. Parents might expect the CAH child to exhibit more masculine behavior, provide the child with more masculine toys and masculine activities, and respond more favorably to masculine behavior displayed by the child. The child herself also might be more comfortable engaging in masculine activities because of her own awareness of the exposure to male hormones. It is difficult to disentangle this issue from the research.

The evidence for the effects of prenatal hormones on boys' gender-role behavior is mixed, at best (Collaer & Hines, 1998). It may be that gender-role behavior is more fluid in society for girls than boys so that boys feel stronger pressures to adhere to the male role, overcoming the impact of any prenatal hormone exposure. This would be consistent with the notion of erotic plasticity discussed in Chapter 3.

If androgens have a "masculinizing" effect on girls, do estrogens have a "feminizing" effect? Most of the research addressing this question has come from exposure to a synthetic estrogen, diethylstilbestrol (DES). DES was prescribed to pregnant women in the 1960s to prevent miscarriage, but its use was discontinued when it was linked to cancer. In a review of the literature, Collaer and Hines (1998) report that exposure to DES seems to be ssociated with increased **lateralization** of language (i.e., distinct to one hemisphere of the brain) but has no effect on play behavior or cognitive abilities. DES also is associated with a bisexual or homosexual orientation in women (Collaer & Hines, 1998; Veniegas & Conley, 2000), but again, these studies also demonstrate that the majority of women exposed to DES are heterosexual. Exposure to DES seems to have little effect on males. Perhaps exposure to DES does not have the psychosocial consequences that exposure to CAH does because parents do not expect DES to influence gender-role behavior, as there is no physical evidence of the effects of DES as there is with CAH.

In summary, most of the studies examining relations of hormones to cognition or social behavior are correlational and, thus, problematic. One cannot determine cause and effect. If one finds a relation between testosterone and aggression, does testosterone lead to aggression or does behaving aggressively increase one's testosterone levels? It appears that the strongest evidence for the role of hormones in gender-role behavior is the link of prenatal androgens to play behavior and the link of

both prenatal androgens and estrogens to sexual orientation. In both cases, these effects are apparent only for girls. There is very limited evidence that prenatal exposure to sex hormones influences cognitive abilities.

The Brain

If genes and hormones can't explain sex differences in cognition and behavior, perhaps the brain can. Isn't it true that women are "right-brained" and men are "left-brained"? Or, is it the reverse? It is true that different areas of the brain are responsible for different cognitive functions. For example, spatial abilities are located in the right hemisphere and verbal abilities in the left hemisphere. Aha! So it must be that males are right-hemisphere-dominant and females are left-hemisphere-dominant. Unfortunately, this theory does not hold up for long. The left hemisphere also is responsible for analytical skills, those required in math; thus, if females are left-hemisphere-dominant, they should be better than males at math.

Another theory of how the brain influences sex differences has to do with the communication between right and left hemispheres. One possibility is that women's brains are more bilateral than those of men; that is, women are more likely than men to use either hemisphere of their brain for a specific function. Men, by contrast, are said to be more lateralized, meaning that the two hemispheres of the brain have more distinct functions. In support of this theory, there is some evidence that the size of the corpus callosum, the structure that connects the right and left hemispheres, may be larger in women. This may reflect greater opportunity for communication between hemispheres for women compared to men (Kimura, 1992).

To test whether there are sex differences in lateralization, Springer and Deutsch (1981) reviewed the effects of damage to the left versus the right hemisphere of the brain on men's and women's cognitive abilities. They found that the particular hemisphere that was damaged had distinct effects on men but not on women. Damage to the right hemisphere affected men's spatial abilities, whereas damage to the left hemisphere affected men's language abilities. The less distinct effects on women led them to conclude that women's abilities could be located in either hemisphere. Further evidence came from a study that used functional magnetic resonance imaging to show which aspects of the brain were activated during language tasks (B. Shaywitz et al., 1995). Among women, both right and left hemispheres were activated; by contrast, men showed greater activation in the left than the right hemisphere. In addition, the location of the activation was more variable among women.

However, the evidence for sex differences in brain lateralization is not conclusive. For example, one study showed that damage to the right hemisphere was associated with a decrease in spatial abilities in both men and women (Kimura, 1992). If men were more lateralized than women, one would expect a greater adverse effect on men's spatial abilities. Hiscock and colleagues (Hiscock, Israelian, Inch, Jacek, & Hiscock-Kalil, 1995) reviewed the evidence on sex differences in brain lateralization and found that the difference was small, accounting for only between 1% and 2% of the variability in brain lateralization. Most studies do not find a sex difference in brain lateralization, but among the ones that do, women appear to be more lateralized than men.

Some argue that differential brain lateralization contributes to the emotional differences between men and women (Guerrero & Reiter, 1998). The right hemisphere is the more emotional half of the brain, whereas the left hemisphere is the more cognitive half of the brain. Women are said to use the right hemisphere more than men when processing emotions.

In total, researchers have investigated the brain in various ways, by examining differences in hemispheres and differences in structures. By examining all of the aspects of the brain, it is not surprising that some sex differences appear. The question remains as to whether these differences in brain anatomy or structure have any functional significance. No one has been able to clearly link these differences to cognition or behavior.

Summary

Biology certainly plays a role in the production of sex differences in cognition and behavior. The role is limited, however. Evidence from twin studies leads to the conclusion that there is a genetic contribution to cognitive and social abilities. Research on hormones has demonstrated relations of sex hormones to sex-related behavior, but those relations are complicated; there is certainly not a one-to-one correspondence between a particular hormone and a gender-role behavior. The strongest evidence lies in the relation of male and female hormones (androgens and estrogens) to male gender-role behavior in women. Why aren't hormones as strongly implicated in gender-role behavior among men? The answer is unclear. One possibility is that the societal pressures on men to behave in gender-role-congruent ways are stronger than those faced by women. In any case, these findings suggest that hormones alone cannot explain sex differences in gender roles or sex differences in cognition and social behavior. Studies of the brain reveal some differences in structure, but the meaning of those differences is unclear. In sum, biological explanations leave open to explanation much variability in the behavior of men and women.

EVOLUTIONARY THEORY AND SOCIOBIOLOGY

We typically think of evolution as explaining how humans developed from simpler organisms, not why men behave in masculine ways and women in feminine ways. Evolutionary psychology applies the principles of evolution to the study of cognition and behavior. Sociobiology examines the biological origins of social behavior—in other words, how social behavior evolved over time to perpetuate the species. Both evolutionary psychology and sociobiology are extensions of Darwin's theory of evolution, which states that we behave in ways to ensure the survival of our genes. The idea is that different behaviors may have evolved in men and women because it was adaptive for their survival (Buss & Kenrick, 1998).

People often confuse the fields of sociobiology and evolutionary psychology. Although there is a great deal of overlap, there are some distinctions. One is that evolutionary psychology is not limited to the study of social behavior, as is sociobiology. Thus, evolutionary psychology might be the more appropriate term to use in the study of gender. There are other, more philosophical distinctions, such as whether the replication of genes is a goal (sociobiology, yes; evolutionary psychology, no) that motivates behavior. These distinctions are beyond the scope of this text, but I refer the interested reader to David Buss's (1999) textbook *Evolutionary Psychology* for an elaboration of these issues.

Sexual Behavior

Buss (1995) argues that we can observe sex differences in behaviors that historically presented men and women with different challenges. One such domain is sexual behavior. First, men and women face different challenges during pregnancy. Because conception takes place inside of the female, males face the challenge of establishing paternity. The challenge that females face is to safely get through nine months of pregnancy and a period of lactation. Thus, males will behave in ways to increase their chances of paternity and females in ways to ensure the survival of themselves and their infant. Second, men and women face different challenges to successful reproduction. For men to reproduce successfully, it is in their best interest to have sexual intercourse with as many women as possible and to mate with women who are more likely to be fertile (i.e., young). For women to reproduce successfully, it is in their best interest to be selective in choosing a man who has the resources to help ensure the survival of the children.

This theory can explain some differences in sexual behavior, for example, why men have more favorable attitudes toward casual sex (Oliver & Hyde, 1993). The theory conflicts, however, with the finding that the sex difference in number of sexual partners is small (Oliver & Hyde, 1993). Why don't men have 10 times as many partners as women? Evolutionary psychologists point out that when men and women are asked how many partners they desire, males report desiring more sexual partners (on average 18) than women (on average 4 or 5; Buss & Schmitt, 1993). The development of contraceptive methods such as the birth control pill might have decreased the size of the sex difference in actual number of sexual partners (Oliver & Hyde, 1993). This is one way culture could alter behavior that evolved for biological reasons. The socio-biological view of sex differences in sexual behavior assumes that sexual intercourse will lead—or is intended to lead—to reproduction. Today, with the introduction of effective contraceptives, sexual behavior does not always lead to reproduction, and the fact that contraceptives are so commonly used suggests that reproduction might not always be the intention of sex. My guess is that most times it is not. I doubt that the majority of men are thinking about establishing paternity and the majority of women are thinking about their partner's ability to support a child when deciding whether or not to engage in sex.

Mate Selection

Evolutionary psychology also can address the issue of mate preference. Women place a greater value than men on financial success in a partner. This finding has been replicated in 37 cultures around the world (Buss, 1989). Men, by contrast, emphasize reproductive fertility in their selection of mates (Buss, 1989; Buss & Kenrick, 1998). Men have been found to have a preference for a waist-to-hip ratio in women that is indicative of reproductive capacity and general good health.

Evolutionary theory also can explain why women prefer older men and men prefer younger women. Men's financial resources generally do not diminish and may, in fact, increase with age. However, women's reproductive resources do diminish with age. In fact, men with financial resources may be attracted to women with reproductive resources. In a study of a computer dating service in Germany, men with the highest personal income were the most likely to desire younger partners (Grammer, 1992).

Has culture influenced mate selection as it has sexual behavior? You might expect that women today are less likely to desire men with financial resources because they are more likely to have their own source of income. Not true. Women who have a high status or their own resources continue to prefer men with a higher status and more resources (Townsend, 1989). This may seem peculiar given their lesser need for resources. Buss and Kenrick (1998) argue that women's historical need for men's resources to take care of children has led to cognitive and emotional changes in women that persist. Thus, women continue to prefer men with resources, regardless of their ability to provide for themselves.

The evolutionary view of mate selection is not this clear-cut. It is true that women are more likely than men to prefer a mate with a good earning potential, and men are more likely to prefer a mate who is physically attractive. Yet, women and men find other traits in their partners more important than earning potential or physical attractiveness, respectively (Buss & Barnes, 1986). At least in the United States, both men and women first said that they preferred mates who were kind and understanding, and women actually rated physical attractiveness as more important than earning capacity. Thus, men may value physical attractiveness more than women, and women may value earning potential more than men, but men and women both agree that other attributes are more important than either physical attractiveness or earning potential. The similarities in mate preferences seem to outweigh the differences.

Jealousy

Evolutionary theory suggests that the different challenges men and women face in reproduction lead to sex differences in the situations that evoke jealousy. To test this idea, college students were asked which of the following two scenarios would be more upsetting: your partner forming a deep emotional attachment to someone else, or your partner having passionate sex with someone else (Buss, Larsen, Westen, & Semmelroth, 1992). Because women are more concerned with keeping men's resources available to them and their children, women should be more upset when men form a deep emotional bond with another woman. The idea is that men would be more likely to leave their partner if they formed an emotional bond with another women than if they had passionate sex with another women. Because men are more concerned with establishing paternity, they should be more upset by their partner engaging in sexual intercourse with another man than forming an emotional attachment to another man. Indeed, these are the results the investigators obtained. As shown in Figure 4.1, more men than women were distressed by their partner being sexually unfaithful, and more women than men were distressed by their partner being emotionally unfaithful. In a subsequent experiment, the investigators also

found physiological effects that paralleled the self-reports of distress. Men were more physiologically reactive when they imagined their partner to be sexually rather than emotionally unfaithful, whereas women were more physiologically reactive when they imagined their partner to be emotionally rather than sexually unfaithful.

One problem with this area of research is whether men and women view sexual infidelity and emotional infidelity as distinct. It is possible that men link sexual infidelity with emotional fidelity, not believing that their partner would have intercourse with someone else unless she were in love. Research in Chapter 8 shows this to be the case. Thus, the sexual infidelity cue may be evoking both sexual and emotional jealousy in men.

The Hunter-Gatherer Society

Sex differences in social behavior and cognition have been linked to the hunter-gatherer society, from which aggression in men and nurturance in women could have evolved. Aggression was required to hunt and feed the family; nurturance was required to take care of children. Evolutionary psychologists suggest that women are more emotionally expressive and sensitive to the emotions in others because they are the primary caretakers of children; it is important for women to be sensitive to the distress of others so that they can nurture them. Because men's traditional roles involved hunting, it was important for them to conceal their emotions; a successful hunter would need to be quiet and maintain a stoic demeanor to avoid being detected by prey.

Evolutionary theory claims that women are more likely than men to be the primary caretakers of children because they have a greater investment in their offspring: women

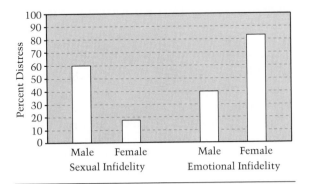

FIGURE 4.1 Sex differences in cues for sexual jealousy. When asked to choose which of two situations would be more upsetting, more men choose sexual infidelity than emotional infidelity. More women choose emotional infidelity than sexual infidelity. *Source:* Adapted from Buss et al. (1992).

have a finite number of eggs, whereas men have an infinite number of sperm; they have to carry the infant for nine months; and they are certain of their genetic link to the infant. With the women caring for children, men were left to hunt.

Sex-related differences in cognition also could have evolved from the hunter-gatherer society. Men's greater spatial skills and geographic knowledge may stem from their traveling more than women and venturing further from the home when hunting (Dabbs et al., 1998). Women's greater ability to locate objects may be linked to their having to keep track of objects close to home; foraging for food, in particular, required women to remember the location of objects (Silverman & Eals, 1992).

Some people find sociobiology and evolutionary theory distasteful as an explanation for sex-related differences in cognitive and social behavior, in part because these theories make sex-related differences seem unchangeable and to view traditional roles as "natural." The concern is that men's and women's different roles must have been—and still are—desirable if they led to survival. Buss and Kenrick (1998) argue against this interpretation. They suggest that evolutionary psychology is not deterministic but interactionistic: it interacts with the environment. Behavior that evolved for survival reasons can be influenced by the culture, such as the example of the influence of birth control pills on sexual behavior. Buss and Kenrick suggest that evolutionary psychology is useful for understanding the mechanisms behind behavior. To change behavior, one must understand its causes.

Psychoanalytic Theory

The first name that comes to mind in response to psychoanalytic theory is Sigmund Freud. Freud (1924, 1925), a psychiatrist, emphasized family dynamics in the development of gender roles. The basic premise of psychoanalytic theory is that gender roles are acquired by identifying with the same-sex parent. In infancy, the mother is the primary object of both boys' and girls' affections. As notions of gender develop, boys and girls take different pathways. According to Freud, the penis plays an instrumental role in gender-role development—for both boys and girls.

At about the time boys become aware that they are distinguished from the other sex by the presence of their penis, they develop an Oedipal complex. The Oedipal complex describes the boy's being sexually attracted to his mother while viewing his father as a rival for her affections. The boy wishes to get rid of his father and subsequently fears castration by his father because of that wish. As the boy realizes that he cannot compete with his father, he resolves the Oedipal complex by repressing his feelings toward his mother and identifying with his father. The "if you can't beat him, join him" metaphor might describe the approach. Thus, the boy acquires his gender identity by identification with the father.

Girls, by contrast, realize that they have no penis and are envious. Girls face the Electra complex, wherein they reject their mother because they believe she is responsible for their lack of a penis. By contrast, girls become attracted to their father and want to bear their father's child, thought to be a substitute for a penis. The Electra complex is not resolved, as is the Oedipal complex: girls continue to feel inferior due to their own lack of a penis. This deficiency leads the girl to identify with the mother, the less powerful of the two parents.

According to Freud, how boys and girls resolve these issues has implications for sexuality and future interpersonal relationships. There are several difficulties with this theory of gender-role acquisition. Most important, there is no way for it to be evaluated from a scientific standpoint because the ideas behind it are unconscious, according to Freud. One must be even more cautious in taking this theory seriously when one realizes that Freud developed it by studying people who sought him out for therapy.

A more modern version of psychoanalytic theory, referred to as object-relations theory, was applied to the acquisition of gender roles by Nancy Chodorow (1978) in her book *The Reproduction of Mothering.* Chodorow's theory emphasizes the importance of early relationships in establishing gender identity. She agrees with other psychoanalytic theorists in emphasizing the importance of sexuality, but she believes the family structure and the child's early social experiences, rather than unconscious processes, determine sexuality. A crucial tenet of her theory is that women are the primary caretakers of children in our society; thus, boys' and girls' first primary relationship is with their mothers, a relationship that affects boys' and girls' sense of self, future relationships, and attitudes toward women.

According to Chodorow (1978), girls acquire their gender identity by connecting with the one person with whom they are already attached: their mother. This explains why females focus on relationships and define themselves through their connection to others. Boys, by contrast, acquire their gender identity by rejecting the one person with whom they have become attached, by separating or individuating themselves from their mother. Thus, males learn to repress relationships and define themselves through separation from others. With whom do boys identify? Because fathers are less of a presence than mothers in children's lives,

there are fewer models available to boys; thus, boys come to identify masculinity as "not being feminine," or not being like mother. Whereas girls learn the feminine role by observing mother on a day-to-day basis, boys may find themselves identifying with cultural images of masculinity to learn their gender role.

Because girls identify with mother, their tendency to mother "reproduces" itself. Chodorow (1978) argues that women have a greater desire than men to be parents because they are more likely to have identified with a parenting role. According to Chodorow, the fact that women are the primary caretakers of children in our society leads directly to the division of labor (i.e., men working outside the home and women working inside the home) and the subsequent devaluation of women in society. The only way these roles can change, according to Chodorow, is for men to become more involved in raising children.

Social Learning Theory

There are two ways we learn behavior, according to social learning theory (Bandura & Walters, 1963; Mischel, 1966). First, we learn behavior that is reinforced; second, we learn behavior that is modeled. These are the primary principles of social learning theory and they apply to the acquisition of gender-role behavior as they do to any other domain of behavior (Mischel, 1966).

Reinforcement

Reinforcement theory no doubt sparks images of Pavlov's dog salivating at the bell, the cue that signifies a reward is coming. With respect to gender-role acquisition, the nature of the bell is different for boys and girls. We reward boys and girls for different behaviors, and the consequences of a behavior determine whether the child performs it again. The cartoon "Jump Start" (Figure 4.2) illustrates how parents reinforce behavior. Imagine that a girl plays with a doll; a parent may smile, play with her, or buy her another doll. Now imagine that a boy plays with a doll; a parent may ignore the behavior, take the doll away, frown, or even scold the boy and say "Only girls play with dolls." Consequences, however, do not actually have to occur to influence be-

havior; the child may infer that a consequence is likely to occur. For example, men do not have to wear high heels to know ahead of time that the consequences will be negative.

We are less tolerant of and more likely to punish cross-sex behavior among boys than among girls. We do not mind if women wear ties or suits, but we mind if men wear dresses; we do not mind if daughters are athletic, but we are less enthusiastic about sons who are graceful; we

FIGURE 4.2 Cartoon illustrates parents reinforcing toughness in boys. Jump Start cartoon by Robb Armstrong, March 7, 1999, "Kiss, Smooch, Smack, Wak . . ." Jump Start reprinted by permission of United Feature Syndicate, Inc.

are even less tolerant of attraction to a member of the same sex in men than in women. Homosexuality is viewed as a greater violation of the male gender role than the female gender role; that is, men are more likely than women to be punished for being homosexual.

Observational Learning or Modeling

A second way children develop gender roles is by patterning their behavior after models in the social environment. Modeling, or observational learning, is "the tendency for a person to reproduce the actions, attitudes, and emotional responses exhibited by real-life or symbolic models" (Mischel, 1966, p. 57). Observational learning may occur from exposure to television, books, or people. Gender roles are constructed and altered by exposure to new and different models.

Whom will children imitate? At first, children may not be very discriminating and may model anyone's behavior. Eventually, they pay attention to the way others respond to their imitative behavior. If others reward the behavior, it is likely to be repeated. Thus, modeling and reinforcement interact with each other to influence behavior. If a little boy sees someone on television punching another person, he may try out this behavior by punching his sibling or a toy. Although the parent may show disapproval when the boy punches his sibling, the parent may respond to punching the toy with mixed reactions. If everyone in the room laughs because they think that the boy's imitation of the television figure is cute, the boy will respond to this reinforcement by repeating the behavior. Observational learning also is more likely to occur if the consequences of the model's behavior are positive rather than negative. Children

should be more likely to imitate an aggressor on television who is glorified rather than punished. And many television aggressors are glorified, Power Rangers and the X-Men, for example. Children also should be more likely to imitate a person who excels in math or gymnastics if the person receives praise rather than ridicule from peers. Some of the conditions that influence observational learning are shown in Table 4.2.

Initially, social learning theory suggested that one way children become sex-typed is by imitating the same sex. But children do not always imitate the same sex (Maccoby & Jacklin, 1974). They are more likely to imitate same-sex behavior that is perceived as typical for the person's sex (Jacklin, 1989; Perry & Bussey, 1979). Children can easily figure out that women are more likely than men to be nurses and men are more likely to be engineers. This explains why a girl is more likely to imitate a mother who is a nurse rather than a mother who is an engineer. A girl whose mother is an engineer may still perceive that only men are engineers because the majority of people in the field of engineering are male.

Is there evidence that the roles parents enact influence children's perceptions of gender roles? One study examined whether parents' traditional or nontraditional roles

TABLE 4.2 Conditions That Influence Observational Learning

Observational learning increases:

If there is a positive relationship between observer and model.

If the consequences of model's behavior are positive rather than negative.

If the model is in a position of power.

If the model is the same sex and behaves in a gender-role-congruent way.

influenced college students' perceptions of men and women (Broverman et al., 1972). They compared college students who came from households where the mother was a housewife to those whose mother was employed outside the home. The investigators predicted that perceptions of men and women would be more similar among college students whose mothers worked outside the home because they were exposed to mothers and fathers who held similar roles; because both parents worked outside the home, fathers would have participated more in the work inside the home. The investigators found that female students' conceptions of women and men were more similar on measures of masculinity (i.e., competence) and femininity (i.e., expressiveness) when their mothers worked outside the home than when their mothers were housewives. College males' perceptions of women and men were more similar on measures of femininity but not masculinity when their mothers worked outside the home. Thus, most of the theory was supported. Yet, it is interesting that college males perceived men and women to differ in masculinity even when their mothers enacted a masculine role.

The application of social learning theory to sex-related differences suggests that as the norms change and the role models (e.g., in the media) of a culture change, sex differences will change. Think of how the traditional male gender role has been influenced by different models. In the 1950s, a model of the male gender role was John Wayne, a cowboy who smoked cigarettes. It is unlikely that this is the aspiration of most young men today. In the 1970s, the macho male gave way to sensitive and caring images like those portrayed by Alan Alda in *MASH* and Michael Landon in *Little House on the Praire*. In the 1980s, a model was Detective Sonny Crockett (played by Don Johnson) of the television show *Miami Vice*, whose unshaven face became the decade's symbol of masculinity. Today, an image of masculinity that comes to mind is the traditional male depicted by Tim Allen of *Home Improvement* and Ray Romano of *Everybody Loves Raymond*.

Social learning theory has contributed to the change in occupational aspirations among children, in particular girls. More women have entered the workforce and more women have jobs that were once held only by men. These changes are depicted in the media. Along with these changes, girls have come to modify their occupational aspirations. In one study, second-graders were asked what kind of job they would want as an adult (Helwig, 1998). They were then asked this same question in fourth and sixth grade. Helwig found that girls' preferences for stereotypical female occupations (e.g., nurse) decreased over time and their preferences for stereotypical male occupations (e.g., physicians) increased over time. This no doubt reflects the fact that more women are entering what were once regarded as exclusively male occupations. In addition, the total range of occupations that girls selected increased over time. Boys' behavior, however, became more stereotypical over time: they increased their preference for male-typical occupations. The reality is that the range of occupations has increased more for women than it has for men.

Social learning theory can explain why some of the sex differences in cognition and behavior have diminished over time. As men become more involved in child care and more models of men as parents appear, sex differences in empathy and nurturance may be reduced. As women become more involved in sports, sex differences in spatial skills could become smaller.

There is already some support for the role of social learning theory in the development of spatial skills. A meta-analysis revealed that experience with spatial activities is related to spatial ability (Baenninger & Newcombe, 1989). Thus, one reason that men have superior spatial skills compared to women might be that boys are more likely than girls to be given toys that require spatial abilities. For example, building blocks, math toys, and sports all require spatial skills, and these activities are encouraged more in boys. The meta-analysis even found that experimental studies of spatial training improved spatial skills. Spatial training typically involved repeated exposure to a spatial skills task or specific instructions on how to perform spatial tasks. There was a moderate effect of spatial training on spatial ability, ranging from .37 to .67, depending on the length of training provided. The effects of training were similar for men and women, meaning that men and women were equally likely to benefit from spatial skills training. This meta-analysis pointed a strong finger at the role of the environment in sex differences in spatial skills.

A central tenet of social learning theory is that the child is a passive agent on whom society is impacting. Behavior is determined by observing others and responding to rewards and punishments in the environment. Observing and performing behavior leads one to develop a gender identity; the gender identity does not lead to the behavior. According to social learning theory, cognitive changes follow behavioral changes. Social learning theory describes what influences behavior.

GENDER-ROLE SOCIALIZATION

Social learning theory is believed to be the basis for gender-role socialization theory. According to social learning theory, behavior is a function of rewards and observational learning. According to gender-role socialization, different people and objects in the child's environment provide rewards and models that shape behavior to fit gender-role norms. Agents in the environment encourage men to be agentic and women to be communal, to take on the male and female gender roles. J. Block (1973) suggested that the difference in how boys and girls are socialized is a primary contributor to sex differences in social behavior. Boys are taught to be assertive and to control their expression of feelings, whereas girls are taught to express concern for others and to control their assertion. This encouragement may take the direct form of reinforcement or the indirect form of modeling.

Gender-role socialization may not only contribute to actual sex differences in behavior but could contribute to the *appearance* of sex differences. Recall that sex differences in empathy were much larger for self-report measures than for more objective measures. Could this be due to the fact that women know they are supposed to be empathic and men know that they are not supposed to be empathic? The issue is one of response bias. Men and women may be distorting their behavior in ways to make them appear more consistent with traditional gender roles, which would artificially inflate the size of sex differences.

It is not surprising that the response bias issue could exaggerate sex differences in empathy. But could a response bias influence something that would appear to be much less subjective, such as spatial ability? There is evidence that when you disguise the nature of a spatial skills task in terms of masculinity and femininity, sex differences in spatial ability disappear. Sharps, Welton, and Price (1993) either emphasized or de-emphasized the spatial nature of the mental rotation task. As shown in Figure 4.3, men outperformed women when the spatial nature of the task was

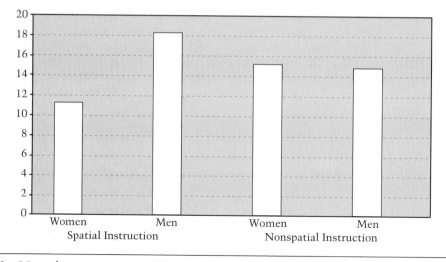

FIGURE 4.3   Mental rotation score. When the spatial nature of the mental rotation task was emphasized, men outperformed women. When the spatial nature of the task was de-emphasized, there was no sex difference in performance. *Source:* Adapted from Sharps et al. (1993).

emphasized, whereas no sex differences were observed when the spatial nature of the task was de-emphasized. These findings illustrate how people's views of a task can alter their performance. To the extent that men and women view a particular task as one in which men or women are expected to excel, participants may respond in a way to confirm this expectation. Test this idea yourself in Exercise 4.2.

Gender-role socialization may explain sex-related differences in emotion. Gender roles are associated with the expression of different emotions. Women's concerns with relationships may lead them to express emotions that strengthen relationships and inhibit emotions that could harm relationships (Timmers et al., 1998). Thus, women may express sadness to another person because they believe sharing such an experience will increase the closeness of the relationship. Women may be reluctant to express anger directly toward another person because of the potential damage to

the relationship. Men, by contrast, are motivated to express emotions that yield power and control and are reluctant to express emotions that suggest low power and vulnerability. Sadness and fear are "low-power" emotions, whereas anger and pride are "high-power" emotions.

To test these ideas, college students were presented with vignettes of four different emotions (anger, disappointment, sadness, fear) and asked how they would express these emotions (Timmers et al., 1998). Students were presented with different options for the expression of each emotion (e.g., cry, walk away, yell, be silent). Women were more likely than men to say that they would respond to sadness, fear, and disappointment by verbally expressing their feelings. Men were more likely to say that they would respond to these three emotions by keeping their feelings to themselves. Both men and women are behaving in ways that fit their motivations with regard to relationships. Women's verbal expression of feelings is

EXERCISE 4.2
Can Perceptions Alter Sex Differences?

1. Ask 20 people to complete two tasks, one being a test of spatial skills and one being a test of verbal skills. Come up with your own two tasks.

2. Before asking people to complete the tasks, randomly assign them to one of the following two conditions:

   Condition 1: This is the control group. Give no particular instructions.

   Condition 2: This is the experimental group. Manipulate respondents into perceiving that the spatial task is one in which females excel and the verbal task is one in which males excel. Think about what information you can provide to alter people's perceptions. You might provide fake statistics that show one sex performs better than the other sex. You might describe the type of person who excels on the task in masculine versus feminine terms.

3. After people have completed the task, have them rate how they view each task on a number of scales, two of which are:

   Not at all　　　　　　　　Very
   masculine　1　2　3　4　5　masculine

   Not at all　　　　　　　　Very
   feminine　1　2　3　4　5　feminine

   You may include other rating scales so that respondents will not detect which items you are really interested in. You also could use other terms besides masculine and feminine, such as those that appear on the masculinity and femininity scales.

4. Compare male and female performance on the two tasks in the two different conditions.

likely to increase the intimacy of a relationship. Men refrain from such expressions because revealing vulnerabilities would reduce their power in the relationship.

Men's motive to express power and control and women's motive to maintain relationships can be seen in how students said they would respond to anger. Their responses depended on whether the person with whom they were talking was or was not the target of the anger. As shown in Figure 4.4, the investigators found that men said they would be more likely to yell if the person was the target of their anger than if the person was not. Women said they would be more likely to yell if the person was *not* the target of their anger. The authors suggested that men express anger directly to the target because the goal is to change or control the other person's behavior. Women are unlikely to express anger directly to the target of their anger because it would threaten the relationship. Men are unlikely to express anger to someone who is not the target because the goal of this emotional expression would be to obtain comfort and support, a goal consistent with relationship maintenance.

There is more evidence that gender roles influence the expression of emotions. College students viewed slides of an emotion, reported their feelings, and had their physiological response measured (heart rate and EMG; Grossman & Wood, 1993, Study 2). Students were either given no instructions, instructions to enhance their emotional response, or instructions to inhibit their emotional response. In the no-instructions condition, women reported more extreme emotional responses to the slides than did men, replicating the results of an earlier study (Grossman & Wood, 1993, Study 1). In the instructions condition, however, sex differences in self-reports of emotions disappeared in favor of the instructions. In other words, people

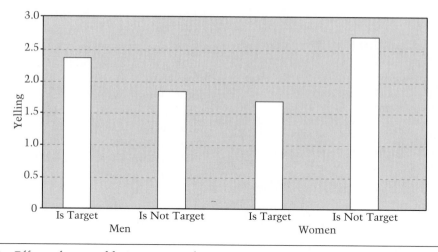

FIGURE 4.4 Effect of sex and being target of anger on expression of anger. Men are more likely to express anger to the person who is the target of the anger than to someone who is not the target of the anger. Women, by contrast, are less likely to express anger to someone who is the target of the anger than to someone who is not the target of the anger. *Source:* Timmers et al. (1998).

behaved as they were told with regard to the expression of emotion, either enhancing or inhibiting their emotional responses. In the absence of instructions, sex differences were observed; however, instructions to behave in a different way were able to override the implicit instructions to adhere to gender roles. The authors concluded that their study supported the idea that social roles, in particular gender roles, shape the experience and expression of emotion.

Now we turn to the question of who or what in the environment influences the acquisition of gender roles.

The Influence of Parents

Differential Treatment of Boys and Girls. Parents are prime candidates for contributing to gender-role socialization. However, evidence for parents treating boys and girls differently has been inconsistent. One of the early studies in this area was conducted by J. Rubin, Provenzano, and

Luria in 1974. They showed that parents stereotyped newborns by perceiving girls as pretty, little, and soft in comparison to boys. They also found that fathers stereotyped their children more than mothers. Twenty years later, investigators tried to replicate these findings (Karraker, Vogel, & Lake, 1995). Parents were asked to freely describe their infant and then rate their infant on a series of dimensions at two different times, postdelivery in the hospital and one week later at home. Results showed that there was absolutely no difference in the open-ended descriptions of boys and girls at either time. There were a few differences on the dimensions evaluated: parents viewed girls as having finer features, as less strong, and as more delicate than boys. Unlike the J. Rubin et al. study, there was no difference between mothers' and fathers' perceptions of their children.

What about the way parents treat their sons and daughters? Maccoby and Jacklin (1974) concluded from their review of the literature that parents treat boys and girls similarly: they encourage independence in both, discourage aggression in both, and display similar amounts of affection to both. Maccoby and Jacklin acknowledged that parents play rougher with boys, use physical punishment with boys more than girls, and provide boys and girls with different toys and activities. However, they argued that these differences are not important and certainly not able to account for sex differences in cognition, behavior, or emotion.

J. Block (1973) reached very different conclusions. She examined studies of parents' socialization practices and found that parents emphasize achievement and competition for boys and close relationships for girls. Parents offer comfort and reassurance to girls and encourage girls to talk about their problems and to show affection to others. Parents discourage boys from expressing feelings and are concerned that boys learn to conform to rules. J. Block also concluded from her review that fathers were more likely than mothers to differ in how they treated sons and daughters.

More recently, two meta-analyses of how parents treat sons and daughters were conducted. The first, conducted by Siegal (1987), concluded that mothers and fathers do treat children differently. Siegal found that the largest differences were in the areas of physical involvement with children (e.g., touch, physical play) and discipline: parents were stricter with boys and engaged in more physical play with boys. The differences in the treatment of boys and girls were larger among fathers than mothers.

By contrast, Lytton and Romney (1991) conducted a more comprehensive meta-analytic review of 172 studies that evaluated parents' socialization practices with children, and concluded that parents' overall treatment of boys and girls was similar. There was only one way in which parents were found to treat boys and girls differently: parents encouraged sex-typed toys $(d = +.34)$. There were trends that showed parents encouraged achievement, were more restrictive, and were more strict with boys; by contrast, parents encouraged dependence and were warmer with girls. These effects were small, however, and did not reach statistical significance.

How do we resolve this discrepancy? Lytton and Romney (1991) examined whether the methodology of a study influenced the results. Studies that included more objective methods, such as experiments and observational studies, showed larger differences in the way parents treated boys and girls than studies that used more subjective methods, such as questionnaires and interviews. In other words, parents did not report treating sons and daughters differently, but their behavior suggested otherwise. In general, the higher-quality studies showed larger differences in the way parents treated sons and daughters.

Lytton and Romney (1991) also found that parents' differential treatment of children seemed to decline with the child's age. This is not surprising, as parents gain more target-based information and are less likely to rely on category-based (stereotypical) information as the child's age increases. The authors noted, in agreement with J. Block (1973) and Siegel (1987), that fathers were more likely than mothers to treat sons and daughters differently.

Another reason Lytton and Romney's (1991) meta-analysis did not reveal a sex difference in parents' treatment of children is that some behaviors were overlooked. Parents' different treatment of boys and girls may be subtle. Even Maccoby and Jacklin (1974) agreed with this position. For example, an observational study found that the physical environments that parents created for boys and girls ages 5, 13, and 25 months differed vastly (A. Pomerleau, Bolduc, Malcuit, & Cossette, 1990). Children were visited in their home by a trained observer, who noted the children's toys, how the children were dressed, and the décor of the children's rooms. Girls were more likely than boys to have dolls, kitchen appliances, and child's furniture, whereas boys were more likely to have tools, sports equipment, and vehicles. Boys were more likely to wear blue and red clothing, whereas girls were more likely to wear pink clothing. Boys' rooms were more likely to contain blue bedding and curtains, whereas girls' rooms were more likely to contain yellow curtains. The question remains as to the impact of these very early differences in boys' and girls' environments. Exposure to certain classes of toys could lead to later preferences for those toys. Does exposure to some kinds of toys foster particular skills that might advantage one sex over the other? If you think that the toys that boys and girls have today are similar, visit a nearby toy store: the aisles of girls' toys are noticeable from 50 feet away because of all the blinding pink packaging. Examine boys' and girls' toys by visiting a toy store with Exercise 4.3.

EMOTION.   One area in which parents may treat children differently is emotion. There is a great deal of evidence that parents discuss emotions and use more emotion words with daughters than sons (Brody & Hall, 1993; Malatesta et al., 1989). For example, Kuebli and Fivush (1992) visited parents and children in their homes on three occasions and found that both mothers and fathers used a greater number and a greater variety of emotion words with their daughters than with their sons.

What are the implications of parents using more emotion words with daughters? Several longitudinal studies have demonstrated that parents' language is associated

---

EXERCISE 4.3
Toy Store Visit

Visit a toy store or the children's section of a department store. Take notes on what you see. Can you tell which are the girls' toys and which are the boys' toys? If so, how? Pay attention to location in the store, packaging, color, and the nature of the toy. How are the toys different? How are the toys similar? Compare these toys to the ones you had during your childhood. Observe the shoppers, particularly as their behavior relates to gender.

---

with children's subsequent use of language. J. Dunn, Bretherton, and Munn (1987) observed mothers' and siblings' natural conversations with 18-month-olds in the home. They found that mothers and siblings were more likely to use words that described feeling states (sad, angry, happy), states of consciousness (awake, tired), and sensations (hungry, cold) with girls than with boys. By the time these children were 24 months old, the girls were using more feeling state words in their language than were the boys. Two other longitudinal studies found that parents' use of more emotion words with girls contributed to girls' subsequent use of more emotion words relative to boys (S. Adams, Kuebli, Boyle, & Fivush, 1995; Kuebli, Butler, & Fivush, 1995). In both studies, parents used more emotion words and a greater variety of emotion words with 40-month-old daughters than sons, despite the lack of sex differences in the children's initial use of emotion words. By 70 months, the girls were responding with a greater variety of emotion words than were the boys.

One possibility is that parents are using more emotion words with girls because they are responding to differences in the language that girls and boys already use.

That is, perhaps there is a biological basis to girls' greater use of emotion words, which then prompts parents to respond similarly. But the longitudinal studies have ruled out this hypothesis. In the previous study (Kuebli et al., 1995), the children's language did not influence the mothers' language over time. Thus, parents are not merely responding to inherent differences in children's use of emotion words.

There also is evidence that parents use different emotion words with sons and daughters. When talking about an event that the parent and child both experienced (e.g., a holiday, a trip), parents were more likely to recount the sad parts of the event to daughters than to sons. However, they were equally likely to mention the happy parts of the event with sons and daughters (Kuebli & Fivush, 1992). For example, parents might be more likely to remind their daughter that it rained on the day they were supposed to go to the beach or that they had to wait in line for hours at the amusement park. But parents would be equally likely to remind their son and daughter that they won a stuffed animal at the fair. Another study found that a greater proportion of emotion words were positive (happy) with sons than daughters, and a greater proportion of emotion words were negative (sad) with daughters than sons (Kuebli et al., 1995). The authors suggested that these differences could have implications for the way men and women cope with stressful events: mothers are teaching daughters to talk about negative emotions and teaching sons not to dwell on negative emotions. A study of mother-child communication reached a similar conclusion. Fivush (1989) found that mothers are more likely to discuss and elaborate on a specific emotion with daughters but to focus on the causes and consequences of the emotional state with sons. The author suggests that mothers may be helping sons to identify the causes

and consequences of an emotion in order to gain control over emotions but encouraging daughters to focus or even dwell on the emotional state itself. These ideas fit with a finding discussed later in the text concerning men's and women's different styles of coping with negative events: women cope by ruminating about the event and men cope by distracting themselves (Nolen-Hoeksema, 1987).

Parents' reactions to emotional expressions also may influence whether children express emotion. Females are socialized to express their emotions, whereas males are socialized to conceal their emotions. In a study of first-, fourth-, and sixth-graders, girls expected more favorable reactions from parents to the expression of sadness compared to boys (Fuchs & Thelen, 1988). Girls were equally likely to express sadness at all three ages, whereas boys expressed less sadness with increasing age. Perhaps older boys became more aware of others' reactions.

GENDER-ROLE BELIEFS. The last issue I would like to address concerns the impact of parents' gender-role beliefs on children's gender-role socialization. That is, do parents with more egalitarian beliefs have children who are less rigid in their gender roles? This issue was examined in a variety of different families in the 1960s and 1970s, including single mothers, people who were living together but not married, people who lived in communes or groups, and people with more traditional marital arrangements (Weisner & Wilson-Mitchell, 1990). The families differed in the extent to which they de-emphasized gender-role stereotypes. When the children in these families were age 6, they were brought into the lab. The extent to which the children were sex-typed was measured by objective ratings, by parent ratings, and through interviews with the children. Appearance, activities and interests, personality, and relationship preferences (i.e., play with same-sex peers) were considered. Overall, the investigators found that the extent to which the family de-emphasized gender stereotypes was rarely related to how sex-typed the child was. There was no relation of the family arrangement to the children's activities, personality, or relationship preferences. However, parents who de-emphasized gender stereotypes had children who were less sex-typed in physical appearance and occupational preferences. The authors also found that girls were less likely to display sex-typed behavior than boys.

SUMMARY. Overall, it appears that parents treat sons and daughters in more similar than different ways. One way parents treat boys and girls differently is in the provision of sex-typed toys and sex-typed environments (e.g., clothing, décor of bedrooms). The debate is over the impact such behavior has. Another important difference is in the way that parents communicate with sons and daughters, particularly with respect to emotion. The long-term consequences of this behavior have not been investigated. It is not clear if parents treat sons and daughters differently with respect to other behaviors, such as encouraging nurturance in girls and independence in boys. There are a couple of reasons why the evidence is not clear on this issue. First, it is difficult to measure these kinds of behaviors. One large meta-analytic review suggested that differences existed on objective measures (observation) but not subjective measures (parents' self-report). Second, differential treatment is more likely to occur among younger than older children. It is not a surprise that as a child gets older, parents respond to the individual child rather than the child's sex. Third, the differential socialization of children may be a product of other people and other environmental

factors rather than parents. I now turn to these other sources of influence.

The Influence of Other People

If parents treat boys and girls in a fairly similar way, who treats them differently? One possibility is that it is other people, such as relatives, teachers, friends, and neighbors, rather than parents who treat children differently (Jacklin & Baker, 1993). Recall that we are more likely to stereotype people we do not know very well. Thus, parents may be less likely than friends or relatives to use category-based information when interacting with their children.

This line of thinking is similar to that of Judith Harris (1998), who concluded that parents have largely no effect on the development of a child's personality. (This was a great relief to me, as the book appeared shortly after I had my daughter.) She wrote a controversial book entitled *The Nurture Assumption: Why Children Turn Out the Way They Do: Parents Matter Less Than You Think and Peers Matter More.* The title says it all. Harris argues that the source of influence on children comes from outside the home, in particular, from the peer group. Her conclusion is partly based on the fact that children raised by the same parents in the same environment often turn out to have very different personalities. However, one can debate whether the same home and the same parents constitute the same environment for each child. Harris's theory is called group socialization and emphasizes the child's experience outside the home. According to her theory, children learn behavior inside the home but then test it on others outside the home to see if it is going to be accepted or rejected. Others' reactions determine if the behavior is repeated.

Is there evidence that peers influence sex differences? Certainly the influence of peers, in particular, same-sex peers, could lead to differences in emotional expression (Brody & Hall, 1993). Boys play in larger groups, which have the potential for conflict and aggression. In boys' groups, the potential for the expression of anger is high, but the potential for the expression of emotions that make one vulnerable to peers, such as fear and sadness, is low. Girls play in small groups, which minimize conflict and emphasize cooperation. In girls' groups, the potential for the expression of emotions that foster relationships, such as sadness and fear, is high. The influence of same-sex social interactions on boys' and girls' behavior is addressed in detail in Chapter 6.

So, is there anything that parents can do, according to Harris (1998)? Yes: parents should choose to live in a good neighborhood. This is because it is the peers in the neighborhood who are going to influence the child. But one wonders: What is the cause of the neighborhood children's behavior?

Another socializing agent that may influence children's gender-role behavior is teachers. One study found that nursery school teachers responded differently to male and female infants (Fagot, Hagan, Leinbach, & Kronsberg, 1985): the teachers gave attention to the boys who were assertive and the girls who were communicative. At the beginning of the study, boys and girls displayed equal amounts of assertive and communicative behavior; one year later, the boys were more aggressive and the girls were more communicative with the teacher. Thus, a self-fulfilling prophecy seems to have occurred; that is, teachers elicited the behavior they expected. The influence of teachers on boys' and girls' achievement-related behavior is discussed in depth in Chapter 5.

Other Features of the Environment

TOYS. The toys children play with may influence sex differences in cognition and behavior. Toys may directly reinforce sex differences in cognitive abilities. As recently as 1992, the Mattel Corporation produced the Teen Talk Barbie, who said, among other things, "Math class is tough" (Sadker & Sadker, 1994). Boys and girls play with different toys: boys overwhelmingly play with vehicles, machines, construction sets (e.g., building blocks), whereas girls play with dolls and domestic toys (Tracy, 1987). Are these differences important? One possibility is that boys' toys are more likely than girls' toys to foster the development of spatial skills, and girls' toys are more likely than boys' toys to foster the development of verbal skills (F. Hughes, 1991). However, there is no evidence that playing with boys' toys actually leads to greater spatial ability, or that playing with girls' toys improves verbal skills. If toys are linked to spatial skills and verbal abilities, the sex differences would be amenable to change. However, it is also plausible that children with better spatial skills are drawn to boys' toys and children with better verbal skills are attracted to girls' toys (F. Hughes, 1991).

BOOKS. The books that children read also may model and encourage gender-role-appropriate behavior. A writer of children's books, Mem Fox (1993), points out that everything we read, from advertisements to magazines to books, shapes who we are by the images of men and women that are presented. She comments that if girls can do anything, "Why is it, then, that in children's literature they are still portrayed more often than not as acted upon rather than active? As nurturers rather than adventurers? As sweetness and light rather than thunder and lightning?" (pp. 84–85). The same can be said of boys. Fox remarks, "Why is it that ballet dancing and painting are seen as less fit occupations for them than being machine gunners, for example, or baseball players? Why should they live, as most of them do, with the idea that it is, in the main, their crippling responsibility to provide for a family when they become grown-up boys?" (p. 85).

A group known as Women on Words and Images conducted a content analysis of 134 elementary school readers in 1972 and 84 readers in 1975. They found that men were portrayed in more active roles than women and women were portrayed in more passive and domestic roles than men. The main character of the majority of the stories was a male. More recently, 62 readers used in three cities in Texas were evaluated (Purcell & Stewart, 1990). There was a clear change in the portrayal of males and females: the books were less likely to focus on a male and included a wider range of roles for both male and female characters. However, although women were now shown as doctors, they were still less likely than men to be shown as hunters or explorers. The investigators also noted that females were more likely than males to be rescued in the stories, in particular by a pet. The authors noted that not a single story portrayed a boy being rescued by an animal.

Ernst (1995) was not so optimistic in her assessment of the children's books that appeared in the 1990s. The title of the books indicated that twice as many books are about boys as girls; two to three times as many biographies are about boys. This pattern even occurred among award-winning children's books. Ernst argued that the prevalence of male characters leads to the conclusion that men are more important than women, and what men do is more worth writing and reading about. In addition, Ernst found that children's books continued to depict men and women in traditional roles. Male characters have an impact on and change the world; female characters follow the lead of others. Examine portrayals of gender roles in children's books on your own in Exercise 4.4

EXERCISE 4.4
How Are Men and Women Portrayed in Children's Books?

Review 10 children's storybooks. Record the sex of all the characters and how they are portrayed. What are they doing? Are they good characters or bad characters? What are their personality traits?

TELEVISION. Television is also a source of information about gender roles. Recent studies of current television shows and commercials do not show as much change in gender roles as one might think. Depictions of men and women on the most popular sitcoms (as indicated by Nielson ratings) were examined from 1950 to 1996 (B. Olson & Douglas, 1997). More recent sitcoms differed from earlier sitcoms in that they showed quite a bit of variability in men's and women's roles. For example, gender roles were fairly equal on *The Cosby Show* but were very traditional on the even more recent *Home Improvement*.

An analysis of television commercials shows that men are still the dominant force. Commercials from the 1950s and early 1960s were compared to those from the 1980s (Allan & Coltrane, 1996). The main character was predominantly male on the old commercials (61%) as well as the more recent commercials (67%). The narrator was male nearly all of the time (old: 93%; recent: 91%). However, women's roles seem to have changed much more than men's roles. When women were shown in commercials in the 1980s, they were less likely to be shown in traditional roles; for example, women were shown in parenting roles 33% of the time in the old commercials but only 9% of the time in more recent commercials. In addition, the range of occupations women hold has sharply increased.

The depiction of men in commercials, however, has not changed as much; for example, men are rarely depicted in parenting roles (old: 7%; recent: 10%).

Males also dominate children's advertisements (B. Browne, 1998). Boys and girls are shown in traditional roles: boys appear aggressive, dominant, and active, whereas girls appear shy, giggling, and deferent (B. Browne, 1998). Gender roles are most distinct in advertisements featuring toys; for example, the most sex segregation occurs in children's toy advertisements (Rajecki, Dame, Creek, Barrickman, & Reid, 1993). Only 30% of toy advertisements showed both a male and a female, whereas 76% of food advertisements and 89% of other advertisements showed both sexes. In an analysis of children's toy advertisements in the United States and Australia, no commercials depicted girls playing with traditional "boy toys" such as trucks, and no commercials depicted boys playing with traditional "girl toys" such as dolls (B. Browne, 1998).

Most of the recently published studies examined television in the 1980s and early 1990s. Have their been further changes? Conduct your own analysis of recent television shows in Exercise 4.5.

EXERCISE 4.5
How Men and Women Are
Portrayed on Television

Watch one episode each of the 10 most popular television shows. You may limit your analysis to comedies or dramas or compare the two. What is the sex of the main character/characters? Describe the personality characteristics, behavior, and occupation of the characters in the shows. Are roles traditional or nontraditional? In what ways?

Conclusion

In conclusion, gender-role socialization may influence sex differences in behavior, cognition, and emotion by teaching and encouraging gender-role-appropriate behavior. Sources of gender-role socialization include parents, teachers, peers, neighbors, and the media. One positive aspect of gender-role socialization theory is that if these practices contribute to sex differences, society is then capable of providing the training or skills that men and women require to remedy any deficiencies. The socialization perspective is supported by data that suggest the size of some sex differences in cognitive performance has diminished over the years as society has recognized men and women to have more equal roles (Richardson, 1997).

SOCIAL ROLE THEORY

According to social role theory, differences in men's and women's behavior are a function of the different roles men and women hold in our society. This is a variant of gender-role socialization theory. It is not specific people that shape behavior, but societal role structures that influence behavior. The idea here is that the way labor is divided between men and women in society accounts for why men become agentic and women become communal. The theory differs from gender-role socialization in that it focuses more on the abstract social conditions of society rather than the concrete ways that people in the environment behave toward men and women. Men are primarily responsible for work outside the home, which leads to an agentic orientation. Women, even when employed, are primarily responsible for work inside the home, which leads to a communal orientation. According to Eagly (1987b), when the roles that men and women hold are similar, sex differences are minimized. For example, in one study, homemakers, regardless of whether they were male or female, were perceived to be more communal and less agentic than people who held full-time jobs outside the home (Eagly & Steffen, 1984).

The roles that men and women possess in society, men being agentic and women being communal, have been used to explain sex differences in influenceability, nonverbal behavior, and behavior in small groups (Eagly, 1987b). Women may be more easily influenced or more conforming than men because they want to appear agreeable and maintain group harmony. The nonverbal behaviors in which women engage more than men—smiling, laughing, gazing, and nodding—may reflect women's desire to foster the development of relationships. Finally, women's tendency to be more agreeable in small groups can be construed as behavior that aims to enhance group relations.

Social role theory states that the roles men and women hold in society are responsible for sex differences in behavior. Social role theory does not specify that men must be agentic and women must be communal. However, most societies have organized men's and women's roles in a way so that they develop these characteristics.

There are other roles that men and women occupy in society besides work and family roles that influence gender-role behavior. For example, men are more likely than women to occupy military roles and athletic roles. These roles may contribute to sex differences in aggression. Men and women also are likely to hold different occupational roles that may contribute to sex differences in aggression. Men hold occupations in the business world that require competitiveness, whereas women hold service occupations such as nursing and teaching, which require nurturance and are incompatible with aggression.

Another difference between men's and women's social roles lies in their differential status. Men and women do not have equal statuses in our society. Thus, any differences in behavior observed between men and women may be due to the status differences in their roles rather than the roles per se. For example, men's higher status may explain why men are less influenceable than women. Sex differences in nonverbal behavior also may be due to status; women may smile and gaze more than men because a low-status person needs to appear attentive and agreeable to a high-status person.

Moskowitz, Suh, and Desaulniers (1994) tested whether status versus the male and female social roles would influence displays of gender-role behavior. Community volunteers recorded their social interactions with supervisors and supervisees at work over 20 days. When participants interacted with supervisees, more agentic (dominant) behavior was displayed, regardless of participant's sex. When participants interacted with supervisors, less agentic behavior was displayed, regardless of participant's sex. Thus, the status of the participant relative to the interaction partner explained agentic behavior; sex did not. However, the investigators also found that women behaved more communally than men across the interactions, regardless of whether they were supervisors or supervisees. Thus, status predicted agentic behavior, but sex predicted communal behavior. As you will learn in Chapter 6, both status and social roles influence men's and women's behavior.

Cross-Cultural Research

One way to determine the contribution of society to gender roles is to examine practices across cultures. One of the most extensive cross-cultural studies of gender roles was conducted by Whiting and Edwards

(1988). They observed the way that children ranging in age from a few months to 10 years from 12 different communities (described in Table 4.3) interacted with other children and adults. The investigators' main hypothesis was that the environments of men and women differ and that these different environments contribute to sex differences in behavior. In general, their hypothesis was supported.

Whiting and Edwards (1988) studied several interpersonal behaviors and found sex differences in two of them: nurturance (helping) and egoistic dominance (coercion, competition). In both cases, Whiting and Edwards concluded that the differences in behavior were due to the different settings. The different settings provided girls with more practice in nurturance and boys with more practice in egoistic dominance. This interpretation of sex differences is consistent with social role theory.

Nurturance was defined in this study as helping behavior. Examples of nurturant behavior included consoling, smiling, and offerings of toys or food. The investigators discovered that girls interacted more than boys with younger children, and interactions

TABLE 4.3   Communities Where Children's Social Interaction Was Observed

Location	National Affiliation	Linguistic Affiliation	Type of Settlement	Population
New Samples				
Kienn-taa	Liberia	Kpelle, Mende	Section of a town	200
Kowet				
Western Province	Kenya	Kipsigis, Nilo-Hamitic	Farm homesteads	447
Kisa				
Western Province	Kenya	Abaluyia	Farm homesteads	3,000
Kariobangi, Nairobi				
Central Province	Kenya	Abalyayia	Housing estate in a city	13,000
Ngeca				
Central Province	Kenya	Kikuyu, Bantu	Village surrounded by farm homesteads	6,000
Bhubaneswar				
Orissa	India	Oriya	City	50,000
Six Culture Samples				
Nyansongo				
Western Province	Kenya	Gusii, Bantu	Farm homesteads	208
Juxtlahuacca				
Oaxaca	Mexico	Mixtecan	Barrio, Indian section of a town	600
Tarong, Luzon	Phillipines	Iloco	Scattered hamlets	259
Taira	Okinawa		Hokan and Japanese village	700
Khalapur				
Uttar Pradesh	India	Hindu	Town, clustered	5,000
Orchard Town				
New England	U.S.A.	English	Part of a town	5,000

Source: Adapted from Whiting and Edwards (1988).

with younger children demanded nurturance. In particular, "lap children," defined as children less than 1 year old, seem to elicit nurturance with their cries, smiles, and vocalizations. Both boys and girls demonstrated more nurturance toward lap children than any other age group of children. There was no evidence that girls were more nurturant than boys when one controlled for the greater amount of time that girls spent with lap children. Because girls did spend more time with lap children, however, they developed the necessary caretaking skills to a greater extent than did boys.

Egoistic dominance was defined as attempts to change another person's behavior to suit one's own needs; coercion, insults, and competitive behavior are examples of egoistic dominance. Boys interacted more with peers than did girls, and interactions with peers were characterized by displays of greater egoistic dominance. Boys were especially more likely to interact with older children of the same sex. Older boys are more likely than older girls to behave in egoistic dominant ways with younger children. Thus, boys had greater experience than girls with egoistic dominant interactions.

Whiting and Edwards (1988) also observed that parents treated boys and girls differently. Although mothers behaved in equally sociable and nurturant ways to both, they were more likely to assign child care and household chores to girls. Why do mothers ask girls rather than boys to take care of children? Is it because mothers believe that girls have a greater capacity for caretaking than boys? Is it because mothers believe that girls are more interested in caretaking than boys? Or, is it because mothers believe that caretaking is not suitable for boys—is inconsistent with the male gender role? Mothers also were more likely to give commands to girls than to boys. At younger ages, these commands involved how to behave appropriately in terms of hygiene and etiquette; at older

ages, these commands involved requests for help with household and child care tasks. Whiting and Edwards remark, "Girls work while boys play" (p. 125). Mothers exerted more controlling behavior over boys in terms of punishments and reprimands for misbehavior, a finding consistent with empirical studies conducted in the United States. The investigators suggest that this difference in treatment of boys and girls was due to boys being less compliant than girls with mothers. Girls were more likely to comply with their mothers' commands perhaps because girls spend more time with their mothers or perhaps because boys are aware of their higher status compared to girls.

The differential treatment of boys and girls was greatest in societies where the status of men and women was most unequal. Physical autonomy of girls—for example, their ability to venture far from the house—was most restricted in communities with the greatest status difference between men and women. Whiting and Edwards (1988) stated, "The power of mothers to assign girls and boys to different settings may be the single most important factor in shaping gender-specific behaviors in childhood" (p. 86). I guess Judith Harris, author of *The Nurture Assumption: Why Children Turn Out the Way They Do: Parents Matter Less Than You Think and Peers Matter More,* would disagree.

In conclusion, the authors point out that the different environment of boys and girls does not say anything about the cause of those differences. Are boys and girls genetically hardwired to select different environments? Or, do adults' beliefs about the differences between men and women lead them to place boys and girls in different environments? More specifically, is there a genetic predisposition in girls to interact with lap children and in boys to interact with peers, which then causes these differences in nurturance and egoistic dominance? Or, do societies assign boys and girls to different settings, which then elicit these behavioral differences?

Cross-cultural research on emotion provides evidence that cultural factors override gender roles. In a study of college students from 37 countries spanning five continents, sex differences in expression were larger in countries with *less* traditional gender roles (A. Fischer & Manstead, 2000). The authors argue that less traditional countries, such as the United States, have an individualistic orientation; the emphasis is on individual expression of feelings. In an individualistic country, individual differences in terms of gender roles may appear. In collectivist countries, which are often more traditional, behavior, including the expression of emotion, is determined more by the environment: the norms of the culture, the other people in the situation. Thus, people (men and women) behave more similarly in terms of emotional expression in collectivist cultures.

COGNITIVE DEVELOPMENT THEORY

Social learning theory, gender-role socialization, and social role theory all emphasize the effect of the environment on the child's skills and behaviors. In contrast, cognitive development theory states that the acquisition of gender roles takes place in the child's head. "It stresses the active nature of the child's thoughts as he organizes his role perceptions and role learnings around his basic conceptions of his body and his world" (Kohlberg, 1966, p. 83). An assumption of cognitive development theory is that the child is an active interpreter of the world. Learning occurs because the child cognitively organizes what he or she sees; learning does not occur from reinforcement or from conditioning. That is, the child is acting on his or her environment, the environment is not acting on the child.

Cognitive development theory also suggests that there are a series of stages of development that eventually lead to the acquisition of gender roles. First, children develop a **gender identity** (Kohlberg, 1966). By age 2 or 3, children learn the labels "boy" and "girl" and apply these labels to themselves and other people. The labels are based on superficial characteristics of people rather than biology, however. If someone has long hair, she must be a girl; if someone is wearing a suit, he must be a man; and if you put a dress on the man, he becomes a she. That is, children at this age believe a person's sex can change—including their own sex. A boy may believe he can grow up to be a mother.

Children do not use the labels "boy" and "girl" correctly until age 4 and 5. Children learn **gender constancy** by age 5. That is, they can categorize themselves as male or female and realize that they cannot change their category. But, even at age 5, children may not use biological distinctions as the basis for categorization. They are more likely to classify people as male or female by their size, strength, or physical appearance. I experienced an example of this confusion one day when I was taking my 2-year-old daughter to day care. Another girl, about 4 or 5 years old, came over and asked, "Is she a boy?" I was a bit surprised because my daughter was wearing a Minnie Mouse outfit. I told the little girl that she was a girl. In some frustration, the little girl replied, "Then why is she wearing boy shoes?" My daughter was wearing blue sandals. Conduct your own experiment with young children to try to identify how they decide that someone is male versus female (see Exercise 4.6). By age 5, children also learn the content of gender categories and become aware of the different roles that men and women possess in society.

According to cognitive development theory, gender identity determines gender-role attitudes and values. Once children

> **EXERCISE 4.6**
> **How Children Determine Gender**
>
> Interview five children: a 2-year-old, a 3-year-old, a 4-year-old, a 5-year-old, and a 6-year-old. If the class is involved in this assignment, you can pool the results. Try to find out how each child determines whether someone is male or female. You can do this through a set of open-ended interview questions. For example, is the teacher male or female? How do you know? Are you male or female? How do you know? Is Santa Claus male or female? How do you know? You can also do this by presenting each child with a series of pictures, perhaps from storybooks, and ask the child to indicate whether the character is male or female and to explain why. Whichever method you choose, be sure to standardize it so that you are using the same procedure for each child.

acquire their gender identity, they have a high internal motivation to behave in ways that are consistent with their self-concept. Their self-concept as male or female expands as they take in new information from the environment. The child identifies the self as male or female and wants to behave in ways consistent with this self category.

One limitation of Kohlberg's theory is that he states gender constancy must be achieved before children will value and seek out behavior that fits their gender role. Yet, studies have shown that children who have not achieved gender constancy still choose sex-typed behavior (Bussey & Bandura, 1992). Bandura (1986; Bussey & Bandura, 1999) has advanced the notion of **social cognitive theory,** which states that cognitive development is one factor in gender-role acquisition but that there are social influences as well, such as parents and peers.

According to social cognitive theory, external sources have the initial influence on behavior. For example, the promise of a reward or the threat of punishment influences behavior. Later, however, children shift from relying on external sources to internal standards to guide behavior. Social cognitive theory emphasizes the interplay between psychological and social influences.

GENDER SCHEMA THEORY

You are probably familiar with the following puzzle: A little boy and his father get into an automobile accident. The father dies, but the little boy is rushed to the hospital. As soon as the boy gets to the emergency room, the doctor looks down at him and says, "I cannot operate. This boy is my son."

How can this be? Didn't the boy's father die in the accident? The solution, of course, is that the physician is the boy's mother. Why is it that we presume the physician is male? Because being male is part of our schema for the category "physician."

A **schema** is a construct that contains information about the features of a category as well as its associations with other categories. We all have schemas for situations (e.g., parties, funerals), for people at school (e.g., the jocks, the nerds), for objects (e.g., animals, vegetables) and for subjects in school (e.g., chemistry, psychology). The content of a schema varies among people. Those of you who are psychology majors have more elaborate schemas for psychology than those of you who are not psychology majors. You know that there are differences among clinical psychology, social psychology, and physiological psychology; a nonpsychology major may not know of these distinctions and think that all fields of psychology are alike. Those of you who are avid football fans have more elaborate football schemas, including all of the rules of the game, the players on the different teams, and the current status of each team, compared to those of you who are not interested in football.

Schemas can be helpful in processing information. Whenever you encounter the object or the setting for which you have a schema, you do not have to relearn the information. So, those of you who have rich football schemas can use your knowledge of what happened in last week's playoffs to understand the games that are being played this coming weekend.

A gender schema includes your knowledge of what being male and female means and what behaviors, cognitions, and emotions are associated with these categories. When buying a toy for a newborn, one of the first questions we ask is if the baby is a boy or a girl. This category will guide our choice of clothing or of a toy. When looking over the personnel at the dry cleaners, we presume that the seamstress is the female clerk and not the male clerk because sewing is consistent with the female gender role, not the male gender role. When hiring a secretary, we interview only female applicants because "secretary" is part of our female gender-role schema, not our male gender-role schema. In fact, to have male secretaries, we have come up with a new term: administrative assistant.

What does it mean to be gender schematic? Someone who is gender schematic uses the gender category to make decisions about what to wear, how to behave, what career to pursue, what leisure interests to pursue, and what emotions to present to others. Someone who is **gender aschematic** does not consider gender when making these decisions.

To understand this more clearly, let's take an example of another variable on which people vary in terms of schematicity: religion. For some of you, religion is central

to your identities and one of the first things that you will notice about a person: whether the person is religious and, if so, to which religion he or she belongs. You will notice whether a person observes religious practices and has any religious belongings in the home. Religious holidays will influence your behavior. That is, you are religious schematic. For others of you, religion is not central to your self-concept, and you are religious aschematic; you will not notice whether a person engages in religious practices ("Did we say prayers before the meal at Joe's house? I really can't recall"), not notice if religious symbols are in a person's home, and fail to notice religious holidays. Being religious aschematic does not mean that you are not religious; it just means that religion is not something you think about and not something that influences your behavior. A strong atheist can still be religious schematic; an atheist may be well aware of religious practices and go to great lengths to ignore religion. This person is still letting religion influence behavior.

It is likely that all of us are gender schematic, to some extent. Bem (1981) argues that gender is a pervasive dichotomy in society that guides our thinking about what clothes to wear, what toys to play with, and what occupations to pursue. But there is variability among us in how readily we think of gender when processing information. The person who does not rely on male/female categories as a way of organizing the world is gender aschematic. This person is less likely to be concerned with the gender category when deciding how to think, feel, or behave. It does not occur to the person that a secretary cannot be male, that it is not OK for a male to wear a barrette, or that girls should not play with trucks.

Gender schema theory is a theory about the *process* by which we acquire gender roles; it is not a theory that describes the content of those roles. The theory simply states that we divide the world into masculine and feminine categories. The culture defines those categories. Gender schema theory combines elements of both social learning theory and cognitive development theory in describing how we acquire gender roles. Social learning theory explains how we acquire the features of the male and female gender categories and what we associate with those categories. Cognitive development theory describes how we begin to encode new information into these cognitive categories to maintain consistency. The child learns to invoke this gender-role category or schema when processing new information.

A construct that you may be more familiar with than gender schema theory is **androgyny.** Recall that the androgynous individual has both masculine and feminine attributes (Bem, 1981). Bem linked gender schematicity to the construct of androgyny. Because the gender aschematic person does not use gender as a guiding principle when thinking about how to behave, Bem suggested that this person would incorporate both traditionally masculine and traditionally feminine qualities into his or her self-concept, or be androgynous. Bem presumed that the gender aschematic person would have the flexibility to develop both masculine and feminine qualities. By contrast, gender schematic people were thought to be sex-typed, that is, masculine if male and feminine if female. Theoretically, cross-sex-typed people (masculine females, feminine males) are also gender schematic; they would still use gender as an organizing principle, but would be concerned with adhering to behavior that is consistent with the norms for the other sex.

Bem (1984) advanced her gender schema theory by showing that sex-typed people engage in gender schematic processing. For example, in one study, she flashed

the 60 attributes of the Bem Sex Role Inventory on a screen. College students were asked to decide whether the attribute described them. The dependent variable in this experiment was how quickly the student made the judgment. Bem hypothesized that sex-typed respondents, compared to androgynous respondents, would decide more quickly that a sex-appropriate attribute described them and that a sex-inappropriate attribute did not describe them. For example, a feminine female could quickly decide that yes, she is "helpful" and that no, she is not "loud." Sex-typed respondents also were expected to take longer to reject a sex-appropriate attribute and to take longer to accept a sex-inappropriate attribute compared to androgynous individuals. So that same feminine female would take longer to admit that no, she does not cook and yes, she is competitive. The results confirmed the hypothesis. The left half of Figure 4.5 indicates how quickly people endorsed terms that were consistent with gender-role schemas compared to terms that were neutral. It appears that sex-typed individuals were faster in making schema-consistent judgments than cross-sex-typed, androgynous, and undifferentiated individuals. The right half of Figure 4.5 indicates how quickly people endorsed terms that were inconsistent with gender-role schemas compared to terms that were neutral. Sex-typed individuals were slower in making schema-inconsistent judgments, especially relative to cross-sex-typed, androgynous, and undifferentiated individuals. In other studies, Bem found that sex-typed individuals were more likely to categorize a list of attributes in terms of gender and more likely to organize groups of others in terms of gender compared to androgynous persons.

Bem also found support for her theory by demonstrating that sex-typed individuals prefer to engage in behavior that is

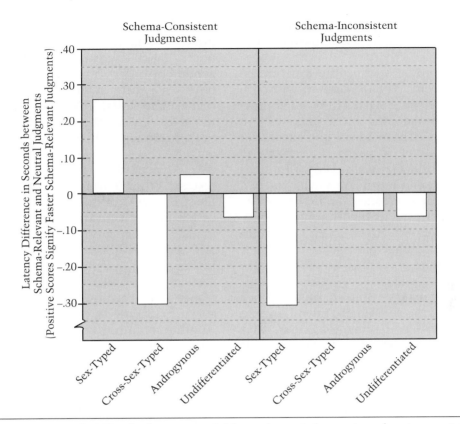

FIGURE 4.5 Sex-typed individuals more quickly endorse information that is consistent with their gender-role schemas than cross-sex-typed, androgynous, or undifferentiated individuals. Sex-typed individuals are slower to endorse information that is inconsistent with their gender-role schemas than the other three groups of individuals. *Source:* S. L. Bem (1981). Gender schema theory: A cognitive account of sex typing. *Psychological Review, 88*(4), 354–364.

consistent with their gender role. In one study, college students were asked to choose which of two activities they would prefer to perform and then to engage in a gender-role-inconsistent activity (Bem, 1984). Sex-typed individuals were more likely than androgynous individuals to choose behaviors that were consistent with their gender role and to feel more uncomfortable performing the gender-role-inconsistent behavior.

One difficulty with gender schema theory is its relation to androgyny. The an-

drogynous person is supposed to be gender aschematic. Being gender aschematic implies that the person does not think of the world in sex-related terms; yet, androgyny is defined in terms of gender-related traits. Bem (1981) acknowledges that this measure of androgyny may not imply the flexibility in behavior that she had hoped. Androgyny can be restrictive in the sense that the person has two ideals to meet: a masculine one and a feminine one. Androgyny also does not rid society of the two culturally defined gender categories, which was Bem's ultimate aim. Bem really advocated gender aschematicity, not androgyny.

How could one become gender aschematic? Bem (1984) suggests how to raise a gender aschematic child using practices that she adopted in raising her son and daughter. These ideas are shown in Table 4.4. Her basic position is that you teach your child that sex is only a biological category, and that the only way you can know whether someone is male or female is to see the person naked. Because society associates sex with much more than biology, the parent must go to some lengths to make sure that prevailing stereotypes are not instilled in the child. This includes altering storybooks so that all men are not viewed as having short hair and all women are not viewed as having long hair; that all men are not viewed as heroes and all women are not rescued; that all men are

TABLE 4.4 Bem's Ideas on How to Raise a Gender Aschematic Child

1. Teach what sex is: a biological distinction. (You cannot tell if someone is male or female unless you see the person naked.)

2. Teach what sex is not: get rid of the cultural correlates of sex.

    Provide child with both male and female toys and clothes.

    Censor books and television for depictions of men and women in traditional roles.

    Eliminate own gender-stereotyped behavior (e.g., mom only washes dishes, dad only washes car).

3. Counter cultural stereotypes with counterexamples (e.g., Child: "Only men can be doctors." Parent: "But your Aunt Jean is a doctor.")

4. Teach that society's view of gender is not only different from the one you are teaching but that it is incorrect.

not depicted in blue and all women in pink. The parent would provide the child with a range of toys and not let the child's gender influence the choice of toys; both boys and girls would be given blocks, trucks, and dolls. There would be no such thing as "girl clothes" and "boy clothes"; both could wear shirts, pants, dresses, and barrettes.

Boys in dresses?! Boys wearing barrettes?! When I first present Bem's (1984) ideas in class, these remarks are the most commonly made. Students are all for letting girls wear any clothes and play with any toys, but someone usually draws the line at seeing a boy in a dress. Because I find dresses fairly uncomfortable, my personal response is to remove dresses from the category of clothing for both men and women. Another common reaction that students have is that a child should choose whom he or she wants to be and how he or she wants to behave—that parents shouldn't force the child to be gender schematic or gender aschematic. Bem would respond that a child is never "free" to behave as he or she pleases because society will provide clear messages about how to behave, and those messages will be sexist. Thus, if parents do not inoculate their children against gender schemas, society will impose those schemas. For those of you who are interested in the results of Bem's child-rearing practices, she has published an autobiography describing her egalitarian marriage and her gender aschematic child rearing (Bem, 1998). At the end of her book, her children comment favorably on the way that they were raised. And, yes, Bem's grown son still occasionally wears a dress.

Bem's (1984) gender schema theory obviously has some political overtones. Historically, Bem has advocated the minimization of differences between men and women—basically reducing the differences to biology alone. She has suggested that society should rid itself of the social construction of gender that is associated with biological sex. In such a culture, there would be no need for the terms masculinity and femininity; the term androgyny would be meaningless. Sex would be viewed as having a very limited influence on us, no more influence then, say, eye color.

More recently, Bem (1995) has realized that her utopian ideals are not reachable. She has suggested an alternative strategy for minimizing sex differences, or what she now refers to as "turning down the volume on sex differences." Her new strategy is to "turn *up* the volume on sex differences." By this, she means that we should have 1,000 categories for sex instead of only two. She suggests starting with a modest 18 categories, derived from all possible combinations of sex (male, female), gender role (masculine, feminine, androgynous), and sexual orientation (heterosexual, homosexual, bisexual). By having so many categories, it would be difficult to have clear-cut boundaries between any two categories. The categories would become fluid and, ultimately, the distinctions among them less important if not meaningless.

CONSIDERING THE CONTEXT: DEAUX AND MAJOR'S MODEL

All of the theories discussed so far emphasize how biological or social forces alone or in conjunction with one another could have led to sex differences in cognition or behavior or could have shaped the traditional male and female gender roles. Instead of focusing on how gender-related behavior is acquired, like the other theories reviewed in this chapter, Deaux and Major (1987) focused on the conditions that create the *display* of gender-related behavior. That is, they emphasized the proximal, or more immediate, causes of whether a sex difference is observed rather than the

distal, or more distant, factors such as biology and socialization.

From a social psychological perspective, the theories discussed so far in this chapter are fundamentally flawed (Deaux & LaFrance, 1998) because they do not take the situation, the context, into account. Deaux and Major (1987) noted that one reason men's and women's behavior is inconsistent across studies is that the situation has a strong impact on behavior. Thus, they incorporated the situation into their model of sex differences.

Deaux and Major's (1987) model emphasizes three determinants of whether a sex difference in behavior is displayed: (1) the perceiver's expectancies, (2) the target's (i.e., person who may or may not display the sex difference) self-concept, and (3) the situation. I review how each of these contributes to the display of sex differences.

Perceiver

The perceiver is the person observing the behavior. The perceiver has an expectation about whether a person, the target, will display a behavior. This expectation is likely to be confirmed by either **cognitive confirmation** or **behavioral confirmation.** Cognitive confirmation is the idea that we see what we want to see; it explains how two people can see the same behavior and interpret it differently. Have you ever watched a baseball game with a person who is rooting for the other team? What happens during those instant replays? You are sure the person on your team is safe and your friend is sure the person is out. The two of you actually see the same replay but interpret the behavior differently and, not surprisingly, in line with what you hoped to see. Behavior is often subject to multiple interpretations, especially social behavior. Thus, the person who believes baby boys are more active than baby girls will probably maintain this belief despite numerous counterexamples because he or she is free to interpret a wide range of behavior as active or inactive.

Behavioral confirmation is the process by which a perceiver's expectation actually alters the target's behavior. The target then confirms the perceiver's expectancy. Imagine that a mother believes that boys are not as capable as girls of taking care of small children. This mother is likely to give her daughter more opportunities to take care of the new baby in the family. Thus, it will not be surprising if the daughter becomes more skillful than the son at feeding and entertaining the baby!

Target

The target in an interaction is the person whose behavior is of interest. The target of an interaction influences whether he or she displays behavior consistent with stereotypes about sex differences by two processes: **self-verification** and **self-presentation.** Self-verification is our concern with behaving in ways consistent with our self-concept. If you are a member of the National Rifle Association (NRA), you may not be able to keep yourself from speaking about the importance of the Second Amendment. If you are a very traditional male, it may be important to you not to express emotions in any situation. Self-presentation is our concern with how our behavior appears to others. The NRA member may find it inappropriate to voice concerns about Second Amendment rights to a mother whose child was accidentally killed by a gun. The traditional male may realize that there are situations that call for emotional expression, such as a funeral.

There are individual differences in concerns with self-presentation and self-verification. **Self-monitoring** is an individual

difference variable that describes the extent to which one is more concerned with self-presentation or self-verification (Snyder, 1979). A high self-monitor is someone who changes his or her behavior to fit the situation. This person will be outgoing at a party, yet serious during a study session. This person will be both supportive of a woman's right to an abortion when talking to a group of feminists but sympathetic to the plight of the unborn child when talking to a priest. This person is very much concerned with self-presentation. A low self-monitor typically behaves the same from one situation to the next. If this person is serious, he or she will be serious at a party, serious at a study session, serious at a movie, and serious during a hike. If in favor of reducing social security, this person will state his or her beliefs whether talking to a 30-year-old or a 70-year-old. The low self-monitor is most concerned with self-verification. The situation, however, also will influence whether we are more concerned with self-verification or self-presentation. Now, I turn to the importance of the situation.

Situation

In some situations, you may be more concerned with adhering to your principles and values and want to behave in a way that is consistent with them. What will determine this? The strength of your values is one determinant. If the issue is something you care strongly about, you will stand firm in your beliefs no matter what the situation. If I believe that hunting is a valuable sport, I will voice this opinion to a group of people who I expect will disagree with me, such as vegetarians. In other areas, however, I may be less certain about an issue. I may be able to see both the pros and cons of day care for children; thus, I will not be outspoken in advocating or rejecting day care in any situation.

In some situations, you will be very much concerned with how you appear to others. These situations include ones in which other people have power over you and situations in which you need something from these other people. If you are a Democrat and you discover that your professor is a Republican, you may decide to conceal your political views. Why? Because you want the professor to like you, especially if you feel that grades are going to be subjective. Obviously there are exceptions. If you feel strongly about being a Democrat or are a low self-monitor, you may share your political views with the professor anyway.

The following personal example illustrates how self-verification may operate in some situations and self-presentation may operate in others. In most situations, if someone asked "Do you mind if I smoke?" I would say yes. I would be behaving true to my self-concept as a nonsmoker and one not very fond of smoke. However, several years ago, I was in a situation where I was surrounded by a half dozen male physicians who I was hoping would refer patients to a study I was conducting. The chief among the group, who was sitting next to me, started the meeting by turning to me and asking, "Do you mind if I smoke?" I found myself quickly replying, "No, I don't mind at all!" In this particular situation, self-presentation won out over self-verification; my goal of behaving in ways consistent with my self-concept was not as strong as my goal of not offending the physician so that I would receive patient referrals.

Other aspects of the situation will influence behavior. Some situations have high behavioral constraints; they provide strong cues as to how to behave. In these situations, most people will behave in accordance with those cues. For example,

church is a situation with high behavioral constraints. Most people, regardless of individual difference variables, will behave in the same way during a church service: sit quietly, listen, try to stay awake, sing when others are singing, and recite passages when others recite passages. There is a set script for behavior. Deviations from these behaviors, such as giggling, are quite noticeable. Other situations are low in behavioral constraints. A party is such a situation. Some people will be loud and mingle with the crowd; others will sit quietly with one other person and talk for hours. Either behavior is acceptable. What situations are high and low in behavioral constraints with respect to gender? A wedding is a situation that is high in behavioral constraints. There are clear guidelines for how the bride and groom are to dress and behave and the guidelines are quite different for the two of them. The classroom is a situation that is low in behavioral constraints with respect to gender. There are clear guidelines for behavior (sit quietly, take notes, raise hand to answer a question), but these guidelines do not differ much for men and women.

Deaux and Major's (1987) model of sex differences, shown in Figure 4.6, shows how these three components—perceiver, target, and situation—interact to determine whether sex differences are observed. Let's go through the model, step by step, with an example. In this example, the perceiver is a father, the target is his 3-year-old daughter, and the situation is that they are playing with toys at a day care.

Box A: This box represents the father's beliefs about men and women, that is, whether he has gender-role stereotypes, specifically about the toys that are appropriate for a girl to play with. As the father gets to know the daughter more, he will be less likely to rely

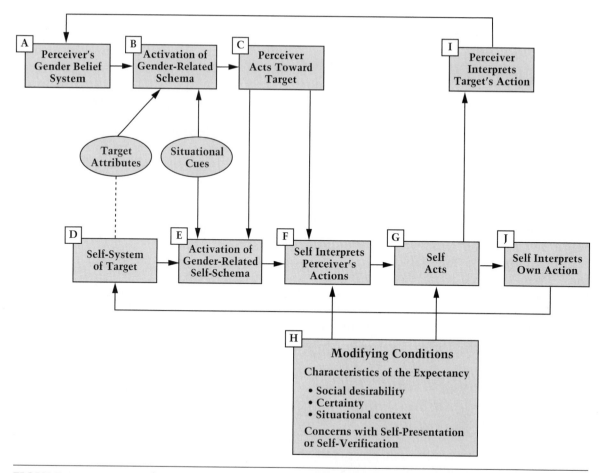

FIGURE 4.6 Deaux and Major's (1987) model of social interaction for gender-related behavior. This model explains how the perceiver, the target, and the situation determine whether sex differences in behavior are displayed in a given situation. *Source:* K. Deaux and B. Major (1987). Putting gender into context: An interactive model of gender-related behavior. *Psychological Review, 94,* 369–389.

on gender-role stereotypes (category-based information) and more likely to respond to target-based information (the attributes of his daughter).

Box B: This box represents whether a gender schema is activated in the father's mind. A recent event could activate a gender schema. For example, on the way to the day care, the father could have heard a story on the news about differences in social abilities between boys and girls. Attributes of the

daughter or the situation could activate a gender schema. Is his daughter dressed quite differently from the boys at the day care? Is she wearing a pink, frilly dress? Or, is the daughter wearing a shirt and pants that does not distinguish her from the other children? The day care also may make gender salient, if the teacher has the boys on one side of the room and the girls on the other side of the room, or if it appears that children are playing only with members of their same sex.

Box C: Here the father behaves toward his daughter. If he is highly gender schematic and has had gender schemas recently activated, perhaps he will offer his daughter a doll to play with. If he is gender aschematic and has not had gender schemas activated, he might offer his daughter the toy that looks most interesting to him or the toy that he knows will be of most interest to her.

Box D: This box represents the target's self-concept, part of which is whether the daughter is gender schematic. In this example, the daughter is likely to know that she is a girl and probably has noticed that boys and girls play with different toys. The daughter, however, has her own unique interests in the toys. Let's imagine that her favorite toy is a remote-control car and that she does not like playing with dolls.

Box E: The same things that activated the father's gender-related schema in Box B can activate the daughter's gender-related schema in Box E. This also includes how the father behaves toward her. Why did he offer her a doll when she never plays with dolls?

Box F: Here the daughter interprets the father's behavior, which is that he has just offered her a doll when she was about to play with the remote-control car. Now she has to decide whether to play with the doll, which would be behavior consistent with self-presentation (pleasing the father), or to play with the car, which would be behavior consistent with self-verification.

Box G: The daughter behaves. The interesting part of this story is that re-gardless of whether the daughter plays with the doll or the car, the father's gender belief system (Box A) and the daughter's self-system (Box D) are likely to remain intact. If the daughter plays with the car, she will confirm her belief that she likes cars (Box J), which fits with her self-system (Box D). The father is likely to make a situational attribution for the behavior, such as "The car is novel, but in time she will return to the dolls" (Box I). Thus, the father's belief system (Box A) also remains intact. Alternatively, if the daughter plays with the doll, the father naturally sees that the behavior fits his belief system (Box I). The daughter will realize that she is playing with the doll so that she can play with her dad and discount her aberrant behavior (Box J). She does not have to alter her self-system either.

Box H: This box has to do with the characteristics of the situation that might influence behavior. Is the behavior socially desirable? In our example, playing with a doll or car is socially desirable behavior. But what is socially desirable may differ for males and females. Is it socially desirable for a boy to play with a doll? The certainty of the perceiver and target self-concepts will influence the outcome. In our example, the 3-year-old is likely to have a quite malleable concept of what toys are appropriate for boys and girls. If the father has spent little time around the daughter, he, too, might be less certain about the toys she will like. Those who have the strongest stereotypes are most likely to have them confirmed. The situation also determines constraints on behavior. Playtime at day care is likely to be a situation with low behavioral constraints. Finally, the extent to which the target is concerned with self-presentation (i.e., pleasing her father) versus adhering to her self-concept (i.e., playing with what she really likes) will influence behavior.

Although the diagram may seem complicated at first glance, the interaction we just described is actually overly simplified. In every interaction, the perceiver is also a target and the target is also a perceiver. So we could talk about how the daughter influences her father's behavior. We could also talk about how the other children and the teacher influence the father-daughter interaction. Each person has expectancies for self and others. The point is that in any given situation, there are many proximal variables that determine whether a behavior occurs, specifically whether men and women display differences in behavior.

CONSTRUCTIONIST AND POSTMODERN PERSPECTIVES

The constuctionists have difficulty with the subject of comparing men and women. They view gender as a dynamic force rather than a static, individual difference variable. Questions about sex differences and sex similarities do not make sense because sex cannot be studied apart from its context. Men's and women's behavior does not exist in a vacuum: it always occurs in a specific place and time. Thus, the constructionists argue that sex comparisons cannot be made with empirical methods.

Perception is the critical feature of the postmodern perspective. According to the constructionists, we cannot discover reality because we construct it (Hare-Mustin & Marecek, 1988). Empirical methods are based on the idea that reality can be observed and that truth and facts can be distinguished from values. Construction-

ism maintains, however, that values determine reality. Thus, the constructionists maintain that we cannot truly understand the nature of gender or sex.

As part of the constructionists' perspective, Hare-Mustin and Marecek (1988) make the point that research showing sex differences and research showing sex similarities are both biased. The former line of research is subject to an alpha bias (in which actual similarities are overlooked), and the latter is subject to a beta bias (in which actual differences are overlooked). The maximalists are most likely to fall victim to the alpha bias and the minimalists to fall victim to the beta bias. The constructionists are not in favor of either approach. They state, "All knowledge is influenced by the standpoint of the knower" (p. 427). Instead of arguing which approach is correct (which can never truly be known), the constructionists examine the consequences of each approach for the study of gender.

An important negative consequence of the alpha bias—of emphasizing men and women as fundamentally different—is that the influence of status, power, and the different roles men and women hold in society are neglected. Differences are attributable to biological sex and the role of environmental variables is ignored. A positive consequence of the alpha bias is that feminine traits are valued. But does valuing women—specifically, their relationship orientation—mean we are affirming the low status and low power of women that led to these characteristics? This presumes, of course, that status and power explain the relationship orientation of women.

An important negative consequence of the beta bias—believing men and women are more similar than they really are—is that treating men and women similarly can be problematic if, in fact, they are different. Hare-Mustin and Marecek (1988) give the example of parental leaves: Should the same parental leave be granted to men and women if the demands on men and women are not the same? In addition, the beta bias would ignore the differential status of men and women in society. A positive consequence of the beta bias is that opportunities for women may increase if people treat men and women equally.

The constructionist perspective and the social psychological perspective share an emphasis on the context. This text takes largely a social psychological perspective rather than a constructionist perspective in understanding sex similarities and differences and the implications of gender for relationships and health. However, this is not to say that the cautions the constructionists make about the limits of our empirical methods should be ignored.

SUMMARY

I reviewed the different theories that explain the origins of the sex differences discussed in Chapter 3 as well as how gender roles are acquired. Biological theories of sex differences focus largely on the role of hormones in gender-related behavior and the effects of the structure of the brain on sex differences in cognition. The evidence for each of these subject areas is fairly controversial. The role of hormones is difficult to study because we cannot manipulate hormone levels in human beings; thus, we are left to rely on correlational research among humans and experimental research on animals. Evolutionary psychology and sociobiology are theories that introduce evolutionary principles to explain cognitive and social behavior. Although a number of social behaviors, such as mate selection and sexual behavior, can be explained by sociobiology, it is difficult to test this theory experimentally. Psychoanalytic theory began with Freud, but has been updated by Chodorow. The basis of the

theory, whether traditional or modern, is how identification with the same-sex parent influences the acquisition of gender roles. Social learning theory states that reinforcement and modeling apply to the acquisition of gender-role behavior just as they do to any other behavior. The principles of social learning theory have been applied directly to gender-role acquisition in the form of gender-role socialization theory. Gender-role socialization emphasizes the role that social agents, in particular, parents, play in the development of children's gender roles. The evidence for parents' differential treatment of sons and daughters is contradictory; put simply, parents treat sons and daughters more similarly than differently, but the few differences may have a large impact. In particular, parents provide sons and daughters with different toys, ones suitable for their gender role. Social role theory is similar to gender-role socialization in that it emphasizes the social forces that shape gender-role behavior. However, social role theory examines those forces at a higher level, for example, by claiming that the division of labor between men and women in society (men working, women caring for children) fosters agentic and communal behavior. Interesting cross-cultural research confirms the notion that the different opportunities societies present to boys and girls can lead to the development of gender-distinct behavior. By contrast, cognitive development theory emphasizes the child as an active processor of the environment rather than a passive recipient of modeling and reinforcement. Gender schema theory integrates the principles of social learning theory (and gender-role socialization) with cognitive development theory. The principles of social learning theory are responsible for the content of the gender categories in society, and cognitive development theory is responsible for our acting in accordance with those categories. Gender schema theory is really a theory of process, rather than content; people who are gender schematic behave in ways consistent with the gender schema of a given society; people who are gender aschematic do not use gender as a guiding principle for behavior.

Finally, Deaux and Major offer a theory that describes the more proximal determinants of sex differences. According to Deaux and Major, characteristics of the perceiver, the target, and the situation will determine at any given moment how people behave and whether a sex difference is observed. The constructionist perspective also emphasizes the importance of the situation or the context in determining behavior, but views gender as a meaningless category that is so subjective and value-laden that it cannot be subject to empirical scrutiny.

Obviously, no one theory is correct in terms of explaining all sex differences, or in terms of explaining how men and women come to possess male and female gender roles. Some theories have more evidence than others. Some theories are more easily testable than others. Some theories are more relevant to one aspect of gender than others; for example, hormones may play a greater role in aggression than in verbal ability. Each of these theories appears throughout this text, but the predominant theories discussed are ones that focus on social or environmental contributors to the impact of gender on relationships and health.

DISCUSSION QUESTIONS

1. Discuss the strengths and weaknesses of each of the theories of gender introduced in this chapter.
2. Which of the theories of gender is most difficult to test? Easiest to test?
3. If you were going to develop a study to determine whether parents treat sons and daughters differently, how would

you go about developing this study? In particular, what specific behaviors would you measure?
4. How are gender roles portrayed in the media?
5. How do the roles men and women hold in society contribute to agentic and communal behavior?
6. Distinguish between social learning theory and cognitive development theory. How does gender schema theory integrate the two?
7. Debate the advantages and disadvantages of raising a gender aschematic child.
8. Apply Deaux and Major's model to a specific behavior. Review each of the steps in the model shown in Figure 4.6.

SUGGESTED READING

Bem, S.L. (1998). *An unconventional family.* New Haven, CT: Yale University Press.

Block, J.H. (1973). Conceptions of sex role: Some cross-cultural and longitudinal perspectives. *American Psychologist, 2,* 512–526.

Buss, D.M. (1995). Psychological sex differences: Origins through sexual selection. *American Psychologist, 50*(3), 164–168.

Chodorow, N. (1978). *The reproduction of mothering: Psychoanalysis and the sociology of gender.* London: University of California Press.

Deaux, K., & Major, K. (1987). Putting gender into context: An interactive model of gender-related behavior. *Psychological Review, 94,* 369–389.

Eagly, A.H. (1987b). *Sex differences in social behavior: A social role interpretation.* Hillsdale, NJ: Erlbaum.

Lytton, H., & Romney, D.M. (1991). Parents' differential socialization of boys and girls: A meta-analysis. *Psychological Bulletin, 1991,* 267–296.

Whiting, B.B., & Edwards, C.P. (1988). *Children of different worlds.* Cambridge, MA: Harvard University Press.

KEY TERMS

Androgens—Male sex hormones (e.g., testosterone).

Androgyny—The incorporation of both traditionally masculine and traditionally feminine qualities into one's self-concept.

Behavioral confirmation—The process by which a perceiver's expectation actually alters the target's behavior so that the target comes to confirm the perceiver's expectancy.

Cognitive confirmation—The idea that individuals see what they want to see.

Estrogens—Female sex hormones.

Gender aschematic—Someone who does not use the gender category as a guiding principle in behavior or as a way of processing information about the world.

Gender constancy—The categorization of the self as male or female, and the realization that this category cannot be changed.

Gender identity—The label determined by biological sex that is applied either to the self or other people.

Lateralization—The distinction of an ability (e.g., language) to one hemisphere of the brain.

Schema—A category that contains information about the features of the category as well as its associations with other categories.

Self-monitoring—A variable that describes the extent to which one is more concerned with self-presentation or self-verification.

Self-presentation—The concern individuals have with how their behavior appears to others.

Self-verification—The concern individuals have with behaving in ways consistent with their self-concepts.

Social cognitive theory—States that cognitive development is one factor in gender-role acquisition but that there are social influences as well.

5

Achievement

Samantha and Austin are enamored with elementary school. Their strongest subject is math. By eighth grade, Samantha prefers math over reading, whereas Austin is torn between reading and math. His primary leisure interest is reading. They have similarly high scores on standardized tests of math ability, but Austin's verbal ability score exceeds Samantha's. By the end of high school, Samantha lags slightly behind Austin in math. As college approaches, Samantha is prepared to declare a major in elementary education. Austin decides to pursue engineering.

What happened? Why did Samantha's math scores decline? Why didn't Samantha pursue a career that involved more math? Why did Austin pursue engineering? Is his favorite leisure interest still reading? This is a likely scenario in some senses but not others. During elementary school, girls typically receive higher grades than boys, even in the traditionally masculine subjects of math and science. Yet today, women are still less likely than men to pursue careers in these subject areas. Why? Do

women have lower math aptitude? If so, why are their math grades higher than or the same as boys prior to high school? Perhaps women are less likely than men to pursue careers that involve math because they are less interested in math. We know that girls are less likely than boys to choose to take extra math courses in high school. Do parents, teachers, and peers do anything to influence girls' pursuit of math? Girls may have different beliefs about the cause of their high math grades than boys. Perhaps, boys believe that they have a natural talent and girls believe that they have to work really hard to get those good grades. If so, where do those different beliefs originate? Remember the talking Barbie who said "Math is hard"? What happened to Austin's interest in reading? Did he choose engineering because he had high math ability or because he believed that engineering was a more suitable career for a man than English literature?

Men and women excel in different areas. As discussed in Chapter 3, women perform better in verbal domains and men in math domains. What are some of the reasons for the differences in performance and the pursuit of different areas of achievement even when performance is the same? There are still a number of fields, notably math and science, in which women have lagged behind men. Although women have reached the same educational level of men in terms of undergraduate degrees, women are still 50% less likely to receive their doctorates (U.S. Census Bureau, 1999). In 1960, twice as many men as women graduated from college, over twice as many men received master's degrees, and nine times as many men received their doctorates. The gap has completely closed for bachelor's and master's degrees; however, by 1996, men were still more likely to receive their doctorates. Thus, at the highest levels, women are not achieving as much as men. What are some of the reasons women are less likely to realize their achievement potential? The purpose of this chapter is to answer these questions.

In the first section of the chapter, I explore a number of individual difference explanations for men's and women's different areas and levels of achievement. These explanations pertain to characteristics of men and women. Men and women may be motivated to achieve in different domains and may have different beliefs about their abilities, which could influence their motivations. There also are a variety of explanations as to why women do not realize their achievement potential, including ideas that women fear success, lack self-confidence, and in general have lower self-esteem.

In the second section of the chapter, I explore social explanations for sex differences in achievement. How do other people's expectations and beliefs—those of parents, teachers, and peers—influence men's and women's achievement? Finally, I conclude the chapter by examining the recent literature on one solution to the problem of women's lower levels of achievement compared to men: single-sex education.

INDIVIDUAL DIFFERENCE FACTORS

The Achievement Motive

Look at the picture of the two acrobats flying through the air depicted in Figure 5.1. What do you see? What kind of story would you write about the two acrobats? If you wrote about how hard the two people had worked to become acrobats, about all they had given up for their profession, about how successful they were, and about the difficult feats they were trying to accomplish, you might be considered to have a high motive for achievement. At least, this is one way the need for achievement has been measured.

David McClelland and colleagues (McClelland, Atkinson, Clark, & Lowell, 1953) described the **achievement motive** as a stable personality characteristic that reflects the tendency to strive for success. The achievement motive was measured by people's responses to scenes from Thematic Apperception Test (TAT) cards like the one depicted in Figure 5.1. People would view the scene on the card and write a story about it. The content of the story was then coded for themes related to the achievement motive. Mentions of success, striving, challenge, and accomplishment would reflect themes of achievement. People who scored high in achievement motivation were found to persist longer at tasks and to actually reach higher levels of achievement. Those people were men. Achievement motivation did not predict these same outcomes in women. Some people suggested that women did not have as great a desire or need for achievement.

FIGURE 5.1 Adaptation of a Thematic Apperception Test (TAT) card depicting two acrobats flying through the air.

There were several problems with this conclusion. First, the domains of achievement studied (or depicted by the TAT cards) may have been more relevant to men than women, especially in the 1950s and 1960s. For example, viewing a TAT card that depicted two scientists in a laboratory may not have aroused the achievement motive in women because there were few women in science laboratories at the time. Women may not have been able to see themselves as a scientist in a laboratory, or women may not have had any desire to be a scientist in a laboratory. Also, men and women might have valued achievement in different areas (A. Stein & Bailey, 1973). One factor that determines whether someone pursues success in an area is the value the person attaches to success in that area (J. Eccles, 1994). An achievement domain that might have been more relevant to women, especially in the 1950s, is achievement in more traditionally female roles, such as the caretaker role. Evidence that traditional roles might have something to do with women's achievement motivation comes from a comparison of African American and Caucasian female college students (S. Harris, 1993). In this study, African American women scored higher on achievement motivation than Caucasian women. One reason might be that the traditional role for African American women has incorporated the paid worker role for a longer period of time than has the traditional role for Caucasian women.

Another difficulty with the study of achievement motivation in women is that the characteristics that defined the motive (assertiveness, independence, competitiveness) conflicted with the characteristics of the female gender role. Thus, another reason women did not fit into the theory of achievement motivation is that women recognized that achievement-related behavior would be inconsistent with their gender role.

What did women do, and what do women do, when they have a high need for achievement but believe achievement conflicts with their gender role? One response is to conceal achievements. Female students may tell their peers that they scored lower on an exam than they really did (Stein & Bailey, 1973). Another response is to compensate for the threat to the female gender role that achievement poses by adopting extremely feminine dress and manner. Another option is for a woman to master both roles: the role of high achiever and of traditional housewife. Thus, high-achievement women may spend enormous amounts of energy both at work and at home to demonstrate that achievement does not conflict with or undermine femininity. One area of research that has addressed how women reconcile a need for achievement with a need to adhere to the female gender role is the fear of achievement or fear of success literature.

Fear of Achievement

HISTORICAL LITERATURE. In the early 1970s, another explanation emerged as to why women who scored high in achievement motivation did not always reach high levels of achievement. The reason was that women feared achievement. The notion that women had a "fear of success" was developed by Matina Horner (1972). She noted that women faced a dilemma when achieving. Competence, independence, and intellectual achievement were inconsistent with the norms for femininity but consistent with the norms for masculinity. Thus, women might withdraw from achievement behavior because they are concerned with the threat that achievement poses for their gender role.

Horner (1972) defined the **fear of success** as the association of negative consequences with achievement. For women, the negative consequences were feeling unfeminine and experiencing social rejection. A woman who believes that graduating at the top of the class will bring respect from peers and parents does not have a fear of success. Conversely, a woman who believes that graduating at the top of the class will lead people to dislike, tease, or avoid her may have a fear of success. Horner included one more prerequisite for the fear of success: the individual must believe that achievement is possible. People who realize that they have no way of reaching a goal will not be concerned with the negative consequences of reaching the goal. Thus, someone may believe that getting an A on an exam will alienate friends but also know that there is no possible way to get an A on the exam; this person will not be worried about the negative consequences associated with success. By contrast, the person who is capable of getting an A and who believes this achievement will lead to rejection by peers is likely to have a fear of achievement. The person could respond to this fear by either decreasing the amount of effort put into the task (i.e., study less) or by hiding the achievement from peers.

To summarize, there are two requirements for a fear of success: first, the person must perceive achievement as possible, if not likely; second, the person must associate achievement with negative consequences. A fear of success is *not* the same as a desire to fail. The person who fears achievement does not seek out failure but is simply more likely to avoid situations that might lead to high achievement and to expend less effort so that high achievement is not realized.

What was Horner's (1972) evidence for a fear of achievement among women? She used a projective storytelling method. She gave college students the first sentence of a story and asked them to complete it. For example, female students were told "Anne is at the top of her class in medical school," whereas male students were told "John is at the top of his class in medical school." Students were then asked to complete the story. Horner reasoned that anyone who wrote a story that showed conflict about the success, denied credit for the success, or associated negative consequences with the success showed a fear of success. The majority of men (90%) wrote positive stories in response to this cue. A substantial portion of the women (65%) wrote troubled stories that showed some conflict or negative consequences associated with Anne's achievement. For example, some women wrote stories about Anne purposely not performing well the next semester or dropping out of medical school. Other women wrote stories about Anne being alienated by friends and family and being very unhappy.

Horner (1972) conducted this first study in 1964 and replicated the findings over the next six years with other samples of college students and with high school and junior high school students. Interestingly, she noted a trend over time for the fear of success to increase among *men*. Men began to write stories that associated male achievement with selfishness and egoism. Conceptually, the fear of success is the same in men and women: the association of negative consequences with achievement. However, the fear of achievement was associated with quite distinct negative consequences for men and women. For women, the major negative consequence was social rejection; for men, the major negative consequence was self-absorption. Both led to unhappiness. Interestingly, these two concerns map onto the two gender-related traits discussed in Chapter 2: unmitigated agency and unmitigated communion. The fear of success among women seems as though it would characterize someone who possessed the features of unmitigated communion: overly concerned with others and their opinions. The fear of success among men seems as though it would characterize someone who possessed the features of unmitigated agency: overly absorbed with the self to the exclusion of others.

Horner (1972) found other indicators of women's fears of success. She noted that women who scored high in fear of success performed worse on a task when working with men than when working with women. These women seemed to perceive achievement in the presence of males as especially aversive. Women who scored high in fear of success admitted that they would prefer to tell a male that they received a C rather than an A on an exam. Horner found that women who were high in fear of success were more likely than women who were low in fear of success to switch from nontraditional to traditional college majors. For example, high fear of success women who were planning to become physicians or lawyers changed their career paths to become teachers or housewives.

Horner's (1972) work has been criticized on many levels. Some have suggested that her projective test actually indicates a discomfort with gender-role-incongruent behavior rather than a fear of success (M. Zuckerman & Wheeler, 1975). It turns out that *both* men and women write more

negative stories in response to Anne rather than John graduating at the top of the class (M. Zuckerman & Wheeler, 1975). Men and women may write negative stories because they are uncomfortable with the idea of women being successful or because they realize that successful women face obstacles.

CONTEMPORARY LITERATURE. The studies on fear of success were conducted mostly in the 1960s and the 1970s. Is there any evidence of a residual fear of achievement in women or men today? Do today's college women feel uncomfortable outperforming men? Do women hide their good exam performances from friends, especially male friends? Do women continue to associate achievement with negative interpersonal consequences? In the 1980s, this issue was taken up again by Susan Pollak and Carol Gilligan (1982).

Pollak and Gilligan (1982) set out to document that a fear of achievement continues to characterize women and a fear of affiliation or intimacy continues to characterize men in our society. They used projective methods similar to those used by Horner (1972). College students were asked to write a story in response to TAT cards. Some of the cards had clear achievement themes, such as the picture of two women in a science laboratory; some had clear relationship or affiliation themes, such as a man and woman sitting next to each other on a bench by a river. For other pictures, the theme was less clear. To determine whether a particular situation aroused fear in students, outside raters coded the stories for indicators of violence. Violence included someone dying, an accident or injury, and personal harm. If women feared success and men feared affiliation, Pollak and Gilligan reasoned that women's achievement stories would contain more violence than their affiliation stories, and men's affiliation stories would contain more violence than their achievement stories. This is exactly what happened, leading Pollak and Gilligan to conclude that there is still a tendency for women to fear achievement and men to fear affiliation.

As you can imagine, quite a debate ensued after these results were published. In particular, Benton and colleagues (Benton et al., 1983; Weiner et al., 1983) were concerned that the findings upheld "common and repressive stereotypes." Thus, politics again entered into the picture. The early 1980s was not the time to be pronouncing sex differences. Benton and colleagues took issue with aspects of Pollak and Gilligan's (1982) methodology, conducted their own experiment, and failed to replicate Pollak and Gilligan's findings.

In other words, they found no sex differences in fears of achievement or affiliation. At the center of the debate was a single TAT card showing a male acrobat in the air about to catch a female acrobat. This is the card shown in Figure 5.1. Because the acrobats' hands were touching, Pollak and Gilligan (1982) classified the card as affiliation. Benton and colleagues (1983) argued that the card had clear themes of achievement. In fact, students later reported that they viewed the card as containing more elements of achievement than affiliation (Benton et al., 1983; Helgeson & Sharpsteen, 1987). The classification of this card was important because it elicited the most violent imagery and was really responsible for the sex difference that Pollak and Gilligan found.

During graduate school, a fellow student, Don Sharpsteen, and I became fascinated with this back-and-forth debate. We decided to conduct our own experiment with the controversial acrobat TAT card (Helgeson & Sharpsteen, 1987; see Figure 5.1). We led one group of students to view the card as achievement-related by emphasizing the achievement aspects of

the acrobats' work. We led another group to view the card as affiliation-related by emphasizing the acrobats' close relationship. Our findings supported Pollak and Gilligan's (1982) claim: women were more likely to write stories that contained violence when we emphasized the achievement elements of the picture than when we emphasized the affiliation aspects of the picture. The reverse occurred among men: men were more likely to write stories that contained violence when we emphasized the affiliation elements of the picture than when we emphasized the achievement aspects.

There is one very important qualification to these findings. The vast majority of students did *not* write stories that contained any violence in response to the acrobat card. Only 8% of women wrote stories containing violence, and only 18% of men wrote stories containing violence. Pollak and Gilligan (1982) also obtained very low rates of violence across a variety of TAT cards. Although there was a sex difference in the distribution of violent imagery across the achievement and affiliation situations, the vast majority of men and women did not write stories that contained violence in response to either cue. Thus, most women and men do not have a fear of either achievement or affiliation.

In sum, the series of studies seemed to demonstrate that (1) most people, men and women, do not fear achievement or affiliation; (2) men are about twice as likely as women to write stories containing violence; and (3) among the minority of people who fear either achievement or affiliation, there is a sex difference in the direction of women fearing achievement and men fearing affiliation.

Several questions about this area of research are probably running through your mind. To take any of it seriously, you have to endorse the assumption that writing stories in response to pictures reflects our unconscious motivations. Does writing a story about a tragic death in response to a picture reflect fear of the situation in the picture, or does it reflect general creativity and imagination? Even if you do not believe that it reflects fear directly, you still have to wonder why men and women would be more likely to write violent stories in response to one cue than another. One answer is that men and women are revealing their knowledge about gender-role stereotypes rather than their personal fears (Ishiyama & Chabassol, 1985). Men are simply revealing a discomfort with a situation that is incongruent with the male gender role: intimacy. Men may also be acknowledging that intimacy is a situation in which men have difficulties. Likewise, women are either revealing a discomfort or acknowledging a difficulty with a situation that is incongruent with the female gender role: achievement.

Other studies have developed more objective measures of the fear of achievement. Sample items from three of these scales are shown in Table 5.1. The core of all three scales is that they measure a concern with the emotional and social consequences of success. These consequences include a concern with negative reactions by peers, social isolation, alienation of others, feelings of pressure to live up to others' expectations, and discomfort with praise. Higher scores on these self-report instruments are associated with lower levels of achievement motivation (Ho & Zemaitis, 1981; Zuckerman & Allison, 1976) and poorer performance (Ho & Zemaitis, 1981; Zuckerman & Allison, 1976).

On the first two measures shown in Table 5.1, female college students score higher than male college students (Ishiyama & Chabassol, 1984; Zuckerman & Allison, 1976), and female marketing managers score higher than their male counterparts

TABLE 5.1   Sample Items from Fear of Success Scales

Fear of Success Scale (Zuckerman & Allison, 1976)

1. Often, the cost of success is greater than the reward.
2. In an attempt to do better than others, I realize I may lose many of my friends.
3. I am happy only when I am doing better than others.*
4. I believe that successful people are often sad and lonely.

Fear of Success Consequence Scale (Ishiyama & Chabassol, 1984)

1. If I became one of the best students at school, I'd worry about losing friendly acceptance by my peers.
2. I'd be concerned about making my friends feel threatened if I became a superior student to others.
3. If people would tell me how excellent I am in certain subjects, I might feel nervous.
4. I'd rather pass unnoticed by others who might be giving me many words of recognition for my accomplishment.

Concern over the Negative Consequences of Success Scale (Ho & Zemaitis, 1981)

1. I have a tendency to fear that others might like me only for what I could do for them due to my competency in a certain field.
2. I sometimes do less than my very best so that no one will feel threatened.
3. I don't worry that I may become so knowledgeable that others will not like me.*
4. If I get a high grade on a work assignment I tend to feel that I fooled the teacher.

* Item is reverse scored.

(Fried-Buchalter, 1997). On the last measure, there are no sex differences (Ho & Zemaitis, 1981). However, gender-role differences were found on this measure: people who scored higher on fear of achievement scored lower in masculinity (Ho & Zemaitis, 1981).

A measure similar to the ones depicted in Table 5.1 was developed for a group of college students in China (Wang & Creedon, 1989). Chinese women scored higher on the measure than men, but both Chinese men and women scored higher than U.S. samples. The greater fear of success in China compared to the United States may reflect a greater concern with relationships on the part of the Chinese.

Thus, the question remains: Is there still a trend toward a sex difference in fear of achievement and fear of affiliation? Try Exercise 5.1 using Horner's (1972) projective

method and some objective questions to test the findings in your own school.

Some studies of early adolescents suggest that girls still associate success with some negative consequences. In a couple of studies, A. Bell (1989, 1996) held weekly discussions with elementary school girls to identify barriers to their success. She found that girls felt that achievement and affiliation were opposites, that one could not do both. She referred to this as the "smart versus social" dilemma. The girls feared that achievement would jeopardize their relationships. This is exactly the theme that underlies the historical fear of success literature. Girls also identified a second dilemma, "silence versus bragging." The girls said that they often hide their success because talking about it is like bragging and might make other people feel bad. Thus, a concern for others and relationships keeps the girls from announcing their achievements. This is reminiscent of Horner's (1972) work where she reports that high fear of success girls often hide their good grades from others. The girls also stated that they felt uncomfortable being singled out by a success because their concerns were with establishing connections to others, not with differentiating themselves from others. The following exchange between the group leader and one of the girls illustrates these ideas (A. Bell, 1996, p. 422):

JANE (after receiving a compliment on a science prize): Well, I don't feel that great when you say that to me because I feel like everybody's equal and everybody should have gotten a prize no matter what they did. I think Chris should have gotten it.

MYRA: OK Jane, tell the group why you didn't say "I feel good about winning the prize."

JANE: Well I feel like um, like everybody's looking at me and um saying, "Oh, she

---

EXERCISE 5.1
Do Women Fear Achievement, and
Do Men Fear Affiliation?

Try out Horner's projective test. Ask a group of students to write a story in response to the following sentence: "＿＿ is at the top of her (his) class in medical school."

You choose the name. You might try a name that can be perceived as either male or female, such as Pat. Or, you might have half of each sex respond to a male target and half to a female target. After participants have completed the story, have them respond to a few of the items shown in Table 5.1 to get a more objective measure of the fear of success.

Before you code the stories for violent imagery, come up with your own specific definition. Ideally, you would find another coder and evaluate the stories independently. Make sure the stories are anonymous with respect to sex when you rate them.

Are there sex differences in fears of success on the projective measure? On the objective measure? How do the objective and projective measures compare?

shouldn't have won that prize, I should have won" and everybody's gonna be mad at me because um, I won and they didn't.

MYRA: Is there any situation that you could think of where you won an honor that you were deserving of and felt good about?

JANE: If other people won also.

Other studies show that high levels of achievement have negative consequences for girls' self-image. In one study, achievement in math and science predicted an increase in social self-image (i.e., feeling accepted by others) from sixth to seventh grade for both boys and girls, but predicted an increase in social self-image from seventh to eighth grade only among boys (L. Roberts & Petersen, 1992). Girl's social self-image improved most if they received Bs in math rather than Cs or even As. These results especially applied to girls who indicated that they valued being popular in school more than they valued getting good grades. Thus, the authors concluded that girls feel more accepted if they are *not* at the top of their math class, especially if the girls are socially oriented.

Similar findings were obtained in another study of sixth- through eighth-graders (L. Roberts, Sarigiani, Petersen, & Newman, 1990). Achievement, as measured by final course grades, was associated with a positive self-image for both male and female sixth-graders. However, between sixth and seventh grade, the relation between achievement and self-image became weaker for girls but stronger for boys. The authors proposed that girls begin to feel a conflict between achievement and peer acceptance at this time, so their self-esteem is no longer as closely tied to achievement.

SWITCHING MAJORS.   One facet of the historical literature on women's fear of success is that high-achievement women would switch from traditionally masculine pursuits to traditionally feminine pursuits. Switching college majors is an area of research that has been examined more recently. Interestingly, women are as likely as men to begin college as a math major and slightly more likely than men to begin college as a life science major, but women are more likely than men to switch out of these majors (Seymour, 1995). In the end, women are underrepresented in science, math, and engineering.

What are women's reasons for switching out of these traditionally masculine majors? Seymour (1995) interviewed college students from seven diverse universities who had high math SAT scores and switched out of science, math, and engineering. It was not the case that women switched out of these areas more than men due to inferior performance level. In fact, it was the men more than the women who complained about the fast pace of the courses, the heavy workload, the competitive atmosphere, and the disappointment over grades that did not reach expectations. The major reason for switching cited by both men and women was a loss of interest in the field. After that, however, reasons for men and women diverged. Men identified instrumental reasons for leaving math, science, and engineering, such as deciding that other majors would improve career prospects or realizing that they would receive a poor monetary return on their investment of time and energy. Women seemed to switch for personal reasons, such as finding another major more appealing or realizing that the lifestyle that accompanied a career in their major was not appealing. Women were more concerned than men about making sure that their career would accommodate family needs. You will see later in the chapter that other people have a strong influence on women's interests in traditionally masculine fields. After switching majors, women said that family and friends were more supportive of their switch compared to men. Others were especially more supportive of women when personal satisfaction was the motivation for switching to another major. Although women are nearly as likely as men to be part of the paid labor force after college, women do not face the same pressures to be the family breadwinner. Thus, as a society, we may afford women the luxury of choosing a career that interests them, and men may face more barriers than women in leaving traditionally masculine majors.

During the course of the interviews and in several focus groups, Seymour (1995) reports anecdotal evidence of women voicing concerns that Horner first raised in 1972. Women still seemed concerned that being successful, especially in math and science, is viewed as not feminine and might have interpersonal costs. Some of these women reported that they hid their good grades from their male peers. The women also reported difficulties in working with their male peers. The men who majored in math, science, and engineering validated women's concerns. These men reported that they considered intelligence and physical attractiveness to be mutually incompatible in women. The men viewed women in math, science, and engineering as pursuing majors that were "unnatural." Find out on your own why men and women switch from nontraditional to traditional majors with Exercise 5.2.

SUMMARY. The fear of success literature was, and still is, quite controversial. People debate the validity of the projective tests that were first used to identify a fear of success in women. Despite these concerns, even self-report instruments show that women are more likely than men to associate achievement with negative consequences. The basic concern is that achievement is inconsistent with the female gender role. Females are concerned that attaining high

> **EXERCISE 5.2**
> **Reasons for Switching from Nontraditional to Traditional Majors**
>
> Conduct interviews with both men and women who switched from nontraditional to traditional majors and from traditional to nontraditional majors. First, you will have to decide what the traditional majors for men and women are. For example, you might find five women who switched from science, math, or engineering to nursing, and five men who switched from the liberal arts to business. To gather more data on this issue, this could be used as a class project with the interview format standardized.
>
> Ask a series of open-ended questions to find out why people initially chose their major, why they switched, if they had any difficulties switching, and how others reacted to their switch. Then, you might follow up with some closed-ended questions to make sure the issues you are interested in are addressed. For example, you might have some specific statements about negative peer reactions or fears of negative consequences associated with success (see the items in Table 5.1).

levels of achievement will have social costs. Many of the older and more recent studies have been conducted with college students, a population in which one would not expect to find high levels of fear of achievement. Findings from more recent studies of adolescents and college students suggest that girls still have concerns that there are interpersonal costs to success.

Self-Confidence

Do women have less confidence in themselves compared to men? Interestingly, women will defend other women's abilities but not necessarily their own. Collis (1991) refers to this as the "We can but I can't" paradox. In general, women are more likely than men to underestimate their abilities and less likely to expect success (J. Eccles, 1994; Lenney, 1977). This is problematic because when one expects not to succeed in a certain domain, one will choose an easier task, give up more easily on a given task, and pursue activities in other domains.

In a review of the literature on men's and women's self-confidence in achievement settings, the conclusion was that women are not less self-confident than men in *all* settings (Lenney, 1977). Women's lower levels of self-confidence compared to men were dependent on (1) the nature of the task, (2) the ambiguity of the feedback, and (3) the social cues in the situation. I discuss how each of these three factors influences women's self-confidence.

FACTORS AFFECTING SEX DIFFERENCES IN SELF-CONFIDENCE. *The nature of the task* is an important determinant of sex differences in self-confidence (Lenney, 1977). Women are less self-confident than men about their performance on masculine tasks, such as those that involve spatial abilities. However, on feminine tasks, such as those that involve social skills or verbal abilities, women are either more self-confident than men or there are no sex differences in self-confidence. Sex differences in self-confidence can be influenced by whether a gender-neutral task is presented as one in which men outperform women or one in which women outperform men. Men will be more self-confident in the former case and women will be more self-confident in the latter case.

Another determinant of sex differences in self-confidence is whether clear feedback about performance has been provided. Women have lower expectancies for performance than men when they have

been given *ambiguous feedback* or no feedback about their performance (Lenney, 1977). However, in studies where clear feedback about performance has been provided, there are no sex differences in performance expectancies.

Sex differences in self-confidence also are influenced by the *social cues* present in the situation. Women are less self-confident compared to men when they perceive that their work will be compared to others or will be evaluated by others (Lenney, 1977). In studies where the experimenter conveys the performance of the "average" participant, women report lower self-confidence than men. In studies where women have to state their expectancies out loud, women also appear less self-confident than men. These kinds of social cues may inspire women to appear modest.

Women may appear modest because they are concerned about another person's self-esteem. One study showed that women underestimate their abilities to preserve other people's self-esteem (Heatherington et al., 1993). College students were asked to predict their GPA privately or publicly. Women estimated lower GPAs than men in the public condition but not in the private condition. Thus, women were not actually less self-confident than men, but they were more concerned than men with how they presented themselves to others. Women are not merely concerned with how others view them, however. Rather, they are concerned that their good performance might make someone else feel bad. The same set of investigators demonstrated this in a second study (Heathington et al., 1993). Students predicted their GPA either privately, publicly to a nonvulnerable other, or publicly to a vulnerable other. The vulnerable other was someone who had received a low GPA in college; the GPA of the nonvulnerable other was not mentioned. Men and women gave similar GPA estimates in the private condition and in the public nonvulnerable other condition. However, when faced with a person who had a low GPA, women estimated lower GPAs than men. Thus, women underestimate their performance in public because they don't want to injure another person's self-esteem, not because they are concerned with how others view them. The focus of concern is on others rather than on themselves.

A subsequent set of studies showed that women are more likely than men to believe their public expression of achievement affects other people's self-esteem. College students were led to believe that they outperformed a peer (91st percentile versus 42nd percentile) and were asked to either make a modest disclosure (told peer that they performed above the 50th percentile) or an immodest disclosure (told peer their specific score; Daubman & Sigall, 1997). Women believed that the peer felt better and liked them more when they made a modest compared to an immodest disclosure. The nature of the disclosure did not affect men's impressions of how the peer felt. In a follow-up study, the investigators examined whether women believed an achievement disclosure affected only other women (Daubman & Sigall, 1997). Female respondents thought that female peers would like them better and feel more confident when they made modest compared to immodest disclosures. However, the nature of the disclosure did not affect female respondents' perceptions of how male peers would react. Male respondents also did not expect that their disclosure would affect male peers' reactions. However, male respondents thought that female peers would like them more when they made immodest compared to modest disclosures. In sum, women seem to be concerned that revealing a high level of achievement would make other women feel bad about themselves but would not affect

men. By contrast, men believe that disclosing a high level of achievement would not affect other men but would have a positive effect on other women.

One reason women believe revealing an achievement affects others is that women's own evaluations of themselves are affected by others' disclosures of achievement. In one study, women's evaluations of their performance depended on the ability level of their partner, whereas men's did not (Lenney, Gold, & Browning, 1983). College students completed a practice task and were led to believe that they would be interacting with a person of high, average, or low ability for the actual task. Women's self-evaluations of their performance were lower than those of men *only* when the women expected to interact with a high-ability partner. Men's self-evaluations were not influenced by their partner. However, a subsequent study tested the same idea in a setting where the partner was physically present rather than hypothetical (Sleeper & Nigro, 1987). In this case, both men's and women's evaluations of their performance were influenced by the ability level of their partner. When a partner's performance is made salient, both men's and women's self-evaluation are equally influenced by the attributes of the partner.

WOMEN'S UNDERCONFIDENCE OR MEN'S OVERCONFIDENCE? The literature on self-confidence typically has been interpreted in terms of a female disadvantage: that women's self-confidence is *lower* than that of men. Do women underestimate their abilities, or do men overestimate their abilities? One way to address this question is to compare men's and women's confidence to their actual performance. If someone expects to receive a 90 on a test and receives an 80, the person is overconfident. If someone expects to receive an 80 and receives a 90, the person is underconfident. College students' confidence and performance on an exam were evaluated (Lundeberg, Fox, & Puncochar, 1994). The investigators found that both men and women were overconfident about their exam performance. However, when correct and incorrect responses were distinguished, women's confidence levels were more closely tied to their exam performance. In other words, women were more confident on items that they answered correctly than on items they answered incorrectly. Men were equally overconfident on correct and incorrect items.

Another set of studies examined whether the nature of the task influences men's and women's confidence levels (Beyer, 1990). Students were asked how many questions on a quiz they expected to answer correctly, and confidence levels were compared to accuracy levels. The quizzes contained masculine questions, feminine questions, or gender-neutral questions. On the masculine task, males were overconfident in one study and accurate in the second study. Females underestimated their performance on the masculine task in both studies. On the feminine and the gender-neutral tasks, males and females were typically equally accurate. Thus, once again, sex differences in confidence levels are most apparent for the masculine task. In that case, part of the sex difference is due to male overconfidence and part is due to female underconfidence. The parallel does not appear for the feminine task; for that task, men and women are accurate rather than overconfident or underconfident.

SUMMARY. Women are less self-confident than men in situations where the feedback is ambiguous or in situations of uncertainty. This suggests that men are more likely than women to confront a novel task with a higher expectation to succeed. The answer is unclear as to whether men's self-confidence then leads to a higher rate of success. Women also are less self-confident than men when there are social cues that inspire women to be concerned with the effect of their achievements on others' self-esteem. Women expect that their achievements will affect others' feelings because their own beliefs about their abilities are affected by others' achievements.

The major factor that influences sex differences in self-confidence is the nature of the task. Sex differences in self-confidence seem to be limited to masculine tasks; it is here that women tend to underestimate their performance and lack self-confidence. Lack of self-confidence could be a contributing factor to the underrepresentation of women in masculine areas of achievement, specifically math and science. Later in the chapter, we explore ways in which the environment may influence women's lack of self-confidence in these areas.

Response to Evaluative Feedback

I began college with a major in journalism, despite the fact that my math SAT score was 200 points higher than my verbal SAT score. I took some psychology classes along the way. Two things happened to make me switch from journalism to psychology: first, I discovered that all of my journalism assignments—news stories, feature stories, editorials, and investigations—were on psychological topics; second, not one of my journalism professors took me aside and told me that I was a gifted writer. Receiving As on papers was not enough to make me think I could be a successful journalist; I was waiting for the tap on the shoulder. Ironically, after I switched my major to psychology in my junior year, a journalism professor did take me aside and told me what I had wanted to hear. By then it was too late, and I had already developed a passion for psychology.

Recently, a similar experience occurred, but this time I was the one tapping someone else's shoulder. I had taken aside an undergraduate who was torn between art and psychology, and within psychology, torn between clinical work and research. I told her that I thought she had all of the skills needed to make a fine researcher: clear conceptual thinking, a strong methodological knowledge base, and creativity in experimental design. I didn't think twice about this conversation until she told me the following semester that it had influenced her to switch her focus to research. The interesting part of this story—and here is where it becomes relevant to the chapter—is that she shared the experience with her boyfriend and he was befuddled. He couldn't understand why what I had said had made any difference.

Women may be more influenced than men by the feedback they receive about their performance. This could stem from a lack of self-confidence on the part of women, or it could stem from an openness to others' opinions; the sex difference can easily be cast in a positive or negative light. In either case, when women are told that they have performed poorly or that they lack ability, they may be more likely than men to take the feedback to heart. Studies of adults and children show that females react more negatively to failure feedback than do males (T. Roberts, 1991; Ruble, Greulich, Pomerantz, & Gochberg, 1993). When told a performance is outstanding, women may be more likely than men to take this feedback seriously as well. Women's thoughts about themselves, including beliefs about their abilities, are more influenced by other people's appraisals of their abilities compared to men. The direction of the influence could be positive or negative, depending on whether the feedback is positive or negative.

Evidence for these ideas comes from a series of studies conducted by Tomi-Ann Roberts and Susan Nolen-Hoeksema. In one study, they asked college students to imagine being a manager of an organization and giving a presentation (T. Roberts & Nolen-Hoeksema, 1989, Study 1). The students then were asked to imagine receiving positive or negative feedback after the presentation. The investigators asked students to report how much they thought the feedback would influence their own evaluations of their performance. As shown in Table 5.2, women reported greater influence compared to men, especially after negative feedback. Specifically, men reported being more influenced by positive than negative feedback, whereas women reported being equally influenced by positive and negative feedback. Students also were asked how informative they expected such feedback to be. Women found negative feedback to be more informative than men did, but both men and women viewed positive feedback as more informative than negative feedback.

In a follow-up study, the investigators conducted an experimental test of their hypothesis to see if feedback actually influenced women's more than men's perceptions of their abilities (T. Roberts & Nolen-Hoeksema, 1989, Study 2). Students were asked to solve a series of cognitive tasks and then were provided with positive feedback ("You are doing very well"; "Your

TABLE 5.2   Degree of Influence Feedback Would Have on Own Evaluation of Performance

	Positive Feedback	Negative Feedback
Men	7.60	6.35
Women	7.87	7.58

Source: Adapted from Roberts & Nolen-Hoeksema (1989, Study 1).

performance is above average") or negative feedback ("You are not doing very well"; "Your performance is below average"). Students were asked how confident they were that they could perform the task and how satisfied they were with their performance before and after receiving the feedback. As shown in Figure 5.2, females' confidence clearly changed in the direction of the feedback, whereas males' confidence was largely unaffected by the feedback. Similarly, males' satisfaction with their performance was unaffected by the feedback, whereas females were much less satisfied with their performance after the negative compared to the positive feedback (see Figure 5.3). The investigators also compared the number of correctly solved tasks to the number of tasks respondents estimated that they solved correctly. It appeared that males overestimated their performance, especially in the negative feedback condition, and females underestimated their performance.

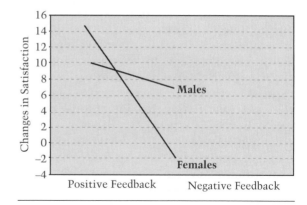

FIGURE 5.3 Effect of feedback on satisfaction. Female college students were more satisfied with their performance after receiving positive feedback and less satisfied after receiving negative feedback. Male college students' satisfaction with their performance was relatively unaffected by the feedback. *Source:* Adapted from Roberts and Nolen-Hoeksema (1989, Study 2).

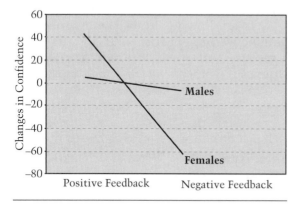

FIGURE 5.2 Effect of feedback on self-confidence. Female college students become more confident about their ability to perform a task after receiving positive feedback and less confident after receiving negative feedback. Male college students' self-confidence did not change and was unaffected by the nature of the feedback that they received. *Source:* Adapted from Roberts and Nolen-Hoeksema (1989, Study 2).

Females' greater responsiveness to evaluative feedback was replicated in a subsequent experiment by the same investigators. They asked college students to give a speech to a group of three other students who were confederates of the experimenter (T. Roberts & Nolen-Hoekema, 1994). One of the confederates provided positive feedback, negative feedback, or gave no feedback. Prior to the feedback, women reported higher performance expectancies compared to men, possibly because giving a speech is considered to be a more feminine task. The results of the study showed that women's evaluations of their speech were more affected by the feedback than those of men. As shown in Figure 5.4, women's evaluations of their speech became more positive in the positive feedback condition and more negative in the negative feedback condition, whereas men's evaluations were much less affected by the feedback. Women

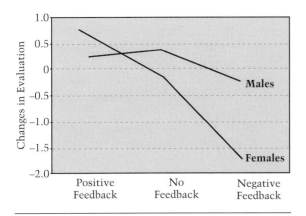

Changes in Evaluation

1.0
0.5
0
-0.5
-1.0
-1.5
-2.0

Positive Feedback | No Feedback | Negative Feedback

Males

Females

FIGURE 5.4 Effect of feedback on evaluation. Women evaluated their speech as more positive after receiving positive feedback and more negative after receiving negative feedback. Men's evaluations of their speech were relatively unaffected by the nature of the feedback they received. *Source:* Adapted from Roberts and Nolen-Hoeksema (1994, Study 2).

were not more responsive to the feedback because they were less confident than men. Recall that women actually had higher initial expectancies than men. Women also were not more responsive to the feedback because they wanted to appear agreeable to the confederates; the evaluations were confidential. Females indicated that the feedback was more accurate than males did. Thus, the authors concluded that women are more responsive to feedback than men because they find the feedback to be more informative about their abilities.

One concern about these studies is that they are all conducted with college students and the feedback is given by peers rather than authority figures. One would expect people to be more responsive to feedback from those judged to be more knowledgeable. An undergraduate and I tested whether there were sex differences in responsiveness to feedback in a real-

world setting (Johnson & Helgeson, 2000). We measured the self-esteem of bank employees before and after they met with their supervisor for their annual performance evaluation. Women's self-esteem slightly improved on receiving a positive evaluation and substantially declined on receiving a negative evaluation, whereas men's self-esteem was largely unaffected by the nature of the feedback. Women also took the evaluation process more seriously, regarded the feedback as more accurate, and viewed their supervisors as credible sources. Men who received negative feedback appeared to psychologically prepare themselves for the upcoming evaluation by derogating the source of the feedback ("My supervisor isn't that smart") and the feedback system ("The evaluation process is not fair"). In general, the results of this study supported the laboratory findings.

Self-Esteem

Do women's lower self-confidence and greater responsiveness to evaluative feedback reflect a lower level of self-esteem? The answer to that question partly depends on the age of the respondents.

A meta-analysis of sex differences in self-esteem found a small difference in favor of males ($d = +.21$; Kling, Hyde, Showers, & Buswell, 1999). Effect sizes varied greatly by age, with the largest sex difference emerging during adolescence ($d = +.33$ for 15- to 18-year-olds). Effect sizes were smaller for younger and older respondents. The few studies that examined self-esteem among respondents over 60 found no sex difference. The effect size was significant in studies of exclusively White samples ($d = +.20$) but not significant among studies of exclusively Black samples ($d = -.04$). Caucasian adolescent girls seem to have the lowest self-esteem (e.g., Simmons & Rosenberg, 1975).

What are some of the reasons that females, especially adolescent White females, have lower self-esteem than males? One reason is that these girls have less favorable attitudes than boys toward their gender role (Simmons & Rosenberg, 1975). We saw in Chapter 2 that girls were more likely than boys to want to become the other sex and that boys viewed changing their sex as a negative event, whereas girls viewed changing their sex as more of an opportunity. A second reason for girls' lower self-esteem compared to boys is girls' greater emphasis on popularity. Girls, in particular Caucasian girls, place a greater value on popularity than do boys. Being concerned with how others view oneself leads to a fragile self-esteem, because one's self-worth is dependent on others.

Support for both of these explanations was obtained in a study of two cohorts of adolescents, one in 1968 and one in 1975 (D. Bush, Simmons, Hutchinson, & Blyth, 1977–1978). In both cohorts, females had lower self-esteem than males. Females in both cohorts also had less favorable views of their gender role than males. Females placed greater emphasis on popularity and less emphasis on competence compared to males, but these sex differences appeared to diminish in the 1975 cohort.

One aspect of self-esteem that is particularly relevant to adolescents is body image. Males' and females' satisfaction with their body may begin to change with the onset of puberty. In a study of adolescents from two different communities, boys had a more favorable body image compared to girls and were more satisfied with their weight compared to girls (Richards, Boxer, Petersen, & Albrecht, 1990). In a cross-sectional study of fifth-, eighth-, and twelfth-graders, boys and girls were asked how their physical appearance affects their feelings about themselves (Polce-Lynch, Myers, Kilmartin, Forssmann-Falck, & Kliewer, 1998). Girls were more likely than boys to identify positive and negative effects. Boys in all grades were most likely to say that their physical appearance had no effect on their self-esteem. Eighth-grade girls, who are at the onset of puberty, reported the most negative effects. Thus, another reason that sex differences in self-esteem emerge during adolescence is that physical appearance is changing and girls become dissatisfied with their appearance. Interestingly, African American girls attach less importance to physical appearance and are more satisfied with their appearance than Caucasian girls (Molloy & Herzberger, 1998; Simmons & Rosenberg, 1975). This supports the lack of sex differences in self-esteem among African Americans.

There are multiple aspects of self-esteem in addition to body image. It may be less informative to compare men's and women's overall self-regard because men and women have high self-esteem in different domains. In one study of children, adolescents, and young adults, there was an overall sex difference in self-esteem favoring males (Marsh, 1989). But an examination of different domains of self-esteem revealed that males had higher self-regard in some areas and females in others. Females had higher self-esteem in the domains of verbal skills, reading, school, and morality (honesty, spirituality), whereas males had higher self-esteem in the domains of math, problem solving, physical abilities, and appearance. A study of Chinese 10- and 13-year-olds revealed no sex differences in individual domains of self-esteem among the 10-year-olds but a number of differences among the 13-year-olds (Watkins, Dong, & Xia, 1997). The older girls had lower self-esteem in four areas: physical abilities, reading, math, and general self-concept. The authors attributed the development of sex differences in self-esteem to the onset of puberty.

The relation of gender role to self-esteem is much more clear and consistent than the relation of sex to self-esteem. Masculinity, as measured with the PAQ or BSRI, is strongly positively related to self-esteem. Femininity, by contrast, is not related to one's overall self-regard but may be related to components of self-esteem (see Helgeson, 1994c, for a review). Femininity, or communion, is often related to the social aspects of self-esteem, such as feeling comfortable and competent in social situations. Femininity is correlated with self-esteem in domains reflecting honesty, religion, and parental relationships, whereas masculinity is correlated with self-esteem in domains reflecting physical abilities and problem solving, as well as general self-esteem (Marsh & Byrne, 1991).

In summary, there is little evidence for an overall sex difference in self-esteem (Hattie, 1992). On some measures of general self-concept, males score higher than females, but the size of the difference is very small. There are sex differences on some dimensions of self-esteem. To the extent that sex differences do emerge, they are more likely to be found among adolescents than other age groups. One dimension of self-esteem that is particularly relevant to adolescent females is body image. Adolescent girls are more unhappy with their body than adolescent boys, which may partly account for adolescent girls' lower levels of self-esteem. Finally, gender-related traits, such as agency and communion, seem to show more consistent relations to self-esteem than sex per se.

Conceptions of the Self

Cross and Madson (1997) argue that many of the sex differences we observe in behavior are due to the different ways men and women define themselves: men maintain an independent sense of self that is separate from others; women, by contrast, maintain an interdependent sense of self, in which others are integrated into the self. They note that men are more likely to describe themselves in terms of their independence from others (e.g., emphasizing personal attributes and skills) and that women are more likely to describe themselves in terms of their connection to others (e.g., emphasizing roles, relationships to others). See if this is true at your school with Exercise 5.3.

Cross and Madson (1997) cite evidence of women's relationship focus by noting that women think more about other people, pay more attention to others, and have greater recall for information about others. Other evidence for sex differences in self-construal comes from Frey and Ruble (1987). They found that girls were less likely than boys to congratulate themselves after a good performance at school but

---

EXERCISE 5.3
Self-Conceptions

Have a group of students respond to the question "Who am I?" Then, review each of the attributes and categorize them as emphasizing separation from others or connection to others or neither. Make sure you are blind to the respondent's sex when you categorize the attributes.

Is it true that females define themselves more in terms of connection to others, and males define themselves more in terms of their separation from others?

Administer a measure of gender-related traits and see if agency, communion, unmitigated agency, or unmitigated communion are related to these categories. What would you predict?

more likely to congratulate peers following their good performance.

How are these different self-definitions related to self-esteem? There is evidence that agentic self-definitions are related to men's self-esteem and communal self-definitions are related to women's self-esteem. In a study of 17- to 19-year-olds, agency, defined as perceived opportunities for the future, predicted increased self-esteem over a four-year period among men but not women (J. Stein, Bentler, & Newcomb, 1992). Communion, defined as the quality of relationships, predicted increased self-esteem over the same time period among women but not men. In studies of adolescents, being popular is more important to girls' than boy's self-esteem, and being smart is more important to boys' than girls' self-esteem (Rosenberg, 1989).

One study showed that independence is related to self-esteem in men and interdependence is related to self-esteem in women (Josephs, Markus, & Tafarodi, 1992). College students identified their best skill or ability in four domains (social, athletic,

academic, creative) and then estimated the percentage of college students who were as good as they in those domains. The investigators hypothesized that men's self-esteem would be linked to perceiving themselves as unique—to believing that few others were as good as they in a domain—but that women's self-esteem would not. Men were thought to derive their self-esteem from distinguishing or separating themselves from others. In each of the four domains, high-self-esteem males perceived themselves to be more unique than low-self-esteem males, high-self-esteem females, and low-self-esteem females. These results are shown in Figure 5.5a for academic ability and Figure 5.5b for social ability. You can see that the high-self-esteem males estimate that the fewest other students have their level of ability. Women apparently do not need to perceive themselves as different from others to feel good about themselves.

By contrast, interdependence was most strongly linked to women's self-esteem. These same investigators showed

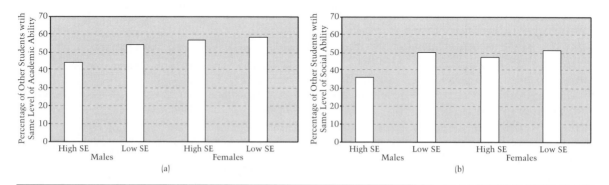

FIGURE 5.5 Effect of self-esteem and sex on perception of other's academic and social ability. This study showed that men's self-esteem is linked to feeling distinct from others. High-self-esteem males perceived themselves to be more unique (i.e., they reported that there were fewer other students with their same level of ability) than low-self-esteem males, high-self-esteem females, and low-self-esteem females. Figure 5.5a demonstrates this finding for academic ability and Figure 5.5b demonstrates this finding for social ability. *Source:* Adapted from Josephs et al. (1992).

college students a word and asked them to construct a sentence in which the word interacts with either you, the group with whom you most highly affiliate, your best friend, or Ronald Reagan (Josephs et al., 1992). The authors hypothesized that women with high self-esteem would be more likely than women with low self-esteem or men in general to later recall words from sentences that referred to the best friend or the group. This is because women's self-concepts are linked to important others. This is exactly what happened. High-self-esteem women recalled more words that were linked to the best friend (see Figure 5.6a) and to the important group (see Figure 5.6b) than did low-self-esteem women, high-self-esteem men, or low-self-esteem men. The authors reasoned that women have more elaborate knowledge structures about others than do men because they derive their self-worth through their connections to others.

Men's and women's different sources of self-esteem were also examined by asking college students how important each of the following was in terms of making them feel good about themselves: reflected appraisals (e.g., having others think highly of you), social comparisons (e.g., doing a better job than someone else), and self-perceived competence (e.g., getting a lot of work done; Schwalbe & Staples, 1991). Men found social comparison information more important than did women, which is consistent with the finding from the Josephs et al. (1992) study of men's need for uniqueness. Women found reflected appraisal information more important than did men, indicating women's greater concern with how they appear to others. Men and women found self-perceived competence to be equally important to their self-esteem.

A study of "autophotographical essays" supported the idea that women view themselves in interdependent terms and men view themselves in independent terms. College students were asked to take 12 photographs that described who they were (S. Clancy & Dollinger, 1993). Women were more likely than men to take pictures that showed other people and that showed

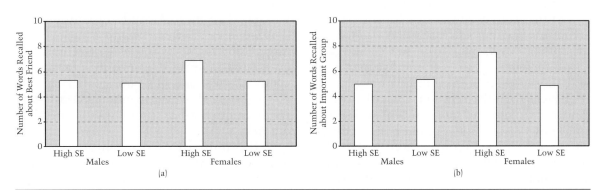

FIGURE 5.6 Effect of self-esteem and sex on words recalled about best friend and important group. This study showed that women's self-esteem is linked to their connections to others. High-self-esteem women recalled more words related to other people than low-self-esteem women, high-self-esteem men, and low-self-esteem men. Figure 5.6a demonstrates this finding for words recalled about a best friend and Figure 5.6b demonstrates this finding for words recalled about an important group of people. *Source:* Adapted from Josephs et al. (1992).

themselves with other people. Men were more likely to take pictures that showed themselves alone, showed themselves engaged in some physical activity, and showed themselves with an object, such as a motor vehicle.

Thus, the evidence for men basing their self-esteem on independence and women basing theirs on interdependence seems clear. However, there are people who have taken issue with this conclusion. The primary criticism is over the definition of interdependence. Baumeister and Sommer (1997) argue that there are two kinds of interdependence: **relational interdependence** and **collective interdependence.** The relational aspects of the self are those that emphasize close relationships with other people. The collective aspects of the self are those that are derived from group memberships and affiliations. What appears to be men's desire for independence and separation may really be their desire to form broader social connections with others, such as that achieved by power and status. Baumeister and Sommer argue that men and women are equally social but they are sociable in different spheres: women invest in a small number of relationships and men orient themselves toward the broader social structure and embed themselves in larger groups. Men's emphasis on power and status, for example, can be viewed as men separating themselves from others or wanting to have a certain relation toward others. Another example of men's interdependence that Baumeister and Sommer cite comes from the helping literature. Recall that the meta-analysis on helping showed that men were more helpful than women (Eagly & Crowley, 1986). One criticism of that meta-analysis is that the studies often assessed helping strangers. The conclusion to be drawn is that men help people they don't know, which is akin to helping society at large, whereas women help people they do

know and with whom they have a relationship, such as family and friends.

The distinction between relational and collective interdependence was examined in a series of studies (Gabriel & Gardner, 1999). In one study, students were asked to respond to the question "Who am I?" Responses showed that men identified more collective aspects of the self (e.g., fraternity member) than did women, and women identified more relational aspects of the self (e.g., daughter). In another study, students were asked to recall a happy or sad event. For both events, women's recollections were more likely than men's to be relational (e.g., death of family member) and men's recollections were more likely to be collective (e.g., losing an important sporting event).

To this point, I have been emphasizing differences. It is important to point out that there are also similarities in the sources of self-esteem for men and women. For example, feeling accepted by others is associated with feeling good about the self and feeling rejected by others is associated with feeling bad about the self for both men and women (Leary, Tambor, Terdal, & Downs, 1995). However, the associations are stronger for women than men. A study of Chinese undergraduates showed that men and women largely derived their self-esteem from similar sources: family relationships, family responsibilities, and personal goals (Watkins & Yu, 1993). However, women did rate family relationships as more important than did men.

It is quite likely that cultural and ethnic factors influence the sources of self-esteem for men and women. Although Western cultures emphasize individualism, achievement, and success, there are people whose opportunities to achieve are limited—by poverty or by discrimination. African Americans, in particular, may derive self-esteem from other domains.

Because the family is central to the identity of African Americans, partly as a buffer against racism, African Americans may derive more of their self-esteem from relationships. In one study, school achievement was linked to self-esteem among White adolescents but not among Black adolescents (M. Hughes & Demo, 1989). In a study of college students, Blacks scored higher on a measure of collectivism than did Whites (Oyserman, Gant, & Ager, 1995.)

Attributions for Performance

What might you say after failing an exam? "The test was unfair." What might you say after acing an exam? "It's a good thing I studied." What might you say after losing a tennis match? "I feel like I'm coming down with something." What might you say after winning a tennis match? "I just got lucky." All of these responses are referred to as attributions for performance. An **attribution** is the cause that we assign to a behavior.

DIMENSIONS OF CAUSALITY. Attributions can be classified along the two dimensions shown in Figure 5.7 (Weiner et al., 1971). The first dimension represents the locus of the cause, internal or external. An **internal attribution** is located within the person, and an **external attribution** is located in the environment. If I trip as I walk into the classroom, an internal attribution would be that I am clumsy; an external attribution would be that there was a catch in the carpet. The second dimension is stability. A cause can be **stable,** meaning that it does not change over time, or **unstable,** meaning that it may change with the time, day, or place. Being clumsy would be a stable attribution because we think of personality traits as relatively enduring. If I had been drinking tequila before class, the

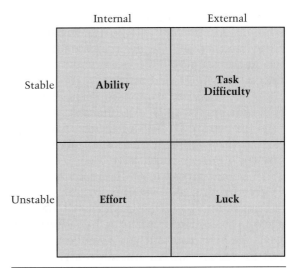

FIGURE 5.7 Two dimensions on which attributions (causes) can be classified: Locus (internal vs. external) and stability (stable vs. unstable).

attribution would be unstable because the state is changeable.

Now let's apply these two dimensions to the study of achievement. Return to Figure 5.7. Imagine that you take a test. An internal, stable attribution for performance would be your ability or lack thereof. An internal, unstable attribution for your performance would be how much effort you put into the task, presumably by studying. An external, stable attribution for your performance would be the difficulty of the test, an unchangeable, inherent characteristic of the task. An external, unstable attribution for your performance would be luck or some transient environmental factor, such as the weather.

The locus of causality dimension has implications for self-esteem. An internal attribution for failure (I am stupid) will decrease self-esteem, whereas an internal attribution for success (I am a brain) will increase self-esteem. An external attribution for failure will preserve self-esteem (It wasn't my fault that my computer crashed), whereas an external attribution for success does not confer any self-esteem (The teacher must not have been paying attention when she graded my essay).

The stability dimension has implications for persistence. An unstable attribution for failure (I did not study) may lead one to try harder or to try to change the environment. A stable attribution for failure (I do not have the ability) may lead one to give up. A stable attribution for success (The teacher is an easy grader) will encourage one to continue with the behavior or to keep the environment the same (e.g., don't switch teachers). An unstable attribution for success (The teacher didn't have her glasses on) merely tells you that the performance may not be repeated, so you will need to continue to exert the same level of effort or keep the environmental conditions the same (e.g., hide the teacher's glasses).

SEX COMPARISONS. Given that attributions for success and failure have implications for self-esteem and persistence in performance, it is important to know if men and women differ in their attributions for success and failure. Early studies demonstrated sex differences in attributions for performance. For example, Deaux and Emswiller (1974) showed that people made different attributions for men's and women's performance even when the level of performance was the same. College students were asked to make attributions for the success of a hypothetical male or female on a masculine or feminine task. When the task was masculine, men's success was attributed to ability and women's to luck. Thus, men's success was attributed to an internal factor, which increases self-esteem, whereas women's success was attributed to an external factor, which detracts from self-esteem. When the task was feminine,

however, there were no sex differences in attributions for performance.

Similar results have been obtained for men's and women's beliefs about their own performance. In one study, respondents performed an anagram task that was labeled as either masculine or feminine by telling participants that one sex outperforms the other on the task (Deaux & Farris, 1977). When the task was presented as masculine, men made stronger attributions to ability compared to women. There were no sex differences in attributions when the task was labeled feminine. Regardless of the task, however, females were more likely than males to make attributions to luck.

In 1984, Kay Deaux examined the literature on sex differences in attributions for performance and created a model that explained these differences in terms of people's expectancies about men's and women's performance. This model is shown in Figure 5.8. The first part of the model states that we attribute behavior to stable and internal causes if it matches our expectancy (i.e., a person fails whom we expect to fail or a person succeeds whom we expect to succeed; Weiner et al., 1971). Thus, if we expect men to perform well on masculine tasks, we should attribute their success to ability; similarly, if we expect women to perform well on feminine tasks, we should attribute their success to ability. In addition, if we expect women to fail at masculine tasks, we should attribute their failure to lack of ability. The second part of the model states that if a behavior violates our expectations, we attribute it to unstable causes. Thus, if we expect women to fail at a masculine task, we should attribute their success to effort and good luck. If we expect men to succeed at a masculine task, we should attribute their failure to lack of effort and bad luck. This model strongly suggests that the nature of the task should influence attributions for performance, as it did in the couple

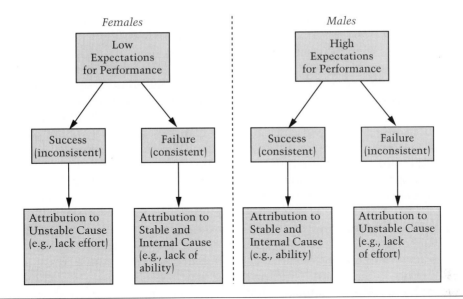

FIGURE 5.8 Expectancy model of attributions: Actors. This model shows that when performance fits our expectations (success following high expectations for performance, failure following low expectations for performance), we attribute the cause to stable factors. When performance does not fit our expectations (success following low expectations for performance, failure following high expectations for performance), we attribute the cause to unstable factors. *Source:* K. Deaux (1984). From individual differences to social categories: Analysis of a decade's research on gender. *American Psychologist, 39,* 105–116.

of studies previously described. In those studies, when the task was masculine, men attributed success to the stable cause of ability and women attributed success to the unstable causes of effort and luck.

Sex differences in attributions for performance have been replicated in other cultures. Wang and Creedon (1989) showed that Chinese women were more likely than Chinese men to attribute success to luck and to attribute failure to lack of ability. Chinese men were more likely than Chinese women to attribute failure to lack of effort.

Many of these studies were conducted 10 or 20 years ago, and not all of the more recent studies have supported this pattern of sex differences in attributions for performance. Swim and Sanna (1996) conducted a meta-analysis of people's attributions for

men's and women's performance. The majority of studies (36 of the 58; 62%) were conducted with college students. Across the studies, there were no sex of perceiver differences in attributions, meaning that men and women tended to make the same attributions for other men's and women's performance. However, perceivers made different attributions for men's and women's performance on *some* tasks, in particular, masculine tasks (e.g., those involving math abilities). However, most studies examine only masculine tasks. On masculine tasks, perceivers attributed women's success to effort and men's success to ability. Thus, perceivers are attributing men's success to a stable cause and women's success to an unstable cause, implying that men's success is more likely than women's to be repeated.

On masculine tasks, perceivers attributed men's failure to unstable causes, that is, lack of effort and bad luck, whereas perceivers attributed women's failure to the difficulty of the task. Again, perceivers are attributing men's failure to unstable causes that will not necessarily be repeated but women's failure to a stable cause that implies the failure will be repeated. The meta-analysis showed fewer differences in the attributions made for men's and women's performance on feminine tasks (e.g., those involving verbal abilities).

Across the individual studies described and the meta-analysis, it appears that there are fewer sex differences in attributions for performance on feminine than masculine tasks. It also appears that people perceive men's and women's performance to be the same when the task is feminine but men to outperform women when the task is masculine. Why do different perceptions exist on masculine tasks but not feminine tasks? One answer is that feminine tasks are perceived to be easier for everyone than masculine tasks, even when the experimenter is employing the same task and manipulating people's perceptions of it (Deaux, 1984).

Although the sex of the perceiver did not influence the attributions made for men's and women's performance in the meta-analysis, some studies have shown that personality characteristics of the perceiver influence attributions. For example, Garland and Price (1977) found that college students with more positive attitudes toward women attributed the success (i.e., promotion) of hypothetical female managers to ability and effort. By contrast, students with negative views of women attributed the success of hypothetical female managers to luck or the ease of the task. Thus, people who had a high regard for women gave the female managers credit for their success, whereas people who had a

low regard for women gave the credit to other sources.

IMPLICATIONS FOR ACHIEVEMENT. What are the implications of sex differences in attributions for performance? If you fail an exam because you believe you do not have the ability, what do you do? You might give up on the subject, drop the class, and decide not to pursue other classes in that area. If you fail an exam and believe it was due to lack of effort (i.e., you did not try hard enough), what do you do? The answer is obvious: you try harder next time. Thus, the difference in attributions for failure can influence whether one persists in an area or gives up completely.

One study examined the implications of third-graders' and junior high school students' attributions for performance on an important math exam (Stipek & Gralinski, 1991). Students' expectancies about the exam were assessed before the exam, and students' attributions for performance were measured after. Despite the fact that boys and girls performed equally well on the exam, boys expected higher grades than did girls. In addition, boys and girls made different attributions for their performance. When performance on the exam was good, boys were more likely than girls to attribute their success to ability. When performance on the exam was poor, girls were more likely than boys to attribute their failure to lack of ability. The implications? Despite their similar performances, boys had higher expectations for their performance on the next exam compared to girls, and girls were more likely than boys to say that they wish they could avoid math. The differing expectations and intentions undoubtedly reflect the students' beliefs about the cause of their performance.

Another study of elementary school children showed how attributions for failure in one situation affected students' expectancies to succeed in another situation (Dweck, Goetz, & Strauss, 1980). Fifthgraders were given failure feedback on four trials of the same task. The investigators' interest was in whether students expected to succeed on the fifth trial. The nature of this trial was manipulated: it was either a different task, a new person evaluating the same task, a new person evaluating a different task, or the same person evaluating the same task. The investigators hypothesized that boys would be more likely to expect success on the fifth trial if the evaluator was changed because boys are likely to attribute task failure to an external cause, such as the evaluator. The investigators hypothesized that girls would be more likely to expect success on the fifth trial if the task was changed because girls are likely to attribute task failure to an internal cause, such as lack of ability for the task. The results showed that all students' expectancies for success declined over the first four trials with the failure feedback. However, the decline was greater among girls than boys. Consistent with the investigators' hypothesis, boys' expectancies recovered (i.e., they began to expect success again) when the evaluator changed, but girls' expectancies did not. Girls' expectancies recovered on the fifth trial when the task changed, but so did boys' expectancies. In other words, boys' expectancies bounced back when either the task or the evaluator was changed, whereas girls' expectancies bounced back only when the task was changed.

Attributions for performance may influence the difficulty of the tasks that males and females undertake. One study showed that males chose more difficult goals than females, and that males were more likely to believe that ability as opposed to luck contributed to the achievement of this goal (P. Levy & Baumgardner, 1991). The investigators suggested that girls may choose less difficult goals than boys because they are less confident of their success and believe that luck rather than ability determines their performance.

SUMMARY. At least for masculine tasks, which are basically achievement-related, males and females make different attributions for their own performance. They also perceive the causes of other males' and females' performance to differ. These attributions about performance seem to be a function of our expectancies for men's and women's successes and failures. In general, men's success is attributed to internal causes, in particular, ability, and women's success is attributed to internal, unstable causes (e.g., effort) or external causes (e.g., luck). The implications are that men's success will be repeated but women's will not. By contrast, men's failure is attributed to external causes or internal, unstable causes (e.g., lack of effort) and women's failure is attributed to internal, stable causes (e.g., lack of ability). The implications here are that men's failure will not necessarily be repeated but women's will. People's beliefs about the causes of their performance have implications for their future efforts in that area. If one attributes the cause of a failure to lack of ability, such as the case of females in math or males in English, one is less likely to pursue work in that area. If one attributes the cause of a success to an unstable factor, such as females believing they have to put considerable effort into math to do well, one also is less likely to pursue work in that area. We are more likely to pursue areas of interest for which we believe we have the ability.

SOCIAL FACTORS

In grade school, there is a paradox between girls' and boys' performance and their beliefs about their performance. For example, despite the fact that girls either perform better than or equal to boys in areas such as math, girls rate their ability lower and have more negative attitudes toward math compared to boys (D. Yee & Eccles, 1988). What are the reasons for these discrepancies? One answer concerns the beliefs that other people hold about boys' and girls' abilities. Despite the failure of research to establish clear sex differences in most intellectual domains (see Chapter 3), people continue to believe that men and women have different abilities. I begin this next section of the chapter by describing the expectancy/value model of sex differences in achievement. This model rests heavily on gender-role socialization. Then I examine several sources of social influence. First, I examine the role of parents in influencing children's beliefs about their abilities; then I examine the role of teachers in influencing children's attributions for success and failure. Both parents and teachers may communicate to children different beliefs about the abilities of boys and girls and provide boys and girls with different experiences. Finally, I conclude this section by examining a third source of influence: the neighborhood in which one lives.

Expectancy/Value Model of Achievement

If girls perform better than boys in school, including in math and science at younger ages, why don't more women have careers in math and science? This question puzzled Jacquelynne Eccles and her colleagues, so they developed a theory to account for the discrepancy between men's and women's school performance and career choices. Their **expectancy/value model of achievement** suggests that men's and women's

achievement-related choices are a function of their performance expectancies ("Will I succeed?") and the value they attach to the area ("Is this important?"; "Do I care about it?"; J.E. Eccles et al., 1983; J.S. Eccles, 1984, 1987). Performance expectancies and values influence the decision to engage in an activity, the decision to persist in the activity, and ultimately performance in the activity. Performance expectancies and values are influenced by gender-role socialization. People in children's environments—parents, teachers, peers—influence males and females to value different areas. Performance expectancies and values also are shaped by the experiences children have and by their interpretations of those experiences. For example, boys and girls might have the same math grades but interpret them differently. If girls believe that their high grades are due to considerable effort and boys believe that their high grades are due to inherent ability, boys will be more likely than girls to believe they will succeed in math in the future. It is the self-perception of ability rather than the actual ability that predicts whether students pursue a given domain (Updegraff, Eccles, Barber, & O'Brien, 1996).

Numerous studies have been conducted in support of this theory. In a longitudinal study of fifth- through twelfth-graders, boys said they had greater math ability than did girls. Boys also had higher expectancies for future success in math than did girls, despite the fact that there were no sex differences on any objective indicator of math performance (J.S. Eccles, 1984). In addition, boys and girls agreed that math was more useful for boys. In other words, boys had higher expectancies for success and attached greater value to the domain of math. In addition, sex differences in expectancies and values increased with age and eventually predicted the number of math courses taken. Girls' perceptions of their math ability declined with increasing age. Girls also attached less value to math with increasing age. Boys' attitudes toward their math ability and the value boys placed on math were stable across time. These differences in expectations and values contributed to girls taking fewer math courses than boys by the end of twelfth grade. Other studies have confirmed that the expectancy/value model predicts course selection and occupational aspirations (J.S. Eccles, Barber, & Jozefowicz, 1999; Updegraff et al., 1996).

One of the features of the expectancy/value model is that achievement-related behavior is understood as a choice between at least two behaviors (J.S. Eccles et al., 1999). In other words, a boy who has equally good grades in all subject areas knows that he will pursue a career in only one area. Even if the boy's grades in math and English are the same and he equally values math and English in elementary school, at some point he is likely to choose between the two areas and value one more than the other. Gender-role socialization may lead him to value math over English. Parents, teachers, and counselors all have the opportunity to encourage or discourage pursuits in a given area.

There is plenty of research to suggest that men and women do value different pursuits. In a study of high school seniors, girls rated family and friends as more important than did boys (J.S. Eccles et al., 1999). Girls also were more interested than boys in having people-oriented jobs. This may explain why girls are underrepresented in computer science majors. In 1995, females received 28% of the computer science undergraduate degrees and 18% of the computer science PhDs (American Association of University Women, 2000). Girls are likely to be attracted to occupations that involve interactions with other people, and the computer scientist often is depicted as a nerd who works in isolation from others. In a series of focus groups with middle and high school girls from 70 different schools,

girls expressed a lack of interest in computer science (American Association of University of Women, 2000). These girls did not say they lacked the ability; in fact, they were often offended at the suggestion. The investigators suggested that the girls' responses could be summarized by the phrase "We can, but I don't want to." Girls perceived the computer scientist to be male and antisocial; the career simply did not appeal to them.

The Influence of Parents

Parents have stereotypes about the subject areas in which boys and girls excel, and parents have opinions about the subject areas in which it is important for boys and girls to excel. Specifically, parents rate girls' math ability as lower than that of boys and believe math is more difficult for girls than for boys—despite equal performance by boys and girls in math during elementary school (Eccles-Parsons, Adler, & Kaczala, 1982; Yee & Eccles, 1988). Parents believe girls are more competent in English and boys are more competent in sports (J.S. Eccles, Jacobs & Harold, 1990). Parents also believe that math and athletics are less important for girls than for boys and that English is less important for boys (Eccles-Parsons, Adler, et al., 1982; Yee & Eccles, 1988).

Rather than assume a bias on the part of parents, is it possible that their beliefs about their sons' and daughters' different abilities are accurate? It is difficult to assess whether one person has more inherent ability than another. If a sex difference appears on an objective indicator of performance, does this mean that one sex has greater natural talent than the other? Not necessarily. Boys and girls may have had different experiences, which led to different performances. For example, men and women may have equal abilities in math, but different experiences provided by teachers, parents, relatives, and peers may lead boys to outperform girls. Even when more objective indicators of performance are taken into consideration (e.g., test scores, teachers' ratings of students, grades), parents still hold sex-differentiated beliefs about their children's abilities that exceed any observed differences in performance (J.S. Eccles et al., 1990). It also turns out that parents who hold stronger stereotypes about men and women are more likely to translate those stereotypes into their beliefs about their individual daughters and sons.

Parents hold different beliefs about boys' and girls' abilities in different cultures. Mothers in Minneapolis, Taiwan, and Japan all indicated that their kindergarten girls were better at reading than their boys and that their boys were better at math than their girls (Lummis & Stevenson, 1990). There were no objective sex differences in ability among these children. It is interesting that parents have sex-differentiated beliefs for children at this early age, because at this age level neither boys nor girls have received any formal instruction in reading or math.

Parents also make different attributions for boys' and girls' success in different subject areas. In one study, parents made different attributions for their junior high boys' and girls' successes and failures in math despite the fact that there were no differences in math performance, as indicated by either grades or standardized tests (Yee & Eccles, 1988). Mothers of girls thought their child was less talented in math than did mothers of boys. Moreover, fathers of girls had lower expectations for their child's math performance than did fathers of boys. In addition, mothers were more likely to attribute boys' success in math to talent (an internal, stable attribution) and girls' success in math to effort (an internal, unstable attribution). Parents also

said that talent was more important than effort for success in math, which would imply that boys should be more successful at math than girls. Parents attributed math failure to lack of effort for both boys and girls, no doubt to preserve a positive image of their child. However, mothers were more likely to attribute girls' failure to the task being too difficult. A subsequent study confirmed this difference in parents' beliefs about their children's math ability and attributions for their children's success in math (J.S. Eccles et al., 1993). In summary, parents appear to be less confident about their girls' than their boys' math abilities.

Are the different attributions for male and female math performance justified? Perhaps girls do have less talent in math compared to boys and compensate by expending more effort. This would explain why boys and girls have similar math grades. However, in a summary of studies, J.S. Eccles et al. (1990) report that boys and girls report spending the same amount of time studying math.

We now know that parents have different beliefs about their children's abilities. The next question is whether those beliefs influence the children's own ability perceptions. This question was addressed in one study by measuring mothers' stereotypes of boys' and girls' abilities, mothers' beliefs about their own children's abilities, children's own perceptions of their abilities, and teachers' perceptions of children's abilities (Jacobs & Eccles, 1992). Mothers' stereotypes of boys and girls were translated into beliefs about their own children's abilities. That is, mothers who held stronger gender-role stereotypes were more likely to perceive differences in their sons' and daughters' abilities. More important, parents' perceptions of their children's abilities influenced the children's own self-perceptions more than did the teachers' ratings of the children's abilities. In other words, children based their beliefs about their math, sports, and social ability more on what their parents thought than what their teachers thought. The conclusions that can be drawn from this study are limited, however, because it was cross-sectional. Thus, one cannot say for certain whether parents' perceptions influenced children's perceptions or children's perceptions influenced parents' perceptions.

The direction of the relation between parents' and children's beliefs has been addressed in at least two longitudinal studies. One found that parents' perceptions of children's abilities affected the children's perceptions rather than vice versa (J.S. Eccles et al., 1993). Another study found that parent's perceptions of their children's math and English ability had a stronger influence on children's perceptions 18 months later than children's own grades in these subjects (Frome & Eccles, 1998). Parents' beliefs about their children's abilities may have affected how children interpreted their grades.

The next question is whether parents' beliefs influence the children's actual abilities, not just the children's perceptions of their abilities. In other words, do parents' stereotypes about boys and girls become self-fulfilling prophecies so that their sons and daughters differ in the abilities as parents expect? We do not have the definitive answer to this question yet, but one can imagine many ways in which parents' beliefs could influence children's actual abilities. For example, parents can provide their children with different opportunities and encourage their children to pursue different activities. Parents who believe boys are better than girls at math might buy a son a calculator, play math games with him, or teach him how to calculate baseball averages. They also might work with a son on math homework and express high praise to him for good math performance and

great disappointment for poor math performance. These same parents may not provide a daughter with math-related opportunities, not encourage her to spend time on math homework, and show indifference to reports of high or low grades in math. These overt behaviors and indirect affective reactions convey to the child whether the subject area is important and worthy of pursuit.

On a final note, investigators in this area have taken issue with the conclusions drawn from some of the studies showing sex differences in math performance. Benbow and Stanley (1980) argue that the sex differences in math performance obtained in the Study of Mathematically Precocious Youth are due to male aptitude. They favor a natural talent explanation over a differential experience explanation because boys and girls have similar backgrounds in math at that age, meaning that boys and girls have taken a similar number of math courses. J.S. Eccles and Jacobs (1986) dispute the point that boys and girls have similar backgrounds in math at any age. Given the evidence on how parents' beliefs may influence children's self-perceptions and behavior, could boys and girls really be said to have similar backgrounds in math?

This study of highly talented youth is also of concern to investigators in this area because of the media attention it received. The media coverage influenced parents' perceptions of their children's abilities (J.S. Eccles & Jacobs, 1986). Mothers who had heard recent media reports about this study were compared to mothers who had not heard of the study in terms of their beliefs about how difficult math was for their sons and daughters. Mothers who had heard the reports said that math was harder for their daughters than for their sons. Mothers who were unaware of the report stated that math was equally difficult for their sons and daughters. This finding was particularly troublesome because the study focused on a very select population: highly talented boys and girls. Thus, the findings did not pertain to the children of most of the parents in the study.

There is another way parents can influence their children's achievement. Parents' gender-role attitudes and own career choices do influence children's choices of achievement. For example, there is a strong relation between father's career and son's career choices (Barling, 1991). Mothers' gender-role attitudes are linked to daughters' gender-role attitudes as well as daughters' career choices (Steele & Barling, 1996). Mothers who held nontraditional attitudes about gender roles had daughters who shared these attitudes and who chose careers that were less likely to be pursued by females. These relations were stronger when the daughter identified with the mother.

The Influence of Teachers

Teachers can influence children's beliefs about their abilities by the attention and instruction they provide to students and by the nature of the feedback they provide about performance.

ATTENTION. Attention and instruction were examined by videotaping the interactions second-grade teachers had with their students during reading and math classes (Leinhardt, Seewald, & Engel, 1979). Interactions were coded as academic if they focused on the instructional material. The investigators found that reading teachers had more academic contacts and spent greater amounts of time with girls than with boys. By contrast, math teachers had more academic contacts and spent greater amounts of time with boys. These differences in interactions are important because the amount of instructional time each student received in math and reading

was correlated with his or her achievement in those subject areas.

Teacher-student interactions were examined in a meta-analysis of 81 studies (A. Kelly, 1988). Results showed that females participated in fewer interactions overall than males, whether the teacher or the student initiated the interaction. When the specific classes were examined, it appeared that females showed especially low involvement in science and social studies classes. However, males and females engaged in similar numbers of interactions in math classes. The sex of the teacher also influenced interactions: male teachers were especially less likely to interact with female compared to male students. Interestingly, teachers typically endorsed equal treatment of males and females and were often unaware that they were responding to them differently.

The extent of teachers' influence depends not only on the amount of time teachers spend with students but also on how they use that time. One study evaluated the amount of praise and criticism teachers gave students in 17 fifth- through ninth-grade math classes (Eccles-Parsons, Kaczala, & Meece, 1982). Overall, boys received more criticism than girls. Your intuition may be that criticism is harmful, but in this study, criticism was positively correlated with belief in greater math ability, belief that math was not difficult, and expecting to perform well in math in the future.

The nature of interactions also was evaluated in the meta-analysis (A. Kelly, 1988). As shown in Figure 5.9, females and males were given equal amounts of praise, but males were given more criticism than females. Of the criticism males received, proportionally more of it was directed at their behavior than their academic performance. Because so much of the criticism that boys receive is unrelated to their academic work, boys may be able to discount

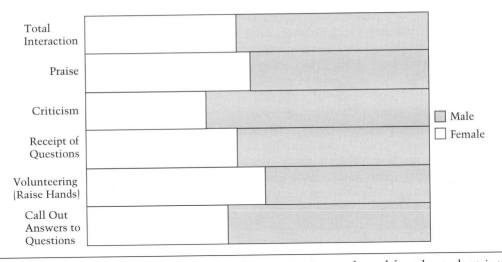

FIGURE 5.9   Results from a meta-analysis of studies comparing male and female student inter-actions with teachers. Teachers interacted with males, praised males, and criticized males more than females. Teachers also directed more questions toward males than females. Females were more likely than males to volunteer to answer a question in class (i.e., raise their hands). Males were more likely than females to call out the answer to a question. *Source:* Adapted from Kelly (1988).

negative feedback from teachers. There were other differences in the interactions shown in Figure 5.9: more questions were directed at males than females; females raised their hands more than males; and males called out answers more.

In 1994, Sadker and Sadker published a book entitled *Failing at Fairness: How America's Schools Cheat Girls.* In this book, they documented the results of extensive observational studies of teacher-student in-teractions in rural, urban, and suburban set-tings across the United States. In 1995, Brady and Eisler reviewed the literature on teacher-student interactions in the class-room, examining both observational and self-report studies. Both of these sets of in-vestigators reached the same conclusions: from elementary school through graduate school, teachers interact more with boys than girls and give boys better feedback. Teachers call on boys more often than girls, ask boys higher-level questions, and expand

on boys' comments more than girls' com-ments. For example, one study found that when students gave incorrect answers, teachers were more likely to persist with boys than with girls by giving the boys hints and encouraging greater effort (Becker, 1981). In college, professors give men more nonverbal attention than they give women: making greater eye contact with men and waiting longer for men to answer a question (Sadker & Sadker, 1994). Girls are inter-rupted more than boys, and boys receive more criticism from teachers (Brady & Eisler, 1995). Sadker and Sadker found that teachers, especially male teachers, are reluc-tant to criticize girls because they fear up-setting them. However, recall that there are benefits of criticism.

Brady and Eisler (1995) also noted in their meta-analysis that self-report studies show fewer differences than observational studies; that is, girls and boys do not report being treated very differently by teachers.

The one exception is that boys report receiving more negative treatment than girls. This self-report finding has been corroborated by observational data (J.S. Eccles & Blumenfeld, 1985). One investigator compared self-reports to observational data from her own classroom (Lundeberg, 1997). She found a discrepancy between student self-reports and observer ratings: objective raters noted that boys talked more than girls, but students reported that the discussion seemed to be equal. Thus, students are unaware of some of the differences in the way teachers treat men and women in the classroom. Conduct your own observational study of a classroom in Exercise 5.4 to see if gender bias exists.

FEEDBACK. Researchers also have investigated the nature of the feedback teachers provide to students. In an observational study, two raters observed instances of evaluative feedback given to children (Dweck, Davidson, Nelson, & Enna, 1978). The observers noted whether the feedback was positive or negative and whether it pertained to the children's intellectual performance or to nonintellectual aspects of performance. Feedback about nonintellectual aspects often pertained to conduct, as in "Johnny, please settle down and sit in your chair," or appearance, "Mary, you have a lovely outfit on today."

One reason girls do not receive as much attention as boys is that girls behave well in school and do not demand as much attention as boys do. While the girls are behaving themselves, the teachers are spending time with the "difficult" boys. In other words, these girls suffer from benign neglect. Meanwhile, the boys' bad behavior is reinforced because it receives the teacher's attention. The investigators found that there was no difference in the amount of positive or negative feedback given to boys and girls, but that there was

---

EXERCISE 5.4
Classroom Behavior

Conduct your own observational study of classroom behavior. Record some or all of the following, noting whether the interaction involved a male or female student. Are there other features of teacher-student interactions that are worth observing?

1. Teacher calling on student.
2. Teacher giving praise.
3. Teacher criticizing.
4. Length of time teacher waits for a response after calling on student.
5. Nature of teacher's response to a student's response (praise, criticism, expands on, ignores).
6. Number of times teacher interrupts student.
7. Number of times student interrupts teacher or another student.
8. Student raising hand.
9. Student shouting out answer.

After conducting your observational study, you might also administer a questionnaire to the teacher and the students asking whether they observed different frequencies of behavior with male and female students. You can then compare your observational data to the student and teacher self-report data.

---

an important difference in whether the feedback pertained to intellectual or nonintellectual aspects of the children's performance. For girls, 70% of their negative feedback pertained to intellectual aspects of their performance and 30% pertained to nonintellectual aspects. For boys, 33% of their negative feedback pertained to intellectual aspects of their performance and 67% to nonintellectual aspects. The authors suggested that these differences make negative feedback a very salient indicator of poor performance for girls but an unclear indicator of poor performance for boys. When girls receive negative feedback, it is more likely to be related to their schoolwork than work-irrelevant domains, such as conduct or appearance; thus, girls take negative feedback seriously. Boys, by contrast, are able to discount negative feedback because it usually has nothing to do with the intellectual aspects of their performance. Thus, when boys receive negative feedback about their work, they can reason "The teacher doesn't like me. She is always criticizing me. She tells me to dress neater and to be quieter. What does she know about whether or not I can read?"

In the same study, positive feedback typically pertained to intellectual aspects of performance for both boys and girls. However, when compared to the positive feedback boys received, proportionally more of girls' positive feedback concerned nonintellectual aspects of their performance. Thus, positive feedback is a clear indicator of good performance for boys but is not as meaningful for girls because it sometimes has to do with nonintellectual aspects of their performance. Girls, then, are unsure whether to take positive feedback about their work seriously because teachers are providing positive feedback about other domains not relevant to work, such as their appearance or behavior. Here, girls may conclude, "The teacher just likes me. She likes how neat I keep my desk and that I don't cause trouble. That's why I received an A on my homework." The investigators also found that teachers made different attributions for boys' and girls' failures: teachers were more likely to make attributions to motivational factors, such as lack of effort, for boys than for girls.

The investigators conducted an experiment to test their theory that the kind of feedback boys receive in the classroom leads boys to attribute failure to lack of effort, and the kind of feedback girls receive leads girls to attribute failure to lack of ability. Sixty fifth-graders were asked to solve 20 anagrams, 10 of which were solvable and 10 of which were unsolvable. No success feedback was ever provided. The manipulations had to do with failure feedback. One condition was created to mimic the feedback boys received (the "teacher-boy" condition). In this condition, failure feedback about intellectual aspects of the work (i.e., correctness of the anagram) was provided on five trials in which the student failed, and failure feedback on the nonintellectual aspects of the work was provided on five other trials (regardless of the child's performance). Thus, these students received failure feedback that was relevant to the problem half of the time and irrelevant to the problem the other half. There were two "teacher-girl" conditions; in both, failure feedback was always relevant to the problem. In the first condition, failure feedback about the correctness of the problem was provided on five trials in which the student failed. In the second condition, failure feedback about the correctness of the problem was provided on 10 trials in which the student failed. Thus, in both teacher-girl conditions, all of the failure feedback students received was relevant to the intellectual aspects of their work. The first version matched the teacher-boy condition in terms of amount of failure feedback assigned to intellectual aspects of performance (five trials). The second version matched the teacher-boy condition in terms of the total amount of failure feedback given (10 trials). (Note that students of both sexes participated in all three conditions.)

Students were then given a second puzzle to solve and were told that they did poorly. The investigators were interested in the attributions the children made for this poor performance. The children opened an envelope that contained a piece of paper that asked them to indicate why they thought the experimenter told them they did poorly on this puzzle. Children had the option of checking one of three responses: (1) I didn't try hard enough (lack of effort); (2) The man was fussy (an external attribution); or (3) I'm not good at this (lack of ability).

The results are shown in Figure 5.10. Both boys and girls in the teacher-boy condition were more likely to make attributions to lack of effort than lack of ability. Students in the two teacher-girl conditions were more likely to make attributions to lack of ability than lack of effort. Hardly any students blamed the teacher. The few that did were in the teacher-boy condition, which fits with the idea of blaming external factors for failure.

The investigators concluded that boys are more likely than girls to attribute success to ability because the positive

FIGURE 5.10 Attributions for failure. Boys and girls were randomly assigned to the "teacher-boy" condition, in which they received the kind of feedback boys normally receive in the classroom (i.e., failure on both the intellectual and nonintellectual aspects of performance), or the "teacher-girl" condition, in which they received the kind of feedback girls normally receive in the classroom (i.e., failure feedback on only the intellectual aspects of performance). There were two teacher-girl conditions; the first matched the teacher-boy condition in terms of the amount of failure feedback on intellectual aspects of performance and the second matched the teacher-boy condition in terms of the total amount of failure feedback. Both boys and girls who were assigned to the teacher-boy condition were more likely to make attributions for failure to effort than to ability. Both boys and girls who were assigned to either of the teacher-girl conditions were more likely to make attributions for failure to ability than to effort. *Source:* Adapted from Dweck et al. (1978).

feedback they receive is almost always tied directly to their work, whereas the positive feedback girls receive can be tied to intellectual or nonintellectual aspects of performance. Regarding failure feedback, girls should be more likely to take this feedback seriously because negative feedback is more likely to be tied exclusively to work for girls than for boys. Boys receive more negative feedback about nonintellectual aspects of their work, which makes boys more able to discount negative feedback. The end result is that boys can maintain a belief in their abilities despite negative feedback from teachers.

What are the implications of these results for how teachers and parents should provide feedback to children? Should we start criticizing girls for behavior that is unrelated to their work so they can discount negative feedback and make external attributions for failure? That would not seem to be an optimal answer. Alternatively, we could make sure that we are providing positive feedback to females about areas that are relevant only to work, so that the positive feedback is salient and directly tied to their performance. The idea here is to eliminate the positive feedback about performance-irrelevant domains such as appearance. If we take Dweck and colleagues' (1978) results seriously, the idea of complimenting or praising someone to soften the blow before providing negative feedback is not a very good idea.

Girls' experiences in the classroom with positive feedback for work-irrelevant aspects of performance may make girls more vulnerable than boys to other situations in which positive feedback undermines attributions to ability. One such situation is flirting. Satterfield and Muehlenhard (1997) examined the impact of flirting on college students' perceptions of their abilities. They were concerned that an authority figure who gives positive feed-

back in the context of flirting could change someone's internal attribution for success to an external attribution; that is, the flirting detracts from the genuineness of the feedback. The individual reasons, "This person is praising my skill in this area only because he/she likes me."

In a study to test these ideas, college women and men were exposed to an experimenter and an authority figure confederate who praised the student's creative abilities (Satterfield & Muehlenhard, 1997). The authority figure provided this feedback in either a nonflirtatious or flirtatious manner. The flirtatious condition included winking, eye contact, and compliments about the student's appearance. As shown in Figure 5.11, in the flirtatious condition, women's ratings of their creativity decreased from before to after the feedback. In the nonflirtatious condition, women's creativity ratings were unchanged. Thus, positive feedback from a flirtatious authority figure was discounted and actually led women to lower their perceptions of their abilities. Men's ratings of their creativity were unaffected by whether the positive feedback was provided by a flirtatious or a nonflirtatious authority figure. In either case, men's ratings did not change from before to after the feedback. The reason women's beliefs about their abilities were affected by the flirtatious confederate and men's were not may be due to women having a greater history of receiving praise for domains unrelated to ability (Dweck et al., 1978).

EFFECTS ON PERFORMANCE. Teachers' beliefs about students' abilities have been shown to influence student performance. In one study, sixth-grade students were followed over the course of a year to determine the effect of teacher's initial expectations on students' subsequent performance in math (Jussim & Eccles, 1992).

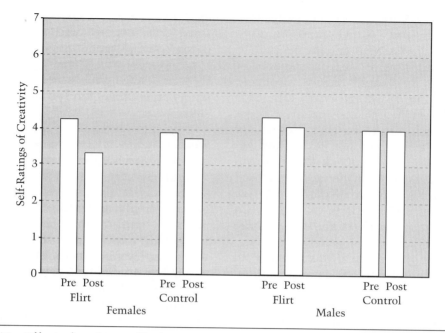

FIGURE 5.11 Effect of evaluator flirting on women's and men's beliefs about their creative ability. Flirting undermines the feedback provided by an evaluator for women but not men. Women's beliefs about their creative ability decreased when the evaluator flirted with them but did not change in the control condition. Men's beliefs about their creative ability were unaffected by whether or not the evaluator flirted with them. *Source:* Adapted from Satterfield and Muehlenhard (1997).

The investigators studied 98 teachers and 1,731 students. Although boys and girls performed equally well in math, teachers perceived that girls performed better and tried harder but that boys had more talent. In other words, the teachers attributed girls' performance to greater effort. Teacher's attributions to effort appeared to be erroneous because girls did not report expending greater effort on math than did boys. What is important is that teacher's perceptions of students' math ability predicted the change in math achievement from fifth to sixth grades. In other words, a student's math achievement improved between fifth and sixth grade when teachers started out believing

the student had high math ability. It appears that teachers' expectations influenced students' performance.

Teachers also have different expectations for the performance of different racial groups, which may influence performance. Teachers have especially low expectations for Black males' performance (Simms, Knight, & Dawes, 1993). This is a problem because teachers' expectancies predict students' academic behavior. Thus, one reason Black males have a negative view of school is that teachers' expectations have been communicated to them. Black males receive more negative feedback and more mixed (positive and negative) feedback than Black females or White students.

Although teachers attribute failure to external causes for White males, they attribute failure to internal causes for Black males (Simms et al., 1993).

The Neighborhood

Characteristics of the neighborhood also have been investigated as a source of influence on boys' and girls' achievement. In 1982, one group of investigators studied 20 first-grade classes, each from a different school, and followed the students for eight years (Entwisle, Alexander, & Olson, 1994). There were no sex differences in math reasoning skills at any grade. The income level of the neighborhood and the educational level of the parents in the school were associated with boys' but not girls' math scores on standardized tests. Why would the education and prosperity level of the neighborhood have a greater influence on boys' than girls' math abilities? The authors suggest that there is a greater opportunity for characteristics of the neighborhood to influence boys than girls because boys spend more time outdoors than girls; boys are more likely than girls to play outside the home and to work after school. Thus, boys have opportunities to take advantage of financial resources that an affluent neighborhood can provide (e.g., access to computers, stores where one can make monetary transactions, and organized team sports). On the other hand, boys also are more likely than girls to suffer from the lack of resources available in poor neighborhoods.

Even broader than the neighborhood, society sends messages to boys and girls about their abilities and the areas of achievement they ought to value. A nonprofit organization called Dads and Daughters is aimed at monitoring the media and identifying advertising and marketing strategies that trivialize girls' achievement. One of the most recent incidents they brought to the public's attention was that the Mattel Barbie computer aimed at girls was not equipped with the same educational programs provided on the Mattel Hotwheels computer aimed at boys (Dads and Daughters, 2000). The response from Mattel was that the fashion program on the Barbie computer did not permit enough space for educational programs. The Dads and Daughters organization remarked that Mattel must think boys need mental stimulation and girls need new outfits.

The Single-Sex Classroom Debate

I have reviewed the evidence that teachers treat boys and girls differently in the classroom. This line of research has been referred to as "gender bias in the classroom." In 1992, the American Association of University Women (AAUW) published a report, *How Schools Shortchange Girls*, which concluded that there is a pervasive gender bias in the classroom. Much of the evidence for this conclusion already has been reviewed in this chapter. The question now to be addressed is whether the single-sex classroom is the remedy to these problems for girls.

The rationale for placing males and females in single-sex classrooms is that somehow one sex suffers from being combined with the other. In elementary school, a concern is that boys suffer from being placed in classes with girls because they lack the physical maturation of girls. During adolescence, the issues become more complex. Some might argue that boys are at a disadvantage compared to girls because of the difference in physical maturity. Boys are more likely than girls to get into trouble at school and boys receive lower grades than girls. Ironically, the inferior performance of boys could have an adverse effect on girls: girls may decrease their academic effort to ensure their popularity with boys. During the later years, particularly junior high, high school, and college, the concern is that boys receive more attention than girls.

According to the 1998 AAUW report, single-sex education is not the answer to the problem of gender bias in the classroom. In 1997, the AAUW convened researchers in the field to discuss research on single-sex education. Although female students rate single-sex classes favorably and report that such classes help them to learn, there does not appear to be any evidence that single-sex classes influence achievement; in fact, there are some indications of adverse effects (Haag, 1998). One concern with single-sex schools is that they do not prepare students adequately to interact and achieve in a world that is coeducational (V. Lee, 1998).

The AAUW (1998), however, noted that the topic is difficult to study. First, there are few single-sex schools. Because of the legal difficulties in instituting a single-sex school in the United States, few exist and most that do are private. Second, single-sex education can take various forms, ranging from single-sex schools to single-sex classes within a coeducational school. Even single-sex classes are varied, ranging from one single-sex class that meets five days a week to one or two full days of single-sex classes. This variability in single-sex format makes it difficult to compare findings across studies.

A major difficulty with the evaluation of single-sex education is that there is a selection bias in who attends single-sex schools (Haag, 1998). A rigorous test of single-sex education would require a control group. It would be difficult to randomly assign someone to have a single-sex versus coeducational school experience. Instead, investigators compare the people who attend single-sex schools to the people who attend coeducational schools. But the two groups of students are not the same. In cases where females who attend a single-sex school attain higher levels of achievement than females who attend a coeducational school, the difference disappears when socioeconomic status is taken into consideration (Haag, 1998). In other words, the higher level of achievement of females who attend single-sex schools is accounted for by the fact that these females come from more educated and wealthier families. It also is likely to be the case that the kind of student who attends a single-sex school is more achievement-oriented.

Another problem with the study of single-sex education is how to define effectiveness or success. Success is typically defined by grades and by scores on standardized tests. Are there other outcomes in which we should be interested? What about how an individual functions as a member of society? What about subsequent career success? These kinds of outcomes are much more difficult to assess, but they may be the outcomes for which single-sex education provides an advantage.

There does seem to be some evidence that single-sex schools are beneficial for females of a lower socioeconomic status (Riordan, 1998). The AAUW (1998) researchers concluded that the single-sex school requires that lower-socioeconomic-status females focus more on academics than they normally would if they were attending a coeducational school. Coeducational schools place a relatively high value on sports and recreation, which might be more distracting to girls with a lesser academic interest.

Even when single-sex education is successful, investigators suggest that the factors responsible for the positive effects are ones that could be applied to coeducational schools. For example, single-sex schools may have teachers with higher qualifications than coeducational schools. Single-sex schools also are likely to have smaller classrooms, a feature that would benefit students in coeducational schools.

Summary

In the first part of the chapter, I examined a number of individual difference variables that might explain men's and women's different levels of achievement. The early work in this area suggested that women had a lower need for achievement compared to men. This hypothesis was later dismissed by suggesting that women's lack of achievement compared to men stemmed from women's "fear of success." The fear of success literature was and continues to be fairly controversial, in part due to the projective nature of the fear of success measures. Recent studies, however, suggest that there is still a concern among some women that success may have negative implications for relationships. Another reason women are thought to achieve less than men is that women have lower levels of self-confidence compared to men or even lower levels of general self-esteem. Women's lower self-confidence and lower self-esteem are limited to certain circumstances; for example, women are less self-confident than men about an upcoming task when it is ambiguous in nature, a task such as that employed in a typical laboratory study. Women also seem to be less self-confident than men when the task is in a masculine domain. In regard to self-esteem, it is more accurate to say that men and women have different beliefs about their strong points and derive their self-esteem from different sources. There is evidence that men derive self-esteem more from individuating themselves from others (i.e., feeling unique in comparison to others), whereas women derive self-esteem from their connection to others.

A final individual difference factor that may have implications for men's and women's achievement has to do with the way they explain their successes and failures. Women are more likely than men to attribute success to effort or luck (unstable causes), whereas men are more likely to attribute success to ability (an internal, stable cause). Women are more likely to attribute failure to stable causes, such as a lack of ability or task difficulty, whereas men are more likely to attribute failure to unstable causes, such as lack of effort or bad luck. These differences in attributions, however, are largely limited to masculine tasks. Sex differences in attributions for performance on feminine tasks are less clear. Importantly, the different attributions men and women make for performance may have implications for the decisions they make about how hard to try in an area or even whether to pursue a particular area of achievement.

In the second half of the chapter, I explored social factors that might contribute to men's and women's beliefs about their abilities as well as their attributions for performance. According to the expectancy/value model, people pursue achievement in an area in which they expect to succeed and that they regard as important and interesting. Children's expectancies and values, however, are a function of gender-role socialization. One source of socialization is parents. Parents often have stereotyped views of boys' and girls' abilities, believing boys have greater math ability and girls have greater verbal ability, which they translate into beliefs about their specific sons' and daughters' abilities. Parents seem to hold these sex-differentiated beliefs even when boys and girls receive the same grades in school. There is some evidence that parents' beliefs about their children's abilities influence children's own self-perceptions and may actually influence children's actual abilities. In other words, parents' stereotypes about boys' and girls' abilities may become self-fulfilling prophecies. The feedback and experiences that parents provide to their children may lead the children to develop the different abilities parents initially expected.

A second source of influence on children's beliefs about their abilities is teachers. Teachers pay more attention to boys than girls in the classroom. This may be due, in part, to boys' misbehavior demanding more attention. Teachers are more likely to criticize boys than girls; interestingly, criticism is linked to greater self-confidence. More important, the nature of the feedback that teachers provide to boys and girls differs. Boys seem to receive a great deal of negative feedback about work-irrelevant domains, which then leads boys to discount negative feedback and maintain a belief in their abilities. Girls, by contrast, seem to receive more positive feedback about work-irrelevant domains, which, unfortunately, leads girls to discount positive feedback and make more unstable attributions for success.

A final source of social influence that I briefly examined was the neighborhood. An intriguing study suggested that the affluence of a neighborhood may have a greater effect on boy's than girls' levels of achievement because boys spend more time outside in the neighborhood compared to girls.

Finally, the chapter concluded with an evaluation of one potential solution to the unequal treatment girls receive in the classroom and to women's lower levels of achievement, particularly in math and science. This solution is the single-sex classroom. To date, however, research shows no advantage in achievement levels for single-sex education compared to coeducation.

One must interpret this conclusion cautiously, however, because studies on this issue are difficult to conduct and more research is needed.

DISCUSSION QUESTIONS

1. Discuss the evidence in favor of and against a "fear of success" in women. What would be a good way to examine this issue today?
2. Of all the ideas discussed in this chapter, which do you find to be most convincing as an explanation of why women haven't reached the same level of achievement in society as men?
3. Which is more adaptive: men's or women's style when it comes to response to evaluative feedback?
4. Under what circumstances would you expect men and women to make similar versus different attributions for their performance?
5. Considering the results from the studies on evaluative feedback and the work by Dweck on teachers' attributions for performance, what is the best way to provide feedback to children? To adults?
6. Given what you have learned about the different ways men and women define their core selves, what would you predict would influence men's versus women's self-esteem?
7. What are the two components of the expectancy/value model of achievement?
8. What are some of the *specific* ways in which parents' beliefs about their children's abilities could influence their children's actual abilities?
9. What do you believe are the major advantages and disadvantages of single-sex classrooms?
10. What could be done to reduce gender bias in the classroom?

SUGGESTED READING

Deaux, K. (1984). From individual differences to social categories: Analysis of a decade's research on gender. *American Psychologist, 39,* 105–116.

Dweck, C.S., Davidson, W., Nelson, S., & Enna, B. (1978). Sex differences in learned helplessness: II. The contingencies of evaluative feedback in the classroom; III. An experimental analysis. *Developmental Psychology, 14,* 268–276.

Eccles, J.S. et al. (1993). Parents and gender-role specialization during the middle childhood and adolescent years. In S. Oskamp & M. Constanzo (Eds.), *Gender issues in contemporary society* (pp. 59–83). Newbury Park, CA: Sage Publications.

Lenney, E., Gold, J., & Browning, C. (1983). Sex differences in self-confidence: The influence of comparison to others' ability level. *Sex Roles, 9,* 925–942.

Roberts, T.-A. (1991). Gender and the influence of evaluations on self-assessments in achievement settings. *Psychological Bulletin, 109,* 297–308.

Sadker, M., & Sadker, D. (1994). *Failing at fairness: How America's schools cheat girls.* New York: Charles Scribner's Sons.

KEY TERMS

Achievement motive—A stable personality characteristic that reflects the tendency to strive for success.

Attribution—The cause assigned to a behavior.

Collective interdependence—Connection to others derived from group membership.

Expectancy/value model of achievement—Theory that achievement-related choices are a function of one's expectancy for success and one's value of the area.

External attribution—Cause assigned to a behavior that originates in the environment.

Fear of success—The association of negative consequences with achievement.

Internal attribution—Cause assigned to a behavior that originates within the person.

Relational interdependence—Emphasis on close relationships.

Stable attribution—Cause for a behavior that does not change over time.

Unstable attribution—Cause for a behavior that may change with time, day, or place.

6
Communication

"Fragile Communication Between the Sexes." (*USA Today*)

"Talking Trouble." (*Working Woman*)

"Good Women, Bad Marriages." (*Redbook*)

"Why Men and Women Cannot Be Like Each Other." (*Glamour*)

"17 Things Men Hate to Tell Women; 17 Things Women Hate to Tell Men." (*Glamour*)

"Are You Missing His Message?" (*Mademoiselle*)

"What's a Nice Couple Like You Doing in a Fight Like This? Why Guys and Girls Can't Talk." (*Mademoiselle*)

These are some of the headlines in recent years that suggest men and women have difficulties communicating with each other. In 1990, Deborah Tannen wrote a popular book entitled *You Just Don't Understand: Women and Men in Conversation*. From this book, it would appear that men and women have completely different styles of conversation, completely different styles of nonverbal communication, and completely different styles of interacting with one another. Indeed, many of the conversational excerpts provided in her book will ring true. But the book is largely based on anecdotal evidence of men's and women's interactions. The stories ring true because they are consistent with our schemas about how men and women interact and because it is easier to recall schema-consistent information than schema-inconsistent information. The research evidence, however, shows that men's and women's communication patterns are much more varied. Communication is influenced by many more variables than the person's sex. Communication is influenced by the sex of the person with whom one is interacting, by the situation in which people find themselves, by the goal or purpose of the interaction, and by the status of the interaction partners.

This is the first chapter in the section on gender and relationships. Before discussing specific aspects of men's and women's friendships, romantic relationships, and work relationships in the next chapters, here I review the literature on how men and women interact with one another. This chapter focuses on both verbal and nonverbal communication. I begin by describing the research on men's and women's interaction styles in childhood and adulthood and the variables that influence those styles. I then turn to the literatures on verbal behavior—the language men and women use—and nonverbal behavior, such as touching, gazing, and smiling. I also discuss two specific kinds of interactions that make gender salient: one in which men or women provide support to one another, and one in which men and women visit a physician. Next, I examine a particular interaction style, one in which one person is trying to influence another. Who is more likely to influence and be influenced? I briefly address the topic of leadership by examining who is likely to become a leader, what style the person uses, and how he or she is evaluated. Then I review several theories that might explain the previously discussed differences in interaction patterns, verbal and nonverbal behavior, and influenceability: sex-segregated interactions in early life, status or power, and social role theory. You should recognize the latter two theories from their earlier introduction in this text.

INTERACTION STYLES IN CHILDHOOD

Two children are sitting quietly at a table in the family room working on a jigsaw puzzle and talking about why they were fighting the previous day. A group of children are playing soccer in the backyard, shouting at one another to get to the ball. Who are the children at the table? In the backyard? Boys? Girls? Both? Can you tell?

There are certainly some differences in the ways boys and girls play. For example, girls are likely to play in dyads and boys

are likely to play in a group. However, regardless of the two distinct situations I just described, you should notice that they share something in common: the children are not playing alone, they are playing with each other. How much do other children influence play style? A recurring theme of this book is that the situation influences behavior. To discuss how males and females interact with one another without taking the situation into consideration would be senseless. Interactions, by definition, do not occur in isolation but in the context of other people. One of the things that you will learn in this chapter is that to understand how men and women interact and communicate, you need to know with whom they are interacting.

Maccoby (1990) examined children's interaction styles and argued that the primary determinant of how boys and girls interact with one another is their peer group. From very early on, children tend to prefer and seek out interactions with same-sex peers. Maccoby argues that same-sex play, in and of itself, becomes a socializing agent that ultimately leads men and women to have different interaction styles. According to Maccoby, parents do not promote these styles; parents merely respond to the styles that emerge from same-sex play.

What is the evidence for same-sex play preferences? Do you recall playing with children of the same sex or children of the other sex? At what age? At ages 1 and 2, there are no preferences for same- or other-sex peers, but by age 3 there is a clear same-sex preference in girls (Maccoby, 1998). A year later, boys' same-sex preference emerges. The preference to interact with same-sex peers peaks between the ages of 8 and 11 (Maccoby, 1998). Maccoby and Jacklin (1987) observed 100 preschool children at two different ages. They found children age 4½ played with peers of the same sex 3 times as often as peers of the other sex. By age 6½, children played with same-sex peers 11 times as often as other-sex peers. They concluded that sex segregation is widespread and that children prefer to play with members of the same sex even when engaging in gender-neutral activities.

By age 5, the same-sex preference is stronger in boys than in girls, even though girls initiate that preference. Boys' groups are more exclusionary of the other sex than are girls' groups. Boys view other boys who play with girls as feminine, and boys do not tolerate feminine behavior in another boy. It is important for boys' sense of masculinity to demonstrate that they are not feminine and to reject all associations with femininity. Girls, however, do not feel the same need to reject masculinity. Girls are more accepting of masculine behavior in another girl (Maccoby, 1998).

Why do children prefer to play with others of the same sex? Maccoby (1990, 1998) provides two reasons. First, she argues that children have different styles of play that are not very compatible. Second, she argues that girls find it difficult to influence boys, which makes interactions with boys less desirable. I discuss the evidence for each of these reasons.

Children's Styles of Play

Boys' play and girls' play are very different (Maccoby, 1998). Boys play in large groups, whereas girls are more likely to play with only one or two friends. Boys' play is rough, competitive, and emphasizes dominance; girls' play is quiet, often conversational, and involves more structured activities (e.g., drawing or painting). Boys' play is boisterous, activity-oriented, and takes up a good deal of space (i.e., the street, the entire yard). Boys are more likely to play outdoors, whereas girls are more likely to play inside

the house or stay within their yards. Even boys' and girls' fantasy play differs. Girls are more likely to pretend to play house or school, where one person enacts the role of teacher or parent and the other enacts the role of student or child; boys, by contrast, are more likely to emulate heroic characters, such as Power Rangers. No wonder Maccoby (1990, 1998) argued that the two play styles are not very compatible.

Boys and girls also have different conversational styles, which map onto their distinct styles of play (Maccoby, 1998). Boys' conversation is motivated to establish dominance, whereas girls' conversation serves to foster connection. Boys interrupt each other, threaten each other, refuse to comply with one another, try to top one another's stories, and call each other names; girls express agreement with one another, take turns when speaking, and acknowledge one another's feelings. Boys are more likely to order someone to do something ("Pick up the ball!"), whereas girls are more likely to make a polite suggestion ("Maybe you should pick up the ball").

These differences in conversational style were demonstrated in a study of third-graders playing checkers with either first-graders or other third-graders who were the same sex (McCloskey, 1996). The study showed that boys brag to and insult their partner, a behavior McCloskey labeled **egoistic dominance.** By contrast, girls were more likely to instruct their partner on how to play the game, especially when the partner was a first-grader. McCloskey labeled this behavior **prosocial dominance.** These findings are consistent with the cross-cultural research discussed in Chapter 4 that showed boys and girls hold distinct roles (Whiting & Edwards, 1988).

Conflict manifests itself in different ways during boys' and girls' play. It is not the case that girls' play is free from social conflict, it is just that conflict takes a different form among girls than boys. Among boys, the conflict is overt and can become physically aggressive; conversely, conflict may be subtle with girls. Boys may shout at one another, argue, or become physical, whereas girls use social alienation (Maccoby, 1998) or **relational aggression** (Crick & Grotpeter, 1995; Crick et al., 1999). Relational aggression is hurting or threatening to hurt a relationship with another person (Crick et al., 1999). That is, girls display aggression by excluding someone from an activity or threatening not to be the person's friend any more.

Crick and Grotpeter (1995) found evidence of boys' and girls' different expressions of conflict in a study of aggressive behavior among third- through sixth-graders. Children nominated classmates who displayed different kinds of aggressive behavior. Boys were found to use more overt aggression than girls, such as hitting and yelling. Girls were found to use more relational aggression than boys, such as excluding people from their group and threatening not to like someone. This sex difference in the kind of aggression boys and girls use has been replicated in other studies (Crick, Bigbee, & Howes, 1996; Rys & Bear, 1997) including children as young as preschool (Crick, Casas, & Mosher, 1997). Cross-cultural studies in Russia, China, and Finland also provide support for sex differences in relational aggression (Crick et al., 1999).

Although relational aggression is perceived as hurtful and harmful by children (Crick et al., 1996), girls evaluate relational aggression as a better strategy to use than do boys, and boys evaluate overt aggression as a better strategy to use (Crick & Werner, 1998). There is some evidence that relational aggression has greater negative consequences for girls than for boys (Crick et al., 1999). In two studies, relational aggression was associated with greater peer rejection among girls but not boys (Crick & Grotpeter, 1995; Rys & Bear, 1997), but in one study relational aggression was associated with peer rejection in both boys and girls (Crick et al., 1997).

Girls' Difficulty in Influencing Boys

A second reason children prefer to play with same-sex peers is that girls find it difficult to influence boys. According to Maccoby (1990), girls attempt to influence others by making polite suggestions, whereas boys are more likely to make demands. Boys are not responsive to girls' polite suggestions; thus, girls' tactics are effective with others girls and with adults but not with boys. Maccoby does not explain why it is that boys are unresponsive to girls.

The differences in interaction styles and influence styles explain why it appears that girls spend more time in close proximity to authority figures (e.g., teachers) than do boys. It was first thought that girls stayed closer to teachers because of the affiliative nature of their gender role. However, Maccoby (1990) points out that girls stand near teachers only in the presence of boys. She suggests that girls are hoping that an adult authority figure will temper boys' dominant behavior.

Explaining the Same-Sex Play Preference

The different ways boys and girls play, interact, and attempt to influence one another might explain why boys and girls prefer to play with peers of their own sex. But what is the source of boys' and girls' divergent play styles? Why is boys' play louder and more aggressive than girls' play? Maccoby (1998) discusses three primary reasons.

First, she suggests that *biology* may play an important role in shaping children's play behavior. She notes that boys' rough-and-tumble play and girls' interest in caretaking can be observed in other nonhuman primates, such as monkeys. There also appears to be some evidence for differences in the rates at which male and female brains mature (Maccoby, 1998). It is possible that females develop language abilities and the ability to regulate emotions earlier than males. If true, this could explain why girls' relationships focus more on language and are more emotionally controlled (i.e., less noisy and less volatile).

Maccoby (1998) suggests that sex hormones might be linked to play styles. However, she acknowledges that a hormonal explanation cannot fully account for the differences in play styles because boys' and girls' play is also influenced by the situation. Many of the differences in boys' and girls' play stem from the people with whom they are interacting rather than from some dispositional trait. For example, boys are more active than girls only when boys are in the company of other boys; when alone, boys are not necessarily more active than girls. If hormones do influence play styles, they would have to predispose males and females to respond differently to each other.

Second, Maccoby (1998) takes up the *socialization* hypothesis. She believes socialization has little to offer in the way of explaining why children develop a same-sex preference. Maccoby argues that adults do not encourage children to play with the same sex; however, there is no evidence on this issue. It seems quite likely that parents select same-sex neighborhood playmates for their children. That is, parents may simply provide a greater opportunity for same-sex play. Think about who is usually invited to a 2-year-old's birthday party, or to a 3- or 4-year-old's party. The question is: Do parents seek out same-sex peers for their children to play with before the children are old enough to have strong preferences? Maccoby also states that children do not learn same-sex play from parents because most of parents' interactions are with each other—the other sex. However, if children distinguish friendship from romantic relationships, they may notice that Mom and Dad are "friends" with people of the same sex.

Perhaps it isn't parents who encourage same-sex play. Perhaps it is other people in the child's environment. I remember when we first moved into our current neighborhood that the neighbors remarked on how lucky we were because there were a lot of other girls for our daughter to play with. Teachers also may reinforce the gender dichotomy. I observed a group of 8- to 10-year-olds playing Red Rover at a day care. The teachers were distraught because the girls kept losing to the boys. There were about 7 girls on one team and 12 boys on the other. It just didn't occur to the teachers that boys and girls could be on the same team. Instead, the teachers tried to find ways to give the girls advantages to "even out" the teams.

If same-sex play were innate, one should find sex segregation across different cultures. In a study of children ages 18 months through 9 years in a rural Kenyan community, there was no sex segregation until age 6 (Harkness & Super, 1985). The authors note that sex segregation begins in this culture at the same time that boys and girls are assigned different chores and become aware of distinct gender roles. In a study of children from 10 different cultures, sex segregation was found to be largest among cultures that provide children with the greatest freedom to choose playmates by allowing them to range further from the home (Whiting & Edwards, 1988). In cultures where children are required to stay closer to home, sex segregation is less, presumably because there are fewer choices of playmates. These findings suggest that children *prefer* to play with same-sex peers. In sum, the jury is still out on how much sex segregation is actually shaped by society.

It also is possible that people treat boys and girls differently so that they develop different play styles, which then leads to sex segregation. Maccoby (1998) acknowledges that the way parents treat children might have something to do with why boys and girls develop different interaction styles. Parents handle girls more gently, talk more about emotions with girls, are more tolerant of fighting among boys, and are more likely to use physical punishment with boys. In addition, parents give children sex-typed toys and reinforce sex-typed behavior. These "small" differences in behavior could lead boys' play to be rougher and girls' play to center more on emotions. The question is whether parents' differential treatment of boys and girls leads to different play styles, or whether the different play styles of boys and girls lead parents to treat them differently.

Third, Maccoby (1998) addresses the question of whether *cognitive differences* between boys and girls lead to differences in play styles. Cognitive-developmental theory suggests that as children acquire a gender identity, they begin to prefer similar others, which would consist of same-sex children. Children learn to behave in ways appropriate for their sex and to interact with others who are behaving in a similar way. However, children's gender-role stereotyping is unrelated to their preference to interact with same-sex peers. That is, children who have weaker stereotypes are just as likely as children who have stronger stereotypes to play with same-sex peers. Maccoby argues that children's different interaction styles are

learned before stereotypes are learned; thus, the stereotypes could not lead to the interaction styles. Is that true? Children prefer same-sex peers at ages 3 or 4. Are 3- and 4-year-olds unaware of gender stereotypes? Even children this young have some knowledge of gender-role stereotypes.

Little research has tried to differentiate boys and girls who have stronger and weaker same-sex peer preferences. This may shed some light on the origin of same-sex play preferences. Conduct your own research on the issue by trying Exercise 6.1.

Summary

There is a great deal of evidence that boys and girls engage in different styles of play and that there is a strong preference to play with members of the same sex. Maccoby (1998) makes the case that the same-sex play preference emerges from boys' and

---

EXERCISE 6.1
Observational Study of Same-Sex and Cross-Sex Play

Visit a day care or a preschool. Pick several boys and girls to observe over several days (or several sessions). Note the frequency of same-sex versus other-sex play. Can you identify any variables that differentiate children who are more or less likely to engage in same-sex play?

You might also interview the children to measure variables that could distinguish those who play more or less frequently with the same sex, such as gender-role attitudes and parents' traditionality. Ask Johnny why he plays with Joe but not Mary. Ask Joan why she plays with Samantha but not Paul.

girls' different styles of play and girls' difficulty in influencing boys. It is not clear, however, what accounts for the emergence of same-sex play preferences. Maccoby discusses a potential role for biology and cognition. Although she argues against socialization, this hypothesis has not been adequately tested. Are we really ready to say that our culture doesn't have a role in leading boys to play with boys and girls to play with girls?

INTERACTION STYLES IN ADULTHOOD

There are parallels between the sex differences in interaction styles observed among children and adults (Aries, 1996). However, rather than examine how adult men and women play together, we examine how men and women work together. Much of the research on adult interaction styles comes from studies of how people behave in small groups. This research shows that men's behavior is more directive, more dominant, more hierarchical, and more task-focused; by contrast, women's behavior is more supportive, cooperative, and egalitarian. Studies of group interactions show that females engage in more **positive social acts,** such as agreeing with others, showing group solidarity, encouraging others to talk, and making positive comments (Smith-Lovin & Robinson, 1992; W. Wood & Rhodes, 1992). Women also are likely to reciprocate positive social acts. In other words, women help to escalate positive social behavior. Men talk more in groups compared to women (Smith-Lovin & Robinson, 1992), and men engage in more **task behavior,** such as asking for and offering opinions and suggestions (W. Wood & Rhodes, 1992). Men even respond to positive social acts with task behavior rather than a reciprocation of positive social behavior (W. Wood & Rhodes, 1992). Thus,

unlike women, men are not interested in encouraging positive social behavior. Men also engage in more **negative social behavior,** such as disagreement and antagonism, and help to escalate negative social behavior (i.e., respond to negative social behavior with more negative social behavior; W. Wood & Rhodes, 1992).

Given this brief summary of quite distinct interaction styles, I now must caution the reader that sex differences in interaction styles are not that clear-cut. The way men and women behave with one another is qualified by a host of other variables (Aries, 1996).

One factor that is often overlooked is the behavior of the person with whom one is interacting. For example, one sex difference that has been found in interactions is that men are more likely to interrupt women than women are to interrupt men. However, Natale, Entin, and Jaffe (1979) found that interruptions were best predicted by how long the partner spoke rather than the listener's sex. Listener's sex accounted for 7% of the variance in interruptive behavior, whereas the partner's length of speaking accounted for 63% of the variance. In other words, the best way to predict whether or not Mary will be interrupted by Joe is how long Mary speaks, rather than any characteristic of Joe.

Another aspect of the situation is the nature of the task. Men are more task-oriented in masculine situations, whereas women are more task-oriented in feminine situations. A task orientation includes making suggestions and providing information. Thus, a certain degree of confidence in or knowledge of the situation is required before one engages in task behavior. Men and women are likely to be more confident in situations relevant to their own sex, which enables them to make suggestions and provide information. In one study, men showed more task behavior in group interactions when they enacted the role of airplane pilot, whereas women showed more task behavior when they enacted the role of nurse (Yamada, Tjosvold, & Draguns, 1983). Because masculine situations are more often studied, it may only appear that men are more task-oriented than women.

A major determinant of men's and women's interaction styles is the sex of the person with whom they are interacting. For example, Carli (1989) found that women displayed more positive social behavior (e.g., agreeing with their partner) and men displayed more task-oriented behavior and disagreement when they were interacting with members of the same sex. However, Carli also found that both men and women used more feminine behavior (e.g., agreement) with female partners and more masculine behavior (e.g., disagreement) with male partners. In other words, men and women accommodated to each other. As shown in Figure 6.1, women engaged in more masculine behavior (task behavior) when they were paired with men than with women and men engaged in less masculine behavior when they were with women than with men. As shown in Figure 6.2, women engaged in less feminine behavior (positive social behavior) when they were paired with men, and men engaged in more feminine behavior when they were paired with women. Thus, men and women behave most differently from each other when they are with members of their same sex.

Sex differences in interaction styles also tend to be greater when the interaction is brief and among strangers (Aries, 1996). This is the typical laboratory study. When we have little information about others besides their sex, we will rely more on that information when making judgments or deciding how to behave. As people get to know one another and understand each other's abilities, sex becomes less important as a determinant of interaction behavior. This is the distinction between category-based and target-based expectancies.

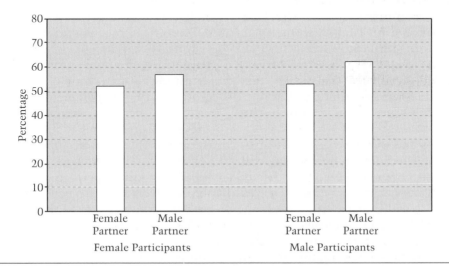

FIGURE 6.1 Task behavior. Both men and women display more task behavior when they interact with a male than a female. Numbers represent the percentage of all behaviors displayed in a particular dyad. *Source:* Adapted from Carli (1989).

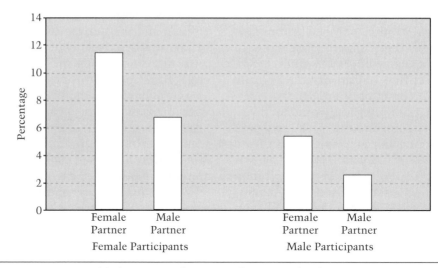

FIGURE 6.2 Positive social behavior. Both men and women display more positive social behavior when they interact with a female than a male. Numbers represent the percentage of all behaviors displayed in a particular dyad. *Source:* Adapted from Carli (1989).

One limitation to this line of research is that many of the studies have been conducted on White, middle-class persons, often college students. The homogeneity of the people studied may make men as a group look more similar to each other than they really are and may make women as a group look more similar to each other than they really are (Aries, 1996). When one examines people of different races, ages, and socioeconomic statuses, there is likely to be greater variability in male and female interaction styles.

Do men's and women's different interaction styles affect their performance in groups? A group's performance may depend on the match between the members' interaction styles and the task with which the group is faced (Hutson-Comeaux & Kelly, 1996). Groups that have task-oriented goals will perform better when members show task-oriented behavior. Groups that are focused on a social activity or an activity that

requires consensus will perform better if members display more positive social behavior. In a meta-analytic review of the literature, W. Wood (1987) showed that male groups perform better on task outcomes and female groups perform better on social outcomes. A recent study found data consistent with that conclusion. Male groups outperformed female groups when the task required the generation of ideas, and female groups outperformed male groups when the task required the group to reach consensus (Hutson-Comeaux & Kelly, 1996). One limitation of these studies is that sex—but not sex-specific interaction styles—is being linked to group performance. We assume that male groups are performing better on task outcomes because they are displaying task-oriented behavior and that female groups are performing better on social outcomes because they are displaying more positive social behavior. It would be more helpful to know that task behavior contributes to better outcomes in groups where the mission is to solve a problem and that positive social behavior contributes to better outcomes in groups that require members to come to an agreement.

In general, there are clear differences in the styles men and women exhibit when interacting in small groups. Women engage in more positive social behavior (e.g., agreement), and men engage in more task behavior (e.g., providing or asking for information). However, these differences are influenced by whether the group is composed of same-sex or other-sex persons. Men and women tend to accommodate to each other. In addition, these differences have largely been found among laboratory studies of people who do not know each other. Interaction styles among people in ongoing relationships may be influenced by other factors much more than sex.

LANGUAGE

Imagine the following interaction:

PERSON A: I haven't talked to you in so long. What's up?

PERSON B: I've been really stressed out lately. Things are kind of weird at home.

PERSON A: What's been going on?

PERSON B: It's my brother.

PERSON A: Uh-huh.

PERSON B: It's never anything specific, but he's just really, really annoying me and there's nothing I can do about it. You know?

PERSON A: That sounds tough.

PERSON B: I've even been having dreams where he's doing something really awful.

PERSON A: It's probably a good thing that you don't have to live with him anymore, don't you think? But it seems like it still haunts you. It must still bother you if you have dreams about him a lot and stuff.

Now consider the following interaction:

PERSON A: Pat still hasn't given me back that money I lent him.

PERSON B: I never would have lent it to him in the first place.

PERSON A: Normally I wouldn't have, but he was in a bind and . . .

PERSON B: Man, you just don't get it. I told you a long time ago: You never lend money to that guy. Never. I've known him twice as long as you have, so I know all about it.

The two interactions are both same-sex interactions. Can you tell which one is between two women and which is between two men? How? There are aspects of language that can distinguish men's and women's speech—but usually only when they interact with each other. The language used in mixed-sex interactions is much harder to distinguish. The two same-sex interactions above are very stereotypical. The first interaction was between two women, and the second was between two men. The speaking styles differed on a number of dimensions that are discussed in this section.

One of the most common perceptions we have about the differences between men's and women's language is that women use more of it! That is, women talk more than men. In the interactions just described, the women's conversation was longer than the men's. Does this stereotype have a basis in reality? James and Drakich (1993) conducted a literature review on talking among adults to find out. They discovered just the opposite: of the 56 studies reviewed, 24 showed that men talked more than women, 10 showed that men talked more on some measures, 16 showed no sex differences in talking, 4 revealed mixed findings, and only 2 showed that women talked more than men.

Why do men talk more than women? The traditional explanation is based on status theory: men have a higher status than women, so they are able to be the more dominant force in conversation. James and Drakich (1993) offered a different explanation. They argued that men's task behavior involves more talking than women's socioemotional behavior. For example, giving advice to someone is likely to take longer than agreeing with someone. In fact, James and Drakich found that many studies showed that men and women spoke the same number of times or had the same number of turns in talking but that men's turns took longer.

If men talk more than women, why do people perceive that women talk more? One answer has to do with the setting in which talking is examined. James and Drakich (1993) found that men were especially more likely than women to talk when the setting was structured or formal. In informal conversations, such as the ones above, men's talking advantage appears to be smaller. Informal conversations often involve more socioemotional behavior and less task behavior. In addition, to whom one is talking influences the length of conversation. Our images of women in conversation depict women talking to other *women*. Although our perceptions of sex differences in talking are based on same-sex interactions, much of the research is based on mixed-sex interactions. Try Exercise 6.2 to figure out the conditions under which people *perceive* that men and women talk equally, men talk more, or women talk more.

Aside from general amount of talking, what are the specific differences in the language men and women use? Features of language that have been studied are shown

---

EXERCISE 6.2
Perceptions of Talking

Develop a survey about perceptions of talking and administer it to a group of people. The class could divide into groups so that each group administers the survey to a different age group: children (10 to 12), early adolescents (13 to 15), later adolescents (16 to 18), college students, middle-age adults, the elderly. Ask about people's perceptions of who talks more (men or women) across a variety of settings, for example: conversations at work, informal conversations among friends, discussions of male problems, discussions of female problems, conversations with strangers, conversations about politics, conversations about family. Come up with a set of variables that might influence talking: sex composition of dyad (same-sex vs. mixed-sex), nature of relationship (friend vs. relative), topic of conversation (current events, work), setting (work vs. school). You could ask about either other people's perceptions or people's personal experiences.

---

in Table 6.1. Mulac (1998) reviewed the literature on sex differences in language use and concluded that (1) men were more likely than women to refer to quantity in language (e.g., "That house is as large as a football field"; "I had to walk four times as far to school as my son does"), to use directives, and to make reference to themselves (i.e., use "I"); and (2) women were more likely than men to use intensive adverbs (e.g., so, really), refer to emotions in language, use longer sentences, ask questions, and use hedges (e.g., sort of, kind of, maybe). Some of these differences can be found in the example interactions I provided.

TABLE 6.1   Features of Language

Feature	Example	Sex Difference
Self-reference	"I"	Male
Directive/imperative	"Close the door"	Male
Quantity terms	"Five miles"	Male
Intensive adverb	"so"; "really"	Female
Use emotions	"afraid"; "loved"	Female
Ask questions	"Why?"	Female
Hedges	"sort of"; "kind of"; "maybe"	Female
Minimal response	"OK"; "uh-huh"	Female
Qualifiers	"unless"	Female
Disclaimers	"I could be wrong, but"	Female

The differences in the language that men and women use has been considered to reflect different emphases on relationships. Women are said to talk in ways that maintain relationships (Maltz & Borker, 1982); they encourage others to communicate by asking questions and making responses that encourage conversation. For example, one feature that is more prominent in women's than men's language is the use of the **minimal response,** such as saying "uh-uh," "OK," and nodding. These responses encourage the speaker to continue. Men's language is less facilitative of relationships. Men interrupt others, challenge others, disagree, ignore others' comments by delayed use of the minimal response or giving no response, and make declarations of fact and opinion (Maltz & Borker, 1982).

Sex differences in language also have been considered to reflect a lack of assertion on the part of women (Smith-Lovin & Robinson, 1992). Women use more tentative and deferential language compared to men. Women use more hedges, qualifiers (e.g., "I

perform well, *unless* I don't get enough sleep"), and disclaimers (e.g., "*I could be wrong,* but I believe . . .").

To better understand the language men and women use, we can classify it along three dimensions (Mulac, 1998). First, language is direct or indirect. Men's language is more direct because they use directives; women's language is more indirect because they ask questions and use hedges. Second, language can be succinct or elaborative. Women's longer sentences and use of intensive adverbs makes their language more elaborative. Third, language can be instrumental or affective. Men's reference to quantity is instrumental and women's use of emotion words is affective. Thus, men's language can be said to be instrumental, succinct, and directive, whereas women's language is affective, elaborative, and indirect.

However, these conclusions about sex differences in language are overly simplistic. Sex differences in language use are not always consistent. One factor that influences the language men and women use is the sex of the person with whom one is talking. Women's greater use of "polite" language, for example, may take place only in their interactions with men. One study found that women used more disclaimers, tag questions, and hedges with men than with women (Carli, 1990).

Language also can serve different purposes. Take interruptions as an example. Most people believe that men interrupt more than women, but it may depend on the context. One of the first observational studies to examine this issue was conducted by D. Zimmerman and West (1975). They recorded conversations of people in their natural environments. In other-sex dyads, men accounted for 96% of the interruptions, but in same-sex dyads men and women interrupted each other equally often. Men and women may interrupt each other for different reasons. Maltz and

Borker (1982) contend that men interrupt to assert themselves and gain the floor, whereas women interrupt to request elaboration or clarification from the speaker. The setting also influences interruptive behavior (Aries, 1996). During informal conversations, women interrupt more than men. Also, women often talk at the same time as one another, completing each other's sentences and agreeing with one another. These interruptions convey enthusiasm and involvement in the conversation rather than dominance. Thus, interruptions have a different meaning in informal settings. In more formal conversations that have a task focus (which are often the situations in the laboratory), men interrupt more than women. These may be the kinds of interruptions that convey dominance; for example, one person interrupts another to change the subject.

The difference in the meaning of interruptive behavior is illustrated in a study of patient-physician interactions (Hall, Irish, Roter, Ehrlich, & Miller, 1994). Interruptions were associated with lower patient satisfaction when either patient or physician was male but greater patient satisfaction when both patient and physician were female. The investigators concluded that interruptions conveyed dominance when a male was involved in the interaction and enthusiasm when the interaction took place between two women. It may be that the setting was viewed as more formal for men than women, or it may be that the nature of interruptive behavior is different among men and women.

Another example of language that has different purposes is the tag question, a question tacked on at the end of a sentence (e.g., "He's right, *isn't he?*"). It used to be thought that women use tag questions more than men, but the sex difference in tag questions is not clear. One reason is that tag questions have a number of different

functions (Aries, 1996). One function is to convey uncertainty, as in "He likes the soup, doesn't he?" This is the kind of tag question that falls under the label of tentative language. Another function is to facilitate conversation, as in "Still sick, are you?" Polite tag questions that soften directives ("You shouldn't eat that, should you?") also facilitate conversation. Interestingly, men appear to be more likely to use tag questions that convey uncertainty, whereas women are more likely to use tag questions that facilitate conversation.

Language also may be more strongly influenced by gender roles than by sex. What we have referred to as female language—the minimal response, hedges, intensive adverbs—is really communal language. What we have referred to as male language—directives and imperatives—is really agentic language. Leaper (1987) found that gender role had implications for communication among mixed-sex dyads. Specifically, agency (as measured by the PAQ) was related to less use of tentative language (e.g., fewer qualifiers).

If men and women speak so differently, we should be able to decipher whether a talk was given by a male or a female. But this is not always the case. In one study, speakers were asked to talk about a topic and the conversation was audiotaped and transcribed (Mulac, 1998). Raters blind to respondent's sex could not judge the sex of the speaker better than chance. In this study, however, speakers were not allowed to choose the topic they discussed. When people are allowed to choose their topic, college students are able to judge the sex composition of the dyad talking (R. Martin, 1997). Students used profanity and slang terms to identify the sex composition, but the feature used most often to identify the dyad was the topic discussed, as reflected in the title of the article "Girls Don't Talk about Garages." Male same-sex dyads talked about sports, women, being trapped in relationships, and drinking; female same-sex dyads talked about relationships, men, clothes, and feelings. Recall the interactions described at the beginning of this section. How did you know that the first interaction was between two women and the second was between two men? One way you distinguished the conversations may have been the topic. The topic of the first interaction was a relationship problem and the topic of the second was money. Perceivers were more accurate in identifying same-sex dyads than cross-sex dyads. The greatest confusion was between female-female dyads and cross-sex dyads. The conversations and language used in cross-sex dyads may actually be more similar to that used in female same-sex dyads. As you will see in the next chapter, men are more likely than women to change their behavior when interacting with the other sex.

Do the features of language previously discussed and shown in Table 6.1 clue us in on the sex of the speaker? Find out for yourself with Exercise 6.3 if your classmates can identify the storyteller.

EXERCISE 6.3
Sex Differences in Language Usage

Have five male friends and five female friends write stories about a specific topic—but the same topic (current relationship problem, how they feel about school, relationships with parents, earliest memory). See if your classmates can guess the sex of the writer better than chance (i.e., more than 50%). Ask what information they used to identify the sex of the speaker. Also, ask them to rate the stories on the use of the language features shown in Table 6.1. Compare the accurate guesses to the inaccurate guesses to see which information was more diagnostic.

Regardless of whether men and women speak differently, people do interpret the same speech as different if displayed by a man versus a woman. In one study, perceivers viewed the same language differently when they thought the speaker was male versus female (Mulac, Incontro, & James, 1985). College students were given actual transcripts of men and women describing landscapes. In one condition, no information about the speaker's sex was given. In that condition, respondents perceived females' speech to be more aesthetic and males' speech to be more dynamic. This finding suggests that there are actual sex differences in speaking style. In another condition, respondents were given correct information about speaker sex in half of the cases and incorrect information in the other half. Respondents rated speeches as more aesthetic when they thought the speaker was female and more dynamic when they thought the speaker was male, regardless of whether the correct sex had been assigned to the speech. In other words, students rated a speech as more aesthetic and less dynamic when they thought the speaker was female, even when the speaker was actually male. The sex of the person that students *thought* wrote the speech influenced their perception of the speech.

There is some evidence that language influences perceptions of women more than men. One study showed that a woman's use of feminine speech detracted from her credibility, but that the nature of the speech used by a man did not influence perceptions of his credibility (Bradley, 1981). In this study, either a male or a female confederate argued a position with which four other people in the group disagreed. In the speech, the confederate either used or did not use qualifying phrases. The female confederate who used qualifiers was viewed as less intelligent and less knowledgeable than the female confederate who did not use qualifiers. That finding is not surprising. However, using qualifying phrases did not detract from a man's credibility: the male confederate was viewed as equally intelligent and knowledgeable, regardless of his use of qualifying phrases. In both conditions, the male confederate was viewed as more intelligent and more knowledgeable than the female who used qualifying phrases. Thus, the combination of being female and using feminine speech detracts from credibility.

Another study also showed that language influenced perceptions of women but not men (Wiley & Eskilson, 1985). College students read one of two job interviews. One version contained "powerless" speech, including hedges and hesitations; the other did not. A picture of either a female or a male was attached to the job interview. The same job interview was interpreted differently when the applicant was thought to be male versus female. Students found the female applicant to be warmer than the male applicant even though the job interview was the same. The nature of the speech used affected how students felt about the female applicant but did not affect their liking of the male applicant. Female students liked the female who used more rather than less powerful speech; male students, by contrast, liked the female who used less rather than more powerful speech. In addition, male students viewed the female applicant who used powerful speech as more aggressive than the male applicant who used powerful speech. (Recall our discussion in Chapter 2 of stereotype-inconsistent information being viewed as more extreme.) In general, male students responded more favorably to a woman who used a more feminine way of speaking.

Thus, women are presented with an interesting dilemma when facing a male audience. Women are viewed more favorably in terms of likability when they use

"feminine" speech but at the expense of being viewed as less competent. This contradiction is supported in another study. Carli (1990) showed that men like more, and are more influenced by, a woman who uses tentative rather than assertive speech. However, men also view the woman who uses tentative speech as less competent than the woman who uses assertive speech. Does this mean that men like less competent women?

The same concern that I raised about the brevity of interactions for the study of interaction styles applies to the study of language. Sex differences in language are more likely to be found in shorter interactions. In experimental settings, participants are strangers and interactions are brief. This is just the kind of situation in which sex is salient and stereotypes are likely to operate. Sex differences in communication disappear when longer interactions are examined. A study that supported this idea involved same-sex and mixed-sex dyads meeting for three or four 90-minute sessions (Wheelan & Verdi, 1992). During the first session, the investigators found sex differences in communication consistent with previous research; after that, however, sex differences disappeared. Thus, as men and women become familiar with each other, their speech may become similar.

To the extent that sex differences in language are due to socialization, these differences may not generalize to other cultures with different socialization practices. There is a fairly large literature comparing U.S. communication to communication in Japan (V. Waldron & DiMare, 1998). Many of the sex differences in language found in this chapter do not generalize to Japan. For example, sex differences in assertive language found in the United States are not found in Japan (C. Thompson, Klopf, & Ishii, 1991). In general, the language that the Japanese use is more similar to the language used by women in Western cultures (e.g., the United States; Wetzel, 1988). Parallels have been drawn between Japanese versus Western language and female versus male language. The Japanese as a culture value language that communicates sensitivity to others' needs, language that includes empathy and agreement (Wetzel, 1988). Whereas people from Western cultures would view this language as "powerless" language, the Japanese do not. Power, in and of itself, is viewed differently by the two cultures. Americans, for example, view power as an attribute of a person, so a person can use more or less powerful language; the Japanese view power as an attribute of a social role or a position. Thus, the position confers power, regardless of the language used. It does not make sense to talk about powerful language in Japan. In fact, language that is viewed as dominant in the United States—being assertive, interrupting someone, challenging someone—is viewed as childish in Japan.

Nonverbal Behavior

Recall the two interactions described in the previous section on language. Now, imagine you can see the people talking. What aspects of their behavior—other than their language—provide you with more information about the interaction? Is it only people's verbal response that indicates whether they are listening? What about eye contact? What about posture? Do you feel as if people are really paying attention when they yawn?

A lot more information is contained in an interaction besides the language used. Aspects of communication that do not include words are referred to as nonverbal behavior. The domains of nonverbal behavior that scientists have investigated, especially with respect to gender, are smiling, gazing,

accuracy in interpreting emotion (decoding), accuracy in conveying emotion (sending), and touching.

In 1984, Judith Hall conducted a meta-analytic review of the literature on nonverbal behavior, which she updated in 2000 (Hall, Carter, & Horgan). From both reviews, she concluded: (1) females smile and gaze more than males; (2) females stand closer to others, face others more directly, and are more likely to touch other people; (3) males have more expansive body movements than females; (4) females are more accurate in interpreting others' emotional expressions and are better able to convey emotions than males. Interestingly, college students' perceptions of sex differences in nonverbal behavior correspond with the sex differences found in the meta-analytic reviews (Briton & Hall, 1995). Thus, people's beliefs about sex differences in nonverbal behavior appear to be fairly accurate.

Smiling

Several meta-analyses indicate that females smile more than males (Hall, 1984; Hall et al., 2000; LaFrance & Hecht, 2000). In one review, the effect size was moderate ($d = -.40$; LaFrance & Hecht, 2000), and in another review, the effect was somewhat larger ($d = -.70$; Hall et al., 2000). There does not seem to be a consistent sex difference in smiling among children, although studies of children are fewer (Hall, 1984; Kolaric & Galambos, 1995). An interesting study of yearbook pictures of males and females from 14 different schools in kindergarten through college showed that the sex difference in smiling became significant by second grade, peaked in fourth grade, and remained the same through college (Dodd, Russell, & Jenkins, 1999). These findings are cross-sectional, however, making it difficult to determine if the effect is due to age or cohort. Students from one of the schools were followed over time. The results were the same, suggesting that the sex difference really does emerge at a certain age rather than characterizing different cohorts of students. The authors suggested that the yearbook picture was viewed differently by males and females. For females, the picture was an opportunity to present an attractive self; for males, the picture was an opportunity to project an image of seriousness, consistent with masculinity.

The sex difference seems to be especially large in social settings. Smiling, however, seems to be more strongly correlated with other personality variables, such as sociability, nurturance, and femininity, than it is with sex (Hall, 1998). There also is evidence of greater female than male smiling in Japan (M. Bond & Young Ho, 1978).

Gazing

Gazing is a difficult nonverbal behavior to interpret. In general, gazing is thought to convey interest and attention; thus, it is not surprising that sex differences in gazing have been found in the direction of women gazing more than men ($d = -.33$; Hall, 1984). Furthermore, sex differences in gazing (female more than male) are typically larger when the situation evaluated is a friendly one. Yet, in other situations, gazing can convey a different message, in particular, a message related to status. A high-status person, for example, may gaze intently at the person to whom he or she is speaking. To confuse matters even more, sex differences in gazing do not generalize to all other cultures. For example, in Japan, it appears that women make less eye contact than men, especially during interactions with other women (M. Bond & Young Ho, 1978). Eye contact here may convey dominance.

Decoding

Females seem to be more sensitive than males to nonverbal cues, meaning that they can more accurately interpret the meaning of nonverbal behavior (Hall, 1984, 1987, 1998). Females are better able to understand the meaning behind such nonverbal cues as facial expression, vocal intonation, and body position. This finding seems to generalize to people in other countries, such as Malaysia, Japan, Hungary, Mexico, New Zealand, Hong Kong, and Israel (Hall, 1984; Hall et al., 2000). It also generalizes to infants, children, and adolescents (McClure, 2000). Furthermore, the sex of the target does not make a difference in decoding accuracy; that is, females are more accurate than males in decoding both men's and women's emotions. This female advantage is stronger for nonverbal facial behavior than for nonverbal body movements or auditory cues. The one exception is deception: females are not more accurate than males at detecting deception. If females' decoding ability is oriented toward promoting relationships, the finding for deception is not that surprising. Detecting deception is not always a behavior that would foster relationship development, whereas accurately interpreting another's emotions certainly is.

Sending

The counterpart to understanding another's emotions is the ability to accurately convey one's own emotions. Sending reflects the capacity to convey one's emotions without intentionally doing so. Because emotional expressiveness is central to the female gender role, it is not surprising that women are better senders than men (Hall, 1984; Hall et al., 2000). That is, others are better able to judge the emotions of a woman than of a man. Again, the difference is larger when judging facial expressions than vocal cues. It is not clear whether a sex difference in sending occurs among children.

Touching

There have been at least two reviews of the literature on touching (Major, 1981; Stier & Hall, 1984). Both suggest that when self-reports of touching are examined, men initiate touch more than women; however, observational studies reveal a different pattern of findings, depending on whether the interaction is cross-sex or same-sex. Major found that males were more likely than females to initiate touch in cross-sex encounters but not in same-sex encounters. However, Stier and Hall found quite different results: there was no sex difference in touch initiation in cross-sex interactions, and females were more likely than males to initiate touch in same-sex interactions. Both Major and Stier and Hall agreed that

women received more touch than men and that there was more touching in female-female interactions than male-male interactions.

There are a variety of factors that influence sex differences in touch, such as the sex composition of the dyad. In an observational study of touch across a variety of settings, women were significantly more likely than men to receive touching, consistent with the two previous reviews (Major, Schmidlin, & Williams, 1990). There was a trend for men to be more likely to initiate touch, but the effect was not significant. Both of these findings, however, are misleading because touching was best understood by considering both the sex of the initiator and the sex of the recipient. As shown in Figure 6.3a, there was greater cross-sex than same-sex touch. Within cross-sex dyads, males were more likely to touch females than females were to touch males. Within same-sex dyads, women were more likely to touch each other than were men. These findings were more in line with Major's (1981) review. It

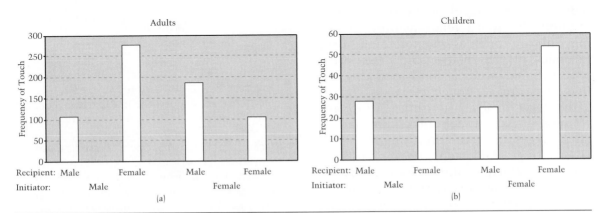

FIGURE 6.3 Among adults, there is greater cross-sex than same-sex touching. Among children, there is greater same-sex than cross-sex touching. Adults are shown in Figure 6.3a and children are shown in Figure 6.3b. *Source:* Adapted from Major, Schmidlin, and William (1990).

was true that males were more likely to initiate touch and females to receive touch, but these two findings, in and of themselves, are misleading. Sex differences in touch need to be understood in the context of both the sex of the initiator and the sex of the recipient.

Investigators have also examined the effects of some contextual factors on touch, such as age and relationship status. For example, the pattern reported above characterizes only interactions among adults (Major et al., 1990). Interactions among children show greater same-sex than cross-sex touching (see Figure 6.3b). Among children, it appeared that females were more likely to initiate touch, but this was due to the high proportion of touching in the female-female dyad compared to the other three dyads. In an observational study of touch among teenagers and adults, men initiated touch toward women among the younger group, but with increasing age, the sex difference reversed such that women initiated touch toward men (Hall & Veccia, 1990). The authors point out, however, that age is confounded with relationship status; younger people are likely to be in less-developed relationships, in which men may initiate touch to indicate their control of the relationship. In more developed relationships, women may initiate touch as an expression of the intimacy of the relationship. Two other observational studies confirmed the fact that men initiate touch more during the early stages of a relationship (dating) and women initiate touch more during the later stages of a relationship (marriage; Guerrero & Andersen, 1994; Willis & Briggs, 1992). An evolutionary explanation for this behavior is that men use touch to seduce a woman into a sexual relationship during the early stages and that women use touch to preserve the intimacy of the relationship during the later stages.

Conduct your own observational study of touch in Exercise 6.4 to see what variables influence touch.

As in research on verbal communication, sex differences in nonverbal behavior really cannot be fully understood without considering the sex of the person with whom one is interacting. Hall (1987) concluded that men and women accommodate to each other. The sex difference in smiling, gazing, distance, and touch is much larger when comparing same-sex dyads to mixed-sex dyads. For example, the most smiling will be observed between two women and the least smiling will be observed between two men. Two females will stand closest to one another, two males will stand farthest from one another, and a male/female dyad will fall somewhere in between.

It is possible that gender role rather than sex per se is related to nonverbal behavior. In 1992, Gallaher had college students observe their friends' nonverbal behavior over several days. Students reported that women were more expressive than men, which included gesturing more frequently, having more variable facial expressions, and

---

EXERCISE 6.4
Observational Study of Touching

Conduct an observational study of touching. Choose a setting, for example, the cafeteria, an airport, the mall, a bar. Have the class break into groups so that each group can observe a different setting. Record instances of touch. Record sex of initiator and sex of recipient. Come up with a list of other variables to record that may help you understand touching, such as type of touch, intention of touch, length of touch, age of participants, and relationships status.

using greater speech inflections. Men appeared to be more expansive than women, as evidenced by men sitting and standing with their legs apart, speaking in a loud voice, and having elbows and hands away from their body. All of these findings were consistent with Hall's (1984) meta-analysis on nonverbal behavior. But Gallaher also measured the gender roles of the people being observed with two items, one ranging from "not at all masculine" to "extremely masculine" and one ranging from "not at all feminine" to "extremely feminine." Femininity was associated with being more expressive and masculinity was associated with being more expansive.

Summary

There are fairly robust sex differences in nonverbal behavior. Women smile more, gaze more, are better able to express an emotion, and are better able to read another person's emotions. It is difficult to summarize the sex comparisons on touch because the direction of the difference depends on so many variables, including the age of the respondent and the relationship between the two people. One reason findings are so variable is that touch has many meanings; it can be used to indicate status or to express intimacy.

SUPPORT PROVISION IN INTERACTIONS

Deborah Tannen (1990) begins one section of her popular book, *You just don't understand*, by relaying the following interaction (p. 49):

> Eve had a lump removed from her breast. Shortly after the operation, talking to her sister, she said that she found it upsetting to have been cut into, and that looking at the stitches was distressing because they

left a seam that had changed the contour of her breast. Her sister said, "I know. When I had my operation I felt the same way." Eve made the same observation to her friend Karen, who said, "I know. It's like your body has been violated." But when she told her husband, Mark, how she felt, he said, "You can have plastic surgery to cover up the scar and restore the shape of your breast."

Eve did not find her husband's remarks reassuring. Of course, Mark was not trying to offer reassurance. He was offering her advice, which he thought would make her feel better.

One way that men's and women's interaction styles may differ is how they respond to one another's problems. According to Tannen (1990), men are more likely to respond to problems by providing advice and women by providing sympathy. Women do not wish to receive advice any more than men wish to receive sympathy. Women inquire about a person's problems to show their concern, whereas men do not inquire about a person's problems out of respect for the person's privacy. According to Tannen, these differences in support provision and support expectancies make for a great deal of conflict between men and women.

Maltz and Borker (1982) also suggested that men and women have a different orientation to problems. Women share problems to connect with one another and to express emotions. Men prefer not to share problems unless they need help solving them. Thus, men respond to women's problems by either giving advice or by minimizing the problem ("Don't worry. It is not that big a deal"). Women respond to men's problems by empathizing or sharing a similar experience; they believe that sharing their own stories will help to make a connection. However, men do not perceive women's empathy and sharing as a way of connecting; instead, they perceive that women are turning the discussion around to focus on their own problems.

Maltz and Borker (1982) point out a series of miscommunications that may occur between men and women because of their different orientations toward problems. An interesting one is the minimal response ("OK"). Maltz and Borker suggest that the minimal response is a sign of listening among women, that they are following the conversation. For men, the minimal response indicates agreement. This would explain why women think men are not listening when men fail to give minimal responses. In actuality, it may be that men are just indicating that they do not necessarily agree. Because women use the minimal response frequently, men overestimate the extent to which women agree with them. See if Maltz and Borker are correct about this miscommunication between men and women by trying Exercise 6.5.

Is there evidence behind Tannen's (1990) and Maltz and Borker's (1982) thinking? Do men and women provide different kinds of support? There have now been a number of experimental studies conducted in the laboratory that examine supportive exchanges between men and women. There is not much correspondence in the results across studies, but one thing is clear: there is little support for the claim that men provide more advice, and only modest support for the idea that women provide more empathy.

In one study, college students were presented with seven different situations in which someone was disclosing a problem (Hall & Veccia, 1990). Students were asked to respond to the problem out loud into a tape recorder. The investigators found that women's responses were longer than those of men and were both more emotion-focused (helping to describe the person's emotional reactions) and more action-focused (giving advice on how to solve the problem). Thus, there is no evidence from this study that men are more likely than women to provide advice but some evidence that women are more likely to provide emotional support. The authors also found that men were more likely than women to deny the problem, which fits with the notion that men prefer not to talk about problems.

I was involved in a study that examined actual support exchanges in the laboratory, although the interactions observed were among strangers (Mickelson et al., 1995). One member of the dyad shared a problem with the other, and the other had the opportunity to respond. Objective coders rated these responses from transcripts of the audiotaped conversations. Dyad members also indicated what kind of support they provided and received. According to coders, male participants received more negative responses (i.e., minimization, changing the subject) than did female participants; that is, both men and women responded negatively to men sharing a problem. (No wonder men choose not to share their problems!) There

---

EXERCISE 6.5
Interpretation of the Minimal Response

Create two conversational vignettes. Keep the vignettes the same but manipulate the use of the minimal response. You could also manipulate the sex composition of the dyad, hold it constant, or omit any information about participants' sex. Then, ask a group of men and women to rate the conversations on a number of dimensions, such as how much the partner appeared to be listening to the speaker and how much the partner seemed to agree with the speaker. Your goal is to find out if the minimal response is interpreted as listening or agreement.

was no evidence that men provided more advice than women according to coders' ratings or self-reports. Female listeners reported that they provided more emotional support than male listeners, but coders did not confirm this difference; in other words, women report providing more emotional support than men do, but outside observers do not agree. Knowledge of gender-role stereotypes and norms may have influenced participants' reports: participants may be responding according to how they expect themselves to behave rather than according to how they actually behave. It is also possible that women are truly providing more emotional support than men, but that objective coders cannot accurately code such subjective behavior.

Sex differences in supportive interactions also have been examined in the context of ongoing relationships. In one study, pairs of same-sex and cross-sex friends discussed how their relationship had changed since college (Leaper, Carson, Baker, Holliday, & Myers, 1995). Conversations were audiotaped and transcribed, and the responses of the listener were coded. There were twice as many "active understanding" responses in the female-female dyad than any other dyad. Active understanding reflects emotional support, specifically, acknowledging the speaker's feelings and encouraging the speaker to reflect on issues. There were no dyad differences in advice giving. In another study of college students, same-sex and cross-sex friends shared a problem with one another in the laboratory (Fritz, Nagurney, & Helgeson, 2000). The participants and objective coders agreed that women provided more emotional support than men—to both men and women. Men, in general, did not provide more advice than women, but men provided more advice to other men; that is, the greatest amount of advice occurred in the context of the male-male dyad. Finally,

a study of newlywed couples showed no sex differences in instrumental behavior (advice) or emotional behavior (reassurance, encouragement) during problem disclosure (Pasch, Bradbury, & Davila, 1997).

Thus, despite people's perceptions, there is not much evidence from laboratory-based studies that men and women respond differently to problems; there is some evidence that women provide more emotional support, but little evidence for sex differences in advice-sharing. McWilliams and Howard (1993), however, point out that men's and women's advice may be perceived differently. Specifically, male advice may be interpreted as instrumental and female advice as communal. The gist of this is that men's advice would be taken as a serious attempt to tell someone what to do and women's advice would be viewed as an attempt to help or convey concern about the problem. It also is possible that gender roles rather than sex may be more strongly related to support provision. In the laboratory study of friends sharing problems discussed above (Fritz et al., 2000), the gender-related traits of the partner were associated with the kind of support he or she provided. Communal partners provided more emotional support and agentic partners provided more advice. In this study, communion and agency were better predictors of support provision than sex.

PHYSICIAN-PATIENT INTERACTIONS

One particularly interesting interaction to study from a gender perspective is the interaction between a patient and a physician. The physician-patient interaction is by definition one of unequal status. When the physician is male and the patient is female, the status difference in roles (physician vs. patient) is congruent with the status difference in sex (male vs. female). But today, it is no longer the case that the physician is always male. How will the interactions between patient and physician differ if the physician is female, especially if the patient is male? Because physician and patient roles are highly structured, with a clearly established hierarchy, male and female physicians might communicate similarly and male and female patients might respond similarly. In other words, the clear-cut demands of these roles may override any sex differences in communication style previously discussed. The research, however, does *not* support this idea.

Hall et al. (1994) investigated patient and physician communication by videotaping 100 routine medical visits. They videotaped 50 male and 50 female physicians interacting with one male patient and one female patient. Both verbal and nonverbal communication was coded. Female physicians had longer visits, made more positive statements, made more partnership statements (i.e., working together on a problem), asked more questions, gave more back-channel responses (e.g., uh-huh, I see, OK), smiled more, and nodded more compared to male physicians. Patients, in turn, talked longer, provided more medical information, and made more partnership statements to female than male physicians. This suggests that female physicians were more successful than male physicians in making patients feel comfortable and encouraging them to talk. The female physicians' style was effective because the patients provided more information to them compared to male physicians. Hall and colleagues concluded that female physicians worked at being good listeners and were more relationship-focused than male physicians. These differences are especially interesting, as physicians were aware that they were being videotaped.

Female-female interactions were the longest of the four dyads and contained the greatest self-disclosure. Physicians in this dyad gave the greatest amount of **back-channel responses,** which include sentence completions, brief questions of clarification, head nods, and use of the minimal response. Back-channel responses facilitate self-disclosure. These responses must have been effective because patients in this dyad conveyed the greatest amount of information about their condition.

The female physician–male patient dyad revealed some complicated communication patterns. During these interactions, the physician's voice was the least friendly and the most anxious, yet the physician appeared the most interested and the most dominant compared to the other dyads. In addition, this dyad was characterized by the most physician smiling. In this case, smiling may have been an indicator of nervousness rather than friendliness. Thus, female physicians' behavior in the presence of a male patient seems to be inconsistent. Male patients in these interactions made the most partnership statements and spoke in the most bored and most dominant voice compared to the other dyads. Hall and colleagues (1994) concluded that there may have been difficulties establishing a rapport in this dyad due to the status incongruity of the roles that physician and patient held.

Another study found similar differences in the nature of patient visits with female versus male physicians. Roter, Lipkin, and Korsgaard (1991) audiotaped the visits patients made to 101 male and 27 female physicians at 11 sites across the United States and Canada. The investigators found that patient's sex had little effect on the nature of the interactions; however, physician's sex had strong effects. Visits with female physicians were longer than visits with male physicians. The longest visit was the female patient with the female physician and the shortest was the female patient with the male physician. The greatest amount of talking occurred with female physicians, and both physicians and patients contributed to this. When the content of the interaction was examined, female physicians engaged in more positive talk (laughter, agreement), made more partnership statements (asked for patient opinion), asked more questions, and provided more information. Patients of female physicians, in turn, responded with positive talk, more partnership statements, more questions, and more information—both medical and personal information.

Taken collectively, these two studies and others (see Roter & Hall, 1997, for a review) seem to show that the effects of patient's sex on the interaction are much smaller than the effects of physician's sex. Female physicians spend a longer amount of time with patients than do male physicians, are more likely to involve patients in decisions, and are more likely to provide both informational support and emotional support. In response, patients, male or female, provide more information to the female physician. There is a small tendency for women to have better experiences with their physicians because they receive more emotional and informational support.

INFLUENCEABILITY

An important behavior that occurs in the context of social interactions is interpersonal influence. Recall that one reason children play with members of the same sex is that girls find it difficult to influence boys. Does this difficulty hold up among adults? Are men more influential than women? Are men or women more susceptible to influence? Do men or women exert influence in the same ways?

Who Is Influenced?

Maccoby and Jacklin (1974) concluded in their narrative review that there were no sex differences in susceptibility to influence. But how does one measure influence? There appear to be two different ways to study influence. In persuasion studies, one person states his or her view and provides supporting arguments. In conformity studies, one or more persons make known their view, but there are no supporting arguments—no attempts at persuasion. In some conformity studies, participants' give their response to the issue in public (group pressure), and in others, the response is made privately (no group pressure). In 1978, Eagly reported a narrative review of sex differences in influenceablity and concluded that there is little evidence of a sex difference among persuasion studies or conformity studies without group pressure. However, in group pressure conformity studies, there was clear evidence that women were more easily influenced than men. Eagly also found that sex differences were more apparent in studies conducted before rather than after 1970. In addition, there was more evidence for women's greater influenceability compared to men when the topic was one with which women were less familiar or less interested (e.g., government, politics).

Later, Eagly and Carli (1981) conducted a meta-analytic review of the literature and concluded that there is a small effect in the direction of women being more susceptible to influence compared to men in all three kinds of studies: persuasion ($d = -.16$), group pressure conformity ($d = -.32$), private response conformity ($d = -.28$). One of the most interesting findings from this review was that the sex of the researchers was related to the size of the sex difference in conformity: sex differences were larger in studies authored primarily by men rather than women ($d = -.34$ vs. $d = -.02$). In addition, sex differences in conformity were more likely to be found in studies where masculine topics were discussed; in other words, females were especially vulnerable to influence when the topic was masculine.

Eagly et al. (1981) investigated the idea that sex differences in conformity appear under public but not private conditions. They suggested that women may conform more than men when others can scrutinize their behavior because women are concerned with maintaining group harmony. To test this idea, they brought college students into the laboratory and led them to discuss a controversial issue with three other students. Because they had obtained students' opinions via a pretest questionnaire, they were able to make sure that the three other students always disagreed with the participant. After the participant viewed the other group members' opinions on the issue of interest, the student was asked to indicate his or her own opinion on the issue. Students who changed their opinion in the direction of the other group members were said to be influenced. Students were randomly assigned to either a surveillance condition, in which they thought others would see their opinion on the issue, or a nonsurveillance condition, in which they thought they would give their opinion privately.

The results revealed an overall sex difference in attitude change, suggesting that women were more conforming than men. Women were more likely than men to change their opinions on the issue and agree with the confederates. However, when men and women in the surveillance versus nonsurveillance conditions were compared, an interesting pattern of findings emerged. As shown in Figure 6.4, women's level of conformity was unaffected by surveillance versus nonsurveillance, whereas men exhibited much *less* conformity in the surveillance than the nonsurveillance condition. Thus, it was not women's concern with maintaining group harmony that accounted for the sex difference in public conformity but men's concern with appearing independent and not susceptible to influence. This led the men to

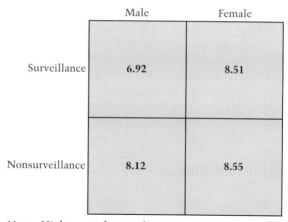

	Male	Female
Surveillance	6.92	8.51
Nonsurveillance	8.12	8.55

Note: Higher numbers indicate greater agreement or conformity.

FIGURE 6.4 Sex differences in conformity under public and private conditions. There were no sex differences in conformity when students reported their opinion privately (nonsurveillance condition). There was a sex difference when students reported their opinion publicly, but this was due to men being more independent rather than women being more conforming. It may be that men are more concerned with appearing independent from others rather than that women are concerned with appearing agreeable to others. *Source:* Adapted from Eagly, Wood, and Fishbaugh (1981).

resist attitude change. Thus, it is not so much that women are susceptible to influence as that men resist influence.

Sex differences in influenceability also are a function of the interaction styles people adopt when interacting with men versus women. Carli (1989) examined men's and women's interaction styles and linked them to influence. She placed 64 men and 64 women into either same-sex or mixed-sex dyads. Prior to the experiment, she obtained participants' opinions on two issues: lowering the drinking age and providing free day care for working parents. She then asked two people who disagreed about one of these issues to discuss the topic for 10 minutes.

One of the partners in each dyad was randomly assigned to try to persuade the partner. The discussion was videotaped and later coded for number of task contributions (giving suggestions or opinions), agreements, disagreements, questions, negative social behaviors (showing negative affect), and positive social behaviors (showing positive affect; see Table 6.2 for examples of codes). After the discussion, each member of the dyad indicated privately what his or her opinion was on the topic. The change in opinion from before to after the discussion was the measure of influence.

Neither task behavior nor positive social behavior was related to attitude change. Disagreement was related to *less* attitude change, or influence. The only interaction style that was associated with greater influ-

ence was agreement. People who interacted with a partner who expressed at least some agreement were more likely to change their attitudes in the direction of the partner than people who interacted with a partner who expressed complete disagreement. It makes sense that we are more receptive to the ideas of someone who finds a way to agree with us; disagreement puts us on the defensive. However, our intuition is to disagree with someone to change the person's mind. When people were randomly assigned to the persuade condition, they used more disagreement, less agreement, and more task behavior—but only with males, not with females. Unfortunately, this is exactly opposite of the kind of behavior that does persuade. Thus, it is not surprising that men and women were more successful in persuading females than males. Influence does not have as much to do with women's behavior as with the way people behave toward women; others express agreement with women, and agreement leads to influence. Figure 6.5 illustrates the process by which women come to be more easily influenced than men.

Carli (1989) concluded that women are more easily influenced than men due to the behavior that people use with women: agreement. People use ineffective influence strategies with men (e.g., disagreement) but display more agreement with women. And agreement is what leads to influence. Thus, women are not more easily influenced than men due to some

TABLE 6.2 Sample Interaction Styles

Task Behavior

"You should ask your roommate not to drink in your room."

Agreement

"I agree that alcoholism is an important problem in our society."

Disagreement

"I disagree that lowering the drinking age will solve any of our problems."

Questions

"Why do you think lowering the drinking age would decrease rates of alcoholism?"

Negative Social Behaviors

"If you think it is OK to drink any alcohol and drive, then you are an idiot."

Positive Social Behavior

"We all have to figure out how to deal with people who drink and drive."

Q: Why are women more easily influenced than men?

A: Because people (both men and women) agree more with women and agreement facilitates influence.

Being female ⟶ Others express agreement ⟶ Influence

FIGURE 6.5 Model of influence process.

fundamental female trait, but due to the fact that people feel more comfortable in interactions with women and thus display agreeable behavior.

Who Is Influential?

Men are more influential than women, partly because men are viewed as more credible sources. Would women be as influential as or more influential than men if their credibility were enhanced? Pugh and Wahrman (1983) addressed this question by giving college students a gender-neutral task and leading them to believe they were working with a member of the other sex who disagreed with them on how to solve the problem. Pugh and Wahrman found that women were more likely than men to defer to their partner's ideas. Although the task was thought to be gender-neutral, the investigators considered the possibility that respondents viewed men as more capable than women on the task. Thus, the investigators repeated the procedure in a second study by making sure students perceived the task as gender-neutral. They added a statement that men and women typically perform the same on the task. This addition did not alter the findings; men still were more influential than women. Finally, in a third study, Pugh and Wahrman convinced students that women perform better on the task than men by having them observe superior female performance on a related task. In this third study, there were no sex differences in influence. In other words, in the absence of information or when merely told that men and women have the same abilities, men are viewed as more influential than women. When it is made obvious that women are more skilled than men in an area (and, thus, more credible sources), men and women are then viewed as equally influential. In none

of the conditions were women more influential than men.

Are women less influential than men because of their language? Language cannot account for women's lack of influence. In fact, Carli (1990) found that women who use more traditional language can be more influential than women who use less traditional language. She instructed college students to listen to a speech that was either assertive or tentative and given by either a male or female confederate. The tentative version of the speech included tag questions, hedges, and disclaimers, whereas the assertive version did not. In the speech, the confederate argued that the college bus should begin charging a fare, an issue with which all participants disagreed. As shown in the left half of Figure 6.6, female speakers had a greater influence on female respondents when the speech was assertive rather than tentative; however, female speakers had a greater influence on male respondents when their speech was tentative rather than assertive. As shown in the right half of Figure 6.6, male speakers had a similar influence on respondents regardless of the style of their speech.

Interestingly, both male and female respondents rated the female tentative speaker as less competent and less knowledgeable than the female assertive speaker. Why were male respondents more influenced by a less competent speaker? Carli (1990) suggests that the first thing a person of lower status must convey to a person of higher status is that he or she is not trying to compete for status. Using tentative language communicates this. Thus, male respondents may have been more receptive to the female tentative speaker's arguments because they did not have to be concerned with status issues. The female assertive speaker might have been perceived as challenging the men's higher status. Thus,

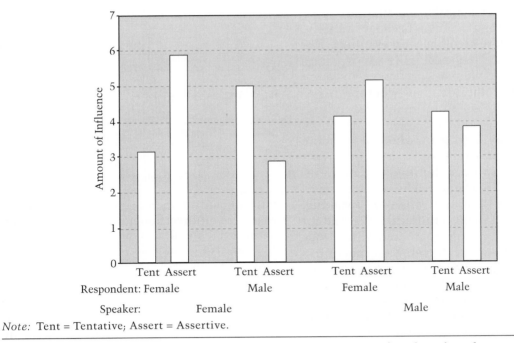

Note: Tent = Tentative; Assert = Assertive.

FIGURE 6.6   Female speakers were more effective in influencing females when they used assertive rather than tentative language. However, female speakers were more effective in influencing males when they used tentative rather than assertive language. Male speakers' influenceability was not affected by the nature of the language they used toward either a male or a female audience. *Source:* Adapted from Carli (1990).

women may have to adopt a more stereotypical style to influence men.

Another study showed that the same language or influence style may have different effects depending on whether it is displayed by a male or a female. College students were asked to view a videotape of either a male or a female speaker who discussed a position on an issue in either a sociable or task-oriented style. After the speech, students rated how much they liked the speaker and how much they agreed with the speaker's position on the issue. Male students found the male speaker with a task-oriented style more influential than the female speaker with a task-oriented style. As in the previous study, male students found the female speaker with a sociable style to be more influential than the female speaker with a task-oriented style. Female students, however, were equally influenced by task-oriented and sociable styles regardless of the speaker's sex (Carli, LaFleur, & Loeber, 1995). Both male and female students found the sociable speaker to be more likable than the task speaker. For male students, likability was strongly related to influence when the speaker was female but not when the speaker was male. Thus, for male students, the likability of a female speaker led to influence, and a sociable style but not a task-oriented style was associated with likability and influence. Again, men are more influenced by women who use a feminine rather than a masculine style of speaking.

In sum, it appears that men are more influential than women because they are viewed as more credible sources of information. It is difficult to enhance women's credibility. A woman's language may enhance her credibility, but whether it enhances her ability to influence depends on the sex of the audience. Women are more influenced by a woman who uses a more assertive, competent style, but men react negatively to this style. Men are more influenced by a woman who uses a traditional, more feminine style of speaking, largely because she is more likable. And for men, likability more than credibility leads to influence—if the person doing the influencing is female. Again, women are faced with a dilemma when interacting with men: if they behave in a way that enhances their competence in the eyes of men, it may also reduce men's liking for them and receptivity to their ideas. One explanation is that such behavior on the part of women challenges men's status.

Influence Strategies

Another reason women are more easily influenced and less influential than men may have to do with the ways men and women try to influence others. Some studies have found that men and women use different influence strategies. Falbo and Peplau (1980) examined influence strategies among 100 heterosexual and 100 homosexual college students. Students were asked to write essays about how they get their partner to do what they want. Strategies were coded on the two dimensions shown in Figure 6.7. One dimension ranges from direct, such as asking your partner to do something, to indirect, such as hinting about what you want your partner to do. The second dimension ranges

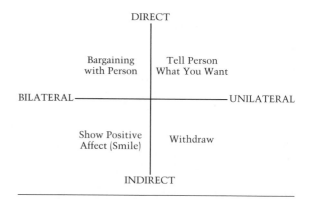

FIGURE 6.7 Two dimensions of influence. Examples of direct unilateral, direct bilateral, indirect unilateral, and indirect bilateral influence strategies are shown. *Source:* Adapted from Falbo and Peplau (1980).

from bilateral, such as trying to persuade your partner of your position, to unilateral, such as ignoring your partner's position and doing your own thing.

Falbo and Peplau (1980) found sex differences in influence strategies among heterosexuals only: men were more likely than women to engage in bilateral and direct strategies; women were more likely to engage in unilateral and indirect strategies. These sex differences were linked to the power differential between men and women. Heterosexuals of either sex who reported having greater power in their relationship were more likely to say that they used direct and bilateral influence strategies. Interestingly, there was no difference between the influence strategies that gay men and lesbians used with their partners. Perhaps this is because gay men and lesbians are with partners of the same sex, which reduces power differences.

Other studies have found more similarities than differences in the influence strategies men and women used

(Buss, Gomes, Higgins, & Lauterbach, 1987; Steil & Weltman, 1992). Power may have a greater effect on influence strategies than respondent's sex. In one study, college students imagined they were interacting with a same-sex or other-sex person and had more power (an expert), less power (a novice), or power similar to the person (Sagrestano, 1992). Students were asked how they would influence their partner. Men and women reported similar influence strategies regardless of whether their partner was male or female. Both men and women were most likely to use direct and bilateral strategies. However, the power relation between participant and partner affected influence strategies; direct and unilateral strategies were used more often by participants who were experts, and bilateral strategies were used more often by participants who were equal in power to their partner.

There is cross-cultural evidence that power is a stronger predictor of influence strategies than sex. Influence strategies were investigated among U.S., Japanese, and Korean students attending a U.S. college (Steil & Hillman, 1993). The three most frequently used strategies by all three groups were direct influence strategies: stating the importance of one's position, reasoning, and convincing the partner. The three least frequently used strategies by all three groups were indirect influence strategies: acquiescing, evading, and using an advocate. The investigators found that power, but not sex, was associated with strategy use. People who said they had greater power in their relationships were less likely to use indirect influence tactics. There were minor cultural differences in that Japanese and Korean students tended to endorse more polite tactics than U.S. students. For example, Japanese and Korean students said they were more likely to

acquiesce and less likely to try to convince their partner compared to U.S. students.

Is it also possible that personality characteristics that are correlated with sex determine influence strategies? Steil and Weltman (1992) examined whether personality variables (e.g., nurturance and dominance) were associated with influence strategies. They found that women engaged in more indirect bilateral strategies than men, but that personality characteristics accounted for this sex difference. Greater nurturance and less dominance were associated with the use of indirect bilateral strategies.

Another variable that has been shown to account for sex differences in influence strategies is self-confidence. College students enacted the role of supervisor and attempted to influence the work of their subordinates (Instone, Major, & Bunker, 1983). Men exerted a greater number of influence attempts than women. Men were more self-confident than women, and self-confident people exerted a greater number of influence attempts than people who lacked self-confidence. There were few sex differences in the nature of the influence.

In short, it appears that there is little evidence from the recent literature that men and women use different influence strategies. However, the majority of this research is based on self-reports. Observational studies of how men and women exert influence in the real world might reveal more differences. It also may be that the traits linked to sex, such as nurturance and dominance, are stronger predictors of influence strategies than sex per se. Because sex differences in influence strategies seem to be small to nonexistent, it is unlikely that influence strategies can explain why men are more influential or women are more easily influenced.

LEADERSHIP

Who Emerges as a Leader

Who is more likely to emerge as a leader in these group interaction studies: a man or a woman? Eagly and Karau (1991) conducted a meta-analysis on studies that evaluated who emerged as the leader of a group. Leadership was measured by both objective indicators of group participation as well as respondents' reports of who appeared to be the group leader. Across laboratory and field studies and across both measures of leadership, men were more likely than women to emerge as leaders. Men contributed more to the group and were more likely to be perceived and chosen as leaders. But the nature of the leadership role influenced who emerged as a leader. Men were especially likely to emerge as leaders when task leadership was needed ($d = +.41$). When the nature of the task was not specified, men also were more likely to emerge as leaders, but the effect was smaller ($d = +.29$). When social leadership was necessary, there was a small effect for women to be more likely to emerge as leaders ($d = -.18$).

There are two methodological limitations of this research. First, the majority of the studies were conducted with college students in the laboratory. More studies are needed in the field to see who actually emerges as a leader in an organization. Second, the laboratory interactions are brief; in the real world, we usually have more than 30 minutes to determine who will be the chairperson of an organization. In their meta-analytic review, Eagly and Karau (1991) found that the length of the interaction influenced who emerged as a leader: males were more likely to emerge as leaders when the group interaction lasted less than 20 minutes ($d = +.58$), but there was no sex difference if the group lasted over

one session ($d = +.09$). Again, this suggests that when people have little information about one another, gender-role stereotypes influence behavior. With more time, and presumably more information, stereotypes have less impact on behavior.

Perhaps more important than sex, certain personality characteristics predict the emergence of a leader. In a study of college students enrolled in a business course, masculinity, but not femininity (as measured with the BSRI), was associated with self-perceptions of leadership and the group's perception of leadership in work groups (Kent & Moss, 1994). Self-esteem, dominance, and other traits related to masculinity also seem to predict leadership (Aries, 1996). However, it is unclear whether these same traits predict leadership in women. Masculine traits are a stronger predictor of leadership in men because the traits are congruent with men's gender role.

One masculine trait that has been associated with leadership is dominance. Men may be more likely than women to emerge as leaders because they behave in a more dominant manner. Nyquist and Spence (1986) paired high- and low-dominant persons together in same-sex and cross-sex dyads, as shown in Figure 6.8. The dyad was first asked to decide who would be the leader on a gender-neutral task (a board game). In same-sex dyads, the high-dominant person was chosen to be the leader 73% of the time. In dyads where the male was high in dominance and the female was low in dominance, the high-dominant male was chosen to be the leader in 90% of the cases. Yet, in dyads where the female was high in dominance and the male was low in dominance, the high-dominant female was chosen to be the leader only 35% of the time. Thus, when the role of dominance was congruent with sex, the choice of leader was clear: male. But was the male chosen because of his sex or because of his dominance? When the male was low in

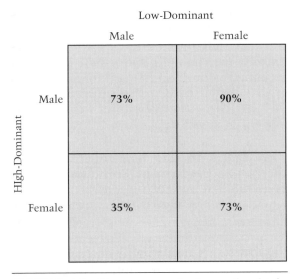

Low-Dominant

	Male	Female
Male	73%	90%
Female	35%	73%

High-Dominant

FIGURE 6.8 Percentage of times the high-dominant person was chosen to be the leader. High- and low-dominant people interacted in same-sex or cross-sex dyads. The person who was high in dominance was most likely to emerge as the leader when the high-dominant person was male or when the dyad consisted of two women. When a high-dominant woman interacted with a low-dominant man, the man rather than the high-dominant person was more likely to emerge as a leader. This study showed that sex was more important than dominance in determining who was chosen to be a leader. *Source:* Adapted from Nyquist and Spence (1986).

dominance and the female was high in dominance, the male was still chosen. In this case, sex appeared to be more important than dominance in establishing who was to be the leader.

The emergence of the male as the leader in groups composed of a high-dominant female and a low-dominant male was examined more closely by B. Davis and Gilbert (1989). They wondered if men emerged as leaders in these dyads because the dyad members did not know each other

and therefore had no information on which they could base their choice of leader. Hence, the participants relied on stereotypes. To address this issue, B. Davis and Gilbert conducted a similar experiment but first had dyad members work together on a task that would reveal the personality trait of dominance. When participants were asked to choose a leader for a subsequent task, the high-dominant person was chosen to be the leader regardless of sex. In dyads with a high-dominant male and a low-dominant female, the high-dominant male was chosen to be leader 75% of the time. In dyads with a high-dominant female and a low-dominant male, the high-dominant female was chosen to be leader 71% of the time.

Taken together, these two studies show that we are more likely to rely on stereotypes in the absence of other information about people. But once we obtain more information, we are likely to use that information when deciding how to behave. This is the distinction I have previously made between category-based expectancies and target-based expectancies.

Leadership Styles

Do men and women have different styles of leadership? Eagly and Johnson (1990) conducted a meta-analytic review of sex differences in leadership style. Three leadership styles were evaluated: task-oriented, socioemotional, and democratic/autocratic. The task-oriented leader lays out plans, articulates rules, and organizes how a task will be accomplished. The socioemotional leader is focused on maintaining group harmony, concentrates on helping people in the group, and explains problems in a friendly manner. The democratic leader encourages others to participate in the group's decision, whereas the autocratic leader discourages others' participation. Eagly and Johnson found no sex difference in task orientation ($d = .00$) or interpersonal orientation ($d = +.04$). Females, however, were found to be more democratic than males ($d = -.22$). The investigators examined the setting in which each study was conducted. They reasoned that sex differences in leadership style would be minimal in organizational settings where participants know one another, their roles are clear, and the nature of the task is clear. By contrast, the authors predicted that sex differences would appear in laboratory studies where participants are strangers and the task is ambiguous, a context in which gender roles would be salient. The results supported the hypothesis. Men and women did have different leadership styles in laboratory studies (men task-oriented and women socioemotional) but not in organizational studies. However, the sex difference in democratic leadership was consistent across the two types of studies.

It is possible that sex differences in leadership style appear only during the initial stages of an interaction when sex is salient. As people get to know one another, the leader, whether male or female, may modify his or her style to fit the needs of the group. To test this idea, undergraduates were placed in small groups to work on group projects (Spillman, Spillman, & Reinking, 1981). The small groups met four times over the semester. During the initial two meetings, women were more likely than men to use both a socioemotional and a task-oriented style of leadership. By the third and fourth meetings, however, sex differences in leadership style disappeared.

It is difficult to study sex differences in leadership style because our stereotypes about how men and women should behave may influence how we perceive the same behavior. Stereotypes also may influence self-perceptions. Snodgrass and Rosenthal (1984) found that female leaders perceived themselves to be less dominant than did male leaders, despite the fact that outside judges and subordinates perceived male and female leaders to be equally dominant.

Views of Leaders

The leadership role is incongruent with the female gender role. So how do people view women as leaders? Do people judge women leaders less harshly because they have overcome gender-role stereotypes? Or, do people evaluate women leaders more negatively because they are behaving in a way inconsistent with norms? Eagly et al. (1992) conducted a meta-analysis on studies that evaluated leaders to determine if people were biased for or against women. These studies typically presented people (often college students) either with written vignettes that manipulated the sex of a described leader or with confederates who enacted a leadership role. The meta-analysis found a very small effect indicating a bias against female leaders. People perceived female leaders to be less competent than male leaders ($d = +.09$) and were less satisfied with female compared to male leaders ($d = +.10$). The bias against female leaders was larger when they used a more masculine style of leadership (i.e., autocratic and directive). In addition, male respondents judged female leaders more harshly than did female respondents. This finding fits with other research reported in this chapter that women are not viewed favorably, especially by men, when they behave in ways that are inconsistent with the female gender role.

One study showed that people's nonverbal responses are more negative to female than male leaders. College students participated in groups led by male or female confederates (D. Butler & Geis, 1990). Judges observed students' nonverbal behavior in response to the leaders' behavior. Students provided more positive responses (smiling, nods of agreement) to male leaders and more negative responses (furrowing brows, nods of disagreement) to female leaders. These different responses occurred even though the leader's behavior was scripted and standardized.

However, studies of people in the workforce do not support a bias against female leaders. Three studies of employees' evaluations of their managers in business, industry, government, and health care found no bias against female leaders (Bass, Avolio, & Atwater, 1996). Subordinates were either more satisfied with female managers or equally satisfied with male and female managers. Across the three studies, female managers were rated as more charismatic, or as better role models, compared to male leaders. In a recent study of 2,482 managers from 459 organizations across the United States, women managers were perceived by their bosses and their employees to be better leaders in terms of communal characteristics (e.g., communication, feedback, and empowerment) as well as agentic characteristics (e.g., goal setting, decisiveness, and planning; Pfaff, 1999). In some occupations, a feminine leadership style is the most highly valued. For example, international managers are most effective if they have strong interpersonal and cooperative skills. Ironically, few women hold those positions (2% to 15%; H. Harris, 1998).

How do we reconcile the different findings from the laboratory and the field? Perhaps we should dismiss the laboratory studies because the tasks are not realistic. However, we should also realize that the men and women who are leaders in organizations are not necessarily a representative sample of men and women. It may take a certain kind of woman to emerge in a leadership role in the real world.

Like the research on language and influence, the way a woman behaves may have an effect on how she is viewed. One field study showed that the leadership style a woman manager uses has a strong impact on how she is perceived. Women leaders were evaluated more favorably when they used a socioemotional rather than a task-oriented leadership style (Callan, 1993). In this study, the most successful female leaders used a transformational style of leadership, which is a style that promotes development and growth among subordinates. These findings are similar to the one reported earlier in the chapter with respect to language: that language influences perceptions of women's credibility but does not have an impact on perceptions of men's credibility.

Summary

Gender and leadership is one area of research where the findings from laboratory studies may not generalize to the field. Men are more likely than women to emerge as leaders in laboratory studies where participants are often strangers and have only a brief opportunity to interact. Yet, even laboratory research has shown that this sex difference disappears when interactions are longer. More important than sex may be personality traits that go along with sex, such as dominance. In the real world, it is more likely that the dominant person will emerge as the leader regardless of sex. Of course, men are more likely than women to be dominant. Differences in men's and women's leadership style also appear to be more apparent in laboratory studies than in field studies; with longer contacts, sex differences in leadership styles disappear. Men and women are likely to be responding to the situation, which includes the other people in the group.

Differences in perceptions of men and women as leaders also seem to be stronger in laboratory than field studies. In laboratory studies, there is a small but consistent negative bias against female leaders. The bias is especially strong among men. In the field, however, people view women leaders favorably, sometimes even more favorably than men. Thus, this is one area of research where it is especially important that we maximize the external validity of our controlled laboratory studies.

EXPLANATIONS FOR SEX DIFFERENCES IN COMMUNICATION

There are a variety of explanations for the differences I have discussed in this chapter on male and female communication. The first explanation states that differences in communication evolve from children's tendencies to play with same-sex peers. The second theory, status theory, suggests that any differences in communication between men and women are due to their unequal status. Once one controls for the status or power differential in relationships, sex differences disappear. Third is social role theory, which argues that the roles men and women hold in society are responsible for sex differences in communication. In particular, the female role emphasizes connections to others, whereas the male role emphasizes separation from others. I discuss the data that support each theory, including studies that pit status and social role theory against one another.

Sex-Segregated Interactions in Early Life

INTERACTION STYLES.   Maccoby (1990) suggests that children's style of interacting with same-sex peers is responsible for the sex differences in interaction styles that emerge in adulthood. Boys' interactions are hierarchical, oriented toward establishing dominance. Girls' interactions are more lateral, oriented toward providing mutual support. These differences could account for the task-oriented style of men and the socioemotional style of women.

LANGUAGE.   Men and women may use different language because different kinds of language were functional during same-sex play in childhood. Maltz and Borker (1982) argue that boys and girls grow up in different cultures and these cultures contribute to sex differences in language. It is not that boys and girls are socialized to talk in different ways; rather, different kinds of conversation have evolved in same-sex girls' groups compared to same-sex boys' groups. Recall that boys play in larger groups, often outdoors, and with a background of noise and a tone of competition. This kind of play requires assertive language and the use of demands rather than requests. Girls' play is often quieter, more cooperative, nonhierarchical, and takes place in smaller groups. This kind of play is more consistent with the use of polite suggestions. According to Maltz and Borker, sex differences in language are larger among children than adults. As adults, we learn how to interact with the other sex and accommodate our behavior accordingly.

Status Theory

Sex is inherently confounded with status. Men have a higher status and more power than women. Below, I describe how status may explain sex differences in interaction styles, in language, in nonverbal behavior, and in influenceability.

INTERACTION STYLES.   One theory of how status influences behavior is **expectations states theory.** According to this theory, group members form expectations about their own and others' abilities, which are based on the value they assign to people in the group. We expect the high-status person to contribute more and the low-status person to facilitate the contributions of the high-status person (Meeker & Weitzel-O'Neill, 1985; Smith-Lovin & Robinson, 1992). Because men have a higher status than women, we have higher expectations of men's abilities compared to women's abilities. This theory suggests that sex differences in interaction styles stem from our more positive evaluation of men's abilities compared to women's. In other words, in the absence of any other information about men's and women's abilities, sex will be interpreted as status during a group interaction.

One study that supported this theory was conducted by W. Wood and Karten (1986). College students were assigned to four-person, mixed-sex groups, which met to discuss a task. In half of the groups, one male and one female were randomly assigned to have a high-status position and the other male and female to have a low-status position. Status was manipulated by revealing either high or low scores on a fake aptitude test. The other half of the groups did not have status manipulated, and group members were aware only of each other's sex. Group members were asked to discuss a dilemma and resolve it. When status was not manipulated, group members perceived men as more competent than women. Men also talked more than women in the groups. In the right half of Figure 6.9, you can see that men engage in more task behavior than women. Status had no meaning in this condition because it was not manipulated. For analysis purposes, the investigators arbitrarily divided people into a high- and a low-status group. As shown in the left half of Figure 6.9, when status was manipulated, high-status people engaged in more task behavior than low-status people regardless of sex. Further, group members perceived high-status people, regardless of sex, as more competent than low-status people. As shown in the left half of Figure 6.10, low-status people engaged in more positive social behavior

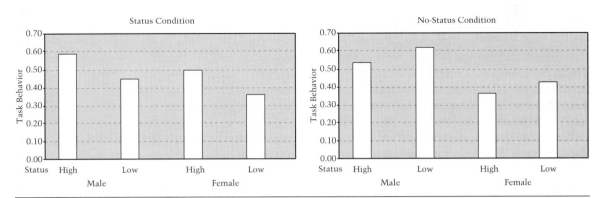

FIGURE 6.9 Effect of sex and status on task behavior. When status was manipulated (status condition), the high-status person, male or female, was more likely to engage in task behavior than the low-status person. When status was not manipulated (no-status condition), men were more likely than women to engage in task behavior. (In the latter case, people were randomly placed into high- and low-status groups for the purpose of data analysis; status had no meaning.) *Source:* Adapted from Wood and Karten (1986).

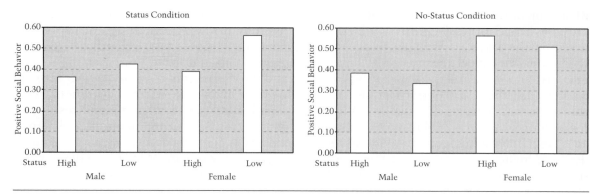

FIGURE 6.10 Effect of sex and status on social behavior. When status was manipulated (status condition), the low-status person, male or female, was more likely to engage in positive social behavior than the high-status person. When status was not manipulated (no-status condition), women were more likely than men to engage in positive social behavior. *Source:* Adapted from Wood and Karten (1986).

than high-status people. However, when status was not manipulated (right half of Figure 6.10), women engaged in more positive social behavior than did men. This study shows that status is responsible for people's tendency to perceive men as more competent than women and that status is responsible for some of the sex differences in interaction styles.

Status theory also was tested by a field study of adults in the community (Moskowitz et al., 1994). Participants monitored their interactions with their boss, coworkers, and subordinates over 20 days. For each interaction, respondents rated whether dominant versus submissive behavior and agreeable versus quarrelsome behavior occurred. The former category of behavior was referred to as agency and the latter as communion. The status of the work role (whether the person was a supervisor or subordinate or coworker) but not sex predicted agentic behaviors. People were more dominant when they were supervisors and more submissive when they were supervisees, regardless of sex. However, sex, but not the status of the work role, predicted communal behavior: women behaved more

communally than men regardless of the status of their interaction partners. Thus, this study partly supported status theory and partly supported social role theory.

Expectations states theory says that we have higher expectations for the contributions of the high-status person. However, the relevance of the task to men and women may alter peoples' expectations about capabilities. We expect men to be more competent than women on masculine tasks, and we expect women to be more competent on feminine tasks. Yet, the sex difference in interaction styles does not necessarily disappear or reverse itself when feminine tasks are studied (Meeker & Weitzel-O'Neill, 1985). Thus, status based on expectations states theory alone cannot explain sex differences in interaction styles.

LANGUAGE. If a male talks more, interrupts more, and uses fewer hedges in an interaction with a female, one cannot discern whether the difference is due to sex or status. This issue was addressed in a study that measured relative status within a couple and also included same-sex couples, where sex is held constant (Kollock,

Blumstein, & Schwartz, 1985). Among heterosexual couples, communication styles were largely similar among men and women who had equal power. Among heterosexual and homosexual couples with unequal power, the investigators found that the more powerful person talked more, interrupted more, used fewer tag questions, and used fewer back-channel responses. (Recall that back-channel responses include sentence completion, brief questions of clarification, and the minimal response.) In other words, the more powerful person used the more powerful language.

Another study compared the effects of sex and status on language and found that status accounted for differences in verbal communication but that sex accounted for differences in nonverbal communication (C. Johnson, 1994). Undergraduates role-played three-person organizations, in which one member was assigned to be a leader and two were assigned to be employees. Four groups were examined: male manager with male employees, male manager with female employees, female manager with male employees, and female manager with female employees. Overall, managers engaged in more talking, used less back-channel communication, and used fewer qualifiers compared to employees—regardless of manager's sex, employees' sex, or the sex composition of the group. Thus, status rather than sex was linked to differences in language. Nonverbal behavior, specifically, smiling and laughing, was not predicted by status but was predicted by sex: in general, females laughed more than males, regardless of their position in the organization. Surprisingly, the most smiling was by males in mixed-sex groups regardless of whether they were managers or employees; the least smiling occurred among males in same-sex groups.

NONVERBAL BEHAVIOR. Henley (1977) was one of the first to argue that differences in nonverbal behavior imply power or status.

She argued that the greater social sensitivity of women was due to their low status. She suggested that women compared to men would be better decoders of emotions, regardless of the sex of the person expressing the emotion. According to status theory, the reason women would have better decoding skills than men and engage in some nonverbal behaviors more frequently than men (e.g., smiling) is that women are in a lower-status position in society. It is important for low-status people to monitor the environment because other people have influence over them. Henley suggested that her theory applied to racial comparisons in nonverbal behavior. She argued that Black people would be better decoders of emotion than White people because Black people are in a lower-status position. (I would like to point out that there is no evidence to date to support these kinds of racial differences in nonverbal behaviors—which calls a general theory of status into question.)

Status theory was tested as an explanation of women's greater interpersonal sensitivity compared to men. Women may be more sensitive to others' feelings because it is more important for the low-status person in a relationship to pay attention to the high-status person's feelings than vice versa. After all, the high-status person controls the resources and usually has a greater influence on the low-status person's life. To test this hypothesis, a study was designed in which one person from a group of same-sex and mixed-sex dyads taught the other person finger spelling (Snodgrass, 1985). Thus, status was manipulated by assigning one person to be the teacher and one person to be the student. Two sensitivity scores were calculated: the first measure reflects how aware one is of another person's view of oneself; the second reflects the accuracy of one's view of the partner. Snodgrass found that low-status people (students) were more sensitive than high-status people (teachers) at perceiving how they were viewed by others. However, there was no difference between high- and low-status people's ability to accurately characterize their partner. Sex was not related to either measure of interpersonal sensitivity. Snodgross concluded that "women's intuition" should be renamed "subordinate's intuition." She reasoned that it was more important for a subordinate to know how the leader feels about the subordinate than it was for the leader to know how the subordinate feels about the leader. Snodgrass did find that females were more sensitive to males than to females whether they were assigned to the high-status or the low-status role. Males were equally sensitive to males and females.

One problem with the Snodgrass (1985) study is that one cannot tell if subordinates were more accurate in their perceptions of how the leaders felt about them because of the subordinate's sensitivity or because of the high-status person's greater ability to convey accurate information. Later, Snodgrass and her colleagues addressed this issue (Snodgrass, Hecht, & Ploutz-Snyder, 1998). They found interpersonal sensitivity to be more strongly associated with the leader being expressive than the subordinate being an accurate perceiver. Therefore, the reason subordinates are more sensitive to the leader's feelings about the subordinate have more to do with the leader clearly expressing those feelings than with the subordinate being especially sensitive to those feelings. In sum, there is little evidence that subordinates have more intuition than leaders about each other's feelings or are more motivated than leaders to accurately decode the other person's feelings.

There are additional problems with the status theory of decoding ability. When status is measured in terms of socioeconomic status, lower status is either unrelated or associated with worse decoding ability (Hall, Halberstadt, & O'Brien, 1997). If the reason for sex differences in nonverbal behavior were entirely due to status, the findings would generalize to other indicators of status besides sex, such as income or race.

Status has been related to other nonverbal behaviors, such as smiling, but the relation is complicated. Status is not related to the mere tendency to smile but to the freedom to smile. Hecht and LaFrance (1998) assigned undergraduates to interact in dyads in which members were either equal or unequal in power. In the equal condition, the two people engaged in a conversation to get to know one another. In the unequal condition, one person was randomly assigned to enact the role of interviewer and the other to enact the role of job applicant. These five-minute interactions were videotaped and smiling was coded every five seconds. The status of the person did not predict smiling. There was more total smiling in the equal power condition than the unequal power condition. In terms of sex differences, females engaged in more smiling than males, but only in the equal power condition. Interestingly, smiling was positively correlated with reports of positive affect for the interviewer but not for the applicant. In other words, the interviewer appeared to smile when he or she was feeling positive, whereas the applicant's smiling was unrelated to how he or she was feeling. Smiling was also positively correlated with positive affect for those in the equal power condition. The investigators suggested that people in positions of low power have constraints imposed on them in terms of how they behave; they are not as free as those in higher-power positions to express their feelings.

Status also has been associated with touch. A review of the literature concluded that people in high-power positions were more likely to initiate touch than people in low-power positions (Stier & Hall, 1984). However, this conclusion was tempered by the fact that status has been measured quite loosely in many studies. The one study with an exceptionally good measure of status found the opposite pattern of results. Touch among male state legislators was observed (Goldstein & Jeffords, 1981). Status was measured objectively, based on the length of time the legislator had served and the committees to which he had been assigned. The investigators observed a trend for low-status people to initiate more touch toward high-status people than vice versa. The authors point out that they never saw the governor touch one of the legislators but they frequently observed legislators touching the governor.

One way to resolve the discrepancies of whether status is related to touch is to examine the nature of the touch. In an observational study of people at an academic conference, status was related to different kinds of touch (Hall, 1996). High-status people were observed to engage in more affectionate touching, such as touching an arm or shoulder, whereas low-status people were more likely to engage in formal touching, such as a handshake. In this study, status was measured in terms of age, rank at the institution, reputation of the institution, and number of articles published in the previous few years. The authors concluded that high- and low-status persons may be equally likely to engage in touching but that they initiate touch for different reasons: high-status people may touch to display their power, whereas low-status people may touch to gain power (Stier & Hall, 1984).

INFLUENCEABILITY. Sex differences in influenceability may be due to status. Drawing on expectations states theory, Lockheed and Zelditch (1985) argued that the high-status person is more influential because

we have higher expectations for this person's performance. If the task is masculine or gender-neutral, we will have higher expectations for men's performance and confer men greater status. If the task is feminine, we will have higher expectations for women's performance and confer women greater status. In a review of 64 studies on influenceability in mixed-sex groups, 45 showed men to have greater influence, 11 showed no difference, and 8 showed women to have greater influence (Lockheed & Zelditch, 1985). Sex differences in influenceability were strongest when the task was masculine, when we presumably assign men a high status. On feminine tasks, there was typically no sex difference in influenceability, but some studies showed a female advantage.

Status also may explain who is more susceptible to influence during an interaction. Eagly and Wood (1982) had college students read vignettes in which one person was trying to influence another. In the experimental condition, information about the dyad members' respective statuses was manipulated by providing job titles. In the control condition, no information except the dyad members' sex was given. In the control condition, students perceived females as lower in status and more susceptible to influence than males. In the experimental condition, students perceived the low-status person as being more susceptible to influence than the high-status person regardless of sex.

Status and social role explanations were compared to one another in a study of the influence strategies used among gay, lesbian, and heterosexual couples (Howard, Blumstein, & Schwartz, 1986). The investigators measured status characteristics of each member of the couple, such as education, income, physical attractiveness, and commitment to the relationship. The person who had less income was more likely to use the weaker tactics of supplication (e.g., pleading, crying, acting helpless) and manipulation. The person who was less physically attractive and more dependent on the relationship was more likely to use supplication. Finally, the person who was more committed to the relationship was more likely to use manipulation and bullying. The investigators concluded that positions of strength were associated with strong influence tactics and positions of weakness were associated with weak influence tactics. Status alone did not account for all of the differences in influence tactics, however. Sex and gender role also were associated with some of the influence tactics. Men were found to use more disengagement than women. People who scored higher on femininity and lower on masculinity were more likely to use supplication. Lower masculinity scores were associated with greater bargaining (reasoning, compromising). Thus, both status and social role were associated with influence strategies. Sexual orientation had no effect on influence strategies.

SUMMARY.   Status theory suggests that sex differences in communication are due to the status differences between men and women. The best tests of this theory have been laboratory studies in which men and women are randomly assigned to high- and low-status positions. These kinds of studies have made a convincing case that sex differences in interaction styles are largely due to status. Especially with respect to task behavior or agentic behavior, there is evidence that this behavior is displayed by the high-status person regardless of sex. There also is evidence that many of the sex differences in language are due to status. It is the lower-status person rather than the female person who uses qualifying phrases and tentative language. Status theory has much more difficulty explaining sex differences in nonverbal behavior. Status does not

seem to be a good explanation of women's better decoding ability, of women's smiling, or of touch. In regard to influenceability, status theory certainly plays a role in why we perceive men as more influential and why women are more easily influenced. Status is related to some sex differences in influence strategies but not others.

Social Role Theory

Social role theory suggests that our expectations about male and female behavior stem from our stereotypes about the different social roles men and women hold in society. Women are more likely than men to hold domestic roles, for example. Even within the work setting, men and women are likely to hold different roles; for example, men are more likely to be the leaders and the supervisors, whereas women are more likely to be the subordinates. Gender roles are an important social role that men and women hold, leading men to behave in agentic or instrumental ways and women to behave in communal or relationship-maintaining ways. To the extent that other roles become more salient than gender roles, people's behavior will be more influenced by other roles than gender roles.

INTERACTION STYLES.   Social role theory has been applied to sex differences in interaction style by Parsons and Bales (1955). They first observed that small group interactions were characterized by two forms of group behavior: task behavior and social behavior. They argued that both kinds of behavior were important to the viability of the group but that the two were incompatible. In other words, different people were needed to serve the two distinct functions. This idea was confirmed by Bales and Slater (1955), who observed that the best-liked person in the group was not the person who was considered to have the best ideas. The person with the best ideas gave suggestions and opinions: task-oriented behavior. The person who was best-liked made statements indicating group solidarity, made statements that relieved group tension, and asked for opinions and suggestions: socioemotional behavior.

Parsons and Bales (1955) suggested that families were small groups, and that husbands and wives held different roles within the family. The father is responsible for task behavior, such as providing for the family, whereas the mother is responsible for socioemotional behavior, such as raising children. Parsons and Bales linked men's and women's traditional family roles to group interactions. They suggested that all groups had two functions: to accomplish the goals of the group and to preserve the group as a unit. They suggested that the first function fit with men's instrumental roles and the second fit with women's socioemotional roles.

Other people have more directly argued that men and women display different interaction styles because of the way they are socialized in our society (W. Wood & Rhodes, 1992). Females are socialized to be communal, whereas males are socialized to be agentic. A communal personality is likely to lead to positive social behavior during group interactions, whereas an agentic personality is likely to lead to instrumental social behavior during group interactions.

The study previously described by Carli (1989) supports a social role rather than a status interpretation of interaction styles. She found that the largest differences in task behavior and social behavior were in comparisons of men and women in same-sex dyads rather than mixed-sex dyads. If sex differences in interaction were due to status, one would expect larger differences in interaction styles in mixed-sex or unequal status dyads as opposed to same-sex dyads.

LANGUAGE. It has been debated whether women's language is related to women's lower status or to the female gender role's greater emphasis on relationships. Some aspects of women's language are related to status and some are related to relationship maintenance. Hedges and disclaimers may reflect women's lower status compared to men, but intensifiers and verbal reinforcers may reflect women's socioemotional orientation. These ideas were examined in a study of same-sex and mixed-sex dyads' discussions of a topic on which the partners disagreed (Carli, 1990). Women used more disclaimers and hedges in mixed-sex than in same-sex dyads, which suggests that status played a role in the behavior. However, women used more intensifiers and verbal reinforcers compared to men in same-sex dyads, which is the kind of language that serves to maintain relationships.

NONVERBAL BEHAVIOR. Many of the nonverbal behaviors in which women engage can be viewed as behaviors that promote and foster good relationships. Smiling at others, gazing at others, and standing close to others can all be viewed as affiliative behavior. Recall that the study conducted by C. Johnson (1994) showed that sex rather than status was related to nonverbal behavior, such as smiling and laughing. A recent study by Hall and Friedman (1999) also showed that status could not explain sex differences in nonverbal behavior. Employees engaged in two tasks with one other employee. Videotapes of these interactions showed that women were warmer, more expressive, smiled more, nodded more, and interrupted less compared to men. The individual's status within the organization or relative to the partner did not explain these sex differences. It is women's relationship orientation that may explain why women are better able to detect another's emotion and better able to convey emotion, but not necessarily more able to detect deception.

SUMMARY. Social role theory states that the differences in men's and women's communication styles have to do with the different social roles men and women hold in our society, the male role being agentic and the female role being communal. Social role theory makes some contribution to all of the sex differences discussed in this chapter. Men's task behavior and women's positive social behavior fit their social roles. There are some aspects of language that fit men's goal of gaining control over the interaction (e.g., directives) and some aspects that fit women's goal of encouraging communication (e.g., back-channel responses). Social role theory is most helpful in explaining sex differences in nonverbal behavior. Women's smiling, touching (in some contexts), decoding ability, and expressions of emotions are all aimed at fostering relationships.

SUMMARY

Boys and girls clearly have different styles of interacting with one another. Boys play in groups that are loud, boisterous, and hierarchical, whereas girls play in dyads that are quiet, conversational, and egalitarian. A strong preference to play with same-sex peers likely exacerbates the difference in play styles. The source of the different styles—biology versus socialization and cognition—is not clear. The distinct play styles map onto the differences in adult interaction styles. In general, studies of small groups show that men are more task-oriented and women are more socioemotional. However, these general findings are qualified by a number of variables: the

nature of the task, the sex of the interaction partner, and the length of the interaction. Sex differences are strongest for gender-typed tasks, for interactions with same-sex people, and when interactions are brief.

Men and women differ in their use of some features of language. Men's language is more instrumental, succinct, and directive, whereas women's language is more affective, elaborative, and indirect. Women's language has been described as promoting relationships but also as being unassertive. Women's style of speaking appears to have negative implications when used by women but not men. In particular, men like—but view as less competent—a woman who uses feminine rather than masculine language.

There are a number of sex differences in nonverbal behavior: women smile more, gaze more, are better at conveying emotion, and better at decoding others' emotions compared to men. Sex differences in touch are more complicated. Among children, touch is more frequent among same-sex peers than cross-sex peers. Among adults, touch is more frequent among cross-sex dyads than same-sex dyads. Within adult cross-sex dyads, touch is determined by relationship status: men initiate touch during the early stages of a relationship, and women initiate touch during the later stages. In general, sex differences in nonverbal behavior are more frequently observed among same-sex dyads than cross-sex dyads. In addition to sex, gender roles may influence nonverbal behavior. However, these effects have rarely been explored.

I examined two specific kinds of interactions in which gender may be quite salient. There is a pervasive conception that men and women provide different kinds of support when sharing problems. Men are thought to provide advice and women to provide sympathy. Laboratory studies, however, have revealed more support for the latter than the former. Gender also has been considered an important variable that influences the communication between patient and physician. Female physicians provide more emotional support but also more information; in response, patients provide more information to female than male physicians. The interaction between the female physician and the male patient is awkward, most likely because the status of the roles is incongruent with gender.

Research on social influence generally shows that men are more influential and women are more easily influenced. Men are more influential partly due to their being viewed as more credible sources of information. There is some evidence that women are more influential when they adopt a feminine, less assertive way of speaking than when they adopt a more masculine, self-confident style—at least when the audience is male. Studies have shown that susceptibility to influence depends on the nature of the task, whether responses are made in private or public, and even whether the article is authored primarily by men or women! If women are more easily influenced than men, a primary reason seems to be the way people interact with women. People are nicer to women, more agreeable; people argue with men. Agreement leads to influence, but disagreement does not. Do sex differences in influence have anything to do with the styles men and women use? Early studies indicated that men use more direct influence tactics compared to women. However, more recent studies show that other variables, such as the personality trait of dominance and relationship characteristics, are better predictors of influence strategies.

If men are more influential, it follows that men are more likely to assume the role of leader in a group. Men are more likely to emerge as leaders, especially when the task is masculine, when interactions are brief, and when men behave in ways congruent with their gender role (i.e., dominant). Sex differences in leadership style depend heavily on whether the study is conducted in the laboratory or the field. In laboratory studies where interactions are brief and participants do not know each other, sex differences appear. In studies of organizations in real-world settings, sex differences disappear, with the exception that women are more democratic than men. Are male and female leaders viewed differently? Laboratory studies indicate a bias against women, whereas field studies indicate a bias in favor of women. Some research shows the same style may be viewed differently when displayed by a man versus a woman. Again, women seem to benefit from using a more gender-congruent, socioemotional style than a gender-incongruent, task-oriented style of leadership.

There are three primary explanations for sex differences in communication: sex-segregated interactions in early life, status, and social role. Boys' and girls' tendencies to interact with same-sex peers leads to divergent play styles that include different forms of communication. According to status theory, men's communication is a function of their higher status and women's communication is a function of their lower status. A number of compelling studies show that men and women behave the same when status is held constant. Evidence for status theory is especially strong in studies of group interactions. According to social role theory, men's communication is a function of their instrumental orientation, and women's communication is a function of their expressive orientation. Support for this theory comes largely from studies showing that nonverbal differences between men and women persist across situations, including different statuses.

DISCUSSION QUESTIONS

1. Compare laboratory and field research on sex differences in communication. For which domains might different conclusions be reached?
2. Discuss boys' and girls' different play styles and explanations as to their origins.
3. What are some of the factors that influence men's and women's interaction styles?
4. Which sex differences in language and nonverbal behavior are best explained by status theory, and which are best explained by social role theory?
5. Imagine that you are studying patient-physician communication. What other variables would be important to know besides the sex of the participants?
6. What trait variables and what situational variables lead to being influenced?
7. What is the best leadership style for women to adopt? Under what circumstances?
8. Do men and women respond to problems differently?

SUGGESTED READING

Aries, E. (1996). *Men and women in interaction.* New York: Oxford University Press.

Carli, L.L. (1989). Gender differences in interaction style and influence. *Journal of Personality and Social Psychology, 56,* 565–576.

Canary, D.J., & K. Dindia (Eds.), *Sex differences and similarities in communication: Critical essays and empirical investigations of sex and gender in interaction.* Mahwah, NJ: Erlbaum.

Fischer, A.H. (1997). *Gender and emotion.* New York: Cambridge University Press.

Maccoby, E.E. (1998). *The two sexes: Growing up apart, coming together.* Cambridge, MA: Harvard University Press.

KEY TERMS

Back-channel response—Response that facilitates communication, including sentence completion and use of the minimal response.

Egoistic dominance—Interaction style characterized by verbal aggression that intends to demonstrate superiority over other participants in the interaction.

Expectations states theory—States that group members form expectations about their own and others' abilities which influence the nature of interactions.

Minimal response—A response that encourages the speaker to continue, such as "uh-huh" or "OK."

Negative social behavior—Behavior during group interaction that could harm a relationship, such as disagreement and provoking conflict.

Positive social acts—Social behaviors engaged in during group interactions that are intended to maintain group harmony.

Prosocial dominance—Interaction style characterized by providing instruction or assistance that intends to foster connection between those involved in the interaction.

Relational aggression—An aggressive interaction behavior usually expressed by girls that is characterized by social alienation tactics such as excluding someone from an activity or threatening not to be a person's friend anymore.

Task behavior—Social behavior, such as asking questions and offering suggestions, that is directed toward achieving a specific goal.

7

Friendship

Who symbolizes friendship to you? What are some famous pairs of friends? Batman and Robin, Sherlock Holmes and Watson, Tom Sawyer and Huckleberry Finn, Butch Cassidy and the Sundance Kid, the Lone Ranger and Tonto. What do all these pairs of friends have in common? They are men. When I asked some students if they could think of a famous pair of female friends, the best anyone could come up with was Laverne and Shirley. Does the bond between two men epitomize friendship? As you will see in this chapter, it depends on what constitutes friendship.

Much of this chapter focuses on friendships between men and friendships between women, or same-sex friends. Although romantic partners can certainly be friends (in fact, I hope they are!), studies on friendship typically focus on platonic, nonromantic relationships. However, platonic friendship does exist between men and women. This area of research is referred to as cross-sex friendship, and I discuss it toward the end of the chapter. Today, one arena in which cross-sex friendships are likely to form is in the workplace. Because women are almost

as likely as men to work outside the home and because women are more likely to work in jobs that were once held exclusively by men, men and women are more likely to come into contact with one another at work. I examine the scant literature on friendships at work. The literature on same-sex friendship and cross-sex friendship typically assumes heterosexuality. Therefore, I also review the research on friendship among gay men and lesbians.

There are at least two levels of analyses to the study of gender and friendship (P. Wright, 1989). First, there is the **dispositional level of analysis,** which emphasizes the characteristics of the person as a determinant of friendship. What characteristics of a person predict friendship? One attribute of a person is his or her sex, another is his or her gender role. An example of a dispositional analysis is the research showing that women's relationships are more intimate than those of men because women are more likely than men to self-disclose. The analysis focuses on a characteristic of women: their tendency to self-disclose. There is also a **structural level of analysis** that emphasizes the different positions of men and women in society. One position or role in society that men traditionally have held more than women is the work role. An example of a structural level of analysis is the research showing that men have more cross-sex friendships than women because men are more likely than women to work outside the home. The structural level of analysis also calls attention to the impact of situational variables on gender and friendship.

In reviewing research on friendship, I begin with a brief description of the nature of children's friendships, then describe in more detail the nature of adult friendship. I discuss specific aspects of friendship such as self-disclosure, intimacy, and conflict. The structural level of analysis appears as I describe how friendship changes across the life span. Then I turn to the literature on cross-sex friendship. I compare cross-sex friendship to same-sex friendship, describe the unique features of cross-sex friendship, and discuss changes in the structure of cross-sex friendship across the life span. The literature on cross-sex friendship leads into the literature on friendship at work. Finally, I conclude the chapter with a discussion of the nature of friendship among gay men and lesbians.

CHILDREN'S FRIENDSHIP

Are boys' and girls' friendships similar or different? Most studies show that boys and girls have a network of friends that is similar in size and structure (Belle, 1989; Urberg, Degirmencioglu, Tolson, & Halliday-Scher, 1995). As described in the previous chapter, there are some structural differences in boys' play versus girls' play that may lead to differences in friendship. Boys may have a larger network of friends compared to girls, due to their involvement in large groups, in particular, team sports.

However, as girls become increasingly involved in team sports, we may observe even fewer differences in boys' and girls' friendship networks with time. Girls are more likely to interact in dyads and to spend time talking to one another, whereas boys are more likely to spend time in large groups that are focused on some activity. Girls are more likely to have a best friend (Golombok & Fivush, 1994; Urberg et al., 1995) and to distinguish between a friend and a nonfriend. In fact, girls' relationships are more exclusive than boys' (T. Berndt, 1982). It is more difficult to join a girls' group than a boys' group, perhaps because girls' groups are smaller and more intimate. In a study of sixth- through twelfth-graders, girls were more likely than boys to be in a clique (Urberg et al., 1995).

The nature of male and female friendship becomes more distinct with increasing age. Buhrmester and Furman (1987) studied second-, fifth-, and eighth-graders and showed how friendship changed over time. Among second-graders, there were no differences between the amount of time that boys and girls spent talking and sharing feelings with friends. By fifth grade, girls spent significantly more time than boys talking and sharing feelings, and by eighth grade the difference between boys and girls became even larger.

During adolescence, this difference in the nature of male and female friendship remains. Girls spend time talking with their friends and boys spend time sharing activities. Boys view friendship as instrumental: a friend is someone with whom you do things. Girls view friendship as more emotional: a friend is someone with whom you connect. Adolescent girls rate their friendships as more satisfying than do adolescent boys. In a study of sixth- through twelfth-graders, adolescent girls rated their same-sex and cross-sex friendships (which could have been romantic) as more intimate, a greater source of companionship, and a greater source of instrumental aid compared to adolescent boys (Lempers & Clark-Lempers, 1993). In a study of 15- through 18-year-olds from the Netherlands, female adolescents reported talking more intimately with their best friends compared to male adolescents (Verkuyten & Masson, 1996).

Female and male adolescents may have different standards for friendship. In a study of seventh- and eighth-graders, boys and girls differed in the extent to which friends met their expectations for empathetic understanding (i.e., helps me when I am in trouble, someone I can talk to about personal problems; M. Clark & Ayers, 1993). Boys reported that their friends provided more empathetic understanding than they expected, whereas girls reported that their friends provided less empathetic understanding than they expected. It turned out that boys' and girls' friends probably provided the same amount of empathy, but girls had higher expectations than boys for empathetic understanding from friends. In terms of loyalty (i.e., friend would stand by me), both boys and girls reported that their three best friends exceeded their expectations.

During adolescence, boys and girls also begin to interact more with each other and to form friendships with the other sex. Some of those friendships will evolve into romantic relationships. Adolescent boys' friendships with males and females are very different, whereas adolescent girls' friendships with males and females are quite similar. Female friendship involves conversation and self-disclosure whether the partner is male or female; thus, the partner's sex does not lead females to alter their friendship style. However, males do alter their friendship style when with females. Adolescent boys' friendships with males involve more shared activities, whereas their friendships with females involve more self-disclosure. As you will see, this finding is true in the adult literature as well.

Friendships with females involve high levels of self-disclosure. In a study of self-disclosure among fifth- through twelfth-graders, boys self-disclosed equally to their male and female friends, but girls self-disclosed more to their female than male friends (Dolgin & Kim, 1994). The authors also found that older boys were especially likely to self-disclose to girls; girls were equally likely to self-disclose at all ages. Another study found that adolescent boys actually rated their friendships with female friends as more rewarding than their friendships with male friends (P. Wright & Keple, 1981). Thus, females seem to be a source of emotional support for both adolescent boys and girls (Aukett, Ritchie, & Mill, 1988).

These sex differences in friendship may be larger for the person who is considered a best friend. In one study (Dolgin & Kim, 1994), sex differences in self-disclosure were much smaller for friends who were not the best friend. In another study, there was no sex difference in self-disclosure to friends who were not designated a best friend (Verkuyten & Masson, 1996).

In sum, there are similarities and differences between boys' and girls' friendships. Children, male or female, place equal value on friendship and have a similar number of friends. With increasing age, the nature of male and female friendship seems to grow more distinct. Boys emphasize doing things and girls emphasize talking. When interacting with the other sex, however, boys modify their style more than girls. It appears that both boys and girls turn to girls to self-disclose and share confidences. Many of these differences are maintained in adulthood.

ADULT FRIENDSHIP

In examining men's and women's friendships, we can take a look at how friendship differs in terms of quantity and quality.

Quantity refers to the number of friends or the size of the network. Quality refers to the nature of the friendship. Is it close? Is it intimate? What functions does the friendship serve? These are the issues I address in this section.

Network Size

Do men and women have the same number of friends? The answer is unclear. Studies of college students have shown that there are no sex differences in number of friends (M. Caldwell & Peplau, 1982; Parker & de Vries, 1993) or that women report a greater number of close friends than men (D. Jones, Bloys, & Wood, 1990). M. Caldwell and Peplau asked college students how many "intimate," "good," and "casual" friends they had. Definitions of each category were provided: an intimate friend was defined as someone with whom the person can talk and share confidences; a good friend was defined as someone with whom the person enjoys sharing activities but does not discuss personal matters; a casual friend was defined as someone primarily with whom the person engages in shared activities, and conversation centers on those activities. Men and women did not differ in total number of friends or in the number of friends they named in each of the three categories. This is especially surprising, because the nature of the intimate friend was defined as self-disclosure and the nature of the other two friendships was defined in terms of shared activities. As you will see in the following sections, these are the dimensions of friendship on which men and women are found to differ. However, one must bear in mind that these findings resulted from a study of college students. One reason to expect that men and women would have a similar network in college is that college is a time when men's and women's roles are structurally similar. Men and women have similar access to friends and similar amounts of time to spend with friends. The structure of older adults' lives leads to differences in status and in social roles. These differences may have implications for the availability of friends to adult men and women.

However, even studies of noncollege adults are inconclusive with respect to sex differences in network size. Some studies show that women have more friends, some studies show that men have more friends, and other studies show no sex difference in number of friends (D. Wright, 1999). One reason it is difficult to determine if there are sex differences in the size of friendship networks is that the *concept* of friend may differ for men and women. For example, L. Rubin (1985) found that women used the term "friend" more selectively than men, with men being more willing than women to identify as friends people they knew less well (e.g., coworkers, neighbors, or golf partners). Rubin also found that 66% of the women that men named as close friends did not agree that "close friend" characterized their relationship. If men and women mean something different by the word "friend," it is difficult to compare the size of their networks.

Despite the finding in L. Rubin's (1985) study that women were more selective in naming friends, single women were more likely than single men to identify a best friend. Seventy-five percent of women but only 33% of men identified a best friend. In addition, both men and women were more likely to say their best friend was female than male. Rubin's interviews with adult men and women as well as Levinson's (1978) interviews with men led to the same conclusion: friendship plays a greater role in the lives of adult women. According to Rubin, the women who could not name a best friend were upset about this absence from their lives, whereas the men seemed unconcerned about not being able to identify a best friend. Levinson reports that friends were rarely mentioned in his interviews with adult men and that the topic of friendship was most noted for its absence from men's lives.

Closeness of Friendship

Regardless of the size of men's and women's social networks, are men and women equally close to their friends? At one time, men's friendships were regarded as stronger than women's friendships. In 1969, Lionel Tiger maintained that men were biologically predisposed to develop superior friendships compared to women. Tiger suggested that the male-male bond was as important to the survival of the species as the male-female bond was for reproduction. Men depended on other men for defense of their territory, for gathering food, and for maintaining social order in the community. In support of his claim, Tiger cites another author, who says:

> Woman is an eminently unsociable being and refrains from forming unions on the basis of like interest, remaining centered in the kinship group based on sexual relations and the reproductive function. Associations created or even joined by women on equal terms with the men are rare and must be considered weak imitations of the exclusively male association. (Schurtz, cited in Tiger, 1969, p. 128)

Perhaps these ideas are why the friendships that have been depicted in the media (identified at the beginning of the chapter) involve men.

More recently, L. Rubin (1985) distinguished the bonding that often characterizes men's friendships from the intimacy that typically characterizes women's friendships. According to Rubin, bonding is an emotional connection between two people that ties them together. It is nonverbal and does not require self-disclosure. Among men, she suggests that bonding comes from a shared sense of "maleness" or having similar experiences in life. Intimacy, Rubin says, requires the sharing of feelings, or what we typically call self-disclosure.

Given this distinction, the more recent consensus has been that women's relationships are closer than those of men. Women report that their relationships are more intimate than men do (Auckett et al., 1988; Veniegas & Peplau, 1997); women characterize their friendships as involving more self-disclosure, appreciation, empathy and authenticity compared to men (Parker & de Vries, 1993); and women are more satisfied than men with their friendships (D. Wright, 1999). Reisman (1990) found in two samples (15- to 17-year-olds, 20- to 29-year-olds) that women were closer and more satisfied with their same-sex friendships than were men.

Many studies of friendship have employed the Acquaintance Description Form to assess different dimensions of friendship (ADF; P. Wright, 1985). These dimensions are shown in Table 7.1. Two scales measure friendship strength, five scales assess rewards one receives from friendship, one is a conflict scale, and four scales assess variables expected to differ across different relationships. The instrument also contains a general favorability scale that assesses one's tendency to view a relationship positively across all dimensions.

In a study of college students using the ADF, women reported an overall more positive view of their same-sex friendships than men (Duck & Wright, 1993). In a study of nonstudent volunteers, P. Wright (1985) compared men's and women's same- and cross-sex best friendships using the ADF.

TABLE 7.1 Scales from Acquaintance Description Form

Friendship Strength

Voluntary interdependence: degree to which one commits free time to one another.

Person-qua-person: viewing one person as unique and genuine.

Relationship Values or Rewards

Utility value: friend uses time and resources to provide assistance.

Ego support value: friend regards one as competent.

Stimulation value: friend is interesting, stimulating, expands one's knowledge.

Self-affirmation: friend recognizes valued attributes.

Security value: regards friend as safe and non-threatening.

Relationship Stress or Conflict

Maintenance difficulty: time spent resolving conflicts.

Relationship Differentiation

Exclusion: claim access to interactions with friend.

Permanence: difficult to dissolve, permanently binding.

Salience of emotional expression: expression of positive affect central to relationship.

Degree of social regulation: relationship influenced by social norms.

General Favorability

Tendency to respond to friendship favorably.

Source: P. H. Wright. (1985). The acquaintance description form. In S. Duck and D. Perlman (Eds.), *Understanding personal relationships: An interdisciplinary approach* (pp. 39–62). Beverly Hills, CA: Sage.

Women rated their female friendships as higher on voluntary interdependence (an indicator of relationship strength) compared to their male friendships. Men did not differentiate between their same-sex and cross-sex friendships on this dimension.

Both men and women rated social regulation as higher for cross-sex friends than for same-sex friends. Social regulation reflects a concern with societal norms for friendship; men and women are more concerned with how their friendship appears to others when it involves the other sex. This issue is addressed more fully in the section on cross-sex friendship.

Thus, studies using the ADF seem to show that women have closer friendships than men and that friendships with women are closer than friendships with men. One must consider the nature of the dimensions reflected on the ADF. Are they biased in the direction of tapping female aspects of friendship? Males may rate their same-sex friendships as lower on these dimensions compared to females, but are males less satisfied with their same-sex friendships?

One way to address this question is to examine men's and women's conceptions of an ideal friend using the ADF. Elkins and Peterson (1993) had college students rate their actual as well as their ideal same-sex friend and cross-sex (nonromantic) friend on each of the dimensions of the ADF. The male-male friendship received the lowest actual and lowest ideal ratings, as shown in Figures 7.1a and 7.1b. Thus, the male-male friendship may be the least close as measured by the ADF, but this study showed that males are *not* dissatisfied with this state of affairs. The discrepancy between actual and ideal friendship was the same for males and females in same-sex and cross-sex friendships.

Another way that researchers have examined the closeness of men's and women's friendships is with a method called the Rochester Interaction Record (RIR). Researchers from the University of Rochester developed the RIR to describe the nature of social interactions on a day-to-day or moment-to-moment basis (Wheeler, Reis, & Nezlek, 1983). Participants complete an

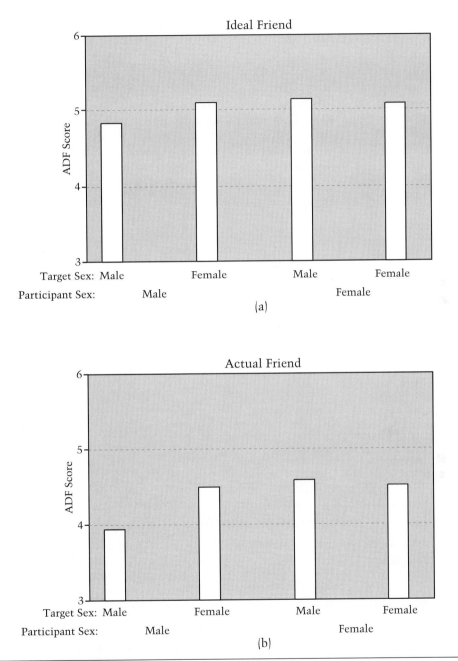

FIGURE 7.1 Ratings of ideal friend and actual friend on measure of relationship strength (ADF). Men rated their ideal male friend lower than they rated their ideal female friend or than women rated their ideal male or female friend. Men also rated their actual male friend lower than they rated their actual female friend or than women rated their actual male or female friend. Although the male-male friendship is less close than other friendships, it is held to a lower standard. *Source:* Adapted from Elkins and Peterson (1993).

RIR for every 10-minute interaction they have over the course of a day. This may seem quite cumbersome, but many of our daily interactions are much briefer, lasting only a minute or two. People typically report about seven or eight 10-minute interactions during an average day. The RIR, shown in Figure 7.2, contains questions about who was involved in the interaction as well as rating scales of the quality of the interaction.

In one study, college students completed the RIR for every 10-minute interaction they had every day for two consecutive weeks (Wheeler et al., 1983). As shown in Figure 7.3a, they found a consistent sex difference in the meaningfulness of interactions, measured as the average of each interaction's intimacy, self-disclosure, other-disclosure, pleasantness, and satisfaction (i.e., the first five ratings

scales shown in Figure 7.2). Men's same-sex interactions were significantly less meaningful than women's, even when interactions with a best friend were examined. All interactions involving at least one female (female-female, male-female) were equally meaningful, and were more meaningful than those involving only males. This study showed that friendship closeness is due not only to a dispositional variable, sex of the person, but to a structural difference, the sex of the friend with whom the person is interacting. Men do not always display less intimacy than women in their interactions with friends. In fact, when men's interactions involve a woman, they can be just as intimate as women's interactions. Men's interactions are less intimate than women's only when they involve another man. Other research has shown that male-male friendships score lower on appreciation,

LONELINESS

Date _____ Time _____ AM ___ Length _____ Hrs ___ Mins ___
PM ___
Initials _____ If More Than 3 Others:
Sex _____ # Of Females _____ # Of Males _____
Intimacy: Superficial 1 2 3 4 5 6 7 Meaningful
I Disclosed: Very Little 1 2 3 4 5 6 7 A Great Deal
Other Disclosed: Very Little 1 2 3 4 5 6 7 A Great Deal
Quality: Unpleasant 1 2 3 4 5 6 7 Pleasant
Satisfaction: Less Than Expected 1 2 3 4 5 6 7 More Than Expected
Initiation: I Initiated 1 2 3 4 5 6 7 Other Initiated
Influence: I Influenced More 1 2 3 4 5 6 7 Other Influenced More
Nature: Work Task Pastime Conversaton Date

FIGURE 7.2 Rochester Interaction Record. *Source:* L. Wheeler, H. Reis, and J. Nezlek (1983). Loneliness, social interaction, and sex roles. *Journal of Personality and Social Psychology, 45,* 943–953.

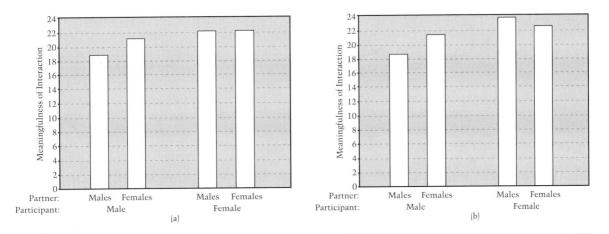

FIGURE 7.3 Meaningfulness of interactions with men and women. A daily diary study showed that men's interactions with men were rated as less meaningful than men's interactions with women or women's interactions with men or women. The results of the study by Wheeler et al. (1983) are depicted in Figure 7.3a. The results were replicated by Reis et al. (1985) and are shown in Figure 7.3b. *Sources:* Adapted from Wheeler et al. (1983) and Reis et al. (1985).

empathy, responsibility, and connectedness compared to female-female and male-female friendships (Parker & de Vries, 1993).

The finding that men's interactions with other men are the least meaningful was replicated by a study that explored several explanations for it (see Figure 7.3b; Reis, Senchak, & Solomon, 1985). The investigators examined whether men were simply more selective than women about the people with whom they are intimate. As in the previous study, RIR interactions with the best friend only were examined. Women rated their interactions with their best friend as more meaningful compared to men. Students also provided a written account of their most recent meaningful conversation with their same-sex best friend. Judges reviewed the narratives and determined that women's accounts were more intimate than those of men. Thus, it did not appear that men were being more selective than women.

Reis and colleagues (1985) also asked whether men's friendships lacked intimacy because men were not capable of intimacy or because men preferred not to behave in intimate ways. Students and their best same-sex friends were asked to engage spontaneously in a conversation about something that was important to them. A female graduate student rated videotapes of these interactions and found that men's interactions were as intimate as women's, as demonstrated by men and women self-disclosing at similar levels. However, a panel of undergraduates found that males discussed less intimate topics than females did. The authors concluded that men and women are equally capable of intimacy but men prefer not to behave as intimately as women.

Rather than sex, gender role may be a better predictor of friendship closeness or intimacy. Femininity is related to social self-esteem and relationship satisfaction

(Helgeson, 1994c). Femininity also has been associated with friendship closeness in men. Narus and Fischer (1982) examined how well college men understood their closest friends, and how often they shared confidences with those friends. Androgynous men said it was easier to understand one another compared to masculine and undifferentiated men. Androgynous men also were more likely than masculine or undifferentiated men to say that they confided in their friends. Androgynous men differ from masculine and undifferentiated men in that they have higher femininity scores.

Barriers to Closeness in Male Friendship. Why are male same-sex friendships less intimate and sometimes less satisfying than female same-sex friendships? Mazur and Olver (1987) suggested that men see danger in affiliations with other men. Drawing on Pollak and Gilligan's (1982) work, they demonstrated that men fear affiliation with men. They presented undergraduates with a series of situations involving same-sex characters. Each situation had a structured and unstructured version. For example, an unstructured situation was two men (or women) sitting together on a bench; a structured situation was two men (or women) sitting together on a bench waiting for their turn at bat. The investigators suggested that men would feel more comfortable in a structured situation in which an activity (in this case, playing baseball) serves as the basis for the interaction. They hypothesized that men would either respond negatively to the unstructured situation or impose structure on the situation to reduce the potential for closeness. The results showed that men responded to the unstructured cue by writing stories that contained negative affect and by imposing structure (i.e., came up with a reason that the people were sitting together on the bench) more so than did women. There was no sex difference in negative affect in response to the structured cue. Mazur and Olver argued that men's emphasis on shared activities is a way to impose structure on a relationship and reduce the potential for closeness.

One fear that men have in relationships with other men is homophobia. **Homophobia** is defined as the fear of homosexuality or the fear of appearing to be homosexual. Homophobia limits intimacy in men's friendships with other men. Men who score higher in homophobia report less trust, less understanding, fewer expressions of caring, and less empathy in their relationships with other men (Devlin & Cowan, 1985). Because men do not want to appear to be homosexual, they limit their physical contact and their emotional closeness with other men, reserving those kinds of contacts for romantic relationships with women (P. Stein, 1986).

A study of college students demonstrated how men limit their physical contact with other men and how both men and women view physical contact between two men as abnormal (Derlega, Lewis, Harrison, Winstead, & Costanza, 1989). Students were asked to role-play a situation in which they were greeting either by same-sex friend, a cross-sex friend, or a romantic partner at the airport (Derlega et al., 1989). Four levels of tactile intimacy were coded: $0 =$ No touch; $1 =$ Handshake, or touch on head, arm, back; $2 =$ Light hug, hold hands; and $3 =$ Solid hug, kiss. Men were less intimate greeting men than they were greeting women. Men also were less intimate greeting men than were women greeting women. In a second study, the investigators examined college students' attitudes toward different levels of touch between same-sex and cross-sex dyads. Students were shown a picture of a pair of people either not touching, hugging, or putting their arms around each other's waist. They were told that the pair consisted of two men, two women, or a man and a woman. Students rated increasing levels of touch as less normal when they thought the pair was two men. All forms of touch were rated as normal when the pair was depicted as a man and a woman. When the photo was thought to consist of two women, level of touch partly affected perceptions of normalcy. Women with arms around each other's waist was rated as abnormal, but women hugging each other was rated as normal. Students also indicated that an arm around another's waist was an indication of a sexual relationship in all three dyads. Hugging, however, was an indicator of a sexual relationship only in the male-male dyad.

Another barrier to male friendship is competition. Men's friendships are more overtly competitive than women's friendships. Competition limits intimacy because it is difficult to be close to someone with whom you are in competition; one would not reveal weaknesses, inadequacies, or difficulties to a competitor (P. Stein, 1986). In addition, competition among men makes them feel threatened by one another's achievements. In general, men are more sensitive than women to status features in relationships. In a meta-analytic review of the literature, Feingold (1988) found greater matching on physical attractiveness among male-male friendships than female-female friendships. Feingold argued that physical attractiveness is a status cue. In a study of junior high school students, male friends were more similar to one another on status cues (e.g., niceness of clothes) than were female friends (M. Clark & Ayers, 1992).

However, competition may not be limited to male friendship. L. Rubin (1985) suggests that both men's and women's friendships are competitive but the nature of the competition is different. Competition among men is overt and direct, whereas competition among women is covert. The overt expression of competition in relationships is viewed as unfeminine;

women resort to more subtle tactics. For example, a friend of mine told me of an occasion when her aunt was so concerned about being the best-dressed person at a party that she refused to answer her friends when they asked her what she intended to wear. My mother was once accused of leaving out a key ingredient of a dessert recipe that she passed on to a friend. Both of these situations are examples of covert competition. Thus, competition may undermine friendships for both men and women but in different ways. Investigate this issue with Exercise 7.1.

A third factor is emotional inexpressiveness. Men tend to express less emotion in relationships. Inexpressiveness may help to maintain power but at the expense of closeness.

A recent study compared the different explanations for the lack of intimacy in men's relationships (Bank & Hansford, 2000). College men reported less intimate and less supportive same-sex friendships than did college women. Homophobia and emotional restraint explained a good portion of this sex difference. In this study,

---

EXERCISE 7.1
Male versus Female Competition

Interview your friends to find out how competition manifests itself in their friendships. Ask for examples of competitive behavior in their friendships with men and their friendships with women. Over what things do people compete: money? status? physical attractiveness? grades? romantic partners? Are the behaviors that men identify different from the behaviors that women identify? Are the behaviors that people identify about men different from the behaviors that people identify about women?

men and women scored similarly on measures of competition, so competition could not explain why men's friendships were less close than those of women.

The Nature of Friendship

There is a large literature concluding that women's friendships are closer than men's and that friendships with women are closer than friendships with men. But how do men's and women's friendships really differ? Now I turn to the literature on the nature of men's and women's friendships. There are fundamental ways in which the nature of friendship differs for men and women, which may explain the sex difference in closeness. However, there also are important ways in which men and women view friendship similarly.

SEX DIFFERENCES. How does the nature of men's and women's friendships differ? In her interviews with adult men and women, Lillian Rubin (1985, p. 61) provides the following example of a woman describing her friendship: "There are a lot of people I can play with, but the people I call my real friends are the ones I can talk to also. I mean, they're the people I can share *myself* with, not just my time." Here is an example provided by a man: "We go to the pool hall and shoot pool, maybe hit a bar or two and drink and tell stories and all that kind of stuff—just raise a little hell."

There is research evidence that support these two anecdotes. Women's friendships are communal and men's friendships are agentic (P. Wright, 1989). When college students were asked whether they preferred to "just talk" to their friends or to "do some activity," more men than women chose the activity, and more women than men chose talking (M. Caldwell & Peplau, 1982). Students were also asked to describe three things they did with their best friend

that defined their relationship; again, men were more likely to name shared activities and women to name talking. When given a choice, men were more likely than women to say they preferred that their friends "did the same things," whereas women were more likely than men to say they preferred that their friends "felt the same about things." Men identify shared activities as a more important feature of friendship than do women, whereas women rate self-disclosure and empathy as more important features of friendship compared to men (Parker & de Vries, 1993). P. Wright (1982) found that men were better friends if they agreed on day-to-day activities, whereas women were better friends if they agreed on deep personal values. Similarity seems to provide the basis of friendship for women more than men. In a study of 15- to 18-year-olds in the Netherlands, boys reported that they were less similar to their friends than girls did (Verkuyten & Masson, 1996). When asked to provide a description of their best friend, boys were more likely to identify social characteristics (e.g., nationality, group affiliations) and girls to identify personal characteristics (e.g., honest, understanding). P. Wright (1982) concluded that female friendships are "face-to-face" relationships that require personal knowledge of one another, and male friendships are "side-by-side" relationships that are activity-focused.

Female friendship also appears to be more holistic than male friendship (P. Wright, 1982). Men tend to compartmentalize their friends, having different friends for different activities. Men have one friend for golfing, one for studying, and one for hanging out. By contrast, women are more likely to have friends that cut across different areas of their lives (Buhrke & Fuqua, 1987). Women talk to, have fun with, and study with the same person. However, both men's and women's *best* friendships are holistic (P. Wright, 1982).

Women also may be more likely than men to have reciprocal relationships. Reciprocity has a number of meanings. A reciprocal relationship can be a "give-and-take" relationship, one in which you provide support and receive support in return. Using this definition of reciprocity, college students reported that their friendships with women were more reciprocal than their friendships with men (Parker & de Vries, 1993). Specifically, there was a greater mutual exchange of self-disclosure and empathy in female than in male friendships. A reciprocal relationship also can be defined as one in which both people define the relationship similarly, that is, they agree that there is a friendship. A nonreciprocal relationship is one in which only one person identifies the other as a friend. Using this definition, a study of junior high school students and a study of sixth- through twelfth-graders found that boys were less likely than girls to have reciprocal relationships (M. Clark & Ayers, 1992; Urberg et al., 1995). This finding is reminiscent of L. Rubin's (1985) interviews with adults in which many adult men reported that a woman was a close friend but the woman did not agree.

SEX SIMILARITIES.   Although I have focused on sex differences, there are also similarities between men's and women's friendships. One way in which men's and women's friendships are similar is in terms of what men and women want from a friend. Both rate trust and authenticity as the most important dimensions of friendship (Parker & de Vries, 1993). Men and women also have similar views of their ideal friendships (Sapadin, 1988); that is, they want the same things from friendship. Although men's same-sex friendships are less intimate and less supportive than women's, intimacy and support are equally associated with how much men and women enjoy spending time with their friends (Bank & Hansford, 2000).

Egalitarianism is an important feature of friendship for both men and women. Friendship by definition implies equal status. It stands to reason that people would find friendships more satisfying when they are of equal rather than unequal status. In one study, college students described a same-sex friendship in which the power distribution was equal and one in which the power distribution was unequal (Veniegas & Peplau, 1997). Both men and women evaluated the equal power relationship more favorably.

Although men and women may differ in how important they perceive a feature of a friendship to be, they often agree on which attributes of a relationship are more or less important. For example, women may self-disclose in same-sex relationships more than men or view self-disclosure as more important in relationships, but both men and women may still rate self-disclosure as more important than activity sharing. This idea was supported in a study in which men and women rated how important eight different communication skills were to same-sex friendship (Burleson, Kunkel, Samter, & Werking, 1996). Some of the skills reflected the affective aspects of relationships (comforting one another, making a person feel good about himself or herself), whereas other skills reflected the instrumental aspects of communication (entertaining one another, casual conversations, conveying information). Women rated the affective aspects as more important than did men, and men rated the instrumental aspects as more important than did women. Aha, differences again! But both men and women agreed that the affective aspects of friendship were more important than the instrumental aspects of friendship.

A similar pattern of findings was detected when undergraduates defined intimacy in their close friendships (Monsour, 1992). Although women were more likely to identify self-disclosure and men were more likely to identify shared activities, the rank order of the most to least frequently mentioned features was the same. The most frequent response among both men and women was self-disclosure. After that was emotional expression, support, physical contact, trust, and mutual activities. In other words, both men and women were more likely to identify self-disclosure as a feature of intimacy than shared activities. When asked about the purpose of meeting with a same-sex friend, both men and women say that meeting to talk is the primary purpose of getting together with a friend (Duck & Wright, 1993). Other studies have shown that the same characteristics of a friendship predict satisfaction in both men and women, in particular, self-disclosure (Reisman, 1990).

In sum, the primary difference in the nature of men's and women's friendships is that an activity is the focus of men's interactions and conversation is the focus of women's interactions. However, it is not the case that men and women have different views of what is important to a relationship. Both men and women view self-disclosure, empathy, trust, and expressions of support as the most important features of a friendship.

Self-Disclosure

Self-disclosure is the aspect of friendship that has caused the most controversy over whether women's relationships are closer than those of men, and whether there are sex differences in the meaning of friendship. Do women self-disclose more than men? To whom: other women or men?

SEX OF DISCLOSER.   Dindia and Allen (1992) conducted a meta-analysis on sex differences in self-disclosure. They found a small effect $(d = -.18)$ indicating that women

self-disclose more than men. The size of the sex difference was similar across self-report $(d = -.17)$ and observational $(d = -.22)$ studies. However, the sex difference was larger for studies that relied on other people's reports of someone's behavior $(d = -.44)$. That is, other people view the difference between men's and women's self-disclosure to be larger than it really is. Gender-role stereotypes must be influencing people's reports of others' behavior.

Sex differences in self-disclosure may be more apparent when the nature of the topic is examined. Several studies show that women are especially more likely than men to self-disclose about personal issues, such as relationship problems or areas of personal weakness. One study found that women were more likely than men to discuss intimate topics and problems with their same-sex friends, but that there were no sex differences in self-disclosure about less intimate topics (Tschann, 1988). Hacker (1981) asked men and women how comfortable they felt revealing strengths and weaknesses to their friends. The majority of men and women said that they would reveal both strengths and weaknesses to same-sex and cross-sex friends. However, there was one difference: none of the women said they would reveal *only* strengths and none of the men said they would reveal *only* weaknesses. A compelling example of men's unwillingness to discuss intimate topics comes from an early study by L. Walker and Wright (1976). They asked college men and women to discuss either intimate or nonintimate topics with an acquaintance. Half of the male students refused to discuss the intimate topics.

Parents of undergraduates were asked to indicate how often and in what depth they discussed 17 topics with a same-sex friend (Aries & Johnson, 1983). Women discussed personal topics more frequently than did men (e.g., personal problems, doubts and fears, family problems, and relationship problems). Women also discussed daily activities and hobbies more. The only topic men discussed more frequently than women was sports. Women talked more in depth about personal problems and family activities than men, whereas men discussed sports and work more in depth than did women. There were no sex differences for the topics of religion/morality, finances, sex, and social/political issues.

Aside from the different topics of self-disclosure, men and women may have different motives for self-disclosure. Women may self-disclose for the sole purpose of sharing feelings, whereas men may self-disclose to get help in solving a problem. This idea was tested by asking college students to write a story about two friends who met for lunch, one of whom is worried (Mark & Alper, 1985). Stories were coded for whether self-disclosure took place for the sole purpose of sharing feelings or for some other reason such as getting help to solve the problem. Over 52% of the women reported self-disclosure for the purpose of sharing feelings, whereas only 19% of the men wrote such stories. In addition, 25% of women but none of the men wrote that the person felt better after disclosing. The results from this study fit with the idea in Chapter 6 that men and women might desire different kinds of support when sharing problems.

SEX OF RECIPIENT.   Who is more likely to be on the receiving end of self-disclosure? The answer depends in part on the sex of the discloser. Women are clearly more likely than men to be the recipients of female disclosure. The question is: To whom do men self-disclose? The research is not clear on this issue. In one study, college students rated how much they disclosed to their same-sex and cross-sex (nonromantic) friends (Dolgin, Meyer, & Schwartz, 1991).

On all of the dimensions (i.e., attitudes, opinions, personality, body, work), women reported that they self-disclosed more to women than to men. Men reported that they disclosed equally to men and women, with the exception of finances, which they discussed more with men. Yet, an earlier study of college males showed that they disclosed more about a variety of topics to women than to men (Komarovsky, 1974). In this study, male college students were asked how much they disclosed information on personal attitudes, work or studies, money, personality, and body to their mother, father, brothers, sisters, male friends, and female friends. Female friends were the primary confidants for all areas except money; parents were the primary confidants for money. The greater self-disclosure to female friends occurred for the more intimate topics (e.g., personality, body). Men also disclosed more to their mothers than to their fathers.

Dindia and Allen's (1992) meta-analytic review supports the findings of both studies. There was a sex of target effect that indicated people are more likely to self-disclose to women than to men but also more likely to self-disclose to the same sex than to the other sex. For women, a same-sex target is another woman, so the result is clear: women are more likely to self-disclose to women than to men. For men, a same-sex target is not a woman; thus, the recipient of male self-disclosure is not always clear. There may be some topics that men discuss with men and others that men discuss with women. There is evidence that men and women prefer to talk to men about task-oriented problems and to women about relationship problems (Derlega, Barbee, & Winstead, 1994). These preferences likely have to do with the support people expect men and women to provide. Task-oriented problems may require more advice and relationship problems may require emotional support. Explore this issue with Exercise 7.2.

SITUATIONAL VARIABLES. There are situational variables that affect self-disclosure. Studies have shown that men's levels of self-disclosure can be increased if they are motivated to self-disclose. Two studies showed that men are more likely to self-disclose when the instrumental aspects of the situation are made salient. In one study, college men and women were led to believe that they would be interacting on a task with a male or female they had just met (Derlega, Winstead, Wong, & Hunter, 1985). Respondents were told to provide a description of themselves to their partner. The descriptions were coded for intimacy of self-disclosure. As shown in Figure 7.4, men's disclosures to women were more intimate than their disclosures to men, and more intimate than women's disclosures to either men or women. The authors concluded that men self-disclose to women during the initial stages of a relationship to advance the relationship.

This idea was further tested in another study by manipulating whether participants believed there was the possibility

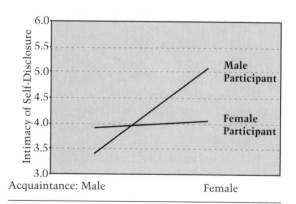

FIGURE 7.4 Self-disclosure to male or female acquaintance. There are conditions under which men may self-disclose. One such condition is on meeting a woman. Men's disclosures to a woman they had just met were more intimate than their disclosures to a man they had just met. Men's disclosures to a woman were also more intimate than women's disclosures to a man or a woman. Women self-disclosed equally to a man or a woman they had just met. *Source:* Adapted from Derlega et al. (1985).

of a future interaction with the other person in the experiment (Shaffer, Pegalis, & Bazzini, 1996). The investigators predicted that men would be especially likely to self-disclose to women if they believed there was the possibility of a future interaction. They also expected that this effect would be strongest for traditionally masculine men.

Shaffer and colleagues (1996) had undergraduates work on a first task with a partner and then led them to believe that they would be working on a second task with or without their partner. This was the manipulation of future interaction. The initial task was discussing four different topics (the most important decision I ever made, sacrifices I made for others, aspects of personality I dislike, past and present

---

EXERCISE 7.2
Sex Differences in Self-Disclosure

Come up with a list of topics. Ask a group of men and women to report how frequently they discuss each topic with their same-sex friends and cross-sex friends. You could have them pick their best same-sex friend and best cross-sex friend. Divide the topics into two groups: more intimate and less intimate. Is there a sex of participant difference in self-disclosure? Is there a sex of target difference? Does it depend on the topic?

things of which I am ashamed) with a stranger who was really a confederate. Conversations were audiotaped and evaluated by two raters for intimacy of self-disclosure. Women were more intimate when they disclosed to female than male targets. Men's self-disclosure was influenced by their masculinity scores, the sex of the target, and the possibility of future interaction. As shown in the right panel of Figure 7.5, men who scored high on masculinity self-disclosed more to female than male targets, but only when there was the possibility of a future interaction (PFI). When there was no possibility of a future interaction (NPFI; left panel of Figure 7.5), high-masculine men self-disclosed equally to male and female targets.

Are highly masculine men increasing their self-disclosure to female targets when they expect to interact with them again? Or, are highly masculine men decreasing their self-disclosure to male targets when they expect to interact with them again? Highly masculine men may be especially uncomfortable disclosing to other men if they think they will see them again. Indeed, comfort level did explain the results from this study. High-masculine men reported greater comfort and were more interested in establishing a relationship with the female than the male target when there was the potential for future interaction. In general, female respondents were more comfortable and more interested in establishing a relationship with the female than the

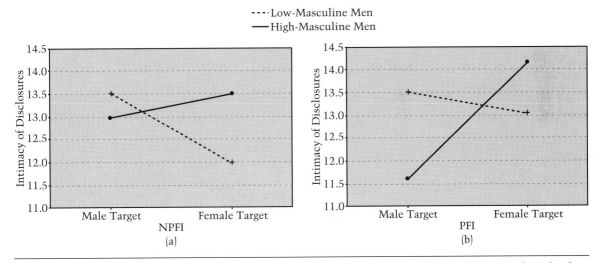

FIGURE 7.5 Men who score high on masculinity are motivated to self-disclose to a female they have just met and with whom they have the possibility of forming a relationship. High-masculine men self-disclosed more intimately to a female than a male target, *only* when there was the possibility of a future interaction (PFI). Where there was no possibility of a future interaction (NPFI), high-masculine men's disclosures were equally intimate toward a male or female target. *Source:* D. R. Shaffer, L. J. Pegalis, and D. G. Bazzini (1996). When boy meets girl (revisited) gender, gender-role orientation, and prospect of future interaction as determinants of self-disclosure among same and opposite sex acquaintances. *Personality and Social Psychology Bulletin, 22,* 495–506.

male target. Thus, it appears that both women and masculine men self-disclosed most to female targets when there was the possibility of a future interaction because they felt comfortable and wanted to establish a relationship.

There are other situational variables that affect sex differences in self-disclosure. Age is one. For example, in one study, females self-disclosed more to women than men among adolescents, but females disclosed equally to men and women among young adults (Reisman, 1990). Adolescent men self-disclosed equally to men and women, but by young adulthood they disclosed more to women than men. Thus, with age, both males and females increased their disclosure to the other sex.

Marital status also affects men's and women's self-disclosure to friends, but not in the same way. Marriage inhibits men but not women from self-disclosing to friends. In one study, married men were less likely than married women or unmarried persons of either sex to discuss intimate topics or personal problems with same-sex friends (Tschann, 1988). Married women were more likely than married men to disclose to friends, and were equally likely to self-disclose to a friend and to a spouse. Married men reserve their intimate disclosures for their spouse.

Social class also may influence self-disclosure. Hacker (1981) found that working-class women had higher levels of self-disclosure to friends than middle-class women. Working-class men had especially low levels of self-disclosure to same-sex friends. However, class level did not affect men's self-disclosure to women.

Barriers to Male Self-Disclosure. Men may be less likely to self-disclose than women because self-disclosure involves revealing weaknesses and vulnerabilities, which is inconsistent with the male gender role. Two aspects of the male gender role—inhibiting affection and restricting emotions—were associated with less self-disclosure of emotion among male and female college students (Snell, Miller, Belk, Garcia-Falconi, & Hernandez-Sanchez, 1989). There is some evidence that men who self-disclose are not viewed as favorably as women who self-disclose. A meta-analysis of the studies that examined the relation of self-disclosure to liking showed that the relation was stronger for female disclosers ($d = +.30$) than male disclosers ($d = +.11$; Collins & Miller, 1994). This finding held for both male and female respondents. In other words, both men and women liked a woman who disclosed more than a man who disclosed.

Men who self-disclose also might be viewed as having more problems than women who self-disclose. This idea was supported by a study that had college students read several vignettes in which one person either did or did not disclose a personal problem (a mental illness or a car accident; Derlega & Chaikin, 1976). The sex of the discloser and the sex of the recipient were varied. Men were rated as better adjusted under nondisclosure than disclosure conditions, whereas women were rated as better adjusted under disclosure than nondisclosure conditions. The sex of the disclosure recipient did not influence the results. In addition, participants liked the female discloser better than the female nondiscloser but liked the male discloser and nondiscloser equally. Regardless of sex, the discloser was rated as more feminine than the nondiscloser. Thus, self-disclosure was viewed as part of the female gender role.

In sum, both men and women view self-disclosure in a male unfavorably. Self-disclosure seems to be linked to femininity, and men who behave in a feminine manner are not highly regarded. If people have negative views of men who disclose their problems, then it is not surprising that men are reluctant to ask for help.

Definition of Intimacy

I have reviewed research showing that women's friendships are closer than those of men. I also have shown that women self-disclose more than men. Because the intimacy of a relationship is often measured by self-disclosure, the logical conclusion is that women's relationships are more intimate than those of men. Recently, researchers have called into question this definition of intimacy and suggested that self-disclosure may be a "feminine" definition. Some have argued that both men and women desire meaningful, close relationships, but that they follow different pathways to achieve this. Women may be more likely to express intimacy through self-disclosure, and men may be more likely to express intimacy through participation in shared activities.

Do men and women define intimacy differently? Swain (1989) found that the vast majority of men mentioned activities rather than self-disclosure when describing their most meaningful experience with a friend. He documents a "covert intimacy" in men, which he defines as "behavior in the context of a friendship that connotes a positive and mutual sense of meaning and importance to the participants" (p. 72). This covert intimacy reflects the comfort that men feel in each other's presence, a comfort that stems from shared experiences and mutual understandings. He suggests that intimacy for men comes from action rather than self-disclosure: men feel connected to other men who choose them to share an activity, who provide them with assistance, and who joke around about ideas or histories that are common to only the pair. This covert intimacy sounds similar to L. Rubin's (1985) concept of bonding.

Yet, other research has shown that men and women agree that self-disclosure is more central to intimacy than shared activities. In one study, college students were asked to define the terms closeness and intimacy in the context of their current same-sex and cross-sex (nonromantic) relationships (Parks & Floyd, 1996). The most frequently cited definition of closeness for both men and women was self-disclosure, although females were more likely than males to identify self-disclosure (76% vs. 64%). The second definition was support provision; again, females identified this feature (45%) more than males (27%). Sharing activities was the third most frequent definition, and it was identified by an equal number of males (35%) and females (28%). Although men and women have different experiences of intimacy (women's being more affective and men's being more instrumental), the two sexes may agree on the definition of intimacy. In another study, both men and women defined intimacy as involving self-disclosure and trust (Oroson & Schilling, 1992).

One study seemed to resolve the issue by showing that self-disclosure is the most central feature of intimacy for both men and women, but shared activities contribute to intimacy for men. The relation of self-disclosure and shared activities to intimacy was examined among two cohorts of eighth-graders (Camarena, Sarigiana, & Petersen, 1990). Students rated their relationship with a close friend (usually a same-sex friend) on emotional closeness (acceptance, understanding), self-disclosure, and shared experiences/activities. Girls rated their close friendships higher in emotional closeness and self-disclosure than did boys. There were no sex differences for shared experiences. However, the predictors of emotional closeness differed for boys and girls. Both self-disclosure and shared experiences predicted emotional closeness for boys, whereas only self-disclosure predicted emotional closeness for girls. Yet, even for boys, the relation of self-disclosure to emotional closeness was much stronger than the relation of shared experiences to emotional closeness.

To determine whether men and women had similar or different conceptions of intimacy, I conducted a study of people's conceptions of intimacy in their same-sex friendships (Helgeson, Shaver, & Dyer, 1987). College students were asked to describe a time when they felt intimate with a person of the same sex. My colleagues and I read these descriptions, made a list of all of the features identified in the stories, and constructed a frequency distribution of those features. In general, we found that there were more similarities than differences in men's and women's intimate experiences. The most frequently identified features of intimacy for both men and women revolved around feelings and expressions of appreciation for one's partner. Talking about personal topics and sharing activities were also features of intimacy

but differed in the frequency with which they were named by men and women. As shown in Figure 7.6, men were equally likely to mention talking about personal topics and sharing activities during their intimate episodes, whereas women were more likely to mention talking about personal topics and less likely to mention sharing activities. Another frequently mentioned feature of intimacy episodes for both men and women involved sharing problems: the partner listening, offering support and understanding.

The question remains: Do men and women define intimacy differently? It appears that self-disclosure is an important, if not the most important, feature of intimacy for both men and women. However, men are more likely than women to incorporate shared experiences into their conceptualizations of intimacy. In studies of intimacy, researchers have neglected the fact that one

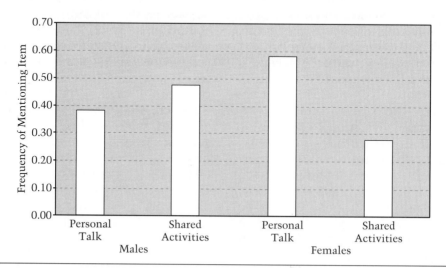

FIGURE 7.6 Conceptions of intimacy: Personal talk and sharing activities. Both men and women define intimacy in terms of self-disclosure, but men also include shared activities in their definitions. Men were equally likely to report personal talk and shared activities in their episodes of intimacy with a friend. Women were more likely to report personal talk than shared activities. *Source:* Adapted from Helgeson et al. (1987).

can be engaged in self-disclosure and shared activities simultaneously. Two men may be discussing problems with their girlfriends while fixing a car: How are these episodes classified—as self disclosure or as shared activities? How do men and women classify this experience?

According to Reis and Shaver (1988), intimacy involves revealing one's innermost self, which can be accomplished via self-disclosure or shared activities. Intimacy is not a static state but a process. This means that self-disclosure alone is not sufficient to establish intimacy. The partner's response to the self-disclosure is just as important as the self-disclosure itself to the intimacy of an interaction. Reis and Shaver suggest that intimate interactions are ones that lead to feeling understood, validated, and cared for. Both self-disclosure and shared activities could accomplish this.

Conflict in Friendship

I have focused on the positive aspects of friendships. But relationships do not always run smoothly. What produces conflict in men's and women's friendships? In the previously described study on conceptions of intimacy (Helgeson et al., 1987), my colleagues and I also investigated conceptions of distance, a time when people felt detached from their friends. Feelings of distance may stem from conflict. The primary feature of distance for both men and women was disapproval of a partner's behavior. Students reported feeling distant from their friends when their friends betrayed them, engaged in immoral behavior, or embarrassed them. Other notable features of distance were not spending time together and feeling as if the partner did not understand when there was a problem. Thus, distance was partly defined as the opposite of intimacy: a lack of understanding. Overall, men and women had similar conceptions of distance. Moreover, both sexes reported feelings of anger more often than feelings of hurt.

Although the same events may lead to conflict for men and women, do they respond to conflict in similar ways? One way they respond to conflict similarly is that men and women are equally likely to terminate a friendship following conflict (P. Wright, 1982). However, there also are some differences in the way men and women manage conflict in their same-sex friendships. Women are more direct than men in bringing up conflict and discussing it with their same-sex friends (P. Wright, 1982). (As you will see in Chapter 8, this finding also holds for romantic relationships.) Men are not direct in the sense of bringing up an issue, but when men do bring up conflict, they are direct in terms of how it is discussed. For example, men are more likely than women to express anger to their friends. In the study reported above (Helgeson et al., 1987), men were more likely than women to report having argued with their partners. Women may be more concerned than men with the threat that such expressions bring to relationships.

A study of children confirmed the idea that males and females are both direct in confronting conflict, but do so in a different manner. Third- and fourth-graders played a game with either someone from class whom they identified as a friend or someone from class whom they did not identify as a friend (Hartup, French, Laursen, Johnston, & Ogawa, 1993). Conflict was instigated by providing each member of the dyad with different rules about how to play the game. (This could be really fun to do with adults!) Conflict was coded from videotapes and defined as one person objecting to the other person's behavior. Results showed no sex differences in the amount of conflict;

that is, conflict was equally likely to be observed among boys and girls. Conflict was more likely to occur among friends than nonfriends. Girls were more likely to respond to the conflict by asserting themselves and providing a rationale, whereas boys were more likely to respond to the conflict by asserting themselves without providing a rationale. In other words, girls would say "You can't move that piece because . . ." and boys would leave it at "You can't move that piece!" The authors concluded that men issue orders without providing justification because they are concerned with their status in relationships: high status alone should be enough to justify an order. Women provide justification because they are concerned with maintaining the relationship and acquiring their partner's agreement. In this study, boys and girls were equally likely to acquiesce to their partner and equally likely to compromise.

One source of conflict is deceit. De-Paulo, Epstein, and Wyer (1993) examined men's and women's deceitful behavior with friends. They asked college students to record all of their social interactions over a one-week period, including every time they told a lie. How many times do you lie to a friend in an average day? You may be surprised to learn that students recorded two lies a day, one lie for every four social interactions. There were no sex differences in lying behavior. Both men and women lied less often to close friends than to casual friends. There also were no sex differences in distress about lying. However, women reported greater discomfort than men *during* the lie. After the lie, men's discomfort decreased, whereas women's did not. In a second study, women reported taking lies more seriously than men. Women said they were more upset when telling a lie and when being told a lie compared to men. Women also reported being more engaged in investigating others' lies, such as looking for evidence and talking to other people.

To recap, there are similar sources of conflict in men's and women's friendships. Both men and women are equally likely to confront their friends about conflict, but confrontation may take different tones. Men are more likely to be direct in the confrontation and express anger; women are more likely to confront the conflict by discussing the issue. Men and women may think about conflict resolution differently. One study suggested that men think that the person who is violated determines whether a conflict is resolved, whereas women think that the person who provoked the conflict determines conflict resolution.

ETHNIC AND CROSS-CULTURAL RESEARCH ON FRIENDSHIP

Ethnic differences in friendship have been found in the United States. One study compared Asian American, African American, and European White American college students' (all living in California) goals in helping a friend with a problem (Samter, Whaley, Mortenson, & Burleson, 1997). Emotion-focused goals involved talking and letting the other person express himself or herself, and problem-focused goals involved helping the person solve the problem and giving advice. Men and women in all three ethnic groups rated emotion-focused goals as more important than problem-focused goals. However, Asian American men rated emotion-focused goals as more important than did African American men, with Caucasian men scoring in the middle. Caucasian women rated emotion-focused goals as more important than did African American women, with Asian American women scoring in the middle. The authors suggested that providing emotional support to friends is more central to White women's than Black women's same-sex friendships.

Within the African American community, Franklin (1992) concluded that the friendships of working-class Black men differ from the friendships of more upwardly mobile Black men. The friendships of upwardly mobile Black men are similar to White men's friendships: activity-based, lacking in self-disclosure, and work-focused. Franklin argued that upwardly mobile Black men discover that the way to get ahead is to behave like successful White men, which means that relationships with other men are competitive and friends are kept at a distance. The friendships of working-class Black men, however, are closer because of shared feelings of oppression and victimization. They seem to understand each other in ways that White men and upper-class Black men do not. They have a "stick together—it is us against them" mentality. Because these friendships involve a great deal of trust and loyalty, working-class Black men react harshly toward a friend who violates these principles. The relation of social class to friendship is a topic worth more investigation. Start with Exercise 7.3.

Cross-cultural research on friendship has confirmed a number of findings on gender and friendship already discussed in this chapter. In a study in New Zealand, college women rated their same-sex friendships as closer than did men (Aukett et al., 1988). Women emphasized self-disclosure, and men emphasized shared activities as the basis of their friendship. The study also showed that women preferred a few close friends (75%) over many less intimate friends (25%). Men, however, were equally divided between the two options, with 53% indicating a preference for a greater number of less intimate friends. In

---

> ### EXERCISE 7.3
> ### Social Class and Friendship
>
> First, decide what dimensions of friendship might vary by social class (e.g., self-disclosure, shared activities, trust, competition). Develop questions to measure these aspects of friendship. Have your friends' parents complete the questionnaire with respect to their current friendships. Record whether the parent is a blue-collar worker or a white-collar worker to see if there are class differences in friendship.

addition, women reported more emotional support from their same-sex than cross-sex friends, whereas men reported more emotional support from their cross-sex friends. Both men and women said that they discuss personal problems with women. A study of college students in Hungary also revealed that men said that it was easier to talk to and feel close to women than men (Reisman, 1990).

Other cross-cultural research suggests that many of the sex differences in friendship are a Western phenomenon. The intimacy of college students' friendships in the United States were compared to those in Germany, the Netherlands, Hong Kong, and Jordan (Reis, 1998). The size of the sex difference in intimacy (female greater than male) varied by culture. The difference was largest in the United States ($d = -.95$), followed by Germany ($d = -.70$) and then the Netherlands ($d = -.39$) and Hong Kong ($d = -.34$). In Jordan, there was no sex difference in intimacy ($d = +.12$). In the three Western cultures, men were more intimate with women than with men. In Jordan and Hong Kong, men were equally intimate with men and women. Thus, the link of intimacy to women appears to be a facet of Western culture.

One might expect men's friendships in countries with a less individualistic focus to differ from men's friendships in the United States. The friendships of college students in the United States were compared to those of students in India (J. Berman, Murphy-Berman, & Pachauri, 1988). The conception of the ideal male in India is quite different from that in the United States. The ideal male in India is social, interdependent, and expressive, rather than competitive, independent, and nonexpressive; these differences should have implications for men's friendships with other men. Students in both countries were asked to complete a self-disclosure scale, a liking scale, and a loving scale in regard to their same-sex best friend. In the United States, women reported greater disclosure than men; in India, there was no sex difference in self-disclosure. In the United States, women spent more time than men on private conversations; there were no differences in how men and women spent time with their same-sex friends in India. There was no sex difference in liking of the best friend for students in either the United States or India; however, women indicated higher loving scores than men in the United States but not India. Thus, in societies that emphasize interdependence, men's and women's friendships are more similar.

CHANGES OVER THE LIFE SPAN

Age has a curvilinear relationship to the amount of time spent with friends. Verbrugge (1983b) surveyed over 1,000 adults and asked them about the frequency of contact with their three best friends. The greatest contact occurred among young adults and the elderly. Middle-age adults had less contact with friends, most likely because they were heavily involved with work or family.

More than chronological age, life events affect friendship. Getting married, becoming a parent, building a career, retiring, and widowhood are all examples of structural issues that may influence friendships for men and women. Some of these life events are more likely to be experienced by one sex than the other or are more likely to have an effect on the friendships of one sex than the other. For example, widowhood is more likely to affect women than men because women live longer than men. However, widowhood may have a stronger effect on men's friendships than women's friendships because wives are often the sole source of support and connection to other relationships for men. Retirement may have a stronger impact on men's friendships than women's friendships because men's friends are more likely than women's to be found in the workplace. Below, I examine some of the structural factors that influence men's and women's friendships in early and later adulthood.

Early Adulthood: Marriage and Family

Historically, men's friendships were based at work and women's were based at home (Wellman, 1992). Women were the social organizers of the couple's friendships, often arranging social activities with other couples. In an early study, C. Fischer (1979) found that young married men had a larger social network than young married women because men had opportunities to meet people at work, whereas women's opportunities to meet people were restricted by having to stay home with children. Men also identified more people in their network available to help them compared to women during the early years of marriage and adulthood (C. Fischer & Oliker, 1983). The investigators attributed this difference to men's greater contact with coworkers.

Today, the majority of women work outside the home, even when they have children. Women who work in male-dominated professions, however, still have fewer opportunities than men for friendship at work due to the lack of available women. The opportunities that work presents for increasing friendships among women may be offset by the fact that women who work are often responsible for housework and child care, which leaves little time for friends. Thus, it is not surprising that parenthood is associated with fewer friendships for women but not men (C. Fischer & Oliker, 1983), presumably because child care takes up a larger portion of women's than men's time. (This issue is addressed again in Chapter 11.)

More recent studies have shown that both the number of friends and the frequency of interaction with friends decrease for men and women during adulthood due to career development and increased time spent with family. Never-married adults have more frequent contact with friends than married adults (Verbrugge, 1983b; Wall, Pickert, & Paradise, 1984). Men spend less time with friends after they get married, in part because they have more familial obligations and in part because friends perceive that they should not spend time with them now that they are married (T. Cohen, 1992). In one study, younger men (25 to 34) were more satisfied with their friendships than were older men (35 to 50; Wall et al., 1984), probably because younger men were less likely to be married

or to be heavily involved with careers. Thus, both family and work obligations limit friendship. However, career development seems to have a greater effect on men's decreased contact with friends, and parenthood seems to have a greater effect on women's decreased contact with friends (P. Wright, 1989). The different positions held by men and women at work and in the family create unique opportunities for and place specific constraints on friendship formation.

Late Adulthood: Retirement and Empty Nest

With advancing age, friendships may increase for women and decrease for men, due to differences in the structural opportunities for friendship (C. Fischer & Oliker, 1983). As women get older, they experience the departure of their children from home, which leads to a decrease in their household responsibilities. Thus, older women are left with more time for friends. For men, increased age brings retirement, which may be associated with a loss of friends if many of their connections are made through work. Aging is also associated with reduced mobility and increased health problems, which will create barriers to friendship for both men and women.

Marital status has a great impact on friendship among the elderly (Akiyama, Elliott, & Antonucci, 1996), especially elderly men. Married men have more people in their social network compared to unmarried men. Marital status has no effect on the number of friends that women have because women maintain a network of friends outside their marital relationship. For men, women are often their link to social relationships. Among the elderly, both men and women have more women friends than men friends (Akiyama et al., 1996). Because men die younger than women, elderly women are more available as friends.

CROSS-SEX FRIENDSHIP

Can men and women be friends? This is the question that was taken up by the characters played by Meg Ryan and Billy Crystal in the movie, *When Harry Met Sally.*

Sally told Harry that they would just be friends. Harry, however, insisted that they could not be friends because men and women can never be friends—sex always gets in the way. Even when Sally said that she had a number of male friends, Harry argued that sex is somehow involved in the relationship—if not on her part than on the part of the men. Of course, as you might imagine, a friendship emerges between Harry and Sally that then blossoms into a romantic relationship.

Many people today, especially college students, would disagree with Harry. Even noncollege samples show on average that 40% of men and 30% of women are able to identify at least one cross-sex friend (P. Wright, 1989). However, Harry may have a point about sex interfering with friendship. I elaborate on this later.

Most relationship research either focuses on same-sex friendship or romantic relationships. Cross-sex friendship is a relatively new area of research. A cross-sex friendship is typically defined as a friendship with someone of the other sex that is not romantic, sexual, or familial. Cross-sex friendships are not uncommon, but they are much less common than same-sex friendships (Monsour, 1997; O'Meara, 1994). Historically, cross-sex friendships among adults were rare; the traditional division of labor in society did not provide many opportunities for men and women to interact with one

another. The changing nature of male and female roles in society has made members of the other sex more available as potential friends.

Comparisons to Same-Sex Friendship

The first studies of cross-sex friendship appeared in the 1980s. Most of those studies focused on comparing cross-sex friends to same-sex friends. Thus, we know quite a bit about how the two types of friendships compare.

On average, cross-sex friendships are less intimate than same-sex friendships (Lempers & Clark-Lempers, 1993; Werking, 1997a). This description is more accurate for women than it is for men, however. Women are closer to their same-sex friends than their cross-sex friends, but it is not clear if men are equally close to cross-sex and same-sex friends or are closer to cross-sex friends (Monsour, 1997; Werking, 1997a). This finding is similar to the conclusion reached about sex differences in self-disclosure to men and women.

In a study of 156 professional men and women, women rated their same-sex friendships as higher in quality and more intimate than their cross-sex friendships (Sapadin, 1988). Men rated their cross-sex friendships as higher on enjoyment and quality compared to same-sex friendships, but rated both friendships as equally intimate. Similar results were obtained with undergraduates (Buhrke & Fuqua, 1987). Women rated their same-sex friendships as closer than men did, whereas men rated their cross-sex friendships as closer than women did. Men self-disclose more in cross-sex compared to same-sex friendships (Werking 1997b).

P. Wright and Scanlon (1991) found that women were closer to same-sex than cross-sex friends, but that men were equally close to both types of friends. They asked adults in their 20s through 50s to complete the ADF for their best same-sex and best cross-sex friend. They found that women's friendships with women were closer than either women's friendships with men or men's friendships with either men or women. Women rated their same-sex friendship as higher on almost all of the dimensions on the ADF compared to their cross-sex friendship. Yet, there was one exception: women reported that their male friendship was higher in social regulation than their female friendship. Social regulation describes one's concern with the social norms regarding relationships. Men, by contrast, gave equivalent ratings to their same-sex and cross-sex friendships on all of the dimensions except one: men rated their male friendship as higher in voluntary interdependence than their female friendship. Voluntary interdependence, one of the two measures of relationship strength, reflects a willingness to commit time to the friend.

Thus, it appears that the female-female relationship is especially strong (P. Wright & Scanlon, 1991). Women clearly are closer to their same-sex than cross-sex friends. It is not clear if men are closer to same-sex or cross-sex friends.

Gender roles may determine whether men are closer to cross-sex or same-sex friends. One study found that masculine men were more expressive in their cross-sex than same-sex friendships, but that androgynous men were equally expressive in both (Narus & Fischer, 1982). Recall the results from the study on self-disclosure (Shaffer et al., 1996), which was depicted in Figure 7.5: highly masculine men self-disclosed more to women than men. It may be that masculine men are inhibited in relationships with men but not in relationships with women. Androgynous people may relate more similarly to cross-sex friends and

same-sex friends because the friend's sex does not influence their behavior. Investigate this issue further by conducting your own experiment in Exercise 7.4.

Similarity is a principle of attraction for same-sex friends. That is, "Birds of a feather flock together." Do cross-sex friends have similar interests and attitudes? Cross-sex friends, like same-sex friends, have a great deal of demographic similarity (Booth & Hess, 1974). Cross-sex friends tend to be similar in age and education. However, when there is a discrepancy, it is more likely that the male is older and more educated than the female. There may be less similarity in cross-sex compared to same-sex friendship. College students said that it was easier to relate to same-sex friends and that they discussed and did different things with same-sex versus cross-sex friends (Parks & Floyd, 1996). Thus, same-sex friends may have more in common than cross-sex friends.

What functions do cross-sex friendships serve for men and women? Men and women might derive different resources

---

EXERCISE 7.4
Gender Roles in Cross-Sex Friendship

Find out how gender roles are related to cross-sex friendship. How do masculine, feminine, androgynous, and undifferentiated people compare on number of cross-sex friends? How is gender role related to the nature of the relationship with a cross-sex friend? Do they spend time talking or engaging in activities? Administer one of the gender-role instruments described in Chapter 2. Examine the relation between one of the gender-related traits and number of cross-sex friends as well as nature of cross-sex friendship.

from cross-sex than from same-sex friendships. Some studies have found that men derive more emotional support from cross-sex friends. For example, one study showed that men found more intimacy and acceptance but less companionship from their cross-sex friends compared to same-sex friends (S.M. Rose, 1985). Another study found that cross-sex friends provided men with a source of nurturance, intimacy, and emotional support typically not available from same-sex friends (Werking, 1997b). For women, cross-sex friendship provides companionship and a sense of relief from the intensity of their same-sex friendships. Women have more conflict with their same-sex friends than their cross-sex friends (Werking, 1997b; P. Wright, 1982). These findings suggest that both men and women are deriving emotional support from their friendships with women and companionship from their friendships with men.

Cross-sex friendships may serve some functions better than same-sex friendships. Cross-sex friends can give insight into the other sex and can validate one's attractiveness to the other sex (Monsour, 1997; Sapadin, 1988; Werking, 1997b). Cross-sex friendship also provides relief from the competitive nature of same-sex friendship for both men and women.

Obstacles

O'Meara (1989) identified five challenges that cross-sex friendships face; these are listed in Table 7.2. First is the **emotional bond challenge,** in which friends question the nature of the relationship. Is the closeness called friendship or romantic love? This is the question that was taken up by the movie *When Harry Met Sally.* According to the movie, cross-sex friendship cannot really exist; even their friendship ultimately evolved into a romantic relationship. Second

TABLE 7.2   Challenges of Cross-Sex Friendship

Emotional bond:	Is this friendship or romantic love?
Sexual:	Is there sexual attraction?
Equality:	Is this relationship equal?
Audience:	How is this relationship viewed by others—and do I care?
Opportunity:	Are there other-sex people in my life available as friends?

Source: O'Meara (1989).

is the **sexual challenge.** We are socialized to view members of the other sex as potential romantic and sexual partners. Is there a sexual attraction? This is the issue with which Harry was initially most concerned. Third is the **equality challenge.** Equality is central to friendship, and men and women have an unequal status. Will the relationship be equal? Fourth is the **audience challenge.** Friends may be concerned with the public's perception of their relationship. In fact, people often view cross-sex friendships with suspicion and wonder if they are not in fact romantic relationships. Fifth is the **opportunity challenge.** Cross-sex friendships are less common and more difficult to establish than same-sex friendships due to the fact that women and men are often not together in situations that would allow them to become friends.

The prevalence of challenges in college students' cross-sex friendships (both good and casual) was examined with a series of open-ended questions and closed-ended questions that reflected these challenges (Monsour, Harris, Kurzweil, & Beard, 1994). The primary conclusion was that the majority of relationships did not suffer from any of these strains. The greatest challenge was the emotional bond challenge, and it was more of a problem with good relationships than with casual relationships. There were no sex differences in the sexual challenge, although more men than women admitted that they thought about sex. The sexuality challenge was mentioned more often by students who were single compared to students who were involved in a romantic relationship. The fewest problems were reported regarding the equality challenge. Theoretically, the equality challenge should be a major issue for cross-sex friends, for friendship by definition is based on equality. There may be an imbalance of power in cross-sex friendship, and people are more satisfied with friendships that are equal in power (Veniegas & Peplau, 1997). The audience challenge was related to students' scores on a personality variable known as self-monitoring. Recall from Chapter 4 that high self-monitors are very aware of their environment and concerned about the impression they make on others. Thus, high self-monitors reported more audience challenge problems.

The authors concluded that researchers have overestimated the degree to which cross-sex friendships face these challenges. However, it is also possible that respondents described only the cross-sex friendships that did not suffer from these challenges. A cross-sex friendship that is facing any one of these challenges might not be the one that comes to mind when researchers ask about friendship. Cross-sex friendships that do face these challenges may be less close than ones that do not. In addition, it would be important for future research to obtain both persons' perceptions of a cross-sex friendship; one person may not be facing the emotional bond challenge or sexual challenge, but the other may. Clearly, more research is needed on this topic.

Despite Monsour et al.'s (1994) results, several studies have shown that sexual tension is a problem in cross-sex friendship, especially for men (Parks & Floyd, 1996). In a study of professional men and women, both identified sexual tension as a problem in their cross-sex friendships, and men did so more than women (Sapadin, 1988). Men were more likely to flirt with their cross-sex friends and to believe that the relationship could become sexual. Male college students reported more sexual attraction than female college students to their cross-sex friends (D. Kaplan & Keys, 1997). Interestingly, in that study, men with romantic partners reported greater sexual attraction to their cross-sex friends than did men without partners. This is exactly the opposite of what Monsour et al. found. The investigators reasoned that men involved in relationships may be more inclined toward intimacy and sexuality.

There is little longitudinal data on cross-sex friendships. It would be interesting to know how likely they are to develop into romantic relationships, how likely they are to dissolve, and what instigates their termination. Does getting married or becoming involved in a romantic relationship influence cross-sex friendship? A local radio station in Pittsburgh invited listeners to call in and share how they would feel if a future husband or wife had a cross-sex friend stand up for them at their wedding. Listeners, especially women, were appalled. This was not exactly a representative sample, however. The people who called in to this station are likely to have had strong feelings about the issue one way or the other. Explore the future of cross-sex friendship in Exercise 7.5.

Changes over the Life Span

It appears that age has a curvilinear relation to the frequency of cross-sex friendship. Cross-sex friendship is rare in childhood, peaking during later adolescence and young adulthood, and rare in old age (Werking,

---

EXERCISE 7.5
Future of Cross-Sex Friendship

Interview 10 of your fellow students about their current and past cross-sex friendships. Find out what happened to the past relationships: Did they end? Did any of them evolve into romantic relationships? Examine the reasons for the relationship ending, including O'Meara's (1989) challenges.

Examine how certain life events influenced these friendships, such as the development of a romantic relationship. In other words, when one person developed a romantic relationship, did that alter the cross-sex friendship? How did the romantic partner view the cross-sex friendship? Are men and women equally accepting of their partner's cross-sex friends?

1997a). There are few cross-sex friendships in childhood (Winstead, Derlega, & Rose, 1997). Children may not have the opportunity to make friends with members of the other sex because boys and girls are often pitted against each other. In school, there may be the boys lunch line and the girls lunch line. Often, teams are formed by having the girls compete against the boys. In addition, children, especially boys, are often teased if they play with the other sex.

Cross-sex friendships are more common in adolescence and young adulthood (Winstead et al., 1997). In college, there is more opportunity for cross-sex friendships due to the availability of potential friends and the similar status that men and women hold in college. Furthermore, cross-sex friendships likely lead to dating relationships.

Among adults, marital status influences cross-sex friendship. A number of studies have shown that married people are less likely than unmarried people to have cross-sex friends (Booth & Hess, 1974; Werking, 1997a). Marriage may be a deterrent from friendly relations with the other sex. However, recall that married people also have fewer same-sex friends than unmarried people. In a survey of over 800 adults age 45 and over, marital status altered the nature of cross-sex friendship (Booth & Hess, 1974). Married people confided more in same-sex than in cross-sex friends, whereas unmarried people confided more in cross-sex than in same-sex friends. The authors suggested that married people were pressured to confide in their spouse rather than someone else of the other sex.

The survey study also showed that work status influenced women's but not men's cross-sex friendships (Booth & Hess, 1974). Women who worked had more cross-sex friends than women who did not work, whereas work status had little to do with men's cross-sex friendship. Due to the prevalence of men in the workplace at the time, work may have provided women more so than men with greater opportunities for interactions with the other sex. The authors also found that white-collar workers had more cross-sex friends than did blue-collar workers. Blue-collar work is much more likely than white-collar work to be sex-segregated. Thus, there are more people of the other sex available as potential friends to white-collar workers.

Cross-sex friendship declines with age among adults (Winstead et al., 1997). Elderly women, in particular, avoid cross-sex friendships because there is a strong norm against dating among the elderly (R. Adams, 1985). Only 17% of a group of White, nonmarried, elderly women identified a friend of the other sex. The majority of respondents assumed that cross-sex friendships were romantic relationships; when asked why they did not have any cross-sex friends, the most common response had to do with not wanting to get married. Participants mentioned that there were strong norms against dating at their age. The following example illustrates just how foreign the concept of cross-sex friendship is to an elderly woman. My widowed mother-in-law lives in an apartment building that houses mostly senior citizens, who are mostly women. There is a single, elderly man who often sits by himself at a picnic table outside the building. Even though my mother-in-law is an extremely friendly and sociable person, she does not feel comfortable talking to this man unless she is in the company of other women. If the person at the picnic table were a woman, I have no doubt that my mother-in-law would be sitting right beside her.

The question is whether this finding is an age effect or a cohort effect. When today's college students reach senior citizen status, will they also find strong norms against cross-sex friendships?

FRIENDSHIP AT WORK

Because men and women spend so much time at work and because work is so central to our lives, it is not surprising that some of our friendships are based at work. In survey studies that have involved over 500 full-time workers, S. Marks (1994) found that 50% of respondents identified at least one coworker who was a close friend, 48% said they discussed important matters with at least one coworker, and 50% said they get together outside of work with at least one coworker. There were no sex differences in these measures of coworker friendship. There was a strong preference, however, for coworkers to be same-sex friends, especially among men.

Work is a good setting to study cross-sex friendships. Although the workplace is still sex-segregated, there is increasing opportunity for men and women to work together. A study in Helsinki found that engineers, teachers, factory workers, and secretaries had more cross-sex friendships when their jobs were not sex-segregated (Haavio-Mannila, Kauppinen-Toropainen, & Kandolin, 1988). Cross-sex friendships also were more likely to form among people who were doing the same kind of work. Thus, men and women are more likely to develop cross-sex friendships at work if they actually perform similar jobs.

Friendships at work usually follow a developmental course. Relations at work begin on an instrumental level: both people are working on a task. One person then chooses whether to make the relationship more affective. "Friendly relations at work" must be distinguished from friendship at work (Bridge & Baxter, 1992). Friendly relations are people at work with whom one is sociable. Being friendly with each other at work promotes cooperation and getting the job done. Friendly relations lack the intimacy of friendship and do not involve the obligations of friendship.

There are advantages and disadvantages to having cross-sex friends at work (Lobel, Quinn, St. Claire, & Warfield, 1994). In survey studies, men and women report that these friendships can improve group productivity when they enhance team building. This would apply to same-sex friendships at work as well. However, drawbacks to cross-sex friendships that may not apply to same-sex friendships at work also were reported. For example, men and women are often self-conscious about how their friendship appears to others; others may gossip or be jealous of a strong friendship at work, which can have a negative impact on office collegiality.

Bridge and Baxter (1992) refer to friendships at work as "blended friendships" because they require the merging of two roles: coworker and friend. Because a friendship at work involves two roles, it is vulnerable to **role conflict,** which occurs when the demands of one role are inconsistent with the demands of another role. You might have found yourself suffering from role conflict when your role as student required that you study for an upcoming exam and your role as a member of some organization (band, fraternity/sorority) required that you work on the upcoming festivities at your school. Bridge and Baxter interviewed nonacademic university employees as well as adult students and found evidence for four different kinds of role conflict among friends at work. They did not examine the issue of gender, however, so I will speculate as to whether gender ought to be an important factor in these kinds of conflicts. You can test these ideas in Exercise 7.6.

Impartiality versus favoritism: As a friend, one expects special treatment and favoritism, but the workplace typically requires treating people equally. Is there any reason to believe that men or women would be more likely to suffer from this role conflict?

Openness versus closedness: Friendships require open, honest communication. At work, one may be expected to hold confidences. Because the literature shows that women self-disclose to friends more than men do, one might predict that women would be more likely than men to suffer from this role conflict. However, sex differences in self-disclosure are clearer when the topic is a personal one. It is not clear if there would be sex differences in refraining from self-disclosure when the topic is work-related.

Autonomy versus connectedness: Work provides a way of connecting to one another, which should foster friendship. Difficulties arise when one feels a lack of autonomy in a friendship because one spends so much time with a friend (i.e., seeing the person daily at work). Because autonomy is central to the male gender role, one might expect that men are more likely than women to suffer from this form of role conflict.

Judgment versus acceptance: An important attribute of friendship is mutual acceptance. The work role might require one person to critically evaluate the other. The literature on women's responsiveness to evaluative feedback suggests that women take feedback to heart more than men do, which could lead to more conflict in women's than men's friendships. In fact, women supervisors become nervous when providing feedback to women (M. Johnson, 1999). One reason could be that some of these

---

EXERCISE 7.6
Role Conflict at Work

Develop items to measure the forms of role conflict discussed by Bridge and Baxter (1992). Administer the items to men and women who have a close friend at work. Determine if there are sex differences. Also, develop a set of open-ended questions to assess role conflict at work.

supervisor-supervisee relationships are friendships. Alternatively, one might predict that men suffer from this form of role conflict more than women because criticizing someone or evaluating someone creates a status differential in a relationship, and men are more sensitive than women to status in friendship.

Friendships at work are usually formed among peers, people who are working at similar job levels (Winstead, Derlega, Montgomery, & Pilkington, 1995). In fact, if only one person in a friendship is promoted, the friendship may disintegrate (D. Wright, 1999). Another kind of friendship at work is an unequal status one, the friendship between one person and his or her mentor. There is a benefit and a cost to friendships between a supervisor and a supervisee. On the down side, such friendships make disciplinary action more difficult for the supervisor; on the up side, such friendships may encourage greater cooperation and facilitate getting the job done. If the subordinate is female and the supervisor is male, people are often suspicious of the nature of the relationship.

There has been some research on women's friendships with other women at work. When there were few women in the workplace and women were considered "tokens," women viewed other women with suspicion and often participated in the derogation of women (O'Leary, 1988). Women may have been competitive with one another for what they viewed as the few "women" positions.

Relationships with a female boss seem to be viewed as especially problematic, as evidenced by an entire book devoted to the issue: *How to Work for a Woman Boss* (Bern, 1987). This book provides employees with dozens of strategies on how to work for a female boss. Some are quite humorous today, and others seem as though they would be equally useful when working for a male boss (see Table 7.3 for sample strategies). It is not clear whether women prefer male or female bosses; there seem to be reasons for both choices (O'Leary, 1988). There is some evidence that women prefer to work for male bosses because men typically have more power and can acquire more resources. On the other hand, there is also evidence that women prefer to work for female bosses because women typically treat them with more respect and more often involve them in decisions.

CROSS-RACE FRIENDSHIP

There is little research on cross-race friendship. Such friendships are less common among Whites than among African Americans, largely because African Americans are more likely to be in the minority in their environment, which means more Whites are available for friendship. In a study of junior high school students, 25% of the White students had cross-race friendships, whereas 50% of the Black students had cross-race friendships (M. Clark & Ayers, 1992). Cross-race friendships were more common than cross-sex friendships. The largest barrier to cross-race friendship is prejudice (S. Rose, 1996b). Friendship by definition involves an equal-status relationship; thus, one reason African Americans may be leery of friendships with White people is that they are not typically treated by Whites as peers (Rose, 1996b). Although people today are less overtly prejudiced than in past decades, there are more covert forms of prejudice, such as preferring not to live in a neighborhood with people of

TABLE 7.3   Tips on How to Work for a Woman Boss

1. Forget your anger and quit demanding that your boss have qualities that she doesn't possess at the present time. If she's astute, she's going to realize her deficiencies pretty quickly and overcome the problem.

2. Assuming that you have a good relationship with your woman superior, tactfully suggest that a few workshops might be helpful for achieving greater understanding between her and the men and women in her department. She may view this as a fine idea and present it to the president. Many excellent training programs are available and are quite effective for lessening a tension-filled workplace atmosphere.

3. Be enthusiastic and optimistic. These two personality traits will take you very far with little effort on your part. Moreover, they will make you visible, especially when your passive boss practices being invisible.

4. If your boss is the token woman manager within the company, practice patience. She might be acting passive deliberately in order not to make waves or call attention to herself. If you are a woman, remember an important point: businesses that have appointed one female manager are often slow to promote another woman to an equal position. Play it cool; otherwise, you will threaten not only your woman boss but her male superiors as well.

5. And most important, don't discuss your weaknesses with her, for she'll never let you forget them and will continually use them to further intimidate you.

6. Let her open the door and hold it for you if she reaches it first.

7. Let her light her own cigarette, pour her own drink, and carry her own packages.

8. Allow her to put on her own coat, but help her if she's overburdened with papers and briefcase. In the reverse situation, allow her to help you.

Source: P. Bern. (1987). *How to work for a woman boss: Even if you'd rather not.* New York: Dodd, Mean.

another race and preferring not to have your child marry a person of another race.

FRIENDSHIPS OF LESBIANS AND GAY MEN

The nature of friendship as typically defined by heterosexuals is similar for homosexuals. However, friendship holds a different place in the lives of homosexuals. Friendships often replace or take greater precedence over familial relationships among homosexuals because homosexuals have less support from family than heterosexuals do (Nardi & Sherrod, 1994). Yet, there is surprisingly little research on friendships among homosexuals. The research that does exist does not examine whether the friends are heterosexual or homosexual.

The obvious question is Do gay men's and lesbians' friendships differ in the same way that heterosexual men's and women's friendships do? Do gay men focus on shared activities? Do lesbians focus on self-disclosure? Nardi and Sherrod (1994) addressed these questions by sending out a survey on friendship to men and women who participated in gay and lesbian organizations. The sample was predominantly White, educated, and professional. Respondents were asked to evaluate three kinds of friends: casual (more than an acquaintance but not a close friend), close (mutual commitment to one another, talk openly with one another), and best friend (greatest commitment to one another, talk the most openly with one another, accepts you as you are). The best friend could not be the respondent's partner.

First, Nardi and Sherrod (1994) found that there were no sex differences in number of friends: gay men and lesbians named the same number of people in each of the three categories. They also found no sex differences in self-disclosure, activities shared over the previous two months, or social support. Thus, unlike studies of friendship among heterosexuals, homosexual men's and women's friendships were more similar in terms of how they spent their time together. These data suggest that the agentic/communal distinction that characterizes sex differences in the heterosexual friendship literature does not reflect sex alone. In the friendships of gay men and lesbians, the male/female distinction does not apply.

There were no differences in the amount of conflict gay men and lesbians reported in their friendships. However, there were sex differences in how important it was to resolve conflict. Lesbians said it was more important to resolve conflict and were more bothered by conflict than were gay men. This difference is consistent with the heterosexual literature. In addition, lesbians were more likely than gay men to report expressing emotion when resolving conflict, but lesbians and gay men were equally likely to talk about or ignore the conflict.

Does the role of sexuality differ in the friendships of gay men and lesbians? Nardi and Sherrod (1994) suggested that sexuality will be more integral to gay men's friendships than to lesbian's friendships because men in general are more likely to use sex to achieve intimacy. They found that the majority of gay men (62%) reported having had sex with one or more of their casual friends, whereas a minority of lesbians (34%) reported having had sex with one or more of their causal friends (Nardi, 1992). The discrepancy was not as large for close friends: 76% of gay men reported having had sex with one or more of their close friends, whereas 59% of lesbians reported having had sex with one or more of their close friends (Nardi, 1992). Because homosexuals'

romantic partners are of the same sex as their friends, the line between friendship and romantic relationship may be more blurred for homosexuals than for heterosexuals. Homosexuals' same-sex friendship may be more similar to heterosexuals' cross-sex friendship.

SUMMARY

There are some similarities and some differences between boys' and girls' friendship. Friendship seems to be equally important to them, but with age, sex differences in the nature of friendship emerge, such that boys emphasize the instrumental aspects of friendship (shared activities) and girls emphasize the emotional aspects of friendship (self-disclosure). These differences persist into adulthood.

Studies on adult friendship do not reveal consistent differences in the number of friends that men and women have. However, women's friendships seem to be closer than those of men. In addition, men's and women's friendships with women are often closer than men's and women's friendships with men. One reason for this is the nature of male and female friendship: men's relationships are agentic—activity-focused—and women's relationships are communal—emotion-focused. Women emphasize self-disclosure in their relationships, and both men and women view self-disclosure as central to intimacy. The intimacy of men's friendships is restricted by homophobia and emotional inhibition.

Do women self-disclose more than men? The answer is yes, and the sex difference increases as the topic of disclosure becomes more personal. One reason for this sex difference is that both men and women view self-disclosure as a feminine activity and view men who self-disclose less favorably than women who self-disclose. Women are more likely to receive self-disclosure from women, but men reserve some disclosures for women and some for men. Aside from sex, there are a host of other variables that influence self-disclosure, such as gender roles, situational variables, age, and marital status.

Does self-disclosure equal intimacy? Traditionally, intimacy has been defined by self-disclosure, but this has been a subject of contention. Some people maintain that self-disclosure is a feminine version of intimacy and that men define intimacy through shared experiences. Research shows that self-disclosure is important to both men's and women's conceptions of intimacy, but men's conceptions may also include shared activities. For both men and women, an intimate interaction is one in which they feel understood, cared for, and appreciated. These feelings may come from self-disclosure, shared activities, or some combination of the two.

Friendships are not only a source of affection, intimacy, and support but also can be a source of conflict. Men and women report similar sources of conflict in their friendships but handle conflict somewhat differently. Women are more likely to confront conflict directly with the intent of resolution and in a way that does not harm the relationship; men raise the issue of conflict, but with less concern about its effect on the relationship.

The study of friendship is greatly limited by its focus on middle-class White people. Interesting differences appear in the nature of friendship due to ethnicity, social class, and cultural ideology. Friendship also is affected by age and by stage in the life cycle—being married, having children, working. All of these factors influence the availability of friends as well as the place of friendship in life.

An emerging area of research is on cross-sex friendship. Although cross-sex friends are not as common as same-sex friends, cross-sex friendship is not unusual. Women still rate same-sex friends as closer than cross-sex friends. However, men are sometimes closer to cross-sex friends. Cross-sex friendship can serve important functions for men and women, such as insight into the other sex, a source of emotional support for men, and relief from the intensity and conflict of same-sex friendship for women. A number of barriers to cross-sex friendship have been postulated, but there is little empirical evidence that these barriers actually pose serious difficulties. To be fair, however, little research has been conducted on the topic and it is difficult to study. One controversial area is sexual attraction. There is some evidence that this is more of a problem for men than for women in cross-sex friendship. Data are meager on the outcome of cross-sex friendship: Do they last, dissolve, or evolve into romantic relationships? Cross-sex friendship is most common among young adults and least common among children and older adults. There are social norms and structural barriers that discourage children from playing with the other sex, that discourage married adults from spending time with the other sex, and that inhibit the elderly from developing relationships with the other sex.

One arena in which cross-sex friendship can arise is the workplace. Friends at work are becoming increasingly common, especially among people who are peers and have similar job responsibilities. I discuss several difficulties that friendships at work face due to the inherent conflict between the roles of friend and coworker.

I conclude the chapter by introducing the understudied issues of cross-race friendship and friendships among gay men and lesbians. Dimensions of friendship used to evaluate heterosexual friendship apply to homosexual friendship, with the exception of sexuality, which may play a greater role among the friendships of gay men. Because of the potential for sexual attraction, studies of friendship among gay men and lesbians may benefit from comparisons to cross-sex friendship among heterosexuals.

DISCUSSION QUESTIONS

1. Whose relationships are closer: men's or women's? Why?
2. How should one determine the answer to the previous question? How would you define a friend?
3. What does P. Wright (1982) mean when he describes men's friendships as "side-by-side" relationships and women's as "face-to-face" relationships?
4. What person and situation variables influence self-disclosure?
5. What inhibits men's self-disclosure to other men?
6. Describe how a culture's view of men, women, and their roles could affect friendship.
7. How do cross-sex friends compare to same-sex friends for men and women?
8. What are the challenges that cross-sex friendship face?
9. What does the research on same-sex friendship and cross-sex friendship predict about friendship among gay men and lesbians?
10. How does marriage and work affect men's and women's friendship?

SUGGESTED READING

Bliezner, R., & Adams, R.G. (1992). *Adult friendship.* Newbury Park, CA: Sage.

Dindia, K., & Allen, M. (1992). Sex differences in self-disclosure: A meta-analysis. *Psychological Bulletin, 112,* 106–124.

Helgeson, V.S., Shaver, P., & Dyer, M. (1987). Prototypes of intimacy and distance in same-sex and opposite-sex relationships. *Journal of Social and Personal Relationships, 4,* 195–233.

Nardi, P.M., & Sherrod, D. (1994). Friendship in the lives of gay men and lesbians. *Journal of Social and Personal Relationships, 11,* 185–199.

Rubin, L.B. (1985). *Just friends: The role of friendship in our lives.* New York: Harper & Row.

Winstead, B., Derlega, V.J., & Rose, S. (1997). *Gender and close relationships.* Thousand Oaks, CA: Sage Publications.

KEY TERMS

Audience challenge—The concern that cross-sex friends have about how their relationship is viewed by others.

Autonomy versus connectedness—Conflict encountered by friends at work when the regular exposure to one another required by the work relationship begins to interfere with individual feelings of autonomy.

Dispositional level of analysis—Emphasizes the characteristics of the person as a determinant of friendship.

Emotional bond challenge—Challenge faced by cross-sex friendship whereby the friends must decide if the closeness they feel toward one another is friendship or romantic love.

Equality challenge—Challenge faced by cross-sex friendships due to the fact that the equality that is central to friendship conflicts with the status hierarchy typically associated with male-female relationships.

Homophobia—Fear of homosexuality or fear of appearing to be homosexual.

Impartiality versus favoritism—Situation encountered by friends at work when the desire to give a friend special treatment conflicts with the necessity to treat all workers the same.

Judgment versus acceptance—Difficulty experienced by friends at work when the mutual acceptance expected of friendship conflicts with the requirement that one friend critically evaluate the other.

Openness versus closedness—Situation encountered by friends at work when the expectation of the honest communication central to friendship conflicts with the necessity to keep professional confidences.

Opportunity challenge—Difficulty experienced when attempting to establish a cross-sex friendship that results from the fact that members of the same sex are generally more accessible.

Role conflict—Situation that occurs when the demands of one role are inconsistent with the demands of another role.

Sexual challenge—Challenge faced by cross-sex friendship whereby the friends must ask themselves if there is a sexual attraction between them that could lead to a romantic relationship.

Structural level of analysis—Emphasizes the different positions or roles men and women hold in society as a determinant of friendship.

8

Romantic Relationships

My husband had a number of friends from work with whom we occasionally got together. One of these friends was Bill. My husband had known Bill for about a year, and to his knowledge (or anyone else's), Bill was not romantically involved with anyone. Bill was from India and had gone home for a two-week vacation. When Bill returned, he was married.

This was an arranged marriage, a concept foreign to people in the Western world. Marriage without love? Without romance? It may surprise you to know that romantic relationships are a relatively recent phenomenon even in the United States (Murstein, 1974). Historically, people turned to friends and relatives rather than a spouse for love and emotional support. The functions of marriage were specific: economic security and procreation. Love was not among these functions. One reason love did not play a significant role in marriage is that it was thought to threaten the bonds with family, which were more important at that time for position in society. Even a few hundred years ago, love was largely independent of

and antithetical to marriage. If two people fell in love, this was regarded as a problem. Parents were concerned about controlling this "dangerous passion." In the nineteenth century, spouses were polite to one another and, hopefully, compatible but led largely separate lives. Even by the mid-nineteenth century, love was not a prerequisite to marriage. Love was expected to follow rather than precede marriage. When individual choice did emerge in the nineteenth century, people generally chose their partner based on the same characteristics with which their parents were concerned: character, health, religious morals, financial stability. Choosing a partner based on physical passion was not at all acceptable. During the latter part of the nineteenth century and in the twentieth century, the idea of marriage based on love developed. This coincided with the greater freedoms that women accrued in American society and the higher status conferred on women. It is the twentieth century that is really known as the century of the "love marriage." Today, the practical functions of marriage have been

311

replaced with more emotional functions (Murstein, 1974).

The focus of this chapter is romantic relationships, what men and women want from relationships and how men and women behave in relationships. I focus on how men and women construe the positive aspects of romantic relationships, such as intimacy, love, and sexuality, and also how men and women manage the conflict in their relationships. Research focuses on dating couples, often college students, as well as married couples.

The majority of research focuses on relationships between men and women, or heterosexual relationships. However, there is a growing literature on same-sex romantic relationships or homosexual relationships. Studying homosexual relationships not only allows us to test whether our existing theories about relationships generalize to homosexuals but also provides us with insight into gender. Are differences in heterosexual men's and women's behavior in relationships due to the structure of the relationship (i.e., it consists of a male and a female), or due to inherent differences between men's and women's personality? Examining same-sex romantic relationships allows us to address this question.

RELATIONSHIP DEVELOPMENT

Interest in Relationships

Men and women are definitely interested in romantic relationships. In a survey of over 2,000 freshmen from 101 colleges and universities in the United States, 96% said that they expected to marry (Steinberg, 1998). Among people over 30 who have not yet married, men indicate a greater desire to marry than women (Frazier, Arikian,

Benson, Losoff, & Maurer, 1996). The investigators of this study suggested that unmarried men's greater desire for marriage may be due to their lack of social support. In this study, men reported less social support than women, and lacking social support was associated with greater interest in marriage.

What do men and women want from romantic relationships? Support and companionship seem to be the primary reason both men and women become involved in romantic relationships. College men and women said they were most interested in a romantic relationship "to have a good time" and "to have a friend" (Peplau & Gordon, 1985). A study of sixth-graders, eleventh-graders, and college students showed that males and females of all age groups were interested in dating for purposes of recreation and companionship (Roscoe, Diana, & Brooks II, 1987). Thus, the motivations for involvement in romantic relationships are similar to the motivations for friendship. Another study of college students found that men and women wanted more from romantic relationships than friendship: they expected their love relationships to include closeness, security, mutual self-disclosure, and sexual exclusivity (Cochran & Peplau, 1985). There are differences in men's and women's motivations for developing romantic relationships. Men view sexual activity as a greater motivation than do women, and women view love and intimacy as a greater motivation than do men (Peplau & Gordon, 1985; Roscoe et al., 1987). We will return to this issue later in the chapter.

People have two primary concerns in romantic relationships: concerns about closeness (e.g., sexual exclusivity and relationship permanence), which is called dyadic attachment, and concerns about independence, which is called personal autonomy and egalitarianism (Cochran &

Peplau, 1985). You are probably thinking that women are more concerned with dyadic attachment and men with autonomy. Not true! In a study of college students, men and women both rated dyadic attachment as more important than personal autonomy in a romantic relationship (Cochran & Peplau, 1985). In addition, women were *more* concerned than men with personal autonomy and egalitarianism. Why? The reason may have to do with the differential emphasis society places on autonomy for men and women. Autonomy may be taken for granted by men; we expect men to have interests and activities separate from their partners, and men probably have no difficulty achieving this kind of autonomy. Because women are socialized to focus on relationships, they may find it more difficult to develop interests separate from their partner. Women may fear that self-interests threaten the relationship.

Standards for Relationships

In general, men and women have similar reasons for entering romantic relationships. But when involved in a romantic relationship, do men and women have different expectations of what the relationship should provide or different standards by which a good relationship is measured? As you will discover later in the chapter, women are less satisfied with their romantic relationships, including marriage, than men. Different expectations have been postulated as an explanation for women's greater unhappiness with relationships. Women may have higher relationship standards than men, which could result in relationships being less likely to meet women's standards. Alternatively, men and women may have the same standards, but relation-

ships could provide more resources to men than to women. If true, men are more likely to have their standards met because they get more out of relationships than women. The first reason focuses on women: their relationship standards. The second reason focuses on the relationship: how its characteristics meet more of men's needs than women's needs. There is evidence to support both views.

Tornstam (1992) concluded that women have higher expectations than men for romantic relationships. In a study of approximately 3,000 men and women in Sweden, ages 18 to 80, younger women (under 50) had higher expectations for intimacy (defined as mutual trust, openness, and understanding) compared to men. This is shown in Figure 8.1. Among adults 50 and over, there was no sex difference in intimacy expectations; with increasing age, women's expectations for intimacy de-

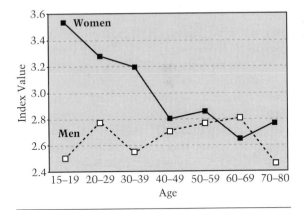

FIGURE 8.1 Expectations of intimacy. Among younger people, women have higher expectations for intimacy than men. Among adults age 50 and over, men and women have similar expectations for intimacy. *Source:* L. Tornstam (1992). Loneliness in Marriage. *Journal of Social and Personal Relationships, 9,* 197–217. Copyright 1992. Reprinted by permission of Sage Publications, Ltd.

clined over time to match those of men. Interestingly, married women under 50 were lonelier than married men in that same age group. Tornstam reasoned that these women were lonelier than men because they expected their relationships to provide more intimacy.

Do women change their intimacy expectations as they grow older? Because this is a cross-sectional study, we do not know if women adjust their expectations for marriage downward over time or whether the women in the older cohort are different in some way from the women in the younger cohort. The older cohort could consist of a more traditional group of women who had lower expectations from the start. It is also possible that the young women with high expectations for intimacy divorce before reaching the older cohort.

Vangelisti and Daly (1997) reached conclusions opposite to Tornstam's (1992). They found that women do not have different standards for relationships than men, but women's standards are less likely than men's to be met. They asked 122 adults enrolled in continuing education courses to rate how important 30 standards were to successful relationships and how much their current relationship met each standard. These 30 standards were grouped into seven categories: (1) relational identity (spending time together, being known as a couple); (2) integration (accepting each other's weaknesses, recognizing that there is conflict in relationships); (3) affective accessibility (self-disclosure, expressing feelings); (4) trust (being faithful, committed, honest); (5) future orientation (sharing similar plans for the future); (6) role fulfillment (each person fulfills his or her roles); and (7) flexibility (adapting to one another).

There was a sex difference in the importance of only one of the seven standards, trust, which women regarded as more important than did men. There were no sex differences in the importance of the other six standards, suggesting that men and women held similar expectations for relationships. For all of the standards except trust, women reported that their current relationship was less likely to have fulfilled their standards compared to men. These results are shown in Figure 8.2; one line indicates the importance of the standard and the other indicates whether the standard is fulfilled in the current relationship. You can see that there is a discrepancy between the two lines for women but not men. The discrepancy between the importance of the standard and the relationship having met the standard was strongly associated with marital dissatisfaction for both men and women. This study suggests that men and women have similar views of what is important for a relationship and are equally unhappy when their relationship does not meet their expectations, but that women's expectations are less likely than men's to be met.

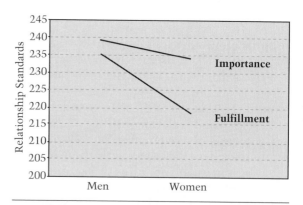

FIGURE 8.2 Sex differences in importance of and fulfillment of relationship standards. Men and women report that a set of relationship standards are similarly important to them. However, women perceive that their relationships are less likely to have fulfilled these standards compared to men. *Source:* Adapted from Vangelisti and Daly (1997).

Characteristics Desired in a Mate

Read the following personal ads taken from a recent edition of a local newspaper (Mac-Dowell, 1999):

Women Seeking Men

Educated, attractive, creative SWF, 29, 5'5", 120 lbs., long brown hair, seeks handsome, articulate *SWPM,* 29–39, 6'+, gentleman, *higher education (Doctorate/Master's a must),* who enjoys politics, arts, medicine. Multilingual a plus.

SF, 5'3", 135 lbs., blonde/brown, enjoys reading, music, concerts, movies, hanging out with friends. Seeking *SM, with good work ethic,* but can also be romantic, spontaneous, for LTR.

Men Seeking Women

SM, 29, 6'1", 190 lbs., enjoys all outdoor athletic activities, stimulating conversation. *Seeking well-built lady, 30–40, with sense of humor. Redheads a plus.*

Seeking attractive, down-to-earth, emotionally well-adjusted (the elusive criterion) SWF, late 20–30s, independent not disinterested, sense of humor (shares mine). Me: attractive, tall, fit, *educated (master's), employed, condo/car-owning SWM, 32.*

Affectionate, loving, honest, compliant, *hard-working,* handsome WM, 39, enjoys affection, music, clubbing, chats, movies. Seeking the perfect lady to share eternity and dreams, romance, passion; for lasting, loving relationship.

Not surprisingly, the women seeking men are providing information about their personal attractiveness and seeking men with education and a good work ethic. The men seeking women are interested in finding an attractive mate and providing information about their financial status and work ethic. Now consider the following ad:

> *Extremely good-looking SWM, 24, blond/blue, seeks financially stable female, age/race open for possible LTR.*

As you can see, there are exceptions to the stereotype. If you more carefully review all of the ads, you will see that there are other qualities besides physical attractiveness and work status that are desired in a mate. What else are people seeking? They are looking for someone who shares their interests, has a sense of humor, is affectionate, and is romantic.

EVIDENCE. Despite the previous personal ads, research shows that in general, men and women desire the same characteristics in their partners: honesty, affection, kindness, and someone to share activities. However, there also are some sex differences in desires that are consistent with stereotypes. As indicated in the personal ads, men desire physical attractiveness in a partner, whereas women desire intelligence or occupational status (Peplau & Gordon, 1985; D. Wright, 1999). Men and women are quite aware of these differences. Studies of personal ads like the ones shown here show that men tend to emphasize their status (i.e., financial security) and women tend to emphasize their physical attributes (A. Harrison & Saeed, 1977).

A study consisting mostly of college students showed that men and women tend to agree that some features are more important for women to possess and some are more important for men to possess (Regan & Sprecher, 1995). Participants indicated how important five personal attributes were for them to possess and how important those same attributes were for their partner to possess. Men and women both reported that it was more important for the man than the woman to have a prestigious career and a high-paying job. Men thought it was more important that their partner was physically attractive than that they themselves were physically attractive; women thought physical attractiveness was equally important for both people to possess. Both men and women believed it was more important for the male than the female to be athletic. Both men and women agreed that the female's chores inside the home were more valuable than her chores outside the home, whereas the male's chores outside the home were more valuable than his chores inside the home. Both men and women agreed that it was equally important for they and their partners to show love to one another. In general, men and women agreed on what was important for them to contribute and for their partners to contribute. However, men and women believed that the areas in which men should contribute differed from the areas in which women should contribute.

Feingold (1992) conducted a meta-analysis of the studies that evaluated sex differences in the characteristics desired in a mate. He found that females were substantially more likely than males to emphasize socioeconomic status ($d = -.69$) and ambition ($d = -.67$), but only somewhat more likely to emphasize intelligence ($d = -.30$) and character ($d = -.35$). There was no sex difference in the value attached to personality. Feingold (1990) also conducted a meta-analysis of sex differences in the importance attached to a mate's physical attractiveness. Across five different methodologies, Feingold found that men were more likely than women to emphasize physical attractiveness. The size of the effect was much larger in studies that used self-report methods (ds in the +.50 range) than in those that examined behavior (ds in

the +.30 range). A meta-analysis of mate preferences across 37 cultures confirmed the findings (Buss, 1989): women were more likely than men to emphasize socioeconomic status ($d = -.73$) and ambition ($d = -.40$) and men were more likely to emphasize physical attractiveness ($d = +.61$).

Since these meta-analyses, a more recent study has confirmed that men focus on youth and attractiveness in mate selection and women focus on status and earning potential (Sprecher, Sullivan, & Hatfield, 1994). In a national survey of adults ages 19 to 35, participants were asked how willing they would be to marry someone who had one of 12 characteristics. Women were more likely than men to say that they would marry someone five years older, someone who earned more money than they, someone who was more educated than they, someone who was not attractive, and someone who already had children. Men were more likely than women to say that they would marry someone who was five years younger, someone who did not have a steady job, someone who earned less than they, someone who was less educated, and someone of a different race. There were no sex differences in willingness to marry someone who was previously married or of a different religion. These results again show that women are more concerned with financial security than physical attractiveness, and men are more concerned with physical attractiveness than financial assets.

Some of the sex differences varied by race (Sprecher, Sullivan, et al., 1994). As shown in the left half of Figure 8.3, both Black and White women were less likely than Black or White men to marry someone who did not have a steady job. However, this sex difference was stronger among White respondents because White women were especially unlikely to marry someone without a steady job. Black women may

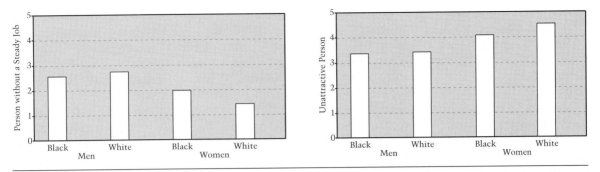

FIGURE 8.3 Willingness to marry someone without a steady job and someone who is unattractive. Black and White women said they would be less willing to marry someone without a steady job than Black and White men. Black and White women said they would be more willing to marry someone who was unattractive than Black and White men. The sex difference for both of these characteristics was stronger among White respondents because White women were especially unwilling to marry someone without a steady job and especially willing to marry an unattractive person. *Source:* Adapted from Sprecher, Sullivan, et al. (1994).

be more tolerant of a mate not holding a steady job because African American men are, in fact, less likely to have steady jobs compared to White men. By contrast, as shown in the right half of Figure 8.3, White women were the most willing to marry someone who was unattractive.

Although these studies clearly conclude that there are sex differences in preferences for a mate to be physically attractive and to have high status, they do not address how important either of these two characteristics are to men's and women's mate preferences. Two studies that evaluated the importance of a variety of characteristics show physical attractiveness and status to be relatively *unimportant.*

In a study of college students, Buss and Barnes (1986) asked students to rate the desirability of 76 characteristics in a partner. The top 10 characteristics were good companion, considerate, honest, affectionate, dependable, intelligent, kind, understanding, interesting, and loyal. Women rated a good earning capacity and ambition as more important than did men, and men rated physical attractiveness, a good cook,

and being frugal as more important than did women. It is important to note that these sex differences appeared on characteristics that were *not* rated as the most important. This is another example of similarities outweighing differences between men and women but differences capturing our attention.

A study of sixth-graders, eleventh-graders, and college students confirmed this finding (Roscoe et al., 1987). Students rated the importance of 30 characteristics when selecting a date. Women rated money and having a good job as more important than did men, whereas men rated physical attractiveness as more important than did women. Again, these three traits were *not* the most highly valued characteristics. Internal characteristics (kind, confident) were rated as more important than external characteristics (race, money) by both men and women.

One factor that is likely to influence sex differences in mate preferences is the nature of the relationship. Kenrick and colleagues (Kenrick, Groth, Trost, & Sadalla, 1993) compared men's and women's mate preferences for a variety of relationships. They had undergraduates report the minimum acceptable level of 24 traits (e.g., kind, physically attractive) for a single date, for a steady date, for marriage, and for a one-night stand. Overall, women required higher levels of each of the traits compared to men, meaning women were more particular about the traits their mates should possess regardless of the nature of the relationship. The characteristics that were most highly valued by both men and women were emotional stability and agreeableness. The expected sex differences appeared on items deemed less important: women held higher standards for status-related characteristics, such as ambition and earning capacity, and men held higher standards for physical attractiveness. The most sex differences in mate preferences occurred for the one-night stand and the fewest sex differences occurred for dating and marriage. Thus, in terms of serious relationships, men's and women's mate preferences are similar. This shows how important it is to consider the nature of the relationship when evaluating sex differences.

It appears that men and women agree on the most important characteristics a partner should possess, especially for a serious relationship such as marriage. Physical attractiveness and earning potential are less important characteristics in a mate but ones that men and women differentially emphasize, especially for dating relationships. Some of these findings generalize across cultures. Hatfield and Sprecher (1995) had students from the United States, Russia, and Japan rate how much they cared whether their partner possessed the 12 positive traits shown in Figure 8.4. First, they found that students in all three countries, men and women alike, valued internal characteristics about a person (e.g., kind and understanding, sense of humor, expres-

sive and open) more than external (e.g., athletic, physically attractive, status). The rank order of the characteristics, as shown in Figure 8.4, was quite similar for men and women. When a specific trait was compared between men and women, however, differences emerged for 7 of the 12 traits. Across the three cultures, men valued physical attractiveness more than women did. Women valued resources, such as ambition, potential for success, money, and intelligence, more than men did, but also traits such as kindness and expressivity. In fact, across the three countries, there was a sex difference in "choosiness," such that women rated all of the traits, on average, as more important than did men. This finding appeared in the previous study of mate preferences in different kinds of relationships (Kenrick et al., 1993). Thus, women appear to be more selective about the characteristics of a mate compared to men. In addition, students from the United States were choosier than students from Russia, who were choosier than students from Japan.

EXPLANATIONS. What is the explanation for men's preference for physically attractive women and women's preference for financially secure men? One explanation comes from evolutionary theory, according to which, men and women behave in ways that will maximize the survival of their genes. Men value physical attractiveness and youth in their mates because these are indicators of fertility (Buss, 1994). Women prefer mates who have a high occupational status because financial resources will help to ensure the survival of their offspring. These ideas are based on the parental investment model (Buss, 1989), which states that women will invest more in their offspring than will men because they have less opportunity than men to reproduce.

If this theory is true, women who are physically attractive should be more likely

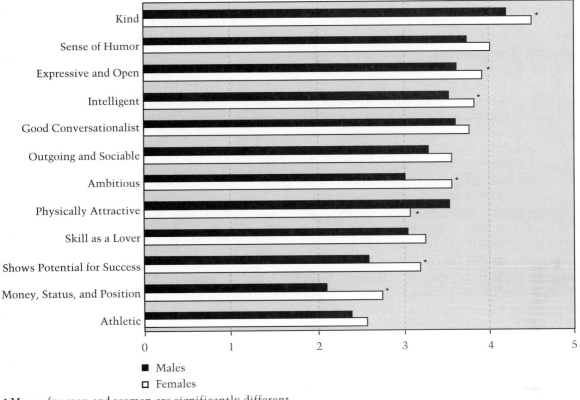

FIGURE 8.4   Trait preferences in men and women. Students from the United States, Russia, and Japan rated how important these characteristics were in a mate. Across the three cultures, women were the "choosier" sex, meaning that they valued almost all of the traits more than men did. The one exception was physical attractiveness, which men regarded as more important than women did. *Source:* Adapted from Hatfield and Sprecher (1995).

than women who are physically unattractive to secure a mate who is financially stable. A study of personal advertisements showed that physically attractive women in fact may feel entitled to a partner with financial security. Women who emphasized their physical attractiveness in the ad indicated that they desired partners who were financially secure (A. Harrison & Saeed, 1977). There are vivid instances of young attractive women paired with wealthy older men; Hugh Hefner and Donald Trump

are examples. However, a test of this theory revealed no support that this linkage occurs. In a study of 129 newlywed couples, there was no evidence that physically attractive women were more likely than physically unattractive women to be paired with a financially well-off mate (G. Stevens, Owens, & Schaefer, 1990). Instead, there was strong support that mates matched on physical attractiveness and education.

Eagly and Wood (1999) have argued that social role theory provides a better explanation than evolutionary theory for sex differences in mate selection. They suggest that a society's emphasis on a distinct division of labor between the sexes will be directly linked to sex differences in mate selection. In other words, females will value a mate with high earning capacity and males will value a mate with domestic skills in societies where men's role is to work outside the home and women's role is to work inside the home. Eagly and Wood tested the hypothesis that more egalitarian cultures would show smaller sex differences in mate preferences. They reanalyzed the data that Buss, Abbott, Angleitner, and Asherian (1990) had collected on mate selection preferences from 37 cultures around the world. First, they confirmed Buss et al.'s finding that women were more likely than men to value a mate with high earning capacity and men were more likely than women to value a mate who was physically attractive. However, they also pointed out that men were more likely to value a mate who was a good cook and a good housekeeper. This sex difference was as large as the previous two. Evolutionary theory would not lead to this prediction, but social role theory would. Second, sex differences in preferences for a mate with high earning capacity were highly correlated with sex differences in preferences for good domestic skills. Therefore, cultures in which high earning capacity is valued more by women are the same cultures in which domestic skills are valued more by men. Finally, the gender equality of a culture (as measured by the percent of women in administrative, technical, and professional positions; the percent of women in political office; and the percent of men's salary the average woman earns) was inversely related to the size of the sex difference in earning capacity preference and domestic skill preference, but not physical attractiveness preference. That is, sex

differences in earning capacity and domestic skill preference were higher in more traditional cultures. The traditionality of a culture did not have anything to do with the sex difference in the value attached to physical attractiveness. Eagly and Wood conclude that sex differences in mate preferences can be directly tied to a culture's emphasis on distinct social roles for men and women. Their theory, however, does not explain the sex difference in preference for physical attractiveness.

There are other cultural reasons that men and women may value different attributes in a mate. First, women have less access to economic resources; thus, it is not surprising that women more than men value a mate's access to economic resources. In addition, women are socialized to believe that their financial security does not depend on themselves alone. Second, men and women are socialized to value different attributes in a mate; it is more acceptable for men than women to discuss the physical attractiveness of the other sex.

Because it is more acceptable for men to say they want a relationship with a physically attractive person, this sex difference in mate preference could be an exaggeration. There is some evidence that men and women are equally likely to value physical attractiveness in a partner (Feingold, 1990; Sprecher et al., 1994). A study of personal advertisements found that both men and women who were physically attractive indicated that they desired a partner who also was physically attractive (A. Harrison & Saeed, 1977). In the personal ads that appeared in this chapter, the men were equally as likely to emphasize their own physical attractiveness as they were to indicate a desire for a physically attractive mate. It was the women who did not indicate that they desired physical attractiveness in a mate—again, perhaps because it is less appropriate for women to voice this desire. Recall that the meta-analysis on mate preferences revealed that partners tended to match on level of physical attractiveness (Feingold, 1990). There also is evidence that both men's and women's physical attractiveness has an influence on interactions among strangers. In a study of dyadic interaction among strangers, the physical attractiveness of either the male or the female was associated with partners getting more involved in the interaction (e.g., smiling more, talking more; Garcia, Stinson, Ickes, Bissonnette, & Briggs, 1991). However, the woman's physical attractiveness did have a stronger impact on the interactions than the man's physical attractiveness. The importance of men's physical attractiveness is often overlooked in research.

One limitation of many of these studies is that people, usually college students, are asked to *imagine* what features are important to a relationship. One's preferences in the abstract for a hypothetical mate may not be the same as one's preferences in an actual mate. More useful information would be gained by examining whom people actually choose for romantic partners. Studies of married couples tend to show similarity on a range of characteristics (Feingold, 1988; G. Stevens et al., 1990). Feingold conducted a meta-analysis on 34 samples that evaluated the similarity of a couple's physical attractiveness. He found evidence for matching, meaning that partners were similar in their levels of physical attractiveness. Explore preferences for a hypothetical versus an actual mate further in Exercise 8.1.

SUMMARY. There are more similarities than differences between what men and women want in a romantic partner. The similarities exist for the most important attributes desired in a mate: honesty, trust, kindness, and a good sense of humor; the differences exist for characteristics that are

---

EXERCISE 8.1
Differences in Mate Preferences among People With and Without a Partner

Identify 10 characteristics of a potential mate. Make sure that half are internal characteristics (e.g., trustworthy) and half are external (e.g., physically attractive). Have 10 friends who are not seriously involved with someone rate how important each characteristic is in a potential mate. Then have 10 friends who are involved in a serious relationship do the same. Do the two groups of people have different ideas about what is important in a mate? One might find more sex differences (e.g., men valuing physical attractiveness) among the people without partners than those with partners.

---

regarded as less important. Those differences are consistent with stereotypes: men weigh physical attractiveness more heavily than do women, and women weigh economic resources more heavily. These differences are consistent across cultures and across time, meaning that they have been found even in recent studies. They can be explained by evolutionary theory as well as by social role theory. The weakness of evolutionary theory is that it cannot explain men's preferences for women with domestic skills; the weakness of social role theory is that it cannot explain men's preferences for attractive mates. Both theories, however, can explain why women prefer a mate with greater economic resources.

We also know that the nature of the relationship influences mate preferences. Sex differences are more likely to appear when the relationship is less serious; men's and women's preferences are most similar in serious relationships and in actual relationships.

Relationship Initiation

Do you remember your first date? How did it come about? Did one person call the other person? Who decided what to do?

How do men and women become involved in romantic relationships? Traditionally, the male has taken the initiative in these relationships. Today, it is more acceptable for women to invite men on a date, and there are more forums set up for female initiation; there are dances in high school and parties in college where females are intended to initiate. Yet, men still shoulder more of the responsibility for relationship initiation. In a recent study of college students, both men and women said they were equally capable and successful in initiating a romantic relationship, but men recalled doing so more frequently than women (C. Clark, Shaver, & Abrahams, 1999). Men and women also reported different strategies for relationship initiation. Men used more direct strategies, such as directly asking the person for a date or making physical contact with the person; women used more indirect strategies, such as hinting or waiting for the other person to make the first move. Gender roles may be more strongly tied to relationship initiation than sex. In the study of college students, masculinity was related to the use of direct initiation strategies (C. Clark et al., 1999); femininity, however, was not related to the use of direct or indirect strategies.

To examine the nature of relationship development, S. Rose and Frieze (1993) asked college students to describe a hypothetical and an actual first date. The investigators were trying to identify first date **scripts.** A script is a schema or cognitive representation for a sequence of events. They found that both men and women conceptualized the man's role as proactive and the woman's as reactive. For example, men and women reported that the man

was typically responsible for asking the woman out for the date, for deciding what to do on the date, for confirming plans, for picking up the date, and for kissing the date goodnight. By contrast, the woman was getting ready for the date, being nervous about the date, worrying about the date, waiting for the date, and accepting or rejecting the date's advances. Although participants were told to describe what they did on a first date, women included some actions that were performed by the partner; by contrast, men focused almost exclusively on their own actions. The authors suggested that this indicated that women view the course of a first date as more dependent on the behavior of their partner. Men's first date scripts consisted of more gender-stereotypical behavior (e.g., asking for date, initiating sex) than women's first date scripts, which may indicate that the script for a first date is more rigid for men than for women. There also was quite a bit of agreement between men and women as to how the course of a first date unfolds. Scripts for hypothetical dates were similar to scripts for actual dates. In short, both men and women agreed that men initiated behaviors on a first date and women reacted to those behaviors.

THE NATURE OF ROMANTIC RELATIONSHIPS

Romantic relationships are expected to provide closeness or intimacy, love, and sexual exclusivity. I examine each of these aspects.

Intimacy

I remember interviewing a couple several months after the husband had suffered a heart attack. I spoke to the two individually. During the course of the separate conversations, I learned that each person had a different conceptualization of "closeness." The wife told me of an occasion when the two of them were sitting together in the living room and watching television. She wasn't very interested in the television program and he wasn't talking to her, so she went into the other room and called a friend. The husband told me about the same interaction, but it held a different meaning for him. He told me that the two of them were sitting comfortably together watching television, something he defined as a moment of closeness. Then, all of a sudden, she disrupted this moment by leaving the room and calling a friend. They were both upset by the sequence of events but for different reasons. These two people had different definitions of intimacy. She defined intimacy by talking or self-disclosure; because the two of them weren't talking, she didn't consider the interaction very meaningful, so she called a friend. He defined intimacy more as a feeling of comfort in the other's presence and physical proximity. She disrupted this connection by leaving the room.

Lillian Rubin wrote a book in 1983 called *Intimate Strangers*. In this book, she argued that men and women define intimacy differently. From her interviews of adult men and women, L. Rubin argued that women define intimacy in terms of self-disclosure and men define intimacy in terms of physical proximity, the culmination of which is sex.

Although my anecdote fit her vivid descriptions of adult male and female intimacy, empirical research has not suggested that overall conceptualizations of intimacy differ for men and women. My colleagues and I investigated sex differences in intimacy in the prototype study of intimacy described in the previous chapter (Helgeson, Shaver, et al., 1987). We asked college students to recall a time when they felt intimate or close to a person of the other sex.

We constructed frequency distributions of all of the features identified in these episodes. In general, men's and women's experiences of intimacy were quite similar. For both men and women, intimacy episodes largely revolved around feelings and expressions of love and appreciation, feelings of happiness and contentment, and self-disclosure. There was some indication that men regarded physical contact as more central to intimacy than women did. Men were more likely than women to include physical contact and sex in their intimacy episodes, but these were not prominent features of intimacy even for men.

This study is limited in two ways. The first is the self-report nature of the methodology; both men and women may have been concerned about how the experimenter would view their conceptions of intimacy if their stories had revolved around sex. A second limitation is the age and education of the sample; perhaps conceptions of intimacy are different among older men and women. I recall sitting in an airplane reviewing these intimacy episodes when an older man sitting next to me inquired about what I was doing. When I explained that I was trying to find out how people define intimacy by asking them about times that they felt intimate or close to another person, he remarked, "You mean sex? You are asking people to describe sex?" Here was anecdotal support for L. Rubin's (1983) theory. The point is that definitions of intimacy may vary among younger and older respondents. When I reported the results of this study to students in my gender course, one man made a very interesting comment: "If intimacy doesn't mean sex, then why do they call it 'intimate apparel'?" I thought he had a very good point.

The results of the study on prototypes of intimacy are similar to results from studies of mate selection. On the whole, men and women are in agreement on what they want in a mate and how they define an intimate relationship. However, there are some differences between men and women on the more peripheral features desired in a mate or required in an intimate encounter.

One feature of intimacy that seems to be more relevant to women than men is self-disclosure. In the prototype study, women were more likely than men to identify self-disclosure as a feature of intimacy (Helgeson, Shaver, et al., 1987). Kilmartin (1994) suggests that romantic relationships will pose a conflict for men because the behaviors required in an intimate relationship—self-disclosure and expressiveness—are inconsistent with the male gender role. Among married couples, women self-disclose more than men (S. Hendrick, 1981). However, this sex difference may be less applicable to African American couples. In a study of Black and White married couples, White men were less likely than White women to self-disclose, but there were no sex differences in self-disclosure among Black couples (Oggins, Veroff, & Leber, 1993). Black men appear to feel more comfortable self-disclosing to spouses than do White men.

Love

What is love? Many people have shared poetic thoughts ("Beauty and Love Quotes," 2000):

> "To love a thing means wanting it to live." (Confucious, Analects, 6th century B.C., 12.10, translated by Ch'u Chai and Winberg Chai)

> "As selfishness and complaint pervert and cloud the mind, so love with its joy clears and sharpens the vision." (Helen Keller, *My Religion,* 1927)

> "The simple lack of her is more to me than others' presence." (Edward Thomas, 1878–1917, English poet)

Even second-graders have strong opinions about love. Here are a few comments they made (Noel, 1997):

> "When someone comes over, or you're hanging around someone, you know when you're in love. After you love someone, you play with the person you love for a long time." (male)

> "When you're in love, you're very nervous. When he or she is very nice and sweet to you for a long time and you are never fighting, you know you're going to be in love and hope it will last a long time." (female)

> "When a girl hugs you or kisses you, you know when you're in love. When the girl gives a ring to a boy and the girls says 'I love you.' Then you go out to dinner." (male)

> "When you meet someone who likes you, and you like them, then you know you're in love. Then you go on dates. Then it's marriage time, and you might have a baby." (female)

From distinguished poets to second-graders, the ideas of love for men and women have been adequately captured. All of the elements are there: wanting to spend time together (a very long time), feeling nervous, showing affection, and putting the other person first.

When it comes to matters of the heart, who is more romantic: men or women? Despite the fact that we view women as more relationship-oriented than men, research suggests that men are more likely than women to have romantic ideals.

For example, in a study conducted several decades ago, Kephart (1967) asked over 1,000 college students "If a boy (girl) had all the other qualities you desired, would you marry this person if you were not in love with him (her)?" The majority of the men

(65%) but only a small portion of the women (24%) said no. In fact, one of the women remarked, "I'm undecided. It's rather hard to give a 'yes' or 'no' answer to this question. If a boy had all the other qualities I desired, and I was not in love with him—well, I think I could talk myself into falling in love!" (p. 473). This study concluded that men view love as more central to marriage than women do. In this sense, men could be considered the more romantic sex. One reason men are more romantic than women has to do with the historical relationship between the sexes. Women were marrying not just a man, but a way of life; thus, women were taught to be practical in mate selection. Men could "afford" to fall in love. This idea was conveyed by a mother to her daughter in the movie *Moonstruck*, when the mother asked about her future son-in-law, "Do you love him, Loretta?" When the daughter replied "No," the mother responded, "Good, if you love 'em they drive you crazy cause they know they can."

More recent studies, however, have suggested that men and women are equally romantic when it comes to marriage. The "Kephart question" (1967) was presented to undergraduates in 1976 and 1984 (Simpson, Campbell, & Berscheid, 1986). Men's and women's responses were the same: over 80% of both said they would not marry the person if they were not in love with him or her. This is not surprising because the basis for the sex difference in romanticism has changed. Women are more likely to be economically independent today than they were 30 years ago; thus, women, too, can afford to base marriage on love. In another study, responses to the Kephart question were compared among college students in the United States, Japan, and Russia (Sprecher, Aron, et al., 1994). As shown in Figure 8.5, in the United States and Japan, men's and women's responses were similar

and again exceeded 80%. However, in Russia, women were less likely than men to view love as a basis for marriage. Russians, in general, had less romantic ideals than the Japanese or Americans. Ask this question today (Exercise 8.2) at your college to see if the findings hold.

Today, it appears that men and women are equally romantic in that they view love as the basis for marriage. However, there are other ways to assess whether men or women have more romantic notions about love. Sprecher and Metts (1989) developed a romanticism scale that consists of four beliefs: (1) love finds a way or conquers all; (2) there is only one true love for a person; (3) one's partner is ideal; and (4) one can fall in love at first sight. The items measuring each of these beliefs are shown in Table 8.1. Men score higher than women on this romantic beliefs scale. Other research shows that men are more likely than women to believe in love at first sight and to endorse "love conquers all" (Frazier & Esterly, 1990; Peplau & Gordon, 1985; Z. Rubin, Peplau, & Hill, 1981). Men are more likely than women to say that a desire to fall in love is a reason for beginning a relationship (C. Hill, Rubin, & Peplau, 1976), and men fall in love more quickly compared to women (Peplau & Gordon, 1985). By contrast, women are more likely to have a practical view of relationships, believing that it is possible to love more than one person and that economic security is more important than passion to a relationship (Frazier & Esterly, 1990; Peplau & Gordon, 1985; Z. Rubin et al., 1981). Thus, on more subtle indicators, men may still hold more romantic ideals than women. Although women have achieved greater economic independence over the past several decades, it is probably still true that women expect they will not be the sole income provider. Thus, women may still have some reason to be more practical when it comes to love.

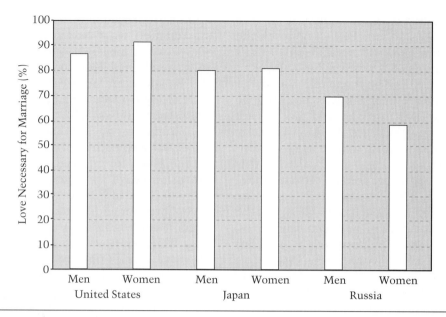

FIGURE 8.5 Students in the United States, Japan, and Russia were asked the "Kephart question" (whether they would marry someone who had all the qualities they desired in a mate but they were not in love with the person). Men and women in the United States and Japan were equally likely to say they would *not* marry the person, that love was the basis for marriage. Only in Russia were women less likely than men to view love as necessary for marriage. *Source:* Adapted from Sprecher, Aron, et al. (1994).

EXERCISE 8.2
Who Is More Romantic in Love?

Ask 10 men and 10 women the following question: "If a man (woman) had all the other qualities you desired, would you marry this person if you were not in love with him (her)?"

Either have a scale of response options (yes, no, unsure) or create a 5-point scale ranging from 1, definitely no, to 5, definitely yes. What other variables besides sex might be associated with responses? Does age matter? Does parents' marital status matter? What about gender roles?

Another way that men's and women's approaches to love has been addressed is by examining "styles" of loving. C. Hendrick and Hendrick (1986) developed a typology of love styles based on J. Lee's (1973) theory of love. According to Lee, there are three primary love styles: **eros,** or romantic love; **storge,** or friendship love; and **ludus,** or game-playing love. There are also three blends of these love styles: **mania,** or manic love, is a blend of eros and ludus; **pragma,** or practical love, is a blend of storge and ludus; **agape,** or pure love, is a blend of eros and storge. The love styles are depicted in Figure 8.6 and sample items are shown in Table 8.2.

TABLE 8.1 Romantic Beliefs Scale

Love Finds a Way

1. If I were in love with someone, I would commit myself to him or her even if my parents and friends disapproved of the relationship.
2. If I love someone, I know I can make the relationship work, despite any obstacles.
3. If I love someone, I will find a way for us to be together regardless of the opposition to the relationship, physical distance, or any other barrier.
4. If a relationship I have was meant to be, any obstacle (e.g., lack of money, physical distance, career conflicts) can be overcome.
5. I expect that in my relationship, romantic love will really last; it won't fade with time.
6. I believe if another person and I love each other we can overcome any differences and problems that may arise.

One and Only True Love

1. Once I experience "true love," I could never experience it again, to the same degree, with another person.
2. I believe that to be truly in love is to be in love forever.
3. There will be only one real love for me.

Idealization of Partner

1. I'm sure that every new thing I learn about the person I choose for a long-term commitment will please me.
2. The relationship I will have with my "true love" will be nearly perfect.
3. The person I love will make a perfect romantic partner; for example, he or she will be completely accepting, loving, and understanding.

Love at First Sight

1. I am likely to fall in love almost immediately if I meet the right person.
2. When I find my "true love" I will probably know it soon after we meet.
3. I need to know someone for a period of time before I fall in love with him or her.

Source: Adapted from Sprecher and Metts (1989).

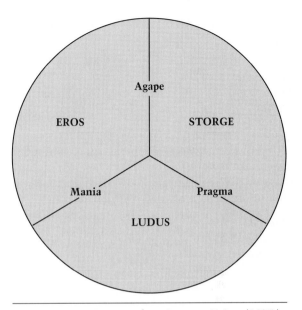

FIGURE 8.6 Love styles. *Source:* J. Lee (1973).

Sex differences appear on some of these love styles. Women typically score higher than men on pragma and storge, and men score higher on ludus (Dion & Dion, 1993; Frazier & Esterly, 1990; C. Hendrick & Hendrick, 1986; S. Hendrick & Hendrick, 1995; Rotenberg & Korol, 1995). The sex difference in pragma is consistent with the previously reviewed research showing women are more practical than men when it comes to love. The sex difference in ludus is certainly consistent with our stereotypes that men are less willing than women to commit to a relationship.

It is not clear whether there are sex differences in mania (Dion & Dion, 1993; S. Hendrick & Hendrick, 1995; Rotenberg & Korol, 1995) or eros (Dion & Dion, 1993; S. Hendrick & Hendrick, 1995; Rotenberg & Korol, 1995). Rarely have sex differences been found on agape (Dion & Dion, 1993; S. Hendrick & Hendrick, 1995); although a couple of studies of college students showed that men scored higher (Frazier &

TABLE 8.2 Love Styles

Eros

My lover and I have the right physical "chemistry" between us.

I feel that my lover and I were meant for each other.

Ludus

I try to keep my lover a little uncertain about my commitment to him or her.

I enjoy playing the "game of love" with a number of different partners.

Storge

It is hard to say exactly where friendship ends and love begins.

The best kind of love grows out of a long friendship.

Pragma

I consider what a person is going to become in life before I commit myself to him or her.

An important factor in choosing a partner is whether or not he or she will be a good parent.

Mania

When my lover doesn't pay attention to me, I feel sick all over.

When I am in love, I have trouble concentrating on anything else.

Agape

I would endure all things for the sake of my lover.

I cannot be happy unless I place my lover's happiness before my own.

Source: Hendrick and Hendrick (1986).

Esterly, 1990; Rotenberg & Korol, 1995). Most of the research on love styles has been conducted with college students. Perhaps in this population, men and women have more similar beliefs about romantic love.

It also is not clear to what extent these findings generalize to other cultures. Sprecher, Aron, et al. (1994) examined sex differences in love styles among college students in the United States, Russia, and Japan. Men scored higher on ludus and women on pragma, but only in the U.S. sample. Women scored higher than men on mania in the United States and Russia, but men scored higher on mania in Japan. In addition, students from the United States were more likely to endorse eros and storge and less likely to endorse ludus and mania than were students from Russia or Japan.

In summary, there are more similarities than differences in men's and women's notions of love. Historically, women had a more practical view of love and men had a more romantic view. Today, the sex differences are smaller. There is still some indication that men are more romantic than women, but this finding does not generalize across all measures of romanticism. There also is still some evidence that women are more practical than men when it comes to love, but women's notions of love seem to include romanticism as well as practicality.

Sexuality

SEXUAL SELF-SCHEMAS.   One way to examine sexuality in men's and women's relationships is to ask how men and women view themselves as sexual beings. Barbara Andersen has examined women's sexual self-schemas (B. Andersen & Cyranowski, 1994) and men's sexual self-schemas (B. Andersen, Cyranowski, & Espindle, 1999). A **sexual self-schema** is a set of beliefs about past and current sexual experiences that includes guides to sexual behavior. Andersen constructed sexual self-schemas by having a group of college students rate the extent to which 300 adjectives described a sexual male or a sexual female. The items that were most relevant to a sexual being were then rated by a second group of undergraduates who reported how descriptive the items were of themselves. A factor analysis was conducted on the items to determine which clustered together. A **factor analysis** is a statistical procedure that groups items together based on how strongly they are related to one another.

There were three clusters of items, or three factors, that described both men's and women's sexual self-schemas. The four or five items that most represent each of the three factors for women and men are shown in Tables 8.3 and 8.4. The male sexual self-schema and the female sexual self-schema had one overriding factor in common: the largest cluster of items for both related to being a passionate, romantic, and loving person. These items are shown in the first section of Tables 8.3 and 8.4. For men, a second factor related to aggression and power; this factor resembled the traditional male gender role, or agency. Both men and

TABLE 8.4   Male Sexual Self-Schema

| *Passionate-Loving* |
| Compassionate |
| Warm-hearted |
| Passionate |
| Loving |
| Sensitive |
| |
| *Powerful-Aggressive* |
| Aggressive |
| Powerful |
| Outspoken |
| Experienced |
| Exciting |
| |
| *Open-Minded/Liberal* |
| Conservative (not) |
| Liberal |
| Open-minded |
| Broad-minded |

Source: B. Andersen, Cyranowski, and Espindle (1999).

TABLE 8.3   Female Sexual Self-Schema

| *Passionate-Romantic* |
| Romantic |
| Passionate |
| Unromantic (not) |
| Warm |
| Loving |
| |
| *Open-Direct* |
| Direct |
| Straightforward |
| Frank |
| Outspoken |
| Broad-minded |
| |
| *Embarrassed-Conservative* |
| Embarrassed |
| Conservative |
| Cautious |
| Self-conscious |
| Timid |

Source: B. Andersen and Cyranowski (1994).

women also evidenced a third factor that reflected openness, but it had a different orientation for men and women: for women, the openness factor reflected being direct and straightforward; for men, it reflected being open-minded and liberal. One difference between the sexual self-schemas of men and women concerned the emotional valence of the items: for men, 89% of the items were positive, whereas for women, only 69% of the items were positive. A negative factor emerged for women that reflected being embarrassed and conservative; this factor was related to neuroticism and anxiety in women and is likely to be a deterrent to sexual behavior. There was no corresponding deterrent factor or negative factor in men's sexual self-schemas.

ATTITUDES TOWARD SEX. People have become more accepting of sexual intercourse before marriage. T. Smith (1994) examined people's perceptions between 1972 and 1991. The number of people who believed that sex before marriage was acceptable increased between 1972 and 1982 but has remained the same since 1982. In 1982, 38% of people said that sex before marriage was *always* wrong and 23% said that sex before marriage was only sometimes wrong; thus, the majority of people were accepting of premarital sex at least sometimes. In a recent survey of over 2,000 college students from 201 colleges and universities in the United States, 68% said that sex before marriage was acceptable if the two people loved each other (Steinberg, 1998).

Do men and women have similar attitudes about sex? In general, men have more permissive standards compared to women (Sprecher & McKinney, 1993). However, sex differences in attitudes toward sex depend on the degree of commitment in the relationship. Sprecher and Hatfield (1996) examined attitudes toward sexual intercourse among college students in the United States, Russia, and Japan. They asked students how acceptable it was to have intercourse on a first date, a casual date, when seriously dating, when preengaged, and when engaged. Students rated acceptability for themselves, for a typical male, and for a typical female. Not surprisingly, students in all three countries rated sexual intercourse as more acceptable as the commitment of the relationship increased. People in all three cultures agreed that sexual intercourse was not acceptable during the early stages of a relationship. As shown in Figure 8.7, in all countries, men viewed sexual intercourse as more acceptable than did women during the early stages of the relationship, but there were no sex differences in acceptability during the later stages of the relationship. When engaged, about 90% of respondents gave at least some approval to sexual intercourse. Americans were more permissive than

the Japanese, and Russians fell between the two groups. These cultural differences were strongest among the more committed relationships.

This study also showed that men hold a double standard regarding the acceptability of engaging in sex, at least during the early stages of a relationship. Men said that sexual intercourse is more acceptable among men than women during the early stages of a relationship. By the later stages, men viewed sexual intercourse as equally acceptable among men and women. Women in the United States showed no evidence of a double standard, but Russian and Japanese women held a double standard. Does a double standard exist in your school? Find out with Exercise 8.3.

Although men and women view sexual intercourse as more acceptable in serious compared to casual relationships, do men and women have positive views of people who have had sex? A recent study of college students showed that both men and women view a dating partner and a marriage partner as more desirable when he or she has not had any sexual experience (Sprecher, Regan, McKinney, Maxwell, & Wazienski,1997). In addition, some experience was viewed more favorably than extensive experience.

EXERCISE 8.3
Sexual Double Standard

Ask a group of men and women to rate the acceptability of sexual intercourse for a man and a woman involved in various levels of relationship commitment (e.g., met at a party, dating for six months, engaged). Do men or women hold a double standard (i.e., believe sex is more acceptable for men than for women) at any particular stage of a relationship?

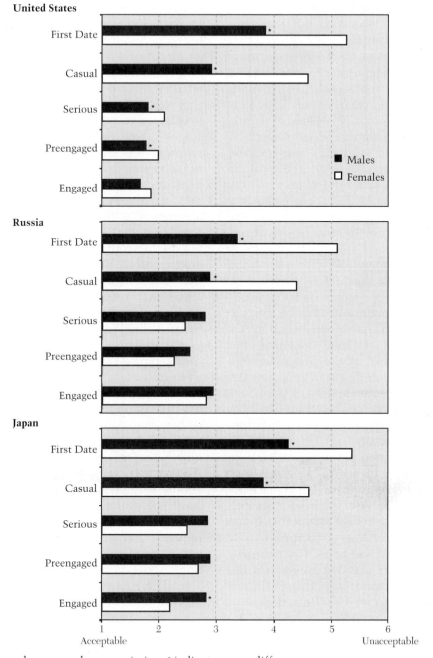

Note: Higher numbers mean less permissive; * indicates a sex difference.

FIGURE 8.7 Sexual standards. Among students from the United States, Russia, and Japan, men have more permissive standards for sexual intercourse than do women when the relationship is more casual. In serious relationships, men and women view sexual intercourse as equally acceptable. *Source:* Adapted from Sprecher and Hatfield (1996).

Attitudes toward people with sexual experience also may depend on whether they *intended* to have sex. One study showed that women viewed sexual intercourse as more acceptable in an uncommitted relationship if the woman was not prepared to have sex than if she was prepared (Hynie, Lydon, & Taradash, 1997). This may seem a little odd at first, as sexual preparedness is a way to reduce the chances of pregnancy and sexually transmitted diseases. However, a woman who engages in sexual intercourse is still viewed more positively if it appears that she was overwhelmed by passion than if she had planned her behavior. In this study, undergraduate women read a story about a woman who had sexual intercourse with a man and used a condom that was either provided by her (prepared) or her partner (not prepared). She was either in a committed or an uncommitted relationship. As shown in Table 8.5, who supplied the condom did not alter women's perceptions of the target woman when she was in a committed relationship. However, the target woman was perceived more negatively if she rather than her partner supplied the condom when the relationship was uncommitted.

Both college men and women are concerned that being prepared for sex may have a negative impact on the relationship. Galligan and Terry (1993) found that college men and women were reluctant to discuss the use of a condom or to actually use a condom with a casual or new partner because they thought this would inhibit the spontaneity of a romantic relationship. Respondents also perceived that discussing or using a condom would undermine the trust in a relationship. Men were more likely to use a condom when they were concerned about the risk of disease; disease risk did not influence women's behavior. Even when men and women intended to practice safe sex, behavior usually fell short of expectations, especially in the case of women.

We have been discussing how men and women view sex in the context of a romantic relationship. We have not yet addressed how men and women view extramarital sex. Although men are more permissive than women, the vast majority of both men and women disapprove of extramarital affairs (Christopher & Sprecher, 2000). In one study, college students viewed a hypothetical relationship between a single friend and a married person (Sprecher, Regan, & McKinney, 1998). Students perceived the female married person as more committed to the affair, as more in love, as more likely to marry the single friend, and as less likely to have other affairs than the male married person. Men and women had similar views on this issue. These findings suggest that people believe women have affairs only when they are in love with another person but that men have affairs without necessarily loving the person. It is also possible that people perceive male extramarital affairs as more common than female extramarital affairs and, thus, less meaningful. In fact, men are more likely than women to have extramarital affairs (Laumann et al., 1994; Sprecher & McKinney, 1993).

The research on perceptions of extramarital affairs provides some support for the idea that men separate sex from love and women view sex and love as occurring together. One study supported this idea by showing that men and women perceive different justifications for extramarital affairs (S. Glass & Wright, 1992). In this study, married people rated four different justifications for extramarital affairs: sexual pleasure and excitement, romantic love, emotional

TABLE 8.5 Niceness Ratings of Female Target

	Male Has Condom	Female Has Condom
Committed	5.20	5.25
Uncommitted	5.16	4.75

Source: Adapted from Hynie et al. (1997).

intimacy (understanding, companionship, mutual respect), and extrinsic reasons (career advancement, revenge on spouse). Nearly a third (30%) of women and 20% of men said that none of these reasons justified an extramarital affair, indicating an overall intolerance for the behavior. However, when justified, men and women disagreed as to the reasons. Women rated romantic love as a greater justification compared to men, and men rated sexual pleasure as a greater justification than women. Women found romantic love to be the strongest justification for extramarital affairs and sexual pleasure to be the weakest justification. Men rated all of the justifications equally.

MOTIVES FOR SEX.   I just reviewed some research that suggested men are more likely than women to separate sex from love. Does this mean that men and women have different motives for engaging in sex? DeLameter (1987) concluded that men have a recreational orientation toward sex in which physical gratification is the goal and a relationship is not required. By contrast, women have a relational orientation toward sex in which sex is integrated into the relationship as a way to convey intimacy. Research, largely based on college students, suggests that men are more likely than women to engage in sexual intercourse for reasons having to do with physical pleasure, and women are more likely than men to engage in sexual intercourse for emotional intimacy and love (Regan & Berscheid, 1999; Sprecher & McKinney, 1993). In one study, college men and women were asked what caused sexual desire in men and women (Regan & Berscheid, 1999). Love was cited as a cause of sexual desire in women by 42% of respondents and in men by 10% of respondents. Respondents also thought that the physical environment, such as a romantic setting, was more likely to lead to sexual desire in women than in men. By contrast, sexual desire in men was viewed as being affected less by the interpersonal aspects of the situation and more by internal motivations. Whereas 66% of respondents identified personal causes of sexual desire in men, such as physical need, hormones, and alcohol, only 33% identified these factors as causes of sexual desire in women.

Research among older adults (ages 22 through 57) confirms this idea (Sprague & Quadagno, 1989). The investigators asked men and women what their primary reason was for engaging in sexual intercourse. Responses were categorized into physical (i.e., tension release) versus emotional (i.e., to show love). Overall, women's reasons were more likely to be emotional than physical and men's reasons were more likely to be physical than emotional. However, the age of the respondent influenced the results. As age increased, sex differences in the reasons for engaging in sex disappeared and almost reversed themselves; there was some evidence that older women emphasized physical motives and older men emphasized emotional motives for sexual intercourse. Thus, the idea that men separate sex from love may be a better descriptor of younger men.

These sex differences have been replicated among homosexuals. In one study, both heterosexual and homosexual men compared to women were more interested in having sex for pure pleasure, to relieve sexual tension, and to please their partner (Leigh, 1989). Heterosexual and homosexual women compared to men were more interested in having sex to express emotional closeness. Thus, the difference in motives for sex is a function of people's sex rather than sexual orientation.

FIRST SEXUAL EXPERIENCES.   On average, men and women have their first sexual experience around age 16 or 17 (Netting, 1992; Sprecher, Barbee, & Schwartz, 1995). A study in Canada showed that the percentage of college students who have not had sexual intercourse has declined over 10 years for women but has remained the same for men (Netting, 1992). In 1980, 27% of college men reported having had no sexual partners; in 1990, 23% of men reported no sexual partners. In 1980, 41% of college women reported having had no sexual partners; in 1990, 21% of women reported no sexual partners. The nature of the relationship for first sexual intercourse has also changed over time. As shown in Figure 8.8, proportionally more sexual relations were with serious rather than casual partners in 1990 compared to 1980.

More recent data revealed that the percentage of virgin ninth- through twelfth-graders has increased during the 1990s among men but remained the same among women (Centers for Disease Control & Prevention, 1998d). Women are more likely to report pride in their virginity, whereas men are more likely to report embarrassment (Sprecher & Regan, 1996). However, between 1991 and 1995, men have begun to take more pride in their virginity. Sprecher and Regan examined the reasons nearly 300 college students gave for maintaining their virginity. There were similarities and differences for men and women. One of the most important reasons for both concerned not having found the right relationship. Women rated this reason as more important than did men. The next most important category of reasons concerned fears: men and women were equally likely to cite fears of AIDS and sexually transmitted diseases as a deterrent to sex, but women were

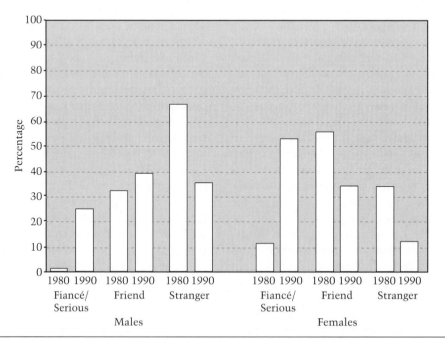

FIGURE 8.8 Percentage of sexual relations with serious partner, acquaintance, and stranger. In 1990, both men and women were more likely to have sexual relations with a serious partner than with an acquaintance or stranger compared to 1980. *Source:* Adapted from Netting (1992).

more likely than men to mention fears of pregnancy. Men and women were equally likely to endorse religious or moral beliefs as reasons for sexual abstinence. The only reason that men endorsed more than women was feeling shy or embarrassed to initiate sex. A lack of desire for sex was identified as the least important reason by both.

What is the first sexual experience like for men and women? First, women are more likely than men to have had their first sexual experience take place within the context of a more intimate relationship (DeLamater, 1987). Second, men report more positive reactions than do women to their first sexual experience. In one study, college students rated the amount of pleasure, anxiety, and guilt they felt during their first sexual experience (Sprecher et al., 1995). Both men and women agreed that they experienced more anxiety than pleasure or guilt; however, men indicated that they experienced more pleasure than women did, and women indicated that they experienced more guilt than men did. One factor that accounted for the sex difference in pleasure was that men were more likely than women to experience orgasm during their first sexual experience. In addition, both men and women reported more pleasure if the relationship was serious rather than casual. Men and especially women recalled more pleasure if that relationship was still intact at the time of the study (which was true in fewer than 25% of the cases). This finding could be due to a recall bias, however; men and women may be recalling more pleasure from their first sexual experience *because* the relationship lasted.

SUMMARY. Men and women have similar views of their own sexuality, with the one difference being that women have slightly more negative associations. Women's reports of being embarrassed, cautious, and self-conscious about sex are no doubt related to their more frequent negative experiences with sex. Women rate their first sexual experience less positively than men do. In terms of attitudes toward sex, men and women are equally accepting of sex in serious relationships. In more casual relationships, men are more accepting of sex. However, there is a double standard regarding sex in casual relationships, such that it is more acceptable for a man than a woman to engage in premarital sex. In other cultures, both men and women share the double standard, but in the United States, only men hold the double standard. The double standard may be expressed in subtle forms in the United States; for example, one study showed that women judge a woman negatively who has sex in a casual relationship when she is prepared for sex (i.e., had a condom available). Both men and women are disapproving of extramarital sex, but women show stronger disapproval than men do.

There also is some evidence that sex may have different meanings for men and women, especially among younger people. Men have a more recreational view of sex and women a more relational view. This may explain why both men and women perceive that a woman who has an extramarital affair is more serious about the relationship partner than a man who has an extramarital affair.

MAINTAINING RELATIONSHIPS

Consider the following book titles that appeared in the 1990s:

Relationship Rescue: A Seven-Step Strategy for Reconnecting with Your Partner (Phillip C. McGraw, 2000)
Fighting for Your Marriage: Positive Steps for Preventing Divorce and

Preserving a Lasting Love (Scott Stanley, 1996)

Communication Miracles for Couples: Easy and Effective Tools to Create More Love and Less Conflict (Jonathan Robinson, 1997)

Light His Fire: How to Keep Your Man Passionately and Hopelessly in Love with You (Ellen Kreidman, 1991)

How One of You Can Bring the Two of You Together: Breakthrough Strategies to Resolve Your Conflicts and Reignite Your Love (Sue Ellen Page, 1998)

The Highly Sensitive Person in Love: How Your Relationships Can Thrive When the World Overwhelms You (Ellen Kreidman, 1992)

What do these books have in common? First and foremost, they are all geared toward the preservation or maintenance of relationships. And toward whom are these books geared? Only *Light His Fire* makes this explicit, but my bet is that the intended audience is women. (For your own amusement, survey the sex of the person browsing through this section of your local bookstore.) In *How One of You Can Bring the Two of You Together*, my bet is that the "one of you" is a woman. As you will see in this section of the chapter, women are typically regarded as the caretakers of relationships.

Maintenance Strategies

What do people do to keep a relationship going? Canary and Stafford (1992) had married couples spend two weeks keeping a daily record of how frequently they employed 29 relationship-maintenance strategies. These strategies reflected five categories: (1) positivity (acting in a positive manner toward the spouse); (2) openness (self-disclosure); (3) assurance (assure partner of commitment to relationship); (4) network (involve family and friends in relationship); and (5) tasks (sharing household chores). Sample items from each of these strategies are shown in Table 8.6. The relative order of the strategies used was the same for men and women. That is, both men and women used strategies in the following order, from most frequent to least frequent: tasks, positivity, assurance, network, and openness. However, women were

TABLE 8.6 Maintenance Strategies

Positivity

Attempt to make our interactions very enjoyable.

Try to build up spouse's self-esteem, including giving him or her compliments, etc.

Do not criticize spouse.

Openness

Encourage spouse to disclose thoughts and feelings to me.

Simply tell spouse how I feel about the relationship.

Like to have periodic talks about our relationship.

Assurances

Stress my commitment to spouse.

Imply that our relationship has a future.

Show my love for spouse.

Network

Focus on common friends and affiliations.

Show that I am willing to do things with spouse's friends or family.

Include our friends or family in our activities.

Tasks

Help equally with tasks that need to be done.

Share in the joint responsibilities that face us.

Do my fair share of work we have to do.

Source: Adapted from Canary and Stafford (1992).

found to use more maintenance strategies than men; specifically, wives recorded more openness, networks, and shared tasks than men. Wife assurance was the strongest predictor of husband and wife commitment to the relationship. These results underscore the idea that wives more than husbands are responsible for maintaining relationships. No wonder the popular books are aimed toward women.

One specific way that wives maintain relationships is to accommodate their own preferences to match those of their husband. In a study of newly married couples, men's and women's preferences for who participates in child care activities were uncorrelated (E. Johnson & Huston, 1998); two years later, after parenthood, their preferences were highly correlated. Who changed? Husband's later preferences were largely a function of their earlier preferences and were not affected much by wife's early preferences. By contrast, wife's later preferences were a function of husband's early preferences, but only under one condition: when she reported high levels of love toward her spouse. Thus, one way wives who are highly in love reduce conflict is to adjust their preferences to match those of their husbands.

It is not only wives who maintain relationships. Partners of either sex who score high on expressivity or psychological femininity are likely to be concerned with relationship maintainence. Both husbands and wives who score higher on expressivity put more effort into improving the relationship (Huston & Houts, 1998).

Marital Satisfaction

Similar background variables and personality characteristics predict marital satisfaction in men and women (Karney & Bradbury, 1995). For example, a history of parental divorce and neuroticism predicts lower marital satisfaction among both men and women. Agreeableness and higher education levels predict higher marital satisfaction among both men and women.

Below, I discuss a set of personality characteristics (gender roles) and relationship characteristics (power distribution, equity) that predict marital satisfaction for both men and women.

GENDER ROLES.   If men are socialized to be masculine and women to be feminine, do the happiest couples consist of a masculine husband and a feminine wife? The literature on this issue is clear: couples with traditional gender roles have the least relationship satisfaction (Ickes, 1993). Instead, the happiest and the longest-lasting relationships are ones in which one partner is either androgynous or feminine regardless of the partner's gender role (Antill, 1983). This is also true for gay and lesbian relationships (Kurdek & Schmitt, 1986). Thus, it is femininity rather than masculinity that is most strongly tied to relationship satisfaction. This is not surprising as femininity reflects a focus on others, involving warmth, caring, and understanding—all attributes that one would expect to foster good relationships. If one person in the couple has sufficient feminine attributes, it means that one person is paying attention to and taking care of the relationship. The following studies illustrate this point.

In a study of distressed and nondistressed couples, the most frequent gender-role pairing among nondistressed couples was an androgynous husband with an androgynous wife (Peterson, Baucom, Elliott, & Farr, 1989). The most frequent gender-role pairing among distressed couples was two undifferentiated people: people who lacked both masculine and feminine qualities. In addition, husband femininity, wife femininity, and wife masculinity were all positively related to marital adjustment. Thus, both masculinity and femininity were associated with marital satisfaction, but the effects for femininity were stronger.

In a study of married and cohabiting couples, femininity was associated not only with relationship satisfaction but with adaptive ways of negotiating conflict (Burger & Jacobson, 1979). When couples were asked to discuss a conflict, femininity was associated with positive problem-solving strategies, such as approval, coming up with solutions, and paraphrasing the partner's remarks. Thus, femininity was related to providing both emotional and instrumental support. Femininity was inversely related to negative problem-solving strategies, such as making negative remarks and issuing commands. Masculinity was not associated with relationship satisfaction or problem-solving strategies.

People recognize the value of feminine traits in relationships. In a study of college students, men and women perceived a potential mate to be more desirable if he or she was androgynous (possessed both masculine and feminine characteristics) as opposed to sex-typed or undifferentiated (B. Green & Kenrick, 1994). However, students rated the feminine characteristics as more important than the masculine characteristics. Vonk and van Nobelen (1993) found that both men and women rated themselves as behaving in a more feminine way and a less masculine way when they were with their partner than when they were by themselves. This indicates that both men and women recognize the importance of femininity to relationships. Moreover, people who behaved in feminine ways with their partner also reported the highest relationship satisfaction.

One way that femininity may be linked to relationship satisfaction is through interpersonal skills. In a study of college students, femininity was associated with greater competence in providing support and self-disclosing (Lamke, Sollie, Durbin, & Fitzpatrick, 1994). These domains of expressive competence accounted for the relation of femininity to relationship satisfaction.

Is there a role for masculinity in relationship satisfaction? In the previous study, masculinity was associated with domains of instrumental competence, such as initiating relationships and bringing up issues of conflict (Lamke et al., 1994). However, instrumental competence was not associated with relationship satisfaction. Two studies of married couples examined the implications of both positive and negative masculine and feminine attributes for marital satisfaction (Bradbury, Campbell, & Fincham, 1995). In the first study, both positive masculine attributes (i.e., agency) and positive feminine attributes in the husband predicted an increase in the wife's marital satisfaction over the year. In the second study, negative masculine attributes in the husband (i.e., unmitigated agency, which includes being hostile, greedy, and arrogant) predicted a decline in the wife's marital satisfaction. Attributes of the wife did not influence the husband's marital satisfaction in either study. These findings underscore the importance of distinguishing positive from negative masculine traits. They also support the idea that characteristics of the husband influence the wife's psychological well-being but the reverse is not true. This finding is discussed in more detail in a later section.

Other studies have examined the relation of gender-role attitudes rather than gender-related traits per se to marital satisfaction. Women tend to have less traditional attitudes toward their relationships compared to men (Peplau & Gordon, 1985). However, there is a high level of correspondence between men's and women's attitudes toward gender roles within a couple; that is, egalitarian women tend to pair off with egalitarian men and traditional women tend to pair off with traditional men.

But whose relationships are more satisfying: those who have traditional views of relationships or those who have egalitarian views? In a study of married couples in Sydney, Australia (Antill, Cotton, & Tindale, 1983), wives were more satisfied when the husband had an egalitarian view of marriage, regardless of the wife's own view (traditional or egalitarian). Husbands were dissatisfied only when they held a traditional view of marriage and their wife held an egalitarian view of marriage.

The bottom line seems to be that femininity rather than masculinity is most strongly related to relationship satisfaction. Femininity is related to providing support, self-disclosure, and effectively managing conflict in relationships. In terms of gender-role attitudes, it is not clear whether egalitarian or traditional attitudes predict relationship satisfaction. This depends, in part, on whether one person's attitude matches the partner's. For example, traditional men married to egalitarian women are not happy with their relationships.

POWER DISTRIBUTION.   One way gender-role attitudes manifest themselves in marriage is in how power is distributed between husband and wife. What is the difference in the power that men and women hold in relationships? Felmlee (1994) reasoned that younger men and women should have more equal power in relationships because they are less likely to adhere to traditional roles. College men and women in particular have a similar status and similar access to resources. It is not until entry into the workforce that there is a sex difference in access to resources. Thus, there is reason to predict that power will be distributed equally in college relationships.

However, in a study of over 400 heterosexual college students, fewer than half (46%) said that they and their partner had similar levels of power in their dating relationship (Felmlee, 1994). Over a third (37%) said that the man had more power and 17% said that the woman had more power. Men and women did not perceive the power distribution similarly: female respondents were most likely to say the power distribution was equal, and male respondents were most likely to say that they had more power than their partner. Another study of college dating couples found similar results. Most couples reported an imbalance of power in their relationship, usually in the direction of the male having more power (Sprecher & Felmlee, 1997). Again, men were more likely to suggest this than women.

In a study of 3,500 married couples, Blumstein and Schwartz (1983) found that 64% said that the balance of power was equal in their relationship. When the balance was unequal, 27% of men and 28% of women reported that the man had more power, and 9% of men and 8% of women reported that the woman had more power. Thus, it appears that the balance of power is equal in the majority of families, and when it is not, power is in favor of the male. These findings may not generalize to all families, however; the respondents in this study were almost all White, young, and college graduates.

What is the balance of power among other ethnic groups? The stereotype about African American families is that women have more power in the family than men. Peplau and Campbell (1989) refer to this idea as the **myth of matriarchy.** The reason for the myth is that people are confusing two issues: the large number of Black households in which a woman is the head because there is no man, and the idea that women dominate in Black families. Data support the first issue but not the second. Studies show that the majority of Black families report equal power relations, similar to those of White families (Peplau & Campbell, 1989). There is some research that shows men are more likely to dominate among lower-socioeconomic-status Black families, but the majority of low- and middle-income Black families still report equal power relations.

An ethnic group in which men are perceived as dominant is the Hispanic family. Peplau and Campbell (1989) refer to this as the **myth of male dominance.** Certainly, you can see the direction in which we are heading: research has shown that most of these families also report equal power relations. Mexican and Mexican American families are assumed to be patriarchal. However, one study found that most couples held egalitarian views (Hawkes & Taylor, 1975). Couples were asked who makes decisions in a number of domains: when to visit friends, where the family lives, whether the wife works, the number of children to have, the discipline used with children, and how money is spent. In all cases except one, the majority of couples said that both partners contributed to making decisions; the exception was that half of the couples said the husband decides where the family lives.

One of the difficulties with these studies of the distribution of power in the family is that they are based on self-report. A more creative methodology to assess power in relationships was developed and examined across several cultures (W. Wagner, Kirchler, Clack, Tekarslan, & Verma, 1990). The investigators asked men and women in Austria, the United States, India, and Turkey to imagine that they bought a fairly expensive product and that their spouse either approved or disapproved of the purchase. Respondents were asked to rate how good or bad they would feel in each situation. The discrepancy between how the person felt when the spouse disapproved versus approved represented

"dependence on the other's agreement," which would reflect low power. In other words, if you feel really good when you buy something of which your spouse approves and really bad when you buy something of which your spouse disapproves, you have low power in the relationship. By contrast, if your feelings are relatively unaffected by whether your spouse approves or disapproves of your purchase, you have high power in the relationship.

As expected, in families in which the husband was dominant, men were less dependent than women. This means that men were less affected than women by whether their spouse approved or disapproved of their purchase. In egalitarian families, men and women were equally dependent. Interestingly, these findings only held for the two Western cultures, Austria and the United States. There was actually *less* dependence in the traditional patriarchal cultures of India and Turkey. If the families are more patriarchal, meaning that husbands are dominant, why aren't wives more affected by their husband's approval versus disapproval? The authors explain that the traditional gender roles in India and Turkey are independent roles: men's and women's roles are distinct from one another and they function in those roles independent of one another. This means that each person has great control over his or her domain but little control over the spouse's domain. They grant each other this power. If one person makes a purchase, the other would have little to say about it. Determine the level of "dependence" in your own and your peers' relationships in Exercise 8.4.

Thus far, the evidence is that power is most likely to be shared between husbands and wives across a variety of ethnic groups. However, there is a problem in the way an equal power relationship has been conceptualized in these studies. There are two ways in which people can report an equal power relationship. First, power can be equal because the two people share responsibility for all domains; this is the definition of a true egalitarian relationship. Second, power can be equal such that one person has exclusive power in some domains and the other person has exclusive power in other domains; thus, there is an *average* balance of power. This is the situation that characterized the Turkish and Indian marriages. Are these egalitarian relationships? They can be, but often they are not. If the domains of power are divided along traditional gender-role lines, such that women have power over child care matters and men have power over economic resources, it is unlikely that the relationship is truly egalitarian.

How is power distribution related to marital satisfaction? The answer is not clear. In the study of college dating couples, perceptions of a power imbalance were unrelated to relationship satisfaction (Sprecher & Felmlee, 1997). In an earlier study of college students, the power differential in the relationship predicted relationship dissolution (Felmlee, 1994). The longest-lasting relationships were *not* the most equitable relationships; instead, the more power men had relative to women, the less likely the relationship was to dissolve. Couples who were most likely to break up were those in which the female had more power than the male.

Studies of married couples show that the highest marital satisfaction occurs among couples in which power is shared (i.e., egalitarian couples), but husband-dominant couples are a close second (Gray-Little & Burks, 1983). The authors point out that the happiness of egalitarian couples may be exaggerated in this study because some traditional couples are inappropriately classified as egalitarian for the reasons discussed above. A truly egalitarian couple is one in which power is shared *across* domains. However, couples could define themselves as egalitarian because the sum total of power is shared: he has power outside the home and she has power inside the home. Thus, it is not completely clear from these studies whether egalitarian couples are really happier than male-dominant couples.

One finding is clear. Both self-report and observational studies show that the least happy couples are those in which the wife is dominant (Gray-Little & Burks, 1983). These couples may be unhappy because they are so sharply violating traditional norms. The authors also provide another explanation for the distress in wife-dominant couples. Perhaps the couples are unhappy because the wife is forced to be dominant due to her husband's passivity. In this case, the wife resents having to take on responsibilities that he refuses, and the husband resents her dominance. Future studies should not only examine who has more power in the relationship but what couples' preferences are for power distribution.

EQUITY.　One determinant of relationship satisfaction for both men and women is **equity** (Cahn, 1992). An equitable relationship is one in which a person feels that what he or she puts into and gets out of a relationship is equal to what the partner puts into and gets out of the relationship. People who report that they are overbenefited (receive more from the relationship than their partner) or underbenefited (receive less from the relationship than their partner) are dissatisfied in relationships, whether male or female (Cahn, 1992). Think about one of your relationships, current or past. What did you put into the relationship (e.g., time, money, effort listening to problems, effort helping with chores)? What did you get out of the relationship (e.g., love, trust, caring, affection, someone to talk to about problems, someone to do things with)? Now, ask yourself these same questions about your partner: What did he or she put into and get out of the relationship? You are likely to be satisfied with the relationship if you perceive the balance to be equal. But does equity determine satisfaction, or does satisfaction determine equity? Both are probably true. Equity is a subjective judgment. If you are happy in the relationship, you will probably perceive what you and your partner put into and get out of the relationship to be equal. For example, even Hugh Hefner claims that his relationship with his four girlfriends is equal. Here is an excerpt from an interview with Hugh Hefner (by Terry Gross) on National Public Radio (November 29, 1999):

GROSS: Now, here's something I sometimes wonder about couples in which there is a really big age disparity between them. . . . Like, if you're 52 years older than the woman you're seeing, she . . . In some ways, she couldn't possibly be your equal because you've lived a long time, you've been very successful, you've amassed a fortune, and published this world-renowned magazine, whereas they're not even out of college yet. So, it just wouldn't be possible for them to function as your equal.
HEFNER: Is that of some importance?
GROSS: Well, if I was the woman in the relationship, it would be important to me.
HEFNER: Well, I think—quite frankly—that people are attracted to one another for a variety of reasons. There is more than one kind of equality. And in my relationship with the women that I am seeing right now, there is a very real equality in terms of who makes the decisions in the relationship in what we do and how we spend our time, etc. But, I would say that the relationships are more complementary than equal. Each of us brings something different to the relationship. I bring the experience and the years and the wisdom and whatever. And they bring a very special joy, [they] relate to life that is not so sophisticated, not so cynical, and very refreshing.

Which kind of inequity is worse: putting in more than your partner or getting out more than your partner? Sprecher (1992) asked college students to imagine being overbenefited and being underbenefited. Students were more distressed by the prospect of being underbenefited, especially women. However, women also were more likely than men to say that they would try to rectify the inequity. If underbenefited, women were more likely than men to say they would ask their partner to put more resources into the relationship. If overbenefited, women were more likely than men to say they would increase what they put into the relationship.

Just because a relationship is equitable, however, does not mean that men and women provide and receive the *same* resources from marriage. Traditionally, fairness in marriage meant that the male assumed responsibility for the traditionally masculine tasks, primarily earning money, and the female assumed responsibility for the traditionally feminine tasks, primarily raising children. Rabin (1998) argues that the concept of fairness in marriage has changed and that both men and women regard the emotional aspects of relationships as more important than these instrumental aspects. Today, the ideal marriage is based more on friendship and intimacy than functionality. Both men and women are often involved in earning money and raising children. When men and women are asked what they want from their relationship, they both want emotional support rather than someone to cook a hot meal or mow the lawn.

CHARACTERISTICS OF HIM BUT NOT HER. Although there are common characteristics of people (e.g., femininity) and relationships (e.g., equity) that influence both husband and wife marital satisfaction, there also is evidence that the husband influences the wife's marital satisfaction more than the reverse. For example, Blum and Mehrabian (1999) examined the relation of temperament to marital satisfaction. A positive temperament included feeling affectionate and excited, whereas a negative temperament included feeling nasty and enraged. They found that men's marital satisfaction was linked more to their own temperament than their wife's temperament. By contrast, women's marital satisfaction was equally influenced by their own and their husband's temperament. Also, recall

the study on gender roles (Bradbury et al., 1995) that showed the husband's gender roles influenced the wife's marital satisfaction but the reverse was not true.

Wives are also more influenced than husbands by their spouse's psychological state. In a study where husbands and wives recorded their emotions periodically throughout the day, the husband's emotions influenced the wife's emotions but the wife's emotions had no impact on the husband's (Larson & Pleck, 1998). In particular, depression in the husband seems to affect the wife. In one study, husbands' depression was associated with their wife's depression, but wives' depression had no effect on their husband's depression (Whiffen & Gotlib, 1989). In another study, husbands' depression was associated with both husband and wife low marital satisfaction, but wives' depression was not associated with husband or wife marital satisfaction (J. Thompson, Whiffen, & Blain, 1995). Finally, one study showed that wives' marital satisfaction was influenced by whether or not their husband had a chronic illness but was not influenced by whether they had the chronic illness themselves (Hafstrom & Schram, 1984).

All of these studies show that whatever is going on with the husband—being depressed, scoring low on femininity, feeling nasty, or having a chronic illness—influences the wife's marital satisfaction, but these same attributes of the wife do not influence the husband's marital satisfaction. One reason might be that poor health and well-being detract from a husband's being able to attend to the relationship but do not detract from a wife's being able to attend to the relationship.

Research has supported the idea that women are more likely than men to focus on and attend closely to others in their environment. M. Ross and Holmberg (1992) showed that women have better memory for relationship events compared to men. They asked husbands and wives to describe three episodes from their past: first date, shared vacation, and recent argument. Descriptions were audiotaped, transcribed, and coded for vividness. Women reported more vivid memories than men for all of the events. This finding was not due to women's descriptions being longer than men's. In fact, the descriptions contained the same number of words.

Acitelli (1992) found support for the idea that wives attend to relationships in a study of "relationship awareness." She interviewed couples and measured relationship awareness by the frequency of relationship statements made during the interviews. Relationship statements were those that mentioned an interaction between the husband and wife or comparisons of one member of the couple to the other. During the interview, couples spent, on average, about half of the time talking about the relationship. Although men and women spoke for the same amount of time, women made more relationship statements. Neither husband's nor wife's relationship talk predicted husband's marital satisfaction, but husband's relationship talk was related to wife's marital satisfaction. These findings suggest that wives are more attentive to the relationship than husbands, and that husbands' relationship attentiveness may have an impact on satisfaction. Wives are especially happy when their husband is more involved in the relationship.

Other studies have shown that husbands' attention to relationships is more strongly related than wives' attention to relationships to spouse marital satisfaction. For example, spouse social support is more strongly tied to wives' than husbands' marital satisfaction (Acitelli & Antonucci, 1994).

Even in the domain of sexual relations, characteristics of the husband predict the wife's sexual satisfaction, but the reverse is not true. In one study, the extent to which husbands understood their wife's sexual preferences predicted higher wife sexual satisfaction and fewer wife sexual difficulties (Purnine & Carey, 1997). However, the extent to which wives understood their husband's sexual preferences was unrelated to husband sexual satisfaction or sexual difficulties.

Why are women affected by what is happening with men—their temperament, their well-being, their involvement in the relationship, their understanding of sexual preferences—but men are relatively unaffected by these same characteristics of women? Aspects of the male and female gender roles provide some clues. Women are socialized to focus on others, which may explain why others' feelings and behavior influence women's feelings and behavior. By contrast, men are socialized to focus on the self, which may explain why it is only attributes of the self that determine men's feelings and behavior. In addition, women may have greater skills than men in detecting another's emotions, which makes them more responsive to another's emotion (Larson & Pleck, 1998).

SUMMARY.   Features of the person (dispositional level of analysis) and features of the environment or situation (structural level of analysis) influence marital satisfaction. One feature of the person is the level of femininity. People who score higher on femininity have more satisfying relationships. Perhaps more important, as long as one person in the relationship scores high on femininity, the relationship is satisfying. This means that at least one person is attending to the relationship. However, there may be a downside to psychological femininity: femininity or a communal orientation may be responsible for women being more affected by the psychological and physical state of their partner.

Two other factors that influence relationship satisfaction are features of the situation or the relationship: the power balance of the relationship and whether the two people perceive the relationship as equitable. In general, more egalitarian relationships and more equitable relationships are associated with relationship satisfaction for both men and women. Research in both of these areas suffers from some measurement difficulties. Egalitarianism may mean joint participation or separate but equal participation. The latter may not be a truly egalitarian philosophy. Because equity is a subjective perception, it is not clear whether equity determines satisfaction, satisfaction determines equity, or both occur. Measurement issues are important because it is not always clear whether it is the egalitarian or the male-dominant relationship that is the most satisfying and stable.

Conflict

Areas of Conflict

Popular books suggest that men and women experience a good deal of conflict. John Gray's best-seller *Men Are from Mars, Women Are from Venus* (1992) suggests that men's and women's relationships are destined to be full of conflict because the two sexes have completely different styles of relating to people. The title of Lillian Rubin's (1983) popular book, *Intimate Strangers*, certainly implies that men and women face considerable conflict. In my opinion, both of these books, as well as many others, exaggerate the difference between men and women as well as their potential for conflict. However, as is often the case, there is a kernel of truth in some of these ideas.

L. Rubin (1983) describes why men and women have relationship problems, largely based on the ideas of Nancy Chodorow (1978). Recall Chodorow's psychoanalytic theory of gender-role development from Chapter 4. According to Chodorow and Rubin, men's and women's difficulties in relating to each other stem from their earliest relationship to their primary caretaker, usually the mother. Because girls grow up identifying with the person who is their primary attachment, girls find it easy to make connections to one another but find it difficult to separate from one another. Conversely, because boys grow up being forced to reject the person with whom they have identified (mother) in favor of someone who plays a smaller role in the home (father), boys are adept at separation and have difficulty with connection.

Is there any evidence that men and women report distinct areas of conflict in romantic relationships that map onto these ideas? L. Baxter (1986) examined conflict in couples by asking undergraduates who had broken up during the previous 12 months to write an essay on why their relationship ended. From these essays, eight reasons for the breakup were identified: (1) autonomy (feeling trapped), (2) similarity (lack of similar interests and attitudes), (3) supportiveness (lack of support), (4) openness (lack of open communication), (5) loyalty/fidelity, (6) shared time (not enough time together), (7) equity, and (8) romance (lacked "magical" quality). Women were more likely than men to name reasons involving issues of autonomy, openness, and equity. It is not a surprise that women identified openness as a problem because women desire greater disclosure than men. It may be surprising that women more than men cited lack of autonomy as a problem, but this finding has been confirmed by other research. Studies of college dating couples have found that women are more likely than men to say that their desire for independence is a problem in the relationship (Cochran & Peplau, 1985; C. Hill et al., 1976). A study of divorced couples also showed that women identified more problems over independence than men did (Newcomb, 1984). These studies seem to show that issues of autonomy and separation are more likely to be issues in relationships for women than for men.

Women's desire for autonomy may seem to be inconsistent with the ideas of Chodorow (1978); she argued that women desire connections and are adept at forming them. Women's problems with autonomy may come from their difficulty at achieving it. Women may be concerned that asserting their independence detracts from the relationship. Whereas men are expected to pursue independent activities outside of the relationship, the expectations for women are not that clear. For these reasons, women may desire more autonomy than they have achieved.

Men's areas of conflict may reflect difficulty with connection. In the study of divorced couples, the only reason for breaking up that men cited more often than women was lack of romance (Newcomb, 1984). This underscores the idea that men are more romantic than women. In the study of dating couples (C. Hill et al., 1976), the only problem that men cited more frequently than women was living too far from one another. This is evidence for L. Rubin's (1983) claim that men define intimacy in terms of physical proximity.

A study of married and cohabiting couples revealed that issues related to both independence and dependence were a source of stress (J. Cunningham, Braiker, & Kelley, 1982). Married and cohabiting men were more likely than women to complain that their partner was too dependent and passive. Married men were the least likely

to complain that their partner was too independent. Thus, when the findings of this study are compared to the findings in previous studies, it appears that both women and men agree that the woman needs to be more independent. In the present study (J. Cunningham et al., 1982), married women were more likely than men and even cohabiting women to say that they did not receive enough attention from their partner. The women are concerned with their husband's lack of attempts at connection. Thus, it appears that women's relationship concerns have to do with connection and autonomy. Women are concerned with their lack of autonomy and their partner's lack of connection.

It is important to point out that men and women, married or cohabiting, agreed that a lack of attention from one's partner was the most serious relationship concern. Thus, even if the nature of conflict differs for men and women, there may be a great deal of agreement on which conflicts are important. Even among divorced couples, men and women seem to agree on which problems are more and less important (Newcomb, 1984).

I also found that the nature of conflict was largely the same for men and women in a prototype study of experiences of distance that I conducted (Helgeson et al., 1987). College students were asked to recall times when they felt distant from their romantic partner. The core feature of distance episodes for both men and women was disapproval of a partner's behavior. The disapproval was often in response to behaviors that threatened the relationship, such as a partner showing interest in or dating others. Other precursors to feelings of distance were lack of communication and physical separation. The episodes were emotionally intense for both men and women, characterized by feelings of anger, hurt, and confusion. Men and women differed only on some of the details. For example, women were more likely than men to mention feelings of hurt, and men were more likely to mention having an argument. In general, men's and women's conceptions of distance in relationships were similar.

Conflict Management

When conflict arises, how do men and women handle it? Some differences exist. For example, men are more likely than women to avoid conflict. In one study, high school students were asked how often they engaged in a series of tactics when they had an important conflict with their romantic partner (Feldman & Gowen, 1998). Men were more likely than women to use distraction. However, if men are engaged in conflict, they tend to use more coercion, aggression, and control tactics compared to women (Cahn, 1992). These findings are consistent with the differences in conflict management among friends described in Chapter 7.

One way conflict management has been studied is by observing couples' behavior in the laboratory as they discuss a conflict. Distressed spouses in general display more disagreement and more criticism than nondistressed spouses, but this difference is more apparent among women than men (Baucom, Notarius, Burnett, & Haefner, 1990). Women are more negative than men during discussions of conflict (Carstensen, Gottman, & Levenson, 1995). However, it may be that women are just more emotionally expressive than men. In one study, women displayed more positive and negative affect than men (Carstensen et al., 1995). In another study, distressed women exhibited higher rates of negativity compared to distressed men, but there were no differences in negativity between nondistressed women and men (Notarius, Benson, Sloane, Vanzetti, & Hornyak, 1989). This is one reason that women have been referred to as the "emotional barometer" of relationships (Floyd & Markman, 1983): if the woman is displaying high negativity, the relationship is likely to be in distress.

Another study confirmed that the key to identifying a distressed couple seems to lie with the wife. Floyd and Markman (1983) studied the behavior of men and women in distressed and nondistressed couples. The couples discussed two conflicts, each for 15 minutes. Following the discussions, they rated each other's behavior; in addition, observers rated videotapes of the interactions. In nondistressed couples, husbands and wives perceived each other's behavior in similar terms. In distressed couples, wives rated husband's behavior as more negative than husbands rated wife's behavior. Yet, observers viewed distressed wives' behaviors as the most negative. Observers even rated distressed wives' behavior as more negative than distressed husbands did. Thus, the behavior of a wife in a distressed couple is especially negative, and a distressed wife interprets her husband's behavior as negative.

The display of negative affect may not reflect distress as much as the management of that affect. Whereas nondistressed women are able to resist negative reciprocity (i.e., responding to negative affect with more negative affect), distressed women seem to have a difficult time doing so (Notarius et al., 1989). When distressed couples come into the laboratory, the wife often sees it as an opportunity to resolve a conflict; thus, she confronts the conflict, which includes displays of negative affect. The husband's goal, by contrast, is to keep the conflict from escalating; thus, he responds to her negative affect with displays of either neutral or positive affect: he tries to smooth over things. Rather than perceiving his response as a positive one, she is frustrated that he is not becoming engaged in this conflict. In other words, she perceives her husband's lack of negative affect as a sign that he is not engaged in the interaction. Women then responded by intensifying their negative behavior, in essence escalating the conflict.

The following exchange illustrates this sequence of events:

WIFE: Let's talk about why you don't help out more with the children. (confrontation of conflict with negative affect)

HUSBAND: You do such a good job with the children that it doesn't seem like this is really an issue of conflict. (attempt to neutralize the affect with positive statement)

WIFE: You just don't get it, do you? If you spent more time with the children, you could do a good job too. (more negative affect, or reciprocity of negative affect)

Both members of a couple are better at reciprocating negative than positive affect. One study found that men and women wanted to reciprocate both positive and negative feelings during a discussion of conflict but were successful only in reciprocating negative feelings (Gaelick, Bodenhausen, & Wyer, 1985). This occurred because couples were accurate in perceiving each other's displays of negative affect (i.e., hostility) but were not accurate in detecting displays of positive affect.

These investigators also found that men and women distorted information in different ways. Men interpreted women's failure to express love as hostility. In other words, men had a **negativity bias.** The authors argued that men do not expect women to be hostile; they expect them to be loving. Therefore, when women do not

behave in loving ways, men infer hostility. By contrast, women displayed a **positivity bias:** women interpreted men's lack of hostility as love. The authors explained this finding also in terms of women's expectations: women expect men to be hostile, and when they are not, positive affect is inferred.

The results of this study lead to a pessimistic outlook on couple interactions. If wives do not convey love, husbands will infer hostility. Because negative affect is likely to be reciprocated, negative affect will escalate. If husbands are not hostile, wives will infer love and may reciprocate with positive affect. However, recall that displays of positive affect, such as love, are less likely to be accurately perceived. Thus, husbands cannot reciprocate that which is not perceived.

We now know about the kinds of interactions that characterize distressed couples. Are these same kinds of interactions associated with marital satisfaction? One provocative longitudinal study found that the kinds of interactions that predicted short-term marital satisfaction differed from the kinds that predicted long-term marital satisfaction. Gottman and Krokoff (1989) found that wife displays of positive verbal behavior (i.e., agreement) were associated with high marital satisfaction, and wife or husband displays of conflict (i.e., disagreement and criticism) were associated with low marital satisfaction. This is as one would expect. However, wife positive verbal behavior predicted a *decline* in marital satisfaction over the next three years, and engagement in conflict by either husband or wife predicted an *increase* in marital satisfaction over the next three years. The authors concluded that confronting problems may cause distress in the short run but be adaptive for couples in the long run. By contrast, wives' positive relationship behavior may smooth out disagreements in the short-term but could have negative consequences in the long-term if it means that important issues are not being addressed.

Although the results of the study are fascinating, a methodological feature of the design might have led the results to be a statistical artifact (Woody & Constanzo, 1990). Couples were selected to participate in the study based on having either very high or low marital satisfaction scores. Marital satisfaction scores are likely to regress toward the mean three years later; that is, marital satisfaction will tend to decline over time in highly satisfied couples and improve over time in highly distressed couples. It may only appear that conflict is associated with improvements in marital satisfaction because couples who were distressed at the start of the study can only improve over time. Similarly, positive verbal behavior may only appear to be associated with declines in marital satisfaction because happy couples can only deteriorate over time. This phenomenon is known as **regression to the mean.**

Gender roles (masculinity vs. femininity) may play a larger role than sex (husband vs. wife) in determining how couples discuss conflict. Not surprisingly, femininity is associated with more positive and fewer negative communication behaviors (Baucom et al., 1990; Burger & Jacobson, 1979). However, a couple of studies have shown that wife femininity is associated with more negative interactions in distressed couples (Baucom et al., 1990; Sayers & Baucom, 1991). One study showed that wife femininity was associated with less negative behavior in happy marriages but more negative behavior in unhappy marriages (Huston & Geis, 1993). In unhappy marriages, these wives may be attempting to keep the husbands engaged in the conflict. If that is the case, wife femininity could appear to be harmful in the short-run but helpful in the long run. Baucom and Aiken (1984) found

that wife femininity predicted an increase in marital satisfaction following therapy.

Demand/Withdraw Pattern

Imagine the following argument:

PERSON A: Why don't you spend a little more time working inside the house?
PERSON B: What? What do you mean?
PERSON A: You are never at home and when you are at home, you spend all of your time reading. I have to clean up everything.
(silence)
PERSON A: You could at least read Mandy a bedtime story.
(still no response; in fact, the sound of a newspaper opening up can be heard)

LINKS TO GENDER.   Man or woman? Who do you believe is more likely to be Person A? Person B? This episode is an example of the **demand/withdraw pattern.** It is characterized by one person demanding, if not nagging, and the other person not responding, or withdrawing. The demander is more likely to initiate problem discussion, whereas the withdrawer is more likely to avoid problem discussion (Christensen & Heavey, 1993). Among distressed and nondistressed couples, the demander is more likely to be a woman and the withdrawer to be a man (Christensen & Heavey, 1993; Gottman, 1994; Markman, Silvern, Clements, & Kraft-Hanak, 1993). This demand/withdraw pattern has been present in marriage since the early part of the twentieth century (Gottman & Carrere, 1994). In public, women are more likely to appear deferential and polite, but in the private sphere of marriage, women confront and demand (Gottman & Carrere, 1994).

Christensen and Heavey (1993) have conducted numerous studies of married couples that rely on either couples' self-reports of demand and withdraw behavior or on coders' observations of such behavior while couples discuss problems. There is a great deal of agreement between the two measures of demand and withdraw behavior. Apparently couples know who demands and who withdraws. Across their studies, Christensen and Heavey conclude that about 60% of couples are characterized by wife demand/husband withdraw, 30% by husband demand/wife withdraw, and 10% by an equal proportion of both demanding and withdrawing.

EXPLANATIONS. Why do wives tend to be the demanders and husbands tend to be the withdrawers? Christensen and Heavey (1993) suggest that husbands and wives have a fundamental conflict: women prefer closeness and men prefer independence. This is the basic dilemma identified by L. Rubin (1983) and Chodorow (1978). Men can achieve independence on their own, but women require the support of their partner to achieve closeness. This fundamental conflict leads men and women to employ different strategies in relationships. Women need to demand to obtain closeness, whereas men can withdraw to achieve independence. Christensen and Heavey measured conflict over closeness versus independence and found that this type of conflict within a couple is associated with greater demand/withdraw behavior. In addition, the person who wanted greater closeness (usually the woman) was more likely to be the demander and the person who wanted greater independence (usually the man) was more likely to be the withdrawer.

Christensen and Heavey (1993) suggested that the wife demand/husband withdraw pattern is most likely to appear in situations when the wife wants the change. Theoretically, when the husband wants change, there should be more husband than wife demanding. To test this idea, Christensen and Heavey had married couples with children talk about an area in which the mother wanted a change and an area in which the father wanted a change. The two interactions were videotaped. Self-reports and observer ratings of demand/withdraw behavior showed that the typical wife demand/husband withdraw pattern was found when the issue was one in which the mother desired a change. This is shown on the left side of each of the figures in Figure 8.9. When the issue was one in which the father desired a change (the right half of the figures), there was less mother demanding and more father demanding, but the pattern did not completely reverse itself. Instead, for the father issue, there was no sex difference in the demand/withdraw pattern. If you compare the data for the father's issue to those for the mother's issue, you can see that mother demand/father withdraw decreased and father demand/mother withdraw increased for the father's issue compared to the mother's issue. Christensen and Heavey (1990) suggest that the previous literature could be overestimating the female demand/male withdraw pattern because the conflicts most often discussed in the laboratory are probably "wife issues": issues in which the wife wants the change. Women are less satisfied in marriage and report more problems compared to men (Antonucci & Akiyama, 1987; Bernard, 1972).

When husbands want change, why isn't there more evidence that husbands demand and wives withdraw? Christensen and Heavey (1990, 1993) suggest that couples are likely to have a history of resolving men's issues compared to women's issues in marriage. This occurs for two reasons. First, men desire less change in relationships; thus, men raise fewer issues. Second, men have greater power in relationships; thus, the issues that men raise are addressed.

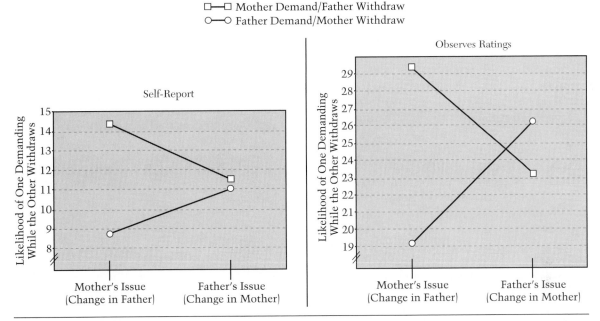

FIGURE 8.9 Demand/withdraw pattern. When the issue being discussed is one in which mothers are concerned, the typical wife demand/husband withdraw pattern is observed. There is little husband demand/wife withdrawal. When the issue being discussed is one in which fathers are concerned, wife demand/husband withdrawal decreases and husband demand/wife withdrawal increases. However, the pattern does not completely reverse itself. Thus, the wife demand/husband withdraw pattern is not only a function of wives having more concerns in the relationship. *Source:* A. Christensen and C. L. Heavy (1993). Gender differences in marital conflict: The demand/withdraw interaction pattern. In S. Oskamp and M. Constanzo (Eds.), *Gender issues in contemporary society* (Vol. 6, pp. 113–141). Beverly Hills, CA: Sage.

Because men's issues are addressed, there is less likelihood of getting into any kind of demand/withdraw cycle. Women's issues are less likely to be resolved than men's issues, so there is more opportunity for conflict. This may lead to a propensity on the part of women to demand and a propensity on the part of men to withdraw. The demand/withdraw cycle is self-perpetuating. The more one person demands, the more the other withdraws; the more one withdraws, the more the other demands. Thus, the female demand/male withdraw pattern can be explained partly in terms of men's and women's personality predispositions and partly in terms of the situations in which men and women find themselves in marriage (e.g., women have lower power, women perceive more problems).

One criticism of the Christensen and Heavey (1993) study is that the issues mothers and fathers chose were in the domain of parenting. Thus, even the husband's issue could be viewed as one in which the wife was highly invested. The findings were replicated in another study in which the husband and wife were able to choose among a number of issues, not all of which had to do with parenting (Heavey, Layne, & Christensen, 1993). The findings paralleled those shown in Figure 8.9: for the wife issue, there was greater female demand and male withdrawal; the pattern changed but did not reverse itself for the husband issue.

Yet, another study found that the demand/withdraw pattern did completely reverse itself when an issue in which husbands desired a change was discussed (Klinetob & Smith, 1996). In this study, couples were allowed to choose the topic they would discuss rather than choose from a predetermined list provided by the experimenter, as in the Heavey et al. (1993) study. Thus, husbands may have discussed issues that were more relevant to them than in previous studies. One concern is that the couples in the Klinetob and Smith study had been married for a shorter period of time. The asymmetry in the demand/withdraw pattern may appear only after years of having a greater history of resolving "his" rather than "her" problems. Klinetob and Smith also suggest that their couples scored quite high in marital satisfaction. Perhaps the demand/withdraw pattern is more balanced in healthier couples. Examine the demand/withdraw pattern in couples you know in Exercise 8.5.

Another argument as to why women demand and men withdraw is that women have a greater tolerance for the physiological arousal that conflict produces (Gottman, 1994; Levenson, Carstensen, & Gottman, 1994). Gottman has suggested that men may avoid situations that produce an increase in physiological arousal because their bodies recover more slowly from arousal than women's bodies. Recall from Chapter 3 that men are more in touch with their internal physiology than women are. Thus, men may find the physiological arousal that conflict produces

---

EXERCISE 8.5
Demand/Withdraw Pattern

Come up with you own self-report measure of demand and withdraw behavior. Some sample items adapted from Christensen and Heavy (1993) are shown below. Measure the frequency that such behavior occurs among dating couples that you know by asking them to complete your survey. Is there evidence that women demand more? Men withdraw more? Is the length of the relationship related to the pattern?

Sample Demand/Withdraw Items

One person nags and the other person refuses to discuss the topic.

One person makes demands and the other person is silent.

One person criticizes and the other person withdraws.

One person tries to start a conversation about a problem and the other person tries to avoid the topic.

---

more aversive than women do and withdraw from it. One study found a greater correspondence between negative affect and physiological arousal among men than women (Levenson et al., 1994). The investigators had 156 couples discuss a conflict while their physiological arousal was measured. Physiological measures included heart rate, skin conductance, and body temperature; interactions were videotaped. Each member of the couple viewed the videotape and used a rating dial to indicate their affect over the course of the discussion. As predicted, men's physiological arousal was correlated with their self-reports of negative affect during the conflict discussion; that is, when men reported greater negative affect, they also had higher arousal. For women, physiological arousal was unrelated to their reports of affect.

One problem with the arousal explanation for male withdraw behavior is that numerous studies show that women become more physiologically aroused than men during discussion of conflict. This will be explored in more detail in Chapter 10. Gottman's (1994) response to this might be that men's withdraw behavior is effective in that it keeps men from becoming aroused.

Noller (1993) suggests that there are cultural reasons for the demand/withdraw pattern. Men withdraw because they are socialized to resist pressure and maintain their independence; withdrawing maintains a position of power. Women are socialized to be relationship experts. Because women have experience managing conflict, they are less disturbed by it.

IMPLICATIONS FOR RELATIONSHIPS. What are the implications of the demand/withdraw pattern for marital satisfaction? Not surprisingly, high rates of demand/withdraw behavior are associated with reports of lower marital satisfaction. However, it also appears to depend on who is engaging in the demanding and who is engaging in the withdrawing. One study found that wife demand/husband withdraw behavior was associated with declines in wife satisfaction over one year, but husband demand/wife withdraw behavior was associated with *improvements* in wife satisfaction over the year (Heavey et al., 1993). These findings were largely replicated in a second study (Heavey, Christensen, & Malamuth, 1995). Why would husband demand behavior be associated with an improvement in wife marital satisfaction? One theory is that demanding behavior reflects engagement in the relationship and wives are happy that

husbands are engaged. In both studies, demand/withdraw behavior did not predict changes in husbands' marital satisfaction, which is consistent with previous research on the predictors of marital satisfaction. Characteristics of the spouse or relationship affect wives but not husbands.

Although Lloyd (1987, 1990) didn't study the association of demand/withdraw behavior per se to marital satisfaction, she examined the association of two related ideas: conflict repetition and conflict resolution. Couples kept a daily record of conflicts. Men's marital satisfaction was a function of conflict repetition, and women's marital satisfaction was a function of conflict resolution. Men were more dissatisfied with the relationship when they reported that their wives continued to bring up the same conflict; this sounds an awful lot like demand behavior. Women were more satisfied with their marriages when the conflicts they initiated were resolved; this likely reflects the absence of husband withdrawal. Women also saw a relation between conflict repetition and conflict resolution; they continued to raise conflicts that were not resolved. Men, however, did not see a relation between conflict repetition and conflict resolution; the men were unhappy with the repetition but saw no connection between their wife bringing up the issue over and over again and the fact that the issue was unresolved.

There also has been research on the demand/withdraw pattern in abusive relationships, and it appears that the pattern is exacerbated in these couples. One study compared demand and withdraw behavior among couples in which the husband was and was not abusive (Berns, Jacobson, & Gottman, 1999). There was greater wife demand behavior and greater husband withdraw behavior in abusive than nonabusive couples. However, there also was greater husband demand behavior in abusive than nonabusive couples. The investigators suggested that the high level of demand behavior among husbands reflected their dissatisfaction with the relationship and attempts to control their wife's behavior. Although the abusive husbands demanded change in their wife, husbands were withdrawing from any attempts their wife made to change the husband's behavior.

SUMMARY. The demand/withdraw behavior pattern has been linked to gender. Women are more likely to demand and husbands are more likely to withdraw. There are several explanations for this pattern. One is that men and women have a basic conflict in that women want connection, which requires cooperation from a partner, and men want autonomy, which they can achieve on their own. Second is that women identify more problems in a relationship than men do. To resolve problems, confrontation or demanding behavior may be necessary. In fact, there is evidence that when husbands have problems in a relationship, their rate of demand behavior increases and their rate of withdraw behavior decreases. There also may be more fundamental reasons that the demand/withdraw pattern is linked to gender, which are related to the power structure in relationships and the lower status of women. Demanding behavior may be an attempt to improve one's status, whereas withdraw behavior may be an attempt to maintain the status quo.

In general, the demand/withdraw pattern is associated with lower levels of marital satisfaction. In fact, this pattern is more pronounced in abusive relationships. One exception is that there seems to be some modest evidence that husband demand behavior has positive implications for women's marital satisfaction. Demand behavior relative to withdraw behavior shows

involvement in the relationship, and women want men to be involved.

Jealousy

In the context of romantic relationships, jealousy is the concern that there is a rival for the other's affections. Are men or women more jealous? There is little evidence for sex differences in jealousy (D. Wright, 1999). When a difference is found, it is usually in the direction of women being more jealous than men. One concern with this research is that men may be less likely than women to admit jealousy. Research that has examined different dimensions of jealousy supports this idea. In a study of 66 married couples, men and women were equally likely to have jealous thoughts and to experience jealous feelings, but women were more likely to communicate jealousy (Guerrero, Eloy, Jorgensen, & Andersen, 1993). Men have been socialized to keep jealous feelings to themselves; admitting jealousy implies weakness and vulnerability. Women may be more likely than men to communicate their feelings about jealousy because they are concerned with preserving the relationship.

There may be different events that inspire jealousy in men and women. S. Glass and Wright (1985) found that women having sex with other men provoked jealousy in men, whereas men spending time with other women (not necessarily having sex) provoked jealousy in women. These findings map onto Buss's (1994) evolutionary theory of sex differences in jealousy. He argues that different situations should provoke jealousy in women and men due to evolutionary reasons. Because men are uncertain of the paternity of their offspring, they should be extremely upset by marital infidelity: Sexual infidelity could jeopardize the chance of their genes surviving.

A husband's sexual infidelity should not disturb women as much because male infidelity does not threaten a female's genetic link to her offspring. Instead, women should be more upset by their partner falling in love with someone else, or emotional infidelity. Emotional infidelity could lead the husband to take his resources elsewhere and invest in children with someone else; thus, emotional infidelity threatens the viability of the female's offspring. To test this idea, Buss et al. (1992) asked college students to choose which of the two would be more disturbing to them, sexual or emotional infidelity. The exact wording of the questions is contained in Table 8.7.

They found that women were more distressed by emotional than sexual infidelity and that men were more distressed by sexual than emotional infidelity. However, these results were not replicated in another study in the United States, a study in the Netherlands, or a study in Germany (Buunk, Angleitner, Oubaid, & Buss, 1996). These three other studies did confirm that

TABLE 8.7 Emotional versus Sexual Infidelity

Imagine that you discover that the person with whom you've been seriously involved became interested in someone else. What would upset or distress you more (please circle only one in each set):

Set A

(A) Imagining your partner forming a deep emotional attachment to that person.

(B) Imagining your partner enjoying passionate sexual intercourse with that other person.

Set B

(A) Imagining your partner trying different sexual positions with that other person.

(B) Imagining your partner falling in love with that other person.

Source: Buss et al. (1992).

men were more distressed than women by sexual infidelity. However, the majority of men in Germany and the Netherlands and about half of the men in the United States said emotional infidelity was more distressing than sexual infidelity. Thus, men are more distressed than women by sexual infidelity, but sexual infidelity is not as distressful as emotional infidelity. One difficulty with this area of research is the extent to which sexual infidelity and emotional infidelity are intertwined. Perhaps men view sexual infidelity as implying emotional infidelity. Men might think "If my wife was unfaithful, she must *really* be in love with someone else." Recall that both men and women perceive that women connect sex with love. Explore the link between emotional and sexual infidelity in Exercise 8.6.

Evolutionary theory also can explain another pattern of sex differences in jealousy. Sharpsteen (1995) reported that men were more jealous over an infidelity if they perceived their partner as a good parent rather than a bad parent, whereas women were more jealous over an infidelity if they perceived their partner as a bad parent rather than a good parent. Men might be more jealous when their partners are good parents because they are losing a valuable resource to raise their offspring. Women might be more jealous when their partners are bad parents because they know that bad parents are less likely than good parents to contribute to the economic welfare of their children.

GAY AND LESBIAN RELATIONSHIPS

There are three major reasons for studying gay and lesbian relationships. First, gay men and lesbians are an important population in their own right. Second, studying homosexual relationships enables us to test

EXERCISE 8.6
Relations Between Sexual and Emotional Infidelity

Ask a group of people who are in a steady dating relationship to imagine that their partner has become interested in someone else. Read the first item under Set A in Table 8.7 (the item that indicates emotional infidelity). Now have these people rate how likely they would be to think their partner had sexual relations with the other person.

Similarly, have another group of people read the second item under Set A in Table 8.7 (the item that indicates sexual infidelity). Have the people rate how likely they would be to think their partner had fallen in love with the other person.

1. Is sexual infidelity linked to emotional infidelity?
2. Is emotional infidelity linked to sexual infidelity?
3. Do the answers to these questions depend on the sex of the respondent?

relationship theories that were largely established on heterosexual relationships; it is important to know whether relationship theories generalize across a variety of relationships. Third, and more important to this book, studying gay men and lesbians can increase knowledge about how gender roles operate in relationships. For example, do men have more power than women in heterosexual relationships because they are male or because they often make more money than women? By examining power distributions in homosexual relationships, we can answer these questions.

There has been much less research on gay and lesbian relationships compared to heterosexual relationships. Instead, target

issues have been the origins of homosexuality and its pathology (Peplau, 1991). One reason for the lack of attention to homosexual relationships is that there are a number of myths about them. People tend to believe that homosexual relationships are unhappy, dysfunctional, deviant, and transient. Research shows that these beliefs are simply untrue (Peplau & Spalding, 2000). Homosexual relationships can be long-lasting. In Eldridge and Gilbert's (1990) study, 90% of lesbian couples lived together and the average relationship lasted 5.4 years, with some lasting as long as 20 years. Studies also have shown that the majority of gay and lesbian relationships are close and mutually satisfying (Peplau, Cochran, Rook, & Padesky, 1978). Another myth about gay men and lesbians is that they are unhappy people and have low self-esteem. Research that has evaluated gay men and lesbians and compared them to heterosexuals also has contradicted that assumption (Bringle, 1995; Eldridge & Gilbert, 1990; Peplau & Garnets, 2000). Another reason for the lack of research on gay and lesbian relationships is that the gay and lesbian community has been reluctant to participate in psychological research. Historically, there has been good reason for homosexuals to mistrust psychologists: until 1973, the American Psychological Association classified homosexuality as a mental disorder (J. Conger, 1975).

It is difficult to study gay and lesbian relationships because all homosexuals are not open about their sexual orientation. Many of the studies of gay men and lesbians described in this chapter were conducted by recruiting participants from advertisements in college newspapers, from gay and lesbian publications, from contacting gay and lesbian organizations, and by word of mouth from one study participant to another. Obviously, the participants in these studies are not representative of the population; gay men and lesbians who are less open about their sexuality or less involved in the homosexual community are under-represented.

More recently, research on gay and lesbian relationships has become more visible. This is likely due to the advent of AIDS. AIDS increased the awareness of homosexuality, and the loss of life through AIDS increased awareness of the closeness of homosexual relationships.

Relationship Development

CHARACTERISTICS DESIRED IN A MATE. Do gay men and lesbians show the same differences in mate preferences as heterosexual men and women? To address this question, Gonzales and Meyers (1993) compared the personal advertisements of heterosexual and homosexual men and women. They found that gay men were most likely to emphasize the importance of a partner's physical appearance in their advertisements, and lesbians were least likely to emphasize physical appearance. Heterosexual women indicated stronger preferences for attractiveness and were more likely to emphasize their own attractiveness compared to homosexual women. In another study of personal advertisements, gay men more than lesbians were found to indicate a preference for a physically attractive partner, whereas lesbians were more likely to indicate personality preferences (e.g., sense of humor) than were gay men (Hatala & Prehodka, 1996). Thus, the finding that men emphasize physical attractiveness more than women in heterosexual relationships seems to be even more extreme in homosexual relationships. This suggests that the attractiveness preference is linked to being male: men prefer attractive partners, whether the partner is male or female.

By contrast, the sex difference in preference for financial security is exaggerated in heterosexual compared to homosexual relationships (Gonzales & Meyers, 1993). Heterosexual men were more likely than homosexual men to offer financial security in their advertisements. Heterosexual women were more likely than homosexual women to express a desire for financial security. Another study found that heterosexual women are more concerned with their partner's status than either homosexual women or both groups of men (Bailey, Gaulin, Agyei, & Gladue, 1994).

RELATIONSHIP INITIATION. The initiation of a relationship may be more awkward for homosexuals than heterosexuals (Peplau & Spalding, 2000). One way that a relationship may develop is out of friendship. Lesbian relationships, in particular, are likely to develop out of friendship (S. Rose, Zand, & Cini, 1993). Although it seems straightforward—two women fall in love during the course of a friendship—even this progression can be difficult in lesbian relationships (S. Rose et al., 1993). Traditionally, women are not used to taking the initiative in the development of romantic relationships. Thus, it may take time for the relationship to move beyond friendship to a romantic relationship. Lesbian friendships may face the emotional bond challenge that confronts cross-sex friendship among heterosexuals: When does the relationship cross over from friendship to romantic love, and are the feelings mutual?

Formation of relationships has been studied by using the methodology of S. Rose and Frieze (1993) to elicit first date scripts among gay men and lesbians (Klinkenberg & Rose, 1994). Homosexual scripts for a first date show that gay men place a greater emphasis on sexuality and lesbians place a greater emphasis on intimacy. More men than women expected sex on a first date. Nearly half of men (48%) but only a small portion of women (12%) had sex on a recent first date. Lesbian scripts were more likely to emphasize the affective aspects of the date, such as thinking about how one felt about the person.

Thus, many of the sex differences in first date scripts observed among heterosexuals also appeared among homosexuals. More than half of the first date script features identified by homosexuals were also found by S. Rose and Frieze (1993). Common features included grooming for the date, discussing plans for the date, initiating physical contact, the actual date activity (movie, dinner), and feelings of nervousness. Another parallel between heterosexual and homosexual first date scripts is that men paid more attention to the physical aspects of intimacy (sex) and women paid more attention to the emotional aspects of intimacy. These similarities suggest that sex differences in emphasis on physical versus emotional intimacy are truly related to being male versus female because they generalize across heterosexual and homosexual relationships. Another way in which homosexual first date scripts were similar to heterosexual scripts is that men were more proactive than women: gay men were more likely than lesbians to discuss making arrangements for the date. One way that homosexual scripts were quite different from heterosexual scripts is in the lack of attention to physical appearance: neither gay men nor lesbians included concerns about their own physical appearance. With the exception of men being more proactive than women, homosexual scripts did not have stereotypical gender roles; the features of the first date were equally likely to be tied to either partner.

Intimacy and Sexuality

If women's friendships are closer than those of men and women are more relationship-focused than men, it seems likely that a romantic relationship between two women will be closer or more intimate than a romantic relationship that involves at least one man. Kurdek (1998) tested this idea by comparing the intimacy level of the relationships of lesbians, gay men, and heterosexual married people. Intimacy was measured in terms of the amount of time spent together, perception of closeness, and including "partner" in one's self-definition. The hypothesis was confirmed: lesbians reported greater intimacy than heterosexual married people.

If men are more likely than women to define intimacy through sexuality, one would expect the most sexual behavior to occur among two gay men and the least to occur among two lesbians. Two studies of personal advertisements show that gay men emphasize sexuality more than lesbians and heterosexual men and women (Gonzales & Meyers, 1993; Hatala & Prehodka, 1996). Compared to heterosexual men, homosexual men have fewer exclusive relationships, report more sexual relationships outside of their current relationship in the prior year, and report a greater number of romantic partners (Bringle, 1995). In one study, homosexual men were 7 times as likely as heterosexual men to have had sex outside of their current relationship (79% vs. 11%; Blumstein & Schwartz, 1983). Within the current relationship, however, homosexual and heterosexual men engage in sex with equal frequency (Blumstein & Schwartz, 1983). Thus, the two groups of men were equally sexually active, but the homosexual men were more accepting of sex outside the relationship.

Because sexual exclusivity does not seem to be as central to homosexual men's relationships, it is not surprising that homosexual men experienced and expressed less sexual jealousy compared to heterosexual men (Bringle, 1995). When a partner had a sexual encounter, homosexual men were more likely than heterosexual men to act as if nothing had happened and were less likely than heterosexual men to confront their partner.

How has AIDS affected the behavior of homosexual men? The study by Blumstein and Schwartz (1983) was conducted before the AIDS epidemic. Bringle (1995) compared two cohorts of homosexual and heterosexual men, one in 1980 and one in 1992. He found greater sexual exclusivity in 1992 compared to 1980 for both heterosexual and homosexual men, but the increase was larger for homosexual men.

Sexual exclusivity is not synonymous with a happy relationship for gay men. It is important to point out that lack of monogamy in gay men's relationships is not necessarily associated with lower relationship satisfaction or commitment. One study of gay men found that there were no differences in satisfaction or commitment between monogamous and nonmonogamous relationships (Blasband & Peplau, 1985). Another study showed that lack of monogamy was unrelated to relationship satisfaction and commitment among gay men, but was associated with lower relationship commitment among heterosexuals and lesbians (Blumstein & Schwartz, 1983).

There appear to be parallels between heterosexual and homosexual romantic relationships in terms of women's emphasis on emotional intimacy and men's emphasis on sexual intimacy. Monteflores and Schultz (1978) found that gay men emphasized sex before emotional intimacy and lesbians emphasized emotional intimacy before sex. This distinction is emphasized in the popular literature on gay men and lesbian romantic relationships. S. Rose (1996a) examined the depiction of homosexual relationships in popular fiction and found that gay men's relationships emphasized adventure, independence, the physical attractiveness of the partner, but difficulties with intimacy. By contrast,

lesbian relationships emphasized romance, emotional intimacy, and commitment. Thus, sexual behavior is not necessarily the best criterion for distinguishing between friendships and romantic relationships among lesbians (S. Rose et al., 1993). The extent to which two women identify as a couple might be a better marker of a romantic relationship (S. Rose et al., 1993).

Relationship Satisfaction

Are homosexuals as satisfied as heterosexuals with their relationships? Kurdek and Schmitt (1986) compared the relationships of heterosexual married couples, heterosexual cohabiting couples, gay couples, and lesbian couples. Among the four couples, heterosexual cohabitors were the least satisfied. There was no difference in relationship satisfaction among the other three couples, and they found no differences in reports of love for one's partner across the couples. Although studies of heterosexual relationships often find that men are more satisfied than women, in a study of gay and lesbian couples without children, there was no sex difference in relationship satisfaction (Kurdek, 1996). Other research has confirmed the idea that gay men and lesbians are as satisfied as heterosexuals with their relationships (Peplau & Spalding, 2000) and that the satisfaction of their relationship changes over time, similar to that of heterosexuals (Kurdek, 1998). Thus, the sex difference in marital satisfaction pertains more to the nature of male-female relationships than to sex (i.e., being male or female).

In general, the same kinds of variables that are associated with relationship satisfaction among heterosexuals are associated with relationship satisfaction among homosexuals. Moreover, the same relationship theories that apply to heterosexual relationships also apply to homosexual relationships. Commitment to a relationship is typically a function of the positive forces that attract one to a relationship and the barriers to leaving a relationship. This commitment process largely functions the same among heterosexuals and homosexuals. Kurdek (1992) found that relationship satisfaction increased over a four-year period to the extent that gay men and lesbians derived more rewards, perceived fewer costs, and increased their emotional investment in the relationship. There seem to be no differences between heterosexuals and homosexuals in the forces that attract to a relationship. However, Kurdek (1991a, 1998) found that homosexuals face fewer barriers to relationship dissolution that heterosexuals. For example, homosexual marriage is typically not recognized by the law, homosexuals are less likely to have children, and homosexuals are less likely to have the support of family to maintain the relationship. Thus, homosexuals have fewer barriers to leave a relationship.

Social exchange theory suggests that relationship satisfaction is partly determined by the benefits gained and costs incurred in a relationship. Benefits may be love and support as well as the partner's income. Costs may be time, money, and effort in maintaining the relationship. One predictor from social exchange theory is that the person who is more dependent on the relationship will have less power in the relationship; the person who has greater personal resources (education, income) will have more power in the relationship. This theory seems to hold well across heterosexual and gay men's relationships (Peplau & Spalding, 2000). The link of resources to power among lesbians is less clear. In one study, lesbian partners who were less dependent on the relationship and had greater personal resources (education, income) also had greater power in their relationships (M. Caldwell & Peplau, 1984). However, other research suggests that income is less likely to be related to power in lesbian relationships compared to gay men's and heterosexual relationships (Blumstein & Schwartz, 1983).

Equality seems to be especially important to the relationship satisfaction of lesbians, who report that equality is more important more than gay men do (Kurdek, 1995). This is interesting because we know that women are more focused than men on equality in heterosexual relationships. The importance of egalitarianism to lesbians is supported by research that shows shared decision making and equal power is higher among lesbian couples than gay male or heteroexual couples (Kurdek, 1998; Kurdek & Schmitt, 1986). M. Caldwell and Peplau (1984) found that the vast majority of lesbians (97%) endorsed egalitarian standards, reporting that both members of the couple should have an equal say in the relationship. However, in that study, a substantial portion of lesbians (39%) reported that their own relationship was not egalitarian. Not surprisingly, perceptions of unequal power were associated with less relationship satisfaction.

Sex versus Status

Sex and status are confounded in a heterosexual relationship. Research on homosexual relationships can help tease apart sex differences from status differences. For example, is the sex difference in influence tactics due to sex or power? Falbo and Peplau (1980) compared the influence tactics of gay men, lesbians, and heterosexuals. They observed a sex difference in influence tactics only among heterosexuals: men were more direct and women were more indirect. They did not find a sex difference in influence tactics when comparing gay men to lesbians. In addition, for all relationships, the person who had the greater power in the relationship used the more direct influence tactics of persuasion and bargaining. Another study found similar results: the person who had less power in the relationship used weaker influence tactics than the person who had more power (Howard et al., 1986). These findings held across heterosexuals, gay men, and lesbians. Sex differences in conflict engagement also may be due to status. Kurdek (1996) found no sex differences in conflict engagement or withdrawal behavior when comparing gay men and lesbians.

By contrast, some domains of behavior seem to be more strongly linked to sex than to status or power. Sexuality is one of those (Peplau & Garnets, 2000). In heterosexual and homosexual relationships, men place greater emphasis on sex compared to women (Peplau, 1991). Both homosexual and heterosexual men express more interest in casual sex and greater frequency of casual sex than do heterosexual and homosexual women (Bailey et al., 1994). Blumstein and Schwartz (1983) showed that sex is most frequent among gay males and least frequent among lesbians. Sexual exclusivity also was least common among gay males. In terms of sexual activity, heterosexual relationships seem to be a compromise.

Mind reading is another behavior that may be more strongly linked to sex than to status. Mind reading is the expectation that one's partner can sense one's moods without that person making an overt request. Kurdek and Schmitt (1986) predicted that gay male couples would be characterized by more mind reading compared to lesbians or heterosexual couples because mind reading is associated with the male gender role, as men are more reluctant than women to

express their feelings. The investigators did find the most mind reading among gay men.

A Note on Minorities

There is very little literature on homosexual relationships among minorities. The literature on gay and lesbian relationships has not examined minorities and the literature on minority relationships has not examined homosexuals. One exception is Peplau, Cochran, and Mays' (1997) survey of over 700 homosexual Black men and women who were involved in relationships. Again, this study disconfirmed the myth of transient homosexual relationships, as the average relationship lasted over 2 years and ranged from several months to 35 years.

Over 33% of these couples were involved in interracial relationships, usually with a White person. The percentage of interracial relationships is larger among Black homosexuals than Black heterosexuals. It is more difficult for Black homosexuals than Black heterosexuals to find partners of the same race. Men were more likely than women to be involved in an interracial relationship (42% vs. 30%). The sex difference in interracial relationships is even larger among heterosexuals.

Peplau and colleagues (1997) examined the characteristics participants preferred in a serious partner. Respondents rated internal characteristics (e.g., honesty, kindness) as more important than external characteristics (e.g., physical attractiveness, income). This finding is similar to that found among heterosexuals. There was no sex difference in the importance assigned to a partner's physical attractiveness or income, unlike the findings for heterosexuals. These findings even contradict the research just reviewed showing that gay men are more likely than lesbians to ascribe importance to physical attractiveness. That research, however, focused largely on White homosexuals. With respect to partner income, it is not surprising that White and Black homosexuals find it less important than do heterosexuals; both partners are more likely to be working outside the home in homosexual relationships compared to heterosexual relationships, in part because homosexuals are less likely to have children at home. Whereas research on heterosexuals finds that men are more satisfied than women and research on White homosexuals finds no sex difference in relationship satisfaction, this study of Black homosexuals found that women were more satisfied than men with their relationships.

Similar to the findings from research on White homosexual relationships, men reported being more likely than women to have had sex on the first date with their current partner (31% vs. 18%). About half of the men and half of the women said they had agreed to be monogamous in their current relationship. Blumstein and Schwartz (1983) found that 36% of gay men and 71% of lesbians said it was important to be monogamous in their relationship. The greater emphasis on monogamy among Black gay men may be due to the fact that the study of Black homosexuals was conducted at a later date than the study of White homosexuals; AIDS is likely to have encouraged greater monogamy. Peplau and colleagues (1997) asked respondents if they had engaged in sex outside the relationship; more men had done so (65%) than women (46%). Again, the sex difference was sharper in the Blumstein and Schwartz study (82% vs. 28%).

In conclusion, there appears to be more similarity in the behavior of Black male and female homosexuals than White male and female homosexuals. There was greater correspondence in preference for mate characteristics and emphasis on sexual exclusivity among Black homosexual respondents.

COHABITING RELATIONSHIPS

Cohabitation is becoming increasingly common. In 1997, over 4 million men and women cohabited, whereas in 1980 the figure was just over 1.5 million (U.S. Census Bureau, 1998). In the late 1980s, 7% of 25- to 29-year-olds were cohabiting; five years later, in the early 1990s, this percentage nearly doubled (13%; Waite, 1995). Waite also reports that nearly 25% of unmarried people between the ages of 25 and 34 are currently cohabiting. In a national survey conducted in 1970, 11% of people reported that they had lived with their partner before marriage; in 1990, nearly 50% reported living with their partner before marriage (Bumpass, Sweet, & Cherlin, 1991). Cohabitation has even increased among the elderly (Chevan, 1996). In 1960, cohabitation did not exist among those 60 years of age and older; by 1990, 2.4% were cohabiting.

There are racial differences in cohabitation. Black people are less likely than White people to marry or cohabit (Waite, 1995), but Black people are proportionally more likely than White people to choose cohabitation over marriage. To be more specific, Black women are twice as likely as White women to have their first union be cohabitation as opposed to marriage (Raley, 1996).

The increase in cohabitation largely accounts for the decline in marriage rates (Bumpass & Sweet, 1989). However, cohabitation has merely delayed rather than replaced marriage. In 1970, the median age of marriage for men was 23; it was 21 for women. In 1994, the median age of marriage for men was 27; it was 24.5 for women (Costello, Miles, & Stone, 1998). When first cohabitation and first marriage are conceptualized as first unions, the age at first union has not changed much (Bumpass et al., 1991).

Cohabitation is not only more common today, it is much more widely accepted, especially among younger people (J. Cunningham & Antill, 1995). For example, the majority of today's high school seniors have positive attitudes toward cohabitation (Lye & Waldron, 1997). Cohabitation is partly more accepted because premarital sex is more widely accepted. Cohabitation also may be more common because people are leery of the high divorce rate (Popenoe & Whitehead, 1999). People who cohabit are more likely to have experienced parental divorce (J. Cunningham & Antill, 1995). Cohabitation often is viewed as a way to test a relationship before marriage; the most common reason that men and women report for cohabiting is to see if they are compatible before marriage (Bumpass et al., 1991). The development of the women's movement and the increased number of women in the workforce also may account for some of the rise in cohabitation. Women are less likely to rely on marriage for economic support and may associate marriage with traditional gender roles. A cohabiting relationship may seem like a more egalitarian alternative.

Who Cohabits

People often associate cohabitation with the college experience. However, cohabitation is more common among less-educated people and poorer people (Bumpass & Sweet, 1989; Bumpass et al., 1991). A common reason for cohabiting is to share living expenses; people who have financial constraints may view cohabitation as an alternative to marriage. Economic reasons are undoubtedly responsible for the increase in

cohabitation among the elderly (Chevan, 1996). Marriage increases income taxes and reduces social security payments. Elderly people, who are often on a fixed income, do not want to become involved in an arrangement that will reduce their income. Further evidence for the role that income has in cohabitation comes from research that shows higher-income people who cohabit are more likely to have plans to marry (Bumpass et al., 1991).

Cohabitation also is more common among previously married persons than never-married persons (Bumpass & Sweet, 1989; Bumpass et al., 1991). In a study of people in their early 30s, half of never-married people had cohabited, whereas two-thirds of previously married people had cohabited (Bumpass & Sweet, 1989). In fact, previously married couples are slightly more likely than never-married couples to enter cohabitation without any plans of marriage. Thus, the decline in rates of remarriage is partly due to an increase in cohabitation.

People assume that cohabiting couples are childless. This is not the case, especially when one of the persons has been previously married. Children are present in 39% of cohabiting households (Bumpass et al., 1991). The cohabiting couple are the birth parents in only 33% of those cases.

Outcomes of Cohabitation

Cohabiting relationships are usually of short duration; most cohabiting couples marry or terminate their relationship rather than remain in a long-term cohabiting relationship (Waite, 1995). The majority of cohabiting relationships end in marriage. Bumpass and Sweet (1989) reported that 60% of first cohabiting relationships ended in marriage and 50% did so within four years. Most cohabiting couples expect to marry. In one study,

47% of people said that they have definite marriage plans (Bumpass et al., 1991). In another study, 75% reported some plans to marry (S. Brown & Booth, 1996). Interestingly, women were less likely than men to expect to marry their partner.

Remember that people view cohabitation as a way to test the relationship before marriage. Does it work? Is cohabitation the solution to the rising divorce rates? The evidence suggests not. Married couples who cohabited before marriage are *more* likely to break up than married couples who did not cohabit (Booth & Johnson, 1988; Popenoe & Whitehead, 1999). In one study, people who cohabited before marriage were 50% more likely to become divorced (Bumpass & Sweet, 1989). In a more recent study, people who cohabited before marriage were over 200% as likely to divorce (Krishnan, 1998).

Why does cohabiting appear to lead to less successful marriages? One answer lies in the kind of people who choose to cohabit. There is a selection bias in comparing marriages among people who did and did not cohabit; after all, people are not randomly assigned to cohabit or not. The kind of person who cohabits has less traditional views of gender roles, less traditional views of marriage, is more accepting of divorce, and is less religious (Clarkberg, Stolzenberg, & Waite, 1995; J. Cunningham & Antill, 1995; C. Hill & Peplau, 1998). Each of these factors is associated with divorce.

Women who cohabit before marriage are likely to be more career-oriented and less reliant on marriage for economic support than women who do not (Clarkberg et al., 1995). By contrast, men who cohabit are more likely to be less financially successful than men who do not. People who cohabit before marriage also are less attached to their families than people who do not (Clarkberg et al., 1995). Thus, there are a number of differences between those who do and do not

cohabit that could explain the higher divorce rate among former cohabitors.

Other explanations have been offered as to why the marriages of cohabiting couples do not fare well. Aside from a difference in the kinds of people who enter into cohabiting relationships, cohabiting relationships may differ qualitatively from marital relationships. It is possible that people enter cohabiting relationships instead of marriage because they are more tentative about the relationship; that tentativeness could be a sign of a less well-functioning relationship. There is a great deal of evidence that cohabiting relationships are not as healthy as marital relationships; cohabiting couples are less committed to their relationship, less satisfied with their relationship, and report more problems in their relationship compared to married couples (Bumpass et al., 1991; S. Brown & Booth, 1996) and gay and lesbian couples (Kurdek & Schmitt, 1986). Similar to the data for marriage, there is some evidence that women are more likely than men to cite difficulties in cohabiting relationships (Bumpass et al., 1991). There also is a higher incidence of domestic violence and child abuse in cohabiting compared to marital relationships (J. Cunningham & Antill, 1995; Popenoe & Whitehead, 1999). The lower quality of cohabiting relationships may extend into marriage. People who cohabited before marriage report lower marital quality than people who did not cohabit before marriage (Booth & Johnson, 1988). These effects remain throughout the duration of the marriage.

Finally, a third reason cohabitation may have adverse effects on marriage is the possibility that the cohabitation experience itself has a negative effect on the relationship that makes it less viable after marriage. People who cohabit have a different set of roles than people who marry and it may be difficult to change those roles. For example, people who cohabit experience less commitment to their relationship and a greater degree of freedom in their activities (Popenoe & Whitehead, 1999). Upon marriage, the low commitment level and high freedom level may persist and cause difficulties. In addition, longitudinal studies have shown that people who cohabit become more accepting of divorce over time (J. Cunningham & Antill, 1995). Thus, there is some evidence that cohabitation is altering people's beliefs about marriage.

The outlook for cohabiting relationships is not entirely gloomy. Researchers have failed to consider the possibility that the divorce rate would be even higher if all people who cohabited had married instead (J. Cunningham & Antill, 1995). Cohabiting relationships are heterogeneous, and there may be a subset of couples who are successful. Some people cohabit as a prelude to marriage, whereas others cohabit as an alternative to marriage; the negative effects of cohabiting may characterize the latter more than the former. Couples who cohabit as a prelude to marriage and do so for a very short time may be less vulnerable to the negative effects of cohabitation (Popenoe & Whitehead, 1999). For example, S. Brown and Booth (1996) found that when cohabiting couples who had plans to marry were distinguished from those who did not, the couples with marriage plans were as satisfied with their relationship as married couples. People who cohabit for longer periods of time end up having the least successful marriages (J. Cunningham & Antill, 1995).

SUMMARY

Men and women are equally interested in romantic relationships and generally expect to get the same things out of a romantic relationship: love, companionship, intimacy, and sex. Men and women also have fairly similar standards for romantic relationships, but it appears that women's standards are less likely than men's to be met. This is not surprising, as women voice more dissatisfaction with relationships compared to men. Men and women also desire similar characteristics in a partner; both value internal characteristics, such as trustworthiness and kindness, more than external characteristics, such as money and physical appearance. There is an overall sex difference such that women attach more importance to most characteristics compared to men, which implies that women are choosier. There also are consistent sex differences in preferences for some of the less important characteristics; across cultures, men attach greater importance to the physical appearance of their partner and women attach greater importance to the financial status of their partner. Evolutionary theory and social role theory provide explanations for these differences.

Romantic relationships are characterized by intimacy, expressions of love and caring, self-disclosure, and sexuality for both men and women. There is little evidence that men and women define intimacy in their relationship differently. There is some evidence that men hold more romantic beliefs about relationships compared to women, and there are some sex differences in styles of love. Men tend to adopt a more game-playing strategy of love, whereas women tend to adopt a more practical and friendship-based approach. Men and women largely perceive their sexuality in terms of romance and passion. Women hold slightly more negative attitudes toward sexuality. Men have more permissive attitudes toward sex, but these differences are limited to less serious relationships. Men can separate sex from love, but women are more likely to see the two as co-occurring. In fact, men are more likely than women to seek sex for physical pleasure, whereas women are more likely to seek sex for emotional intimacy.

Who are the happiest couples? Research on gender roles shows that there is a clear link between femininity and relationship satisfaction. As long as one member of the couple possesses feminine traits, someone is attending to the relationship. Research on power shows that couples who share power and couples in which the man is dominant are satisfied with the relationship. The least happy couples are ones in which the wife is dominant. Regardless of what one puts into a relationship, men and women are most happy when they perceive their contributions as equitable. It also turns out that characteristics of men (gender roles, personality traits, well-being) are related to women's relationship satisfaction, whereas characteristics of women have little impact on men's relationship satisfaction.

Connection versus separation is a source of conflict for men and women. Women express more concerns about autonomy in a relationship, and men complain that women are too dependent on them. Women also express concerns about a lack of communication with men. The primary way conflict has been examined has been laboratory studies of conflict discussions; these studies show quite divergent styles of interactions among distressed couples: women are more negative than men and remain engaged in the conflict, whereas men withdraw from the conflict and try to de-escalate it with positive behavior. Because the behavior of women is so different in distressed versus nondistressed relationships, women have been referred to as the "emotional barometers" of relationships. Much research has focused on a particular conflict pattern of behavior known as the demand/withdraw pattern. Research suggests that women are more likely to demand and men to withdraw, largely because women desire more change in relationships than men do.

Jealousy is equally likely to be evoked in men and women. Some research has distinguished between jealousy over sexual infidelity versus emotional infidelity, arguing that men are more upset by the former and women by the latter. However, the extent to which sexual infidelity and emotional infidelity are linked in the minds of men and women has not been investigated.

The majority of research in this chapter is limited to White, middle-class adults and college students. Relationships in other cultures may operate differently depending on the values of the culture and the way gender roles are arranged in the relationship. Studies of gay male and lesbian relationships have shown that there are many features of relationships that span both heterosexual and homosexual relationships (e.g., how relationships develop, the forces that attract one to a relationship, and how relationships dissolve). These studies also have shown: (1) that some of the sex differences in behavior in heterosexual relationships are more likely to be a function of status than of sex; (2) that some mate preferences and ways of behaving in relationships are a function of both sex and sexual orientation; and (3) that men's greater emphasis on sex in relationships pervades both heterosexual and homosexual relationships.

Finally, the chapter concludes with a discussion of cohabiting relationships. Cohabiting relationships are of a lower quality than marital relationships, and cohabitation prior to marriage is predictive of divorce. The negative outcomes of cohabitation may be due to the kinds of people who enter into cohabitation, the nature of the cohabiting relationship itself, or to actual adverse effects of cohabitation on people's relationships.

Discussion Questions

1. What is the "approach/avoidance" dance in L. Rubin's (1983) book?
2. Why do women demand and men withdraw?
3. Knowing what you do about gender roles in relationships, how would you predict that gay men's relationships would differ from lesbians' relationships?
4. What kinds of problems might be unique to homosexual couples? Heterosexual couples?
5. If the majority of men held the male gender role and the majority of women held the female gender role, regardless of sexual orientation, describe the nature of lesbian relationships, gay relationships, and heterosexual relationships.
6. What are the similarities and differences in men's and women's mate preferences?
7. How do men and women view the relation of sex to love?
8. Which sex is more romantic? Why?
9. What are the differences in the way men and women interact when discussing conflict?
10. What does it mean that women are the "emotional barometer" in a relationship?

Suggested Reading

Christensen, A., & Heavy, C.L. (1993). Gender differences in marital conflict: The demand/withdraw interaction pattern. In S. Oskamp & M. Constanzo (Eds.), *Gender issues in contemporary society* (Vol. 6, pp. 113–141). New York: Sage.

Dickson, L. (1993). The future of marriage and family in Black America. *Journal of Black Studies, 23*(4), 472–491.

Kurdek, L., & Schmitt, J.P. (1986). Relationship quality of partners in heterosexual married, heterosexual cohabiting, and gay and lesbian relationships. *Journal of Personality and Social Psychology, 51,* 711–720.

Peplau, L.A. (1994). Men and women in love. In D.L. Sollie & L.A. Leslie (Eds.), *Gender, families, and close relationships: Feminist research journeys* (pp. 19–49). Thousand Oaks, CA: Sage.

Peplau, L.A., & Spalding, L.R. (2000). The close relationships of lesbians, gay men, and bisexuals. In C. Hendrick & S.S. Hendrick (Eds.), *Close relationships: A sourcebook* (pp. 111–123). Thousand Oaks, CA: Sage.

Sprecher, S., & McKinney, K. (1993). *Sexuality.* Newbury Park, CA: Sage.

Winstead, B.A., Derlega, V.J., & Rose, S. (1997). *Gender and close relationships.* Thousand Oaks, CA: Sage.

Key Terms

Agape—Pure love, a blend of eros and storge.

Demand/withdraw pattern—An interaction episode characterized by one person demanding and the other person not responding or withdrawing.

Equity—State of a relationship in which the ratio of what one puts in and gets out of a relationship equals that of the partner.

Eros—Romantic love.

Factor analysis—A statistical procedure that groups items together based on how strongly they are related to one another.

Ludus—Game-playing love.

Mania—Manic love, a blend of eros and ludus.

Mind reading—Expectation that other person can sense one's moods and feelings.

Myth of male dominance—Inaccurate belief that men dominate the family; applied to Hispanic families.

Myth of matriarchy—Belief that women have more power than men in African American families.

Negativity bias—Distorted perception of behavior whereby men interpret their wife's failure to express love as hostility.

Positivity bias—Distorted perception of behavior whereby women interpret their husband's lack of hostility as love.

Pragma—Practical love, a blend of storge and ludus.

Regression to the mean—The idea that extreme scores will become less extreme (regress to the mean) over time.

Script—A schema or cognitive representation for a sequence of events.

Sexual self-schema—A set of cognitions about past and current sexual experiences that includes guides to sexual behavior.

Social exchange theory—Theory that relationship satisfaction is partly a function of the rewards and costs in the relationship.

Storge—Friendship love.

9

Sex Differences in Health: Evidence and Explanations

Women are sicker than men. They report spending more days in bed during the year due to illness compared to men, report more pain, are more depressed, perceive their health as less good, and report more physical symptoms than men. Yet, women live longer than men! In fact, men are more likely than women to die from each of the 10 leading causes of death in the United States. This is the great paradox of gender and health. Women have higher rates of **morbidity** (i.e., illness), but men have higher rates of **mortality.** There are a number of reasons for this paradox, each of which is reviewed in this chapter.

This chapter begins the final section of the book, which focuses on the implications of gender for health. A large section of the book is devoted to health issues because health is one domain in which there are pervasive and sizable sex differences, such as those described above. I construe health broadly, as emotional well-being (psychological distress, life satisfaction, happiness), behavioral problems (aggression, alcohol abuse), and physical problems (physical

symptoms, coronary heart disease). The goal of this chapter is to provide an overview of the sex differences in health as well as the common classes of explanations for these sex differences. First, I describe the sex differences in mortality rates and then differences in morbidity rates. Then, I review numerous explanations for these differences. Subsequent chapters focus on specific health problems. Some of the explanations for sex differences in health described in this chapter appear in later chapters when specific health problems are evaluated.

SEX DIFFERENCES IN MORTALITY

Life Span

Men die younger than women at all points during the life span. Although 106 boys are born for every 100 girls (Stillion, 1995; Strickland, 1988), more boys than girls die at every age. There are not an equal number of males and females in the United States until age 18. After that, there are a greater number of females than males. The ratio of male to female mortality for each age group is shown in Table 9.1. For every 34 girls who die between the ages of 1 and 4, 43 boys die, resulting in a sex ratio of 1.26. You can see that the sex difference peaks during adolescence and young adulthood.

There is some suggestion that males are more likely than females to die even before birth. Researchers have suggested that 120 to 160 boys are conceived for every 100 girls (Stillion, 1995; Strickland, 1988), which would imply a high death rate for boys if only 106 boys to 100 girls are actually born. More recently, the sex difference in the number of males to females conceived has been called into question. I. Waldron (1998) contends that the number of males and females conceived as well as the number of males and females who die during the first 8 weeks after conception is unknown. Estimates of a higher male:female rate of conception is based on the finding that more male *fetuses* die compared to female fetuses, yet more

males than females are born. However, the term fetus is not applied until after the eighth week of gestation, and by far the highest mortality rate before birth occurs during those first 8 weeks. Technically, it is plausible that more females than males are conceived but that a very high proportion of those females die during the first 8 weeks of pregnancy, resulting in a higher male:female ratio of infants.

After birth, it is certain that males have higher death rates at all ages. Thus, it comes as no surprise that women live longer than men. In 1997, people in the United States reached a record long life expectancy of 76 years (Hoyert, Kochanek, & Murphy, 1999; World Almanac, 1998). However, men did not live as long as women. In 1997, life expectancy at birth for White women was 79.8 and for White men was 74.3. Life expectancies at birth for Black people lagged behind, but the sex difference persisted: 76.7 for Black women and 69.9 for Black men. Thus, women outlive men by about six years.

Sex differences in longevity have existed throughout the twentieth century, but their size has varied. The average length of life for men and women during each decade of the twentieth century is shown in Table 9.2. In 1900, the average man lived to be 46 and the average woman 48; the sex difference in mortality was only two years. This gap widened during the middle of the century, peaking in 1979 (Hoyert et al., 1999), when women outlived men by nearly eight years (7.8). Life spans lengthened for both men and women over the course of the century due to better nutrition, better health care, and the development of vaccines (J. Harrison, 1978). The sex difference in longevity widened during the middle of the century due to the reduction in women's mortality during childbirth and the increase in men's mortality from heart disease and lung cancer. The

TABLE 9.1   Number of Deaths per 100,000 in 1996

Age	Male	Female	Male:Female Ratio
1–4	43	34	1.26
5–14	26	18	1.44
15–24	132	46	2.87
25–34	180	75	2.40
35–44	301	146	2.06
45–54	577	325	1.78
55–64	1,397	831	1.68
65–74	3,248	1,989	1.63
75–84	7,271	4,879	1.49
85 and over	17,580	14,441	1.22
All ages	900	852	1.06

Source: Adapted from U.S. Census Bureau (1998).

TABLE 9.2   Life Expectancies over the Twentieth Century

	Men	Women	White Men	White Women	Black Men	Black Women
1997	73.6	79.2	74.3	79.8	69.9	76.7
1990	71.8	78.8	72.9	79.4	67.0	75.2
1980	70.0	77.5	70.7	78.1	65.3	73.6
1970	67.1	74.7	68.0	75.6	61.3	69.4
1960	66.6	73.1	67.4	74.1	61.1	66.3
1950	65.6	71.1	66.5	72.2	59.1	62.9
1940	60.8	65.2	62.1	66.6	51.5	54.9
1930	58.1	61.6	59.7	63.5	47.3	49.2
1920	53.6	54.6	54.4	55.6	45.5	45.2
1910	48.4	51.8	48.6	52.0	33.8	37.5
1900	46.3	48.3	46.6	48.7	32.5	33.5

Source: Adapted from *World Almanac Book* (1998).

increase in men's lung cancer can be directly tied to smoking.

More recently, the sex gap in mortality has narrowed. In the 1980s and 1990s, sex differences in life expectancy grew smaller. The narrowing has been attributed to a greater proportionate decrease in heart disease mortality among men than women and to a greater increase in the incidence of lung cancer among women than men. Between 1979 and 1986, lung cancer increased 7% for men and 44% for women (J. Rodin & Ickovics, 1990). These statistics can be directly tied to changes in smoking patterns. Women's smoking rates increased during the second half of the twentieth century, and women were less likely than men to quit smoking (I. Waldron, 1995b).

As you can see in Table 9.2, there are large race differences in mortality. Furthermore, the size of the sex difference in mortality is greater for Black than White persons. This is largely because the mortality rates of Black men are substantially higher than for White men or women of either race. Black men are the only group whose life expectancy remained relatively unchanged for the 10-year period 1985 to 1995. Staples (1995) suggests that the spread of AIDS, drug abuse, and violence among the Black community may "wipe out" the Black race in another 100 years. Although Black people constitute only 12% of the population, they make up 48% of murder victims (Staples, 1995). Among men ages 15 to 34, Black men are 7 times more likely than White men to become a victim of murder (Staples, 1995).

Sex differences in life expectancy are similar in other nations of the world. Table 9.3 shows sex differences in life expectancies in Western and Eastern Europe (Macintyre, 1993a). The sex difference is larger in the East (7 years) than the West (6.5 years). The sex difference is more variable in third world countries where the life span is much shorter. Some examples are shown in Table 9.3.

One country that has seen a dramatic decline in life expectancy toward the end of the twentieth century is Russia (Notzon et al., 1998). While life expectancy was increasing in the United States during the 1990s, life expectancy declined in Russia.

TABLE 9.3   Life Expectancies Around the World

	Year	Male	Female	Difference (F > M)
East				
Bulgaria	1987	68.4	74.6	6.2
Poland	1988	66.3	74.2	7.9
Romania	1984	67.9	73.2	5.3
USSR	1987	66.0	74.5	8.5
West				
Denmark	1987	71.7	77.5	5.8
France	1987	72.3	80.6	8.3
Ireland	1987	71.3	76.8	5.5
Netherlands	1987	73.2	79.8	6.6
Portugal	1988	70.5	77.6	7.1
Third World Countries				
Afghanistan	1998	47.8	46.8	−1.0
Botswana	1998	39.4	40.4	1.0
Haiti	1998	49.5	53.9	4.4
Laos	1998	52.6	55.9	3.3
Madagascar	1998	52.0	54.5	2.5
Nepal	1998	58.5	58.4	0.1
Rwanda	1998	40.8	41.8	1.0
Somalia	1998	44.7	47.9	3.2
Zimbabwe	1998	38.8	38.9	0.1

Source: Macintyre (1993a); Central Intelligence Agency (1998).

In 1990, Russian men lived to be 63.8 years old and Russian women 74.4 years old. By 1994, only four years later, the life expectancy for men had declined to 57.7 and for women to 71.2; the decline for men was twice that for women. Three-quarters of the decline was due to the increase in death of people ages 25 to 64 due to heart disease, injuries, suicide, and homicide. The primary reason for the decline in life expectancy was the economic and social instability that resulted from the breakup of the Soviet Union, which was associated with an increase in poverty, a decline in income, an increase in stress, and a rise in alcohol intake—all of which might be related.

Leading Causes of Death

At the turn of the twentieth century, men and women were most likely to die from infectious diseases, such as tuberculosis, influenza, pneumonia, and diphtheria. Today, with the exception of AIDS, people are less likely to die from communicable diseases. Instead, people die from diseases in which lifestyle factors play a role. The leading causes of death in the United States are shown in Table 9.4. The leading cause of death for both men and women, White and Black, is coronary heart disease. The second leading cause of death is cancer, followed by accidents, cerebrovascular disease (i.e., stroke), and chronic obstructive pulmonary disease (COPD; i.e., emphysema). Many of the risk factors for these diseases include behavioral factors, such as smoking, drinking, and driving while intoxicated. The most noteworthy feature of Table 9.4 is that the death rates for the top 13 of the 14 causes are higher in males than females. This pattern holds across White and Black people. The one exception is Alzheimer's disease, which has a higher death rate for women than men among Whites. The largest sex differences appear for accidents, suicide, homicide, and HIV. Men are over twice as likely as women to die from accidents. Although injuries at work are not among the leading causes of death, men are 10 times as likely as women to die from injuries at work. Men are over 4 times more likely than women to die from suicide, 3.8 times more likely to die from homicide, and 3.5 times more likely to die from HIV (Hoyert et al., 1999).

The causes of death for young people differ from those for older people (Hoyert et al., 1999). The leading cause of death among people under 44 is accidents. The leading cause of death among 45- to 64-year-olds is cancer, and the leading cause of death

TABLE 9.4 Age-Adjusted Death Rates (per 100,000) for the Leading Causes of Death

Causes of Death	Male/Female All	Ratio	White Male	Female	Black Male	Female
Heart disease	166.1	1.68	206.2	120.0	303.0	198.9
Cancer	125.6	1.40	145.9	106.0	214.8	131.2
Accidents	30.1	2.41	42.0	17.5	54.2	20.4
Cerebrovascular disease	25.9	1.15	25.7	22.5	48.6	37.9
COPD	21.1	1.47	26.5	18.5	24.5	12.7
Diabetes mellitus	13.5	1.19	13.4	10.6	29.2	28.5
Pneumonia and influenza	12.9	1.54	15.5	10.2	23.0	13.1
Suicide	10.6	4.24	18.4	4.4	11.2	1.9
Homicide	8.0	3.79	7.0	2.3	48.3	9.3
Liver disease	7.4	2.33	10.3	4.4	12.9	5.3
HIV	5.8	3.50	5.6	1.0	38.5	13.3
Kidney disease	4.4	1.46	4.8	3.2	11.7	8.5
Septicemia	4.2	1.23	4.0	3.2	11.5	8.9
Alzheimer's disease	2.7	.89	2.6	3.0	2.0	1.9

Source: Adapted from Hoyert et al. (1999).

among people age 65 and over is heart disease. Sex differences in heart disease and cancer account for most of the sex difference in mortality among older adults. Sex differences in accidents, suicide, homicide, and HIV account for most of the sex difference in mortality among younger people.

In general, the leading causes of death are the same for White and Black people (Hoyert et al., 1999). However, as shown in Table 9.4, Black men and women have higher death rates from most of the leading causes than White men and women. The only exceptions are COPD, suicide, and Alzheimer's disease. There are a few important differences between the profiles of leading causes of death for Black and White persons. Black people have substantially higher rates of HIV and homicide, which is the fifth leading cause of death for Black men, but the tenth leading cause among White men. Across both sexes, Black persons

are 6 times more likely to die from homicide. Black persons also are 7.5 times more likely to die from HIV. For both HIV and homicide, Black men are at the highest risk. Some of the race differences in death rates are larger within certain age groups. For example, the leading cause of death for White persons under age 45 is accidents; the leading cause for Black persons ages 15 through 24 is homicide and for Black persons ages 25 through 44 is HIV.

SEX DIFFERENCES IN MORBIDITY

Morbidity reflects illness. Whereas mortality rates have decreased and the life span has lengthened, morbidity rates have increased. People are living longer but partly because they are living with diseases rather than dying from them. During the early part of the twentieth century, the leading causes of death were from infectious diseases. The causes of these diseases were relatively simple to understand; typically, there was a single causal agent, the germ. With the development of penicillin and vaccinations, people began to live longer; thus, they had more time to develop and subsequently die from chronic diseases. Whereas an acute illness lasts a short time and is either fatal (a possibility in the case of tuberculosis or pneumonia) or nonfatal (the common cold), a chronic illness is long-lasting and typically does not disappear. A chronic illness can be fatal or nonfatal; rheumatoid arthritis is an example of a nonfatal chronic illness, and cancer and heart disease are examples of chronic illnesses that can be fatal—in fact, they are now the two leading causes of death. The increase in chronic disease accounts for the increase in morbidity, that is, the increase in illness, disability, and activity restriction among the U.S. population.

Women have higher morbidity rates than men. Although men have higher incident rates (i.e., men contract the diseases more than women do) and death rates from the two leading causes of death (heart disease and cancer), women suffer from more acute illnesses and more nonfatal chronic illnesses compared to men (Verbrugge, 1989). Thus, at any given point in time, women are more likely than men to be ill and to be living with a chronic disease. Among nonfatal chronic illnesses, women suffer higher rates of arthritis, immune disorders, and digestive conditions compared to men (Verbrugge, 1989). Women suffer from more painful disorders compared to men, such as migraines, tension headaches, musculoskeletal pain, back pain, abdominal pain, carpal tunnel syndrome, irritable bowel syndrome, rheumatoid arthritis, multiple sclerosis, and Raynaud's disease (Berkley, 1997; Macintyre, Hunt, & Sweeting, 1996; Unruh, 1996). Women also report

more psychological and physical symptoms than men (Gijsbers van Wijk, Huisman, & Kolk, 1999; Macintyre et al., 1996; Mechanic, 1976). In fact, women score worse than men on most indicators of health (Lahelma, Martikainen, Rahkonen, & Silventoinen, 1999).

Women also perceive their health to be worse than men's. Subjective health perceptions are typically measured by a single item that asks respondents to rate their health as poor, fair, good, very good, or excellent. A 1998 nationwide survey of adults in the United States revealed this sex difference (Division of Adult and Community Health, 1998): as shown in Figure 9.1, men were more likely than women to report that their health was excellent, whereas women were more likely than men to give the remaining responses. Even among the elderly, women report worse health perception than men (Arber & Ginn, 1993). The report of worse health by women is not limited to the United States; women also have worse self-reports of health in Scotland (Macintyre et al., 1996) and Britain (Arber & Ginn, 1993).

Women also report more **illness behavior** than men. Illness behaviors are those that signify illness; for example, women report more days spent in bed due to illness, more days in which they restricted their activities due to illness, and greater use of prescription drugs (Kandrack, Grant, & Segall, 1991; Verbrugge, 1989). Even among the elderly, women report greater functional disability than men (Arber & Ginn, 1993).

One aspect of illness behavior is seeking medical care. Women report a greater use of health services compared to men (C. Green & Pope, 1999; Verbrugge, 1989), which is often taken as an indication of women being sicker than men. Sex differences in the use of health care services peak during women's childbearing years. When reproductive-related reasons are

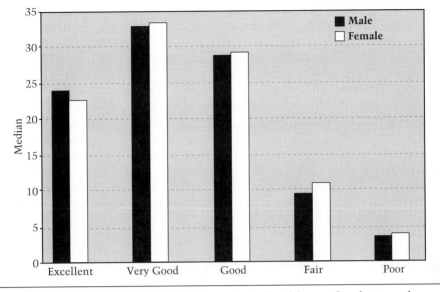

FIGURE 9.1 Perceived health. Men perceive their health to be better than women do. *Source:* Adapted from Division of Adult and Community Health (1998).

taken into consideration, sex differences in hospitalization become more similar, but women still receive greater outpatient care than men (Verbrugge, 1985). One study found that women's greater health care in the prior year compared to men was due to women having a greater number of chronic conditions (Cleary, Mechanic, & Greenley, 1982). Some of women's higher morbidity rates are related to their gynecological problems, but again, even when these problems are taken into consideration, women have higher rates of morbidity compared to men (Cleary et al., 1982). Some researchers have concluded that women's excess morbidity is strongest among illnesses that have more psychological aspects to them (Macintyre et al., 1996).

I have identified many ways in which women come to be classified as the "sicker sex." Now let me give you an example of a typical study on sex differences in morbidity. Verbrugge (1989) asked 589 adults in Detroit to keep a daily health record for six weeks. On average, women rated their health as poorer compared to men. On 67 indicators of health (e.g., self-rated health status, number of sick days in prior two weeks, number of days restricted due to injury, number of symptoms, number of days in bed), women scored worse than men on 60 and significantly so on 42. In general, women felt worse than men. Over the six weeks, women reported more psychological and physical symptoms of illness, had greater restricted activity days, and spent a greater number of days in bed due to illness. However, women also reported greater preventative care. When asked about the prior year, women reported more disability days than men but also more visits to the doctor for preventative health care. Clearly, the use of health care services should not always be taken as an indicator of poor health; some of women's physician visits may be due to their greater illness compared to men, but some of the visits are also due to women having more routine checkups compared to men.

Interestingly, sex differences in morbidity do not appear until adolescence. For example, chronic illnesses, such as asthma and migraine headaches, are more prevalent among boys than girls during childhood; by early adolescence, however, this sex difference reverses itself (Sweeting, 1995). Health care utilization rates reflect these differences. During childhood, boys visit health care professionals more frequently than girls do, but during adolescence, girls visit health care professionals more. It is difficult to link health care utilization in childhood to children's behavior, however, because adults are more likely than children to be making the decision to seek health care. Thus, it may be that parents, in particular, mothers, are more likely to take boys than girls to see a doctor when they are young. Parents might take boys' complaints more seriously because they expect boys to be less likely than girls to complain of symptoms; admitting illness violates gender-role norms for boys.

EXPLANATIONS FOR SEX DIFFERENCES IN HEALTH

Below, I examine seven classes of explanations for sex differences in morbidity and mortality. First, I examine biological factors that might contribute to sex differences in health, focusing on the role of genes and hormones. Second, I examine whether socioeconomic status variables are differentially related to health for men and women: Is women's poor health a function of their lower income? Third, I consider the role of artifacts in sex differences in health. **Artifacts** are factors that cause sex differences to appear that do not really exist.

Physician bias is an example of an artifact; perhaps physicians treat men and women differently so that it appears that women are sicker but men and women are actually equally healthy or unhealthy. Fourth, I consider the role of health behaviors, such as preventive health care, smoking, drinking, drug use, diet, and exercise; there are sex differences for most of these behaviors. Fifth, I consider aspects of the male and female gender roles that might influence health. Aspects of the male gender role can be linked to specific health behaviors and to general risk-taking behavior; aspects of the female gender role can be related to greater concerns with health but also to risks associated with involvement in relationships. Sixth, I discuss whether men and women perceive symptoms similarly or whether women have a lower threshold for symptoms which makes it appear that women are sicker than men. Finally, I consider whether men and women respond to symptoms in similar ways in terms of taking care of themselves and seeking medical attention.

Biology

GENES. Women may have a greater genetic resistance to some diseases compared to men. Women may be genetically predisposed to better health because they have a second X chromosome (Travis, 1988). The X chromosome carries more information on it than the Y chromosome. In females, an abnormality on an X chromosome is not necessarily a problem because there is a second X chromosome to suppress it; the abnormality is usually recessive. Thus, a female will simply be a carrier of the abnormality but will not manifest it. The male, however, has a Y chromosome, which cannot override an abnormality on an X chromosome. This may explain why there are more males than females with some congenital disorders, such as hemophilia, meningitis, muscular dystrophy, and mental retardation (Travis, 1988).

HORMONES. Estrogen plays a significant role in women's health. Whereas estrogen protects women from cardiovascular disease, it plays a hazardous role in the development of some cancers (breast cancer, endometrial cancer) and may be linked to osteoarthritis (Strickland, 1988). Estrogens also may play a role in autoimmune diseases, but the effects are not consistently beneficial nor detrimental (Schuurs & Verheul, 1990). Thus, hormones certainly play a role in men's and women's health, but which hormones are responsible for the effects and the direction of the effects are not clear.

IMMUNE SYSTEM. Recently, it has been suggested that the nature of men's and women's immune systems differ. Whitacre, Reingold, O'Looney, and the Task Force on Gender (1999) suggested that women's immune system responds better than men's to viruses. A substantial body of work has shown that females are more resistant than males to infections, but much of the early work focused on mice (Goble & Konopka, 1973). Among humans, men have lower rates of immunoglobulin M (a protein involved in immune function), which may be a source of men's greater vulnerability to disease (Schuurs & Verheul, 1990; I. Waldron, 1983a). Recent work has shown that women are less likely than men to develop infections during hospitalization following severe injuries (Offner, Moore, & Biffl, 1999).

There is a paradox in the nature of men's and women's immune functioning. Although women's immune system may be more likely than men's to fight off infection, women are more vulnerable to diseases specific to the immune system, such as lupus and rheumatoid arthritis. Overall, there may be differences in the way men's and women's immune systems operate (Whitacre et al., 1999).

OTHER FACETS OF BIOLOGY. One aspect of women's biology that contributes to women's higher morbidity rates compared to men is women's reproductive capabilities. Pregnancy, for example, is likely to be related to a number of morbidity indices, such as disability, restricted activity days, visits to the physician, and hospitalization. However, even when reproductive events are taken into consideration, women continue to have higher rates of morbidity compared to men.

Socioeconomic Status

Socioeconomic status (SES) clearly is related to health. With every increase in income, even among people who are middle to upper class, health improves. Do men have a higher SES than women? If SES is measured by earnings, men have a higher status than women. If SES is measured by education, today men and women have a relatively equal status. It does not appear that differences in men's and women's SES can explain sex differences in either mortality or morbidity.

Another question is whether SES shows the same relation to health for men and women. Past research has shown that SES has a stronger relation to health for men than for women, but several recent studies have called this finding into question. In a group of young adults, the relation of SES to health was similar for men and women (Matthews, Manor, & Power, 1999). The relation of SES to health in men and women may depend on the health outcome. In a study of the elderly in Britain, higher income and social class were equally associated with better health for men and women when health was measured in terms of physical functioning. However, SES was more strongly related to men's than women's health when health was measured in terms of subjective health perceptions (Arber & Ginn, 1993).

One reason the relation of SES to women's health has been inconsistent across studies may have to do with how SES is measured in women. Some studies use the woman's occupation and income to represent SES, whereas other studies use the husband's occupation and income to represent the woman's SES. The relation of SES to health in women was evaluated with both methodologies by Arber and Ginn (1993). They found that women's health was equally predicted by their own or their husband's SES when health was measured in terms of physical functioning. However, women's subjective health perceptions were better predicted by their husband's SES than their own SES. The authors suggest that husband's occupation is likely to have contributed more than wife's occupation to the couple's standard of living. One's standard of living might lead to better health perceptions. In a study that followed people for nearly 20 years, SES was associated with reduced mortality among women regardless of how it was measured (McDonough, Williams, House, & Duncan, 1999). Both own income and spouse income predicted reduced mortality among women. Among men, however, only their own income was associated with reduced mortality; for men, spouse income was associated with *increased* mortality. This finding is consistent with some of the research reviewed in Chapter 11 that shows men's mental health may be adversely affected by wives who work and have a high income. A woman's high contribution to family income may threaten the man's role as family provider, causing an increase in men's

distress. In addition, men who are married to women with high income also might suffer because the women are not tending to the men's health care needs (McDonough et al., 1999). As discussed in the next chapter, one reason men benefit from marriage is that wives take care of the family's health. A wife who works full-time in a high-powered job is going to be less likely than other wives to make physician appointments for her husband, to remind him of physician appointments, to buy healthy food for him, or to cook healthy meals.

Status, as measured in other ways besides financial, has been associated with both men's and women's health. In one study, the status of women in each of the 50 states was calculated by the number of women who participated in politics and the number of women who worked outside of the home (Kawachi, Kennedy, Gupta, & Prothrow-Smith, 1999). States in which women had a higher status were associated with lower mortality rates and lower rates of activity limitations among women. Interestingly, men also benefited from women's high status: men who lived in states where women had a higher status had reduced mortality rates. This finding may seem contradictory to the one reported in the previous paragraph. However, the previous study was about the amount of income women made (McDonough et al., 1999), whereas this study simply evaluates whether women work or not. As you will see in Chapter 11, women's employment does *not* detract from men's health. There may be an underlying SES variable that is contributing to both men's and women's health in states where women are involved in government.

Artifacts

One class of explanations for sex differences in health is that the differences are not real but are due to artifacts. Recall that artifacts are methodological variables that might lead to the *appearance* of sex differences in health even when differences do not exist. Mortality is an objective index of health; thus, it would be difficult to find an artifactual explanation for sex differences in mortality. However, many of the indices of morbidity are subjective and may be influenced by the way they are assessed. Thus, sex differences in morbidity may be influenced by artifacts.

PROXY. One very uninteresting reason women may report greater morbidity than men is that respondents in surveys are more likely to be women than men; that is, women report on behalf of themselves and their spouse. Respondents, whether male or female, report greater symptoms for themselves than for others. Each of us is certainly more aware of our own heath idiosyncracies than we are of another person's. Thus, survey research may underestimate men's illness if women are allowed to report on behalf of men. We know that the use of a proxy response is problematic because sex differences in morbidity are larger when women report on behalf of their spouses (Nathanson, 1978). Today, people are aware of this bias, so more recent studies do not permit proxy responses.

PHYSICIAN BIAS. Physicians may respond to men and women differently so that it appears that women have higher rates of morbidity than men. Here, I examine how physicians might contribute to the appearance of greater psychological problems among women.

Women are more likely than men to receive prescriptions for psychotropic drugs, such as tranquilizers, antidepressants, and sedatives, following a visit to a hospital clinic (Morabia, Fabre, & Dunand, 1992). There are a number of possible reasons for this difference. First, it is possible that

women are more psychologically distressed than men; support is provided for this hypothesis in Chapter 12. It also is possible that psychotropic drugs are overprescribed to women because women's symptoms are more likely to be attributed to psychological causes.

There is some evidence that physicians are more likely to attribute problems to psychological causes in women than in men. Physicians attribute women's complaints to psychological causes even when there is an organic cause (Lennane & Lennane, 1973). This kind of bias has implications for the kinds of treatment men and women receive. Women's higher rates of medication usage compared to men may reflect physicians overprescribing antidepressants and tranquilizers to women. An examination of patient medical records across the nation revealed that women were more likely than men to receive antidepressants and antianxiety drugs, even when they had similar symptoms (Hohmann, 1989). These differences in prescribed medication could be due to physician bias. However, it also is possible that female patients are more likely than male patients to request medication for anxiety and depression (Hohmann, 1989).

The tendency of physicians to misattribute women's problems to psychiatric causes may be more likely to occur during ambiguous situations. When men and women make a psychological complaint explicit, physicians respond similarly. Bernstein and Kane (1981) gave general practitioners vignettes of hypothetical patients and found that they were equally likely to make a psychiatric diagnosis among males (23%) and females (29%) when the patient disclosed a personal problem. These findings are shown in Figure 9.2. However, when there was no disclosure of a personal problem, physicians were much more likely to diagnose a female than a male with a psychiatric disorder (14% vs.

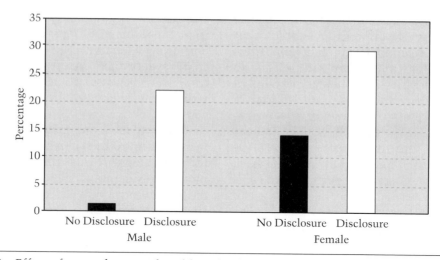

FIGURE 9.2 Effect of sex and personal problem disclosure on psychiatric diagnosis. When patients disclosed a personal problem, psychiatrists were equally likely to diagnose males and females with a psychiatric problem. When there was no disclosure of a personal problem, psychiatrists were more likely to assign females than males a psychiatric diagnosis. *Source:* Adapted from Bernstein and Kane (1981).

2%). These rates also are shown in Figure 9.2. Both male and female physicians responded in the same way, although there were many fewer female than male physicians in the sample. The authors concluded that the expression of a personal problem had a greater impact on physicians' perceptions of men than of women. Because men disclose personal problems less often than women, physicians may take men's disclosures quite seriously.

Other research has shown that physicians are more likely to diagnose a mental disorder in men than in women who complain of mental distress. Verbrugge (1984) conducted a national survey of physician visits that involved an adult whose primary complaint was mental distress. Physicians not only were more likely to diagnose a mental disorder among men, but also viewed men's complaints as more severe. Verbrugge suggested that men's complaints may have been viewed as more

severe because physicians do not expect men to seek help or complain of mental distress, so when they do, it must be serious. Research on people's view of the severity of personality disorders in men and women is consistent with this idea. Personality disorders that are more common to women than men, such as dependency, are viewed as more severe when they appear in men, whereas personality disorders that are more common to men, such as antisocial behavior, are viewed as more severe when they appear in women (Sprock, 1996).

Although men's mental disorders were viewed as more severe than women's in the Verbrugge (1984) survey, women actually ended up receiving more treatment by physicians, at least among general practitioners. Psychiatrists tended to treat men and women similarly, but other physicians prescribed different treatments. Other physicians were more likely to prescribe drugs and to request follow-up care for women than for men; men were more likely to be referred elsewhere or to not be asked to return for a follow-up visit. Thus, the physician who understands the most about mental illness (the psychiatrist) treats men and women most similarly. Physicians who understand less about mental illness may be relying more on gender-role stereotypes to guide their behavior. In total, women received a greater amount of care and attention from physicians in response to emotional distress. This is the kind of bias that could artificially inflate women's morbidity rates relative to those of men. The source of the differential treatment, however, is not clear. Physicians may perceive women with emotional problems as needing more care than men, or women with emotional problems may request greater care.

Physician bias not only has been applied to the diagnosis of psychiatric disorders, such as depression, but also to alcohol usage. According to Bickel (1997), alcohol problems are underdiagnosed in women compared to men because the criteria used to identify such problems are more relevant to men. Common signs of alcohol problems in men are difficulties with the law, problems at work, and general disruptive behavior. Women with alcohol problems may be less likely to show symptoms that are disruptive to society. Thus, alcohol problems in women may be less easily detected by others.

Health Behaviors

One class of variables that may explain sex differences in mortality and morbidity are health behaviors. These include risky behaviors, such as smoking, alcohol abuse, and drug abuse, as well as healthy behaviors, such as preventive health care, exercise, and diet. I. Waldron (1995b) argues that sex differences in behavior are the

major reason men die younger than women, and that these behavioral factors contribute to sex differences in the leading causes of death. Behaviors are implicated in heart disease, lung cancer, COPD, accidents, suicides, homicides, liver disease, and AIDS. Now that people are living longer and dying of chronic disease, behavioral factors may play a larger role than biology in sex differences in mortality.

In this section, I focus on the relation of gender to specific health behaviors. However, some studies have examined indices of health behavior that average across a range of distinct behaviors and found links to gender roles; first, I review those studies.

HEALTH BEHAVIOR INDICES. Gender roles have been associated with indices of health behavior. Masculinity and femininity were both associated with good health behavior among undergraduates (i.e., smoking, drinking, exercise, and safety habits; Shifren & Bauserman, 1996). In another study, masculinity was associated with good health behaviors (e.g., diet, exercise, seat belt use, smoking, alcohol), but masculine gender-role stress was associated with poor health behaviors (Eisler, Skidmore, & Ward, 1988). Recall that masculine gender-role stress reflects appraising as stressful situations that threaten the male role. Such situations include being outperformed by the other sex and expressing emotions. These studies underscore the idea that there are multiple aspects of masculinity that may have different relations to health behaviors. The male gender role is examined as an explanation for sex differences in morbidity and mortality at the end of this chapter. Conduct Exercise 9.1 to see how gender roles are related to health behavior.

PREVENTIVE HEALTH CARE. Women are more likely than men to believe in the value of preventive health care (Cleary

---

EXERCISE 9.1
Gender Roles and Health Behavior

First, develop an inventory of health behaviors. Then, choose some measures of gender roles discussed in Chapter 2. You might choose gender-related traits (agency, communion, unmitigated agency, unmitigated communion), measures of gender-role stress, or attitudes toward gender roles. Ask a group of your peers to complete one of the gender role inventories along with the health behavior inventory.

How are gender roles related to health behaviors? Are the relations different for men and women?

EXERCISE 9.2
Do You Have a Doctor?

Interview 10 male and 10 female college students to find out if they have a regular physician. You might ask, "If you become sick, is there a specific physician you would call?" To really be certain that people have a physician, you might even ask for the physician's name. If a person does not have a physician, ask why.

Then, interview 20 older adults (10 male, 10 female) and ask the same question. You might interview the same students' parents, staff, or faculty.

Are there sex differences in having a physician? Does it depend on age? What are the reasons for not having a physician? Do men and women provide different reasons?

---

et al., 1982). Women are more likely to have a regular physician and over twice as likely to have had a regular check-up in the prior year (Kandrack et al., 1991; Muller, 1990). Women also are more likely to return to the doctor's office for follow-up care (Muller, 1990). Women expect to have a regular physician, whereas men do not. When men do not have a regular physician, they report it is because they have no need for one; when women report that they do not have a regular physician, it is because they have not found the right one (Muller, 1990). Using Exercise 9.2, find out if your male and female peers have a physician and examine their reasons.

One reason women have a regular physician and have better preventive care habits centers on reproductive issues. Women regularly visit the doctor for pap smears, mammograms, birth control, pregnancy, and postmenopausal symptoms. Men do not have the same regular life events or health issues early in life that require the establishment of a regular physician or routine physician visits. However, even when reproductive visits are excluded

from analyses, women still visit the doctor more frequently than men do (I. Waldron, 1983b). In a sense, it is difficult to completely account for reproductive reasons when examining sex differences in the use of health care services. One can certainly count the number of visits that can be attributed to reproductive issues, such as pregnancy or contraception. However, one also must consider the fact that women are more likely than men to become involved in the health care system in the first place because of reproductive issues. Thus, when it comes to getting a flu shot, getting a regular physical, and seeking medical attention in response to a complaint, women are more likely to have a resource available and to be familiar with turning to that resource. Thus, in a sense, reproductive issues could still explain why women are more likely than men to visit a physician.

One group of women do not receive greater health care compared to men:

lesbians. Both lesbians and gay men may be underserved by the health care system (T. Mann, 1996). Lesbians are less likely than heterosexual women to have health insurance from a spouse's employment. Lesbian households also have lower income, which is associated with lower use of health services, in particular lower rates of screening for breast cancer (Rankow & Tessaro, 1998b). Despite the fact that lesbians have just as high a risk for cervical cancer as heterosexual women, they are less likely to obtain pap smears (Rankow & Tessaro, 1998a). Both lesbians and gay men report feeling uncomfortable dealing with a health care system that is not sensitive to homosexuality (T. Mann, 1996; Rankow & Tessaro, 1998a). Gay men are stigmatized by the association of homosexuality with AIDS, and this association may make them unwilling to deal with the health care system.

What are the implications of heterosexual women's greater use of medical services for prevention compared to men? Theoretically, if women visit the doctor more frequently than men do, women's illnesses should be diagnosed at an earlier stage than men's. Early intervention may keep minor illnesses from developing into fatal ones. Routine office visits provide physicians with an opportunity to detect disease and provide patients with an opportunity to disclose problems. Although this is a compelling explanation for sex differences in mortality, there is no evidence that women's greater use of health services leads to earlier detection of disease (Verbrugge, 1985). In fact, heart disease is detected later in women than men and women delay longer in seeking treatment for symptoms of heart disease and cancer.

SMOKING.   Smoking has been referred to as the single most preventable cause of death (American Cancer Society, 1999b). Smoking is associated with the leading causes of death: heart disease, COPD (e.g., emphysema), stroke, and cancer.

Smoking accounts for about 30% of deaths from heart disease (Strickland, 1988). Smoking reveals a dose-response relation to heart disease, meaning that the more one smokes, the greater the risk of heart disease (Rich-Edwards, Manson, Hennekens, & Buring, 1995). When people quit smoking, the risk of heart disease decreases dramatically. Within three to five years after quitting, heart disease rates are similar to those of a nonsmoker. Smoking also is more strongly linked to heart disease in women than in men. In a prospective study of healthy men and women, smoking predicted the incidence of a heart attack 12 years later (Prescott, Hippe, Schnohr, Hein, & Vestbo, 1998). Women who smoked had 2.24 times the risk of a heart attack as women who did not smoke; the relative risk for men was 1.43. These findings held even when the number of cigarettes smoked was taken into consideration.

Smoking is most strongly linked to lung cancer. The increased rates of men smoking in the middle of the twentieth century can be directly tied to the dramatic rise in lung cancer and heart disease among men and the subsequent widening of the sex difference in mortality at that time (I. Waldron, 2000). The increased rates of smoking among women in the 1960s and 1970s can be directly tied to the increased rate of lung cancer that emerged among women 20 to 30 years later. In 1987, lung cancer surpassed breast cancer as the leading cause of cancer death among women.

Smoking accounts for half of the sex difference in mortality (I. Waldron, 1995a). The increase in smoking among women and the lower quit rates among women have contributed to the recent narrowing of the sex gap in longevity. Smoking also is riskier for women than men in terms of lung cancer. Given the same level of smoking, women are more susceptible than men to lung cancer (Ernster, 1996). Women may have a genetic predisposition to develop lung cancer, making smoking especially harmful to women (Shriver et al., 2000).

Besides heart disease and lung cancer, there are a variety of other health problems that smoking poses for men and women. Women who smoke are vulnerable to osteoporosis, early menopause, decreased fertility, and complications during pregnancy. Men and women who smoke are at increased risk for other cancers, such as cancer of the mouth, pancreas, bladder, and kidneys (B. Berman & Gritz, 1991).

Prevalence among Adults. The most recent data from a national health survey of people in the United States show that 26% of White people, 27% of Black people, and 18% of Hispanic people smoke (U.S. Department

of Health and Human Services, 1998c). As shown in Figure 9.3, among the three most prevalent ethnic groups in the United States, men are more likely than women to smoke. A 1998 random-digit dialing survey of smoking in each of the 50 states showed that the median smoking prevalence across the states was 24% (Centers for Disease Control and Prevention, 1999d). The prevalence for men was 25% and for women 21%. The rates ranged from a low of 14% in Utah to a high of 31% in Kentucky.

Sex differences in smoking have changed over the latter half of the twentieth century (I. Waldron, 1997; 2000). In the early part of the century, men smoked more than women because smoking was not viewed as socially acceptable among women. In 1955, 25% of women smoked compared to 52% of men (Chesney & Nealey, 1996). In the 1960s and 1970s, the health hazards of smoking became publicized, but smoking also

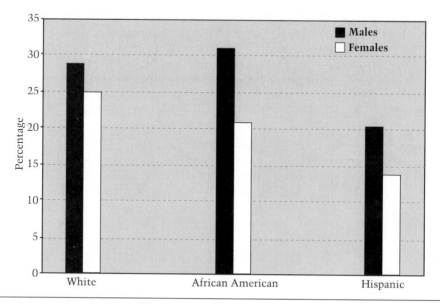

FIGURE 9.3 Current smoking in the United States. These are the percentages of White, African American, and Hispanic adults who report that they currently smoke. In all three ethnic groups, more men than women smoke. *Source:* Adapted from U.S. Department of Health and Human Services (1998c).

became more socially acceptable for women (I. Waldron, 1991; 2000). Smoking among women increased with the rise of the women's movement and came to be associated with women's fight for equality. In 1977, women's rates of smoking peaked at 40% (Chesney & Nealey, 1996). Thus, in the 1960s and 1970s, men's rates of smoking initiation were lower than those of women. In addition, patterns of smoking cessation differed by sex. In the latter part of the century, more men than women began to quit smoking. Today, men still have higher quit rates than women. Along with the sex differences in smoking patterns, the sex differences in lung cancer shifted. In 1950, the male:female ratio of lung cancer was 4.6; in 1960, it was 6.7; in 1990, it was 2.3 (I. Waldron, 2000). Because lung cancer occurs two to three decades following smoking, the changes in men's and women's rates of lung cancer can be directly tied to the changes in their rates of smoking.

Smoking rates have declined in all three ethnic groups among both men and women since the 1970s (U.S. Department of Health and Human Services, 1998c). The decline has been consistent among African American and Hispanic men but leveled off for White men in the 1990s. For women, the decline was consistent among all three ethnic groups until the 1990s; then, the rates of smoking seem to have remained unchanged among all groups of women. Figures for White and Black men and women are shown in Figure 9.4.

Prevalence among Adolescents and Children. Smoking is particularly important to study among children and adolescents. First, the majority of smokers begin to smoke during adolescence or early adulthood; more

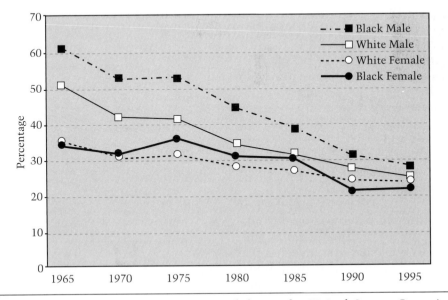

FIGURE 9.4 Changes in smoking rates among adults in the United States. Over time, rates of smoking have declined for men and women, but the decline has been steeper among men. Rates of smoking also have leveled off in the 1990s. *Source:* Adapted from U.S. Department of Health and Human Services (1998c).

than 80% of adult smokers started smoking before the age of 18 (Centers for Disease Control and Prevention, 2000e). In a study of over 6,000 young adults who were one to two years out of high school, 27% of women and 23% of men reported that they smoked (Pirie, Murray, & Luepker, 1991). These rates are comparable to those of adults. Second, there is some evidence that smoking slows lung development among adolescents (Gold et al., 1996). These effects are stronger among females than males.

Although smoking rates have declined among adults, smoking rates have recently increased among children and adolescents. In the 1990s, smoking rates increased among middle school and high school students (Centers for Disease Control and Prevention, 1999b; U.S. Department of Health and Human Services, 1998a). Among eighth-graders, boys' rates increased from 8% in 1991 to 9% in 1997; girls' rates increased from 6% to 9%. Among tenth-graders, boys' rates increased from 12% in 1991 to 17% in 1997; girls' rates increased from 13% to 19%. Among twelfth-graders, boys' rates increased from 29% to 37%; girls rates increased from 28% to 35%. Two recent studies assessed adolescents when they were in eighth grade and followed them to twelfth grade to see who began to smoke (Flay, Hu, & Richardson, 1998; K. Griffin, Botvin, Doyle, Diaz, & Epstein, 1999). In both studies, by twelfth grade, 25% to 33% of adolescents smoked irregularly and 12% were regular smokers.

As you can see, the sex difference in rates of smoking has narrowed among adolescents. For the first time, a nationwide study of high school students revealed that White girls were more likely than White boys to have smoked in the prior month (40% vs. 37%; Centers for Disease Control and Prevention, 1996). Among African American students, however, over twice as many boys as girls smoked (28% vs. 12%).

More boys than girls smoked among Hispanic students also (35% vs. 33%).

There are ethnic differences in smoking among adolescents. The rates of smoking and experimenting with cigarettes are higher among White and Hispanic than African American adolescents (Flay et al., 1998; Siddiqui, Mott, Anderson, & Flay, 1999; U.S. Department of Health and Human Services, 1998c). Race differences in smoking increased during the 1980s, largely due to a greater decrease in smoking among African American and Hispanic compared to White youth. In the 1990s, smoking rates increased among all three groups. Between 1991 and 1997, smoking rates increased 80% among African Americans, 34% among Hispanics, and 28% among White students (Centers for Disease Control and Prevention, 1998c). These rates are shown in Figure 9.5. Although the rates of smoking have increased substantially for African American students, their rates are still much lower than those of Whites or Hispanics. Recent data collected on younger adolescents reveal no race differences in

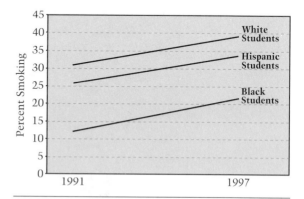

FIGURE 9.5 Overall prevalence of current cigarette smoking among high school students. Smoking rates have increased among White, Black, and Hispanic high school students in the 1990s. *Source:* Adapted from Centers for Disease Control and Prevention (1998c).

smoking. The first national survey of middle school children (grades 6 through 8) showed that 9.2% of children smoke, and these rates are similar for boys and girls and for White, Black, and Hispanic students (Centers for Disease Control and Prevention, 2000e).

Do boys and girls have different concerns about smoking? Although both are equally aware of the disadvantages of smoking, they are differentially concerned with specific disadvantages. Both boys and girls perceive health consequences as the major disadvantage, but this is regarded as more important by boys (W. Taylor et al., 1999). Girls focus more on the moral (i.e., smoking is wrong) and the aesthetic consequences of smoking (e.g., yellow teeth, bad breath; W. Taylor et al., 1999; I. Waldron, 1991). Boys are more concerned with the effects of smoking on athletic performance (I. Waldron, 1991). Black children are more likely than White children to be concerned about the ethics of smoking. Black children also are more likely than White children to perceive parents as a deterrent to smoking.

Smoking Cessation. Although more men than women smoke, more men than women also have quit smoking. Men's higher rates of smoking cessation holds across all ages (Centers for Disease Control and Prevention, 1994) and pertains to Black as well as White persons (Lockery & Stanford, 1996). There also is evidence that when both men and women try to quit smoking, men's attempts are more often successful. In three randomized clinical trials to test the effectiveness of the nicotine patch, men were more successful than women in quitting smoking regardless of whether they received the real nicotine patch or the placebo patch (Wetter et al., 1999b). At the end of the treatment, 45% of men had quit compared to 29% of women.

At six-month follow-up, 25% of men had remained quitters compared to 12% of women. In a community smoking cessation trial, men and women were equally likely to try to quit, but men were more successful (Royce, Corbett, Sorensen, & Ockene, 1997). In an intervention program using nicotine gum, men were more likely than women to have quit at 12 months (29% vs. 25%) and at 36 months (22% vs. 18%; Bjornson et al., 1995). However, a couple of recent studies have found no sex differences in success rates in response to a smoking cessation intervention (Frederick, Hall, Humfleet, & Munoz, 1996; Whitlock, Vogt, Hollis, & Lichtenstein, 1997). Although the majority of the evidence suggests that men are more successful in quitting, adolescent men and women are equally confident that they can quit (Sussman et al., 1998).

There are several theories as to why it may be more difficult for women to quit smoking. One theory is that smoking is associated with negative affect and depression (Covey, 1999; Wetter et al., 1999b) and women are more likely than men to be depressed. Distress is clearly associated with smoking. People with a history of depression or anxiety disorders are more likely to smoke than are people without such histories (Covey, 1999). Even among adolescents, depression has been linked to the frequency of smoking (Simons-Morton et al., 1999). Depression also is associated among adults and adolescents with being less able to quit smoking (Zhu, Sun, Billings, Choi, & Malarcher, 1999). In one study, depressed people were 40% less likely to quit smoking than nondepressed people (Anda et al., 1990). Depression is not only associated with difficulty quitting, but when people with a history of depression quit, their depression increases (R. Glass, 1990). To recap, one reason women may be less able to quit smoking is that depression interferes with cessation and women are more likely than men to be depressed.

Another theory as to why women might have more difficulty quitting smoking is that women are more likely to be physiologically addicted to smoking. Female smokers are more likely than male smokers to report behaviors indicative of physiological addiction, including smoking a cigarette within 10 minutes of waking, smoking when sick, being upset about having to go a whole day without a cigarette, and reporting "not feeling right" if one goes too long without smoking (Royce et al., 1997; Sussman et al., 1998). The Fagerstrom Tolerance Questionnaire, shown in Table 9.5, is a widely used measure of physiological addiction to nicotine (Heatherton, Kozlowski, Frecker, & Fagerstrom, 1991). If you have friends who smoke, conduct Exercise 9.3 to see who is more strongly addicted to smoking.

Another way physiological addiction is measured is by self-reports of withdrawal symptoms when quitting smoking. Withdrawal symptoms include depressed mood, insomnia, irritability, anxiety, difficulty concentrating, restlessness, decreased heart rate, and increased appetite (American Psychiatric Association, 1994). It is not clear from these self-reports whether men or women experience more withdrawal symptoms. The methodology of a study influences whether sex differences in withdrawal symptoms appear. Prospective studies (conducted during cessation) show no sex differences, whereas retrospective studies (conducted after cessation) show that women recall more symptoms than men. Is it that women recall more symptoms than they actually experience, or that men recall fewer symptoms? The latter seems to be the case. C. Pomerleau, Tate, Lumley, and Pomerleau (1994) compared prospective and retrospective reports of withdrawal symptoms. They asked men

TABLE 9.5   Revised Fagerstrom Tolerance Questionnaire

1. How soon after you wake up do you smoke your first cigarette?
   a. After 60 minutes.
   b. 31–60 minutes.
   c. 6–30 minutes.
   d. Within 5 minutes.

2. Do you find it difficult to refrain from smoking in places where it is forbidden?
   No   Yes

3. Which cigarette would you hate to give up?
   a. The first one in the morning.
   b. Any other.

4. How many cigarettes per day do you smoke?
   a. 10 or fewer
   b. 11–20
   c. 21–30
   d. 31 or more

5. Do you smoke more frequently during the first hours after waking than during the rest of the day?
   No   Yes

6. Do you smoke if you are so ill that you are in bed most of the day?
   No   Yes

Source: T. F. Heatherton, L. T. Kozlowski, R. C. Frecker, and K. O. Fagerstrom (1991). The Fagstrom test for nicotine dependence: A revision of the Fagerstrom Tolerance questionnaire. *British Journal of Addiction, 86,* 1119–1127. Copyright 1991. Reprinted by permission of Taylor & Francis.

EXERCISE 9.3
Who Is More Physiologically Addicted to Smoking?

Administer the Fagerstrom Tolerance Questionnaire shown in Table 9.5 to 10 male and 10 female smokers. Is one sex more addicted than the other? Can you predict addiction from any other variables, such as age or depression?

and women to first recall their experience of four common withdrawal symptoms (anxiety, anger/irritation, difficulty in concentrating, hunger) from previous attempts to quit smoking and then to report prospectively their experience of these symptoms over the first few days that they quit smoking. Men recalled fewer symptoms in the past than they actually experienced during their present attempt; in other words, men's recall of symptoms underestimated the extent to which they actually experienced symptoms. For example, only 5% of men said that they experienced difficulty concentrating during past attempts to quit smoking, but 58% reported this symptom during the present attempt. Women's retrospective reports of difficulty concentrating were more similar to their prospective reports (40% vs. 56%). The main finding is that there were no sex differences in any of the prospective reports of symptoms. Thus, retrospective methodologies may suggest that women experience more withdrawal symptoms due to men's tendency to recall fewer symptoms than they actually experienced. According to self-reports of current withdrawal symptoms, men and women experience similar withdrawal symptoms, which means similar levels of physiological addiction.

Perkins (1996; Perkins, Donny, & Caggiula, 1999), however, has argued that women are *less* likely than men to be physiologically addicted to nicotine. They base their argument on research that shows nicotine replacement therapies are less effective for women (Perkins et al., 1999). In one study, nicotine replacement therapy influenced an objective measure of withdrawal symptoms among men but not women (Wetter et al., 1999a). The objective measure was a physiological recording of sleep quality. Men and women who had quit smoking were randomly assigned to receive a nicotine patch or a placebo patch and their sleep quality was measured physiologically. Men who received the nicotine patch had better sleep quality, as indicated by physiological recordings of sleep duration and sleep awakenings, than men who did not receive the patch. However, the patch did not influence women's sleep quality. Thus, the nicotine patch was effective in helping men to sleep but had no effect on women's sleep quality. Wetter et al. concluded that their findings supported Perkins's theory that men are more physiologically addicted to nicotine.

In general, research on people who quit smoking shows that men choose to use more nicotine replacement therapies (e.g., nicotine sprays) than women do (Perkins et al., 1999). These findings suggest that men find nicotine more rewarding and more relieving of withdrawal symptoms. Men are also better than women at discriminating different doses of nicotine (Perkins, 1999). If women are not as physiologically addicted to nicotine, what is the basis of women's addiction? Perkins and colleagues suggest that smoking is more of a sensory experience for women than for men: women enjoy the visual and olfactory experiences of smoking more than men do.

A third theory as to why women have greater difficulty quitting smoking is that women are more concerned with the potential for weight gain. Fear of weight gain is a deterrent to smoking cessation especially among women. In a study of men and women one to two years out of high school, women smokers were more likely to express concerns about weight gain if they quit smoking (Pirie et al., 1991). In fact, women were more likely than men to say that they experienced weight gain and a desire to eat when they tried to quit smoking. The previous study on prospective versus retrospective reports of withdrawal symptoms (C. Pomerleau et al., 1994) showed that women are overly concerned with weight issues; the one withdrawal symptom that women overestimated in that study was hunger. Over three-quarters (76%) of women said they had experienced hunger during past attempts but only 44% reported hunger during the present attempt. Men, again, underestimated their experience of hunger, retrospective (37%) versus prospective (53%). Thus, women overestimate the extent to which they will experience hunger if they quit smoking.

There is a basis for the concern that smoking leads to weight gain, but the weight gain is not as large as one might expect. According to the U.S. Surgeon General (U.S. Department of Health and Human Services, 1990), the average weight gain after smoking cessation is 5 pounds. Some more recent studies have reported more substantial weight gains (Hudmon, Gritz, Clayton, & Nisenbaum, 1999; Nides et al., 1994); and some show larger gains for women than men (Frederick et al., 1996).

There may be a methodological difficulty with some of these estimates of weight gain after smoking cessation. Some studies rely on people's self-reports of smoking before and after quitting, such as the one by Hudmon et al. (1999) that reported a large weight gain. It has been shown that people underestimate how much they weighed before they quit smoking. In one study, people underestimated their precessation weight by 3.5 pounds (Peterson, 1999); 66% of respondents underestimated their weight before quitting by 6.6 pounds. Thus, people may think that they gain more weight than they actually do after they quit smoking.

What causes men and women to quit smoking? I. Waldron (1997) suggests that they quit smoking for different reasons: men quit smoking for physical fitness reasons; women are likely to quit smoking when they become pregnant. However only

10% of these women remain abstinent after childbirth (I. Waldron, 1991).

In summary, various theories have been put forth to explain why women have more difficulty than men when they try to quit smoking. One theory is that women are more depressed and depression interferes with smoking cessation; there is some evidence to support this. Another theory is that women are more physiologically addicted to smoking, but the evidence in support of this theory is completely contradictory. On some self-report measures of physiological addiction, women appear more dependent than men on nicotine; on others, there are no sex differences; yet another group of investigators suggests that men are more physiologically addicted because nicotine patches are more effective in relieving men's withdrawal symptoms than those of women. A third theory is that women are more concerned than men with the weight gain that follows smoking cessation. The evidence suggests that women do have this concern but it is not clear whether the concern interferes with cessation efforts. The concern about weight gain is valid, as people do gain weight when they quit smoking but probably not as much as they expect.

Prediction of Smoking. Demographic characteristics as well as features of the social environment influence the onset of smoking. Higher education and income are associated with lower smoking among White and Black adults (Lockery & Stanford, 1996). Education influences rates of smoking and quitting (U.S. Department of Health and Human Services, 1998c): more educated people are less likely to start smoking and more likely to quit if they start. The relation of education to smoking may be stronger among men than women. There have been greater declines in smoking among men with more education than less education, but the association of education to smoking is smaller among women. Racial differences in smoking rates change when education is taken into consideration. Although Hispanic men are less likely than White men to smoke as adults, this difference becomes even larger when comparing Hispanic and White men at the same educational level.

Parents' attitudes toward smoking and parents' smoking behavior also influence children's smoking. Living with a parent who smokes is associated with the onset of smoking (Flay et al., 1998), the frequency of smoking (Simons-Morton et al., 1999), and lower rates of quitting smoking (Zhu et al., 1999). Parents' attitudes toward smoking is associated with smoking in both boys and girls (Flay et al., 1998), but the relation may be stronger for girls (K. Griffin et al., 1999; Siddiqui et al., 1999) and stronger for Black and Hispanic than White adolescents (Siddiqui et al., 1999). Compared to White persons, minority persons may place relatively greater importance on family than peers.

Attitudes and behaviors of peers also influence smoking. Adolescents are more likely to smoke if their friends smoke (Abdelrahman, Rodriguez, Ryan, French, & Weinbaum, 1998). Studies have shown that the number of friends who smoke predicts the onset of and frequency of smoking (Flay et al., 1998). In one study, friends' smoking and siblings' smoking had a stronger impact on smoking among girls than among boys (K. Griffin et al., 1999). Friends' attitudes toward smoking also are associated with smoking behavior in both boys and girls (Flay et al., 1998; Simons-Morton et al., 1999). Some studies suggest that friends' attitudes have a greater impact on girls than boys because girls are more easily influenced by the opinions of others (K. Griffin et al., 1999). In a study in Britain, smoking was linked to popularity among girls but not boys. Girls who were in the most popular cliques smoked (Michell & Amos, 1997). The popular boys were reluctant to smoke because it conflicted with their involvement in sports. Given that parents' attitudes toward smoking had a stronger effect on minority than White adolescents, it is not surprising to find that peers' attitudes toward smoking has a stronger effect on White than minority adolescents (Siddiqui et al., 1999).

Summary. Smoking is the health behavior that can be most strongly tied to the leading causes of death, and smoking contributes greatly to sex differences in mortality. Lung cancer is the best illustration of how changes in smoking behavior have influenced changes in mortality rates. Men smoke more than women, have higher rates of lung cancer than women, and die younger than women. There is a parallel with heart disease. However, more men also have quit smoking, and women's rates of smoking have not decreased to the extent that men's have, resulting in an increase in lung cancer among women and a reduction in the sex difference in longevity. Among adults, men still smoke more than women and men are still quitting more than women. Among children and adolescents, boys smoke more than girls, but the sex gap is narrowing, and in some age groups, there may be exceptions. Demographic factors, such as education, and environmental factors, such as parents' and peers' smoking behavior, influence the initiation of smoking. There is some evidence that these environmental factors have a stronger influence on girls than on boys.

ALCOHOL. The relation of moderate alcohol intake to health is mixed. On the one hand, alcohol in moderation is protective against heart disease and appears to provide immunity from the common cold (Rich-Edwards et al., 1995). However, alcohol in moderation also may be associated with breast cancer (American Cancer Society, 1999a).

Large quantities of alcohol are clearly harmful to health. Heavy use of alcohol is associated with increased risk of heart disease, cancer, cirrhosis of the liver, accidents, suicide, homicide, and male impotence (American Cancer Society, 1999b; Rich-Edwards et al., 1995; I. Waldron, 1995b). Alcohol is linked to motor vehicle accidents; in 1998, 38% of motor vehicle fatalities involved alcohol (Centers for Disease Control and Prevention, 1999a). Alcohol use also has been associated with accidents more generally, especially among men. In a national sample, moderate to heavy drinking was associated with injuries in men but not women (Cherpitel, 1993). Men who sustained more injuries during the prior year were more likely to be moderate or heavy drinkers. Alcohol abuse also has economic and social consequences. It has been linked to loss of jobs as well as loss of relationships (Lex, 1991) and is associated with antisocial behaviors, such as aggression (Hull & Bond, 1986).

Alcohol has different physiological consequences for men and women (Frezza et al., 1990; I. Waldron, 1997). It takes proportionally less alcohol to have the same effect on a woman as a man; even if a man and a woman of similar weight drink the same amount of alcohol, the woman will have a higher blood-alcohol level. The ratio of fat to water in a woman's body is greater than that in a man's body; in other words, men have more water available in their systems to dilute consumed alcohol. In addition, more of the alcohol is metabolized by enzymes in the stomach for men compared to women (Frezza et al., 1990). Thus, men and women who drink the same amount of alcohol in proportion to their body weight will not have the same blood-alcohol levels. This may be one reason alcohol is more

strongly associated with cirrhosis of the liver in women than in men (Frezza et al., 1990; Lex, 1991). Thus, women are more vulnerable than men to both acute and chronic (long-lasting) effects of alcohol.

Prevalence. In general, men drink more alcohol than women (C. Robbins & Martin, 1993; I. Waldron, 1995b). Among problem drinkers, men also drink more alcohol (Lex, 1991). In a national study of over 8,000 persons age 12 and over, men were more likely than women to report getting drunk and more likely to lose control when drinking, as evidenced by blackouts and becoming aggressive (C. Robbins & Martin, 1993). There is cross-cultural support for these findings. In a study of 10 countries (Australia, Canada, Czech Republic, Estonia, Finland, Israel, Russia, Sweden, Netherlands, United States), men drank alcohol more frequently, consumed higher amounts of alcohol at one time, had more heavy episodes of drinking, and were more likely to suffer adverse consequences of drinking (e.g., health problems, criticism by others, losing control; Wilsnack, Vogeltanz, Wilsnack, & Harris, 2000).

According to the findings from the 1998 National Household Survey of Drug Abuse, 59% of males and 45% of females age 12 and over used alcohol in the prior month (U.S. Department of Health and Human Services, 1999a). This survey also showed that 23% of males and 9% of females reported "binge" drinking at least once in the prior month, defined as consuming five or more drinks on the same occasion (U.S. Department of Health and Human Services, 1999b). Binge drinking is most common among 18- to 25-year-olds. Among this group, 42% of men and 21% of women reported binge drinking in 1998.

The sex difference in alcohol usage occurs at all ages but is smaller among adolescents than adults (C. Robbins & Martin,

1993; U.S. Department of Health and Human Services, 1999a). According to the Monitoring the Future Study of adolescents and young adults, 54% of eighth-graders, 72% of tenth-graders, and 82% of twelfth-graders had tried alcohol in 1997 (U.S. Department of Health and Human Services, 1998a). Sex differences were small among adolescents but became larger among college students and young adults.

Although men are more likely than women to develop a drinking problem, the time course between using alcohol and developing a drinking problem is different for men and women. Women are more likely to start drinking at a later age than men (Lex, 1991) but progress more rapidly from the onset of drinking to problem drinking (Orford & Keddie, 1985). Several explanations have been proposed. Orford and Keddie suggest that drinking may be more social for men than for women, so men are social drinkers for a longer time. It is not clear whether problem drinking is more easily recognized in women or men. On the one hand, alcoholism is more stigmatized among women, so perhaps women problem drinkers are more easily identified. On the other hand, the adverse consequences of problem drinking may be more visible among men; alcoholic men are more likely to lose their jobs or get into trouble with the law.

One reason women drink less heavily than men has to do with society's attitudes toward drinking (I. Waldron, 1997). Society disapproves of heavy drinking in women, which is thought to interfere with the female role of being responsible for children. Another reason women drink less than men is that women are more involved in religion, which deters drinking. However, sex differences in drinking have decreased since the middle part of the twentieth century (I. Waldron, 1997). Find out about your peers' attitudes toward men and women drinking in Exercise 9.4.

EXERCISE 9.4
Attitudes toward Men and Women Drinking

Create several scenarios of a person at a party drinking varying amounts of alcohol, ranging from none to moderate to a lot (i.e., so much that he or she gets sick or blacks out). Create two versions of these surveys by using a male name and a female name. Develop a set of items to measure people's attitudes toward the person in the scenario. Are men and women who do not use alcohol viewed similarly? Are men and women who drink alcohol viewed similarly? Does it depend on the level? Finally, do the answers to these questions depend on the sex of the respondent?

Prediction. Alcohol usage is associated with other problems, including poor grades among adolescents (Abdelrahman et al., 1998) and family conflict in adolescent females (Hops, Davis, & Lewin, 1999). These studies do not determine cause and effect, however. Does drinking alcohol lead to these other problems, or do other problems lead to alcohol usage?

Family members' use of alcohol is associated with children's use of alcohol and subsequent development of alcohol problems (Abdelrahman et al., 1998). Children of alcoholics are 4 to 5 times more likely to become alcoholics (Lex, 1991). Peer usage of alcohol also is associated with adolescents' use of alcohol (Abdelrahman et al., 1998).

Alcohol use is associated with drug usage and depression in both adolescents and adults. Some studies find the association of alcohol to depression to be stronger among men than women (Berger & Adesso, 1991). In a prospective study of problem drinking, Horwitz and White (1991) found that depression at age 21 predicted alcohol problems in men at age 24; depression did not predict problem drinking in women. By contrast, in another study, problem drinking was equally associated with depression among adult men and women, but was more strongly associated with depression among adolescent women than adolescent men (C. Robbins & Martin, 1993). Thus, it is not clear if the link between alcohol and depression is stronger in males or females.

Drinking alcohol is associated with characteristics of the male gender role. The traditional male not only drinks alcohol but prides himself on being able to drink large quantities without losing control. McCreary, Newcomb, and Sadava (1999) distinguished among several male gender-role characteristics to see which were associated with drinking alcohol among a group of recently graduated college students. Masculine gender-role stress, which reflects distress when facing situations inconsistent with the male gender role, was associated with more alcohol-related problems. Agency, however, as measured by the PAQ, was associated with fewer alcohol-related problems. Having traditional attitudes about men was associated with reports of greater alcohol consumption. Studies of adolescents also have linked traditional attitudes toward gender roles to the use of alcohol and alcohol problems (Huselid & Cooper, 1992; Pleck, Sonenstein, & Ku, 1993a). However, the relation of traditional gender-role attitudes to alcohol usage differs for men and women: more traditional attitudes are associated with greater usage for males but less usage for females (Huselid & Cooper, 1992). These findings support the idea that alcohol use is consistent with traditional masculinity but inconsistent with traditional femininity.

Thus, it appears that there are characteristics of the male gender role that are advantageous and disadvantageous with respect to drinking alcohol. Masculine traits that reflect a healthy sense of self (i.e., agency) are associated with fewer alcohol problems. However, having traditional attitudes toward gender roles is associated with greater alcohol problems in males.

DRUGS. The health consequences of substance abuse can be severe; the most severe consequence is death. However, substance abuse also can lead to other problems, such as complications with pregnancy, health problems in children born to addicted mothers and fathers, and sexual difficulties (M. Griffin, Weiss, & Mirin, 1989). Use of IV drugs has been linked to AIDS (I. Waldron, 1995b).

Prevalence. Men use more drugs than women do. According to findings from the 1998 National Household Survey on Drug Abuse, the rate of drug use has declined for both men and women since the late 1970s and stabilized in the 1990s (U.S. Department of Health and Human Services, 1999b). These findings are based on persons age 12 and over using illicit drugs within the prior month. As shown in Figure 9.6, the sex difference in drug use also has narrowed. Table 9.6 shows the rates of drug use for males and females in different age groups in 1998 (U.S. Department of Health and Human Services, 1999a). Males have nearly twice the rate of drug use as females except between the ages of 12 and 17, when rates are similar. Rates are similar for Whites and Hispanics, but African Americans have slightly higher drug usage, largely due to greater usage among males (U.S. Department of Health and Human Services, 1999a).

A study that provides substantial information about drug usage among younger adolescents, older adolescents, college students, and young adults (age 19 to 32) is the

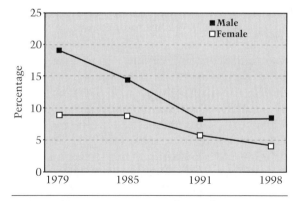

FIGURE 9.6 Percentages of people age 12+ reporting use of any illegal drug during the prior month. The rate of illicit drug use has declined and the sex gap has narrowed. *Source:* Adapted from U.S. Department of Health and Human Services (1999b).

Monitoring the Future Study (U.S. Department of Health and Human Services, 1998a, 1998b). This study has tracked drug use among thousands of high school seniors since 1975 and among thousands of eighth- and tenth-grade students since 1991. Between

TABLE 9.6   Percentage of People Using Illicit Drugs in Prior Month, 1998

Age/Gender	Percentage
12–17	
Male	10.3
Female	9.5
18–25	
Male	20.5
Female	11.7
26–34	
Male	9.8
Female	4.3
≥ 35	
Male	4.4
Female	2.4

Source: Adapted from U.S. Department of Health and Human Services (1999a).

the late 1970s and 1990, drug usage declined dramatically among twelfth-graders, college students, and young adults. During the 1990s, however, drug usage rose among adolescents. For example, marijuana use during the prior year increased from 6% in 1991 to 18% in 1997 among eighth-graders, increased from 15% in 1992 to 35% in 1997 among tenth-graders, and increased from 22% in 1992 to 39% among twelfth-graders. Similar trends were observed for other illicit drugs. There are few sex differences in drug usage among eighth- and tenth-graders. The increase in drug use during the 1990s among adolescents occurred for both males and females. Adolescents today are less disapproving of drugs than they were a decade ago. In 1997, 29% of eighth-graders, 47% of tenth-graders, and 54% of twelfth-graders had used an illicit drug at least once. Consistent with the previous report, the Monitoring the Future Study did not find increases in drug usage among young adults (19- to 28-year-olds). Drug usage among this group has remained stable throughout the 1990s.

Although there are no sex differences in drug use among eighth- and tenth-graders, males use more illicit drugs than females among high school seniors, college students, and young adults. Among young adults, 30% of males and 25% of females used an illicit drug in the prior year. Among college students, 38% of males and 31% of females did so. What do we make of the sex difference among older students and adults but the similar rates of drug use among younger students? At this point, it is difficult to tell whether the age differences are cohort effects or age effects. With increasing age, will drug use increase more among males than females to produce the sex difference? Or, are the younger students living in a different era in which the behavior of males and females is more similar? If so, drug use will increase with age for both males and females, which will result in a larger proportion of female adults using drugs than ever before.

Males use more of almost all kinds of drugs compared to females. The only drug that females tend to use more than males is sedatives; this finding holds for all age groups. Averaging across studies, sex differences in the use of specific drugs are shown in Table 9.7. Men are more likely than women to use illegal drugs, but women are more likely to use prescription tranquilizers and sedatives.

Racial differences in drug use depend on age. The Monitoring the Future study found that African American adolescents have lower rates of drug usage compared to Whites (U.S. Department of Health and Human Services, 1998a, 1998b). Hispanic students have the highest rates of drug use. These data contrast with the previously mentioned finding among adults, in which African Americans demonstrated higher rates of drug usage compared to Whites. Somewhere between adolescence and adulthood, drug usage among African Americans increases much more than it does among Whites.

TABLE 9.7   Sex Differences in Substance Abuse

Substance	Abuse Ratio
Alcohol	Males higher (5:1)
Amphetamine	Males higher (3–4:1)
Caffeine	Males higher
Cannabis	Males higher
Cocaine	Similar
Hallucinogens	Males higher (3:1)
Inhalants	Males higher
Nicotine	Males higher
Opioids	Males higher (3–4:1)
Sedatives	Females higher

Source: Adapted from the American Psychiatric Association (1994).

Despite males greater use of drugs compared to females, estimates of those who are dependent on drugs are similar for men and women. Among illicit drug users, 17% of men and 19% of women are dependent on the drugs they use (U.S. Department of Health and Human Services, 1999b). These estimates are based on clinical interviews with respondents. In 1991, the rates of men and women visiting the emergency room for a drug-related episode were equal, but by 1998 more men than women visited the emergency room (Drug Abuse Warning Network Series, 1999). Between 1991 and 1998, the rates of emergency room visits had increased for women by 19% and for men by 38%.

Men are more likely than women to die from drug abuse: 75% of all deaths from drugs in 1997 occurred among males (Drug Abuse Warning Network Series, 1999). Among drug-related deaths, cocaine is the most frequently cited substance, involved in nearly half (45%) of drug-related deaths in 1997 (Drug Abuse Warning Network Series, 1999). Proportionally more of men's drug-related deaths are accidental or unexpected compared to women's (59% vs. 48%). Proportionally more of women's drug-related deaths are due to suicide (25% vs. 16%).

Prediction. Substance abuse is related to environmental factors. In a study of seventh- and eighth-graders, substance abuse was predicted by several variables related to the family: family history of substance abuse, family conflict, parental divorce, and no rules in the home about substance abuse (Abdelrahman et al., 1998). In another study, family conflict among children ages 7 to 9 predicted drug usage seven years later (Hops et al., 1999); this relation was significant for females but not males. In a study of seventh- through twelfth-graders, easy access to marijuana at home predicted usage (Resnick et al., 1997). Although the family clearly has a role in substance abuse, one study found that peer usage was more strongly related to substance abuse than demographic, family, or school variables (Abdelrahman et al., 1998). Like cigarettes and alcohol, poor grades also predict substance abuse (Abdelrahman et al., 1998; Resnick et al., 1997). One study showed that academic difficulties and social difficulties among 7- to 9-year-olds predicted more deviant forms of drug use seven years later (Hops et al., 1999). Social difficulties, such as getting along with peers, were more predictive than academic difficulties. In addition, the nature of these social difficulties differed for males and females. For boys, the problem was aggression; for girls, the problem was withdrawal from social interaction.

OVERWEIGHT AND OBESITY.   Obesity itself is a risk factor for heart disease and some cancers. Obesity also predisposes one to a number of other risk factors for heart disease, such as hypertension (high blood pressure), high cholesterol, and adult-onset diabetes (non-insulin-dependent). Obesity takes different forms in men and women (Wing & Klem, 1997). Men are more likely to have **android obesity:** the apple shape, which consists of extra weight collected around the abdomen. Women are more likely to have **gynoid obesity:** pear shape, which consists of extra weight around the hips. Android obesity poses greater risks to health than does gynoid obesity, meaning that obesity poses a greater risk for men than for women. Android obesity is measured by the ratio of waist to hip size. A ratio of more than 1.0 is a significant risk factor for men and a ratio of more than .8 is a significant risk for women (Wing & Klem, 1997).

Obesity has been linked to mortality among both men and women, but the association is stronger among men (Calle,

Thun, Petrelli, Rodriguez, & Heath, 1999). The association also is stronger among Whites than Blacks; the link of obesity to mortality is weakest among Black women (Calle et al., 1999).

Aside from physical health problems, there are social, psychological, and economic consequences of obesity. These consequences are more severe for women than for men (Wing & Klem, 1997). In a longitudinal study of 370 people, overweight women were less likely to marry, completed fewer years of school, had lower incomes, and were more likely to live in poverty seven years later than women who were not overweight (Gortmaker, Must, Perrin, Sobol, & Dietz, 1993). Similar consequences were detected among men, but the effects were not as strong. The investigators of this study compared the effects of being overweight to the effects of having other chronic health conditions, such as asthma, diabetes, and arthritis. They found that these other conditions had none of the social or economic consequences that obesity had.

Definition. What does it mean to be overweight or obese? Researchers often define obesity as the extreme end of overweight. There are different ways to measure whether a person is overweight or obese. Obesity is typically measured by a combination of weight and height, which can be judged by using the standard weight and height tables that are used by insurance companies. More recent studies assess obesity with the **body**

TABLE 9.8   Body Mass Index (BMI)

$$\text{BMI calculation:} \frac{\text{Weight (kilograms}}{\text{Height}^2 \text{ (meters)}}$$

BMI = 19–24   → Ideal
BMI = 25–29   → Moderately overweight
BMI = over 31   → Severely obese

mass index (BMI), a ratio of height to weight. Table 9.8 shows how to calculate and interpret your BMI. An even better measure of obesity requires a measure of body fat such as a skin-fold test. Because weight and body fat are correlated, researchers often use the BMI to reflect obesity.

Prevalence. The prevalence of obesity changes depending on the definition. Most recent reports indicate that 33% (Wing & Klem, 1997) to 50% (National Center for Health Statistics, 1999) of Americans are overweight. Women are more likely than men to be overweight, and Blacks are more likely than Whites to be overweight. The race difference is larger among women than men. In one study, 49% of Black women compared to 33% of White women were overweight (Kuczmarski, Flegal, Campbell, & Johnson, 1994).

Did the health craze of the 1980s and 1990s lead to lower rates of obesity in the United States? Four national studies of obesity have been conducted between 1960 and 1991 (Kuczmarski et al., 1994).

These studies included surveys, in-person interviews, and physical exams of people representative of the United States. In these studies, being overweight was defined as a body mass index over 27.8 for men and 27.3 for women. The four surveys indicated that the incidence of obesity is *increasing* in the United States. As shown in Figure 9.7, the percentage of overweight Americans remained the same between 1960 and 1980, around 25%. However, in the 1988 to 1991 survey, one-third of Americans were overweight (31% of men and 35% of women). Obesity appears to have increased 8% between 1980 and 1990. The incidence was especially high for Mexican American women (47%) and Black women (49%). Rates of obesity were similar among non-Hispanic White men and women.

More recent estimates of obesity suggest that increases have continued to occur in the 1990s. One study compared rates of obesity in 1991 to rates in 1998 (Mokdad et al., 1999). A more stringent definition of obesity was used in this study compared to

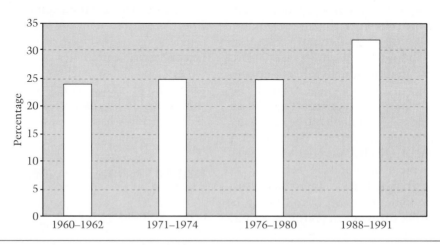

FIGURE 9.7   Percentage of overweight Americans from four national surveys. The most recent national survey of obesity showed that the obesity rate, which had remained steady, has increased since 1988. *Source:* Adapted from Kuczmarski et al. (1994).

the one used in the four national surveys. Obesity was defined as a BMI over 30. In 1991, using this definition, obesity rates for both men and women were 12%; in 1998, rates for both men and women were 18%, which is a 50% increase.

In a recent national survey undertaken in the United States in 1997 (National Center for Health Statistics, 1999), overweight was distinguished from obesity. Overweight was defined as a BMI of more than 25 and obesity was defined as a BMI of more than 30. This survey relied on self-reports of height and weight. The study showed that 62% of men and 47% of women were overweight, and that 19% of men and 19% of women were obese. The incidence of overweight and obesity increased with age, peaking in 45- to 64-year-olds and declining after that. There were racial differences in overweight and obesity, especially among women. Whereas 65% of Black women and 57% of Hispanic women were overweight, 43% of White women and only 25% of Asian women were overweight. Among men, fewer Asians were overweight (35%) compared to the other three groups (ranges from 62% to 65%).

Why are women more likely than men to suffer from obesity? First, women engage in a lower level of physical activity than men (Wing & Klem, 1997). Second, there are life events specific to women that are associated with obesity: women are most likely to gain weight when they get married, when they have a child, and during menopause (Wing & Klem, 1997).

Obesity is more common among people of lower SES (Flynn & Fitzgibbon, 1998). People of lower SES have poorer diets and are less likely to exercise (Flynn & Fitzgibbon, 1998); they may also have a less negative view of being overweight because historically, weight symbolized wealth. Low income may explain part of the racial differences in obesity.

There are also cultural factors associated with racial differences in obesity. Among Black and White women with similar incomes, Black women are still more likely than White women to be obese. Black and White women have been found to have different standards for beauty (Flynn & Fitzgibbon, 1998). When Black and White women view the same image of a person's body, Black women view the image as slimmer than do White women; Black women are less influenced than White women by society's association of attractiveness with thinness. Black women view these images as applying to White women. Black women are more satisfied with their bodies than are White women, even when they are overweight (Flynn & Fitzgibbon, 1998). Across a range of studies, between 0 and 60% of overweight Black women say they have a normal weight; the comparable figure for White women is between 0 and 8%.

On the positive side, Black women are less likely than white women to be diagnosed with eating disorders. Interestingly, Black women with higher SES are more likely to have eating disorders and less likely to be satisfied with their body (Flynn & Fitzgibbon, 1998). That is, they are more likely to take on the characteristics of White women. On the negative side, Black women are more likely than White women to be obese, which poses a serious risk factor to physical health. In addition, obese Black women are less likely than obese White women to view their weight as a problem.

Etiology. There are genetic predispositions to obesity, but behavioral factors also are involved, such as diet and exercise. In a national survey of adults age 18 and over, 66% of overweight adults who were trying to lose weight said they were using physical activity to do so (Centers for Disease Control and Prevention, 2000c). However, only

20% of those actually met the national guidelines for physical activity (30 minutes five times a week). There are no data to show that psychological characteristics lead to obesity (Wing & Klem, 1997).

Summary. The rates of obesity have increased in recent years. Although obesity increases with age, the period in life in which people are most likely to gain weight is young adulthood. There is a sex difference in obesity, with women having higher rates than men. However, men and women demonstrate different kinds of obesity, and the kind of obesity that is more likely to characterize men, android obesity, poses greater risks to health. Sex differences in obesity are influenced by and confounded with race. Women have higher rates of obesity than men among African Americans and Hispanics but not necessarily among Caucasians. The highest rates of obesity are found among African American and Hispanic women. There are socioeconomic and cultural explanations for ethnic differences in obesity. These ethnic groups have a lower income and low income is associated with obesity. Culturally, however, being thin is not as valued among the African American as the Caucasian community. These cultural differences have advantages and disadvantages; on the positive side, the rate of eating disorders among African American women is lower, but on the negative side, obesity has negative physical health consequences for African American women.

EXERCISE. Physical activity has been related to lower mortality rates (U.S. Department of Health and Human Services, 1996). Specifically, physical activity is associated with reduced heart disease, hypertension, some cancers (e.g., colon cancer), and adult-onset diabetes. Exercise may be associated with a reduced incidence of osteoporosis in women.

Among adolescents, young adults, and older adults, men are more likely than women to engage in leisure-time physical activity (U.S. Department of Health and Human Services, 1996). White people also are more likely to engage in physical activity than Black or Hispanic people. Among adults, rates of leisure exercise increased in the 1970s and 1980s (I. Waldron, 1997). In the 1990s, rates of leisure physical activity appear to have decreased. In 1990, 26% of adult women and 23% of adult men reported that they had *no* leisure physical activities (Centers for Disease Control and Prevention, 2000a). In 1994, slightly more men (27%) and women (31%) reported no leisure physical activities (Centers for Disease Control and Prevention, 1997).

Rates of physical activity among children have decreased dramatically. In 1984, 62% of children engaged in vigorous activity, whereas in 1990, only 37% of children did so (Centers for Disease Control and Prevention, 1992). Vigorous activity was defined as exercising for a minimum of 20 minutes three times a week, such that breathing was heavy and heart rate increased. Rates of vigorous activity differed by race: 39% White, 35% Hispanic, and 29% Black.

What are some of the reasons for the reduced rates of physical activity among children? One answer is that technological advances have made sedentary activities more appealing; these include television, video games, and the computer. In a nationally representative sample of children ages 8 through 16, watching television was inversely associated with exercise and positively associated with obesity (R. Andersen, Crespo, Bartlett, Cheskin, & Pratt, 1998). Children who watched more than four hours of television a day were at particular risk for obesity and lack of exercise. The relation of television to lack of exercise was especially strong among non-Hispanic Black persons and Mexican Americans. The authors suggest that one reason rates of exercise are low in these ethnic groups is that children do not go outside to play because parents are concerned about the safety of their neighborhood. Other studies have found links of television and computer usage to obesity. In Japan, obesity in children has been linked to playing TV games (Shimai, Yamada, Masuda, & Tada, 1993). In one study, increases in BMI over a one-year period among 9- to 14-year-olds were associated with television watching and video and computer game usage (Berkey et al., 2000).

Throughout childhood, boys are more physically active than girls. In the 1990 national survey of high school children, 50% of boys and 25% of girls said they engaged in vigorous activity (Centers for Disease Control and Prevention, 1992). One reason boys get more exercise is that boys are more likely to participate in sports, espe-

cially team sports (U.S. Census Bureau, 1998). In a recent study of adolescents ages 13 through 16, 66% of boys and 50% of girls participated in sports (K. Miller, Sabo, Farrell, Barnes, & Melnick, 1998). As shown in Figure 9.8, the sex difference in participation in sports is smaller for White than Black or Hispanic children. There are some similarities and differences in the barrier to physical activity for girls compared to boys. In a study of ninth- and eleventh-graders, girls and boys identified similar barriers to physical activity, but girls rated several barriers as more important than boys did (Allison, Dwyer, & Makin, 1999). The top four barriers to physical activity were (1) lack of time due to schoolwork, (2) lack of time due to other interests, (3) lack of time due to family activities, and (4) mood. Thus, it appears that girls are less likely than boys to engage in physical activity because they regard other

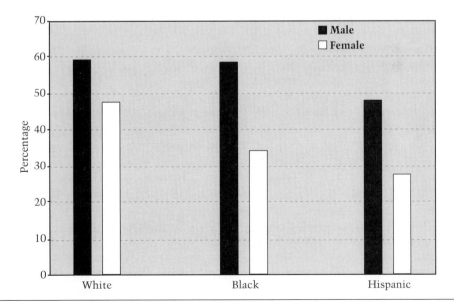

FIGURE 9.8 Participation in team sports among high school students. Across three ethnic groups (White, Black, Hispanic), more boys than girls are likely to participate in team sports. The sex difference is smaller among Whites compared to Blacks and Hispanics. *Source:* Adapted from U.S. Census Bureau (1998).

activities as more important, namely, schoolwork, other interests, and time with family.

In recent years, girls have become more involved in athletics (U.S. Census Bureau, 1998). Whereas high school boys' rates of participation in sports remained unchanged between 1971 and 1997, girls' rates increased dramatically. In 1997, roughly 3.7 million high school boys were involved in sports; in 1971, only slightly fewer boys participated (3.66 million). The rate of participation for girls increased eight-fold over this same time period. In 1971, fewer than 300,000 high school girls participated in sports; in 1997, almost 2.5 million girls participated. During the 1996 to 1997 school year, the leading sports for boys were football, basketball, track and field, and baseball; the leading sports for girls were basketball, track and field, volleyball, and softball.

Physical activity in childhood is important because these patterns persist into adulthood. Physical activity may be especially important to adolescent girls for two reasons. First, physical activity has been linked to an improved body image, which may reduce the risk of eating disorders (Richards, Boxer, Petersen, & Albrecht, 1990). Second, physical activity is a deterrent to sexual behavior among girls. In a study of nearly 700 13- through 16-year-olds, girls who participated in athletics were less sexually active (K. Miller et al., 1998). Among boys, there was a trend for athletic participation to be related to greater sexual activity. The investigators suggested that gender roles might explain the different associations of athletic activity to sexual behavior among boys and girls. For males, athletic behavior is part of the male gender role, as is sexual activity; for females, athletic behavior signifies independence and is inconsistent with the passive nature of the female gender role. In addition, women gain status by participation in athletics. Thus, girls who participate in athletics may be better able to resist sexual pressures.

The kinds of exercise in which men and women engage also differ (I. Waldron, 1997). Men are more likely to be involved in team sports, whereas women are more likely to be involved in noncompetitive exercise. The motives for exercise may differ also (I. Waldron, 1997); men are motivated by competition, whereas women are motivated by concerns about appearance and weight control.

Men's and Women's Social Roles

If gender roles contribute to sex differences in health, fewer sex differences should exist when roles are more similar. Leviatan and Cohen (1985) tested this hypothesis by studying men and women in a setting where their roles were more equal: a kibbutz. A kibbutz is a community in Israel characterized by a collective lifestyle whereby everyone contributes to the welfare of the community. On a kibbutz, there is equal access to health care, all men and women work inside and outside of the home, and all participate in community decisions. However, roles are not perfectly equal even on a kibbutz. It is still true that women tend to take care of household chores more than men, and that the kinds of jobs men and women hold are different and sex-stereotypical. Women are more likely to be employed in education and service industries, whereas men are more likely to be employed in agriculture and industry. Nonetheless, Leviatan and Cohen found that sex differences in life expectancies on the kibbutz were smaller than those in the general population, largely due to an increase in men's life expectancy. Leviatan and Cohen suggest that men may have had more social support on the kibbutz and may have been faced with fewer sources of male gender-role strain.

The same hypothesis was tested in a second study of people on a kibbutz (Anson, Levenson, & Bonneh, 1990). A wide array of health outcomes were examined, and sex differences appeared on only two of them—in the direction opposite that previously observed. Women rated their subjective health as higher than men, and women were less disabled than men. There were no sex differences in psychological distress, physical symptoms, health behaviors, chronic illnesses, restricted activity days, doctor visits, or use of medication. These two studies suggest that when men's and women's social roles are more similar, sex differences in health diminish.

Studies also have measured people's gender roles and examined their relation to health. Masculinity, or agency, has been associated with greater perceived health, fewer physical symptoms, reduced psychological distress, reduced psychiatric problems, and better physical health (Helgeson, 1994c). By contrast, femininity, or communion, is typically unrelated to psychological or physical health (Helgeson, 1994c). Thus, some of men's lower morbidity rates compared to women may be explained by the male gender-related trait of agency, but women's higher morbidity rates cannot be linked to the female gender-related trait of communion.

It is important to keep in mind the different facets of gender roles. In my dissertation research, I distinguished the positive from the negative aspects of masculinity by measuring agency and unmitigated agency among a group of people who had sustained their first heart attack. Unmitigated agency was associated with more severe heart attacks, whereas agency was associated with less severe heart attacks (Helgeson, 1990). Aspects of the female gender role also are

multifaceted; feminine traits, or communion, are typically unrelated to health, but unmitigated communion is associated with poor health, especially psychological distress (Helgeson, 1994c; Helgeson & Fritz, 1996, 1998). The implications of these traits for specific health problems are addressed in later chapters.

What are some specific features of men's and women's social roles that might be linked to health? Men's social roles include risky behavior, such as working at hazardous jobs and driving. Risk-taking behavior, in general, is part of the male gender role. The female social role includes attending to one's own health concerns. However, the female gender role also is associated with taking care of others, which could have negative implications for health. Below, I review some aspects of the male and female social roles that have implications for health.

JOB CHARACTERISTICS. One social role that men and women occupy is their work role. Men work at more hazardous jobs compared to women (Verbrugge, 1989). According to the Bureau of Labor Statistics, only 8% of job-related fatalities reported between 1992 and 1996 were women, despite the fact that only slightly less than 50% of the workforce was female (U.S. Department of Labor, 1998). The sex difference in fatalities likely reflects men working in riskier jobs than women, such as the construction industry. Because men are more likely than women to be employed in manual labor positions, men are more likely to sustain physical injuries in the form of accidents at work (I. Waldron, 1997). Job hazards also have been linked to lung cancer and accidents, which men suffer more than women (I. Waldron, 1995b). Men are more likely to be exposed to dangerous toxins, such as asbestos, which has been linked to cancer. Black males are especially likely to be exposed to hazardous substances at work (Staples, 1995).

Men's labor at home also includes more risks than women's labor at home. For example, men are more likely to be the ones who repair electrical problems and climb on the roof to fix a leak.

DRIVING. In 1998, there were 1.6 fatalities for every 100 million miles driven in the United States (U.S. Department of Transportation, 1999). The total number of persons killed in motor vehicle accidents was 41,471 in 1998, which is a decline since the peak of 54,589 in 1972. The decline in motor vehicle accidents and motor vehicle fatalities has been linked to improved safety measures, including the use of seat belts and lower rates of drinking and driving (I. Waldron, 2000). The peak age for male and female victims is between 16 and 24, although the rate peaks again after age 74.

Driving is part of men's social role. Men drive more than women, and when men and women are together, the man typically drives the car. Thus, men are much more likely than women to be the drivers of fatal driving accidents. Men also constitute 67% of fatalities from driving accidents. A number of factors contribute to this. Men drive more miles than women. However, per mile, men are still more likely than women to have fatal accidents. Why? Men drive faster and take more risks while driving. Although there were no sex differences in use of seat belts in 1980, by 1990, women were more likely than men to buckle up (I. Waldron, 1997).

One link to motor vehicle fatalities is alcohol. The percentage of fatalities that involved alcohol declined from 1982 (57%) to 1998 (38%; U.S. Department of Transportation, 1999). On holidays, however, the percentage of fatalities involving alcohol is still around 50%. Men are twice as likely as women to drive after using drugs or alcohol

(U.S. Department of Transportation, 1998); this sex difference holds across White, Black, and Hispanic people.

The sex difference in mortality from motor vehicle accidents has declined over time. In 1950, men were 3.4 times as likely as women to die in a motor vehicle accident; in 1990, the figure was 2.5. In 1950, men were 5.8 times as likely as women to die as the driver of a motor vehicle; in 1990, the figure was 3.4. The primary reason for the decrease in the size of the sex difference is a modification of the female gender role: women increased their rates of driving.

RISKY BEHAVIOR. Many differences in health can be explained by a single aspect of the male gender role: risk-taking behavior (I. Waldron, 1997). Men's activities are inherently riskier than women's, and men take more risks than women during these activities. Men engage in more risky behavior at work, at home, and during leisure activities (Veevers & Gee, 1986). We have seen that men's jobs are more hazardous than those of women. We also have seen that men are more likely to find themselves in the driver's seat of a car and to take more risks when driving. Men also are more likely to engage in risky leisure activities such as downhill skiing, skydiving, and mountain climbing (Veevers & Gee, 1986). Men also are more likely to own guns (I. Waldron, 1995b). Conduct Exercise 9.5 to see if there are sex differences in risky leisure activities among college students and if risky activities can be linked to gender roles.

There have been a number of studies on risk-taking behaviors. In a study of high school and college students, men reported being more likely than women to engage in risky behavior, such as jumping off a moving vehicle (Langhinrichsen-Rohling et al., 1998). A meta-analysis of 150 risk-taking behavior studies revealed that men were

EXERCISE 9.5
Risky Leisure Activities

Develop a list of leisure activities that vary in their level of risk. Ask a group of men and women if they have ever engaged in the activity and, if so, how often. You might also ask respondents how willing they would be to engage in each activity. Also, administer a measure of gender roles; agency, communion, unmitigated agency, and traditional gender-role attitudes are good candidates.

Is there a sex difference in willingness to engage in risky activities? Is there a sex difference in having engaged in risky activities? Compare responses to risky behaviors and nonrisky behaviors to make sure that any differences you find are not a reflection of one sex being more willing to engage in any behavior than the other sex. Are differences in risky behavior linked to gender roles?

higher risk-takers than women $(d = +.13)$. This effect held across a range of behaviors that included sex, drinking, using drugs, risky driving, risky physical activities, and gambling. The authors also found that the size of the sex difference decreased over time. Comparison of studies conducted between 1964 and 1980, and between 1981 and 1997 showed a marked decrease in effect size $(d = +.20$ vs. $d = +.13)$. Men score higher than women on sensation seeking (D. Zuckerman, 1994), which is the tendency to seek novel and stimulating experiences. Sensation seeking is associated with a number of risky health behaviors among adolescents, such as drinking alcohol, smoking, and having a greater number of sexual partners (Kraft & Rise, 1994).

Participation in violent sports is a risky behavior that is consistent with the traditional male gender role. Masculinity is not only connected to sports but also to playing sports while in pain or while injured (P. White, Young, & McTeer, 1995). Playing through pain and injury in sports is not only tolerated but encouraged among men. Playing while injured is a sign of emotional toughness and physical strength; in fact, taking care of oneself after an injury is viewed as weak behavior that undermines masculinity. The athlete who continues to play while injured is afforded high status.

Another way to evaluate risk-taking behavior is to study accidents and injuries. Boys sustain more injuries than girls, and boys' injuries are more severe than those of girls (Rosen & Peterson, 1990). The kinds of behaviors that are risk factors for injuries include a high activity level, a desire to engage in daring behavior, impulsiveness, and antisocial behavior—all of which characterize boys more than girls (Rosen & Peterson, 1990). Rosen and Peterson suggest that one reason boys may be more likely to be injured is that boys receive less supervision than girls. If true, this would be an indication that risk-taking is encouraged in boys more than girls.

Because of men's risk-taking behavior, men have higher rates of all kinds of accidents compared to women, including driving, work, and recreational (I. Waldron, 1997). Men are more likely to drown from swimming and boating; men's greater use of guns contributes to a greater number of fatal gun accidents. Until recently, only men participated in the armed services, risking death from combat.

CONCERNS WITH HEALTH. So far, we have discussed a number of characteristics of the male gender role that might account for men's higher mortality rates: hazardous jobs, driving, and risky behavior in general. What aspects of the female gender role relate to women's lower mortality rates and higher morbidity rates? One aspect of the female gender role that may be related to both is women's concern with health (Verbrugge, 1989; I. Waldron, 1997), which could lead to more physician visits and a greater awareness of symptoms, resulting in the appearance of a higher morbidity rate for women. Theoretically, women's greater concern with health could lead to better health care, which then would reduce mortality.

Studies have shown that women are more interested than men in health matters (C. Green & Pope, 1999; Hibbard & Pope, 1983). For example, women report that they think about health and read about health in newspapers and magazines more often than men do. In some newspapers, health-related articles appear in the Women's Section. Women are designated as the persons responsible for the family's health care. However, it is not the case that women's concerns with health lead them to engage in all health-promoting behaviors; for example, women exercise less than men and have been more reluctant than men to quit smoking.

NURTURANT ROLES.   There is also an aspect of the female gender role that poses a risk to women's health and may account for some of women's higher morbidity rates compared to men: women's nurturant role. Women are socialized to take care of others, and taking care of others has its costs. Although there are obvious health benefits to involvement in social networks, reviewed in detail in Chapter 10, there is a down side to such involvement for women. For one, social networks increase exposure to infectious disease; thus, women may sustain more minor illnesses than men, such as colds and flu, because they spend more time around people, in particular children, compared to men.

A specific hypothesis about how women's involvement in relationships could be hazardous to their health is the **nurturant role hypothesis:** that women have greater morbidity than men because of their nurturant roles (Gove, 1984; Gove & Hughes, 1979). According to the nurturant role hypothesis, women's roles require them to attend to the needs of others, and taking care of others interferes with taking care of oneself. First, the nurturant role leads to caretaking behavior, which results in fatigue and vulnerability to illness. Second, the nurturant role leads to greater exposure to communicable diseases. Finally, once sick, the nurturant role prevents one from taking care of oneself.

In one survey, Gove and Hughes (1979) found that women suffered greater health problems than men due to their nurturant roles. Specifically, women were more likely than men to say that they did not get enough sleep and did not eat properly when taking care of others. Women also reported that they were more likely to catch others' illnesses and did not take care of themselves when they were ill (i.e., continued with chores, did not get proper rest). Married women suffered more of these problems than married men, and the differences were even greater when the people had children. This is because married women, especially mothers, have greater nurturant role obligations. Among married couples without children, 14% of men and 21% of women said they were unable to rest when they were sick; among married couples with children, 16% of men and 44% of women said they were unable to rest when they were sick. Among unmarried individuals who lived alone, there were no sex differences in these nurturant role problems. Nurturant role problems, in particular the inability to rest when ill, were associated with poor physical health and accounted for most of the sex differences in physical health.

The nurturant role hypothesis has not gone without criticism. For example,

Marcus and Seeman (1981) point out that married women are healthier than single women, which would seem to contradict the nurturant role hypothesis because married women have more nurturant roles. Women with seemingly more role obligations, such as women who work and women who have children, report less illness and less disability. In one study, women with more role responsibilities were less likely to restrict activities, give up responsibilities, or seek heath care when ill, whereas the number of role responsibilities was unrelated to the way men responded to illness (Hibbard & Pope, 1983).

How can these contradictory ideas be reconciled? Are nurturant roles related to less illness or more illness among women? One possibility is that nurturant roles actually do lead to more illness but also lead to less *reporting* of illness. People who have more nurturant role responsibilities may be less able to restrict activities and seek health care. Thus, the nurturant role hypothesis is a viable explanation for women's higher rates of morbidity compared to men. As you will see in Chapter 10, marriage and social networks confer fewer health benefits to women than to men, and one reason is that there are health costs to involvement in social networks for women.

Symptom Perception

One explanation of why women suffer greater morbidity compared to men is that women are more sensitive to changes within their body. That is, women have a lower threshold for noticing and reporting symptoms.

EVIDENCE.   Some evidence suggests just the opposite. In a study of cold symptoms, men were more likely than women to take note of symptoms (Macintyre, 1993b). Volunteers were randomly assigned to receive either a cold virus or a placebo and later provided self-reports of cold symptoms. Clinicians also assigned each person a severity score based on the symptoms they observed, such as fever and swollen glands. Men's self-reports of symptoms were more severe than those rated by clinicians, whereas women's self-reports showed greater correspondence to clinicians' reports. These findings suggest that men are exaggerating their symptoms compared to women. If true, this means that sex differences in morbidity are really an underestimate: men report fewer symptoms, but men's reports are an exaggeration. One problem with this study is that physicians were not blind to participant sex. The investigator pointed out that clinicians may perceive the same symptom as more severe in women compared to men; thus, the possibility of clinician bias cannot be completely ruled out. In no way, however, did the study support the idea that women have a lower threshold for reporting symptoms compared to men.

A recent study also concluded that, if anything, women underreport their symptoms (Macintyre, Ford, & Hunt, 1999). When men and women are asked a general question as to whether they have any long-standing illness or disability, they give similar responses; that is, an equal number of men and women admit to a condition. The illnesses reported also are similar in severity. However, when men and women are provided with a list of conditions and asked if they have any of these, women report more conditions. In other words, women need more prompting than men to report an illness. This suggests that women underreport illness when asked open-ended questions.

Other research has directly challenged the idea that women are more in touch with their bodies compared to men. Recall the research discussed in Chapter 3 about the basis of men's and women's emotions.

Those studies (Cox et al., 1985; Pennebaker & Watson, 1988) showed that men were more accurate in predicting their physiological state when environmental cues were removed from the situation. That line of research would suggest that men are more sensitive than women to symptoms.

Thus, there is really no evidence that women are more able than men to *perceive* symptoms. However, it is important, though difficult, to distinguish symptom perception from symptom reporting. Women may be more likely to report a symptom once it is perceived. Sex differences in reports of symptoms are smaller when objective measures of symptoms are used, when symptoms are more tangible, and when symptoms are more incapacitating (Mechanic, 1976).

One area of research that has aimed to address symptom perception is pain research. Researchers have suggested that women have a lower threshold of pain compared to men (Feine, Bushnell, Miron, & Duncan, 1991; Otto & Dougher, 1985). In a review of the literature, Berkley (1997) concluded that there were clear sex differences in response to experimentally induced pain. In laboratory studies, a pain stimulus is applied to the respondent at a very low level and intensity is gradually increased. These studies tend to show that women have lower thresholds of pain, report greater intensity of pain, have lower tolerance levels for pain, and are better able to discriminate different levels of pain. However, Berkley also acknowledged that the size of these sex differences was small, that sex differences were not always consistent across studies, and that they were influenced by a variety of situational variables.

Consistent with the experimental work, studies of people in the real world show that women report more pain than men. Women report more severe pain, more frequent pain, and longer episodes of pain (Unruh, 1996), although findings are not always consistent, even within a given study.

Do sex differences in pain perceptions and pain reports influence how men and women are treated? In a review of the literature, Unruh (1996) concluded that women were given less medication than men in response to pain. Thus, women's pain seems to be taken less seriously than men's, or men's pain is taken more seriously than women's.

EXPLANATIONS.   Although sex differences in pain perception are far from clear, this has not stopped investigators from speculating on the cause of differences. Is there a biological basis to sex differences in pain? A recent study found that men are less sensitive to pain and that men's higher blood pressure accounted for the difference (Sheffield, Biles, Orom, Maixner, & Sheps, 2000); high blood pressure somehow interfered with pain perception. One reason biological factors have been thought to play a role in sex differences in pain perceptions is that women are more responsive than men to some classes of painkillers. In one study, analgesics were more effective in reducing pain from wisdom teeth removal among women than men (Gear et al., 1999). Men and women were randomly assigned to receive either a placebo or an analgesic. There was no sex difference in pain reports among patients who received the placebo, but men reported greater pain than women when receiving some of the analgesics.

Social factors, too, may influence reports of pain. Family members who experience and frequently express pain may serve as "pain models" for children. In one study, women reported a greater number of pain models than men, and pain models were associated with reports of greater pain symptoms (Koutantji, Pearce, & Oakley, 1998). Reports of pain also are vulnerable to the demand characteristics of the situation. In one study, the sex of the experimenter was manipulated and influenced pain reports (F. Levine & de Simone,

1991). Men reported less pain in response to the cold pressor test (i.e., putting a hand in ice water) when the experimenter was an attractive female rather than an attractive male. Women reported similar amounts of pain to male and female experimenters. In fact, there was a trend for women to report *more* pain to male than to female experimenters. Thus, men were less likely and women were more likely to admit pain when gender roles were made salient, that is, when the experimenter was of the other sex.

Gender roles are likely to be an important factor in pain reports. The male gender role is associated with strength and emotional inhibition, both of which are consistent with minimizing reports of pain. In one study, the male gender role was associated with higher pain thresholds and pain tolerance. A pain stimulus was applied to respondents' middle finger and slowly increased in intensity (Otto & Dougher, 1985). Respondents were asked to report when they first became aware of pain, their degree of discomfort at various stages of intensity, and when the pain became intolerable. Men had higher pain tolerances than women, meaning that men endured higher levels of pain before reporting that it was intolerable. However, masculinity also was associated with higher pain tolerances. Although there were no sex differences in pain thresholds (i.e., men and women were aware of pain at the same point), masculinity was associated with higher pain thresholds in men and was unrelated to pain thresholds in women.

Illness Behavior

Illness behavior is often referred to as adopting the "sick role," or labeling a symptom as illness and responding to it. Sick role behavior includes restricting activities, getting bed rest, taking medication,

and seeking the help of health care professionals. These are all activities that women do more than men.

IMPLICATIONS FOR MORBIDITY. The sick role behaviors just identified are frequently included in indices of morbidity. Thus, one reason women have higher rates of morbidity compared to men is that women are more likely to adopt the sick role (Nathanson, 1978). One study showed that women were more likely to have restricted their activities for at least half of a day in response to headache pain (14% vs. 8%; Celentano et al., 1990). Even when the severity of pain was taken into consideration, the sex difference in activity restriction remained. The authors argue that it is more socially acceptable for women than men to reduce their activities when ill.

The **sick role hypothesis** suggests that sex differences in medical care utilization are due to women's greater tendency to adopt the sick role. If men and women are equally ill but women are more likely to seek help for symptoms, sex differences in morbidity are really artifactual.

One reason women may be more willing to adopt the sick role is that women have fewer **fixed role obligations** than men (Marcus & Seeman, 1981). A fixed role is one that is structured and difficult to reschedule (Gove, 1984). Men are likely to have two fixed roles: worker and head of household. Performance in these roles is visible. Historically, women were likely to have only one role, that of housewife, a role relatively unstructured and invisible. A housewife has few deadlines and can easily put chores off from one day to the next; thus, women have fewer constraints on their time and are freer to restrict their activities and take care of themselves when ill. That is, women's social role can accommodate illness (Mechanic, 1976). A recent study found that adopting the sick role (e.g., restricted activity days, days in bed, taking medication, visiting a doctor) was associated with symptoms among women but not men (Gijsbers van Wijk et al., 1999). The authors concluded that women's roles are more flexible, allowing them to respond to symptoms. One tenet of the fixed role obligations hypothesis is that men's fixed roles keep them task-focused, whereas women's lack of fixed roles allows them time to ruminate about their problems. This would explain why women perceive their health as worse than men and why women report more symptoms than men.

In a test of the fixed role hypothesis, Marcus and Seeman (1981) examined the relation of role obligations to health problems. Fixed role obligations were measured in terms of financial responsibility (how much the person contributes to family income), status as head of household, and employment status. They found that men had greater fixed role obligations than women, and women had greater restricted activity days and more chronic illnesses than men. In addition, fixed role obligations were associated with fewer restricted activity days and fewer chronic illnesses. Fixed role obligations accounted for the sex differences in restricted activity days, suggesting that women had more restricted activities than men because they had fewer fixed roles. One interpretation of this study is that men's higher number of fixed roles prevented them from adopting the sick role. However, it also is possible that good health allowed the men and women to have more fixed roles. Because the study is correlational, the causal relation between fixed roles and health cannot be determined.

Other research findings are consistent with the fixed role hypothesis. In one study, sex differences in physician visits were reduced when fixed roles (employment status and contribution to family income) were taken into consideration (Marcus & Siegel, 1982). Men were less

likely than women to visit physicians, possibly because they were employed and their jobs contributed substantially to the household income. The finding that unemployed people report greater physical and psychological symptoms of distress is also consistent with the fixed role obligations hypothesis (Klonoff & Landrine, 1992).

Today, however, it is not the case that men necessarily have more fixed roles than women. The implications of the fixed role hypothesis is that women who have a large number of role obligations, such as women with children or women who work, would be less likely to adopt the sick role. Are changes in women's roles associated with changes in their health? If women now have more fixed roles, there should be fewer sex differences in morbidity. This hypothesis was tested by examining whether sex differences in morbidity changed as women's roles changed in Denmark, Finland, Norway, and Sweden (Haavio-Mannila, 1986). Consistent with the fixed role hypothesis, women had higher morbidity rates than men in countries where there was a greater proportion of women staying at home. Morbidity was measured in terms of illness rates and hospitalization rates. In addition, sex differences in morbidity were larger during periods of history when a greater proportion of women stayed at home. It may be that women who stay home have fewer fixed roles and are thus able to take on the sick role. However, it also is possible that women with fewer roles are less healthy.

Illness behavior may be encouraged in women and discouraged in men. Research suggests that boys become socialized not to complain about illness and not to seek help for illness or injury. In a study of 6- to 12-year-olds, sex differences in stoicism (being unemotional during illness) were larger among older than younger children (Campbell, 1978). At all ages, boys were less emotional than girls, and with increasing age, both boys and girls became less emotional during illness. However, the age effect was much stronger among boys than girls: boys were especially likely to become unemotional during illness as they grew older.

Who encourages these different responses to illness? Parents are an obvious choice. L.S. Walker and Zeman (1992) found that girls were more likely than boys to say that parents encouraged illness behaviors, such as missing school and taking medication. The parents, however, reported that they encouraged these behaviors equally in sons and daughters. In a study of third- through twelfth-graders, females more than males said that their family thought and talked about health matters (R. Cohen et al., 1990).

IMPLICATIONS FOR MORTALITY. Just as women's illness behaviors may account for their greater morbidity compared to men, these same illness behaviors may account for women's longer life span. Perhaps women respond to acute symptoms of illness more quickly, which makes it appear at a given point in time that women are sicker than men. However, women's early response to symptoms could prevent a minor illness from developing into a more serious one.

Once a symptom is perceived, is there evidence that men and women respond to the symptom differently? Responses to illness can be tied to gender roles. Help-seeking behavior is inconsistent with the male gender role; admitting illness may be construed as admitting weakness or vulnerability. Thus, men may be less likely to admit that they are ill.

However, many studies show that men and women respond to symptoms in a similar way. One study found no difference in men's and women's reports of how they would respond to symptoms (Kandrack et al., 1991). Men and women were equally likely to say they would respond to a symp-

tom by ignoring it, by taking care of themselves, or by visiting a physician. These are self-reports of hypothetical behavior, however. In a survey of White married individuals who experienced at least one symptom in the prior week, respondents were asked to indicate how they actually responded to this symptom (Meininger, 1986); respondents could have treated themselves, asked someone other than a doctor for advice, or visited a health care professional. There was no sex difference in responses. In addition, similar variables predicted responses to symptoms for men and women: believing that a physician could alleviate a symptom was associated with visiting a physician; having a symptom for a longer period of time was associated with visiting a physician. Another study found that women reported more physical symptoms than men did, but that men and women were equally likely to have visited a physician in the prior month in response to each symptom (Wyke, Hunt, & Ford, 1998). Thus, there is no evidence from these studies that women respond differently to symptoms. In particular, there is no evidence that women are more likely to seek medical attention in response to a symptom.

There are exceptions to this conclusion, however. In one study, elderly people (ages 62 through 94) were asked to keep a daily diary of their physical symptoms and their responses to symptoms for two weeks (Rakowski, Julius, Hickey, Verbrugge, & Halter, 1988). Women were more likely than men to take action in response to symptoms, either by seeking the attention of medical professionals, by restricting activities, or by self-medication. In a study of headache pain, women were more likely to have consulted a doctor about the pain in the prior year (Celentano et al., 1990). The sex difference in help seeking remained when sex differences in severity were taken into consideration.

One variable that influences sex differences in response to symptoms is the severity of the symptom. Research suggests that men's and women's help-seeking responses are more similar when symptoms are severe; sex differences in physician visits are greater for minor complaints. Women are more likely than men to visit the doctor for minor conditions, but there are no sex differences in visits to the doctor for serious illness (Dracup et al., 1995; I. Waldron, 1995b, 1997). Although it appears that women are more interested than men in health and more concerned with prevention, there is no evidence that women seek care for problems earlier than men (Muller, 1990). Studies of people who have had heart attacks find that there is a tendency for women to delay longer than men before seeking help for symptoms (Dracup et al., 1995). Delay behavior is associated with mortality following a heart attack (Turi et al., 1986). Because heart disease is associated with being male, it is possible that women are less sensitive than men to symptoms of this disease. However, a study of patients with colon and rectal cancer found no sex differences in delay behavior among rectal cancer patients and longer delays for women than men among colon cancer patients (Marshall & Funch, 1986). That women visit the physician more frequently than men for minor but not severe symptoms suggests that women may have a lower tolerance for symptoms or feel more comfortable seeking help for minor illness. Find out if your male and female peers respond similarly to symptoms in Exercise 9.6.

One source of help that men may be more reluctant to seek compared to women is help for psychological problems. In four national surveys, Kessler, Brown, and Broman (1981) found evidence to support this.

EXERCISE 9.6
Responses to Symptoms

Develop a list of responses to illness. Your list should include visiting a physician, taking medication, and restricting activities. Ask 10 men and 10 women to recall the last time they were ill and have them indicate how they responded to their illness by checking the responses that apply from your list. Also, ask them to state the nature of the illness or injury so that you can determine its severity. Do men and women respond to illness in similar ways? Does it depend on the severity of the illness or symptom?

CONCLUSIONS

I have reviewed a number of classes of explanations for sex differences in morbidity and mortality. Which has the greatest explanatory power? A number of investigators have reviewed the literature and compared different classes of explanations. I. Waldron (1995b) concluded that sex differences in behavior are the major cause of sex differences in mortality, and Verbrugge (1985) concluded that sex differences in health behaviors explained a large portion of sex differences in morbidity and mortality.

Health behaviors are limited in their ability to explain sex differences in morbidity (Verbrugge, 1989). Men have worse health behaviors than women, yet women have higher morbidity rates. When health behaviors are taken into consideration, sex differences in morbidity actually increase (Verbrugge, 1985). Health behaviors also cannot account in total for the sex difference in mortality. Men may smoke and drink more than women, but women exercise less and have a greater incidence of obesity than men.

It may be that different classes of explanations affect men's and women's health. Denton and Walters (1999) argue that health behaviors play a greater role in men's health, whereas social structural factors play a greater role in women's health. In terms of subjective health status and physical functioning, behavioral factors, such as smoking and drinking, contribute to men's poor health. Social structural factors, such as support from network members and caretaking responsibilities, contribute to women's health. Support is an advantage, whereas caretaking responsibilities are a disadvantage for women. Thus, the class of explanations that describe men's health and women's health may differ.

SUMMARY

Men have higher mortality rates than women, but women have higher morbidity rates than men. In this chapter, I reviewed the different classes of explanations for this paradox. Although biological factors certainly contribute to health, biology alone cannot explain the increase in the size of the sex difference in life expectancy that has occurred over the twentieth century. SES factors contribute to health, but again are unable to explain sex differences in health. Sex differences in morbidity may be overestimated to the extent that women report on men's health and to the extent that physicians overdiagnose psychiatric problems in women.

A major contributor to sex differences in morbidity and mortality is health behavior. Women engage in more preventive health care compared to men. Although this difference should theoretically lead to women's lower mortality rates, there is

no evidence to support this conjecture. Instead, women's preventive behavior gets counted as physician visits in indices of morbidity. Smoking is a major contributor to mortality. That men smoke more than women accounts for a portion of the sex difference in mortality as well as the sex difference in specific diseases (e.g., coronary heart disease, lung cancer). That women have increased their rates of smoking during the last half of the twentieth century accounts for the fact that the sex difference in life expectancy has narrowed. Men also have higher rates of alcohol and drug usage compared to women. All three risk factors for early mortality (smoking, alcohol, and drugs) are interrelated and are associated with other problems, such as depression and antisocial behavior. Relations to depression are often stronger among women, and relations to antisocial behavior are often stronger among men.

Other health behaviors pose greater risks to women's than men's health: obesity and lack of exercise. More women than men are obese in the United States, and the sex difference is particularly striking among Blacks. Women also exercise less than men. Sex differences in exercise may change in the future as the number of female children becoming involved in sports increases.

Another explanation for sex differences in mortality and morbidity focused on the contribution of men's and women's social roles. One of men's social roles is working outside the home, and men are exposed to more hazards at work compared to women. It also is men's social role to drive: men drive more than women, drive less safely, and are involved in more driving accidents. In general, many of the behaviors that pose dangers for men's health can be conceptualized as general risk-taking behavior. Men's work, home, and leisure activities are riskier than those of women, which undoubtedly contributes to men's higher death rates from accidents.

The female social role has the advantage of making women more concerned with health matters but the disadvantage of making women the caretakers of other people's health. The nurturant role exposes women to more illness, is a source of fatigue among women, making them more susceptible to illness, and prevents women from taking care of themselves when they are ill.

Other explanations for sex differences in morbidity have to do with women being more sensitive than men to symptoms, more likely to enact the sick role, and more likely to seek medical care. Women appear to have a lower threshold and tolerance for pain in experimental studies of pain perception as well as community surveys. The explanation for this sex difference is not clear. It does not appear that women are more sensitive than men to changes within their bodies. However, women are more likely to respond to symptoms by restricting their activities and taking care of themselves, in other words, enacting the sick role. One explanation for this sex difference is that women have fewer fixed role obligations than men, and fewer role obligations are associated with a greater willingness to respond to health problems. Women use health services more frequently than men, but the sex difference is limited to minor symptoms. In the case of serious illness, men and women are equally likely to seek the attention of a health care professional.

Taken collectively, different explanations are more and less relevant to men and women. A few health behaviors explain a good portion of men's higher mortality rates compared to women. These health behaviors can be construed in terms of a larger framework reflecting men's risk-taking behavior. Women's higher morbidity rates are more likely to reflect women's social roles than their health behaviors.

DISCUSSION QUESTIONS

1. How do sex and race influence the leading causes of death?
2. When examining the relation of SES to health, whose SES should be used: that of the husband? The wife? Both? Why? What are the advantages and disadvantages?
3. Under what conditions do you believe physicians are more or less likely to make a similar diagnosis in a male and a female who present with the same symptoms?
4. Discuss how sex differences in smoking, drinking alcohol, and drug usage have changed over time.
5. Given our culture's increasing health consciousness, in particular, the emphasis on diet and exercise, why do you think rates of obesity have increased?
6. Which health behaviors are more strongly related to health in men, and which are more strongly related to health in women?
7. In what ways are men's behaviors riskier than women's? What are the specific health implications?
8. Why are nurturant roles hazardous to health?
9. Discuss how to determine if men and women actually perceive symptoms differently.
10. In what ways are men's and women's responses to illness similar and different?

SUGGESTED READING

Berkley, K.J. (1997). Sex differences in pain. *Behavioral and Brain Sciences, 20,* 371–380.

Gove, W.R., & Hughes, M. (1979). Possible causes of the apparent sex differences in physical health: An empirical investigation. *American Sociological Review, 44,* 126–146.

Helgeson, V.S. (1994c). Relation of agency and communion to well-being: Evidence and potential explanations. *Psychological Bulletin, 116,* 412–428.

Hibbard, J.H., & Pope, C.R. (1983). Gender roles, illness orientations and use of medical services. *Social Science and Medicine, 17*(3), 129–137.

Marcus, A.C., & Seeman, T.E. (1981). Sex differences in reports of illness and disability: A preliminary test of the "fixed role obligations" hypothesis. *Journal of Health and Social Behavior, 22,* 174–182.

Verbrugge, L.M. (1989). The twain meet: Empirical explanations of sex differences in health and mortality. *Journal of Health and Social Behavior, 30,* 282–304.

Waldron, I. (1997). Changing gender roles and gender differences in health behavior. In D. S. Gochman (Ed.), *Handbook of health behavior research: I. Personal and social determinants* (pp. 303–328). New York: Plenum Press.

KEY TERMS

Android obesity—Extra weight around the abdomen.

Artifact—A confounding variable that leads an effect to appear that doesn't really exist.

Body mass index—Measure of obesity that takes into consideration the ratio of weight to height.

Fixed role obligations—Responsibilities specific to one's defining role that are structured and difficult to reschedule.

Gynoid obesity—Extra weight around the hips.

Health behavior—Any activity that either promotes good health (e.g., preventive health care, exercise, healthy diet) or contributes to bad health (e.g., smoking, alcohol, and drug use).

Illness behavior—The condition of labeling a symptom as illness and responding to it as such; adopting the "sick role."

Morbidity—The presence of illness or disease.

Mortality—Death rate.

Nurturant role hypothesis—Supposition that women's roles require them to attend to the needs of others, which results in fatigue, exposure to illness, and not taking care of oneself when sick.

Sick role hypothesis—Suggestion that sex differences in medical care utilization are due to women's greater tendency than men to adopt the "sick role."

10

Relationships and Health

In 1977, James Lynch wrote *The Broken Heart*. The broken heart was a metaphor for the effects of relationships on health, specifically coronary heart disease. Lynch claimed there are

> few conditions in life that do not involve some type of human contact, and so in one sense it would be remarkable if human contact did not influence our hearts. Like the air we breathe, it envelops every aspect of our lives. A simple visit to your doctor, arguments, reassurance and praise, sexual activity, social gatherings, competitive sports, the loss of a friend or loved one, jealousies, humiliations, human triumphs, the cuddling of a child in your lap, the silent hand-holding between two lovers, the quiet comforting of a dying patient—all these affect the heart. (p. 12)

Lynch demonstrated an association between markers of social isolation (e.g., high mobility) and high mortality rates from heart disease. Since then, numerous studies have demonstrated links between aspects

of social relationships and health (S. Cohen & Wills, 1985).

The goal of the present chapter is to examine the implications of relationships for men's and women's health. We know that the female gender role involves a relationship orientation. Does this mean that women benefit more than men from social relationships? Or does men's lack of a relationship orientation make relationships all the more important to their health? In the first part of the chapter, I focus on the implications of a primary social relationship for health: marriage. I focus on marriage because there is quite a bit of evidence that marriage affects men's and women's health in different ways. I also focus on marriage because it is one of the most important relationships (if not *the* most important relationship) to men and women. I also explore the health implications of the loss of a primary relationship through the death of a spouse and relationship dissolution (e.g., divorce). Next, I examine the health implications of the *quality* of marriage for men's and women's health. One central aspect of quality is how household chores and child care are divided in the family. Thus, I describe the division of labor, examine predictors of the division of labor, and discuss the implications of the division of labor for relationship satisfaction and well-being.

Although marriage is an important relationship, it is not the only relationship that influences health. In the last section of the chapter, I review the social support literature to determine how other relationships influence men's and women's health.

EFFECTS OF MARRIAGE ON HEALTH

"I now pronounce you man and wife." Those are the words of the traditional marriage ceremony. Historically, marriage for women has meant that they become defined by their relationship to their husband; marriage for men has meant that they have someone to take care of the home and the children. Today, however, marriage may have a more similar meaning for men and women: gaining a partner, a person with whom to share one's life. Today, the minister or officiator is more likely to say "I now pronounce you husband and wife," reflecting the similarity of marriage for men and women.

One characteristic of modern marriage is that it is less likely to last. People have increasing expectations of marriage, and marriage may be less likely to meet those expectations. It also is much easier to dissolve a marriage and society is more tolerant of marital breakups. While the marriage rate has decreased over the past three decades, the divorce rate has steadily increased. The divorce rate is higher among African Americans than Whites (Kposowa, 1998). Today, 47% of Black marriages but only 17% of White marriages will end after 15 years. The decline of the two-parent family also is increasing, especially among African Americans. In 1998, 81% of White families consisted of a husband and a wife, 14% were headed by women, and 5% were headed by men (U.S. Census Bureau, 1999). Among Black families, 47% consisted of a husband and a wife, 47% were headed by women, and 7% were headed by men. Dickson (1993) cites a shift in cultural values in the United States as contributing to the decline of the Black family, but this shift also could explain the decline of all families. Today, there is a greater emphasis on individual and personal fulfillment, which means that people may be less likely to tolerate or stay in relationships that are not satisfying. There also are greater expectations for relationships: marriage is expected to provide a source of intimacy, sexuality, and companionship.

In response to the "breakdown of the family," traditional marriage has received recent support by the Southern Baptists. They adopted a resolution during their 1998 convention that a wife must "submit herself graciously" to her husband and allow her husband to be the leader (Warner, 1998). Recall from Chapter 8, however, that traditional roles in families do not necessarily lead to greater happiness.

Regardless of the divorce statistics, the majority of men and women must find some value in getting married. In 1998, 60% of persons over 18 in the United States were married (U.S. Census Bureau, 1999). The figure for White people is larger than for Blacks (62% vs. 42%). The vast majority, 97% of men and 95% of women, have been married at some point in their life (U.S. Bureau of the Census, 1999).

Marriage is a right that is currently conferred only to heterosexual men and women. In fact, in 1996, President Clinton signed into law the Defense of Marriage Act (DOMA), which states that marriage consists of a legal union between a man and a woman. DOMA also indicates that states do not have to recognize same-sex civil unions that are legal in other states. This turned out to be an important feature of DOMA, as Vermont became the first state to allow homosexual civil unions in 2000. The civil union in Vermont provides homosexual partners with health care benefits (although taxable) and the right for one partner to make medical decisions for another. Although individual states may sanction same-sex civil unions, these unions are not recognized by the federal government. Thus, civil unions do not provide for social security benefits and immigration status, which are directly tied to the institution of marriage.

The research on marriage and health has focused on heterosexual relationships. Sociologists often use marriage as a proxy for social support, which would suggest that marriage benefits men's and women's health. Does marriage benefit men and women equally?

Evidence

In 1957, Hannah Lees wrote the book *How to Help Your Husband Stay Alive.* She expressed concern at the fact that men die younger than women and that the sex difference in longevity was widening. She argued that it was the duty of women to help lengthen the life span of their husband. Lees points out that there are "a hundred different ways" a woman can contribute to a man's happiness and asks "What is it men need in their marriages that not enough women are giving them today?" Lees said that wives should provide support to husbands, make husbands' lives easier, help husbands cope with the pressures and frustrations they face in the working world, provide opportunities for husbands to relax, and help husbands take care of their health.

Lees (1957) may have been too critical of wives. It turns out that women do help men live longer. Numerous studies have shown that being married is advantageous to psychological and physical health but that men reap greater rewards from marriage than women do (Bernard, 1972; C. Ross, Mirowsky, & Goldsteen, 1990). The importance of marriage to men was best articulated by Bernard. He said that the proportion of men who are married in a society is a social indicator of how the society is operating, just as the unemployment rate is an economic indicator of how the society is operating.

The greater health benefits of marriage for men compared to women come from large epidemiological studies in which men's and women's marital status and health status are measured and then followed for many years. In three such studies, men who were married were less likely to die than men who were unmarried over the 9 to 15 years they were followed (Berkman & Syme, 1979; House, Robbins, & Metzner, 1982; Shye, Mullooly, Freeborn, & Pope, 1995). Marital status did not predict mortality among women in any of these studies. In a study of over 2,000 men and women, Schoenbach, Kaplan, Fredman, and Kleinbaum (1986) found that marital status predicted decreased mortality among White and Black men and White women but not Black women.

It is not clear whether men's deriving greater health benefits from marriage than women do reflects marriage being a greater source of distress for women or whether being unmarried is a greater source of distress for men. Marriage is often construed as less beneficial for women because married women are more distressed than married men, but unmarried women and men do not differ in distress (Ensel, 1986). However, others have suggested that it is not that marriage is associated with increased distress for women, but that the state of being unmarried is more distressing for men. In a survey of over 500 adult men and women, people who lived with a partner were less lonely than people who lived alone (de Jong-Gierveld, 1986). However, men who lived alone were more lonely than women who lived alone, whereas there was no difference in the loneliness of men and women who lived with a partner. Thus, this study showed that men suffered more than women from the lack of a relationship.

There is cross-cultural support for the idea that marriage confers greater benefits to men's than women's health. In a study of 17 countries (e.g., France, Netherlands, Japan, Norway, Australia), marriage was associated with decreased loneliness and greater perceived health in 16 of the nations (S. Stack, 1998b). Overall, these effects were stronger among men than women. These nations were all Western cultures, however. In a study that compared the health benefits of marriage in India and the United States, marriage was associated with decreased distress among people from the United States (especially men) but was unrelated to distress among people from India (Sastry, 1999). The author suggested that the cultural differences in how marriage is construed explain why marriage is associated with health benefits in the United States but not India. In the United States, marriage is based on love and mutual support, whereas in India, marriage is based on tradition and family obligations; the family rather than the spouse is the primary source of support in India.

A study of African Americans concluded that marriage was good for health, but only when compared to people whose marriages had ended through separation, divorce, or widowhood (D. Brown, 1996). D. Brown found that men's health varied more across these marital statuses than did women's health. The least distressed men were married or never married; widowed

men had the highest distress, with divorced and separated men in between the two groups. Although there were clear differences in distress among men in different marital statuses, marital status was only weakly related to women's health. Women who never married, were married, or divorced had equally low distress. The highest distress was observed among separated women; widowed women fell between the two groups. Thus, there is substantial evidence that marriage has more benefits for men's than women's health.

Is it marriage per se that leads to health benefits, or is it the presence of a partner? Several studies have examined the effects of heterosexual cohabitation on health. It is not clear whether cohabitation provides the same benefits as marriage. In one study, Horwitz and White (1998) measured alcohol problems in a group of unmarried people and then followed them for seven years. After the seven years, people were classified as married, unmarried, or cohabiting. Although the three groups started out with similar levels of alcohol problems, cohabiting and single persons had an increase in alcohol problems over the seven years compared to married persons—especially among men. Thus, it appeared that marriage reduced the incidence of alcohol problems over time, but cohabitation did not. By contrast, in a cross-sectional study, married people reported higher levels of happiness and less depression than cohabiting people, but cohabiting people reported higher levels of happiness and less depression than people who lived without another adult (Kurdek, 1991b). Yet another study showed that married people and cohabiting people had less distress than people who did not live with their partner or people without partners (C. Ross, 1995). In this study, cohabiting and married people benefited equally from the presence of a partner. Clearly, more research is needed on this issue. It may be that cohabiting relationships that result in marriage have benefits on health, whereas cohabiting relationships that do not result in marriage provide no benefits or fewer benefits.

Literature on the relation of marital-like relationships to the health of gay men and lesbians is even more sparse. One older study showed that gay men and lesbians who were living with their sexual partner in a marital-like relationship were less lonely, less depressed, and had higher self-acceptance than other homosexuals (A. Bell & Weinberg, 1978).

Explanations

There are many theories as to why marriage benefits health. Marriage is presumed to affect health through a set of physiological processes. What is it about marriage that affects those physiological processes? There are two categories of variables that might affect physiology: psychological and behavioral. Marriage may provide one with a sense of identity, a source of self-esteem, and a companion to share activities, all of which should promote a positive psychological state. Marriage also may promote good health behavior (e.g., exercising), decrease risk behavior (e.g., smoking), and promote early detection of disease (e.g., routine physical exam). These effects of marriage on health are referred to as direct effects, or **main effects** (S. Cohen & Wills, 1985). In each case, marriage is directly linked to a psychological state or behavior that influences health. An alternative hypothesis is that marriage indirectly affects health by providing resources to cope with stress. These effects are referred to as **buffering effects;** marriage is buffering one against the negative effects of stressors (S. Cohen & Wills, 1985). During times of stress, marriage may help one to perceive a stressful event as less troublesome and may

provide resources to cope with stress (e.g., emotional support, financial support, concrete assistance). In the face of an illness, marriage may help one to make the health behavior changes necessary for a successful recovery.

The distinction between the main effects and buffering effects hypotheses is shown in Figure 10.1. In the left half of Figure 10.1, the main effects hypothesis shows that married people are less distressed than unmarried people, regardless of the level of stress. The magnitude of the difference between the two lines is similar. Of course, stress leads to an increase in distress among married and unmarried people. In the right half of Figure 10.1, the stress-buffering hypothesis shows that stress is associated with a larger increase in distress among unmarried people than married people. That is, married people who face high levels of stress are protected from the large increase in distress that unmarried people face. Here, the magnitude of the difference between the two lines is greater under high levels of stress.

Below, I review some of the research on these psychological and behavioral links of marriage to health.

SOCIAL SUPPORT.   One explanation for the effects of marriage on health concerns social support. Married men and women report higher levels of support than unmarried persons (Ensel, 1986; C. Ross, 1995). Marriage may confer a greater health benefit to men compared to women because marriage is a greater source of support for men (Stroebe & Stroebe, 1983). This is especially the case for emotional support. Husbands report receiving more emotional support from their spouse than wives do (Vanfossen, 1981), and husbands are more likely than wives to name their spouse as their primary confidant (Tower & Kasl, 1996). Women are more likely than men to name someone else as their primary confidant. Thus, marriage

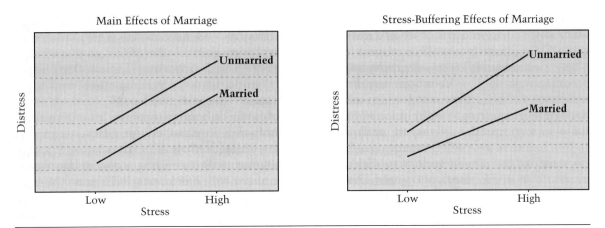

FIGURE 10.1 Main effects of marriage (left panel): married people are less distressed than unmarried people, regardless of their levels of stress. Stress-buffering effects of marriage (right panel): married people are especially less distressed than unmarried people when they face high levels of stress. In other words, marriage buffers people from the deleterious effects of stress.

may be a greater source of emotional support for men.

One kind of support from marriage that might benefit women more than men is financial support. In one study, the only women whose health improved from marriage were unemployed women (I. Waldron, Hughes, & Brooks, 1996). The increase in family income that marriage brought to these women accounted for part of this health benefit. Another study found that the decreased psychological distress of mothers who were married compared to unmarried (either never married or divorced) was associated with fewer financial difficulties (Hope, Power, & Rodgers, 1999).

STRESSFUL LIFE EVENTS. Another reason for the differences in distress among people of different marital statuses has to do with the occurrence of negative life events (Ensel, 1986). The state of being unmarried is associated with stressful life events. Separation, divorce, and widowhood are often experienced as negative life events in and of themselves, but they also can lead to other negative life events, such as changes in one's social network. It is these negative life events that may be producing an increase in distress rather than marriage being responsible for a lowered level of distress. Ensel found that when social support and life events were taken into consideration, there was no difference in distress between married and unmarried people.

Marriage is not only related to the occurrence of fewer stressful life events but also is a buffer against the stress from life events. This buffer appears to be stronger for men than for women. J. Siegel and Kuykendall (1990) examined the effect of the death of a close family member (not a spouse) on depression among elderly men and women. Marriage protected men but not women against the depression associated with the loss. Widowed men who suffered the loss of a close family member were especially depressed. In another study, social support from wives buffered men from the distress associated with work (Vanfossen,

1981). When men were having problems with work, social support from wives was strongly related to reduced depression.

HEALTH BEHAVIOR. Marriage has a positive effect on both men's and women's health behavior, but the effects are particularly strong for men (Schone & Weinick, 1998; Umberson, 1987). Wives take more responsibility for husband's health than husbands take for their wife's health. Marriage has a stronger beneficial effect on the eating and sleeping patterns of men and is a greater deterrent to drinking and drug problems for men than for women (Umberson, 1987). In a study of over 4,000 married and widowed senior citizens, married men were more likely to have had their blood pressure checked in the prior year, were more likely to engage in physical activities, and were less likely to smoke than widowed men. Marriage benefited women in that married women were more likely to eat breakfast and more likely to use seatbelts than widowed women. In a study of people who visited a family medicine clinic, men were twice as likely as women to say that they visited the clinic because someone of the other sex encouraged them to do so (Norcross, Ramirez, & Palinkas, 1996); this person was typically a spouse. Getting married also seems to have adverse effects on women's weight but no effects on men's weight. In a phone survey, nearly 2,500 adults reported their marital status and weight and were followed for one year (Rauschenbach, Sobal, & Frongillo, 1995). A change in marital status over the year (becoming married, getting separated or divorced) did not affect men's weight; however, women who married over that year gained more weight than women who did not get married that year.

MARITAL SATISFACTION. Another reason marriage may be more health beneficial for

men is that women, in general, are more dissatisfied with their marriages (Antonucci & Akiyama, 1987; Bernard, 1972). Women report more problems in marriage, more negative feelings about marriage, and more frequent thoughts of divorce.

One reason marriage may present more problems for women is that women's roles change more after marriage compared to those of men. Historically, women conformed more than men to what their spouse expected of them (Bernard, 1972). Because women were more dependent than men on marriage for financial security, women had more at stake in maintaining the marriage. Thus, there was greater motivation for women to accommodate to their spouse's wishes. In addition, according to Gove and Tudor (1973), the housewife role is inherently frustrating: it lacks status, structure, and recognition because "accomplishments" often go unnoticed. Gove and Tudor argue that the lack of structure in the housewife role left women with time to ruminate about their problems. Today, however, women are more likely to take on other roles besides housewife and are better equipped to take care of themselves financially. Thus, men's and women's roles are now more similar in marriage. If the difference in roles is the explanation for why marriage is more health beneficial for men, we may expect to see more similar effects of marriage on men's and women's health in the future.

SELECTION HYPOTHESIS. I have been discussing ways in which marriage could influence health, but it also is possible that health influences marriage. This is referred to as the **marital selection hypothesis.** This hypothesis suggests that healthier people are "selected" into marriage. To examine the marital selection hypothesis, a longitudinal study must be conducted to determine whether initial health influences subsequent marriage and whether initial marital status influences subsequent health.

Evidence for the selection hypothesis comes from a 10-year longitudinal study of people who were single at the start of the study and either remained single or married (Hope, Rodgers, & Power, 1999). Those who got married began the study with lower levels of distress. This was especially the case for men. Thus, psychological health predicted getting married. In this study, there was no evidence that marriage influenced health; 10 years later, those who married and those who remained single reported similar changes in distress.

By contrast, another study provided evidence for a reciprocal relation between marriage and health. This longitudinal study of women showed that marriage leads to improvements in health but also that health leads to marriage for some groups of women (I. Waldron et al., 1996). The initial health status of unemployed women and women employed part time predicted whether they would marry and, if married, whether they would divorce. Unemployed and part-time employed women who had health problems were less likely to get married and more likely to divorce if already married. The initial health status of women who held full-time jobs did not predict entry into or exit from marriage. However, it was also the case that married women ended up with better health than unmarried women.

The bidirectional relation of marriage to health also was examined by Horwitz and White (1991). They focused on two health indicators: depression and problem drinking. They suggested that depression was a female form of distress and that alcohol problems were a male form of distress. They hypothesized that marriage would reduce depression in women and reduce problem drinking in men. They also examined whether depression and problem drinking

influenced the likelihood of getting married. Nearly 400 participants were enrolled in the study at age 21 and followed for three years. Just over 25% of participants became married during that time. The investigators found a reciprocal relation between marriage and alcohol problems, meaning that marriage was associated with reduced alcohol problems but also that people with alcohol problems were less likely to get married. There was no relation between marriage and depression; depression did not predict marriage and marriage did not predict depression. The investigators were somewhat surprised that marriage was not associated with declines in depression and speculated that these benefits of marriage may take more time to appear.

Summary

Marriage benefits health for both men and women but the effects are stronger for men. It is true that healthier people are more likely to get married, but marriage still benefits health above and beyond the selection effect. There are a number of reasons why marriage exerts greater protective effects on men's health: marriage is a greater source of emotional support, is more likely to alleviate stress, and encourages better health behavior for men than for women. In addition, men are more satisfied with marriage compared to women, partly due to the receipt of more social support resources.

EFFECT OF BEREAVEMENT ON HEALTH

If marriage is good for health, presumably losing a spouse has negative effects on health. These negative effects could stem from the loss of resources that the deceased spouse provided as well as the general experience of bereavement. Determining the effects of bereavement on health is not easy. Two kinds of studies have been conducted to address this issue: cross-sectional and longitudinal. Cross-sectional studies evaluate people who are widowed at a single point in time. The advantage of this methodology is that large representative samples can be studied. The disadvantage is that causality cannot be inferred. In other words, one will not know if widowhood caused the decline in health or if unhealthy people were more likely to be widowed. At first glance, this latter possibility may seem highly unlikely. However, recall that people are attracted to similar others and marry people who are similar to themselves. One characteristic on which matching could occur is health. It is possible, then, that less healthy people might be more likely to lose a spouse. Another problem with cross-sectional studies is that the healthiest people are more likely to remarry after widowhood. Thus, the people who remain widowed are not representative of all widowed people and may be more unhealthy than the widowed who have remarried.

An important methodological issue to keep in mind when evaluating studies of the effect of widowhood on health is whether an appropriate comparison group of nonwidowed persons was used. This is especially important when evaluating sex differences in the effects of widowhood on health. Why? If widowed men and widowed women show equal health profiles, can we conclude that widowhood has the same effects on the health of men and women?

No, because men and women who are not widowed differ in health. For example, married women are more depressed than married men. A study that shows no sex differences in depression among widowed men and women could imply that widowhood increased men's distress levels to those of women or lowered women's distress levels

to those of men. In other words, widowhood could have very different effects on men's and women's distress. Let's take another example. In general, men have higher suicide rates compared to women. A study that shows no sex differences in suicide rates among the widowed could imply that widowhood increased women's suicide rates to those of men or decreased men's suicide rates to those of women. The most appropriate comparison group to use in a study of widowhood is married men and women because both widowed and married people share the experience of having entered into marriage. It would not be appropriate to compare widowed persons to never-married persons because we know that there are differences between the kinds of people who do and do not get married.

The second way to examine the effects of widowhood on health is to conduct a longitudinal study. Longitudinal studies typically examine people shortly after widowhood and then follow them over time to assess changes in their health. The disadvantage of this methodology is that we do not know people's level of health before widowhood. The advantage, however, is that we know people's initial health status immediately after widowhood so we can truly examine changes in health over time.

The ideal study of widowhood would use a **prospective design** in which people's health is examined before and after widowhood. Imagine how difficult this study would be to conduct. One would have to enroll a large group of people into a study and follow them for a long enough time so that a sufficient number of people lose a spouse. Thus, you can imagine that there are few prospective studies on widowhood. One way to conduct a prospective study is to identify people who are at risk for losing a spouse or a partner. One such group of people may be men who have HIV. Indeed, prospective studies of gay men have shown negative health effects of bereavement. In one study, the number of persons lost to AIDS was associated with an increase in psychological distress and recreational drug use (J. Martin, 1988). In another study of HIV+ men who were asymptomatic, those who had negative expectations about their illness were more likely to experience the development of HIV symptoms if they had lost a partner to AIDS over the course of a year (Reed, Kemeny, Taylor, & Visscher, 1999). These studies showing adverse effects of partner loss are important because of their prospective nature.

Evidence

With the exception of the two studies just cited, the vast majority of research on bereavement has examined married couples. Stroebe and Stroebe (1983) reviewed the literature on the impact of widowhood on a wide range of health indicators among men and women. This literature was largely cross-sectional; they evaluated only studies that compared widowed men and women to married men and women. With respect to depression, studies either showed that men are more depressed than women after widowhood or that there is no sex difference in depression. Both of these findings contrast with the sex differences in depression among married men and women: married women are more depressed than married men. Thus, the authors concluded that widowhood was associated with relatively greater increases in distress for men than women. Similar results appeared for rates of mental and physical illness. Widowed persons suffered poorer health compared to married persons, but the differences were larger among men than women. Widowhood had even stronger effects on the mortality of men compared to women. Although men

have higher mortality rates in general, widowhood was associated with a much higher increase in mortality among men than among women. Widowhood also was associated with sharper increases in the suicide rate of men compared to women.

Recall that studies that examine only the currently widowed may overestimate their degree of distress because the healthiest people have already remarried. This is especially a problem in examining widowed men's health because men are more likely than women to remarry and to do so quickly. Umberson, Wortman, and Kessler (1992) addressed this issue by comparing men and women who had *ever* been widowed to those who had *never* been widowed. Thus, people who had remarried were included in the widowed group. The investigators found that being ever widowed was associated with a greater increase in depression for men than women. By retaining in the analysis the widowed people who had remarried, the authors were being conservative in the test of their hypothesis about the effects of widowhood on health.

Not only do healthier people remarry, but remarriage also provides benefits to health. Remarriage after widowhood has greater protective effects on widowed men's than widowed women's health. In a 12-year longitudinal study of widowed persons, widowed men who remarried had lower mortality rates than men who did not remarry (Helsing, Szklo, & Comstock, 1981). There were no differences in mortality between widowed women who did and did not remarry.

Explanations

STRAINS.   One explanation for sex differences in health following the loss of a spouse is that men and women face different strains or stressors. Umberson et al.

(1992) hypothesized that women suffer financial strains, whereas men suffer strains from household chores. They found that the sex difference in depression after widowhood (men greater than women) was primarily accounted for by strains from household chores. Thus, the primary reason that men were more distressed than women after widowhood was that they had to cope with household chores. Women's increased distress upon widowhood was mostly accounted for by increased financial strains.

The different strains men and women experience during widowhood may explain why the period of health vulnerability following widowhood differs for each. Men are at increased risk of death, including suicide, within the first six months following widowhood, whereas women face their greatest risk of death during the second year of widowhood (Stroebe & Stroebe, 1983). An important strain for men is the loss of social support, which would have an immediate effect. An important strain for women is the loss of financial resources, which may take a few years to have negative health consequences. It also is possible that men's health appears to suffer more during the early than the late phases of widowhood because many men have remarried by the later phases.

SOCIAL SUPPORT.   A major strain associated with widowhood is the loss of social support. **Interpersonal protection theory** has been used to explain why men suffer more than women upon widowhood (Stroebe & Stroebe, 1983). Interpersonal protection theory implies that there are differences in social support across the marital statuses and that social support buffers one from distress. Marriage increases men's more than women's social support, and widowhood results in a greater loss of support among men than women, especially emotional support

(Stroebe & Stroebe, 1983; Umberson et al., 1992). Recall that men are more likely than women to rely on their spouse as the sole source of emotional support; women, by contrast, receive less support from marriage compared to men and often obtain support from other network members. Women also may have more support available to them following widowhood because it is more acceptable for women to seek support from others. Men suffer a greater loss of support from other network members after widowhood because it is typically the wife who arranges social affairs and maintains contacts with friends and family. In addition, widowed men have a smaller reference group compared to widowed women. Because women outlive men, widowed women have a larger peer group available than do widowed men. Thus, men lose more in terms of receiving support from a spouse and support from other network members following widowhood. Finally, there is one additional support-related reason that widowhood is associated with less distress for women. For women, marriage has costs in terms of support provision. Because women are often the sole providers of emotional support to men, marriage may be associated with some support burden for women. Widowhood relieves this burden. Thus, there are multiple reasons why marriage is a greater source of social support for men. This is a prominent explanation for why men suffer more ill effects of marital loss.

Summary

A number of methodological issues must be considered when studying the effects of widowhood on health. Because we rarely know the status of people's health prior to widowhood, it is important to compare widowed people to an appropriate group of nonwidowed individuals, ideally, married couples.

Such studies overwhelmingly show that widowhood is associated with greater adverse effects on men's than women's health across an array of indicators. The reasons for this sex difference have to do with the different strains men and women face and the greater loss of support that a spouse's death poses for men compared to women.

EFFECT OF RELATIONSHIP DISSOLUTION ON HEALTH

The evidence clearly suggests that marriage is associated with greater health benefits for men than for women and that the loss of marriage through widowhood is associated with greater harm to men's than women's health. Can we conclude that the breakup of relationships has more adverse effects on men's health? The answer is not as clear. First, we examine the breakup of dating relationships and then the breakup of marital relationships.

Breakup of Dating Relationships

In general, women seem to adjust better than men to the breakup of dating relationships (Choo, Levine, & Hatfield, 1996; Sprecher, 1994). One of the most noteworthy studies to shed light on men's and women's perspectives of how relationships dissolve is the Boston Couples Study. In 1972, just over 200 couples who were juniors and seniors in college enrolled in the study (C. Hill, Rubin, & Peplau, 1976). Two years later, 45% of the couples had broken up. There was some evidence that men were more distressed by the breakup compared to women.

These findings were replicated in a more recent study of college student dating relationships that I conducted (Helgeson,

1994a). This study focused on long-distance romantic relationships, mostly among freshmen college students. Just over 100 students enrolled in the study at the beginning of fall and were followed for one semester. Women adjusted better than men to physical separation from their partner; for example, women construed more benefits from the separation compared to men. At the end of the semester, 36% of the couples had broken up. Across an array of measures, women showed better adjustment to the breakup compared to men. As shown in Figure 10.2, at the beginning of the study, when the couples were together (Time 1), women were more distressed than men. At the end

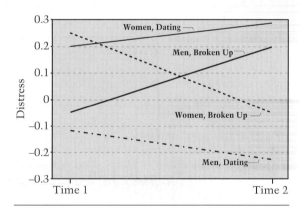

FIGURE 10.2 At the beginning of the semester, when relationships were intact (Time 1), women were more distressed than men. By the end of the semester, when a third of couples had broken up (Time 2), women's distress levels did not significantly differ from those of men. This is because women were more distressed than men among couples who remained together but were less distressed than men among couples who had broken up. Women's distress level decreased following breakup, whereas men's distress level increased following breakup. *Source:* V. S. Helgeson (1994). Long distance romantic relationships: Sex differences in adjustment and breakup. *Personality and Social Psychology Bulletin, 20,* 254–265.

of the semester, when a third of the couples had broken up (Time 2), there was no sex difference in distress among people who had broken up, but women were more distressed than men when the relationship still existed. An alternative way of viewing these findings is that men who broke up became more distressed, whereas women who broke up became less distressed. Women also reported better adjustment to the breakup than men did.

Relationship dissolution has been studied almost exclusively among heterosexuals. One study of breakups among gay men and lesbians showed no sex differences in adjustment to the breakup and no sex differences in the reasons for the breakup (Kurdek, 1991a). The reasons gay men and lesbians cited for their breakup were similar to the reasons cited among heterosexuals: partner not responding to needs, and partner's emotional distance.

Breakup of Marriage: Separation and Divorce

There is some evidence that separation and divorce do not have as many negative effects on women as on men. A longitudinal study of women found that those who were married at the start of the study and became separated or divorced over a 10-year period did not show any health changes and had similar health to women who remained married over a 10-year period (I. Waldron, Weiss, & Hughes, 1997). D. Brown (1996) found that separated and divorced women perceived benefits from marital dissolution; women were more likely than men to say that being unmarried was better than being married.

There are exceptions, however. One study showed that the effects of marital dissolution were similar in magnitude for men and women. In a survey of 757 community residents, men and women who were separated or divorced were more distressed than those who were married (Gerstel, Riessman, & Rosenfield, 1985). Another study found that the effect of divorce on psychological distress was greater for women than men. In a 10-year longitudinal study, married people who remained married were compared to those who divorced (Hope, Rodgers, & Power, 1999). Divorced men and women had greater distress than those who remained married, but the difference was larger for women.

Riessman and Gerstel (1985) argued that marital dissolution might affect different indicators of health for men and women. Men appear to suffer more ill effects of divorce and separation in terms of mortality, hospitalizations for physical health problems, and psychiatric hospitalizations. By contrast, women suffer more ill effects in terms of restricted activity days, acute conditions, and depression. These are exactly the health problems in which sex differences appear regardless of marital status. Thus, divorce or separation may exacerbate preexisting vulnerabilities in men and women.

Some researchers have argued that distress may take different forms in men and women and that other indicators of distress besides depression, such as problem drinking, should be examined. In one study (Horwitz, White, & Howell-White, 1996), investigators measured depression and problem drinking in adolescents who were 12, 15, or 18 years old and then followed them for 13 years. Men and women who had separated or divorced during that period were more depressed and had more alcohol problems than those who remained married. The question arises as to whether these problems were a *result* of marital dissolution or *caused* the marriages to dissolve. To address this question, the investigators compared the baseline rates of depression and alcohol use in the people who remained married to those who separated or divorced. They found evidence that the relation between marital dissolution and distress indicators was reciprocal. Taking initial levels of depression and alcohol use into consideration, separation and divorce increased distress in both areas for men and women alike. However, it was also the case that women who began the study depressed were more likely to end up separated or divorced. Surprisingly, initial alcohol problems did not predict marital dissolution. There was no evidence that marital dissolution was associated with unique sources of distress for men and women.

Studies of marital dissolution have grouped together separated and divorced individuals. This may be problematic because there is some evidence that separation and divorce have different effects on men and women. Ensel (1986) found that separation is more difficult for women and divorce is more difficult for men. In one study, women who were separated had more restricted activity days and more limitations in daily activities than women who were divorced, but the reverse occurred for men (Riessman & Gerstel, 1985).

Other studies have found a different pattern of results by comparing distress before and after separation. In one study, women were more distressed than men prior to the separation, but after the separation, women immediately began to perceive benefits and were better adjusted than men (Bloom, Hodges, & Caldwell, 1983). By eight months after the separation, men began to perceive benefits from the separation and caught up to women's levels of adjustment. Four other studies showed that women were more distressed prior to the separation, whereas men were more distressed shortly after the separation (Bloom & Caldwell, 1981).

One reason that the findings across studies are inconsistent may be how separation is defined and when during the process of separation men and women are studied. In general, it appears that women are more distressed than men during the early phases of relationship dissolution and men are more distressed than women during the later stages of dissolution.

Is there evidence of sex differences in adjustment to marital dissolution in other cultures? In a study of nine countries (United States, Canada, Puerto Rico, Germany, Taiwan, Korea, Lebanon, France, New Zealand), Weissman et al. (1996) found that separated and divorced individuals were two to four times more likely to have major depression than married individuals, but the difference was greater for men than women in all of the countries except Canada and Taiwan. This is not to say that divorce is without consequences for women. In Israel, divorce is associated with considerable psychological distress and severe economic problems for women (Al-Krenawi & Graham, 1998). In a study that compared Anglo, Chicana, and Mexicana women's reaction to separation and divorce, Chicana women experienced the highest levels of distress (Parra, Arkowitz, Hannah, & Vasquez, 1995). The Chicana women had a Mexican heritage but were living in the United States. Thus, the impact of divorce on women may be particularly stressful when living in a different culture.

Explanations

COPING STYLES.   Men and women may respond differently to separation and divorce due to differences in coping styles (Riessman & Gerstel, 1985). As we saw in Chapter 8, women are more likely to confront problems and express their emotions, whereas men are more likely to withdraw and avoid dealing with problems. These differences may explain why the earlier stages of separation are more difficult for women and the later stages of separation or divorce are more difficult for men. During separation, women are confronting their distress and men are avoiding their distress. By the time a divorce is granted, women will be further along than men in coming to terms with the dissolution of the relationship.

STRAINS. Separation and divorce may be associated with different strains for men and women. In one study, marital dissolution was associated with a greater disruption to men's than women's social networks (Gerstel et al., 1985). For example, men who were separated or divorced were especially unlikely to report having a confidant. The impact of separation or divorce on social ties explained the increase in distress for both men and women, but to a greater extent for men. By contrast, marital dissolution meant a loss of income and an increase in parental obligations for women. Women who separated or divorced reported a greater loss in income than did men. The greater distress of separated or divorced women compared to married women was due to this decline in income. The drop in income was especially large for women who retained custody of children. Men's income did not decline as much as women's; in fact, because men's household size was more likely to decrease, men experienced a relative *increase* in income following divorce. The one study that found greater adverse effects of divorce on women than men (Hope et al., 1999) showed that the primary explanation had to do with socioeconomic factors. The women most adversely affected were those with parental responsibilities and those who experienced a decline in SES.

One conclusion we can draw from these studies is that the dissolution of traditional marriages will have a stronger negative effect on men and women than the dissolution of egalitarian marriages. In egalitarian marriages, women are less likely to be dependent on their spouse for financial support and men are less likely to be dependent on their spouse alone for emotional support. Thus, the financial and support strains following divorce or separation should be less in egalitarian than in traditional marriages.

Because the different strains associated with marital dissolution do not occur at the same time, men and women may be distressed at different times after separation and divorce. Financial strains for women who are parents occur immediately on separation; this may explain why some studies show that women experience separation as more stressful than men. Women who are not parents may experience less financial strain. The effects on social ties may take some time to be noticed, which may explain why men adjust more poorly than women to the later stages of marital dissolution.

SOCIAL NETWORK. I have discussed social support as a loss that men might be more likely than women to suffer upon marital dissolution. A study of newly divorced men and women found that men had less support available two months after the separation but that men and women had similar levels of support six months after separation (R. Caldwell & Bloom, 1982). The long-term effects of marital separation on social support may appear in the shape of the social network. Gerstel (1988) suggested that men's and women's social networks take different forms after separation or divorce. From her interviews with over 100 separated and divorced men and women, Gerstel concluded that marital dissolution leads to an increase in interactions with other network members for both men and women. However, the specific "other network members" are different for men and women. Marital dissolution leads women to spend more time with old friends. The women in this study reported that marriage had interfered with existing friendships; when the marriage dissolved, women renewed their old friendships. Marital dissolution led men to develop new relationships. Although men and women reported similar network sizes after separation and divorce, a greater proportion of women's network members were old friends and relatives and a greater proportion of men's network members were new relations. Men are afforded greater opportunities to pursue new relationships as compared to women due to the nature of the strains women experience following divorce (i.e., custody of children, loss of income; Gerstel, 1988).

Although men may form more new relationships than women following marital dissolution, this does not necessarily mean that men and women have equivalent support resources. The new relationships in men's networks may not provide the support that the older relationships of women's networks do. After divorce, women have multiple categories of helpers available to them that men do not; these include children, friends, and health care professionals (Chiriboga, Coho, Stein, & Roberts, 1979). However, when men and women are asked who would ideally be the most helpful support source after divorce, men are more likely than women to name their spouse (27% compared to 16%).

WOMEN INITIATE BREAKUP. One explanation for cases where women do adjust better to the breakup of a dating relationship or the dissolution of a marriage might be that women are more likely to initiate relationship dissolution. Women are more likely than men to consider separation and divorce (Levenson, Carstensen, & Gottman, 1993) and to initiate the breakup of marriage

(Bloom et al., 1983). In the Boston Couples Study (C. Hill et al., 1976), as well as in my study of long-distance romantic relationships (Helgeson, 1994a), women were more likely than men to initiate the breakup of dating relationships.

One might expect that the person who initiates a breakup would adjust better because he or she is the one who wanted the relationship to end. This may be the case for men, but not for women. In the two studies of dating relationships, men initiated the breakup when they were less involved or less happy with the relationship, but not so for women (Helgeson, 1994a; C. Hill et al., 1976). Women initiated the breakup regardless of who was more involved or who was more unhappy with the relationship, probably because they perceived problems with the overall relationship. This may explain why who initiated the breakup was associated with men's but not women's adjustment in one of these studies (Helgeson, 1994a). As shown in Figure 10.3, men were better adjusted when they initiated the breakup than when their partner initiated the breakup. However, who initiated the breakup was unrelated to women's adjustment. Women were equally well off, regardless of who initiated the breakup.

Why weren't women upset when their partner initiated the breakup? One reason has to do with being prepared. Women reported that they had thought about and talked about the possibility of a breakup, regardless of who ultimately initiated it. Men thought about and talked about the possibility of a breakup only when they ended up initiating it. Thus, women seem to have been more psychologically prepared for the breakup than men. This finding was supported in the Boston Couples Study (C. Hill et al., 1976). Women more than men reported that the breakup process was gradual. These findings are also consistent

FIGURE 10.3 Women adjusted positively to the breakup regardless of who initiated it. Men adjusted positively to the breakup *only* when they initiated it. *Source:* Adapted from Helgeson (1994a).

with those from a study of midlife divorced couples. Hagestad and Smyer (1982) found that women viewed the disintegration of the relationship as a long, slow process, whereas men viewed the breakup as abrupt. Thus, women may adjust better than men to the dissolution of a relationship because they are more prepared for it.

Summary

Studies of dating and married couples generally show that the dissolution of the relationship is a greater source of distress for men than for women. There are inconsistencies, however, which may have to do with the phase of the dissolution evaluated. Some research suggests that women experience more distress than men during the early phase of dissolution; this may reflect women being more aware of problems in the relationship or aware of problems at an earlier point in the relationship. Women

are more likely to initiate a breakup and are more prepared for a breakup. The dissolution of a relationship is associated with different strains for men and women and has distinct effects on the character of men's and women's social networks.

EFFECT OF MARITAL QUALITY ON HEALTH

I have been discussing the effects of marital status—whether one is single, married, widowed, or divorced—on health. Does marital status alone determine one's health? Surely, all marriages are not the same or provide the same health benefits. Is a distressed marriage better for health than no marriage at all? A couple of studies suggest that the answer is no: unmarried persons have better health than unhappily married persons (Helgeson, 1991; C. Ross, 1995). Thus, it is important to consider the quality of the relationship when evaluating the health implications of marriage.

Many of the explanations as to why marriage benefits men's health more than women's pertain to the quality of the marital relationship. For example, a primary explanation for sex differences in the effects of marriage and widowhood on health has to do with marriage providing relatively more social support to men. This explanation suggests that the quality of the marital relationship is different for men and women. Perhaps marriage benefits men's health more because the relationship is more satisfying to men than to women. In fact, we know that men are more satisfied in marriage than are women. To thoroughly understand the effects of marriage on health, one needs to examine the quality of the relationship.

Two types of studies examine the nature of marital relationships. In survey studies, men and women complete various marital satisfaction or marital strain inventories. The relation of these self-report measures of marital quality to men's and women's health is then examined. In laboratory studies, men and women engage in some sort of marital interaction (usually, a discussion of a conflict) that is videotaped, recorded, and analyzed. The relation of specific interaction patterns to health is examined. I review both kinds of studies.

Evidence

SURVEY STUDIES. Numerous survey studies have found that the quality of the marital relationship is more strongly related to women's than men's health (e.g., Husaini, Neff, Newbrough, & Moore, 1982). In a study of Chinese men and women in Hong Kong, marital satisfaction was more strongly associated with fewer health symptoms, greater life satisfaction, and greater perceived health among women than among men (Shek, 1995). Levenson et al. (1993) showed that the relation between marital satisfaction and health was stronger for women than men: in satisfied marriages, men and women had similar levels of health; in unhappy marriages, women had worse psychological and physical health than men. In a longitudinal study of 300 dual-earner couples, a rewarding marriage was associated with a reduction in distress for both men and women, but the effect was stronger among women (Barnett, Raudenbush, Brennan, Pleck, & Marshall, 1995). A high-quality marriage also has been shown to be more effective in buffering women than men from depression after a severe life event (Edwards, Nazroo, & Brown, 1998).

A couple of studies have focused on the negative aspects of marital relationship (i.e., conflict) rather than the positive aspects (i.e., social support). Two studies showed that conflict with the spouse had a greater effect on women's than men's psychological well-being (Horowitz, McLaughlin, & White, 1998; H. Turner, 1994). In one of the studies, conflict with family and friends was evaluated and also was found to be more strongly related to women's than men's psychological well-being (Horowitz et al., 1998). Thus, the quality of relationships in general may be more important to women's than men's health.

It appears that what is important for men is the mere presence of a spouse, but what is important for women is the support of the spouse or the quality of the relationship. A review of the literature led to the conclusion that the quality of the marriage is associated with women's health, whereas simply being married is associated with men's health (Hess & Soldo, 1985). This may be because women are more adept than men at providing the features of social interactions that benefit health. Thus, the mere existence of a relationship with a woman is health-protective, whereas the nature of the relationship with a man must be considered for health benefits to occur.

A study of college students revealed results that fit these conclusions. Students kept diaries of their social interactions for two weeks (Wheeler et al., 1983). For both men and women, time spent with women was related to less loneliness, whereas time spent with men was unrelated to loneliness. However, the meaningfulness of students' interactions with men was associated with reduced loneliness. Thus, mere time with women was health-protective, but the nature of the time with men had to be considered for health benefits to appear.

One reason that more time with women might be health-beneficial is that women are more effective support providers than men. A recent study supported this conclusion (Glynn, Christenfeld, & Gerin, 1999). College students underwent a stressful task (giving a speech) and received support from either a supportive or nonsupportive confederate. The confederate was either male or female. Support from a female decreased both men's and women's cardiovascular reactivity (i.e., increases in blood pressure), whereas support from a male had no effect.

Many of the studies relating marital quality to health are cross-sectional; thus, one must be concerned about the direction of causality: Does marital quality influence health, or does health influence marital quality? In a study of newlyweds, the reciprocal relation between marital satisfaction and depression was examined over 18 months (Fincham, Beach, Harold, & Osborne, 1997). Initial marital satisfaction had no impact on subsequent depression for men but predicted depression in women. This fits with previous research showing that the quality of marriage affects women's but not men's health. By contrast, initial depression predicted a decline in marital satisfaction among men but did not predict changes in marital satisfaction among women. Thus, men's rather than women's initial psychological state seems to influence the quality of marriage. The authors suggested that men respond to depression by withdrawing from relationships and having a negative attitude toward relationships, which ultimately affects the quality of their marriage. Women's depression, however, appears not to affect their relationships. Women may be more likely to hide their depression and keep it from interfering with attending to the relationship.

It is not only the woman's perception of her marriage that influences her health, but her husband's perception of the marriage also affects her well-being. We know from Chapter 8 that characteristics of husbands influence wives' relationships, but characteristics of wives do not influence husbands' relationships. Is the same true for husbands' and wives' health? There is some evidence that husbands' marital satisfaction influences wives' well-being more than wives' marital satisfaction influences husbands' well-being. Whiffen and Gotlib (1989) examined couples in which the husband, the wife, both, or neither was dissatisfied with the marriage. They found that husband marital satisfaction was associated with wife marital satisfaction and wife depression; that is, wives were more unhappy with their marriage and more depressed if their husband was unhappy. By contrast, wife satisfaction was not associated with husband marital satisfaction or husband depression; husbands were equally satisfied with their marriage and had the same level of depression regardless of their wife's level of marital satisfaction. Another study found that husbands' marital satisfaction, psychological well-being, and physical health all were associated with wives' psychological well-being, but characteristics of wives were not associated with husbands' well-being (Quirouette & Gold, 1992). Finally, a study of chronic pain patients showed no difference in marital satisfaction between male and female patients, but female spouses were less satisfied than male spouses (Flor, Turk, & Rudy, 1989). The authors suggested that women were more affected than men by their spouse's illness.

This idea also has been supported by longitudinal research. In a 10-year longitudinal study, changes in husbands' well-being influenced wives' well-being, but changes in wives' well-being did not influence husbands' well-being (Ferraro & Wan, 1986). In a study of depression and alcohol consumption, husbands' alcohol consumption predicted an increase in depression among wives, and husbands' depression predicted an increase in alcohol consumption among wives 12 months later. However, wives' alcohol consumption and depression did not influence husbands.

LABORATORY STUDIES. The studies I reviewed on marital quality and health rely on people's self-reports of marital satisfaction or distress. Another way to examine the link between features of the marital relationship and health is to examine the specific behaviors that occur during marital interactions. Because communication is central to the quality of a relationship, numerous studies have couples come into the laboratory and observe how they communicate. Topics of conflict are usually the subject matter. Health is measured in terms of physiological responses to the interactions, such as blood pressure, heart rate, hormone production, and immune function.

These studies tend to show that women are more physiologically reactive to conflict discussions than are men. In one study, patients with hypertension discussed an area of disagreement with their partner for 10 minutes (Ewart, Taylor, Kraemer, & Agras, 1991). Female patients' blood pressure increased more than male patients' blood pressure. In addition, only women's blood pressure was influenced by the quality of the communication; hostile interactions (e.g., criticism, disagreement) were associated with an increase in blood pressure for women. In another study of personal conflict discussions, the amount of negative interaction influenced wives' but not husbands' physiological reactivity (Gottman & Levenson, 1992).

Immune and endocrine changes during conflict discussion also have been examined. Ninety newlywed couples engaged in a 30-minute conflict discussion (Kiecolt-Glaser et al., 1993). Negative and hostile

behavior during the interaction was associated with changes in immune function and elevations in blood pressure in both men and women, but women showed more negative immune changes than men. Endocrine function was later examined in these same couples (Kiecolt-Glaser et al., 1996). Husbands' behavior during the interaction influenced the production of hormones in wives; for example, when husbands withdrew from conflict, wives' cortisol increased, and when husbands provided validation, wives' stress hormones decreased. The behavior of wives was not related to men's hormone levels. All of these findings are consistent with Floyd and Markman's (1983) idea that women are the emotional barometers of relationships. Women's bodies are responding physiologically to the nature of marital interactions, whereas men's are not.

Disagreement in general seems to affect women's but not necessarily men's physiology. In one study, the disagreement was not even about the relationship. Married couples were brought into the lab and assigned to take the same side or opposing sides of an issue (T. Smith, Gallo, Goble, Ngu, & Stark, 1998). The latter was expected to provoke disagreement. The issues concerned rent control in the city and university admission standards. Disagreement increased the cardiovascular reactivity of women but not men. As shown in Figure 10.4, wives had higher reactivity when they disagreed rather than agreed at two different time periods: preparation for the task and during the task discussion. Disagreement did not influence husbands' reactivity.

The greater physiological responsiveness of women compared to men in these studies directly contradicts Gottman's (1994) explanation for why men withdraw from discussions of conflict. Recall from Chapter 8 that he argued that men withdraw because

FIGURE 10.4 Effects of disagreement on systolic blood pressure (SBP) reactivity. Men and women were brought into the lab and randomized to take similar sides (agreement) or opposing sides (disagreement) of an issue. During the preparation for the discussion and during the discussion, women's blood pressure reactivity increased more when they disagreed with their husband than when they agreed. Men's reactivity was not affected by whether they disagreed or agreed with their wife. *Source:* T. Smith, L. C. Gallo, L. Goble, L. Q. Ngu, and K. A. Stark (1998). Agency, communion and cardiovascular reactivity during marital interaction. *Health Psychology 17*(6), 537–545.

they are more physiologically reactive to stress and less able than women to tolerate such physiological changes. These studies suggest that it is women who are more physiologically reactive.

These studies have not produced uniform results. One study showed that conflict discussions were related to greater negative affect in women than men but greater physiological reactivity in at least a subgroup of men compared to women (G. Miller, Dopp, Myers, Stevens, & Fahey, 1999). In this study, married couples discussed a conflict for 15 minutes. Women reported more anger and sadness during the discussions than did men. Men were not more reactive overall compared to women but were reactive only if they became angry. Anger was unrelated to reactivity among women but was associated with increased blood pressure among men. In

addition, cynicism affected the relation of anger to reactivity among men; anger was associated with reactivity in terms of blood pressure, immune function, and cortisol only among cynical men. Thus, in this study, men were more reactive to the conflict discussion if they were cynical and if they became angry. This study suggests that there may be a subgroup of men who react physiologically to marital interactions.

Another study showed that discussing a conflict increased men's more than women's physiological reactivity, but this discussion was unrelated to the relationship and unrelated to anything of personal relevance (P. Brown & Smith, 1992). In that study, couples were given a problem to solve: 8 out of 12 school specialists had to be laid off and they were to argue for retaining 4 specific specialists. In one condition, each spouse was told separately that there was the potential for monetary reward if they successfully influenced their partner. Discussions did not influence wives' cardiovascular reactivity, regardless of whether they received the influence manipulation. However, men's cardiovascular reactivity increased, especially in the influence condition. Other research suggests that men's reactivity increases when they attempt to influence wives (Ewart et al., 1991).

There is one important way in which this last study (P. Brown & Smith, 1992) differed from the others discussed: these couples were not discussing a conflict in their marital relationship or even discussing a topic with personal relevance such as rent control as in the T. Smith et al. (1998) study. Thus, women may have been less reactive than men because the topic did not involve the relationship.

Explanations

The quality of marriage may have greater implications for women's than men's health because women view the marital role as more self-relevant and self-defining. However, some research shows that men and women rate their marital role as equally important (Thoits, 1992). Thus, one might expect that future studies will show similar effects of marital quality on men's and women's health. In a study of young dual-earner couples (ages 25 to 40), men and women derived similar positive effects from having a high-quality marital role (Barnett, Brennan, Raudenbush, & Marshall, 1994). Marital role quality was related to reduced psychological distress in both men and women. Barnett et al. concluded that marriage is equally important to men's and women's identity in dual-earner couples. Another reason that discussions about conflict may produce greater physiological

changes in women compared to men is that such discussions are more threatening to women. Relationships are central to the female gender role and conflict is a threat to relationships.

Summary

Whereas simply being married influences men's more than women's health, the quality of marriage has a greater effect on women's health. The evidence that supports the latter claim is based on surveys of self-reported marital quality as well as laboratory studies of actual marital interactions. The nature of those interactions is linked to physiological changes in women but not men. Explanations for these findings have to do with relationships being more central to women's than men's roles.

DIVISION OF LABOR

In the fourth century B.C., unmarried women from the Sarmatian tribe shared many activities with men, both leisure and work. To get married, a woman even had to kill a man in battle. However, once married, women were delegated to the domestic sphere of life. Marriage led to the enactment of traditional roles in this very primitive culture.

This is a characteristic of marriage that is still with us today. Today, traditional roles are enacted by a sex-segregated division of labor: men working outside the home and women working inside the home. Who does what in the family, or the division of labor, is an important aspect of marital relationships that may have effects on psychological and physical health. The way work inside and outside the home is divided affects the quality of the marital relationship as well as general psychological distress. Below, I examine the literature on who does what in the family and show how the division of labor is associated with marital satisfaction and well-being.

Who Does What?

"A man may work from sun to sun, but a woman's work is never done." Is there any truth to this old adage? According to Hochschild (1989), there is. She refers to employed women's work at home as "the second shift": women work one shift at work and a second shift at home. Hochschild interviewed 50 couples and found that women worked on average 15 hours a week longer than men, including paid employment, household chores, and child care. In a year, she remarked that this extra time added up to one month of 24-hour days.

Even when women are employed, they still contribute more to household labor than men do. Household labor includes preparing meals, cleaning, yard work, household repairs, grocery shopping, washing clothes, paying bills, automobile maintenance, and running errands. A national survey of over 3,000 couples showed that women spent twice as much time as men on household chores (Blair & Lichter, 1991). Women spent 33 hours a week on household

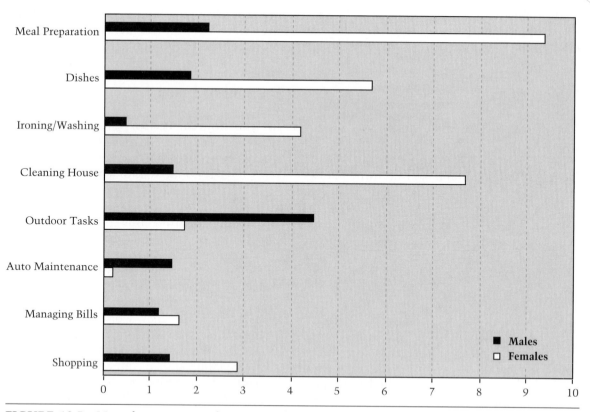

FIGURE 10.5 Mean hours per week spent on household tasks by sex. Women spend more time than men on all household tasks except auto maintenance and outdoor tasks. *Source:* Adapted from Blair and Lichter (1991).

labor, and 66% of that time was devoted to meal preparation and household cleaning; men spent 14 hours a week on household labor, and 33% of that time was devoted to outdoor tasks. Men's and women's participation in specific household chores is shown in Figure 10.5. As you can see, with the exception of auto maintenance and outdoor tasks, women spent more time than men on household tasks. Similar findings were reported in a study of over 1,000 employed people in Australia; women spent twice the number of hours as men on household labor (28 vs. 14 hours).

However, the size of the difference in household labor and child care has drastically decreased over the past four decades, mostly due to women spending less time on such activities and partly due to men spending more time on such activities (Robinson & Godbey, 1999). As shown in Figure 10.6, women spent almost four times the number of hours on household

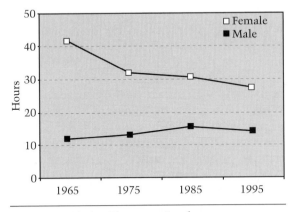

FIGURE 10.6 Changes in hours spent on household chores and child care. Since 1965, men's participation in household labor has increased slightly and women's has decreased dramatically. A large portion of the decrease among women can be accounted for by their increased participation in the paid labor force. *Source:* Adapted from Robinson and Godbey (1999).

labor and child care as men in 1965. By 1995, the sex difference was closer to twofold. The fewer hours women spend on family chores is largely accounted for by the increase in women's employment; in 1995, women who were employed spent seven hours less on household chores and child care than women who were not employed.

Do women spend more time than men on household chores only when married? No, but the largest sex difference in division of labor occurs among married individuals. Men and women come to have more traditional attitudes toward gender roles after marriage, regardless of whether they become parents (MacDermid, Huston, & McHale, 1990). A national survey of over 13,000 families examined the division of household labor among men and women across a variety of marital statuses: never married, cohabiting, married, divorced, and widowed (South & Spitze, 1994). As shown in Figure 10.7, across all five statuses, women spent more time than men on household labor. Women spent an average of 33 hours per week on household tasks, whereas men spent an average of 18 hours per week. However, the largest sex difference appeared in the married group: married women spent substantially more time on household labor than unmarried women. In fact, among women, the highest rate of household labor was among the married, followed by cohabiting and then divorced persons. Widowed and never-married women spent the least time on household labor. The amount of time men spent on household labor did not vary as much by marital status. Cohabiting, married, and never-married men spent similar amounts of time on household labor; divorced and widowed men spent the largest amount of time on household labor.

About half of the sex difference in the division of labor among married

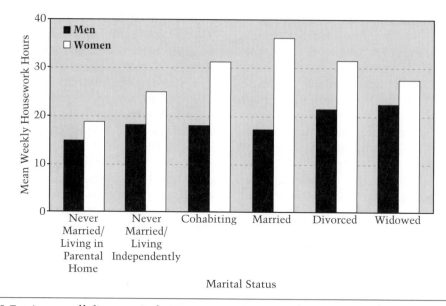

FIGURE 10.7   Across all five marital statuses, women spend more time than men on household labor. The largest sex difference appears among married men and women. *Source:* S. J. South and G. Spitze (1994). Housework in marital and nonmarital households. *American Sociological Review, 59,* 327–347. Copyright 1994 by the American Sociological Association. Reprinted by permission.

respondents was accounted for by the presence of children in the home and by women working fewer hours than men outside the home (18 compared to 32 hours). The other half of the sex difference in division of labor was unexplained. South and Spitze (1994) maintain that men and women "do gender" when they marry. This means that marriage leads men and women to enact traditional gender roles. One study showed that men's and women's total work hours were the same when work inside and outside the home were summed (Barnett & Shen, 1997).

How do people from different ethnic groups divide the household labor in the family? A national survey of over 13,000 households examined ethnic differences in the division of labor (John, Shelton, & Luschen, 1995). White men re-

ported spending less time on household tasks compared to Black men. White men also were more likely than Black men to say that the division of labor in their household was unfair to their wives. Thus, White men seem to be aware of their lack of participation in household labor. Other research also shows that Black men contribute more to household chores than White men (Greenstein, 1996). The sex difference in division of labor is typically higher among Hispanic than non-Hispanic couples (Golding, 1990). Hispanic women and men are less likely than White or Black women and men to espouse egalitarian views of the division of labor (John et al., 1995). Hispanic women and men are more likely to believe that men should support the family and women should support the home.

What Determines Who Does What?

GENDER-ROLE ATTITUDES.   One would expect that whether the couple endorses traditional versus egalitarian views of marriage would influence the household division of labor. A study of employed adults throughout Australia (J. Baxter, 1992) and a study of married couples in Sydney (Antill et al., 1983) showed that husbands' traditional versus egalitarian gender-role attitudes were more predictive of the division of labor than wives' gender-role attitudes. When the husband had an egalitarian view of marriage, he contributed more and she contributed less compared to other couples. Wives' egalitarian scores were unrelated to either husbands' or wives' household contributions.

By contrast, another study found that it was the interaction between husbands' and wives' views that predicted the division of labor. In a U.S. survey of approximately 2,700 married couples under age 65, Greenstein (1996) found that men increased their participation in household chores if *both* husband and wife had egalitarian views. If either the wife or the husband held traditional views, the husband contributed little to the division of labor. Both studies agree that husbands must have an egalitarian view of marriage for them to participate more in household chores.

Gender-role attitudes are multidimensional (Hochschild, 1989), however, so they may not predict the division of labor: attitudes toward behavior in one domain may not predict behavior in another domain. For example, a man who appears to have an egalitarian gender-role ideology may support his wife working outside the home but strongly object to her mowing the lawn and his having to cook dinner.

Rabin (1998) points out that men's and women's gender-role attitudes are changing and undergoing some negotiation. She refers to the **gender tension line** as the point at which people feel uncomfortable with further change: "The gender tension line is that point beyond which the person can no longer change in terms of gender role and still feel masculine or feminine enough" (p. 182). For example, a man may have egalitarian views and believe that both mothers and fathers should change a child's diapers. When at home, the man is willing to change the child's diaper; when in public, however, the man is not willing to take the child into the men's room to change the diaper. Public displays of such behavior cross the line for this man. Similarly, a woman may have egalitarian views of her marriage and work full time; however, when it comes to deciding who retrieves a sick child from school, the woman feels more comfortable having the school contact her than her husband. See if you can determine what your own gender tension lines are in Exercise 10.1.

EXERCISE 10.1
Determine Your Gender Tension Line

This exercise involves some in-depth self-analysis. First, think carefully about the behaviors that characterize the other sex in which you would be willing to engage. Start with a domain of behavior, such as appearance. For example, "I am a woman and I would be willing to wear a suit." Then, keep upping the stakes until you find a behavior that "crosses the line" for you. For example, "I would be unwilling to have hair transplanted into my face so that I could have a beard." Do the same for at least two other domains, such as leisure interests, how you behave in relationships with friends or with a romantic partner, how you would divide the household chores in your family, and so on.

POWER. There are indicators of power in the marital relationship that may affect the division of labor in the family. Two such indicators are education and income. Several studies have shown that husbands contribute more to household labor when wives have higher education and higher income (Blair & Lichter, 1991). J. Baxter (1992) found that as the income gap increased (men more than women), women spent more time on child care and household chores. A more equal contribution to income was associated with a more egalitarian division of labor in terms of household chores and child care. The income gap, however, influenced men's participation rates more than women's. In other words, high-income men were especially unlikely to spend time on household labor. One study showed that the effect of income disparity on men's participation in household chores depended on the nature of men's job (Arrighi & Maume, 2000). When men's and women's earnings were similar, men who held subordinate positions at work were especially unlikely to participate in household chores. When the nature of men's jobs threatens their masculinity (i.e., lack of autonomy, lack of control), they may be reluctant to perform tasks at home that are viewed as part of the female role. When men had much higher income than women (affirming their masculinity), job subordination had less effect on participation in household chores.

Blair and Lichter (1991) point out that even among the most highly educated couples and among couples in which the wife has a high income, division of labor is still sex-segregated. Thus, there may be other societal bases of power differences between men and women that explain why the division of labor at home is unequal when employment, income, and education are equal.

WORK OUTSIDE THE HOME. Who does what inside the home is bound to be influenced by who does what outside the home. If one partner works full time (usually the husband) and one works part time or not at all (usually the wife), would a 50/50 split on household chores really be an equitable arrangement? Several studies have found that the number of hours people work outside the home influences the division of labor at home. One study showed that the amount of time husbands and wives spent at work influenced the amount of time husbands spent on household chores (Greenstein, 1996). The more hours husbands worked outside the home, the fewer hours they worked inside the home. The more hours wives worked outside the home, the more hours husbands worked inside the home. By contrast, another study found that only the husband's employment influenced the division of labor within the home (Blair & Lichter, 1991); the number of hours a wife worked outside the home had no effect on the division of labor. A study of dual-earner couples employed in either an academic or a business setting revealed findings consistent with both of these studies. Among academics, the longer one spouse worked, the more the other spouse engaged in child care (Biernat & Wortman, 1991). Among the business couples, however, only the husband's hours at work influenced the amount of time spent on child care. The academic couples may have had less traditional gender-role attitudes than the business couples. Thus, hours of paid employment may interact with other variables such as gender-role attitudes to predict division of labor.

It is important to distinguish child care tasks from other household tasks when evaluating the effect of employment on the division of labor, at least for women. In a study of over 1,000 employed people in Australia, the number of hours women worked outside the home was unrelated to the overall division of labor at home, because work outside the home was related to more time spent with children and less time spent on household chores (J. Baxter, 1992). The authors suggested that employed women who spent considerable time at work may have compensated for their lack of time at home by spending proportionally more home time with children. These women spent less time on household chores, so less housework was completed. The more hours men worked outside the home, the less time they spent with children and the less time they spent on household chores.

SEXUAL ORIENTATION.   One way to understand whether there are universal gender roles with respect to the division of labor is to study homosexual couples. Is it always the case that one person performs the traditionally masculine chores (e.g., mow the lawn, take out the garbage) and one person performs the traditionally feminine chores (e.g., prepare the meal, wash the dishes)?

Kurdek (1993) found that there was no variable in homosexual relationships that determined the division of labor to the extent that sex did in heterosexual relationships. Division of labor does not appear to be divided into two distinct roles among lesbian and gay couples. Each partner may specialize in a set of tasks, but it is unlikely that those tasks will be divided up between the two in terms of gender roles (i.e., one person performs all of the masculine tasks; Peplau, 1991). For example, in one study of lesbians, participation in traditionally masculine tasks (e.g., driving, household repairs) was unrelated to participation in traditionally feminine tasks (cooking, cleaning; M. Caldwell & Peplau, 1984). If one person in the couple performed all of the masculine tasks and the other performed all of the feminine tasks, one would expect a high negative correlation between the two domains. Instead, there was zero correlation.

There seems to be a more equal division of labor for household chores among homosexual than heterosexual couples. Kurdek (1993) found that gay and lesbian couples were more likely than heterosexual couples to share tasks by evenly dividing the chores. In addition, lesbians were more likely than gay men or heterosexuals to share tasks in a second way: by performing the tasks together, for example, by going grocery shopping together.

Two studies have examined the division of labor among lesbian couples with children. One study showed an inequity in the division of labor between biological and nonbiological mothers with respect to child care but not with respect to household labor (Patterson, 1995). Biological mothers spent more time on child care than nonbiological mothers, and nonbiological mothers spent more time on paid employment than biological mothers. Any inequity that exists among lesbian couples may still be smaller than that which exists among heterosexual couples. In a second study, the division of labor among lesbian couples was compared to heterosexual couples (R. Chan, Brooks, Raboy, & Patterson, 1998). Both couples had a child via insemination from an anonymous donor. Lesbian parents had more equal rates of participation in child care compared to heterosexual couples. The investigators noted that heterosexual women preferred greater involvement on the part of their partner, but heterosexual men were satisfied with their level of child care participation. Thus, the importance of equality in the division of labor may be more a function of sex (being female) than of sexual orientation.

These findings indicate that the differential status of men and women in heterosexual couples may contribute to the uneven division of labor. In homosexual couples, the status of one's partner based on gender is equal and the division of labor is more evenly divided. In Kurdek's (1993) comparison of heterosexual and homosexual couples, men's and women's income was associated with lower participation in household chores among heterosexual couples but was unrelated to household chores among homosexual couples. Insofar as income implies status, status seems to have a greater influence on the division of labor in heterosexual than homosexual couples.

Satisfaction

Are men and women satisfied with an unfair division of labor? Apparently not, at least among women. Cohabiting and married women are more likely than their male counterparts to cite division of labor as a problem in their relationship (J. Cunningham et al., 1982). In a study of dual-income couples, more men than women were satisfied with the division of labor when it was unequal (77% vs. 55%; Fish, New, & Van Cleave, 1992).

Studies suggest that an equal division of labor is more important to women's than men's marital satisfaction. In a study of married couples in Israel, an egalitarian division of labor predicted wives' marital satisfaction but was unrelated to husbands' marital satisfaction (Rabin & Shapira-Berman, 1997). The amount of housework conducted by men is directly related to women's marital commitment (Canary & Stafford, 1992) and marital conflict (Perry-Jenkins & Folk, 1994). Hochschild (1989) found that couples were happier when men participated more in household labor, regardless of couples' gender-role ideology. Even in preindustrial societies, role sharing is a strong predictor of marital quality (Hendrix, 1997).

Not all women value an equal division of labor. In a study that compared middle-class men and women to working-class men and women, working-class men and women reported less conflict in their relationship when the woman performed more household chores (Perry-Jenkins & Folk, 1994). By contrast, middle-class women, but not men, had more conflict if they perceived the division of labor as unfair. Women who work part time may be more comfortable with an uneven division of labor at home. In one study, an unequal division of labor was associated with feeling unsupported by the husband and with more depression among women who worked full time but not women who worked part time (Pina & Bengtson, 1993). The gender-role attitudes of the couple also determine whether a traditional division of labor is a source of distress. Pina and Bengtson found that traditional women who worked outside the home did not seem upset by an unequal division of labor. By contrast, employed women with egalitarian views felt unsupported by their husband, had less marital satisfaction, and were more depressed if the division of labor was unequal. Interestingly, a more equal division of labor is associated with more conflict in families where husband and wife have traditional attitudes (MacDermid et al., 1990). Thus, lower-class women, women who work part time, and women with traditional gender-role attitudes may not be as upset by an unequal division of labor.

The concept of an equitable division of labor may differ for men and women. In one study of married couples in Israel, both men and women reported that women did more around the home compared to men, but men viewed this relationship as egalitarian and women did not (Rabin & Shapira-Berman, 1997). Wives' concept of fairness meant equal decision making and equal participation in household chores. By contrast, men's concept of fairness meant that men had more power in decision making and did fewer household chores. This is an impossible situation. If men's and women's definitions conflict in this way, marriage will never seem fair to both men and women.

Although women are generally happier when men contribute to household chores, men do not have to perform half of the chores for women to be satisfied. In fact, rarely is household labor divided 50/50, even when men and women work equally outside the home. Why are women satisfied with an "unequal" division of labor? One answer has to do with women's comparison referents (Hawkins, Marshall, & Meiners, 1995; Hochschild, 1989; L. Thompson, 1991). Women compare their own household participation rate to those of other women rather than that of their husband. One comparison referent for women is the "superwoman," the woman who does it all, who works full time without disrupting family and household responsibilities (L. Thompson, 1991). Women compare their husband's participation rate to those of other men. They may be satisfied that their husband performs 25% of the household chores because the neighbor's husband doesn't participate in *any* household chores. Wives' evaluations of husbands' assistance at home may become even more favorable if the comparison referents become men of previous generations: fathers or grandfathers. Thus, one reason women are not as dissatisfied with the division of labor as one would expect is that they do not directly compare themselves to men. When women are forced to compare their own participation rate to that of their husband, satisfaction decreases (Hawkins et al., 1995). Test this idea yourself in Exercise 10.2.

Effects on Well-Being

There are two contrasting views on how the division of labor should be related to psychological well-being. One view says that the more power we have, the less depressed

---

EXERCISE 10.2
Comparison Referents

Interview a few college students who are involved in a romantic relationship with someone they live with. These people can be married or cohabiting. First, try to find out who does what in the relationship. Second, try to find out the rationale for this division of labor. Third, ask about their perceptions of fairness: Is the division of labor fair? How do they decide if it is fair? Ask about comparison referents; that is, to whom do they compare themselves when judging the fairness of how much time they spend on household tasks?

---

we are. If that is the case, we should be happiest and least distressed when we are responsible for no household chores. An alternative view that may make more sense in the context of relationships is that an equitable or fair distribution of power is related to less distress. There was some evidence for both views in a national sample of married couples (Mirowsky, 1985). Greater power, in terms of deciding where to live, where to take a vacation, and whether to move was associated with less depression—up to a point. At that point, too much power was not healthy because it reflected greater inequity in the relationship.

If the division of labor has stronger implications for women's marital satisfaction, one would expect that the division of labor also would have stronger implications for women's health. Hochschild (1989) suggests that women suffer from the "second shift" in terms of fatigue, sickness, and emotional exhaustion. In a study of Hispanic and non-Hispanic White men and women, amount of housework was associated with household strain for women but not men. However, household strain was associated with depression for both men and women (Golding, 1990). In another study, women's greater participation in household labor was associated with depression in women and accounted for part of women's higher rates of depression compared to men (Bird, 1999). The amount of time women spent on housework was not as strongly related to depression as their perception of equity. What is important to women is not an equal division of labor but the perception of an equitable or fair division of labor.

If men do not contribute to household chores, they pay a price for women conducting the second shift (Hochschild, 1989). The price may take the form of wives' resentment, of negative effects on the marital relationship, and of husbands being shut out from relationships with children.

Again, it is important to distinguish household chores from child care. One study showed that participation in child care was associated with less distress among fathers (Ozer, Barnett, Brennan, & Sperling, 1998). The relation of child care to distress for mothers was more complicated. On the one hand, time spent with children was associated with less distress among mothers. However, the more time mothers spent with children compared to fathers, the lower mothers' marital satisfaction, which then had the effect of increasing mothers' distress.

Summary

The sex difference in the division of labor has decreased over the past 40 years, largely due to the increase of women in the employed labor force. Yet, even when women work outside the home, they spend more time than men on household labor and child care. One determinant of the division of labor is people's gender-role attitudes, and the husband's attitude is a stronger predictor than the wife's. For the division of labor to be more equal, the husband must have an egalitarian gender-role attitude. Power is a major determinant of the division of labor. The person who makes more money, works more hours outside the home, and has a higher education typically participates less in household labor, especially when that person is male. However, power is inherent in gender roles. This is one reason why women perform more household labor than men even when men's and women's social roles are the same. This also explains why the husband's gender-role attitudes, income, hours of work outside the home, and education are more predictive of the division of labor than those same attributes of the wife. The linking of the division of labor to gender roles occurs in heterosexual couples but not homosexual couples; homosexual couples adopt a more egalitarian division of labor and do not divide tasks along gender lines.

The inequity in the division of labor is a prominent source of marital distress for women and may be a source of ill health. What is surprising is that women aren't more dissatisfied with this state of affairs. Women do not necessarily want an equal division of labor; they want an equitable or fair division of labor, and a 50/50 split may not be necessary for women to perceive fairness. One source of information that women use to derive estimates of fairness is social comparison. Women do not compare their husband's contributions to their own contributions; instead, women compare their husband's contributions to those of other men. This kind of comparison usually results in a more favorable view of men and leaves women more satisfied.

EFFECT OF SOCIAL SUPPORT ON HEALTH

So far in this chapter we have examined the relation of marriage or marital-like relationships to health. However, people have relationships with individuals other than their spouse or partner, such as family, friends, and neighbors. These relationships act as sources of social support. Do men and women differ in the amount of support they receive from these other network members? Does support from network members produce the same health benefits for men and women? First, I review the literature that compares the amount and nature of men's and women's social support. Then, I turn to the question of how support is related to health for men and women.

Sex Comparisons

Social support has a wide variety of meanings. To compare men's and women's social support, we need to distinguish among these different meanings. First, there are quantitative dimensions of support and qualitative dimensions of support. Quantitative dimensions are referred to as **structural** measures of support; these measures typically assess the size of a social network or the number of social relations. Qualitative dimensions are referred to as **functional** measures of support because they address the question of what functions networks serve; network members may provide emotional support (love, caring, concern), instrumental support (concrete assistance, such as running an errand), or informational support (guidance, advice). In a review of the literature on gender and support, Belle (1987) concluded that women's networks were more "intensive" but men's networks were more "extensive." This would suggest that women come out ahead on the functional aspects of support but men come out ahead on the structural aspects of support.

STRUCTURAL SUPPORT. It is unclear whether there are sex differences in structural measures of support. Some studies show that men have larger social networks compared to women (Berkman, Vaccarino, & Seeman, 1993), but other studies show just the opposite. A study of college students found that women identified a greater number of supportive network members compared to men (Wohlgemuth & Betz, 1991). Notice that network members were defined as "supportive" in this last study. Some of the inconsistencies across studies may have to do with how structural aspects of social networks are defined. Do investigators ask how many friends someone has, how many "supportive" relations someone has, or how many people someone talks to in an average week? You can see by the differences in the way the question might be worded that qualitative aspects of support could be embedded in some of these structural measures.

FUNCTIONAL SUPPORT. Sex differences in support functions are more clear. Women are more likely than men to receive support (Belle, 1987) and to perceive that support is available from network members (T. Butler, Giordano, & Neren, 1985; Wohlgemuth & Betz, 1991). Women also are more satisfied than men with the support they receive from network members (Antonucci & Akiyama, 1987; Belle, 1987; Wohlgemuth & Betz, 1991). Sex differences in the functional aspects of support seem to be notably strong for emotional support. Men are especially less likely than women to have someone available to talk to when they are distressed (Matthews, Stansfeld, & Power, 1999). In a study of undergraduates, there were no sex differences in receipt of instrumental or informational support, but women reported greater emotional support (Stokes & Wilson, 1984). Even among the elderly, women report greater emotional support (Seeman et al., 1994).

Sex differences in perceptions of, receipt of, and satisfaction with support may have to do with the female gender role more than female sex. Femininity, or communion, has been related to perceived support (Burda, Vaux, & Schill, 1984; Helgeson & Fritz, 1996) and to support satisfaction (Krames, England, & Flett, 1988).

SEEKING SUPPORT.   Women of all ages are more likely than men to seek support during times of stress (Belle, 1987; T. Butler et al., 1985). Women report that they are more likely than men to confide in others (Antonucci & Akiyama, 1987). Support from other network members may offset a lack of support from a spouse for women. In one study, women with a poor quality marriage were less distressed following a severe life event if they sought support from other network members (Edwards et al., 1998). For men, seeking support outside the marriage was associated with an *increase* in depression (Edwards et al., 1998); thus, men seem to suffer if they have to turn to others for support aside from their spouse. This is consistent with other research that shows men in happy marriages self-disclose to their spouse, but men in unhappy marriages self-disclose to no one (Gottman, 1994). Wives, by contrast, self-disclose to others aside from their spouse despite their level of marital satisfaction. Thus, women have other sources of support available to them besides their spouse.

When men do seek support, it is most likely to be from a woman. College males reported that they received more emotional support from their female than male friends (Burda & Vaux, 1987). Medical students,

both male and female, were more likely to identify female than male support sources (Flaherty & Richman, 1989). In married couples, men are more likely than women to name their spouse as a primary confidant, whereas women are more likely than men to turn to family and friends for support (Berkman et al., 1993). The selection of a woman as a confidant is not limited to married respondents. In a community sample, men were more likely to choose a woman as their primary confidant than women were to choose a man at two different time periods across all marital statuses (Lin, Woelfel, & Dumin, 1986). The consistency in choosing an other-sex confidant for men and women is shown in Figure 10.8. Chiriboga et al. (1979) found that men were more likely than women to name their spouse as their most helpful source of support even after divorce!

If both men and women are turning to women for support, then it is not surprising that women are more likely than men to report that they provide support to others (Belle, 1987; Wethington, McLeod, & Kessler, 1987). Even professionally, women are more likely to be involved in caregiving; for example, women are more likely than men to be teachers, social workers, and nurses.

EXPLANATIONS.   Why don't men have as much support available to them compared to women? One reason is that men are more reluctant to ask for help. The male gender role's emphasis on independence and invulnerability may inhibit men from asking for help when they need it. In a study of male college students, traditionally masculine attitudes were associated with perceiving less support to be available and receiving less support from network members (Burda & Vaux, 1987). Another study showed a link between the female gender role and asking for help. Femininity,

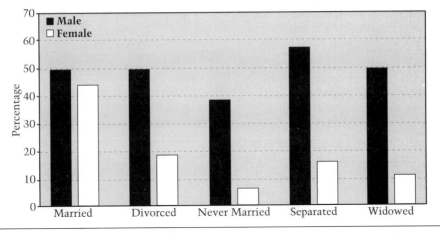

FIGURE 10.8 Consistent choice of other sex as a confidant at two time periods. At two different time periods, men and women in five different marital statuses were asked the sex of their primary confidant. Men were more likely than women to choose someone of the other sex at both time periods. *Source:* Adapted from Lin, Woelfel, and Dumin (1986).

as measured by the PAQ, was associated with greater requests for support during a stressful event (T. Butler et al., 1985).

Another reason men may receive less support may have to do with the perceptions that others hold about men's and women's needs for support. Men and women may assume that men do not want or need support and be less likely to offer support to men (Barbee et al., 1993). Thus, women may be more likely than men to receive unsolicited support.

A third reason men lack support compared to women concerns social skills. Men may be less skilled in activating support from network members (Barbee et al., 1993). Because men have been reluctant to ask for help in the past, they may be unsure about how to obtain help when they really need it. Some evidence for women's greater social skills comes from laboratory studies. In a study of college student dyadic interactions, coders rated women as more socially competent than men (Sarason, Sarason, Hacker, & Basham, 1985). Competence was defined

as friendly facial expressions, maintaining eye contact, making relevant contributions to the interaction, and making communicative as opposed to nervous gestures. Determine why men and women at your school do not seek support in Exercise 10.3.

EXERCISE 10.3
Social Support Seeking

Is it true that men are less likely than women to seek support when they are having problems? If so, why? Have a group of men and women recall the last time they experienced a stressful event. Then ask them to rate how much they sought the help of others. If they check a response that indicates they did not seek help or did not seek much help, ask why. Tally your responses to see if men's and women's reasons for not seeking help differ.

Evidence: Relations to Health

STRUCTURAL INDICES. A number of large epidemiological studies have evaluated the relation of social network indices to health. These studies typically evaluate men's and women's initial health status, measure aspects of their social networks (group membership, church attendance, frequency of contact with neighbors, and sometimes marital status), and then measure physical health years later. A number of these studies show stronger health benefits of social networks for men than women. In a study of 2,754 men and women from Tecumseh County, Michigan, men who reported more social relationships and more activities (e.g., attending voluntary associations and going out to social events) were less likely to die 9 to 12 years later (House et al., 1982). There were weak trends in the same direction for women, but they were not significant. In a study of over 13,000 people in eastern Finland, a social network index composed of marital status, contact with friends and relatives, and involvement in social activities predicted lower mortality 5 years later among men but not women (G. Kaplan et al., 1988). A study of elderly men and women, ages 70 to 79, showed that the number of social ties was related to better neuroendocrine function among men but not women (Seeman et al., 1994). In a study that followed over 2,000 men and women for 13 years, the social network index predicted mortality among White men but not White women, Black men, or Black women (Schoenbach et al., 1986).

Some studies even show adverse effects of social networks on women's health. For example, Schoebach et al. (1986) found that their social network index was associated with greater mortality among White women under 60. In a study in Sweden, a social network index was related to reduced mortality for both men and women with one exception: for women between the ages of 65 and 74, the social network index was associated with heightened mortality (Orth-Gomer & Johnson, 1987). In another study, a greater number of social ties and contacts was associated with *worse* mental health for Italian and Polish women living in the United States (Cohler & Lieberman, 1980). Finally, one study showed that women were more distressed when they lived with another person than when they lived alone, whereas men were more distressed when they lived alone than when they lived with another person (R. Page & Cole, 1992). These results are shown in Figure 10.9.

EXPLANATIONS. Taken collectively, these studies show consistent benefits of social networks on men's health but less consistent evidence that social network variables have a positive effect on women's health (Berkman et al., 1993; Shumaker & Hill, 1991). In fact, some studies showed harmful effects for women. The explanations for the lack of effects and adverse effects on women's health often revolve around women's social roles. For example, R. Page and Cole (1992) argued that women did not benefit from living with someone because living with others imposed demands on them. Cohler and Lieberman (1980) argued that the Italian and Polish women with a large number of social ties in their study also had greater social obligations. Thus, the presence of a social network for women is a double-edged sword (Belle, 1982): it means that more people are available to help women but also that more people will turn to women for help. For example, what happens in marriage when one person has a chronic illness? Women are expected to take care of the family whether they are the caregiver or the patient (Revenson, 1994).

Social networks also may expose women to additional sources of stress (Belle, 1982). Women are more likely than men to

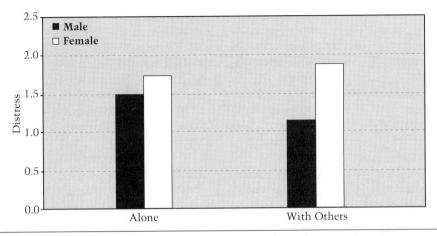

FIGURE 10.9   Women reported higher levels of distress when they lived with someone than when they lived alone, whereas men reported higher levels of distress when they lived alone than when they lived with someone. *Source:* Adapted from R. Page and Cole (1992).

report stressful life events that involve other people. For example, both a husband and a wife may have a neighbor with cancer; the event occurs to both of them, but when asked about recent stressors, the wife is more likely than the husband to identify the neighbor's illness as a personal stressor. One study showed that both men and women were affected by stressors that afflicted their spouse and children, but women were more likely than men to be affected by stressors that affected other network members (Wethington et al., 1987). Find out if women are more likely than men to report stressors that involve others in Exercise 10.4.

In sum, it appears that women are more likely than men to reap the benefits of a social network but also to suffer the costs of network involvement. Women are not only more likely to have social support available but also are more likely to have problematic social relations and conflict (H. Turner, 1994). H. Turner concluded that the positive and negative effects of social networks for women seem to cancel each other out in terms of health: supportive

> **EXERCISE 10.4**
> **The Nature of Stress**
>
> Find out if women are more likely than men to report stressful events that involve other network members. Create a stressful events checklist (e.g., failed an exam, got into a car accident, mother became ill, pet died, sister divorced). Ask a group of people to circle all of the events that happened to them over the past year. Divide the stressful events into ones that the individuals experienced themselves (e.g., car accident) and ones that other people experienced but that affected the individuals (sister divorced). Is there a sex difference?

relations decrease depression, but unsupportive relations and caregiver burden increase depression.

FUNCTIONAL INDICES.   There is some evidence that the functional aspects of support are more strongly related to reduced psychological distress among women than men (Bird, 1999). A study of undergraduates found that perceptions of support were associated with lower blood pressure in women but not men (Linden, Chambers, Maurice, & Lenz, 1993). A study of medical students showed that emotional support was associated with less depression and less anxiety in women but not men (Flaherty & Richman, 1989). Another study of undergraduates showed that satisfaction with support and perceptions of support were associated with lower physical symptoms among women but not men (Wohlgemuth & Betz, 1991). One study, however, showed that emotional support had greater benefits for men than women. In a study of elderly men and women (ages 70 to 79), emotional support was related to multiple markers of neuroendocrine function among men but not women (Seeman et al., 1994).

A prospective study of initially healthy people found that feeling isolated, which is similar to a lack of emotional support, predicted mortality from cancer among women but not men (P. Reynolds & Kaplan, 1990). In a study of lung, colorectal, and breast cancer patients, perceived adequacy of emotional support predicted survival only for a subgroup of women—those with localized disease—but not any subgroup of men (Ell, Nishimoto, Mediansky, Mantell, & Hamovitch, 1992). Thus, two studies show links of emotional support to mortality among women but not men.

EXPLANATIONS. The evidence suggests that the qualitative dimensions of support are more strongly related to women's than men's health. Why would this be? The explanation may be similar to the one that explains why marital quality is more strongly related to women's than men's health. Women's identities more than men's are based on their connection to others. Thus,

variability in an identity-relevant domain is more likely to have implications for health. It also may be that supportive networks benefit women more than men because they facilitate women's coping with distress. Women are more likely to seek support during times of stress; thus, if others are supportive, women's needs are met.

SUMMARY

Marriage is associated with better health for both men and women. Longitudinal research shows that initial health also influences the likelihood of getting married; however, even adjusting for these selection effects, marriage benefits health. The effect of marriage on health is stronger among men, because marriage is a greater source of support for men, because marriage promotes better health behavior in men, and because men are more satisfied with the state of marriage compared to women.

The loss of marriage through widowhood seems to have more adverse effects on men's than women's health. The effects of widowhood on health can be understood in terms of the different strains men and women suffer when they lose their spouse. The primary reason widowhood has stronger effects on men's health has to do with men's loss of support; women have alternative sources of support available after widowhood. Men are more likely than women to remarry after widowhood and to do so sooner; remarriage is associated with health benefits for men but not women.

Both men's and women's health suffers upon relationship dissolution. There is some evidence that men suffer greater ill effects than women. Marital dissolution seems to be associated with different strains for men and women and to have different consequences for men's and women's social networks. The exact timing of the ill effects of marital dissolution on men's and women's health is not clear. However, it is clear that women are more distressed than men prior to the relationship breakup and that women are more likely to have thought about the breakup and to actually initiate it. Women's greater mental preparation for the breakup may explain why some studies show women adjust more easily to the dissolution of a relationship.

Although there is consistent evidence that marital status benefits men more than women, when the quality of marriage is examined, women are more strongly affected than men. Studies consistently show that reports of marital satisfaction and marital conflict have greater implications for women's than men's health. Marital interaction studies also show that communication patterns influence women's more than men's physiology, especially when those communications have to do with discussing a marital conflict.

One important aspect of the marital relationship that has implications for relationship satisfaction as well as health is how labor is divided in the family. In general, women contribute more to household labor regardless of their employment status. Sex differences in the division of labor are greatest among married couples. Factors that influence how labor is divided are based on power and status, such as gender, income, education, and hours worked outside the home. Gender-role attitudes also influence the division of labor within the family. In general, all of these factors have stronger implications for household labor when they characterize men; that is, it is men's gender-role attitudes, income, and hours working outside the home that influence how much they participate in tasks inside the home. Women's gender-role attitudes, income, education, and hours of work outside the home come into play only in the context of more egalitarian relationships.

Further evidence that status and power influence the division of labor in the heterosexual family comes from studies of homosexual couples, where household labor is divided more equally.

In general, the more men contribute to household labor, the more satisfied women are. In fact, the division of labor in the family seems to have a stronger effect on women's than men's marital satisfaction and well-being. However, men do not have to participate equally in household chores for women to be satisfied. It is perhaps remarkable that more women are not dissatisfied with the current state of affairs. A primary reason has to do with the fact that women make within-sex rather than between-sex social comparisons.

Other relationships besides marriage influence health. I distinguished between the structural and functional dimensions of support. It is not clear if there are sex differences in the structural dimensions of support, but women perceive and receive greater support functions. Supportive relations are a double-edged sword for women: the mere existence of social relationships means that women have more support available to them but also that women have greater caregiving burdens. This is a likely explanation for why structural measures of support are more consistently related to men's health than women's health. However, the functional aspects of support seem to be more strongly related to women's than men's health.

Taken collectively, the findings on sex differences in the association of marriage to health and sex differences in the association of other social relations to health are quite similar. Simply being married and having social ties is more beneficial to men than women. For women, the quality of marriage and the quality of support derived from other network members is more strongly tied to health.

Discussion Questions

1. What is the marital selection hypothesis?
2. Why does marriage have a stronger effect on men's than women's health?
3. What are some of the methodological issues to consider when examining the effect of widowhood on men's and women's health?
4. Given what you know about how men and women behave in marriage and what men and women get out of marriage, what predictions would you make about how men and women adjust to separation and divorce?
5. What aspects of marriage influence women's health more than men's health? Why?
6. What determines household division of labor?
7. What is the gender tension line and how has it changed over the past 20 years?
8. What determines men's and women's perceptions of an equitable division of labor?
9. Why do women have more support compared to men?
10. Why are structural indices of support more strongly related to men's health than women's health?

Suggested Reading

Barbee, A.P., Cunningham, M.R., Winstead, B.A., Derlega, V.J., Gulley, M.R., Yankeelov, P.A., & Druen, P.B. (1993). Effects of gender role expectations on the social support process. *Journal of Social Issues, 49*(3), 175–190.

Blair, S.L., & Lichter, D.T. (1991). Measuring the division of household labor: Gender segregation of housework among American couples. *Journal of Family Issues, 12*(1), 91–113.

Gove, W., Hughes, M., & Style, C.B. (1983). Does marriage have positive effects on the psychological well-being of the individual? *Journal of Health and Social Behavior, 24,* 122–131.

Hochschild, A.R. (1989). *The second shift.* New York: Avon Books.

Shumaker, S.A., & Hill, D.R. (1991). Gender differences in social support and physical health. *Health Psychology, 10*(2), 102–111.

Stroebe, M.S., & Stroebe, W. (1983). Who suffers more? Sex differences in health risks of the widowed. *Psychological Bulletin, 93,* 279–301.

Key Terms

Buffering effects—The link of social support to health only under conditions of high stress.

Functional measures (of support)—Qualitative dimensions of support, such as the type of support offered by network members.

Gender tension line—The point at which one feels uncomfortable with the adoption of some aspect of the other gender role.

Interpersonal protection theory—Suggests that social support differs across marital statuses and that social support buffers one from distress.

Main effects—The direct link of social support to health, regardless of level of stress.

Marital selection hypothesis—Suggestion that healthier people are "selected" into marriage.

Prospective design—Research method in which the dependent variable (e.g., health) is measured before and after exposure to the independent variable (e.g., widowhood).

Structural measures (of support)—Quantitative dimensions of support, such as the size of a social network or the number of social relations.

11

Multiple Roles and Health

Life was pretty simple for June and Ward Cleaver of *Leave It to Beaver.* Every morning, Ward, in a suit, kissed his wife and left for work. June, in a dress, took care of the children and had a hot meal waiting for Ward's return from work. The routine was the same for Margaret and Jim Anderson, the married couple on *Father Knows Best.* These two popular television shows from the late 1950s depicted the traditional nuclear family, where men worked outside the home and women worked inside the home.

Contrast that scenario with today's single-parent families where a woman might be responsible for the emotional, practical, and economic support of her children. Television shows of the 1980s and 1990s reflected this changing state of the family by offering alternatives to the traditional families of the 1950s, such as in the sitcom *Grace Under Fire,* where a divorced woman raises three children and works full time in an oil refinery with all male coworkers. Even the media images of two-parent families reflect a move from the traditional.

Consider two shows from the 1980s, *The Cosby Show* and *Growing Pains,* in which mothers have jobs and fathers are very involved with the children. Today, more and more, families are sharing responsibilities. Women, even mothers, often work outside the home and men are more involved in parenting. There are societal signs of this shift. For example, even the U.S. Congress, traditionally all male, began to install women's bathrooms; public places have begun to create "family restrooms" where both men and women can change children's diapers. Both men and women juggle *multiple roles,* in particular the roles of spouse, paid employee, and parent.

A **role** is defined as a position in society governed by a set of norms. **Norms** are expectations for behavior. One role you have is the role of student. There is a set of norms that dictates how a student should behave. What are these norms? One norm is to study; another norm is to attend class; still another norm is to socialize with your peers. A person may have only a couple of roles or many roles. Other roles that you might possess are daughter/son, boyfriend/ girlfriend, friend, worker, volunteer, and organizational member. In the literature on men's and women's health, three primary roles have been studied: the spouse role, the parent role, and the worker role. In the previous chapter, I discussed how the presence of the spouse role and the quality of the spouse role is associated with health. In this chapter, I focus on the implications of the work role and the parent role for men's and women's health. Regardless of whether men and women stay home with children or receive monetary compensation for employment, I realize that they work. For simplicity, in this chapter, the work role refers to paid employment.

First, I discuss how the mere possession of the work role influences health; then I discuss how the quality of the work role affects health. One important aspect of this role that pertains to gender is discrimination. Second, I discuss family roles, in particular, the parenting role, again addressing the influence of the mere possession of this role as well as the quality of this role on health. Because the effects of one role on an individual do not necessarily occur in isolation of the impact of other roles, I address the interactive effects of family roles (spouse, parent) and work roles. An important question that the literature on roles has tried to address is whether having more roles or fewer roles is better for health. This is the multiple roles question. I examine how particular combinations of roles influence health. Whereas research has shown that the benefits of one role can be used to offset the costs of another role (role buffering), it is also true that problems in one role can exacerbate difficulties in another role. Evidence for both role buffering and role exacerbation is presented.

One reason it is important to study the effects of different roles on men's and women's health is that sex differences in the possession of roles may explain sex differences in health. Are women more depressed than men because they hold fewer roles, hold different roles, or value different roles? There are two questions we can ask about the effects of roles on men's and women's health: Do differences in the kinds of roles men and women possess explain sex differences in health, and do roles have different effects on health for men and women? These two questions are known as the differential exposure and the differential vulnerability hypotheses, respectively (Pugliesi, 1995). The **differential exposure hypothesis** suggests that men and women possess different roles, and different roles are associated with different stressors and different resources. For example, if we agree that work is an economic resource, one explanation for sex differences in health is that men are more likely than women to possess the work role and thus have access to this resource. If we decide that the housewife role is a source of stress for women, to the extent that women possess this role more than men, women may suffer greater distress. The **differential vulnerability hypothesis** suggests that a specific role has different effects on men's and women's health. For example, being a parent might be more valued by women than men and have greater consequences for women's than men's health. I examine both of these hypotheses in this chapter. With regard to work, I address whether men and women who work outside the home have similar health (differential exposure) or whether work has different effects on men's and women's health (differential vulnerability). With regard to family, I address whether men and women who are parents have similar health (differential exposure) or whether parenting has a different impact on men's and women's health (differential vulnerability).

WORK ROLE

Women's participation in the labor force has steadily increased over the course of the twentieth century. In 1948, 32.7% of women age 16 and over worked; in 1975 the rate was 46.3%, and in 1996 the rate was 59.3% (Costello et al., 1998).

Whereas women's labor force participation has increased since 1975, the participation rate for men has decreased. The reason is unemployment (i.e., not enough jobs are available to accommodate the number of men who wish to work). Historically, women had higher unemployment rates than men, but by 1996, the rates were the same for White men and women (4.7%) as well as for Black men and women (11.1% and 10%; Costello et al., 1998). Notice, however, that the unemployment rate for Blacks is twice that for Whites. However, the racial disparity really only applies to men. The percentage of White men who are employed exceeds that of Black men (75.8% vs. 68.7%), but the percentage of White and Black women employed is more equal (59.1% vs. 60.4%; Costello et al., 1998).

What is the effect of paid employment on men's and women's health? There is reason to assume that both the differential exposure and differential vulnerability hypotheses explain sex differences in the effects of the work role on health. Men are more likely to possess this role than women, especially if the work role is limited to those who are employed full time. To the extent that the work role is associated with good health, men are more likely than women to reap the benefits. This is the differential exposure hypothesis. As a society, we attach greater importance to men working outside the home compared to women; thus, the effect of the work role on health may be stronger for men. This is the differential vulnerability hypothesis.

There is strong evidence that the work role influences the health of both men and women. In general, paid employment is associated with better health for both (Gore & Mangione, 1983; C. Ross, Mirowsky, & Goldsteen, 1990; Verbrugge, 1983a). It is difficult to evaluate the differential effects of employment on men's and women's health because we expect men to work outside the home; we do not have the same expectations of women. When we compare working men to nonworking men, we are typically studying the effect of unemployment on health. Women who do not work outside the home are not necessarily unemployed; they may choose to be housewives. Thus, if we compare working women to nonworking women, we are typically comparing employed women to women who choose to be housewives. Only a small percentage of the nonworking women will be "unemployed."

The changes in the employment and unemployment rates over the latter part of the twentieth century have been examined in relation to men's and women's health. Apparently, sex differences in distress have decreased in recent years due to a combination of women's increasing rates of employment and men's decreasing rates of employment (McLanahan & Glass, 1985). This is evidence for the differentiated exposure hypothesis. Between the 1960s and the 1980s, overall distress levels increased in the United States, Canada, and Sweden. Yet, sex differences in distress decreased. Researchers have recognized that women's increased employment has had a positive effect on their levels of distress but have neglected to attend to the fact that men's employment rates have decreased and have been associated with strong psychological costs. During the 1960s, 1970s, and 1980s, the increase in women working contributed to a decrease in women's distress, but the decrease in men working contributed to an increase in men's distress. Data from a survey administered to men and women in 1957 and in 1976 showed that men's employment rates decreased due to a rise in the unemployment rate and an increase in disability and early retirement (McLanahan & Glass, 1985). Being employed was associated with less distress for both men and women, but the effect was larger among men. This is evidence for the differential vulnerability hypothesis.

First, I examine the effect of work on men's health by reviewing the literature on unemployment and then by reviewing the literature on retirement. Then, I examine the effect of work on women's health. To do so, I compare employed women to employed men as well as compare employed women to housewives. I also examine the effect of women working on men's health. After evaluating the effects of the mere possession of the work role on health, I turn to the implications of the more qualitative aspects of the work role for health.

Unemployment

A recent meta-analytic review of 16 longitudinal studies (G. Murphy & Athanasou, 1999) showed that losing one's job has negative effects on mental health ($d = +.36$) and becoming employed has positive effects on mental health ($d = +.54$). Unemployment may lead to physical health problems, as prolonged unemployment has been shown to have lasting negative effects on health behaviors, such as diet, exercise, and smoking (Wadsworth, Montgomery, & Bartley, 1999).

Because men have historically been employed outside the home at higher rates than women, studies of unemployment have often focused exclusively on men. These studies show that unemployment poses a serious risk to men's psychological and physical well-being. In one study, 40

blue-collar workers and 40 white-collar workers who lost their jobs were compared to a control group of men with similar jobs who remained employed (Liem & Rayman, 1982). Psychological distress increased among the men who lost their jobs, and was reduced among the men who became reemployed. It is important to note that initial distress upon losing the job was the same for men who became reemployed and those who remained unemployed. This rules out the possibility that distress kept men from becoming reemployed. Instead, unemployment increased distress.

However, another study showed that health does influence unemployment and reemployment. In a four-year longitudinal study in Norway, physical health in 1989 did not predict unemployment in 1993, but mental health did (Mastekaasa, 1996). Men who were more psychologically distressed in 1989 were more likely to lose their job by 1993. However, it is possible that some people expected to be laid off in 1989, which increased their distress before unemployment. There also was some suggestive evidence that the psychological and physical health of the unemployed influenced reemployment, such that the healthiest people were most likely to become reemployed.

Retirement

Imagine that you are 55 years old, work full time, and make $100,000 a year. Your boss calls you into her office and says that you can stop working, keep your salary for two years, and then earn two-thirds of your salary for the rest of your life. Would you retire? The incentives to retire can be strong in some industries.

As a greater portion of our population moves into retirement, this period of life is receiving more attention. Retirement now can take a variety of forms. Some people phase in their retirement by reducing the hours they work, whereas others engage in an abrupt retirement. The most common form of retirement today is an abrupt end to the job at age 65 (Shaw, Patterson, Semple, & Grant, 1998). Yet, because people are living longer, elderly people can consider working after age 65. A greater proportion of the elderly in the workforce, however, would reduce the number of jobs available to younger people. This is one reason that many organizations have offered incentives to retire early. In 1930, 5.4% of the population was over 65; today, 12% of the population is over 65 (Shaw et al., 1998). As shown in Figure 11.1, in 1950, 46% of men over 65 were employed, whereas in 1992, only 16% of men over 65 were employed (Manheimer, 1994). The decline in labor force participation among the elderly is largely due to the increased benefits offered for retirement. The number of women over 65 who have remained employed has stayed at about 10% over this same period. The increase in women retiring has been offset by the increase in the number of women working.

If work is associated with good health, what is the effect of retirement on health? One determinant will be whether the person chooses to retire or feels forced to retire. The force to retire may come from the employer but also could come from family obligations. Another determinant of the effect of retirement on health will probably be whether the person has other activities to occupy his or her time.

Much of the early work on retirement focused on men, as men historically made up the larger portion of the workforce. Studies conducted in the 1970s that did compare men and women showed that women were more satisfied than men with retirement (Quick & Moen, 1998). These women had been in the labor force a shorter period of time and in a less steady fashion compared to men. Because the male gender

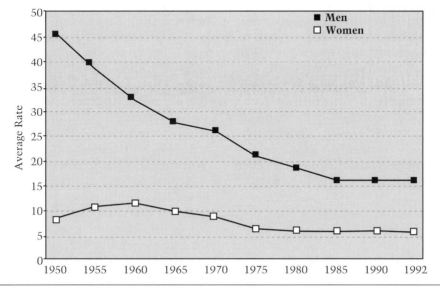

FIGURE 11.1 Changes in labor force participation rate of people age 65+. The labor force participation rate of men over age 65 has substantially declined. Although women's rates of participation are the same, there has been a substantial increase in the number of women who work outside the home. *Source:* Adapted from Manheimer (1994).

role was so heavily tied to work, one concern that men faced when retiring was a loss of masculinity (Gradman, 1994). To the extent that work is tied to the masculine role, retirement might be viewed as a threat to that role. Gradman examined this issue in a study of men who had retired from a large company. Contrary to expectations, he found that the men who best adjusted to retirement were the ones who most strongly identified with their jobs. Thus, it appears that men adjust successfully to retirement by maintaining their work role as a part of their self-concept.

More recent research shows that men are more satisfied with retirement compared to women (Quick & Moen, 1998). One reason is that retirement today takes place in a different context for men and women (Szinovacz & Washo, 1992). For example, retirement often takes place in the context of other life events, such as the death of a spouse or an illness of self or family member. Women are more likely than men to experience these kinds of life events before they retire (Szinovacz & Washo, 1992). Women often retire to assume a caregiving responsibility, and women who retire to meet family needs at the expense of being able to pursue leisure activities are dissatisfied with retirement (Szinovacz, 1987). Upon retirement, life events seem to have a stronger relation to women's than men's adjustment (Szinovacz & Washo, 1992). It may be that these life events are more likely to entail caregiving responsibilities for women than for men.

Women's Employment

A historical explanation of why women were more distressed and had worse health than men was that women were less likely to possess the work role (Gove & Tudor, 1973). As we have just seen, the data on

unemployment clearly indicate that the work role is beneficial to health. However, when women entered the workforce, people began to consider the negative effects of employment on health. People were concerned that women who combined work and family roles would suffer role strain and role overload. People also were concerned that women working would detract from the time women spent taking care of husband and family. Thus, in this section, I examine the implications of women working for their own health and then the implications of women working for men's health.

EFFECTS ON WOMEN'S HEALTH. There are multiple ways to evaluate the effects of work on women's health. Some studies compare the health of employed men to employed women. It is difficult to evaluate the outcome of such a comparison because women, in general, are more distressed than men. Studies that have made this comparison show contradictory findings. One study found no differences in distress between employed men and women (Gore & Mangione, 1983), and one study found that employed women were less distressed than men (Rosenfield, 1980). If women are ordinarily more distressed than men, then these studies suggest that work is beneficial to women's health. However, another study found that employed women were still more distressed than employed men (Aneshensel, Frerichs, & Clark, 1981).

Some studies have compared the health of men and women who work outside the home to men and women who do not work outside the home to evaluate whether work has similar effects on men's and women's health. These studies tend to show that the work role is associated with health for men and women, but the effects are stronger for men. For example, Thoits (1992) found that the work role was more strongly related to symptoms for men than for women. As stated previously, however, this kind of study is problematic because employed men are being compared to unemployed men. It is likely that more of the nonworking men than the nonworking women wish to be employed.

Another way the effect on health of women working has been evaluated is to compare women who are employed outside the home to those who are housewives. When working women are compared to housewives, there is a wealth of evidence that employed women report better psychological and physical health than nonemployed women (Baruch, Biener, & Barnett, 1987; Kandel, Davies, & Raveis, 1985; Kessler & McRae, 1982; Khlat, Sermet, & Le Pape, 2000; Rosenfield, 1980). Even among women with children, the weight of the evidence is that employed mothers are healthier than nonemployed mothers (Gore & Mangione, 1983). However, there may be cultural differences in the benefits of work for women. For example, a study in India found no differences in psychological well-being between women who did and did not work outside the home (Andrade, Postma, & Abraham, 1999).

Most of these studies focused on the psychological benefits of the employed worker role for women's health. Are there implications of work for women's physical health? One study found that mortality rates are higher among housewives than among employed women (Passannante & Nathanson, 1985), but another study found similar mortality rates (Kotler & Wingard, 1989). When women entered the workforce, one question raised was whether women would begin to suffer some of the same physical health problems that men do, in particular, coronary heart disease. If roles influence health, and men's and women's roles are becoming more similar, will women end up with the same health problems as men?

The development of heart disease was studied among 387 working women, 350 housewives, and 580 men who were initially healthy when they enrolled in the study between 1965 and 1967 (Haynes & Feinleib, 1980). Participants were followed for eight years. There were no differences in rates of heart disease between working women and housewives, and men had higher rates of heart disease than both groups of women. Thus, work per se did not elevate women's risk of heart disease. However, there were features of work that were linked to heart disease among women. Women working in clerical positions (as opposed to white-collar positions) had twice the rate of heart disease as housewives. The authors argued that clerical positions are likely to be stressful due to a lack of control and autonomy. Thus, the nature of the work role may have stronger implications for women's health than the mere possession of the work role. The quality of work is examined in detail in the next section of the chapter.

One problem with studies that compare the health of employed women to housewives is that they are often cross-sectional, meaning that the people are studied at a single point in time. (The study on heart disease discussed above is an exception.) Thus, we don't know if employment leads to an improvement in health or if healthier people are more likely to be employed. This is the basis of the **selection effect.** A one-year longitudinal study of 2,436 men and women addressed this issue (C. Ross & Mirowsky, 1995). There was evidence that physical health and employment were reciprocally related. First, full-time employment had a benefit on health: the health of men and women who were employed full time did not change over the year, but men and women who were employed part time showed a significant decline in physical health over the year; women who were housewives also showed a significant decline in physical health over the year. Second, health influenced employment: men and women who had better physical functioning were more likely to find a full-time job during the year. Housewives were an exception; physical functioning did not affect whether housewives stayed in that role or became part of the paid labor force. The authors concluded that full-time employment "keeps healthy people healthy." That is, healthy people are more likely to be employed and employment keeps health from deteriorating. The one exception is the homemaker role; there was no evidence that health caused people to select this role, but there was an effect of this role on poor health.

EXPLANATIONS.   There are a number of reasons the employee role benefits women's health. Employment increases self-esteem, instills a sense of accomplishment, and provides more social contacts. One study showed that employment had stronger effects on the health of women who lacked other sources of self-esteem (e.g., women who lacked education) and other social contacts (e.g., women without family roles; Nathanson, 1980). This study underscores the idea that work may have important links to self-esteem and social contacts for women.

One explanation for the effects of work on women's health focuses on perceptions of control (Rosenfield, 1989). Feeling in control over one's life is consistently related to better health. To the extent that employment increases women's sense of control, it should be helpful. However, if employment decreases women's sense of control, it may be harmful. One study examined the implications of job control on women's health. Employed women were less distressed than housewives when they had high job control but more distressed than housewives when they had low job control (Lennon & Rosenfield, 1992).

Not only is it important whether one's job is characterized by control; employment, in and of itself, has implications for feelings of control over life in general (Rosenfield, 1989). On the one hand, employment may increase women's economic resources and thus power within the family, which should enhance feelings of control. On the other hand, employment may make it more difficult for women to manage household responsibilities, which would detract from their sense of control. Thus, work has the potential to increase resources for women in one area but decrease resources in another. Each of these resources has implications for control. This model is shown in Figure 11.2.

This model has been supported by three different studies (Rosenfield, 1989). In all three, women who were susceptible to high family demands (i.e., women with children and employed full time) were more distressed than men, whereas women with fewer demands (women with children and who worked part time or women without children and who worked full time) had levels of distress similar to men's. If demands were low, employed women were less distressed than housewives. Employment increased women's perceptions of control when it increased their relative income in the family. Women with higher relative incomes had a heightened sense of control and, subsequently, reduced distress. In total, the healthiest women in this study were those who had children or who were employed part time. These women gained some advantage from an increase in relative income that was not offset by an increase in demands. However, other research has shown that part-time employment does not provide the same health benefit that full-time employment does for women (Wethington & Kessler, 1989).

According to this model, the best way for full-time employed women to manage their psychological health is to decrease

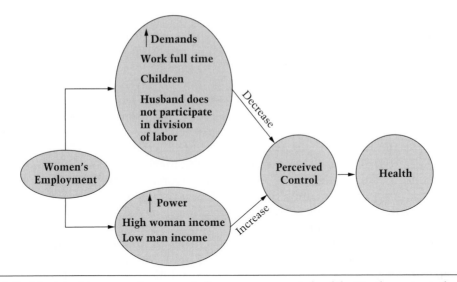

FIGURE 11.2 Model of how employment influences women's health. To the extent that employment increases women's household demands, employment reduces perceptions of control and harms health. To the extent that employment increases women's relative income in the family, employment increases perceptions of control and benefits health. *Source:* Adapted from Rosenfield (1989).

family demands by increasing husbands' involvement in the division of labor. Alternatively, full-time employed women may be able to pay someone to assist them with household labor. One study showed that the work role was beneficial to women's health only when they could afford services to assist them with child care and household labor (Khlat et al., 2000). Thus, the work role may be more beneficial to middle-class than lower-class women because middle-class women are more able to pay for such services. In addition, lower-class women are more likely to be married to husbands who are unwilling to participate in household labor (Arrighi & Maume, 2000).

EFFECTS ON MEN'S HEALTH. It probably would not occur to us to investigate the effects of men working on women's health. The vast majority of men work and society clearly agrees that working is a good thing

for men to do. In addition, men working clearly provides women with economic resources. However, there may be costs to women in terms of men's employment when the work hours are long and when work detracts from family time. These issues have rarely been explored.

Nonetheless, there has been much interest in the effects of women working on men's health. First, do men support their wife working? In general, yes. Men are more likely to support their wife participating in the labor force than they are to support an egalitarian division of labor at home (Kane & Sanchez, 1994). Many men and women still believe that women's primary responsibility is child care and men's primary responsibility is paid employment. In a 1997 study of dual-earner couples, 41% agreed that "it is much better for everyone involved if the man earns the money and the woman takes care of the home and children" (J. Bond, Galinsky, & Swanberg,

1998). However, in 1977, the corresponding figure was 64%.

One study showed that the only instance in which husbands had a generally unfavorable view of wives working was when there were children under 3 in the home (Spitze & Waite, 1981). In that study, Black men had more favorable attitudes than White men, and in fact, Black women were more likely than White women to be working. One study found that men with high self-esteem supported women working, whereas men with low self-esteem opposed it (Valentine, 1998). Men with low self-esteem may feel that their sense of masculinity is threatened when wives work. Conduct Exercise 11.1 to find out what the attitudes at your college are toward married women working.

EXERCISE 11.1
Men's Support of Working Wives

Interview a group of men about whether they would be in favor of their wife working. Start out by asking the very simple question "If you get married, how much would you want or not want your wife to work?" Use a scale such as 1 = I really do NOT want my wife to work; 5 = I really DO want my wife to work.

Then, see if you can figure out what conditions influence these men's responses. Ask if men would support their wife working if they had children. What if there were three children? What if there was a child under 1 year old? What if she worked more than 40 hours per week? What if she made more money than her husband did? Come up with some of your own qualifications. The goal is to try to describe how supportive men are today of wives working and what limitations there are to men's support.

Even if husbands support their wife working, do they reap any rewards from it? The effect on men's health of women working is unclear. Several older studies have found negative effects. For example, Rosenfield found that women were more depressed than men when wives did not work, but men were more depressed than women when wives worked. Wives working may be particularly distressful to couples who have traditional attitudes toward gender roles. One study showed that only men with traditional sex roles were adversely affected by wives working (Kessler & McRae, 1982). A study conducted in India, where sex roles are more traditional than they are in the United States, showed that men whose wives worked perceived their health to be worse than men whose wives did not work (Andrade et al., 1999). There are several reasons why traditional couples might not benefit from wives working: a wife working detracts from the husband's role as family breadwinner, and wives in traditional couples may be working out of economic necessity rather than desire (McLanahan & Glass, 1985).

Fendrich (1984) conducted a meta-analysis of five studies and showed that there was no overall effect of wife employment on men's health. Fendrich also conducted his own study and replicated the null effect finding. However, he also found that the effect of wife employment on men's health depended on the husband's income level: if husbands had a high income level, wife employment was associated with lower husband self-esteem. These husbands may have felt that their wife's employment undermined their role as the family breadwinner. The effect of wife employment depended on the extent to which her income detracted from his income. Men's health was more likely to suffer if their wife's contributions to family income were substantial.

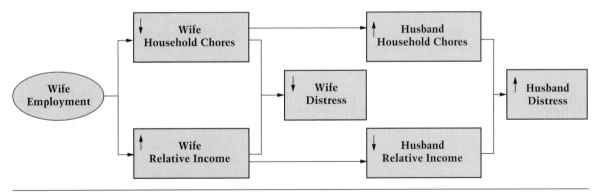

FIGURE 11.3 The dilemma behind women's employment. At the same time that women's employment reduces household demands for women, it increases them for men. Because household demands are associated with increased distress, women benefit and men suffer. At the same time that women's employment increases women's relative power in the family, it decreases men's relative power. Because relative income is associated with a decrease in distress, women benefit and men suffer.

The same theory about work's implications for resources and family demands that explained the effect of women working on women's health has been used to explain the effect of women working on men's health (Rosenfield, 1992). A wife working will increase a husband's distress to the extent that it decreases his resources (relative income) and increases his family demands (household responsibilities). According to this theory, a wife working presents the twofold dilemma for men and women depicted in Figure 11.3. If wife employment increases the husband's family demands and decreases the wife's family demands, husbands will be more distressed and wives will be less distressed—because family demands are associated with increased distress. To the extent that wife employment decreases husband's relative income and increases wife's relative income, husbands will be more distressed and wives will be less distressed—because relative income is associated with reduced distress.

To test this theory, Rosenfield (1992) examined psychological distress in 172 married couples. Women were more distressed than men. There were no differences in the distress levels of husbands whose wife worked versus husbands whose wife did not work. Thus, wife employment per se did *not* affect men's distress. However, to the extent that wives' employment decreased husband's relative income, men's distress levels increased. Men's distress levels also increased if they shared household chores. The effect of family demands was greater than the effect of reduced relative income on men's distress. Thus, wives' employment alone did not influence husbands' distress, but to the extent that wives' employment decreased husbands' relative income and increased husbands' family demands, husbands' distress increased. Rosenfield also noted that relative income and household demands were inversely related, meaning that those who had more power (i.e., higher relative income) probably used that power to avoid household tasks.

Summary

Studies of both men and women show that paid employment has a positive effect on health. The effects may be stronger among men, supporting the differential vulnerability hypothesis, but this difference may be due to the fact that the two groups of nonworking men and women are not alike. Nonworking men are likely to be unemployed, whereas nonworking women are likely to be homemakers. There also is some evidence of a selection effect such that the healthiest people are likely to become employed.

The effect of retirement on health depends on whether the person chooses to retire and has alternative activities to substitute for retirement. Most recently, retirement has appeared to be a less pleasant experience for women, but that is largely because retirement takes place in the context of other life stressors that entail caregiving responsibilities for women.

There is no overall effect on men's health of women working, but there are conditions under which men may be adversely affected. The effect of women working on both women's and men's health depends on the extent to which women's employment affects the division of labor in the family and alters men's and women's relative incomes.

QUALITY OF WORK ROLE

One reason it is difficult to evaluate the effects of work on men's and women's health is that the nature of the work role differs for men and women. For example, men and women are not employed in the same kinds of jobs. Table 11.1 shows the percentage of women employed in a number of jobs in 1983 and 1996. Women also are more likely than men to be employed in part-time positions. In 1996, 74% of employed women held full-time jobs compared to 89% of men. However, Black women are almost equally likely to be employed full time as Black men; 82% of employed Black women hold full-time jobs versus 72% of White women (Costello et al., 1998). Men and women also report different job conditions. Thus, to compare employed men and women, one needs to know more about the characteristics of their jobs to see if the two

TABLE 11.1   Women as a Percentage of Workers in Selected Occupations in 1983 and 1996

Occupation	Percent of Workers Who Are Female	
	1983	*1996*
Airplane pilots and navigators	2.1	1.4
Auto mechanics	0.5	1.2
Clergy	5.6	12.3
Computer programmers	32.5	30.8
Dental assistants	98.1	99.1
Economists	37.9	54.4
Financial managers	38.6	54.0
Firefighters	1.0	1.8
Lawyers and judges	15.8	29.0
Librarians	87.3	82.7
Physicians	15.8	26.4
Registered nurses	95.8	93.3
Social workers	64.3	68.5
Teachers, college and university	36.3	43.5
Teachers, elementary school	83.3	83.3
Welders	5.0	5.0

Source: Adapted from Costello et al. (1998).

groups really are comparable. In the following section, I examine characteristics of work.

Work Strains

Are men and women equally satisfied with their work? The answer to this question is not clear. Two studies reported that men were more satisfied than women with their job (Lai, 1995; C. Ross & Bird, 1994), whereas two other studies found that men and women were equally satisfied (Cleary & Mechanic, 1983; Hibbard & Pope, 1993).

Do men or women work under more stressful conditions? If the measure of stress is the sheer number of hours worked, then men are under more stress because men work more hours compared to women (Roxburgh, 1996). However, on a variety of other indicators of job strain, women fare poorly compared to men. Thus, one reason work may not always have clear benefits on women's health is that women are more likely than men to face negative work conditions (Lennon, 1987). Compared to men, women report that their jobs require less skill (Hughes & Galinsky, 1994a), are characterized by less complexity (Lennon, 1987; Roxburgh, 1996), are more monotonous (Matthews, Hertzman, Ostry, & Power, 1998), and are less controllable (Hibbard & Pope, 1993; Hughes & Galinsky, 1994a; Roxburgh, 1996). Women also report more unfavorable work environments than men (e.g., hot, cold, wet; Lennon, 1987).

Status plays a role in the different work environments of men and women. Women report having less job opportunity and less job mobility compared to men (Matthews et al., 1998). Women are less likely than men to have mentoring relationships at work, which can lead to career enhancement (Kram, 1988). Women also complain of sexual harassment and discrimination, both of which are reviewed in more detail later in the text. Women are especially likely to report these latter sources of strain in work environments that are predominately male (Gardiner & Tiggemann, 1999). Yet, work provides women with a resource that it does not equally provide men: women receive more support at work compared to men. In a study of Canadian workers, women were more likely than men to report support from coworkers (Roxburgh, 1996).

I have focused on the different conditions men and women face in paid employment, but how does the work environment of employed women differ from that of housewives? Can the differences in the paid work environment and the home environment explain why employed women are healthier than housewives? Housewives report less support (Matthews, Stansfield, et al., 1999) and greater stress than employed women (Baruch et al., 1987). Housewives' work lacks structure and control. The traditional female role is to see to it that others in the family (husbands, children) are happy; it is difficult to have control over another individual's happiness. Housewives also complain of a greater burden in taking care of children (Goldsteen & Ross, 1989). This may be surprising because housewives spend more time with children than do employed women. However, the expectations differ for a housewife's and a working woman's time with children. Housewives are always available to children and children know that. Goldsteen and Ross found that women who did not work outside the home said their children made more demands of them and that they had less privacy than women who were employed. Because housewives are better integrated into the neighborhood than employed women, neighbors also are more likely to expect housewives than employed women to help out with their children (Goldsteen & Ross, 1989).

The housewife role is not entirely negative, however. There are advantages and disadvantages compared to employment. In a national survey, housewives reported greater job autonomy, fewer time pressures, and less responsibility for things outside of their control compared to women who held paid positions of employment (e.g, being held responsible for others' behavior; Lennon, 1994). However, housewives also reported more interruptions, more physical effort, and more job routinization. The job characteristics that were associated with depression—routinization and responsibility for things outside of one's control—had opposite effects on housewives. Housewives' psychological health benefited from having less responsibility for things outside of their control but worsened from job routinization. Thus, it is not a surprise that there was no overall difference in depression between housewives and employed women in this study.

Effects on Health

Does the quality of one's work role have the same implications for men's and women's health? Some studies have shown that aspects of the work role are more strongly related to men's psychological and physical well-being compared to women. In one study, aspects of the work role were more strongly related to employed men's than employed women's self-esteem (Reitzes & Mutran, 1994). In another study, job satisfaction was more strongly related to reduced depression among men than women (Cleary & Mechanic, 1983). Finally, in a third study, the relation of long work hours and frequent work deadlines to symptoms of stress was stronger among men than women (G. Sorenson et al., 1985). Aspects

of work also were associated with men's health behavior. Job mobility was associated with less exercise and higher blood pressure among men but not women. These studies show that the quality of the work role has a stronger effect on men's than women's health. However, there are exceptions. One study showed that job routinization was more strongly related to women's than men's distress (Roxburgh, 1996).

It is difficult to compare the impact of job quality on men's and women's health because the men and women who are being compared to one another may differ in the other roles they possess. Perhaps work is less related to women's than men's health because more of the women in the study work part time compared to the men. Or, the women in the study were more likely than the men to have family roles (spouse, parent). Four fairly recent studies of dual-earner couples concluded that job role quality had equal effects on men's and women's health. Two of these were cross-sectional and showed that job role quality was equally associated with decreased psychological distress for both men and women (Barnett, Marshall, Raudenbush, & Brennan, 1993; Barnett et al., 1994). A longitudinal study of 300 dual-earner couples showed that job role quality predicted changes in distress for both men and women (Barnett et al., 1995). Finally, a fourth investigation of dual-earner couples showed that aspects of the work environment had similar effects on men's and women's health cross-sectionally (Barnett & Brennan, 1995) and were equally likely to predict changes in health over a three-year period (Barnett & Brennan, 1997). In this last investigation, the two aspects of work that were associated with men's and women's health were job monotony and job strain. Having a challenging, as opposed to a monotonous, job was associated with health benefits, whereas role overload and role conflict were associated with health declines.

These four studies focused on men and women who possessed both work and family roles. The findings from these studies support social role theory—that when men's and women's roles are more similar (both married and work full time), the relation between the quality of that role and health is similar.

In sum, it appears that in more recent studies where men and women have comparable roles, aspects of the work role have similar effects on men's and women's health. In actuality, however, men and women do not always have similar roles; thus, aspects of work may be more strongly related to men's health. The nature of the health outcome evaluated also may influence the relation of job role quality to men's and women's health. For example, low job complexity was more strongly related to high levels of distress among women than men, but was more strongly associated with drinking problems among men than women (Lennon, 1987).

Discrimination

One important work condition that has implications for men's and women's psychological and physical well-being is discrimination. There are two kind of discrimination: access discrimination and treatment discrimination. **Access discrimination** occurs when hiring decisions are made. If men or women are not offered a job or are offered a lesser job because of their sex, this is access discrimination. Access discrimination is more likely to occur when the qualifications for a job are ambiguous (R.F. Martell, 1996). If a person of either sex is clearly well-qualified for a job, access discrimination is unlikely to occur. Yet, there are some high-status jobs that are less accessible to women than to men. For example, women are less represented than men in the executive branch of government. In the year 2000, 9 of 100 (9%) U.S. senators were women, and 58 of 435 (13%) U.S. representatives were women. The occupations in Table 11.1 show that the proportion of women in some jobs has remained the same over time. For example, nearly all dental assistants were women and nearly all firefighters were men in both 1983 and 1996. By contrast, the percentage of women who are economists and physicians has increased over time.

Treatment discrimination occurs after the person has the job and takes the form of reduced salary or reduced opportunities for promotion. In 1999, the Massachusetts Institute of Technology released a report admitting treatment discrimination (Koerner, 1999). The report concluded that female faculty received lower pay and fewer resources than male faculty. Women were even allocated only half the office space of men. In this rare case, the women did not sue MIT; instead, the school responded to the accusations by conducting their own investigation and substantiating the women's claims.

The **glass ceiling** is a form of treatment discrimination that refers to barriers to the advancement of women and minorities in organizations. In the early 1990s, only 4.5% of the corporate directors of Fortune 500 companies were women (DiMona & Herndon, 1994). In 1996, 996 of the top 1,000 corporations in the United States were headed by men and 4 were headed by women (Valian, 1998). A new concept that has been introduced into the literature is the **glass escalator,** which refers to the ability of men to be promoted quickly when they take positions in traditionally female fields, such as nursing, social work, or education (C. Williams, 1998).

One kind of treatment discrimination is **pay disparity.** In 1997, women who worked full time earned 74% of men's median salary (World Almanac, 1998). In 1970, the comparable figure was 62% (Costello et al., 1998). The wage gap has historically been and still is smaller among Black and Hispanic persons than White persons (Costello et al., 1998). Calculating the wage gap is difficult: using weekly salaries neglects the fact that women's work week is shorter than men's, and using annual salaries neglects the fact that women work fewer weeks per year than men. In 1995, among those employed over 20 hours per week, men worked on average 42 hours per week and women worked on average 37 hours per week (Robinson & Godbey, 1999). A study of men and women who worked at least 35 hours per week also showed a four-hour discrepancy (men 51 hours, women 47 hours; J. Bond et al., 1998).

In a review of 41 publications on the wage gap during the 1970s, 1980s, and 1990s, Stanley and Jarrell (1998) concluded that the wage gap is becoming smaller with time and is smaller yet for people just entering the workforce. One study of the wage gap at career entry found that women earned 84% of men's salaries (Marini & Fan, 1997).

There are different theories that explain the wage gap. **Supply-side theory,** or human capital theory, emphasizes the difference characteristics of *workers* that may contribute to the wage gap (D. Dunn, 1996); thus, the focus is on the person. Today men and women tend to have more similar job qualifications, such as education and experience. The other explanation for the wage gap is referred to as **demand-side theory,** or discrimination, which emphasizes the different ways men and women are treated (D. Dunn, 1996); the focus here is on the environment. The effects of discrimination are typically estimated by the proportion of the wage gap that cannot be explained by all of the personal characteristics that distinguish men and women (i.e., supply-side theory). Discrimination is difficult to estimate, and

its accuracy is fully dependent on whether all of those other factors are taken into consideration.

COMPARABLE WORTH. One primary contribution to pay disparity is the jobs that men and women enter. In a study of college graduates, college major accounted for about half of the pay disparity between men and women because it was related to occupational choice (C. Brown & Corcoran, 1997). Men entered occupations that paid more than women.

Why do the occupations men enter pay more than the occupations women enter? One theory is that sex is used as a factor to determine the wage of an occupation. The proportion of women in a given occupation is directly and inversely related to the wage (D. Dunn, 1996). In other words, a job is worth less if women are more likely than men to be found in that job. This problem has led to the **comparable worth** policy, which states that men and women in different jobs should be paid the same wage for comparable work. The difficulty comes in identifying comparable work. Some of the factors that are considered in developing comparable worth standards are job activities, responsibilities, environmental conditions/hazards, knowledge required, education required, skill involved, and experience needed (Barker, 1996). Many of these job features are quite subjective, making it difficult to develop rigorous guidelines. Try to develop your own comparable worth standards in Exercise 11.2 to see if you can identify comparable jobs.

When jobs are comparable, do men and women receive similar pay? The statistics in Table 11.2 show that women still receive less money than men when they have similar jobs. A number of studies have directly compared the salaries of men and women with the same jobs. In a study

By contrast, a study of young physicians showed a pay disparity between men
and women that was accounted for by supply-side factors (Baker, 1996). In 1991, male
physicians under age 45 made 41% more
than their female counterparts. However,
this sex difference in salary completely disappeared when medical specialty, practice
setting, number of hours worked, education, experience, and the characteristics of
the community were considered. This is
certainly optimistic news for the issue of
pay disparity. Among older physicians (i.e.,
those with more than 10 years of experience), however, men earned more than
women even when the previously mentioned factors were taken into consideration. There were some specialties in which
men earned more than women, such as internal medicine, regardless of age.

One reason men may start out with
higher salaries than women is that they
negotiate a higher salary. In a study of over
200 students who recently received their
MBAs, men and women were equally likely
to negotiate for a higher salary when offered a position, but women received less
from the negotiation than men (Gerhart &
Rynes, 1991). Men's negotiations led to a
4.3% salary increase, whereas women's negotiations led to a 2.7% salary increase. Is
this because employers are more receptive
to negotiation among men than women?
Or, is it because men were actually better
negotiators than women? The answers to
these questions are not known.

of men and women business managers,
women were paid less than men (Tsui,
1998). There were reasons for men's higher
salaries, however: men were more likely to
have graduated from a selective college, had
higher SAT scores, and were more likely to
hold a graduate degree. Women, however,
earned higher grades in college. When all of
these factors were taken into consideration
(supply-side theory), a pay disparity still
emerged between men and women.

FAMILY TIES.   Another reason for the wage
gap between the sexes may be that employers believe they can pay women less because women are less likely to leave their
position for more money. Women are less
mobile than men because family ties keep
women in the area. In a phone survey of
married couples, Bielby and Bielby (1992)
asked men and women how willing they

**TABLE 11.2   1997 Weekly Earnings in Dollars for
Full-Time Employees**

	Men	Women
Managerial and professional	875	632
Sales	603	352
Service	372	282
Mechanics and repairers	581	489
Construction	538	445

Source: U.S. Bureau of Labor Statistics (1998).

would be to take a much better job in a city that was 100 miles away; 57% of men and 89% of women expressed some reluctance to move. The majority of women's reasons concerned family ties (56%), whereas only 16% of men named family as a reason for their reluctance. As shown in Figure 11.4, when the spouse earned more, people expressed more concerns about moving due to family reasons. This was especially the case for women. Women who were married to men with high incomes expressed a great

reluctance to move. Women with traditional beliefs about gender roles were especially unlikely to move for their own job if their husband had a substantial income. Traditional men, however, were willing to relocate for their own job, regardless of how much their wife made. (The spike when spouse earnings is 0 is a statistical anomaly from the logarithmic transformation used to calculate these lines.)

The presence of children contributes to the pay disparity. One study compared the 1991 wages of men to women who did and did not have children (Waldfogel, 1997b). As shown in Figure 11.5, the wages of mothers were substantially lower than nonmothers. Nonmothers made 95% of men's wages, whereas mothers made 77% of men's wages. Men had higher wages than women overall ($11.24 vs. $9.40), but the difference was due to the comparison of men with women who were mothers ($8.65) rather than with women who were not mothers ($10.71). Parental status accounted for over half of the sex difference in pay.

Some of the effects of parental status on women's salaries are tangible, in that women lose experience and time at work when they have children. Women are more likely than men to take time off from work when having children and to take care of children (Schneer & Reitman, 1990). This loss of employment has negative implications for salary. Yet, even when the money lost from taking time off is taken into consideration, parenthood still has a negative effect on women's salaries (Schneer & Reitman, 1990; Waldfogel, 1997a). One reason mothers have a lower hourly wage than nonmothers is that mothers are more likely to be employed in part-time positions, which are associated with lower hourly wages (Waldfogel, 1997a).

A study of graduates from a prestigious law school demonstrated the dramatic effect that having children has on

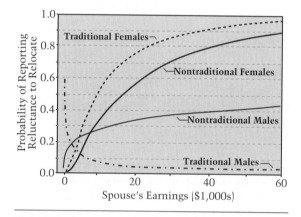

FIGURE 11.4 Women were more reluctant than men to move if they were offered a better job. Women's reluctance was a function of how much money their husband earned and of how traditional they were. The more money the husband earned, the more reluctant women were to relocate if they were offered a better job. This was especially the case for women who held traditional beliefs about gender roles. Men's reluctance to move was not influenced at all by their wife's earnings if they held traditional views of gender roles. Nontraditional males' reluctance to move was modestly affected by how much money their wife earned. *Source:* W. T. Bielby and D. D. Bielby (1992). I will follow him: Family ties, gender-role beliefs, and reluctance to relocate for a better job. *American Journal of Sociology,* 97(5) 1241–1267. Copyright 1992. Reprinted by permission of the University of Chicago Press.

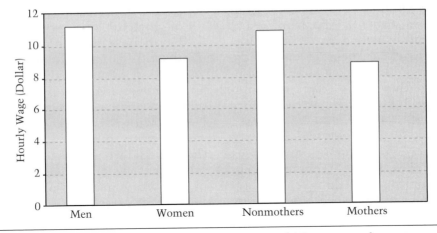

FIGURE 11.5   Men's and women's wages in 1991. Men earn higher wages than women, but the difference is largely due to comparisons to women who are mothers. The hourly wage of men was quite similar to the hourly wage of women who were not mothers. *Source:* Adapted from Waldfogel (1997b).

women's wages (R. Wood, Corcoran & Courant, 1993). Women earned 93% of men's wages during the first year after graduation. Fifteen years later, however, women received 62% of men's wages. Nearly half of the pay disparity was accounted for by women's time off from work to have and take care of children. Again, the cost of having children was not accounted for by the sheer amount of time lost at work. Having children had some indirect effects on women's salaries; for example, women change jobs more often than men, which has negative effects on their earnings, and women may choose positions that are more accommodating to families (more flexible hours, less travel) at the expense of higher salaries. Although few men reduced their full-time status to have children, the wage penalty was actually costlier for men than for women.

One group of women who may not suffer from the wage gap is lesbians. It used to be thought that gay men and lesbians earn less money for comparable work than their heterosexual counterparts due to discrimination (e.g., Badgett, 1995). This may be true in the case of gay men, but more recent research suggests that lesbians do not suffer from the wage gap. Black, Makar, Sanders, and Taylor (1998) found that gay men earned less than heterosexual men but that lesbians earned *more* than heterosexual women. Their explanation of why lesbians women earned more than heterosexual women was based on **human capital accumulation theory.** Heterosexual women limit their market skills more than lesbians do because they expect to be part of a traditional family where a second income will exist. Lesbians do not limit their market skills because they are less certain of a second income. In addition, lesbians have greater freedom to pursue their career because they do not have the constraints of a husband and are less likely to have children. The authors acknowledge, however, that treatment discrimination may still exist for lesbians, which would mean that their pay should be higher than it is.

Whereas family ties detract from a heterosexual woman's opportunities at work, there is evidence that family ties benefit heterosexual men. In one study, men and women were asked in 1990 and in 1996 whether they had received a promotion in the prior two years. At both times of assessment, men who were married were more likely than men who were unmarried to receive a promotion, whereas women who were married were less likely than women who were unmarried to receive a promotion (Cobb-Clark & Dunlop, 1999). It is possible that there are differences in the work behavior of married and unmarried men and women. However, it also may be the case that employers believe it is more worthwhile to reward single women than married women because single women are less likely to let family obligations interfere with work and are more likely to seek a job elsewhere that pays more money.

DENIAL OF DISCRIMINATION. Despite the difference in pay between men and women, it is perhaps surprising that women do not seem more unhappy with this state of affairs. Women, on average, perceive that *other* women are victims of discrimination but not themselves. Faye Crosby (1984) asked women the following three questions in several studies (p. 371):

1. Do you currently receive the benefits from your job that you deserve to receive?
2. Are you at present the victim of sex discrimination?
3. Are women discriminated against?

The vast majority of women say yes to question 1 and no to question 2. They believe that they receive the benefits they deserve and that they do not suffer personal discrimination. However, the majority of women also answer yes to question 3: they believe other women are victims of discrimination. Crosby argues that women are **denying their disadvantage.** She demonstrated this denial in a study of men and women who reported equal satisfaction with their salary but actually received quite different salaries. Although the men and women were matched to each other in terms of the prestige of their job, their education, their job experience, the number of hours worked, their age, and their marital status, the women received between $5,000 and $8,000 less than the men. Despite their denial of disadvantage, the vast majority of the women (and men) agreed that women in general are subject to discrimination and that women do not receive the same salary as men for comparable work. The women in this study suffered discrimination, perceived that discrimination existed, but denied that they were victims of discrimination. See if this phenomenon appears among your peers in Exercise 11.3.

Why do women deny personal discrimination? Crosby (1984) offers a couple of explanations. First, she suggests that it is difficult for a person to infer discrimination on the basis of a single case. We can always find another reason why we did not receive the job, the promotion, or the salary increase: other people had more experience, education, or knowledge. It is difficult for a single person to compare himself or herself to a group of individuals. Second, perceiving discrimination arouses discomfort. If an individual suffers discrimination, there is someone specific to blame. Perceiving that a group of people suffer discrimination (i.e., all women) does not cause as much discomfort because the source of the discrimination is more diffuse: society as a whole.

Another reason women do not perceive personal discrimination is that women feel

10 that the tendency of women to compare themselves to women rather than men was also used to explain why women are satisfied with an unequal division of household responsibilities.

This tendency to make **in-group** (within-sex) rather than **out-group** (between-sex) social comparisons when evaluating wages was demonstrated in an experimental study by Bylsma and Major (1994). Groups of six college students participated in an experiment that involved reviewing college applicants and predicting who would be successful. Participants were told that they would be paid based on their performance. The groups were assigned to one of three conditions: a condition in which same-sex peers were paid more than other-sex peers, a condition in which other-sex peers were paid more than same-sex peers, and a condition in which no comparison information was available. In the first two conditions, the social comparison information was made available by a set of receipts that were left on the table. Participants were asked to rate their performance and indicate how much they thought they should be paid. As shown in Figure 11.6, participants gave estimates of higher pay when they thought same-sex peers were paid more than other-sex peers, and lesser pay when they thought other-sex peers were paid more than same-sex peers. Pay ratings of the people in the no social comparison condition fell between the two groups. These findings held for both men and women. Women also rated their performance as superior when they thought same-sex peers were paid more compared to when they thought other-sex peers were paid more. Men's ratings of their performance were not affected by the social comparison information. On average, men rated their performance across the conditions as better than women did.

Thus, both men's and women's judgments of entitlement were determined by

entitled to less pay than men. In two laboratory studies, female college students paid themselves less for the same task than male college students (Desmarais & Curtis, 1997). One reason women feel less entitled to equal pay is because they compare their earnings to those of other women rather than those of other men (Major, 1989). Because work is often segregated by sex, women find other women more suitable sources of comparison. A basic principle of social comparison theory is that we compare ourselves with "similar others." Women perceive similar others to be women in general and other people in the same job, who are typically women. However, when women do compare themselves to men, they become less satisfied. Recall from Chapter

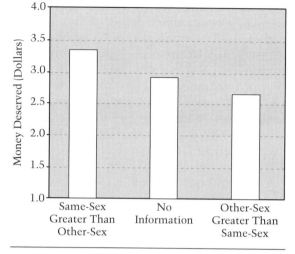

FIGURE 11.6 Men's and women's entitlement to pay as a function of social comparison information. Both male and female participants in an experiment said they should receive more pay when they thought that same-sex people were paid more compared to when they thought other-sex people were paid more. *Source:* Adapted from Bylsma and Major (1994).

what the in-group had received. Women's actual ratings of their performance also were influenced by what the in-group was paid. This latter finding is consistent with research that shows women's perceptions of their abilities are responsive to feedback and other environmental information. The implications of these findings are that members of disadvantaged groups, in this case women, will be satisfied with unfair treatment and may even judge that they deserve it. For women to be dissatisfied with less pay than men, comparisons to men need to be made salient and relevant.

Another reason women may feel entitled to less pay than men reflects how women view their jobs. L. Thompson (1991) points out that women may place a greater value on their husband's job than their own. Even when women work, they typically perceive their husband as the breadwinner. It is only when women perceive their job as essential to the economic status of the family that women might become dissatisfied with unequal pay at work and an unequal division of labor at home.

SUMMARY. There seem to be a variety of factors that account for the sex difference in wages. One factor is that the occupations men enter are associated with higher salaries than the occupations women enter. However, sex differences in wages still appear among men and women in the same occupation, although the size of the disparity is smaller. A second factor is children. Women take more time off from work for children, and this differential work experience accounts for a sizable difference in earnings. Even when differences in work experience are taken into consideration, women who have children still earn less money than men. Finally, when all of these sex differences in training, experience, job characteristics, and family situations are considered, a sex difference in wages still exists, pointing toward some evidence of sex discrimination (Waldfogel, 1997a; R. Wood et al., 1993).

Remarkably, women are not all that dissatisfied with the pay disparity. Whereas women perceive that women as a group are victims of discrimination, the majority of women do not perceive themselves as victims. Thus, women do not recognize a personal pay disparity. One reason is that women compare their salary to those of other women rather than those of men. When comparisons to men are made salient, women become less satisfied with their pay.

FAMILY ROLES

During the eighteenth and nineteenth centuries, men were regarded as the ultimate source of moral influence on children

(Pleck, 1987). If marriages dissolved, men retained custody of the children. Fathers' custody of children was partly due to the fact that fathers were in greater proximity to work and children were involved in work. This connection was especially strong with sons. During the nineteenth and twentieth centuries, the role of mother in the family expanded. Women were regarded as pure and innocent, thus possessing the ideal qualities to raise children. In addition, society began to regard infancy and childhood as critical times of development, times in which a mother's role was especially important. It was at this time that it became the norm to award mothers custody of children in the event of divorce. Fathers were still regarded as the moral authority but became more far removed from children, in part due to industrialization shifting fathers' work farther from home.

Family roles again shifted in the middle of the twentieth century, specifically after World War II, when women moved into the workforce. The roles of mothers and fathers in the family are not as clearly distinct as they once were. Today, fathers are more involved in families. Fathers, however, are still typically regarded as the economic providers of a family and mothers are regarded as the primary caretakers of children. For example, the arrival of children in the family is more likely to bring maternity leave than paternity leave.

In this section, I examine the implications of family roles—in particular, the parent role—on health. Because parenting is a subject of controversy in the gay and lesbian community, I devote a separate section to this issue.

Effects of Parental Status on Health

In general, we tend to believe that having children is good for one's overall life satisfaction and well-being. This is evidenced by the fact that over 90% of women plan to have children (U.S. Bureau of Census, 1993). However, one review of the literature concluded that there is no evidence that the presence of children in the home improves psychological well-being or physical health (C. Ross et al., 1990). In fact, there is some evidence that children at home may be detrimental to health. In a nationally representative study of adults, there was a trend for the presence of children in the home to be associated with greater depression (C. Ross, 1995). In a survey in Sweden, people with children reported a lower quality of life than people without children (Willen & Montgomery, 1996). A study of women found that the parent role was associated with role overload, role conflict, and anxiety (Barnett & Baruch, 1985). The benefits of parenting that do occur seem to appear after children leave the home (C. Ross et al., 1990).

More recent studies suggest that there may be a benefit of parenthood on health, or at least no adverse effect on health. A study of dual-earner couples showed that parents were less distressed than nonparents (Barnett et al., 1994). This relation held for both men and women. Barnett et al. suggested that parenthood may have had similar effects on men's and women's health in this sample because men's and women's roles were similar; both men and women had family and work roles. A study of employed married men in dual-earner families (Barnett, Marshall, & Pleck, 1992), a study of working women (Barnett & Marshall, 1991), and a study of working men and women (J. Bond et al., 1998) all concluded that parental status is unrelated to psychological well-being.

The effect of parental status on health also may differ across cultures. In a cross-cultural study of representative samples from 17 nations around the world, being a parent was associated with less loneliness but was unrelated to health (S. Stack, 1998b). The effects on loneliness were stronger for men than for women. In a comparison of the United States and India, the presence of children in the home was associated with lower satisfaction with home life among U.S. women but higher satisfaction with home life among Indian women (Sastry, 1999). The author suggested that having children is more closely tied to a woman's identity in India than in the United States, where the presence of children often leads to role conflict because women assume other roles.

One must consider the nature of the health outcome when evaluating the effects of parental status on health. Umberson and Gove (1989) found that parents demonstrated lower well-being and greater psychological distress than nonparents, but parents also scored higher on life meaning than nonparents. The increase in distress was most apparent when children were still at home. When children had moved away from home, parents had higher well-being, lower distress, and higher life meaning than nonparents. Thus, having children at home may lead to strains that induce more frequent feelings of anxiety or distress; however, having children may enhance other aspects of life.

Regardless of the mixed effects of parenthood on different psychological outcomes, there may be a benefit of parenthood on mortality. In an analysis of U.S. census data, married parents had lower mortality rates than married nonparents (Kobrin & Hendershot, 1977). The benefit was slightly larger for women. One recent study, however, found no relation of parental status to mortality for men or women (Hibbard & Pope, 1993).

What are some of the reasons that having children influences health? C. Ross and colleagues (1990) cite two reasons for adverse effects on health. First, children are a financial strain. One study found that the adverse effects of parenthood on health were accounted for by the increased economic strains that children present (C. Ross, 1995). Second, children detract from the emotional support available to a spouse. The latter argument is elaborated later in the chapter when I address the interaction among roles, specifically, how parental status influences the quality of marriage.

One reason for the benefits of parenthood on health, in particular, reduced mortality, may be that the presence of children discourages poor health behavior. One study found that the presence of children in the home was associated with lower rates of substance abuse (e.g., marijuana, alcohol; Umberson, 1987). The benefits on health behavior were similar for mothers and fathers. Thus, parenthood, like marriage, may encourage good health behavior.

There are also selection effect issues to consider when evaluating the effect of parental status on health (Kobrin & Hendershot, 1977). Healthier people are more likely than less healthy people to become parents. In addition, parenthood may influence how health is reported. If health is measured as restricted activity days, parents may report better health than nonparents. It is much more difficult for a parent than a nonparent to take on the sick role because of the responsibilities for child care; a parent may be less likely to stay in bed when sick because child care demands do not permit him or her to do so.

Quality of Parental Role

One reason for the contradictory findings regarding the effects of parental status on health is that there are so many features of the parent role that must be considered: the age of the child, the number of children, the work status of the parents, and the quality of the relationship with children. In this section, I examine some of these characteristics and their implications for health.

FAMILY STRAINS.   Do men and women have the same experiences in the parenting role? One study found that married employed men, married employed women, and housewives were equally satisfied with their role as parents (Cleary & Mechanic, 1983), but another study found that fathers were less satisfied with their parent role than were mothers (S. Rogers & White, 1998). A number of studies have shown that women report more parental strain and role overload than men, regardless of marital status (Hibbard & Pope, 1993; Simon, 1992). In fact, parental strain is one explanation for women's greater distress than men (Simon, 1992). Women also report greater commitment to the parental role than men do. In one study, it was the committed parents whose psychological health was most responsive to parental strains (Simon, 1992). In that study, women reported greater commitment to parenting than men did, but the important finding is that committed parents, male or female, were equally vulnerable to the strains of parenting.

EFFECTS ON HEALTH.   The quality of the parent role is more important in predicting health than whether someone is a parent. In a study of women, being a parent was associated with role overload, role conflict, and anxiety, but parents who derived more rewards from their parent role reported less role overload, less role conflict, and less anxiety (Barnett & Baruch, 1985).

The quality of the parental role affects both men's and women's health. A study of married men in dual-earner couples showed that rewards from the parent role were associated with reduced distress (Barnett, Marshall, & Pleck, 1992), and a study of employed women showed that rewards from the parent role were associated with enhanced psychological well-being (Barnett & Marshall, 1991). One study showed that satisfaction with the parent role was related to reduced depression among both women and men, but the effects were stronger among employed married women than among housewives or employed married men (Cleary & Mechanic, 1983). Consistent with this finding, a study of employed persons found that commitment to the parental role was more strongly related to women's than men's self-esteem (Reitzes & Mutran, 1994). Employed women may be particularly sensitive to the quality of their relationship with children.

Becoming a parent may have different consequences for men's and women's health to the extent that it has different consequences for men's and women's other roles. Research suggests that parenthood is accompanied by more changes in women's than men's lives (McBride, 1990), due in part to the fact that women assume more responsibilities for child care and adjust their work schedules accordingly. Thus, we may understand more about the effects of parenthood on health when we consider it in the context of other roles.

Parenting among Homosexuals

I devote a separate section to parenting among homosexuals because issues about parenting have arisen for homosexuals that do not arise for heterosexuals. The first issue concerns whether homosexual persons are fit to be parents. The second issue concerns the effects of a parent's homosexuality on children: effects on the children's gender-role development, sexual orientation, and psychological adjustment. Each of these issues has been raised during custody disputes over whether children should be allowed to reside with a homosexual parent.

More and more children are being raised by gay and lesbian parents. It is difficult to determine the exact number of children because it is difficult to estimate the number of gay and lesbian people. Parents who are homosexual may be less likely to report their sexual orientation because they are concerned about losing custody or contact with their children. Estimates have been made that 6 to 8 million children have a homosexual parent (Patterson, 1995).

There are two groups of homosexual parents. The first and largest group consists of homosexual persons who were once married, had children, and then divorced, often due to the discovery or acceptance of homosexuality. A second growing group of parents consists of homosexual couples who choose to have children. In the case of lesbian couples, one partner may become pregnant through the use of a donor sperm. In the case of a gay couple, the most likely avenue is adoption. Alternatively, a lesbian and gay man may decide to have a child together.

In the following sections, I briefly address whether there is any evidence that homosexual parents are inferior to heterosexual parents and the effect of a homosexual parent on a child's gender-role development, sexual orientation, and psychological adjustment.

PARENTING SKILLS. There is no evidence that homosexual parents differ from heterosexual parents in levels of self-esteem, psychological distress, or emotional stability (Golombok & Tasker, 1994; Patterson, 1995). Not surprisingly, lesbian parents are more likely than heterosexual mothers to be involved in feminist organizations (Patterson, 1995). Among people who have divorced, one advantage that homosexual parents seem to have over heterosexual parents is that they have fewer difficulties with their divorced partner (Golombok & Tasker, 1994; Patterson, 1995). This means that children of a homosexual parent have more contact with both parents than other children whose parents have divorced. In terms of actual parenting skills, one study found that lesbian parents were better than heterosexual mothers at coming up with solutions to hypothetical child difficulties (Flaks, Ficher, Masterpasqua, & Joseph, 1995). Few studies have compared gay fathers to heterosexual fathers; one reason may be that custody disputes typically revolve around whether a lesbian mother rather than a gay father is a fit parent. The woman's sexual orientation is more in question because the norm is for women to retain custody of children.

GENDER-ROLE DEVELOPMENT. There does not appear to be any effect of being raised by a lesbian versus heterosexual mother on the development of children's gender role (Golombok & Tasker, 1994; Patterson, 1995). That is, children in both kinds of family are equally likely to develop traditional roles.

SEXUAL ORIENTATION. Children raised by heterosexual and homosexual parents report similar levels of attraction to persons of the same sex (Golombok & Tasker, 1994; Patterson, 1995). However, children raised by homosexual parents are more likely than children raised by heterosexual parents to act on homosexual feelings. Undoubtedly, being raised by a homosexual parent will lead children to feel freer to express homosexuality.

PSYCHOLOGICAL ADJUSTMENT. It is difficult to study the effects of being raised by a homosexual parent on children's psychological well-being because many of these children also come from divorced families.

Thus, adjustment difficulties could stem from the divorce rather than from the parent's sexual orientation. When children being raised by a homosexual parent are compared to children whose parents are divorced, no differences are found in cognitive functioning, self-esteem, psychological distress, psychiatric disorders, or quality of friendships (Flaks et al., 1995; Golombok & Tasker, 1994; Patterson, 1995). However, children who have homosexual parents are more likely to be teased about their sexuality (Golombok & Tasker, 1994). In cases of divorce, the father's response to the mother's homosexuality may influence the children's adjustment. In one study, children had lower self-esteem when fathers were not accepting of the mother's homosexuality (Patterson, 1995).

SUMMARY.   There seems to be very little evidence that heterosexual and homosexual parents differ in their adjustment levels or parenting abilities. There also is very little evidence that a parent's sexual orientation influences children's gender-role development, sexual orientation, or psychological adjustment. This field of research challenges psychoanalytic theory and social learning theory, which maintain that it is important for children to be raised by both a male and a female. Psychoanalytic theory would suggest that children's gender-role development will be impeded without mother and father in the home because both parents are necessary for the successful resolution of the Oedipal conflict. Social learning theory suggests that children model their parents' sexual orientation, which does not appear to be true; otherwise, there would be no homosexual children with heterosexual parents. However, the fact that children with homosexual feelings are more likely to act on them if they are raised by a homosexual parent may be explained by social learning theory: the

parent's sexual orientation is influencing the child's perceptions of the appropriateness of behavior.

INTERACTIVE EFFECTS AMONG ROLES

It is difficult to examine the implications of a single role on health in isolation from other roles. The mere possession of one role may influence the quality of another role; for example, parenthood has been shown to have a negative effect on marital satisfaction. The quality of one role also may influence the quality of another role; strains at work may carry over to the home. In this section, I first examine specific interactive effects among roles: the implications of the work role for marriage, the implications of parenthood for work roles, and the implications of parenthood for marriage. Then, I examine how strain from work and family roles carry over or spill over into one another.

Effect of Work on Marriage

There are a number of ways in which work and family roles are intertwined. First, the work role may be linked to marriage. In a study of 12 nations, a country's employment rate was positively associated with its marriage rate and negatively associated with its divorce rate (Lester, 1996). For women, there are features of the work role that may be linked to marital status. In a study of about 2,500 employed men and women, long work hours, high job mobility, and job absorption were associated with being single for women but were not associated with marital status for men (G. Sorenson et al., 1985). Because most men are in the labor force, the implications of employment status for marriage has largely focused on women. Studies of men instead focus on the marital implications of the loss of work through unemployment or retirement. First, I address the effect of women's employment on marriage and then I examine the effect of men's retirement on marriage.

WOMEN WORKING. In a previous section of the chapter, I concluded that women working benefited women's health and had no overall effects on men's health. There were some conditions, however, under which men's health suffered. The relation of women's employment to marital satisfaction is similar. One study found no relation of wife employment to husband's marital satisfaction, which is consistent with there being no overall effect on husbands' health of wives' working (Fendrich, 1984). However, there are some conditions under which a wife working has negative effects on marriage.

Women's employment detracts from marriage when there are a greater number of children in the home, and women's employment benefits marriage when the family is small (S. Rogers, 1996). When women work more than 40 hours a week, there are negative effects on marriage (Hyde, DeLamater, & Hewitt, 1998; S. Rogers, 1996).

One aspect of marriage that has been studied is sexual functioning. The sexual functioning of couples was studied among women who were housewives, employed part time, employed full time, or employed "high" full time, (i.e., 45 or more hours a week; Hyde et al., 1998). There was one effect of wives' work status on husbands' sexual functioning: husbands of women employed high full time reported less sexual satisfaction and less frequency of sex than husbands of the other three groups of women. However, in this study, the quality of the work role was a stronger predictor of sexual outcomes for men and women than the sheer number of hours worked. Men had the highest sexual satisfaction when husband and wife had rewarding jobs.

Another feature of women's work that has implications for the marriage is whether the couple wants the woman to be working. Women's employment has a negative effect on marital satisfaction when the couple has traditional values about gender roles but the wife is required to work outside the home due to the family's financial situation (C. Ross et al., 1990). Women are unhappy with their marriages if they are employed out of economic necessity rather than choice (Perry-Jenkins, Seery, & Crouter, 1992). However, women also are unhappy with their marriage when they are not employed, wish to be employed, but their husbands do not want them to be employed (Feinauer & Williams-Evans, 1989). Thus, marriages may suffer if employed women do not wish to work and if housewives prefer to be employed.

One feature of women's employment that has implications for marital satisfaction is the wife's income, especially relative to the husband's income. Recall that relative income influenced men's and women's health. In one study, changes in the income disparity between husband and wife over a two-year period had no implications for wives' marital satisfaction but strong implications for husbands' marital satisfaction (Brennan, Barnett, & Gareis, in press). A decrease in the disparity in income (men higher than women) was associated with a decrease in men's marital satisfaction, especially among men who said they valued the monetary aspects of their jobs. Thus, the implications of women's salaries for men's marital satisfaction appear to depend on whether men identify with the breadwinner aspect of the male gender role.

In sum, there are features of women's work that can have a negative impact on marriage: long work hours, high income relative to husbands, and greater number of children in the home. A major effect on marital satisfaction of women working is whether the couple has traditional or egalitarian gender-role attitudes.

MEN RETIRING. Many couples enjoy more leisure time together after retirement. Couples who are satisfied with the husband's retirement and spend more time together following retirement report greater marital satisfaction (Vinick & Ekerdt, 1989). A common complaint that wives have about retired husbands is that they are "underfoot" and disrupt their routine. These complaints are minor annoyances, however, and characterize only the first weeks or months of retirement (Vinick & Ekerdt, 1989).

The one situation in which men's retirement seems to have negative implications for the quality of the marriage is when wives continue to work (G. Lee & Shehan, 1989). In one study, the husband's retirement had a negative effect on marriage if the wife worked many hours outside the home or had a higher income (S. Myers & Booth, 1996). That is, when retirement resulted in role reversal—the woman becoming the breadwinner of the family—retirement had a negative effect on marriage.

Wives who continue to work are especially unhappy when their husband retires and fails to participate in household labor (G. Lee & Shehan, 1989). Three studies have shown that husband's participation in household chores is positively linked to wife's marital satisfaction and satisfaction with husband's retirement (S. Myers & Booth, 1996; Vinick & Ekerdt, 1989). When wives continue to perform the majority of household chores, marital quality suffers.

Effect of Parenthood on Work

What are the implications of parenthood for work? The effects differ for men and women. Becoming a parent leads to a decrease in the amount of hours women work outside the home but not the number of hours that men work outside the home (MacDermid et al., 1990). Women are more likely than men to take time off from work for child-related reasons. Women are more likely to take time off during pregnancy, after a child is born (i.e., maternity leave), and when children are sick. These job interruptions have implications for women's salary, as previously discussed. A recent study suggested that parenthood might have different consequences for men's work depending on whether men have sons or daughters. In a study of over 2,000 men, Lundberg and Rose (1999) found that men who had sons worked more hours and had higher salaries than men who had daughters. They suggested that men might construe their role differently depending on the sex of their children.

Effect of Parenthood on Marriage

It is not clear whether parenthood adversely affects marital satisfaction (Grote, Frieze, & Stone, 1996) or has no impact on marital satisfaction (L. White & Booth, 1985), but there is little evidence that parenthood improves marital satisfaction. Parenthood does seem to deter separation and divorce (L. White & Booth, 1985). The decline in marital satisfaction is largely explained by the shift in the family division of labor. The division of labor becomes more traditional with the arrival of children (Grote et al., 1996; MacDermid et al., 1990). Women may quit working or cut back on working. Regardless of the division of labor prior to the arrival of children, women increase their contributions to household tasks when they become parents.

Is there less conflict in the marriage when fathers become involved in child care—when the traditional division of labor is resisted? In cross-sectional studies, the relations of father involvement in child care to marital quality are mixed. However, in longitudinal studies, there seems to be more clear evidence that father involvement in child care is associated with good marriages. A longitudinal study of dual-earner couples showed that greater father participation in child care was associated with lower levels of distress in mothers and fathers (Ozer et al., 1998).

Yet, a traditional division of labor is not always associated with conflict. In fact, a nontraditional division of labor causes conflict in couples who have traditional views of gender roles (MacDermid et al., 1990). This situation occurs among parents who believe that wives should take care of the home and family and that husbands should be economic providers, but the wife works out of economic necessity and the husband shares household responsibilities because the wife is not always available.

The division of labor is not the only source of conflict among parents. Another reason parenthood is associated with a decline in marital satisfaction is that the couple simply spend less time together (C. Ross et al., 1990). The time that is spent together is often child-focused. Thus, there is less time for the couple to engage in mutually supportive activities. In a longitudinal study of married couples, those who ultimately became parents spent less time together (that was not child-focused) than nonparents (MacDermid et al., 1990). All couples reported a decline in the amount of leisure time they spent with their spouse, but this decline was greater among parents than nonparents. Parents spent a large proportion of their time together in child-focused activities rather than in leisure activities.

Is there any reason to be concerned with a selection bias in cross-sectional studies that find parenthood associated with lower marital satisfaction? Would you expect people who are less happy with their marriage to have children, or people who are more happy with their marriage to refrain from becoming parents? At least one study ruled out a selection effect. There were no differences between people who eventually did and did not become parents in terms of marital quality or marital problems (L. White & Booth, 1985).

Role Spillover

To this point, I have discussed specific interactive effects among roles, how women's entry into and men's exit from the workforce influences marriage, how parenthood influences work, and how parenthood influences marriage. However, I have not specifically addressed how the aspects of one role might carry over to the other role on a day-to-day basis. Strains from work influence stress at home; strains from home influence stress at work; similarly, rewards from work can enhance home life, and rewards from home can enhance work life. This phenomenon is known as role **spillover:** what happens in one role "spills over" to affect the other role. When what happens to one person affects another person, such as the husband's job influencing the wife's marital satisfaction, the phenomenon is known as role **crossover.** Spillover and crossover effects can be positive or negative. Negative spillover occurs when concerns in one role adversely affect the other role; positive spillover occurs when rewards from one role benefit the other role.

SPILLOVER BETWEEN WORK AND FAMILY. Several studies have shown that strains at work spill over to family life. Three studies showed that stress at work was associated with withdrawal from interactions with children and spouse: one study with women (Repetti & Wood, 1997); one study with men (Repetti, 1994); and one study with both men and women (Repetti, 1989). Two other studies showed that greater pressures at work were associated with more negative moods at home and more marital tension (D. Hughes & Galinsky, 1994b; Repetti, 1993). A study of Mexican immigrants found that conflict at work increased marital strains (Santos, Bohon, & Sanchez-Sosa, 1998). In immigrant families, work conflicts are a threat to the family's economic stability.

Studies also have shown positive spillover from work to home. In one study, having an enriching job (high skill, high authority) was associated with a more positive mood at home and less marital tension (D. Hughes & Galinsky, 1994b).

Spillover from work to family may be stronger among men than women. One study found that fathers' stress at work spills over to the family, but mothers' stress at work does not (Larson & Almeida, 1999). Another study examined the relation between single mothers' mood and their adolescent children's mood at home by having respondents wear watches that beeped randomly throughout the day. Mothers' negative mood at work did not influence adolescents' mood at home (Larson & Gillman, 1999).

The reciprocal effects of home and work strains were examined by having 166 married couples complete daily diaries of their interactions for 42 days (Bolger, DeLongis, Kessler, & Wethington, 1989). Greater stress at work was associated with subsequently greater stress at home for both men and women. However, on one indicator of stress—role overload (e.g., having too much to do)—men's stress at work was associated with a *reduction* in stress at home. Men who were overwhelmed with demands at work returned home to find their wife had assumed more of the household responsibilities; the wives were no doubt trying to reduce their husband's role overload. There was no indication that wife role overload at work was associated with husbands increasing household responsibilities.

The reverse also occurred: greater stress at home was associated with greater stress at work, but only among men. This finding is somewhat counterintuitive:

people expect stress at home to interfere with work more for women than for men. Why does home stress affect men's work but not women's work? The authors argue that men are not used to dealing with home stress, so they have more difficulty containing it. In fact, men reported less stress at home than at work, whereas women reported equal levels of stress at home and at work. Other studies have found similar results (Kirchmeyer, 1993). Even a study in China showed that conflict at home was related to dissatisfaction with work, but only for men (Lai, 1995). Thus, it seems that employers' concerns that women will be unable to keep conflicts at home from interfering with work is unfounded.

Crossover effects between work and home have been studied by examining whether one spouse's mood influenced the other spouse's mood (Chan & Margolin, 1994). Wives' negative affect and fatigue at work were associated with husbands' fatigue at home, presumably because these husbands had to assume more household responsibilities. Husbands' mood at work, however, did not predict wives' mood at home. Thus, husbands but not wives were affected by their spouse's experiences at work. One spouse's mood at home predicted the other spouse's mood at work the next day, but the effects of husbands' home mood on wives' mood at work the next day was stronger. Thus, wives are affected by husbands' mood at home but not at work, whereas husbands are affected by wives' mood at home and at work.

SPILLOVER IN FAMILY ROLES. Do relationships with children and relationships with a spouse affect one another? Almeida, Wethington, and Chandler (1999) examined tension in marital interactions and tension in parental interactions by having over 100 couples record their daily interactions over 42 days. For both men and women, marital tension on one day predicted tension with children the next day. This suggests that conflict in one relationship can affect the nature of other relationships. Only among men did tension with children on one day predict subsequent tension with a spouse the next day; thus, parenthood strains affected marital strains only among men. This is consistent with other research that shows men's relationships with their children are more strongly tied to the quality of their marriage than are women's relationships with their children (S. Rogers & White, 1998). The reciprocal relations between marital tension and child tension in the Almeida et al. study were especially strong among men whose wife worked and among men who had other stressors in their lives. These men may have had to contribute more to child care than they desired, which had a negative impact on their marital interactions.

In sum, strains at work spill over to the home, and problems at home can be disruptive to work. Strains in family roles also can spill over to one another. Interestingly, all of these effects seem to be stronger for men than for women. In addition, men are more affected by their wife's strains at home and work than are women.

Combining Roles

Historically, men have easily combined the roles of worker, spouse, and parent. Today, more women are combining these roles. The labor force participation rates of married women are as high as, or even higher than, those of unmarried women. This is especially true for Black women. In 1996, 61% of married White women were employed compared to 67% of married Black women and 53% of married Hispanic women (Costello et al., 1998). An increasing number of women who have children

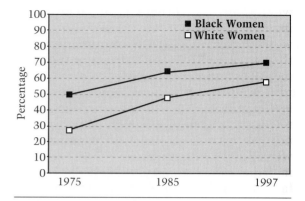

FIGURE 11.7 Changes in the percentage of women with children under age 1 who are employed. *Source:* Adapted from U.S. Bureau of Labor Statistics (1998).

remain employed. As shown in Figure 11.7, as of 1997, 59% of White women and 70% of Black women with children under 1 year old worked. In 1975, the comparable figures were 29% for White women and 50% for Black women.

What are the consequences of women holding the same roles as men? One argument is that sex differences in health would disappear. The **social roles hypothesis** suggests that men and women who take on the same roles should have similar health. This is also the differential exposure hypothesis. However, the same role (e.g., parent) may place different demands on men and women, which could have different consequences for men's and women's health. This is the differential vulnerability hypothesis. A specific form of differential vulnerability is the **gender-role hypothesis,** which suggests that roles are perceived differently by men and women in a way that is consistent with gender roles. Thus, men and women who assume the same roles will not necessarily display the same health.

These two hypotheses were evaluated by comparing the distress levels of men and women who held various marriage and work statuses (Aneshensel et al., 1981). The investigators concluded that men's and women's distress levels were similar when their roles were most similar. For example, men and women who possessed the work role but no family roles reported similar levels of distress. This supports the social roles hypothesis. However, these people not only possessed the same role but also were likely to be faced with similar demands from that role because they lacked family roles. Aneshensel and colleagues argued that the demands on men and women in their work and family roles will be most different when there are children in the household. In fact, a comparison of employed women with children to employed men with children revealed that the women were more distressed. Even though the employed men and women possessed the same roles, they were faced with different demands. This supports the gender-role hypothesis.

Gore and Mangione (1983) also found support for both the social roles and the gender-role hypothesis. Their findings on depression supported the social roles hypothesis. Women were more depressed than men, in part because women had fewer roles than men; men were more likely than women to be married and to work full-time. However, gender roles provided a better explanation for their findings on physical symptoms. Among married people with children, employed women reported more physical symptoms than employed men. The gender-role hypothesis argues that the same social role is associated with different demands for men and women. The presence of children had a different effect on physical symptoms for women due to the different demands children place on women and men. Another study also supported the gender-role hypothesis by showing that employed married women were more distressed than employed married men because of greater demands associated with family roles (Hughes & Galinsky, 1994a). Employed women reported greater inequity in the division of labor and child care and greater difficulties arranging child care. Thus, there seems to be some evidence that both social roles and gender roles explain the effects of multiple roles on men's and women's health.

In this section of the chapter, I first examine the effects of multiple roles on health. I devote a separate section to women's combining work and family roles because the effects on health are dependent on so many factors. I then discuss the difficulties men and women face when combining work and family roles.

The Multiple Roles Question

The question is: Are multiple roles good for health? There are two main hypotheses about the effects of multiple roles on health, which make opposite predictions. The **role scarcity hypothesis** suggests that multiple roles will have a negative effect on health because time and resources are limited and additional roles tap resources. The scarcity hypothesis predicts that there are two kinds of strain that stem from the possession of multiple roles: **role overload** refers to the difficulties in fulfilling obligations for all of one's roles because time is limited; **role conflict** refers to the demands of one role conflicting with the demands from another role. You are suffering from role overload when you feel stressed because you have three exams on Monday, a party to plan for Saturday, and a fundraising event to attend on Sunday. You suffer from role conflict when your grandmother turns 90 and your best friend turns 21 on the same Saturday, and family obligations prevent you from celebrating the occasion with your best friend. In either case, having more roles is problematic because it is difficult to meet all of the demands of multiple roles.

By contrast, the **role expansion hypothesis** suggests that there are benefits to be gained from having diverse roles. The additional resources gained by multiple roles outweigh the increase in strains that might arise from more roles. In the early 1970s, when women were just beginning to move into the workforce, Gove and Tudor (1973) used the expansion hypothesis to explain why men were psychologically healthier than women. At that time, women were less likely than men to hold multiple roles. Gove and Tudor argued that work would provide women with resources that would reduce their distress. A more specific version of the expansion hypothesis is the **stress-buffering hypothesis,** which articulates the exact benefits of multiple roles: resources from one role are used to buffer the strains arising from another role. For example, social support from coworkers may help to alleviate distress arising from family problems.

What is the evidence for the scarcity and expansion hypotheses? Are multiple roles healthful or harmful? A number of studies have shown that the healthiest people, men or women, are the ones who possess all three roles: spouse, parent, and worker (Kandel et al., 1985; Kotler & Wingard, 1989; Thoits, 1992; Verbrugge, 1983a). The most distressed people possess none of these roles. A couple of studies have found a comparative advantage of multiple roles for men over women (Adelmann, 1994; Aneshensel et al., 1981). Thus, additional roles may be more likely to create a burden among women than men. As will be discussed later, men's work and family roles are more easily integrated than women's work and family roles.

It may not be the mere accumulation of roles, but the particular combination of roles that is beneficial. One role may "enhance" the effects of another role; for example, the parent role may be adaptive only if one possesses the worker role. In one study, being the primary parent was associated with good health only if one possessed the worker role (Thoits, 1992). The healthiest men were fathers who worked, regardless of their marital status. The least healthy women were mothers who did not work and were either married or divorced. Thus, the worker role is critical to health in the presence of children. The parent role also may be beneficial to health only if one possesses the spouse role, at least for women. Two studies showed that the parent role benefits women's health only if they also possess the spouse role. One study found that having children was associated with physical health benefits if the women were married but mental health detriments if the women were unmarried (Khlat et al., 2000). Another study found that mothers without partners had higher mortality rates than mothers with partners (Weitoft, Haglund, & Rosen, 2000). Unmarried mothers may feel overwhelmed with raising children because they lack the emotional and financial support of a spouse.

Each addition of a role does not necessarily have the same health benefit. Some research suggests that the added benefits of a work or family role have a stronger effect on women's health when they lack other roles. Several studies have shown that employment has stronger effects on women's health if they lack family roles (spouse, parent; Nathanson, 1980; I. Waldron, Weiss, & Hughes, 1998). Employment has less effect on women's health if they are married and have children (Nathanson, 1980). Similarly, marriage has a stronger benefit for women's health when they are unemployed than employed (I. Waldron et al., 1998). Thus, the work role is more beneficial to women who lack family roles and a family role is more beneficial to women who lack the work role. Both of these effects can be explained by income: marriage provides unemployed women with increased income and employment provides unmarried women with increased income.

Among work and family roles, is there any evidence that one role has a stronger impact on men's and women's health? If one is talking about the sheer possession of a role, the work role appears to have the strongest effects on men's and women's health. Two studies showed that the work role had a stronger effect on health than family roles (spouse, parent) for both men and women (Nathanson, 1980; Verbrugge, 1983a).

When one examines the implications of role strains for health, however, which role has the most potential to harm health is not clear. In a study of married women, family role strains were more strongly related to depression than job role strains (Kandel et al., 1985). In a study of men, job role strains were more strongly associated with physical health than were marital strains (Barnett & Marshall, 1993). However, among men who were fathers, parental role strain was the strongest predictor of health. A study of married employed people in China revealed that men's mental health was more affected by work strains than family strains, whereas women's mental health was equally affected by both (Lai, 1995). Finally, in a study of dual-earner couples, job role quality, parent role quality, and marital role quality all affected men's psychological distress and the magnitude of the relations for each was similar (Barnett, Marshall & Pleck, 1992). Thus, it is not clear that work or family strains have a greater impact on health. There certainly is *not* support for the notion that family strains have a stronger effect on women and work strains have a stronger effect on men.

Working Mothers

One reason the effects of multiple roles on women's health seem to be more complicated than they are for men's health is that women suffer more role conflict than men when they combine work and parenting roles. As discussed earlier in the chapter, women are more likely than men to take time off from work to take care of children; thus, the parenting role has the potential to interfere with the work role for women. In that case, can work still be advantageous?

Society provides women with mixed messages about whether they should work when they have children (Lewis & Cooper, 1983). Working mothers receive the message that it is acceptable to work and to be a parent—as long as parenting is the number one priority. That is, work should never interfere with parenting. Women who opt not to work while raising children, however, may receive a different message from society. Today, these mothers often feel the need to justify why they are not working outside the home. In this section, I examine whether paid employment benefits mothers.

Whether working outside the home is beneficial for women with children depends on a number of factors, including salary earned, number of children, availability of child care, and husband's participation in household and child care activities (C. Ross et al., 1990). Two studies showed that a greater number of children in the home detracts from the health benefits of employment. One of these studies found that having three or more children increased the risk of heart disease among working women but not housewives (Haynes & Feinleib, 1980). The other study found that the number of minors in the household was related to increased distress for employed married women but was not related to distress for housewives (Cleary

& Mechanic, 1983). Yet, another study reached opposite conclusions: the number of children in the home had no effect on the mortality of working women, but housewives with four or more children had higher mortality (Kotler & Wingard, 1989). In one study, having more children was associated with poor health only among working women with low incomes. Having a higher income would provide working women with resources to cope with the increased demands of combining work and family roles (Cleary & Mechanic, 1983). Thus, one cannot say that the effect of work on women's health depends on the sheer number of children in the home; it depends on what resources are available to assist the woman in caring for her children.

Access to resources, whether the resource is income, child care, or a supportive husband, influences whether mothers benefit from work. In one study, mothers who worked outside the home were distressed when they had difficulty with child care arrangements and received no support from their husband in terms of help with household labor (C. Ross & Mirowsky, 1995). Other studies have shown that employment benefits women's health when husbands share child care responsibilities (Kessler & McRae, 1982; Ozer, 1995).

Another factor that may influence the effect on women's health of combining work and family roles is the traditionality of the field in which women work. It may be easier for women to combine work and family roles if they are employed in a field that by tradition is inhabited by women rather than men. A study of women who were either librarians (traditionally female occupation) or held MBAs (traditionally male occupation) found that librarians had an easier time combining the two roles (J. Olson, Frieze, & Detlefson, 1990). On the other hand, traditional jobs for women, such as nurses, secretaries, and teachers,

may have less flexibility than higher-status positions to accommodate family needs. One of the attributes of a high-status position is that the person often sets his or her own hours.

Difficulties in Combining Roles

Simon (1995) argues that to understand the effect of multiple roles on well-being, we need to understand what the individual roles mean to men and women. In support of the gender-role hypothesis, she says that the same role places different demands on men and women. Historically, there have been greater interrelations between work and family roles for men than for women. A man's family role is to provide economic support, an obligation he can fulfill through paid employment. A woman's family role is to provide emotional support, a function that is not served by paid employment. Thus, men's work and family roles are intertwined: they serve the same function. By contrast, women's work and family roles are independent: the woman's work role does not facilitate the function of her family role and may even detract from it.

To examine these issues, Simon (1995) interviewed 40 couples about how they experienced the relations between their work and family roles. More men than women defined their family role in terms of economic support, and more women than men defined their family roles in terms of emotional support. Women indicated that they felt guilty combining work and family roles, whereas no man in the study mentioned guilt. This is an indication that combining roles is more difficult for women. Another indication that work and family roles were less intertwined for women is that women suffered greater interrole conflict than men: women were more likely than men to report conflicts in combining work with family. The nature of the conflicts men and women reported also differed. Women were more likely to report vague and diffuse conflicts such as "not being there," whereas men reported specific conflicts, such as missing a child's soccer game. More women than men were concerned that they neglected the marital relationship. Although women were concerned that they did not pay enough attention to their spouse, women were not concerned that their husband did not pay enough attention to them. Men agreed. In other words, both men and women were concerned that wives' employment caused the women to neglect the marriage; yet, neither was concerned that men's employment led men to neglect the marriage. A third indication that work and family roles were more independent for women is differences in satisfaction at combining roles. Whereas 90% of the men felt adequate in their family roles as husbands and fathers, 70% of women felt *inadequate* as mothers and wives. The one situation in which men felt inadequate was when their wife worked but both wished she did not have to work; in this instance, men's work role did not completely fulfill the family role of economic provider.

A number of difficulties arise in families where both men and women work. Hochschild (1989) identified three kinds of tension in dual-earner couples. The first tension exists when men and women have different views about who should do what work outside the home and inside the home. I discussed in Chapter 10 how disagreement about the division of labor in the family is associated with marital unhappiness, especially for women. The second tension occurs when men and women have the desire for traditional roles but their economic status does not permit them to enact those roles. In other words, both husband and wife prefer that the wife takes care of the home and the husband is employed outside of the home, but lack of financial resources requires that the woman be employed outside the home. In this instance, the husband may contribute to household chores, but neither the husband nor the wife is satisfied with this arrangement.

The third tension is one that pervades egalitarian couples who are heavily involved in work outside the home. Husbands and wives in these couples jointly devalue family responsibilities to justify spending more time on their career. The egalitarian philosophy leads such couples to share responsibilities such that less time is devoted to home and family—less time on housework, less time with children, less time with each other. And someone is hired to take care of most household tasks (cooking, cleaning, and child care). The ideas about what a family needs change to accommodate the couple's egalitarian focus on careers. Hochschild (1989) calls it a hollow victory "if the work of raising a family becomes devalued because women have become equal to men on traditionally male terms" (p. 211). The homemaker role is now being devalued by both men and women. Hochschild suggests that a primary way to increase the value of this role is for men to become involved in household labor.

EXERCISE 11.4
Combining Roles

Interview a group of men and women who have combined work and family roles—preferably, people who have children and work outside the home. Ask questions similar to the ones Simon (1995) asked. Come up with some of your own questions to determine the unique difficulties men and women face.

Find out for yourself what difficulties men and women face when combining work and family roles in Exercise 11.4.

Summary

Multiple roles are good for both men's and women's health. Employment benefits women's health even in the presence of children. However, the presence of children adds to the complexity of understanding the conditions under which work is beneficial to women. To understand the interactive effects among roles, one needs to consider what roles mean to men and women and what the demands are in each of the roles. The traditionality of the couple and their SES are important determinants of role meaning and role demands. Although there is evidence that "more is better" in terms of roles, it also is the case that one role has a stronger effect on well-being when the person lacks other roles: employment has a stronger effect on the health of men and women who lack family roles, and family roles have a stronger effect on the health of women who lack employment. Roles provide resources, and having more roles may buffer one from the strains that arise in any one role. The fewer roles one has, the greater the effect that strain in any one role will have on health.

FAMILY-SUPPORTIVE WORK ENVIRONMENT

Because there is the potential for both role overload and role conflict when work and family roles are combined, many employers have taken action to support families. There are ways that work can provide resources to cope with family issues. Pleck (1993) discusses three family-supportive workplace policies. First, employers can provide child care support, in terms of on-site day care or monetary subsidies. Second, employers can provide flexible hours. One organization instituted flexible work hours and found that similar numbers of men and women took advantage of this opportunity (Pleck, 1993). Flextime may be one unrecognized way that men accommodate work schedules to family needs. Pleck points out that employers and coworkers assume that men are adjusting their work hours out of personal preference rather than to accommodate family needs, and men allow others to maintain this belief. In other words, men do not advertise that family roles are responsible for the changes they make in their work schedule.

A third policy that employers can institute is paternity leave. This has been implemented to a limited extent in workplaces in the United States. To date, very few men take advantage of paternity leave, but the rate is increasing (Pleck, 1993). Although there is no national paternity leave policy, in 1993 President Clinton signed into law the Family and Medical Leave Act. Because of this Act, employees may take a 12-week unpaid leave of absence from work to care for a child or an ill relative without fear of losing their job.

In Sweden, national paternity leave has been in existence since 1974 (Haas, 1993). Both parents are provided with paid leave for childbirth at a minimum of 90% of their salary. During the first years that paternity leave was provided, only 3% of men took advantage of it; by 1991, 44% of men in Sweden used some form of paternity leave. Also, by 1991, the paternity leave policy provided the combination of mothers and fathers with up to 12 months of paid leave. Mothers still take off more days than fathers (260 compared to 43 days).

Why don't more men in the United States take advantage of paternity leave? First, there are a couple of differences between the policies that exist in the United States and Sweden. In the United States, paternity leave is unpaid, whereas in Sweden it is paid. In Sweden, mothers and fathers are allocated a total amount of time, which they can distribute in any way between themselves. Typically, mothers take the first part of the leave and fathers take the second part. In a study of over 500 women and their partners in the United States, Hyde (1995) found that women took an average of 8.5 weeks of leave, whereas men took an average of 5 days. Men typically used their vacation days or personal days to cover this leave. Men with more egalitarian gender-role attitudes took longer leaves. The primary reason men did not take longer leaves was loss of salary; half of the men said they would take a longer leave if they received 50% of their salary.

Pleck (1993) argues that there are other, perhaps more important reasons why men in the United States do not take paternity leave: employers and coworkers have a negative attitude toward paternity leave; men who take advantage of paternity leave are viewed as unmasculine and lacking a commitment to work; there seems to be an unwritten policy not to take paternity leave. Often, organizations provide for paternity leave to avoid sex discrimination charges, but do not expect or encourage men to take advantage of it. In fact, since President Clinton signed the Family and Medical Leave Act, two lawsuits have been filed by fathers who said they were discriminated against when they tried to take a family leave to care for a newborn. In 1999, Kevin Knussman, a former Maryland state trooper, was awarded $375,000 in the first sex discrimination case associated with the Act (Morse, 1999). Knussman requested an extended leave because his wife had a complicated pregnancy and was not able to take care of the baby. Knussman claimed that his request was denied. In 1999, a second

suit was filed by David Roberts, a former South Carolina state trooper, who complained that he was fired for requesting family leave to care for his newborn daughter (American Civil Liberties Union, 1999). He requested family leave because his wife had not worked long enough to accrue paid leave and he wanted to offer her the opportunity to advance in her position. His supervisor responded by telling him that it was a mother's duty to take care of the children. The sharp criticism he received from his supervisors made him withdraw the request, but three months later he was terminated. The suit is still pending.

Pleck (1993) argues that men do not take formal paternity leave because they take "informal" paternity leave. The vast majority of men (87% in one study) take some time off after the birth of a child. In one study, the average man took 5.3 days off (Pleck, 1993). Men typically use vacation days or sick days to compensate them for this time so that they do not lose pay. Most men and employers feel uncomfortable referring to this time off as paternity leave.

ROLE BUFFERING AND ROLE EXACERBATION

I have shown that multiple roles are generally good for health despite their challenges, and that particular combinations of roles are especially beneficial. A primary explanation for why multiple roles benefit health is that the resources gained by one role can be used to buffer one from the distress associated with strains in another role. Is this true? Do work roles buffer men and women from the strains of family roles? Do family roles buffer men and women from the strains of work roles? Alternatively, strains in one role may exacerbate the negative effects of stressors in another role; for example, work stress could make one less able to tolerate difficulties with children. In this section, I examine whether work and family roles buffer or exacerbate stress from other roles.

Does Work Role Buffer or Exacerbate Family Stress?

A number of studies have shown that the work role buffers one from stressors at home. A longitudinal study of caregivers found that work buffers the psychological distress associated with caregiving (Pavalko & Woodbury, 2000). Caregivers' health declined more if they were not working than if they were working. Work also buffers the negative effects of marital difficulties. Two studies showed that the relation of marital distress to depression was smaller among women who worked outside the home than women who were housewives (Cleary & Mechanic, 1983; Kandel et al., 1985). One reason work buffers family distress is that it provides access to social support. A study of working-class mothers with children found that work buffered distress if they had social support (Parry, 1986). In response to a stressful life event, as shown in Figure 11.8, employed mothers were less distressed than nonemployed mothers when they had support available. If a stressful event occurred, employment alleviated women's distress in the presence of social support; in the absence of social support, employment exacerbated the negative effects of a stressor. The author noted that the majority of employed women who faced a major stressful life event did have social support; thus, the majority of women who faced a major life stressor benefited from employment.

There is no evidence that work per se exacerbates family stress, but there is evidence that strains at work exacerbate

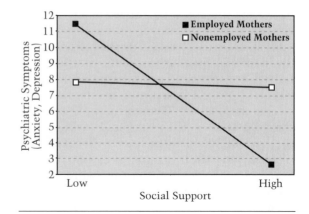

FIGURE 11.8   Effect of social support and employment on mothers' response to a major stressful life event. Employed mothers had fewer psychiatric symptoms than nonemployed mothers following a major stressful event *if* they had high levels of support. Under conditions of low support, employed mothers had more psychiatric symptoms than nonemployed mothers. In the majority of cases, employment benefited women because most mothers reported high levels of social support. *Source:* Adapted from Parry (1986).

family stress. In one study of women, low control at work was associated with greater distress when family demands were high (i.e., greater number of children; Lennon & Rosenfield, 1992). A study of men and women found that work strain was associated with marital strain and that these relations were stronger under conditions of high family demands (D. Hughes & Galinsky, 1994a). High family demands included having children under age 13 or having a spouse who did not help with household tasks.

Thus, it appears that the work role, in and of itself, buffers women from family stressors. In this way, work can be viewed as a resource for women. There is no evidence as to whether the work role buffers men from family distress, as most men possess the work role. However, stressors at work can exacerbate strains in the family for both men and women.

Do Family Roles Buffer or Exacerbate Work Stress?

The stress-buffering hypothesis also suggests that the presence of family roles buffers one from the distress associated with job difficulties. Two studies showed that either family role—spouse or parent—buffers one from the deleterious effects of work-related stress. In a longitudinal study of employed women, being a spouse or a parent buffered women from the impact on mental health of stress at work (Barnett, Marshall, & Singer, 1992). Changes in job role quality over time were more strongly associated with distress for women who did not have partners than women who had partners and for women who did not have children than women who had children. In fact, the subgroup of women who showed the strongest relation between changes in job role quality and changes in distress were women who did not have partners or children. These findings are consistent with the stress-buffering hypothesis that access to resources in one role buffers one from the distress of another role. A study of both men and women by Maslach and Jackson (1985) reached similar conclusions. They found lower job burnout scores among federal service employees who were either married or had children. The investigators of both studies point out that strains at work may have less impact on people with family roles because these people are less invested in their jobs than people without family roles. Employees with other roles may view their job differently. It also is

possible that coping skills acquired from one role can be used to address stressors arising from another role.

Not only the presence of family roles, but also the quality of family roles may buffer distress from the work role. A study of male air traffic controllers showed that wife support buffered husbands from the deleterious effects of work stress (Repetti, 1989). In a study of working women, the quality of the job was more strongly related to distress among women who reported unhappy marriages and among women who had a poor relationship with their children (Barnett, 1994). The same results were found for men (Barnett, Marshall, & Pleck, 1992). In fact, when the two samples were combined, high marital quality and high parental quality equally buffered men and women from distress arising from jobs (Barnett, 1994).

Family roles also may exacerbate the effects of work stress. There is evidence that work strains have a greater impact on women who hold the parent role. One study showed that the relation of work strains to depression was stronger among women who were parents than nonparents (Kandel et al., 1985). Another study of women showed that dissatisfaction with salary was associated with physical symptoms among parents but not nonparents (Barnett, Davidson, & Marshall, 1991). A low salary may be particularly distressful if there are children in the home. The one study of men showed that being a parent did not influence the relation of job role quality to distress (Barnett, Marshall, & Pleck, 1992).

Thus, family roles buffer strains at work for men and women but also have the potential to exacerbate strain at work for women. This latter finding may reflect the greater difficulty women have combining work and family roles.

SUMMARY

In this chapter, I evaluated the effect of work and family roles on men's and women's health. The work role is associated with health benefits for both men and women, but the effects are stronger among men. There is no overall effect on men's health of women working, but there may be some conditions under which it has negative implications for men. A primary way in which women working influences both men's and women's health has to do with its effect on resources and demands. To the extent that women working increases women's economic resources and detracts from men's economic resources, women benefit and men suffer. To the extent that women's work increases men's and decreases women's participation in household chores, women benefit and men suffer. Thus, it is not the case that men are necessarily worse off if their wife works—it is only under certain conditions that men may suffer. This presents a challenge for couples in which husbands and wives both work.

One reason it is difficult to compare the effect of work on health for men and women is that men and women have different work experiences. Women report more strains in their job role, which may explain why work is not always associated with good health for women. In some studies, aspects of the work role have a stronger relation to men's than women's health. When men's and women's roles are similar (i.e., dual-earner couples), the association of job role quality to health is similar for both.

One aspect of the work role that has consequences for women's well-being is discrimination. I distinguished between access and treatment discrimination: access discrimination reflects the differential opportunities men and women have to hold certain jobs; once hired, treatment discrimination occurs in the form of the glass ceiling and pay disparity. There is still evidence that women make less money than men when characteristics of men and women such as education and experience are taken into consideration. However, the wage gap is closing. One factor that contributes to the wage gap is taking care of children. Women with children earn less than women without children, and there are both concrete and abstract explanations for this difference. Interestingly, women are not as dissatisfied with pay disparity as one would expect. Although women believe that other women suffer discrimination, the majority of women deny any personal discrimination; this phenomenon is referred to as the denial of personal disadvantage. One theory of why women deny disadvantage involves social comparison theory: women compare themselves to other women rather than to men.

The effects of the parent role on men's and women's health are unclear. Early research showed largely negative effects of parenthood on health, but more recent studies hint that there may be benefits or at least that benefits equal costs. The mixed effects are due to the fact that there are so many factors that qualify the effect of parenthood on health: ages and number of children, whether the children live in the home, income, and other roles that parents possess. Women report more strains in the parent role and greater commitment to the parent role than do men. The quality of this role influences both men's and women's health, but the relation may be stronger among women. The quality of parenting has become an important issue for homosexuals, especially lesbian mothers. However, research shows few differences between heterosexual and homosexual parents and few differences among the children they raise.

It is difficult to evaluate the effects on health of one role in isolation from other roles because roles influence one another: whether one works might influence the likelihood of possessing family roles, as well as the quality of those roles; becoming a parent has consequences for time spent at work (at least for women) and for time that husbands and wives spend together. Features of one role also can spill over to influence the quality of another role. Spillover studies show that mood at work influences mood at home and mood at home influences mood at work. There is some evidence that both of these spillover effects are stronger among men.

There are contrasting theories as to whether multiple roles are associated with health benefits or health hazards, particularly with respect to women. The role-scarcity hypothesis suggests that additional roles tap resources, which are finite. The role-expansion hypothesis suggests that additional roles provide more resources, in particular, resources that can be used to buffer one from the strains that occur in a particular role (i.e., stress-buffering hypothesis). Taken collectively, there is more evidence for the role-expansion hypothesis than the role-scarcity hypothesis. More roles seem to be associated with better health for men and women, but this does not mean that role strains do not occur. Women, in particular, face difficulties combining work and family roles when there are children at home. These women do not necessarily suffer, however, when they have resources to cope with the increased demands—resources in terms of a high income or a husband who shares household responsibilities. There is also evidence that the addition of a role has a stronger influence on health when people lack other roles; thus, multiple roles may be especially beneficial at the lower end of the continuum of roles. As the number of roles increases, additional roles have less incremental benefits.

One way multiple roles are associated with health is that the resources provided by one role buffer one from the strains in another role. There is good evidence that work buffers men and women from the strains of family roles and that family roles buffer men and women from the strains of work roles. Yet, the positive aspects of one role not only can offset the negative aspects of another role, but the negative aspects of one role can exacerbate the negative aspects of another role. Difficulties at work can lead to increased strains at home, and demanding family roles can exacerbate strains at work. There is more evidence that the latter occurs than the former.

DISCUSSION QUESTIONS

1. Is there evidence that work roles have a stronger effect on men's health and family roles have a stronger effect on women's health?
2. What are the conditions under which employment is most strongly related to good health for women? To poor health for women?
3. What is the difference between access discrimination and treatment discrimination?
4. Why do women deny personal discrimination?
5. To the extent that parenthood has a negative effect on marriage, what are the explanations?
6. Generate some examples of positive and negative spillover.
7. Distinguish between the role-expansion and role-scarcity hypotheses.
8. What are the different predictions that social role theory and gender-role theory make about the association of roles to health?
9. What are some of the difficulties men and women face when combining work

and family roles? How could these be alleviated?

10. Give an example of the role-buffering hypothesis with respect to work and family roles.

Suggested Reading

Bolger, N., DeLongis, A., Kessler, R., & Wethington, E. (1989). The contagion of stress across multiple roles. *Journal of Marriage and the Family, 51,* 175–183.

Crosby, F. (1991). *Juggling.* New York: Free Press.

Crosby, F. (1984). The denial of personal discrimination. *American Behavioral Scientist, 27*(4), 371–386.

Haynes, S.G., & Feinleib, M. (1980). Women, work and coronary heart disease: Prospective findings from the Framingham heart study. *American Journal of Public Health, 70*(2), 133–141.

Major, B. (1989). Gender differences in comparisons and entitlement: Implications for comparable worth. *Journal of Social Issues, 45*(4), 99–115.

Rosenfield, S. (1989). The effects of women's employment: Personal control and sex differences in mental health. *Journal of Health and Social Behavior, 30,* 77–91.

Simon, R.W. (1995). Gender, multiple roles, role meaning, and mental health. *Journal of Health and Social Behavior, 36,* 182–194.

Key Terms

Access discrimination—Situation in which an individual is not offered a given job or is offered a lesser job because of some defining characteristic (e.g., sex).

Comparable worth—Policy that states that men and women in different jobs should be paid the same wage for comparable work.

Crossover—Phenomenon in which what happens to one person affects another person.

Demand-side theory—Explanation for the wage gap that emphasizes the different ways men and women are treated.

Denial of disadvantage—Condition in which women perceive that discrimination exists, but deny that they personally are victims of it.

Differential exposure hypothesis—Proposition that men and women possess different roles, which are associated with different stressors and different resources.

Differential vulnerability hypothesis—Proposition that a specific role has different effects on men's and women's health.

Gender-role hypothesis—Perspective that roles are perceived differently by men and women in a way that is consistent with gender roles; a specific form of the differential vulnerability hypothesis.

Glass ceiling—Label applied to barriers to the advancement of women and minorities in organizations.

Glass escalator—Term referring to the ability of men to be promoted quickly when they take positions in traditionally female fields.

Human capital accumulation theory—A job and the salary associated with the job is a function of the person's characteristics or "human capital," such as skills, experience, and education (see supply-side theory).

In-group comparison—Evaluation of oneself based on the condition of similar others (e.g., within-sex comparison).

Norms—Expectations for behavior.

Out-group comparison—Evaluation of oneself based on the condition of dissimilar others (e.g., between-sex comparison).

Pay disparity—Type of treatment discrimination in which women are paid less than men for doing comparable work.

Role—A position in a society governed by a set of norms.

Role conflict—Condition in which the demands of one role are at odds with the demands of another role.

Role expansion hypothesis—Idea that there are benefits to be gained from having diverse roles.

Role overload—Condition that arises when time limitations create difficulties in fulfilling obligations for one's roles.

Role scarcity hypothesis—Idea that multiple roles will have a negative effect on health because time and resources are limited and additional roles tap resources.

Selection effect—The potential for healthier people to choose certain roles, which then leads to difficulties in determining whether those roles influence health.

Social roles hypothesis—Suggestion that men and women who take on the same roles should have similar health (see differential exposure hypothesis).

Spillover—Phenomenon in which the quality of one role spills over to affect another role.

Stress-buffering hypothesis—Proposition that resources from one role can be used to buffer one from the strains arising from another role; a more specific version of the role expansion hypothesis.

Supply-side theory—Explanation for the wage gap that emphasizes the different characteristics of male and female workers.

Treatment discrimination—Situation in which an individual receives a reduced salary or reduced opportunities for promotion compared to other individuals having the same job.

12

Mental Health

In 1998, 130 million prescriptions were written for antidepressant medications in the United States (Moore, 1999). Prozac, a common antidepressant, is third on the list of highest-earning drugs, topping $1 billion in 1998 (IMS Health, 1999). Mental health, in particular, depression, is clearly an important problem in our country. Some important public figures have brought attention to mental health problems, with the effect of reducing their stigma and permitting more people to seek help for them. Tipper Gore, for example, publicly declared her battle with depression and championed mental health during her tenure as spouse of Vice President Al Gore. Several years ago, Great Britain's Princess Diana acknowledged depression and an eating disorder. Tina Turner admitted in her autobiography that she tried to kill herself with an overdose of Valium (1986). Mental health problems do not afflict men and women equally. There is substantial evidence that women are more likely than men to suffer from depression and are more likely to have an eating disorder.

The primary focus of this chapter is on depression, but I also examine two other mental health problems: eating disorders and suicide. Suicide has a paradoxical link to gender; although women attempt suicide more often than men, more men actually kill themselves.

SEX DIFFERENCES IN DEPRESSION

There seems to be a large and pervasive sex difference in depression, such that women suffer more depression than men. There are critics, however, who argue that definitional and methodological problems make this difference less clear. I begin this section by reviewing the evidence for sex differences in depression. Then, I examine the extent to which methodological artifacts can account for this difference. The rest of my discussion of depression is devoted to theoretical explanations for the sex difference. These theories have biological, psychological, social, and cultural underpinnings. No one theory can completely

500

account for women being more depressed than men. But many theories have female gender-role socialization at their core. Theories differentially emphasize the following ideas: (1) women are led to perceive less control over their environment than men; (2) women adopt a pessimistic way of explaining events; (3) women and men cope differently with stress; and (4) women and men face different stressors. One reason gender-role explanations are so viable is that sex differences in depression emerge during adolescence when gender-role norms become salient. Thus, I conclude with some remarks about the challenges of adolescence and how they might spark the sex difference in depression.

Before we examine the incidence of depression in men and women, it is important to distinguish between depressive symptoms, which all of us experience to some extent at one time or another, and major depressive disorder or clinical depression, which is a diagnosable mental health problem. Instruments that measure depressive symptoms include items such as feeling sad or blue, feeling depressed, having crying spells, difficulty concentrating, and loss of interest in things. Perhaps you have completed such an instrument during college. A widely used self-report measure of depression, the Center for Epidemiological Studies in Depression scale (CES-D; Radloff, 1977), is shown in Table 12.1.

The criteria for a major depressive disorder, as diagnosed by the *Diagnostic and Statistical Manual of Mental Disorders* (*DSM-IV*; APA, 1994), are shown in Table 12.2. The critical feature of a major depressive disorder is that the person must have experienced a set of depressive symptoms for a period no shorter than two weeks. Major depressive disorder is often referred to as **clinical depression.**

How do we determine the frequency of depressive symptoms or the incidence of

TABLE 12.1   Center for Epidemiological Studies in Depression Scale (CES-D)

1. I was bothered by things that usually don't bother me.
2. I did not feel like eating; my appetite was poor.
3. I felt that I could not shake off the blues even with the help of my family or friends.
4. I felt that I was just as good as other people. *
5. I had trouble keeping my mind on what I was doing.
6. I felt depressed.
7. I felt that everything I did was an effort.
8. I felt hopeful about the future. *
9. I thought my life had been a failure.
10. I felt fearful.
11. My sleep was restless.
12. I was happy. *
13. I talked less than usual.
14. I felt lonely.
15. People were unfriendly.
16. I enjoyed life. *
17. I had crying spells.
18. I felt sad.
19. I felt that people disliked me.
20. I could not get "going."

* These items are reverse scored.
Source: Radloff (1977).

clinical depression? Two different methods are used. Depressive symptoms are typically evaluated with community surveys. The strength of this methodology is that large, representative samples of men and women can be obtained to identify the frequency of depression. The weakness of this methodology is that depression is measured by self-report instruments, which are vulnerable to demand characteristics. For example, if men are less willing than women to report depression, community surveys may underestimate men's levels of

TABLE 12.2 Major Depressive Episode Criteria from *DSM-IV*

Five or more of these symptoms present for two weeks.

One symptom must be depressed mood or loss of interest.

1. Depressed mood most of the day, nearly every day.
2. Markedly diminished interests in activities.
3. Significant weight loss.
4. Insomnia.
5. Psychomotor agitation or retardation.
6. Fatigue or loss of energy.
7. Feelings of worthlessness.
8. Diminished ability to think or concentrate or indecisiveness.
9. Recurrent thoughts of death.

Source: APA (1994).

depression. Information on clinical depression is typically obtained from treatment facilities. The strength of this methodology is that depression can be evaluated with more sophisticated measures employed by trained clinicians. The weakness is that respondents are not randomly selected and are not representative of the population. To the extent that men are less likely than women to seek help for depression, studies of people in clinics also may underestimate men's rates of depression.

These two methodologies have provided a wealth of evidence that women experience more depressive symptoms than men in the general population and that women are more likely than men to be diagnosed with clinical depression (Weissman & Klerman, 1977). Epidemiological studies have found the rate of depressive symptoms to be twice as high among women as men (Culbertson, 1997; Nolen-Hoeksema, 1987). The sex difference in major depressive disorder is even higher, on the order of 4 to 1 (Culbertson, 1997).

Findings among adolescents are comparable (Compas et al., 1997).

Previously, I noted the advantages and disadvantages of surveying the general population versus studying the clinic population. It was not until the early 1990s that the two methods were combined. In an extensive undertaking, clinical interviews were conducted with a representative sample of over 8,000 people ages 15 to 54 in the United States (Kessler, McGonagle, Zhao, et al., 1994). The sex difference in major depressive disorder confirmed previous research. The findings, shown in Figure 12.1, revealed a 2:1 sex difference. Women were nearly twice as likely as men to report a history of major depressive disorder and to report the occurrence of major depression

FIGURE 12.1 National survey of major depression. Clinical interviews of a representative sample of over 8,000 people ages 15 to 54 in the United States revealed that women are more likely than men to report a history of major depression and to have had an episode of major depression in the past year. The sex difference is on the order of 2:1. *Source:* Adapted from Kessler, McGonagle, Zhao, et al. (1994).

over the prior year. The sex difference in depression was similar across the different age ranges (Kessler, McGonagle, Swartz, Blazer, & Nelson, 1993; Kessler, McGonagle, Nelson, et al., 1994).

Sex differences in depression are found not only in the United States. There is a great deal of cross-cultural support for sex differences in depression (McGrath, Keita, Strickland, & Russo, 1990). Women are between two and three times more likely than men to be depressed in countries such as Sweden, Germany, Canada, New Zealand, Puerto Rico, and Korea (Klerman & Weissman, 1989). One study evaluated the incidence of lifetime depression (i.e., an experience of clinical depression at any time during one's life) across 10 countries (United States, Canada, Puerto Rico, France, Italy, West Germany, Lebanon, Taiwan, Korea, and New Zealand; Weissman et al., 1996). As shown in Figure 12.2, rates of lifetime depression were higher among women than men in every country. The ratio of female:male depression ranged from

a low of 1:6 in Lebanon and Taiwan to a high of 3:1 in West Germany. The ratio in the United States was 2:6.

There are some populations in which sex differences in depression are less likely to be found. Although the sex difference in depression consistently appears in developed countries, sex differences in depression do not appear in underdeveloped countries (Nolen-Hoeksema, 1990). In addition, sex differences in depression are often not found in homogeneous populations, such as studies of college students (Bryson & Pilon, 1984; Hammen & Padesky, 1977) and medical students (D. Clark & Zeldow, 1988). There also appear to be no sex differences in depression among the Amish. Depression was examined in the Amish community by interviewing residents to see if there was a consensus that certain people in the community appeared "disturbed" (Egeland & Hostetter, 1983). There was no difference in the number of men and women who were identified as depressed. However, the methodology of the study is somewhat

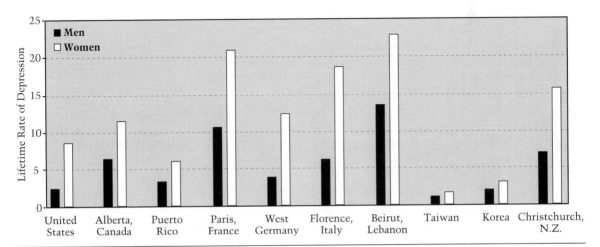

FIGURE 12.2 Incidence of major depression across cultures. Across a variety of cultures, women are more likely than men to have experienced an episode of major depression in their lifetime. *Source:* Adapted from Weissman et al. (1996).

troublesome. Only people who *appeared* to be depressed were referred to the investigator. People who suffered from less observable forms of depression would not have been identified. Another population that shows no sex difference in depression is the widowed. As discussed in Chapter 10, this is largely because rates of depression increase among men more than women following widowhood.

The sex difference in depression emerges during adolescence and is fairly consistent across the life span. Thus, one may wonder whether the same men and women remain depressed throughout their life or if, at any given point, women are twice as likely as men to become depressed. The answer to this question is not completely clear. One longitudinal study supported the idea that women are twice as likely as men to become depressed at any given time (Coryell, Endicott, & Keller, 1992), whereas another longitudinal study suggested that the sex difference in depression arose from a greater recurrence of depression in women than men (Amenson & Lewinsohn, 1981). Two cross-sectional studies have found few sex differences in self-reports of recurrence of depression (Kessler et al., 1993; Kornstein et al., 1995). However, a longitudinal study that follows people over time is better able to detect a true recurrence. Thus, there is some evidence that at any given point in time, women are more likely than men to become depressed among those without a history of depression. However, there also is some evidence that depression is more likely to recur among women than men among those with a history of depression.

Although the sex difference in depression is consistent across a variety of samples and a variety of methodologies, the size of the difference in the United States appears to have decreased in recent years, largely due to a rise in male depression rather than a decline in female depression

(Culbertson, 1997; Klerman & Weissman, 1989; McGrath et al., 1990). A recent study in Scotland also found a decrease in the sex difference in depression. The sex difference in hospital admission rates for depression decreased from 1:9 in 1980 to 1:5 in 1995 (Shajahan & Cavanagh, 1998). However, in Scotland, the change was due to both an increase in male depression and a decrease in female depression.

METHODOLOGICAL ARTIFACTS

Some investigators have contested these seemingly indisputable data that a sex difference in depression exists. Three sets of methodological problems or artifacts could explain why women "appear" to be more depressed. First, there may be a bias on the part of clinicians, such that depression is overdiagnosed among women and underdiagnosed among men. Second, there may be a response bias on the part of depressed persons; men may be less likely than women to admit depression or to seek help for depression. Third, men and women may manifest depression in different ways, and instruments are biased in the direction of tapping female depression.

Clinician Bias

One source of bias is the clinician's judgment. Perhaps clinicians are more likely to interpret a set of symptoms as depression when the patient is female. Why might this be? First, clinicians are undoubtedly aware of the sex difference in depression. Thus, clinicians' mental illness schema for a female patient is more likely to contain depression than their mental illness schema for a male patient. When a female patient comes into the office, depression-related schemas are more likely to be activated.

The clinician may be more likely to look for features of depression in a female patient than a male patient. Ambiguous symptoms such as feeling tired or lacking energy may be more likely to be interpreted as a depressive symptom in a female patient.

The research evidence on clinician bias is not completely clear. One study refuted the idea of clinician bias by showing that interviewers were equally likely to diagnose clinical depression in men and women with the same symptoms (Amenson & Lewinsohn, 1981). However, a recent study of primary care physicians showed that they were less likely to detect depression in men compared to women, and in African Americans and Hispanics compared to Caucasians (Borowsky et al., 2000). In that study, physicians' detection of mental health problems among over 19,000 patients was compared to independent screening of depression. The comparison showed more men's than women's depression went undetected by physicians. Research also has shown that physicians are more likely to prescribe antidepressants and antianxiety drugs to women than to men, even when they have similar diagnoses (Simoni-Wastila, 1998). Thus, there is some evidence that physicians are either eager to identify depression in women or reluctant to identify depression in men. With Exercise 12.1, see if your peers are more predisposed to identify depression in a female than a male.

Response Bias

There are a number of ways that people can distort their reports of depression. A common concern is that men may be less likely than women to report depression because depression is inconsistent with the male gender role. The term depression has feminine connotations; it implies a lack of

---

EXERCISE 12.1
Identifying Depression

Create a description of a depressed person. Make the symptoms subtle. Do not say the person is depressed. Use items from Tables 12.1 and 12.2 to help you. Create two versions of this description, one with a male name and one with a female name. Randomly distribute one of the two versions to 20 people. Ask each respondent to identify the person's problem.

Compare the percentages of people who identify depression in the female and male vignettes.

---

self-confidence, a lack of control, and passivity—all of which contradict the traditional male gender role.

Men might be less willing than women to report depression because they are concerned that others will view them negatively (Hammen, 1982). This concern has some basis in fact. Research shows that depressed men are viewed more negatively than depressed women. In one study, college students read a description of a male or a female who was having difficulties with academic work and relationships (Hammen & Peters, 1977). In one version, the target was depicted as depressed; in two other versions, the target was depicted as anxious or having flat affect. Although all three targets were rated as equally impaired, depressed male targets were more strongly rejected than depressed female targets. A study of college roommates found that depressed men were evaluated more negatively by their roommates than were depressed women (S. Siegel & Alloy, 1990). In addition, roommates of depressed men reported more negative affect than roommates of depressed women, suggesting that depression in men was more likely than depression in women to evoke adverse emotional reactions. Another investigation evaluated loneliness rather than depression and found that lonely men and women were rated as less well-adjusted than nonlonely men and women, but the negative effects of loneliness were more noticeable for male targets (Lau & Gruen, 1992).

Are men and women equally harsh in their views of depressed men? The roommate study evaluated only same-sex pairs, so that study could not address this question. The other studies, however, showed that women were more negative than men in their evaluations of depressed male targets (Hammen & Peters, 1978; Lau & Gruen, 1992). This is ironic because men are more likely to disclose depression to a female than to a male.

I have suggested reasons why men might want to deny being depressed. Is there evidence that men do, in fact, underreport depression? One study showed that men may be leery of admitting depressive symptoms. Men were more likely to endorse

depressive items on an instrument that was labeled "hassles" than an instrument that was labeled "depression" (S. Page & Bennesch, 1993). As shown in Figure 12.3, the label did not affect women's reports of depression. However, another study showed that men and women who had the same depressive symptoms score were equally likely to describe themselves as depressed (Amenson & Lewinsohn, 1981). Still, this study does not completely rule out a response bias on the part of males. The men and women in this study had to at least be willing to report depressive symptoms. What this study actually shows, then, is that men and women who acknowledge depressive symptoms will label them accordingly. Thus, the possibility remains that men may underreport depression.

A response bias related to men's unwillingness to report depression is men's unwillingness to seek help for depression. This issue is important to studies of depression conducted in clinics. Even if men and women are equally willing to admit

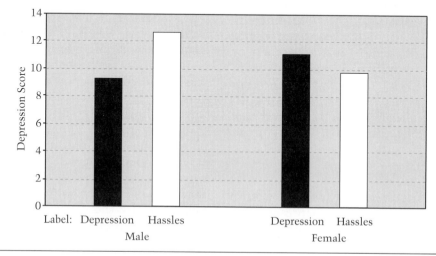

FIGURE 12.3 Effects of questionnaire label on self-report of depression. Men were more likely to report symptoms of depression on a questionnaire that was labeled "hassles" rather than "depression." The label attached to the questionnaire did not influence women's reports of depressive symptoms. *Source:* Adapted from S. Page and Bennesch (1993).

depression on an inventory, men may be less likely to seek help for depression (Hartung & Widiger, 1998). Recall that the size of the sex difference in major depressive disorder in clinic populations is larger than that found in surveys of the general population.

There are other response biases besides men's unwillingness to report and seek help for depression that might influence sex differences in depression. K. Clancy and Gove (1974) investigated the "naysaying" bias, the tendency to say no (or yes) to an item regardless of how it is worded. They found a tendency for women to engage in more naysaying than men. When this difference was taken into consideration, the sex difference in depression increased! That is, if women were not naysaying so much, they would admit to even more symptoms of depression.

Finally, a more subtle response bias is that men are less likely than women to realize that they are depressed or to interpret their symptoms as depression. I once interviewed a man following coronary bypass surgery who complained of a lack of energy, a loss of interest in leisure activities, and a desire to stay in bed all day. He was perplexed by these symptoms but completely denied any feelings of depression on a questionnaire that I administered. One study showed that men were less likely than women to recognize depression depicted in a series of vignettes (Yoder, Shute, & Tryban, 1990). Thus, men may underreport their depression because they do not recognize depressive symptoms.

Different Manifestations of Depression

A difficulty in examining sex differences in depression, or any other disorder, is that symptoms of depression may differ for men and women. This is a general problem associated with the classification of many mental illnesses (Hartung & Widiger, 1998). For example, histrionic personality disorder is more common among women than men. In an earlier version of the manual used to diagnosis this disorder (the *DSM-III-R*), a feature of the disorder was "overconcern with physical attractiveness." There was some concern that this feature biased the disorder in favor of women. In a more recent version of the manual (*DSM-IV*), this feature was changed to "physical appearance draws attention to the self." Undoubtedly, this change in wording reduced the extent to which the disorder was linked to women. However, the change in wording also altered the actual feature of the disorder. If a feature of a disorder is linked to male or female gender roles, should it be altered so that it is equally endorsed by both sexes? One certainly would not change the features of medical illnesses such as prostate cancer or breast cancer so that they are equally represented among both men and women.

With respect to depression, some people argue that men and women are equally "distressed," but that they manifest it in different ways. There is a concern that instruments that measure depression are more likely to tap female than male symptoms. One of the most widely used self-report instruments, the Beck Depression Inventory, was examined to see if men and women who reported similar levels of general depression would be more or less likely to endorse particular items (Hammen & Padesky, 1977). The item that most characterized female as opposed to male depression was indecisiveness. The item that most characterized male as opposed to female depression was social withdrawal. If withdrawal is a key feature of depression for men, men may be less likely than women to seek help for depression. Find out if your peers perceive depression differently among men and women in Exercise 12.2.

EXERCISE 12.2
**Perceptions of Depression in
Men and Women**

Interview five people. Ask each of them
to describe how they identify depression
in a series of people, for example, their
partner, a parent, a sibling, a friend, a
work associate, and a stranger. Be sure to
record the sex of each of these target people. On average, do people perceive depression differently when it is displayed
by a male versus a female?

The idea that some items are more
likely to be associated with a trait, such as
depression, among men versus women is
referred to as **differential item functioning.**
Crying is a depression item that may be
susceptible to differential item functioning. Crying is a symptom of depression that
women are more likely to engage in than
men, even among women and men who are
equally depressed. This item could cause
depression to be overdiagnosed in women.
The construct of differential item functioning has been applied to the domain of negative affectivity, which reflects negative
emotions such as depression, anxiety, and
anger. Some items on a widely used measure of negative affectivity were more
likely to be endorsed by men and some
were more likely to be endorsed by women
(L. Smith & Reise, 1998). In particular,
women were more likely to endorse items
that indicated oversensitivity and hurt
feelings; men, by contrast, were more likely
to endorse items that indicated irritation
and moodiness. Interestingly, regardless of
whether an item was more sensitive to
male or female negative affectivity, women
were more likely than men to endorse all of
the items. Thus, the sex difference in negative affectivity is real; it is not an artifact of

a response bias. However, the size of the
sex difference in negative affectivity depends on whether an instrument contains
items that are more sensitive to male or female negative affectivity. In some cases,
the sex difference could be exaggerated.

Other investigators argue that men
and women manifest depressive symptoms
in completely different ways and that male
depression is not even tapped by existing
instruments. Supporters of this view argue
that women display symptoms of depression, such as sadness, lethargy, and crying,
whereas men are more likely to turn to alcohol when depressed. A study of people diagnosed with major depressive disorder
found that depressed men were more likely
than depressed women to have a history of
alcohol and drug abuse (Kornstein et al.,
1995).

The idea that alcohol and drug problems are manifestations of depression in
men is not easily refuted. In some sense,
the reasoning is circular because depression
ends up being defined as the mental health
problem that men and women exhibit. Even
if men and women do manifest distress
in different ways, one can still ask why
women are more depressed than men and
why men have more drinking problems
than women. I now turn to the different
theories that have been developed to account for sex differences in depression.

THEORIES OF DEPRESSION

Sex differences in depression can be understood by distinguishing between two sets
of factors: susceptibility factors and precipitating factors (Radloff & Rae, 1979). **Susceptibility factors** are innate, usually biological
factors that place women at greater risk for
depression than men. Hormones or genes
that are unique to women would be susceptibility factors. Gender-role socialization,

however, also could be a susceptibility factor; if we learn that women are socialized in different ways than men that make them more at risk for depression, their learning history would be a susceptibility factor. **Precipitating factors** are environmental events that trigger depression. If there are certain environmental factors that induce depression—and that women face more than men—such as poverty or high relationship strain, depression might be triggered more in women than in men.

One fact that any theory of sex differences in depression must take into consideration is that sex differences in depression do not appear until adolescence (Nolen-Hoeksema, 1990). Before age 13 or 14, sex differences in depression are rarely found (Nolen-Hoeksema & Girgus, 1994). This fact suggests that any theory of sex

differences in depression must take one of three forms (Nolen-Hoeksema & Girgus, 1994). These three perspectives are depicted in Figure 12.4.

The **same cause theory** suggests that the same factor causes depression in both males and females, but that factor must increase during adolescence for women only. For example, imagine that a poor body image was equally associated with depression in boys and girls but that a poor body image increased among girls but not boys during adolescence.

The **different cause theory** says that there are different causes of girls' and boys' depression and that only the cause of girls' depression increases during adolescence. For example, imagine that a poor body image is associated with depression only among girls and being a poor athlete is associated with

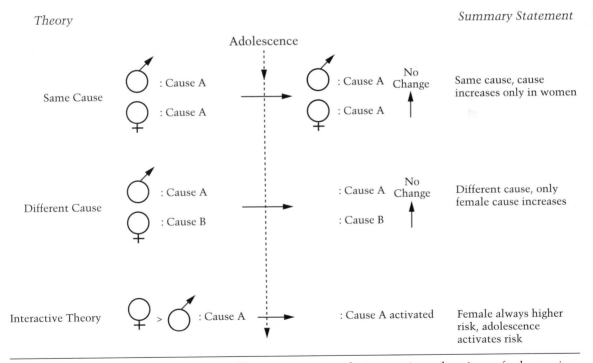

FIGURE 12.4 The same cause, different cause, and interactive theories of depression. *Source:* Adapted from Nolen-Hoeksema and Girgus (1994).

depression only among boys. This theory could explain the emergence of sex differences in depression during adolescence if it were true that a negative body image (i.e., women's risk factor for depression) becomes more prevalent during adolescence, but poor athletic ability (i.e., men's risk factor for depression) does not change over time.

The **interactive theory** suggests that being female always poses a risk for depression, but the events of adolescence activate that risk factor. For example, imagine that females are more concerned than males with their relationships and that unsatisfying relationships are more strongly related to girls' than boys' distress. Concern with relationships would be the "female risk factor." This concern could interact with events that are likely to occur during adolescence such as interpersonal conflict. Because females are more relationship-focused than males, girls will be more likely than boys to react to interpersonal conflict with depression.

In sum, these theories suggest either that the cause of depression is the same for men and women, that there are different causes for male and female depression, or that environmental factors interact with predisposing factors to predict depression. Each of the theories below supports one of these perspectives.

Biology

GENES. If there is a genetic explanation for the sex difference in depression, one would expect the depression risk factor to lie on the X chromosome. That being the case, one would predict that depressed fathers would be more likely to pass on their depressive gene to daughters than sons because fathers give daughters their X chromosome and sons their Y chromosome. However, there are more father-son pairs who are depressed than

father-daughter pairs (Nolen-Hoeksema, 1987). Thus, sex-linked genes alone cannot explain depression.

Because genes are present at birth, a genetic theory of depression has difficulty explaining the emergence of depression in females during adolescence. Genetic theories could only suggest that women are at risk for depression and that the events of adolescence interact with that risk. At least one study supports this theory. A study of 8- to 16-year-old twins found a higher concordance rate of depression in monozygotic than dizygotic twins but only among females who had reached puberty (Silberg et al, 1999). The investigators suggested that there may be a latent genetic factor involved in women's depression that is activated at puberty.

HORMONES. In contrast to genes, hormones do change over the life span and there is a great deal of hormonal fluctuation during adolescence, when sex differences in depression emerge. Thus, hormones would seem to be an ideal candidate to explain sex differences in depression. However, there is no consistent evidence that the changes in hormones during puberty are associated with the onset of depression in adolescent females (Brooks-Gunn & Warren, 1989; Nolen-Hoeksema & Girgus, 1994). In one study of 10- to 14-year-old girls, negative affect was associated with rapid rises in hormone levels, but even that association was weak (Brooks-Gunn & Warren, 1989). One review of the literature concluded that there is no consistent or simple relation of hormones to depression in adolescents (Buchanan, Eccles, & Becker, 1992). However, hormones may interact with other environmental factors, supporting the interactive theory of depression.

Aside from the hormonal changes during adolescence, researchers have attempted to link hormonal changes to depression at other times in women's lives. Although fluctuations in women's hormones, in particular, estrogen, prior to menstruation and after the birth of a child are related to depression, these effects are not nearly large enough to account for the sex difference in depression (Weissman & Klerman, 1977). In addition, it has been difficult to pinpoint exactly which hormonal change is associated with depression (Nolen-Hoeksema, 1987). Increases in a particular hormone are linked to higher rates of depression at some times and lower rates at other times. It is easier to link a general pattern of hormonal fluctuation to depression than to a specific change in a particular hormone.

Researchers have often focused on the hormonal fluctuations of the menstrual cycle and attempted to link these fluctuations to mood. One difficulty with much of the research linking mood to the menstrual cycle is that women are aware of their cycle when completing mood questionnaires. A woman who is about to begin her period may attribute normal mood changes to her menstrual cycle. A student of mine conducted a study to show the effects of expectancy on mood (Long, 1992). College women were either told that research has shown that premenstrual symptoms (PMS) are most likely to occur after their period (false expectancy) or were given no information, assuming they would expect premenstrual symptoms to occur before their period. Women completed a PMS questionnaire four days before, four days during, and four days after menstruation. As predicted, women reported more PMS on the days they expected symptoms to occur.

Some research has focused on the protective effects of testosterone, the male hormone, in regard to depression. However, even that relation is not a simple one. In one study, testosterone showed a curvilinear relation to depression, such that people with extremely low or extremely high levels of testosterone were depressed (Booth, Johnson, & Granger, 1999). The relation of high testosterone to depression appeared to be accounted for by its relation to antisocial behavior. High testosterone men were more likely to engage in antisocial behavior, which was linked to depression. This research is consistent with the idea that men and women manifest depression in different ways. In this study, low testosterone levels were associated with the more stereotypical female form of depression, whereas high levels were associated with the more stereotypical male form of distress: acting-out behavior.

A more recent theory of hormonal influences on depression has focused on oxytocin (R. Turner, Altemus, Enos, Cooper, & McGuinness, 1999). Oxytocin increases during puberty and has been shown to promote affiliative behavior in women (Frank & Young, 2000). Affiliative behavior, in and of itself, should not lead to depression. However, affiliative behavior might interact with some of the events during adolescence to place women at risk for depression. Specifically, changes in oxytocin regulation during puberty may cause females to be more reactive to interpersonal stressors. High levels of oxytocin have been associated with greater interpersonal problems among women, such as being intrusive in relationships and being anxious about relationships (R. Turner et al., 1999).

Taken collectively, biological factors alone are not sufficient to explain sex differences in depression (McGrath et al., 1990). However, much more research is needed on this issue. Hormones, in particular, may play a role, but their effect is not a direct one. The role of oxytocin in depression is a promising avenue of research. Hormones probably have their greatest explanatory power when they are examined within the context of environmental events.

Learned Helplessness

Learned helplessness is the sense of giving up because one perceives that there is nothing that can be done to alter a situation. If you have ever studied long hours for a class without improving your grade, you might have experienced learned helplessness. Learned helplessness is the product of three events (Seligman, 1992). First, one learns that an outcome is beyond one's control; second, one responds by giving up or ceasing to respond; third, one generalizes this response to new situations—perceives that future responses cannot influence future outcomes. A model of learned helplessness is shown in Figure 12.5. According to the model, the chain of events is instigated by an environmental event rather than by a characteristic of the perceiver. That is, something in the environment leads to the perception of uncontrollability. For example, you exercise daily and eat a healthy diet for six months without losing any weight. Your word processing program won't work and after four hours of trying different tactics, your computer won't even turn on. After the environmental event occurs, it is the cognitive expectation that future responses will not influence outcomes

that leads to the behavior of giving up. Recall your own experiences of learned helplessness in Exercise 12.3.

Is there any evidence that women are more susceptible than men to learned helplessness? There is some evidence that women receive more "helplessness training" than men. Women are more likely to find themselves in situations in which they do not have control, partly due to their lower status. During childhood, girls learn that they cannot influence boys,

---

EXERCISE 12.3
Personal Experience of Learned Helplessness

Review the model of learned helplessness in Figure 12.5. Think about a time when you exerted a response over and over again and found that it had no effect on the outcome. Did you give up? After how long? Why? What were the effects of this experience? Specifically, did this lead you to give up on subsequent tasks—related or unrelated to the present one? What were the short-term effects? The long-term effects?

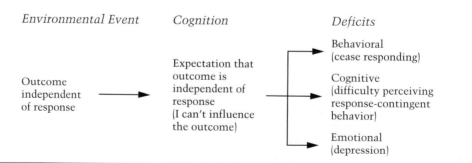

FIGURE 12.5   A model of learned helplessness. An environmental event leads to a cognition, which produces behavioral, cognitive, and emotional deficits. *Source:* Adapted from Seligman (1992).

which is one reason girls play with other girls rather than boys (Maccoby, 1998). Girls receive less attention from teachers, which may teach them that there is little they can do to influence their environment. In a study of 1,000 community residents, women scored lower on feelings of control than did men, and reduced feelings of control were associated with depression (Nolen-Hoeksema, Larson, & Grayson, 1999). The female stereotype includes passivity, dependence, and needing others' protection (Radloff & Monroe, 1978). This image of women is conveyed by the media, by parents, by teachers, and by therapists (Radloff & Monroe, 1978).

Susceptibility to learned helplessness has been linked to gender roles. In a study of undergraduate women, those who were low in masculinity were least likely to choose to control their environments, especially after an experience of learned helplessness (Baucom, 1983). Women performed a task in which either accurate or inaccurate (helpless condition) feedback was provided to assist them with solving the task. Women who were exposed to the helpless condition were especially unlikely to choose to exert control on a subsequent task, especially if they were low in masculinity. Another laboratory study found that women who scored high in femininity were less likely to exert control when given the opportunity and to feel depressed after being faced with a control task (Sayers, Baucom, & Tierney, 1993).

The learned helplessness theory of depression is supported by the fact that other demographic variables linked to a lack of control besides sex are associated with depression. Low income, lack of education, and unemployment are also associated with depression (Amenson & Lewinsohn, 1981). One factor that gender and these other demographic variables have in common is a lack of control or helplessness in

influencing the environment (Radloff, 1975). However, even when these other demographic factors are taken into consideration, women are still more depressed than men (Amenson & Lewinsohn, 1981). The learned helplessness theory of depression is appealing, but there are not good studies that test whether this theory accounts for sex differences in depression. The evidence is largely circumstantial.

Attributional Styles

Recall from Chapter 5 that men and women generally make different attributions for success and failure. One particular attributional style has been linked to learned helplessness and depression: a pessimistic attributional style. A **pessimistic, or depressive, attributional style** occurs when one makes internal, stable, and global attributions for negative events (Abramson, Seligman, & Teasdale, 1978). For example, a man who responds to his girlfriend breaking up with him by saying "I am not a very interesting, fun, attractive, or worthwhile companion, partner, or friend anyway and I never will be" is displaying a pessimistic attributional style. You can certainly see why someone who had this response would be depressed! This person is clearly making internal attributions for the event by blaming himself. The attributions are global because he is generalizing across an array of traits and an array of relationships (friend, partner, companion). The attributions are stable because he says that there is no hope for change. A person who responds to a success experience, such as receiving an A on an exam, by saying "I just got lucky. My luck will wear out. It is only one exam. I am sure that I will flunk the rest of them" is also exhibiting a depressive attributional style. This person is attributing the success to outside forces (luck) that are unstable (will wear out) and specific (only this exam).

Each dimension of the pessimistic attributional style—internality, stability, globality—has been linked to depression (Peterson & Villanova, 1988; Whitley, 1991). Use of the pessimistic attributional style for the interpretation of negative events is more strongly related to depression than its use for the interpretation of positive events (Whitley, Michael, & Tremont, 1991).

Some research has suggested that a pessimistic attributional style may lead to the occurrence of stressful events, which then cause depression. In a cross-sectional study, a pessimistic attributional style was unrelated to the occurrence of independent stressful events but was related to reporting more dependent stressful life events (Simons, Angell, Monroe, & Thase, 1993). A dependent stressful event is one in which one's own behavior might have brought about the event, such as the loss of a job. An independent stressful event is one that occurs independent of behavior, such as the death of a relative.

Are women more likely than men to exhibit the pessimistic attributional style? The evidence is mixed. In two studies of college students, women were more likely to make internal, stable, and global attributions for negative events (Boggiano & Barrett, 1991). However, in another study of college students, few sex differences in attributions for negative events appeared (S. Berndt, Berndt, & Kaiser, 1982). In a study of fifth- through eleventh-graders, there was weak support for sex differences in the pessimistic attributional style (J. Parsons, Meece, Alder, & Kaczala, 1982). However, some important sex differences in attributions did emerge: girls were more likely than boys to attribute success to effort and failure to lack of ability, whereas boys were more likely than girls to attribute

success to ability and failure to lack of effort. Recall from Chapter 5 that sex differences in attributions for success and failure depend on a number of variables, including the nature of the task. Because it is unclear how strongly the pessimistic attributional style is linked to sex, this theory is inadequate for explaining sex differences in depression.

Coping

GENERAL COPING STRATEGIES. There are many different ways of coping with stressful life events. One distinction that has been made in the literature is between emotion-focused coping and problem-focused coping (Lazarus & Folkman, 1984). **Problem-focused coping** refers to attempts to actually alter the stressor itself. Finding a solution to the problem, seeking the advice of others as to how to solve the problem, and coming up with a plan to approach the problem are all problem-solving methods. **Emotion-focused coping** refers to ways in which we accommodate ourselves to the stressor. There are a variety of emotion-focused coping strategies that are quite distinct from one another. Distracting oneself from the stressor, avoiding the problem, and denying that the problem exists are all ways that we change our reaction to the stressor rather than altering the stressor itself. Talking about the problem to relieve distress, accepting the problem, and putting a positive spin on the problem are also emotion-focused ways of coping.

Investigators frequently suggest that women cope with stressful events by engaging in emotion-focused strategies and men cope by engaging in problem-focused strategies. Some research has supported this claim (Stone & Neale, 1984). Although the conceptual distinction between problem-focused coping and emotion-focusing coping is a useful one for the study of coping, this distinction may be less useful when studying gender. When coping strategies are placed into these two broad categories, sometimes expected sex differences appear (i.e., women more emotion-focused, men more problem-focused), sometimes no sex differences appear, and sometimes sex differences appear in the opposite direction (i.e., women more problem-focused). The broad categories of emotion-focused coping and problem-focused coping collapse across distinct coping strategies, and only some of these may show sex differences. For example, researchers often hypothesize that men are more likely than women to engage in problem-focused coping. Yet, one primary problem-focused coping strategy is to seek the advice of others, and we know that women are more likely than men to seek out others for help. There are different kinds of help that a person can seek, however. If people seek others' advice, they are engaging in problem-focused coping; if people seek others in order to express feelings, they are engaging in emotion-focused coping. In the latter case, the person is trying to reduce distress rather than alter the stressor. Researchers do not always distinguish between these two kinds of support-seeking strategies. However, it is possible that women are more likely than men to do both.

Thus, to evaluate sex differences in coping it is important to turn to specific coping strategies. Below, I briefly review the evidence for sex differences in the use of six commonly studied ways of coping with stress. Examples of each kind of coping are shown in Table 12.3.

SPECIFIC COPING STRATEGIES. *Avoiding* the stressor or distracting oneself from the stressor seems to be a coping strategy employed by men more than women (Kleinke, Staneski, & Mason, 1982; Kohlmann, Weidner, Dotzauer, & Burns, 1997), but there are

TABLE 12.3 Sample Coping Strategies

Avoidance	I read a book or watch TV to think less about the problem.
Self-blame	I blame myself for what happened.
Wishful thinking	I wish that the problem would go away.
Seek social support	I find someone to talk to about the problem.
Problem-focused coping	I figure out what to do to solve the problem.
Positive reappraisal	I try to find the good in the situation.

studies that show women are more likely than men to engage in avoidant behaviors (Ptacek, Smith, & Dodge, 1994; Ptacek, Smith, & Zanas, 1992). Sex differences in avoidance probably depend on the particular kind of avoidant behavior. Men are more likely than women to engage in escape behaviors such as smoking marijuana (Kleinke et al., 1982) and distraction behaviors such as exercise (Kleinke et al., 1982; Thoits, 1991).

The majority of studies show that women engage in more *self-blame* than men do (Kleinke et al., 1982; Ptacek et al., 1992, 1994; Vingerhoets & Van Heck, 1990). Women also have been shown to be more likely than men to engage in *wishful thinking* (Ptacek et al., 1994; Vingerhoets & Van Heck, 1990).

The most pervasive sex difference in coping is in *seeking social support*. Women are more likely than men to cope by seeking support (Vingerhoets & Van Heck, 1990; L. Archer, Keever, Gordon, & Archer, 1991; Ptacek et al., 1992, 1994; Thoits, 1991). Again, the majority of research has failed to distinguish whether women are seeking support for emotion-focused or problem-focused reasons.

Despite the hypothesis that men engage in more *problem-focused coping* than women, there is little research to support this claim. The majority of studies do not find sex differences in problem-focused coping (Ptacek et al., 1994). Often, problem-focused coping is the most frequently employed coping strategy by both men and women (Ptacek et al., 1992). Finally, sex differences in *positive reappraisal* are unclear (Vingerhoets & Van Heck, 1990; L. Archer et al., 1991).

A recent meta-analytic review of the literature on sex differences in coping (Tamres, Janicki, & Helgeson, under review) has shown that women are more likely than men to engage in nearly all of the coping strategies, problem-focused and emotion-focused. This is consistent with the results of most of the studies described above. The sizes of these sex differences are all small, however. The largest differences appeared for seeking support, rumination, and positive self-talk (i.e., encouraging oneself). Notice that all of these strategies involve the expression of feelings, either to oneself or to someone else.

One difficulty in interpreting the literature on gender and coping is that women may report more of all kinds of coping simply because women are more distressed than men and more distressed people try a greater range of strategies. Women use more coping strategies than men (Thoits, 1991). Thus, many of the observed sex differences in coping (women greater than men) may be methodological artifacts of women simply being more distressed than men.

One way to address the issue of people's distress influencing their coping is to evaluate **relative coping,** which refers to how likely men or women are to use one strategy compared to another. Instead of comparing the frequency with which men

and women engage in a specific kind of coping, we compare the frequency with which men engage in one coping strategy compared to another strategy and the frequency with which women engage in one coping strategy compared to another strategy. Within the range of coping responses, are men relatively more likely to use a strategy compared to women? For example, imagine that both men and women report engaging in problem-focused coping with equal frequency: "some of the time." For men, this may be the most frequently employed strategy, whereas women may report engaging in other strategies "almost all of the time." In that case, men would engage in problem-focused coping relatively more often than women. In fact, research has shown that men engage in *relatively* more problem-focused coping than women (Ptacek et al., 1992; Tamres et al., under review).

A rarely investigated topic is the extent to which coping strategies are tied to gender roles rather than sex per se. In one study, masculinity was associated with greater problem-focused and less emotion-focused coping (Nezu & Nezu, 1987). Problem-focused coping strategies included actively trying to solve the problem, which is typically adaptive, whereas emotion-focused coping was defined as avoiding the problem, a strategy that is typically maladaptive. These coping strategies explained the link of masculinity to reduced depression. Studies of specific coping strategies would benefit from a focus on gender roles.

TEND AND BEFRIEND. Recently, one team of researchers has argued that women's general response to stress is different from that of men. Historically, the general response to stress has been described as "fight or flight." However, Taylor et al. (2000) argue that this response may apply only to men and that women's response to stress may be better understood as "tend and befriend." Is this true? We have seen so far that one of the most consistent sex differences in coping is that women seek the support of others, which may be consistent with the tend and befriend idea. We also have some evidence that men may engage in more avoidant coping or distraction, consistent with "flight," and it is clear that men are more physically aggressive than women, consistent with "fight."

Taylor and colleagues (2000) also argue that women's response to stress may have biological underpinnings. In particular, they emphasize the role of oxytocin. Oxytocin may inhibit the flight response and encourage the tending to relationships in women. Oxytocin helps to calm one down during times of stress and promotes affiliative behavior (McCarthy, 1995). Positive physical contact, in the form of touch or hugging, releases oxytocin, which then reduces the stress response (Uvnas-Moberg, 1997). The amount of oxytocin released during stress is greater in women than men (Jezova, Jurankova, Mosnarova, Kriska, & Skultety-ova, 1996), which may explain why women respond to stress by seeking rather than withdrawing from others.

Although this theory explains why women may cope differently with stress than men, it does not explain why women are more depressed than men. The tend and befriend idea, however, does suggest that women will be more involved in relationships than men. To the extent that relationships are a source of stress (an idea expanded on later in the chapter), women's tendency to tend and befriend may have some negative outcomes.

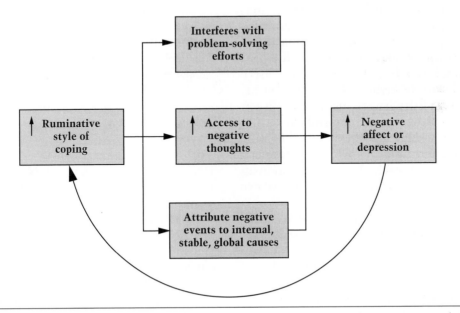

FIGURE 12.6 Nolen-Hoeksema's rumination and depression model. A ruminative style of coping leads to interference with problem-solving efforts, increased access to negative thoughts, and a pessimistic style of thinking (i.e., attribute negative events to internal, stable, global causes)—all of which increase negative affect or depressive symptoms. Negative affect or depressive symptoms also lead to more ruminative coping.

RUMINATION. A large program of research on sex differences in depression has emerged that focuses on two specific kinds of coping strategies: rumination and distraction. Susan Nolen-Hoeksema (1987, 1994) has argued that women are more depressed than men because women ruminate about their feelings after negative events and men distract themselves. She argues that rumination increases depression in three ways, each of which is depicted in Figure 12.6. First, rumination interferes with instrumental behavior, which might reduce depression. For example, if you are dwelling on a poor grade from a first exam, your distress may keep you from studying for the next exam—which ultimately will lead to another failure experience and further depression. Second, rumination about negative feelings makes other negative feelings and negative memories more salient, which will reinforce depression. After failing an exam, other failure experiences may become increasingly vivid. Third, rumination leads people to make pessimistic explanations for negative events, such as the ones characterized by the pessimistic attributional style described above. In a study of bereaved adults, rumination was associated with an increase in pessimistic thinking (Nolen-Hoeksema, Parker, & Larson, 1994). Sample rumination and distraction items from Nolen-Hoeksema's Responses to Depression Questionnaire are shown in Table 12.4.

In a number of studies, Nolen-Hoeksema (1987) has shown that women are more likely than men to respond to depression by talking about and trying to figure out their negative feelings: rumination. By contrast, men are more likely than women to respond to depression by playing sports and by avoiding thoughts about the reasons for their depression: distraction. The sex difference in rumination is more consistent than the sex difference in distraction

TABLE 12.4   Nolen-Hoeksema's Responses to Depression Questionnaire

Sample Rumination Scale Items

- Think about how alone you feel.
- Think "I won't be able to do my job/work because I feel so badly."
- Think about your feelings of fatigue and achiness.
- Think, "Why can't I get going?"
- Go away by yourself and think about why you feel this way.
- Write down what you are thinking about and analyze it.
- Think about how sad you feel.
- Analyze your personality and try to understand why you are depressed.
- Listen to sad music.

Sample Distraction Scale Items

- Help someone else with something in order to distract yourself.
- Remind yourself that these feelings won't last.
- Go to a favorite place to get your mind off your feelings.
- Concentrate on your work.
- Do something you enjoy.

Source: Nolen-Hoeksema and Morrow (1991).

(Nolen-Hoeksema, Morrow, & Fredrickson, 1993; Strauss, Muday, McNall, & Wong, 1997). See if there are sex differences in rumination and distraction at your school with Exercise 12.4.

What is the evidence that rumination leads to depression? Numerous studies have shown that people who tend to ruminate in response to a stressful event end up more distressed. In a study of people in San Francisco just after the 1989 earthquake, ruminators were more depressed seven weeks after the earthquake than nonruminators (Nolen-Hoeksema & Morrow, 1991). In a study of men who had lost their partner

EXERCISE 12.4
**Sex Differences in Rumination
and Distraction**

Ask 10 men and women to think about how they respond when they are depressed about an achievement-related failure (e.g., failing an exam) and a relationship-related failure (e.g., relationship breakup). You choose the two specific failure experiences. Then, ask people how they responded to each failure experience by having them answer the items in Table 12.4. Feel free to supplement these sample rumination and distraction items with questions of your own.

Is there a sex difference in rumination and distraction? Does it depend on the situation?

Much of the research discussed is compelling because it was conducted in the field with people facing actual stressful life events; thus, the research has good external validity. However, recall that the cost of field research is often a loss of internal validity. Is rumination an actual cause of depression? The reciprocal nature of the relation between rumination and depression shows that depression also causes rumination. One way to address the causal issue is to conduct an experiment in a controlled laboratory setting.

Just such an experiment was conducted and showed that inducing depressed people to ruminate increases their depression and inducing depressed people to distract reduces their depression (Lyubomirsky & Nolen-Hoeksema, 1993). Rumination and distraction were manipulated in the laboratory by having depressed and nondepressed college students either think about their feelings and why they are the kind of person they are (rumination condition) or think about external events (distraction condition). Among depressed students, rumination increased depressed mood and distraction reduced depressed mood. However, rumination and distraction had no effect on nondepressed students' moods. There also was evidence that the rumination manipulation interfered with the potential for instrumental behavior among depressed students. Depressed students who were induced to ruminate about themselves reported that they were less likely to engage in a list of pleasant activities (e.g., go to dinner with friends, play favorite sport) than the other students.

to AIDS, rumination and self-analysis one month after the partner's death predicted reduced positive mood and increased depression 12 months later. In a one-year longitudinal study of over 1,000 community residents (Nolen-Hoeksema et al., 1999), women reported a greater tendency than men to ruminate and rumination explained women's increased depression.

Nolen-Hoeksema and colleagues (1999) argue that individuals get involved in a cycle of rumination and depression. This cycle is depicted in Figure 12.6. Rumination increases depression, which then increases rumination. The reciprocal relation between rumination and depression has been demonstrated in longitudinal studies of bereaved adults (Nolen-Hoeksema et al., 1994) and community residents (Nolen-Hoeksema et al., 1999). Rumination also leads episodes of depression to last longer (Nolen-Hoeksema et al., 1993).

Why are women more likely than men to ruminate in response to stressful events? One possibility is that people encourage women to ruminate more than men. A study that supported this idea showed that college students gave more ruminative advice (i.e., figure out why you are depressed) to women than to men (Ali & Toner, 1996).

Students were equally likely to give distracting advice to men and women. One reason people might encourage women to ruminate is that they do not perceive rumination to be maladaptive. Despite the evidence, college students perceive rumination strategies (e.g., talking with someone, determining the cause of one's feelings) as more effective in alleviating depression than distraction strategies (Strauss et al., 1997).

Does a ruminative response style explain why depression emerges only among women during adolescence? Nolen-Hoeksema (1994) views rumination as an interactive cause of sex differences in depression. She argues that females are more likely than males to ruminate even before adolescence but that the negative events that occur to adolescent women make their ruminative response more detrimental. The negative events that occur to women during adolescence involve negative body images, difficulties in relationships, and awareness of the limits of the female gender role (i.e., role inconsistent with independence and achievement). These difficulties are addressed at the end of the section on depression.

PRIVATE SELF-CONSCIOUSNESS. Private self-consciousness, or one's awareness of the self, is typically considered a personality trait rather than a way of coping. Because self-awareness or self-consciousness is so closely linked to rumination, I discuss it here. Private self-consciousness reflects attending to one's inner thoughts and feelings. Sample items from the private self-consciousness scale are "I'm always trying to figure myself out" and "I generally pay attention to my inner feelings" (Fenigstein, Scheier, & Buss, 1975). Private self-consciousness has been linked to depression cross-sectionally in adolescents (Allgood-Merten, Lewinsohn, & Hops, 1990) and longitudinally in a study of middle-age women (Bromberger & Matthews, 1996).

Private self-consciousness can provide an explanation for sex differences in depression only if women score higher than men in private self-consciousness. The early studies in this area showed no sex differences in private self-consciousness (Fenigstein et al., 1975). However, two more recent studies of adolescents suggest that girls focus more on their inner feelings than boys do (Allgood-Merten, et al., 1990; Sethi & Nolen-Hoeksema, 1997). In one of the studies, children were asked to write down whatever came to mind (Sethi & Nolen-Hoeksema). Girls' statements contained more references to the self and to relationships, whereas boys' statements contained more references to external stimuli, such as movies, music, and sports. The authors concluded that girls engaged in more internal focusing and relationship focusing, whereas boys engaged in more external focusing. It may be this dispositional difference in styles of thinking that then leads women to ruminate and men to distract when depressed.

Even if there is not an overall sex difference in private self-consciousness, there could be a sex difference in the tendency to react to environmental events by engaging in private self-consciousness. In other words, private self-consciousness could fall into the category of interactive theories of depression. In the study of middle-age women, private self-consciousness interacted with chronic strains, such that women who were high in private self-consciousness and high in chronic strains were especially distressed (Bromberger & Matthews, 1996). In other words, private self-consciousness was linked to depression among women only when stressful circumstances existed about which they could ruminate.

Other research has shown that women may be more vulnerable than men to situational cues that evoke private self-consciousness. In one study, women's levels of private self-consciousness increased in response to a self-focusing cue, a mirror, whereas men's levels of private self-consciousness decreased in response to the same cue (Ingram, Cruet, Johnson & Wisnicki, 1988). These findings are shown in Figure 12.7. Unexpectedly, women's levels of private self-consciousness also increased in response to a quite different cue, a video of another person. Because women define themselves partly through their connections to others, seeing another person may have led women to think of themselves and their connections to others. Gender roles also were associated with responses to self-focusing cues. In response to a self-focusing cue, high levels of masculinity were associated with a decrease in self-focusing, whereas low levels of masculinity were associated with an increase in self-focusing.

In sum, the tendency to engage in private self-consciousness provides an explanation for sex differences in depression, partly due to its overlap with rumination. It also is an interactive theory of depression because it predicts that women are more likely than men to respond to certain cues by becoming introspective.

Stressful Life Events

Instead of focusing on how men and women cope with stress, some investigators have evaluated differences in the amount of stress that men and women experience. A recent meta-analytic review of the literature on sex differences in stressful life events showed that across 119 studies there was a small tendency for females to report more stressful events than males ($d = +.12$; M. Davis, Matthews, & Twamley, 1999). The size of this effect is extremely small and there were a number of variables that influenced the size of the relation. One factor that influenced the effect size was how stress was measured. Researchers who

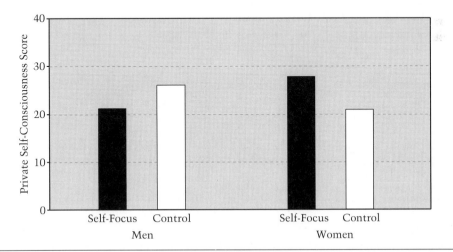

FIGURE 12.7 Effects of sex and self-focusing cue on private self-consciousness. Women's private self-consciousness increased in response to a self-focusing cue, a mirror, whereas men's private self-consciousness decreased in response to the same cue. *Source:* Adapted from Ingram et al. (1988).

study stressful life events typically ask respondents to indicate whether an event happened and/or to rate the level of stress associated with an event. That is, ratings are made of *stress exposure, stress impact,* or both. When these two kinds of ratings were distinguished from one another in the meta-analysis, the sex difference in exposure was smaller than the sex difference in impact ($d = +.08$ vs. $d = +.18$). Thus, women may appraise stressors as more severe than men, but women and men do not necessarily experience a different number of stressors. The age of the sample also influenced the size of the relation. The sex difference in stress was larger among adolescent samples compared to children and adult samples, supporting Nolen-Hoeksema's (1994) claim that adolescent females face more stress than adolescent males.

One reason the overall sex difference in exposure to stress is small may be that women and men experience stressors in different domains. The meta-analysis examined whether sex differences appeared for different kinds of stressors. The sex difference for interpersonal stressors was larger than the sex difference for noninterpersonal stressors ($d = +.17$ vs. $d = +.07$). There was no category of stressor on which men scored higher than women.

There is a great deal of research on adolescents that supports the meta-analysis finding that females report greater interpersonal stress than males. In a study of preadolescent (ages 8 to 12) and adolescent (ages 13 to 18) boys and girls, there was no sex difference in the total number of stressful events, but females reported greater interpersonal stress and males reported greater noninterpersonal stress (Rudolph & Hammen, 1999). As shown in the left half of Figure 12.8, adolescent girls reported higher levels of interpersonal stress than preadolescent girls, preadolescent boys, or adolescent boys. As shown in the right half of Figure 12.8, adolescent boys experienced greater noninterpersonal stress than the other three groups. In another study of adolescents ranging in age from junior high to college, females were more likely than males to report stressful events that involved relationships and events that occurred to people in their network (B. Wagner & Compas, 1990). In a study of ninth-, tenth-, and eleventh-graders, girls reported

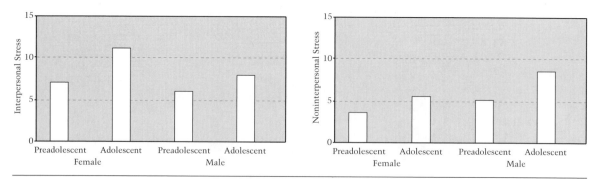

FIGURE 12.8 Sex comparisons of interpersonal and noninterpersonal stress among preadolescents and adolescents. Adolescent females reported higher levels of interpersonal stress compared to adolescent males and either group of preadolescents. Adolescent males reported higher noninterpersonal stress compared to adolescent females and either group of preadolescents. *Source:* Adapted from Rudolph and Hammen (1999).

more events that occurred to family and friends, and boys reported more personal events (Gore, Aseltine, & Colten, 1993). In one study, college students were asked to indicate at the end of the day for 10 consecutive days whether they were depressed and, if so, to identify a cause. Women were more likely than men to identify relationship causes, and men were more likely than women to identify academic causes (P. Robbins & Tanck, 1991).

Studies of noncollege adult populations confirm these findings. In a study of married couples, men reported more negative events involving work and finances, whereas women reported more negative events that involved relationships (R. Conger, Lorenz, Elder, Simons, & Ge, 1993). In addition, men reported greater distress than women in response to work and financial stressors, whereas women reported greater distress than men in response to relationship stressors. There was no sex difference in the reporting of events that involved personal illness or others' illness. A study of physically disabled people found no difference in the number of stressful events that happened to the self but found that women were more likely than men to report events that occurred to others (R. Turner & Avison, 1989).

Thus, it appears that there is only slight evidence for a sex difference in overall stress exposure and more evidence that there is a sex difference in the kinds of stressors experienced. Women are more likely than men to report stressful events that involve relationships and that actually occur to others. Although both of these events are sometimes referred to as relationship stressors, there is a difference. In the first case, investigators are finding that women are more likely to report problems within relationships, such as conflicts, breakups, or losses. In the second case, research is showing that women perceive

stressful events that occur to others as their own personal stressors. Further investigate the distinction between these two kinds of stressors with Exercise 12.5.

Investigators have asked whether sex differences in depression are due to **differential exposure** to stressful events or **differential vulnerability** to stressful events. Differential exposure suggests that women are more depressed than men because they experience more of a certain kind of stressful event. Differential vulnerability implies that certain stressful events are more strongly associated with distress among women than

---

EXERCISE 12.5
Sex Differences in Stressful Life Events

Develop a list of stressful life events that are relevant to the population you are sampling. Classify these events into categories, such as personal events and relationship events. Have 10 men and 10 women:

1. Indicate if the event occurred to them in the previous year.
2. If the event occurred, have them rate how much the event affected them (none, a little bit, a lot).
3. Indicate if the event happened to someone they know in the previous year.
4. If the event occurred to someone else, rate how much the event personally affected them (none, a little bit, a lot).

Are there sex differences in exposure to different kinds of life events? Are there sex differences in exposure to events that occur to others? Are there sex differences in the magnitude of response to (impact of) personal events? Others' events?

men. This distinction is partly captured by the difference between stress exposure and stress impact ratings. R. Turner and Avison (1989) stated nicely the distinction between women's greater exposure to interpersonal stress and greater vulnerability to interpersonal stress: "Women may care about more people or care more about the people they know, or both" (p. 450). The first part of the sentence pertains to exposure and the second part pertains to vulnerability.

Studies have compared the differential exposure and differential vulnerability hypotheses and come in on the side of vulnerability. One example is a study that examined whether men or women were more vulnerable to stressful events that occurred to themselves versus stressful events that occurred to others. Stressful events that occurred to the self were equally associated with depression in men and women, but stressful events that happened to others were more strongly associated with depression in women than men (R. Turner & Avison, 1989). Thus, with respect to stressful events that occurred to others, women were more vulnerable than men.

Kessler and McLeod (1984) examined evidence from five epidemiologic studies of men's and women's exposure and vulnerability to life events. Six categories of events were examined: income loss, separation/divorce, other love loss, ill health, death of a loved one, and other network events. Men reported more life events in the categories of income loss and ill health; women reported more life events in the categories of death of a loved one and other network events. Thus, men and women were exposed to different kinds of stressors. However, these events also showed different relations to distress for men and women. Income loss, separation/divorce, and other love loss showed similar relations to distress for men and women. However, ill health, death of a loved one, and network

events were more strongly related to distress among women. Thus, women were not more vulnerable to the effects of all negative events, but to a portion of events that involved social networks. When the effect of women's exposure to network events was compared to the effect of women's vulnerability to network events, vulnerability appeared to account for more of women's depression.

Taken collectively, these studies show that the reason women are more depressed than men has less to do with the stressful events they face and more to do with how strongly they respond to those events. And women are especially affected by stressors that involve others. Why are women more vulnerable to stressful events that affect network members? This question is addressed next, when I examine the female gender role as an explanation of sex differences in depression.

The Female Gender Role

There are a variety of ways in which one can examine the relation of the female gender role to depression. Because sex differences emerge during adolescence, any good theory of sex differences in depression must start with adolescence. Is there a reason to believe that the female gender role makes adolescent girls vulnerable to depression? I believe the answer is yes.

GENDER INTENSIFICATION. During adolescence, gender roles become salient for men and women. Adolescence has been referred to as a time of **gender intensification** (J. Hill & Lynch, 1983). During adolescence, boys become increasingly concerned with adhering to the male gender role and girls become increasingly concerned with adhering to the female gender role. These concerns arise in part from outside forces: adolescents feel increasing pressure from society to adhere to their gender roles.

Gender intensification theory was partly supported in one study that examined changes in gender roles and gender-role attitudes from sixth- to eighth-grade (Galambos, Almeida, & Petersen, 1990). At all ages, boys scored higher than girls on masculinity, or agency, but the largest sex difference appeared in the oldest group (e.g., eighth-graders). Boys' masculinity scores increased more than girls' with age. Girls always scored higher than boys on femininity, or communion, but these scores did not change with age. Sex differences in gender-role attitudes increased with age: girls became more egalitarian and boys became more traditional.

Other evidence for gender intensification comes from studies that show females' interpersonal orientation increases during adolescence. In a study of 9- to 15-year-olds, older girls spent increasingly more time with friends than did younger girls (Larson & Richards, 1991). By contrast, older boys spent more time alone than did younger boys. In a study of fifth- through ninth-graders, older girls spent more time in social activities, on the phone with friends, and talking with friends than did younger girls. In addition, girls' conversations began to have a more interpersonal focus as they grew older (Raffaelli & Duckett, 1989). These same behavioral differences were not observed between older and younger boys. A study of fifth-, eighth-, and twelfth-graders showed that as boys increased in age, they found it more difficult to share their feelings with others, whereas girls found it easier to share feelings with others as age increased (Polce-Lynch et al., 1998). Thus, there is some evidence for gender intensification during adolescence.

Why would gender intensification lead to depression? There is some evidence that depression is heightened among women who realize the limiting value of the female gender role. One study examined cohorts of women over the entire twentieth century and found that those who reached adolescence when a high proportion of women were graduating from college in comparison to when their mother graduated from college were more depressed (Silverstein & Perlick, 1991). Among cohorts of women who reached adolescence when the proportion of women graduating from college was similar to that in their mother's time, there were no sex differences in depression. The investigators argue that the discrepancy between the graduation rates of women and their mothers made the first group of women more aware of the limiting factors of the female gender role. This point also was illustrated by a study that showed women who had concerns about their mother's limited achievement (e.g., felt their mother was limited by being female, felt guilty for having more opportunities than their mother) were twice as likely to be depressed than women who did not express these concerns (Silverstein, Perlick, & Clauson, 1993). In addition, women who felt they were limited by being female and wished they were a male were at increased risk for depression.

Although intelligence and achievement orientation in childhood or adolescence exert protective effects on men's mental health, there is evidence that these qualities pose risks for women's mental health. IQ scores have been associated with ambition, productivity, persistence, and self-satisfaction in young adult men (ages 18 and 23), but introspection, anxiety, rumination, and guilt among young adult women (J. Block & Kremen, 1996). In a longitudinal study, higher IQ scores during preschool predicted greater depression among female 18-year-olds but less depression among male 18-year-olds (J. Block, Gjerde, & Block, 1991). Five years later, similar results were obtained when predicting depression among the 23-year-olds (Gjerde, 1995).

Other evidence is consistent with the idea that high achievement has positive mental health consequences for men but not women. In a six-year longitudinal study of people without a history of mental illness, men who attended college were less likely to become depressed than men who did not attend college. By contrast, women who attended college were more likely to become depressed than women who did not (Coryell et al., 1992). In a study of patients hospitalized for depression, a high achievement orientation was associated with recovery from depression among men but a lack of recovery from depression among women (Veiel, Kuhner, Brill, & Ihle, 1992). Another study showed that women are distressed when they don't achieve the goals they set for themselves. Women who had not attained by 1992 the goals they set in 1975 showed an increase in depression over this period (Carr, 1997).

Thus, adolescence is a time when gender roles become salient for men and women. This is troublesome for some women because they realize the female gender role is inconsistent with achievement.

COMMUNION AND AGENCY. The gender intensification hypothesis can explain sex differences in depression only if aspects of the female gender role can be linked to depression. The female gender role is typically measured with communion scales of the BSRI or PAQ, which reflect a positive focus on others. These scales include traits such as being helpful, kind, and caring. Communion, however, is unrelated to depression. Two meta-analytic reviews of the literature show that communion is virtually unrelated to depression, and that agency is associated with a lack of depression (Bassoff & Glass, 1982; Whitley, 1984). Recall that agency reflects a positive focus

on the self. A recent study of college students in Hong Kong also showed that agency was associated with a lack of depression and communion was unrelated to depression (Cheng, 1999). Longitudinal data reveal protective effects of agency and null effects of communion. In a longitudinal study of middle-age women, a lack of agency predicted an increase in depression three years later (Bromberger & Matthews, 1996). Communion did not predict depression. In a longitudinal study of medical students, agency was associated with less depression, whereas communion was unrelated to depression (D. Clark & Zeldow, 1988).

Thus, there appear to be no data linking the female gender role trait of communion to depression. Instead, it seems that features of the male gender role (agency) protect against depression. However, gender roles are multifaceted. I argue that there is an aspect of the female gender role that is related to depression: unmitigated communion.

UNMITIGATED COMMUNION. Recall that unmitigated communion is defined as a focus on others to the exclusion of the self (Helgeson, 1994c; Helgeson & Fritz, 1998). Unmitigated communion has been associated with depression in studies of college students, cardiac patients, healthy adolescents, adolescents with diabetes, and healthy adults (Helgeson & Fritz, 1998). In addition, unmitigated communion accounts for sex differences in depression. For example, in a study of adolescents with diabetes, unmitigated communion was more strongly related to depression than respondent's sex and there were no sex differences in depression once levels of unmitigated communion were considered (Helgeson & Fritz, 1996).

The primary explanation of why unmitigated communion is linked to depression pertains to the focus on others. People characterized by unmitigated communion become overly involved in others' problems and take on others' problems as their own. Recall from the section on stressful life events that women are more likely than men to report stressful events that occur to other people. Unmitigated communion also has been linked to reporting stressful events that occurred to others. Unmitigated communion may be associated with exposure to others' problems because such individuals seek out others to help. However, the person who scores high on unmitigated communion also may be more likely than others to interpret another person's problem as his or her own. For example, two people may both be exposed to a neighbor going through a divorce, but only the unmitigated communion person defines this stressful event as his or her own personal stressor.

Getting involved in others' problems can take its toll. In the study of adolescents with diabetes, older adolescents (ages 15 through 18) who scored high on unmitigated communion reported being more upset by stressful events that involved others. These stressors explained the link of unmitigated communion to depression (Helgeson & Fritz, 1996). Thus, unmitigated communion may explain why some women experience interpersonal events as stressful.

Unmitigated communion also is associated with *worrying* about other people's problems. Thus, unmitigated communion is associated with rumination, consistent with Nolen-Hoeksema's (1994) theory—but the rumination is not about one's own problems, but about other people's problems. Two laboratory studies showed that people high in unmitigated communion ruminate about others' problems (Fritz & Helgeson, 1998). In each study, one person disclosed a problem to another. In one study, the two people discussing the problem were friends. In the other study, a confederate of the experimenter disclosed a problem to the research participant. Listen-

ers who scored high on unmitigated communion reported more intrusive thoughts about the discloser's problem two days later, whether the discloser was a friend or a stranger.

A study of adolescents reveals support for the unmitigated communion hypothesis, although unmitigated communion per se was not measured in that study. Female adolescents were more depressed than male adolescents, and those who were characterized by a high interpersonal orientation were more vulnerable to depression (Gore et al., 1993). The two-item interpersonal orientation scale closely resembles items on the unmitigated communion scale: "I worry a lot about the people that are close to me" and "It hurts me a lot when people I love are unhappy." The interpersonal orientation accounted for sex differences in depression.

CAREGIVING. Aside from the personality trait of unmitigated communion, there is a general caregiving aspect of the female gender role that may be linked to depression. It is true that people characterized by unmitigated communion may be more likely to be caregivers; however, people can end up in the caregiver role regardless of their level of unmitigated communion. Events such as a spouse becoming ill, parents growing older and needing care, and children becoming sick can happen to anyone. Women traditionally shoulder more of the burden of these caregiving responsibilities. Caregiving also is more likely to lead to distress in women than in men. In a recent review of the literature, women and men caregivers were compared to non-caregivers (J. Yee & Schulz, 2000). Studies showed that caregiving was associated with a greater increase in distress among women than men. There are a number of reasons that caregiving may be associated with more distress in women. First, women spend more time than men on caregiving activities, especially the day-to-day activities (J. Yee & Schulz, 2000). A longitudinal study of women showed that caregiving led some women to decrease or cease employment (Pavalko & Woodbury, 2000). Men, by contrast, are more likely to obtain assistance with caregiving (J. Yee & Schulz, 2000). Second, the nature of the caregiving relationship may affect men and women differently. One study found that female caregivers of spouses, children, or parents were more likely to be distressed than female noncaregivers, but male caregivers were more distressed than male noncaregivers only when the person they were taking care of was a spouse (W. Marks, 1998).

It is the caregiving role that may explain why social ties are not as protective against depression among women as they are among men. Recall from Chapter 10 that social relations are a double-edged sword for women. On the one hand, social ties are a source of support, support is related to reduced distress, and women have more support available to them than men do. However, social relations are a source of stress for women as well (Belle, 1982). For example, one study determined that the number of social roles was directly related to fewer mental health problems among men but showed a curvilinear relation to mental health problems among women (Weich, Sloggett, & Lewis, 1998). That is, women with the fewest social roles and women with the most social roles had higher levels of mental distress. Women who have many social roles may find that the stresses to which they are exposed outweigh the support that they receive.

CHALLENGES OF ADOLESCENCE

The consensus seems to be that sex differences in depression begin to appear at around age 13, the time of transition from elementary or junior high school to high school. In a longitudinal study, 300 adolescents were evaluated in the sixth, seventh, eighth, and twelfth grades (Petersen, Sarigiani, & Kennedy, 1991). The investigators found that sex differences in depression began to emerge in the eighth grade and increased by the twelfth grade. There were no sex differences in depression among the early adolescents (sixth or seventh grade). Many of the theories of sex differences in depression posit that female vulnerabilities interact with the challenges of adolescence. Cyranowski, Frank, Young, and Shear (2000) state: "Pubertal maturation sensitizes females to the depressogenic effects of negative life events" (p. 22). In this section of the chapter, I examine some of the events of adolescence that might lead to an increase in depression among young women.

Puberty

Because the emergence of sex differences in depression coincides with puberty, researchers have investigated whether the physical changes that accompany puberty are associated with depression in women. In a longitudinal study of adolescents, depression was associated with *early* pubertal changes (i.e., development of breasts; Petersen et al., 1991). When adolescents reached their peak pubertal height before they made the transition from elementary school to high school, depression increased. This was a phenomenon that largely occurred among girls, as boys are less likely to reach puberty this early.

However, other research has shown that it is reaching puberty that is associated with sex differences in depression, regardless of its timing (Angold, Costello, & Worthman, 1998). Two studies have shown that puberty is more strongly linked than age to the sex difference in depression

(Angold et al., 1998; Patton et al., 1996). One way in which pubertal changes may be associated with depression is through their impact on adolescents' body image.

Body Image

A negative body image is associated with depression in both males and females (Allgood-Merten et al., 1990). However, women have a more negative body image than men, which may make them more vulnerable to depression.

In a study of ninth- through twelfth-graders, girls had lower self-esteem and more negative body image than boys in all grades (Allgood-Merten et al., 1990). Girls' low self-esteem and negative body image accounted for a large portion of the sex difference in depression. Interestingly, body image was more strongly associated with global self-esteem among girls than among boys. When the relations of both body image and self-esteem to depression were compared, self-esteem had the stronger relation to depression. This finding suggests that the impact of a negative body image on girls' depression operates through adverse effects on their overall feelings of self-worth.

A recent study of African American sixth- through ninth-graders showed that girls were more depressed than boys and that girls had more negative body image than boys (Grant et al., 1999). In addition, the negative body image accounted for the sex difference in depression. This study is important because it suggests that a negative body image may play a role in African American girls' depression. Historically, Black women have been less concerned with their weight than have White women; the findings from this study suggest that these ethnic differences may be disappearing. The increased dissatisfaction with body image among young Black women may be due to the acculturation of Black women into the middle class and to the increased availability of thin Black models in the media (Grant et al., 1999).

Self-Esteem

Sex differences in self-esteem were reviewed in Chapter 5 and led to the conclusion that there were few overall sex differences among adults but measurable differences in adolescents. A study of high school students found that girls had lower self-esteem than boys and were more depressed than boys (Avison & McAlpine, 1992). Furthermore, self-esteem accounted for sex differences in depression. A study of sixth- and seventh-graders showed that girls received lower scores on a variety of domains of self-esteem: global self-worth, physical appearance, and athletic ability (Ohannessian, Lerner, Lerner, & von Eye, 1999). Because there was no sex difference in depression among sixth-graders but a sex difference in depression among seventh-graders, the authors argued that the sex difference in self-esteem preceded the sex difference in depression. In addition, sex differences in these domains of self-esteem accounted for the sex difference in depression.

The self-concepts that adolescents are expected to develop may have different implications for men's and women's mental health. Men are expected to develop an achievement-oriented self-concept, whereas women are expected to develop an interdependent self-concept (Gore & Colten, 1991). The former can be achieved on one's own, whereas the latter can be achieved only with the help of others. This may make women's self-esteem and overall mental health more vulnerable to environmental factors, which may explain why women are more vulnerable than men to stressful events that happen to others.

Parental Relations

Adolescence is a time of challenge for and conflict with parents (Arnett, 1999). The move from childhood to adulthood involves a separation from parents and an identification with peers. There is some evidence that parental relations have a stronger impact on depression among girls than among boys. Good relations with mother were associated with less depression for sixth- and seventh-grade girls but not boys (Ohannessian, Lerner, von Eye, & Lerner, 1996). Support from mother influenced the relation of stressful life events to depression for adolescent girls but not adolescent boys (Ge, Lorenz, Conger, Elder, & Simons, 1994). One study found that mothers and fathers were more overprotective of girls and that an overprotective father accounted for part of the sex difference in depression (Avison & McAlpine, 1992). Thus, parental relations are strained during adolescence and these strains have a greater effect on girls.

Different Manifestations of Depression

I have pointed out that sex differences in depression emerge during adolescence, but an alternative theory is that boys and girls begin to *manifest* depression differently by adolescence. Some studies have examined the personality traits that characterize depressed adolescent males and females and find them to be quite different. In one study, clinicians observed 18-year-olds in a variety of settings and rated them on a number of personality characteristics (Gjerde, Block, & Block, 1988). Depressed men were viewed as aggressive and disagreeable, whereas depressed women were viewed as introspective and ruminating. That is, depressed men showed more **externalizing**

behavior and depressed women showed more **internalizing behavior.** However, the depressed men and women reported views of themselves that were slightly different from the views the clinicians held. Depressed men reported being aggressive but also reported worrying and feeling vulnerable—internalizing characteristics that were not recognized by the clinicians. Depressed women reported being aggressive and unrestrained—externalizing characteristics that were not recognized by the clinicians. Either the men and women were less likely to manifest the gender-role-incongruent forms of depression to clinicians, or the clinicians were less likely to perceive them.

Studies also have sought to identify the childhood precursors of adolescent and adult depression and found that those characteristics differed for boys and girls. In a longitudinal study of children followed from the age of 3 to 18, personality characteristics and behaviors were coded by teachers and clinicians (J. Block et al., 1991). Boys who ended up depressed were characterized in childhood by **allocentric,** or outward-directed, behavior (anger, aggression), whereas girls who ended up depressed were characterized in childhood by **autocentric,** or inward-directed, behavior (introspection). The allocentric/autocentric distinction is quite similar to the distinction between externalizing and internalizing behavior. Similar findings emerged when participants turned 23 (Gjerde, 1995); that is, the same sex difference in childhood predictors of depression was found.

Thus, a variety of events that occur during adolescence—body image changes, challenges to relationships with parents and peers—may pose a greater risk for depression in girls than in boys. However, it also is possible that the sex difference in manifestations of depression emerges during adolescence, with girls' greater internalizing behavior recognized as depression but boys' externalizing behavior construed as another problem behavior.

EATING DISORDERS

Princess Diana, Jane Fonda, Elton John, Joan Rivers, and Cathy Rigby—What do they all have in common? They all have admitted to eating disorders ("A Debilitating Obsession," 1992).

Definitions and Prevalence

There are three major eating disorders: anorexia nervosa, bulimia nervosa, and binge eating disorder (Pike & Striegel-Moore, 1997). Although the three disorders can be clearly defined and distinguished from one another, people can have degrees of any one of them. In fact, various degrees of binge eating exist in the normal population (Attie, Brooks-Gunn, & Petersen, 1990).

ANOREXIA NERVOSA. Of the three, **anorexia nervosa** is the most life-threatening eating disorder. The primary feature of this disorder is the continual pursuit of thinness. The anorexic person has a distorted body image and refuses to maintain a normal weight. One of the diagnostic features of anorexia is that the anorexic person weighs less than 85% of what is considered normal for that person's age and height. A common symptom of anorexia in women is amenorrhea (cessation of menstrual cycling).

There are two kinds of anorexia nervosa: (1) restricting, which consists of dieting, fasting, and exercising but not bingeing and purging, and (2) binge-eating/purging, which, as the name implies, consists of bingeing and purging. Ironically, anorexia is more common in industrialized societies, where food is plentiful (APA, 1994). The majority of cases of anorexia (90%) are found in women (APA, 1994; Pike & Striegel-Moore, 1997), and about 1% of the female population has anorexia nervosa (Pike & Striegel-Moore, 1997). The onset of anorexia typically occurs between the ages of 13 and 18 (APA, 1994).

BULIMIA NERVOSA. **Bulimia nervosa** is characterized by recurrent binge eating followed by vomiting, laxatives, diuretics, enemas, and/or exercising. By far the most common method of purging is vomiting (APA, 1994). Although any food can be consumed during a binge, foods typically consist of sweets and fats. During the binge, the person usually feels a loss of control. This person constantly thinks about food and weight control. The typical person with bulimia is of average weight but may have been overweight prior to the onset of the disorder (APA, 1994). The low weight of an anorexic person is a feature that distinguishes him or her from the bulimic.

There are two types of bulimia: (1) purging, which involves vomiting and using laxatives, diuretics, and enemas, and (2) nonpurging, which involves dieting and exercise and not the other, more extreme methods. As with anorexia, the majority of bulimia cases are also found among women (Pike & Striegel-Moore, 1997), and between 1% and 2% of women have bulimia (Pike & Striegel-Moore, 1997). The onset of bulimia is somewhat later than anorexia, during late adolescence to early adulthood (Pike & Striegel-Moore, 1997). The incidence of bulimia has increased over the past several decades, whereas the rate of anorexia has stabilized (Rolls, Fedoroff, & Guthrie, 1991).

BINGE-EATING DISORDER. **Binge-eating disorder** is a newly defined category of eating disorders (APA, 1994). It is characterized by recurrent binge eating without purging or fasting. Binge eating also is more common among women than men but not to the same extent as anorexia or bulimia. Binge eating can be found in about 2% of women, and half of those women are obese. The typical onset of binge-eating disorder is during young adulthood.

DISTURBED EATING BEHAVIOR. Because the prevalence rate of eating disorders in the general population is so small, investigators often study symptoms of bulimia or anorexia. These symptoms are referred to as disturbed eating behavior. One of the most frequently used instruments to assess disturbed eating is the Eating Disorder Inventory (Garner, Olmstead, & Polivy, 1983). There are three subscales of this inventory that have been linked to eating disorders, such as anorexia and bulimia: drive for thinness, bulimia, and body dissatisfaction. The items from each of these scales are shown in Table 12.5. Many of the studies reviewed in this section have used this instrument or a similar one.

Consequences

The consequences of eating disorders range from minor to severe (Pike & Striegel-Moore, 1997). Dental problems may occur from repeated vomiting. Gastrointestinal problems and colon problems may result from repeated use of laxatives. Bone problems may occur with anorexia and place one at risk for osteoporosis. Women with eating disorders are likely to have problems getting pregnant. People with anorexia are likely to suffer from hypotension (low blood pressure), which could cause cardiovascular problems. A recent study reported that there may be long-term effects of anorexia on the structure of the brain, some

TABLE 12.5   Eating Disorder Inventory

Drive for Thinness

1. I eat sweets and carbohydrates without feeling nervous.*
2. I think about dieting.
3. I feel extremely guilty after overeating.
4. I am terrified of gaining weight.
5. I exaggerate or magnify the importance of weight.
6. I am preoccupied with the desire to be thinner.
7. If I gain a pound, I worry that I will keep gaining.

Bulimia

1. I eat when I am upset.
2. I stuff myself with food.
3. I have gone on eating binges where I have felt that I could not stop.
4. I think about bingeing (overeating).
5. I eat moderately in front of others and stuff myself when they are gone.
6. I have thought of trying to vomit in order to lose weight.
7. I eat or drink in secrecy.

Body Dissatisfaction

1. I think that my stomach is too big.
2. I think that my thighs are too large.
3. I think that my stomach is just the right size.*
4. I feel satisfied with the shape of my body.*
5. I like the shape of my buttocks.*
6. I think my hips are too big.
7. I think that my thighs are just the right size.*
8. I think that my buttocks are too large.
9. I think that my hips are just the right size.*

* These items are reverse scored.

Source: Garner et al. (1983).

of which are reversible upon recovery and some of which may not be reversible (Katzman, Zipursky, Lambe, & Mikulis, 1997).

About 40% of people with anorexia recover completely, 30% improve, and 20% to 25% remain chronically ill (Rolls et al., 1991; Steinhausen, Rauss-Mason, & Seidel, 1991). The prognosis is more favorable if anorexia is caught early. Anorexia can result in death due to starvation; the mortality rate ranges from 4% to 20% (Crisp, Callender, Halek, & Hsu, 1992; Rolls et al., 1991). In two cohorts of anorexic patients followed for 20 years, the mortality rate was 4% in one study and 13% in the other (Crisp et al., 1992); deaths were due to self-starvation and suicide. Compared to the mortality rates expected for women this age, women with anorexia were 1.36 times more likely to die in one cohort and 4.71 times more likely to die in the other cohort. Another longitudinal study of 30 adults found that anorexia nervosa was associated with an 18-fold increase in mortality (Norring & Sohlberg, 1993), which would make it the psychiatric disorder with the highest death rate.

Etiology

The etiology of eating disorders is unclear. Researchers have examined genetic links, demographic factors that may predispose one to eating disorders, social factors, and a variety of psychological factors, including difficulties with achievement and lack of control.

GENES. The heritability component of eating disorders is questionable (Pike & Striegel-Moore, 1997). Some twin studies have found higher rates of anorexia in monozygotic than dizygotic twins (APA, 1994). One study found a 55% concordance rate of eating disorders among monozygotic twins and only a 7% concordance rate among dizygotic twins (Crisp, Hall, & Holland, 1985). Because monozygotic twins share 100% of their genes and dizygotic twins share only half of their genes, a higher concordance rate among monozygotic than dizygotic twins is evidence for a genetic influence. However, another study found a co-occurrence of anorexia and bulimia among twins, but co-occurrence rates were similar for monozygotic and dizygotic twins (Walters & Kendler, 1995).

DEMOGRAPHICS. Anorexia nervosa has often been characterized as an illness of the upper class. The desire for thinness is associated with higher income and higher social class. Eating disorders are more prevalent among people of a higher social class, among college students, and among people in certain professions, such as dancers, actors, models, and athletes (Attie et al., 1990; Rolls et al., 1991; Walters & Kendler, 1995). Among men, eating disorders are especially prevalent among athletes who have strict weight limitations placed on them, such as wrestlers and jockeys (Rolls et al., 1991; R. Thompson & Sherman, 1999). In the late 1990s, three college wrestlers died because of the extreme behaviors they used to lose weight before a match (R. Thompson, 1998); two were working out in rubber suits and one was riding an exercise bike and refused to drink water.

More recently, eating disorders have been studied among homosexual men and women. Eating disorders are more common among gay men than among heterosexual men (Lakkis, Ricciardelli, & Williams, 1999; I. Williamson & Hartley, 1998). The rate of eating disorders among gay men appears to be more similar to that of heterosexual women, and in one study exceeded that of heterosexual women (Schneider,

O'Leary, & Jenkins, 1995). Interestingly, the rate of eating disorders is lower among lesbians than heterosexual women (Lakkis et al., 1999).

Much of the research on eating disorders has taken place in the United States, Canada, and England. One interesting study compared the rate of eating disturbances among college women in the United States to the rate in Japan. Despite the fact that the Japanese women were thinner on average than the American women, the rate of eating disturbances was similar (Mukai, Kambara, & Sasaki, 1998). The authors suggested that eating disorders may become more prevalent in countries that internalize Western culture's association of thinness with physical attractiveness. It also may be that countries that embody the stereotypical female and male gender roles are more at risk for eating disorders. A study that compared body shape preferences in Denmark and Portugal found that the Portuguese, who hold more traditional attitudes toward gender roles, preferred more traditional bodies in men and women (V-shaped males and hour-glass females; Furnham & Nordling, 1998). The authors speculated that these preferences could be linked to eating disorders.

FEMALE GENDER ROLE. Eating disorders have been linked to features of the female gender role. The female gender role is multifaceted. Communion, the aspect of the role that emphasizes a positive orientation toward others, has not been implicated in eating disorders. However, an aspect of the female gender role referred to as negative femininity might play a role in the development of eating disorders. Negative femininity includes being dependent, weak, timid, and needing others' approval. In two studies that evaluated positive and negative aspects of masculinity and femininity, only negative femininity emerged as a predictor

of disordered eating behavior (Lakkis et al., 1999; Paxton & Sculthorpe, 1991). One of these studies evaluated male and female heterosexual and homosexual college students and found that negative femininity predicted disordered eating in all four groups (Lakkis et al., 1999).

The female gender role also is involved in the development of eating disorders to the extent that it is tied to a concern with physical appearance. College women who score high on femininity and low on masculinity are less satisfied with their appearance (L. Jackson, Sullivan, & Rostker, 1988). In fact, women reduce the amount of food they eat in front of the other sex in order to appear more feminine (Pliner & Chaiken, 1990). Women with eating disorders score higher on a measure of female gender-role stress compared to women with other psychiatric problems and healthy women in the general population (Martz, Handley, & Eisler, 1995). One aspect of this measure of female gender-role stress is a fear of physical unattractiveness; thus, women with eating disorders seem concerned with adhering to the ideal female role, which entails physical attractiveness.

SOCIETAL FACTORS. One perspective on eating disorders places the blame on society's obsession with dieting and the pressure for thinness among women (Rolls et al., 1991). Not surprisingly, dieting appears to be an antecedent to eating disorders (Cogan & Ernsberger, 1999). The majority of women in the United States are currently dieting or have dieted in the past. About 40% of women and 24% of men report that they are currently dieting (Wing & Klem, 1997). Between 50% and 80% of high school women have been on a diet (Attie et al., 1990; Smolak & Striegel-Moore, 1996), and up to 40% of elementary school girls have tried to lose weight (Smolak & Levine, 1996). Studies of children show that girls are less satisfied with their bodies than are boys (Rolls et al., 1991). One problem with dieting is that it causes metabolism to decrease over time, making it increasingly difficult to lose weight. Thus, after the initial pounds are shed, more extreme methods are required to achieve the same rate of weight loss.

U.S. society's image of the ideal woman is an extremely thin form, really without shape. Today, young women are surrounded by media exposure to thinness through magazines and television. Patients with anorexia and bulimia often recall models in magazines as motivators to lose weight (M. Levine & Smolak, 1996). Toy models such as Barbie display unrealistic body shapes. When the measurements of Barbie were compared to the actual measurements of a sample of 18- to 35-year-old women, the chances of finding Barbie's measurements in this population were estimated to be less than 1 in 100,000 (Norton, Olds, Olive, & Dank, 1996).

The standards for thinness have grown increasingly strict and have become more unrealistic over the past three to four decades (Siever, 1996). The changing standards for women were illustrated in a study that showed *Playboy* centerfolds and Miss America contestants have become increasingly thin between 1957 and 1978 (Garner, Garfinkel, Schwartz, & Thompson, 1980). The standards of the ideal male body also have changed. One group of investigators examined changes in male action figures over the past 30 years, in particular, G.I. Joe and *Star Wars* characters (H. Pope, Olivardia, Gruber, & Borowiecki, 1999). Over time, the figures have grown more muscular. Again, if the dimensions of these figures were translated into human beings, only the rare adult male would meet these specifications. The authors contend that changes in these action toys reflect changing standards of the male body image and

that these changes could be linked to eating disturbances in men.

Over the twentieth century, eating disorders have risen at the same time that the media have given greater attention to thinness (M. Levine & Smolak, 1996). Exposure to media, including magazines and television, is associated with disordered eating and lower body satisfaction (M. Levine & Smolak, 1996; J. Thompson & Heinberg, 1999). However, much of this research is correlational, meaning that cause and effect cannot be determined. It is not clear whether the media's attention to thinness increases the prevalence of eating disorders, whether people who have eating disorders pay more attention to the media, or some third variable causes eating disorders and sensitivity to media attention to thinness. Several laboratory studies, however, have shown that exposing people to magazine spreads and photographs of thin models leads to more dissatisfaction with one's body (J. Thompson & Heinberg, 1999).

Concerns about thinness also come from sources other than the media, such as family and friends, who are often dieting themselves. Eating disorders are associated with families who express concerns about weight and with families in which parents are overly critical of weight and appearance (Pike & Striegel-Moore, 1997). Mothers' attitudes toward their own body and toward their daughter's body have been related to daughters' eating disorders (Attie et al., 1990).

Because peers have such an influence on adolescents' behavior, one would expect eating disorders to be more common when there are peer pressures to diet. In one study, sorority members' bingeing behaviors were correlated with one another (Crandall, 1988). Over time, the relations became stronger; presumably, sorority members' relationships strengthened and they grew to have a stronger influence on one another. In addition, friends' bingeing behavior at the beginning of the study predicted participants' subsequent bingeing behavior one year later. In one sorority, popularity was directly linked to greater reports of bingeing.

If peers can promote eating disturbances, one would also expect that peers could help one another avoid eating disorders. One set of researchers tried to capitalize on this idea by designing a peer support group intervention to deter eating disorders among college women (T. Mann, Nolen-Hoeksema, Huang, & Burgard, 1997). Women were randomly assigned to a control group or an intervention group. In the intervention group, peers who had recovered from an eating disorder shared their experiences and provided information. At the end of the study, much to the investigators' surprise, the intervention group showed *more* symptoms of eating disorders than the control group. The authors reasoned that listening to peers discuss eating disorders normalized the behavior and reduced the stigma associated with eating disorders. Studies such as this one show the impact that peers can have on eating disorders.

Social factors also might explain why eating disorders are more prevalent among gay than heterosexual men and less prevalent among lesbians than heterosexual women. Gay men report more dissatisfaction with their body compared to heterosexual men, whereas lesbians report greater satisfaction with their body compared to heterosexual women (Lakkis et al., 1999; I. Williamson & Hartley, 1998). In a study of gay and heterosexual men, body dissatisfaction and low self-esteem were associated with eating disturbances among gay men but not heterosexual men (I. Williamson & Hartley, 1998). There are several reasons that body image is important to gay men. First, the gay community emphasizes youth, thinness, and physical attractiveness (I. Williamson, 1999). Second, the

partners of gay men are also men, and it is men more than women who value physical attractiveness in their partner.

PSYCHOLOGICAL FACTORS. A general psychological theory of eating disorders is that they stem from feelings of a lack of autonomy, a lack of control, and a lack of a sense of self in combination with a striving for perfection and achievement (Attie et al., 1990; Rolls et al., 1991). Weight loss is one way to fulfill these needs: losing weight is a way to gain control over one's body and has the potential to enhance self-esteem. Eating disorders have been linked to a high need for others' approval and a concern with pleasing others (Leary, Tchividjian, & Kraxberger, 1994), even in Japanese college women (Mukai et al., 1998). Many investigators have argued that eating disorders emerge in women during adolescence because it is during this time that girls feel a loss of control, become concerned with others' views of them, and become aware of the limitations of the female gender role with respect to achievement (Attie et al., 1990; Silverstein & Perlick, 1995). One way of responding to these challenges is to exert control over weight.

Some have suggested that eating disorders are more common among women who have high need for achievement (Silverstein & Perlick, 1995). In one study, women with nontraditional gender roles were twice as likely as women with traditional gender roles to report purging or bingeing behavior (Silverstein, Carpman, Perlick, & Perdue, 1990). Women who wished they were male also were more likely to show symptoms of eating disorders.

Eating disorders have been linked to a host of other problems that female adolescents suffer, such as anxiety and depression (APA, 1994; Silverstein & Perlick, 1995; Walters & Kendler, 1995). Eating disorders are one way that distress manifests itself among these girls. However, the sex ratio of eating disorders is much larger than the sex difference in depression; thus, eating disorders must be more than a manifestation of psychological distress.

Research also has examined whether eating is used as a way to cope with negative affect. In a study of women in Japan and the United Kingdom, emotional eating behavior was associated with eating disturbances among women in the United Kingdom but not women in Japan (Waller & Matoba, 1999). Interestingly, there was a small association of emotional eating to eating disturbances among a third group, Japanese women living in the United Kingdom. This may reflect some degree of acculturation on the part of the Japanese into Western culture.

In summary, it is not surprising that eating disorders emerge during adolescence, or that nearly all of the theories just reviewed focus on adolescence. It is during adolescence that girls experience body changes, in particular, an increase in fat. It is also during this time that girls become dissatisfied with their bodies and become increasingly concerned with their appearance and how others view them. Finally, during adolescence, girls recognize limiting factors associated with the female gender role.

SUICIDE

In 1994, Kurt Cobain, 27 years old and lead singer of the popular alternative rock band Nirvana, committed suicide by shooting himself. In 1993, Vince Foster, a White House aide to President Clinton, committed suicide also by shooting himself. Cobain had a history of depression, drug abuse, and suspected suicide attempts. He left a suicide note indicating that he lacked the excitement for creating music and felt guilty that the roar of the crowd no longer had an effect on him (Love, 1994). Foster had recently started taking antidepressants. It is alleged that he left a suicide note indicating a sense of failure in his role in Washington (Carlson, 1993). There are some similarities between these two cases: both used firearms; both had a history of mental health problems; both were men.

Despite the fact that women are more depressed than men, men actually commit suicide more frequently. There is an even more interesting paradox: men commit suicide more frequently than women, but women attempt suicide more frequently than men. In this section of the chapter, I provide statistical information on suicide rates and attempts, and then discuss some of the factors that have been associated with suicide and suicide attempts in men and women.

Incidence

In 1997, 24,492 men and 6,043 women committed suicide. The suicide rate is much higher among men (18.7 per 100,000) than women (4.4 per 100,000). As shown in Figure 12.9, the size of this sex difference is relatively stable across the life span until old age. Among the elderly, there is a dramatic increase in men's suicide rates, which increases the magnitude of the sex difference (Canetto & Sakinofsky, 1998; Coren & Hewitt, 1999). Men account for 86% of the suicides that occur among persons age 65 and older (Coren & Hewitt, 1999). The sex difference is also a bit larger among the younger cohorts: among 15- to 19-year-olds and 20- to 24-year-olds, men are about 6 times as likely as women to commit suicide. The size of the sex difference is similar among White and non-White persons in the United States (Canetto & Lester, 1995).

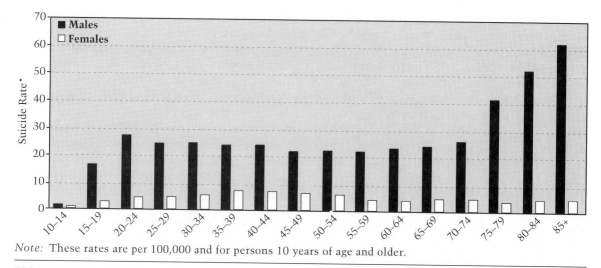

Note: These rates are per 100,000 and for persons 10 years of age and older.

FIGURE 12.9   Suicide rates by sex and age. Men have higher suicide rates than women at all ages. The sex differential is particularly high among young people and the elderly. *Source:* Adapted from the Bureau of Justice Statistics' *Sourcebook of Criminal Justice Statistics* (1997).

Sex differences in suicide extend across cultures (Pampel, 1998). The sex difference (male:female ratio) in suicide rates for 18 countries is shown in Table 12.6. In a study of 70 countries, men had higher suicide rates than women in all countries except China and Papua New Guinea (Canetto & Lester, 1995). The size of the sex difference was smaller in Asian countries.

Men and women use different methods to commit suicide: men are more likely to use guns and women are more likely to use poisons. The first method is more decisive than the latter. However, the difference in methods does not account for the sex difference in suicide rates. Even within a given method, suicide attempts are more likely to be fatal among men compared to women (Canetto & Lester, 1995).

Pampel (1998) examined suicide rates from 1953 to 1992. Sex differences in suicide decreased from the 1950s to the 1970s but then rose again in the 1980s. The increase was due to a greater increase in suicide

TABLE 12.6   Sex Differences in Suicide

Nation	Male:Female Suicide Ratio
Australia	2.84
Austria	2.75
Belgium	2.50
Canada	3.28
Denmark	2.03
Finland	4.41
France	2.92
Germany	2.31
Ireland	2.97
Italy	2.51
Japan	1.65
Netherlands	1.78
New Zealand	2.92
Norway	3.29
Sweden	2.78
Switzerland	2.84
United Kingdom	2.00
United States	3.59

Source: Pampel (1998).

among men relative to women. The suicide rates of adolescents have increased over the past several decades (Centers for Disease Control and Prevention, 1995, 1998b). Between 1952 and 1992, the rate of suicide among adolescents tripled; a large portion of this increase was accounted for by the availability of firearms. Although the suicide rate is still highest among White males, the greatest rate of increase more recently has been among Black males: between 1980 and 1995, adolescent Black males' suicide rates doubled. Firearms accounted for two-thirds of Black male suicide.

Suicide rates are not as easy to estimate as you might think. The official statistics on suicide rates are likely to be underestimates because some suicides are mistakenly classified as other causes of death. This misclassification may lead to a greater underestimation of female than male suicide because women are more likely to use ambiguous methods, such as poisoning, which are less easily classified as suicide (Canetto & Lester, 1995). Men, by contrast, are more likely to use guns; it is easier to determine that a self-inflicted gunshot was a suicide.

Attempts

Although men commit suicide more frequently than women, women attempt suicide more often than men and express more suicidal thoughts than men. This paradox holds across most Western societies (Canetto & Sakinofsky, 1998). Among adolescents, females also report more suicidal thinking and more suicide attempts than males (Rich, Kirkpatrick-Smith, Bonner, & Jans, 1992). In a 1995 nationwide study of over 10,000 high school students, 24% of adolescents said they had seriously considered attempting suicide in the prior year (Centers for Disease Control and Prevention,

1996); the percentage of girls was greater than that of boys (30% vs. 18%). Twice as many girls as boys reported actually attempting suicide (12% vs. 6%). Suicide attempts that required medical attention were reported by 6% of girls compared to 1% of boys.

One estimate is that about 5 million persons in the United States attempt suicide in a year (J. McIntosh, 1985). Suicide attempts are difficult to estimate; for example, an overdose of drugs can be interpreted as a suicide attempt or as an accident. Some have suggested that men's suicide attempts are underreported (Canetto & Sakinofsky, 1998). Both attempting suicide and not succeeding are considered weak behaviors that are inconsistent with the strength and decisiveness of the male gender role; thus, men themselves may not admit to making a suicide attempt, and clinicians may be less likely to consider the possibility that a drug overdose in a man was a suicide attempt.

The Gender Paradox

One methodological explanation for the paradox of men's higher suicide rates and women's higher suicide attempts is that men's attempts are underreported and women's actual suicides are underestimated because they are classified as other causes of death (e.g., accidental).

A theoretical explanation behind the gender paradox lies in gender-role socialization. According to Canetto and Sakinofsky (1998), "Women and men will tend to adopt the self-destructive behaviors that are congruent with the gender scripts of their cultures" (p. 17). Suicide is considered masculine behavior, but suicide attempts are considered feminine behavior. Among men, committing suicide is considered to be a powerful response to some kind of failure; attempting but not completing a suicide is often construed as weak behavior and thus is viewed negatively, especially in men. Males are more likely than females to report being concerned with societal disapproval of suicide (Rich et al., 1992), which may explain why their suicide attempts are successful. The gender paradox in suicide attempts and suicide rates is most prominent among adolescents and young adults, the very people who are most concerned with adhering to gender roles (Canetto & Sakinofsky, 1998).

Factors Associated with Suicide among Adults

Among adults, suicide and suicide attempts have been linked to substance abuse and depression. The link of suicide to depression is problematic, however, because a suicide attempt might lead to a diagnosis of depression. There is evidence in the United States and from other cultures that the link between suicide and alcohol abuse is stronger in men than in women (Canetto & Lester, 1995). By contrast, the link between suicide and depression appears to be stronger among women. Predictors of suicide *attempts* may differ. A study of suicidal thinking and suicide attempts revealed just the opposite sex difference: depression was a stronger predictor of suicidal thinking and suicide attempts among men, and antisocial behavior predicted suicidal thinking and suicide attempts among women but not men (Wannan & Fombonne, 1998).

We often associate suicide with the breakup of a relationship. There is some evidence to support this thinking. In the United States, the divorce rate is positively correlated with the suicide rate, and the marriage rate is negatively correlated with the suicide rate (Lester & Yang, 1998). In other words, as more people are married, fewer people commit suicide; as more people become divorced, more people commit

suicide. These findings generalize to other countries (Lester & Yang, 1998). In a study of 29 nations, divorce rates were positively associated and marriage rates were negatively associated with suicide rates (Lester & Yang, 1998). In addition, the association with divorce rates was stronger than the association with marriage rates. Divorce rates also are more strongly associated with suicide rates for men than women across a variety of countries (Lester & Yang, 1998). This finding supports the research reviewed in Chapter 10 that marriage is more health-protective for men than for women. Suicide rates are higher among single, widowed, and divorced men compared to married men (Canetto & Lester, 1995).

Marital status also influences how people view suicide. Suicide is viewed as less acceptable by married than unmarried people. This finding appears in 15 different countries, including the United States, Australia, and many European nations (S. Stack, 1998a). Across these countries, the difference in views of suicide by married and unmarried people is greatest among men, meaning that married men find suicide the least acceptable. Findings regarding people's acceptability of suicide are important because these views are linked to suicide attempts and suicide completions (S. Stack, 1998a).

Thus, suicide rates in men are linked, in part, to the absence of marriage, which may signify the absence of emotional support. Women's greater integration into social relationships may protect them against suicide. Women not only receive support from network members but provide support to them as well. The fact that women have people to take care of, such as a husband and children, may make them less likely to commit suicide (Canetto & Lester, 1995).

Suicide rates also increase as unemployment increases. This finding holds in the United States as well as in other nations (Lester & Yang, 1998). Suicide rates are more strongly tied to unemployment rates among men than among women. In a study of 15 countries, unemployed people were more accepting of suicide than were employed people (S. Stack, 1998a).

Among men, suicide is associated with divorce and unemployment; among women, suicide seems to be related to their status. In countries where the status of women is low, such as China, India, and Japan, the suicide rates of women are relatively high (Canetto & Lester, 1995). In countries where women have a low status and are frequently abused by husbands, suicide among women is almost considered acceptable. Suicide by a woman in these societies (such as Papua New Guinea) is construed as an assertive act of rebellion by the woman (Counts, 1987). The husband suffers from public humiliation because her act of assertion undermines his authority and power in the family.

Gender roles also have been implicated in suicide. In a study of the elderly in the United States, the suicide rate of men and women in each state was examined in relation to agentic variables (indicators of financial and social status, such as income and education) and communal variables (indicators of social stability and social environment stress, such as moving and crowding; Coren & Hewitt, 1999). The investigators found that agentic variables more strongly predicted suicide among elderly men than women, and communal variables more strongly predicted suicide among elderly women.

There are some similarities and differences in how men and women view suicide. In a study of adults in the United States and Germany, men and women were equally likely to view committing suicide as an act of mental illness (Domino & Groth, 1997). However, men were more likely than women to view suicide as impulsive, which contradicts the stereotype that women are the ones who make impulsive attempts at suicide. In addition, women were more likely than men to view suicide as aggression, to believe that people have a right to die, and to associate suicide with a lack of religion.

Factors Associated with Suicide among Adolescents

Not surprisingly, suicide and suicide attempts in adolescents are associated with other mental disorders, in particular, depression and substance abuse (Lester & Yang, 1998; Rich et al., 1992). In one study, 80% of those who attempted suicide could have been classified as having mental disorders, such as major depression, alcohol dependence, drug dependence, or disruptive behavior disorders (Andrews & Lewinsohn, 1992). It is not clear whether suicide and suicidal behavior are more strongly associated with depression in males or females. Two studies showed a stronger link in males (Andrews & Lewinsohn, 1992; Wannan & Fombonne, 1998), and two showed a stronger link in females (Brent, 1995; Prigerson & Slimack, 1999). One study suggested that depression may be directly linked to suicide in females but indirectly linked to suicide in males through substance abuse (Metha, Chen, Mulvenon, & Dode, 1998). However, the literature also is not clear as to whether alcohol use is more strongly linked to suicidal behavior in males or females (Brent, 1995; Wannan & Fombonne, 1998) and whether antisocial behavior is more strongly linked to suicidal behavior in males or females (Brent, 1995; Prigerson & Slimack, 1999; Wannan & Fombonne, 1998). In one study, investigators examined suicidal thinking in a high-risk group: adolescents who had a friend commit suicide in the prior six years. Aggressive behavior predicted suicidal thinking among adolescent boys and depression predicted suicidal thinking among adolescent girls (Prigerson & Slimack, 1999).

Social relationships also play a role in adolescent suicide. In a one-year longitudinal study of fifth-graders and their mothers, poor family functioning, as indicated by mothers, was associated with increased suicidal ideation over the year (Garber, Little, Hilsman, & Weaver, 1998). Lack of support from and troubled relationships with family and friends have been associated with a greater risk of suicide (D'Attilio, Campbell, Lubold, Jacobson, & Richard, 1992), greater suicidal ideation, and more frequent suicide attempts (Dubow, Kausch, Blum, Reed, & Bush, 1989; Wannan & Fombonne, 1998). In a study of depressed adolescents, suicide attempts were predicted by a lack of family support and a loss of support over the prior three months (Morano, Cisler, & Lemerond, 1993). Loss of support was measured by asking respondents if they had lost anyone in the prior three months who had been important to them. Suicide among adolescents also has been associated with the breakup of romantic relationships. In one study, investigators interviewed family members of adolescents who had committed suicide to find out what kinds of life events occurred in the prior year. Compared to a control group of adolescents, family members of suicide victims reported that the adolescents were more likely to have experienced problems in romantic relationships, including breakups (Brent et al., 1993).

SUMMARY

There is a consistent and pervasive sex difference in depression in the United States population that extends to other cultures. The difference is on the order of 2:1 (female:male) but may be larger in studies of people with major depressive disorder. Sex differences in depression emerge during adolescence and persist over the life span. Sex differences in depression may be affected by a response bias on the part of clinicians and respondents; clinicians may be more likely to recognize or interpret symptoms as depression in women than in men. Because depression is inconsistent with the male gender role, men may be more reluctant than women to admit, report, or seek help for depression.

There are numerous theories of sex differences in depression, tapping biological, psychological, and social factors. There is little evidence that genes can explain sex differences in depression. Although hormonal changes have been associated with mood changes, the evidence is inconsistent as to which hormone is protective or harmful at what time. The evidence that hormonal changes during puberty are linked to the onset of depression is weak.

Psychological theories of depression suggest that women are socialized in ways that lead them to perceive less control than men over their environment. Thus, women are more vulnerable to learned helplessness, which can lead to depression. Consistent with this theory, women may be more likely than men to interpret negative events in a pessimistic light. The attributional style theory of depression suggests that women are more likely than men to exhibit a pessimistic attributional style; the evidence for this suggestion, however, is not compelling.

Other theories of sex differences in depression focus on the stressors that men and women face and how they cope with them. The coping literature distinguishes between problem-focused and emotion-focused coping, which may not be useful when studying gender. Research suggests that women may be more likely than men to engage in most coping strategies, which may be a result of rather than a cause of women's distress. One promising theory of sex differences in depression focuses on a particular maladaptive form of coping, rumination. There is a great deal of evidence that women are more likely than men to respond to stressful events by ruminating about them, and rumination is linked to depression.

There is little evidence that women experience more stressful life events than men, but women do experience more of a specific kind of stressor: relationship stressors. Women report more stressful events that involve relationships and the association of relationship stressors to distress is stronger for women than for men. It is women's differential vulnerability to stress rather than differential exposure to stress that best explains depression.

The last theory of depression focused on the female gender role. Two aspects of the female gender role must be distinguished: communion and unmitigated communion. Whereas communion is unrelated to depression, unmitigated communion is consistently associated with depression. People characterized by unmitigated communion seem to take on others' problems as their own and become overly involved in helping others. Aside from this specific personality trait, caregiving more broadly has been linked to the female gender role and may be linked to depression.

Regardless of which theory best explains sex difference in depression, the onset during adolescence must be addressed. Several challenges of adolescence were reviewed that might explain this onset, including body image changes and strains in relationships. These events might activate depression in girls who are at risk for depression.

A second mental health problem discussed in this chapter was eating disorders.

Eating disorders are more common in women than in men and more likely to arise during adolescence than at any other time in life. Many of the theories of eating disorders are linked to adolescence. During adolescence, women's bodies change and women become more aware of societal pressures to be thin. It also is during adolescence that women recognize the limitations placed on the female gender role and on their control more generally. Eating disorders may be a manifestation of attempts to exert control.

The last mental health problem reviewed was suicide. Men commit suicide more frequently than women at all ages and across most cultures, but women contemplate suicide and attempt suicide more frequently than men. Substance abuse, depression, and impaired social relations all play a role in suicidal behavior among adolescents and adults.

DISCUSSION QUESTIONS

1. In what populations are there less likely to be sex differences in depression?
2. Which methodological bias do you believe is most likely to undermine sex differences in depression?
3. What kind of experiences during childhood, adolescence, and adulthood do females face compared to males that might instill learned helplessness?
4. Give an example of a pessimistic attributional explanation for catching a cold.
5. Distinguish between problem-focused and emotion-focused coping. Are there sex differences in either of these?
6. Explain *how* rumination leads to depression.
7. What is the difference between the differential exposure and the differential vulnerability hypotheses concerning the relation of stressful events to depression?

8. Which aspect of gender roles are related and unrelated to depression?

9. Why is the desire for high achievement associated with greater depression in women?

10. What are some of the reasons that sex differences in depression emerge during adolescence?

11. How does society contribute to the development of eating disorders in women?

12. Discuss how the difficulties in documenting suicide rates and suicide attempts might alter the sex difference in suicide and suicide attempts.

13. What social factors are associated with suicide in males and females?

Suggested Reading

Block, J.H., Gjerde, P.F., & Block, J.H. (1991). Personality antecedents of depressive tendencies in 18-year-olds: A prospective study. *Journal of Personality and Social Psychology, 60*(5), 726–738.

Canetto, S.S., & Lester, D. (1995). Gender and the primary prevention of suicide mortality. *American Association of Suicidology, 25*(1), 58–69.

Culbertson, F.M. (1997). Depression and gender: An international review. *American Psychologist, 52*(1), 25–31.

Helgeson, V.S., & Fritz, H.L. (1998). A theory of unmitigated communion. *Personality and Social Psychology Review, 2*, 173–183.

Nolen-Hoeksema, S. (1990). *Sex differences in depression*. Stanford, CA: Stanford University Press.

Pike, K.M., & Striegel-Moore, R.H. (1997). Disordered eating and eating disorders. In S.J. Gallant, G.P. Keita, & R. Royak-Schaler (Eds.), *Health care for women: Psychological, social, and behavioral influences* (pp. 97–114). Washington, DC: American Psychological Association.

Silverstein B., & Perlick, D. (1995). *The cost of competence: Why inequality causes depression, eating disorders, and illness in women.* New York: Oxford University Press.

Key Terms

Allocentric—Outward-directed behavior, such as aggression.

Anorexia nervosa—Eating disorder characterized by the continual pursuit of thinness, a distorted body image, and refusal to maintain a weight that is more than 85% of what is considered normal for the person's age and height.

Autocentric—Inward-directed behavior, such as introspection.

Binge-eating disorder—Eating disorder characterized by recurrent binge eating without purging or fasting.

Bulimia nervosa—Eating disorder characterized by recurrent binge eating followed by purging via vomiting, laxatives, diuretics, enemas, and/or exercising.

Clinical depression—Another name for major depressive disorder, the critical feature of which is that the person must have experienced a set of depressive symptoms for a period no shorter than two weeks.

Different cause theory—Suggestion that there are different causes of girls' and boys' depression and that the cause of girls' depression increases during adolescence.

Differential exposure—Idea that men and women are exposed to a different number of or kinds of stressors.

Differential item functioning—Idea that some items are more likely to be associated with a trait, such as depression, among men versus women.

Differential vulnerability—Idea that certain stressors are more strongly linked to distress in one sex than the other.

Emotion-focused coping—Approach to stressful situations in which individuals attempt to accommodate themselves to the stressor.

Externalizing behavior—Aggressive and disagreeable behavior.

Gender intensification—Idea that gender roles become salient during adolescence, causing boys and girls to more strongly adhere to these roles.

Interactive theory—Suggestion that being female always poses a risk for depression but the events of adolescence activate that risk.

Internalizing behavior—Introspective and ruminating behavior.

Learned helplessness—Learning that one's actions are independent of outcomes, which then leads one to stop responding (give up) in other situations.

Pessimistic (depressive) attributional style—Tendency to make internal, stable, and global attributions for negative events.

Precipitating factors—Environmental events that trigger the emergence of a disorder (e.g., depression).

Problem-focused coping—Approach to stressful situations in which one attempts to actually alter the stressor itself.

Relative coping—Likelihood that men or women use one coping strategy compared to another strategy.

Same cause theory—Suggestion that the same factor could cause depression in both men and women but that the factor increases during adolescence only for girls.

Susceptibility factors—Innate, usually biological, factors that place one group (e.g., women) at greater risk for a disorder (e.g., depression) than another group.

13

Aggression

On September 15, 1999, Larry Gene Ashbrook, age 47, killed seven worshippers and then himself in a Baptist church in Tennessee ("Latest Shootings," September 17, 1999).

On July 29, 1999, Mark Barton, a 44-year-old securities day trader, killed his wife, his 12-year-old son, and his 7-year-old daughter in his home. He then went on a rampage, killing nine other people in two office buildings in Atlanta before killing himself (Sack, 1999).

On April 20, 1999, Eric Harris and Dylan Klebold, two teenagers, killed 12 classmates and wounded 23 others within 16 minutes and then killed themselves at Columbine High School in Littleton, Colorado. They had intended to kill 488 people in the cafeteria with two bombs ("Sheriff Releases," May 16, 2000).

On October 16, 1991, George Hennard drove his pickup truck through the window of Luby's Cafeteria in Texas, killed 23 people, and then shot himself ("Mass Murders," April 26, 1996).

On February 29, 2000, a 6-year-old boy who was living in a crack house brought a gun to school and killed a 6-year-old girl, Kayla Rolland, at an elementary school in Michigan. The boy was determined to be too young to prosecute (Barboza, 2000).

Finally, in the small town where I grew up (Bradley, Illinois), Timothy Buss at age 13 murdered and then mutilated the body of a 5-year-old girl in 1981. Fourteen years later, in 1995, after being released from prison on parole, Buss returned to the area and brutally murdered a 10-year-old boy (Cotliar, 1996).

What do all of these atrocities have in common? They were horrendous acts of violence that received a great deal of media attention, causing us, as a nation, to question the sources of such behavior. They also all involved male perpetrators. The public has taken note of such incidences, especially the Columbine massacre, as the perpetrators were children. In the past couple of years, books that address the subject of troubled boys who become involved in violence have been best-sellers, such as *Lost Boys: Why Our Sons Turn Violent and How We Can Save Them* by James Garbarino (1999), *Raising Cain: Protecting the*

Emotional Life of Boys by Dan Kindlon and Michael Thompson (1999), and *Real Boys: Rescuing Our Sons from the Myths of Boyhood* by William Pollack (1998).

In Chapter 3, I pointed out that there were sex differences in aggression. The purpose of this chapter is to expand on that issue. You may wonder why the topic of aggression appears in the health section of this text. There are several reasons. First, some people consider aggressive behavior to be a manifestation of psychological distress. Second, aggression is hazardous to the victim, leaving physical and/or psychological scars. In this chapter, I discuss research on aggression and present criminal statistics on acts of aggression. Not only are men more likely than women to be the perpetrators of aggression, men are much more likely to be the victims of aggression as well; we often lose sight of this latter fact. Aggression also has important implications for male-female relationships, in part due to the power imbalance in those relationships. Thus, I discuss three forms of aggression that most commonly take place in the context of male-female relationships: rape, domestic abuse, and sexual harassment. In each section of the chapter, I present different theories of aggression, many of which focus on aspects of male gender-role socialization.

AGGRESSION/VIOLENCE

The subject of this chapter is one particular kind of aggression, **hostile aggression,** defined as behavior motivated by anger that has the primary intention of harming someone. Hostile aggression must be distinguished from **instrumental aggression,** which is the use of aggression as a means to an end (Berkowitz, 1993). For example, punching someone you dislike is hostile aggression; slapping a child's hand as the child reaches to touch a hot burner is instrumental aggression. The second behavior may be aggressive, but the overall goal of the behavior was not to inflict harm; in this case, it was intended to keep the person from being harmed.

In this first section, I review the research evidence that compares rates of male and female aggression. Then, I review the field evidence (i.e., crime statistics) on rates of male and female violence.

Research Evidence

Research on aggression has overwhelmingly emphasized the sex of the perpetrator, but some research has examined the sex of the victim. I address each of these issues separately.

SEX OF PERPETRATOR.   In 1986, Eagly and Steffen conducted a meta-analysis of studies that evaluated sex differences in aggression among adults. They restricted their analysis to studies that used behavioral measures of aggression; in other words, self-report studies were omitted. The meta-analysis included laboratory experiments, which were often based on the teacher-learner paradigm (i.e., participant is teacher and shocks learner for incorrect response), and field studies, in which people were typically exposed to some frustrating event. On average, men displayed greater aggression than women ($d = +.29$). Sex differences were larger for physical measures of aggression compared to verbal measures. Sex differences also were larger in laboratory studies than field studies, but many fewer field studies existed. Hyde (1984) conducted a meta-analysis around the same time and reached similar conclusions. However, she included self-report studies and noted that they showed a larger effect ($d = +.55$) than behavioral studies ($d = +.25$). This difference in effect size may be explained by the vulnerability of self-reports of aggression to demand characteristics: it is more socially desirable for men than women to report acts of aggression.

More recent studies of college students as well as noncollege adults confirm that men report greater physical aggression than women (M. Harris, 1996; M. Harris & Knight-Bohnhoff, 1996b). Sex differences in verbal aggression, however, are less consistent (M. Harris, 1996; M. Harris & Knight-Bohnhoff, 1996b). One meta-analysis revealed no sex differences in verbal aggression in the field ($d = +.03$) and only a small sex difference in the laboratory, in the direction of men being more aggressive than women ($d = +.13$; Bettencourt & Miller, 1996).

We noted in Chapter 3 that most sex differences are influenced by a variety of situational variables. The study of aggression is no exception. One important situational factor is *provocation*. A meta-analysis of experimental studies on aggression was conducted to examine whether provocation influenced sex differences (Bettencourt & Miller, 1996). Provocation may release women from the constraints the female gender role places on aggressive behavior. Across 107 tests of sex differences, the meta-analysis revealed that men were more aggressive than women. The size of the effect ($d = +.24$) was similar to that found by Eagly and Steffen (1986). Again, the sex difference was larger for physical than verbal aggression. In addition, provocation led to greater aggression than nonprovocation, and provocation altered the size of the sex difference in aggression; the sex difference was smaller under provocation conditions ($d = +.17$) than under neutral conditions ($d = +.33$). In addition, a judge's rating of the intensity of a provocation was negatively correlated with sex differences in aggression; in other words, the stronger the provocation,

the smaller the sex difference. There was only one type of provocation to which men reacted much more strongly than women: receiving negative feedback on intelligence. In those studies, the sex difference in aggression was larger ($d = +.55$). Does this mean that woman are not as upset as men when they receive negative feedback about their intelligence? Not necessarily. The investigators suggest that men and women may respond to failure feedback with different emotions; failure feedback may evoke anger in men and sadness in women. Recall the research from Chapter 5 showing that women take negative evaluative feedback more personally than men do.

Other features of the situation may contribute to sex differences in aggression. Eagly and Steffen (1986) found that sex differences in aggression were larger when women felt more guilt and anxiety than men and when women found the situation more dangerous than men did. These two findings accounted for most of the sex differences in aggression. In other words, women were less likely than men to behave aggressively when they viewed the situation as dangerous and when they felt more anxious and guilty about the situation. Another factor that influences sex differences in aggression, related to the danger of the situation, is whether women fear retaliation. One meta-analysis showed that sex differences in aggression were larger when women had greater fears of retaliation (Bettencourt & Miller, 1996). Thus, danger and fears of retaliation are stronger deterrents of aggression for women than for men, whereas provocation is more likely to release women's inhibitions to behave aggressively.

Another point noted in Chapter 3 pertaining to many sex differences is that they seem to be getting smaller over time. Is that true of aggression? As men's and women's roles have become more similar, have rates of aggression become more similar? As women have become more assertive, have they also become more aggressive? Research findings on this issue are contradictory. One meta-analysis showed that sex differences in aggression were getting smaller over time (Hyde, 1984). However, another meta-analysis revealed just the opposite: sex differences in aggression seem to be getting larger over time (Knight, Fabes, & Higgins, 1996).

One problem with comparing the early to the later studies is that research methodologies have changed over time (Knight et al., 1996). Recent studies are more likely to have used nonexperimental methods such as field designs, and these methods have produced larger sex differences than laboratory studies. In one meta-analysis, the size of the sex difference for nonexperimental studies was larger than that for experimental studies ($d = +.77$ vs. $d = +.37$; Knight et al., 1996). When differences in the research methodologies used in the early and later studies were taken into consideration, the year of publication was unrelated to the size of the sex difference in aggression. In the end, we have no evidence that sex differences in aggression have changed over time. We only know that researchers today are using different methods to study aggression.

The limitations of self-report methods are obvious. Are observations of behavior any more objective? We know from previous chapters that the same behavior may be construed differently when it is observed in a man or a woman. Is aggressive behavior viewed the same when the perpetrator is male versus female? One study showed that we view the same behavior as more aggressive when it is displayed by a male, and we also view the same behavior as more aggressive when it is displayed *toward* a female (M. Harris & Knight-Bohnhoff, 1996a). In this study, college students and a group of people working on a military base were presented with an aggressive scenario in which the sex of the perpetrator and the sex of the victim were varied. Respondents viewed the same aggressive behavior as more serious when the perpetrator was a man and when the victim was a woman. People may perceive aggression to be more serious when committed by a male and more serious when directed toward a female because of the differences in physical strength between the sexes. In other words, people perceive the same aggressive act to have different consequences depending on the sex of the perpetrator and sex of the victim. Test this out yourself with Exercise 13.1.

It is important to point out that the focus of this chapter is on *physical* aggression. Recall that the previous meta-analyses showed less support for sex differences in verbal aggression (Bettencourt & Miller, 1996; Eagly & Steffen, 1986). When more indirect forms of aggression, such as relational aggression (described in Chapter 6), are considered, sex differences may disappear (Crick et al., 1999). In fact, women may be more likely than men to engage in

---

EXERCISE 13.1
Perceptions of Aggressive Behavior

Create two different scenarios of aggressive behavior. For each scenario, manipulate the sex of the perpetrator and the sex of the victim. You will have four different versions. The scenarios should be identical, with the exception that the sex of the perpetrator and victim are different. Ask a group of men and women to rate the aggressive behavior in terms of severity. Does the sex of the perpetrator, sex of the victim, or sex of the respondent influence perceptions?

indirect forms of aggression (Bjorkqvist & Niemela, 1992).

SEX OF VICTIM.   Men also are more likely than women to be victims of aggression. Eagly and Steffen's (1986) meta-analysis found an effect for the sex of the victim ($d = +.13$). Sex differences were larger for physical than verbal aggression and larger in laboratory than field studies. More recent studies have confirmed this finding. Men are more likely than women to report being victims of physical aggression. In a study of college students, men were twice as likely to report having been kicked, bitten, hit by a fist, and hit by another object (M. Harris, 1996). Men were three times as likely to report being threatened with a gun or knife.

The sex of the perpetrator and the sex of the victim may be interrelated. A study of elementary school children found that boys were more aggressive toward other boys than toward girls, but girls were equally aggressive to boys and girls (A. Russell & Owens, 1999). However, the kind of aggression that girls used with boys and girls differed; girls tended to be physically aggressive with boys but used verbal and indirect aggression with girls.

Crime Statistics

One concern with the experimental research on aggression, both laboratory and field, is that it is not clear if one person is *intending* to harm another. In the teacher-learner paradigm, the participant believes shocking the confederate is supposed to aid learning; in other words, the person's ultimate goal is not to hurt the other person. A critical component of hostile aggression is the intention to harm. An important source of information on hostile aggression is crime statistics. We can be certain that intent to harm is present in most criminal acts.

As with aggressive acts in general, men are more likely than women to commit violent crimes, and men are much more likely than women to be the victims of violent crimes. The one exception is rape (United States Department of Justice, 1994). Thus, men are more likely than women to be assaulted, robbed, and threatened with violence. Although Black people constitute only 12% of the population, they constitute 48% of murder victims. Among people age 15 to 34, Black men are seven times more likely than White men to die as the result of an act of violence (Staples, 1995).

Men are clearly more likely than women to be the perpetrators and victims of homicide. It is rare that women commit murder. Imagine how society would have reacted if the two teenagers at Columbine High School were girls instead of boys. Multiple homicides also are much more likely to be committed by men than women (N. Wilson, 1993). In 1997, both perpetrator and victim were male in 88% of the homicide cases (Federal Bureau of Investigation, 1997b). When women were victims, they were nine times more likely to be murdered by a male than a female. The female perpetrator/female victim category is a rare one and mainly comprises mothers killing female infants (C. Mann, 1993; N. Wilson, 1993). In addition, female infants are more likely than male infants to be killed (C. Mann, 1993).

We often imagine murder as involving a stranger. Many of the mass killings such as those described at the beginning of the chapter draw a great deal of publicity and involve a person killing strangers. However, nearly half (48%) of people who are murdered know the perpetrator (Federal Bureau of Investigation, 1997b). Only 14% of murders are committed by strangers, and the relationship is unknown in 38% of cases. The perpetrator's relationship to the victim differs for men and women. Women are more likely than men to be killed by someone they know. In 1997, 29% of the women who were murdered were killed by husbands or boyfriends, whereas only 3% of the men who were murdered were killed by wives or girlfriends (Federal Bureau of Investigation, 1997b). However, keep in mind that men are much more likely than women to be murdered, so an equal number of men and women may be killed by someone they know.

Women also are proportionally more likely than men to kill someone with whom they have a relationship. Women are more likely to kill a family member than a stranger, in particular, a husband (Silverman, Vega, & Danner, 1993). Women are next most likely to kill boyfriends and children. Men, by contrast, are more likely to kill acquaintances and strangers than people they know. Again, keep in mind that men are much more likely than women to commit murder, so an equal number of men and women may kill someone they know. In fact, this was shown to be true in a study of intimate homicide patterns in Chicago between 1965 and 1993 (C. Block & Christakos, 1995). During that period, 2,556 intimate homicides occurred: in 1,271 cases, women murdered their male partner; in 1,227 cases, men murdered their female partner; and in 58 cases, a gay person was murdered by his partner. Thus, nearly the same number of men and women killed their partner. However, this statistic is slightly misleading, because there were substantial ethnic differences. Among Black couples, a greater number of women than men killed their partner. Among non-Hispanic White and Hispanic couples, a greater number of men than women killed their partner. In addition, the risk of intimate homicide was greater among Black than White (Hispanic and non-Hispanic) families. Other research has confirmed that there is a higher rate of females killing male partners in African American families (Ucko, 1994).

Has the number of intimate homicides changed over time? Between 1976 and 1987, the rate of marital homicide decreased (A. Browne & Williams, 1993). Both men and women were less likely to kill their spouses. However, the rate of homicide among male perpetrators in unmarried couples increased over that same period. The rate of homicide among female perpetrators in unmarried couples fluctuated and did not show a distinct pattern of change. What happened over this 12-year interval to cause a decrease in men killing their spouse but an increase in men killing their girlfriend? People began to delay marriage and were more likely to live together before or instead of marrying. Thus, the apparent "good news" decrease in marital homicide is offset by a "bad news" increase in cohabitation homicide—at least for male perpetrators.

THEORIES OF AGGRESSION

Biological Theories

Proponents of biological theories argue that there is a biological—genetic or hormonal—predisposition in men to be aggressive.

GENES.   An early genetic theory of aggression focused on the role of an extra Y chromosome in men. Some studies found that there was a higher than average proportion of men with the XYY configuration in prison than in the normal population. However, more recent studies have called this finding into question. Even if the XYY pattern is linked to aggression, it also is the case that the vast majority of the criminal population do not have this extra Y chromosome and the vast majority of people with the extra Y chromosome are not prisoners (Manning, 1989). Studies have shown that boys with the XYY pattern are more irritable and have more temper tantrums than boys without that configuration (Manning, 1989). However, it also is the case that parents of these children are aware of the extra Y chromosome and the potential link to aggression. It is possible that these parents respond to their child's behavior differently, which may further encourage aggressive behavior.

Regardless of whether aggression can be tied to a specific chromosome, there is a hereditary component to criminal behavior. Studies of twins have found a much stronger correlation of aggressive behavior between monozygotic than dizygotic twins. The authors of one study estimated that genetics accounted for 39% of aggression and environment accounted for 61% (Rushton, 1986). Another study of twins found that genetics accounted for between 24% and 94% of aggression depending on the specific aggressive behavior (Ghodsian-Carpey & Baker, 1987). The heritability component of aggression was estimated to be .94 when extreme forms of aggression were examined but .24 when minor instances of aggression, such as noncompliance, were examined. A genetic link to aggression has also been found in adoption studies. One study compared the rate of criminal behavior between adopted children and their biological and adoptive parents (Mednick, Gabrielle, & Hutchings, 1984). The children's criminal behavior was related to that of their biological parents but not of their adoptive parents. However, when *violent* criminal behavior was examined, there was no link to either set of parents. The authors also note that adoptive parents were likely to be aware of the biological parents' criminal behavior, which could have led them to expect such behavior on the part of their children. Expectations can have strong effects on behavior.

HORMONES. Hormonal explanations for male violence often center on the male hormone, testosterone. Testosterone has been linked to frustration, impatience, high levels of physical activity, and rough-and-tumble play (Miedzian, 1991). Interestingly, testosterone decreases with age, just as aggression decreases with age (Rushton, 1986).

Is there any evidence that testosterone is linked to violence? Several studies of prisoners confirm a relation (J. Archer, 1991). One study found that testosterone levels were higher among male prisoners who committed personal crimes of sex and violence than property crimes of burglary, theft, or drugs (Dabbs, Carr, Frady, & Riad, 1995). In addition, prisoners with high testosterone levels were more likely to have violated prison rules. Another study showed that testosterone was higher among prisoners who had committed violent crimes and those rated as tougher on fellow inmates (Dabbs, Frady, Carr, & Besch, 1987). Finally, one study found that prisoners who committed violent crimes and prisoners who had established dominance in the prison system had higher levels of testosterone than other prisoners (Ehrenkranz, Bliss, & Sheard, 1974). The levels of testosterone for these three groups of prisoners are shown in Figure 13.1. Testosterone also has been linked to aggressive behavior in hockey players (Scaramella & Brown, 1978) and found to increase upon victory of a competitive sport (Kemper, 1990).

Thus, there is a relation between aggression and testosterone, but the evidence is far from clear that testosterone plays any causal role in aggression (J. Archer, 1991; Kemper, 1990). One problem is that aggression and dominance are often confounded. Testosterone is linked to dominance, which may be achieved through aggressive behavior; for example, testosterone clearly rises with the establishment of dominant hierarchies in monkeys (Kemper, 1990). Kemper suggests that

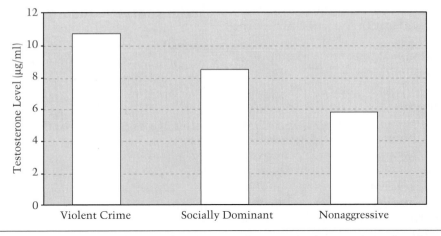

FIGURE 13.1 Testosterone levels in male prisoners. Prisoners who committed violent crimes and prisoners who had established dominance in the prison system had higher levels of testosterone than other prisoners. *Source:* Adapted from Ehrenkranz et al. (1974).

there may be a stronger relation of testosterone to aggression among people of a lower social class because they are in less dominant positions.

There also may be sex differences in the linking of testosterone to aggression. One study of women showed no difference in testosterone levels between dominant and submissive women (Rejeski, Parker, Gagne, & Koritnik, 1990). In addition, women's testosterone did not increase in response to a stressful task, as it typically does in men.

One difficulty with this area of research is that it is largely correlational. Does testosterone cause aggression, or does behaving aggressively lead to a rise in testosterone? Aggressive and competitive interactions have been linked to increases in testosterone (J. Archer, 1991). Testosterone also might lead to dominant behavior, which could increase aggression, or dominance may increase both testosterone and aggression. Even if hormones are linked to aggressive behavior, it is more likely that hormones interact with situational factors

to produce aggression rather than directly causing aggression (Herbert, 1989).

SOCIOBIOLOGY. Recall that sociobiology is the theory that social behavior can be explained by evolutionary principles. Sociobiologists argue that men are aggressive because they are in competition with each other for women and the opportunity to reproduce. This view is supported by studies that found that a large number of violent acts are committed by men who are trying to establish dominance among a group of men (Daly & Wilson, 1988; M. Wilson & Daly, 1985). A study of the nature of urban homicide in the United States concluded that the most prevalent urban homicides were due to conflicts over status (Daly & Wilson, 1988). These conflicts were often minor, such as one person insulting another (M. Wilson & Daly, 1985). The men who were most likely to commit acts of violence were the ones who had not established dominance: young men and poor men. Although these findings suggest that status and dominance may play a role in instigating male violence, they do not establish that competition over women is the precipitating factor.

Evolutionary theory also can be used to explain violence in families (Daly & Wilson, 1988). At first glance, familial violence would seem to violate the basic principles of evolutionary theory. However, the majority of homicides within families occur between spouses who are genetically unrelated to each other rather than between blood relatives. Women, but not men, are at greatest risk for being murdered when they try to end the relationship. Consistent with evolutionary theory, the primary motive men have for killing their spouse is sexual jealousy. Also consistent with evolutionary theory is the fact that *young* wives are most likely to be murdered, perhaps because youth is a sign of fertility, and fertility would make a woman more attractive to male rivals. Although young men are the individuals most likely to commit murder, the wife's age is a better predictor than the husband's age of a wife being murdered. Evolutionary theory also has been applied to the study of violence toward children. Among parents who abuse or kill their children, the incidence is higher among stepparents than biological parents. In sum, some patterns of violence are consistent with evolutionary principles.

SUMMARY. There is clearly a biological basis for aggressive behavior. Both genes and hormones have been linked to aggression but do not explain all of aggression. Biological factors are more likely to predispose men to violence rather than cause men to be violent. Men may have a lower threshold for behaving violently compared to women due to biological factors. However, it is likely that social factors interact with biological factors to produce violence. I now turn to those social factors.

Social Learning Theory

Social learning theory suggests that there are two principles that influence behavior: *modeling* and *reinforcement*. There is evidence that both modeling of aggressive behavior and reinforcement of aggressive behavior influence aggression (Bandura, 1973).

A primary source of modeling and reinforcement is the family. Studies of families show that there is some stability to aggression across generations. One study found that aggression was transmitted across three generations (Huesmann & Eron, 1984). Nearly 600 boys were enrolled in a study at the age of 8 and followed for 22 years. Boys who were aggressive at age 8 (according to their peers) were more likely to be involved in criminal behavior, spousal abuse, and physical aggression at age 30. These boys' aggression levels were correlated with the aggression levels of their sons 22 years later. There was correspondence in aggression among the study participants, their parents, and their eventual children. In a study of domestic abuse (to be discussed in detail later), a pattern of violence also was found across three generations (Straus, Gelles, & Steinmetz, 1980). Couples who were violent were more likely to have had violent parents and to behave violently toward their children.

MODELING. Models of aggression abound. Think of *Rambo, The Terminator, The Matrix, Natural Born Killers,* and even *Home Alone. Natural Born Killers* is a movie about a young couple who murder 52 people while on a road trip across the United States. There have been numerous reports of "copycat" killings based on this movie. One victim was shot and paralyzed by a couple who said they were inspired by the movie (Swerczek, 1999). The victim even tried to sue Oliver Stone, the film's director.

Aggression is modeled in movies, television, and video games. A content analysis of popular video games revealed that 80% included violence as part of the strategy, and 50% contained violence directed at specific others (Dietz, 1998). Even toy commercials provide models of aggression. A study of toy commercials found that this modeling was aimed at boys (Sobieraj, 1998). In 69% of the toy commercials depicting only boys, physical aggression, verbal aggression, or both were involved. Usually, violence was portrayed in the context of boys' interactions with action figures. Not one of the toy commercials featuring only girls involved either physical or verbal aggression.

Why do examples of aggressive behavior lead people to imitate them? Witnessing another's behavior not only teaches one how to perform the behavior, but a model suggests that the behavior must be appropriate or it would not exist. There is evidence that children who grow up in aggressive homes are more likely to behave aggressively (Miedzian, 1991; Widom, 1989a, 1989b). Sons who have aggressive fathers are more likely to be aggressive (Huesmann & Eron, 1984), and children who witness violence between parents are more likely to become aggressive. Children who are direct victims of violence by parents also are more likely to become aggressive (Dodge, Bates & Pettit, 1990). One study found that children who were identified by court records as abused or neglected by age 11 were more likely to have juvenile crime records and to commit violent crimes 20 years later (Widom, 1989a). It should be noted that this study showed that being abused by a parent was linked to committing violent crimes among men but not women. Other research has linked the experience of physical punishment in the home to subsequent aggression among adolescents (S. Feshbach, 1989).

One reason being abused leads to aggressive behavior is that abuse alters the way a child processes information about the world. This theory was tested by presenting children who had and had not been abused with a videotape of an ambiguous provocation (e.g., one child knocks another child's blocks over; Dodge et al., 1990). The abused children were more likely to attribute hostile intentions to the behavior. The authors concluded that the children misinterpreted the relevant social cues surrounding these videotaped negative events.

However, it also is the case that the majority of aggressive adults do *not* come from violent homes, and the majority of people who come from violent homes do *not* become violent adults (Bandura, 1973; Widom, 1989a, 1989b). Thus, growing up in a violent home can be identified as only one potential cause of violence.

REINFORCEMENT.   Families are more likely to reinforce than model violence. There are many ways parents can reinforce aggressive behavior. Some parents may overtly encourage aggression; they may encourage their sons to fight with other children as a way to settle arguments. Other parents encourage aggression in subtle ways; they verbally declare that fighting is not appropriate, but at the same time beam with pride when their child emerges the victor of a fight. Comparisons of boys who do and do not display aggressive and antisocial behavior find that aggressive behavior is reinforced in families of the former (Bandura, 1973). Parents may encourage aggression toward peers and even other adults.

Boys are more likely than girls to be reinforced for aggressive behavior (S. Feshbach, 1989). Parents and teachers ignore aggression in girls and respond negatively to aggression in boys (Fagot et al., 1985). But attention, even if it is negative, is reinforcing. One study showed that both teachers and other students were more likely to react negatively to aggression in boys than girls (Fagot & Hagan, 1985). These findings are shown in Figure 13.2. As you can see, negative responses are more common than positive responses, especially by teachers. Girls' aggression is most likely to be ignored by teachers and peers. Not responding to the aggression was more likely to terminate the episode, whereas attention (negative or positive) made the episode last longer. Thus, both teachers' and peers' responses to aggression led girls to stop their behavior and boys to continue their behavior. Interview your peers about their childhood experiences of how people respond to aggression in Exercise 13.2.

Modeling and reinforcement interact to influence aggression. Laboratory research on modeling has shown that boys are more likely than girls to imitate an aggressive model (Bandura, 1973). However, when the model is rewarded for the aggressive behavior, boys and girls imitate the model with equal frequency.

EXERCISE 13.2
Childhood Experiences of Responses to Aggression

Interview five male and five female college students. Ask them to recall times when they behaved aggressively during childhood. First, ask them to recall a time when they displayed any physical aggression, such as hitting another person. Ask them who witnessed or found out about the aggression and how they responded. Second, ask them to recall a time when they displayed verbal aggression, such as insulting someone or yelling at someone. Again, ask them who witnessed or found out about the aggression and how they responded. Try to develop a coding system to categorize others' responses. Did others respond positively, negatively, or not at all? Did others respond the same to aggression in boys and girls?

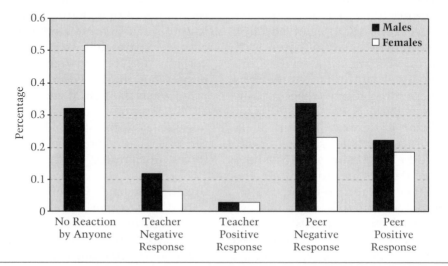

FIGURE 13.2 Response to toddlers' aggression. Peers and teachers are more likely to respond negatively to aggression in boys. Peers and teachers are more likely to ignore aggression in girls than boys. *Source:* Adapted from Fagot and Hagan (1985).

Families may contribute to aggression in ways other than modeling and reinforcement. They may produce the frustrating events that trigger aggression. Children who come from families that are rejecting and show little affection may not develop the positive bonds with people that normally inhibit aggression (S. Feshbach, 1989). Children who are neglected may show higher rates of violence than children who are abused (Widom, 1989b).

PEER INFLUENCE.   Peers may also contribute to aggression through modeling and reinforcement. Whereas aggression in younger children is associated with being rejected by peers, there is some recent evidence that aggression can confer status among preadolescents and adolescents. One study selected children who were rejected by peers (i.e., peers said they did not like them) and followed their social status for two years (Sandstrom & Coie, 1999). The aggressive children were more likely to improve their social status two years later. This status improvement of aggressive children was more strongly observed among boys than girls. Another study of inner-city ninth-graders, the majority of whom were ethnic minorities, showed that children who engaged in aggressive and disruptive behavior (e.g., picks on other kids, gets into fights, loses temper easily, teases other children) were more popular with their peers than nonaggressive children (Luthar & McMahon, 1996). Why do aggressive children, in particular boys, become liked by their peers? Some social cliques are based on aggression. During adolescence, aggressive behavior may come to be viewed as powerful and glamorous. Particularly among inner-city youth, aggressive behavior may be viewed as an acceptable and effective way to achieve goals (Luthar & McMahon, 1996).

The aggressive adolescents who become more popular may be characterized by what has been referred to as **proactive aggression** compared to **reactive aggression** (Poulin & Boivin, 2000b). Reactive aggression is an angry, impulsive response to threat or provocation. Proactive aggression, by contrast, is not provoked, is planned, and is socially motivated. Groups of children form alliances, partly based on their aggressive behavior (Coie, Terry, Zakriski, & Lochman, 1995). These alliances are based on proactive rather than reactive aggression (Poulin et al., 1997). Proactive aggressive groups may gang up on and target a specific individual. These children expect to be rewarded for their behavior. Perhaps this is why reactive aggression has been associated with peer rejection, but proactive aggression has been associated with peer acceptance (Poulin & Boivin, 2000a). Through proactive aggression, peer groups promote and reinforce aggressive behavior.

There may be cross-cultural differences in peer support of aggression. In a study that compared European American, Chinese American, and two groups of Chinese (Taiwan, China) seventh- and eighth-graders, European American children were more approving of aggressive and antisocial behavior (i.e., fighting, damaging property) than the two Chinese groups (Chen, Greenberger, Lester, Dong, & Guo, 1998). The Chinese American (Chinese living in California) children's approval of antisocial behavior fell between the two groups, indicating some acculturation into American society. Across all four cultures, boys were more approving than girls.

Gender Role Theories

Eagly and Steffen (1986) concluded that aggressive behavior can be understood within a social-role framework: the male gender role encourages aggression and the female gender role limits aggressive behavior.

Aggression has been linked to the male gender role by Myriam Miedzian (1991) in her book *Boys Will Be Boys: Breaking the Link between Masculinity and Violence.* Miedzian argues that one cannot study violence without considering the fact that men are so much more likely than women to commit acts of violence. Linking violence to men, however, often makes people feel uncomfortable. Some argue that women commit acts of violence too. According to Miedzian, to study violence without linking it to being male is missing a central piece of the puzzle. Where would AIDS researchers be if they did not consider the fact that the incidence was much higher among gay men and intravenous drug users? To ignore these facts would have certainly impeded research.

It goes without saying that not all men are violent. However, because men are more prone to violence, it is important to identify predisposing factors. Miedzian (1991) argues that the **masculine mystique** plays a major role in criminal and domestic violence. The masculine mystique consists of toughness, dominance, emotional detachment, callousness toward women, eagerness to seek out danger, and competition. The masculine mystique is instilled in boys by society. Miedzian argues that we not only tolerate violence in males, but we encourage it. War is an example: we associate war with maleness and we associate avoiding war with a lack of masculinity; we glorify war with toys, books, television, and movies; political leaders affirm their masculinity by engaging in war. Miedzian points out that the media claimed former President George Bush proved his manhood and overcame his image as a "wimp" by going to war with Iraq; Bush's approval ratings hit an all-time high during the Persian Gulf War and plummeted after the war was over.

Miedzian (1991) also argues that men grow up in a culture of violence. Hollywood offers an abundance of models of men committing violent acts, and some of these models become heroes (e.g., Sylvester Stallone, Jean-Claude Van Damme). Themes of violence pervade music, sports, video games, and toys geared toward boys. Miedzian says, "He is learning to sacrifice his body unnecessarily and to hide all feelings of fear and vulnerability, however warranted they may be. He is also being taught to sacrifice the bodies of others" (p. 201).

Miedzian (1991) points out that the masculine mystique is more dangerous for lower-class than upper-class boys. Upper-class boys are provided with legitimate pathways to validate their masculinity through achievement; lower-class boys have more difficulty attaining achievement levels that will garner dominance and respect. Black males, in particular, are denied legitimate opportunities to validate their masculinity through achievement and economic success; thus, Black men may resort to other means. Staples (1995) argues that higher rates of violence in Black communities may stem from "relative deprivation." The highest rates of violence occur in communities where the income gap between Blacks and Whites is largest.

An alternative way to view aggression from a gender-role perspective is to consider the facets of the female gender role that might inhibit aggression. Empathy is a primary candidate. Empathy involves taking another person's perspective and being able to experience vicariously another person's feelings. Empathy is inversely related to aggression and has been used as a principle to intervene with aggression. Children 7 to 11 years old from Los Angeles who attended an empathy training program showed a decrease in aggression (N. Feshbach, 1989).

Miedzian (1991) suggests that one way to foster empathy in men is to increase nurturant behavior, such as by having men become more involved in raising children. She suggests an innovative program whereby both boys and girls receive child care training that begins in elementary school and extends through high school. I find it interesting that this is one lifetime duty for which neither men nor women are adequately prepared; women are "expected" to know how to take care of and raise children (the maternal instinct), and men are excused for not knowing how to do these things. By introducing child care skills early in life, boys and girls would not only gain useful knowledge about how to parent, but would grow up to view child care as an essential element of both men's and women's roles. Taking care of children should promote nurturance and empathy and reduce aggression. In her book, Miedzian describes programs that introduce child care training in the school system and reports promising effects in terms of reduced violence, delinquency, and teenage pregnancy.

Is there any evidence that traditional gender roles are associated with aggression? In one study, college men who endorsed more traditional beliefs about the male gender role were more likely to report using psychological violence in their relationships with women and were more likely to endorse violent beliefs (i.e., believing that rape is the fault of the woman; Good, Hepper, Hillenbrand-Gunn, & Wang, 1995). In a laboratory study, traditional masculinity was associated with aggressive behavior against a competitor (Weisbuch, Beal, & O'Neal, 1999). In a study that distinguished the negative from the positive aspects of masculinity (i.e., unmitigated agency vs. agency), only unmitigated agency was associated with an index of acting-out behavior, which included misdemeanors, school misbehavior, and physical fights (Spence et al., 1979).

This issue was examined at a cultural level by relating the gender equality of a state to the state's homicide rate (Weisheit, 1993). Gender equality was measured by a series of economic, political, and legal indices. If traditional gender roles are associated with violence, states whose citizens do not display distinct gender roles should have lower rates of violence; alternatively, the more equal men's and women's roles, the more similar their behavior. If women's roles become similar to those of men, do women become *more* violent? The study showed that states with the highest gender equality were associated with the lowest female-male homicide rate (Weisheit, 1993). Gender equality of a state was unrelated to the male homicide rate, however. Thus, traditional roles at a state level are associated only with greater violence among women. Aggressive behavior on the part of women in states with traditional roles may stem from their low status in those states.

Cognitive Theories

There are a number of cognitive theories of aggression. However, most of these theories do not specifically address why aggression is more prevalent in boys than girls; thus, I describe only some of these theories.

A popular theory of aggression is that it stems from low self-esteem. However, recent research suggests that this theory may not have a scientific basis. Baumeister and colleagues (Baumeister, Bushman, & Campbell, 2000) point out that aggressive people often have *high* self-esteem. They suggest that aggressive behavior stems from **threatened egoism:** holding a positive view of oneself and reacting with aggression toward anyone who threatens that view. This theory was supported in two studies of college students who wrote an essay and either received insulting remarks or compliments by a confederate pretending to be another participant. The students were then given the opportunity to aggress against the confederate by sounding a loud blast of noise. The most aggressive behavior came from students who were high on narcissism (had grandiose views of the self) who had been insulted. This group constituted those who had threatened egoism. However, the students who were high on narcissism were no more aggressive than other students—*unless* they had been provoked. As further support of their theory, the authors note that prisoners who have committed felonies score higher on narcissism than people who have not been in prison (Baumeister et al., 2000). You may be thinking that people who are narcissistic really have low self-esteem and that they are just using their sense of superiority to mask deep-seated insecurities. This idea may be intuitively appealing, but to date there is no evidence to support to it.

Another cognitive theory of aggression emphasizes the child as an active processor of information about the world. The child possesses cognitive scripts for aggression, which are learned early in life (Huesmann & Eron, 1992). Exposure to models of and reinforcement of aggression shapes those scripts, which then guide behavior in response to events that occur. For example, a child may have a script for how to behave when a person doesn't get his or her own way; the script may say that fighting is the way to remedy this situation.

Environmental Factors

A social psychological perspective on aggression suggests that aggressive behavior results from the combination of person and environment. The theory of threatened egoism is an example of this perspective: a certain kind of person (narcissist) responds aggressively when provoked. A variety of environmental characteristics have been associated with aggression. In addition to provocation, aggressive behavior has been associated with alcohol, exposure to television violence, and playing violent video games (Ballard & Lineberger, 1999; Bushman & Anderson, 1998). In each situation, the environment alone does not produce aggression; however, in combination with other factors, such as personality, aggressive behavior might take place.

One important environmental cue is a weapon. The **weapons effect** refers to the idea that people are more likely to behave aggressively in the presence of a weapon than in the absence of one. For example, in one field study, a confederate pretended to stall a truck at a traffic light with or without a military rifle in the back window of the truck (C. Turner, Layton, & Simons, 1975, Study 2). Motorists in the rifle condition were more likely to honk than motorists in the no-weapon condition. A meta-analysis has shown that the weapons effect appears in both laboratory ($d = +.17$) and field studies ($d = +.21$; Bushman & Anderson, 1998).

In the following sections of this chapter, I examine three particular cases of aggression: rape, domestic abuse, and sexual harassment. These forms of aggression have several things in common: first, men are more likely than women to be perpetrators and women are more likely than men to be victims; second, they are forms of aggression that are difficult to define and difficult to measure. These two problems are related to one another. Estimates vary widely, depending on how conservative or liberal the definitions.

RAPE AND OTHER FORMS OF SEXUAL COERCION

Rape is an act of violence with numerous physical and mental health consequences. Physical injuries range from minor bruises to life-threatening injuries to death. Mental health consequences range from fear, anxiety, and depression, to posttraumatic stress syndrome (Wallace, 1999). Rape also has been associated with impairments in sexual functioning (Wallace, 1999). In this section, I first define rape and then report on studies that examine the incidence of rape and other forms of sexual coercion. I devote a specific section to studies among college students because the findings may differ from those of the general population. I discuss characteristics of the perpetrator and victim: Who rapes and who is likely to be raped? Finally, I discuss theories of rape.

Definitions

You might expect that rape is a straightforward concept with a straightforward definition. However, there are many definitions of rape (D. Russell, 1990). Definitions vary regarding the specific behavior that distinguishes rape from other sexual acts. Of concern is how *nonconsent* to engage in sexual behavior is determined, and whether force is required (Muehlenhard, Powch, Phelps, & Giusti, 1992). The most conservative definition of rape restricts the behavior to vaginal-penile penetration. More liberal definitions include other forms of sexual contact, such as kissing, fondling, oral sex, and anal sex. Definitions also vary in how nonconsent is determined. What is an adequate indicator of victim nonconsent? Some definitions refer to rape as sexual behaviors that are undesired by the victim. Other definitions require evidence of victim resistance. There are other situations in which a person is unable to give informed consent, such as being under age, being mentally ill, or being intoxicated. Consent also may be obtained under duress. Many definitions refer to the sexual behavior as being forced on the recipient, but

defining force is difficult. Does there have to be evidence of physical injury? Are verbal threats sufficient?

In addition, men and women may have different definitions of rape. In one study, college students were given a vignette and asked if rape occurred (McLendon et al., 1994). Women were more likely than men to perceive the behavior as rape.

One kind of rape that especially suffers from these definitional issues is spousal rape. Some people still believe that rape cannot occur in marriage, because sexual intercourse between husband and wife is a right of marriage (D. Russell, 1990). Historically, rape laws in the United States contained in their definitions of rape what is known as the **marital rape exemption** clause. This exemption can be found in the following definition of rape: "the forcible penetration of the body of a woman, not the wife of the perpetrator" (p. 17, D. Russell, 1990). It was not until 1993 that all 50 states had deleted the marital rape exemption clause. However, some other countries still employ some form of marital rape exemption. Interestingly, there is a high rate of conviction among offenders charged with wife rape (D. Russell, 1990); this is probably due to the fact that only the extreme cases of spousal rape are reported.

The definitions of sexual assault or sexual coercion are even more varied. Sexual coercion has been defined as pressure or force to have sexual contact (George, Winfield, & Blazer, 1992; S. Sorenson & Siegel, 1992), pressure or force to have sexual relations (Struckman-Johnson & Struckman-Johnson, 1994), and, even more broadly, as engaging in sexual activities against one's wishes (Muehlenhard & Cook, 1988). Sexual coercive acts are susceptible to some of the same definitional problems as rape. What behaviors constitute sexual coercion? How are force, pressure, and nonconsent determined?

Incidence

POPULATION STUDIES. In 1997, 96,122 cases of rape were reported (Federal Bureau of Investigation, 1997a). The incidence of rape among women varies widely; most studies report an incidence between 8% and 27% (Koss, 1993). The rates for male victims are much lower, ranging from less than 1% to 7%. One difficulty with estimating the prevalence of rape is that rape is underreported. Unlike other crimes, rape can be reported only by the victim; bystanders may report other assaults but are unlikely to witness and report a rape. Many victims do not report rape because they feel guilty, feel a sense of shame, doubt that people will believe them, and/or do not want to share their personal sexual history with strangers. Even surveys of rape may underestimate its incidence (Koss, 1993). The majority of surveys ask individuals a single question about whether they have been raped and use only the term rape. However, some individuals do not apply the label of rape to experiences that would qualify as rape; people often do not include oral sex or anal penetration when thinking of rape. In addition, people may not include rape attempts as rape. When multiple questions about rape are asked in surveys, the incidence of rape increases (Koss, 1993).

Estimates of the prevalence of sexual assault among women vary even more than estimates of rape, from 15% to 50% (George et al., 1992). In an interview study of over 3,000 persons in the Los Angeles area, 17% said they had been sexually assaulted (S. Sorenson & Siegel, 1992). In that study, sexual assault was defined as someone pressuring or forcing them to have sexual contact. More women than men reported sexual assault (17% vs. 9%), and the rate was much higher among non-Hispanic White people (20%) than Hispanic people (8%). In an interview study of over 1,000 persons from North Carolina, only 6% of respondents reported having been sexually assaulted, which was defined as pressure or force to have unwanted sexual contact (George et al., 1992). The authors attributed their substantially lower rate of sexual assault to characteristics of the geographic region: the people in this area are more politically conservative, have lower rates of alcohol abuse, and have higher involvement in religious practices.

What is the incidence of spousal rape? In a random sample of adults from the San Francisco area, 14% of people who had ever been married reported being a victim of spousal rape or attempted spousal rape (D. Russell, 1990). In that study, rape was defined as forced oral, anal, digital, or penile-vaginal penetration. In the majority of cases (85%), the rape was vaginal-penile penetration. In 31% of the cases, the rape was isolated, occurring only once. In 37%, rape occurred between 2 and 20 times; in 31% of the cases, rape occurred more than 20 times. Alcohol was involved in 20% to 25% of the incidents.

An extreme view of the incidence of rape was offered by S. Griffin (1971). She maintains that all women are victims of rape in a sense—not necessarily because someone has attempted to rape them but because all women have to deal with the fear of rape. Women's day-to-day behavior reflects this fear. Women are more fearful than men of living alone, of walking alone at night, and of leaving a window open at night (S. Griffin, 1971). People chastise women for walking alone at night but don't think twice about men being by themselves. In Chapter 1, I mentioned a study in which I asked college students to imagine a typical day if they were of the other sex; one of the most frequent remarks that men made was that they would have to call campus security to get to their dorm because they would be afraid to walk alone at night.

By contrast, women reported that they felt a sense of freedom in being able to go where they want when they want. These findings suggest that both men and women are well aware that women are more fearful than men of rape.

STUDIES OF COLLEGE STUDENTS.   Studies of college students report higher incidences of sexual assault, but definitions are often more liberal. In a national survey of female college students, 54% of the 3,187 women reported some form of sexual victimization: 16% rape, 12% attempted rape, 11% sexual coercion, and 15% sexual contact (Ullman, Karabatsos, & Koss, 1999). In over half of the cases (53%), women said the offender used alcohol; in 42% of the cases, the women reported using alcohol. Use of alcohol was not only common during sexual assault but was associated with the severity of the assault. The more severe cases of assault (i.e., rape, attempted rape) were associated with alcohol usage by both offender and victim. Forty percent of the sexual assaults occurred during the course of a date.

We typically think of women as the victims of rape and sexual assault; in fact, criminal statistics define rape as something that occurs only to women. There are no criminal statistics on male victims of rape. Though rape may be rare among men, sexual coercion may not.

Studies of college students have examined the frequency of sexual coercion among men. In a study of 1,000 college students, 63% of men and 46% of women reported engaging in sex against their wishes (Muehlenhard & Cook, 1988). The high rate of sexual coercion reported by men may be surprising. However, men may find it difficult to refuse sex because the expectation of the male gender role is that men are always ready and willing to have sex.

The men and women in this study responded quite differently to pressures to have sex. The majority of women refused sex when they received pressure from their partner, whereas the majority of men had sex when they received pressure. The men who engaged in coercive sex reported doing so because their partner enticed them, they were intoxicated, or they felt pressure from peers. Even among students as young as tenth grade, males have more difficulty than females saying no to sex. In one study, tenth-grade boys and girls were asked how confident they were that they could refuse sex if someone tried to pressure them (R. Zimmerman, Sprecher, Langer, & Holloway, 1995). Whereas 61% of females said that they "definitely" could say no, only 32% of males gave this response. Males cited peer pressure as their primary reason for having difficulty refusing.

Another study of college men found that 34% reported at least one "forced sexual experience" (Struckman-Johnson & Struckman-Johnson, 1994), defined as the use of pressure or force to have sexual contact or sexual intercourse. This definition is a little more stringent than the one used to define sexual coercion in the previous study, which may account for the lower frequency rate among men. Most of these forced sexual experiences involved women and occurred with an acquaintance or a friend rather than a stranger. When women initiated these coercive episodes, men reported that the women typically used persuasion or alcohol. When other men initiated these coercive episodes, men reported that the men used persuasion, bribery, alcohol, or physical threats and restraints. Men rated sexual coercion by men more negatively than sexual coercion by women.

It is difficult to evaluate what these episodes of sexual coercion mean to college men. In one study, their occurrence was unrelated to men's current well-being (Struckman-Johnson & Struckman-Johnson, 1994). In that study, 50% of the men said a female coercive episode had no impact on them at all; in only 23% of the cases was there a strong negative impact. By contrast, the impact of coercion initiated by a male had a strong negative impact on men nearly 50% of the time.

Thus, it appears that both men and women college students may be victims of sexual coercion. However, sexual coercion seems to mean something different to men and women. Men feel less able to refuse sex, so they don't; women feel more able to refuse, so when victimization occurs, they suffer more serious consequences.

Characteristics of Perpetrator

Most of us tend to perceive rape as occurring by a stranger, but in the majority of cases the two people know each other (D. Russell, 1990; Ward, 1995). One study reported that only 22% of women were raped by a stranger (Kilpatrick, Edmunds, & Seymour, 1992). One reason rape is underreported and not given more serious attention is that people have more sympathy for victims who do not know their attackers. Yet, in the majority of cases, victims do know their attackers. We also perceive rape as involving physical force, but rape often involves verbal threats (Ward, 1995), and we have less sympathy for victims who do not show physical signs of abuse. To make matters worse, strangers are more likely to use physical force, and known others are more likely to use verbal threats (Cleveland, Koss, & Lyons, 1999). Thus, the most common occurrence of rape—a known other who uses verbal threats—evokes the least sympathy from the community.

Perpetrators have been found to have two primary motives for rape (Groth,

Burgess, & Holmstrom, 1977). **Power rape** occurs when the person is seeking to control and exert power over the victim. The rapist with this motive may be more likely to suffer from low self-esteem and, if male, to feel inadequate in his gender role. **Anger rape** occurs when the perpetrator is expressing hostility or hate toward the victim; the motivation here is to harm the victim. Anger rape among men may be viewed as revenge against a particular woman or all women in general. Men who rape and behave in sexually aggressive ways toward women typically are more likely to hold hostile attitudes toward women (Lisak, 1991). These men are more likely to report being hurt by women through deception, betrayal, or manipulation, and to feel put down and belittled by women (Lisak & Roth, 1988).

Perpetrators often hold myths about women and rape. Brownmiller (1975) identified four basic rape myths: (1) that all women want to be raped; (2) that a women cannot be raped against her will; (3) that a woman who is raped is asking for it; and (4) that if a woman is going to be raped, she might as well enjoy it. Numerous scales have emerged to measure rape myths. Items from one of the most widely used scales (Burt, 1980) are shown in Table 13.1. See how many people today endorse these myths with Exercise 13.3.

Rape myths are likely to be endorsed by people who have strong gender-role stereotypes, people who are more accepting of interpersonal violence, and people who are less educated (Burt, 1980). People who endorse rape myths are more likely to blame the victim and less likely to blame the perpetrator (Kopper, 1996). Women are less likely than men to endorse these rape myths (Kopper, 1996; Ward, 1995). In a study of college students, men who were in fraternities and men who were athletes were more likely to endorse rape myths,

TABLE 13.1 Sample Items from Rape Myth Acceptance Scale

1. Any healthy woman can successfully resist a rapist if she really wants to.

2. When women go around braless or wearing short skirts and tight tops, they are just asking for trouble.

3. In the majority of rapes, the victim is promiscuous or has a bad reputation.

4. Women who get raped while hitchhiking get what they deserve.

5. Many women have an unconscious wish to be raped, and may then unconsciously set up a situation in which they are likely to be attacked.

Source: Burt (1980).

such as "Women pretend not to want sex but want to be forced" and "Women secretly want to be raped" (Boeringer, 1999). Fraternity membership also has been directly linked to sexual aggression (Lackie & de Man, 1997).

Traditional masculinity also has been directly linked to sexual aggression (Lackie & de Man, 1997). In a study of seventh-, ninth-, and eleventh-graders, students who

---

EXERCISE 13.3
Endorsement of Rape Myths

Administer the items in Table 13.1 to a group of men and women to establish the prevalence of rape myths. Feel free to add a few items of your own. What other variables do you expect to be associated with rape myths: traditional attitudes toward gender roles, gender-related traits (agency, communion, unmitigated agency, unmitigated communion), socioeconomic status? Measure one of these other variables and see if it is associated with rape myths in men and women.

---

held more traditional attitudes toward gender roles were more tolerant of sexual violence on the part of males and females in dating relationships (Price & Byers, 1999). In a study of college students, hypermasculinity was associated with sexual aggression (Lackie & de Man, 1997), and in a study of adolescent males, traditional attitudes toward men's roles were associated with sexual coercive behavior (Pleck, Sonenstein, & Ku, 1993a).

Characteristics of Victim

In general, victims of rape and sexual assault span all age ranges and all educational backgrounds. However, rape and sexual assault are more likely to occur among younger people (i.e., ages 13 to 24), among Black people, and among people of a lower SES (George et al., 1992). By contrast, more-educated people report a higher incidence of sexual assault (George et al., 1992). This latter finding is difficult to interpret because definitions of sexual assault vary; more-educated people may define sexual assault in more liberal terms or be more likely to report sexual assault.

Demographic variables, such as social class, ethnicity, and age, are generally not associated with being a victim of spousal rape (D. Russell, 1990). Attitudes toward gender roles also are not associated with being a victim of spousal rape. However, attitudes toward gender roles are associated with one's *response* to spousal rape. Women with more traditional attitudes are more likely to blame themselves and to stay in the relationship than women with more egalitarian attitudes. In one study, 22% of wives stayed with their husbands after rape (D. Russell, 1990). The women who stayed were more likely to have minimized the trauma of the rape, to report that it was an isolated occurrence, to have fewer economic resources, and to blame themselves for the rape. Of these variables, the strongest predictor of staying in the relationship was self-blame. Race also was a predictor of staying in the relationship. Whereas 13% of White women remained in the relationship, 42% of Black, Asian, and Latina women stayed in the relationship. Members of minority groups may have lacked economic resources.

Theories

The early theories of rape focused on characteristics of the perpetrator (Donat & D'Emilio, 1992). The rapist was considered to be someone who was mentally ill and sexually perverted. Thus, in a sense, researchers focused on the plight of the perpetrator rather than the plight of the victim. In addition, rape was considered a form of sexually deviant behavior and thus tied to sex rather than aggression. Later, theorists began to focus on characteristics of the victim. As women's sexuality became more accepted during the middle of the twentieth century, people came to wonder what role women played in rape. People asked what the woman could have done to cause or prevent the rape: What was she wearing? Did she fight back? Was there evidence of physical harm? The next phase in history appeared with the development of the women's movement. Rape was reconceptualized as an act of violence rather than an act of sex. Feminists maintained that rape was a "means of enforcing gender roles in society and maintaining the hierarchy in which men retained control" (Donat & D'Emilio, 1992, p. 14). In her best-selling book *Against Our Will: Men, Women, and Rape,* Susan Brownmiller (1975) defined rape as "a conscious process of intimidation by which all men keep all women in a state of fear" (p. 15).

Today, people generally regard rape as an act of violence rather than sex (Wallace, 1999). Men are socialized to be aggressive, to be dominant over women, and to view women as sexual conquests. However, rape also may be related to an important situational variable: misperceptions of sexual intentions and behavior.

Men interpret sexual behavior differently than women, perhaps because men are more likely than women to assume that others are interested in sex (Sprecher & McKinney, 1993). Several studies of college students demonstrated that men are more likely than women to interpret neutral behavior in more sexual terms. In one study, college students were shown a videotape in which a man and a woman were either acting friendly toward one another or conveying sexual interest (Shotland & Craig, 1988). Both men and women were able to discriminate the friendly interaction from the sexual interest interaction. However, for both interactions, college men perceived greater sexual interest on the part of the people in the vignettes than did college women. A second set of investigators conducted three separate studies of college students observing men and women engaging in social interactions (Saal, Johnson, & Weber, 1989). Across all three studies, men were more likely than women to view people's behavior as flirtatious and seductive. In these three studies as well as the previous one, the overinterpretation of sexual behavior was larger for female targets than male targets. Taken collectively, this means that men are especially likely to view women's behavior in sexual terms.

In general, men may have a lower threshold for viewing behavior in sexual terms. However, it is unlikely that this pertains to all men. One study of college students found that men were more likely than women to view a female's behavior as sexual, but this sex difference was largely due to men who endorsed a high number of rape myths (Abbey & Harnish, 1995). That is, men who hold misperceptions about rape are the ones who are most likely to interpret a woman's neutral behavior in sexual terms. Thus, rape may be a function of the person and the situation: rape may be more likely to occur in certain situations among people who have predisposing characteristics.

DOMESTIC ABUSE

Historically, men were permitted to hit their wives without sanction from the community, let alone the legal system. In fact, folklore claims that the phrase "rule of thumb" came out of legal reform in the area of wife beating: husbands were prohibited from hitting their wives with an instrument that was thicker in diameter than their thumb (H. Kelly, 1994). Today, "rule of thumb" has no meaning because men are not legally permitted to abuse their wives. This does not mean, however, that violence does not occur in families.

The subject of domestic abuse really came to the public's attention in the 1970s with the development of the women's movement. Shelters for battered women appeared then and in the 1980s. In 1985, Surgeon General C. Everett Koop proclaimed that violence against women was the number one health problem afflicting women. More recent attention was brought to the subject of battered women by the 1994–1995 trial of O.J. Simpson for the murder of his wife, Nicole Brown Simpson. Although Simpson was acquitted of the murder, the evidence was clear that there had been a history of domestic violence in the relationship.

Domestic abuse has been associated with physical, mental, and financial consequences (Wallace, 1999). Domestic abuse results in physical symptoms and physical injuries. Psychological distress may take the form of anxiety and depression. In more severe cases, domestic abuse has been associated with suicide among women—in the United States as well as in other countries (Krane, 1996). There are also economic costs associated with domestic abuse in terms of lost days of work, legal fees, and health care costs.

I titled this section "Domestic Abuse" rather than "Battered Women," in recognition of the fact that both husbands and wives can be abused. Isn't it true, though, that women are more likely than men to be the subjects of violence in families? Some people argue that adopting gender-neutral language ("domestic abuse" vs. "battered woman") ignores the linking of gender and power to the occurrence of violence in families (e.g., Kurz, 1998). The subject is politically charged. I begin this section of the chapter by examining the incidence of spousal abuse. Then I examine characteristics of people likely to engage in spousal abuse as well as characteristics of people who suffer abuse. I conclude this section by reviewing theories of domestic violence.

Incidence

It is difficult to calculate the incidence of domestic abuse, in part because abuse can be physical or verbal. In keeping with the theme of this chapter, I focus more on physical abuse. Yet, even estimates of physical abuse are difficult to obtain. Researchers have relied on surveys and police and physician reports to estimate abuse. Obviously, police and physicians underestimate the incidence of abuse because they will be made aware of only the most extreme cases. However, even surveys may underestimate abuse because poor people and non-English-speaking people are underrepresented in surveys (A. Browne, 1993).

The first national survey of domestic violence was conducted in 1976 and involved 2,143 families (Straus et al., 1980). Rates of violence were so high that the phrase "the marriage license as a hitting license" was coined. The investigators found that 28% of families had engaged in at least one incident of violence over the course of their relationship, and 16% of families had done so in the prior year. Violent acts include punching, kicking, biting, hitting, beating, shooting, and stabbing. I present the items that were used to measure violence in this study in Table 13.2 because this definition of violence has been used in many subsequent studies. In 1985, a second national survey of 6,002 families revealed the annual incidence of abuse to be 16% (Straus & Gelles, 1990a). The investigators estimated that domestic violence occurs in 8.7 million families per year (Straus & Gelles, 1990a). In a randomized sample of women surveyed from the San Francisco area, a slightly higher figure was reported: 21% of women reported that their husband had been violent with them (D. Russell, 1990).

The rates for some acts of violence declined slightly between the 1975 and 1985 national surveys (Straus & Gelles, 1990b). This decline may have been due to the development of women's shelters, the increased public attention the problem received, and the development of policies to handle the abusive person (Straus & Gelles, 1990b; Wallace, 1999). More recent statistics show an increase in violence. Surveys of domestic abuse among women revealed that 14% of women said that their husband or boyfriend had been violent with them at some point during 1992 (Klein, Campbell, Soler, & Ghez, 1997). By 1994, the percentage had risen to 24%, and by 1995, 30%. A survey conducted in Canada in 1995 provided comparable figures (H. Johnson & Sacco, 1995); in that study, the incidence of domestic violence was 29%. Other, more recent studies have reported rates ranging from 28% to 33% (J. White & Kowalski, 1998).

Thus, recent estimates of domestic abuse are in the range of 30%. Physical violence among dating couples appears to be equally prevalent, about 32% (J. White & Kowalski, 1998). The rate of violence in marriages that ultimately dissolve may be higher. In a study of 129 divorced mothers, 66% reported experiencing violence at some time during their marriage (Kurz, 1998).

Are men and women equally likely to engage in domestic violence? In 1998, Currie reviewed 30 studies and showed that men and women were equally violent against their partner. The two nationally representative studies I described, one conducted in 1975 (Straus et al., 1980) and one in 1985 (Straus & Gelles, 1990a), showed that both men and women were violent 50% of the time, only the male was violent 25% of the time, and only the female was violent 25% of the time. In those studies, acts of violence were defined as throwing, pushing, grabbing, shoving, and slapping, as well as more severe aggressive acts such as kicking, biting, punching, and beating (see Table 13.2).

At first glance, these figures may be surprising: they suggest that violent acts are committed equally by husbands and wives. However, the context in which violence occurs needs to be considered, such

TABLE 13.2   Indicators of Violence

Threw something at the other one.

Pushed, grabbed, or shoved the other one.

Slapped the other one.

Kicked, bit, or hit with a fist.

Hit or tried to hit with something.

Beat up the other one.

Threatened with a knife or gun.

Used a knife or gun.

Source: Adapted from Straus et al. (1980).

as who initiated the violence and what was the outcome (Kurz, 1998; Straus et al., 1980; Straus & Gelles, 1990a). Men are more likely to initiate domestic abuse, and women are more likely to act in self-defense (DeKeseredy & Schwartz, 1998). In addition, women suffer greater physical injuries than men. When the consequences of violence from the 1985 national survey were examined, the degree of violence was more strongly associated with psychological symptoms (i.e., depression, stress), physical injury (i.e., need for medical care), and time off from work for women than for men (Stets & Straus, 1990).

In addition, men's and women's reports of violence may be influenced by what Currie (1998) refers to as "gendered expectations about appropriate behavior." Women expect men to be aggressive, and men expect women to be passive. Thus, women may be less likely to interpret a man's behavior as violent, and men may be more likely to interpret a woman's behavior as violent. A study of college students supports this idea (Currie, 1998). Both men and women minimized violent acts committed by men. Women often justified men's violence and even blamed themselves. Men, by contrast, exaggerated violent acts committed by women. Recall from previous research that the sex of the person engaging in a behavior determines how it is interpreted. Thus, men and women may be equally likely to report that their partners commit violent acts when in actuality men are more violent than women. Violent acts of men may be underreported and violent acts of women may be overreported.

Finally, another distinction that might help to shed light on why rates of violence appear to be equal among men and women is the distinction between **common couple violence** and **patriarchal terrorism** (M.P. Johnson, 1995). This distinction may help to explain why statistics showing equal rates of victimization among men and women do not fit with our intuition that women are more likely than men to be the victim. Patriarchal terrorism refers to violence on the part of men that stems from their attempts to control women. It involves the systematic repetition of violence. Common couple violence, by contrast, refers to the occasional episodes of violent behavior on the part of husbands and wives that are precipitated by stressful events; it is not linked to the power imbalance between men and women. Common couple violence occurs in an attempt to control the particular situation, whereas patriarchal terrorism is a response to control the relationship more generally. The control tactics that are involved in patriarchal terrorism are depicted in Figure 13.3. M.P. Johnson (1995) argues that this distinction may help us understand why large-scale surveys have found similar incidences of violence on the part of husbands and wives despite the fact that the people who appear at shelters are predominantly women: the surveys do not distinguish patriarchal terrorism from common couple violence.

Characteristics of Perpetrator

The person who engages in domestic abuse can be identified by a number of characteristics (Wallace, 1999). Abusive men are more likely to have a lower SES, to be young, and to be unemployed (Straus et al., 1980). Abusers typically have stereotypical views of men and women and have authoritarian personalities. Abusers also often have low self-esteem and use violence as a means to elevate their self-esteem (Gondolf & Hanneken, 1987). In addition, abusers often have a deficit in verbal skills, using violence as one way to handle disagreements.

People who engage in domestic abuse are often exposed to violence as a child, as either the subject of or a witness to violence. Men who abuse their wife are more

VIOLENCE

PHYSICAL

SEXUAL

Using Coercion and Threats

Making and/or carrying out threats to do something to hurt her • threatening to leave her, to commit suicide, to report her to welfare • making her drop charges • making her do illegal things

Using Intimidation

Making her afraid by using looks, actions, gestures • smashing things • destroying her property • abusing pets • displaying weapons

Using Economic Abuse

Preventing her from getting or keeping a job • making her ask for money • giving her an allowance • taking her money • not letting her know about or have access to family income

Using Emotional Abuse

Putting her down • making her feel bad about herself • calling her names • making her think she's crazy • playing mind games • humiliating her • making her feel guilty

Power and Control

Using Male Privilege

Treating her like a servant • making all the big decisions • acting like the "master of the castle" • being the one to define men's and women's roles

Using Isolation

Controlling what she does, who she sees and talks to, what she reads, where she goes • limiting her outside involvement • using jealousy to justify actions

Using Children

Making her feel guilty about the children • using the children to relay messages • using visitation to harass her • threatening to take the children away

Minimizing, Denying, and Blaming

Making light of the abuse and not taking her concerns about it seriously • saying the abuse didn't happen • shifting responsibility for abusive behavior • saying she caused it

PHYSICAL

SEXUAL

VIOLENCE

FIGURE 13.3   Control tactics involved in patriarchal terrorism. *Source:* E. Pence and M. Paymar (1993). *Education groups for men who batter: The Duluth model.* Copyright 1993. Reprinted by permission of Springer Publishing Co.

likely to have witnessed violence between their parents, been abused by their parents, or suffered physical punishment by their parents (Hampton & Gelles, 1994; Straus et al., 1980; Straus, 1990a).

Rates of domestic violence are higher among Hispanic families than among other families in the United States. In the 1985 national survey, domestic violence occurred in 25% of Hispanic families compared to

16% of all families (Straus & Smith, 1990). The rates of violence again were similar for men and women. The high rate of violence in Hispanic families was linked to their lower income, younger age, and tendency to live in urban areas. When these three factors were taken into consideration, there were no differences in rates of violence between Hispanic and non-Hispanic families.

Rates of violence are also higher in Black families than White families, as evidenced in both the 1976 national survey (Straus et al., 1980) and the 1985 national survey (Hampton & Gelles, 1994). In the latter survey, Black women were over twice as likely as White women to experience severe violence. Although low income was associated with violence and accounted for some of the racial differences in violence, domestic abuse remained higher in Black families compared to White families with similar incomes.

As well as specific characteristics associated with an abuser, there are defining features associated with the abuse itself (Wallace, 1999). First, abuse is often accompanied by attempts to socially isolate the victim from family and friends, so that the victim cannot gain feedback from others about the abuse. Second, the victim is typically economically dependent on the abuser. Third, alcohol is often associated with abuse; however, despite the link between alcohol and violence, alcohol alone is not sufficient to provoke violence (National Institute on Alcohol Abuse and Alcoholism, 1997). Finally, there is a cycle to the abuse (L.E. Walker, 1979). There is a tension-building phase, characterized by minor battering in which the victim tries to calm the abuser and accommodate her behavior to him, but eventually withdraws. This phase is followed by an explosion, or acute battering episode, which is then followed by a calm and loving period in which the abuser tries to make amends, asks forgiveness, and

promises to never hurt the victim again. It is this positive period that convinces the victim that she can change the abuser's behavior. Ultimately, however, the abuser becomes irritated, the victim again engages in accommodation, and then the victim withdraws. The tension escalates until another violent episode is precipitated. This cycle is depicted in Figure 13.4.

Characteristics of Victim

Women who are abused tend to be younger, less educated, and have a lower income status (Birns, 1998). No personality characteristics have been associated with being a victim of abuse (Wallace, 1999). There is no evidence that the experience of abuse or witnessing abuse as a child is associated with becoming a victim of abuse (Hampton & Gelles, 1994).

An often asked question is: Why do women who are abused remain in the relationship? The answer depends more on features of the situation than characteristics of the victim. A good predictor of whether someone stays in or leaves a relationship is not how satisfied the person is with the relationship but whether the person has alternatives to that relationship. In one study, women who had experienced violence from their husband said that they stayed in the relationship because they did not have anywhere to go and did not have a job (Kurz, 1998). Women who are more financially dependent on their husband are more tolerant of abuse in their relationship (Wallace, 1999).

Theories

Some researchers view men's abuse of women as an extreme form of the stereotypical relationship that exists between men

Tension-Building Phase

- Minor battering
- Victim accommodation
- Victim withdrawal

Calm/Loving Period

- Abuser asks forgiveness
- Victim tries to change abuser
- Abuser becomes irritated

Acute Battering Episode

FIGURE 13.4   Cycle of domestic abuse. *Source:* Adapted from Walker (1979).

and women (Goldner, Penn, Sheinberg, & Walker, 1990). Spousal abuse is viewed as men's attempt to establish control and to restore dominance to their relationships with women (Birns, 1998; A. Browne & Williams, 1993). In support of this theory, women who are abused report that violence seemed to occur when they acted independently. Women say that their husband tries to control their behavior by isolating them from friends and family. Thus, control and dominance seem to be the primary motivations behind abuse. This description of abuse is consistent with the definition of patriarchal terrorism (M. Johnson, 1995). The theory that spousal abuse is a form of power and a way to exert dominance is supported by data showing that the lowest levels of violence occur in families where power and decision making are shared (Straus et al., 1980; Wallace, 1999). A cross-cultural study of domestic violence in 90 societies

revealed that the lowest rates of domestic violence occurred in the more egalitarian societies (Levinson, 1989).

Abuse also has been linked to stress. The 1985 national survey showed that the number of stressful life events recently experienced was associated with violence among both men and women (Straus, 1990b). Stress also interacts with personality variables to predict abuse. Straus found that men who believed husbands should be dominant in the family were 1.5 to 3 times more likely to assault their wife than other men *if* they were under high stress. In addition, men who were socially isolated were more likely to assault their wife *if* they were under high stress. Thus, stressful circumstances might combine with other factors, such as personality traits or environmental conditions, to produce family violence. This may reflect the common couple form of abuse (M. Johnson, 1995).

Sexual Harassment

In 1991, the Tailhook Association, an organization for Navy aviators, convened at the Hilton Hotel in Las Vegas for their annual convention. The convention was known for its memorable parties and rowdy behavior, but this year things got out of hand—or, this year, people got caught. Women who were on vacation, as well as women who were members of the association, walked in on the third-floor party to find the halls lined with men (known as the "Banister") who proceeded to grab and fondle various body parts and remove clothing despite the women's screams and attempts to fight the men off. The final report that was sent to the Navy contained incidents of verbal abuse, physical abuse, and sexual molestation (Ballingrud, 1992).

Not nearly as famous as Tailhook but equally as devastating was the Eveleth Mines Case (Tevlin, 1998). In 1993, sixteen female mine workers successfully sued Oglebay Norton Corp. in the first ever hostile sexual work environment class-action lawsuit in the United States ("The Eveleth Mines," 1998). The mine was decorated with pornography, obscene graffiti, and sexual objects. One woman went to discuss these issues with her supervisor but found a picture of a vagina on his desk. The women were subjected to dirty jokes, sexual propositions, fondling, and groping on a daily basis. One woman even found semen on the clothes in her locker. Although the courts agreed that the women suffered sexual harassment, the case is still pending because there is disagreement as to the degree of injury sustained and the amount of compensation the women should be awarded.

Sexual harassment is associated with adverse effects on work quality and on health (Gutek & Done, 2000). In terms of work quality, people who are harassed are unhappy with their job, have more difficulty performing their job, and are less committed to their job. People who are harassed may quit their job, be fired, or lose career opportunities. Health outcomes range from psychological distress, such as loss of self-esteem, anxiety, and depression, to physical symptoms, such as headaches and gastrointestinal problems. Sexual harassment also may affect people's ability to trust others. People who are harassed may withdraw from social interactions.

In this section of the chapter, I define sexual harassment, examine its incidence, and describe characteristics of perpetrators and victims. Then, I review some theories of sexual harassment.

Definitions

The following is the Equal Employment Opportunity Commission's (EEOC, 1980, p. 74677) definition of sexual harassment:

> Unwelcome sexual advances, requests for sexual favors, and other verbal or physical conduct of a sexual nature constitute sexual harassment when (1) submission to such conduct is made either explicitly or implicitly a term or condition of an individual's employment, (2) submission to or rejection of such conduct by an individual is used as the basis for employment decisions affecting such individual, or (3) such conduct has the purpose or effect of unreasonably interfering with an individual's work performance or creating an intimidating, hostile, or offensive working environment.

The EEOC defines two types of sexual harassment: (1) **quid pro quo,** which means that one person offers work benefits (e.g., promotion) or threatens work repercussions (e.g., loss of job) in exchange for sexual favors, and (2) **hostile environment,** which means that the person is faced with a hostile, intimidating work environment. Quid pro quo, which can be translated as "this for that," is likely to occur among two people of different status. Hostile environment sexual harassment, which frequently consists of pervasive pornographic material, sexual language, and displays of sexual behavior, is more likely to occur among coworkers; this type of harassment was the subject of the Eveleth Mines case.

It is difficult to define sexual harassment exclusively in terms of behavior because a given behavior can be construed as harassment in some instances and not others. Although some behaviors can be clearly defined as sexual harassment, such as a sexual bribe, others cannot be objectively classified as harassment in an absolute sense. How can you tell whether a comment or a look is flirting or harassment? Paludi and Barickman (1998) have suggested that one way to determine whether a behavior is harassment is to examine whether the recipient has the freedom to pursue the relationship. If the person feels free to pursue or not pursue the relationship, the behavior is not harassment; if the person feels that he or she has no choice, the behavior is harassment. A second way to determine whether a behavior is harassment is to examine the effect of the behavior on the person. If the behavior makes one feel good and even attractive, the behavior is not harassment; if the behavior makes one feel uncomfortable, the behavior is harassment.

One problem is that these definitional distinctions rely on the recipient's interpretation of the behavior. Another problem is that these are not *legal* definitions of harassment. Much of the research relies on people's interpretation of sexual harassment when examining prevalence rates, but one must keep in mind that not all of these forms of sexual harassment are illegal.

There is some consensus across studies of undergraduates and adult populations on the behaviors that clearly are sexual harassment and the behaviors that clearly are not (Frazier, Cochran, & Olson, 1995). Yet, on average, undergraduates are less likely than other adults to view behaviors as sexual harassment (Frazier et al., 1995). Sexual propositions, sexual coercion, and sexual touching are viewed as sexual harassment by most everyone. Sexist comments, jokes, coarse language, flirting, and staring, however, are typically not viewed as harassment. There is more agreement that harassment has occurred when behaviors are physical (e.g., petting, pinching) rather than verbal (e.g., sexual comments, innuendoes).

Fitzgerald, Gelfand, and Drasgow (1995) have defined three levels of sexual harassment. In order from least to most severe, they are (1) gender harassment (e.g., sexist comments, suggestive stories), (2) unwanted sexual attention (e.g., leering, attempts at touching, repeated requests for dates), and (3) sexual coercion (e.g., bribes and threats involving sex, negative consequences for refusals to have sex). The first two levels are more similar to hostile environment sexual harassment, whereas the third reflects quid pro quo sexual harassment (Gutek & Done, 2000). There is more agreement that harassment has occurred at the most severe levels.

Do men and women define sexual harassment in the same way? There clearly is a difference. Women are more likely than men to perceive a behavior as harassment (Frazier et al., 1995; Ivy & Hamlet, 1996) and to view sexual harassment as a problem in the workplace (Gutek & O'Connor, 1995). A meta-analysis showed that women were more likely to define a situation as harassing, but the effect size was small to moderate ($d = +.35$; J. Blumenthal, 1998). However, differences between men's and women's interpretations of a behavior are most likely to emerge for more ambiguous behaviors, such as staring or sexist remarks. Men and women clearly agree that a sexual proposition is sexual harassment.

One behavior that men and women view differently is touching. According to Gutek (1985), a man views a woman touching him on the shoulder in sexual terms, but the same man does not view his touching a woman on the shoulder in sexual terms. Even when men interpret an event in a sexual way, they do not necessarily construe the behavior as harassment. In a survey of over 1,000 working people, 58% of men and 84% of women said that sexual touching was harassment (Gutek, 1985).

Even a sexual proposition is not *personally* defined by both men and women as harassment. In the same study conducted by Gutek (1985), participants were asked how they would feel if they were propositioned by the other sex at work; 67% of men said that they would be flattered, whereas only 17% of women gave this response. However, both men and women still agree that a man propositioning a women at work is sexual harassment.

Sex differences in perceptions of sexual harassment are not universal. College students from the United States, Australia, Germany, and Brazil read a story about a college professor who invited a student from his seminar to dinner (Pryor et al., 1997). Only in the United States were women more likely than men to view the behavior as sexual harassment. As shown in Figure 13.5, in Brazil, men were more likely than women to view the behavior as harassment, there were no sex differences in perception of harassment in Australia and Germany, and in the United States, women were more likely than men to view the behavior as harassment. Notice that the sex difference in the United States was not due to U.S. women being more likely than women in other countries to interpret a behavior as harassment but was due to U.S. men being *less* likely than men from other countries to perceive the behavior as harassment.

The situation also may influence whether a behavior is interpreted as sexual harassment. One feature of the situation that may influence perceptions is the status differential between the two people. In quid pro quo sexual harassment, the harasser has a higher status than the person

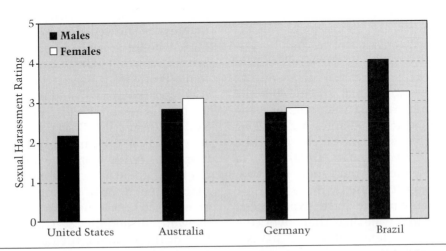

FIGURE 13.5   College students' perceptions of sexual harassment. In the United States, women were more likely than men to interpret a behavior as sexual harassment. In Australia and Germany, there were no sex differences in perceptions of sexual harassment. In Brazil, men were more likely than women to interpret a behavior as sexual harassment. *Source:* Adapted from Pryor et al. (1997).

being harassed. Thus, one might perceive the same behavior as harassment if the harasser has a high rather than a low status. Research has shown this to be true. A meta-analysis revealed a medium effect for status on perceptions of harassment ($d = +.65$; J. Blumenthal, 1998), such that a behavior was more likely to be labeled harassment when there was a status difference between perpetrator and target.

However, one study showed that status has a more complicated relation to perceptions of harassment. Although status is associated with power, which leads to a behavior being interpreted as harassment, status also is associated with perceiving the high-status person as desirable and wanting to be associated with the person, which leads to a behavior not being interpreted as harassment (Sheets & Braver, 1999). Thus, if a high-status person engages in an ambiguous behavior, such as making sexual innuendoes, one will be less likely to interpret the behavior as harassment if one knows and likes the person than if one does not know and/or does not like the person.

Incidence

In 1992, 10,532 charges of sexual harassment were filed with the EEOC (2000). In 1995, there was an increase of almost 50%: 15,549 charges were filed. Since 1995, the number of charges filed has remained the same. The majority of charges are filed by women, but the number of charges filed by men is increasing. In 1992, 9% of charges filed were by men, and in 1998, 13% of charges filed were by men.

How many people have experienced sexual harassment during their working history? The prevalence of sexual harassment is typically measured with surveys. One methodological difficulty with the survey method is that all of the respondents to

whom surveys are sent do not complete them. The people who complete the survey could differ from the people who choose not to complete the survey. The kind of person who responds to a survey is likely to be interested in the topic, and it makes sense that the people who will be most interested in the topic of sexual harassment are those who have experienced it. There is evidence that such a response bias exists. Gruber (1990) found that studies with low response rates (i.e., a smaller percentage of people returning the survey) revealed higher rates of sexual harassment. This finding suggests that the people who do not respond to surveys are less likely to have been harassed. Thus, to obtain a good estimate of the frequency of sexual harassment, it is very important to have a representative sample of participants and a high response rate.

Good studies with representative samples show that the incidence of sexual harassment ranges between 42% and 53% (J. White & Kowalski, 1998), with an average of 44% (Gruber, 1990). Higher percentages occur for milder forms of sexual harassment, such as sexual remarks. A study of sexual harassment among federal employees showed that 42% of women reported being sexually harassed within the prior two years (United States Merit Systems Protection Board, 1981). The study was repeated in 1987 and in 1994, and similar results were found (United States Merit System Protection Board, 1988, 1995). In a survey of 5,225 randomly selected Navy personnel (with women oversampled), sexual harassment was reported by 44% of enlisted women, 33% of women officers, 8% of enlisted men, and 2% of men officers (Newell, Rosenfeld, & Culbertson, 1995). Few of these people filed a complaint: only 8% of enlisted women and 6% of women officers. Again, the most frequent types of sexual harassment were the milder forms, such as unwanted looks and sexual jokes. People typically responded to harassment by either avoiding the perpetrator or confronting the perpetrator and asking him or her to stop.

The prevalence of sexual harassment is influenced by the way the question is asked. When men and women are asked about specific behaviors at work, they report comparable levels of sexual harassment (Gutek, 1985). For example, in a study of 1,000 working people, similar percentages of men and women reported that a person of the other sex had made insulting comments (19% men, 23% women), given insulting looks (19% men, 20% women), touched them sexually (33% men, 33% women), and made socializing or dating part of their job (8% men, 12% women). The only exception was that twice as many women as men said they were required to have sex with someone at work as part of their job (8% vs. 4%).

Although men and women reported similar rates of most specific behaviors, when asked if they had been sexually harassed, more women than men said yes (53% vs. 37%). To further examine whether the behaviors men and women reported could be construed as harassment, independent coders rated the behaviors and classified them as definitely sexual harassment, probably sexual harassment, uncertain, probably not sexual harassment, and definitely not sexual harassment. The coders largely agreed with participants' own perceptions; coders said sexual harassment had definitely or probably occurred among 59% of women and 28% of men.

What does the discrepancy between reports of specific behaviors and perceptions of sexual harassment mean? Are the categories of behaviors too broad to capture whether a behavior is harassment? Does the context within which a behavior takes place affect whether a behavior is interpreted as

harassment? If so, part of that context may be the sex of the victim, that is, being female.

What is the incidence of sexual harassment among men? The United States Merit Systems Protection Board surveys (1981, 1988, 1995) showed that between 14% and 19% of men had experienced sexual harassment in the prior 24 months. In her review of the literature, Gutek (1985) concluded that between 9% and 35% of men experience sexual harassment (depending on the definition) by women at some point in their working life. Men may be even less likely than women to report sexual harassment. Men are expected to handle these kinds of situations on their own; admitting to harassment means admitting to victim status, which is inconsistent with the male gender role. Being the subject of harassment by another man would be especially threatening to men. Thus, it is not surprising that men are even less likely to report sexual harassment by other men (Dziech & Hawkins, 1998).

What is the incidence of sexual harassment on college campuses? In an examination of nine campus surveys, between 20% and 30% of college women reported being sexually harassed by male faculty (Dziech & Weiner, 1990). In a recent study of 824 undergraduates, 68% of women and 25% of men said they had been victims of sexual harassment by peers (Ivy & Hamlet, 1996). One study distinguished between undergraduate and graduate students' experiences with sexual harassment (Cammaert, 1985). Slightly more undergraduate than graduate women reported sexual harassment (30% vs. 23%). The source of the harassment differed somewhat: female undergraduates were most likely to experience sexual harassment from peers, whereas female graduate students were equally likely to experience sexual harassment from peers and authority figures (i.e., faculty). The majority of harassment incidents consist of verbal behaviors, such as lewd comments, sexual innuendoes, and remarks about body parts. Despite the difference in men's and women's experiences of sexual harassment, the majority of both viewed sexual harassment as a problem on campus (Ivy & Hamlet, 1996). Still, the percentage was higher for women than men (81% vs. 64%). Conduct your own study of sexual harassment on campus with Exercise 13.4.

Characteristics of Perpetrator

There are few distinctive demographic characteristics of men who sexually harass women. Sexual harassment is usually not related to a man's age, marital status, physical attractiveness, or occupation (Gutek, 1985; Paludi & Barickman, 1998). If anything, men who harass are more likely to be married and are older (Gutek, 1985; U.S. Merit Systems Protection Board, 1981). Harassers are more likely to be coworkers than supervisors (Bondurant & White, 1996), in part because people have more coworkers than supervisors, which means that hostile

---

EXERCISE 13.4
Prevalence of Sexual
Harassment on Campus

First, you must decide on a definition of sexual harassment. Then, you must decide on the behaviors that constitute sexual harassment. Administer a survey to 10 men and 10 women on campus and ask them how frequently they have experienced each behavior. After the frequency ratings are made, you might ask the respondents to evaluate whether they perceive each of these behaviors as sexual harassment.

---

environment harassment is more common than quid pro quo harassment.

Although male harassers cannot be distinguished by demographic characteristics, psychological characteristics are linked to those who harass. Pryor (1998) has developed the Likelihood to Sexually Harass (LSH) scale to identify the person who is most likely to engage in sexual harassment. This scale consists of a series of situations that create the opportunity for quid pro quo sexual harassment to occur. Following each scenario, respondents are asked how likely they would be to engage in a number of behaviors. A sample scenario is shown in Table 13.3. Men who score high on this scale say that they would respond to the series of scenarios by engaging in sexual behavior. These men also endorse rape myths and link sexuality and sexual harassment to power (Deaux & Lafrance, 1998). The male who has a high tendency to sexually harass women endorses stereotypical masculine beliefs and has traditional attitudes toward women (Paludi & Barickman, 1998; Pryor, Giedd, & Williams, 1995). These men equate masculinity with high status, appearing tough, and being dominant. You might expect that men who sexually harass women are likely to interpret neutral behavior in sexual terms. Some research shows this to be true (Deaux & LaFrance, 1998), but other research has strongly refuted this idea (Saal, 1996).

It is not surprising that personality characteristics can be linked to the person who engages in sexual harassment because incidents of harassment are usually not isolated. The male harasser usually approaches more than one woman and the women are aware of this (Gutek, 1985).

Characteristics of Victim

Younger and unmarried women are more likely to be harassed than older and married

TABLE 13.3   Likelihood to Sexually Harass Scenario

Imagine that you are a college professor. You are 38 years old; you teach in a large, Midwestern university; you are a full professor with tenure; you are renowned in your field (abnormal psychology) and have numerous offers for other jobs. One day, following the return of an examination to a class, a female student stops in your office. She tells you that her score is one point away from an A and asks you if she can do an extra credit project to raise her score. She tells you that she may not have a sufficient grade to get into graduate school without the A. Several other students have asked you to do extra credit assignments and you have declined to let them. This particular woman is a stunning blonde. She sits in the front row of the class every day and always wears short skirts. You find her extremely sexy. How likely are you to do the following things in this situation?

a. Would you let her carry out a project for extra credit (e.g., write a paper)?

   Not at all likely   1   2   3   4   5   Very likely

b. Assuming that you are very secure in your job and the university has always tolerated professors who make passes at students, would you offer the student a chance to earn extra credit in return for sexual favors?

   Not at all likely   1   2   3   4   5   Very likely

c. Given the same assumptions as in the question above, would you ask her to join you for dinner to discuss the possible extra credit assignments?

   Not at all likely   1   2   3   4   5   Very likely

Source: Pryor (1998).

women (Gutek, 1985; Gutek & Done, 2000). Unmarried men also are more likely than married men to be sexually harassed (Gutek, 1985).

Women's occupations also are linked to sexual harassment. Women employed in male-dominated positions are more likely to be harassed than women employed in traditional occupations (Bondurant & White, 1996; Gutek, 1985), in part because these women have greater contact with men. For example, in a 1988 survey of sexual harassment among active duty military, 64% of women reported an incident of sexual harassment in the prior year (Martindale, 1990). This is a much higher incidence than that reported in nationally representative samples.

Women's occupations also influence the type of sexual harassment. Women in traditional occupations are likely to suffer quid pro quo sexual harassment, whereas women in nontraditional occupations are likely to suffer from hostile environment harassment (Lach & Gwartney-Gibbs, 1993). When women are in nontraditional jobs, they are perceived by male peers as a threat to their job.

Among college students, sexual harassment occurs most often among minority women, graduate rather than undergraduate women, women in classes with small faculty: student ratios, women in traditionally male majors (e.g., engineering), and women from low-income families (Dziech & Weiner, 1990).

Theories

One theory of sexual harassment is that it is a natural and normal part of male-female relationships (Tangri, Burt, & Johnson, 1982; Tangri & Hayes, 1997). Sexual harassment may be viewed as the product of male hormones or as a normal part of male courting behavior. One motive for sexual harassment may be to seek sexual intimacy. The behavior becomes a problem, however, when it is not desired on the part of the female.

Another theory of sexual harassment is that it is a manifestation of patriarchy—men's dominance over women. According to this view, harassment is a form of men asserting their power over women and has more to do with power than sex (Sandler & Shoop, 1997; Tangri et al., 1982; Tangri & Hayes, 1997). With quid pro quo harassment, certainly power is an important factor. However, even with hostile environment harassment between coworkers, some would argue that assertion of power is the underlying motivation (Sandler & Shoop, 1997).

A social psychological perspective conceptualizes sexual harassment as the product of both person factors and situational factors. Sexual harassment is a behavior that occurs among some of the people some of the time (Pryor et al., 1995). Characteristics of people who harass are addressed with Pryor's (1998) LSH scale. What are the environmental conditions that foster sexual harassment? In one study, priming men with a sexist film was associated with gender harassment (i.e., number of sexist questions asked of a female during a mock job interview; Pryor, Hesson-McInnis, Hitlan, Olson, & Hahn, 2000). In another study, men whose masculinity was threatened by being outperformed by a female on a masculine task were more likely to engage in the same form of sexual harassment (Pryor et al., 2000).

Sexual harassment is most likely to occur in situations where it is perceived as acceptable or tolerated (Pryor et al., 1995). In organizations where management condones sexual harassment, the frequency increases. A study conducted by the Department of Defense (Martindale, 1990) nicely illustrates this finding. They compared women's reports of sexual harassment to men's reports of the commanding officers' attitudes toward sexual harassment. Thus, estimates of sexual harassment and environmental acceptability were derived from separate sources. In locations where men said the atmosphere was more accepting of sexual harassment, women reported more harassment. Sexual harassment also may be more likely to occur when there is a power imbalance between supervisors and supervisees (Tangri et al., 1982).

Another theory of sexual harassment that emphasizes the contribution of situational variables is the **sex-role spillover theory,** which suggests that expectations about men's and women's roles carry over to the workplace when they are not appropriate or are irrelevant (Tangri & Hayes, 1997). This theory implies that sexual harassment is more likely to occur when gender is salient (Gutek & Done, 2000), when men are in the clear majority and women are in the minority (Gutek, 1985): because of women's minority status, their gender role rather than their work role become salient. Sexual harassment is also more likely to occur to women whose occupation is consistent with the female gender role, such as waitresses and secretaries (Gutek & Done, 2000); again, their sex is salient. This theory also applies to men: men who work with a large number of women are more likely to experience sexual harassment (Gutek & Done, 2000).

According to Gutek (1985), work conditions are conducive to the sexual harassment of women in two ways. First, attractiveness is valued in female workers more than male workers. In a study of over 1,000 working persons, 50% of the women said that physical attractiveness was at least somewhat important in their job; 20% said that their attractiveness was very important to their job. Second, women are often in lower job positions than men.

SUMMARY

Experimental studies, field research, and crime statistics all lead to the same conclusion: men are more likely than women to be the perpetrators of aggressive acts. Men also are more likely to be the victims of aggression. Biological theories of aggression focus on the role of genetics, testosterone, and evolutionary principles. Although biological factors may predispose men to aggression, they are likely to interact with social factors to produce aggression. Social learning theory has demonstrated that modeling and reinforcement produce aggressive behavior. Children who grow up in aggressive homes, either by witnessing or experiencing violence, are more likely to become aggressive. However, the majority of children from aggressive homes do not become violent, and the majority of violent people do not come from aggressive homes. During adolescence, peers may become an important socializing force for aggression. Gender-role theories of aggression focus on the idea that we socialize men to be aggressive by our glorification of war and aggressive sports, by the toys we provide to boys, and by the heroes on television and in the media whom boys are taught to emulate.

Specific acts of violence are examined in this chapter: rape, domestic abuse, and sexual harassment. I defined these behaviors and provided data on their incidence. In the vast majority of cases, the perpetrator is male and the victim is female. Characteristics of perpetrators have been identified; men who hold more traditional attitudes toward women are more likely to be perpetrators of these acts. With the exception of sexual harassment, indicators of low status have been associated with aggression toward women. There are fewer characteristics of

victims. Youth and indicators of low status have been linked to becoming a victim of rape and abuse. Characteristics of victims are more likely to predict how they respond to the experience, rather than the experience itself.

Each of these instances of aggressive behavior has been viewed in terms of the power structure of male-female relations. Men who rape, abuse, and harass women may be trying to establish or reestablish power in these relations. It also is clear that personality factors interact with situational factors to precipitate these aggressive acts. Men who have traditional views of male-female relations may be more likely to respond to situational cues with aggression toward women; for example, dominant men are more likely to abuse their wife under conditions of high stress. Another example of the interaction between personality and environment is that men who score high in the tendency to sexually harass women do so when their masculinity is undermined.

DISCUSSION QUESTIONS

1. What are some moderator variables of sex differences in aggression?
2. Give some specific examples of how our culture models and reinforces violence.
3. What is the masculine mystique?
4. What do you think would be the best way to measure the prevalence of rape? How would you define rape?
5. Are men and women equally likely to be victims of abuse?
6. What are the differences between common couple violence and patriarchal terrorism?
7. Do men and women define sexual harassment differently?
8. Describe rape, domestic abuse, and sexual harassment from a social psychological perspective: offer an explanation

that takes into consider both dispositional and situational factors.

SUGGESTED READING

Brownmiller, S. (1975). *Against our will.* New
York: Bantam Books.

Eagly, A.H., & Steffen, V.J. (1986). Gender and
aggressive behavior: A meta-analytic review
of the social psychological literature. *Psychological Bulletin, 100,* 309–330.

Gutek, B.A. (1985). *Sex and the workplace: Impact of sexual behavior and harassment on
women.* San Francisco: Jossey-Bass.

Koss, M.P. (1993). Detecting the scope of rape: A
review of prevalence research methods. *Journal of Interpersonal Violence, 8*(2), 198–222.

Miedzian, M. (1991). *Boys will be boys: Breaking the link between masculinity and violence.* Thousand Oaks, CA: Sage.

Pryor, J.B., Giedd, J.L., & Williams, K.B. (1995).
A social psychological model for predicting
sexual harassment. *Journal of Social Issues,
51*(1), 69–84.

Straus, M.A., Gelles, R.J., & Smith, C. (Eds.).
(1990). *Physical violence in American families: Risk factors and adaptations to violence in 8,145 families.* Portland, OR: Book
News, Inc.

KEY TERMS

Anger rape—Type of rape that occurs when
the perpetrator is expressing hostility or
hate toward the victim.

Common couple violence—Occasional
episodes of violent behavior on the part of
husbands and wives that are precipitated by
stressful events.

Hostile aggression—Behavior that has the
purpose of intending to harm someone.

Hostile environment—Type of sexual harassment in which one person is creating a
hostile, intimidating work environment for
the other.

Instrumental aggression—Behavior in which
aggression is used as a means to an end.

Marital rape exemption clause—Clause
that once appeared in state definitions of
rape that excluded forced intercourse with
one's wife.

Masculine mystique—Image of masculinity
upheld by society that consists of toughness, dominance, emotional detachment,
callousness toward women, eagerness to
seek out danger, and competition.

Patriarchal terrorism—Violence on the part
of men that stems from their attempts to
control women.

Power rape—Type of rape that occurs when
the perpetrator is seeking to control and
exert power over the victim.

Proactive aggression—Aggressive behavior
that is planned and is generally socially
motivated.

Quid pro quo—Type of sexual harassment
in which one person offers work benefits or
threatens work repercussions in exchange
for sexual favors.

Reactive aggression—Aggressive behavior
that takes the form of an angry, impulsive
response to threat or provocation.

Sex-role spillover theory—Suggestion that
expectations about men's and women's
roles carry over to the workplace when
they are not appropriate or are irrelevant.

Threatened egoism—Theory of aggression
that suggests that some people who hold
positive views of themselves may react
with aggression toward anyone who threatens that view.

Weapons effect—Idea that people are more
likely to behave aggressively in the presence of a weapon than in the absence of
one.

REFERENCES

Abbey, A., & Harnish, R. J. (1995). Perception of sexual intent: The role of gender, alcohol consumption, and rape supportive attitudes. *Sex Roles, 32,* 297–313.

Abdelrahman, A. I., Rodriguez, G., Ryan, J. A., French, J. F., & Weinbaum, D. (1998). The epidemiology of substance use among middle school students: The impact of school, familial, community and individual risk factors. *Journal of Child and Adolescent Substance Abuse, 8*(1), 55–75.

Abramson, L. Y., Seligman, M. E. P., & Teasdale, J. D. (1978). Learned helplessness in humans: Critique and reformulation. *Journal of Abnormal Psychology, 87,* 49–74.

Acitelli, L. K. (1992). Gender differences in relationship awareness and marital satisfaction among young married couples. *Personality and Social Psychology Bulletin, 18,* 102–110.

Acitelli, L. K., & Antonucci, T. C. (1994). Gender differences in the link between marital support and satisfaction in older couples. *Journal of Personality and Social Psychology, 67,* 688–698.

Adams, R. G. (1985). People would talk: Normative barriers to cross-sex friendships for elderly women. *Gerontologist, 25*(6), 605–611.

Adams, S., Kuebli, J., Boyle, P. A., & Fivush, R. (1995). Gender differences in parent-child conversations about past emotions: A longitudinal investigation. *Sex Roles, 33,* 309–323.

A debilitating obsession that doesn't spare celebs. (1992, August 3). *People* [On-line]. Available: http://people.aol.com/people/tribute/diana\archive-all/p920803.html

Adelmann, P. K. (1994). Multiple roles and physical health among older adults: Gender and ethnic comparisons. *Research on Aging, 16*(2), 142–166.

Akiyama, H., Elliott, K., & Antonucci, T. C. (1996). Same-sex and cross-sex relationships. *Journal of Gerontology, 51B*(6), 374–382.

Ali, A., & Toner, B. B. (1996). Gender differences in depressive response: The role of social support. *Sex Roles, 35,* 281–293.

Al-Krenawi, A., & Graham, J. R. (1998). Divorce among Muslim Arab women in Israel. *Journal of Divorce and Remarriage, 29*(3/4), 103–119.

Allan, K., & Coltrane, S. (1996). Gender displaying television commercials: A comparative study of television commercials in the 1950s and 1980s. *Sex Roles, 35,* 185–203.

Allgood-Merten, B., Lewinsohn, P. M., & Hops, H. (1990). Sex differences and adolescent depression. *Journal of Abnormal Psychology, 99,* 53–63.

Allison, K. R., Dwyer, J. J. M., & Makin, S. (1999). Perceived barriers to physical activity among high school students. *Preventive Medicine, 28,* 608–615.

Almeida, D. M., Wethington, E., & Chandler, A. L. (1999). Daily transmission of tensions between marital dyads and parent-child dyads. *Journal of Marriage and the Family, 61,* 49–61.

Amenson, C. S., & Lewinsohn, P. M. (1981). An investigation into the observed sex difference in prevalence of unipolar depression. *Journal of Abnormal Psychology, 90,* 1–13.

American Association of University Women. (1992). *How schools shortchange girls.* Washington, DC: Author.

American Association of University Women. (2000). *Tech-Savvy: Educated girls in the new computer age.* Washington, DC: Author.

American Association of University Women Educational Foundation. (1998). *Gender gaps:*

Where schools still fail our children. Washington, DC: Author.

American Cancer Society. (1999a). *Breast cancer facts and figures 1999–2000.* Atlanta, GA: Author.

American Cancer Society. (1999b). *Cancer facts and figures–1999.* New York: Author.

American Civil Liberties Union. (1999, June 22). *ACLU defends father's right to care for first-born daughter* [On-line]. Available: http://www.alcu.org/news/1999/n062299a.html

American Psychiatric Association. (1994). *Diagnostic and statistical manual of mental disorders* (4th ed.). Washington, DC: Author.

Anda, R. F., Williamson, D. F., Escobedo, L. G., Mast, E. E., Giovino, G. A., & Remington, P. L. (1990). Depression and the dynamics of smoking: A national perspective. *Journal of the American Medical Association, 264,* 1541–1545.

Andersen, B. L., & Cyranowski, J. M. (1994). Women's sexual self-schema. *Journal of Personality and Social Psychology, 67,* 1079–1100.

Andersen, B. L., Cyranowski, J. M., & Espindle, D. (1999). Men's sexual self-schema. *Journal of Personality and Social Psychology, 76,* 645–661.

Andersen, R. E., Crespo, C. J., Bartlett, S. J., Cheskin, L. J., & Pratt, M. (1998). Relationship of physical activity and television watching with body weight and level of fatness among children: Results from the Third National Health and Nutrition Examination Survey. *Journal of the American Medical Association, 279,* 938–942.

Andrade, C., Postma, K., & Abraham, K. (1999). Influence of women's work status on the well-being of Indian couples. *International Journal of Social Psychiatry, 45*(1), 65–75.

Andrews, J. A., & Lewinsohn, P. M. (1992). Suicidal attempts among older adolescents: Prevalence and co-occurrence with psychiatric disorders. *Journal of the American Academy of Child Adolescent Psychiatry, 31,* 655–662.

Aneshensel, C. S., Frerichs, R. R., & Clark, V. A. (1981). Family roles and sex differences in depression. *Journal of Health and Social Behavior, 22,* 379–393.

Angold, A., Costello, E. J., & Worthman, C. M. (1998). Puberty and depression: The roles of age, pubertal status and pubertal timing. *Psychological Medicine, 28,* 51–61.

Anson, O., Levenson, A., & Bonneh, D. Y. (1990). Gender and health on the Kibbutz. *Sex Roles, 22,* 213–231.

Antill, J. K. (1983). Sex role complementarity versus similarity in married couples. *Journal of Personality and Social Psychology, 45,* 145–155.

Antill, J. K., Cotton, S., & Tindale, S. (1983). Egalitarian or traditional: Correlates of the perception of an ideal marriage. *Australian Journal of Psychology, 35*(2), 245–257.

Antonucci, T. C., & Akiyama, H. (1987). An examination of sex differences in social support among older men and women. *Sex Roles, 17,* 737–749.

Arber, S., & Ginn, J. (1993). Gender and inequalities in health in later life. *Social Science and Medicine, 36*(1), 33–46.

Archer, J. (1991). The influence of testosterone on human aggression. *British Journal of Psychology, 82,* 1–28.

Archer, L. R., Keever, R. R., Gordon, R. A., & Archer, R. P. (1991). The relationship between residents' characteristics, their stress experiences, and their psychosocial adjustment at one medical school. *Academic Medicine, 66,* 301–303.

Aries, E. (1996). *Men and women in interaction: Reconsidering the differences.* New York: Oxford University Press.

Aries, E. J., & Johnson, F. L. (1983). Close friendship in adulthood: Conversational content between same-sex friends. *Sex Roles, 9,* 1183–1196.

Aristotle. (1963). *Generation of animals with an English translation by A. L. Peck* (Rev. ed.). Cambridge, MA: Harvard University Press.

Arnett, J. J. (1999). Adolescent storm and stress, reconsidered. *American Psychologist, 54,* 317–326.

Arrighi, B. A., & Maume, D. J., Jr. (2000). Workplace subordination and men's avoidance of housework. *Journal of Family Issues, 21*(4), 464–487.

Arthritis Foundation. (1999). *Practical help from the Arthritis Foundation.* Atlanta, GA: Author.

Ashmore, R. D. (1990). Sex, gender, and the individual. In L. A. Pervin (Ed.), *Handbook of personality: Theory and research* (pp. 486–526). New York: Guilford Press.

Attie, I., Brooks-Gunn, J., & Petersen, A. C. (1990). A developmental perspective on eating disorders and eating problems. In M. Lewis & S. M. Miller (Eds.), *Handbook of developmental psychopathology* (pp. 409–420). New York: Plenum Press.

Aukett, R., Ritchie, J., & Mill, K. (1988). Gender differences in friendship patterns. *Sex Roles, 19,* 57–66.

Averill, J. R. (1982). *Anger and aggression: An essay on emotion.* New York: Springer.

Avison, W. R., & Mcalpine, D. D. (1992). Gender differences in symptoms of depression among adolescents. *Journal of Health and Social Behavior, 33,* 77–96.

Badgett, M. V. L. (1995). The wage effects of sexual orientation discrimination. *Industrial and Labor Relations Review, 48*(4), 726–739.

Baenninger, M., & Newcombe, N. (1989). The role of experience in spatial test performance: A meta-analysis. *Sex Roles, 20,* 327–344.

Bailey, J. M., Gaulin, S., Agyei, Y., & Gladue, B. A. (1994). Effects of gender and sexual orientation on evolutionarily relevant aspects of human mating psychology. *Journal of Personality and Social Psychology, 66,* 1081–1093.

Bakan, D. (1966). *The duality of human existence.* Chicago: Rand McNally.

Bales, R. F., & Slater, P. E. (1955). Role differentiation in small decision-making groups. In T. Parsons & R. F. Bales (Eds.), *Family, socialization, and interaction process* (pp. 259–306). Glencoe, IL: Free Press.

Ballard, M. E., & Lineberger, R. (1999). Video game violence and confederate gender: Effects on reward and punishment given by college males. *Sex Roles, 41*(7/8), 541–558.

Ballingrud, D. (1992). Assaults tarnish Navy group. *St. Petersburg Times* [On-line]. Available: http://proquest.umi.com

Bandura, A. (1973). *Aggression: A social learning analysis.* Englewood Cliffs, NJ: Prentice-Hall.

Bandura, A. (1986). *Social foundations of thought and action: A social cognitive theory.* New York: Cambridge University Press.

Bandura, A., & Walters, R. (1963). *Social learning and personality development.* New York: Holt, Rinehart and Winston.

Bank, B. J., & Hansford, S. L. (2000). Gender and friendship: Why are men's best same-sex friendships less intimate and supportive? *Personal Relationships, 7,* 63–78.

Barbee, A. P., Cunningham, M. R., Winstead, B. A., Derlega, V. J., Gulley, M. R., Yankeelov, P. A., & Druen, P. B. (1993). Effects of gender role expectations on the social support process. *Journal of Social Issues, 49*(3), 175–190.

Barboza, D. (2000, March 3). School copes with slain girl, 6-year-old shooter man, 19, charged with giving boy access to his gun. *Times–Picayune,* p. A8.

Barker, M. (1996). Remedying gender-based wage discrimination: The comparable worth approach. In P. J. Dubeck & K. Borman (Eds.), *Women and work: A handbook* (pp. 375–382). New York: Garland.

Barling, J. (1991). Fathers' employment: A neglected influence on children. In J. V. Lerner & N. L. Galambos (Eds.), *Employed mothers and their children* (pp. 181–209). New York: Garland.

Barnett, R. C. (1994). Home-to-work spillover revisited: A study of full-time employed women in dual-earner couples. *Journal of Marriage and the Family, 56,* 647–656.

Barnett, R. C., & Baruch, G. K. (1985). Women's involvement in multiple roles and psychological distress. *Journal of Personality and Social Psychology, 49*(1), 135–145.

Barnett, R. C., & Brennan, R. T. (1995). The relationship between job experiences and psychological distress: A structural equation approach. *Journal of Organizational Behavior, 16,* 259–276.

Barnett, R. C., & Brennan, R. T. (1997). Change in job conditions, change in psychological distress, and gender: A longitudinal study of dual-earner couples. *Journal of Organizational Behavior, 18,* 253–274.

Barnett, R. C., Brennan, R. T., Raudenbush, S. W., & Marshall, N. L. (1994). Gender and the relationship between marital-role quality and psychological distress. *Psychology of Women Quarterly, 18,* 105–127.

Barnett, R. C., Davidson, H., & Marshall, N. L. (1991). Physical symptoms and the interplay of work and family roles. *Health Psychology, 10,* 94–101.

Barnett, R. C., & Marshall, N. L. (1991). The relationship between women's work and family roles and their subjective well-being and psychological distress. In M. Frankenhauser (Ed.), *Women, work, and health: Stress and opportunities* (pp. 111–136). New York: Plenum Press.

Barnett, R. C., & Marshall, N. L. (1993). Men, family-role quality, job-role quality, and physical health. *Health Psychology, 12,* 48–55.

Barnett, R. C., Marshall, N. L., & Pleck, J. H. (1992). Men's multiple roles and their relationship to men's psychological distress. *Journal of Marriage and the Family, 54,* 358–367.

Barnett, R. C., Marshall, N. L., Raudenbush, S. W., & Brennan, R. T. (1993). Gender and the relationship between job experiences and psychological distress: A study of dual-earner couples. *Journal of Personality and Social Psychology, 64,* 794–806.

Barnett, R. C., Marshall, N. L., & Singer, J. D. (1992). Job experiences over time, multiple roles, and women's mental health: A longitudinal study. *Journal of Personality and Social Psychology, 62,* 634–644.

Barnett, R. C., Raudenbush, S. W., Brennan, R. T., Pleck, J. H., & Marshall, N. L. (1995). Change in job and marital experiences and change in psychological distress: A longitudinal study of dual-earner couples. *Journal of Personality and Social Psychology, 69,* 839–850.

Barnett, R. C., & Shen, Y-C. (1997). Gender, high- and low-schedule-control housework tasks, and psychological distress. *Journal of Family Issues, 18*(4), 403–428.

Baruch, G. K., Biener, L., & Barnett, R. C. (1987). Women and gender in research on work and family stress. *American Psychologist, 42*(2), 130–136.

Bass, B. M., Avolio, B. J., & Atwater, L. (1996). The transformational and transactional leadership of men and women. *Applied Psychology: An International Review, 45*(1), 5–34.

Bassoff, E., & Glass, G. (1982). The relationship between sex roles and mental health: A meta-analysis of 26 studies. *Counseling Psychologist, 10*(4), 105–112.

Baucom, D. H. (1983). Personality process and individual differences: Sex role identity and the decision to regain control among women: A learned helplessness investigation. *Journal of Personality and Social Psychology, 44,* 334–343.

Baucom, D. H., & Aiken, P. A. (1984). Sex role identity, marital satisfaction, and response to behavioral marital therapy. *Journal of Consulting and Clinical Psychology, 52,* 438–444.

Baucom, D. H., Besch, P. K., & Callahan, S. (1985). Relation between testosterone concentration, sex role identity, and personality among females. *Personality processes and individual differences, 48*(5), 1218–1226.

Baucom, D. H., Notarius, C. I., Burnett, C. K., & Haefner, P. (1990). Gender differences and sex-role identity in marriage. In F. D. Fincham & T. N. Bradbury (Eds.), *The psychology of marriage: Basic issues and applications* (pp. 150–171). New York: Guilford Press.

Baumeister, R. F. (1988). Should we stop studying sex differences altogether? *American Psychologist, 43,* 1092–1095.

Baumeister, R. F. (2000). Gender differences in erotic plasticity: The female sex drive as socially flexible and responsive. *Psychological Bulletin, 126,* 347–374.

Baumeister, R. F., Bushman, B. J., & Campbell, W. K. (2000). Self-esteem, narcissism, and aggression: Does violence result from low self-esteem or from threatened egotism? *Current Directions in Psychological Science, 9*(1), 26–29.

Baumeister, R. F., & Sommer, K. L. (1997). What do men want? Gender differences and two spheres of belongingness: Comment on Cross and Madson (1997). *Psychological Bulletin, 122,* 38–44.

Baxter, J. (1992). Power attitudes and time: The domestic division of labour. *Journal of Comparative Family Studies, 23*(2), 165–182.

Baxter, L. A. (1986). Gender differences in the heterosexual relationship rules embedded in break-up accounts. *Journal of Social and Personal Relationships, 3,* 289–306.

Beauty and Love Quotes. (2000). [On-line]. Available: www.cc.gatech.edu/grads/b/Gary.N.Boone/beauty_and_love_quotes.html

Becker, J. R. (1981). Differential treatment of females and males in mathematics classes. *Journal for Research in Mathematics Education, 12*(1), 40–53.

Bell, A. P., & Weinberg, M. W. (1978). *Homosexualities: A study of diversity among men and women.* New York: Simon & Schuster.

Bell, L. A. (1989). Something's wrong here and it's not me: Challenging the dilemmas that block girls' success. *Journal for the Education of the Gifted, 12*(2), 118–130.

Bell, L. A. (1996). In danger of winning: Consciousness raising strategies for empowering girls in the United States. *Women's Studies International Forum, 19*(4), 419–427.

Belle, D. (1982). Social ties and social support. In D. Belle (Ed.), *Lives in stress: Women and depression* (pp. 133–144). Beverly Hills, CA: Sage.

Belle, D. (1985). Ironies in the contemporary study of gender. *Journal of Personality, 53,* 400–405.

Belle, D. (1987). Gender differences in the social moderators of stress. In R. Barnett, L. Beiner, & G. K. Baruch (Eds.), *Gender and stress* (pp. 257–277). New York: Free Press.

Belle, D. (1989). Gender differences in children's social network and supports. In D. Belle (Ed.), *Children's social network and social supports* (pp. 173–188). New York: Wiley.

Bem, S. L. (1974). The measurement of psychological androgyny. *Journal of Consulting and Clinical Psychology, 42*(2), 155–162.

Bem, S. L. (1975). Sex role adaptability: One consequence of psychological androgyny. *Journal of Personality and Social Psychology, 31,* 634–643.

Bem, S. L. (1981). Gender schema theory: A cognitive account of sex typing. *Psychological Review, 88,* 354–364.

Bem, S. L. (1984). Androgyny and gender schema theory: A conceptual and empirical integration. In T. B. Sonderegger (Ed.), *Nebraska symposium on motivation 1984: Psychology and gender* (Vol. 32, pp. 179–226). Lincoln: University of Nebraska Press.

Bem, S. L. (1995). Dismantling gender polarization and compulsory heterosexuality: Should we turn the volume down or up? *Journal of Sex Research, 32*(4), 329–334.

Bem, S. L. (1998). *An unconventional family.* New Haven, CT: Yale University Press.

Benbow, C. P. (1988). Sex differences in mathematical reasoning ability in intellectually talented preadolescents: Their nature, effects, and possible causes. *Behavioral and Brain Sciences, 11,* 169–232.

Benbow, C. P., & Stanley, J. C. (1980). Sex differences in mathematical ability: Fact or artifact? *Science, 210,* 1262–1264.

Benton, C. J., Hernandez, A. C. R., Schmidt, A., Schmitz, M. D., Stone, A. J., & Weiner, B. (1983). Is hostility linked with affiliation among males and with achievement among females? A critique of Pollak and Gilligan. *Journal of Personality and Social Psychology, 45,* 1167–1171.

Berenbaum, S. A., & Hines, M. (1992). Early androgens are related to childhood sex-typed toy preferences. *Psychological Science, 3*(3), 203–206.

Bergen, D. J., & Williams, J. E. (1991). Sex stereotypes in the United States revisited: 1972–1988. *Sex Roles, 24,* 413–423.

Berger, B. D., & Adesso, V. J. (1991). Gender differences in using alcohol to cope with depression. *Addictive Behaviors, 16,* 315–327.

Berkey, C. S., Rockett, H. R., Field, A. E., Gillman, M. W., Frazier, A. L., Camargo, C. A. J., & Colditz, G. A. (2000). Activity, dietary intake, and weight changes in a longitudinal study of preadolescent and adolescent boys and girls. *Pediatrics, 105*(4), E56.

Berkley, K. J. (1997). Sex differences in pain. *Behavioral and Brain Sciences, 20,* 371–380.

Berkman, L. F., & Syme, S. L. (1979). Social networks, host resistance, and mortality: A nine-year follow-up study of Alameda county residents. *American Journal of Epidemiology, 109*(2), 186–204.

Berkman, L. F., Vaccarino, V., & Seeman, T. (1993). Gender differences in cardiovascular morbidity and mortality: The contribution of social networks and support. *Annals of Behavioral Medicine, 15,* 112–118.

Berkowitz, L. (1993). *Aggression.* New York: McGraw-Hill.

Berman, B. A., & Gritz, E. R. (1991). Women and smoking: Current trends and issues for the 1990s. *Journal of Substance Abuse, 3,* 221–238.

Berman, J. J., Murphy-Berman, V., & Pachauri, A. (1988). Sex differences in friendship patterns in India and the United States. *Basic and Applied Social Psychology, 9*(1), 61–71.

Berman, P. W. (1975). *Attraction to infants: Are sex differences innate and invariant.* Paper presented at the 83rd annual convention of the American Psychological Association, Chicago.

Berman, P. W. (1980). Are women more responsive than men to the young? A review of developmental and situational variables. *Psychological Bulletin, 88,* 668–695.

Bern, P. (1987). *How to work for a woman boss: Even if you'd rather not.* New York: Dodd, Mean.

Bernard, J. (1972). *The future of marriage.* New York: World Publishing.

Berndt, S. M., Berndt, D. J., & Kaiser, C. F. (1982). Attributional styles for helplessness and depression: The importance of sex and situational context. *Sex Roles, 8,* 433–441.

Berndt, T. J. (1982). The features and effects of friendship in early adolescence. *Child Development, 53,* 1447–1460.

Berns, S. B., Jacobson, N. S., & Gottman, J. M. (1999). Demand-withdraw interaction in couples with a violent husband. *Journal of Consulting and Clinical Psychology, 67*(5), 666–674.

Bernstein, B., & Kane, R. (1981). Physicians' attitudes toward female patients. *Medical Care, 19*(6), 600–608.

Bettencourt, B. A., & Miller, N. (1996). Gender differences in aggression as a function of provocation: A meta-analysis. *Psychological Bulletin, 119,* 422–447.

Beyer, S. (1990). Gender differences in the accuracy of self-evaluations of performance. *Journal of Personality and Social Psychology, 59,* 960–970.

Biaggio, M. K. (1989). Sex differences in behavioral reactions to provocation of anger. *Psychological Reports, 64,* 23–26.

Bickel, J. (1997). Gender stereotypes and misconceptions: Unresolved issues in physicians' professional development. *Journal of the American Medical, 277,* 1405–1407.

Bielby, W. T., & Bielby, D. D. (1992). I will follow him: Family ties, gender-role beliefs, and reluctance to relocate for a better job. *American Journal of Sociology, 97*(5), 1241–1267.

Biernat, M. (1991). Gender stereotypes and the relationship between masculinity and femininity: A developmental analysis. *Journal of Personality and Social Psychology, 61,* 351–365.

Biernat, M., & Wortman, C. B. (1991). Sharing of home responsibilities between professionally employed women and their husbands. *Journal of Personality and Social Psychology, 60,* 844–860.

Binion, V. J. (1990). Psychological androgyny: A Black female perspective. *Sex Roles, 22,* 487–507.

Bird, C. E. (1999). Gender, household labor, and psychological distress: The impact of the amount and division of housework. *Journal of Health and Social Behavior, 40,* 32–45.

Birns, B. (1998). Battered wives: Causes, effects, and social change. In C. Forden, A. E. Hunter, & B. Birns (Eds.), *Readings in the psychology of women: Dimensions of the female experience* (pp. 280–288). Boston: Allyn & Bacon.

Bjorkqvist, K., & Niemela, P. (1992). New trends in the study of female aggression. In K. Bjorkqvist & P. Niemela (Eds.), *Of mice and women: Aspects of female aggression* (pp. 3–16). San Diego, CA: Academic Press.

Bjornson, W., Rand, C., Connett, J. E., Lindgren, P., Nides, M., Pope, F., Buist, A. S., Hoppe-Ryan, C., & O'Hara, P. (1995). Gender differences in smoking cessation after 3 years in the lung health study. *American Journal of Public Health, 85*(2), 223–230.

Black, D. A., Makar, H. R., Sanders, S. G., & Taylor, L. (1998). *The effects of sexual orientation on earnings.* Unpublished manuscript, Carnegie Mellon University, Pittsburgh, PA.

Blair, S. L., & Lichter, D. T. (1991). Measuring the division of household labor: Gender segregation of housework among American couples. *Journal of Family Issues, 12*(1), 91–113.

Blasband, D., & Peplau, L. A. (1985). Sexual exclusivity versus openness in gay male couples. *Archives of Sexual Behavior, 14*(5), 395–412.

Blee, K. M., & Tickamyer, A. R. (1995). Racial differences in men's attitudes about women's gender role. *Journal of Marriage and the Family, 57*, 21–30.

Block, C. R., & Christakos, A. (1995). Intimate partner homicide in Chicago over 29 years. *Crime and Delinquency, 41*(4), 496–526.

Block, J. H. (1973). Conceptions of sex role: Some cross-cultural and longitudinal perspectives. *American Psychologist, 2*, 512–526.

Block, J. H. (1976). Issues, problems, and pitfalls in assessing sex differences: A critical review of the psychology of sex differences. *Merrill-Palmer Quarterly, 22*(4), 283–308.

Block, J. H., Gjerde, P. F., & Block, J. H. (1991). Personality antecedents of depressive tendencies in 18-year olds: A prospective study. *Journal of Personality and Social Psychology, 60*, 726–738.

Block, J. H., & Kremen, A. M. (1996). IQ and ego-resiliency: Conceptual and empirical connections and separateness. *Journal of Personality and Social Psychology, 70*, 349–361.

Bloom, B. L., & Caldwell, R. A. (1981). Sex differences in adjustment during the process of marital separation. *Journal of Marriage and the Family, 43*, 693–701.

Bloom, B. L., Hodges, W. F., & Caldwell, R. A. (1983). Marital separation: The first eight months. In E. J. Callahan & K. A. McCluskey (Eds.), *Life-span developmental psychology* (pp. 217–239). New York: Academic Press.

Blum, J. S., & Mehrabian, A. (1999). Personality and temperament correlates of marital satisfaction. *Journal of Personality, 67*, 93–125.

Blumenthal, J. A. (1998). The reasonable woman standard: A meta-analytic review of gender differences in perceptions of sexual harassment. *Law and Human Behavior, 22*(1), 33–57.

Blumstein, P., & Schwartz, P. (1983). *American couples.* New York: William Morrow.

Bly, R. (1990). *Iron John: A book about men.* Reading, MA: Addison-Wesley.

Boeringer, S. B. (1999). Associations of rape-supportive attitudes with fraternal and athletic participation. *Violence Against Women, 5*(1), 81–90.

Boggiano, A. K., & Barrett, M. (1991). Gender differences in depression in college students. *Sex Roles, 25*, 595–605.

Bohan, J. S. (1997). Regarding gender: Essentialism, constructionism, and feminist psychology. In M. M. Gergen & S. N. Davis (Eds.), *Toward a new psychology of gender: A reader* (pp. 31–47). New York: Routledge.

Bolger, N., DeLongis, A., Kessler, R. V., & Wethington, E. (1989). The contagion of stress across multiple roles. *Journal of Marriage and the Family, 51*, 175–183.

Bond, J. T., Galinsky, E., & Swanberg, J. E. (1998). *The 1997 national study of the changing workforce.* New York: Families and Work Institute.

Bond, M. H., & Young Ho, H. (1978). The effect of relative status and the sex composition of a dyad on cognitive responses and non-verbal behavior of Japanese interviewees. *Psychologia, 21*, 128–136.

Bondurant, B., & White, J. W. (1996). Men who sexually harass: An embedded perspective. In D. K. Shrier (Ed.), *Sexual harassment in the work place and academia* (pp. 59–78). Washington, DC: American Psychiatric Press.

Booth, A., & Hess, E. (1974). Cross-sex friendship. *Journal of Marriage and the Family, 36*, 38–47.

Booth, A., & Johnson, D. (1988). Premarital cohabitation and marital success. *Journal of Family Issues, 9*(2), 255–272.

Booth, A., Johnson, D. R., & Granger, D. A. (1999). Testosterone and men's depression: The role of social behavior. *Journal of Health and Social Behavior, 40*, 130–140.

Borowsky, S. J., Rubenstein, L. V., Meredith, L. S., Camp, P., Jackson-Triche, M., & Wells, K. B. (2000). Who is at risk of nondetection of mental health problems in primary care?

Journal of General Internal Medicine, 15, 381–388.

Bradbury, T. N., Campbell, S. M., & Fincham, F. D. (1995). Longitudinal and behavioral analysis of masculinity and femininity in marriage. *Journal of Personality and Social Psychology, 68,* 328–341.

Bradley, P. H. (1981). The folk-linguistics of women's speech: An empirical examination. *Communication Monographs, 48,* 73–90.

Brady, K. L., & Eisler, R. M. (1995). Gender bias in the college classroom: A critical review of the literature and implications for future research. *Journal of Research and Development in Education, 29*(1), 9–19.

Brannon, R., & Juni, S. (1984). A scale for measuring attitudes toward masculinity. *JSAS Catalog of Selected Documents in Psychology, 14*(6).

Brennan, R. T., Barnett, R. C., & Gareis, K. C. (in press). When she earns more than he does. *Journal of Marriage and the Family.*

Brent, D. A. (1995). Risk factors for adolescent suicide and suicidal behavior: Mental and substance abuse disorders, family environmental factors, and life stress. *Suicide and Life-Threatening Behavior, 25*(Suppl.), 52–63.

Brent, D. A., Perper, J. A., Moritz, G., Baugher, M., Roth, C., Balach, L., & Schweers, J. (1993). Stressful life events, psychopathology, and adolescent suicide: A case control study. *Suicide and Life Threatening Behavior, 23*(3), 179–187.

Bridge, K., & Baxter, L. A. (1992). Blended relationships: Friends as work associates. *Western Journal of Communication, 56,* 200–225.

Bridgeman, B., & Wendler, C. (1991). Gender differences in predictors of college mathematics performance and in college mathematics course grades. *Journal of Educational Psychology, 83*(2), 275–284.

Briere, J., & Lanktree, C. (1983). Sex-role related effects of sex bias in language. *Sex Roles, 9,* 625–632.

Bringle, R. G. (1995). Sexual jealousy in the relationships of homosexual and heterosexual men: 1980 and 1992. *Personal Relationships, 2,* 313–325.

Briton, N. J., & Hall, J. A. (1995). Beliefs about female and male nonverbal communication. *Sex Roles, 32,* 79–90.

Brody, L. R., & Hall, J. A. (1993). Gender and emotion. In M. Lewis & J. M. Haviland (Eds.), *Handbook of emotions* (pp. 447–460). New York: Guilford Press.

Bromberger, J. T., & Matthews, K. A. (1996). A "feminine" model of vulnerability to depressive symptoms: A longitudinal investigation of middle-aged women. *Journal of Personality and Social Psychology, 70,* 591–598.

Brooks-Gunn, J., & Warren, M. P. (1989). Biological and social contributions to negative affect in young adolescent girls. *Child Development, 60,* 40–55.

Broverman, I. K., Vogel, S. R., Broverman, D. M., Clarkson, F. E., & Rosenkrantz, P. S. (1972). Sex-role stereotypes: A current appraisal. *Journal of Social Issues, 28*(2), 59–78.

Brown, C., & Corcoran, M. (1997). Sex-based differences in school content and the male-female wage gap. *Journal of Labor Economics, 15*(3), 431–465.

Brown, D. R. (1996). Marital status and mental health. In H. W. Neighbors & J. S. Jackson (Eds.), *Mental health in Black America* (pp. 77–94). Thousand Oaks, CA: Sage.

Brown, P. C., & Smith, T. W. (1992). Social influence, marriage, and the heart: Cardiovascular consequences of interpersonal control in husbands and wives. *Health Psychology, 11,* 88–96.

Brown, S. L., & Booth, A. (1996). Cohabitation versus marriage: A comparison of relationship quality. *Journal of Marriage and the Family, 58,* 668–678.

Browne, A. (1993). Violence against women by male partners. *American Psychologist, 48,* 1077–1087.

Browne, A., & Williams, K. R. (1993). Gender, intimacy, and lethal violence: Trends from 1976 through 1987. *Gender and Society, 7*(1), 78–98.

Browne, B. A. (1998). Gender stereotypes in advertising on children's television in the 1990s: A cross-national analysis. *Journal of Advertising, 27*(1), 83–96.

Brownmiller, S. (1975). *Against our will: Men, women, and rape.* New York: Bantam Books.

Bryson, S. E., & Pilon, D. J. (1984). Sex differences in depression and the method of administering the Beck Depression Inventory. *Journal of Clinical Psychology, 40,* 529–534.

Buchanan, C. M., Eccles, J. S., & Becker, J. B. (1992). Are adolescents the victims of raging hormones: Evidence for activational effects of hormones on moods and behavior at adolescence. *Psychological Bulletin, 111,* 62–107.

Buhrke, R. A., & Fuqua, D. R. (1987). Sex differences in same- and cross-sex supportive relationships. *Sex Roles, 17,* 339–352.

Buhrmester, D., & Furman, W. (1987). The development of companionship and intimacy. *Child Development, 58,* 1101–1113.

Bumpass, L. L., & Sweet, J. A. (1989). National estimates of cohabitation. *Demography, 26*(4), 615–625.

Bumpass, L. L., Sweet, J. A., & Cherlin, A. (1991). The role of cohabitation in declining rates of marriage. *Journal of Marriage and the Family, 53,* 913–927.

Burda, P. C., & Vaux, A. C. (1987). The social support process in men: Overcoming sex-role obstacles. *Human Relations, 40*(1), 31–44.

Burda, P. C., Vaux, A., & Schill, T. (1984). Social support resources: Variation across sex and sex role. *Personality and Social Psychology Bulletin, 10,* 119–126.

Burger, A. L., & Jacobson, N. S. (1979). The relationship between sex role characteristics, couple satisfaction and couple problem-solving skills. *American Journal of Family Therapy, 7,* 52–60.

Burleson, B. R., Kunkel, A. W., Samter, W., & Werking, K. J. (1996). Men's and women's evaluations of communication skills in personal relationships: When sex differences make a difference and when they don't. *Journal of Social and Personal Relationships, 13,* 201–224.

Burt, M. R. (1980). Cultural myths and supports for rape. *Journal of Personality and Social Psychology, 38,* 217–230.

Bush, D. E., Simmons, R. G., Hutchinson, B., & Blyth, D. A. (1977–1978). Adolescent perception of sex-roles in 1968 and 1975. *Public Opinion Quarterly, 41,* 459–474.

Bushman, B. J., & Anderson, C. A. (1998). Methodology in the study of aggression: Integrating experimental and nonexperimental findings. In R. G. Geen & E. Donnerstein (Eds.), *Human aggression: Theories, research, and implications for social policy* (pp. 23–48). San Diego, CA: Academic Press.

Buss, D. M. (1989). Sex differences in human mate preferences: Evolutionary hypotheses tested in 37 cultures. *Behavioral and Brain Sciences, 12*(1), 1–49.

Buss, D. M. (1994). *The evolution of desire.* New York: Basic Books.

Buss, D. M. (1995). Psychological sex differences: Origins through sexual selection. *American Psychologist, 50,* 164–168.

Buss, D. M. (1999). *Evolutionary psychology: The new science of mind.* Boston: Allyn & Bacon.

Buss, D. M., Abbott, M., Angleitner, A., & Asherian, A. (1990). International preferences in selecting mates: A study of 37 cultures. *Journal of Cross-Cultural Psychology, 21,* 5–47.

Buss, D. M., & Barnes, M. F. (1986). Preferences in human mate selection. *Journal of Personality and Social Psychology, 50,* 559–570.

Buss, D. M., Gomes, M., Higgins, D. S., & Lauterbach, K. (1987). Tactics of manipulation. *Journal of Personality and Social Psychology, 52,* 1219–1229.

Buss, D. M., & Kenrick, D. T. (1998). Evolutionary social psychology. In D. T. Gilbert, S. T. Fiske, & G. Lindzey (Eds.), *The handbook of social psychology* (pp. 982–1026). New York: Oxford University Press.

Buss, D. M., Larsen, R. J., Westen, D., & Semmelroth, J. (1992). Sex differences in jealousy: Evolution, physiology, and psychology. *Psychological Science, 3*(4), 251–255.

Buss, D. M., & Schmitt, D. P. (1993). Sexual strategies theory: An evolutionary perspective on human mating. *Psychological Review, 100,* 204–232.

Bussey, K., & Bandura, A. (1992). Self-regulatory mechanisms governing gender development. *Child Development, 63,* 1236–1250.

Bussey, K., & Bandura, A. (1999). Social cognitive theory of gender development and differentiation. *Psychological Review, 106*(4), 676–713.

Butler, D., & Geis, F. L. (1990). Nonverbal affect responses to male and female leaders: Implications for leadership evaluations. *Journal of Personality and Social Psychology, 58,* 48–59.

Butler, T., Giordano, S., & Neren, S. (1985). Gender and sex-role attributes as predictors of utilization of natural support systems during personal stress events. *Sex Roles, 13,* 515–524.

Buunk, B. P., Angleitner, A., Oubaid, V., & Buss, D. M. (1996). Sex differences in jealousy in evolutionary and cultural perspective: Tests from the Netherlands, Germany, and the United States. *Psychological Science, 7*(6), 359–363.

Bylsma, W. H., & Major, B. (1994). Social comparisons and contentment: Exploring the psychological costs of the gender wage gap. *Psychology of Women Quarterly, 18,* 241–249.

Cahn, D. D. (1992). *Conflict in intimate relationships.* New York: Guilford Press.

Caldwell, M. A., & Peplau, L. A. (1982). Sex differences in same-sex friendship. *Sex Roles, 8,* 721–732.

Caldwell, M. A., & Peplau, L. A. (1984). The balance of power in lesbian relationships. *Sex Roles, 10,* 587–599.

Caldwell, R. A., & Bloom, B. L. (1982). Social support: Its structure and impact on marital disruption. *American Journal of Community Psychology, 10*(6), 647–667.

Callan, V. J. (1993). Subordinate-manager communication in different sex dyads: Consequences for job satisfaction. *Journal of Occupational and Organizational Psychology, 66,* 13–27.

Calle, E. E., Thun, M. J., Petrelli, J. M., Rodriguez, C., & Heath, C. W., Jr. (1999). Body-mass index and mortality in a prospective cohort of U. S. adults. *New England Journal of Medicine, 341*(15), 1097–1105.

Camarena, P. M., Sarigiana, P. A., & Petersen, A. C. (1990). Gender-specific pathways to intimacy in early adolescence. *Journal of Youth and Adolescence, 19,* 19–32.

Cammaert, L. P. (1985). How widespread is sexual harassment on campus? *International Journal of Women's Studies, 8,* 388–397.

Campbell, J. D. (1978). The child in the sick role: Contributions of age, sex, parental status, and parental values. *Journal of Health and Social Behavior, 19,* 35–51.

Canary, D. J., & Stafford, L. (1992). Relational maintenance strategies and equity in marriage. *Communication Monographs, 59,* 243–267.

Canetto, S. S. (1995). Men who survive a suicidal act: Successful coping or failed masculinity? In D. Sabo & D. F. Gordon (Eds.), *Mens health and illness* (Vol. 8, pp. 292–304). Thousand Oaks, CA: Sage.

Canetto, S. S., & Lester, D. (1995). Gender and the primary prevention of suicide mortality. *American Association of Suicidology, 25*(1), 58–69.

Canetto, S. S., & Sakinofsky, I. (1998). The gender paradox in suicide. *American Association of Suicidology, 28*(1), 1–23.

Carli, L. L. (1989). Gender differences in interaction style and influence. *Journal of Personality and Social Psychology, 56,* 565–576.

Carli, L. L. (1990). Gender, language, and influence. *Journal of Personality and Social Psychology, 59,* 941–951.

Carli, L. L., LaFleur, S. J., & Loeber, C. C. (1995). Nonverbal behavior, gender, and influence. *Journal of Personality and Social Psychology, 68,* 1030–1041.

Carlson, M. B. (1993, August 9). Shreds of evidence. *Time, 142,* pp. 26–27.

Carlson, M. B. (1996, January 29). Public eye: The crying game. *Time, 147.*

Carr, D. (1997). The fulfillment of career dreams at midlife: Does it matter for women's mental health? *Journal of Health and Social Behavior, 38,* 331–344.

Carstensen, L. L., Gottman, J. M., & Levenson, R. W. (1995). Emotional behavior in long-term marriage. *Psychology and Aging, 10*(1), 140–149.

Casey, M. B. (1996). Understanding individual differences in spatial ability within females: A nature/nurture interactionist framework. *Developmental Review, 16,* 241–260.

Casey, M. B., Nuttall, R. L., & Pezaris, E. (1997). Mediators of gender differences in mathematics college entrance test scores: A comparison of spatial skills with internalized beliefs and anxieties. *Developmental Psychology, 33,* 669–680.

Celentano, D. D., Linet, M. S., & Stewart, W. F. (1990). Gender differences in the experience of headache. *Social Science and Medicine, 30*(12), 1289–1295.

Centers for Disease Control and Prevention. (1992). Vigorous physical activity among high school students–United States, 1990. *Morbidity and Mortality Weekly Report, 41*(3), 33–35.

Centers for Disease Control and Prevention. (1994). Surveillance for selected tobacco-use behaviors–United States, 1900–1994. *Morbidity and Mortality Weekly Report, 43,* 1–43.

Centers for Disease Control and Prevention. (1995). Suicide among children, adolescents, and young adults–United States, 1980–1992. *Morbidity and Mortality Weekly Review, 44*(15), 289–291.

Centers for Disease Control and Prevention. (1996). Youth risk behavior surveillance–United States, 1995. *Morbidity and Mortality Weekly Report, 45*(4), 1–83.

Centers for Disease Control and Prevention. (1997). Monthly estimates of leisure-time physical inactivity–United States, 1994. *Morbidity and Mortality Weekly Report, 46*(18), 393–397.

Centers for Disease Control and Prevention. (1998a). Suicide among Black youths–United States. *Morbidity and Mortality Weekly Report, 47*(10), 193–106.

Centers for Disease Control and Prevention. (1998b). Tobacco use among high school students–United States, 1997. *Morbidity and Mortality Weekly Report, 47*(12), 229–233.

Centers for Disease Control and Prevention. (1998c). Trends in sexual risk behaviors among high school students–United States, 1991–1997. *Morbidity and Mortality Weekly Report, 47*(36), 749–752.

Centers for Disease Control and Prevention. (1999a). Alcohol involvement in fatal motor-vehicle crashes–United States, 1997–1998. *Morbidity and Mortality Weekly Report, 48*(47), 1086–1087.

Centers for Disease Control and Prevention. (1999b). Cigarette smoking among high school students–11 States, 1991–1997. *Morbidity and Mortality Weekly Report, 48*(31), 686–692.

Centers for Disease Control and Prevention. (1999c). State-specific prevalence of current cigarette and cigar smoking among adults–United States, 1998. *Morbidity and Mortality Weekly Report, 48*(45), 1034–1039.

Centers for Disease Control and Prevention. (2000a). Prevalence of leisure-time and occupational physical activity among employed adults–United States, 1990. *Morbidity and Mortality Weekly Report, 49*(19), 420–424.

Centers for Disease Control and Prevention. (2000b). Prevalence of leisure-time physical activity among overweight adults–United States, 1998. *Morbidity and Mortality Weekly Report, 49*(15), 326–330.

Centers for Disease Control and Prevention. (2000c). Tobacco use among middle and high school students–United States, 1999. *Morbidity and Mortality Weekly Report, 49*(3), 49–53.

Central Intelligence Agency. (1998). *The world factbook 1999.* Washington, DC: Author.

Chan, C-J., & Margolin, G. (1994). The relationship between dual-earner couples' daily work mood and home affect. *Journal of Social and Personal Relationships, 11,* 573–586.

Chan, R. W., Brooks, R. C., Raboy, B., & Patterson, C. J. (1998). Division of labor among lesbian and heterosexual parents: Associations with children's adjustment. *Journal of Family Psychology, 12*(3), 402–419.

Chen, C., Greenberger, E., Lester, J., Dong, Q., & Guo, M-S. (1998). A cross-cultural study of family and peer correlates of adolescent misconduct. *Developmental Psychology, 34,* 770–781.

Cheng, C. (1999). Gender-role differences in susceptibility to the influence of support availability on depression. *Journal of Personality, 67,* 439–467.

Cherpitel, C. J. (1993). Alcohol, injury, and risk-taking behavior: Data from a national sample. *Alcoholism: Clinical and Experimental Research, 17*(4), 762–766.

Chesney, M. A., & Nealey, J. B. (1996). Smoking and cardiovascular disease risk in women: Issues for prevention and women's health. In P. M. Kato & T. Mann (Eds.), *Handbook of diversity issues in health psychology* (pp. 199–218). New York: Plenum Press.

Chevan, A. (1996). As cheaply as one: Cohabitation in the older population. *Journal of Marriage and the Family, 58,* 656–667.

Chia, R. C., Allred, L. J., & Jerzak, P. A. (1997). Attitudes toward women in Taiwan and China: Current status, problems, and suggestions for future research. *Psychology of Women Quarterly, 21,* 137–150.

Chia, R. C., Moore, J. L., Lam, K. N., Chuang, C. J., & Cheng, B. S. (1994). Cultural differences in gender role attitudes between Chinese and American students. *Sex Roles, 31*(1/2), 23–29.

Chiriboga, D. A., Coho, A., Stein, J. A., & Roberts, J. (1979). Divorce, stress and social supports: A study in helpseeking behavior. *Journal of Divorce, 3*(2), 121–135.

Chisholm, J. F. (2000). Culture, ethnicity, race, and class. In F. Denmark, V. Rabinowitz, & J. Sechzer (Eds.), *Engendering psychology* (pp. 107–139). Boston: Allyn & Bacon.

Chodorow, N. (1978). *The reproduction of mothering: Psychoanalysis and the sociology of gender.* London: University of California Press.

Choo, P., Levine, T., & Hatfield, E. (1996). Gender, love schemas, and reactions to romantic break-ups. *Journal of Social Behavior and Personality, 11*(5), 143–160.

Christensen, A., & Heavey, C. L. (1990). Gender and social structure in the demand/withdraw pattern of marital conflict. *Journal of Personality and Social Psychology, 59,* 73–81.

Christensen, A., & Heavey, C. L. (1993). Gender differences in marital conflict: The demand/ withdraw interaction pattern. In S. Oskamp & M. Constanzo (Eds.), *Gender issues in contemporary society* (Vol. 6, pp. 113–141). New York: Sage.

Christopher, F. S., & Sprecher, S. (2000). Sexuality in marriage, dating, and other relationships: A decade review. *Journal of Marriage and the Family, 62*(4), 999–1017.

Clancy, K., & Gove, W. (1974). Sex differences in mental illness: An analysis of response bias in self-reports. *American Journal of Sociology, 80,* 205–216.

Clancy, S. M., & Dollinger, S. J. (1993). Photographic depictions of the self: Gender and age differences in social connectedness. *Sex Roles, 29*(7/8), 477–495.

Clark, C. L., Shaver, P. R., & Abrahams, M. F. (1999). Strategic behaviors in romantic relationship initiation. *Personality and Social Psychology Bulletin, 25,* 707–720.

Clark, D. C., & Zeldow, P. B. (1988). Vicissitudes of depressed mood during four years of medical school. *Journal of the American Medical Association, 260,* 2521–2528.

Clark, M. L., & Ayers, M. (1992). Friendship similarity during early adolescence: Gender and racial patterns. *Journal of Psychology, 126,* 393–405.

Clark, M. L., & Ayers, M. (1993). Friendship expectations and friendship evaluations: Reciprocity and gender effects. *Youth & Society, 24*(3), 299–313.

Clarkberg, M., Stolzenberg, R. M., & Waite, L. J. (1995). Attitudes, values, and entrance into cohabitational versus marital unions. *Social Forces, 74*(2), 609–634.

Cleary, P. D., & Mechanic, D. (1983). Sex differences in psychological distress among married people. *Journal of Health and Social Behavior, 24,* 111–121.

Cleary, P. D., Mechanic, D., & Greenley, J. R. (1982). Sex differences in medical care utilization: An empirical investigation. *Journal of Health and Social Behavior, 23,* 106–119.

Cleveland, H. H., Koss, M. P., & Lyons, J. (1999). Rape tactics from the survivors' perspective: Contextual dependence and within-event independence. *Journal of Interpersonal Violence, 14*(5), 532–547.

Clifton, A. K., McGrath, D., & Wick, B. (1976). Stereotypes of woman: A single category? *Sex Roles, 2,* 135–148.

Cobb-Clark, D. A., & Dunlop, Y. (1999). The role of gender in job promotions. *Monthly Labor Review, 122*(12), 32–38.

Cochran, S. D., & Peplau, L. A. (1985). Value orientations in heterosexual relationships. *Psychology of Women Quarterly, 9,* 477–488.

Cogan, J. C., & Ernsberger, P. (1999). Dieting, weight, and health: Reconceptualizing research and policy. *Journal of Social Issues, 55*(2), 187–205.

Cohen, J. (1977). *Statistical power analysis for the behavioral sciences.* New York: Academic Press.

Cohen, R. Y., Brownell, K. D., & Felix, M. R. J. (1990). Age and sex differences in health habits and beliefs of schoolchildren. *Health Psychology, 9,* 208–224.

Cohen, S., & Wills, T. A. (1985). Stress, social support, and the buffering hypothesis. *Psychological Bulletin, 98,* 310–357.

Cohen, T. F. (1992). Men's families, men's friends: A structural analysis of constraints on men's social ties. In P. M. Nardi (Ed.), *Men's friendships* (pp. 115–131). Newbury Park, CA: Sage.

Cohler, B. J., & Lieberman, M. A. (1980). Social relations and mental health: Middle-aged and older men and women from three European ethnic groups. *Research on Aging, 2*(4), 445–469.

Coie, J. D., Terry, R., Zakriski, A., & Lochman, J. (1995). Early adolescent social influences on delinquent behavior. In J. McCord (Ed.), *Coercion and punishment in long-term perspectives* (pp. 229–244). New York: Cambridge University Press.

Cole, N. (1997). *The ETS gender study: How females and males perform in educational settings.* Princeton, NJ: Educational Testing Services.

Cole, S. S., Denny, D., Eyler, A. E., & Samons, S. L. (2000). Issues of transgender. In L. T. Szuchman & F. Muscarella (Eds.), *Psychological perspectives on human sexuality* (pp. 149–195). New York: Wiley.

Collaer, M. L., & Hines, M. (1998). Human behavioral sex differences: A role for gonadal hormones during early development. *Psychological Bulletin, 118,* 55–107.

Collins, N. L., & Miller, L. C. (1994). Self-disclosure and liking: A meta-analytic review. *Psychological Bulletin, 116,* 457–475.

Collis, B. (1991). Adolescent females and computers: Real and perceived barriers. In J. Gaskell & A. McLaren (Eds.), *Women and education: A Canadian perspective* (pp. 147–161). Calgary, Canada: Detselig.

Compas, B. E., Oppedisano, G., Connor, J. K., Gerhardt, C. A., Hinden, B. R., Achenbach, T. M., & Hammen, C. (1997). Gender differences in depressive symptoms in adolescence: Comparison of national samples of clinically referred and nonreferred youths. *Journal of Consulting and Clinical Psychology, 65,* 617–626.

Condry, J., & Condry, S. (1976). Sex differences: A study of the eye of the beholder. *Child Development, 47,* 812–819.

Condry, J. C., & Ross, D. F. (1985). Sex and aggression: The influence of gender label on the perception of aggression in children. *Child Development, 56,* 225–233.

Conger, J. J. (1975). Proceedings of the American psychological association, incorporated, for the year 1974: Minutes of the annual meeting of the council of representatives. *American Psychologist, 30,* 620–651.

Conger, R. D., Lorenz, F. O., Elder, G. H., Jr., Simons, R. L., & Ge, X. (1993). Husband and wife differences in response to undesirable life events. *Journal of Health and Social Behavior, 34,* 71–88.

Constantinople, A. (1973). Masculinity-femininity: An exception to a famous dictum? *Psychological Bulletin, 80,* 389–407.

Coren, S., & Hewitt, P. L. (1999). Sex differences in elderly suicide rates: Some predictive factors. *Aging and Mental Health, 3*(2), 112–118.

Coryell, W., Endicott, J., & Keller, M. (1992). Major depression in a nonclinical sample: Demographic and clinical risk factors for first onset. *Archives of General Psychiatry, 49,* 117–125.

Costello, C. B., Miles, S., & Stone, A. J. (Eds.). (1998). *The American woman 1999–2000.* New York: Norton.

Cotliar, S. (1996). Buss gets death in child slaying. *Chicago Sun-Times* [On-line]. Available: http://proquest.umi.com

Counts, D. A. (1987). Female suicide and wife abuse: A cross-cultural perspective. *American Association of Suicidology, 17*(3), 194–204.

Covey, L. S. (1999). Nicotine dependence and it's associations with psychiatric disorders: Research evidence and treatment implications. In D. F. Seidman & L. S. Covey (Eds.), *Helping the hard-core smoker, A clinician's guide* (pp. 23–50). Mahwah, NJ: Erlbaum.

Cox, D. J., Clarke, W. L., Gonder-Frederick, L. A., Pohl, S., Hoover, C., Snyder, A., Zimbelman, L., Carter, W. R., Bobbitt, S., & Pennebaker, J. W. (1985). Accuracy of perceiving blood glucose in IDDM. *Diabetes Care, 8,* 529–536.

Crandall, C. S. (1988). Social contagion of binge eating. *Journal of Personality and Social Psychology, 55*(4), 588–598.

Crick, N. R., Bigbee, M. A., & Howes, C. (1996). Gender differences in children's normative beliefs about aggression: How do I hurt thee? Let me count the ways. *Child Development, 67,* 1003–1014.

Crick, N. R., Casas, J. F., & Mosher, M. (1997). Relational and overt aggression in preschool. *Developmental Psychology, 33,* 579–588.

Crick, N. R., & Grotpeter, J. K. (1995). Relational aggression, gender, and social-psychological adjustment. *Child Development, 66,* 710–722.

Crick, N. R., Werner, N. E., Casas, J. F., O'Brien, K. M., Nelson, D. A., Grotpeter, J. K., & Markon, K. (1999). Childhood aggression and gender: A new look at an old problem. In D. Bernstein (Ed.), *Nebraska Symposium on Motivation and Gender* (pp. 75–141). Lincoln: University of Nebraska Press.

Crick, N. R., & Werner, N. W. (1998). Response decision processes in relational and overt aggression. *Child Development, 69,* 1630–1639.

Crisp, A. H., Callender, J. S., Halek, C., & Hsu, L. K. G. (1992). Long-term mortality in anorexia nervosa: A 20-year follow-up of the St. George's and Aberdeen cohorts. *British Journal of Psychiatry, 161,* 104–107.

Crisp, A. H., Hall, A., & Holland, A. J. (1985). Nature and nurture in anorexia nervosa: A study of 34 pairs of twins, one pair of triplets, and an adoptive family. *International Journal of Eating Disorders, 4*(1), 5–27.

Crosby, F. (1984). The denial of personal discrimination. *American Behavioral Scientist, 27*(3), 371–386.

Crosby, F. J., Todd, J., & Worell, J. (1996). Have feminists abandoned social activism? Voices from the academy. In L. Montada & M. J. Lerner (Eds.), *Current societal concerns about justice* (pp. 85–102). New York: Plenum Press.

Cross, S. E., & Madson, L. (1997). Models of the self: Self-construals and gender. *Psychological Bulletin, 122,* 5–37.

Culbertson, F. M. (1997). Depression and gender: An international review. *American Psychologist, 52,* 25–31.

Cunningham, J. D., & Antill, J. K. (1995). Current trends in nonmarital cohabitation: In search of the POSSLQ. In J. T. Wood & S. Duck (Eds.), *Under-studied relationships: Off the beaten track* (Vol. 6, pp. 148–172). Thousand Oaks, CA: Sage.

Cunningham, J. D., Braiker, H., & Kelley, H. H. (1982). Marital-status and sex differences in problems reported by married and cohabitating couples. *Psychology of Women Quarterly, 6,* 415–427.

Currie, D. H. (1998). Violent men or violent women? Whose definition counts? In R. K. Bergen (Ed.), *Issues in intimate violence* (pp. 97–111). Thousand Oaks, CA: Sage.

Cyranowski, J. M., Frank, E., Young, E., & Shear, M. K. (2000). Adolescent onset of the gender difference in lifetime rates of major depression. *Archives of General Psychiatry, 57,* 21–27.

Dabbs, J. M., Jr., Carr, T. S., Frady, R. L., & Riad, J. K. (1995). Testosterone, crime, and misbehavior among 692 male prison inmates. *Personality and Individual Differences, 18*(5), 627–633.

Dabbs, J. M., Jr., Chang, E-L., Strong, R. A., & Milun, R. (1998). Spatial ability, navigation strategy, and geographic knowledge among men and women. *Evolution and Human Behavior, 19,* 89–98.

Dabbs, J. M., Jr., Frady, R. L., Carr, T. S., & Besch, N. F. (1987). Saliva testosterone and criminal violence in young adult prison inmates. *Psychosomatic Medicine, 49*(2), 174–265.

Dads & Daughters. (2000, January 24). *Make Mattel put brains over Barbie* [On-line]. Available: http://www.dadsanddaughters.org/barbieact.html

Daly, M., & Wilson, M. (1988). Evolutionary social psychology and family homicide. *Science, 242,* 519–524.

D'Attillo, J. P., Campbell, B. M., Lubold, P., Jacobson, T., & Richard, J. A. (1992). Social support and suicide potential: Preliminary findings for adolescent populations. *Psychological Reports, 70,* 76–78.

Daubman, K. A., & Sigall, H. (1997). Gender differences in perceptions of how others are affected by self-disclosure of achievement. *Sex Roles, 37,* 73–89.

Davis, B. M., & Gilbert, L. A. (1989). Effect of dispositional and situational influences on women's dominance expression in mixed-sex dyads. *Journal of Personality and Social Psychology, 57,* 294–300.

Davis, M. C., Matthews, K. A., & Twamley, E. W. (1999). Is life more difficult on Mars or Venus? A meta-analytic review of sex differences in major and minor life events. *Annals of Behavioral Medicine, 21,* 83–97.

Davis, P. J. (1999). Gender differences in autobiographical memory for childhood emotional experiences. *Journal of Personality and Social Psychology, 76,* 498–510.

Davis, T. L. (1995). Gender differences in masking negative emotions: ability or motivation? *Developmental Psychology, 31*(4), 660–667.

Deaux, K. (1984). From individual differences to social categories: Analysis of a decade's research on gender. *American Psychologist, 39,* 105–116.

Deaux, K., & Emswiller, T. (1974). Explanations of successful performance on sex-linked tasks: What is skill for the male is luck for the female. *Journal of Personality and Social Psychology, 29,* 80–85.

Deaux, K., & Farris, E. (1977). Attributing causes for one's own performance: The effects of sex, norms, and outcome. *Journal of Research in Personality, 11,* 59–72.

Deaux, K., & LaFrance, M. (1998). Gender. In D. Gilbert, S. Fiske, & G. Lindzey (Eds.), *Handbook of social psychology* (pp. 788–826). New York: McGraw-Hill.

Deaux, K., & Lewis, L. L. (1983). Assessment of gender stereotypes: Methodology and components. *Psychological Documents, 13,* 25 (MS. No. 2583).

Deaux, K., & Lewis, L. L. (1984). Structure of gender stereotypes: Interrelationships among components and gender label. *Journal of Personality and Social Psychology, 46,* 991–1004.

Deaux, K., & Major, B. (1987). Putting gender into context: An interactive model of gender-related behavior. *Psychological Review, 94,* 369–389.

Defense of Marriage Act. (1996). House Bill text, Available: http://www.hrcusa.org/issues/leg/doma/billtext.html

de Jong-Gierveld, J. (1986). Husbands, lovers, and loneliness. In R. A. Lewis & R. E. Salt (Eds.), *Men in families* (pp. 115–125). Beverly Hills, CA: Sage.

DeKeseredy, W. S., & Schwartz, M. D. (1998). *Woman abuse on campus: Results from the Canadian national survey.* Thousand Oaks, CA: Sage.

DeLamater, J. (1987). Gender difference in sexual scenarios. In K. Kelley (Ed.), *Females, males, and sexuality: Theories and research* (pp. 127–139). Albany: State University of New York Press.

Denton, M., & Walters, V. (1999). Gender differences in structural and behavioral determinants of health: An analysis of the social production of health. *Social Science and Medicine, 48,* 1221–1235.

DePaulo, B. M., Epstein, J. A., & Wyer, M. M. (1993). Sex differences in lying: How men and women deal with the dilemma of deceit. In M. Lewis (Ed.), *Lying and deception in everyday life* (pp. 126–147). New York: Guilford Press.

Derlega, V. J., Barbee, A. P., & Winstead, B. A. (1994). Friendship, gender, and social support: Laboratory studies of supportive interactions. In B. R. Burleson, T. L. Albrecht, & I. G. Sarason (Eds.), *Communication of social support: Messages, interactions, relationships, and* *community* (pp. 136–151). Thousand Oaks, CA: Sage.

Derlega, V. J., & Chaikin, A. L. (1976). Norms affecting self-disclosure in men and women. *Journal of Consulting and Clinical Psychology, 44,* 376–380.

Derlega, V. J., Lewis, R. J., Harrison, S., Winstead, B. A., & Costanza, R. (1989). Gender differences in the initiation and attribution of tactile intimacy. *Journal of Nonverbal Behavior, 13*(2), 83–96.

Derlega, V. J., Winstead, B. A., Wong, P. T. P., & Hunter, S. (1985). Gender effects in an initial encounter: A case where men exceed women in disclosure. *Journal of Social and Personal Relationships, 2,* 25–44.

Desmarais, S., & Curtis, J. (1997). Gender and perceived pay entitlement: Testing for effects of experience with income. *Journal of Personality and Social Psychology, 72,* 141–150.

Devlin, P. K., & Cowan, G. A. (1985). Homophobia, perceived fathering, and male intimate relationships. *Journal of Personality Assessment, 49*(5), 467–473.

Dickson, L. (1993). The future of marriage and family in Black America. *Journal of Black Studies, 23*(4), 472–491.

Dietz, T. L. (1998). An examination of violence and gender role portrayals in video games: Implications for gender socialization and aggressive behavior. *Sex Roles, 38*(5/6), 425–442.

DiMona, L., & Herndon, C. (1994). *The 1995 information please: Women's sourcebook.* Boston: Houghton Mifflin.

Dindia, K., & Allen, M. (1992). Sex differences in self-disclosure: A meta-analysis. *Psychological Bulletin, 112,* 106–124.

Dion, K. L., & Dion, K. K. (1993). Gender and ethnocultural comparison in styles of love. *Psychology of Women Quarterly, 17,* 463–473.

Dittman, R. W. (1997). Sexual behavior and sexual orientation in females with congenital adrenal hyperplasis. In L. Ellis & L. Ebertz (Eds.), *Sexual orientation: Toward biological understanding* (pp. 53–69). Westport, CT: Praeger.

Dittman, R. W., Kappes, M. H., Kappes, M. E., Borger, D., Stegner, H., Willig, R. F., & Wallis, H. (1990). Congenital adrenal hyperplasia. I: Gender-related behavior and attitudes in female patients and sisters. *Psychoneuroendocrinology, 15*(5/6), 401–420.

Division of Adult and Community Health, National Center for Chronic Disease Prevention and Health Promotion, Centers for Disease Control and Prevention. (1998). *Behavioral Risk Factor Surveillance System online prevalence data:* http://www.2.cdc.gov/nccdphp/brfss/index.asp

Dodd, D. K., Russell, B. L., & Jenkins, C. (1999). Smiling in school yearbook photos: Gender differences from kindergarten to adulthood. *Psychological Record, 49,* 543–554.

Dodge, K. A., Bates, J. E., & Pettit, G. S. (1990). Mechanisms in the cycle of violence. *Science, 250,* 1678–1683.

Dolgin, K. G., & Kim, S. (1994). Adolescents' disclosure to best and good friends: The effects of gender and topic intimacy. *Social Development, 3*(2), 146–157.

Dolgin, K. G., Meyer, L., & Schwartz, J. (1991). Effects of gender, target's gender, topic, and self-esteem on disclosure to best and midling friends. *Sex Roles, 25,* 311–329.

Domino, G., & Groth, M. (1997). Attitudes toward suicide: German and U. S. nationals. *Omega: Journal of Death and Dying, 35*(3), 309–319.

Donaldson, M. (1976). Development of conceptualization. In V. Hamilton & M. D. Vernon (Eds.), *The development of cognitive processes* (pp. 277–303). London: Academic Press.

Donat, P. L. N., & D'Emilio, J. (1992). A feminist redefinition of rape and sexual assault: Historical foundation and change. *Journal of Social Issues, 48*(1), 9–22.

Douvan, E., & Adelson, J. (1966). *The adolescent experience.* New York: Wiley.

Doyle, J. A. (1995). *The male experience.* Madison, WI: Brown & Benchmark.

Dracup, K., Moser, D. K., Eisenberg, M., Meischke, H., Alonzo, A. A., & Braslow, A. (1995). Causes of delay in seeking treatment for heart attack symptoms. *Social Science and Medicine, 40*(3), 379–392.

Drug Abuse Warning Network Series. (1999a). Drug abuse warning network annual medical examiner data 1997. *Substance Abuse and Mental Health Services Adminstration, D-12,* 1–83.

Drug Abuse Warning Network Series. (1999b). Year-end 1998 emergency department data from the drug abuse warning network. *Substance Abuse and Mental Health Services Administration, D-11*, 97–114.

Dubow, E. F., Kausch, D. F., Blum, M. C., Reed, J., & Bush, E. (1989). Correlates of suicidal ideation and attempts in a community sample of junior high and high school students. *Journal of Clinical Child Psychology, 18*(2), 158–166.

Duck, S., & Wright, P. H. (1993). Reexamining gender differences in same-gender friendships: A close look at two kinds of data. *Sex Roles, 28*, 709–727.

Dunn, D. (1996). Gender and earnings. In P. J. Dubeck & K. Borman (Eds.), *Women and work: A handbook* (pp. 61–63). New York: Garland.

Dunn, J., Bretherton, I., & Munn, P. (1987). Conversations about feeling states between mothers and their young children. *Developmental Psychology, 23*, 132–139.

Dweck, C. S., Davidson, W., Nelson, S., & Enna, B. (1978). Sex differences in learned helplessness. II: The contingencies of evaluative feedback in the classroom, and III: An experimental analysis. *Developmental Psychology, 14*, 268–276.

Dweck, C. S., Goetz, T. E., & Strauss, N. L. (1980). Sex differences in learned helplessness. IV: An experimental and naturalistic study of failure generalization and its mediators. *Journal of Personality and Social Psychology, 38*, 441–452.

Dziech, B. W., & Hawkins, M. W. (1998). *Sexual harassment in higher education: Reflection and new perspectives:* New York: Garland Press.

Dziech, B. W., & Weiner, L. (1990). *The lecherous professor* (2nd ed.). Chicago: University of Illinois Press.

Eagly, A. H. (1978). Sex differences in influenceability. *Psychological Bulletin, 85*, 86–116.

Eagly, A. H. (1987a). Reporting sex differences. *American Psychologist, 42*, 756–757.

Eagly, A. H. (1987b). *Sex differences in social behavior: A social role interpretation.* Hillsdale, NJ: Erlbaum.

Eagly, A. H. (1995). The science and politics of comparing women and men. *American Psychologist, 50*, 145–158.

Eagly, A. H., & Carli, L. L. (1981). Sex of researchers and sex-typed communication as determinants of sex difference in influenceability: A meta-analysis of social influence studies. *Psychological Bulletin, 90*, 1–20.

Eagly, A. H., & Crowley, M. (1986). Gender and helping behavior: A meta-analytic review of the social psychological literature. *Psychological Bulletin, 100*, 283–308.

Eagly, A. H., & Johnson, B. T. (1990). Gender and leadership style: A meta-analysis. *Psychological Bulletin, 108*, 233–256.

Eagly, A. H., & Karau, S. J. (1991). Gender and the emergence of leaders: A meta-analysis. *Journal of Personality and Social Psychology, 60*, 685–710.

Eagly, A. H., & Kite, M. E. (1987). Are stereotypes of nationalities applied to both women and men? *Journal of Personality and Social Psychology, 53*, 451–462.

Eagly, A. H., Makhijani, M. G., & Klonsky, B. G. (1992). Gender and the evaluation of leaders: A meta-analysis. *Psychological Bulletin, 111*, 3–22.

Eagly, A. H., & Steffen, V. J. (1984). Gender stereotypes stem from the distribution of women and men into social roles. *Journal of Personality and Social Psychology, 46*, 735–754.

Eagly, A. H., & Steffen, V. J. (1986). Gender and aggressive behavior: A meta-analytic review of the social psychological literature. *Psychological Bulletin, 100*, 309–330.

Eagly, A. H., & Wood, W. (1982). Inferred sex differences in status as a determinant of gender stereotypes about social influence. *Journal of Personality and Social Psychology, 43*, 915–928.

Eagly, A. H., & Wood, W. (1999). The origins of sex differences in human behavior: Evolved dispositions versus social roles. *American Psychologist, 54*, 408–423.

Eagly, A. H., Wood, W., & Fishbaugh, L. (1981). Sex differences in conformity: Surveillance by the group as a determinant of male nonconformity. *Journal of Personality and Social Psychology, 40*, 384–394.

Eals, M., & Silverman, I. (1994). The Hunter-Gatherer theory of spatial sex differences: Proximate factors mediating the female advantage in recall of object arrays. *Ethology and Sociobiology, 15*, 95–105.

Eaton, W. O., & Enns, L. R. (1986). Sex differences in human motor activity level. *Psychological Bulletin, 100*, 19–28.

Eccles, J. (1984). Sex differences in achievement patterns. In T. Sonderegger (Ed.), *Nebraska symposium on motivation* (Vol. 32, pp. 97–132). Lincoln: University of Nebraska Press.

Eccles, J., Adler, T. F., Futterman, R., Goff, S. B., Kaczala, C. M., Meece, J. I., & Midgley, C. (1983). Expectations, values and academic behaviors. In J. T. Spence (Ed.), *Achievement and achievement motives* (pp. 75–145). San Francisco: Freeman.

Eccles, J. S. (1987). Gender roles and women's achievement-related decisions. *Psychology of Women Quarterly, 11*, 135–172.

Eccles, J. S. (1994). Understanding women's educational and occupational choices. *Psychology of Women Quarterly, 18*, 585–609.

Eccles, J. S., Barber, B., & Jozefowicz, D. (1999). Linking gender to educational, occupational, and recreational choices: Applying the Eccles et al. Model of Achievement-Related Choices. In W. B. Swann, Jr., J. H. Langlois, & L. A. Gilbert (Eds.), *Sexism and stereotypes in modern society: The gender-science of Janet Taylor Spence* (pp. 153–192). Washington, DC: American Psychological Association.

Eccles, J. S., & Blumenfeld, P. (1985). Classroom experiences and student gender: Are there differences and do they matter? In L. C. Wilkinson & C. B. Marrett (Eds.), *Gender influences in classroom interaction* (pp. 79–114). Orlando, FL: Academic Press.

Eccles, J. S., & Jacobs, J. E. (1986). Social forces shape math attitudes and performance. *Journal of Women in Culture and Society, 11*(2), 367–380.

Eccles, J. S., Jacobs, J. E., & Harold, R. D. (1990). Gender role stereotypes, expectancy effects, and parents' socialization of gender differences. *Journal of Social Issues, 46*, 183–201.

Eccles, J. S., Jacobs, J. E., Harold, R. D., Yoon, K. S., Abreton, A., & Freedman-Doan, C. (1993). Parents and gender-role socialization during the middle childhood and adolescent years. In S. Oskamp & M. Constanzo (Eds.), *Gender issues in contemporary society* (pp. 59–83). Newbury Park, CA: Sage.

Eccles-Parsons, J., Adler, T. F., & Kaczala, C. M. (1982). Socialization of achievement attitudes and beliefs: Parental influences. *Child Development, 53*, 310–321.

Eccles-Parsons, J., Kaczala, C. M., & Meece, J. L. (1982). Socialization of achievement attitudes and beliefs: Classroom influences. *Child Development, 53*, 322–339.

Edwards, A. C., Nazroo, J. Y., & Brown, G. W. (1998). Gender differences in marital support following a shared life event. *Social Science and Medicine, 46*(8), 1077–1085.

Egeland, J. A., & Hostetter, A. M. (1983). Amish Study. I: Affective disorders among the Amish 1976–1980. *American Journal of Psychiatry, 140*, 56–61.

Ehrenkranz, J., Bliss, E., & Sheard, M. H. (1974). Plasma testosterone: Correlation with aggressive behavior and social dominance in man. *Psychosomatic Medicine, 36*(6), 469–475.

Eisenberg, N., & Lennon, R. (1983). Sex differences in empathy and related capacities. *Psychological Bulletin, 94*, 100–131.

Eisler, R. M., & Skidmore, J. R. (1987). Masculine gender role stress: Scale development and component factors in the appraisal of stressful situations. *Behavior Modification, 11*(2), 123–136.

Eisler, R. M., Skidmore, J. R., & Ward, C. H. (1988). Masculine gender-role stress: Predictor of anger, anxiety, and health-risk behaviors. *Journal of Personality Assessment, 52*(1), 133–141.

Ekman, P. (1992). An argument for basic emotion. *Cognition and Emotion, 6*, 169–200.

Eldridge, N. S., & Gilbert, L. A. (1990). Correlates of relationship satisfaction in lesbian couples. *Psychology of Women Quarterly, 14*, 43–62.

Elkins, L. E., & Peterson, C. (1993). Gender differences in best friendships. *Sex Roles, 29*, 497–508.

Ell, K., Nishimoto, R., Mediansky, L., Mantell, J., & Hamovitch, M. (1992). Social relations, social support, and survival among patients with cancer. *Journal of Psychosomatic Medicine, 36*, 531–541.

Ellis, H. (1894). *Man and woman.* London: Scott.

Ensel, W. M. (1986). Sex, marital status, and depression: The role of life events and social support. In N. Lin, A. Dean, & W. M. Ensel (Eds.), *Social support, life events, and depression* (pp. 231–247). Orlando, FL: Academic Press.

Entwisle, D. R., Alexander, K. L., & Olson, L. S. (1994). The gender gap in math: Its possible origins in neighborhood effects. *American Sociological Review, 59,* 822–838.

Equal Employment Opportunity Commission. (1980). Guidelines on discrimination because of sex (sec. 1604.11). *Federal Register, 45,* 74676–74677.

Equal Employment Opportunity Commission. (2000, January). *Sexual harassment charges EEOC & FEPAs combined: FY 1992–FY 1999* [On-line]. Available: http://www.eeoc.gov/stats/harass.html

Erikson, E. H. (1950). *Childhood and society.* New York: Norton.

Ernst, S. B. (1995). Gender issues in books for children and young adults. In S. Lehr (Ed.), *Battling dragons: Issues and controversy in children's literature* (pp. 66–78). Portsmouth, NH: Heinemann.

Ernster, V. L. (1996). Female lung cancer. *Annual Review of Public Health, 17,* 97–114.

Ewart, C. K., Taylor, C. B., Kraemer, H. C., & Agras, W. S. (1991). High blood pressure and marital discord: Not being nasty matters more than being nice. *Health Psychology, 10,* 155–163.

Fabes, R. A., & Martin, C. L. (1991). Gender and age stereotypes of emotionality. *Personality and Social Psychology Bulletin, 17,* 532–540.

Fagot, B. I., & Hagan, R. (1985). Aggression in toddlers: Responses in the assertive acts of boys and girls. *Sex Roles, 1,* 341–351.

Fagot, B. I., Hagan, R., Leinbach, M. D., & Kronsberg, S. (1985). Differential reactions to assertive and communicative acts of toddler boys and girls. *Child Development, 56,* 1499–1505.

Falbo, T., & Peplau, L. A. (1980). Power strategies in intimate relationships. *Journal of Personality and Social Psychology, 38,* 618–628.

Faludi, S. (1991). *Backlash: The undeclared war against American women.* New York: Crown.

Farrell, W. (1993). *The myth of male power: Why men are the disposable sex.* New York: Simon & Schuster.

Federal Bureau of Investigation. (1997a). Forcible rape. *Uniform Crime Reports for the United States* (pp. 25–27). Washington, DC: U. S. Department of Justice.

Federal Bureau of Investigation. (1997b). Murder and nonnegligent manslaughter. *Uniform Crime Reports for the United States* (pp. 15–23). Washington, DC: U. S. Department of Justice.

Fehr, B., Baldwin, M., Collins, L., Patterson, S., & Benditt, R. (1999). Anger in close relationships: An interpersonal script analysis. *Personality and Social Psychology Bulletin, 25,* 299–312.

Feinauer, L. L., & Williams-Evans, L. (1989). Effects of wife employment preference on marital adjustment. *American Journal of Family Therapy, 17*(3), 208–218.

Feine, J. S., Bushnell, M. C., Miron, D., & Duncan, G. H. (1991). Sex differences in the perception of noxious heat stimuli. *Pain, 44,* 255–262.

Feingold, A. (1988). Matching for attractiveness in romantic partners and same-sex friends: A meta-analysis and theoretical critique. *Psychological Bulletin, 104,* 226–235.

Feingold, A. (1990). Gender differences in effects of physical attractiveness on romantic attraction: A comparison across five research paradigms. *Journal of Personality and Social Psychology, 59,* 981–993.

Feingold, A. (1992). Gender differences in mate selection preferences: A test of the parental investment model. *Psychological Bulletin, 112,* 125–139.

Feingold, A. (1994). Gender differences in personality: A meta-analysis. *Psychological Bulletin, 116,* 429–456.

Feldman, S. S., & Gowen, L. K. (1998). Conflict negotiation tactics in romantic relationships in high school students. *Journal of Youth and Adolescence, 27*(6), 691–717.

Felmlee, D. H. (1994). Who's on top? Power in romantic relationships. *Sex Roles, 31,* 275–295.

Fendrich, M. (1984). Wives' employment and husbands' distress: A meta-analysis and a replication. *Journal of Marriage and the Family, 46,* 871–879.

Fenigstein, A., Scheier, M. F., & Buss, A. H. (1975). Public and private self-consciousness: Assessment and theory. *Journal of Consulting and Clinical Psychology, 43,* 522–527.

Ferraro, K. F., & Wan, T. T. H. (1986). Marital contributions to well-being in later life. *American Behavioral Scientist, 29*(4), 423–437.

Feshbach, N. D. (1989). Empathy training and prosocial behavior. In J. Groebel & R. A. Hinde (Eds.), *Aggression and war their biological and social bases* (pp. 101–111). New York: Cambridge University Press.

Feshbach, S. (1989). The bases and development of individual aggression. In J. Groebel & R. A. Hinde (Eds.), *Aggression and war: Their biological and social bases* (pp. 78–90). New York: Cambridge University Press.

Festinger, L. (1954). A theory of social comparison processes. *Human Relations, 7,* 117–140.

Fincham, F. D., Beach, S. R. H., Harold, G. T., & Osborne, L. N. (1997). Marital satisfaction and depression: Different causal relationships for men and women? *Psychological Science, 8*(5), 351–357.

Fischer, A. H., & Manstead, A. S. R. (2000). The relation between gender and emotions in different cultures. In A. H. Fischer (Ed.), *Gender and emotion: Social psychological perspectives.* Cambridge, England: Cambridge University Press.

Fischer, C. S. (1979). *Friendship, gender and the life cycle.* Unpublished manuscript, University of California, Berkeley.

Fischer, C. S., & Oliker, S. J. (1983). A research note on friendship, gender, and the life cycle. *Social Forces, 62,* 124–133.

Fish, L. S., New, R. S., & Van Cleave, N. K. (1992). Shared parenting and dual-income families. *American Journal of Orthopsychiatry, 62*(1), 83–92.

Fiske, S. T., Bersoff, D. N., Borgida, E., Deaux, K., & Heilman, M. E. (1991). Social science research on trial: Use of sex stereotyping research in Price Waterhouse v. Hopkins. *American Psychologist, 46,* 1049–1060.

Fiske, S. T., & Stevens, L. E. (1993). What's so special about sex? Gender stereotyping and discrimination. In S. Oskamp & M. Costanzo (Eds.), *Gender issues in contemporary society* (pp. 173–196). Newbury Park, CA: Sage.

Fiske, S. T., & Taylor, S. E. (1991). *Social cognition* (2nd ed.). New York: McGraw-Hill.

Fitzgerald, L. F., Gelfand, M. J., & Drasgow, F. (1995). Measuring sexual harassment: Theoretical and psychometric advances. *Basic and Applied Social Psychology, 17*(4), 425–445.

Fivush, R. (1989). Exploring sex differences in the emotional content of mother-child conversations about the past. *Sex Roles, 20*(11/12), 675–691.

Flaherty, J., & Richman, J. (1989). Gender differences in the perception and utilization of social support: Theoretical perspectives and an empirical test. *Social Science and Medicine, 28*(12), 1221–1228.

Flaks, D. K., Ficher, I., Masterpasqua, F., & Joseph, G. (1995). Lesbians choosing motherhood: A comparative study of lesbian and heterosexual parents and their children. *Developmental Psychology, 31,* 105–114.

Flay, B. R., Hu, F. B., & Richardson, J. (1998). Psychosocial predictors of different stages of cigarette smoking among high school students. *Preventive Medicine, 27,* A9–A18.

Flor, H., Turk, D. C., & Rudy, T. E. (1989). Relationship of pain impact and significant other reinforcement of pain behaviors: The mediating role of gender, marital status and marital satisfaction. *Pain, 38,* 45–50.

Floyd, F. J., & Markman, H. J. (1983). Observational biases in spouse observation: Toward a cognitive/behavioral model of marriage. *Journal of Consulting and Clinical Psychology, 51,* 450–457.

Flynn, K. J., & Fitzgibbon, M. (1998). Body images and obesity risk among Black females: A review of the literature. *Annals of Behavior Medicine, 20*(1), 13–24.

Fox, M. (1993). Men who weep, boys who dance: The gender agenda between the lines in children's literature. *Language Arts, 70,* 54–88.

Franck, K., & Rosen, E. (1949). A projective test of masculinity-femininity. *Journal of Consulting Psychology, 13,* 247–256.

Frank, E., & Young, E. (2000). Pubertal changes and adolescent challenges. In E. Frank (Ed.), *Gender and its effects on psychopathology* (pp. 85–102). Washington, DC: American Psychiatric Press.

Franklin, C. W., Jr. (1992). Hey home yo, bro: Friendship among Black men. In P. M. Nardi

(Ed.), *Men's friendships* (pp. 201–214). Newbury Park, CA: Sage.

Frazier, P., Arikian, N., Benson, S., Losoff, A., & Maurer, S. (1996). Desire for marriage and life satisfaction among unmarried heterosexual adults. *Journal of Social and Personal Relationships, 13,* 225–239.

Frazier, P. A., Cochran, C. C., & Olson, A. M. (1995). Social science research on lay definitions of sexual harassment. *Journal of Social Issues, 51*(1), 21–37.

Frazier, P. A., & Esterly, E. (1990). Correlates of relationship beliefs: Gender, relationship experience and relationship satisfaction. *Journal of Social and Personal Relationships, 7,* 331–352.

Frederick, S. L., Hall, S. M., Humfleet, G. L., & Munoz, R. F. (1996). Sex differences in the relation of mood to weight gain after quitting smoking. *Experimental and Clinical Psychopharmacology, 4*(2), 178–185.

Freud, S. (1924). The dissolution of the Oedipus complex. *Standard Edition, 19,* 172–179.

Freud, S. (1925). Some physical consequences of the anatomical distinction between the sexes. *Standard Edition, 19,* 243–258.

Frey, K. S., & Ruble, D. N. (1987). What children say about classroom performance: Sex and grade differences in perceived competence. *Child Development, 58,* 1066–1078.

Frezza, M., Di Padova, C., Pozzato, G., Terpin, M., Baraona, E., & Lieber, C. S. (1990). High blood alcohol levels in women: The role of decreased gastric alcohol dehydrogenase activity and first-pass metabolism. *New England Journal of Medicine, 322*(2), 95–99.

Friedan, B. (1963). *The feminine mystique.* New York: Norton.

Fried-Buchalter, S. (1997). Fear of success, fear of failure, and the imposter phenomenon among male and female marketing managers. *Sex Roles, 37*(11/12), 847–859.

Friedman, W. J., Robinson, A. B., & Friedman, B. L. (1987). Sex differences in moral judgments? A test of Gilligan's theory. *Psychology of Women Quarterly, 11,* 37–46.

Fritz, H., Nagurney, A., & Helgeson, V. S. (2000). *Sex and gender-related trait differences in support and cardiovascular reactivity during problem disclosure:* Manuscript submitted for publication.

Fritz, H. L., & Helgeson, V. S. (1998). Distinctions of unmitigated communion from communion: Self-neglect and overinvolvement with others. *Journal of Personality and Social Psychology, 75,* 121–140.

Frome, P. M., & Eccles, J. S. (1998). Parents' influence on children's achievement-related perceptions. *Journal of Personality and Social Psychology, 74,* 435–452.

Fuchs, D., & Thelen, M. H. (1988). Children's expected interpersonal consequences of communicating their affective state and reported likelihood of expression. *Child Development, 59,* 1314–1322.

Fujita, F., Diener, E., & Sandvik, E. (1991). Gender differences in negative affect and well-being: The case for emotional intensity. *Journal of Personality and Social Psychology, 61,* 427–434.

Furnham, A., & Nordling, R. (1998). Cross-cultural differences in preferences for specific male and female body shapes. *Personality and Individual Differences, 25,* 635–648.

Gabriel, S., & Gardner, W. L. (1999). Are there "his" and "hers" types of interdependence? The implications of gender differences in collective versus relational interdependence for affect, behavior, and cognition. *Journal of Personality and Social Psychology, 77*(3), 642–655.

Gaelick, L., Bodenhausen, G. V., & Wyer, R. S., Jr. (1985). Emotional communication in close relationships. *Journal of Personality and Social Psychology, 49,* 1246–1265.

Galambos, N. L., Almeida, D. M., & Petersen, A. C. (1990). Masculinity, femininity, and sex role attitudes in early adolescence: Exploring gender intensification. *Child Development, 61,* 1905–1914.

Gallaher, P. E. (1992). Individual differences in nonverbal behavior: Dimensions of style. *Journal of Personality and Social Psychology, 63,* 133–145.

Galligan, R. F., & Terry, D. J. (1993). Romantic ideals, fear of negative implications, and the practice of safe sex. *Journal of Applied Social Psychology, 23*(20), 1685–1711.

Gallup News Service. (1997, November 7). Family values differ sharply around the world. *Gallup News Service* [On-line]. Available: http://web.lexis-nexis.com

Ganong, L. H., & Coleman, M. (1984). Sex, sex roles, and emotional expressiveness. *Journal of Genetic Psychology, 146*(3), 405–411.

Garbarino, J. (1999). *Lost boys: Why our sons turn violent and how we can save them.* New York: Free Press.

Garbarino, J. (1999, December 20). Some kids are orchids. *Time Magazine, 154* [On-line]. Available: www.time.com/time/magazine/articles/0,3266,35858,00.html

Garber, J., Little, S., Hilsman, R., & Weaver, K. R. (1998). Family predictors of suicidal symptoms in young adolescents. *Journal of Adolescence, 21,* 445–457.

Garcia, S., Stinson, L., Ickes, W., Bissonnette, V., & Briggs, S. R. (1991). Shyness and physical attractiveness in mixed-sex dyads. *Journal of Personality and Social Psychology, 61,* 35–49.

Gardiner, M., & Tiggemann, M. (1999). Gender differences in leadership style, job stress and mental health in male- and female-dominated industries. *Journal of Occupational and Organizational Psychology, 72,* 301–315.

Garland, H., & Price, K. H. (1977). Attitudes toward women in management and attributions for their success and failure in a managerial position. *Journal of Applied Psychology, 62,* 29–33.

Garner, D. M., Garfinkel, P. E., Schwartz, D., & Thompson, M. (1980). Cultural expectations of thinness in women. *Psychological Reports, 47,* 483–491.

Garner, D. M., Olmstead, M. P., & Polivy, J. (1983). Development and validation of a multidimensional eating disorder inventory for anorexia nervosa and bulimia. *International Journal of Eating Disorders, 2*(2), 15–34.

Gastil, J. (1990). Generic pronouns and sexist language: The oxymoronic character of masculine generics. *Sex Roles, 23,* 629–643.

Ge, X., Lorenz, F. O., Conger, R. D., Elder, G. H., Jr., & Simons, R. L. (1994). Trajectories of stressful life events and depressive symptoms during adolescence. *Developmental Psychology, 30,* 467–483.

Gear, R. W., Miaskowski, C., Gordon, N. C., Paul, S. M., Heller, P. H., & Levine, J. D. (1999). The kappa opioid nalbuphine produces gender- and dose-dependent analgesia and antianalgesia in patients with postoperative pain. *Pain, 83,* 339–345.

George, L. K., Winfield, I., & Blazer, D. G. (1992). Sociocultural factors in sexual assault: Comparison of two representative samples of women. *Journal of Social Issues, 48*(1), 105–125.

Gerhart, B., & Rynes, S. (1991). Determinants and consequences of salary negotiations by male and female MBA graduates. *Journal of Applied Psychology, 76*(2), 256–262.

Gerstel, N. (1988). Divorce, gender, and social integration. *Gender and Society, 2*(3), 343–367.

Gerstel, N., Riessman, C. K., & Rosenfield, S. (1985). Explaining the symptomatology of separated and divorced women and men: The role of material conditions and social networks. *Social Forces, 64*(1), 84–99.

Ghodsian-Carpey, J., & Baker, L. A. (1987). Genetic and environmental influences on aggression in 4- to 7-year-old twins. *Aggressive Behavior, 13,* 173–186.

Gibbons, J. L., Stiles, D. A., & Shkodriani, G. M. (1991). Adolescents' attitudes toward family and gender roles: An international comparison. *Sex Roles, 25,* 625–643.

Gijsbers van Wijk, C. M. T., Huisman, H., & Kolk, A. M. (1999). Gender differences in physical symptoms and illness behavior: A health diary study. *Social Science and Medicine, 49,* 1061–1074.

Gillespie, B. L., & Eisler, R. M. (1992). Development of the feminine gender role stress scale: A cognitive-behavioral measure of stress, appraisal, and coping for women. *Behavior Modification, 16*(3), 426–438.

Gilligan, C. (1982). *In a different voice.* Cambridge, MA: Harvard University Press.

Gilligan, C., & Attanucci, J. (1988). Two moral orientations: Gender differences and similarities. *Merrill-Palmer Quarterly, 34*(3), 223–237.

Gilmore, D. D. (1990). *Manhood in the making: Cultural concepts of masculinity.* New Haven, CT: Yale University Press.

Gilroy, F., & Steinbacher, R. (1983). Preselection of child's sex: Technological utilization and feminism. *Psychological Reports, 53,* 671–676.

Gjerde, P. F. (1995). Alternative pathways to chronic depressive symptoms in young adults:

Gender differences in developmental trajectories. *Child Development, 66,* 1277–1300.

Gjerde, P. F., Block, J., & Block, J. H. (1988). Depressive symptoms and personality during late adolescence: Gender differences in the externalization-internalization of symptom expression. *Journal of Abnormal Psychology, 97,* 475–486.

Glass, R. M. (1990). Blue mood, blackened lungs: Depression and smoking. *Journal of the American Medical Association, 264*(12), 1583–1584.

Glass, S. P., & Wright, T. L. (1985). Sex differences in type of extramarital involvement and marital dissatisfaction. *Sex Roles, 12,* 1101–1120.

Glass, S. P., & Wright, T. L. (1992). Justifications for extramarital relationships: The association between attitudes, behaviors, and gender. *Journal of Sex Research, 29*(3), 361–387.

Glick, P., & Fiske, S. T. (1996). The Ambivalent Sexism Inventory: Differentiating hostile and benevolent sexism. *Journal of Personality and Social Psychology, 70,* 491–512.

Glick, P., Zion, C., & Nelson, C. (1988). What mediates sex discrimination in hiring decisions? *Journal of Personality and Social Psychology, 55,* 178–186.

Glynn, L. M., Christenfeld, N., & Gerin, W. (1999). Gender, social support, and cardiovascular responses to stress. *Psychosomatic Medicine, 61,* 234–242.

Goble, F. C., & Konopka, E. A. (1973). Sex as a factor in infectious disease. *Transactions New York Academy of Sciences, 35,* 325–346.

Gold, D. R., Wang, X., Wypij, D., Speizer, F. E., Ware, J. H., & Dockery, D. W. (1996). Effects of cigarette smoking on lung function in adolescent boys and girls. *New England Journal of Medicine, 335,* 931–937.

Goldberg, H. (1976). *The hazards of being male.* New York: New American Library.

Golding, J. M. (1990). Division of household labor, strain, and depressive symptoms among Mexican Americans and Non-Hispanic Whites. *Psychology of Women Quarterly, 14,* 103–117.

Goldner, V., Penn, P., Sheinberg, M., & Walker, G. (1990). Love and violence: Gender paradoxes in volatile attachments. *Family Process, 29*(4), 343–364.

Goldsmith, D. J., & Dun, S. A. (1997). Sex differences and similarities in the communication of social support. *Journal of Social and Personal Relationships, 14,* 317–337.

Goldsteen, K., & Ross, C. E. (1989). The perceived burden of children. *Journal of Family Issues, 10*(4), 504–526.

Goldstein, A. G., & Jeffords, J. (1981). Status and touching behavior. *Bulletin of the Psychonomic Society, 17*(2), 79–81.

Golombok, S., & Fivush, R. (1994). *Gender development.* New York: Cambridge University Press.

Golombok, S., & Tasker, F. (1994). Children in lesbian and gay families: Theories and evidence. *Annual Review of Sex Research, 5,* 73–100.

Gondolf, E. W., & Hanneken, J. (1987). The gender warrior: Reformed batterers on abuse, treatment, and change. *Journal of Family Violence, 2*(2), 177–191.

Gonzales, M. H., & Meyers, S. A. (1993). Your mother would like me: Self-presentation in the personal ads of heterosexual and homosexual men and women. *Personality and Social Psychology Bulletin, 19,* 131–142.

Good, G. E., Dell, D. M., & Mintz, L. B. (1989). Male role and gender role conflict: Relations to help seeking in men. *Journal of Counseling Psychology, 36*(3), 295–300.

Good, G. E., Hepper, M. J., Hillenbrand-Gunn, T., & Wang, L-F. (1995). Sexual and psychological violence: An exploratory study of predictors in college men. *Journal of Men's Studies, 4*(1), 59–71.

Good, G. E., & Mintz, L. B. (1990). Gender role conflict and depression in college men: Evidence for compounded risk. *Journal of Counseling and Development, 69,* 17–21.

Goodman, M. J., Griffin, P. B., Estioko-Griffen, A. A., & Grove, J. S. (1985). The compatibility of hunting among the Agta hunter-gatherers of the Philippines. *Sex Roles, 12*(11/12), 1199–1209.

Gore, S., Aseltine, R. H., Jr., & Colten, M. E. (1993). Gender, social-relational involvement, and depression. *Journal of Research on Adolescence, 3,* 101–125.

Gore, S., & Colten, M. E. (1991). Gender, stress, and distress: Social-relational influences. In

J. Eckenrode (Ed.), *The social context of coping* (pp. 139–163). New York: Plenum Press.

Gore, S., & Mangione, T. W. (1983). Social roles, sex roles, and psychological distress: Additive and interactive models of sex differences. *Journal of Health and Social Behavior, 24,* 300–312.

Gortmaker, S. L., Must, A., Perrin, J. M., Sobol, A. M., & Dietz, W. H. (1993). Social and economic consequences of overweight in adolescence and young adulthood. *New England Journal of Medicine, 329*(14), 1008–1012.

Gottman, J. M. (1994). *What predicts divorce? The relationship between marital processes and marital outcomes.* Hillsdale, NJ: Erlbaum.

Gottman, J. M., & Carrere, S. (1994). Why can't men and women get along? Developmental roots and marital inequities. In D. J. Canary & L. Stafford (Eds.), *Communication and relational maintenance* (pp. 203–229). London: Academic Press.

Gottman, J. M., & Krokoff, L. J. (1989). Marital interaction and satisfaction: A longitudinal view. *Journal of Consulting and Clinical Psychology, 57,* 47–52.

Gottman, J. M., & Levenson, R. W. (1992). Marital processes predictive of later dissolution: Behavior, physiology, and health. *Journal of Personality and Social Psychology, 63,* 221–233.

Gove, W. R. (1984). Gender differences in mental and physical illness: The effects of fixed roles and nurturant roles. *Social Science and Medicine, 19*(2), 77–91.

Gove, W. R., & Hughes, M. (1979). Possible causes of the apparent sex differences in physical health: An empirical investigation. *American Sociological Review, 44,* 126–146.

Gove, W. R., & Tudor, J. F. (1973). Adult sex roles and mental illness. *American Journal of Sociology, 78,* 812–835.

Gradman, T. J. (1994). Masculine identity from work to retirement. In E. H. Thompson, Jr. (Ed.), *Older men's lives* (pp. 104–121). Thousand Oaks, CA: Sage.

Grammer, K. (1992). Variations on a theme: Age dependent mate selections in humans. *Behavioral and Brain Sciences, 15,* 100–102.

Grant, K., Lyons, A., Landis, D., Cho, M. H., Scudiero, M., Reynolds, L., Murphy, J., &

Bryant, H. (1999). Gender, body image, and depressive symptoms among low-income African American adolescents. *Journal of Social Issues, 55*(2), 299–316.

Gray, J. (1992). *Men are from Mars, women are from Venus.* New York: HarperCollins.

Gray-Little, B., & Burks, N. (1983). Power and satisfaction in marriage: A review and critique. *Psychological Bulletin, 93,* 513–538.

Green, B. L., & Kenrick, D. T. (1994). The attractiveness of gender-typed traits at different relationship levels: Androgynous characteristics may be desirable after all. *Personality and Social Psychology Bulletin, 20,* 244–253.

Green, C. A., & Pope, C. R. (1999). Gender, psychosocial factors and the use of medical services: A longitudinal analysis. *Social Science and Medicine, 48,* 1363–1372.

Greenstein, T. N. (1996). Husbands' participation in domestic labor: Interactive effects of wives' and husbands' gender ideologies. *Journal of Marriage and the Family, 58,* 585–595.

Griffin, K. W., Botvin, G. J., Doyle, M. M., Diaz, T., & Epstein, J. A. (1999). A six-year follow-up study of determinants of heavy cigarette smoking among high-school seniors. *Journal of Behavioral Medicine, 22*(3), 271–285.

Griffin, M. L., Weiss, R. D., & Mirin, S. M. (1989). A comparison of male and female cocaine abusers. *Archives of General Psychiatry, 46,* 122–126.

Griffin, S. (1971). Rape: The all-American crime. *Ramparts, 10,* 26–35.

Grossman, M., & Wood, W. (1993). Sex differences in intensity of emotional experience: A social role interpretation. *Journal of Personality and Social Psychology, 65,* 1010–1022.

Grote, N. K., Frieze, I. H., & Stone, C. A. (1996). Children, traditionalism in the division of family work, and marital satisfaction: What's love got to do with it? *Personal Relationships, 3,* 211–228.

Groth, A. N., Burgess, A. W., & Holmstrom, L. L. (1977). Rape: Power, anger, and sexuality. *American Journal of Psychiatry, 134*(11), 1239–1243.

Gruber, J. E. (1990). Methodological problems and policy implications in sexual harassment research. *Population Research and Policy Review, 9,* 235–254.

Guerrero, L. K., & Andersen, P. A. (1994). Patterns of matching and initiation: Touch behavior and touch avoidance across romantic relationship stages. *Journal of Nonverbal Behavior, 18*(2), 137–153.

Guerrero, L. K., Eloy, S. V., Jorgensen, P. F., & Andersen, P. A. (1993). Hers or his? Sex differences in the experience and communication of jealousy in close relationships. In P. J. Kalbfleisch (Ed.), *Interpersonal communication: Evolving interpersonal relationships* (pp. 109–131). Hillsdale, NJ: Erlbaum.

Guerrero, L. K., & Reiter, R. L. (1998). Expressing emotion: Sex differences in social skills and communicative responses to anger, sadness, and jealousy. In D. J. Canary & K. Dindia (Eds.), *Sex differences and similarities in communication: Critical essays and empirical investigations of sex and gender in interaction* (pp. 321–350). Mahwah, NJ: Erlbaum.

Gutek, B. A. (1985). *Sex and the workplace.* San Francisco: Jossey-Bass.

Gutek, B. A., & Done, R. S. (2000). Sexual harassment. In R. K. Unger (Ed.), *Handbook of the psychology of women and gender* (pp. 1–61). New York: Wiley.

Gutek, B. A., & O'Connor, M. (1995). The empirical basis for the reasonable women standard. *Journal of Social Issues, 51*(1), 151–166.

Haag, P. (1998). Single-sex education in grades K–12: What does the research tell us? In S. Morse (Ed.), *Separated by sex: A critical look at single-sex education for girls* (pp. 13–38). Washington, DC: American Association of University Women Educational Foundation.

Haas, L. (1993). Nurturing fathers and working mothers: Changing gender roles in Sweden. In J. C. Hood (Ed.), *Men, work, and family* (pp. 238–261). Newbury Park, CA: Sage.

Haavio-Mannila, E. (1986). Inequalities in health and gender. *Social Science and Medicine, 22*(2), 141–149.

Haavio-Mannila, E., Kauppinen-Toropainen, K., & Kandolin, I. (1988). The effect of sex composition of the workplace on friendship, romance, and sex at work. In B. A. Gutek, A. H. Stromberg, & L. Larwood (Eds.), *Women and*

work: An annual review (Vol. 3, pp. 123–137). Newbury Park, CA: Sage.

Hacker, H. M. (1981). Blabbermouths and clams: Sex differences in self-disclosure in same-sex and cross-sex friendships. *Psychology of Women Quarterly, 5,* 385–401.

Hafstrom, J. L., & Schram, V. R. (1984). Chronic illness in couples: Selected characteristics, including wife's satisfaction with and perception of marital relationships. *Family Relations, 33,* 195–203.

Hagestad, G. O., & Smyer, M. A. (1982). Dissolving long-term relationships: Patterns of divorcing in middle age. In S. W. Duck (Ed.), *Personal relationships. IV: Dissolving personal relationships* (pp. 155–188). London: Academic Press.

Hall, J. A. (1984). *Nonverbal sex differences: Communication accuracy and expressive style.* Baltimore: Johns Hopkins University Press.

Hall, J. A. (1987). On explaining gender differences: The case of nonverbal communication. In P. Shaver & C. Hendrick (Eds.), *Sex and gender* (pp. 177–200). Beverly Hills, CA: Sage.

Hall, J. A. (1996). Touch, status, and gender at professional meetings. *Journal of Nonverbal Behavior, 20*(1), 23–44.

Hall, J. A. (1998). How big are nonverbal sex differences? The case of smiling and sensitivity to nonverbal cues. In D. J. Canary & K. Dindia (Eds.), *Sex differences and similarities in communication: Critical essays and empirical investigations of sex and gender in interaction* (pp. 155–177). Mahwah, NJ: Erlbaum.

Hall, J. A., & Carter, J. D. (1999). Gender-stereotype accuracy as an individual difference. *Journal of Personality and Social Psychology, 77,* 350–359.

Hall, J. A., Carter, J. D., & Horgan, T. G. (2000). Gender differences in nonverbal communication of emotion. In A. H. Fischer (Ed.), *Gender and emotion: Social and pyschological perspectives* (pp. 97–117). New York: Cambridge University Press.

Hall, J. A., & Friedman, G. B. (1999). Status, gender, and nonverbal behavior: A study of structured interactions between employees of a company. *Personality and Social Psychology Bulletin, 25*, 1082–1091.

Hall, J. A., Halberstadt, A. G., & O'Brien, C. E. (1997). Subordination and nonverbal sensitivity: A study and synthesis of findings based on trait measures. *Sex Roles, 37*, 295–317.

Hall, J. A., Irish, J. T., Roter, D. L., Ehrlich, C. M., & Miller, L. H. (1994). Gender in medical encounters: An analysis of physician and patient communication in a primary care setting. *Health Psychology, 13*, 384–392.

Hall, J. A., & Veccia, E. M. (1990). More "touching" observations: New insights on men, women, and interpersonal touch. *Journal of Personality and Social Psychology, 59*, 1155–1162.

Halpern, D. F. (1992). *Sex differences in cognitive education* (2nd ed.). Hillsdale, NJ: Erlbaum.

Halpern, D. F. (2000). *Sex differences in cognitive abilities* (3rd ed.). Mahwah, NJ: Erlbaum.

Hamilton, M. C. (1988). Using masculine generics: Does generic he increase male bias in the user's imagery? *Sex Roles, 19*, 785–799.

Hammen, C. L. (1982). Gender and depression. In A-I. Ihsan (Ed.), *Gender and psychopathology* (pp. 133–152). New York: Academic Press.

Hammen, C. L., & Padesky, C. A. (1977). Sex differences in the expression of depressive responses on the Beck Depression Inventory. *Journal of Abnormal Psychology, 86*, 609–614.

Hammen, C. L., & Peters, S. D. (1977). Differential responses to male and female depressive reactions. *Journal of Consulting and Clinical Psychology, 45*, 994–1001.

Hammen, C. L., & Peters, S. D. (1978). Interpersonal consequences of depression: Responses to men and women enacting a depressed role. *Journal of Abnormal Psychology, 87*, 322–332.

Hampton, R. L., & Gelles, R. J. (1994). Violence toward Black women in a nationally representative sample of Black families. *Journal of Comparative Family Studies, 25*(1), 105–119.

Hare-Mustin, R. T., & Marecek, J. (1988). The meaning of difference: Gender theory, postmodernism, and psychology. *American Psychologist, 43*, 455–464.

Hare-Mustin, R. T., & Marecek, J. (1998). Asking the right questions: Feminist psychology and sex differences. In D. L. Anselmi & A. L. Law (Eds.), *Questions of gender: Perspectives and paradoxes* (pp. 104–108). Boston: McGraw-Hill.

Harkness, S., & Super, C. M. (1985). The cultural context of gender segregation in children's peer groups. *Child Development, 56*, 219–224.

Harris, I., Torres, J. B., & Allender, D. (1994). The responses of African American men to dominant norms of masculinity within the United States. *Sex Roles, 31*, 703–719.

Harris, J. R. (1998). *The nurture assumption: Why children turn out the way they do; Parents matter less than you think and peers matter more*. New York: Free Press.

Harris, M. B. (1996). Aggressive experiences and aggressiveness: Relationship to ethnicity, gender, and age. *Journal of Applied Social Psychology, 26*(10), 843–870.

Harris, M. B., & Knight-Bohnhoff, K. (1996a). Gender and aggression I: Perceptions of aggression. *Sex Roles, 35*, 1–25.

Harris, M. B., & Knight-Bohnhoff, K. (1996b). Gender and aggression II: Personal aggressiveness. *Sex Roles, 35*, 27–42.

Harris, S. M. (1993). The influence of personal and family factors on achievement needs and concerns of African-American and Euro-American college women. *Sex Roles, 29*(9/10), 671–689.

Harris, S. M., & Majors, R. (1993). Cultural value differences: Implications for the experiences of African-American men. *Journal of Men's Studies, 1*(3), 227–238.

Harrison, A. A., & Saeed, L. (1977). Let's make a deal: An analysis of revelations and stipulations in lonely hearts advertisements. *Journal of Personality and Social Psychology, 35*, 257–264.

Harrison, J. (1978). Warning: The male sex role may be dangerous to your health. *Journal of Social Issues, 34*(1), 65–86.

Hartung, C. M., & Widiger, T. A. (1998). Gender differences in the diagnosis of mental disorders: Conclusions and controversies of the *DSM-IV. Psychological Bulletin, 123*, 260–278.

Hartup, W. W., French, D. C., Laursen, B., Johnston, M. K., & Ogawa, J. R. (1993). Conflict and friendship relations in middle childhood: Behavior in a closed-field situation. *Child Development, 64*, 445–454.

Hatala, M. N., & Prehodka, J. (1996). Content analysis of gay male and lesbian personal advertisements. *Psychological Reports, 78*, 371–374.

Hatfield, E., & Sprecher, S. (1995). Men's and women's preferences in marital partners in the United States, Russia, and Japan. *Journal of Cross-Cultural Psychology, 26*(6), 728–750.

Hathaway, S. R., & McKinley, J. C. (1940). A multiphasic personality schedule (Minnesota): Construction of the schedule. *Journal of Psychology, 10*, 249–254.

Hattie, J. (1992). *Self-concept.* Hillsdale, NJ: Erlbaum.

Haugh, S. S., Hoffman, C. D., & Cowan, G. (1980). The eye of the very young beholder: Sex typing of infants by young children. *Child Development, 51*, 598–600.

Hawkes, G. R., & Taylor, M. (1975). Power structure in Mexican and Mexican American farm labor families. *Journal of Marriage and the Family, 37*(4), 807–811.

Hawkins, A. J., Marshall, C. M., & Meiners, K. M. (1995). Exploring wives' sense of fairness about family work: An initial test of the distributive justice framework. *Journal of Family Issues, 16*(6), 693–721.

Haynes, S. G., & Feinleib, M. (1980). Women, work, and coronary heart disease: Prospective findings from the Framingham heart study. *American Journal of Public Health, 70*(2), 133–141.

Heatherington, L., Daubman, K. A., Bates, C., Ahn, A., Brown, H., & Preston, C. (1993). Two investigations of female modesty in achievement situations. *Sex Roles, 29*, 739–754.

Heatherton, T. F., Kozlowski, L. T., Frecker, R. C., & Fagerstrom, K-O. (1991). The Fagerstrom test for nicotine dependence: A revision of the Fagerstrom Tolerance questionnaire. *British Journal of Addiction, 86*, 1119–1127.

Heavey, C. L., Christensen, A., & Malamuth, N. M. (1995). The longitudinal impact of demand and withdrawal during marital conflict. *Journal of Consulting and Clinical Psychology, 63*(5), 797–801.

Heavey, C. L., Layne, C., & Christensen, A. (1993). Gender and conflict structure in marital interaction: A replication and extension. *Journal of Consulting and Clinical Psychology, 61*(1), 16–27.

Hecht, M. A., & LaFrance, M. (1998). License or obligation to smile: The effect of power and sex on amount and type of smiling. *Personality and Social Psychology Bulletin, 24*, 1332–1342.

Hedges, L. V., & Nowell, A. (1995). Sex differences in mental test scores, variability, and numbers of high-scoring individuals. *Science, 269*, 41–45.

Helgeson, V. S. (1990). The role of masculinity in a prognostic predictor of heart attack severity. *Sex Roles, 22*, 755–774.

Helgeson, V. S. (1991). The effects of masculinity and social support on recovery from myocardial infarction. *Psychosomatic Medicine, 53*, 621–633.

Helgeson, V. S. (1993). Implications of agency and communion for patient and spouse adjustment to a first coronary event. *Journal of Personality and Social Psychology, 64*, 807–816.

Helgeson, V. S. (1994a). Long-distance romantic relationships: Sex differences in adjustment and breakup. *Personality and Social Psychology Bulletin, 20*, 254–265.

Helgeson, V. S. (1994b). Prototypes and dimensions of masculinity and femininity. *Sex Roles, 31*, 653–682.

Helgeson, V. S. (1994c). Relation of agency and communion to well-being: Evidence and potential explanations. *Psychological Bulletin, 116*, 412–428.

Helgeson, V. S. (2000). *Unmitigated communion and adjustment to breast cancer.* Unpublished manuscript.

Helgeson, V. S., & Fritz, H. L. (1996). Implications of communion and unmitigated communion for adolescent adjustment to Type I diabetes. *Women's Health: Research on Gender, Behavior, and Policy, 2*(3), 169–194.

Helgeson, V. S., & Fritz, H. L. (1998). A theory of unmitigated communion. *Personality and Social Psychology Review, 2*, 173–183.

Helgeson, V. S., & Fritz, H. L. (1999). Unmitigated agency and unmitigated communion: Distinctions from agency and communion. *Journal of Research in Personality, 33,* 131–158.

Helgeson, V. S., & Sharpsteen, D. J. (1987). Perception of danger in achievement and affiliation situations: An extension of the Pollak and Gilligan versus Benton et al. debate. *Journal of Personality and Social Psychology, 53,* 727–733.

Helgeson, V. S., Shaver, P., & Dyer, M. (1987). Prototypes of intimacy and distance in same-sex and opposite-sex relationships. *Journal of Social and Personal Relationships, 4,* 195–233.

Helsing, K. J., Szklo, M., & Comstock, G. W. (1981). Factors associated with mortality after widowhood. *American Journal of Public Health, 71*(8), 802–809.

Helwig, A. A. (1998). Gender-role stereotyping: Testing theory with a longitudinal sample. *Sex Roles, 38,* 403–423.

Hendrick, C., & Hendrick, S. (1986). A theory and method of love. *Journal of Personality and Social Psychology, 50,* 392–402.

Hendrick, C., Hendrick, S.S., Foote, F. H., & Slapion-Foote, M. J. (1984). Do men and women love differently? *Journal of Social and Personal Relationships, 1,* 177–195.

Hendrick, S. S. (1981). Self-disclosure and marital satisfaction. *Journal of Personality and Social Psychology, 40,* 1150–1159.

Hendrick, S. S., & Hendrick, C. (1995). Gender differences and similarities in sex and love. *Personal Relationships, 2,* 55–65.

Hendrix, L. (1997). Quality and equality in marriage: A cross-cultural view. *Cross-Cultural Research, 31*(3), 201–225.

Henley, N. M. (1977). *Body politics: Power, sex, and nonverbal communication.* Englewood Cliffs, NJ: Prentice-Hall.

Henley, N. M. (1989). Molehill or mountain? What we know and don't know about sex bias in language. In M. Crawford & M. Gentry (Eds.), *Gender and thought: Psychological perspectives* (pp. 59–78). New York: Springer-Verlag.

Herbert, J. (1989). The physiology of aggression. In J. Groebel & R. A. Hinde (Eds.), *Aggression and war: Their biological and social*

bases (pp. 58–77). New York: Cambridge University Press.

Hess, B. B., & Soldo, B. J. (1985). Husband and wife networks. In W. J. Sauer & R. T. Coward (Eds.), *Social support networks and the care of the elderly: Theory, research, and practice* (pp. 67–92). New York: Springer.

Hessini, L. (1994). Wearing the Hijab in contemporary Morocco: Choice and identity. In F. M. Gocek & S. Balaghi (Eds.), *Reconstructing gender in the Middle East* (pp. 40–56). New York: Columbia University Press.

Hibbard, J. H., & Pope, C. R. (1983). Gender roles, illness orientation and use of medical services. *Social Science and Medicine, 17*(3), 129–137.

Hibbard, J. H., & Pope, C. R. (1993). The quality of social roles as predictors of morbidity and mortality. *Social Science and Medicine, 36,* 217–225.

Hill, C. T., & Peplau, L. A. (1998). Premarital predictors of relationship outcomes: A 15-year follow-up of the Boston Couples Study. In T. N. Bradbury (Ed.), *The developmental course of marital dysfunction* (pp. 237–278). New York: Cambridge University Press.

Hill, C. T., Rubin, Z., & Peplau, L. A. (1976). Breakups before marriage: The end of 103 affairs. *Journal of Social Issues, 32*(1), 147–168.

Hill, J. P., & Lynch, M. E. (1983). The intensification of gender-related role expectations during early adolescence. In J. Brooks-Gunn & A. C. Petersen (Eds.), *Girls at puberty* (pp. 201–228). New York: Plenum Press.

Hiscock, M., Israelian, M., Inch, R., Jacek, C., & Hiscock-Kalil, C. (1995). Is there a sex difference in human laterality? II: An exhaustive survey of visual laterality studies from six neuropsychology journals. *Journal of Clinical and Experimental Neuropsychology, 17,* 590–610.

Ho, R., & Zemaitis, R. (1981). Concern over the negative consequences of success. *Australian Journal of Psychology, 33*(1), 19–28.

Hochschild, A. R. (1989). *The second shift.* New York: Avon Books.

Hohmann, A. A. (1989). Gender bias in psychotropic drug prescribing in primary care. *Medical Care, 27*(5), 478–490.

Hope, S., Power, C., & Rodgers, B. (1999). Does financial hardship account for elevated psychological distress in lone mothers? *Social Science and Medicine, 49,* 1637–1649.

Hope, S., Rodgers, B., & Power, C. (1999). Marital status transitions and psychological distress: Longitudinal evidence from a national population sample. *Psychological Medicine, 29,* 381–389.

Hops, H., Davis, B., & Lewin, L. M. (1999). The development of alcohol and other substance use: A gender study of family and peer context. *Journal of Studies on Alcohol, 13,*(Suppl.), 22–31.

Horner, M. S. (1972). Toward an understanding of achievement-related conflicts in women. *Journal of Social Issues, 28,* 157–175.

Horowitz, A. V., McLaughlin, J., & White, H. R. (1998). How the negative and positive aspects of partner relationships affect the mental health of young married people. *Journal of Health and Social Behavior, 39,* 124–136.

Horowitz, A. V., & White, H. R. (1991). Becoming married, depression, and alcohol problems among young adults. *Journal of Health and Social Behavior, 32,* 221–237.

Horowitz, A. V., & White, H. R. (1998). The relationship of cohabitation and mental health: A study of a young adult cohort. *Journal of Marriage and the Family, 60,* 505–514.

Horowitz, A. V., White, H. R., & Howell-White, S. (1996). Becoming married and mental health: A longitudinal study of a cohort of young adults. *Journal of Marriage and the Family, 58,* 895–907.

House, J. S., Robbins, C., & Metzner, H. L. (1982). The association of social relationships and activities with mortality: Prospective evidence from the Tecumseh Community health study. *American Journal of Epidemiology, 116*(1), 123–140.

Howard, J. A., Blumstein, P., & Schwartz, P. (1986). Sex, power, and influence tactics in intimate relationships. *Journal of Personality and Social Psychology, 51,* 102–109.

Hoyert, D. L., Kochanek, K. D., & Murphy, S. L. (1999). *National Vital Statistics Reports* (Vol. 47). Washington, DC: United States Department of Health and Human Services.

Hudmon, K. S., Gritz, E. R., Clayton, S., & Nisenbaum, R. (1999). Eating orientation, postcessation weight gain, and continued abstinence among female smokers receiving an unsolicited smoking cessation intervention. *Health Psychology, 18,* 29–36.

Huesmann, L. R., & Eron, L. D. (1984). Stability of aggression over time and generations. *Development Psychology, 20,* 1120–1134.

Huesmann, L. R., & Eron, L. D. (1992). Childhood aggression and adult criminality. In J. McCord (Ed.), *Facts, frameworks, and forecasts* (pp. 137–156). New Brunswick, NJ: Transaction.

Hughes, D. L., & Galinsky, E. (1994a). Gender, job, family conditions, and psychological symptoms. *Psychology of Women Quarterly, 18,* 251–270.

Hughes, D. L., & Galinsky, E. (1994b). Work experiences and marital interactions: Elaborating the complexity of work. *Journal of Organizational Behavior, 15,* 423–438.

Hughes, F. P. (1991). *Children, play, and development.* Needham Heights, MA: Allyn & Bacon.

Hughes, M., & Demo, D. H. (1989). Self-perceptions of Black Americans: Self-esteem and personal efficacy. *American Journal of Sociology, 95,* 132–159.

Hull, J. G., & Bond, C. F., Jr. (1986). Social and behavioral consequences of alcohol consumption and expectancy: A meta-analysis. *Psychological Bulletin, 99,* 347–360.

Husaini, B. A., Neff, J. A., Newbrough, J. R., & Moore, M. C. (1982). The stress-buffering role of social support and personal competence among the rural married. *Journal of Community Psychology, 10*(4), 409–426.

Huselid, R. F., & Cooper, M. L. (1992). Gender roles as mediators of sex differences in adolescent alcohol use and abuse. *Journal of Health and Social Behavior, 33,* 348–362.

Huston, T. L., & Geis, G. (1993). In what ways do gender-related attributes and beliefs affect marriage? *Journal of Social Issues, 49*(3), 87–106.

Huston, T. L., & Houts, R. M. (1998). The psychological infrastructure of courtship and marriage: The role of personality and compatibility in romantic relationships. In T. N. Bradbury (Ed.), *The developmental course of marital dysfunction* (pp. 114–151). New York: Cambridge University Press.

Hutson-Comeaux, S. L., & Kelly, J. R. (1996). Sex differences in interaction style and group task performance: The process-performance relationship. *Journal of Social Behavior and Personality, 11*(5), 255–275.

Hyde, J. S. (1984). How large are gender differences in aggression? A developmental meta-analysis. *Developmental Psychology, 20,* 772–736.

Hyde, J. S. (1986). Gender differences in aggression. In J. S. Hyde & M. C. Linn (Eds.), *The psychology of gender: Advances through meta-analysis* (pp. 51–66). Baltimore: Johns Hopkins University Press.

Hyde, J. S. (1995). Women and maternity leave: Empirical data and public policy. *Psychology of Women Quarterly, 19,* 299–313.

Hyde, J. S., DeLamater, J. D., & Hewitt, E. C. (1998). Sexuality and the dual-earner couple: Multiple roles and sexual functioning. *Journal of Family Psychology, 12*(3), 1–15.

Hyde, J. S., Fennema, E., & Lamon, S. J. (1990). Gender differences in mathematics performance: A meta-analysis. *Psychological Bulletin, 107,* 139–155.

Hyde, J. S., Fennema, E., Ryan, M., Frost, L. A., & Hopp, C. (1990). Gender comparisons of mathematics attitudes and affect. *Psychology of Women Quarterly, 14,* 299–324.

Hyde, J. S., & Linn, M. C. (1988). Gender differences in verbal ability: A meta-analysis. *Psychological Bulletin, 104,* 53–69.

Hyde, J. S., & McKinley, N. M. (1997). Gender differences in cognition: Results from meta-analysis. In P. J. Caplan, M. Crawford, J. S. Hyde, & J. T. E. Richardson (Eds.), *Gender differences in human cognition* (pp. 30–51). New York: Oxford University Press.

Hynie, M., Lydon, J. E., & Taradash, A. (1997). Commitment, intimacy, and women's perceptions of premarital sex and contraceptive readiness. *Psychology of Women Quarterly, 21,* 447–464.

IMS Health. (1999). Top 20 drugs sell more than $1 billion each. *IMS Health MIDAS* [On-line]: Available: http://www.ims-global.com//insight/news_story/news_story_991005.html

Ingram, R. E., Cruet, D., Johnson, B. R., & Wisnicki, K. S. (1988). Self-focused attention, gender, gender role, and vulnerability to negative affect. *Journal of Personality and Social Psychology, 55,* 967–978.

Instone, D., Major, B., & Bunker, B. B. (1983). Gender, self confidence, and social influence strategies: An organization simulation. *Journal of Personality and Social Psychology, 44,* 322–333.

Isenhart, C. E. (1993). Masculine gender role stress in an inpatient sample of alcohol abusers. *Psychology of Addictive Behaviors, 7*(3), 177–184.

Ishiyama, F. I., & Chabassol, D. J. (1984). Fear of success consequence scale: Measurement of fear of social consequences of academic success. *Psychological Reports, 54,* 499–504.

Ishiyama, F. I., & Chabassol, D. J. (1985). Adolescents' fear of social consequences of academic success as a function of age and sex. *Journal of Youth and Adolescence, 14,* 37–46.

Ivy, D. K., & Hamlet, S. (1996). College students and sexual dynamics: Two studies of peer sexual harassment. *Communication Education, 45,* 149–166.

Jacklin, C. N. (1989). Female and male: Issues of gender. *American Psychologist, 44,* 127–133.

Jacklin, C. N., & Baker, L. (1993). Early gender development. In S. Oskamp & M. Costanzo (Eds.), *Gender issues in contemporary society* (Vol. 6, pp. 41–57). Newbury Park, CA: Sage.

Jackson, L. A., Sullivan, L. A., & Rostker, R. (1988). Gender, gender role, and body image. *Sex Roles, 19,* 429–443.

Jacobs, J. E., & Eccles, J. S. (1992). The impact of mothers' gender-role stereotypic beliefs on mothers' and children's ability perceptions. *Journal of Personality and Social Psychology, 63,* 932–944.

James, D., & Drakich, J. (1993). Understanding gender differences in amount of talk: A critical review of research. In D. Tannen (Ed.), *Gender and conversational interaction* (pp. 281–312). New York: Oxford University Press.

Jezova, D., Jurankova, E., Mosnarova, A., Kriska, M., & Skultetyova, I. (1996). Neuroendocrine response during stress with relation to gender differences. *Acta Neurobiologiae Experimentalis, 56,* 779–785.

John, D., Shelton, B. A., & Luschen, K. (1995). Race, ethnicity, gender, and perceptions of fairness. *Journal of Family Issues, 16*(3), 357–379.

Johnson, C. (1994). Gender, legitimate authority, and leader-subordinate conversations. *American Sociological Review, 59,* 122–135.

Johnson, E. M., & Huston, T. L. (1998). The perils of love, or why wives adapt to husbands during the transition to parenthood. *Journal of Marriage and the Family, 60,* 195–204.

Johnson, H., & Sacco, V. F. (1995). Researching violence against women: Statistics Canada's national survey. *Canadian Journal of Criminology,* 281–304.

Johnson, M. (1999). *Sex differences in response to evaluative feed back.* Unpublished honors thesis, Carnegie Mellon University, Pittsburgh, PA.

Johnson, M., & Helgeson, V. S. (2000). *Sex differences in response to evaluative feedback.* Manuscript submitted for publication.

Johnson, M. E., & Dowling-Guyer, S. (1996). Effects of inclusive vs. exclusive language on evaluations of the counselor. *Sex Roles, 34,* 407–418.

Johnson, M. P. (1995). Patriarchal terrorism and common couple violence: Two forms of violence against women. *Journal of Marriage and the Family, 57,* 283–294.

Jones, D. C., Bloys, N., & Wood, M. (1990). Sex roles and friendship patterns. *Sex Roles, 23,* 133–145.

Jones, E. E., & Davis, K. E. (1965). From acts to dispositions: The attribution process in social psychology. In L. Berkowitz (Ed.), *Advances in experimental social psychology* (Vol. 2, pp. 219–266). New York: Academic Press.

Jones, W. H., Chernovetz, M. E. O. C., & Hansson, R. O. (1978). The enigma of androgyny: Differential implications for males and females. *Journal of Consulting and Clinical Psychology, 46,* 298–313.

Josephs, R. A., Markus, H. R., & Tafarodi, R. W. (1992). Gender and self-esteem. *Journal of Personality and Social Psychology, 63,* 391–402.

Jussim, L., & Eccles, J. S. (1992). Teacher expectations. II: Construction and reflection of student achievement. *Journal of Personality and Social Psychology, 63,* 947–961.

Kahn, S., Zimmerman, G., Csikszentmihalyi, M., & Getzels, J. W. (1985). Relations between identity in young adulthood and intimacy in midlife. *Journal of Personality and Social Psychology, 49,* 1316–1322.

Kandel, D. B., Davies, M., & Raveis, V. H. (1985). The stressfulness of daily social roles for women: Marital, occupational and household roles. *Journal of Health and Social Behavior, 26,* 64–78.

Kandrack, M. A., Grant, K. R., & Segall, A. (1991). Gender differences in health related behaviour: Some unanswered questions. *Social Science and Medicine, 32*(5), 579–590.

Kane, E. W., & Sanchez, L. (1994). Family status and criticism of gender inequality at home and at work. *Social Forces, 72*(4), 1079–1102.

Kaplan, D. L., & Keys, C. B. (1997). Sex and relationship variables as predictors of sexual attraction in cross-sex platonic friendships between young heterosexual adults. *Journal of Social and Personal Relationships, 14*(2), 191–206.

Kaplan, G. A., Salonen, J. T., Cohen, R. D., Brand, R. J., Syme, S. L., & Puska, P. (1988). Social connections and mortality from all causes and from cardiovascular disease: Prospective evidence from eastern Finland. *American Journal of Epidemiology, 128*(2), 370–380.

Karney, B. R., & Bradbury, T. N. (1995). The longitudinal course of marital quality and stability: A review of theory, method, and research. *Psychological Bulletin, 118,* 3–34.

Karraker, K. H., Vogel, D. A., & Lake, M. A. (1995). Parents' gender-stereotyped perceptions of newborns: The eye of the beholder revisited. *Sex Roles, 33,* 687–701.

Katkin, E. S., Blascovich, J., & Goldband, S. (1981). Empirical assessment of visceral self-perception: Individual and sex differences in the acquisition of heartbeat discrimination. *Journal of Personality and Social Psychology, 40,* 1095–1101.

Katzman, D. K., Zipursky, R. B., Lambe, E. K., & Mikulis, D. J. (1997). A longitudinal magnetic resonance imaging study of brain changes in adolescents with anorexia nervosa. *Archives of Pediatric Adolescent Medicine, 151,* 793–797.

Kawachi, I., Kennedy, B. P., Gupta, V., & Prothrow-Stith, D. (1999). Women's status and the health of women and men: A view from the states. *Social Science and Medicine, 48*, 21–32.

Kelly, A. (1988). Gender differences in teacher-pupil interactions: A meta-analytic review. *Research in Education, 39*, 1–23.

Kelly, H. A. (1994). Rule of thumb and the folk-law of the husband's stick. *Journal of Legal Education, 44*(3), 341–365.

Kemper, T. D. (1990). *Social structure and testosterone: Explorations of the socio-bio-social chain.* New Brunswick, NJ: Rutgers University Press.

Kenrick, D. T., Groth, G. E., Trost, M. R., & Sadalla, E. K. (1993). Integrating evolutionary and social exchange perspectives on relationships: Effects of gender, self-appraisal, and involvement level of mate selection criteria. *Journal of Personality and Social Psychology, 64*, 951–969.

Kent, R. L., & Moss, S. E. (1994). Effects of sex and gender role on leader emergence. *Academy of Management Journal, 37*(5), 1335–1346.

Kephart, W. M. (1967). Some correlates of romantic love. *Journal of Marriage and the Family, 29*, 470–474.

Kessler, R. C., Brown, R. L., & Broman, C. L. (1981). Sex differences in psychiatric help-seeking: Evidence from four large-scale surveys. *Journal of Health and Social Behavior, 22*, 49–64.

Kessler, R. C., McGonagle, K. A., Nelson, C. B., Hughes, M., Swartz, M., & Blazer, D. G. (1994). Sex and depression in the National Comorbidity Survey. II: Cohort effects. *Journal of Affective Disorders, 30*, 15–26.

Kessler, R. C., McGonagle, K. A., Swartz, M., Blazer, D. G., & Nelson, C. B. (1993). Sex and depression in the National Comorbidity Survey. I: Lifetime prevalence, chronicity and recurrence. *Journal of Affective Disorders, 29*, 85–96.

Kessler, R. C., McGonagle, K. A., Zhao, S., Nelson, C. B., Hughes, M., Eshleman, S., Wittchen, H-U., & Kendler, K. S. (1994). Lifetime and 12-month prevalence of *DSM-III-R* psychiatric disorders in the United States. *Archives of General Psychiatry, 51*, 8–19.

Kessler, R. C., & McLeod, J. D. (1984). Sex differences in vulnerability to undesirable life events. *American Sociological Review, 49*, 620–631.

Kessler, R. C., & McRae, J. A., Jr. (1982). The effect of wives' employment on the mental health of married men and women. *American Sociological Review, 47*, 216–227.

Khlat, M., Sermet, C., & Le Pape, A. (2000). Women's health in relation with their family and work roles: France in the early 1900s. *Social Science and Medicine, 50*, 1807–1825.

Kiecolt-Glaser, J. K., Malarkey, W. B., Chee, M., Newton, T., Cacioppo, J. T., Mao, H-Y., & Glaser, R. (1993). Negative behavior during marital conflict is associated with immunological down-regulation. *Psychosomatic Medicine, 55*, 395–409.

Kiecolt-Glaser, J. K., Newton, T., Cacioppo, J. T., MacCallum, R. C., Glaser, R., & Malarkey, W. B. (1996). Marital conflict and endocrine function: Are men really more physiologically affected than women? *Journal of Consulting and Clinical Psychology, 64*(2), 324–332.

Kilmartin, C. T. (1994). *The masculine self.* New York: Macmillan.

Kilpatrick, D. G., Edmunds, C. N., & Seymour, A. K. (1992). *Rape in America: A report to the nation.* Arlington, VA: National Victim Center.

Kimura, D. (1987). Are men's and women's brains really different? *Canadian Psychology, 28*, 133–147.

Kimura, D. (1992). Sex differences in the brain. *Scientific American, 267*(3), 119–125.

Kimura, D. (1999). *Sex and cognition.* Cambridge, MA: MIT Press.

Kindlon, D. J., Thompson, M., & Barker, T. (1999). *Raising Cain: Protecting the emotional life of boys.* New York: Ballantine Books.

Kirchmeyer, C. (1993). Nonwork-to-work spillover: A more balanced view of the experiences and coping of professional women and men. *Sex Roles, 28*, 531–552.

Klein, E., Campbell, J., Soler, E., & Ghez, M. (1997). *Ending domestic violence: Changing public perceptions/halting the epidemic.* Thousand Oaks, CA: Sage.

Kleinke, C. L., Staneski, R. A., & Mason, J. K. (1982). Sex differences in coping with depression. *Sex Roles, 8,* 877–889.

Klerman, G. K., & Weissman, M. M. (1989). Increasing rates of depression. *Journal of the American Medical Association, 261,* 2229–2235.

Klinetob, N. A., & Smith, D. A. (1996). Demand-withdraw communication in marital interaction: Tests of interspousal contingency and gender role hypotheses. *Journal of Marriage and the Family, 58,* 945–957.

Kling, K. C., Hyde, J. S., Showers, C. J., & Buswell, B. N. (1999). Gender differences in self-esteem: A meta-analysis. *Psychological Bulletin, 125,* 470–500.

Klinkenberg, D., & Rose, S. (1994). Dating scripts of gay men and lesbians. *Journal of Homosexuality, 26*(4), 23–35.

Klonoff, E. A., & Landrine, H. (1992). Sex roles, occupational roles, and symptom-reporting: A test of competing hypotheses on sex differences. *Journal of Behavioral Medicine, 15*(4), 355–364.

Knight, G. P., Fabes, R. A., & Higgins, D. A. (1996). Concerns about drawing causal inferences from meta-analyses: An example in the study of gender differences in aggression. *Psychological Bulletin, 119,* 410–421.

Kobrin, F. E., & Hendershot, G. E. (1977). Do family ties reduce mortality? Evidence from the United States, 1966–1968. *Journal of Marriage and the Family, 46,* 807–816.

Koerner, B. I. (1999, April 5). The boys' club persists. *U. S. News and World Report.* Available: www.usnews.com/usnews/issue/990405/5mit.html

Kohlberg, L. (1966). A cognitive-developmental analysis of children's sex-role concepts and attitudes. In E. E. Maccoby (Ed.), *The development of sex differences* (pp. 82–173). Stanford, CA: Stanford University Press.

Kohlberg, L. (Ed.). (1981). *The psychology of moral development* (Vol. 2). San Francisco: Harper & Row.

Kohlmann, C-W., Weidner, G., Dotzauer, E., & Burns, L. R. (1997). Gender differences in health behaviors: The role of avoidant coping. *Revue Europeenne de Psychologie Appliquee [European Review of Applied Psychology], 47,* 115–120.

Kolaric, G. C., & Galambos, N. L. (1995). Face-to-face interactions in unacquainted female-male adolescent dyads: How do girls and boys behave? *Journal of Early Adolescence, 15*(3), 363–382.

Kollock, P., Blumstein, P., & Schwartz, P. (1985). Sex and power in interaction: Conversational privileges and duties. *American Sociological Review, 50,* 34–46.

Komarovsky, M. (1974). Patterns of self-disclosure of male undergraduates. *Journal of Marriage and the Family, 36,* 677–686.

Kopper, B. A. (1996). Gender, gender identity, rape myth acceptance, and time of initial resistance on the perception of acquaintance rape blame and avoidability. *Sex Roles, 34,* 81–93.

Kopper, B. A., & Epperson, D. L. (1996). The experience and expression of anger: Relationships with gender, gender role socialization, depression, and mental health functioning. *Journal of Counseling Psychology, 43*(2), 158–165.

Kornstein, S. G., Schatzberg, A. F., Yonkers, K. A., Thase, M. E., Keitner, G. I., Ryan, C. E., & Schlager, D. (1995). Gender differences in presentation of chronic major depression. *Psychopharmacology Bulletin, 31,* 711–718.

Koss, M. P. (1993). Detecting the scope of rape: A review of prevalence research methods. *Journal of Interpersonal Violence, 8*(2), 198–222.

Kotler, P., & Wingard, D. L. (1989). The effect of occupational, marital and parental roles on mortality: The Alameda County Study. *American Journal of Public Health, 79,* 607–612.

Koutantji, M., Pearce, S. A., & Oakley, D. A. (1998). The relationship between gender and family history of pain with current pain experience and awareness of pain in others. *Pain, 77,* 25–31.

Kposowa, A. J. (1998). The impact of race on divorce in the United States. *Journal of Comparative Family Studies, 29*(3), 529–548.

Kraft, P., & Rise, J. (1994). The relationship between sensation seeking and smoking, alcohol consumption and sexual behavior among

Norwegian adolescents. *Health Education Research: Theory and Practice, 9*(2), 193–200.

Kram, K. E. (1988). *Mentoring at work: Developmental relationships in organizational life.* Lanham, MD: University Press of America.

Krames, L., England, R., & Flett, G. L. (1988). The role of masculinity and femininity in depression and social satisfaction in elderly females. *Sex Roles, 19,* 713–721.

Krane, J. E. (1996). Violence against women in intimate relations: Insights from cross-cultural analyses. *Transcultural Psychiatric Research Review, 33,* 435–465.

Kring, A. M., & Gordon, A. H. (1998). Sex differences in emotion: Expression, experience, and physiology. *Journal of Personality and Social Psychology, 74,* 686–703.

Krishnan, V. (1998). Premarital cohabitation and marital disruption. *Journal of Divorce & Remarriage, 28,* 157–170.

Kuczmarski, R. J., Flegal, K. M., Campbell, S. M., & Johnson, C. L. (1994). Increasing prevalence of overweight among U.S. adults. *Journal of the American Medical Association, 272*(3), 205–211.

Kuebli, J., Butler, S., & Fivush, R. (1995). Mother-child talk about past emotions: Relations of maternal language and child gender over time. *Cognition and Emotion, 9*(2/3), 265–283.

Kuebli, J., & Fivush, R. (1992). Gender differences in parent-child conversations about past emotions. *Sex Roles, 27,* 683–698.

Kurdek, L. A. (1991a). The dissolution of gay and lesbian couples. *Journal of Social and Personal Relationships, 8,* 265–278.

Kurdek, L. A. (1991b). The relations between reported well-being and divorce history, availability of a proximate adult, and gender. *Journal of Marriage and the Family, 53,* 71–78.

Kurdek, L. A. (1992). Relationship stability and relationship satisfaction in cohabiting gay and lesbian couples: A prospective longitudinal test of the contextual and interdependence models. *Journal of Social and Personal Relationships, 9,* 125–142.

Kurdek, L. A. (1993). The allocation of household labor in gay, lesbian, and heterosexual married couples. *Journal of Social Issues, 49*(3), 127–139.

Kurdek, L. A. (1995). Developmental changes in relationship quality in gay and lesbian cohabitating couples. *Developmental Psychology, 31,* 86–94.

Kurdek, L. A. (1996). The deterioration of relationship quality for gay and lesbian cohabitating couples: A five-year prospective longitudinal study. *Personal Relationships, 3,* 417–442.

Kurdek, L. A. (1998). Relationship outcomes and their predictors: Longitudinal evidence from heterosexual married, gay cohabiting, and lesbian cohabiting couples. *Journal of Marriage and the Family, 60,* 553–568.

Kurdek, L. A., & Schmitt, J. P. (1986). Relationship quality of partners in heterosexual married, heterosexual cohabitating, and gay and lesbian relationships. *Journal of Personality and Social Psychology, 51,* 711–720.

Kurz, D. (1998). Old problems and new directions in the study of violence against women. In R. K. Bergen (Ed.), *Issues in intimate violence* (pp. 197–208). Thousand Oaks, CA: Sage.

Lacayo, R. (1995, August 28). To hell week and back: A woman's long fight to enter the Citadel withers in the heat, but the controversy marches on. *Time, 146,* 1–3.

Lach, D. H., & Gwartney-Gibbs, P. A. (1993). Sociological perspectives on sexual harassment and workplace dispute recognition. *Journal of Vocational Behavior, 42*(1), 102–115.

Lackie, L., & de Man, A. F. (1997). Correlates of sexual aggression among male university students. *Sex Roles, 37*(5/6), 451–457.

Lacombe, A. C., & Gay, J. (1998). The role of gender in adolescent identity and intimacy decisions. *Journal of Youth and Adolescence, 27*(6), 795–802.

LaFrance, M., & Banaji, M. (1992). Toward a reconsideration of the gender-emotion relationship. In M. S. Clark (Ed.), *Review of personality and social psychology* (Vol. 14, pp. 178–201). Newbury Park, CA: Sage.

LaFrance, M., & Hecht, M. A. (2000). Gender and smiling: A meta-analysis. In A. H. Fischer (Ed.), *Gender and emotion: Social psychological perspectives.* Cambridge, England: Cambridge University Press.

Lahelma, E., Martikainen, P., Rahkonen, O., & Silventoinen, K. (1999). Gender differences in ill health in Finland: Patterns, magnitude and change. *Social Science and Medicine, 48,* 7–19.

Lai, G. (1995). Work and family roles and psychological well-being in urban China. *Journal of Health and Social Behavior, 36,* 11–37.

Lakkis, J., Ricciardelli, L. A., & Williams, R. J. (1999). Role of sexual orientation and gender-related traits in disordered eating. *Sex Roles, 41*(1/2), 1–16.

Lamke, L. K., Sollie, D. L., Durbin, R. G., & Fitzpatrick, J. A. (1994). Masculinity, femininity, and relationship satisfaction: The mediating role of interpersonal competence. *Journal of Social and Personal Relationships, 11,* 535–554.

Landrine, H. (1985). Race x class stereotypes of women. *Sex Roles, 13,* 65–75.

Lang, S. (1996). The procreative and ritual constitution of female, male and other androgynous beings in the cultural imagination of the Bimin-Kuskusmin of Papual New Guinea. In S. P. Ramet (Ed.), *Gender reversals and gender cultures: Anthropological and historical perspectives* (pp. 183–196). London: Routledge.

Langhinrichsen-Rohling, J., Lewisohn, P., Rohde, P., Seeley, J., Monson, C. M., Meyer, K. A., & Langford, R. (1998). Gender differences in the suicide-related behaviors of adolescents and young adults. *Sex Roles, 39,* 839–854.

Larson, R., & Pleck, J. (1998). Hidden feelings: Emotionality in boys and men. In D. Bernstein (Ed.), *The Nebraska Symposium on Motivation: Gender and motivation* (pp. 25–74). Lincoln: University of Nebraska Press.

Larson, R., & Richards, M. H. (1991). Daily companionship in late childhood and early adolescence: Changing developmental contexts. *Child Development, 62,* 284–300.

Larson, R. W., & Almeida, D. M. (1999). Emotional transmission in the daily lives of families: A new paradigm for studying family process. *Journal of Marriage and the Family, 61,* 5–20.

Larson, R. W., & Gillman, S. (1999). Transmission of emotions in the daily interactions of single-mother families. *Journal of Marriage and the Family, 61,* 21–37.

Latest Shootings Demand Nation's Action. (1999, September 17). *Tennessean,* p. 16A.

Lau, S., & Gruen, G. E. (1992). The social stigma of loneliness: Effect of target person's and perceiver's sex. *Personality and Social Psychology Bulletin, 18,* 182–189.

Laumann, E. O., Gagnon, J. H., Michael, R. T., & Michaels, S. (1994). *The social organization of sexuality: Sexual practices in the United States.* Chicago: University of Chicago Press.

Lazarus, R. S., & Folkman, S. (1984). Stress, appraisal and coping. *Journal of Adolescence, 14,* 119–133.

Leaper, C. (1987). Agency, communion, and gender as predictors of communication style and being liked in adult male-female dyads. *Sex Roles, 16,* 137–149.

Leaper, C., Carson, M., Baker, C., Holliday, H., & Myers, S. (1995). Self-disclosure and listener verbal support in same-gender and cross-gender friends' conversations. *Sex Roles, 33,* 387–404.

Leary, M. R., Tambor, E. S., Terdal, S. K., & Downs, D. L. (1995). Self-esteem as an interpersonal monitor: The sociometer hypothesis. *Journal of Personality and Social Psychology, 68,* 518–530.

Leary, M. R., Tchividjian, L. R., & Kraxberger, B. E. (1994). Self-presentation can be hazardous to your health: Impression management and health risk. *Health Psychology, 13*(6), 461–470.

Lee, G. R., & Shehan, C. L. (1989). Retirement and marital satisfaction. *Journal of Gerontology: Social Sciences, 44*(6), S226–S230.

Lee, J. A. (1973). *The colors of love: An exploration of the ways of loving.* Don Mills, Ontario, Canada: New Press.

Lee, V. E. (1998). Is single-sex secondary schooling a solution to the problem of gender inequity. In S. Morse (Ed.), *Separated by sex: A critical look at single-sex education for girls* (pp. 41–52). Washington, DC: American Association of University Women Educational Foundation.

Lees, H. (1957). *Help your husband stay alive!* New York: Appleton-Century-Crofts.

Leigh, B. C. (1989). Reasons for having and avoiding sex: Gender, sexual orientation, and relationship to sexual behavior. *Journal of Sex Research, 26*(2), 199–209.

Leinhardt, G., Seewald, A. M., & Engel, M. (1979). Learning what's taught: Sex differences in instruction. *Journal of Educational Psychology, 71*(4), 432–439.

Lempers, J. D., & Clark-Lempers, D. S. (1993). A functional comparison of same-sex and opposite-sex friendships during adolescence. *Journal of Adolescent Research, 8*(1), 89–108.

Lennane, K. J., & Lennane, R. J. (1973). Alleged psychogenic disorders in women: A possible manifestation of sexual prejudice. *New England Journal of Medicine, 288*(6), 288–292.

Lenney, E. (1977). Women's self-confidence in achievement settings. *Psychological Bulletin, 84*, 1–13.

Lenney, E., Gold, J., & Browning, C. (1983). Sex differences in self-confidence: The influence of comparison to others' ability level. *Sex Roles, 9*, 925–942.

Lennon, M. C. (1987). Sex differences in distress: The impact of gender and work roles. *Journal of Health and Social Behavior, 28*, 290–305.

Lennon, M. C. (1994). Women, work, and well-being: The importance of work conditions. *Journal of Health and Social Behavior, 35*, 235–247.

Lennon, M. C., & Rosenfield, S. (1992). Women and mental health: The interaction of job and family conditions. *Journal of Health and Social Behavior, 33*, 316–327.

Lester, D. (1996). The impact of unemployment on marriage and divorce. *Journal of Divorce and Remarriage, 25*(3/4), 151–153.

Lester, D., & Yang, B. (1998). *Suicide and homicide in the twentieth century: Changes over time.* Commack, AL: Nova Science.

Levenson, R. W., Carstensen, L. L., & Gottman, J. M. (1993). Long-term marriage: Age, gender, and satisfaction. *Psychology and Aging, 8*(2), 301–313.

Levenson, R. W., Carstensen, L. L., & Gottman, J. M. (1994). The influence of age and gender on affect, physiology, and their interrelations: A study of long-term marriages. *Journal of Personality and Social Psychology, 67*, 56–68.

Leveroni, C. L., & Berenbaum, S. A. (1998). Early androgen effects on interest in infants: Evidence from children with congenital adrenal hyperplasia. *Developmental Neuropsychology, 14*(2/3), 321–340.

Leviatan, U., & Cohen, J. (1985). Gender differences in expectancy among Kibbutz members. *Social Science and Medicine, 21*(5), 545–551.

Levin, S. (2000). Plum man plans for 13,000 at Promise Keepers gathering. *Pittsburgh Post-Gazette*, p. B–2.

Levine, F. M., & de Simone, L. L. (1991). The effects of experimenter gender on pain report in male and female subjects. *Pain, 44*(1), 69–72.

Levine, M. P., & Smolak, L. (1996). Media as a context for the development of disordered eating. In L. Smolak, M. P. Levine, & R. Striegel-Moore (Eds.), *The developmental psychopathology of eating disorders* (pp. 235–257). Mahwah, NJ: Erlbaum.

Levinson, D. (1989). *Family violence in cross-cultural perspective.* Newbury Park, CA: Sage.

Levinson, D. J. (1978). *The seasons of a man's life.* New York: Ballantine Books.

Levy, P. E., & Baumgardner, A. H. (1991). Effects of self-esteem and gender on goal choice. *Journal of Organizational Behavior, 12*, 529–541.

Lewis, S., & Cooper, C. L. (1983). The stress of combining occupational and parental roles: A review of the literature. *Bulletin of the British Psychological Society, 36*, 341–345.

Lex, B. W. (1991). Some gender differences in alcohol and polysubstance users. *Health Psychology, 10*, 121–132.

Liem, R., & Rayman, P. (1982). Health and social costs of unemployment: Research and policy considerations. *American Psychologist, 37*, 1116–1123.

Lin, N., Woelfel, M., & Dumin, M. Y. (1986). Gender of the confidant and depression. In N. Lin, A. Dean, & W. M. Ensel (Eds.), *Social support, life events, and depression* (pp. 283–306). Orlando, FL: Academic Press.

Linden, W., Chambers, L., Maurice, J., & Lenz, J. W. (1993). Sex differences in social support, self-deception, hostility, and ambulatory cardiovascular activity. *Health Psychology, 12*, 376–380.

Linn, M. C., & Petersen, A. C. (1985). Emergence and characterization of sex differences in spatial ability: A meta-analysis. *Child Development, 56*, 1479–1498.

Lippa, R. (1991). Some psychometric characteristics of gender diagnosticity measures: Reliability, validity, consistency across domains, and relationship to the Big Five. *Journal of Personality and Social Psychology, 61,* 1000–1011.

Lippa, R. (1995). Gender-related individual differences and psychological adjustment in terms of the Big Five and circumplex models. *Journal of Personality and Social Psychology, 69,* 1184–1202.

Lippa, R., & Connelly, S. C. (1990). Gender diagnosticity: A new Bayesian approach to gender-related individual differences. *Journal of Personality and Social Psychology, 59,* 1051–1065.

Lisak, D. (1991). Sexual aggression, masculinity, and fathers. *Journal of Women in Culture and Society, 16*(2), 238–262.

Lisak, D., & Roth, S. (1988). Motivational factors in nonincarcerated sexually aggressive men. *Journal of Personality and Social Psychology, 55,* 795–802.

Lloyd, S. A. (1987). Conflict in premarital relationships: Differential perceptions of males and females. *Family Relations, 36,* 290–294.

Lloyd, S. A. (1990). A behavioral self-report technique for assessing conflict in close relationships. *Journal of Social and Personal Relationships, 7,* 265–272.

Lobel, S. A., Quinn, R. E., St. Clair, L., & Warfield, A. (1994). Love without sex: The impact of psychological intimacy between men and women at work. *Organizational Dynamics, 23,* 5–16.

Lockery, S. A., & Stanford, E. P. (1996). Physical activity and smoking: Gender comparisons among older African American adults. *Journal of Health Care for the Poor and Underserved, 7*(3), 232–251.

Lockheed, M. E., & Zelditch, M., Jr. (1985). Sex and social influence: A meta-analysis guided by theory. In J. Berger & M. Zelditch, Jr. (Eds.), *Status, rewards, and influence* (pp. 406–429). San Francisco: Jossey-Bass.

Lombardo, W. K., Cretser, G. A., Lombardo, B., & Mathis, S. L. (1983). Fer cryin' out loud: There is a sex difference. *Sex Roles, 9,* 987–995.

Long, R. J. (1992). *Gender roles and the self-report of symptoms.* Unpublished manuscript, Carnegie Mellon University, Pittsburgh, PA.

Love, C. (1994, June 2). A cry in the dark: Love reads Cobain's note to vigil. *Rolling Stone,* 40.

Lummis, M., & Stevenson, H. W. (1990). Gender differences in beliefs and achievement: A cross-cultural study. *Developmental Psychology, 26,* 254–263.

Lundberg, S., & Rose, E. (1999). *The effects of sons and daughters on men's labor supply and wages.* Unpublished manuscript, University of Washington, Seattle.

Lundeberg, M. A. (1997). You guys are overreacting: Teaching prospective teachers about subtle gender bias. *Journal of Teacher Education, 48*(1), 55–61.

Lundeberg, M. A., Fox, P. W., & Puncochar, J. (1994). Highly confident but wrong: Gender differences and similarities in confidence judgments. *Journal of Educational Psychology, 86*(1), 114–121.

Luthar, S. S., & McMahon, T. J. (1996). Peer reputation among inner-city adolescents: Structure and correlates. *Journal of Research on Adolescence, 6*(4), 581–603.

Lye, D. N., & Waldron, I. (1997). Attitudes toward cohabitation, family, and gender roles: Relationships to values and political ideology. *Sociological Perspectives, 40*(2), 199–225.

Lynch, J. J. (1977). *The broken heart.* New York: Basic Books.

Lyons, N. (1983). Two perspectives: On self, relationships, and morality. *Harvard Educational Review, 53,* 125–145.

Lytton, H., & Romney, D. M. (1991). Parents' differential socialization of boys and girls: A meta-analysis. *Psychological Bulletin, 109,* 267–296.

Lyubomirsky, S., & Nolen-Hoeksema, S. (1993). Self-perpetuating properties of dysphoric rumination. *Journal of Personality and Social Psychology, 65,* 339–349.

Maccoby, E. E. (1966). Sex differences in intellectual functioning. In E. E. Maccoby (Ed.), *The development of sex differences* (pp. 25–55). Stanford, CA: Stanford University Press.

Maccoby, E. E. (1990). Gender and relationships: A developmental account. *American Psychologist, 45,* 513–520.

Maccoby, E. E. (1998). *The two sexes: Growing up apart, coming together.* Cambridge, MA: Harvard University Press.

Maccoby, E. E., & Jacklin, C. N. (1974). *The psychology of sex differences.* Stanford, CA: Stanford University Press.

Maccoby, E. E., & Jacklin, C. N. (1987). Gender segregation in childhood. In H. W. Reese (Ed.), *Advances in child development and behavior* (Vol. 20, pp. 239–288). New York: Academic Press.

MacDermid, S. M., Huston, T. L., & McHale, S. M. (1990). Changes in marriage associated with the transition to parenthood: Individual differences as a function of sex-role attitudes and changes in the division of household labor. *Journal of Marriage and the Family, 52,* 475–486.

MacDowell, J. (Ed.). (1999, June 21). Personals. In *Pittsburgh Weekly* (Vol. 16, pp. 58–59).

Macintyre, S. (1993a). Gender differences in longevity and health in Eastern and Western Europe. In S. Platt, H. Thomas, S. Scott, & G. Williams (Eds.), *Locating health: Sociological and historical explorations* (pp. 57–73). Aldershot, Hampshire, England: Avebury.

Macintyre, S. (1993b). Gender differences in the perception of common cold symptoms. *Social Science and Medicine, 36*(1), 15–20.

Macintyre, S., Ford, G., & Hunt, K. (1999). Do women over-report morbidity? Men's and women's responses to structured prompting on a standard question on long standing illness. *Social Science and Medicine, 48,* 89–98.

Macintyre, S., Hunt, K., & Sweeting, H. (1996). Gender differences in health: Are things really as simple as they seem? *Social Science and Medicine, 42*(4), 617–624.

Major, B. (1981). Gender patterns in touching behavior. In C. Mayo & N. M. Henley (Eds.), *Gender and nonverbal behavior* (pp. 15–37). New York: Springer-Verlag.

Major, B. (1989). Gender differences in comparisons and entitlement: Implications for comparable worth. *Journal of Social Issues, 45*(4), 99–115.

Major, B., Schmidlin, A. M., & Williams, L. (1990). Gender patterns in social touch: The impact of setting and age. *Journal of Personality and Social Psychology, 58,* 634–643.

Malatesta, C. Z., Culver, C., Tesman, J. R., & Shepard, B. (1989). The development of emotion expression during the first two years of life. *Monographs of the Society for Research in Child Development, 54*(1/2), 1–104.

Maltz, D. N., & Borker, R. A. (1982). A cultural approach to male-female miscommunication. In J. J. Gumperz (Ed.), *Language and social identity* (pp. 196–216). Cambridge, MA: Cambridge University Press.

Manheimer, R. J. (1994). *Older Americans almanac.* Washington, DC: Gale Research.

Mann, C. R. (1993). Maternal filicide of preschoolers. In A. V. Wilson (Ed.), *Homicide: The victim/offender connection* (pp. 227–246). Cincinnati, OH: Anderson.

Mann, T. (1996). Why do we need a health psychology of gender or sexual orientation? In P. M. Kato & T. Mann (Eds.), *Handbook of diversity issues in health psychology* (pp. 187–198). New York: Plenum Press.

Mann, T., Nolen-Hoeksema, S., Huang, K., & Burgard, D. (1997). Are two interventions worse than none? Joint primary and secondary prevention of eating disorders in college females. *Health Psychology, 16*(3), 215–225.

Manning, A. (1989). The genetic bases of aggression. In J. Groebel & R. A. Hinde (Eds.), *Aggression and war: Their biological and social bases* (pp. 48–57). New York: Cambridge University Press.

Marcia, J. E. (1993). The status of the statuses: Research review. In J. E. Marcia, D. R. Matteson, J. L. Orlofsky, A. S. Waterman, & S. L. Archer (Eds.), *Ego identity: A handbook for psychosocial research* (pp. 22–41). New York: Springer-Verlag.

Marcus, A. C., & Seeman, T. E. (1981). Sex differences in reports of illness and disability: A preliminary test of the fixed role obligations hypothesis. *Journal of Health and Social Behavior, 22,* 174–182.

Marcus, A. C., & Siegel, J. M. (1982). Sex differences in the use of physician services: A preliminary test of the fixed role hypothesis. *Journal of Health and Social Behavior, 23,* 186–197.

Marecek, J. (1995). Gender, politics, and psychology's ways of knowing. *American Psychologist, 50,* 162–163.

Margolis, D. R. (1993). Women's movements around the world: Cross-cultural comparison. *Gender and Society, 7,* 379–399.

Marini, M. M., & Fan, P-L. (1997). The gender gap in earnings at career entry. *American Sociological Review, 62*, 588–604.

Mark, E. W., & Alper, T. G. (1985). Women, men, and intimacy motivation. *Psychology of Women Quarterly, 9*(1), 81–88.

Markman, H. J., Silvern, L., Clements, M., & Kraft-Hanak, S. (1993). Men and women dealing with conflict in heterosexual relationships. *Journal of Social Issues, 49*(3), 107–125.

Marks, N. F. (1998). Does it hurt to care? Caregiving, work-family conflict, and midlife well-being. *Journal of Marriage and the Family, 60*, 951–966.

Marks, S. R. (1994). Intimacy in the public realm: The case of co-workers. *Social Forces, 72*(3), 843–858.

Marsh, H. W. (1989). Age and sex effects in multiple dimensions of self-concept: Preadolescence to early adulthood. *Journal of Educational Psychology, 81*(3), 417–430.

Marsh, H. W., & Byrne, B. M. (1991). Differentiated additive androgyny model: Relations between masculinity, femininity, and multiple dimensions of self-concept. *Journal of Personality and Social Psychology, 61*, 811–828.

Marshall, J. R., & Funch, D. P. (1986). Gender and illness behavior among colorectal cancer patients. *Women Health, 11*, 67–82.

Martell, R. F. (1996). Gender-based bias and discrimination. In P. J. Dubeck & K. Borman (Eds.), *Women and work: A handbook* (pp. 329–332). New York: Garland.

Martell, R. F., Lane, D. M., & Emrich, C. (1996). Male-female differences: A computer simulation. *American Psychologist, 51*, 157–158.

Martin, C. L. (1989). Children's use of gender-related information in making social judgments. *Developmental Psychology, 25*, 80–88.

Martin, J. L. (1988). Psychological consequences of AIDS-related bereavement among gay men. *Journal of Consulting and Clinical Psychology, 56*, 856–862.

Martin, R. (1997). Girls don't talk about garages!: Perceptions of conversation in same and cross-sex friendships. *Personal Relationships, 4*, 115–130.

Martindale, M. (1990). *Sexual harassment in the military: 1988*. Arlington, VA: Department of Defense.

Martz, D. M., Handley, K. B., & Eisler, R. M. (1995). The relationship between feminine gender role stress, body image, and eating disorders. *Psychology of Women Quarterly, 19*, 493–508.

Maslach, C., & Jackson, S. E. (1985). The role of sex and family variables in burnout. *Sex Roles, 12*(7/8), 837–851.

Mass Murders. (1996, April 29). *Chicago Sun-Times*, p. 3.

Mastekaasa, A. (1996). Unemployment and health: Selection effects. *Journal of Community and Applied Social Psychology, 6*, 189–205.

Masters, M. S., & Sanders, B. (1993). Is the gender difference in mental rotation disappearing? *Behavior Genetics, 23*(4), 337–341.

Matthews, S., Hertzman, C., Ostry, A., & Power, C. (1998). Gender, work roles and psychosocial work characteristics as determinants of health. *Social Science and Medicine, 46*(11), 1417–1424.

Matthews, S., Manor, O., & Power, C. (1999). Social inequalities in health: Are there gender differences? *Social Science and Medicine, 48*, 49–60.

Matthews, S., Stansfeld, S., & Power, C. (1999). Social support at age 33: The influence of gender, employment status and social class. *Social Science and Medicine, 49*, 133–142.

Mazur, E., & Olver, R. R. (1987). Intimacy and structure: Sex differences in imagery of same-sex relationships. *Sex Roles, 16*, 539–558.

McAndrew, F. T. (1986). A cross-cultural study of recognition thresholds for facial expressions of emotion. *Journal of Cross-Cultural Psychology, 17*(2), 211–224.

McBride, A. B. (1990). Mental health effects of women's multiple roles. *American Psychologist, 45*, 381–384.

McBurney, D. H., Gaulin, S. J. C., Devineni, T., & Adams, C. (1997). Superior spatial memory of women: Stronger evidence for the gathering hypothesis. *Evolution and Human Behavior, 18*, 165–174.

McCarthy, M. M. (1995). Estrogen modulation of oxytocin and its relation to behavior. In R. Ivel & J. A. Russell (Eds.), *Oxytocin, cellular and molecular approaches in medicine and research* (pp. 235–245). New York: Plenum Press.

McClelland, D. C., Atkinson, J. W., Clark, R. A., & Lowell, E. L. (1953). *The achievement motive.* New York: Appleton-Century-Crofts.

McCloskey, L. A. (1996). Gender and the expression of status in children's mixed-age conversations. *Journal of Applied Developmental Psychology, 17,* 117–133.

McClure, E. B. (2000). A meta-analytic review of sex differences in facial expression processing and their development in infants, children, and adolescents. *Psychological Bulletin, 126,* 424–453.

McCreary, D. R., Newcomb, M. D., & Sadava, S. W. (1999). The male role, alcohol use, and alcohol problems: A structural modeling examination in adult women and men. *Journal of Counseling Psychology, 46*(1), 109–124.

McCreary, D. R., Wong, F. Y., Wiener, W., Carpenter, K. M., Engle, A., & Nelson, P. (1996). The relationship between masculine gender role stress and psychological adjustment: A question of construct validity? *Sex Roles, 34,* 507–516.

McDonough, P., Williams, D. R., House, J. S., & Duncan, G. J. (1999). Gender and the socioeconomic gradient in mortality. *Journal of Health and Social Behavior, 40,* 17–31.

McDougall, J., DeWit, D. J., & Ebanks, G. E. (1999). Parental preferences for sex of children in Canada. *Sex Roles, 41,* 615–626.

McGrath, E., Keita, G. P., Strickland, B. R., & Russo, N. F. (1990). *Women and depression: Risk factors and treatment issues.* Washington, DC: American Psychological Association.

McHugh, M. C., Koeske, R. D., & Frieze, I. H. (1986). Issues to consider in conducting nonsexist psychological research: A guide for researchers. *American Psychologist, 41,* 879–890.

McIntosh, D. N., Keywell, J., Reifman, A., & Ellsworth, P. C. (1994). Stress and health in first-year law students: Women fare worse? *Journal of Applied Social Psychology, 24*(16), 1474–1499.

McIntosh, J. L. (1985). *Research on suicide: A bibliography.* New York: Greenwood Press.

McKenna, W., & Kessler, S. J. (1977). Experimental design as a source of sex bias in social psychology. *Sex Roles, 3,* 117–128.

McLanahan, S. S., & Glass, J. L. (1985). A note on the trend in sex differences in psychological distress. *Journal of Health and Social Behavior, 26,* 328–336.

McLendon, K., Foley, L. A., Hall, J., Sloan, L., Wesley, A., & Perry, L. (1994). Male and female perceptions of date rape. *Journal of Social Behavior and Personality, 9*(3), 421–428.

McLeod, J. D. (1991). Childhood parental loss and adult depression. *Journal of Health and Social Behavior, 32,* 205–220.

McWilliams, S., & Howard, J. (1993). Solidarity and hierarchy in cross-sex friendships. *Journal of Social Issues, 49*(3), 191–202.

Mechanic, D. (1976). Sex, illness, illness behavior, and the use of health services. *Journal of Human Stress, 2,* 29–40.

Mednick, S. A., Gabrielle, W. F., & Hutchings, B. (1984). Genetic influences in criminal convictions: Evidence from an adoption cohort. *Science, 224,* 891–894.

Meeker, B. F., & Weitzel-O'Neill, P. A. (1985). Sex roles and interpersonal behavior in task-oriented groups. In J. Berger & M. Zelditch, Jr. (Eds.), *Status, rewards, and influence* (pp. 379–405). San Francisco: Jossey-Bass.

Meininger, J. C. (1986). Sex differences in factors associated with use of medical care and alternative illness behaviors. *Social Science and Medicine, 22*(3), 285–292.

Messner, M. A. (1997). *Politics of masculinities: Men in movements.* London: Sage.

Metha, A., Chen, E., Mulvenon, S., & Dode, I. (1998). A theoretical model of adolescent suicide risk. *Archives of Suicide Research, 4,* 115–133.

Michell, L., & Amos, A. (1997). Girls, pecking order and smoking. *Social Science and Medicine, 44*(12), 1861–1869.

Mickelson, K. D., Helgeson, V. S., & Weiner, E. (1995). Gender effects on social support provision and receipt. *Personal Relationships, 2,* 221–224.

Miedzian, M. (1991). *Boys will be boys: Breaking the link between masculinity and violence.* Thousand Oaks, CA: Sage.

Miller, C., & Swift, K. (1980). *The handbook of nonsexist writing.* New York: Harper & Row.

Miller, C., Swift, K., & Maggio, R. (1997, September/October). Liberating language. *Ms. Magazine,* 51–54.

Miller, G. E., Dopp, J. M., Myers, H. F., Stevens, S. Y., & Fahey, J. L. (1999). Psychosocial predictors of natural killer cell mobilization during marital conflict. *Health Psychology, 18,* 262–271.

Miller, K. E., Sabo, D. F., Farrell, M. P., Barnes, G. M., & Melnick, M. J. (1998). Athletic participation and sexual behavior in adolescents: The different worlds of boys and girls. *Journal of Health and Social Behavior, 39,* 108–123.

Mirowsky, J. (1985). Depression and marital power: An equity model. *American Journal of Sociology, 91*(3), 557–592.

Mischel, W. (1966). A social-learning view of sex differences in behavior. In E. E. Maccoby (Ed.), *The development of sex differences* (pp. 56–81). Stanford, CA: Stanford University Press.

Mitchell, J. E., Baker, L. A., & Jackson, C. N. (1989). Masculinity and femininity in twin children: Genetic and environmental factors. *Child development, 60,* 1475–1485.

Mokdad, A. H., Serdula, M. K., Dietz, W. H., Bowman, B. A., Marks, J. S., & Koplan, J. P. (1999). The spread of the obesity epidemic in the United States, 1991–1998. *Journal of the American Medical Association, 282*(16), 1519–1522.

Molloy, B. L., & Herzberger, S. D. (1998). Body image and self-esteem: A comparison of African-American and Caucasian women. *Sex Roles, 38*(7/8), 631–643.

Monsour, M. (1992). Meanings of intimacy in cross- and same-sex friendships. *Journal of Social and Personal Relationships, 9,* 277–295.

Monsour, M. (1997). Communication and cross-sex friendships across the life cycle: A review of the literature. *Communication Yearbook, 20,* 375–414.

Monsour, M., Harris, B., Kurzweil, N., & Beard, C. (1994). Challenges confronting cross-sex friendships: Much ado about nothing? *Sex Roles, 31,* 55–77.

Monteflores, C. D., & Schultz, S. J. (1978). Coming out: Similarities and differences for lesbians and gay men. *Journal of Social Issues, 34*(3), 59–72.

Moore, T. J. (1999, October 17). No prescription for happiness. *Boston Globe.* Available: http://www.boston.com/globe/

Morabia, A., Fabre, J., & Dunand, J-P. (1992). The influence of patient and physician gender on prescription of psychotropic drugs. *Journal of Clinical Epidemiology, 45*(2), 111–116.

Morano, C. D., Cisler, R. A., & Lemerond, J. (1993). Risk factors for adolescent suicidal behavior: Loss, insufficient familial support, and hopelessness. *Adolescence, 28*(112), 851–865.

Morgan, B. L. (1996). Putting the feminism into feminism scales: Introduction of a Liberal Feminist Attitude and Ideology Scale (LFAIS). *Sex Roles, 34,* 359–390.

Morse, J. (1999, February 15). Make time for daddy. *Time, 153.* Available: www.time.com/ t . . . zine/articles/0,3266, 19888,00.html

Moskowitz, D. S., Suh, E. J., & Desaulniers, J. (1994). Situational influences on gender differences in agency and communion. *Journal of Personality and Social Psychology, 66,* 753–761.

Muehlenhard, C. L., & Cook, S. W. (1988). Men's self reports of unwanted sexual activity. *Journal of Sex Research, 24,* 58–72.

Muehlenhard, C. L., Powch, I. G., Phelps, J. L., & Giusti, L. M. (1992). Definitions of rape: Scientific and political implications. *Journal of Social Issues, 48*(1), 23–44.

Mukai, T., Kambara, A., & Sasaki, Y. (1998). Body dissatisfaction, need for social approval, and eating disturbances among Japanese and American college women. *Sex Roles, 39*(9/10), 751–763.

Mulac, A. (1998). The gender-linked language effect: Do language differences really make a difference. In D. J. Canary & K. Dindia (Eds.), *Sex differences and similarities in communication* (pp. 127–153). Mahwah, NJ: Erlbaum.

Mulac, A., Incontro, C. R., & James, M. R. (1985). Comparison of the gender-linked language effect and sex role stereotypes. *Journal of Personality and Social Psychology, 49,* 1098–1109.

Muller, C. F. (1990). *Health care and gender.* New York: Russell Sage Foundation.

Murphy, G. C., & Athanasou, J. A. (1999). The effect of unemployment on mental health. *Journal of Occupational and Organizational Psychology, 72,* 83–99.

Murstein, B. I. (1974). *Love, sex, and marriage through the ages.* New York: Springer.

Myers, A. M., & Gonda, G. (1982). Utility of the masculinity-femininity construct: Comparison of traditional and androgyny approaches. *Journal of Personality and Social Psychology, 43,* 514–522.

Myers, S. M., & Booth, A. (1996). Men's retirement and marital quality. *Journal of Family Issues, 17*(3), 336–357.

Naifeh, S., & Smith, G. W. (1984). *Why can't men open up?* New York: Warner Books.

Nardi, P. M. (1992). Sex, friendship, and gender roles among gay men. In P. M. Nardi (Ed.), *Men's friendships* (pp. 173–185). Newbury Park, CA: Sage.

Nardi, P. M., & Sherrod, D. (1994). Friendship in the lives of gay men and lesbians. *Journal of Social and Personal Relationships, 11,* 185–199.

Narus, L. R., Jr., & Fischer, J. L. (1982). Strong but not silent: A reexamination of expressivity in the relationships of men. *Sex Roles, 8,* 159–168.

Natale, M., Entin, E., & Jaffe, J. (1979). Vocal interruptions in dyadic communication as a function of speech and social anxiety. *Journal of Personality and Social Psychology, 37,* 865–878.

Nathanson, C. A. (1978). Sex roles as variables in the interpretation of morbidity data: A methodological critique. *International Journal of Epidemiology, 7*(3), 253–262.

Nathanson, C. A. (1980). Social roles and health status among women: The significance of employment. *Social Science and Medicine, 14,* 463–471.

National Center for Health Statistics. (1999). *Health, United States, 1999 with health and aging chartbook* [On-line]. Hyattsville, MD. Available: http://www.clpgh.org/clp/socsci/collect.html

National Institute on Alcohol Abuse and Alcoholism. (1997). Alcohol alert. *Alcohol, Violence, and Aggression, 38,* 1–6.

National Public Radio. (1999, November 29). *Interview with Hugh Hefner by Terry Gross.*

Netting, N. S. (1992). Sexuality in youth culture: Identity and change. *Adolescence, 27*(108), 961–976.

Newcomb, M. D. (1984). Marital discord and problem areas: Longitudinal personality prediction of sex differences among the divorced. *Journal of Divorce, 8*(2), 67–77.

Newcombe, N., & Arnkoff, D. B. (1979). Effects of speech style and sex of speaker on person perception. *Journal of Personality and Social Psychology, 37,* 1293–1303.

Newell, C. E., Rosenfeld, P., & Culbertson, A. L. (1995). Sexual harassment experiences and equal opportunity perceptions of navy women. *Sex Roles, 32,* 159–168.

Nezu, A. M., & Nezu, C. M. (1987). Psychological distress, problem solving, and coping reactions: Sex role differences. *Sex Roles, 16,* 205–214.

Nichols, J. (1975). *Men's liberation: A new definition of masculinity.* New York: Penguin Books.

Nides, M., Rand, C., Dolce, J., Murray, R., O'Hara, P., Voelker, H., & Connett, J. (1994). Weight gain as a function of smoking cessation and 2-mg nicotine gum use among middle-aged smokers with mild lung impairment in the first 2 years of the lung health study. *Health Psychology, 13,* 354–361.

Niemann, Y. F., Jennings, L., Rozelle, R. M., Baxter, J. C., & Sullivan, E. (1994). Use of free responses and cluster analysis to determine stereotypes of eight groups. *Personality and Social Psychology Bulletin, 20,* 379–390.

Noel, C. (1997, February 12). Springer school students offer definitions of love. *Los Altos Town Crier,* p. 26.

Nolen-Hoeksema, S. (1987). Sex differences in unipolar depression: Evidence and theory. *Psychological Bulletin, 101,* 259–282.

Nolen-Hoeksema, S. (1990). *Sex differences in depression.* Stanford, CA: Stanford University Press.

Nolen-Hoeksema, S. (1994). An interactive model for the emergence of gender differences in depression in adolescence. *Journal of Research on Adolescence, 4,* 519–534.

Nolen-Hoeksema, S., & Girgus, J. S. (1994). The emergence of gender differences in depression during adolescence. *Psychological Bulletin, 115,* 424–443.

Nolen-Hoeksema, S., Larson, J., & Grayson, C. (1999). Explaining the gender difference in depressive symptoms. *Journal of Personality and Social Psychology, 77,* 1061–1072.

Nolen-Hoeksema, S., & Morrow, J. (1991). A prospective study of depression and distress following a natural disaster: The 1989 Loma Prieta earth quake. *Journal of Personality and Social Psychology, 61,* 105–121.

Nolen-Hoeksema, S., Morrow, J., & Fredrickson, B. L. (1993). Response styles and the duration of episodes of depressed mood. *Journal of Abnormal Psychology, 102*(1), 20–28.

Nolen-Hoeksema, S., Parker, L. E., & Larson, J. (1994). Personality processes and individual differences: Ruminative coping with depressed mood following loss. *Journal of Personality and Social Psychology, 67,* 92–104.

Noller, P. (1993). Gender and emotional communication in marriage: Different cultures or differential social power? *Journal of Language and Social Psychology, 12,* 132–152.

Norcross, W. A., Ramirez, C., & Palinkas, L. A. (1996). The influence of women on the health care-seeking behavior of men. *Journal of Family Practice, 43*(5), 475–480.

Norring, C. E. A., & Sohlberg, S. S. (1993). Outcome, recovery, relapse and mortality across six years in patients with clinical eating disorders. *Acta Psychiatrica Scandinavica, 87,* 437–444.

Norton, K. I., Olds, T. S., Olive, S., & Dank, S. (1996). Ken and Barbie at life size. *Sex Roles, 34,* 287–294.

Notarius, C. I., Benson, P. R., Sloane, D., Vanzetti, N. A., & Hornyak, L. M. (1989). Exploring the interface between perception and behavior: An analysis of marital interaction in distressed and nondistressed couples. *Behavioral Assessment, 11,* 39–64.

Notzon, F. C., Komarov, Y. M., Ermakov, S. P., Sempos, C. T., Marks, J. S., & Sempos, E. V. (1998). Causes of declining life expectancy in Russia. *Journal of the American Medical Association, 279*(10), 793–800.

Nyquist, L. V., & Spence, J. T. (1986). Effects of dispositional dominance and sex role expectations on leadership behaviors. *Journal of Personality and Social Psychology, 50,* 87–93.

Offner, P. J., Moore, E. E., & Biffl, W. L. (1999). Male gender is a risk factor for major infections after surgery. *Archives of Surgery, 134,* 935–940.

Oggins, J., Veroff, J., & Leber, D. (1993). Perceptions of marital interaction among Black and White newlyweds. *Journal of Personality and Social Psychology, 65,* 494–511.

Ohannessian, C. M., Lerner, R. M., Lerner, J. V., & von Eye, A. (1999). Does self-competence predict gender differences in adolescent depression and anxiety? *Journal of Adolescence, 22,* 1–15.

Ohannessian, C. M., Lerner, R. M., von Eye, A., & Lerner, J. V. (1996). Direct and indirect relations between perceived parental acceptance, perceptions of the self, and emotional adjustment during early adolescence. *Family and Consumer Sciences Research Journal, 25*(2), 159–183.

O'Leary, V. E. (1988). Women's relationships with women in the workplace. In B. A. Gutek, A. H. Stromberg, & L. Larwood (Eds.), *Women and work: An annual review* (Vol. 3, pp. 189–213). Newbury Park, CA: Sage.

Oliver, M. B., & Hyde, J. S. (1993). Gender differences in sexuality: A meta-analysis. *Psychological Bulletin, 114,* 29–51.

Olson, B., & Douglas, W. (1997). The family on television: Evaluation of gender roles in situation comedy. *Sex Roles, 36,* 409–427.

Olson, J. E., Frieze, I. H., & Detlefson, E. G. (1990). Having it all? Combining work and family in a male and a female profession. *Sex Roles, 23,* 515–533.

O'Meara, J. D. (1989). Cross-sex friendship: Four basic challenges of an ignored relationship. *Sex Roles, 21,* 525–543.

O'Meara, J. D. (1994). Cross-sex friendship's opportunity challenge: Uncharted terrain for exploration. *Personal Relationship Issues, 2,* 4–7.

O'Neil, J. M., Helms, B. J., Gable, R. K., David, L., & Wrightsman, L. S. (1986). Gender-role conflict scale: College men's fear of femininity. *Sex Roles, 14,* 335–350.

Orford, J., & Keddie, A. (1985). Gender differences in the functions and effects of moderate and excessive drinking. *British Journal of Clinical Psychology, 24,* 265–279.

Orlofsky, J. L. (1993). Intimacy status: Theory and research. In J. E. Marcia, D. R. Matteson, J. L. Orlofsky, A. S. Waterman, & S. L. Archer (Eds.), *Ego identity: A handbook for psychosocial research* (pp. 111–133). New York: Springer-Verlag.

Oroson, P. G., & Schilling, K. M. (1992). Gender differences in college students' definitions and perceptions of intimacy. *Women and Therapy, 12*(1/2), 201–212.

Orth-Gomer, K., & Johnson, J. (1987). Social network interaction and mortality: A six-year follow-up of a random sample of the Swedish population. *Journal of Chronic Diseases, 4,* 944–957.

Ostenson, R. S. (1996). Who's in and who's out: The results of oppression. In J. C. Chrisler, C. Golden, & P. D. Rozee (Eds.), *Lectures on the psychology of women* (pp. 23–31). New York: McGraw-Hill.

Otto, M. W., & Dougher, M. J. (1985). Sex differences and personality factors in responsivity to pain. *Perceptual and Motor Skills, 61,* 383–390.

Oyserman, D., Gant, L., & Ager, J. (1995). A socially contextualized model of African American identity: Possible selves and school persistence. *Journal of Personality and Social Psychology, 69,* 1216–1232.

Ozer, E. M. (1995). The impact of childcare responsibility and self-efficacy on the psychological health of professional working mothers. *Psychology of Women Quarterly, 19,* 315–335.

Ozer, E. M., Barnett, R. C., Brennan, R. T., & Sperling, J. (1998). Does child care involvement increase or decrease distress among dual-earner couples? *Women's health: Research on Gender, Behavior, and Policy, 4*(4), 285–311.

Page, R. M., & Cole, G. E. (1992). Demoralization and living alone: Outcomes from an urban community study. *Psychological Reports, 70,* 275–280.

Page, S., & Bennesch, S. (1993). Gender and reporting differences in measures of depression. *Canadian Journal of Behavioural Science, 25,* 579–589.

Paludi, M. A., & Barickman, R. B. (1998). *Sexual harassment, work, and education.* New York: State University of New York Press.

Pampel, F. C. (1998). National context, social change and sex differences in suicide rates. *American Sociological Review, 63,* 744–758.

Parker, S., & de Vries, B. (1993). Patterns of friendship for women and men in same and cross-sex relationships. *Journal of Social and Personal Relationships, 10,* 617–626.

Parks, M. R., & Floyd, K. (1996). Meanings for closeness and intimacy in friendship. *Journal of Social and Personal Relationships, 13,* 85–107.

Parra, E. B., Arkowitz, H., Hannah, M. T., & Vasquez, A. M. (1995). Coping strategies and emotional reactions to separation and divorce in Anglo, Chicana, and Mexicana women. *Journal of Divorce and Remarriage, 23*(1/2), 117–129.

Parry, G. (1986). Paid employment, life events, social support, and mental health in working-class mothers. *Journal of Health and Social Behavior, 27,* 193–208.

Parsons, J. E., Meece, J. L., Alder, T. F., & Kaczala, C. M. (1982). Sex differences in attributions and learned helplessness. *Sex Roles, 4,* 421–432.

Parsons, T., & Bales, R. F. (1955). *Family, socialization and interaction process.* Glencoe, IL: Free Press.

Pasch, L. A., Bradbury, T. N., & Davila, J. (1997). Gender, negative affectivity, and observed social support behavior in marital interaction. *Personal Relationships, 4,* 361–378.

Passannante, M. R., & Nathanson, C. A. (1985). Female labor force participation and female mortality in Wisconsin 1974–1978. *Social Science and Medicine, 21*(6), 655–665.

Patterson, C. J. (1995). Families of the lesbian baby boom: Parents' division of labor and children's adjustment. *Developmental Psychology, 31,* 115–123.

Patton, G. C., Hibbert, M. E., Carlin, J., Shao, Q., Rosier, M., Caust, J., & Bowes, G. (1996). Menarche and the onset of depression and anxiety in Victoria, Australia. *Journal of Epidemiology and Community Health, 50,* 661–666.

Pavalko, E. K., & Woodbury, S. (2000). Social roles as process: Caregiving careers and women's health. *Journal of Health and Social Behavior, 41,* 91–105.

Paxton, S. J., & Sculthorpe, A. (1991). Disordered eating and sex role characteristics in young women: Implications for sociocultural theories of disturbed eating. *Sex Roles, 24*(9/10), 587–598.

Pence, E., & Paymar, M. (1993). *Education groups for men who batter: The Duluth model.* New York: Springer.

Pennebaker, J. W., & Roberts, T. A. (1992). Toward a his and hers theory of emotion: Gender differences in visceral perception. *Journal of Social and Clinical Psychology, 11,* 199–212.

Pennebaker, J. W., & Watson, D. (1988). Blood pressure estimation and beliefs among normotensives and hypertensives. *Health Psychology, 7,* 309–328.

Peplau, L. A. (1991). Lesbian and gay relationships. In J. C. Gonsiorek & J. D. Weinrich (Eds.), *Homosexuality: Research implications for public policy* (pp. 177–196). Newbury Park, CA: Sage.

Peplau, L. A. (1994). Men and women in love. In D. L. Sollie & L. A. Leslie (Eds.), *Gender, families, and close relationships: Feminist research journeys* (pp. 19–49). Thousand Oaks, CA: Sage.

Peplau, L. A., & Campbell, S. M. (1989). The balance of power in dating and marriage. In J. Freeman (Ed.), *Women: A feminist perspective* (pp. 121–137). Mountain View, CA: Mayfield.

Peplau, L. A., Cochran, S. D., & Mays, V. M. (1997). A national survey of the intimate relationships of African American lesbians and gay men: A look at commitment, satisfaction, sexual behavior, and HIV disease. In B. Greene (Ed.), *Ethnic and cultural diversity among lesbians and gay men* (Vol. 3, pp. 11–38). Thousand Oaks, CA: Sage.

Peplau, L. A., Cochran, S. D., Rook, K., & Padesky, C. (1978). Loving women: Attachment and autonomy in lesbian relationships. *Journal of Social Issues, 34*(3), 7–27.

Peplau, L. A., & Garnets, L. D. (2000). A new paradigm for understanding women's sexuality and sexual orientation. *Journal of Social Issues, 56,*(2), 329–350.

Peplau, L. A., & Gordon, S. L. (1985). Women and men in love: Gender differences in close heterosexual relationships. In V. E. O'Leary, R. K. Unger, & B. S. Wallston (Eds.), *Women, gender, and social psychology* (pp. 257–291). Hillsdale, NJ: Erlbaum.

Peplau, L. A., & Spalding, L. R. (2000). The close relationships of lesbians, gay men, and bisexuals. In C. Hendrick & S. S. Hendrick (Eds.), *Close relationships: A sourcebook* (pp. 111–123). Thousand Oaks, CA: Sage.

Perkins, K. A. (1996). Sex differences in nicotine versus nonnicotine reinforcement as determinants of tobacco smoking. *Experimental and Clinical Psychopharmacology, 4*(2), 166–177.

Perkins, K. A. (1999). Nicotine discrimination in men and women. *Pharmacology, Biochemistry and Behavior, 64*(2), 295–299.

Perkins, K. A., Donny, E., & Caggiula, A. R. (1999). Sex differences in nicotine effects and self-administration: Review of human and animal evidence. *Nicotine and Tobacco Research, 1,* 301–315.

Perry, D. G., & Bussey, K. (1979). The social learning theory of sex differences: Imitation is alive and well. *Journal of Personality and Social Psychology, 37,* 1699–1712.

Perry-Jenkins, M., & Folk, K. (1994). Class, couples, and conflict: Effects of the division of labor on assessment of marriage in dual-earner families. *Journal of Marriage and the Family, 56,* 165–180.

Perry-Jenkins, M., Seery, B., & Crouter, A. C. (1992). Linkages between women's provider-role attitudes, psychological well-being, and family relationships. *Psychology of Women Quarterly, 16,* 311–329.

Petersen, A. C., Sarigiani, P. A., & Kennedy, R. E. (1991). Adolescent depression: Why more girls? *Journal of Youth and Adolescence, 20,* 247–271.

Peterson, A. L. (1999). Inaccurate estimation of body weight prior to smoking cessation: Implications for quitting and weight gain. *Journal of Applied Biobehavioral Research, 4*(2), 79–84.

Peterson, C., & Villanova, P. (1988). An expanded attributional style questionnaire. *Journal of Abnormal Psychology, 97*(1), 87–89.

Peterson, C. D., Baucom, D. H., Elliott, M. J., & Farr, P. A. (1989). The relationship between sex role identity and marital adjustment. *Sex Roles, 21,* 775–787.

Pfaff, L. (1999). *Gender, differences in leadership skills.* Unpublished data.

Pike, K. M., & Striegel-Moore, R. H. (1997). Disordered eating and eating disorders. In S. J. Gallant, G. P. Keita, & R. Royak-Schaler (Eds.), *Health care for women: Psychological, social, and behavioral influences* (pp. 97–114). Washington, DC: American Psychological Association.

Pina, D. L., & Bengtson, V. L. (1993). The division of household labor and wives' happiness: Ideology, employment, and perceptions of support. *Journal of Marriage and the Family, 55,* 901–912.

Pirie, P. L., Murray, D. M., & Luepker, R. V. (1991). Gender differences in cigarette smoking and quitting in a cohort of young adults. *American Journal of Public Health, 81*(3), 324–327.

Pleck, J. H. (1987). Men in domestic settings: American fathering in historical perspective. In M. S. Kimmel (Ed.), *Changing men: New directions in research on men and masculinity* (pp. 83–97). Newbury Park, CA: Sage.

Pleck, J. H. (1993). Are family-supportive employer policies relevant to men? In J. C. Hood (Ed.), *Men, work, and family* (pp. 217–237). Newbury Park, CA: Sage.

Pleck, J. H. (1995). The gender role strain paradigm: An update. In R. F. Levant & W. S. Pollack (Eds.), *A new psychology of men* (pp. 11–32). New York: Basic Books.

Pleck, J. H., Sonenstein, F. L., & Ku, L. C. (1993a). Masculinity ideology and its correlates. In S. Oskamp & M. Costanzo (Eds.), *Gender issues in contemporary society* (pp. 85–110). Newbury Park, CA: Sage.

Pleck, J. H., Sonenstein, F. L., & Ku, L. C. (1993b). Masculinity ideology: Its impact on adolescent males' heterosexual relationships. *Journal of Social Issues, 49*(3), 11–29.

Pliner, P., & Chaiken, S. (1990). Eating, social motives, and self-presentation in women and men. *Journal of Experimental Social Psychology, 26,* 240–254.

Pohlman, E. (1969). *The psychology of birth planning.* Cambridge, MA: Schenkman.

Polce-Lynch, M., Myers, B. J., Kilmartin, C. T., Forssmann-Falck, R., & Kliewer, W. (1998). Gender and age patterns in emotional expression, body image, and self-esteem: A qualitative analysis. *Sex Roles, 38*(11/12), 1025–1048.

Pollack, W. S. (1998). *Real boys: Rescuing our sons from the myths of boyhood.* New York: Henry Holt.

Pollak, S., & Gilligan, C. (1982). Images of violence in Thematic Apperception Test stories. *Journal of Personality and Social Psychology, 42,* 159–167.

Pomerleau, A., Bolduc, D., Malcuit, G., & Cossette, L. (1990). Pink or blue: Environmental gender stereotypes in the first two years of life. *Sex Roles, 22,* 359–367.

Pomerleau, C. S., Tate, J. C., Lumley, M. A., & Pomerleau, O. F. (1994). Gender differences in prospectively versus retrospectively assessed smoking withdrawal symptoms. *Journal of Substance Abuse, 6,* 433–440.

Pope, H. G., Jr., Olivardia, R., Gruber, A., & Borowiecki, J. (1999). Evolving ideals of male body image as seen through action toys. *International Journal of Eating Disorders, 26*(1), 65–72.

Popenoe, D., & Whitehead, B. D. (1999). The state of our unions. *The social health of marriage in America* [On-line]. Available:http//marriage.rutgers.edu

Poulin, F., & Boivin, M. (2000a). Reactive and proactive aggression: Evidence of a two-factor model. *Psychological Assessment, 12*(2), 115–122.

Poulin, F., & Boivin, M. (2000b). The role of proactive and reactive aggression in the formation and development of boys' friendships. *Developmental Psychology, 36*(2), 233–240.

Poulin, F., Cillessen, A. H. N., Hubbard, J. A., Coie, J. D., Dodge, K. A., & Schwartz, D. (1997). Children's friends and behavioral similarity in two social contexts. *Behavioral Similarity and Friendship, 6*(2), 224–235.

Powell, B., & Reznikoff, M. (1976). Role conflict and symptoms of psychological distress in college-educated women. *Journal of Consulting and Clinical Psychology, 44,* 473–479.

Pratt, M. W., Golding, G., Hunter, W., & Sampson, R. (1988). Sex differences in adult moral orientations. *Journal of Personality, 56,* 373–391.

Prescott, E., Hippe, M., Schnohr, P., Hein, H. O., & Vestbo, J. (1998). Smoking and risk of myocardial infarction in women and men: Longitudinal population study. *British Medical Journal, 316,* 1043–1047.

Price, E. L., & Byers, E. S. (1999). The attitudes towards dating violence scales: Development and initial validation. *Journal of Family Violence, 14*(4), 351–375.

Prigerson, H. G., & Slimack, M. J. (1999). Gender differences in clinical correlates of suicidality among young adults. *Journal of Nervous and Mental Disease, 187*(1), 23–31.

Pryor, J. B. (1998). The Likelihood to Sexually Harass Scale. In C. M. Davis, W. H. Yarber, R. Bauserman, G. Schreer, & S. L. Davis (Eds.), *Sexuality-related measures: A compendium* (pp. 295–298). Beverly Hills, CA: Sage.

Pryor, J. B., DeSouza, E. R., Fitness, J., Hutz, C., Kumpf, M., Lubbert, K., Pesonen, O., & Erber, M. W. (1997). Gender differences in the interpretation of social-sexual behavior: A cross-cultural perspective on sexual harassment. *Journal of Cross-Cultural Psychology, 28*(5), 509–534.

Pryor, J. B., Giedd, J. L., & Williams, K. B. (1995). A social psychological model for predicting sexual harassment. *Journal of Social Issues, 51*(1), 69–84.

Pryor, J. B., Hesson-McInnis, M. S., Hitlan, R. T., Olson, M., & Hahn, E. J. (2000). *Antecedents of gender harassment: An analysis of person and situation factors.* Unpublished manuscript.

Ptacek, J. T., Smith, R. E., & Dodge, K. L. (1994). Gender differences in coping with stress: When stressor and appraisals do not differ. *Personality and Social Psychology Bulletin, 20,* 421–430.

Ptacek, J. T., Smith, R. E., & Zanas, J. (1992). Gender, appraisal, and coping: A longitudinal analysis. *Journal of Personality, 60,* 747–770.

Pugh, M. D., & Wahrman, R. (1983). Neutralizing sexism in mixed-sex groups: Do women have to be better than men? *American Journal of Sociology, 88,* 746–761.

Pugliesi, K. (1995). Work and well-being: Gender differences in the psychological consequences of employment. *Journal of Health and Social Behavior, 36,* 57–71.

Purcell, P., & Stewart, L. (1990). Dick and Jane in 1989. *Sex Roles, 22,* 177–185.

Purnine, D. M., & Carey, M. P. (1997). Interpersonal communication and sexual adjustment: The roles of understanding and agreement. *Journal of Consulting and Clinical Psychology, 65*(6), 1017–1025.

Quick, H. E., & Moen, P. (1998). Gender, employment, and retirement quality: A life course approach to the differential experiences of men and women. *Journal of Occupational Health Psychology, 3*(1), 44–64.

Quirouette, C., & Gold, D. P. (1992). Spousal characteristics as predictors of well-being in older couples. *International Journal of Aging and Human Development, 34*(4), 257–269.

Rabin, C. (1998). Gender and intimacy in the treatment of couples in the 1990s. *Sexual and Marital Therapy, 13*(2), 179–190.

Rabin, C., & Shapira-Berman, O. (1997). Egalitarianism and marital happiness: Israeli wives and husbands on a collision course? *American Journal of Family Therapy, 25*(4), 319–329.

Radloff, L. (1975). Sex differences in depression: The effects of occupation and marital status. *Sex Roles, 1,* 249–265.

Radloff, L. S. (1977). The CES-D scale: A self-report depression scale for research in the general population. *Journal of Applied Psychological Measurement, 1,* 385–401.

Radloff, L. S., & Monroe, M. K. (1978). *Sex differences in helplessness with implications for depression.* Stanford, CA: Stanford University Press.

Radloff, L. S., & Rae, D. S. (1979). Susceptibility and precipitating factors in depression: Sex differences and similarities. *Journal of Abnormal Psychology, 88,* 174–181.

Raffaelli, M., & Duckett, E. (1989). "We were just talking . . .": Conversations in early adolescence. *Journal of Youth and Adolescence, 18,* 567–582.

Rajecki, D. W., Dame, J. A., Creek, K. J., Barrickman, P. J., & Reid, C. A. (1993). Gender casting in television toy advertisements: Distributions, message content analysis, and evaluations. *Journal of Consumer Psychology, 2*(3), 307–327.

Rakowski, W., Julius, M., Hickey, T., Verbrugge, L. M., & Halter, J. B. (1988). Daily symptoms and behavioral responses: Results of a health diary with older adults. *Medical Care, 26*(3), 278–297.

Raley, R. K. (1996). A shortage of marriageable men? A note on the role of cohabitation in Black-White differences in marriage rates. *American Sociological Review, 61,* 973–983.

Ramet, S. P. (1996). *Gender reversals and gender cultures.* New York: Pointing-Green.

Rankow, E. J., & Tessaro, I. (1998a). Cervical cancer risk and papanicolaou screening in a sample of lesbian and bisexual women. *Journal of Family Practice, 47*(2), 139–143.

Rankow, E. J., & Tessaro, I. (1998b). Mammography and risk factors for breast cancer in lesbian and bisexual women. *American Journal of Health Behavior, 22*(6), 403–410.

Rauste-Von Wright, M., Von Wright, J., & Frankenhaeuser, M. (1981). Relationships between sex-related psychological characteristics during adolescence and catecholamine excretion during achievement stress. *Psychophysiology, 18*(4), 362–370.

Reed, G. M., Kemeny, M. E., Taylor, S. E., & Visscher, B. R. (1999). Negative HIV-specific expectancies and AIDS-related bereavement as predictors of symptom onset in asymptomatic HIV-positive gay men. *Health Psychology, 18,* 354–363.

Regan, P. C., & Berscheid, E. (1999). *Lust: What we know about human sexual desire.* Thousand Oaks, CA: Sage.

Regan, P. C., & Sprecher, S. (1995). Gender differences in the value of contributions to intimate relationships: Egalitarian relationships are not always perceived to be equitable. *Sex Roles, 33,* 221–237.

Reis, H. T. (1998). Gender differences in intimacy and related behaviors: Context and process. In D. J. Canary & K. Dindia (Eds.), *Sex differences and similarities in communication: Critical essays and empirical investigations of sex and gender in interaction* (pp. 203–231). Mahwah, NJ: Erlbaum.

Reis, H. T., Senchak, M., & Solomon, B. (1985). Sex differences in the intimacy of social interaction: Further examination of potential explanations. *Journal of Personality and Social Psychology, 48,* 1204–1217.

Reis, H. T., & Shaver, P. (1988). Intimacy as an interpersonal process. In S. Duck (Ed.),

Handbook of personal relationships: Theory, relationships, and interventions (pp. 367–389). Chichester, England: Wiley.

Reisman, J. M. (1990). Intimacy in same-sex friendships. *Sex Roles, 23,* 65–82.

Reitzes, D. C., & Mutran, E. J. (1994). Multiple roles and identities: Factors influencing self-esteem among middle-aged working men and women. *Social Psychology Quarterly, 57*(4), 313–325.

Rejeski, W. J., Parker, P. E., Gagne, M., & Koritnik, D. R. (1990). Cardiovascular and testosterone responses to contested dominance in women. *Health Psychology, 9,* 35–47.

Renzetti, C. M. (1987). New wave or second stage? Attitudes of college women toward feminism. *Sex Roles, 16,* 265–277.

Repetti, R. L. (1989). Effects of daily workload on subsequent behavior during marital interaction: The roles of social withdrawal and spouse support. *Journal of Personality and Social Psychology, 57,* 651–659.

Repetti, R. L. (1993). Short-term effects of occupational stressors on daily mood and health complaints. *Health Psychology, 12*(2), 125–131.

Repetti, R. L. (1994). Short-term and long-term processes linking job stressors to father-child interaction. *Social Development, 3*(1), 1–15.

Repetti, R. L., & Wood, J. (1997). Effects of daily stress at work on mothers' interactions with preschoolers. *Journal of Family Psychology, 11*(1), 90–108.

Resnick, M. D., Bearman, P. S., Blum, R. W., Bauman, K. E., Harris, K. M., Jones, J., Tabor, J., Beuhring, T., Sieving, R. E., Shew, M., Ireland, M., Bearinger, L. H., & Udry, J. R. (1997). Protecting adolescents from harm. *Journal of the American Medical Association, 278,* 823–832.

Revenson, T. A. (1994). Social support and marital coping with chronic illness. *Annals of Behavioral Medicine, 16*(2), 122–130.

Reynolds, P., & Kaplan, G. A. (1990). Social connections and risk for cancer: Prospective evidence for the Alameda County Study. *Behavioral Medicine, 16,* 101–110.

Rice, T. T. (1957). *The sythians* (2nd ed.). New York: Praeger.

Rich, A. R., Kirkpatrick-Smith, J., Bonner, R. L., & Jans, F. (1992). Gender differences in the psychosocial correlates of suicidal ideation among adolescents. *Suicide and Life-Threatening Behavior, 22*(3), 364–373.

Richards, M. H., Boxer, A. M., Petersen, A. C., & Albrecht, R. (1990). Relation of weight to body image in pubertal girls and boys from two communities. *Developmental Psychology, 26,* 313–321.

Richardson, J. T. (1997). Introduction to the study of gender differences in cognition. In P. J. Caplan & M. Crawford (Eds.), *Gender differences in human cognition* (pp. 3–29). New York: Oxford University Press.

Rich-Edwards, J. W., Manson, J. E., Hennekens, C. H., & Buring, J. E. (1995). Medical progress: The primary prevention of coronary heart disease in women. *New England Journal of Medicine, 332*(26), 1758–1766.

Riessman, C. K., & Gerstel, N. (1985). Marital dissolution and health: Do males or females have greater risk? *Social Science and Medicine, 20*(6), 627–635.

Riordan, C. (1998). The future of single-sex schools. In S. Morse (Ed.), *Separated by sex: A critical look at single-sex education for girls* (pp. 53–62). Washington, DC: American Association of University Women Educational Foundation.

Robbins, C. A., & Martin, S. S. (1993). Gender, styles of deviance, and drinking problems. *Journal of Health and Social Behavior, 34,* 302–321.

Robbins, P. R., & Tanck, R. H. (1991). Gender differences in the attribution of causes for depressed feelings. *Psychological Reports, 68,* 1209–1210.

Roberts, L. J., & Krokoff, L. J. (1990). A time-series analysis of withdrawal, hostility, and displeasure in satisfied and dissatisfied marriages. *Journal of Marriage and the Family, 52,* 95–105.

Roberts, L. R., & Petersen, A. C. (1992). The relationship between academic achievement and social self-image during early adolescence. *Journal of Early Adolescence, 12,* 197–219.

Roberts, L. R., Sarigiani, P. A., Petersen, A. C., & Newman, J. L. (1990). Gender differences in the relationship between achievement and self-image during early adolescence. *Journal of Early Adolescence, 10,* 159–175.

Roberts, T-A. (1991). Gender and the influence of evaluations on self-assessments in achievement settings. *Psychological Bulletin, 109,* 297–308.

Roberts, T-A., & Nolen-Hoeksema, S. (1989). Sex differences in reactions to evaluative feedback. *Sex Roles, 21,* 725–747.

Roberts, T-A., & Nolen-Hoeksema, S. (1994). Gender comparisons in responsiveness to others' evaluations in achievement settings. *Psychology of Women Quarterly, 18,* 221–240.

Robinson, J. P., & Godbey, G. (1999). *Time for life: The surprising ways Americans use their time.* University Park: Pennsylvania State University Press.

Rodin, J., & Ickovics, J. R. (1990). Women's health: Review and research agenda as we approach the 21st century. *American Psychologist, 45,* 1018–1034.

Rogers, S. J. (1996). Mothers' work hours and marital quality: Variations by family structure and family size. *Journal of Marriage and the Family, 58,* 606–617.

Rogers, S. J., & White, L. K. (1998). Satisfaction with parenting: The role of marital happiness, family structure, and parents' gender. *Journal of Marriage and the Family, 60,* 293–308.

Rolls, B. J., Fedoroff, I. C., & Guthrie, J. F. (1991). Gender differences in eating behavior and body weight regulation. *Health Psychology, 10,* 133–142.

Roscoe, B., Diana, M. S., & Brooks, R. H., II. (1987). Early, middle, and late adolescents' views on dating and factors influencing partner selection. *Adolescence, 22*(85), 59–68.

Rose, S. (1996a). Lesbian and gay love scripts. In E. D. Rothblum & L. A. Bond (Eds.), *Preventing heterosexism and homophobia* (pp. 151–173). Thousand Oaks, CA: Sage.

Rose, S. (1996b). Who to let in: Women in cross-race friendships. In J. C. Chrisler, C. Golden, & P. D. Rozee (Eds.), *Lectures on the psychology of women* (pp. 211–226). New York: McGraw-Hill.

Rose, S., & Frieze, I. H. (1993). Young singles' contemporary dating scripts. *Sex Roles, 28,* 499–509.

Rose, S., Zand, D., & Cini, M. A. (1993). Lesbian courtships scripts. In E. D. Rothblum

& K. A. Brehony (Eds.), *Boston marriages* (pp. 70–85). Amherst: University of Massachusetts Press.

Rose, S. M. (1985). Same- and cross-sex friendships and the psychology of homosociality. *Sex Roles, 12,* 63–74.

Rosen, B. R., & Peterson, L. (1990). Gender differences in children's outdoor play injuries: A review and an integration. *Clinical Psychology Review, 10,* 187–205.

Rosenberg, M. (1989). *Society and the adolescent self-image.* Middletown, CT: Wesleyan University Press.

Rosenbloom, A. (2000, April 16). Only a generation ago, the marathon banned women. *Boston Globe,* p. D1.

Rosenfield, S. (1980). Sex differences in depression: Do women always have higher rates? *Journal of Health and Social Behavior, 21,* 33–42.

Rosenfield, S. (1989). The effects of women's employment: Personal control and sex differences in mental health. *Journal of Health and Social Behavior, 30,* 77–91.

Rosenfield, S. (1992). The costs of sharing: Wives' employment and husbands' mental health. *Journal of Health and Social Behavior, 33,* 213–225.

Rosenthal, R. (1966). *Experimenter effects in behavioral research.* New York: Appleton-Century-Crofts.

Rosenthal, R. (1994). Parametric measures of effect size. In H. Cooper & L. V. Hedges (Eds.), *The handbook of research synthesis* (pp. 231–244). New York: Russell Sage Foundation.

Ross, C. E. (1995). Reconceptualizing marital status as a continuum of social attachment. *Journal of Marriage and the Family, 57,* 129–140.

Ross, C. E., & Bird, C. E. (1994). Sex stratification and health lifestyle: Consequence for men's and women's perceived health. *Journal of Health and Social Behavior, 35*(2), 161–178.

Ross, C. E., & Mirowsky, J. (1995). Does employment affect health? *Journal of Health and Social Behavior, 36,* 230–243.

Ross, C. E., Mirowsky, J., & Goldsteen, K. (1990). The impact of the family on health:

The decade in review. *Journal of Marriage and the Family, 52,* 1059–1078.

Ross, M., & Holmberg, D. (1992). Are wives' memories for events in relationships more vivid than their husbands' memories? *Journal of Social and Personal Relationships, 9,* 585–604.

Rotenberg, K. J., & Korol, S. (1995). The role of loneliness and gender in individuals' love styles. *Journal of Social Behavior and Personality, 10*(3), 537–546.

Roter, D., Lipkin, M., Jr., & Korsgaard, A. (1991). Sex differences in patients' and physicians' communication during primary care medical visits. *Medical Care, 29*(11), 1083–1093.

Roter, D. L., & Hall, J. A. (1997). Gender differences in patient-physician communication. In S. J. Gallant, G. P. Keita, & R. Royak-Schaler (Eds.), *Health care for women: Psychological, social, and behavioral influences* (pp. 57–71). Washington, DC: American Psychological Association.

Rothbart, M., & John, O. P. (1985). Social categorization and behavior episodes: A cognitive analysis of the effects of intergroup contact. *Journal of Social Issues, 41*(3), 81–104.

Rothbart, M. K., Hanley, D., & Albert, M. (1986). Gender differences in moral reasoning. *Sex Roles, 15,* 645–653.

Roxburgh, S. (1996). Gender differences in work and well-being: Effects of exposure and vulnerability. *Journal of Health and Social Behavior, 37,* 265–277.

Royce, J. M., Corbett, K., Sorensen, G., & Ockene, J. (1997). Gender, social pressure, and smoking cessations: The community intervention trial for smoking cessation (commit) at baseline. *Social Science and Medicine, 44*(3), 359–370.

Rubin, L. B. (1983). *Intimate strangers.* New York: Harper & Row.

Rubin, L. B. (1985). *Just friends: The role of friendship in our lives.* New York: Harper & Row.

Rubin, Z., Peplau, L. A., & Hill, C. T. (1981). Loving and leaving: Sex differences in romantic attachments. *Sex Roles, 7,* 821–835.

Rubin, J. Z., Provenzano, F. J., & Luria, Z. (1974). The eye of the beholder: Parents' views on sex of newborns. *American Journal of Orthopsychiatry, 44*(4), 512–519.

Ruble, D. N., Greulich, F., Pomerantz, E. M., & Gochberg, B. (1993). The role of gender-related processes in the development of sex differences in self-evaluation and depression. *Journal of Affective Disorders, 29*, 97–128.

Ruble, D. N., & Ruble, T. L. (1982). Sex stereotypes. In A. G. Miller (Ed.), *In the eye of the beholder: Contemporary issues in stereotyping* (pp. 188–252). New York: Praeger.

Rudolph, K. D., & Hammen, C. (1999). Age and gender as determinants of stress exposure, generation, and reactions in youngsters: A transactional perspective. *Child Development, 70*, 660–677.

Rushton, J. P. (1986). Altruism and aggression: The heritability of individual differences. *Journal of Personality and Social Psychology, 50*, 1192–1198.

Russell, A., & Owens, L. (1999). Peer estimates of school-aged boys' and girls' aggression to same- and cross-sex targets. *Social Development, 8*(3), 364–379.

Russell, D. (1990). *Rape in marriage.* Bloomington: Indiana University Press.

Rys, G. S., & Bear, G. G. (1997). Relational aggression and peer relations: Gender and developmental issues. *Merrill-Palmer Quarterly, 43*(1), 87–106.

Saal, F. E. (1996). Men's misperceptions of women's interpersonal behaviors and sexual harassment. In M. S. Stockdale (Ed.), *Sexual harassment in the workplace: Perspectives, frontiers, and response strategies* (Vol. 5, pp. 67–84). Thousand Oaks, CA: Sage.

Saal, F. E., Johnson, C. B., & Weber, N. (1989). Friendly or sexy? It may depend on whom you ask. *Psychology of Women Quarterly, 13*, 263–276.

Sack, K. (1999, July 30). Gunman kills 9, self in Atlanta shootings at 2 brokerages; His wife, 2 children also found dead. *Pittsburgh Post-Gazette*, p. A–1.

Sadker, M., & Sadker, D. (1994). *Failing at fairness: How America's schools cheat girls.* New York: Charles Scribner's Sons.

Sagrestano, L. M. (1992). Power strategies in interpersonal relationships: The effects of

expertise and gender. *Psychology of Women Quarterly, 16*, 481–495.

Samter, W., Whaley, B. B., Mortenson, S. T., & Burleson, B. R. (1997). Ethnicity and emotional support in same-sex friendship: A comparison of Asian-Americans, African-Americans, and Euro-Americans. *Personal Relationships, 4*, 413–430.

Sanchez-Hucles, J. V. (1997). Jeopardy not bonus status for African American women in the work force: Why does the myth of advantage persist? *American Journal of Community Psychology, 25*(5), 565–580.

Sandler, B. R., & Shoop, R. J. (1997). What is sexual harassment? In B. R. Sandler & R. J. Shoop (Eds.), *Sexual harassment on campus: A guide for administrators, faculty, and students* (pp. 1–21). Boston: Allyn & Bacon.

Sandstrom, M. J., & Coie, J. D. (1999). A developmental perspective on peer rejection: Mechanisms of stability and change. *Child Development, 70*, 955–966.

Santos, S. J., Bohon, L. M., & Sanchez-Sosa, J. J. (1998). Childhood family relationships, marital and work conflict, and mental health distress in Mexican immigrants. *Journal of Community Psychology, 26*(5), 491–508.

Sapadin, L. A. (1988). Friendship and gender: Perspectives of professional men and women. *Journal of Social and Personal Relationships, 5*, 387–403.

Sarason, B. R., Sarason, I. G., Hacker, T. A., & Basham, R. B. (1985). Concomitants of social support: Social skills, physical attractiveness, and gender. *Journal of Personality and Social Psychology, 49*, 469–480.

Sastry, J. (1999). Household structure, satisfaction and distress in India and the United States: A comparative cultural examination. *Journal of Comparative Family Studies, 30*(1), 135–152.

Satterfield, A. T., & Muehlenhard, C. L. (1997). The effects of an authority figure's flirtatiousness on women's and men's self-related creativity. *Psychology of Women Quarterly, 21*, 395–416.

Sayers, S. L., & Baucom, D. H. (1991). Role of femininity and masculinity in distressed couples' communication. *Journal of Personality and Social Psychology, 61,* 641–647.

Sayers, S. L., Baucom, D. H., & Tierney, A. M. (1993). Sex roles, interpersonal control, and depression: Who can get their way? *Journal of Research in Personality, 27,* 377–395.

Scaramella, T. J., & Brown, W. A. (1978). Serum testosterone and aggressiveness in hockey players. *Psychosomatic Medicine, 40*(3), 262–265.

Schiedel, D. G., & Marcia, J. E. (1985). Ego identity, intimacy, sex role orientation, and gender. *Developmental Psychology, 21,* 149–160.

Schneer, J. A., & Reitman, F. (1990). Effects of employment gaps on the careers of M. B. A.'s: More damaging for men than for women? *Academy of Management Journal, 33*(2), 391–406.

Schneider, J. A., O'Leary, A., & Jenkins, S. R. (1995). Gender, sexual orientation, and disordered eating. *Psychology and health, 10*(2), 113–128.

Schoenbach, V. J., Kaplan, B. H., Fredman, L., & Kleinbaum, D. G. (1986). Social ties and mortality in Evans County, Georgia. *American Journal of Epidemiology, 123*(4), 577–591.

Schone, B. S., & Weinick, R. M. (1998). Health-related behaviors and the benefits of marriage for elderly persons. *Gerontologist, 38*(5), 618–627.

Schuurs, A. H. W. M., & Verheul, H. A. M. (1990). Effects of gender and sex steroids on the immune response. *Journal of Steroid and Biochemistry, 35*(2), 157–172.

Schwalbe, M. L., & Staples, C. L. (1991). Gender differences in sources of self-esteem. *Social Psychology Quarterly, 54*(2), 158–168.

Sears, D. O. (1986). College sophomores in the laboratory: Influences of a narrow data base on social psychology's view of human nature. *Journal of Personality and Social Psychology, 51,* 515–530.

Seeman, T. E., Berkman, L. F., Blazer, D., & Rowe, J. W. (1994). Social ties and support and neuroendocrine function: The MacArthur studies of successful aging. *Annals of Behavioral Medicine, 16*(2), 95–106.

Seligman, M. E. P. (1992). *Helplessness: On depression, development, and death.* New York: Freeman.

Sethi, S., & Nolen-Hoeksema, S. (1997). Gender differences in internal and external focusing among adolescents. *Sex Roles, 37,* 687–700.

Seymour, E. (1995). The loss of women from science, mathematics, and engineering undergraduate majors: An explanatory account. *Science Education, 79*(4), 437–473.

Shaffer, D. R., Pegalis, L. J., & Bazzini, D. G. (1996). When boy meets girl (revisited): Gender, gender-role orientation, and prospect of future interaction as determinants of self-disclosure among same- and opposite-sex acquaintances. *Personality and Social Psychology Bulletin, 22,* 495–506.

Shajahan, P. M., & Cavanagh, J. T. O. (1998). Admission for depression among men in Scotland, 1980–95: Retrospective study. *British Medical Journal, 316,* 1496–1497.

Sharpe, M. J., & Heppner, P. P. (1991). Gender role, gender-role conflict, and psychological well-being in men. *Journal of Counseling Psychology, 38*(3), 323–330.

Sharps, M. J., Welton, A. L., & Price, J. L. (1993). Gender and task in the determination of spatial cognitive performance. *Psychology of Women Quarterly, 17,* 71–83.

Sharpsteen, D. J. (1995, April). *Sex, attachment, and infidelity: The context of jealousy.* Paper presented at a meeting of the Southwestern Psychological Association, Austin, TX.

Shaw, W. S., Patterson, T. L., Semple, S., & Grant, I. (1998). Health and well-being in retirement: A summary of theories and their implications. In M. Herson & V. B. V. Hasselt (Eds.), *Handbook of clinical geropsychology* (pp. 383–409). New York: Plenum Press.

Shaywitz, B. A., Shaywitz, S. E., Pugh, K. R., Constable, R. T., Skudlarski, P., Fulbright, R. K., Bronen, R. A., Fletcher, J. M., Shankweller, D. P., Katz, L., & Gore, J. C. (1995). Sex differences in the functional organization of the brain for language. *Nature, 373,* 607–608.

Shaywitz, S. E., Shaywitz, B. A., Fletcher, J. M., & Escobar, M. D. (1990). Prevalence of reading disability in boys and girls: Results of the Connecticut longitudinal study. *Journal of the American Medical Association, 264,* 998–1002.

Sheets, V. L., & Braver, S. L. (1999). Organizational status and perceived sexual harassment: Detecting the mediators of a null effect. *Personality and Social Psychology Bulletin, 25,* 1159–1171.

Sheffield, D., Biles, P. L., Orom, H., Maixner, W., & Sheps, D. S. (2000). Race and sex differences in cutaneous pain perception. *Psychosomatic Medicine, 62*(4), 517–523.

Shek, D. T. L. (1995). Gender differences in marital quality and well-being in Chinese married adults. *Sex Roles, 32,* 699–715.

Sheriff releases time line of Columbine shooting: The report from the 13-month investigation seems to counter claims that police officers could have saved lives had they acted more quickly. (2000, May 16). *Star Tribune,* p. 06A.

Shields, S. A. (1975). Functionalism, Darwinism, and the psychology of women: A study in social myth. *American Psychologist, 30,* 739–754.

Shifren, K., & Bauserman, R. L. (1996). The relationship between instrumental and expressive traits, health behaviors, and perceived physical health. *Sex Roles, 34,* 841–864.

Shih, M., Pittinsky, T. L., & Ambady, N. (1999). Stereotype susceptibility: Identity salience and shifts in quantitative performance. *Psychological Science, 10*(1), 80–83.

Shimai, S., Yamada, F., Masuda, K., & Tada, M. (1993). TV game play and obesity in Japanese school children. *Perceptual and Motor Skills, 76*(3, Pt. 2), 1121–1122.

Shotland, R. L., & Craig, J. M. (1988). Can men and women differentiate between friendly and sexually interested behavior? *Social Psychology Quarterly, 51*(1), 66–73.

Shriver, S. P., Bourdeau, H. A., Gubish, C. T., Tirpak, D. L., Gaither Davis, A. L., Luketich, J. D., & Siegfried, J. M. (2000). Sex-specific expression of gastrin-releasing peptied receptor: Relationship to smoking history and risk of lung cancer. *Journal of the National Cancer Institute, 92,* 24–33.

Shumaker, S. A., & Hill, D. R. (1991). Gender differences in social support and physical health. *Health Psychology, 10,* 102–111.

Shye, D., Mullooly, J. P., Freeborn, D. K., & Pope, C. R. (1995). Gender differences in the relationship between social network support and mortality: A longitudinal study of an elderly cohort. *Social Science and Medicine, 41*(7), 935–947.

Siddiqui, O., Mott, J., Anderson, T., & Flay, B. (1999). The application of Poisson random-effects regression models to the analyses of adolescents' current level of smoking. *Preventive Medicine, 29,* 92–101.

Siegal, M. (1987). Are sons and daughters treated more differently by fathers than by mothers? *Developmental Review, 7,* 183–209.

Siegel, J. M., & Kuykendall, D. H. (1990). Loss, widowhood, and psychological distress among the elderly. *Journal of Consulting and Clinical Psychology, 58,* 519–524.

Siegel, S. J., & Alloy, L. B. (1990). Interpersonal perceptions and consequences of depressive-significant other relationships: A naturalistic study of college roommates. *Journal of Abnormal Psychology, 99*(4), 361–373.

Siegfried, J. (2000, January 5). Pitt study links gene to cancer in women. *Pittsburgh Post-Gazette,* p. A-1.

Siever, M. D. (1996). The perils of sexual objectification: Sexual orientation, gender, and socioculturally acquired vulnerability to body dissatisfaction and eating disorders. In C. J. Alexander (Ed.), *Gay and lesbian mental health: A sourcebook for practitioners* (pp. 223–247). New York: Harrington Park Press.

Silberg, J., Pickles, A., Rutter, M., Hewitt, J., Simonoff, E., Maes, H., Carbonneau, R., Murrelle, L., Foley, D., & Eaves, L. (1999). The influence of genetic factors and life stress on depression among adolescent girls. *Archives of General Psychiatry, 56,* 225–232.

Silverman, I., & Eals, M. (1992). Sex differences in spatial abilities: Evolutionary theory and data. In J. H. Barkow, L. Cosmides, & J. Tooby (Eds.), *The adapted mind: Evolutionary psychology and the generation of culture* (pp. 533–549). New York: Oxford University Press.

Silverman, I. S., Vega, M., & Danner, T. A. (1993). The female murderer. In A. V. Wilson (Ed.), *Homicide: The victim/offender connection* (pp. 175–190). Cincinnati, OH: Anderson.

Silverstein, B., Carpman, S., Perlick, D., & Perdue, L. (1990). Nontraditional sex role aspirations, gender identity conflict, and disordered eating among college women. *Sex Roles, 23,* 687–695.

Silverstein, B., & Perlick, D. (1991). Gender differences in depression: Historical changes. *Sex Roles, 28,* 637–653.

Silverstein, B., & Perlick, D. (1995). *The cost of competence: Why inequality causes depression, eating disorders, and illness in women.* New York: Oxford University Press.

Silverstein, B., Perlick, D., & Clauson, J. (1993). Depression combined with somatic symptomatology among adolescent females who report concerns regarding maternal achievement. *Sex Roles, 28,* 673–653.

Simmons, R. G., & Rosenberg, F. (1975). Sex, sex roles, and self-image. *Journal of Youth and Adolescence, 4*(3), 229–258.

Simms, K. B., Knight, D. M., Jr., & Dawes, K. I. (1993). Institutional factors that influence the academic success of African-American men. *Journal of Men's Studies, 1*(3), 253–266.

Simon, R. W. (1992). Parental role strains, salience of parental identity and gender differences in psychological distress. *Journal of Health and Social Behavior, 33,* 25–35.

Simon, R. W. (1995). Gender, multiple roles, role meaning, and mental health. *Journal of Health and Social Behavior, 36,* 182–194.

Simoni-Wastila, L. (1998). Gender and psychotropic drug use. *Medical Care, 36*(1), 88–94.

Simons, A. D., Angell, K. L., Monroe, S. M., & Thase, M. E. (1993). Cognition and life stress in depression: Cognitive factors and the definition, rating, and generation of negative life events. *Journal of Abnormal Psychology, 102,* 584–591.

Simons-Morton, B., Crump, A. D., Haynie, D. L., Saylor, K. E., Eitel, P., & Yu, K. (1999). Psychosocial, school, and parent factors associated with recent smoking among early-adolescent boys and girls. *Preventive Medicine, 28,* 138–148.

Simpson, J. A., Campbell, B., & Berscheid, E. (1986). The association between romantic love and marriage: Kephart (1967) twice revisited. *Personality and Social Psychology Bulletin, 12,* 363–372.

Six, B., & Eckes, T. (1991). A closer look at the complex structure of gender stereotypes. *Sex Roles, 24*(1/2), 57–71.

Skrypnek, B. J., & Snyder, M. (1982). On the self-perpetuating nature of stereotypes about women and men. *Journal of Experimental Social Psychology, 18,* 277–291.

Sleeper, L. A., & Nigro, G. N. (1987). It's not who you are but who you're with: Self-confidence in achievement settings. *Sex Roles, 16,* 57–69.

Smith, L. L., & Reise, S. P. (1998). Gender differences on negative affectivity: An IRT study of differential item functioning on the multidimensional personality questionnaire stress reaction scale. *Journal of Personality and Social Psychology, 75,* 1350–1362.

Smith, P. A., & Midlarsky, E. (1985). Empirically derived conceptions of femaleness and maleness: A current view. *Sex Roles, 12,* 313–328.

Smith, T. W. (1994). Attitudes toward sexual permissiveness: Trends, correlates, and behavioral connections. In A. S. Rossi (Ed.), *Sexuality across the life course* (pp. 63–97). Chicago: University of Chicago Press.

Smith, T. W., Gallo, L. C., Goble, L., Ngu, L. Q., & Stark, K. A. (1998). Agency, communion, and cardiovascular reactivity during marital interaction. *Health Psychology, 17,* 537–545.

Smith-Lovin, L., & Robinson, D. T. (1992). Gender and conversational dynamics. In C. Ridgeway (Ed.), *Gender, interaction, and inequality* (pp. 122–156). New York: Springer-Verlag.

Smolak, L., & Levine, M. P. (1996). Adolescent transitions and the development of eating problems. In L. Smolak, M. P. Levine, & R. Striegel-Moore (Eds.), *The developmental psychopathology of eating disorders* (pp. 207–233). Mahwah, NJ: Erlbaum.

Smolak, L., & Striegel-Moore, R. (1996). The implications of developmental research for eating disorders. In L. Smolak & M. P. Levine (Eds.), *The developmental psychopathology of eating disorders: Implications for research, prevention, and treatment* (pp. 183–203). Mahwah, NJ: Erlbaum.

Snell, W. E., Jr. (1986). The Masculine Role Inventory: Components and correlates. *Sex Roles, 15,* 443–455.

Snell, W. E., Jr., Miller, R. S., Belk, S. S., Garcia-Falconi, R., & Hernandez-Sanchez, J. E. (1989). Men's and women's emotional disclosures: The impact of disclosure recipient, culture, and the masculine role. *Sex Roles, 21,* 467–486.

Snodgrass, S. E. (1985). Women's intuition: The effect of subordinate role on interpersonal sensitivity. *Journal of Personality and Social Psychology, 49,* 146–155.

Snodgrass, S. E., Hecht, M. A., & Ploutz-Snyder, R. (1998). Interpersonal sensitivity: Expressivity or perceptivity? *Journal of Personality and Social Psychology, 74,* 238–249.

Snodgrass, S. E., & Rosenthal, R. (1984). Females in charge: Effects of sex of subordinate and romantic attachment status upon self-ratings of dominance. *Journal of Personality, 52*(4), 355–371.

Snyder, M. (1979). Self-monitoring processes. In L. Berkowitz (Ed.), *Advances in experimental social psychology* (Vol. 12, pp. 85–128). New York: Academic Press.

Snyder, M., Tanke, E. D., & Berscheid, E. (1977). Social perception and interpersonal behavior: On the self-fulfilling nature of social stereotypes. *Journal of Personality and Social Psychology, 35,* 656–666.

Sobieraj, S. (1998). Taking control: Toy commercials and the social construction of patriarchy. In L. H. Bowker (Ed.), *Masculinities and violence* (pp. 15–28). Thousand Oaks, CA: Sage.

Sochting, I., Skoe, E. E., & Marcia, J. E. (1994). Care-oriented moral reasoning and prosocial behavior: A question of gender or sex role orientation. *Sex Roles, 31,* 131–147.

Sorenson, G., Pirie, P., Folsom, A., Luepker, R., Jacobs, D., & Gillum, R. (1985). Sex differences in the relationship between work and health: The Minnesota Heart Survey. *Journal of Health and Social Behavior, 26,* 379–394.

Sorenson, S. B., & Siegel, J. M. (1992). Gender, ethnicity, and sexual assault: Findings from a Los Angeles study. *Journal of Social Issues, 48*(1), 93–104.

South, S. J., & Spitze, G. (1994). Housework in marital and nonmarital households. *American Sociological Review, 59,* 327–347.

Spence, J. T., & Buckner, C. E. (2000). Instrumental and expressive traits, trait stereotypes, and sexist attitudes: What do they signify? *Psychology of Women Quarterly, 24,* 44–62.

Spence, J. T., & Helmreich, R. L. (1972). The Attitudes Toward Women Scale: An objective instrument to measure attitudes toward the rights and roles of women in contemporary society. *JSAS Catalog of Selected Documents in Psychology, 2,* 667–668.

Spence, J. T., Helmreich, R. L., & Holahan, C. K. (1979). Negative and positive components of psychological masculinity and femininity and their relationships to self-reports of neurotic and acting out behaviors. *Journal of Personality and Social Psychology, 37*(10), 1673–1682.

Spence, J. T., Helmreich, R. L., & Stapp, J. (1974). The Personal Attributes Questionnaire: A measure of sex role stereotypes and masculinity-femininity. *JSAS Catalog of Selected Documents in Psychology, 43,* Ms. no. 617.

Spence, J. T., & Sawin, L. L. (1985). Images of masculinity and femininity: A reconceptualization. In V. E. O'Leary, R. K. Unger, & B. S. Wallston (Eds.), *Sex, gender and social psychology* (pp. 35–66). Hillsdale, NJ: Erlbaum.

Spillman, B., Spillman, R., & Reinking, K. (1981). Leadership emergence: Dynamic analysis of the effects of sex and androgyny. *Small Group Behavior, 12*(2), 139–157.

Spitze, G. D., & Waite, L. J. (1981). Wives' employment: The role of husbands' perceived attitudes. *Journal of Marriage and the Family, 43,* 117–124.

Sprague, J., & Quadagno, D. (1989). Gender and sexual motivation: An exploration of two assumptions. *Journal of Psychology and Human Sexuality, 2*(1), 57–76.

Sprecher, S. (1992). How men and women expect to feel and behave in response to inequity in close relationships. *Social Psychology Quarterly, 55*(1), 57–69.

Sprecher, S. (1994). Two sides to the breakup of dating relationships. *Personal Relationships, 1,* 199–222.

Sprecher, S., Aron, A., Hatfield, E., Cortese, A., Potapova, E., & Levitskaya, A. (1994). Love: American style, Russian style, and Japanese style. *Personal Relationships, 1,* 349–369.

Sprecher, S., Barbee, A., & Schwartz, P. (1995). Was is good for you, too?: Gender differences in first sexual intercourse experiences. *Journal of Sex Research, 32*(1), 3–15.

Sprecher, S., & Felmlee, D. (1997). The balance of power in romantic heterosexual couples over time from "his" and "her" perspectives. *Sex Roles, 37,* 361–379.

Sprecher, S., & Hatfield, E. (1996). Premarital sexual standards among U. S. college students: Comparison with Russian and Japanese students. *Archives of Sexual Behavior, 25*(3), 261–288.

Sprecher, S., & McKinney, K. (1993). *Sexuality.* Newbury Park, CA: Sage.

Sprecher, S., & Metts, S. (1989). Development of the Romantic Beliefs Scale and examination of the effects of gender and gender-role orientation. *Journal of Social and Personal Relationships, 6,* 387–411.

Sprecher, S., & Regan, P. C. (1996). College virgins: How men and women perceive their sexual status. *Journal of Sex Research, 33*(10), 3–15.

Sprecher, S., Regan, P. C., & McKinney, K. (1998). Beliefs about the outcomes of extramarital sexual relationships as a function of the gender of the cheating spouse. *Sex Roles, 38,* 301–311.

Sprecher, S., Regan, P. C., McKinney, K., Maxwell, K., & Wazienski, R. (1997). Preferred level of sexual experience in a date or mate: The merger of two methodologies. *Journal of Sex Research, 34*(4), 327–337.

Sprecher, S., & Sedikides, C. (1993). Gender differences in perceptions of emotionality: The case of close heterosexual relationships. *Sex Roles, 28,* 511–530.

Sprecher, S., Sullivan, Q., & Hatfield, E. (1994). Mate selection preferences: Gender differences examined in a national sample. *Journal of Personality and Social Psychology, 66,* 1074–1080.

Springer, S. P., & Deutsch, G. (1981). *Left brain, right brain.* New York: Freeman.

Sprock, J. (1996). Abnormality ratings of the *DSM-III-R* personality disorder criteria for males vs. females. *Journal of Nervous and Mental Disease, 184*(5), 314–316.

Stack, C. B. (1997). Different voices, different visions: Gender, culture, and moral reasoning. In M. B. Zinn, P. Hondagneu-Sotelo, & M. A. Messner (Eds.), *Through the prism of difference: readings on sex and gender* (pp. 51–57). Boston: Allyn & Bacon.

Stack, S. (1998a). Gender, marriage, and suicide acceptability: A comparative analysis. *Sex Roles, 38,* 501–520.

Stack, S. (1998b). Marriage, family, and loneliness: A cross-national study. *Sociological Perspectives, 41*(2), 415–432.

Stangor, C., & McMillan, D. (1992). Memory for expectancy-congruent and expectancy-incongruent information: A review of the social and social developmental literatures. *Psychological Bulletin, 111,* 42–61.

Stanley, T. D., & Jarrell, S. B. (1998). Gender wage discrimination bias? A meta-regression analysis. *Journal of Human Resources, 33*(4), 947–973.

Staples, R. (1978). Masculinity and race: The dual dilemma of Black men. *Journal of Social Issues, 34*(1), 169–183.

Staples, R. (1995). Health among Afro-American males. In D. F. Sabo & D. F. Gordon (Eds.), *Research on men and masculinities series* (Vol. 8, pp. 121–138). Thousand Oaks, CA: Sage.

Steele, J., & Barling, J. (1996). Influence of maternal gender-role beliefs and role satisfaction on daughters' vocational interests. *Sex Roles, 34,* 637–648.

Steering Committee of the Physicians' Health Study Research Group. (1988). Preliminary report: Findings from the aspirin component of the ongoing physicians' health study. *New England Journal of Medicine, 318*(4), 262–264.

Steil, J. M., & Hillman, J. L. (1993). The perceived value of direct and indirect influence strategies: A cross-cultural comparison. *Psychology of Women Quarterly, 17,* 457–462.

Steil, J. M., & Weltman, K. (1992). Influence strategies at home and at work: A study of sixty dual career couples. *Journal of Social and Personal Relationships, 9,* 65–88.

Stein, A. H., & Bailey, M. M. (1973). The socialization of achievement orientation in females. *Psychological Bulletin, 80,* 345–366.

Stein, J. A., Newcomb, M. D., & Bentler, P. M. (1992). The effect of agency and communality on self-esteem: Gender differences in longitudinal data. *Sex Roles, 26*, 465–483.

Stein, P. J. (1986). Men and their friendships. In R. A. Lewis & R. E. Salt (Eds.), *Men in families* (pp. 261–269). Beverly Hills, CA: Sage.

Steinberg, N. (1998, February 8). Class of 2001 has confidence, computer skills. *Chicago Sun-Times*, p. 6.

Steinhausen, H. C., Rauss-Mason, C., & Seidel, R. (1991). Follow-up studies of anorexia nervosa: A review of four decades of outcome research. *Psychological Medicine, 21*, 447–454.

Stephan, W. G., Ageyev, V., Coates-Shrider, L., Stephan, C. W., & Abalakina, M. (1994). On the relationship between stereotypes and prejudice: An international study. *Personality and Social Psychology Bulletin, 20*, 277–284.

Stephan, W. G., & Stephan, C. W. (1993). Cognition and affect in stereotyping: Parallel interactive network. In D. M. Mackie & D. L. Hamilton (Eds.), *Affect, cognition, and stereotyping: Interactive processes in group perception* (pp. 111–136). Santa Barbara, CA: Academic Press.

Stets, J. E., & Straus, M. A. (1990). Gender differences in reporting marital violence and its medical and psychological consequences. In M. A. Straus, R. J. Gelles, & C. Smith (Eds.), *Physical violence in American families: Risk factors and adaptations to violence in 8,145 families* (pp. 151–165). New Brunswick, NJ: Transaction.

Stevens, G., Owens, D., & Schaefer, E. C. (1990). Education and attractiveness in marriage choices. *Social Psychology Quarterly, 53*(1), 62–70.

Stier, D. S., & Hall, J. A. (1984). Gender differences in touch: An empirical and theoretical review. *Journal of Personality and Social Psychology, 47*, 440–459.

Stillion, J. M. (1995). Premature death among males. In D. Sabo & D. F. Gordon (Eds.), *Men's health and illness: Gender, power, and the body* (pp. 46–67). Thousand Oaks, CA: Sage.

Stipek, D. J., & Gralinski, J. H. (1991). Gender differences in children's achievement-related beliefs and emotional responses to success and failure in mathematics. *Journal of Educational Psychology, 83*(3), 361–371.

Stokes, J. P., & Wilson, D. G. (1984). The Inventory of Socially Supportive Behaviors: Dimensionality, prediction, and gender differences. *American Journal of Community Psychology, 12*(1), 53–69.

Stone, A. A., & Neale, J. M. (1984). New measure of daily coping: Development and preliminary results. *Journal of Personality and Social Psychology, 46*, 892–906.

Straus, M. A. (1990a). Ordinary violence, child abuse, and wife beating: What do they have in common? In M. A. Straus, R. J. Gelles, & C. Smith (Eds.), *Physical violence in American families: Risk factors and adaptations to violence in 8,145 families* (pp. 403–424). New Brunswick, NJ: Transaction.

Straus, M. A. (1990b). Social stress and marital violence in a national sample of American families. In M. A. Straus, R. J. Gelles, & C. Smith (Eds.), *Physical violence in American families: Risk factors and adaptations to violence in 8,145 families* (pp. 181–201). New Brunswick, NJ: Transaction.

Straus, M. A., & Gelles, R. J. (1990a). How violent are American families? Estimates from the national family violence resurveyed and other studies. In M. A. Straus, R. J. Gelles, & C. Smith (Eds.), *Physical violence in American families: Risk factors and adaptations to violence in 8,145 families* (pp. 95–112). New Brunswick, NJ: Transaction.

Straus, M. A., & Gelles, R. J. (1990b). Societal change and change in family violence from 1975 to 1985 as revealed by two national surveys. In M. A. Straus, R. J. Gelles, & C. Smith (Eds.), *Physical violence in American families: Risk factors and adaptations to violence in 8,145 families* (pp. 113–131). New Brunswick, NJ: Transaction.

Straus, M. A., Gelles, R. J., & Steinmetz, S. K. (1980). *Behind closed doors: Violence in the American family.* Garden City, NY: Anchor Books.

Straus, M. A., & Smith, C. (1990). Violence in Hispanic families in the United States: Incidence rates and structural interpretation. In

M. A. Straus, R. J. Gelles, & C. Smith (Eds.), *Physical violence in American families: Risk factors and adaptations to violence in 8,145 families* (pp. 341–367). New Brunswick, NJ: Transaction.

Strauss, J., Muday, T., McNall, K., & Wong, M. (1997). Response style theory revisited: Gender differences and stereotypes in rumination and distraction. *Sex Roles, 36,* 771–792.

Strickland, B. R. (1988). Sex-related differences in health and illness. *Psychology of Women Quarterly, 12,* 381–399.

Stroebe, M. S., & Stroebe, W. (1983). Who suffers more? Sex differences in health risks of the widowed. *Psychological Bulletin, 93,* 279–301.

Strong, E. K. J. (1936). Interests of men and women. *Journal of Social Psychology, 7,* 49–67.

Struckman-Johnson, C., & Struckman-Johnson, D. (1994). Men pressured and forced into sexual experience. *Archives of Sexual Behavior, 23*(1), 93–114.

Sussman, S., Dent, C. W., Nezami, E., Stacy, A. W., Burton, D., & Flay, B. R. (1998). Reasons for quitting and smoking temptation among adolescent smokers: Gender differences. *Substance Use and Misuse, 33*(14), 2703–2720.

Swain, S. (1989). Covert intimacy: Closeness in men's friendships. In B. J. Risman & P. Schwartz (Eds.), *Gender in intimate relationships: A microstructural approach* (pp. 71–86). Belmont, CA: Wadsworth.

Sweeting, H. (1995). Reversals of fortune? Sex differences in health in childhood and adolescence. *Social Science and Medicine, 40*(1), 77–90.

Swerczek, M. (1999). Copycat killing suit is facing test. *Times-Picaynue* [On-line]. Available: http://proquest.umi.com

Swim, J. K. (1994). Perceived versus meta-analytic effect sizes: An assessment of the accuracy of gender stereotypes. *Journal of Personality and Social Psychology, 66,* 21–36.

Swim, J. K., Aikin, K. J., Hall, W. S., & Hunter, B. A. (1995). Sexism and racism: Old-fashioned and modern prejudices. *Journal of Personality and Social Psychology, 68,* 199–214.

Swim, J. K., & Sanna, L. J. (1996). He's skilled, she's lucky: A meta-analysis of observers' attributions for women's and men's successes and failures. *Personality and Social Psychology Bulletin, 22,* 507–519.

Szinovacz, M. (1987). Preferred retirement timing and retirement satisfaction in women. *International Journal of Aging and Human Development, 24*(4), 301–317.

Szinovacz, M., & Washo, C. (1992). Gender differences in exposure to life events and adaptation to retirement. *Journal of Gerontology Social Sciences, 47*(4), S191–S196.

Tamres, L. K., Janicki, D., & Helgeson, V. S. (2001). *Sex difference in coping behavior: A meta-analytic review:* Manuscript submitted for publication.

Tangri, S. S., Burt, M. R., & Johnson, L. B. (1982). Sexual harassment at work: Three explanatory models. *Journal of Social Issues, 38*(4), 33–54.

Tangri, S. S., & Hayes, S. M. (1997). Theories of sexual harassment. In W. O'Donohue (Ed.), *Sexual harassment: Theory, research, and treatment* (pp. 112–128). Needham Heights, MA: Allyn & Beacon.

Tannen, D. (1990). *You just don't understand: Women and men in conversation.* New York: William Morrow.

Tavris, C. (1999). The science and politics of gender research: The meanings of difference. In D. Berstein (Ed.), *Gender and motivation* (Vol. 45, pp. 1–23). Lincoln: University of Nebraska Press.

Tavris, C., & Wade, C. (1984). *The longest war: Sex differences in perspective.* San Diego: Harcourt Brace Jovanovich.

Taylor, S. E., & Hall, J. A. (1982). Psychological androgyny: Theories, methods, and conclusions. *Psychological Bulletin, 92,* 347–366.

Taylor, S. E., Klein, L. C., Lewis, B. P., Gruenewald, T. L., Gurung, R. A. R., & Updegraff, J. A. (2000). Biobehavioral responses to stress in females: Tend-and-befriend, not fight-or-flight. *Psychological Review, 107,* 411–429.

Taylor, W. C., Ayars, C. L., Gladney, A. P., Peters, R. J., Jr., Roy, J. R., Prokhorov, A. V., Chamberlain, R. M., & Gritz, E. R. (1999). Beliefs about smoking among adolescents–Gender and ethnic differences. *Journal of*

Child and Adolescent Substance Abuse, 8(3), 37–54.

Terman, L. M., & Miles, C. C. (1936). *Sex and personality: Studies in masculinity and femininity.* New York: McGraw-Hill.

Tevlin, J. (1998, November 29). The Eveleth Mines case. *Star Tribune* [On-line]. Available: http://web.lexis-nexis.com/universe/docu

Thoits, P. A. (1991). Gender differences in coping with emotional distress. In J. Eckenrode (Ed.), *The social context of coping* (pp. 107–138). New York: Plenum Press.

Thoits, P. A. (1992). Identity structures and psychological well-being: Gender and marital status comparisons. *Social Psychology Quarterly, 55*(3), 236–256.

Thompson, C. A., Klopf, D. W., & Ishii, S. (1991). A comparison of social style between Japanese and Americans. *Communication Research Reports, 8,* 165–172.

Thompson, J. K., & Heinberg, L. J. (1999). The media's influence on body image disturbance and eating disorders: We've reviled them, now can we rehabilitate them? *Journal of Social Issues, 55*(2), 339–353.

Thompson, J. M., Whiffen, V. E., & Blain, M. D. (1995). Depressive symptoms, sex and perceptions of intimate relationships. *Journal of Social and Personal Relationships, 12*(1), 49–66.

Thompson, L. (1991). Family work: Women's sense of fairness. *Journal of Family Issues, 12*(2), 181–196.

Thompson, R. A. (1998). The last word. *Eating Disorders, 6,* 207–210.

Thompson, R. A., & Sherman, R. T. (1999). Athletes, athletic performance, and eating disorders: Healthier alternatives. *Journal of Social Issues, 55*(2), 317–337.

Tiger, L. (1969). *Men in groups.* New York: Random House.

Timmers, M., Fischer, A. H., & Manstead, A. S. R. (1998). Gender differences in motives for regulating emotions. *Personality and Social Psychology Bulletin, 24,* 974–985.

Tolson, A. (1977). *The limits of masculinity.* New York: Harper & Row.

Tornstam, L. (1992). Loneliness in marriage. *Journal of Social and Personal Relationships, 9,* 197–217.

Tower, R. B., & Kasl, S. V. (1996). Gender, marital closeness, and depressive symptoms in elderly couples. *Journal of Gerontology, 51B*(3), 115–129.

Townsend, J. M. (1989). Mate selection criteria: A pilot study. *Ethology and Sociobiology, 10,* 241–253.

Tracy, D. M. (1987). Toys, spatial ability and science and mathematics achievement: Are they related? *Sex Roles, 17,* 115–138.

Travis, C. B. (1988). *Women and health psychology: Biomedical issues.* Hillsdale, NJ: Erlbaum.

Tschann, J. M. (1988). Self-disclosure in adult friendship: Gender and marital status differences. *Journal of Social and Personal Relationships, 5,* 65–81.

Tsui, L. (1998). The effects of gender, education, and personal skills self-confidence on income in business management. *Sex Roles, 38,* 363–373.

Turi, Z. G., Stone, P. H., Muller, J. E., Parker, C., Rude, R. E., Raabe, D. E., Jaffe, A. S., Hartwell, T. D., Robertson, T. L., & Braunwald, E. (1986). Implications for acute intervention related to time of hospital arrival in acute myocardial infarction. *American Journal of Cardiology, 58*(3), 203–209.

Turner, C. W., Layton, J. F., & Simons, L. S. (1975). Naturalistic studies of aggressive behavior: Aggressive stimuli, victim visibility, and horn honking. *Journal of Personality and Social Psychology, 31,* 1098–1107.

Turner, H. A. (1994). Gender and social support: Taking the bad with the good? *Sex Roles, 30,* 521–541.

Turner, R. A., Altemus, M., Enos, T., Cooper, B., & McGuinness, T. (1999). Preliminary research on plasma oxytocin in normal cycling women: Investigating emotion and interpersonal distress. *Psychiatry, 62*(2), 97–113.

Turner, R. J., & Avison, W. R. (1989). Gender and depression: Assessing exposure and vulnerability to life events in a chronically strained population. *Journal of Nervous and Mental Disease, 177*(8), 443–455.

Turner, T. (with Loder, K.). (1986). *I, Tina: My life story.* New York: Morrow.

Twenge, J. M. (1997a). Attitudes toward women, 1970–1995. *Psychology of Women Quarterly, 21,* 35–51.

Twenge, J. M. (1997b). Changes in masculine and feminine traits over time: A meta-analysis. *Sex Roles, 36*, 305–325.

Ucko, L. G. (1994). Culture and violence: The interaction of Africa and America. *Sex Roles, 31*, 185–201.

Udry, J. R., Morris, N. M., & Kovenock, J. (1995). Androgen effects on women's gendered behaviour. *Journal of Biosocial Science, 27*, 359–368.

Ullman, S. E., Karabatsos, G., & Koss, M. P. (1999). Alcohol and sexual assault in a national sample of college women. *Journal of Interpersonal Violence, 14*(6), 603–625.

Umberson, D. (1987). Family status and health behaviors: Social control as a dimension of social integration. *Journal of Health and Social Behavior, 28*, 306–319.

Umberson, D., & Gove, W. R. (1989). Parenthood and psychological well-being. *Journal of Family Issues, 10*(4), 440–462.

Umberson, D., Wortman, C. B., & Kessler, R. C. (1992). Widowhood and depression: Explaining long-term gender differences in vulnerability. *Journal of Health and Social Behavior, 33*, 10–24.

Unger, R. K. (1990). Imperfect reflections on reality: Psychology constructs gender. In R. T. Hare-Mustin & J. Marecek (Eds.), *Making a difference: Psychology and the construction of gender* (pp. 102–149). New Haven, CT: Yale University Press.

United States Department of Justice. (1994). *Criminal victimization in the United States.* Washington, DC: Bureau of Justice Statistics.

United States Merit Systems Protection Board. (1981). *Sexual harassment in the federal workplace: Is it a problem?* Washington, DC: U.S. Government Printing Office.

United States Merit Systems Protection Board. (1988). *Sexual harassment in the federal workplace: An update.* Washington, DC: U.S. Government Printing Office.

United States Merit Systems Protection Board. (1995). *Sexual harassment in the federal workplace: Trends, progress, continuing challenges.* Washington, DC: U.S. Government Printing Office.

Unruh, A. M. (1996). Gender variations in clinical pain experience. *Pain, 65*, 123–167.

Updegraff, K. A., Eccles, J. S., Barber, B. L., & O'Brien, K. M. (1996). Course enrollment as self-regulatory behavior: Who takes optional high school math courses? *Learning and Individual Differences, 8*(3), 239–259.

Urberg, K. A., Degirmencioglu, S. M., Tolson, J. M., & Halliday-Scher, K. (1995). The structure of adolescent peer networks. *Developmental Psychology, 31*, 540–547.

U.S. Bureau of Census. (1993). *Current Population Reports.* Washington, DC: United States Government Printing Office.

U.S. Census Bureau. (1998). *Statistical abstracts of the United States: 1998.* Washington, DC: United States Government Printing Office.

U.S. Census Bureau. (1999). *Statistical Abstract of the United States: 1999* (119th ed.). Washington, DC: United States Government Printing Office.

U.S. Department of Health and Human Services. (1990). *The health benefits of smoking cessation (DHHS Publication No. CDC 90–8416).* Rockville, MD: Public Health Service, Center for Disease Control, Center for Chronic Disease Prevention and Health Promotion, Office on Smoking Health.

U.S. Department of Health and Human Services. (1996). *Physical activity and health: A report of the Surgeon General.* Atlanta, GA: U.S. Department of Health and Human Services, Centers for Disease Control and Prevention, National Center for Chronic Disease Prevention and Health Promotion.

U.S. Department of Health and Human Services. (1998a). *National survey results on drug use from the Monitoring the Future study, 1975–1997* (Vol. I Secondary School Students). Rockville, MD: U.S. Department of Health and Human Services, Public Health Service, National Institutes of Health.

U.S. Department of Health and Human Services. (1998b). *National survey results on drug use from the Monitoring the Future study, 1975–1997* (Vol. 2 College Students and Young Adults). Rockville, MD: U.S. Department of Health and Human Services, Public Health Service, National Institutes of Health.

U.S. Department of Health and Human Services. (1998c). *Tobacco use among U.S.*

racial/ethnic minority groups–African Americans, American Indians and Alaska Americans, Asian Americans and Pacific Islanders, and Hispanics: A report of the Surgeon General. Atlanta, Georgia: U.S. Department of Health and Human Services, Centers for Disease Control and Prevention, National Center for Chronic Disease Prevention and Health Promotion, Office on Smoking and Health.

U.S. Department of Health and Human Services, & Substance Abuse and Mental Health Services Administration. (1999a). *National household survey on drug abuse: Population estimates 1998.* Rockville, MD: Author.

U.S. Department of Health and Human Services, & Substance Abuse and Mental Health Services Administration. (1999b). *Summary of findings from the 1998 national household survey on drug abuse.* Rockville, MD: Author.

U.S. Department of Justice, & Bureau of Justice Statistics. (1998). Table 3.142: Suicide rate (per 100,000 persons in each age group) for persons 10 years of age and older. In K. McGuire & A. L. Pastore (Eds.), *Sourcebook of Criminal Justice Statistics* (pp. 299). Washington, DC: U.S. Government Printing Office.

U.S. Department of Labor, & Bureau of Labor Statistics. (1998). Job-related deaths are less likely for women. *Monthly Labor Review* [On-line]. Available: http://stats.bls.gov/opub/ted/tedhome.html

U.S. Department of Transportation. (1998). *Driving after drug or alcohol use: Findings from the 1996 National Household Survey on Drug Abuse.* Rockville, MD: Department of Health and Human Services, Substance Abuse and Mental Health Services Administration.

U.S. Department of Transportation. (1999). *Traffic safety facts 1998.* Washington, DC: National Highway Traffic Safety Administration.

Uvnas-Moberg, K. (1997). Oxytocin linked anti-stress effects–the relaxation and growth response. *Acta Physiologica Scandinavica, 640,* 38–42.

Valentine, S. (1998). Self-esteem and men's negative stereotypes of women who work. *Psychological Reports, 83,* 920–922.

Valian, V. (1998). *Why so slow?: The advancement of women.* Cambridge, MA: MIT Press.

Vanfossen, B. E. (1981). Sex differences in the mental health effects of spouse support and equity. *Journal of Health and Social Behavior, 22,* 130–143.

Vangelisti, A. L., & Daly, J. A. (1997). Gender differences in standards for romantic relationships. *Personal Relationships, 4,* 203–219.

Vazquez-Nuttall, E., Romero-Garcia, I., & de Leon, B. (1987). Sex roles and perceptions of femininity and masculinity of Hispanic women. *Psychology of Women Quarterly, 11,* 409–425.

Veevers, J. E., & Gee, E. M. (1986). Playing it safe: Accident mortality and gender roles. *Sociological Focus, 19*(4), 349–360.

Veiel, H. O. F., Kuhner, C., Brill, G., & Ihle, W. (1992). Psychosocial correlates of clinical depression after psychiatric in-patient treatment: Methodological issues and baseline differences between recovered and non-recovered patients. *Psychological Medicine, 22,* 415–427.

Veniegas, R. C., & Conley, T. D. (2000). Biological research on women's sexual orientations: Evaluating the scientific evidence. *Journal of Social Issues, 56*(2), 267–282.

Veniegas, R. C., & Peplau, L. A. (1997). Power and the quality of same-sex friendships. *Psychology of Women Quarterly, 21,* 279–297.

Verbrugge, L. M. (1983a). Multiple roles and physical health of women and men. *Journal of Health and Social Behavior, 24,* 16–30.

Verbrugge, L. M. (1983b). A research note on adult friendship contact: A dyadic perspective. *Social Forces, 62*(1), 78–83.

Verbrugge, L. M. (1984). How physicians treat mentally distressed men and women. *Social Science and Medicine, 18*(1), 1–9.

Verbrugge, L. M. (1985). Gender and health: An update on hypotheses and evidence. *Journal of Health and Social Behavior, 26,* 156–182.

Verbrugge, L. M. (1989). The twain meet: Empirical explanations of sex differences in health and mortality. *Journal of Health and Social Behavior, 30,* 282–304.

Verkuyten, M., & Masson, K. (1996). Culture and gender differences in the perception of friendship by adolescents. *International Journal of Psychology, 31*(5), 207–217.

Vingerhoets, A. J. J. M., & Van Heck, G. L. (1990). Gender, coping and psychosomatic symptoms. *Psychological Medicine, 20,* 125–135.

Vinick, B. H., & Ekerdt, D. J. (1989). Retirement: What happens to husband-wife relationships? *Journal of Geriatric Psychiatry, 24,* 23–40.

Vonk, R., & van Nobelen, D. (1993). Masculinity and femininity in the self with an intimate partner: Men are not always men in the company of women. *Journal of Social and Personal Relationships, 10,* 627–630.

Voyer, D., Voyer, S., & Bryden, M. P. (1995). Magnitude of sex differences in spatial abilities: A meta-analysis and consideration of critical variables. *Psychological Bulletin, 117,* 250–270.

Wadsworth, M. E. J., Montgomery, S. M., & Bartley, M. J. (1999). The persisting effect of unemployment on health and social well-being in men early in working life. *Social Science and Medicine, 48,* 1491–1499.

Wagner, B. M., & Compas, B. E. (1990). Gender, instrumentality, and expressivity: Moderators of the relation between stress and psychological symptoms during adolescence. *American Journal of Community Psychology, 18*(3), 383–406.

Wagner, W., Kirchler, E., Clack, F., Tekarslan, E., & Verma, J. (1990). Male dominance, role segregation, and spouses' interdependence in conflict. *Journal of Cross-Cultural Psychology, 21*(1), 48–70.

Waite, L. J. (1995). Does marriage matter? *Demography, 32*(4), 483–507.

Waldfogel, J. (1997a). The effect of children on women's wages. *American Sociological Review, 62,* 209–217.

Waldfogel, J. (1997b). Working mothers then and now: A cross-cohort analysis of the effects of maternity leave on women's pay. In F. D. Blau & R. G. Ehrenberg (Eds.), *Gender and family issues in the work place* (pp. 92–126). New York: Russell Sage Foundation.

Waldron, I. (1983a). Sex differences in human mortality: The role of genetic factors. *Social Science and Medicine, 17*(6), 321–333.

Waldron, I. (1983b). Sex differences in illness incidence, prognosis and mortality: Issues and evidence. *Social Science and Medicine, 17*(16), 1107–1123.

Waldron, I. (1991). Patterns and causes of gender differences in smoking. *Social Science and Medicine, 32*(9), 989–1005.

Waldron, I. (1995a). Contributions of biological and behavioural factors to changing sex differences in ishemic heart disease mortality. In A. Lopez, G. Caselli, & T. Valkonen (Eds.), *Adult mortality in developed countries* (pp. 161–178). New York: Oxford University Press.

Waldron, I. (1995b). Contributions of changing gender differences in behavior and social roles to changing gender differences in mortality. In D. Sabo (Ed.), *Men's health and illness: Gender, power, and the body* (pp. 22–45). Thousand Oaks, CA: Sage.

Waldron, I. (1997). Changing gender roles and gender differences in health behavior. In D. S. Gochman (Ed.), *Handbook of health behavior research: I. Personal and social determinants* (pp. 303–328). New York: Plenum Press.

Waldron, I. (1998). Factors determining the sex ratio at birth. In Department of Economic and Social Affairs Population Division (Ed.), *Too young to die: Genes or gender?* (pp. 53–63). New York: United Nations.

Waldron, I. (2000). Trends in gender differences in mortality: Relationships to changing gender differences in behaviour and other causal factors. In E. Annandale & K. Hunt (Eds.), *Gender inequalities in health* (pp. 150–181). Philadelphia: Open University Press.

Waldron, I., Hughes, M. E., & Brooks, T. L. (1996). Marriage protection and marriage selection: Prospective evidence for reciprocal effects of marital status and health. *Social Science and Medicine, 43*(1), 113–123.

Waldron, I., Weiss, C. C., & Hughes, M. E. (1997). Marital status effects on health: Are there differences between never married women and divorced and separated women? *Social Science and Medicine, 45*(9), 1387–1397.

Waldron, I., Weiss, C. C., & Hughes, M. E. (1998). Interacting effects of multiple roles on women's health. *Journal of Health and Social Behavior, 39,* 216–236.

Waldron, V. R., & DiMare, L. (1998). Gender as a culturally determined construct: Communication styles in Japan and the United States. In D. J. Canary & K. Dindia (Eds.), *Sex differences and similarities in communication* (pp. 179–201). Mahwah, NJ: Erlbaum.

Walker, L. E. (1979). *The battered woman.* New York: Harper & Row.

Walker, L. J., de Vries, B., & Trevethan, S. D. (1987). Moral stages and moral orientations in real-life and hypothetical dilemmas. *Child Development, 58,* 842–858.

Walker, L. S., & Green, J. W. (1986). The social context of adolescent self-esteem. *Journal of Youth and Adolescence, 15,* 315–322.

Walker, L. S., & Wright, P. H. (1976). Self-disclosure in friendships. *Perceptual and Motor Skills, 42,* 735–742.

Walker, L. S., & Zeman, J. L. (1992). Parental response to child illness behavior. *Journal of Pediatric Psychology, 17*(1), 49–71.

Wall, S. M., Pickert, S. M., & Paradise, L. V. (1984). American men's friendships: Self-reports on meaning and changes. *Journal of Psychology, 116,* 179–186.

Wallace, H. (1999). *Family violence: Legal, medical, and social perspectives.* Boston: Allyn & Bacon.

Waller, G., & Matoba, M. (1999). Emotional eating and eating psychopathology in nonclinical groups: A cross-cultural comparison of women in Japan and the United Kingdom. *International Journal of Eating Disorders, 26,* 333–340.

Walters, E. E., & Kendler, K. S. (1995). Anorexia nervosa and anorexic-like syndromes in a population based female twin sample. *American Journal of Psychiatry, 152*(1), 64–71.

Wang, T. H., & Creedon, C. F. (1989). Sex role orientations, attributions for achievement, and personal goals of Chinese youth. *Sex Roles, 20,* 473–485.

Wannan, G., & Fombonne, E. (1998). Gender differences in rates and correlates of suicidal behavior amongst child psychiatric outpatients. *Journal of Adolescence, 21,* 371–381.

Ward, C. A. (1995). *Attitudes toward rape.* Thousand Oaks, CA: Sage.

Wark, G. R., & Krebs, D. L. (1996). Gender and dilemma differences in real-life moral judgment. *Developmental Psychology, 32,* 220–230.

Warner, M. (1998). *Love, honor, and obey?* [Online]. Available: http://www.pbs.org/newshour/bb/religion/jan-june98/baptist_6-10.html

Watkins, D., Dong, Q., & Xia, Y. (1997). Age and gender differences in the self-esteem of Chinese children. *Journal of Social Psychology, 137*(3), 374–379.

Watkins, D., & Yu, J. (1993). Gender differences in the source and level of self-esteem of Chinese college students. *Journal of Social Psychology, 133*(3), 347–352.

Weich, S., Sloggett, A., & Lewis, G. (1998). Social roles and gender difference in the prevalence of common mental disorders. *British Journal of Psychiatry, 173,* 489–493.

Weidner, G., & Messina, C. R. (1998). Cardiovascular reactivity to mental stress. In K. Orth-Gomer, M. Chesney, & N. K. Wenger (Eds.), *Women, stress, and heart disease* (pp. 219–236). Mahwah, NJ: Erlbaum.

Weiner, B., Frieze, I., Kukla, A., Reed, L., Rest, S., & Rosenbaum, R. M. (1971). *Perceiving the causes of success and failure.* Morristown, NJ: General Learning Press.

Weiner, B., Stone, A. J., Schmitz, M. D., Schmidt, A., Hernandez, A. C. R., & Benton, C. J. (1983). Compounding the errors: A reply to Pollak and Gilligan. *Journal of Personality and Social Psychology, 45,* 1176–1178.

Weisbuch, M., Beal, D., & O'Neal, E. C. (1999). How masculine ought I be? Men's masculinity and aggression. *Sex Roles, 40*(7/8), 583–592.

Weisheit, R. (1993). Structural correlates of female homicide patterns. In A. V. Wilson (Ed.), *Homicide: The victim/offender connection* (pp. 191–206). Cincinnati, OH: Anderson.

Weisner, T. S., & Wilson-Mitchell, J. E. (1990). Nonconventional family life-styles and sex typing in six-year-olds. *Child Development, 61,* 1915–1933.

Weissman, M. M., Bland, R. C., Canino, G. J., Faravelli, C., Greenwald, S., Hwu, H-G., Joyce, P. R., Karam, E. G., Lee, C-K., Lellouch,

J., Lepin, J-P., Newman, S. C., Rubio-Stipec, M., Wells, J. E., Wickramaratne, P. J., Wittchen, H-U., & Yeh, E-K. (1996). Cross-national epidemiology of major depression and bipolar disorder. *Journal of the American Medical Association, 276,* 293–299.

Weissman, M. M., & Klerman, G. L. (1977). Sex differences and the epidemiology of depression. *Journal of Health and Social Behavior, 26,* 156–182.

Weitoft, G. R., Haglund, B., & Rosen, M. (2000). Mortality among lone mothers in Sweden: A population study. *Lancet, 355,* 1215–1219.

Wellman, B. (1992). Men in networks: Private communities, domestic friendships. In P. M. Nardi (Ed.), *Men's friendships* (pp. 74–114). Newbury Park, CA: Sage.

Werking, K. J. (1997a). Cross-sex friendship research as idealogical practice. In S. Duck (Ed.), *Handbook of personal relationships: Theory, research, and interventions* (2nd ed., pp. 391–410). West Sussex, England: Wiley.

Werking, K. J. (1997b). *We're just good friends: Women and men in nonromantic relationships.* New York: Guilford Press.

Wethington, E., & Kessler, R. (1989). Employment, parental responsibility, and psychological distress. *Journal of Family Issues, 10*(4), 527–546.

Wethington, E., McLeod, J. D., & Kessler, R. S. (1987). The importance of life events for explaining sex differences in psychological distress. In R. C. Barnett, L. Biener, & G. K. Baruch (Eds.), *Gender and stress* (pp. 144–156). New York: Free Press.

Wetter, D. W., Fiore, M. C., Young, T. B., McClure, J. B., de Moor, C. A., & Baker, T. B. (1999a). Gender differences in response to nicotine replacement therapy: Objective and subjective indexes of tobacco withdrawal. *Experimental and Clinical Psychopharmacology, 7*(2), 135–144.

Wetter, D. W., Kenford, S. L., Smith, S. S., Fiore, M. C., Jorenby, D. E., & Baker, T. B. (1999b). Gender differences in smoking cessation. *Journal of Consulting and Clinical Psychology, 67*(4), 555–562.

Wetzel, P. J. (1988). Are powerless communication strategies the Japanese norm? *Language and Society, 17,* 555–564.

Wheelan, S. A., & Verdi, A. F. (1992). Differences in male and female patterns of communication in groups: A methodological artifact? *Sex Roles, 27,* 1–15.

Wheeler, L., Reis, H., & Nezlek, J. (1983). Loneliness, social interaction, and sex roles. *Journal of Personality and Social Psychology, 45,* 943–953.

Whiffen, V. E., & Gotlib, I. H. (1989). Stress and coping in maritally distressed and nondistressed couples. *Journal of Personality and Social Psychology, 6,* 327–344.

Whitacre, C. C., Reingold, S. C., O'Looney, P. A., & the Task Force on Gender, M. S. A. A. (1999). Biomedicine: A gender gap in autoimmunity. *Science, 283,* 1277–1278.

White, J. W., & Kowalski, R. M. (1998). Male violence toward women: An integrated perspective. In R. G. Geen & E. Donnerstein (Eds.), *Human aggression: Theories, research, and implications for social policy* (pp. 203–228). San Diego, CA: Academic Press.

White, L. K., & Booth, A. (1985). The transition to parenthood and marital quality. *Journal of Family Issues, 6*(4), 435–449.

White, P. G., Young, K., & McTeer, W. G. (1995). Sport, masculinity and the injured body. In D. F. Sabo & D. F. Gordon (Eds.), *Men's health and illness: Gender, power, and the body* (pp. 158–182). Thousand Oaks, CA: Sage.

Whiting, B. B., & Edwards, C. P. (1988). *Children of different worlds.* Cambridge, MA: Harvard University Press.

Whitley, B. E., Jr. (1984). Sex role orientation and psychological well-being: Two meta-analyses. *Sex Roles, 12,* 207–225.

Whitley, B. E., Jr. (1991). A short form of the expanded attributional style questionnaire. *Journal of Personality Assessment, 56,* 365–369.

Whitley, B. E., Jr., & Gridley, B. E. (1993). Sex role orientation, self-esteem, and depression: A latent variables analysis. *Personality and Social Psychology Bulletin, 19,* 363–369.

Whitley, B. E., Jr., & Kite, M. E. (1995). Sex differences in attitudes toward homosexuality: A comment on Oliver and Hyde (1993). *Psychological Bulletin, 117,* 146–154.

Whitley, B. E., Jr., Michael, S. T., & Tremont, G. (1991). Testing for sex differences in the relationship between attributional style and depression. *Sex Roles, 24,* 753–758.

Whitlock, E. P., Vogt, T. M., Hollis, J. F., & Lichtenstein, E. (1997). Does gender affect response to a brief clinic-based smoking intervention? *American Journal of Preventive Medicine, 13*(3), 159–166.

Widom, C. S. (1989a). The cycle of violence. *Science, 244,* 160–166.

Widom, C. S. (1989b). Does violence beget violence? A critical examination of the literature. *Psychological Bulletin, 106,* 3–28.

Wiley, M. G., & Eskilson, A. (1985). Speech style, gender stereotypes, and corporate success: What if women talk more like men? *Sex Roles, 12,* 993–1007.

Willen, H., & Montgomery, H. (1996). The impact of wish for children and having children on attainment and importance of life values. *Journal of Comparative Family Studies, 27*(3), 499–518.

Williams, C., & Bybee, J. (1994). What do children feel guilty about? Developmental and gender differences. *Developmental Psychology, 30,* 617–623.

Williams, C. L. (1998). The glass escalator: Hidden advantages for men in the female professions. In M. S. Kimmel & M. A. Messner (Eds.), *Men's lives* (pp. 285–299). Boston: Allyn & Bacon.

Williams, J. E., & Best, D. L. (1990). *Measuring sex stereotypes: A multination study* (Rev. ed.). Newbury Park, CA: Sage.

Williamson, I. (1999). Why are gay men a high risk group for eating disturbance? *European Eating Disorders Review, 7*(1), 1–4.

Williamson, I., & Hartley, P. (1998). British research into the increased vulnerability of young gay men to eating disturbance and body dissatisfaction. *European Eating Disorders Review, 6*(3), 160–170.

Willis, F. N., Jr., & Briggs, L. F. (1992). Relationship and touch in public settings. *Journal of Nonverbal Behavior, 16*(1), 55–63.

Wilsnack, R. W., Vogeltanz, N. D., Wilsnack, S. C., & Harris, T. R. (2000). Gender differences in alcohol consumption and adverse drinking consequences: Cross-cultural patterns. *Addiction, 95*(2), 251–265.

Wilson, M., & Daly, M. (1985). Competitiveness, risk taking and violence: The young male syndrome. *Ethology and Sociobiology, 6,* 59–73.

Wilson, N. K. (1993). Gender interaction in criminal homicide. In A. V. Wilson (Ed.), *Homicide: The victim/offender connection* (pp. 43–62). Cincinnati, OH: Anderson.

Wing, R. R., & Klem, M. L. (1997). Obesity. In S. J. Gallant, G. P. Keita, & R. Royak-Schaler (Eds.), *Health care for women: Psychological, social, and behavioral influences* (pp. 115–131). Washington, DC: American Psychological Association.

Winstead, B. A., Derlega, V. J., Montgomery, M. J., & Pilkington, C. (1995). The quality of friendships at work and job satisfaction. *Journal of Social and Personal Relationships, 12,* 199–215.

Winstead, B. A., Derlega, V. J., & Rose, S. (1997). *Gender and close relationships.* Thousand Oaks, CA: Sage.

Wohlgemuth, E., & Betz, N. E. (1991). Gender as a moderator of the relationships of stress and social support to physical health in college students. *Journal of Counseling Psychology, 38*(3), 367–374.

Wood, R. G., Corcoran, M. E., & Courant, P. N. (1993). Pay differences among the highly paid: The male-female earnings gap in lawyers' salaries. *Journal of Labor Economics, 11*(3), 417–441.

Wood, W. (1987). Meta-analytic review of sex differences in group performance. *Psychological Bulletin, 102,* 53–71.

Wood, W., & Karten, S. J. (1986). Sex differences in interaction style as a product of perceived sex differences in competence. *Journal of Personality and Social Psychology, 50,* 341–347.

Wood, W., & Rhodes, N. (1992). Sex differences in interaction style in task groups. In C. L. Ridgeway (Ed.), *Gender, interaction, and inequality* (pp. 97–121). New York: Springer-Verlag.

Woody, E. Z., & Constanzo, P. R. (1990). Does marital agony precede marital ecstasy? A comment on Gottman and Krokoff's "Martial interaction and satisfaction: A longitudinal view." *Journal of Consulting and Clinical Psychology, 58*(4), 499–501.

Worell, J. (1996). Feminist identity in a gendered world. In J. Chrisler, C. Golden, & P. Rozee (Eds.), *Lectures in the psychology of women* (pp. 759–370). Hillsdale, NJ: Erlbaum.

World Almanac Books. (1998). *The World Almanac and book of facts 1999.* Mahwah, NJ: PRIMEDIA Reference.

Wright, D. E. (1999). *Personal relationships: An interdisciplinary approach.* Mountain View, CA: Mayfield.

Wright, P. H. (1982). Men's friendships, women's friendships and the alleged inferiority of the latter. *Sex Roles, 8,* 1–20.

Wright, P. H. (1985). The acquaintance description form. In S. Duck & D. Perlman (Eds.), *Understanding personal relationships: An interdisciplinary approach* (pp. 39–62). Beverly Hills, CA: Sage.

Wright, P. H. (1989). Gender differences in adults' same- and cross-gender friendships. In R. G. Adams & R. Blieszner (Eds.), *Older adult friendship: Structure and process* (pp. 197–221). Newbury Park, CA: Sage.

Wright, P. H., & Keple, T. W. (1981). Friends and parents of a sample of high school juniors: An exploratory study of relationship intensity and interpersonal rewards. *Journal of Marriage and the Family, 43,* 559–570.

Wright, P. H., & Scanlon, M. B. (1991). Gender role orientation and friendship: Some attenuation, but gender differences abound. *Sex Roles, 24,* 551–566.

Wyke, S., Hunt, K., & Ford, G. (1998). Gender differences in consulting a general practitioner for common symptoms of minor illness. *Social Science and Medicine, 46*(7), 901–906.

Yamada, E. M., Tjosvold, D., & Draguns, J. G. (1983). Effects of sex-linked situations and sex composition on cooperation and style of interaction. *Sex Roles, 9,* 541–553.

Yee, D. K., & Eccles, J. S. (1988). Parent perceptions and attributions for children's math achievement. *Sex Roles, 19,* 317–333.

Yee, J. L., & Schulz, R. (2000). Gender differences in psychiatric morbidity among family caregivers: A review and analysis. *Gerontologist, 40*(2), 147–164.

Yoder, C. Y., Shute, G. E., & Tryban, G. M. (1990). Community recognition of objective and subjective characteristics of depression. *American Journal of Community Psychology, 18*(4), 547–566.

Zammuner, V. L. (1987). Children's sex-role stereotypes: A cross-cultural analysis. In P. S. Shaver & C. Hendrick (Eds.), *Research in personality and social psychology* (Vol. 7, pp. 272–293). Newbury Park, CA: Sage.

Zanna, M. P., & Pack, S. J. (1975). On the self-fulfilling nature of apparent sex differences in behavior. *Journal of Experimental Social Psychology, 11,* 583–591.

Zhu, S. H., Sun, J., Billings, S. C., Choi, W. S., & Malarcher, A. (1999). Predictors of smoking cessation in U.S. adolescents. *American Journal of Preventive Medicine, 16*(3), 202–207.

Zimmerman, D. H., & West, C. (1975). Sex roles, interruptions, and silences in conversation. In B. Thorne & N. Henley (Eds.), *Language and sex: Difference and dominance* (pp. 105–129). Rowley, MA: Newbury House.

Zimmerman, R. S., Sprecher, S., Langer, L. M., & Holloway, C. D. (1995). Adolescents' perceived ability to say no to unwanted sex. *Journal of Adolescent Research, 10*(3), 383–399.

Zuckerman, M., & Allison, S. N. (1976). An objective measure of fear of success: Construction and validation. *Journal of Personality Assessment, 40,* 422–430.

Zuckerman, M., & Wheeler, L. (1975). To dispel fantasies about the fantasy-based measure of fear of success. *Psychological Bulletin, 82,* 932–946.

AUTHOR INDEX

SUBJECT INDEX